Fundamental Accounting Principles

KERMIT D. LARSON
The University of Texas at Austin

WILLIAM W. PYLE

MICHAEL ZIN
University of Windsor
Windsor, Ontario

MORTON NELSON
Wilfrid Laurier University
Waterloo, Ontario

Fifth Canadian Edition

Fundamental Accounting Principles

1987

Homewood, Illinois   60430

© RICHARD D. IRWIN, INC., 1955, 1959, 1963, 1966, 1969, 1972, 1975, 1976, 1978, 1980, 1981, 1984, and 1987

ISBN 0-256-03601-2

Library of Congress Catalog Card No. 86–83105

Printed in the United States of America

5 6 7 8 9 0 DO 4 3 2 1 0 9 8

Preface

Fundamental Accounting Principles is intended to provide the textual materials for the first year-long accounting course at the university and college level. This course typically has a variety of objectives. For many students, the course provides the first educational exposure to many business topics, including forms of business organization, typical business practices, legal instruments such as notes, bonds, and stocks, and financial statements. Specific objectives often include: (1) developing a general understanding of financial reports and analyses that students will find useful in their personal affairs regardless of their fields of specialization, (2) introducing students to managerial decision processes and the use of accounting information by the managers of a business, (3) providing a strong foundation for subsequent courses in business and finance, and (4) initiating the coursework leading to a career in accounting. *Fundamental Accounting Principles* is designed to serve all of these objectives.

The central orientation of the book is to explain how accounting data are accumulated and how the resulting reports are prepared so that students can interpret and use accounting information intelligently and effectively. The concepts and principles that guide the preparation of accounting information are persistently emphasized so that students will be able to generalize and apply their knowledge to a variety of new situations. As new concepts and principles are gradually introduced throughout the book, they are defined, explained, and illustrated with practical applications. Thus, students need not hold abstract concepts in limbo before they see how the concepts are applied. This careful integration of conceptual principles and their application to specific business situations is a hallmark of *Fundamental Accounting Principles*.

This fifth Canadian edition contains substantially more important revisions than one might normally expect to observe in a book that has a successful tradition. Numerous important changes have been introduced to make this edition an exciting, completely up-to-date product. Many of these changes have resulted from extensive input by fourth edition adopters. Because of these changes, the teaching effectiveness of the book should be markedly improved in several areas. In addition, important new topics have been covered. A substantial number of additional exercises, problems, provocative problems, and analytical and review problems also have been added to the book. Yet, with all of these changes, the basic objectives and philosophy of *Fundamental Accounting Principles* have not changed. The goal is to provide a challenging but, at the same time, exceptionally readable teaching package. Consistent with the tradition of this book, extraordinary measures have been taken to minimize errors in the text and all supplementary materials. Students will find the book to be interesting and highly comprehensible. Instructors will find the book to be rigorous and comprehensive.

The book's important changes include the following:

1. The homework material in the book has been extensively revised. The addition of several new exercises, problems, provocative problems, analytical and review problems, and the addition of mini discussion cases and multiple-choice questions have increased the diversity of assignment material. This diversity is most apparent in terms of the varied levels of difficulty contained in the end-of-chapter material.

2. Some instructors prefer to minimize the time devoted to corporations during the first semester. To facilitate this preference, the revised and re-ordered homework material for Chapter 5 includes several assignments that are based on the single proprietorship as well as several that are based on the corporation. Thus, adopters may choose to include or exclude the corporation assignment material throughout the first half of the book.

3. The inclusion of a supplement to Chapter 5, reviews and summarizes in one place the accounting concepts, assumptions and principles.

4. Chapter 6 includes an updated discussion of computerized accounting information systems. The increasing importance of microcomputers in small accounting systems is emphasized.

5. The addition of a present and future values supplement to Chapter 12, with additional problem material, gives an added dimension in terms of flexibility. Again, the instructor can decide the depth of coverage he or she desires.

6. Chapter 13 has been revised to reflect recent changes in the law.

7. Discussion of the corporate form of business organization and the related accounting, continues to emphasize no par value shares. This is consistent with the continuing trend of provinces modelling provincial corporate legislation on the Canada Business Corpora-

tions Act, 1975. Included in this edition is an expanded discussion of convertible preferred shares.

8. Chapter 18 has been substantially revised so that the statement of changes in financial position is presented on a cash and cash equivalent basis. This is in line with the revised CICA Handbook recommendation (Section 1540).

9. The addition of a unique new feature is the ''My Own Company'' practice set included in the text. This set emphasizes the setting up of a new business designed to create a new experience that could not be duplicated by the usual transaction-oriented assignment.

10. Chapter 28 reflects the changes in income tax legislation that have occurred since the previous edition.

11. Of significant importance is the addition of a new 29th chapter. ''Micro-Computer Software for Accounting Applications'' is designed to introduce students to the various types of software currently available. It discusses the application of software as an accounting tool. The authors are indebted to John W. Yu, M.Sc., C.D.P., C.G.A., who prepared this chapter. Mr. Yu's wealth of experience in computer applications is an invaluable addition to the text.

12. The addition of the mini-cases for class discussion to the homework material enables the instructor to illustrate the changing nature of accounting. For many of the cases there is no one correct answer. The response may vary to accommodate a number of possible assumptions.

Several important changes and additions have been made in the supplementary materials for *Fundamental Accounting Principles*. These items include the following:

COMPUTERIZED PRACTICE SETS.   Four computerized practice sets have been written to accompany this edition. All are designed to run on microcomputers and have been extensively class tested. Both LITE FLIGHT and HANALEI BAY by Christine Sprenger, Keith Weidkamp, and Clifford Burns are single proprietorship exercises that may be assigned after coverage of Chapter 6. KC's DEALS ON WHEELS and D-BUG are larger exercises that include more transactions, perpetual inventories, and comparative statements and that covers notes, interest, and depreciation. Either may be assigned after coverage of Chapter 10.

MANUAL PRACTICE SETS.   Two manual practice sets are available for use with *Fundamental Accounting Principles*. Bright Paint Store is intended to be used at the completion of Chapter 8. Ross Manufacturing Company Ltd. may be assigned after coverage of Chapter 21.

INSTRUCTOR'S LECTURE GUIDE.   Another new feature provided for the use of adopting instructors is an *Instructor's Lecture Guide*. This guide will provide suggested course plans, lecture outlines, chapter topics and related assignment materials, suggested objectives and areas for emphasis, and suggested assignments organized into class illustrations, homework, questions, cases, multiple-choice questions, problems, provocative problems, enrichment problems and alternative problems. The authors are extremely grateful to Ray Carroll C.G.A., instructor at Halifax Regional Vocational School and lecturer at Dalhousie University and Mount Saint Vincent University, who has prepared this guide. Mr. Carroll's extensive teaching experience has proved to be a valuable contribution to the teaching package accompanying the text.

WORKING PAPERS.   Separate booklets of working papers for solutions to the problems and alternate problems are available for Chapters 1–14 and Chapters 14–28. Note that Chapter 14 is included in both booklets to increase flexibility in course design.

STUDY GUIDES.   The study guides and solutions for the fifth edition have been revised to include more detailed outlines of each chapter.

ACHIEVEMENT TESTS.   Two alternative series of achievement tests are available in bulk to adopters. Each series includes 10 tests plus two final examinations.

SOLUTIONS MANUAL.   Complete answers and solutions to all of the assignment material at the end of each chapter are provided in the solutions manual. Also included are estimates of the time required by the average student to complete each problem.

TRANSPARENCIES.   Illustrative transparencies for use in teaching is available with the fifth edition. Transparencies of the solutions to selected problem material are also available.

CHECK FIGURES.   A list of key figures in the solutions to problems is available for distribution to students by the instructor.

For those students studying in the French language, my colleague, Professor Jean Collette of the Université de Moncton, has prepared an outstanding translation and adaptation. *Initiation à La Compatibilité Financière et Administrative,* le troisième edition, is as thoroughly up-to-date as this, its English language counterpart.

ACKNOWLEDGMENTS

Literally dozens of colleagues, adoptors of the previous edition, and friends too numerous to mention here, have significantly assisted the authors through their comments, criticisms and thoughtful ideas. We are grateful for these contributions and eagerly invite further commentary from Canadian faculty on this fifth edition.

The authors gratefully acknowledge the comments of users of the previous edition who have pointed out numerical and computational inaccuracies in the text and supplemental package. Every effort has been made to eliminate errors in this edition. In particular, the authors wish to thank Sharon Roth of the University of Windsor, who is also a public accountant, and Lee Parent. Along with the authors, they conducted a very thorough four-stage check of illustrations, problems, and solutions for accuracy.

Further, the authors feel compelled to mention the very significant assistance of several commentators and a reviewer. Lea E. Milner of Capilano College provided a thoughtful and thorough review of the fourth edition. Also, the authors appreciate the comments of Charles A. O. Morris, FCGA, of New Brunswick Community College, Moncton. Several adoptors have assisted with on-going commentary over a number of years. The authors are indebted to Dorothy Curzon of Sheridan College; Robert Bell of British Columbia Institute of Technology; William Gilbert of Durham College; Howard Teall of Wilfrid Laurier University; Megeed A. Ragab of the University of Windsor; and Otto H. Visser. All have provided helpful suggestions.

A special thank you must go to Dean Eric West of the University of Windsor and Dean Alex Murray of Wilfrid Laurier University for their encouragement and cooperative support of the authors.

We gratefully acknowledge the contribution to this volume from the faculty members and the secretarial staff at the University of Windsor and Wilfrid Laurier University, especially Carol Pageau, Sandy Berlasty and Susan Muck.

Michael Zin
Morton Nelson

Contents

Ledger. Disposing of Accrued Items. Cash and Accrual Bases of Accounting. Classification of Balance Sheet Items. Owner's Equity on the Balance Sheet. Arrangement of Balance Sheet Items. Account Numbers.

Work Sheet in the Accounting Procedures. Preparing a Work Sheet. Work Sheet and the Financial Statements. Work Sheet and Adjusting Entries. Closing Entries. Why Closing Entries Are Made. Closing Entries Illustrated. Sources of Closing Entry Information. The Accounts after Closing. The Post-Closing Trial Balance. Accounting for Partnerships and Corporations. The Accounting Cycle.

Revenue from Sales. Cost of Goods Sold. Cost of Goods Sold, Periodic Inventory System. Income Statement of a Merchandising Concern. Work Sheet of a Merchandising Concern. Cost of Goods Sold on the Work Sheet. Completing the Work Sheet. Preparing the Statements. Retained Earnings Statement. Retained Earnings Account. Adjusting and Closing Entries. Closing Entries and the Inventories. Other Inventory Methods. Income Statement Forms. Combined Income and Retained Earnings Statement. Statement of Changes in Financial Position. Debit and Credit Memoranda. Trade Discounts. Supplement 5–A: Review of Accounting Concepts and Principles.

Reducing Writing and Posting Labour. Subsidiary Ledgers. Posting the Sales Journal. Identifying Posted Amounts. Controlling Accounts. Cash Receipts Journal. Posting Rule. Creditor Accounts. Purchases Journal. The Cash Disbursements Journal and Its Posting. Proving the Ledgers. Sales Taxes. Sales Invoices as a Sales Journal. Sales Returns. General Journal Entries. Machine Methods. Computerized Data Processing. Recording Actual Transactions.

PART THREE
Accounting for Assets

Internal Control. Computers and Internal Control. Internal Control for Cash. The Voucher System and Control. The Voucher System and Expenses. Recording Vouchers. The Petty Cash Fund. Petty Cash Fund Illustrated. Cash Over and Short. Reconciling the Bank Balance. Illustration of a Bank Reconciliation. Other Internal Control Procedures. Appendix: Recording Vouchers, Pen-and-Ink System. The Unpaid Vouchers File. The Voucher System Cheque Register. Purchases Returns.

PART FOUR
Accounting for Equities: Liabilities and Partners' Equities

Wages, Hours, and Union Contracts. Other Payroll Deductions. Timekeeping. The Payroll Register. Recording the Payroll. Paying the Employees. Payroll Bank Account. Employee's Individual Earnings Recorded. Payroll Deductions Required by the Employer. Paying the Payroll Deductions. Accruing Expenses Based on Wages. Employee (Fringe) Benefit Costs. Computerized Payroll Systems.

Characteristics of a Partnership. Advantages and Disadvantages of a Partnership. Partnership Accounting. Nature of Partnership Earnings. Division of Earnings. Earnings Allocated on a Stated Fractional Basis. Division of Earnings Based on the Ratio of Capital Investments. Salaries and Interest as Aids in Sharing. Partnership Financial Statements. Addition or Withdrawal of a Partner. Death of a Partner. Liquidations.

PART FIVE
Corporation Accounting

Advantages of the Corporate Form. Disadvantages of the Corporate Form. Organizing a Corporation. Organization Costs. Management of a Corporation. Stock Certificates and the Transfer of Stock. Corporation Accounting. Shareholders' Equity Accounts Compared to Partnership Accounts. Authorization and Issuance of Stock. Sale of Stock through Subscriptions. Rights of Common Shareholders. Par and No-Par Value. Classes of Shares. Why Preferred Stock Is Issued. Stock Values.

Retained Earnings and Dividends. Stock Dividends. Stock Splits. Retirement of Stock. Treasury Stock. Purchase of Treasury Stock. Reissuing Treasury Stock. Appropriations of Retained Earnings. Net Income and Retained Earnings—Additional Factors. Stocks as Investments. Classifying Interests. Accounting for Investments in Stock. Parent and Subsidiary Corporations. Consolidated Balance Sheets. Earnings and Dividends of a Subsidiary. Consolidated Balance Sheets at a Date after Acquisition. Other Consolidated Statements. The Corporation Balance Sheet.

Installment Notes Payable. Borrowing by Issuing Bonds. Why Issue Bonds Instead of Stock? Characteristics of Bonds. The Process of Issuing Bonds. Bonds Sold between Interest Dates. Bond Interest Rates. Bonds Sold at a Discount. Bonds Sold at a Premium. Accrued Bond Interest Expense. Sale of

Bonds by Investors. Redemption of Bonds. Bond Sinking Fund. Restriction on Dividends Due to Outstanding Bonds. Converting Bonds to Stock. Investments in Bonds. Mortgages as Security for Notes Payable and Bonds.

PART SIX
Financial Statements, Interpretation and Modifications

Objective of the SCFP. SCFP Noncash Financing and Investing Activities. Disclosure of the SCFP. Format of the SCFP. Preparation of the SCFP, Cash Basis. Direct Approach. Working Paper Approach. T-Account Approach. Using a Cash Plus Temporary Investments Basis.

Understanding Price-Level Changes. Construction of a Price Index. Using Price Index Numbers. Specific versus General Price-Level Indexes. Using Price Indexes in Accounting. Constant-Dollar Accounting. Constant-Dollar Accounting for Assets. Constant-Dollar Accounting for Liabilities and Shareholders' Equity. Preparing Comprehensive, Constant-Dollar Financial Statements. Constant-Dollar Accounting and Current Values. Current Value Accounting. Current Cost Accounting. *CICA Handbook* Recommendation—Current Cost Information. The Momentum toward More Comprehensive Price-Level Accounting.

Objectives of Financial Reporting. Comparative Statements. Analysis of Working Capital. Standards of Comparison. Other Balance Sheet and Income Statement Relations.

PART SEVEN
Managerial Accounting for Costs

Basic Difference in Accounting. Systems of Accounting in Manufacturing Companies. Elements of Manufacturing Costs. Accounts Unique to a Manufacturing Company. Income Statement of a Manufacturing Company. Manufacturing Statement. Work Sheet for a Manufacturing Company. Preparing a Manufacturing Company's Work Sheet. Preparing Statements. Adjusting Entries. Closing Entries. Inventory Valuation Problems of a Manufacturer.

JOB ORDER COST ACCOUNTING. Job Cost Sheets. The Goods in Process Account. Accounting for Materials under a Job Cost System. Accounting for

Labour in a Job Cost System. Accounting for Overhead in a Job Cost System. Overapplied and Underapplied Overhead. Recording the Completion of a Job. Recording Cost of Goods Sold. PROCESS COST ACCOUNTING. Assembling Costs by Departments. Charging Costs to Departments. Equivalent Finished Units. Process Cost Accounting Illustrated.

Reporting on Broad Business Segments. Departmental Accounting. Departmentalizing a Business. Basis for Departmentalization. Information to Evaluate Departments. Securing Departmental Information. Allocating Expenses. Bases for Allocating Expenses. Mechanics of Allocating Expenses. Departmental Contributions to Overhead. Eliminating the Unprofitable Department. Controllable Costs and Expenses. Responsibility Accounting. Joint Costs.

PART EIGHT
Planning and Controlling Business Operations

Cost Behaviour. Break-Even Point, Break-Even Graph., Sales Required for a Desired Net Income. Margin of Safety. Income from a Given Sales Level. Other Questions. Multiproduct Break-Even Point. Evaluating the Results.

The Master Budget. Benefits from Budgeting. The Budget Committee. The Budget Period. Preparing the Master Budget. Preparation of the Master Budget Illustrated.

Fixed Budgets and Performance Reports. FLEXIBLE BUDGETS. Preparing a Flexible Budget. Flexible Budget Performance Report. STANDARD COSTS. Establishing Standard Costs. Variances. Isolating Material and Labour Variances. Charging Overhead to Production. Establishing Overhead Standards. Overhead Variances. Controlling a Business through Standard Costs. Standard Costs in the Accounts.

Capital Budgeting. Accepting Additional Business. Buy or Make. Other Cost Concepts. Scrap or Rebuild Defective Units. Process or Sell. Deciding the Sales Mix.

Fundamental Accounting Principles

Introduction

PART ONE

Accounting, an Introduction to Its Concepts

1

After studying Chapter 1, you should be able to:

Tell the function of accounting and the nature and purpose of the information it provides.

List the main fields of accounting and tell the kinds of work carried on in each field.

List the accounting concepts and principles introduced and tell the effect of each on accounting records and statements.

Describe the purpose of a balance sheet and of an income statement and tell the kinds of information presented in each.

Recognize and be able to indicate the effects of transactions on the elements of an accounting equation.

Prepare simple financial statements.

Tell in each case the extent of the responsibility of a business owner for the debts of a business organized as a single proprietorship, a partnership, or as a corporation.

Define or explain the words and phrases listed in the chapter Glossary.

Accounting is a service activity. Its function is to provide quantitative information about economic entities. The information is primarily financial in nature and is intended to be useful in making economic decisions. If the entity for which the information is provided is a business, for example, the information is used by its management in answering questions such as: What are the resources of the business? What debts does it owe? Does it have earnings? Are expenses too large in relation to sales? Is too little or too much merchandise being kept? Are amounts owed by customers being collected rapidly? Will the business be able to meet its own debts as they mature? Should the plant be expanded? Should a new product be introduced? Should selling prices be increased?

In addition, grantors of credit such as banks, wholesale houses, and manufacturers use accounting information in answering such questions as: Are the customer's earning prospects good? What is its debt-paying ability? Has it paid its debts promptly in the past? Should it be granted additional credit? Likewise, governmental units use accounting information in regulating businesses and collecting taxes. Labour unions use it in negotiating working conditions and wage agreements, and investors make wide use of accounting data in investment decisions.

WHY STUDY ACCOUNTING

Information for use in answering questions like the ones listed is conveyed in accounting reports. If a person is to use these reports effectively, he or she must have some understanding of how their data were gathered and the figures were put together. He or she must appreciate the limitations of the data and the extent to which portions are based on estimates rather than precise measurements. And, he or she must understand accounting terms and concepts. Needless to say, these understandings are gained in a study of accounting.

Another reason to study accounting is to make it one's lifework. A career in accounting can be very interesting and highly rewarding.

ACCOUNTANCY AS A PROFESSION

Over the past half century, accountancy as a profession has attained a stature comparable with that of law or medicine. Most provinces license *public accountants* just as they license doctors and lawyers. The licensing helps ensure a high standard of professional service. Only individuals who have passed a rigorous examination of their accounting and related knowledge, met other education and experience requirements, and have received a license may designate themselves as public accountants.

In Canada, there are a number of accounting organizations providing education and professional training. These include the provincial Institutes of Chartered Accountants, the Certified General Accountants' Association of Canada, and the Society of Management Accountants *(SMA)*. Successful completion of the prescribed courses of instruction and practical experience lead to the following appellations:

Chartered Accountant (CA)

Certified General Accountant *(CGA)*

Certified Management Accountant (CMA)[1]

An activity of the three accounting organizations that has shaped accounting thought has been the education and the publication program. Each has an extensive educational program and has maintained the publication of journals which enjoy wide readership.

In the past decade reliance on post-secondary accounting education has become a significant part of the educational process and complements the extensive correspondence and lecture programs of both the Certified General Accountants' Association of Canada and the Society of Management Accountants—The Canadian Institute of Chartered Accountants *(CICA)* requires a university degree with specified course content.

Accountancy is the fastest growing of the professions. This growth is in response to the expansion and complexity of the economy, the increasing involvement of the accountant in the process of management decision making, and a growing number of financial reporting activities.

THE WORK OF AN ACCOUNTANT

Accountants are employed in three main fields: (1) in public accounting, (2) in private accounting, or (3) in government.

Public Accounting

Public accountants are individuals who offer their professional services and those of their employees to the public for a fee, in much the same manner as a lawyer or a consulting engineer.

AUDITING. The principal service offered by a public accountant is auditing. Banks commonly require an *audit* of the financial statements of a company applying for a sizable loan, with the audit being performed by a public accountant who is not an employee of the audited concern but an independent professional person working for a fee. Companies whose securities are offered for sale to the public generally must also

---

[1]At this writing legislation pending or passed provides for the use of CMA (Certified Management Accountant) in place of RIA.

have such an audit before the securities may be sold. Thereafter, additional audits must be made periodically if the securities are to continue being traded.

The purpose of an audit is to lend credibility to a company's financial statements. In making the audit, the auditor carefully examines the company's statements and the accounting records from which they were prepared. In the examination, the auditor seeks to assure that the statements fairly reflect the company's financial position and operating results and were prepared in accordance with generally accepted accounting principles from records kept in accordance with such principles. Banks, investors, and others rely on the information in a company's financial statements in making loans, in granting credit, and in buying and selling securities. They depend on the auditor to verify the dependability of the information the statements contain.

MANAGEMENT ADVISORY SERVICES.   In addition to auditing, accountants commonly offer *management advisory services*. An accountant gains from an audit an intimate knowledge of the audited company's accounting procedures and its financial position. Thus, the accountant is in an excellent position to offer constructive suggestions for improving the procedures and strengthening the position. Clients expect these suggestions as a useful audit by-product. They also commonly engage public accountants to conduct additional investigations for the purpose of determining ways in which their operations may be improved. Such investigations and the suggestions growing from them are known as management advisory services.

Management advisory services include the design, installation, and improvement of a client's general accounting system and any related information system it may have for determining and controlling costs. They also include the application of machine and computer methods to these systems plus advice in financial planning, budgeting, forecasting, and inventory control. In fact, they include all phases of information systems and related matters.

TAX SERVICES.   In this day of increasing complexity in income and other tax laws and continued high tax rates, few important business decisions are made without consideration being given to their tax effect. A professional accountant, through training and experience, is well qualified to render important service in this area. The service includes not only the preparation and filing of tax returns but also advice as to how transactions may be completed so as to incur the smallest tax.

Private Accounting

Accountants employed by a single enterprise are said to be in private accounting. A small business may employ only one accountant or it may depend upon the services of a professional accountant and employ none. A large business, on the other hand, may have more than a hundred employees in its accounting department. They commonly work under the supervision of a chief accounting officer, commonly called the ***controller***. The title controller results from the fact that one of the chief uses of accounting data is to control the operations of a business.

The one accountant of the small business and the accounting department of a large business do a variety of work, including general accounting, cost accounting, budgeting, and internal auditing.

GENERAL ACCOUNTING. ***General accounting*** has to do primarily with recording transactions, processing the recorded data, and preparing financial and other reports for the use of management, owners, creditors, and governmental agencies. The private accountant may design or help the professional accountant design the system used in recording the transactions. He or she will also supervise the clerical or data processing staff in recording the transactions and preparing the reports.

COST ACCOUNTING. The phase of accounting that has to do with collecting, determining, and controlling costs, particularly costs of producing a given product or service, is called ***cost accounting***. A knowledge of costs and controlling costs is vital to good management. Therefore, a large company may have a number of accountants engaged in this activity.

BUDGETING. Planning business activities before they occur is called ***budgeting***. The objective of budgeting is to provide management with an intelligent plan for future operations. Then, after the budget plan has been put into effect, it provides summaries and reports that can be used to compare actual accomplishments with the plan. Many large companies have a number of people who devote all their time to this phase of accounting.

INTERNAL AUDITING. In addition to an annual audit by an independent firm of public accountants, many companies maintain a staff of internal auditors. The internal auditors constantly check the records prepared and maintained in each department or company branch. It is their responsibility to make sure that established accounting procedures and management directives are being followed throughout the company.

Governmental Accounting

Furnishing governmental services is a vast and complicated operation in which accounting is just as indispensable as in business. Elected and appointed officials must rely on data accumulated by means of accounting if they are to complete effectively their administrative duties. Accountants are responsible for the accumulation of these data. Accountants also check and audit the millions of income, payroll, and sales tax returns that accompany the tax payments upon which governmental units depend.

And finally, federal and provincial agencies, such as the Board of Transport Commissioners, Restrictive Trade Practices Commission, Security Commissions, and so on, use accountants in many capacities in their regulation of business.

ACCOUNTING AND BOOKKEEPING

Many people confuse *accounting* and *bookkeeping* and look upon them as one and the same. In effect, they identify the whole with one of its parts. Actually, bookkeeping is only part of accounting, the record-making part. To keep books is to record transactions, and a bookkeeper is one who records transactions either manually with pen and ink or with a bookkeeping machine. The work is often routine and primarily clerical in nature. The work of an accountant goes far beyond this, as a rereading of the previous section will show.

ACCOUNTING AND COMPUTERS

Computers are used for many tasks in our modern society, including the processing of accounting data. A computer can accept and store accounting data, sort and rearrange it, perform arithmetic calculations on it, and prepare reports from the data. Furthermore, after accepting data, a computer can process it very rapidly and with little or no human intervention. However, before a computer can do this, a set of detailed instructions must be prepared and entered in the computer to tell it how to process the data. The person who prepares these instructions must have a thorough understanding of accounting procedures and accounting principles. A beginning on that understanding can be gained in the succeeding pages of this text.

ACCOUNTING STATEMENTS

Accounting statements are the end product of the accounting process, but a good place to begin the study of accounting. They are used to convey a concise picture of the profitability and financial position of a business. The two most important are the income statement and the balance sheet.

The Income Statement

A company's *income statement* (see Illustration 1–1) is perhaps more important than its balance sheet. It shows whether or not the business achieved or failed to achieve its primary objective—earning a "profit"

Illustration 1–1

COAST REALTY
Income Statement
For Year Ended December 31, 19—

Revenues:
   Commissions earned $55,150
   Property management fees   1,200
      Total revenues $56,350

Operating expenses:
   Salaries expense $12,800
   Rent expense   6,000
   Utilities expense   915
   Telephone expense   760
   Advertising expense   4,310
      Total operating expenses   24,785
Net income $31,565

or net income. A *net income* is earned when revenues exceed expenses, but a *net loss* is incurred if the expenses exceed the revenues. An income statement is prepared by listing the revenues earned during a period of time, listing the expenses incurred in earning the revenues, and subtracting the expenses from the revenues to determine if a net income or a net loss was incurred.

Revenues are inflows of cash or other properties received in exchange for goods or services provided to customers. Rents, dividends, and interest earned are also revenues. Coast Realty of Illustration 1–1 had revenue inflows from services that totaled $56,350.

Expenses are goods and services consumed in operating a business or other economic unit. Coast Realty consumed the services of its employees (salaries expense), the services of a telephone company, and so on.

The heading of an income statement tells the name of the business for which it is prepared and the time period covered by the statement. Both bits of information are important. However, the time covered is extremely significant, since the items on the statement must be interpreted in relation to the period of time. For example, the item "Commissions earned, $55,150" on the income statement of Illustration 1–1 has little significance until it is known that the amount represents one year's commissions and not the commissions of a week or a month.

The Balance Sheet

The purpose of a *balance sheet* is to show the financial position of a business on a specific date. It is often called a *position statement*.

Financial position is shown by listing the *assets* of the business, its *liabilities* or debts, and the *equity* **of the owner or owners.** (An asset is a property or property right and an equity is a right, claim or interest in an asset or assets.) The name of the business and the date are given in the balance sheet heading. It is understood that the item amounts shown are as of the close of business on that date.

Before a business manager, investor, or other person can make effective judgments based on balance sheet information, he or she must understand balance sheet terminology and several accounting concepts and principles. For a beginning on these understandings, assume that on August 3, Joan Ball began a new business, called World Travel Agency. During the day, she completed these transactions in the name of the business:

Aug. 3 Invested $5,000 of her personal cash in the business.
     3 Rented suitable office space and paid the rent for three months in advance, $1,500. (In exchange for the $1,500 the business gained the right to occupy the office space for three months, an asset called prepaid rent.)
     3 Purchased for cash office equipment costing $2,500.
     3 Purchased on credit office supplies costing $100 and additional office equipment costing $500. (Purchased on credit means purchased with a promise to pay at a later date.)

A balance sheet reflecting the effects of these transactions appears in Illustration 1–2. It shows that after completing the transactions, the agency has four assets, a $600 debt, and its owner has a $5,000 equity in the business.

Observe that the two sides of the balance sheet are equal. This is where it gets its name. Its two sides must always be equal because one side shows the resources of the business and the other shows who supplied the resources. For example, World Travel Agency has $5,600 of resources (assets) of which $5,000 were supplied by its owner and $600 by its creditors. (*Creditors* are individuals and organizations to whom the business owes debts.)

Illustration 1–2

WORLD TRAVEL AGENCY
Balance Sheet
August 3, 19—

Assets		Liabilities	
Cash	$1,000	Accounts payable	$ 600
Office supplies	100	**Owner's Equity**	
Prepaid rent	1,500		
Office equipment	3,000	Joan Ball, capital	5,000
		Total liabilities and owner's	
Total assets	$5,600	equity	$5,600

ASSETS, LIABILITIES, AND OWNER'S EQUITY

The assets of a business are, in general, the properties or economic resources owned by the business. They include cash, amounts owed to the business by its customers for goods and services sold to them on credit (called *accounts receivable*), merchandise held for sale by the business, supplies, equipment, buildings, and land. Assets may also include such intangible rights as those granted by a patent or copyright.

The liabilities of a business are its debts. They include amounts owed to creditors for goods and services bought on credit (called *accounts payable*), salaries and wages owed employees, taxes payable, notes payable, and mortgages payable.

When a business is owned by one person, the owner's interest or equity in the assets of the business is shown on a balance sheet by listing the person's name, followed by the word **capital,** and then the amount of the equity. The use of the word capital comes from the idea that the owner has furnished the business with resources or ''capital'' equal to the amount of the equity.

A liability represents a claim or right to be paid. The law recognizes this right. If a business fails to pay its creditors, the law gives the creditors the right to force the sale of the assets of the business to secure money to meet creditor claims. Furthermore, if the assets are sold, the creditors are paid first, with any remainder going to the business owner. Obviously, then, by law creditor claims take precedence over those of a business owner.

Since creditor claims take precedence over those of an owner, an owner's equity in a business is always a residual amount. Creditors recognize this. When they examine the balance sheet of a business, they are always interested in the share of its assets furnished by creditors and the share furnished by its owner or owners. The creditors recognize that if the business must be liquidated and its assets sold, the shrinkage in converting the assets into cash must exceed the equity of the owner or owners before the creditors will lose.

GENERALLY ACCEPTED ACCOUNTING PRINCIPLES

An understanding of financial statement information requires a knowledge of the generally accepted *accounting principles* that govern the accumulation and presentation of the data appearing on such statements. A common definition of the word **principle** is: ''A broad general law or rule adopted or professed as a guide to action; a settled ground or basis of conduct or practice. . . .'' Consequently, generally accepted accounting principles may be described as broad rules adopted by the accounting profession as guides in measuring, recording, and reporting the financial affairs and activities of a business. They consist of a number of concepts, principles, and procedures that are summarized in the supplement to Chapter 5. They also are referred to again and again throughout this text in order to increase your understanding of the information conveyed by accounting data.

SOURCE OF ACCOUNTING PRINCIPLES

Generally accepted accounting principles are not natural laws in the sense of the laws of physics and chemistry but man-made rules that depend for their authority upon their general acceptance by the accounting profession. They have evolved from the experience and thinking of the accounting profession, influenced by the financial community and governmental regulations. Primary among the organizations that fostered and continue to foster development of accounting principles are the Canadian Institute of Chartered Accountants (CICA), the American Institute of Certified Public Accountants *(AICPA),* the Securities and Exchange Commission, and the American Accounting Association.

Over the years the accounting profession has devoted much time and attention to the problem of generally accepted accounting principles. For three decades prior to 1968, the Accounting and Auditing Committee of the CICA issued bulletins on financial disclosure, accounting principles, terminology, reporting, and auditing procedures. In 1968 these bulletins were consolidated to form a major part of the *CICA Handbook*. Since 1968 the *Handbook* has been constantly updated by the *Accounting Standards Committee* (formerly the Accounting Research Committee) through the issuance of recommendations on various current topics. These recommendations are issued only after due consideration of comments by interested parties on the exposure drafts. Added importance was given these recommendations when the regulations of the Canada Business Corporations Act, 1975, required that financial statements and the auditor's report be prepared in accordance with the recommendations of the CICA set out in the *Handbook*. The *Handbook* and the regulations permit departure from the recommendations in circumstances where departure would achieve a fairer disclosure. The fact of a departure from the recommendations of the *Handbook* and an explanation of the effect of the accounting method or statement presentation used must, however, be clearly set out in the financial statements, in a note thereto, or in a summary of accounting policies. This requirement parallels that of the AICPA's 1964 rule that its members must disclose in footnotes to published financial statements any departure from generally accepted accounting principles as set forth in the *Opinions of the Accounting Principles Board. Opinions* of the *APB* have the same status in the United States as the recommendations in the *CICA Handbook* in Canada. In 1959 the

AICPA established the APB and gave it the authority to issue authoritative expressions of generally accepted accounting principles. In 1973 the APB was replaced by a seven-member Financial Accounting Standards Board *(FASB)*, independent of the AICPA, with authority to formulate rules governing the practice of accounting. In Canada, a move to an independent rules-setting body is under way with the formation of the Accounting Standards Authority of Canada (ASAC).

The American Accounting Association, an organization with strong academic ties, has also been influential in describing and defining generally accepted accounting principles. It has sponsored a number of research studies and has published many articles dealing with accounting principles.

On the international scene, Canadian accounting bodies were in 1973 signatories of an Agreement establishing the International Accounting Standards Committee (IASC). This Agreement (revised in 1977) gave the IASC, now comprising 60 accounting bodies in 48 countries, the authority to "formulate and publish in the public interest, standards to be observed in the preparation of audited financial statements and to promote their world wide acceptance and observance." Canadian agreement to require disclosure of compliance and any material departure from the international standards gave added weight to IASC recommendations. All organizations are continuing active research in accounting theory and the updating of accounting standards. Numerous references to these statements will be made throughout the discussion in this book.

UNDERSTANDING ACCOUNTING PRINCIPLES

Your authors believe that an understanding of *accounting principles* is best conveyed with examples illustrating the application of each principle. The examples must be such that a student can understand at his or her level of experience. Consequently, three *accounting concepts* and two accounting principles are introduced here. Discussions of the others are delayed until later in the text when meaningful examples of their application can be developed.

Business Entity Concept

Under the *business entity concept,* for accounting purposes, every business is conceived to be and is treated as a separate entity, separate and distinct from its owner or owners and from every other business. Businesses are so conceived and treated because, insofar as a specific business is concerned, the purpose of accounting is to record its transactions and periodically report its financial position and profitability. Consequently, the records and reports of a business should not include either the transactions or assets of another business or the personal assets and transactions of its owner or owners. To include either distorts the financial position and profitability of the business. For example, the personally owned automobile of a business owner should not be included among the assets of the owner's business. Likewise, its gas, oil, and repairs should not be treated as an expense of the business, for to do so distorts the reported financial position and profitability of the business.

Cost Principle

In addition to the *business entity concept,* an accounting principle called the *cost principle* should be borne in mind when reading financial statements. Under this principle, all goods and services purchased are recorded at cost and appear on the statements at cost. For example, if a business pays $50,000 for land to be used in carrying on its operations, the purchase should be recorded at $50,000. It makes no difference if the buyer and several competent outside appraisers thought the land "worth" at least $60,000. It cost $50,000 and should appear on the balance sheet at that amount. Furthermore, if five years later, due to booming real estate prices, the land's market value has doubled, this makes no difference either. The land cost $50,000 and should continue to appear on the balance sheet at $50,000 even though its estimated market value is twice that.

In applying the *cost principle,* costs are measured on a cash or cash-equivalent basis. If the consideration given for an asset or service is cash, cost is measured at the entire cash outlay made to secure the asset or service. If the consideration is something other than cash, cost is measured at the cash-equivalent value of the consideration given or the cash-equivalent value of the thing received, whichever is more clearly evident.

Why are assets and services recorded at cost and why are the balance sheet amounts for the assets not changed from time to time to reflect changing market values? The *objectivity principle* and the *continuing-concern concept* supply answers to these questions.

Objectivity Principle

The *objectivity principle* supplies the reason transactions are recorded at cost, since it requires that transaction amounts be objectively established. Whims and fancies plus, for example, something like an opinion of management that an asset is "worth more than it cost" have no place in accounting. To be fully useful, accounting information must be based on objective data. As a rule, costs are objective, since they normally are established by buyers and sellers, each striking the best possible bargain for himself or herself.

Continuing-Concern Concept

Balance sheet amounts for assets used in carrying on the operations of a business are not changed from time to time to reflect changing market values. A balance sheet is prepared under the assumption that the business for which it is prepared will continue in operation, and as a continuing or going concern the assets used in carrying on its operations are not for sale. In fact, they cannot be sold without disrupting the business. Therefore, since the assets are for use in the business and are not for sale, their current market values are not particularly relevant and need not be shown. Also, without a sale, their current market values usually cannot be objectively established, as is required by the *objectivity principle*.

The *continuing-concern* or *going-concern concept* applies in most situations. However, if a business is about to be sold or liquidated, the *continuing-concern concept* and the *cost and objectivity principles* do not apply in the preparation of its statements. In such cases, amounts other than costs, such as estimated market values, become more useful and informative.

The Stable-Dollar Concept

In our country, accounting transactions are measured, recorded, and reported in terms of dollars. In the measuring, recording, and reporting process, the dollar has been treated as a stable unit of measure, like a kilo, a litre or a kilometre. However, unfortunately the dollar, like other currencies, is not a stable unit of measure. When the general price level (the average of all prices) changes, the value of money (its purchasing power) also changes. For example, during the past 10 years, the general price level has approximately doubled, which means that over these years the purchasing power of the dollar has declined from 100 cents to approximately 50 cents.

Nevertheless, although the instability of the dollar is recognized, accountants in their reports continue to add and subtract items acquired in different years with dollars of different sizes. In effect, they ignore changes in the size of the measuring unit. For example, assume a company purchased land some years ago for $10,000 and sold it today for $20,000. If during this period the purchasing power of the dollar declined from 100 cents to 50 cents, it can be said that the company is no better off for having purchased the land for $10,000 and sold it for $20,000 because the $20,000 will buy no more goods and services today than the $10,000 at the time of the purchase. Yet, using the dollar to measure both transactions, the accountant reports a $10,000 gain from the purchase and sale.

The instability of the dollar as a unit of measure is recognized. Therefore, the question is should the amounts shown on financial statements be adjusted for changes in the purchasing power of the dollar. Techniques have been devised to convert the historical dollars of statement amounts into dollars of current purchasing power. Such statements are called *price-level-adjusted statements.* Also, by consulting catalogues and securing current prices from manufacturers and wholesalers, it is possible to determine replacement costs for various assets owned. As a result, such costs could be used in preparing financial statements. However, financial statements showing current replacement costs and also price-level-adjusted statements require subjective judgments in their preparation. Consequently, most accountants are of the opinion that the traditional statements based on the *stable-dollar concept* are best for general publication and use. Nevertheless, they also recognize that the information conveyed by traditional statements can be made more useful if accompanied by replacement cost and/or price-level-adjusted information. This is discussed in a later chapter.

From the discussions of the *cost principle,* the *continuing-concern concept,* and *stable-dollar concept,* it should be recognized that in most instances a balance sheet does not show the amounts at which the listed assets can be sold or replaced. Nor does it show the "worth" of the business for which it was prepared, since some of the listed assets may be salable for much more or much less than the dollar amounts at which they are shown.

BUSINESS ORGANIZATIONS

Accounting is applicable to all economic entities such as business concerns, schools, churches, fraternities, and so on. However, this text will focus on accounting for business concerns organized as single proprietorships, partnerships, and corporations.

Single Proprietorships

An unincorporated business owned by one person is called a *single proprietorship.* Small retail stores and service enterprises are commonly operated as single proprietorships. There are no legal requirements to be met in starting a single proprietorship business. Furthermore, single proprietorships are the most numerous of all business concerns.

In accounting for a single proprietorship, the *business entity concept* is applied and the business is treated as a separate entity, separate and distinct from its owner. However, insofar as the debts of the business are concerned, no such legal distinction is made. The owner of a single proprietorship business is personally responsible for its debts. As a result, if the assets of such a business are not sufficient to pay its debts, the personal assets of the proprietor may be taken to satisfy the claims of the business creditors.

Partnerships

When a business is owned by two or more people as partners, it is called a *partnership*. Like a single proprietorship, there are no special legal requirements to be met in starting a partnership business. All that is required is for two or more people to enter into an agreement to operate a business as partners. The agreement becomes a contract and may be either oral or written, but to avoid disagreements, a written contract is preferred.

For accounting purposes, a partnership business is treated as a separate entity, separate and distinct from its owners. However, just as with a single proprietorship, insofar as the debts of the business are concerned, no such legal distinction is made. A partner is personally responsible for all the debts of the partnership, both his or her own share and the shares of any partners who are unable to pay. Furthermore, the personal assets of a partner may be taken to satisfy all the debts of a partnership if other partners cannot pay.

Corporations

A business incorporated under the laws of a province or the federal government is called a *corporation*. Unlike a single proprietorship or partnership, a corporation is a separate legal entity, separate and distinct from its owners. The owners are called *shareholders* or *stockholders* because their ownership is evidenced by shares of the corporation's *capital stock*. The stock may be sold and transferred from one shareholder to another without affecting the operation of the corporation.

Separate legal entity is the most important characteristic of a corporation. It makes a corporation responsible for its own acts and its own debts and relieves its shareholders of liability for either. It enables a corporation to buy, own, and sell property in its own name, to sue and be sued in its own name, and to enter into contracts for which it is solely responsible. In short, separate legal entity enables a corporation to conduct its business affairs as a legal person with all the rights, duties, and responsibilities of a person. However, unlike a person, it must act through agents.

A corporation is created by securing approval of articles of incorporation from one of the provinces or the federal government. The requirements for incorporation vary; but in general, they call for filing an application with the proper governmental official and paying certain fees and taxes. If the application complies with the law and all fees and taxes have been paid, the articles of incorporation are approved and the corporation comes into existence. At that point, the corporation's organizers and perhaps others buy the corporation's stock and become shareholders. Then, as shareholders they meet and elect a board of directors. The board then meets, appoints the corporation's president and other officers, and makes them responsible for managing the corporation's business affairs.

Lack of shareholder liability and the ease with which stock may be sold and transferred have enabled corporations to multiply, grow, and become the dominant form of business organization in our country. Nevertheless, because of its simplicity, it is best to begin the study of accounting with a single proprietorship.

THE BALANCE SHEET EQUATION

As previously stated, a balance sheet is so called because its two sides must always balance. The sum of the assets shown on the balance sheet must equal liabilities plus the equity of the owner or owners of the business. This equality may be expressed in equation form for a single proprietorship business as follows:

Assets = Liabilities + Owner's equity

When balance sheet equality is expressed in equation form, the resulting equation is called the *balance sheet equation.* It is also known as the *accounting equation,* since all double-entry accounting is based on it. Like any mathematical equation, its elements may be transposed and the equation expressed:

Assets − Liabilities = Owner's equity

The equation in this form illustrates the residual nature of the owner's equity. An owner's claims are secondary to the creditors' claims.

EFFECTS OF TRANSACTIONS ON THE ACCOUNTING EQUATION

A *business transaction* is an exchange of goods or services, and business transactions affect the elements of an accounting equation. However, regardless of what transactions a business completes, its accounting equation always remains in balance. Also, its assets always equal the combined claims of its creditors and its owner or owners. This may be demonstrated with the transactions of Larry Owen's law practice, a single proprietorship business, which follow.

On July 1, Larry Owen began a new law practice by investing $5,000 of his personal cash, which he deposited in a bank account opened in the name of the business, Larry Owen, Lawyer. After the investment, the one asset of the new business and the equity of Owen in the business are shown in the following equation:

Assets   =   Owner's equity

Cash, $5,000 = Larry Owen, capital, $5,000

Observe that after its first transaction, the new business has one asset, cash, $5,000. Therefore, since it has no liabilities, the equity of Owen in the business is $5,000.

To continue the illustration, after the investment (transaction 2), Owen used $900 of the business cash to pay the rent for three months in advance on suitable office space and (transaction 3) $3,700 to buy office equipment. These transactions were exchanges of cash for other assets. Their effects on the accounting equation are shown in color in Illustration 1–3. Observe that the equation remains in balance after each transaction.

Illustration 1–3

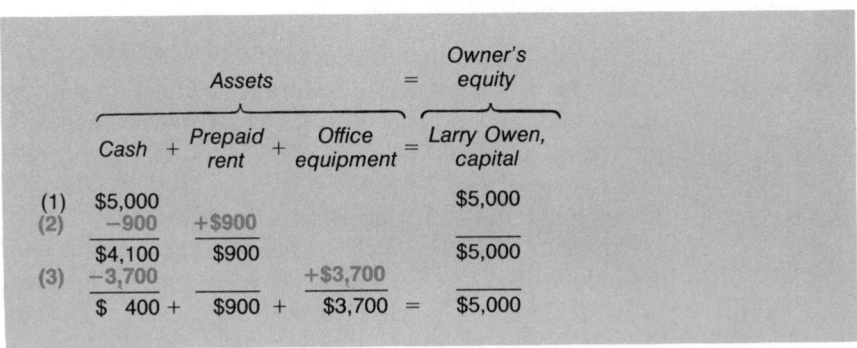

	Cash +	Prepaid rent +	Office equipment =	Larry Owen, capital
(1)	$5,000			$5,000
(2)	−900	+$900		
	$4,100	$900		$5,000
(3)	−3,700		+$3,700	
	$ 400 +	$900 +	$3,700 =	$5,000

Continuing the illustration, assume that Owen needed office supplies and additional equipment in the law office. However, he felt he should conserve the cash of the law practice. Consequently, he purchased on credit from Alpha Company office supplies costing $60 and office equipment that cost $300. The effects of these purchases (transaction 4) are shown in Illustration 1–4. Note that the assets were increased by the purchases. However, Owen's equity did not change because Alpha Company acquired a claim against the assets equal to the increase in the assets. The claim or amount owed Alpha Company is called an *account payable*.

A primary objective of a business is to increase the equity of its owner or owners by earning a profit or a net income. Owen's law practice will accomplish this objective by providing legal services to its clients on a fee basis. Of course, the practice will earn a net income only if legal fees earned are greater than the expenses incurred in earning the fees. Legal fees earned and expenses incurred affect the elements of an

Illustration 1–4

		Assets			= Liabilities +	Owner's equity
	Cash +	Prepaid rent +	Office supplies +	Office equipment =	Accounts payable +	Larry Owen, capital
(1)	$5,000					$5,000
(2)	−900	+$900				
	$4,100	$900				$5,000
(3)	−3,700			+$3,700		
	$ 400	$900		$3,700		$5,000
(4)			+$60	+300	+$360	
	$ 400 +	$900 +	$60 +	$4,000 =	$360 +	$5,000

accounting equation. To illustrate their effects, assume that on July 12, Larry Owen completed legal work for a client (transaction 5) and immediately collected $500 in cash for the services rendered. Also, the same day (transaction 6) he paid the salary of the office secretary for the first two weeks of July, a $400 expense of the business. The effects of these transactions are shown in Illustration 1–5.

Observe first the effects of the legal fee. The $500 fee is a revenue, an inflow of assets from the sale of services. Note that the revenue not only increased the asset cash but also caused a $500 increase in Owen's

Illustration 1–5

		Assets			= Liabilities +	Owner's equity
	Cash +	Prepaid rent +	Office supplies +	Office equipment =	Accounts payable +	Larry Owen, capital
(1)	$5,000					$5,000
(2)	−900	+$900				
	$4,100	$900				$5,000
(3)	−3,700			+$3,700		
	$ 400	$900		$3,700		$5,000
(4)			+$60	+300	+$360	
	$ 400	$900	$60	$4,000	$360	$5,000
(5)	+500					+500
	$ 900	$900	$60	$4,000	$360	$5,500
(6)	−400					−400
	$ 500 +	$900 +	$60 +	$4,000 =	$360 +	$5,100

equity. Owen's equity increased because total assets increased without an increase in liabilities.

Next observe the effects of paying the secretary's $400 salary, an expense. Note that the effects are opposite those of a revenue. Expenses are goods and services consumed in the operation of a business. In this instance, the business consumed the secretary's services. When the services were paid for, both the assets and Owen's equity in the business decreased. Owen's equity decreased because cash decreased without an increase in other assets or a decrease in liabilities.

Note this about earning a net income: A business earns a net income when its revenues exceed its expenses, and the income increases both net assets and the equity of the owner or owners. (*Net assets* are the excess of assets over liabilities.) Net assets increase because more assets flow into the business from revenues than are consumed and flow out for expenses. The equity of the owner or owners increases because net assets increase. A net loss has opposite effects.

To simplify the material and emphasize the actual effects of revenues and expenses on owner's equity, in this first chapter revenues are added directly to and expenses are deducted from the owner's capital. However, this is not done in actual practice. In actual practice, revenues and expenses are first accumulated in separate categories. They are then combined; and their combined effect, the net income or loss, is added to or deducted from owner's capital. A further discussion of this is deferred to later chapters.

REALIZATION PRINCIPLE

In transaction 5, the revenue inflow was in the form of cash. However, revenue inflows are not always in cash because of the *realization principle* (also called the *recognition principle*), which governs the recognition of revenue. This principle (1) defines a revenue as an inflow of assets (not necessarily cash) in exchange for goods or services. (2) It requires that the revenue be recognized (entered in the accounting records as revenue) at the time, but not before, it is earned. (Generally, revenue is considered to be earned at the time title to goods sold is transferred or services are rendered and become billable.) (3) The principle also requires that the amount of revenue recognized be measured by the cash received plus the cash equivalent (fair value) of any other asset or assets received.

To demonstrate the recognition of a revenue inflow in a form other than cash, assume that (transaction 7) Larry Owen completed legal work for a client and billed the client $1,000 for the services rendered. Also assume that 10 days later, the client paid in full (transaction 8) for the services rendered. The effects of the two transactions are shown in Illustration 1–6.

Illustration 1–6

	Cash	+	Accounts receivable	+	Prepaid rent	+	Office supplies	+	Office equipment	=	Accounts payable	+	Larry Owen, capital
													Assets = Liabilities + Owner's equity	
(1)	$5,000												$5,000
(2)	−900				+$900								
	$4,100				$900								$5,000
(3)	−3,700								+$3,700				
	$ 400				$900				$3,700				$5,000
(4)							+$60		+300		+$360		
	$ 400				$900		$60		$4,000		$360		$5,000
(5)	+500												+500
	$ 900				$900		$60		$4,000		$360		$5,500
(6)	−400												−400
	$ 500				$900		$60		$4,000		$360		$5,100
(7)			+$1,000										+1,000
	$ 500		$1,000		$900		$60		$4,000		$360		$6,100
(8)	+1,000		− 1,000										
	$1,500 +		$ 0 +		$900 +		$60 +		$4,000 =		$360 +		$6,100

Observe in transaction 7 that the asset flowing into the business was the right to collect $1,000 from the client, an account receivable. Compare transactions 5 and 7 and note that they differ only as to the type of asset received. Next observe that the receipt of cash (10 days after the services were rendered) is nothing more than an exchange of assets, cash for the right to collect from the client. Also note that the receipt of cash did not affect Owen's equity because the revenue was recognized in accordance with the realization principle and Owen's equity was increased upon completion of the services rendered.

As a final transaction assume that on July 30, Larry Owen paid Alpha Company $100 of the $360 owed for the equipment and supplies purchased in transaction 4. This transaction reduced in equal amounts both assets and liabilities, and its effects are shown in Illustration 1–7.

IMPORTANT TRANSACTION EFFECTS

Look again at Illustration 1–7 and observe that every transaction affected at least two items in the equation; and in each case, after the effects were entered in the columns, the equation remained in balance. The accounting system you are beginning to study is called a *double-entry system.* It is based on the fact that every transaction affects two

Illustration 1–7

	Assets					= Liabilities +	Owner's equity
	Cash +	Accounts receivable +	Prepaid rent +	Office supplies +	Office equipment =	Accounts payable +	Larry Owen, capital
(1)	$5,000						$5,000
(2)	−900		+$900				
	$4,100		$900				$5,000
(3)	−3,700				+$3,700		
	$ 400		$900		$3,700		$5,000
(4)				+$60	+300	+$360	
	$ 400		$900	$60	$4,000	$360	$5,000
(5)	+500						+500
	$ 900		$900	$60	$4,000	$360	$5,500
(6)	−400						−400
	$ 500		$900	$60	$4,000	$360	$5,100
(7)		+$1,000					+1,000
	$ 500	$1,000	$900	$60	$4,000	$360	$6,100
(8)	+1,000	−1,000					
	$1,500	$ 0	$900	$60	$4,000	$360	$6,100
(9)	−100					−100	
	$1,400 +		$900 +	$60 +	$4,000 =	$260 +	$6,100

or more items in an accounting equation, such as that in Illustration 1–7, and requires a "double entry" or, in other words, entries in two or more places. Also, the fact that the equation remained in balance after each transaction is important, for this is a proof of the accuracy with which the transactions were recorded.

BASES OF REVENUE RECOGNITION

Returning to the discussion of revenue recognition, revenue is realized and in most cases should be recognized in the accounting records upon the completion of a sale or when services have been performed and are billable. This is known as the *sales basis of revenue recognition*. Under it, a sale is considered to be completed when assets such as cash or the right to collect cash within a short period of time are received in exchange for goods sold or services rendered. Theoretically, revenue is earned throughout the entire performance of a service or throughout the whole process of securing goods for sale, taking a customer's order, and delivering the goods. Yet, until all steps are completed, and there is a right to collect the sale price, the requirements of the *objectivity principle* are not fulfilled and revenue is not recognized.

An exception to the required use of the sales basis is made for installment sales when payments are to be made over a relatively long period of time and there is considerable doubt as to the amounts that ultimately will be collected. For such sales, when collection of the full sale price is in doubt, revenue may be recognized as it is collected in cash. This is known as the *cash basis of revenue recognition.*

A second exception to the required use of the sales basis applies to construction firms. Large construction jobs often take two or more years to complete. Consequently, if a construction firm has only a few jobs in process at any time and it recognizes revenue on a sales basis (upon the completion of each job), it may have a year in which no jobs are completed and no revenue is recognized even though the year is one of heavy activity. As a result, construction firms may and do recognize revenue on a **percentage-of-completion basis.** Under this basis, for example, if a firm has incurred 40% of the estimated cost to complete a job, it may recognize 40% of the job's contract price as revenue.

Space does not permit a full discussion of the cash basis and the percentage-of-completion basis of revenue recognition. This must be reserved for a more advanced text.

GLOSSARY

Accounting. The art of recording, classifying, reporting, and interpreting the financial data of an organization.

Accounting concept. An abstract idea that serves as a basis in the interpretation of accounting information.

Accounting equation. An expression in dollar amounts of the equivalency of the assets and equities of an enterprise, usually stated Assets = Liabilities + Owner's equity. Also called a **balance sheet equation.**

Accounting principle. A broad rule adopted by the accounting profession as a guide in measuring, recording, and reporting the financial affairs and activities of a business.

Accounting Standards Authority of Canada. The relatively recently formed, broadly based, committee whose declared aim is to become the independent standard-setting body.

Accounting Standards Committee. The committee of CICA charged with developing recommendations for inclusion in the *CICA Handbook.*

Account payable. A debt owed to a creditor for goods or services purchased on credit.

Account receivable. An amount receivable from a debtor for goods or services sold on credit.

AICPA.   American Institute of Certified Public Accountants, the professional association of certified public accountants in the United States.

APB.   Accounting Principles Board, a committee of the AICPA that was responsible for formulating accounting principles.

Asset.   A property or economic resource owned by an individual or enterprise.

Audit.   A critical exploratory review of the business methods and accounting records of an enterprise, made to enable the auditor to express an opinion as to whether the financial statements of the enterprise fairly reflect its financial position and operating results.

Balance sheet.   A financial report showing the assets, liabilities, and owner's equity of an enterprise on a specific date. Also called a **position statement.**

Balance sheet equation.   Another name for the **accounting equation.**

Bookkeeping.   The record-making phase of accounting.

Budgeting.   The phase of accounting dealing with planning the activities of an enterprise and comparing its actual accomplishments with the plan.

Business entity concept.   The idea that a business is separate and distinct from its owner or owners and from every other business.

Business transaction.   An exchange of goods, services, money, and/or the right to collect money.

Capital stock.   Ownership equity in a corporation represented by transferable certificates showing shares of ownership.

CGA–Canada.   Certified General Accountants' Association of Canada.

CICA.   Canadian Institute of Chartered Accountants.

Continuing-concern concept.   The idea that a business is a going concern that will continue to operate, using its assets to carry on its operations and, with the exception of merchandise, not offering the assets for sale.

Controller.   The chief accounting officer of a large business.

Corporation.   A business incorporated under the provincial or federal laws.

Cost accounting.   The phase of accounting that deals with collecting and controlling the costs of producing a given product or service.

Cost principle.   The accounting rule that requires assets and services plus any resulting liabilities to be taken into the accounting records at cost.

Creditor.   A person or enterprise to whom a debt is owed.

Debtor.   A person or enterprise that owes a debt.

Equity.   A right, claim, or interest in property.

Expense.   Goods or services consumed in operating an enterprise.

FASB.   Financial Accounting Standards Board, the seven-member board that currently has the authority to formulate and issue pronouncements of generally accepted accounting principles.

General accounting.   That phase of accounting dealing primarily with recording transactions, processing the recorded data, and preparing financial statements.

Going-concern concept. Another name for the **continuing-concern concept.**

Income statement. A financial statement showing revenues earned by a business, the expenses incurred in earning the revenues, and the resulting net income or net loss.

Internal auditing. A continuing examination of the records and procedures of a business by its own internal audit staff to determine if established procedures and management directives are being followed.

Liability. A debt owed.

Management advisory services. The phase of public accounting dealing with the design, installation, and improvement of a client's accounting system, plus advice on planning, budgeting, forecasting, and all other phases of accounting.

Net assets. Assets minus liabilities.

Net income. The excess of revenues over expenses.

Net loss. The excess of expenses over revenues.

Objectivity principle. The accounting rule requiring that wherever possible the amounts used in recording transactions be based on objective evidence rather than on subjective judgments.

Owner's equity. The equity of the owner (or owners) of a business in the assets of the business.

Partnership. An association of two or more persons to co-own and operate a business for profit.

Position statement. Another name for the **balance sheet.**

Price-level-adjusted statements. Financial statements showing item amounts adjusted for changes in the purchasing power of money.

Public accountant. An accountant who has met requirements as to age, education, experience, residence, and moral character and is licensed to practice public accounting.

Realization principle. The accounting rule that defines a revenue as an inflow of assets, not necessarily cash, in exchange for goods or services and requires the revenue to be recognized at the time, but not before, it is earned.

Recognition principle. Another name for the **realization principle.**

Revenue. An inflow of assets, not necessarily cash, in exchange for goods and services sold.

Shareholder. A person or enterprise owning a share or shares of stock in a corporation. Also called a **stockholder.**

Single proprietorship. A business owned by one individual.

SMA. Society of Management Accountants.

Stable-dollar concept. The idea that the purchasing power of the unit of measure used in accounting, the dollar, does not change.

Stockholder. Another name for a **shareholder.**

Tax services. The phase of public accounting dealing with the preparation of tax returns and with advice as to how transactions may be completed in a way as to incur the smallest tax liability.

QUESTIONS FOR CLASS DISCUSSION

1. What is the nature of accounting and what is its function?
2. How does a business executive use accounting information?
3. Why do the provinces license public accountants?
4. What is the purpose of an audit? What do public accountants do when they make an audit?
5. A public accountant may provide management advisory services. Of what does this consist?
6. What do the tax services of a professional accountant include beyond preparing tax returns?
7. Differentiate between accounting and bookkeeping.
8. What does an income statement show?
9. As the word is used in accounting, what is a revenue? An expense?
10. Why is the period of time covered by an income statement of extreme significance?
11. What does a balance sheet show?
12. Define *(a)* asset, *(b)* liability, *(c)* equity, and *(d)* owner's equity.
13. Why is a business treated as a separate entity for accounting purposes?
14. What is required by the cost principle? Why is such a principle necessary?
15. Why are not balance sheet amounts for the assets of a business changed from time to time to reflect changes in market values?
16. A business shows office stationery on its balance sheet at its $50 cost, although the stationery can be sold for not more than $0.25 as scrap paper. What accounting principles and concept justify this?
17. In accounting, transactions are measured, recorded, and reported in terms of dollars and the dollar is assumed to be a stable unit of measure. Is the dollar a stable unit of measure?
18. What are generally accepted accounting principles?
19. Why are the recommendations of the *CICA Handbook* of importance to accounting students?
20. How does separate legal entity affect the responsibility of a corporation's shareholders for the debts of the corporation? Does this responsibility or lack of responsibility for the debts of the business apply to the owner or owners of a single proprietorship or partnership business?

21. What is the balance sheet equation? What is its importance to accounting students?

22. Is it possible for a transaction to increase or decrease a single liability without affecting any other asset, liability, or owner's equity item?

23. In accounting, what does the realization principle require?

MULTIPLE CHOICE

1. The continuing-concern concept states that:
    a. A selected accounting method or procedure should be applied period after period.
    b. The life of a business is divisible into time periods of equal length.
    c. The purchasing power of the unit of measure used in accounting, the dollar, does not change.
    d. A business is a going company that will continue to operate, using its assets to carry on its operations.
    e. A business is separate and distinct from its owner or owners and from every other business.

2. The accounting rule that defines a revenue as an inflow of assets, not necessarily cash, in exchange for goods or services and requires the revenue to be recognized at the time, but not before it is earned, is the:
    a. Going-concern concept.
    b. Materiality principle.
    c. Realization principle.
    d. Objectivity principle.
    e. Stable-dollar concept.

3. The objectivity principle requires:
    a. That assets and services plus any resulting liabilities be taken into the accounting records at cost.
    b. That revenue be recognized at the time, but not before it is earned.
    c. That wherever possible the amounts used in recording transactions be based on objective evidence rather than on subjective judgments.
    d. That all expenses incurred in earning a revenue be deducted from the revenue in determining net income.
    e. That financial statements and their accompanying notes disclose all information of a material nature relating to the financial position and operating results of the company for which they were prepared.

4. The cost principle:
    a. States that a strict adherence to any accounting principle is not required when adherence is relatively difficult or expensive and lack of adherence will not materially affect reported net income.
    b. Requires that wherever possible the amounts used in recording transactions be based on objective evidence rather than on subjective judgments.
    c. States that all expenses incurred in earning a revenue be deducted from the revenue in determining net income.
    d. Requires assets and services plus any resulting liabilities to be taken into the accounting records at cost.
    e. Requires accountants to be conservative in their estimates and opinions.

5. The going-concern concept is:
    a. Another name for the realization principle.
    b. The idea that a business is a continuing enterprise that will continue to operate.
    c. The idea that the purchasing power of the unit of measure used in accounting, the dollar, does not change.
    d. The idea that a business is separate and distinct from its owner or owners and from every other business.
    e. The idea that the life of a business is divisible into time periods of equal length.

6. Revenue is recognized in most businesses:
    a. When the customer's order is received.
    b. When the production process is complete.
    c. Periodically throughout the production process.
    d. Upon completion of the sale or when services have been performed and are billable.
    e. When cash from a sale is received.

7. An expense is:
    a. Reduction in the marked selling price of an item.
    b. A right, claim, or interest in property.
    c. Goods or services consumed in operating an enterprise.
    d. A property or economic resource owned by an individual or enterprise.
    e. A negative amount of retained earnings.

8. A revenue is:
    a. An intangible asset.
    b. A property or economic resource owned by an individual or enterprise.

c.   An inflow of assets, not necessarily cash, in exchange for goods and services sold.

d.   A debt owed.

e.   A right, claim, or interest in property.

9.   If a parcel of land is offered for sale at $45,000, assessed for tax purposes at $20,000, recognized by its purchasers as easily being worth $36,000, and purchased for $34,000, the land should be recorded in the purchaser's books at:

a. $20,000.

b. $34,000.

c. $36,000.

d. $45,000.

e.   Some other amount.

10.   If the assets of a business increased $15,000 during a period of time and its liabilities increased $6,000 during the same period, owner's equity in the business must have:

a.   Increased $9,000.

b.   Decreased $9,000.

c.   Increased $21,000.

d.   Decreased $21,000.

e.   Changed by some other amount.

MINI DISCUSSION CASES

Case 1–1

In order to realize a lifelong dream, Catherine Swazzee decides to open a video and audio rental and sales business. Catherine worked for such a business on a part-time basis while attending school and learned much about the operation of such a business. However, she needs help setting up the business—especially with determining available sources of financing because her own resources are insufficient to provide for all the necessary assets.

Required:

Prepare for Catherine a possible balance sheet that will show the necessary assets to start the business and the proposed sources of these assets. Support your proposal.

Case 1–2

Studies indicate that 50% of small businesses fail within the first two years of their life. These studies also indicate that the failure rate would be substantially reduced if serious planning preceded the starting of a business.

Required:

Discuss the type of preplanning indicated by the balance sheet and income statement.

Case 1-3   James Haddad located a business he was interested in and started negotiations with the owner, Caspar Fitz, for its purchase. Fitz supplied Haddad with a balance sheet. The balance sheet, which Fitz had prepared personally, listed four assets, two liabilities, and the owner's capital account. The listed assets were cash, accounts receivable, merchandise, and building and equipment.

The purchase was completed, and James Haddad took over with satisfaction and enthusiasm. Sales the first month of operations were up to Haddad's expectation. But prior to the end of the month, Haddad received a disturbing letter from Millie Fitz, which he turned over to a lawyer. A couple of days later he learned from the lawyer that Millie Fitz was indeed the sole owner of the building. Haddad was certain he had purchased the building since it was listed on the balance sheet Caspar Fitz had given him.

Required:

Discuss the GAAP applicable to the situation and what Haddad should have done prior to concluding the purchase.

CLASS EXERCISES

Exercise 1-1   On May 31 of the current year, the balance sheet of Ski Shop, a single proprietorship, showed the following:

Cash	1,500
Other assets	40,000
Accounts payable	15,000
Jack Hill, capital	26,500

On that date, Jack Hill sold the "Other assets" for $20,000 in preparation for ending and liquidating the business of Ski Shop.

Required:

1. Prepare a balance sheet for the shop as it would appear immediately after the sale of the assets.
2. Tell how the shop's cash should be distributed in ending the business and why.

Exercise 1-2   Determine the missing amount on each of the following lines:

Assets = Liabilities + Owner's equity

	Assets	Liabilities	Owner's equity
a.	$32,600	$8,200	?
b.	28,800	?	$15,300
c.	?	7,200	21,500

Exercise 1-3   The effects of five transactions on the assets, liabilities, and owner's equity of Ted Lee in his law practice are shown in the following equation with each transaction identified by a letter. Write a short sentence or phrase telling the probable nature of each transaction.

	Assets				= Liabilities +	Owner's equity
	Cash +	Accounts receivable +	Law library +	Office equipment =	Accounts payable +	Ted Lee, capital
	$800		$3,500	$8,600		$12,900
a.	−100		+100			
	$700		$3,600	$8,600		$12,900
b.				+300	+$300	
	$700		$3,600	$8,900	$300	$12,900
c.		+$500				+500
	$700	$500	$3,600	$8,900	$300	$13,400
d.	−300				−300	
	$400	$500	$3,600	$8,900	$ 0	$13,400
e.	+500	−500				
	$900 +	$ 0 +	$3,600 +	$8,900 =	$ 0 +	$13,400

Exercise 1–4

Determine:

a. The equity of the owner in a business having $96,800 of assets and $15,200 of liabilities.

b. The liabilities of a business having $72,800 of assets and in which the owner has a $51,400 equity.

c. The assets of a business having $6,300 of liabilities and in which the owner has a $31,600 equity.

Exercise 1–5

On October 1 Dale Beck began a new business, a real estate agency. The following accounting equation of the agency was prepared after it had completed four transactions. Analyze the equation and list the four transactions with their amounts.

Cash +	Office supplies +	Office furniture +	Land and building =	Accounts payable +	Mortgage payable +	Dale Beck, capital
$2,500	$250	$7,500	$100,000	$250	$75,000	$35,000

Exercise 1–6

A business had the following assets and liabilities at the beginning and at the end of a year:

	Assets	Liabilities
Beginning of the year	$65,000	$20,000
End of the year	75,000	10,000

Determine the net income or net loss of the business during the year under each of the following unrelated assumptions:

a. The owner of the business made no additional investments in the business and no withdrawals of assets from the business during the year.

b. The owner made no additional investments in the business during the year but had withdrawn $1,500 per month to pay personal living expenses.

c. During the year, the owner had made no withdrawals but had made a $25,000 additional investment in the business.

d. The owner had withdrawn $2,000 from the business each month to pay personal living expenses and near the year-end had invested an additional $10,000 in the business.

Exercise 1–7   Jane Ball began the practice of dentistry and during a short period completed these transactions:

a. Invested $8,000 in cash and dental equipment having a $2,000 fair value in a dental practice.

b. Paid the rent on suitable office space for two months in advance, $1,500.

c. Purchased additional dental equipment on credit, $5,500.

d. Completed dental work for a patient and immediately collected $100 cash for the work.

e. Completed dental work for a patient on credit, $600.

f. Purchased additional dental equipment for cash, $400.

g. Paid the dental assistant's wages, $300.

h. Collected $200 of the amount owed by the patient of transaction (e).

i. Paid for the equipment purchased in transaction (c).

Required:

Arrange the following asset, liability, and owner's equity titles in an equation form like Illustration 1–7: Cash; Accounts receivable; Prepaid rent; Dental equipment; Accounts payable; and Jane Ball, Capital. Then show by additions and subtractions the effects of the transactions on the elements of the equation. Show new totals after each transaction.

Exercise 1–8   On October 1 of the current year, Sue Davis began the practice of law. On October 31, her records showed the following asset, liability, and owner's equity items including revenue earned and expenses. From the information, prepare an October income statement and a month-end balance sheet like Illustration 1–2. Head the statements Sue Davis, Lawyer. (The October 31, $3,500 amount of Sue's capital is the amount of her capital after it was increased and decreased by the October revenue and expenses.)

Cash	$ 400	Sue Davis, capital	$3,500
Accounts receivable	200	Legal fees earned	2,300
Prepaid rent	500	Rent expense	500
Law library	2,500	Salaries expense	800
Accounts payable	100	Telephone expense	50

Exercise 1–9   List a transaction for each of the following that will:

a. Increase an asset and decrease an asset.

b. Increase an asset and increase a liability.

c. Decrease an asset and decrease a liability.

d. Decrease a liability and increase a liability.

e. Increase an asset and increase owner equity.

f. Decrease an asset and decrease owner equity.

PROBLEMS

Problem 1–1

June Cole, Public Accountant, began a public accounting practice and during a short period completed these transactions:

a. Sold for $36,450 a personal investment in IBM stock and deposited $35,000 of the proceeds in a bank account opened in the name of the practice.

b. Purchased for $90,000 a small building to be used as an office. She paid $30,000 in cash and signed a mortgage contract promising to pay the balance over a period of years.

c. Took office equipment from home for use in the practice. The equipment had a $400 fair value.

d. Purchased office supplies for cash, $250.

e. Purchased office equipment on credit, $5,000.

f. Completed accounting work for a client and immediately collected $100 for the work done.

g. Paid a local newspaper $50 for a small notice of the opening of the practice.

h. Completed $750 of accounting work for a client on credit.

i. Made a $500 installment payment on the equipment purchased in transaction (e).

j. The client of transaction (h) paid $500 of the amount he owed.

k. Paid the office secretary's wages, $400.

l. June Cole withdrew $250 from the bank account of the practice to pay personal living expenses.

Required:

1. Arrange the following asset, liability, and owner's equity titles in an equation like Illustration 1–7: Cash; Accounts Receivable; Office Supplies; Office Equipment; Building; Accounts Payable; Mortgage Payable; and June Cole, Capital.

2. Show by additions and subtractions the effects of each transaction on the elements of the equation. Show new totals after each addition or subtraction, as in Illustration 1–7.

Problem 1–2

Jed Hill began a new law practice and completed these transactions during June of the current year:

June 1 Transferred $5,000 from his personal savings account to a chequing account opened in the name of the law practice, Jed Hill, Lawyer.

1 Rented the furnished office of a lawyer who was retiring, and paid cash for three months' rent in advance, $1,500.

1 Purchased the law library of the retiring lawyer for $3,000, paying $1,000 in cash and agreeing to pay the balance in one year.

2 Purchased office supplies for cash, $50.

June 8 Completed legal work for a client and immediately collected $150 in cash for the work done.
9 Purchased law books on credit, $300.
14 Completed legal work for Guaranty Bank on credit, $750.
18 Purchased office supplies on credit, $25.
19 Paid for the law books purchased on June 9.
22 Completed legal work for Apex Realty on credit, $1,000.
24 Received $750 from Guaranty Bank for the work completed on June 14.
30 Paid the office secretary's salary, $950.
30 Paid the monthly utility bills, $80.
30 Recognized that one month's rent on the office had expired and become an expense. (Reduce the prepaid rent and the owner's equity.)
30 Took an inventory of unused office supplies and determined that $25 of supplies had been used and had become an expense.

Required:

1. Arrange the following asset, liability, and owner's equity titles in an equation like Illustration 1–7: Cash; Accounts Receivable; Prepaid Rent; Office Supplies; Law Library; Accounts Payable; and Jed Hill, Capital.
2. Show by additions and subtractions the effects of each transaction on the items of the equation. Show new totals after each transaction.
3. Prepare for the law practice a June 30 balance sheet like Illustration 1–2.
4. Analyze the increases and decreases in the last column of the equation and prepare a June income statement for the practice.

Problem 1–3   The records of Terry Blue, Realtor, show the following assets and liabilities as of the ends of 1986 and 1987:

	December 31	
	1986	*1987*
Cash	$1,200	$ 600
Accounts receivable	800	400
Prepaid rent	600	
Office supplies	200	100
Prepaid insurance	800	1,500
Office equipment	5,200	6,800
Land		25,000
Building		85,000
Accounts payable	500	700
Note payable		10,000
Mortgage payable		75,000

During the last week of December 1987, Mr. Blue purchased in the name of the business, Terry Blue, Realtor, a small office building and moved the business from rented quarters to the new building. The building and the land it occupied cost $110,000. The business paid $35,000 in cash and assumed a mortgage liability for the balance. Mr. Blue had to borrow $10,000 in the name of the business, signing a $10,000 note payable, and invest an additional $20,000 in the business to enable it to pay the $35,000. The business earned a satisfactory net income during 1987, which enabled Mr. Blue to withdraw $2,000 per month from the business to pay personal living expenses.

Required:

1. Prepare balance sheets like Illustration 1–2 for the business as of the ends of 1986 and 1987.
2. Prepare a calculation to show the net income earned by the business during 1987.

Problem 1–4

Ned Hall graduated from the university in June of the current year with a degree in architecture and on July 1 began the practice of his profession by investing $3,000 in a business he called Ned Hall, Architect. He then completed these transactions.

July 1   Rented the furnished office and equipment of an architect who was retiring, paying $1,800 cash for three months' rent in advance.

    1   Purchased drafting supplies for cash, $75.

    2   Purchased insurance protection for one year in advance for cash by paying the premium on two policies, $600.

    5   Completed architectural work for a client and immediately collected $250 cash for the work done.

    8   Completed architectural work for Valley Realty on credit, $750.

   15   Paid the salary of the draftsman, $500.

   18   Received payment in full for the work completed for Valley Realty on July 8.

   19   Completed architectural work for Western Contractors on credit, $800.

   20   Purchased additional drafting supplies on credit, $25.

   23   Completed architectural work for Dale West on credit, $600.

   27   Purchased additional drafting supplies on credit, $50.

   29   Received payment in full from Western Contractors for the work completed on July 19.

   30   Paid for the drafting supplies purchased on July 20.

   31   Paid the July telephone bill, $25.

   31   Paid the July utilities expense, $65.

   31   Paid the salary of the draftsman, $500.

   31   Recognized that one month's office rent had expired and had become an expense. (Reduce the prepaid rent and owner's equity to record the expense.)

   31   Recognized that one month's prepaid insurance, $50 had expired.

   31   Took an inventory of drafting supplies and determined that $60 of drafting supplies had been used and had become an expense.

Required:

1. Arrange the following asset, liability, and owner's equity titles in an equation like Illustration 1–7: Cash; Accounts Receivable; Prepaid Rent; Prepaid Insurance; Drafting Supplies; Accounts Payable; and Ned Hall, Capital.
2. Show the effects of the transactions on the elements of the equation by recording increases and decreases in the appropriate columns. Indicate an increase with a + and a decrease with a − before the amount. *Do not determine new totals for the items of the equation after each transaction.*
3. After recording the last transaction, determine and insert on the next line the final total for each item of the equation and then determine if the equation is in balance.
4. Prepare a July 31 balance sheet for the practice like the one in Illustration 1–2. Head the statement Ned Hall, Architect.
5. Analyze the items in the last column of the equation and prepare a July income statement for the practice.

ALTERNATE PROBLEMS

Problem 1–1A   June Cole secured her broker's license and opened a real estate office. During a short period she completed these transactions:

a. Sold for $31,250 a personal investment in General Electric stock, which she had inherited, and deposited $30,000 of the proceeds in a bank account opened in the name of the business, June Cole, Realtor.
b. Purchased for $80,000 a small building to be used as an office. She paid $25,000 in cash and signed a mortgage contract promising to pay the balance over a period of years.
c. Purchased office equipment for cash, $800.
d. Took from home for use in the business office equipment having a $350 fair value.
e. Purchased on credit office supplies, $50, and office equipment, $3,600.
f. Paid the local paper $110 for advertising.
g. Completed a real estate appraisal for a client on credit and billed the client $125 for the work done.
h. Sold a house and collected a $5,000 cash commission on completion of the sale.
i. June Cole withdrew $1,000 from the business to pay personal expenses.
j. The client paid for the appraisal of transaction (g).
k. Made a $2,000 installment payment on the amount owed from transaction (e).
l. Paid the office secretary's wages, $850.

Required:

1. Arrange the following asset, liability, and owner's equity titles in an equation like Illustration 1–7: Cash; Accounts Receivable; Office Supplies; Office Equipment; Building; Accounts Payable; Mortgage Payable; and June Cole, Capital.
2. Show by additions and subtractions, as in Illustration 1–7, the effects of each transaction on the elements of the equation. Show new totals after each transaction.

Problem 1–2A   Jed Hill graduated from law school in June of the current year and on July 1 began a law practice by investing $3,000 in cash in the practice. He completed these additional transactions during July.

July 1 Rented the furnished office of a lawyer who was retiring and paid two month's rent in advance, $1,200.
      1 Moved law books acquired at university from home to the law office. (In other words, invested the books in the practice.) The books had a $400 fair value.
      2 Purchased office supplies for cash, $60.
      3 Purchased additional law books costing $1,000. Paid $500 in cash and promised to pay the balance within 90 days.
      6 Completed legal work for a client and immediately collected $250 for the work done.

July 12   Completed legal work for Valley Bank on credit, $750.
      16   Purchased additional office supplies on credit, $25.
      22   Received $750 from Valley Bank for the work completed on July 12.
      26   Completed legal work for Vista Realty on credit, $650.
      30   Made $200 installment payment on the law books purchased on July 3.
      31   Paid the July telephone bill, $40.
      31   Paid the office secretary's wages, $950.
      31   Recognized that one month's rent on the office had expired and had become an expense. (Reduce the prepaid rent and the owner's equity.)
      31   Took an inventory of unused office supplies and determined that $35 of supplies had been used and had become an expense.

Required:

1.   Arrange the following asset, liability, and owner's equity titles in an equation like Illustration 1–7: Cash; Accounts Receivable; Prepaid Rent; Office Supplies; Law Library; Accounts Payable; and Jed Hill, Capital.
2.   Show by additions and subtractions the effects of each transaction on the elements of the equation. Show new totals after each transaction.
3.   Prepare a July 31 balance sheet for the law practice. Head the statement Jed Hill, Lawyer.
4.   Analyze the items in the last column of the equation and prepare a July income statement for the practice.

Problem 1–3A   The accounting records of Maria Gomez's dental practice show the following assets and liabilities as of the ends of 1986 and 1987:

	December 31	
	1986	*1987*
Cash	$ 1,200	$ 700
Accounts receivable	2,900	3,500
Prepaid rent	900	
Office supplies	500	400
Prepaid insurance	600	1,500
Office equipment	12,200	14,100
Land		40,000
Building		110,000
Accounts payable	700	800
Note payable		10,000
Mortgage payable		100,000

During the last week of December 1987, Dr. Gomez purchased a small office building in the name of the dental practice, Maria Gomez, DDS, and moved her practice from rented quarters to the new building. The building and the land it occupies cost $150,000; the practice paid $50,000 in cash and assumed a mortgage liability for the balance. Dr. Gomez had to borrow $10,000 in the name of the practice, signing a $10,000 note payable, and invest an additional $25,000 in the practice to enable it to pay the $50,000. The practice earned a satisfactory net income during 1987, which enabled Dr. Gomez to withdraw $2,000 per month from the practice to pay her personal living expenses.

Required:

1. Prepare balance sheets like Illustration 1–2 for the practice as of the ends of 1986 and 1987.
2. Prepare a calculation to show the amount of net income earned by the practice during 1987.

Problem 1–4A Ned Hall graduated from college, completed his internship, and on May 1 of the current year began an architectural practice by investing $3,000 in the practice. He then completed these additional transactions:

May 1 Rented the office and equipment of an architect who was retiring, paying $1,500 cash for two months' rent in advance.
1 Purchased insurance protection for one year by paying the premium on two policies, $660.
2 Purchased drafting supplies for cash, $60.
5 Completed a short architectural assignment for a client and immediately collected $200 cash for the work done.
8 Purchased additional drafting supplies on credit, $40.
10 Completed architectural work for Ajax Contractors on credit, $700.
15 Paid the salary of the draftsman, $600.
18 Paid for the drafting supplies purchased on July 8.
20 Received payment in full from Ajax Contractors for the work completed on July 10.
23 Completed architectural work for Valley Realtors on credit, $550.
26 Purchased additional drafting supplies on credit, $30.
30 Completed additional architectural work for Ajax Contractors on credit, $725.
31 Paid the salary of the draftsman, $600.
31 Paid the July telephone bill, $25.
31 Paid the July electric bill, $70.
31 Recognized that one month's office rent had expired and become an expense. (Reduce the prepaid rent and the owner's equity to record the expense.)
31 Recognized that one month's prepaid insurance, $55, had expired.
31 Took an inventory of the unused drafting supplies and determined that supplies costing $50 had been used and had become an expense.

Required:

1. Arrange the following asset, liability, and owner's equity titles in an equation like Illustration 1–7: Cash; Accounts Receivable; Prepaid Rent; Prepaid Insurance; Drafting Supplies; Accounts Payable; and Ned Hall, Capital.
2. Show the effects of the transactions on the elements of the equation by recording increases and decreases in the appropriate columns. Indicate an increase with a + and a decrease with a − before the amount. *Do not determine new totals for the items after each transaction.*
3. After recording the last transaction, determine and enter on the next line the final total for each item and determine if the equation is in balance.
4. Prepare a May 31 balance sheet for the practice like the one in Illustration 1–2. Head the statement Ned Hall, Architect.
5. Analyze the items in the last column of the equation and prepare a May income statement for the practice.

PROVOCATIVE PROBLEMS

Provocative Problem 1–1, County Fair Stand

Gary West invested $750 in a short-term enterprise, the sale of soft drinks during the county fair in his small rural town. He paid $150 for the right to sell soft drinks in the fair grounds. He constructed a stand from which to make the sales at a cost of $50 for lumber and crepe paper, none of which had any value at the end of the fair. He bought ice for which he paid $40 and purchased soft drinks costing $750. At this point, he had only $510 in cash and could not pay in full for the drinks, but since his credit rating was good, the soft drink company accepted $500 in cash and the promise that he would pay the balance the day after the fair ended. During the fair, he collected $1,540 in cash from sales, and at the end of the fair, he paid a young man $90 for helping with the sales. He had soft drinks left over that cost $35 and could be returned to the soft drink company.

Assemble the information in such a way that will enable you to prepare a balance sheet like Illustration 1–2 for Gary West as of the end of the fair. Also prepare an income statement showing the net income or loss of the enterprise. Assume the fair lasted three days, ending on July 15 of the current year.

Provocative Problem 1–2, Jack's Delivery Service

Jack Ives ran out of money at the end of the first semester of his sophomore year in college. He had to go to work, but he could not find a satisfactory job. However, since he had a motorcycle having a $2,400 fair value, he decided to go into business for himself. Consequently, he began Jack's Delivery Service with no assets other than the motorcycle. He kept no accounting records; and now, at the year-end, he has engaged you to determine the net income earned by the service during its first partial year of 42 weeks. You find that the service has a $700 year-end bank balance plus $50 of undeposited cash. Local stores owe the service $125 for delivering packages during the past month. The service still owns the motorcycle, but its fair value has declined by one fourth due to use in the business. In addition, the service has a new delivery truck that cost $6,800, but that has depreciated $400 through use since its purchase. The service still owes a finance company $4,000 as a result of the truck's purchase. Also, when the truck was purchased, Jack borrowed $1,500 from his father to help make the down payment. The loan was made to the delivery service, was interest free, and has not been repaid. Finally, since the service has been profitable from the beginning, Jack Ives has withdrawn $200 of its earnings each week for the 42 weeks of its existence to pay personal living expenses.

Determine and present a calculation to prove the net income earned by the business during the 42 weeks of its operations.

ANALYTICAL AND REVIEW PROBLEMS

**Problem 1–1
A&R**

Hugh Hope began his Auto-Repair Shop early this month. The balance sheet, prepared by an inexperienced part-time bookkeeper is shown below:

HOPE AUTO-REPAIR SHOP
Balance Sheet
November 30, 1987

Assets		Liabilities and Owner's Equity	
Cash	$ 1,000	Parts and supplies	$ 3,000
Accounts payable	6,000	Accounts receivable	3,000
Building	4,000	Land	1,000
Hugh Hope, capital	3,000	Automotive equipment	2,000
		Mortgage payable	5,000
	$14,000		$14,000

Required:

1. Prepare a correct balance sheet.
2. Explain why the incorrect balance sheet can also be in balance.

**Problem 1–2
A&R**

An analysis of the cash, accounts payable, and capital accounts of Townsend Service for the month of October shows the following:

Cash accounts:
    Beginning balance .... nil
    Joan Townsend, investment $11,000
    Rental payment for October 500
    Automobile purchased 8,000
    Services rendered 2,000
    Wages paid 1,000
    Payment to Townsend 200
Accounts payable account:
    Beginning balance .... nil
    Office supplies purchased .... $ 300
Joan Townsend capital:
    Beginning balance .... nil
    Investment $11,000
    Services rendered 2,000
    Wages paid 1,000
    Withdrawal 200

Required:

1. Describe all the transactions that have occurred in the month of October for Townsend Service as described in the above accounts.
2. Compute the balance for **all** the accounts that should appear on the balance sheet at October 31.
3. Prepare a balance sheet as of October 31.

**Problem 1–3
A&R**

John Anderson is the owner of a television repair shop, Quick T-V Service, which has been in operation for some time. The following statements summarize the shop's operations for October, 198A.

QUICK T-V SERVICE
Income Statement
For the Month of October, 198A

Revenues:
Service fees	$6,000	
Accounts payable	2,000	
Accounts receivable	300	$8,300
Operating expenses:		
Rent expense	$ 900	
Utility and telephone expense	200	
Repair parts and supplies	6,000	7,100
Net income		$1,200

Balance Sheet
October 31, 198A

Assets		Owner's Equity	
Cash	$ 500	John Anderson,	
Repair parts and supplies		capital	$4,600
expense	1,350		
Salaries expense	2,550		
Salaries payable	200		
	$4,600		$4,600

Required:

Prepare corrected income statement and balance sheet for October.

Problem 1–4
A&R
The following notes are excerpted from the financial statements of two companies headquartered in Canada:

> The consolidated financial statements have been prepared by management following accounting policies generally accepted in Canada. Except as indicated in Note 19(a), they are also in conformity, in all material respects, with accounting policies generally accepted in the United States. The consolidated financial statements are presented in U.S. dollars. This currency best reflects the economic environment in which the Company operates and provides for a more meaningful measurement of operating results in consideration of the international scope of its operations. Such presentation also affords a better basis of comparison with major companies in the industry, the larger of which are U.S. based and report their results in U.S. dollars.

and

> The consolidated financial statements have been prepared by management on a historical cost basis in accordance with Canadian generally accepted accounting principles consistently applied and conform in all material respects with International Accounting Standards.

Required:

1. Are there differences between the generally accepted accounting principles or accounting policies in Canada and the United States? May there be differences with the International Accounting Standards? If yes, what in your opinion may account for differences?
2. Do you believe disclosure of any differences is desirable? Why?

PRACTICE SET

MY OWN COMPANY

My Own Company is a practice set designed to give you, the student, an opportunity to simulate the necessary steps involved in:

a. Starting a business.
b. Recording and processing financial data through the accounting cycle.
c. Designing an accounting system for an expanded business.

The focus initially is on the importance of research that must precede any business undertaking. This research must provide answers to questions implicit in the "Planning Chart" illustrated below. Steps in starting a business and completing this project are as follows.

Step 1 Preliminary screening and refinement of ideas and alternatives.
Step 2 Narrow down the types of businesses you are interested in. Prepare a short list of possibilities based on interest and knowledge acquired through work experience, observation, education, and so on.

To limit the number of alternatives to be considered, assume that:

a. Your search for an existing business was fruitless.
b. You did, however, obtain leads on available property suitable for a new beginning.
c. The property is available on a purchase basis.
d. The types of businesses you are considering are:
    (1) A boutique.
    (2) A restaurant/lounge.
    (3) A sports and health equipment store.
    (4) A video rental and record shop.
    (5) Any other business approved by your instructor.

Step 3 Determine the market potential and the necessary strategy to exploit that potential.
Step 4 Prepare a detailed list of resources and quantities required to open up your business. This list will include cash, supplies, inventory, prepayments (e.g., insurance), equipment, building, and so on.
Step 5 Decide how to acquire the assets (resources) determined in Step 4 (e.g., purchase for cash, purchase on a time plan, and

Planning Chart

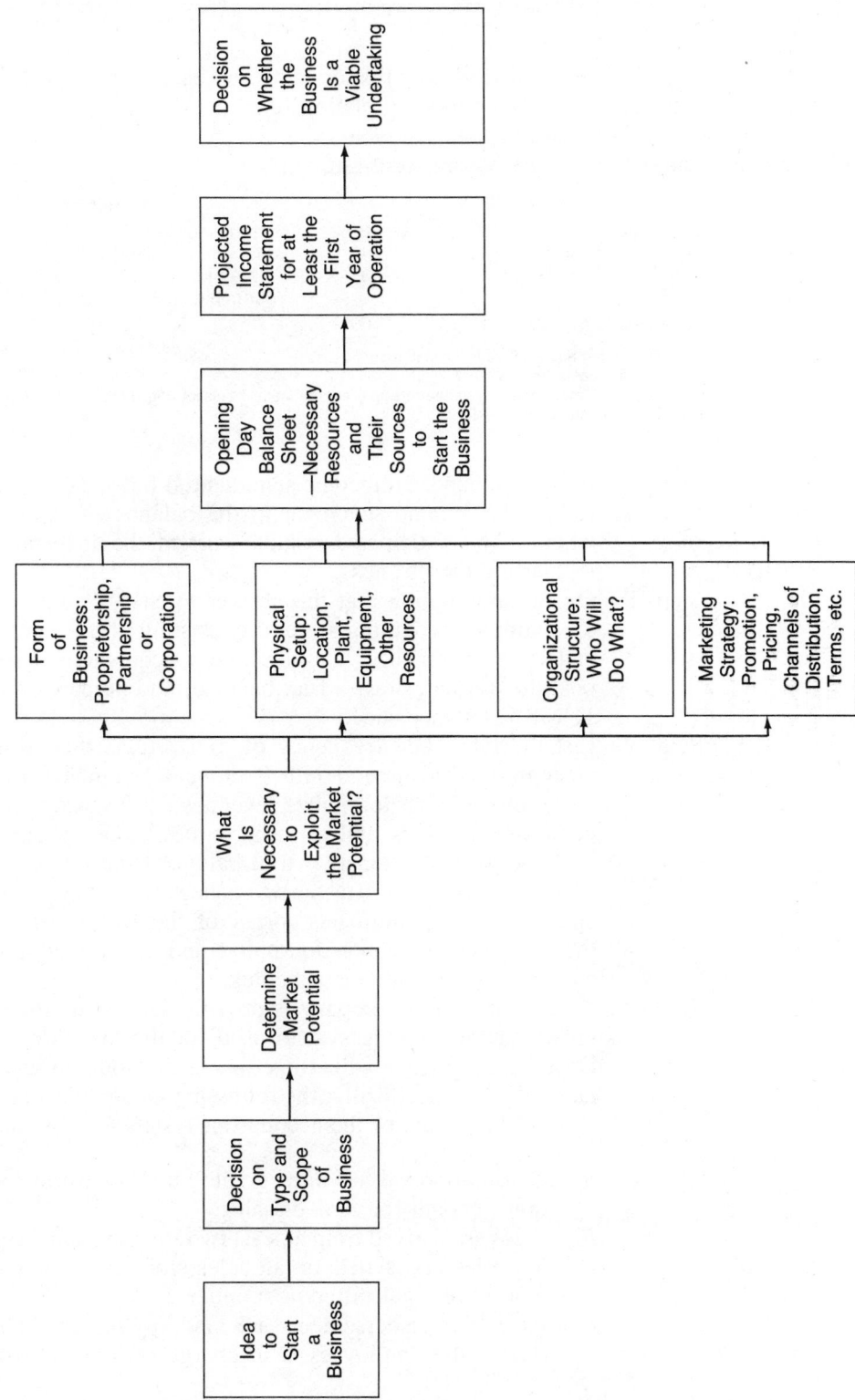

so on) and assume that opening day balance sheet will approximate the following relationships:

October 1, 198A

Assets		Liabilities	
Cash	25%	Current liabilities	20%
Other current assets	40	Long-term liabilities†	
Equipment and buildings*	35	12% mortgage	30
		Your capital	50
Total assets	100%		100%

* Equipment has a 10-year estimated service life.
  Building has a 25-year service life.
  † The 12% mortgage is payable in equal annual installments of one tenth of original amount plus interest on the outstanding balance.

Step 6   Project an expected income statement(s) for one or more years.

Step 7   Relate the income statement to the balance sheet and decide whether the anticipated results warrant the investment, that is, starting the business.

Step 8   On the assumption that the answer to Step 7 is positive, set up a simple accounting system, consisting of a general journal and ledger. Journalize your investment, acquisition of the assets, post the journal, draw a trial balance, and prepare an October 1, 198A, balance sheet.

Step 9   List the types and frequency of transactions that would take place in the first three months (October–December). Journalize these transactions. Journalize revenues (cash sales, rental, etc.) on a weekly basis and all other transactions as they occur. Post the journal. Prepare a trial balance (first two columns of a worksheet). Complete the worksheet (give key to adjusting entries on the bottom left corner of the worksheet). Prepare the financial statements. Journalize and post the adjusting and closing entries. Rule the accounts.

Step 10   Assume that your company is proving successful and has outgrown the accounting system used for the first three months. Design a system that will utilize specialized journals and subsidiary ledgers. Specifically, the following factors must be considered in the design of the accounting system:

    a.   Credit approval has been granted to 100 customers. They now account for 40% of sales.

    b.   Sales are derived from at least two sources, and the prevailing sales tax is 10% on all sales and service revenue.

    c.   You have eight different suppliers.

    d.   All major disbursements are made by cheque. Therefore one of the employees is in charge of a petty cash fund.

Step 11   Repeat Step 9. The period is January 1, 19B, through March
          31, 19B. You should have a *minimum* of eight typical transac-
          tions journalized in each of the specialized journals. Assume
          that cash revenues are journalized weekly as are wages and
          salaries.

Assignment schedule:

1. Steps 1 through 5 should be completed within the first month of
    beginning of course.
2. Steps 6 and 7 should be completed within one week of completion
    of Step 5 and after completion of Chapter 5.
3. Steps 8 through 11 should be completed at the rate of 1 step per
    week.

Processing Accounting Data

PART TWO

Recording Transactions

2

After studying Chapter 2, you should be able to:

Explain the mechanics of double-entry accounting and tell why transactions are recorded with equal debits and credits.

State the rules of debit and credit and apply the rules in recording transactions.

Tell the normal balance of any asset, liability, or owner's equity account.

Record transactions in a General Journal, post to the ledger accounts, and prepare a trial balance to test the accuracy of the recording and posting.

Define or explain the words and phrases listed in the chapter Glossary.

Transactions are the raw material of the accounting process. The process consists of identifying transactions, recording them, and summarizing their effects in periodic reports for the use of management and other decision makers.

Some years ago, almost all companies used pen and ink to manually record and process the data resulting from transactions. Today, only very small companies use this method, companies small enough that their accounting can be done by one person working an hour or two each day. Larger, modern companies use electric bookkeeping machines and computers in recording transactions and in processing the recorded data.

Nevertheless, students normally begin their study of accounting by learning to process accounting data manually with a pen or pencil. By manually processing the data, students can more readily understand the data and the relationships between its parts. Also, almost everything learned through manual methods is applicable to machine and computer methods. Actually, the machines and computer equipment replace pen and ink in processing the data, speeding the work, and taking the drudgery out of the processing.

BUSINESS PAPERS

Business papers provide evidence of transactions completed and are the basis for accounting entries to record the transactions. For example, when goods are sold on credit, two or more copies of an invoice or sales ticket are prepared. One copy is enclosed with the goods or is delivered to the customer. The other is sent to the accounting department where it becomes the basis for an entry to record the sale. Also, when goods are sold for cash, the sales are commonly "rung up" on a cash register that prints the amount of each sale on a paper tape locked inside the register. At the end of the day, when the proper key is depressed, the register prints on the tape the total cash sales for the day. The tape is then removed and becomes the basis for an entry to record the sales. Also, when an established business purchases assets, it normally buys on credit and receives an invoice that becomes the basis for an entry to record the purchase. Likewise, when the invoice is paid, a cheque is issued and the cheque or a carbon copy becomes the basis for an entry to record the payment. Obviously, then, business papers are the starting point in the accounting process. Furthermore, verifiable business papers, particularly those originating outside the business, are also objective evidence of transactions completed and the amounts at which they should be recorded, as required by the **objectivity principle.**

ACCOUNTS

A company with an accounting system based on pen and ink or electric bookkeeping machines uses *accounts* in recording its transactions. A number of accounts are normally required. A separate account is used for summarizing the increases and decreases in each asset, liability, and owner's equity item appearing on the balance sheet and each revenue and expense appearing on the income statement.

In its most simple form, an account looks like the letter "T," is called a *T-account,* and appears as follows:

(Place for the Name of the Item Recorded in This Account)

(Left side)	(Right side)

Note that the "T" gives the account a left side, a right side, and a place for the name of the item, the increases and decreases of which are recorded therein.

When a T-account is used in recording increases and decreases in an item, the increases are placed on one side of the account and the decreases on the other. For example, if the increases and decreases in the cash of Larry Owen's law practice of the previous chapter are recorded in a T-account, they appear as follows:

Cash

Investment	5,000	Prepayment of rent	900
Legal fee earned	500	Equipment purchase	3,700
Collection of account receivable	1,000	Salary payment	400
		Payment on account payable	100

The reason for putting the increases on one side and the decreases on the other is that this makes it easy to add the increases and then add the decreases. The sum of the decreases may then be subtracted from the sum of the increases to learn how much of the item recorded in the account the company has, owns, or owes. For example, the increases in the cash of the Owen law practice were:

Investment	$5,000
Legal fee earned	500
Collection of an account receivable ...	1,000
Sum of the increases	$6,500

And the decreases were:

Prepayment of office rent . . . . $ 900
Equipment purchase   3,700
Salary payment   400
Payment on account payable   100
 Sum of the decreases $5,100

And when the sum of the decreases is subtracted from the sum of the increases,

Sum of the increases $6,500
Sum of the decreases   5,100
 Balance of cash remaining . . . $1,400

The subtraction shows the law practice has $1,400 of cash remaining.

Balance of an Account

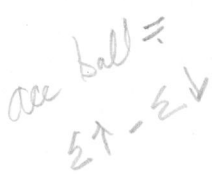

When the increases and decreases recorded in an account are separately added and the sum of the decreases is subtracted from the sum of the increases, the procedure is called determining the *account balance*. The balance of an account is the difference between its increases and decreases. It is also the amount of the item recorded in the account that the company has, owns, or owes at the time the balance is determined.

ACCOUNTS COMMONLY USED

A business uses a number of accounts in recording its transactions. However, the specific accounts used vary from one concern to another, depending upon the assets owned, the debts owed, and the information to be secured from the accounting records. Nevertheless, although the specific accounts vary, the following accounts are common.

Asset Accounts

If useful records of a company's assets are to be kept, an individual account is needed for each kind of asset owned. Some of the more common assets for which accounts are maintained are as follows.

CASH. Increases and decreases in cash are recorded in an account called Cash. The cash of a business consists of money or any medium of exchange that a bank will accept at face value for deposit. It includes coins, currency, cheques, and postal and bank money orders. The balance of the Cash account shows both the cash on hand in the store or office and that on deposit in the bank.

NOTES RECEIVABLE. A formal written promise to pay a definite sum of money at a fixed future date is called a *promissory note*. When amounts due from others are evidenced by promissory notes, the notes are known as notes receivable and are recorded in a Notes Receivable account.

ACCOUNTS RECEIVABLE. Goods and services are commonly sold to customers on the basis of oral or implied promises of future payment. Such sales are known as sales on credit or sales on account; and the oral or implied promises to pay are known as accounts receivable. Accounts receivable are increased by sales on credit and are decreased by customer payments. Since it is necessary to know the amount currently owed by each customer, a separate record must be kept of each customer's purchases and payments. However, a discussion of this separate record is deferred until a later chapter. For the present, all increases and decreases in accounts receivable are recorded in a single account called Accounts Receivable.

PREPAID INSURANCE. Fire, liability, and other types of insurance protection are normally paid for in advance. The amount paid is called a premium and may give protection from loss for one or more years. As a result, a large portion of each premium is an asset for a considerable time after payment. When insurance premiums are paid, the asset prepaid insurance is increased by the amount paid. The increase is normally recorded in an account called Prepaid Insurance. Day by day, insurance premiums expire. Consequently, at intervals the insurance that has expired is calculated and the balance of the Prepaid Insurance account is reduced accordingly.

OFFICE SUPPLIES. Stamps, stationery, paper, pencils, and like items are known as office supplies. They are assets when purchased, and continue to be assets until consumed. As they are consumed, the amounts consumed become expenses. Increases and decreases in the asset office supplies are commonly recorded in an account called Office Supplies.

STORE SUPPLIES. Wrapping paper, cartons, bags, string, and similar items used by a store are known as store supplies. Increases and decreases in store supplies are recorded in an account of that name.

OTHER PREPAID EXPENSES. *Prepaid expenses* are items that are assets at the time of purchase but become expenses as they are consumed or expire. Prepaid insurance, office supplies, and store supplies are examples. Other examples are prepaid rent and prepaid taxes. Each is accounted for in a separate account.

EQUIPMENT.   Increases and decreases in such things as typewriters, desks, chairs, and office machines are commonly recorded in an account called Office Equipment. Likewise, changes in the amount of counters, showcases, cash registers, and like items used by a store are recorded in an account called Store Equipment.

BUILDINGS.   A building used by a business in carrying on its operations may be a store, garage, warehouse, or factory. However, regardless of use, an account called Buildings is commonly employed in recording the increases and decreases in the buildings owned by a business and used in carrying on its operations.

LAND.   An account called Land is commonly used in recording increases and decreases in the land owned by a business. Land and the buildings placed upon it are inseparable in physical fact. Nevertheless, it is usually desirable to account for land and its buildings in separate accounts because buildings depreciate and wear out, but the land on which they are placed is assumed not to do so.

Liability Accounts

Most companies do not have as many liability accounts as asset accounts; however, the following are common:

NOTES PAYABLE.   Increases and decreases in amounts owned because of promissory notes given to creditors are accounted for in an account called Notes Payable.

ACCOUNTS PAYABLE.   An account payable is an amount owed to a creditor. Accounts payable result from the purchase of merchandise, supplies, equipment, and services on credit. Since it is necessary to know the amount owed each creditor, an individual record must be kept of the purchases from and the payments to each. However, a discussion of this individual record is deferred until a later chapter. For the present, all increases and decreases in accounts payable are recorded in a single Accounts Payable account.

UNEARNED REVENUES.   The *realization principle* requires that revenue be earned before it is recognized in the accounts as revenue. Therefore, when payment is received for products or services before delivery, the amounts received are *unearned revenue.* An unearned revenue results in a liability that will be extinguished by delivering the product or service paid for in advance. Subscriptions collected in advance by a magazine publisher, rent collected in advance by a landlord, and legal fees collected in advance by a lawyer are examples. Upon receipt, the amounts collected are recorded in liability accounts such as Unearned Subscriptions, Unearned Rent, and Unearned Legal Fees. When earned by delivery, the amounts earned are transferred to the revenue accounts, Subscriptions Earned, Rent Earned, and Legal Fees Earned.

OTHER SHORT-TERM PAYABLES. Wages payable, taxes payable, and interest payable are other short-term liabilities for which individual accounts must be kept.

MORTGAGE PAYABLE. A *mortgage payable* is a long-term debt for which the creditor has a secured prior claim against some one or more of the debtor's assets. The mortgage gives the creditor the right to force the sale of the mortgaged assets through a foreclosure if the mortgage debt is not paid when due. An account called Mortgage Payable is commonly used in recording the increases and decreases in the amount owed on a mortgage.

Owner's Equity Accounts

Several kinds of transactions affect the equity of a business owner. In a single proprietorship, these include the investment of the owner, his or her withdrawals of cash or other assets for personal use, revenues earned, and expenses incurred. In the previous chapter, the effects of all such transactions on owner's equity were entered in a column under the name of the owner. This simplified the material of the chapter but made it necessary to analyze the items entered in the column in order to prepare an income statement. Fortunately, such an analysis is not necessary. All that is required to avoid it is a number of accounts, a separate one for each owner's equity item appearing on the balance sheet and a separate one for each revenue and expense on the income statement. Then, as each transaction affecting owner's equity is completed, it is recorded in the proper account. Among the accounts required are the following:

CAPITAL ACCOUNT. When a person invests in a business of his or her own, the investment is recorded in an account carrying the owner's name and the word **Capital.** For example, an account called Larry Owen, Capital is used in recording the investment of Larry Owen in his law practice. In addition to the original investment, the *capital account* is used for any permanent additional increases or decreases in owner's equity.

WITHDRAWALS ACCOUNT. Usually a person invests in a business to earn income. However, income is earned over a period of time, say, a year. Often during this period, the business owner must withdraw a portion of the earnings to pay living expenses or for other personal uses. These withdrawals reduce both assets and owner's equity. To record them, an account carrying the name of the business owner and the word **Withdrawals** is used. For example, an account called Larry Owen,

Withdrawals is used to record the withdrawals of cash by Larry Owen from his law practice. The *withdrawals account* is also known as the *personal account* or *drawing account.*

An owner of a small unincorporated business often withdraws a fixed amount each week or month to pay personal living expenses, and often thinks of these withdrawals as a salary. However, in a legal sense they are not a salary because the owner of an unincorporated business cannot enter into a legally binding contract with him or herself to hire and to pay him or herself a salary. Consequently, in law and custom it is recognized that such withdrawals are neither a salary nor an expense of the business but are withdrawals in anticipation of earnings.

REVENUE AND EXPENSE ACCOUNTS.   When an income statement is prepared, it is necessary to know the amount of each kind of revenue earned and each kind of expense incurred during the period covered by the statement. To accumulate this information, a number of revenue and expense accounts are needed. However, all concerns do not have the same revenues and expenses. Consequently, it is impossible to list all revenue and expense accounts to be encountered. Nevertheless, Revenue from Repairs, Commissions Earned, Legal Fees Earned, Rent Earned, and Interest Earned are common examples of revenue accounts. And Advertising Expense, Store Supplies Expense, Office Salaries Expense, Office Supplies Expense, Rent Expense, Utilities Expense, and Insurance Expense are common examples of expense accounts. It should be noted that the kind of revenue or expense recorded in each above-mentioned account is evident from its title. This is generally true of such accounts.

Real and Nominal Accounts

To add to your vocabulary, it may be said here that balance sheet accounts are commonly   *real accounts.* Presumably, this is because most of the items recorded in these accounts exist in objective form. Likewise, income statement accounts are called *nominal accounts* because items recorded in these accounts exist in name only.

THE LEDGER

A business may use from two dozen to several thousand accounts in recording its transactions. Each account is placed on a separate page in a bound or loose-leaf book, or on a separate card in a tray of cards. If the accounts are kept in a book, the book is called a *ledger.* If they are kept on cards in a file tray, the tray of cards is a ledger. Actually, as used in accounting, the word ledger means a group of accounts.

DEBIT AND CREDIT

As previously stated, a T-account has a left side and a right side. However, in accounting, the left side is called the *debit* side, abbreviated "Dr."; and the right side is called the *credit* side, abbreviated "Cr." Furthermore, when amounts are entered on the left side of an account, they are called **debits,** and the account is said to be **debited.** When amounts are entered on the right side, they are called **credits,** and the account is said to be **credited.** The difference between the total debits and the total credits recorded in an account is the **balance of the account.** The balance may be either a **debit balance** or a **credit balance.** It is a debit balance when the sum of the debits exceeds the sum of the credits and a credit balance when the sum of the credits exceeds the sum of the debits. An account is said to be **in balance** when its debits and credits are equal.

The words **to debit** and **to credit** should not be confused with **to increase** and **to decrease.** To debit means simply to enter an amount on the left side of an account. To credit means to enter an amount on the right side. Either may be an increase or a decrease. This may readily be seen by examining the way in which the investment of Larry Owen is recorded in his Cash and capital accounts that follow:

Cash		Larry Owen, Capital	
Investment 5,000			Investment 5,000

When Owen invested $5,000 in his law practice, both the business cash and Owen's equity were increased. Observe in the accounts that the increase in cash is recorded on the left or debit side of the Cash account, while the increase in owner's equity is recorded on the right or credit side. The transaction is recorded in this manner because of the mechanics of *double-entry accounting.*

MECHANICS OF DOUBLE-ENTRY ACCOUNTING

The mechanics of double-entry accounting are such that every transaction affects and is recorded in two or more accounts with equal debits and credits. Transactions are so recorded because the equal debits and credits offer a means of proving the recording accuracy. The proof is, if every transaction is recorded with equal debits and credits, then the debits in the ledger must equal the credits.

The person who first devised double-entry accounting based the system on the accounting equation, $A = L + OE$. He assigned the recording of increases in assets to the debit sides of asset accounts. He then recognized that equal debits and credits were possible only if increases in liabilities and owner's equity were recorded on the opposite or credit sides of liability and owner's equity accounts. In other words, he recognized that if increases in assets were to be recorded as debits, then increases and decreases in all accounts would have to be recorded as follows:

Assets		=	Liabilities		+	Owner's equity	
Debit for increases	Credit for decreases		Debit for decreases	Credit for increases		Debit for decreases	Credit for increases

From the T-accounts it is possible to formulate rules for recording transactions under a double-entry system. The rules are:

1. Increases in assets are debited to asset accounts; consequently, decreases must be credited.
2. Increases in liability and owner's equity items are credited to liability and owner's equity accounts; consequently, decreases must be debited.

At this stage, beginning students will find it helpful to memorize these rules. They should also note that in a single proprietorship there are four kinds of owner's equity accounts: (1) the capital account, (2) the withdrawals account, (3) revenue accounts, and (4) expense accounts. Furthermore, for transactions affecting these accounts, students should observe these additional points:

1. The original investment of the owner of a business plus any more or less permanent changes in the investment are recorded in the capital account.
2. Withdrawals of assets for personal use, including cash to pay personal expenses, decrease owner's equity and are debited to the owner's withdrawals account.
3. Revenues increase owner's equity and are credited in each case to a revenue account that shows the kind of revenue earned.
4. Expenses decrease owner's equity and are debited in each case to an expense account that shows the kind of expense incurred.

TRANSACTIONS ILLUSTRATING THE RULES OF DEBIT AND CREDIT

The following transactions of Larry Owen's law practice illustrate the application of debit and credit rules. They also show how transactions are recorded in the accounts. The number preceding each transaction is used throughout the illustration to identify the transaction in the accounts. Note that most of the transactions are the same ones used in Chapter 1 to illustrate the effects of transactions on the accounting equation.

To record a transaction, it must be analyzed to determine what items were increased or decreased. The rules of debit and credit are then applied to determine the debit and credit effects of the increases or decreases. An analysis of each of the following transactions is given in order to demonstrate the process.

1. On July 1, Larry Owen invested $5,000 in a new law practice.

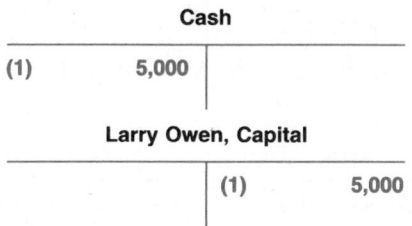

Cash	
(1) 5,000	

Larry Owen, Capital	
	(1) 5,000

Analysis of the transaction: The transaction increased the cash of the practice and at the same time it increased the equity of Owen in the business. Increases in assets are debited, and increases in owner's equity are credited. Consequently, to record the transaction, Cash should be debited and Larry Owen, Capital should be credited for $5,000.

2. Paid the office rent for three months in advance, $900.

Cash	
(1) 5,000	(2) 900

Prepaid Rent	
(2) 900	

Analysis of the transaction: The asset prepaid rent, the right to occupy the office for three months, is increased; and the asset cash is decreased. Increases in assets are debited, and decreases are credited. Therefore, to record the transaction, debit Prepaid Rent and credit Cash for $900.

3. Purchased office equipment for cash, $3,700.

Cash	
(1) 5,000	(2) 900
	(3) 3,700

Office Equipment	
(3) 3,700	

Analysis of the transaction: The asset office equipment is increased, and the asset cash is decreased. Debit Office Equipment and credit Cash for $3,700.

4. Purchased on credit from Alpha Company office supplies, $60, and office equipment, $300.

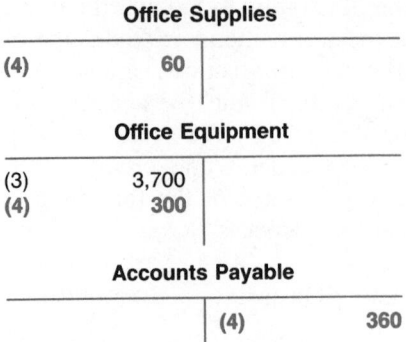

Office Supplies

(4)	60

Office Equipment

(3)	3,700
(4)	300

Accounts Payable

	(4)	360

Analysis of the transaction: This transaction increased the assets office supplies and office equipment, but it also created a liability. Increases in assets are debits, and increases in liabilities are credits; therefore, debit Office Supplies for $60 and Office Equipment for $300 and credit Accounts Payable for $360.

5. Completed legal work for a client and immediately collected a $500 fee.

Cash

(1)	5,000	(2)	900
(5)	500	(3)	3,700

Legal Fees Earned

	(5)	500

Analysis of the transaction: This revenue transaction increased both assets and owner's equity. Increases in assets are debits, and increases in owner's equity are credits. Therefore, Cash is debited; and in order to show the nature of the increase in owner's equity and at the same time accumulate information for the income statement, the revenue account Legal Fees Earned is credited.

6. Paid the secretary's salary for the first two weeks of July, $400.

Cash

(1)	5,000	(2)	900
(5)	500	(3)	3,700
		(6)	400

Office Salaries Expense

(6)	400

Analysis of the transaction: The secretary's salary is an expense that decreased both assets and owner's equity. Debit Office Salaries Expense to decrease owner's equity and also to accumulate information for the income statement, and credit Cash to record the decrease in cash.

7. Signed a contract with Coast Realty to do its legal work on a fixed-fee basis for $300 per month. Received the fee for the first month and a half in advance, $450.

Cash

(1)	5,000	(2)	900
(5)	500	(3)	3,700
(7)	450	(6)	400

Unearned Legal Fees

	(7)	450

Analysis of the transaction: The $450 inflow increased cash, but the inflow is not a revenue until earned. Its acceptance before being earned created a liability, the obligation to do the client's legal work for the next month and a half. Consequently, debit Cash to record the increase in cash and credit Unearned Legal Fees to record the liability increase.

8. Completed legal work for a client on credit and billed the client $1,000 for the services rendered.

Accounts Receivable

(8)	1,000		

Legal Fees Earned

		(5)	500
		(8)	1,000

Analysis of the transaction: Completion of this revenue transaction gave the law practice the right to collect $1,000 from the client, and thus increased assets and owner's equity. Consequently, debit Accounts Receivable for the increase in assets and credit Legal Fees Earned to increase owner's equity and at the same time accumulate information for the income statement.

9. Paid the secretary's salary for the second two weeks of the month.

Cash

(1)	1,000	(2)	900
(5)	500	(3)	3,700
(7)	450	(6)	400
		(9)	400

Office Salaries Expense

(6)	400		
(9)	400		

Analysis of the transaction: An expense that decreased assets and owner's equity. Debit Office Salaries Expense to accumulate information for the income statement and credit Cash.

10. Larry Owen withdrew $200 from the law practice to pay personal expenses.

Cash

(1)	5,000	(2)	900
(5)	500	(3)	3,700
(7)	450	(6)	400
		(9)	400
		(10)	200

Larry Owen, Withdrawals

(10)	200		

Analysis of the transaction: This transaction reduced in equal amounts both assets and owner's equity. Cash is credited to record the asset reduction; and the Larry Owen, Withdrawals account is debited for the reduction in owner's equity.

11. The client paid the $1,000 legal fee billed in transaction 8.

Cash

(1)	5,000	(2)	900
(5)	500	(3)	3,700
(7)	450	(6)	400
(11)	1,000	(9)	400
		(10)	200

Accounts Receivable

(8)	1,000	(11)	1,000

Analysis of the transaction: One asset was increased, and the other decreased. Debit Cash to record the increase in cash, and credit Accounts Receivable to record the decrease in the account receivable, or the decrease in the right to collect from the client.

12. Paid Alpha Company $100 of the $360 owed for the items purchased on credit in transaction 4.

Cash

(1)	5,000	(2)	900
(5)	500	(3)	3,700
(7)	450	(6)	400
(11)	1,000	(9)	400
		(10)	200
		(12)	100

Accounts Payable

| (12) | 100 | (4) | 360 |

Analysis of the transaction: Payments to creditors decreased in like amounts both assets and liabilities. Decreases in liabilities are debited, and decreases in assets are credited. Debit Accounts Payable and credit Cash.

13. Paid the July telephone bill, $30.
14. Paid the July electric bill, $35.

Cash

(1)	5,000	(2)	900
(5)	500	(3)	3,700
(7)	450	(6)	400
(11)	1,000	(9)	400
		(10)	200
		(12)	100
		(13)	30
		(14)	35

Telephone Expense

| (13) | 30 | | |

Heating and Lighting Expense

| (14) | 35 | | |

Analysis of the transactions: These expense transactions are alike in that each decreased cash; they differ in each case as to the kind of expense involved. Consequently, in recording them, Cash is credited; and to accumulate information for the income statement, a different expense account, one showing the nature of the expense in each case, is debited.

THE ACCOUNTS AND THE EQUATION

In Illustration 2–1, the transactions of the Owen law practice are shown in the accounts, with the accounts brought together and classified under the elements of an accounting equation.

Illustration 2–1

Assets				=	Liabilities			+	Owner's equity		
Cash					**Accounts Payable**				**Larry Owen, Capital**		
(1)	5,000	(2)	900		(12)	100	(4)	360		(1)	5,000
(5)	500	(3)	3,700								
(7)	450	(6)	400		**Unearned Legal Fees**				**Larry Owen, Withdrawals**		
(11)	1,000	(9)	400								
		(10)	200				(7)	450	(10)	200	
		(12)	100								
		(13)	30								
		(14)	35						**Legal Fees Earned**		
										(5)	500
Accounts Receivable										(8)	1,000
(8)	1,000	(11)	1,000								
									Office Salaries Expense		
Prepaid Rent									(6)	400	
(2)	900								(9)	400	
Office Supplies									**Telephone Expense**		
(4)	60								(13)	30	
Office Equipment									**Heating and Lighting Expense**		
(3)	3,700								(14)	35	
(4)	300										

PREPARING A TRIAL BALANCE

As previously stated, in a double-entry accounting system every transaction is recorded with equal debits and credits so that the equality of the debits and credits may be tested as a proof of the recording accuracy. This equality is tested at intervals by preparing a *trial balance*. A trial balance is prepared by (1) determining the balance of each account in the ledger; (2) listing the accounts having balances, with the debit balances in one column and the credit balances in another (as in Illustration 2–2); (3) adding the debit balances; (4) adding the credit balances; and then (5) comparing the sum of the debit balances with the sum of the credit balances.

Illustration 2–2

LARRY OWEN, LAWYER
Trial Balance
July 31, 19—

Cash	$1,185	
Prepaid rent	900	
Office supplies	60	
Office equipment	4,000	
Accounts payable		$ 260
Unearned legal fees		450
Larry Owen, capital		5,000
Larry Owen, withdrawals	200	
Legal fees earned		1,500
Office salaries expense	800	
Telephone expense	30	
Heating and lighting expense	35	
Totals	$7,210	$7,210

The illustrated trial balance was prepared from the accounts in Illustration 2–1. Note that its column totals are equal, or in other words, the trial balance is in balance. When a trial balance is in balance, debits equal credits in the ledger, and it is assumed that no errors were made in recording transactions.

THE PROOF OFFERED BY A TRIAL BALANCE

If when a trial balance is prepared it does not balance, an error or errors have been made. The error or errors may have been either in recording transactions, in determining the account balances, in copying the balances on the trial balance, or in adding the trial balance columns. On the other hand, if a trial balance balances, it is assumed that no errors have been made. However, a trial balance that balances is not absolute proof of accuracy. Errors may have been made that did not affect the equality of its columns. For example, an error in which a correct debit amount is debited to the wrong account or a correct credit amount is credited to the wrong account will not cause a trial balance to be out of balance. Likewise, an error in which a wrong amount is both debited and credited to the right accounts will not cause a trial balance to be out of balance. Consequently, a trial balance in balance is only presumptive proof of recording accuracy.

STANDARD ACCOUNT FORM

T-accounts like the ones shown thus far are commonly used in textbook illustrations and also in accounting classes for blackboard demonstrations. In both cases, their use eliminates details and permits the student to concentrate on ideas. However, although widely used in textbooks and in teaching, T-accounts are not used in business for recording transactions. In recording transactions, accounts like the one in Illustration 2–3 are generally used. (Note the year in the date column of the illustrated account. Throughout the remainder of this text, years will be designated 198A, 198B, 198C, and so forth. In all such situations, 198A is the earliest year, 198B is the succeeding year, and so on through the series.)

Illustration 2–3

Cash						ACCOUNT NO. 111
DATE		EXPLANATION	PR	DEBIT	CREDIT	BALANCE
198A July	1		G1	5,000 00		5,000 00
	1		G1		900 00	4,100 00
	3		G1		3,700 00	400 00
	12		G1	500 00		900 00

The account of Illustration 2–3 is called a *balance column account.* It differs from a T-account in that it has columns for specific information about each debit and credit entered in the account. Also, its Debit and Credit columns are placed side by side and it has a third or Balance column. In this Balance column, the account's new balance is entered each time the account is debited or credited. As a result, the last amount in the column is the account's current balance. For example, on July 1, the illustrated account was debited for the $5,000 investment of Larry Owen, which caused it to have a $5,000 debit balance. It was then credited for $900, and its new $4,100 balance was entered. On July 3, it was credited again for $3,700, which reduced its balance to $400. Then, on July 12, it was debited for $500, and its balance was increased to $900.

When a balance column account like that of Illustration 2–3 is used, the heading of the Balance column does not tell whether the balance is a debit balance or a credit balance. However, this does not create a problem because an account is assumed to have its normal kind of balance, unless the contrary is indicated. Furthermore, an accountant is expected to know the *normal balance of any account.* Fortunately, this too is not difficult because the balance of an account normally results from recording in it a larger sum of increases than decreases. Consequently, if increases are recorded as debits, the account normally has a debit balance. Likewise, if increases are recorded as credits, the account normally has a credit balance. Or, increases are recorded in an account in each of the following classifications as shown, and its normal balance is:

Account classification	Increases are recorded as—	And the normal balance is—
Asset	Debits	Debit
Contra asset*	Credits	Credit
Liability	Credits	Credit
Owner's equity:		
Capital	Credits	Credit
Withdrawals	Debits	Debit
Revenue	Credits	Credit
Expense	Debits	Debit

* Explained in the next chapter.

When an unusual transaction causes an account to have a balance opposite from its normal kind of balance, this opposite from normal kind of balance is indicated in the account by entering it in red or entering it in black and encircling the amount. Also, when a debit or credit entered in an account causes the account to have no balance, some bookkeepers place a –0– in the Balance column on the line of the entered amount. Other bookkeepers and bookkeeping machines write 0.00 in the column to indicate the account does not have a balance.

NEED FOR A JOURNAL

It is possible to record transactions by entering debits and credits directly in the accounts, as was done earlier in this chapter. However, when this is done and an error is made, the error is difficult to locate, because even with a transaction having only one debit and one credit, the debit is entered on one ledger page or card and the credit on another, and there is nothing to link the two together.

Consequently, to link together the debits and credits of each transaction and to provide in one place a complete record of each transaction, it is the universal practice in pen-and-ink systems to record all transactions in a *journal.* The debit and credit information about each transaction is then copied from the journal to the ledger accounts. These procedures are important when errors are made, since the journal record makes it possible to trace the debits and credits into the accounts and to see that they are equal and properly recorded.

The process of recording transactions in a journal is called *journalizing transactions.* Also, since transactions are first recorded in a journal and their debit and credit information is then copied from the journal to the ledger, a journal is called a *book of original entry* and a ledger a *book of final entry.*

THE GENERAL JOURNAL

The simplest and most flexible type of journal is a *General Journal.* For each transaction, it provides places for recording (1) the transaction date, (2) the names of the accounts involved, and (3) an explanation of the transaction. It also provides a place for (4) the account numbers of the accounts to which the transaction's debit and credit information is copied and (5) the transaction's debit and credit effect on the accounts named. A standard ruling for a general journal page with two of the transactions of the Owen law practice recorded therein is shown in Illustration 2–4.

The first entry in Illustration 2–4 records the purchase of supplies and equipment on credit, and three accounts are involved. When a transaction involves three or more accounts and is recorded with a general journal entry, a compound entry is required. A *compound journal entry* is one involving three or more accounts. The second entry records a legal fee earned.

Illustration 2–4

GENERAL JOURNAL   PAGE 1

DATE	ACCOUNT TITLES AND EXPLANATION	PR	DEBIT	CREDIT
198A July	5	Office Supplies		60 00	
	Office Equipment		300 00	
	Accounts Payable			360 00
	Purchased supplies and			
	equipment on credit.			
	12	Cash		500 00	
	Legal Fees Earned			500 00
	Collected a legal fee.			

RECORDING TRANSACTIONS IN A GENERAL JOURNAL

To record transactions in a General Journal:

1. The year is written in small figures at the top of the first column.
2. The month is written on the first line in the first column. The year and the month are not repeated except at the top of a new page or at the beginning of a new month or year.
3. The day of each transaction is written in the second column on the first line of the transaction.
4. The names of the accounts to be debited and credited and an explanation of the transaction are written in the Account Titles and Explanation column. The name of the account debited is written first, beginning at the left margin of the column. The name of the account credited is written on the following line, indented about one inch. The explanation is placed on the next line, indented about a half inch from the left margin. The explanation should be short but sufficient to explain the transaction and set it apart from every other transaction.
5. The debit amount is written in the Debit column opposite the name of the account to be debited. The credit amount is written in the Credit column opposite the account to be credited.
6. A single line is skipped between each journal entry to set the entries apart.

At the time transactions are recorded in the General Journal, nothing is entered in the *Posting Reference (Post. Ref. or PR) column.* However, when the debits and credits are copied from the journal to the ledger, the account numbers of the ledger accounts to which the debits and credits are copied are entered in this column. The Posting Reference column is sometimes called the *Folio column.*

POSTING TRANSACTION INFORMATION

The process of copying journal entry information from the journal to the ledger is called *posting.* Normally, near the end of a day, all transactions recorded in the journal that day are posted. In the posting procedure, journal debits are copied and become ledger account debits and journal credits are copied and become ledger account credits.

The posting procedures for a journal entry are shown in Illustration 2–5 (page 73), and they may be described as follows. To post a journal entry:

Illustration 2–5

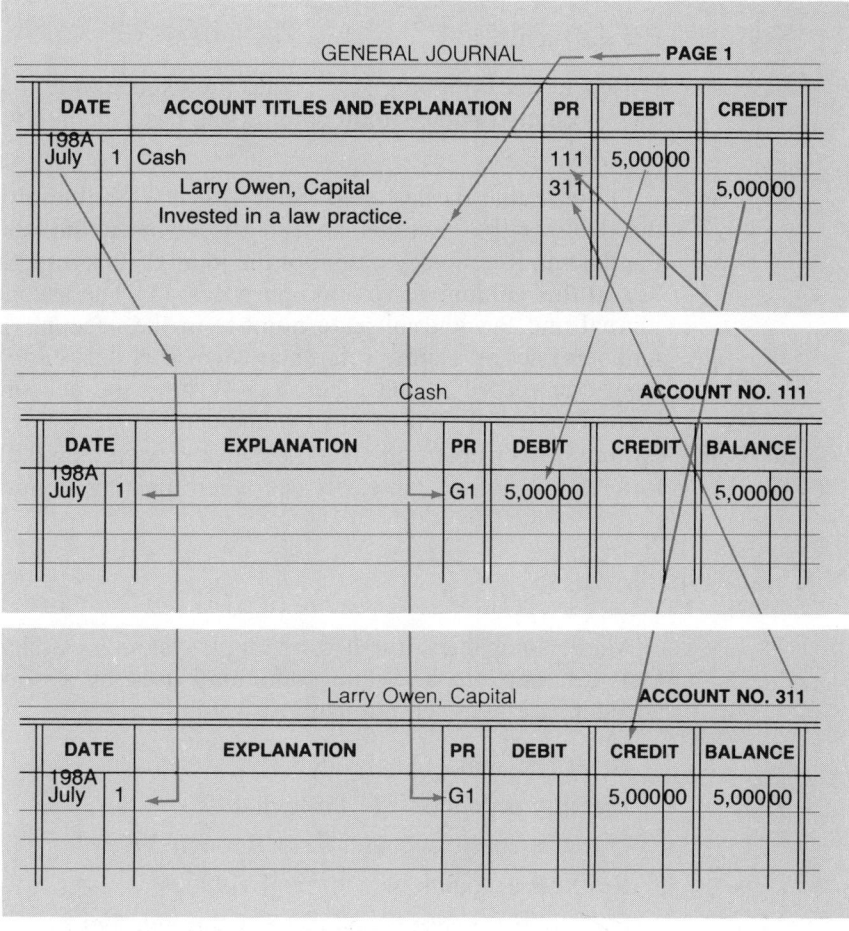

For the debit:

1. Find in the ledger the account named in the debit of the entry.
2. Enter in the account the date of the entry as shown in the journal, the *journal page number* from which the entry is being posted, and the debit amount in the Debit column. Note the letter ''G'' preceding the journal page number in the Posting Reference column of the account. The letter indicates that the amount was posted from the General Journal. Other journals are introduced in Chapter 6, and each is identified by a letter.
3. Determine the effect of the debit on the account balance and enter the new balance.

4.   Enter in the Posting Reference column of the journal the number of the account to which the amount was posted.

For the credit:

Repeat the foregoing steps, with the exception that the credit amount is entered in the Credit column and has a credit effect on the account balance.

Observe that the last step (Step 4) in the posting procedure for either the debit or the credit of an entry is to insert the *account number* in the Posting Reference column of the journal. Inserting the **account number** in this column serves two purposes: (1) The account number in the journal and the journal page number in the account (posting reference numbers) act as a cross-reference when it is desired to trace an amount from one record to the other. (2) Writing the account number in the journal as a last step in posting indicates that posting is completed. If posting is interrupted, the bookkeeper, by examining the journal's Posting Reference column, can easily see where posting stopped.

ACCOUNT NUMBERS

Many companies use a three-digit system in assigning numbers to their accounts. In a system commonly used by service-type concerns, accounts are assigned numbers as follows:

Asset accounts, 111 through 199.
Liability accounts, 211 through 299.
Owner's equity accounts, 311 through 399.
Revenue accounts, 411 through 499.
Operating expense accounts, 511 through 599.

Observe that asset accounts are assigned numbers with first digits of 1, liability accounts are assigned numbers with first digits of 2, and so on. In each case, the first digit of an account's number tells its balance sheet or income statement classification. The second and third digits further identify the account. However, there will be more about this in the next chapter.

LOCATING ERRORS

When a trial balance does not balance, an error or errors are indicated. To locate the error or errors, check the journalizing, posting, and trial balance preparation steps in their reverse order. First check the addition of the columns in the trial balance to see that no error in addition was made. Then check to see that the account balances were correctly copied from the ledger. Then recalculate the account balances. If at this stage the error or errors have not been found, check the posting and then the original journalizing of the transactions.

CORRECTING ERRORS

When an error is discovered in either the journal or the ledger, it must be corrected. Such an error is never erased, for this seems to indicate an effort to conceal something. However, the method of correction will vary with the nature of the error and the stage in the accounting procedures at which it is discovered.

If an error is discovered in a journal entry before the error is posted, it may be corrected by ruling a single line through the incorrect amount or account name and writing in above the correct amount or account name. Likewise, a posted error or an error in posting in which only the amount is wrong may be corrected in the same manner. However, when a posted error involves a wrong account, it is considered best to correct the error with a correcting journal entry. For example, the following journal entry to record the purchase of office supplies was made and posted:

Oct.	14	Office Furniture and Fixtures	15.00	
		Cash		15.00
		To record the purchase of office supplies.		

Obviously, the debit of the entry is to the wrong account; consequently, the following entry is needed to correct the error:

Oct.	17	Office Supplies	15.00	
		Office Furniture and Fixtures		15.00
		To correct the entry of October 14 in which the Office Furniture and Fixtures account was debited in error for the purchase of office supplies.		

The debit of the second entry correctly records the purchase of supplies, and the credit cancels the error of the first entry. Note the full explanation of the correcting entry. Such an explanation should always be full and complete so that anyone can see exactly what has occurred.

BOOKKEEPING TECHNIQUES

Commas and Decimal Points in Dollar Amounts

When amounts are entered in a journal or a ledger, commas to indicate thousands of dollars and decimal points to separate dollars and cents are not necessary. The ruled lines accomplish this. However, when statements are prepared on unruled paper, the decimal points and commas are necessary.

Dollar Signs

Dollar signs are not used in journals or ledgers but are required on financial reports prepared on unruled paper. On such reports, a dollar sign is placed (1) before the first amount in each column of figures and (2) before the first amount appearing after a ruled line that indicates an addition or a subtraction. Examine Illustration 3–5 in Chapter 3, for examples of the use of dollar signs on a financial report.

Omission of Zeros in the Cents Columns

When an amount to be entered in a ledger or a journal is an amount of dollars and no cents, some bookkeepers will use a dash in the cents column in the place of two zeros to indicate that there are no cents. They feel that the dash is easier and more quickly made than the two zeros. This is a matter of choice in journal and ledger entries. However, on financial reports, the two zeros are preferred because they are neater.

Often in this text, where space is limited, exact dollar amounts are used in order to save space. Obviously, in such cases, neither zeros nor dashes are used to show that there are no cents involved.

GLOSSARY

Account. An accounting device used in recording and summarizing the increases and decreases in a revenue, an expense, asset, liability, or owner's equity item.

Account balance. The difference between the increases and decreases recorded in an account.

Account number. An identifying number assigned to an account.

Balance column account. An account having a column for entering the new account balance after each debit or credit is posted to the account.

Book of final entry. A ledger to which amounts are posted.

Book of original entry. A journal in which transactions are first recorded.

Business paper.   A sales ticket, invoice, cheque, or other document arising in and evidence of a transaction.

Capital account.   An account used to record the more or less permanent changes in the equity of an owner in his or her business.

Compound journal entry.   A journal entry having more than one debit or more than one credit.

Credit.   The right-hand side of a T-account.

Debit.   The left-hand side of a T-account.

Double-entry accounting.   An accounting system in which each transaction affects and is recorded in two or more accounts with equal debits and credits.

Drawing account.   Another name for the **withdrawals account.**

Folio column.   Another name for the **Posting Reference column.**

General Journal.   A book of original entry in which any type of transaction can be recorded.

Journal.   A book of original entry in which transactions are first recorded and from which transaction amounts are posted to the ledger accounts.

Journal page number.   A posting reference number entered in the Posting Reference column of each account to which an amount is posted and which shows the page of the journal from which the amount was posted.

Ledger.   A group of accounts used by a business in recording its transactions.

Mortgage payable.   A debt, usually long term, that is secured by a special claim against one or more assets of the debtor.

Nominal accounts.   The income statement accounts.

Normal balance of an account.   The usual kind of balance, either debit or credit, that a given account has and that is a debit balance if increases are recorded in the account as debits and a credit balance if increases are recorded as credits.

Personal account.   Another name for the **withdrawals account.**

Posting.   Transcribing the debit and credit amounts from a journal to the ledger accounts.

Posting Reference (Post. Ref.) column.   A column in a journal and in each account for entering posting reference numbers. Also called a **folio column.**

Posting reference numbers.   Journal page numbers and ledger account numbers used as a cross-reference between amounts entered in a journal and posted to the ledger accounts.

Prepaid expense.   An asset that will be consumed in the operation of a business; and as it is consumed, it will become an expense.

Promissory note.   An unconditional written promise to pay a definite sum of money on demand or at a fixed or determinable future date.

Real accounts.   The balance sheet accounts.

T-account. An abbreviated account form, two or more of which are used in illustrating the debits and credits required in recording a transaction.

Trial balance. A list of accounts having balances in the ledger, the debit or credit balance of each account, the total of the debit balances, and the total of credit balances.

Unearned revenue. A liability that will be extinguished by delivering the product or service a customer has paid for in advance.

Withdrawals account. The account used to record the withdrawals from a business by its owner of cash or other assets intended for personal use. Also known as **personal account** or **drawing account.**

QUESTIONS FOR CLASS DISCUSSION

1. What is an account? What is a ledger?
2. What determines the number of accounts a business will use?
3. What are the meanings of the following words and terms: *(a)* debit, *(b)* to debit, *(c)* credit, and *(d)* to credit?
4. Does debit always mean increase and credit always mean decrease?
5. A transaction is to be entered in the accounts. How do you determine the accounts in which amounts are to be entered? How do you determine whether a particular account is to be debited or credited?
6. Why is a double-entry accounting system so called?
7. Give the rules of debit and credit for *(a)* asset accounts and *(b)* liability and owner's equity accounts.
8. Why are the rules of debit and credit the same for both liability and owner's equity accounts?
9. List the steps in the preparation of a trial balance.
10. Why is a trial balance prepared?
11. Why is a trial balance considered to be only presumptive proof of recording accuracy? What types of errors are not revealed by a trial balance?
12. What determines whether the normal balance of an account is a debit or a credit balance?
13. Can transaction debits and credits be recorded directly in the ledger accounts? What is gained by first recording transactions in a journal and then posting to the accounts?
14. In recording transactions in a journal, which is written first, the debit or the credit? How far is the name of the account credited indented? How far is the explanation indented?
15. What is a compound entry?
16. Are dollar signs used in journal entries? In the accounts?
17. If decimal points are not used in journal entries to separate dollars from cents, what accomplishes this purpose?

18. Define or describe each of the following:
    - *a.* Journal.
    - *b.* Ledger.
    - *c.* Book of original entry.
    - *d.* Book of final entry.
    - *e.* Folio column.
    - *f.* Posting.
    - *g.* Posting Reference column.
    - *h.* Posting reference numbers.

19. Entering in the Posting Reference column of the journal the account number to which an amount was posted is the last step in posting the amount. What is gained by making this the last step?

MULTIPLE CHOICE

1. The right-hand side of a T-account indicates a (an):
   - *a.* Debit.
   - *b.* Increase.
   - *c.* Credit.
   - *d.* Decrease.
   - *e.* Bad debt.

2. Debit is:
   - *a.* An increase in an account.
   - *b.* The right-hand side of a T-account.
   - *c.* A decrease in an account.
   - *d.* The left-hand side of a T-account.
   - *e.* Good.

3. Real accounts are:
   - *a.* Ledger accounts.
   - *b.* Income statement accounts.
   - *c.* Balance sheet accounts.
   - *d.* Nominal accounts.
   - *e.* Journal accounts.

4. While in the process of posting the journal to the ledger, the accountant for X company failed to post a $50 debit to office supplies. The effect of this error will be as follows:
   - *a.* The Office Supplies account balance will be overstated.
   - *b.* The trial balance will not balance.
   - *c.* The error will not affect the debits listed in the journal.
   - *d.* The total debits in the trial balance will be larger than the total credits.
   - *e.* All of the above effects will be caused by the error.

5. A credit is used to record:
   - *a.* A decrease in an expense account.
   - *b.* A decrease in an asset account.
   - *c.* An increase in an unearned revenue account.

    d. An increase in a revenue account.

    e. All of the foregoing.

6. A debit is used to record:

    a. A decrease in an asset account.

    b. A decrease in an expense account.

    c. An increase in a revenue account.

    d. A decrease in the balance of the owner's withdrawals account.

    e. An increase in the balance of the owner's withdrawals account.

7. Tom Janfer, owner of Janfer Book Store, purchased a new automobile that cost $10,000. He made a down payment of $3,000, and signed a note payable for the balance. The entry to record this transaction is:

a.	Cash	3,000	
	Note Payable	7,000	
	Automobile		10,000
b.	Cash	3,000	
	Automobile		3,000
c.	Automobile	10,000	
	Cash		3,000
	Janfer, Capital		7,000
d.	Automobile	3,000	
	Cash		3,000
e.	Automobile	10,000	
	Note Payable		7,000
	Cash		3,000

8. Aimes opened a new business by investing the following assets: Cash, $4,000; Land, $20,000; Building, $80,000. Acre Bank holds a $32,000 mortgage on the land and building. Which Journal entry should be used on the books of the new business to record the investment by Aimes?

a.	Assets	104,000	
	Aimes, Capital		104,000
b.	Assets	104,000	
	Liability		32,000
	Aimes, Capital		72,000
c.	Cash	4,000	
	Land	20,000	
	Building	48,000	
	Aimes, Capital		72,000
d.	Cash	4,000	
	Land	20,000	
	Building	80,000	
	Note Payable		32,000
	Aimes, Capital		72,000
e.	Some other entry.		

9. If Tim Jones, the owner of Jones Hardware proprietorship, uses cash from the business to purchase a family automobile. The business should record this use of cash with an entry to:

    a. Debit salary expense and credit cash.

    b. Debit Tim Jones, salary and credit cash.

    c. Debit cash and credit Tim Jones, withdrawals.

    d. Debit Tim Jones, capital and credit cash.

    e. Debit Tim Jones, withdrawals and credit cash.

10. Of the following errors, the one that by itself will cause the trial balance to be out of balance is:

    a. A $200 salary payment posted as a $200 debit to cash and a $200 credit to salaries expense.

    b. A $100 receipt from a customer in payment of his account posted as a $100 debit to cash and a $10 credit to accounts receivable.

    c. A $75 receipt from a customer in payment of his account posted as a $75 debit to cash and a $75 credit to cash.

    d. A $50 payment for office supplies purchased for cash posted as a $50 debit to office equipment and a $50 credit to cash.

    e. Any one and all of the foregoing errors.

MINI DISCUSSION CASE

Case 2–1   Archibald and Amanda, students in accounting class, were overheard discussing problems they encountered in the first test after Chapter 2. Their problem centered around their inability to understand the rules of debit and credit. They just could not understand why, when they deposit their allowances at the Campus Bank, their accounts are credited, reflecting an increase in the amount of money they have on deposit. When they withdraw money from the bank their accounts are debited, reflecting a decrease in the amount of money they have left on deposit. Yet in their class and in their textbook they are told just the opposite.

    The two students decided to go to their instructor for a resolution of their dilemma. The instructor welcomed them and began to explain their apparent problem.

Required:

    Put yourself in the position of the instructor and explain to Archibald and Amanda the source of their problem and why the rules of debit and credit are correct as stated in the textbook.

CLASS EXERCISES

Exercise 2–1   Prepare the following columnar form. Then (1) indicate the treatment for increases and decreases by entering the words *debited* and *credited* in the proper columns. (2) Indicate the normal balance of each kind of account by entering the word *debit* or *credit* in the last column of the form.

Kind of account	Increases	Decreases	Normal balance
Asset			
Liability			
Owner's capital			
Owner's withdrawals			
Revenue			
Expense			

Exercise 2–2

Place the following T-accounts on a sheet of notebook paper: Cash; Accounts Receivable; Office Supplies; Office Equipment; Accounts Payable; Ted Lee, Capital; Revenue from Services; and Utilities Expense. Then record these transactions by entering debits and credits directly in the accounts. Use the transaction letters to identify amounts in the accounts.

a. Ted Lee began a service business, called Quick Service, by investing $3,000 in the business.
b. Purchased office supplies for cash, $50.
c. Purchased office equipment on credit, $2,500.
d. Earned revenue by rendering services for a customer for cash, $200.
e. Paid for the office equipment purchased in transaction (c).
f. Earned revenue by rendering services for a customer on credit, $750.
g. Paid the monthly utility bills, $25.
h. Collected $250 of the amount owed by the customer of transaction (f).

Exercise 2–3

After recording the transactions of Exercise 2–2, prepare a trial balance for Quick Service. Use the current date.

Exercise 2–4

Ned East began a real estate agency and after completing seven transactions he prepared the trial balance that follows. Analyze the trial balance and prepare a list describing each transaction and its amount. (Hint: T-accounts will help.)

NED EAST, REALTOR
Trial Balance
October 5, 19—

Cash	$ 3,950	
Office supplies	150	
Prepaid rent	1,800	
Office equipment	4,000	
Accounts payable		$ 4,000
Ned East, capital		5,000
Ned East, withdrawals	2,000	
Commissions earned		3,000
Advertising expense	100	
Totals	$12,000	$12,000

Exercise 2–5   Prepare a form on notebook paper with the following three column headings: (1) Error, (2) Amount Out of Balance, and (3) Column Having Larger Total. Then for each of the following errors: (1) list the error by letter in the first column, (2) tell the amount it will cause the trial balance to be out of balance in the second column, and (3) tell in the third column which trial balance column will have the larger total as a result of the error. If the error does not affect the trial balance, write "none" in each of the last two columns.

a. A $70 debit to Office Supplies was debited to Office Equipment.
b. A $90 credit to Office Equipment was credited to Sales.
c. A $60 credit to Sales was credited to the Sales account twice.
d. A $40 debit to Office Supplies was posted as a $45 debit.
e. A $35 debit to Office Supplies was not posted.
f. A $11 credit to Sales was posted as a $110 credit.

Exercise 2–6   A trial balance did not balance. In looking for the error, the bookkeeper discovered that a transaction for the purchase of a calculator on credit for $350 had been recorded with a $350 debit to Office Equipment and a $350 debit to Accounts Payable. Answer each of the following questions, giving the dollar amount of the misstatement, if any.

a. Was the balance of the Office Equipment account overstated, understated, or correctly stated in the trial balance?
b. Was the balance of the Accounts Payable account overstated, understated, or correctly stated in the trial balance?
c. Was the debit column total of the trial balance overstated, understated, or correctly stated?
d. Was the credit column total of the trial balance overstated, understated, or correctly stated?
e. If the credit column total of the trial balance was $96,000 before the error was corrected, what was the total of the debit column?

Exercise 2–7   A careless bookkeeper prepared the following trial balance that does not balance, and you have been asked to prepare a corrected trial balance. In examining the records of the concern you discover the following: (1) The debits to the Cash account total $33,200, and the credits total $30,750. (2) A $75 receipt of cash from a customer in payment of the customer's account was not posted to Accounts Receivable. (3) A $25 purchase of shop supplies on credit was entered in the journal but was not posted to any account. (4) The 1 and the 2 in the balance of the Revenue from Services account, as shown on the bookkeeper's trial balance, were transposed in copying the balance from the ledger to the trial balance.

JOE'S FIXIT SHOP
Trial Balance
December 31, 19—

Cash	$ 2,550	
Accounts receivable		$ 3,175
Shop supplies	3,300	
Shop equipment	6,500	
Accounts payable		600
Joe Sims, capital		8,175
Joe Sims, withdrawals	18,000	
Revenue from services		31,200
Rent expense	7,200	
Advertising expense	325	
Totals	$39,450	$41,575

Exercise 2–8

The following accounts contain seven transactions keyed together with letters. Write a short explanation of each transaction with the amount(s) involved.

Cash					Office Equipment		John Peal, Capital		
(a)	5,000	(b)	1,650	(d)	7,500			(a)	8,000
(e)	300	(c)	50						
		(f)	1,525						
		(g)	60						

Office Supplies			Law Library			Legal Fees Earned		
(c)	50		(a)	3,000			(e)	300
(d)	25							

Prepaid Rent			Accounts Payable				Utilities Expense	
(b)	1,650		(f)	1,525	(d)	7,525	(g)	60

Exercise 2–9

Prepare a general journal form on notebook paper as shown in Illustration 2–4. Then prepare general journal entries to record the following transactions. Omit the year in the journal date column.

May 1 Dale Hall invested $2,000 in cash and an automobile having a $10,000 fair value in a real estate agency called Valley Realty.
    1 Rented furnished office space and paid two months' rent in advance, $1,000.
    2 Purchased office supplies for cash, $60.
  14 Sold a building lot for a client and collected a $2,500 commission on the sale.
  31 Paid for gas and oil used in the agency car during May, $40.

Exercise 2–10

1. Open the following T-accounts on note paper: Cash; Prepaid Rent; Office Supplies; Automobile; Dale Hall, Capital; Commissions Earned; and Gas and Oil Expense.

2. Post the transactions of Exercise 2–9 to the T-accounts. Omit posting reference numbers.

3. Prepare a trial balance of the T-accounts.

PROBLEMS

Problem 2–1

Susan Kent began business as a real estate agent and during a short period completed these transactions:

a. Invested $35,000 in cash and office equipment having a $5,000 fair value in a real estate agency she called Kona Realty.
b. Purchased land valued at $25,000 and a small office building valued at $85,000, paying $30,000 cash and signing a mortgage contract to pay the balance over a period of years.
c. Purchased office supplies on credit, $50.
d. Took her personal automobile, which had a $6,000 fair value, for exclusive use in the business.
e. Purchased additional office equipment on credit, $600.
f. Paid the office secretary's salary, $500.
g. Sold a house and collected a $6,600 cash commission on the sale.
h. Paid $125 for newspaper advertising that had appeared.
i. Paid for the supplies purchased on credit in transaction (c).
j. Gave a typewriter carried in the accounting records at $115 and $700 cash for a new typewriter.
k. Completed a real estate appraisal on credit and billed the client $150 for the appraisal.
l. Paid the secretary's salary, $500.
m. Received payment in full for the appraisal of transaction (k).
n. Susan Kent withdrew $1,000 from the business to pay personal expenses.

Required:

1. Open the following T-accounts: Cash; Accounts Receivable; Office Supplies; Office Equipment; Automobile; Land; Building; Accounts Payable; Mortgage Payable; Susan Kent, Capital; Susan Kent, Withdrawals; Commissions Earned; Appraisal Fees Earned; Office Salaries Expense; and Advertising Expense.
2. Record the transactions by entering debits and credits directly in the accounts. Use the transaction letters to identify each debit and credit amount.
3. Prepare a trial balance using the current date.

Problem 2–2

Dale Hall, Public Accountant, completed these transactions during October of the current year:

Oct. 1 Began a public accounting practice by investing $3,500 in cash and office equipment having a $4,000 fair value.
  1 Paid two months' rent in advance on suitable office space, $1,500.
  2 Purchased on credit office equipment, $350, and office supplies, $65.
  5 Completed accounting work for a client and immediately received $150 cash therefor.
  9 Completed accounting work on credit for Guaranty Bank, $600.
  11 Paid for the items purchased on credit on October 2.
  12 Paid the $625 premium on an insurance policy.
  19 Received payment in full from Guaranty Bank for the work completed on October 9.
  25 Completed accounting work on credit for Hilltop Realty, $400.
  29 Dale Hall withdrew $250 cash from the practice to pay personal expenses.
  30 Purchased additional office supplies on credit, $40.
  31 Paid the October utility bills, $135.

Required:

1. Open the following accounts: Cash; Accounts Receivable; Prepaid Rent; Prepaid Insurance; Office Supplies; Office Equipment; Accounts Payable; Dale Hall, Capital; Dale Hall, Withdrawals; Accounting Revenue; and Utilities Expense.
2. Prepare general journal entries to record the transactions, post to the accounts, and prepare a trial balance. Head the trial balance Dale Hall, Public Accountant.

Problem 2–3   Jerry Marsh began business as an excavating contractor and during a short period completed these transactions:

a. Began business by investing cash, $15,000; office equipment, $1,200; and machinery, $42,500.
b. Purchased land for an office site and for parking machinery, $17,500. Paid $5,500 in cash and signed a promissory note payable for the balance.
c. Purchased for cash a used prefabricated building and moved it onto the land for use as an office, $5,000.
d. Paid the premium on two insurance policies, $725.
e. Completed an excavating job and collected $875 cash in full payment.
f. Purchased additional machinery costing $6,800. Gave $1,800 in cash and signed a note payable for the balance.
g. Completed an excavating job on credit for Western Contractors, $1,200.
h. Purchased additional office equipment on credit, $350.
i. Completed an excavating job for Lakeside Contractors on credit, $950.
j. Received and recorded as an account payable a bill for rent on a special machine used on the Lakeside Contractors job, $150.
k. Received $1,200 from Western Contractors for the work of transaction (g).
l. Paid the wages of the machinery operator, $850.
m. Paid for the office equipment purchased in transaction (h).
n. Paid $125 cash for repairs to a machine.
o. Jerry Marsh wrote a $65 cheque on the bank account of the business to pay for repairs to his personal automobile. (The car is not used for business purposes.)
p. Paid the wages of the machinery operator, $900.
q. Paid for gas and oil consumed by the excavating machinery, $210.

Required:

1. Open the following T-accounts: Cash; Accounts Receivable; Prepaid Insurance; Office Equipment; Machinery; Building; Land; Notes Payable; Accounts Payable; Jerry Marsh, Capital; Jerry Marsh, Withdrawals; Excavating Revenue; Machinery Repairs Expense; Wages Expense; Machinery Rentals Expense; and Gas and Oil Expense.
2. Record the transactions by entering debits and credits directly in the accounts. Use the transaction letters to identify each debit and credit. Prepare a trial balance using the current date and headed Jerry Marsh, Contractor.

Problem 2–4   Nancy Ives completed these transactions during July of the current year:

July 1 Began an architectural practice by investing cash, $4,500; drafting supplies, $150; and office and drafting equipment, $3,750.
1 Paid two months' rent in advance on suitable office space, $1,200.
2 Paid the premium on an insurance policy taken out in the name of the practice, $560.

July 3 Purchased drafting equipment, $475, and drafting supplies, $35, on credit.
8 Delivered a set of plans to a contractor and collected $500 cash in full payment.
15 Completed and delivered a set of plans to Kemper Contractors on credit, $700.
15 Paid the draftsman's salary, $650.
17 Purchased drafting supplies on credit, $40.
18 Paid for the equipment and supplies purchased on July 3.
25 Received $700 from Kemper Contractors for the plans delivered on July 15.
26 Nancy Ives withdrew $200 from the practice for personal use.
27 Paid for the supplies purchased on July 17.
30 Completed architectural work for Kona Realty on credit, $500.
31 Paid the draftsman's salary, $650.
31 Paid the July utility bills, $115.
31 Paid the blueprinting expenses incurred in July, $85.

Required:

1. Open the following accounts: Cash; Accounts Receivable; Prepaid Rent; Prepaid Insurance; Drafting Supplies; Office and Drafting Equipment; Accounts Payable; Nancy Ives, Capital; Nancy Ives, Withdrawals; Architectural Fees Earned; Salaries Expense; Blueprinting Expense; and Utilities Expense.

2. Prepare and post general journal entries to record the transactions. Prepare a trial balance, heading it Nancy Ives, Architect.

Problem 2–5   Ted Lee completed these transactions during May of the current year:

May 1 Began a new law practice by investing $2,500 in cash and law books having a $1,200 fair value.
1 Rented the furnished office of a lawyer who was retiring due to illness, and paid two months' rent in advance, $1,000.
1 Paid the premium on a liability insurance policy giving one year's protection, $420.
2 Purchased office supplies on credit, $40.
8 Completed legal work for a client and immediately collected $250 cash for the work.
12 Paid for the office supplies purchased on July 2.
15 Completed legal work for Evans Realty on credit, $850.
22 Completed legal work for Security Bank on credit, $750.
25 Received $850 from Evans Realty for the work completed on July 15.
27 Ted Lee wrote a $15 cheque on the bank account of the legal practice to pay his home telephone bill.
29 Purchased additional office supplies on credit, $45.
31 Paid the July telephone bill of the office, $25.
31 Paid the salary of the office secretary, $950.
31 Recognized that one month's rent on the office had expired and had become an expense. (Make a general journal entry to transfer the amount of the expense from the asset account to the Rent Expense account.)
31 Recognized that one month's insurance had expired and become an expense.
31 Took an inventory of unused office supplies and determined that supplies costing $30 had been used and had become an expense.

Required:

1. Open the following accounts: Cash; Accounts Receivable; Prepaid Rent; Prepaid Insurance; Office Supplies; Law Library; Accounts Payable; Ted Lee, Capital; Ted Lee, Withdrawals; Legal Fees Earned; Rent Expense; Salaries Expense; Telephone Expense; Insurance Expense; and Office Supplies Expense.

2. Prepare general journal entries to record the transactions, post to the accounts, and prepare a trial balance headed Ted Lee, Lawyer.
3. Analyze the transactions and prepare a May income statement and a May 31 balance sheet for the practice. (The $3,700 trial balance amount of capital for Ted Lee is his May 1 beginning-of-month capital. To determine the May 31 balance sheet amount of his capital, add the net income to his beginning capital and deduct the withdrawal. Show the ending capital as in Illustration 1–2.)

ALTERNATE PROBLEMS

Problem 2–1A   Susan Kent completed these transactions during a short period:

a. Began a real estate agency by investing the following assets at their fair values: cash, $2,500; office equipment, $3,000; automobile, $5,300; land, $25,000; and building, $75,000. A bank holds a $60,000 mortgage on the land and building.
b. Purchased office supplies, $60, and additional office equipment, $350, on credit.
c. Collected a $6,600 commission from the sale of property for a client.
d. Purchased additional office equipment on credit, $425.
e. Paid for advertising that had appeared in the local paper, $125.
f. Traded the agency's automobile and $4,700 in cash for a new automobile.
g. Paid the office secretary's salary, $525.
h. Paid for the supplies and equipment purchased in transaction (b).
i. Completed a real estate appraisal for a client on credit, $175.
j. Collected a $2,500 commission from the sale of a building lot for a client.
k. The client of transaction (i) paid $75 of the amount owed.
l. Paid the secretary's salary, $525.
m. Paid $115 for newspaper advertising that had appeared.
n. Susan Kent withdrew $1,500 from the business for personal use.

Required:

1. Open the following T-accounts: Cash; Accounts Receivable; Office Supplies; Office Equipment; Automobile; Land; Building; Accounts Payable; Mortgage Payable; Susan Kent, Capital; Susan Kent, Withdrawals; Commissions Earned; Appraisal Fees Earned; Office Salaries Expense; and Advertising Expense.
2. Record the transactions by entering debits and credits directly in the accounts. Use the transaction letters to identify the amounts in the accounts.
3. Prepare a trial balance headed Susan Kent, Realtor. Use the current date.

Problem 2–2A   Dale Hall began a public accounting practice and completed these transactions during August of the current year:

Aug. 1 Invested $4,500 in a public accounting practice begun this day.
     1 Rented suitable office space and paid two month's rent in advance, $1,600.
     2 Purchased office supplies, $65, and office equipment, $3,750, on credit.
     3 Paid the premium on a liability insurance policy, $435.
     8 Completed accounting work for a client and immediately collected $175 in cash for the work done.

Aug. 13 Completed accounting work for Valley Bank on credit, $450.
    15 Purchased additional office supplies on credit, $35.
    23 Received $450 from Valley Bank for the work completed on August 13.
    26 Dale Hall withdrew $250 from the accounting practice to pay personal expenses.
    30 Completed accounting work for Kona Realty on credit, $350.
    31 Made an $815 installment payment on the equipment and supplies purchased on August 2.
    31 Paid the August utility bills of the accounting practice, $145.

Required:

1. Open the following accounts: Cash; Accounts Receivable; Prepaid Rent; Prepaid Insurance; Office Supplies; Office Equipment; Accounts Payable; Dale Hall, Capital; Dale Hall, Withdrawals; Accounting Revenue; and Utilities Expense.
2. Prepare general journal entries to record the transactions, post to the accounts, and prepare a trial balance headed Dale Hall, Public Accountant.

Problem 2–3A   Jerry Marsh completed these transactions during a short period:

a. Began business as an excavating contractor by investing cash, $25,000; office equipment, $1,500; and excavating machinery, $45,000.
b. Purchased for $25,000 land to be used as an office site and for parking equipment. Paid $10,000 in cash and signed a promissory note payable for the balance.
c. Purchased additional excavating machinery costing $21,750. Paid $6,750 in cash and signed a promissory note payable for the balance.
d. Paid $4,500 cash for a used prefabricated building and moved it on the land for use as an office.
e. Completed an excavating job and immediately collected $850 in cash for the work.
f. Paid the premium on an insurance policy giving one year's protection, $625.
g. Completed a $1,250 excavating job for Tri-City Contractors on credit.
h. Paid the wages of the equipment operator, $800.
i. Paid $160 cash for repairs to excavating machinery.
j. Received $1,250 from Tri-City Contractors for the work of transaction (g).
k. Completed an $800 excavating job for TVX Contractors on credit.
l. Received and recorded as an account payable a $110 bill for the rent of a special machine used on the TVX Contractors job.
m. Purchased additional office equipment on credit, $525.
n. Jerry Marsh withdrew $500 from the business for personal use.
o. Paid the wages of the equipment operator, $900.
p. Paid the $110 account payable resulting from renting the machine of transaction (l).
q. Paid for gas and oil consumed by the excavating machinery, $225.

Required:

1. Open the following T-accounts: Cash; Accounts Receivable; Prepaid Insurance; Office Equipment; Machinery; Building; Land; Notes Payable; Accounts Payable; Jerry Marsh, Capital; Jerry Marsh, Withdrawals; Excavating Revenue; Machinery Repairs Expense; Wages Expense; Machinery Rentals Expense; and Gas and Oil Expense.
2. Record the transactions by entering debits and credits directly in the accounts. Use the transaction letters to identify each debit and credit. Prepare a trial balance using the current date and headed Jerry Marsh, Contractor.

Problem 2–4A   Nancy Ives completed these transactions during March of the current year:

Mar. 1 Began an architectural practice by opening a bank account in the name of the practice, Nancy Ives, Architect, and deposited $5,000 therein.

1 Rented suitable office space and paid two months' rent in advance, $1,000.

2 Purchased for $4,750 office and drafting equipment under an agreement calling for a $750 down payment and the balance in monthly installments. Paid the down payment and recorded the account payable.

3 Purchased drafting supplies for cash, $175.

9 Completed and delivered a set of plans to a contractor and immediately received $525 cash in full payment therefor.

11 Paid the premium on a liability insurance policy, $480.

12 Purchased on credit additional drafting supplies, $35, and drafting equipment, $115.

15 Paid the salary of the draftsman, $550.

18 Completed and delivered a set of plans to Lakeview Developers on credit, $1,200.

22 Paid in full for the supplies and equipment purchased on March 12.

26 Completed additional architectural work for Lakeview Developers on credit, $350.

28 Received $1,200 from Lakeview Developers for the plans delivered on March 18.

29 Nancy Ives withdrew $200 cash from the practice to pay personal expenses.

31 Paid the salary of the draftsman, $550.

31 Paid the March utility bills, $80.

31 Paid $135 cash for blueprinting expense.

Required:

1. Open the following accounts: Cash; Accounts Receivable; Prepaid Rent; Prepaid Insurance; Drafting Supplies; Office and Drafting Equipment; Accounts Payable; Nancy Ives, Capital; Nancy Ives, Withdrawals; Architectural Fees Earned; Salaries Expense; Blueprinting Expense; and Utilities Expense.

2. Prepare general journal entries to record the transactions, post to the accounts, and prepare a trial balance.

Problem 2–5A   Ted Lee graduated from the University with a law degree in June of the current year, and during July, he completed these transactions:

July 1 Began the practice of law by investing $2,000 in cash and law books acquired at the university and having an $800 fair value.

1 Rented the furnished office of a lawyer who was retiring and paid two months' rent in advance, $950.

2 Purchased law books costing $750 under an agreement calling for a $100 down payment and the balance in monthly installments. Paid the down payment and recorded the remaining $650 as an account payable.

3 Purchased office supplies on credit, $45.

5 Paid the premium on a liability insurance policy giving one year's protection, $360.

9 Completed legal work for a client and immediately collected $300 for the work done.

13 Paid for the office supplies purchased on credit on July 3.

15 Completed legal work for Valley Bank on credit, $850.

23 Ted Lee wrote a $20 cheque on the bank account of the legal practice to pay his home telephone bill.

25 Received $850 from Valley Bank for the work completed July 15.

27 Completed legal work for Hillside Realty on credit, $600.

31 Paid the telephone bill of the legal practice, $30.

31 Paid the salary of the office secretary, $900.

31 Recognized that one month's rent on the office had expired and had become an expense. (Make a general journal entry to transfer the amount of the expense from the asset account to the Rent Expense account.)

July 31 Recognized that one month's insurance had expired and had become an expense.
   31 Took an inventory of unused office supplies and determined that supplies costing $25 had been used and had become an expense.

Required:

1. Open the following accounts: Cash; Accounts Receivable; Prepaid Rent; Prepaid Insurance; Office Supplies; Law Library; Accounts Payable; Ted Lee, Capital; Ted Lee, Withdrawals; Legal Fees Earned; Rent Expense; Salaries Expense; Telephone Expense; Insurance Expense; and Office Supplies Expense.
2. Prepare general journal entries to record the transactions, post to the accounts, and prepare a trial balance headed Ted Lee, Lawyer.
3. Analyze the transactions and prepare a July income statement and a July 31 balance sheet. (The $2,800 trial balance amount of capital for Ted Lee is his July 1 beginning-of-month capital. To determine his July 31 balance sheet amount of capital, add the net income to his beginning capital and deduct the withdrawal. Show the ending capital as in Illustration 1–2.)

PROVOCATIVE PROBLEMS

Provocative
Problem 2–1,
Summer
Concession

Mary Cone, a school teacher, has just completed the first summer's operation of a concession on Blue Lake, at which she rents boats and sells sandwiches, soft drinks, and candy. She began the summer's operation with $3,000 in cash and a five-year lease on a boat dock and a small concession building on the lake. The lease requires a $1,200 annual rental, although the concession is open only from June 1 through August 31. On opening day, Mary paid the first year's rent in advance and purchased four boats at $350 each, paying cash. She estimated the boats would have a five-year life, after which she could sell them for $50 each.

During the summer, she purchased food, soft drinks, and candy costing $6,255, all of which was paid for by summer's end, excepting food costing $150 that was purchased during the last week's operation. By summer's end, she had paid electric bills, $235, and wages of a part-time helper, $880. She had also withdrawn $200 of earnings of the concession each week for 12 weeks for personal expenses.

She took in $1,510 in boat rentals during the summer and sold $12,870 of food and drinks, all of which was collected in cash, except $135 owed by Small Company for food and drinks for an employees' picnic.

On August 31, when she closed for the summer, Ms. Cone was able to return to the soft drink company several cases of soft drinks for which she received a $60 cash refund. However, she had to take home for personal consumption a number of candy bars and a few cans of soft drinks that cost $15 and could have been sold for $30.

Prepare an income statement showing the results of the summer's operations and an August 31 balance sheet. Head the statements Summer Concession. Determine Ms. Cone's ending equity by subtracting the liability from the assets.

Then prepare a different calculation to prove the amount of the equity. (T-accounts will be helpful in organizing the data.)

Provocative Problem 2–2, Bright Glass Service

Ray Black began a window cleaning service by investing $750 in the business, Bright Glass Service. He made a $500 down payment and signed a promissory note payable to purchase a secondhand truck priced at $1,200. He then spent $150 for detergents, sponges, and other supplies to be used in the business. He also paid $60 for newspaper advertising through which he gained a number of customers, who together agreed to pay him approximately $300 per week for his services.

After six months, on June 30 of the current year, his records show he has collected $7,600 in cash from customers for his services and that other customers owe him $250 for washing windows. He has bought additional supplies for cash, $325, which brings the total supplies purchased during the six months to $475. However, supplies that cost $100 are on hand and unused at the period end. He has spent $310 for gas and oil used in the truck. Through payments, he has reduced the balance owed on the truck to $350; but through use, the truck has worn out and depreciated an amount equal to one fourth of its cost. Also, he has withdrawn sufficient cash from the business each week to pay his personal living expenses.

Under the assumption that the business has a $225 balance of cash remaining at the period end, determine the amount of cash Ray has withdrawn from the business. Prepare an income statement for the six months and a balance sheet as of the period-end. Determine Ray's end-of-period equity by subtracting the balance owed on the note payable from the total of the assets. Then prepare a calculation to prove in another way the amount of the ending equity. (T-accounts will be helpful in organizing the data.)

Provocative Problem 2–3, Ted's Lawn Service

Upon graduation from high school last summer, Ted Neal needed a job to earn a portion of his first-year university expenses. He was unable to find anything satisfactory and decided to go into the lawn-care business. He had $350 in a savings account that he used to buy a lawn mower and other lawn-care tools. However, to haul the tools from job to job, he needed a truck. Consequently, he borrowed $800 from a bank, agreeing to pay 1¼% interest per month, and used the entire amount to buy a secondhand truck.

From the beginning, he had as much work as he could do, and after two months, he repaid the bank loan plus two months' interest. On September 5, he ended the business after exactly three months' operations. Throughout the summer, he followed the practice of depositing in the bank all cash received from customers. An examination of his chequebook record showed he had deposited $3,550. He had written cheques to pay $145 for gas, oil, and lubricants used in the truck and mower and a $35 cheque for mower repairs. A notebook in the truck contained copies of credit card tickets that showed the business owed $40 for additional gas and oil used in the truck and mower. The notebook also showed that customers owed Ted $125 for lawn-care services. He estimated that his lawn-care equipment had worn out and depreciated an amount equal to one half its cost, and the truck had worn out and depreciated an amount equal to one fourth its cost.

Under the assumption that Ted had withdrawn $525 from the business during the summer for spending money and to buy clothes, prepare an income statement showing the results of the summer's operations. Also prepare a September 5 balance sheet like Illustration 1–2. Head the statements Ted's Lawn Service. (T-accounts should be helpful in organizing the data. To determine the balance sheet amount of Ted's capital, add the net income to his beginning investment and deduct the withdrawals.)

ANALYTICAL AND REVIEW PROBLEMS

Problem 2–1 A&R

Mary Benn just dismissed her inexperienced bookkeeper and asked you to help out until she finds a replacement. Since you had a few days before your Florida winter break, you agreed to see Benn through a proper trial balance. Benn was grateful for your offer and turned over all the accounting records. You found that the trial balance prepared by the bookkeeper (shown below) was nothing more than a listing of account balances.

BENN COMPANY
Trial Balance
December 31, 198A

Cash	$ 1,480
Accounts receivable	1,020
Equipment	3,000
Prepaid rent	1,200
Accounts payable	560
M. Benn, capital	6,000
M. Benn, withdrawals	720
Service revenue	9,000
Salaries expense	7,000
Insurance expense	1,000
Miscellaneous, expenses	180
Total	$31,160

After classifying the accounts into debit and credit balances, you found that the trial balance did not balance. Consequently, you proceeded to examine the accounting records. In searching back through the accounting records, you discovered that the accounts as listed had normal balances and that the following errors were made by the bookkeeper.

a. An entire entry was not posted. It included a debit to Cash and a credit to Accounts Receivable for $120.
b. In computing the balance of Accounts Payable, a credit of $80 was omitted from the computation.
c. In copying Benn's Capital account, the bookkeeper entered $6,000 instead of $6,080, the correct amount in the ledger.

d. A withdrawal of $60 by Benn was posted as a credit to Benn withdrawal account.

e. Equipment of $200 was debited to Prepaid Rent when purchased.

Required:

Prepare a corrected trial balance for the Benn Company as of December 31, 198A.

Problem 2–2
A&R

The following T-accounts show the October transactions of Cindy Etsell's service business which was organized on the first day of October this year. Since the bookkeeper is very inexperienced, some dates and amounts are missing.

Cash					Accounts Receivable		
Oct. 26	2,000	Oct. 2	3,000		Oct. 6	800	
		10	400				
		15	500				
		30	600				

Office Supplies	
Oct. 5 for cash	100

Building			Land	
Oct. 2	6,000		Oct. 1	2,000

Accounts Payable	
	300

Wages Payable			Mortgage Payable	
	Oct. 31	200		Oct. 2	3,000

Cindy Etsell, Capital	
	Oct. 1	10,000

Service Revenue			Wages Expense	
	Oct. 26	2,000	Oct. 15	500
			30	600

Miscellaneous Expense	
Oct. 10	400
24	300

Required:

1. Prepare journal entries (omit narratives) to reconstruct all transactions for the month of October.
2. Identify the missing data.

Problem 2–3 A&R

Kelly Cleaner Service, owned by Kelly Smyth, has been in operation for a few years. The transactions and trial balance for the month of November are presented below:

Nov. 1 Received from Superior Hotel for cleaning work done in October, $600.
2 Purchased cleaning supplies for cash, $300, to be used for the next three weeks.
5 Bill Caucus Club for cleaning work completed on credit, $800.
6 Cleaning services performed for customers and collected $100 in full payment therefor.
16 Kelly Smyth invested an additional $2,000 cash in the business.
22 Paid advertising, $150.
28 Purchased cleaning supplies to be used for the next few days on credit, $50.
29 Kelly Smyth withdrew $700 from the business.
30 Paid telephone and utility expenses, $100.
30 Paid employees' monthly salary, $500.
30 Cleaning services completed and collected, $700.

KELLY CLEANER SERVICE
Trial Balance
November 1, 198A

Cash	$1,800	
Accounts receivable	800	
Office supplies	100	
Land	5,000	
Accounts payable		$ 250
Mortgage payable		3,000
Kelly Smyth, capital		4,650
Kelly Smyth, withdrawals	700	
Cleaning service revenue		1,600
Salaries expense	500	
Cleaning supplies expense	350	
Advertising expense	150	
Telephone and utility expense	100	
	$9,500	$9,500

Required:

Assuming that Kelly Cleaner Service's accounting period is a month and accordingly follows the practice of preparing monthly financial statements.

1. Open all necessary T-accounts and post the transactions directly to these T-accounts without preparing journal entries.
2. Compute the balance for all the accounts in (1) above.
3. Prepare a trial balance.
4. Compare the trial balance in (3) above with the trial balance presented in the problem, explain the differences between the two trial balances. (All information in the given trial balance is correct.)
5. Which types of accounts tend to have opening balances and why?

Adjusting the Accounts and Preparing the Statements

3

After studying Chapter 3, you should be able to:

Explain why the life of a business is divided into accounting periods of equal length and why the accounts of a business must be adjusted at the end of each accounting period.

Prepare adjusting entries for prepaid expenses, accrued expenses, unearned revenues, accrued revenues, and depreciation.

Prepare entries to dispose of accrued revenue and expense items in the new accounting period.

Explain the difference between the cash and accrual bases of accounting.

Explain the importance of comparability in the financial statements of a business, period after period; and tell how the realization principle and the matching principle contribute to comparability.

Define each asset and liability classification appearing on a balance sheet, classify balance sheet items, and prepare a classified balance sheet.

Define or explain the words and phrases listed in the chapter Glossary.

The life of a business often spans many years, and its activities go on without interruption over the years. However, taxes based on annual income must be paid governmental units, and the owners and managers of a business must have periodic reports on its financial progress. Consequently, a *time-period concept* of the life of a business is required in accounting for its activities. This concept results in a division of the life of a business into time periods of equal length, called *accounting periods.* Accounting periods may be a month, three months, or a year in length. However, **annual accounting periods,** periods one year in length, are the norm.

An accounting period of any 12 consecutive months is known as a *fiscal year.* A fiscal year may coincide with the calendar year and end on December 31 or it may follow the natural business year. When accounting periods follow the natural business year, they end when inventories are at their lowest point and business activities are at their lowest ebb. For example, in department stores, the natural business year begins on February 1, after the Christmas and January sales, and ends the following January 31. Consequently, the annual accounting periods of department stores commonly begin on February 1 and end the following January 31.

NEED FOR ADJUSTMENTS AT THE END OF AN ACCOUNTING PERIOD

As a rule, at the end of an accounting period, after all transactions are recorded, several of the accounts in a company's ledger do not show proper end-of-period balances for preparing the statements. This is true even though all transactions were correctly recorded. The balances are incorrect for statement purposes, not through error but because of the expiration of costs brought about by the passage of time. For example, the second item on the trial balance of Owen's law practice, as prepared in Chapter 2 and reproduced again as Illustration 3–1, is "Prepaid rent, $900." This $900 represents the rent for three months paid in advance on July 1. However, by July 31, $900 is not the balance sheet amount for this asset because one month's rent, $300, has expired and become an expense and only $600 remains as an asset. Likewise, a portion of the office supplies as represented by the $60 debit balance in the Office Supplies account has been used, and the office equipment has begun to wear out and depreciate. Obviously, then, the balances of the Prepaid Rent, Office Supplies, and Office Equipment accounts as they appear on the trial balance do not reflect the proper amounts for preparing the July 31 statements. The balance of each and the balances of the Office Salaries Expense and Legal Fees Earned accounts must be *adjusted* before they will show proper amounts for the July 31 statements.

Illustration 3–1

LARRY OWEN, LAWYER
Trial Balance
July 31, 19—

Cash	$1,185	
Prepaid rent	900	
Office supplies	60	
Office equipment	4,000	
Accounts payable		$ 260
Unearned legal fees		450
Larry Owen, capital		5,000
Larry Owen, withdrawals	200	
Legal fees earned		1,500
Office salaries expense	800	
Telephone expense	30	
Heating and lighting expense	35	
Totals	$7,210	$7,210

ADJUSTING THE ACCOUNTS

Prepaid Expenses

As previously stated, a prepaid expense is an expense that has been paid for in advance of its use. At the time of payment, an asset is acquired that will be used or consumed, and as it is used or consumed, it becomes an expense. For example:

On July 1, the Owen law practice paid three months' rent in advance and obtained the right to occupy a rented office for the following three months. On July 1, this right was an asset valued at its $900 cost. However, day by day the law practice occupied the office, and each day a portion of the prepaid rent expired and became an expense. On July 31, one month's rent, valued at one third of $900, or $300, had expired. Consequently, if Owen's July 31 accounts are to reflect proper asset and expense amounts, the following *adjusting entry* is required:

July	31	Rent Expense	300.00	
		Prepaid Rent		300.00
		To record the expired rent.		

Posting the adjusting entry has the following effect on the accounts:

Prepaid Rent				**Rent Expense**	
July 1	900	July 31	300	July 31	300

After the entry is posted, the Prepaid Rent account with a $600 balance and the Rent Expense account with a $300 balance show proper statement amounts.

To continue, early in July, the Owen law practice purchased some office supplies and placed them in the office for use. Each day the secretary used a portion. The amount used or consumed each day was an expense that daily reduced the supplies on hand. However, the daily reductions were not recognized in the accounts because day-by-day information as to amounts used and remaining was not needed. Also, labor could be saved by recording only a single amount, the total of all supplies used during the month.

Consequently, if on July 31 the accounts are to reflect proper statement amounts, the dollar amount of office supplies used during the month must be determined and recorded. To learn the amount used, it is necessary to count or inventory the unused supplies remaining and to deduct their cost from the cost of the supplies purchased. If, for example, $35 of unused supplies remain, then $25 ($60 − $35 = $25) of supplies were used and have become an expense. The following adjusting entry is required to record this:

July	31	Office Supplies Expense	25.00	
		Office Supplies		25.00
		To record the supplies used.		

The effect of the adjusting entry on the account is:

Office Supplies				**Office Supplies Expense**	
July 5	60	July 31	25	July 31	25

Often, unlike in the two previous examples, items that are prepaid expenses at the time of purchase are both bought and fully consumed within a single accounting period. For example, a company pays its rent in advance on the first day of each month. Each month the amount paid results in a prepaid expense that is entirely consumed by the month's end and by the end of the accounting period. In such cases, it is best to ignore the fact that an asset results from each prepayment because an adjustment can be avoided if each prepayment is originally recorded as an expense.

Other prepaid expenses that are handled in the same manner as prepaid rent and office supplies are prepaid insurance, store supplies, and factory supplies.

Depreciation

An item of equipment used in carrying on the operations of a business in effect represents a "quantity of usefulness." Also, since the equipment will eventually wear out and be discarded, the cost of its "quantity of usefulness" must be charged off as an expense over the useful life of the equipment. This is accomplished by recording *depreciation.*

Depreciation is an expense just like the expiration of prepaid rent. For example, if a company purchases a machine for $4,500 that it expects to use for four years, after which it expects to receive $500 for the machine as a trade-in allowance on a new machine, the company has purchased a $4,000 quantity of usefulness ($4,500 − $500 = $4,000). Furthermore, this quantity of usefulness expires or the machine depreciates at the rate of $1,000 per year [($4,500 − $500) ÷ 4 years = $1,000]. Actually, when depreciation is compared to the expiration of a prepaid expense, the primary difference is that since it is often impossible to predict exactly how long an item of equipment will be used or how much will be received for it at the end of its useful life, the amount it depreciates each accounting period is only an estimate.

Estimating and apportioning depreciation can be simple, as in the foregoing example, or it can become complex. A discussion of more complex situations is unnecessary at this point and is deferred to Chapter 10. However, to illustrate the recording of depreciation, assume that on July 31, the Owen law practice estimated its office equipment had depreciated $40 during the month. The depreciation reduced the assets and increased expenses, and the following adjusting entry is required:

July	31	Depreciation Expense, Office Equipment	40.00	
		Accumulated Depreciation, Office Equipment		40.00
		To record the July depreciation.		

The effect of the entry on the accounts is:

Office Equipment			Depreciation Expense, Office Equipment		
July 3	3,700		July 31	40	
5	300				

**Accumulated Depreciation,
Office Equipment**

July 31	40

After the entry is posted, the Office Equipment account and its related Accumulated Depreciation, Office Equipment account together show the July 31 balance sheet amounts for this asset. The Depreciation Expense, Office Equipment account shows the amount of *depreciation expense* that should appear on the July income statement.

In most cases, a decrease in an asset is recorded with a credit to the account in which the asset is recorded. However, note in the illustrated accounts that this procedure is not followed in recording depreciation. Rather, depreciation is recorded in a *contra account,* the Accumulated Depreciation, Office Equipment account. (A contra account is an account in which the balance is subtracted from the balance of an associate account to show a more proper amount for the item recorded in the associated account.)

There are two good reasons for using contra accounts in recording depreciation. First, although based on objective evidence whenever possible, at its best depreciation is only an estimate. Second, the use of contra accounts better preserves the facts in the lives of items of equipment. For example, in this case, the Office Equipment account preserves a record of the equipment's cost, and the Accumulated Depreciation, Office Equipment account shows its depreciation to date.

A better understanding of the second reason for using contra accounts, along with an appreciation of why the word **accumulated** is used in the account name, can be gained when it is pointed out that depreciation is recorded at the end of each accounting period in a depreciating asset's life. As a result, at the end of the third month in the life of the law practice's office equipment, the Office Equipment and its related *accumulated depreciation* account will look like this:

Office Equipment				**Accumulated Depreciation, Office Equipment**	
July 3	3,700			July 31	40
5	300			Aug. 31	40
				Sept. 30	40

And the equipment's cost and three months' accumulated depreciation will be shown on its September 30 balance sheet thus:

Office equipment	$4,000	
Less accumulated depreciation	120	$3,880

[handwritten margin note: Two reasons contra acc / 1) dep. is an estimate / 2) preserves the facts]

Accumulated depreciation accounts are sometimes found in ledgers and on statements under titles such as Allowance for Depreciation, Store Equipment or the totally unacceptable caption, Reserve for Depreciation, Office Equipment. However, more appropriate terminology is Accumulated Depreciation, Store Equipment and Accumulated Depreciation, Office Equipment. The "Accumulated" terminology is better because it is more descriptive of the depreciation procedure.

Accrued Expenses

Most expenses are recorded during an accounting period at the time they are paid. However, when a period ends there may be expenses that have been incurred but have not been paid and recorded because payment is not due. These unpaid and unrecorded expenses for which payment is not due are called *accrued expenses*. Earned but unpaid wages are a common example. To illustrate:

The Owen law practice has a secretary who is paid $40 per day or $200 per week for a workweek that begins on Monday and ends on Friday. The secretary's wages are due and payable every two weeks on Friday; and during July, they were paid on the 12th and 26th and recorded as follows:

Cash			Office Salaries Expense		
	July 12	400	July 12	400	
	26	400	26	400	

If the calendar for July appears as illustrated and the secretary worked on July 29, 30, and 31, then at the close of business on Wednesday, July 31, the secretary has earned three days' wages that are not paid and recorded because payment is not due. However, this $120 of earned but unpaid wages is just as much a part of the July expenses as the $800 of wages that have been paid. Furthermore, on July 31, the unpaid wages are a liability. Consequently, if the accounts are to show the correct amount of wages for July and all liabilities owed on July 31, then an adjusting entry like the following must be made:

JULY						
S	M	T	W	T	F	S
		1	2	3	4	5	6
7	8	9	10	11	12	13
14	15	16	17	18	19	20
21	22	23	24	25	26	27
28	29	30	31			

July	31	Office Salaries Expense	120.00	
		Salaries Payable		120.00
		To record the earned but unpaid wages.		

The effect of the entry on the accounts is:

Office Salaries Expense		Salaries Payable	
July 12	400	July 31	120
26	400		
31	120		

Unearned Revenues

An unearned revenue results when payment is received for goods or services in advance of their delivery. For instance, on July 15, Larry Owen entered into an agreement with Coast Realty to do its legal work on a fixed-fee basis for $300 per month. On that date, Owen received $450 in advance for services during the remainder of July and the month of August. The fee was recorded with this entry:

July	15	Cash	450.00	
		Unearned Legal Fees		450.00
		Received a legal fee in advance.		

Acceptance of the fee in advance increased the cash of the law practice and created a liability, the obligation to do Coast Realty's legal work for the next month and a half. However, by July 31, the law practice has discharged $150 of the liability and earned that much income, which according to the *realization principle* should appear on the July income statement. Consequently, on July 31, the following adjusting entry is required:

July	31	Unearned Legal Fees	150.00	
		Legal Fees Earned		150.00
		To record legal fees earned.		

Posting the entry has this effect on the accounts:

Unearned Legal Fees				Legal Fees Earned	
July 31	150	July 15	450	July 12	500
				19	1,000
				31	150

The effect of the entry is to transfer the $150 earned portion of the fee from the liability account to the revenue account. It reduces the liability and records as a revenue the $150 that has been earned.

Accrued Revenues

An *accrued revenue* is a revenue that has been earned but has not been collected because payment is not due. For example, assume that on July 20, Larry Owen also entered into an agreement with Guaranty Bank to do its legal work on a fixed-fee basis for $300 per month to be paid monthly. Under this assumption, by July 31, the law practice has earned one third of a month's fee, $100, which according to the *realization principle* should appear on its July income statement. Therefore, the following adjusting entry is required:

July	31	Accounts Receivable	100.00	
		Legal Fees Earned		100.00
		To record legal fees earned.		

Posting the entry has this effect on the accounts:

Accounts Receivable					Legal Fees Earned	
July 19	1,000	July 29	1,000		July 12	500
31	100				19	1,000
					31	150
					31	100

THE ADJUSTED TRIAL BALANCE

A trial balance prepared before adjustments is known as an *unadjusted trial balance,* or simply a trial balance. One prepared after adjustments is known as an adjusted trial balance. A July 31 adjusted trial balance for the law practice appears in Illustration 3–2.

PREPARING STATEMENTS FROM THE ADJUSTED TRIAL BALANCE

An adjusted trial balance shows proper balance sheet and income statement amounts. Consequently, it may be used in preparing the statements. When it is so used, the revenue and expense items are arranged into an income statement, as in Illustration 3–3. Likewise, the asset,

Illustration 3–2

LARRY OWEN, LAWYER
Adjusted Trial Balance
July 31, 19—

Cash	$1,185	
Accounts receivable	100	
Prepaid rent	600	
Office supplies	35	
Office equipment	4,000	
Accumulated depreciation, office equipment		$ 40
Accounts payable		260
Salaries payable		120
Unearned legal fees		300
Larry Owen, capital		5,000
Larry Owen, withdrawals	200	
Legal fees earned		1,750
Office salaries expense	920	
Telephone expense	30	
Heating and lighting expense	35	
Rent expense	300	
Office supplies expense	25	
Depreciation expense, office equipment	40	
Totals	$7,470	$7,470

liability, and owner's equity items are arranged into a balance sheet in Illustration 3–4.

When the statements are prepared, the income statement is normally prepared first because the net income, as calculated on the income statement, is needed in completing the balance sheet's owner's equity section. Observe in Illustration 3–4 how the net income is combined with the withdrawals and the excess is added to Owen's July 1 capital. The income increased Owen's equity, and the withdrawals reduced it. Consequently, when the excess of the income over the withdrawals is added to the beginning equity, the result is the ending equity.

THE ADJUSTMENT PROCESS

The *adjustment process* described in this chapter arises from recognition that the operation of a business results in a continuous stream of transactions. Some of the transactions affect several accounting periods. The objective of the process is to allocate to each period that portion of a transaction's effects applicable to the period. For example, if a revenue is earned over several accounting periods, the adjustment process apportions and credits to each period its fair share. Likewise, if an

Illustration 3-3

LARRY OWEN, LAWYER
Adjusted Trial Balance
July 31, 19—

Cash	$1,185	
Accounts receivable	100	
Prepaid rent	600	
Office supplies	35	
Office equipment	4,000	
Accumulated depreciation, office equipment		$ 40
Accounts payable		260
Salaries payable		120
Unearned legal fees		300
Larry Owen, capital		5,000
Larry Owen, withdrawals	200	
Legal fees earned		1,750
Office salaries expense	920	
Telephone expense	30	
Heating and lighting expense	35	
Rent expense	300	
Office supplies expense	25	
Depreciation expense, office equipment	40	
Totals	$7,470	$7,470

PREPARING THE INCOME STATEMENT
FROM THE ADJUSTED TRIAL BALANCE

LARRY OWEN, LAWYER
Income Statement
For Month Ended July 31, 19—

Revenue:		
Legal fees earned		$1,750
Operating expenses:		
Office salaries expense	$920	
Telephone expense	30	
Heating and lighting expense	35	
Rent expense	300	
Office supplies expense	25	
Depreciation expense, office equipment	40	
Total operating expense		1,350
Net income		$ 400

Illustration 3–4

PREPARING THE BALANCE SHEET
FROM THE ADJUSTED TRIAL BALANCE

LARRY OWEN, LAWYER
Adjusted Trial Balance
July 31, 19—

Cash	$1,185	
Accounts receivable	100	
Prepaid rent	600	
Office supplies	35	
Office equipment	4,000	
Accumulated depreciation, office equipment		$ 40
Accounts payable		260
Salaries payable		120
Unearned legal fees		300
Larry Owen, capital		5,000
Larry Owen, withdrawals	200	
Legal fees earned		1,750
Office salaries expense	920	
Telephone expense	30	
Heating and lighting expense	35	
Rent expense	300	
Office supplies expense	25	
Depreciation expense, office equipment	40	
Totals	$7,470	$7,470

LARRY OWEN, LAWYER
Balance Sheet
July 31, 19—

Assets

Current assets:		
Cash	$1,185	
Accounts receivable	100	
Prepaid rent	600	
Office supplies	35	
Total current assets		$1,920
Plant and equipment:		
Office equipment	$4,000	
Less accumulated depreciation	40	
Total plant and equipment		3,960
Total assets		$5,880

Liabilities

Current liabilities:		
Accounts payable	$ 260	
Salaries payable	120	
Unearned legal fees	300	
Total liabilities		$ 680

Owner's Equity

Larry Owen, capital, July 1, 19—		$5,000
July net income	$400	
Less withdrawals	200	
Excess of income over withdrawals		200
Larry Owen, capital, July 31, 19—		5,200
Total liabilities and owner's equity		$5,880

July net income
from the July
income statement

expense benefits several periods, the adjustment process charges a fair share to each benefited period.

The adjustment process is based on two accounting principles, the realization principle and the *matching principle*. The *realization principle* requires that revenue be assigned to the accounting period in which it is earned, rather than to the period in which it is collected in cash. The matching principle requires that revenues and expenses be matched. As for matching revenues and expenses, it is recognized that a business incurs expenses in order to earn revenues. Consequently, it is only proper that expenses be matched with (deducted on the income statement from) the revenues they helped to produce.

The basic purpose behind the adjustment process, the *realization principle,* and the *matching principle* is to make the information on accounting statements comparable from period to period. For example, the Owen law practice paid its rent for three months in advance on July 1 and debited the $900 payment to Prepaid Rent. Then, at the end of July, it transferred $300 of this amount to its Rent Expense account and the $300 appeared on its July income statement as the July rent expense. At the end of August, it will transfer another $300 to rent expense, and at the end of September, it will transfer the third $300. As a result, the amounts shown for rent expense on its July, August, and September income statements will be comparable.

An unsatisfactory alternate procedure would be to debit the entire $900 to Rent Expense at the time of payment and permit the entire amount to appear on the July income statement as rent expense for July. However, if this were done, the July income statement would show $900 of rent expense and the August and September statements would show none. Thus, the income statements of the three months would not be comparable. In addition, the July net income would be understated $600 and the net incomes of August and September would be overstated $300 each. As a result, a person seeing only the fluctuations in net income might draw an incorrect conclusion.

ARRANGEMENT OF THE ACCOUNTS IN THE LEDGER

Normally, the accounts of a business are classified and logically arranged in its ledger. This serves two purposes: (1) it aids in locating any account and (2) it aids in preparing the statements. Obviously, statements can be prepared with the least difficulty if accounts are arranged in the ledger in the order of their statement appearance. This causes the accounts to appear on the adjusted trial balance in their statement order, which aids in rearranging the adjusted trial balance items into a balance sheet and an income statement. Consequently, the balance sheet accounts beginning with Cash and ending with the owner's equity accounts appear first in the ledger. These are followed by the revenue and expense accounts in the order of their income statement appearance.

DISPOSING OF ACCRUED ITEMS

Accrued Expenses

Several pages back, the July 29, 30, and 31 accrued wages of the secretary were recorded as follows:

July	31	Office Salaries Expense	120.00	
		Salaries Payable		120.00
		To record the earned but unpaid wages.		

When these wages are paid on Friday, August 9, the following entry is required:

Aug.	9	Salaries Payable	120.00	
		Office Salaries Expense	280.00	
		Cash		400.00
		Paid two weeks' wages.		

The first debit in the August 9 entry cancels the liability for the three days' wages accrued on July 31. The second debit records the wages of August's first seven working days as an expense of the August accounting period. The credit records the amount paid the secretary.

Accrued Revenues

On July 20, Larry Owen entered into an agreement to do the legal work of Guaranty Bank on a fixed-fee basis for $300 per month. On July 31, the following adjusting entry was made to record one third of a month's revenue earned under this contract.

July	31	Accounts Receivable	100.00	
		Legal Fees Earned		100.00
		To record legal fees earned.		

And when payment of the first month's fee is received on August 20, the following entry will be made:

Aug.	20	Cash	300.00	
		Accounts Receivable		100.00
		Legal Fees Earned		200.00
		Received legal fees earned.		

The first credit in the August 20 entry records the collection of the fee accrued at the end of July. The second credit records as revenue the fee earned during the first 20 days of August.

CASH AND ACCRUAL BASES OF ACCOUNTING

Under the *cash basis,* no adjustments are made for prepaid, unearned, and accrued items. Revenues are reported as being earned in the accounting period in which they are received in cash. Expenses are deducted from revenues in the accounting period in which cash is disbursed in their payment. As a result, under the cash basis net income is the difference between revenue receipts and expense disbursements. Under the *accrual basis,* on the other hand, adjustments are made for accrued and deferred (prepaid and unearned) items. Under this basis, revenues are credited to the period in which earned, expenses are matched with revenues, and no consideration is given to when cash is received and disbursed. As a result, net income is the difference between revenues earned and the expenses incurred in earning the revenues.

The cash basis of accounting is satisfactory for individuals and a few concerns in which accrued and deferred items are not important. However, it is not satisfactory for most concerns since it results in accounting reports that are not comparable from period to period. Consequently, most businesses keep their records on an accrual basis.

CLASSIFICATION OF BALANCE SHEET ITEMS

The balance sheets in the first two chapters were simple ones, and no attempt was made to classify the items. However, a balance sheet becomes more useful when its assets and liabilities are classified into significant groups. A reader of such a *classified balance sheet* can better judge the adequacy of the different kinds of assets used in the business. The reader can also better estimate the probable availability of funds to meet the various liabilities as they become due.

Illustration 3–5

VALLEY STORE
Balance Sheet
December 31, 198A

Assets

Current assets:

Cash	$ 1,050	
Notes receivable	300	
Accounts receivable	3,961	
Merchandise inventory	20,248	
Prepaid insurance	109	
Office supplies	46	
Stores supplies	145	
Total current assets		$ 25,859

Plant and equipment:

Office equipment	$ 1,500		
Less accumulated depreciation	300	$ 1,200	
Store equipment	$ 3,200		
Less accumulated depreciation	800	2,400	
Buildings	$75,000		
Less accumulated depreciation	7,400	67,600	
Land		24,200	
Total plant and equipment			95,400
Total assets			$121,259

Liabilities

Current liabilities:

Notes payable	$ 3,000	
Accounts payable	2,715	
Wages payable	112	
Mortgage payable (current portion)	1,200	
Total current liabilities		$ 7,027

Long-term liabilities:

First mortgage payable, secured by a mortgage on land and buildings		78,800
Total liabilities		$ 85,827

Owner's Equity

Samuel Jackson, capital, January 1, 198A		$33,721
Net income for the year	$19,711	
Less withdrawals	18,000	
Excess of income over withdrawals		1,711
Samuel Jackson, capital, December 31, 198A		35,432
Total liabilities and owner's equity		$121,259

Accountants are not in full agreement as to the best way in which to classify balance sheet items. As a result, they are classified in several ways. A common way classifies assets into (1) current assets, (2) long-term investments, (3) plant and equipment, and (4) intangible assets. It classifies liabilities into (1) current liabilities and (2) long-term liabilities.

Of the four asset classifications listed, only two, current assets and plant and equipment, appear on the balance sheet of Valley Store, Illustration 3–5. The store is small and has no long-term investments and intangible assets.

Current Assets

Current assets are primarily those to which current creditors (current liabilities) may look for payment. As presently defined, current assets consist of cash and assets that are reasonably expected to be realized in cash or be sold or consumed within one year or within one *operating cycle of the business* whichever is longer. The accounts and notes receivable of Illustration 3–5 are expected to be realized in cash. The merchandise (merchandise inventory) is expected to be sold either for cash or accounts receivable that will be realized in cash. The prepaid insurance and supplies are to be consumed.

The operating cycle of a business is the average period of time between its acquisition of merchandise or raw materials and the realization of cash from the sale of the merchandise or the sale of the products manufactured from the raw materials. In many companies, this interval is less than one year; and as a result, these companies use a one-year period in classifying current assets. However, due to an aging process or other cause, some companies have an operating cycle longer than one year. For example, distilleries must age some products for several years before the products are ready for sale. Consequently, in such companies, inventories of raw materials, manufacturing supplies, and products being processed for sale are classified as current assets, although the products made from the inventories will not be ready for sale for more than a year.

Such things as prepaid insurance, office supplies, and store supplies are called prepaid expenses. Until consumed, they are classified as current assets. Prepaid expenses are not current assets in the sense that they will be converted into cash but in the sense that, if not paid in advance, they would require the use of current assets during the operating cycle. This means that if the prepaid expense items were not already owned, current assets would be required for their purchase during the operating cycle.

The prepaid expenses of a business, as a total, are seldom a major item on its balance sheet. As a result, instead of listing them individually, as in Illustration 3–5, they are commonly totaled and only the total is shown under the caption "Prepaid expenses."

Long-Term Investments

The second balance sheet classification is long-term investments. Stocks, bonds, and promissory notes that will be held for more than one year or one cycle appear under this classification. Also, such things as land held for future expansion but not now being used in the business operations appear here.

Plant and Equipment

Plant assets are relatively long-lived assets of a tangible nature that are held for use in the production or sale of other assets or services. Examples are items of equipment, buildings, and land. The key words in the definition are **long-lived** and **held for use in the production or sale of other assets or services.** Land held for future expansion is not a plant asset. It is not being used to produce or sell other assets, goods, or services.

The words *Plant and equipment* are commonly used as a balance sheet caption. More complete captions are "Property, plant, and equipment" and "Land, buildings, and equipment." However, all three captions are long and unwieldy. As a result, items of plant and equipment will be called plant assets in this book.

The order in which plant assets are listed within the balance sheet classification is not uniform. However, they are often listed from the ones of least permanent nature to those of most permanent nature.

Intangible Assets

Intangible assets are assets having no physical nature. Their value is derived from the rights conferred upon their owner by possession. Goodwill, patents, and trademarks are examples.

Current Liabilities

Current liabilities are debts or other obligations that must be paid or liquidated within one year or one operating cycle, using presently listed current assets in their payment or liquidation. Common current liabilities are notes payable, accounts payable, wages payable, taxes payable, interest payable, and unearned revenues. Also, that portion of a long-term debt due within one year or one operating cycle, for example, the $1,200 portion of the mortgage debt shown in Illustration 3–5, is a current liability. The order of their listing within the classification is not uniform.

Often notes payable are listed first because notes receivable are listed first after cash in the current asset section.

Unearned revenues are classified as current liabilities because current assets will normally be required in their liquidation. For example, payments for future delivery of merchandise will be earned and the obligation for delivery will be liquidated by delivering merchandise, a current asset.

Long-Term Liabilities

The second main liability classification is *long-term liabilities*. Liabilities that are not due and payable for a comparatively long period, usually more than one year, are listed under this classification. Common long-term liability items are mortgages payable, bonds payable, and notes payable due more than a year after the balance sheet data.

OWNER'S EQUITY ON THE BALANCE SHEET

Single Proprietorship

The equity of the owner of a single proprietorship business may be shown on a balance sheet as follows:

Owner's Equity		
James Gibbs, capital, January 1, 198A		$23,152
Net income for the year	$10,953	
Less withdrawals	12,000	
Excess of withdrawals over income		(1,047)
James Gibbs, capital, December 31, 198A		$22,105

The withdrawals of James Gibbs exceeded his net income; and in the equity section, the excess is enclosed in parenthesis to indicate that it is a negative or subtracted amount. Negative amounts are commonly shown in this way on financial statements.

The illustrated equity section shows the increases and decreases in owner's equity resulting from earnings and withdrawals. Some accountants prefer to put these details on a supplementary schedule attached to the balance sheet and called a **statement of owner's equity.** When this is done, owner's equity is shown on the balance sheet as follows:

Owner's Equity	
James Gibbs, capital (see schedule attached)	$22,105

Partnerships

Changes in partnership equities resulting from earnings and withdrawals are commonly shown in a statement of partners' equities. Then, only the amount of each partner's equity and the total of the equalities as of the statement date are shown on the balance sheet, as follows:

Partners' Equities	
John Reed, capital	$16,534
Robert Burns, capital	18,506
Total equities of the partners	$35,040

Corporations

Corporations are regulated by provincial and federal corporation laws. These laws require that a distinction be made between amounts invested in a corporation by its shareholders and the increase or decrease in shareholders' equity due to earnings, losses, and dividends. Consequently, shareholders' equity is commonly shown on a corporation balance sheet as follows:

Shareholders' Equity	
Common stock	$500,000
Retained earnings	64,450
Total shareholders' equity	$564,450

If a corporation issues only one kind of stock (others are discussed later), it is called *common stock*. The $500,000 amount shown here for this item is the amount originally invested in this corporation by its shareholders through the purchase of the corporation's stock. The $64,450 of *retained earnings* represents the increase in the shareholders' equity resulting from earnings that exceeded any losses and any *dividends* paid to the shareholders. (A dividend is a distribution of assets made by a corporation to its shareholders. A dividend of cash reduces corporation assets and the equity of its shareholders in the same way a withdrawal reduces assets and owner's equity in a single proprietorship.)

ARRANGEMENT OF BALANCE SHEET ITEMS

The balance sheet of Illustration 1–2 in the first chapter, with the liabilities and owner's equity placed to the right of the assets, is called an *account form balance sheet*. Such an arrangement emphasizes that assets equal liabilities plus owner's equity. Account form balance sheets are often reproduced on a double page with the assets on the left-hand page and the liabilities and owner's equity on the right-hand page.

The balance sheet of Illustration 3–5 is called a ***report form balance sheet.*** Its items are arranged vertically and better fit a single page. Both forms are commonly used, and neither is preferred.

ACCOUNT NUMBERS

A commonly used three-digit account numbering system was introduced in Chapter 2. In the system, the number assigned to an account not only identifies the account but also tells its balance sheet or income statement classification. In the system, the first digit in an account's number tells its main balance sheet or income statement classification. For example, account numbers with first digits of 1 are assigned to asset accounts. Liability accounts are assigned numbers with first digits of 2, and the accounts in each main balance sheet and income statement classification of a concern selling merchandise are assigned numbers as follows:

111 to 199 are assigned to asset accounts.
211 to 299 are assigned to liability accounts.
311 to 399 are assigned to owner's equity accounts.
411 to 499 are assigned to sales or revenue accounts.
511 to 599 are assigned to cost of goods sold accounts.
611 to 699 are assigned to operating expense accounts.
711 to 799 are assigned to other revenue and expense accounts.

In the system, the second digit further classifies an account. For example, the second digits under each of the following main classifications indicate the subclassification shown:

111 to 199.   Asset accounts
   111 to 119.   Current asset accounts (second digits of 1)
   121 to 129.   Long-term investment accounts (second digits of 2)
   131 to 139.   Plant asset accounts (second digits of 3)
   141 to 149.   Intangible asset accounts (second digits of 4)

211 to 299.   Liability accounts
   211 to 219.   Current liability accounts (second digits of 1)
   221 to 229.   Long-term liability accounts (second digits of 2)

611 to 699.   Operating expense accounts
   611 to 629.   Selling expense accounts (second digits of 1 and 2)
   631 to 649.   General and administrative expense accounts (second digits of 3 and 4)

The third digit of an account's number completes its identification. For example, third digits complete the identification of the following current asset accounts:

111 to 199.   Asset accounts
   111 to 119.   Current asset accounts
      111.   Cash
      112.   Petty Cash
      113.   Notes Receivable
      114.   Accounts Receivable

The sales and cost of goods sold accounts mentioned here are discussed in Chapter 5. The division of the operating expense accounts into selling expense accounts and general and administrative expense accounts is also discussed there. In a service-type business such as the ones described in this chapter, generally all expense accounts are classified as operating expense accounts without subdividing them.

GLOSSARY

Account form balance sheet.   A balance sheet with the assets on the left and the liability and owner's equity items on the right.

Accounting period.   The time interval over which the transactions of a business are recorded and at the end of which its financial statements are prepared.

Accrual basis of accounting.   The accounting basis in which revenues are assigned to the accounting period in which earned regardless of whether or not received in cash, and expenses incurred in earning the revenues are deducted from the revenues regardless of whether or not cash has been disbursed in their payment.

Accrued expense.   An expense that has been incurred during an accounting period but that has not been paid and recorded because payment is not due.

Accrued revenue.   A revenue that has been earned during an accounting period but has not been received and recorded because payment i not due.

Accumulated depreciation.   The cumulative amount of depreciation recorded against an asset or group of assets during the entire period of time the asset or assets have been owned.

Adjusted trial balance.   A trial balance showing account balances brought up-to-date by recording appropriate adjusting entries.

Adjusting entries.   Journal entries made to assign revenues to the period in which earned and to match revenues and expenses.

Adjustment process.   The end-of-period process of recording appropriate adjusting entries to assign revenues to the period in which earned and to match revenues and expenses.

Cash basis of accounting. The accounting basis in which revenues are reported as being earned in the accounting period received in cash and expenses are deducted from revenues in the accounting period in which cash is disbursed in their payment.

Classified balance sheet. A balance sheet with assets and liabilities classified into significant groups.

Common stock. The name given to a corporation's stock when it issues only one kind or class of stock.

Contra account. An account the balance of which is subtracted from the balance of an associated account to show a more proper amount for the item recorded in the associated account.

Current asset. Cash or an asset that may reasonably be expected to be realized in cash or be consumed within one year or one operating cycle of the business, whichever is longer.

Current liability. A debt or other obligation that must be paid or liquidated within one year or one operating cycle, and the payment or liquidation of which will require the use of presently classified current assets.

Depreciation. The expiration of a plant asset's "quantity of usefulness."

Depreciation expense. The expense resulting from the expiration of a plant asset's "quantity of usefulness."

Dividend. A distribution of cash or other assets made by a corporation to its shareholders.

Fiscal year. A period of any 12 consecutive months used as an accounting period.

Intangible asset. An asset having no physical existence but having value because of the rights conferred as a result of its ownership and possession.

Long-term liability. A debt that is not due and payable for a comparatively long period, usually more than one year.

Matching principle. The accounting rule that all expenses incurred in earning a revenue be deducted from the revenue in determining net income.

Natural business year. Any 12 consecutive months used by a business as an accounting period, at the end of which the activities of the business are at their lowest point.

Operating cycle of a business. The average period of time between the acquisition of merchandise or materials by a business and the realization of cash from the sale of the merchandise or product manufactured from the materials.

Plant and equipment. Tangible assets having relatively long lives that are used in the production or sale of other assets or services.

Report form balance sheet. A balance sheet prepared on one page, at the top of which the assets are listed, followed down the page by the liabilities and owner's equity.

Retained earnings.   Shareholders' equity in a corporation resulting from earnings in excess of losses and dividends declared.

Time-period concept.   The idea that the life of a business is divisible into time periods of equal length.

Unadjusted trial balance.   A trial balance prepared after transactions are recorded but before any adjustments are made.

QUESTIONS FOR CLASS DISCUSSION

1. Why are the balances of some of a concern's accounts normally incorrect for statement purposes at the end of an accounting period even though all transactions were correctly recorded?

2. Other than to make the accounts show proper statement amounts, what is the basic purpose behind the end-of-period adjustment process?

3. A prepaid expense is an asset at the time of its purchase or prepayment. When is it best to ignore this and record the prepayment as an expense? Why?

4. What is a contra account? Give an example.

5. What contra account is used in recording depreciation? Why is such an account used?

6. What is an accrued expense? Give an example.

7. How does an unearned revenue arise? Give an example of an unearned revenue.

8. What is the balance sheet classification of an unearned revenue?

9. What is an accrued revenue? Give an example.

10. When the statements are prepared from an adjusted trial balance, why should the income statement be prepared first?

11. The adjustment process results from recognizing that some transactions affect several accounting periods. What is the objective of the process?

12. When are a concern's revenues and expenses matched?

13. Why should the income statements of a concern be comparable from period to period?

14. What is the usual order in which accounts are arranged in the ledger?

15. Differentiate between the cash and the accrual bases of accounting.

16. What is a classified balance sheet?

17. What are the characteristics of a current asset? What are the characteristics of an asset classified as plant and equipment?

18. What are current liabilities? Long-term liabilities?

19. The equity section of a corporation balance sheet shows two items, common stock and retained earnings. What does the sum of the items represent? How did each item arise?

MULTIPLE CHOICE

1. The accounting basis in which revenues are assigned to the accounting period in which earned regardless of whether or not received in cash and expenses incurred in earning the revenues are deducted from the revenues regardless of whether or not cash has been disbursed in their payment is the:

   a. Adjusted basis of accounting.
   b. Cash basis of accounting.
   c. Accrual basis of accounting.
   d. Classified basis of accounting.
   e. Real basis of accounting.

2. An expense which has been incurred during an accounting period but which has not been paid and recorded because payment is not due is a(n):

   a. Intangible expense.
   b. Prepaid expense.
   c. Unearned expense.
   d. Accrued expense.
   e. Net expense.

3. An accrued revenue is:

   a. A revenue that has been received but is not yet earned.
   b. A revenue that has not been earned during an accounting period but has been recorded in advance.
   c. A revenue that has been earned during an accounting period but has not been received or recorded prior to making adjusting entries because payment is not due.
   d. A revenue that has not been earned, received nor recorded.
   e. A revenue that has been earned and received and posted.

4. Payment received in advance for goods or services to be delivered at a later date is a(n):

   a. Accrued revenue.
   b. Retained earnings.
   c. Contra revenue.
   d. Unearned revenue.
   e. Dividend.

5. The accounting rule that all expenses incurred in earning a revenue must be deducted from the revenue in determining net income is the:

   a. Recognition principle.
   b. Cost principle.
   c. Objectivity principle.
   d. Matching principle.
   e. Materiality principle.

6. The average period of time between the acquisition of merchandise or materials by a business and the realization of cash from the materials is the:
    a. Accounting period of a business.
    b. Fiscal year.
    c. Time-period concept.
    d. Operating cycle of a business.
    e. Natural business year.

7. The accounting basis in which revenues are reported as being earned in the accounting period received in cash and expenses are deducted from revenues in the accounting period in which cash is disbursed in their payment is the:
    a. Accrual basis of accounting.
    b. Fiscal basis of accounting.
    c. Cash basis of accounting.
    d. Adjusted basis of accounting.
    e. Current basis of accounting.

8. Journal entries made at the end of an accounting period to assign revenues to the period in which earned and to match revenues and expenses are:
    a. Operating entries.
    b. Balancing entries.
    c. Matching entries.
    d. Adjusting entries.
    e. Contra entries.

9. If throughout an accounting period the fees for legal services paid in advance by clients are recorded in an account called unearned legal fees, the end-of-the-period adjusting entry to record the portion of these fees that has been earned is:
    a. Debit cash and credit legal fees earned.
    b. Debit cash and credit unearned legal fees.
    c. Debit unearned legal fees and credit legal fees earned.
    d. Debit legal fees earned and credit unearned legal fees.
    e. Some other entry.

MINI DISCUSSION CASES

Case 3–1

The president of Seneca Company called in the controller to personally express his displeasure with the length of time the accounting department took to produce the monthly financial statements. The controller replied that he appreciated the president's frustration; however, the month-end adjustments did require time, which was reduced to the absolute minimum. The president responded that he did not know why these adjustments were necessary. In fact, in his opinion, the time spent on adjustments was nothing more than a "make-work" procedure.

It was unnecessary since these adjustments were repetitions of the same items which, if left alone, would cancel out the effects and result in financial statements that were just as accurate. For example, the president continued, with accrued wages payable at the end of each month, why then waste time on adjustments?

Required:

Discuss whether the president's underlying assumptions are realistic and apply equally to all types of adjustments normally encountered at the end of each period.

Case 3–2

Durham Company's president believed that the monthly executive meetings, which considered the results of previous month's activity, could be "pushed up" a couple of days if the financial statements were available. After a discussion with the controller, the president found out that the month-end adjustments were the cause of delays. Consequently, he is contemplating asking the controller to speed up month-end statement preparation without the benefit of month-end adjustments. However, before taking such a step, he asks you to evaluate such an alternative.

Required:

Discuss the short-comings of "unadjusted" financial statements. Focus your discussion on *(a)* compliance with GAAP, *(b)* treatment of such items as supplies and insurance, and *(c)* manipulation of results.

CLASS EXERCISES

Exercise 3–1

A company has two shop employees who together earn a total of $150 per day for a five-day workweek that begins on Monday and ends on Friday. They were paid for the week ended Friday, December 26, and both worked full days on Monday, Tuesday, and Wednesday, December 29, 30, and 31. January 1 of the next year was an unpaid holiday and none of the employees worked, but all worked a full day on Friday, January 2. Give in general journal form the year-end adjusting entry to record the accrued wages and the entry to pay the employees on January 2.

Exercise 3–2

Give in general journal form the year-end adjusting entry for each of the following situations:

a. The Shop Supplies account had a $225 debit balance on January 1; $415 of supplies were purchased during the year; and a year-end inventory showed $120 of unconsumed supplies on hand.

b. The Prepaid Insurance account had a $765 debit balance at the end of the accounting period before adjustment for expired insurance. An examination of insurance policies showed $445 of insurance expired.

c. The Prepaid Insurance account had an $880 debit balance at the end of the accounting period before adjustment for expired insurance. An examination of insurance policies showed $265 of unexpired insurance.

d. Depreciation on shop equipment was estimated at $915 for the accounting period.

e. Four months' property taxes, estimated at $565, have accrued but are unrecorded and unpaid at the accounting period end.

Exercise 3–3   Assume that the required adjustments of Exercise 3–2 were not made at the end of the accounting period and tell for each adjustment the effect of its omission on the income statement and balance sheet prepared at that time.

Exercise 3–4   Determine the amounts indicated by the question marks in the columns below. The amounts in each column constitute a separate problem.

	(a)	(b)	(c)	(d)
Supplies on hand on January 1	$235	$140	$375	?
Supplies purchased during the year	450	530	?	$630
Supplies remaining at the year-end	165	?	215	240
Supplies consumed during the year	?	480	670	560

Exercise 3–5   A company paid the $900 premium on a three-year insurance policy on May 1, 198A. The policy gave protection beginning on that date.

a. How many dollars of the premium should appear on the 198A income statement as an expense?

b. How many dollars of the premium should appear on the December 31, 198A, balance sheet as an asset?

c. Under the assumption that the Prepaid Insurance account was debited in recording the premium payment, give the December 31, 198A, adjusting entry to record the expired insurance.

d. Under the assumption that the bookkeeper incorrectly debited the Insurance Expense account for $900 in recording the premium payment, give the December 31, 198A, adjusting entry. (Hint: Did the bookkeeper's error change the answers to questions [a] and [b] of this exercise?)

Exercise 3–6   a. A tenant rented space in a building on October 1 at $300 per month, paying six months' rent in advance. The building owner credited Unearned Rent to record the $1,800 received. Give the year-end adjusting entry of the building owner.

b. Another tenant rented space in the building at $350 per month on October 1. The tenant paid the rent on the first day of October and again on the first day of November, but by December 31 the December rent had not yet been paid. Give the required adjusting entry of the building owner.

c. Assume the foregoing tenant paid the rent for December and January on January 2 of the new year. Give the entry to record the receipt of the $700.

Exercise 3–7   The adjusted trial balance that follows was taken from the ledger of Mary Luke, a lawyer.

MARY LUKE, LAWYER
Adjusted Trial Balance
December 31, 19—

Cash	$ 1,500	
Accounts receivable	3,200	
Prepaid insurance	700	
Office supplies	100	
Office equipment	10,500	
Accumulated depreciation, office equipment		$ 3,000
Building	110,000	
Accumulated depreciation, building		10,000
Land	40,000	
Salaries payable		200
Unearned legal fees		800
Mortgage payable		95,000
Mary Luke, capital		48,000
Mary Luke, withdrawals	36,000	
Legal fees earned		85,000
Operating expenses (combined)	40,000	
Totals	$242,000	$242,000

Required:

A subtraction of the combined operating expenses from the legal fees earned indicates that the law practice earned $45,000 during the year of the adjusted trial balance. A $5,000 payment on the mortgage is due within one year. Use this information and any relevant information from the adjusted trial balance to prepare a classified year-end balance sheet for the practice.

Exercise 3–8   An inexperienced bookkeeper prepared the first of the following income statements, but forgot to adjust the accounts before its preparation. However, the oversight was discovered and the second statement was prepared. Analyze the statements and prepare the adjusting journal entries that were made between the preparation of the two statements. Assume that one third of the additional property management fees resulted from recognizing accrued fees and two thirds resulted from previously recorded unearned fees that were earned by the date of the statements.

HILLSIDE REALTY
Income Statement
For Year Ended December 31, 19—

Revenues:		
Commissions earned		$54,750
Property management fees		3,000
Total revenues		$57,750
Operating expenses:		
Salaries expense	$11,500	
Rent expense	9,000	
Advertising expense	2,500	
Gas, oil, and repairs expense	500	
Total operating expenses		23,500
Net income		$34,250

HILLSIDE REALTY
Income Statement
For Year Ended December 31, 19—

Revenues:
Commissions earned		$54,750
Property management fees		3,750
Total revenues		$58,500
Operating expenses:		
Salaries expense	$12,000	
Rent expense	9,000	
Advertising expense	2,500	
Gas, oil, and repairs expense	500	
Office supplies expense	100	
Insurance expense	900	
Depreciation expense, office equipment	1,000	
Depreciation expense, automobile	2,000	
Total operating expenses		28,000
Net income		$30,500

Exercise 3–9   Following are data from the records of three single proprietorships. Prepare a year-end balance sheet equity section for each.

a. Frank Hall, capital, January 1, 19— $63,000
    Net income earned during the year 38,000
    Withdrawals during the year 30,000

b. Harry Beal, capital, January 1, 19— $36,000
    Net income earned during the year 15,000
    Withdrawals during the year 18,000

c. George Nash, capital, January 1, 19—...... $48,000
    Net loss incurred during the year 4,000
    Withdrawals during the year 12,000

Exercise 3–10   A corporation had $250,000 of common stock issued and outstanding during all of 198B. It began with $65,000 of retained earnings and it paid $20,000 of cash dividends to its shareholders. It also earned $50,000 net income for 198B. Prepare the equity section of the corporation's year-end balance sheet. (Hint: Net income increases a corporation's assets and retained earnings and dividends and losses reduce its assets and retained earnings. However, only the net amount of a corporation's retained earnings as of the statement date is shown on its balance sheet.)

PROBLEMS

Problem 3–1   The following information for adjustments was available on December 31, the end of a yearly accounting period. Prepare an adjusting journal entry for each unit of information.

a. The Store Supplies account had a $125 debit balance at the beginning of the year, $560 of supplies were purchased during the year, and an inventory of unused store supplies at the year-end totaled $150.

b. An examination of insurance policies showed three policies, as follows:

Policy	Date of purchase	Life of policy	Cost
1.....	October 1 of previous year	3 years	$1,800
2.....	April 1 of current year	2 years	720
3.....	August 1 of current year	1 year	480

Prepaid Insurance was debited for the cost of each policy at the time of its purchase. Expired insurance was correctly recorded at the end of the previous year.

c. The company's two office employees earn $50 per day and $60 per day, respectively. They are paid each Friday for a five-day workweek that begins on Monday. This year December 31 fell on Tuesday, and the employees both worked on Monday and Tuesday.

d. The company owns a building that it completed and occupied for the first time on June 1 of the current year. The building cost $360,000, has an estimated 30-year life, and is not expected to have any salvage value at the end of that time.

e. The company occupies most of the space in its building but it also rents space to two tenants. One tenant rented a small amount of space on September 1 at $400 per month. The tenant paid the rent on the first day of each month September through November, and the amounts paid were credited to Rent Earned. However, the tenant has not paid the rent for December, although on several occasions the tenant said the rent would be paid the next day. *(f)* The second tenant agreed on November 1 to rent a small amount of space at $450 per month, and on that date paid three months' rent in advance. The amount paid was credited to the Unearned Rent account.

Problem 3–2   A trial balance of the ledger of Apex Realty at the end of its annual accounting period carried the items that follow.

APEX REALTY
Trial Balance
December 31, 19—

Cash	$ 1,940	
Prepaid insurance	915	
Office supplies	290	
Office equipment	6,250	
Accumulated depreciation, office equipment ...		$ 1,920
Automobile	12,780	
Accumulated depreciation, automobile		2,150
Accounts payable		225
Unearned management fees		450
Dale Pitts, capital		11,145
Dale Pitts, withdrawals	18,600	
Sales commissions earned		41,280
Office salaries expense	10,300	
Advertising expense	830	
Rent expense	4,800	
Telephone expense	465	
Totals	$57,170	$57,170

Required:

1. Open the accounts of the trial balance plus these additional ones: Accounts Receivable; Office Salaries Payable; Management Fees Earned; Insurance

Expense; Office Supplies Expense; Depreciation Expense, Office Equipment; and Depreciation Expense, Automobile. Enter the trial balance amounts in the accounts.

2. Use the following information to prepare and post adjusting entries:
   a. An examination of insurance policies showed $645 of expired insurance.
   b. An inventory showed $65 of unused office supplies on hand.
   c. The year's depreciation on office equipment was estimated at $780 and (d) on the automobile at $1,800.
   e. and (f) Apex Realty offers property management services and has two contracts with clients. In the first contract (e), it agreed to manage an office building beginning on November 1. The contract calls for a $150 monthly fee, and the client paid the first three months' fees in advance at the time the contract was signed. The amount paid was credited to the Unearned Management Fees account. In the second contract (f), it agreed to manage an apartment building for $100 per month payable at the end of each three-month period. The contract was signed on October 15, and two and a half months' fees have accrued.
   g. The one office employee is paid weekly; and on December 31, three days' wages at $45 per day have accrued.

3. After posting the adjusting entries, prepare an adjusted trial balance, an income statement, and a classified balance sheet.

Problem 3–3   A year-end trial balance of the ledger of Lakeside Moving and Storage follows:

LAKESIDE MOVING AND STORAGE
Trial Balance
December 31, 19—

Cash	$ 2,240	
Accounts receivable	545	
Prepaid insurance	3,580	
Office supplies	320	
Office equipment	3,650	
Accumulated depreciation, office equipment		$ 1,680
Trucks	44,200	
Accumulated depreciation, trucks		11,540
Building	168,000	
Accumulated depreciation, building		28,600
Land	17,500	
Unearned storage fees		1,730
Mortgage payable		120,000
John Hall, capital		54,110
John Hall, withdrawals	24,000	
Revenue from moving services		90,115
Storage fees earned		7,770
Office salaries expense	11,400	
Drivers' and helpers' wages expense	26,630	
Gas, oil, and repairs expense	2,680	
Mortgage interest expense	10,800	
Totals	$315,545	$315,545

Required:

1. Open the accounts of the trial balance plus these additional ones: Salaries and Wages Payable; Insurance Expense; Office Supplies Expense; Depreciation Expense, Office Equipment; Depreciation Expense, Trucks; and Depreciation Expense, Building. Enter the trial balance amounts in the accounts.

2. Prepare and post adjusting journal entries based on the information that follows:

   a. An examination of insurance policies showed $2,350 of expired insurance.

   b. An inventory showed $135 of unused office supplies on hand.

   c. Estimated depreciation on the office equipment, $455; *(d)* on the trucks, $4,420; and *(e)* on the building, $5,600.

   f. The company credits storage fees of customers who pay in advance to the Unearned Storage Fees account. Of the $1,730 credited to this account, $1,420 was earned by the year-end.

   g. Accrued storage fees earned but unrecorded and uncollected at the year-end totaled $260.

   h. There were $610 of earned but unrecorded drivers' and helpers' wages at the year-end.

3. Prepare an adjusted trial balance, an income statement for the year, and a classified year-end balance sheet. A $4,000 installment on the mortgage is due within one year.

Problem 3–4   After all transactions were recorded at the end of its annual accounting period, a trial balance of the ledger of Vista Trailer Park carried the items that follow.

VISTA TRAILER PARK
Trial Balance
December 31, 19—

Cash	$ 2,540	
Prepaid insurance	1,525	
Office supplies	260	
Office equipment	2,450	
Accumulated depreciation, office equipment		$ 815
Buildings and improvements	92,000	
Accumulated depreciation, buildings and improvements		21,350
Land	95,000	
Unearned rent		780
Mortgage payable		118,000
June Lake, capital		41,810
June Lake, withdrawals	18,200	
Rent earned		51,865
Wages expense	10,120	
Utilities expense	825	
Property taxes expense	1,965	
Interest expense	9,735	
Totals	$234,620	$234,620

Required:

1. Open the accounts of the trial balance plus these additional ones: Accounts Receivable; Wages Payable; Property Taxes Payable; Interest Payable; Insurance Expense; Office Supplies Expense; Depreciation Expense, Office Equipment; and Depreciation Expense, Buildings and Improvements. Enter the trial balance amounts in the accounts.

2. Use the following information to prepare and post adjusting journal entries:
   a. An examination of insurance policies showed $1,180 of expired insurance.
   b. An office supplies inventory showed $115 of unused office supplies on hand.
   c. Estimated depreciation on office equipment, $290; and *(d)* on buildings and improvements, $4,600.
   e. The trailer park follows the practice of crediting the Unearned Rent account for rents paid in advance by tenants. An examination revealed that $580 of the balance of this account was earned by the year-end.
   f. A tenant is in arrears on rent payments, and this $85 of accrued revenue was unrecorded at the time the trial balance was prepared.
   g. The one employee of the trailer park works a five-day workweek at $40 per day. The employee was paid last week but has worked three days this week for which he has not been paid.
   h. Three months' property taxes, totaling $655, have accrued. This additional amount of property taxes expense has not been recorded.
   i. One month's interest on the mortgage, $885, has accrued but is unrecorded.

3. Post the adjusting entries and prepare an adjusted trial balance, an income statement for the year, and a classified balance sheet. A $6,000 installment on the mortgage is due within one year.

Problem 3–5   Sue Hall purchased Vagabond Village, a mobile home park, last September 1, and she has operated it four months without keeping formal accounting records. However, she has deposited all receipts in the bank and has kept an accurate chequebook record of payments. An analysis of her cash receipts and payments follows.

	Receipts	Payments
Investment	$42,000	
Purchased Vagabond Village:		
Office equipment .... $ 1,200		
Buildings and improvements 75,000		
Land 85,000		
Total $161,200		
Less mortgage assumed............ 120,000		
Cash paid		$41,200
Insurance premium paid		960
Office supplies purchased		120
Wages paid		3,400
Utilities paid		370
Property taxes paid		1,260
Personal withdrawals of cash by owner		4,000
Mobile home space rentals collected	16,150	
Totals	$58,150	$51,310
Cash balance, December 31		6,840
Totals	$58,150	$58,150

Ms. Hall wants you to prepare an accrual basis income statement for the village for the four-month period she has operated the business and a December 31 balance sheet. You ascertain the following. (T-accounts will be helpful in organizing the data.)

The buildings and improvements were estimated to have a 25-year remaining life when purchased and at the end of that time will be wrecked. It is estimated that the sale of salvaged materials will just pay the wrecking costs and the cost of clearing the site. The office equipment is in good condition. At the time of purchase, Ms. Hall estimated she would use the equipment for three years and would then trade it in on new equipment of like kind. She thought $120 a fair estimate of what she would receive for the old equipment when she traded it in at the end of three years.

The $960 payment for insurance was for a policy taken out on September 1. The policy's protection was for one year beginning on that date. Ms. Hall estimates that one third of the office supplies purchased have been used. She also says that the one employee of the village earns $40 per day for a five-day workweek that ends on Friday. The employee was paid last week but has worked Monday, Tuesday, Wednesday, and Thursday, December 28, 29, 30, and 31, for which he has not been paid.

Included in the $16,150 of mobile home rentals collected is $300 received from a tenant for three months' rent beginning on December 1. Also, a tenant has not paid his $100 rent for the month of December.

The mortgage requires the payment of 12% interest annually on the beginning principal balance and a $4,800 annual payment on the principal. The property tax payment was for one year's taxes that were paid on October 1 for the tax year beginning on September 1, the day Ms. Hall purchased the business.

ALTERNATE PROBLEMS

Problem 3–1A   The following information for preparing adjusting entries was available for the annual accounting period ended December 31 of the current year. Prepare the required adjusting entries.

a. The Store Supplies account had a $115 debit balance at the beginning of the year. Supplies costing $565 were purchased during the year, and an inventory of unused supplies at the year-end totaled $125.

b. An examination of insurance policies showed three policies, as follows:

Policy	Protection began on	Life of policy	Cost
1.....	May 12 of the previous year	3 years	$840
2.....	March 1 of current year	2 years	540
3.....	August 1 of current year	1 year	420

Prepaid Insurance was debited for the cost of each policy at the time of purchase. Expired insurance was correctly recorded at the end of the previous year.

c. The company's two office employees earn $40 per day and $50 per day, respectively. They are paid each Friday for a five-day workweek that begins on Monday. December 31 fell on Wednesday, and the employees both worked on Monday, Tuesday, and Wednesday but have not been paid.

d. The company owns a building that it completed and occupied for the first time on June 1 of the current year. The building cost $450,000, has an estimated 25-year life, and is not expected to have any salvage value at the end of its life.

e. On September 1, the company received its property tax bill for the tax year beginning on October 1. The bill totaled $2,580 and was payable in two equal installments of $1,290 each. The company paid the first installment and debited the amount paid to the Property Taxes Expense account.

f. The company occupies most of the space in its building, but it also rents space to two tenants. One tenant rented a small amount of space on September 1 at $200 per month. The tenant paid the rent on the first day of each month, September through November, and the amounts paid were credited to the Rent Earned account. However, the tenant has not paid the rent for December, although on several occasions has said it would be paid the next day.

g. The second tenant agreed on November 1 to rent a small amount of space at $225 per month and on that date paid three months' rent in advance. The amount paid was credited to the Unearned Rent account.

Problem 3–2A   At the end of its annual accounting period, Pitts Realty prepared from its ledger the trial balance that follows.

PITTS REALTY
Trial Balance
December 31, 19—

Cash	$ 1,940	
Prepaid insurance	915	
Office supplies	290	
Office equipment	6,250	
Accumulated depreciation, office equipment		$ 1,920
Automobile	12,780	
Accumulated depreciation, automobile		2,150
Accounts payable		225
Unearned management fees		450
Dale Pitts, capital		11,145
Dale Pitts, withdrawals	18,600	
Sales commissions earned		41,280
Office salaries expense	10,300	
Advertising expense	830	
Rent expense	4,800	
Telephone expense	465	
Totals	$57,170	$57,170

Required:

1. Open the accounts of the trial balance plus these additional ones: Accounts Receivable; Office Salaries Payable; Management Fees Earned; Insurance Expense; Office Supplies Expense; Depreciation Expense, Office Equipment; and Depreciation Expense, Automobile. Enter the trial balance amounts in the accounts.
2. Use the information that follows to prepare and post adjusting entries:
    a. An examination of insurance policies showed $725 of expired insurance.
    b. An inventory showed $80 of unused office supplies on hand.
    c. The year's depreciation on office equipment was estimated at $815 and *(d)* on the automobile at $1,775.
    e. The December telephone bill arrived after the trial balance was prepared, and its $40 amount was not included in the trial balance amounts. Also, a bill for $110 of newspaper advertising that had appeared in December arrived after the trial balance was prepared and was not included in the trial balance amounts.
    f. A client who was taking a tour around the world signed a contract with Pitts Realty for the management of his apartment building. The contract calls for a $150 monthly fee, and management began on December 1. The client paid three months' fees in advance, and the amount paid was credited to the Unearned Management Fees account.
    g. Pitts Realty agreed to manage the small office building of a second client for $150 per month payable at the end of each three months. The contract was signed on November 15, and one and a half months' fees have accrued.
    h. The one office employee is paid weekly; and on December 31, four days' wages at $40 per day have accrued.

3. After posting the adjusting entries, prepare an adjusted trial balance, an income statement, and a classified balance sheet.

Problem 3–3A A year-end trial balance of the ledger of Corona Moving and Storage follows:

CORONA MOVING AND STORAGE
Trial Balance
December 31, 19—

Cash	$ 2,240	
Accounts receivable	545	
Prepaid insurance	3,580	
Office supplies	320	
Office equipment	3,650	
Accumulated depreciation, office equipment ...		$ 1,680
Trucks	44,200	
Accumulated depreciation, trucks		11,540
Building	168,000	
Accumulated depreciation, building		28,600
Land	17,500	
Unearned storage fees		1,730
Mortgage payable		120,000
John Hall, capital		54,110
John Hall, withdrawals	24,000	
Revenue from moving services		90,115
Storage fees earned		7,770
Office salaries expense	11,400	
Drivers' and helpers' wages expense	26,630	
Gas, oil, and repairs expense	2,680	
Mortgage interest expense	10,800	
Totals	$315,545	$315,545

Required:

1. Open the accounts of the trial balance plus these additional ones: Salaries and Wages Payable; Insurance Expense; Office Supplies Expense; Depreciation Expense, Office Equipment; Depreciation Expense, Trucks; and Depreciation Expense, Building. Enter the trial balance amounts in the accounts.
2. Use the information that follows to prepare and post adjusting entries:
    a. An examination of insurance policies showed $2,815 of expired insurance.
    b. An inventory showed $110 of unused office supplies on hand.
    c. Estimated depreciation on the office equipment, $515; *(d)* on the trucks, $5,220; and *(e)* on the building, $6,200.
    f. The company credits storage fees of customers who pay in advance to the Unearned Storage Fees account. Of the $1,730 credited to this account, $1,325 was earned by the year-end.
    g. Accrued storage fees earned but unrecorded and uncollected at the year-end totaled $345.
    h. There were $135 of earned but unrecorded office salaries and $755 of earned but unrecorded drivers' and helpers' wages at the year-end.
3. Prepare an adjusted trial balance, an income statement for the year, and a

classified year-end balance sheet. A $6,000 installment on the mortgage is due within one year.

Problem 3–4A   At the end of its annual accounting period, after all transactions were recorded, a trial balance of the ledger of Lazy T Trailer Park carried the items that follow:

LAZY T TRAILER PARK
Trial Balance
December 31, 19—

Cash	$ 2,540	
Prepaid insurance	1,525	
Office supplies	260	
Office equipment	2,450	
Accumulated depreciation, office equipment		$ 815
Buildings and improvements	92,000	
Accumulated depreciation, buildings and improvements		21,350
Land	95,000	
Unearned rent		780
Mortgage payable		118,000
June Lake, capital		41,810
June Lake, withdrawals	18,200	
Rent earned		51,865
Wages expense	10,120	
Utilities expense	825	
Property taxes expense	1,965	
Interest expense	9,735	
Totals	$234,620	$234,620

Required:

1. Open the accounts of the trial balance plus these additional ones: Accounts Receivable; Wages Payable; Property Taxes Payable; Interest Payable; Insurance Expense; Office Supplies Expense; Depreciation Expense, Office Equipment; and Depreciation Expense, Buildings and Improvements. Enter the trial balance amounts in the accounts.

2. Use the information that follows to prepare and post adjusting journal entries:
    a. An examination of insurance policies showed $1,235 of expired insurance.
    b. An inventory of office supplies showed $85 of unused supplies on hand.
    c. Estimated depreciation of office equipment, $310; and *(d)* of buildings and improvements, $5,250.
    e. The trailer park credits the Unearned Rent account for rents paid in advance. An examination revealed that $445 of the balance of this account was earned by the year-end.
    f. One tenant is in arrears on rent payments, and this $100 of accrued revenue was unrecorded at the time the trial balance was prepared.
    g. Four months' property taxes expense, estimated at $980, has accrued but was not recorded at the time the trial balance was prepared.
    h. The one employee of the trailer park works a five-day workweek at

$40 per day. He was paid last week but has worked four days this week for which he has not been paid.

  i. Three months' interest on the mortgage, $3,245, has accrued but was unpaid and unrecorded on the trial balance date.

3. Post the adjusting entries and prepare an adjusted trial balance, an income statement for the year, and a classified balance sheet. A $5,500 payment on the mortgage is due within one year.

Problem 3–5A   Walter Swift, a lawyer, has always kept his records on a cash basis; at the end of 198B, he prepared the following cash basis income statement.

WALTER SWIFT, LAWYER
Income Statement
For Year Ended December 31, 198B

Revenues	$69,700
Expenses	28,300
Net income	$41,400

In preparing the statement, the following amounts of accrued and deferred items were ignored at the ends of 198A and 198B.

	End of	
	198A	*198B*
Prepaid expenses	$1,540	$1,215
Accrued expenses	1,730	2,180
Unearned revenues	2,210	3,620
Accrued revenues	3,190	2,440

Required:

Under the assumptions that the 198A prepaid expenses were consumed or expired in 198B, the 198A unearned revenues were earned in 198B, and the 198A accrued items were either paid or received in cash in 198B, prepare a 198B accrual basis income statement for Walter Swift. Attach to your statement calculations showing how you arrived at each 198B income statement amount.

PROVOCATIVE PROBLEMS

Provocative Problem 3–1 Small Appliance Service   Ted Small began Small Appliance Service, a new business, on January 2. After one year's operations, Ted feels the business has done a lot of work during its first year. However, the bank has begun to dishonour its cheques. Its creditors are dunning it for bills it is unable to pay, and Ted just cannot understand why. Consequently he has asked your help in determining the results of the first year's operations.

You find the service's accounting records, such as they are, have been kept by Ted's wife, who has no formal training in record-keeping. However, she has prepared for your inspection the statement of cash receipts and disbursements that follows.

There were no errors in the statement, and you learn these additional facts:

1. The lease contract for the shop space runs for five years and requires rent payments of $250 per month, with the first and last months' rent to be paid in advance. All required payments were made on time.
2. The repair equipment has an estimated six-year life, after which it will be valueless. It has been used a full year.

SMALL APPLIANCE SERVICE
Cash Receipts and Disbursements
For Year Ended December 31, 19—

Receipts:
Investment	$12,000	
Received from customers for services ..	35,565	$47,565
Disbursements:		
Rent expense	$ 3,250	
Repair equipment purchased	5,400	
Service truck expense	10,315	
Wages expense	18,720	
Insurance expense	1,270	
Repair parts and supplies	8,650	47,605
Bank overdraft		$ (40)

3. The service truck expense consists of $9,200 paid for the truck on January 2, plus $1,115 paid for gas and oil. Mr. Small expects to use the truck four years, after which he thinks he will get $1,200 for it as a trade-in on a new truck.
4. The wages expense consists of $3,120 paid the service's one employee who was hired on September 30, plus $15,600 of personal withdrawals by Mr. Small. Also, the one employee is owed $100 of earned but unpaid wages.
5. The $1,270 of insurance expense resulted from paying the premiums on two insurance policies on January 2. One policy cost $550 and gave protection for one year. The other policy cost $720 for two years' protection.
6. In addition to the $8,650 of repair parts and supplies paid for during the year, creditors are dunning the business for $485 for parts and supplies purchased and delivered, but not paid for. Also, an inventory shows $955 of unused parts and supplies on hand.
7. Mr. Small reports that the business does most of its work for cash, but customers owe $375 for repair work done on credit.

Prepare an accrual basis income statement showing the results of the first year's operations of the business and a classified balance sheet showing its year-end financial position.

Provocative
Problem 3–2,
The Fixit Shop

During the first week of January of the current year, Gary Blake began a small repair business he calls The Fixit Shop. He has kept no accounting records, but he does file any unpaid invoices for things purchased by impaling them on a nail in the wall over his workbench. He has kept a good record of the year's receipts and payments, which follows.

Gary would like to know how much the business actually earned during its first year. Therefore, he would like for you to prepare an accrual basis income statement and a year-end classified balance sheet for the shop.

You learn that the shop equipment has an estimated eight-year life, after which it will be worthless. There is a $315 unpaid invoice on the nail over Gary's workbench for supplies received, and an inventory shows $330 of unused supplies on hand. The shop space rents for $200 per month on a five-year lease. The lease contract requires payment of the first and last months' rents in advance, which were paid. The insurance premiums were for two policies taken out on January 2. The first is a one-year policy that cost $220. The second is a two-year policy that cost $540. There are $60 of earned but unpaid wages owed the helper, and customers owe the shop $385 for repair services they have received.

	Receipts	Payments
Investment	$ 5,000	
Shop equipment		$ 4,000
Repair parts and supplies		4,210
Rent payments		2,600
Insurance premiums paid		760
Newspaper advertising paid		250
Utility bills paid		645
Part-time helper's wages paid		6,230
Gary Blake for personal use		15,000
Revenue from repairs	29,955	
Subtotals	$34,955	$33,695
Cash balance, December 31, 19—		1,260
Totals	$34,955	$34,955

Provocative Problem 3–3, Tipton Realty

The 198A and 198B balance sheets of Tipton Realty show the following assets and liabilities at the end of each of the years:

	December 31	
	198A	*198B*
Prepaid insurance	$1,375	$1,010
Property management fees receivable	300	575
Interest payable	415	360
Unearned property management fees	725	850

The concern's records show the following amounts of cash disbursed and received for these items during 198B:

Cash disbursed to pay insurance premiums	$2,320
Cash disbursed to pay interest	1,450
Cash received for managing property	6,280

Present calculations to show the amounts to be reported on Tipton Realty's 198B income statement for (a) insurance expense, (b) interest expense, and (c) property management fees earned.

ANALYTICAL AND REVIEW PROBLEMS

Problem 3–1
A&R

The Salaries Payable account of James Bay Company Limited appears below:

Salaries Payable

Entries during 19A5	74,560	Bal. Jan. 1, 19A5	260
		Entries during 19A5	74,420

The company records the salary expense and related liability at the end of each week and pays the employees on the last Friday of the month.

Required:

Calculate:

1. Salary expense for 19A5.
2. How much was paid to employees in 19A5 for work done in 19A4?
3. How much was paid to employees in 19A5 for work done in 19A5?
4. How much will be paid to employees in 19A6 for work done in 19A5?

Problem 3–2
A&R

The Prepaid Insurance account of Hobby Shops is reproduced below:

Prepaid Insurance

Bal. Jan. 1, 19A5	290	Entry Dec. 31, 19A5	1,050
Entries during 19A5	900		

Required:

Reconstruct the journal entries made by Hobby Shops in 19A5.

Problem 3–3
A&R

Ida M. Smart, the accountant for Longview Company, believes that the need for adjusting entries at the end of the accounting period is caused by the lack of anticipation on the part of the accountant. She holds that if all transactions are recorded properly, with the year-end adjustments fully anticipated at the time the transactions occur, the need for year-end adjustments will be completely eliminated. To prove her point, she cites the following journal entries recorded in the books for the current year.

January 1	Insurance expense	120	
	Prepaid insurance	240	
	Cash		360
	To record the payment of a three-year insurance.		
1	Rent expense	1,200	
	Cash		1,200
	One year's rent paid.		
1	Depreciation expense	600	
	Accumulated depreciation		600
	One-year depreciation for office equipment costing $6,000 with an estimated useful life of 10 years and no salvage value.		

```
July    1    Cash .............................................  1,000
                  Commission earned ..............................           500
                  Commission received in advance  .................           500
                  Receipt of 12 months' commissions.
July    1    Office supplies used ..............................    200
             Office supplies ......................................    200
                  Accounts payable ...............................           400
                  Purchase of office supplies, half of which will
                  probably be used during the year.
```

Required:

1. By anticipating year-end adjustments at the time the transactions are recorded, what problems or difficulties do you think Ms. Smart will most likely encounter at the year-end date?
2. Is it usually true that some adjustments are not susceptible to accurate anticipation? Explain and give examples to support your answer.
3. If you follow Ms. Smart's approach of anticipating adjustments at the time the transactions occur, what entries should you make at the beginning of year two, based on the entries recorded in year one?
4. What is to be gained by Ms. Smart's approach of anticipating adjustments? Explain.

Problem 3–4
A&R

Robert Dufour operates a management consulting firm and uses a cash basis for recording transactions. The trial balance presented below reflects the operations for the first year of business.

ROBERT DUFOUR, MANAGEMENT CONSULTANT
Trial Balance
December 31, 198A

Cash	$ 8,200	
Office equipment	16,000	
R. Dufour, capital		$ 1,000
Management consulting fees		62,000
Office salaries expense	28,000	
Telephone expense	1,000	
Office expense	8,000	
Office supplies expense	1,300	
Miscellaneous expense	500	
	$63,000	$63,000

Additional information:

1. Amount of office supplies still on hand at the end of the year was $50.
2. The office equipment was estimated to have a 10-year useful life with no salvage value.
3. Consulting services rendered for which no payment has been received amounted to $12,000.
4. Telephone bill for the month of December, 198A, was paid in January, 198B, $200.
5. Office expenses incurred but not yet paid for, $800.

6. Golden Ltd. paid $2,000 consulting fee for services to be performed in 198B.

Required:

1. Prepare all necessary adjusting entries (omit narratives) to reflect Dufour's operation on an accrual basis of accounting.
2. Prepare a trial balance on the accrual basis of accounting.
3. What is the difference in net income between the cash and the accrual bases of accounting for Dufour's business?
4. Which basis, in your opinion, more realistically reflects the operations of Dufour? Why?
5. What are the similarities and dissimilarities between the adjusting entries to convert a cash basis to an accrual basis and the adjusting entries for an accrual basis?

Problem 3–5 A&R

Paula Skelton, a local dentist, asked you to help her prepare an income statement that would be acceptable by Revenue Canada. Skelton's secretary/nurse maintained all the records and had developed the following statement for the year ended December 31, 1987.

DR. PAULA SKELTON
Income and Expense Statement
1987

Dental fees collected		$95,800
Expenses paid:		
Rent for office	$ 7,200	
Rent for dental equipment	18,000	
Utilities	600	
Telephone	360	
Supplies	2,500	
Wages of secretary/nurse	16,000	44,660
Profit for the year		$51,140

Since the statement was prepared on a 100% cash basis you realized that it would not be acceptable by Revenue Canada. Consequently, you conducted an investigation of records of the current year as well as of the previous year. You discovered the following:

a. Of the $95,800 of fees collected in 1987, $3,800 was for work performed in 1986.
b. On December 31, 1987, uncollected fees for work performed during 1987 were $1,700.
c. When Skelton started her dental practice in 1986, she entered into a 10-year agreement with Universal Dental Supply, Inc. Under the agreement Skelton obtained all the necessary equipment for a monthly rental of $1,500. The payments are made on the 15th of each month.
d. Office rent is paid at the rate of $600 on the 1st of each month.
e. On December 31, 1987, a count of supplies indicated $300 were on hand. It was estimated that on January 1, 1987, supplies of $400 were on hand.

    f. The secretary/nurse started working in February 1987 and on December 31, 1987, wages amounting to $500 remained unpaid.

    g. Unpaid utilities and telephone for December 1987 were expected to be greater by $50 and $60 respectively than for December 1986.

Required:

Prepare an income statement for 1987 on an accrual basis. Support all changes in amounts from the statement prepared by the secretary/nurse.

The Work Sheet and Closing the Accounts of Proprietorships, Partnerships, and Corporations

4

After studying Chapter 4, you should be able to:

Explain why a work sheet is prepared and be able to prepare a work sheet for a service-type business.

Explain why it is necessary to close the revenue and expense accounts at the end of each accounting period.

Prepare entries to close the temporary accounts of a service business and prepare a post-closing trial balance to test the accuracy of the end-of-period adjusting and closing procedures.

Explain the nature of the retained earnings item on corporation balance sheets.

Explain why a corporation with a deficit cannot pay a legal dividend.

Prepare entries to close the Income Summary account of a corporation and to record the declaration and payment of a dividend.

List the steps in the accounting cycle in the order in which they are completed.

Define or explain the words and phrases listed in the chapter Glossary.

As an aid in this work, accountants prepare numerous memoranda, analyses, and informal papers that serve as a basis for the formal reports given to management or to their clients. These analyses and memoranda are called *working papers* and are invaluable tools of the accountant. The work sheet described in this chapter is such a working paper. It is prepared solely for the accountant's use. It is not given to the owner or manager of the business for which it is prepared but is retained by the accountant. Normally, it is prepared with a pencil, which makes changes and corrections easy as its preparation progresses.

WORK SHEET IN THE ACCOUNTING PROCEDURES

In the accounting procedures described in the previous chapter, at the end of an accounting period, as soon as all transactions were recorded, recall that adjusting entries were entered in the journal and posted to the accounts. Then, an adjusted trial balance was prepared and used in making an income statement and balance sheet. For a very small business, these are satisfactory procedures. However, if a company has more than a few accounts and adjustments, errors in adjusting the accounts and in preparing the statements are less apt to be made if an additional step is inserted in the procedures. The additional step is the preparation of a *work sheet.* A work sheet is a tool of accountants upon which they (1) achieve the effect of adjusting the accounts before entering the adjustments in the accounts, (2) sort the adjusted account balances into columns according to whether the accounts are used in preparing the income statement or balance sheet, and (3) calculate and prove the mathematical accuracy of the net income. Then, after the work sheet is completed, (4) accountants use it in preparing the income statement and balance sheet and in preparing adjusting and closing entries. (Closing entries are discussed later in this chapter.)

PREPARING A WORK SHEET

The Owen law practice of previous chapters does not have sufficient accounts or adjustments to warrant the preparation of a work sheet. Nevertheless, since its accounts and adjustments are familiar, they are used here to illustrate the procedures involved.

During July, the Owen law practice completed a number of transactions. On July 31, after these transactions were recorded but **before any adjusting entries were prepared and posted,** a trial balance of its ledger appeared as in Illustration 4–1.

Illustration 4–1

LARRY OWEN, LAWYER
Trial Balance
July 31, 19—

Cash	$1,185	
Prepaid rent	900	
Office supplies	60	
Office equipment	4,000	
Accounts payable		$ 260
Unearned legal fees		450
Larry Owen, capital		5,000
Larry Owen, withdrawals	200	
Legal fees earned		1,500
Office salaries expense	800	
Telephone expense	30	
Heating and lighting expense	35	
Totals	$7,210	$7,210

Notice that the trial balance is an **unadjusted trial balance.** The accounts have not been adjusted for expired rent, supplies consumed, depreciation, and so forth. Nevertheless, this unadjusted trial balance is the starting point in preparing the work sheet for the law practice, which is shown in Illustration 4–2.

Note that the work sheet has five pairs of money columns and that the first pair is labeled "Trial Balance." In this first pair of columns is copied the unadjusted trial balance of the law practice. Often when a work sheet is prepared, the trial balance is prepared for the first time in its first two money columns.

The second pair of work sheet columns is labeled "Adjustments." The adjustments are entered in these columns. Note they are, with one exception, the same adjustments for which adjusting journal entries were prepared and posted in the previous chapter. The one exception is the last one, *(e),* in which the two adjustments affecting the Legal Fees Earned account are combined into one compound adjustment. They were combined because both result in credits to the same account.

Note that the adjustments on the illustrated work sheet are keyed together with letters. When a work sheet is prepared, after it is completed, the adjusting entries still have to be entered in the journal and posted to the ledger. At that time, the key letters help identify each adjustment's related debits and credits.

Some accountants follow the practice of providing a key to adjustments on the lower left-hand corner of the work sheets as shown in Illustration 4–2.

Illustration 4–2

LARRY OWEN, LAWYER
Work Sheet for Month Ended July 31, 19—

ACCOUNT TITLES	TRIAL BALANCE DR.	TRIAL BALANCE CR.	ADJUSTMENTS DR.	ADJUSTMENTS CR.	ADJUSTED TRIAL BALANCE DR.	ADJUSTED TRIAL BALANCE CR.	INCOME STATEMENT DR.	INCOME STATEMENT CR.	BALANCE SHEET DR.	BALANCE SHEET CR.
Cash	1,18500				1,18500				1,18500	
Prepaid rent	90000			(a) 30000	60000				60000	
Office supplies	6000			(b) 2500	3500				3500	
Office equipment	4,00000				4,00000				4,00000	
Accounts payable		26000				26000				26000
Unearned legal fees		45000	(e) 15000			30000				30000
Larry Owen, capital		5,00000				5,00000				5,00000
Larry Owen, withdrawals	20000				20000				20000	
Legal fees earned		1,50000		(e) 25000		1,75000		1,75000		
Office salaries expense	80000		(d) 12000		92000		92000			
Telephone expense	3000				3000		3000			
Heating & lighting expense	3500				3500		3500			
	7,21000	7,21000								
Rent expense			(a) 30000		30000		30000			
Office supplies expense			(b) 2500		2500		2500			
Depr. expense, office equip.			(c) 4000		4000		4000			
Accum. depr., office equip.				(c) 4000		4000				4000
Salaries payable				(d) 12000		12000				12000
Accounts receivable			(e) 10000		10000				10000	
			73500	73500	7,47000	7,47000	1,35000	1,75000	6,12000	5,72000
Net income							40000			40000
							1,75000	1,75000	6,12000	6,12000

Key to adjustments:
Adjustment (a): To adjust for the rent expired.
Adjustment (b): To adjust for the office supplies consumed.
Adjustment (c): To adjust for depreciation of the office equipment.
Adjustment (d): To adjust for the accrued secretary's salary.
Adjustment (e): To adjust for unearned and accrued revenue.

Provision of a key to adjustments is to be encouraged especially in the early stages of study. A key to adjustments is not shown on work sheets other than Illustration 4–2 because of the limited space on a page in this textbook.

Each adjustment on the illustrated work sheet required one or two additional account names to be written in below the original trial balance. These accounts did not have balances when the trial balance was prepared. Consequently, they were not listed in the trial balance. Often, when a work sheet is prepared, the effects of the adjustments are anticipated and any additional accounts required are provided without amounts in the body of the trial balance.

When a work sheet is prepared, after the adjustments are entered in the Adjustments columns, the columns are totaled to prove the equality of the adjustments.

The third set of work sheet columns is labeled "Adjusted Trial Balance." In preparing a work sheet, each amount in the Trial Balance columns is combined with its adjustment in the Adjustments columns, if any, and is entered in the Adjusted Trial Balance columns. For example, in Illustration 4–2, the Prepaid Rent account has a $900 debit balance in the Trial Balance columns. This $900 debit is combined with the $300 credit in the Adjustments columns to give Prepaid Rent a $600 debit in the Adjusted Trial Balance columns. Rent Expense has no balance in the Trial Balance columns, but it has a $300 debit in the Adjustments columns. Therefore, no balance combined with a $300 debit gives Rent Expense a $300 debit in the Adjusted Trial Balance columns. Cash, Office Equipment, and several other accounts have trial balance amounts but no adjustments. As a result, their trial balance amounts are carried unchanged into the Adjusted Trial Balance columns. Notice that the result of combining the amounts in the Trial Balance columns with the amounts in the Adjustments columns is an adjusted trial balance in the Adjusted Trial Balance columns.

After the combined amounts are carried to the Adjusted Trial Balance columns, the Adjusted Trial Balance columns are added to prove their equality. Then, the amounts in these columns are sorted to the proper Balance Sheet or Income Statement columns according to the statement on which they will appear. This is an easy task that requires answers to only two questions: (1) is the item to be sorted a debit or a credit, and (2) on which statement does it appear? As to the first question, an adjusted trial balance debit amount must be sorted to either the Income Statement debit column or the Balance Sheet debit column. Likewise, a credit amount must go into either the Income Statement credit or Balance Sheet credit column. In other words, debits remain debits and credits remain credits in the sorting process. As to the second question, it is only necessary in the sorting process to remember that revenues and expenses appear on the income statement and assets, liabilities, and owner's equity items go on the balance sheet.

After the amounts are sorted to the proper columns, the columns are totaled. At this point, the difference between the totals of the Income Statement columns is the net income or loss. The difference is the net income or loss because revenues are entered in the credit column and expenses in the debit column. If the credit column total exceeds the debit column total, the difference is a net income. If the debit column total exceeds the credit column total, the difference is a net loss. In the illustrated work sheet, the credit column total exceeds the debit column total, and the result is a $400 net income.

After the net income is determined in the Income Statement columns, it is added to the total of the Balance Sheet credit column. The reason for this is that with the exception of the balance of the capital account, the amounts appearing in the Balance Sheet columns are "end-of-period" amounts. Therefore, it is necessary to add the net income to the Balance Sheet credit column total to make the Balance Sheet columns equal. Also, adding the income to this column has the effect of adding it to the capital account.

Had there been a loss, it would have been necessary to add the loss to the debit column. This is because losses decrease owner's equity, and adding the loss to the debit column has the effect of subtracting it from the capital account.

Balancing the Balance Sheet columns by adding the net income or loss is a proof of the accuracy with which the work sheet was prepared. When the income or loss is added in the Balance Sheet columns and the addition makes these columns equal, it is assumed that no errors were made in preparing the work sheet. However, if the addition does not make the columns equal, it is proof that an error or errors were made. The error or errors may have been either mathematical, or an amount may have been sorted to a wrong column.

Although balancing the Balance Sheet columns with the net income or loss is a proof of the accuracy with which a work sheet was prepared, it is not an absolute proof. These columns will balance even when errors have been made if the errors are of a certain type. For example, an expense amount carried into the Balance Sheet debit column or an asset amount carried into the debit column of the income statement section will cause both of these columns to have incorrect totals. Likewise, the net income will be incorrect. However, when such an error is made, the Balance Sheet columns will balance, but with the incorrect amount of income. Therefore, when a work sheet is prepared, care must be exercised in sorting the adjusted trial balance amounts into the correct Income Statement or Balance Sheet columns.

WORK SHEET AND THE FINANCIAL STATEMENTS

As previously stated, the work sheet is a tool of the accountant and is not for management's use or publication. However, as soon as it is completed, the accountant uses it in preparing the income statement and balance sheet that are given to management. To do this, the accountant rearranges the items in the work sheet's Income Statement columns into a formal income statement and rearranges the items in the Balance Sheet columns into a formal balance sheet.

WORK SHEET AND ADJUSTING ENTRIES

Entering the adjustments in the Adjustments columns of a work sheet does not get these adjustments into the ledger accounts. Consequently, after the work sheet and statements are completed, adjusting entries like the ones described in the previous chapter must still be entered in the General Journal and posted. The work sheet makes this easy, because its Adjustments columns provide the information for these entries. All that is needed is an entry for each adjustment appearing in the columns.

As for the adjusting entries for the illustrated work sheet, they are the same as the entries in the previous chapter, with the exception of the entry for adjustment *(e)*. Here a compound entry having a $150 debit to Unearned Legal Fees, a $100 debit to Accounts Receivable, and $250 credit to Legal Fees Earned is used.

CLOSING ENTRIES

After the work sheet and statements are completed, in addition to adjusting entries, it is also necessary to prepare and post *closing entries*. Closing entries clear and close the revenue and expense accounts. The accounts are cleared in the sense that their balances are transferred to another account. They are closed in the sense that they have zero balances after closing entries are posted.

WHY CLOSING ENTRIES ARE MADE

The revenue and expense accounts are cleared and closed at the end of each accounting period by transferring their balances to a summary account called *Income Summary*. Their summarized amount, which is the net income or loss, is then transferred in a single proprietorship to the owner's capital account. These transfers are necessary because—

a.   Revenues actually increase the owner's equity and expenses decrease it.

b.   However, throughout an accounting period these increases and decreases are accumulated in revenue and expense accounts rather than in the owner's capital account.

c. As a result, closing entries are necessary at the end of each accounting period to transfer the net effect of these increases and decreases out of the revenue and expense accounts and on to the owner's capital account.

In addition, closing entries also cause the revenue and expense accounts to begin each new accounting period with zero balances. This too is necessary because—

a. An income statement reports the revenues and expenses incurred during just **one accounting period** and is prepared from information recorded in the revenue and expense accounts.

b. The revenue and expense accounts are not discarded at the end of each accounting period but are used in recording the revenues and expenses of succeeding periods.

c. Consequently, if at the end of a period the balances of these accounts are to reflect only a single period's revenues and expenses, the accounts must begin the period with zero balances.

CLOSING ENTRIES ILLUSTRATED

At the end of July, after its adjusting entries were posted but before its accounts were cleared and closed, the owner's equity accounts of Owen's law practice had the balances shown in Illustration 4–3. (An account's Balance column heading as a rule does not tell the nature of an account's balance. However, in Illustration 4–3 and in the illustrations immediately following, the nature of each account's balance is shown as an aid to the student.)

Observe in Illustration 4–3 that Owen's capital account shows only its $5,000 July 1 balance. This is not the amount of Owen's equity on July 31. Closing entries are required to make this account show the July 31 equity.

Note also the third account in Illustration 4–3, the Income Summary account. This account is used only at the end of the accounting period in summarizing and clearing the revenue and expense accounts.

Closing Revenue Accounts

Before closing entries are posted, revenue accounts have credit balances. Consequently, to clear and close a revenue account, an entry debiting the account and crediting Income Summary is required.

Illustration 4–3

Larry Owen, Capital — Credit

Date		Explanation	Debit	Credit	Balance
July	1			5,000	5,000

Larry Owen, Withdrawals — Debit

Date		Explanation	Debit	Credit	Balance
July	26		200		200

Income Summary

Date	Explanation	Debit	Credit	Balance

Legal Fees Earned — Credit

Date		Explanation	Debit	Credit	Balance
July	12			500	500
	19			1,000	1,500
	31			250	1,750

Office Salaries Expense — Debit

Date		Explanation	Debit	Credit	Balance
July	12		400		400
	26		400		800
	31		120		920

Telephone Expense — Debit

Date		Explanation	Debit	Credit	Balance
July	31		30		30

Heating and Lighting Expense — Debit

Date		Explanation	Debit	Credit	Balance
July	31		35		35

Rent Expense — Debit

Date		Explanation	Debit	Credit	Balance
July	31		300		300

Office Supplies Expense — Debit

Date		Explanation	Debit	Credit	Balance
July	31		25		25

Depreciation Expense, Office Equipment — Debit

Date		Explanation	Debit	Credit	Balance
July	31		40		40

The Owen law practice has only one revenue account, and the entry to close and clear it is:

July	31	Legal Fees Earned..........................	1,750.00	
		Income Summary		1,750.00
		To clear and close the revenue account.		

Posting the entry has this effect on the accounts:

Legal Fees Earned				Credit		**Income Summary**				Credit
Date	Explanation	Debit	Credit	Balance	Date	Explanation	Debit	Credit	Balance
July 12			500	500	July 31			1,750	1,750
19			1,000	1,500					
31			250	1,750					
31		1,750		–0–					

Note that the entry clears the revenue account by transferring its balance as a credit to the Income Summary account. It also causes the revenue account to begin the new accounting period with a zero balance.

Closing Expense Accounts

Before closing entries are posted, expense accounts have debit balances. Consequently, to clear and close a concern's expense accounts, a compound entry debiting the Income Summary account and crediting each individual expense account is required. The Owen law practice has six expense accounts, and the compound entry to clear and close them is:

July	31	Income Summary	1,350.00	
		Office Salaries Expense		920.00
		Telephone Expense		30.00
		Heating and Lighting Expense		35.00
		Rent Expense		300.00
		Office Supplies Expense		25.00
		Depreciation Expense, Office Equipment . . .		40.00
		To close and clear the expense accounts.		

Posting the entry has the effect shown in Illustration 4–4. Turn to Illustration 4–4 and observe that the entry clears the expense accounts of their balances by transferring the balances in a total as a debit to the Income Summary account. It also causes the expense accounts to begin the new period with zero balances.

Closing the Income Summary Account

After a concern's revenue and expense accounts are cleared and their balances transferred to the Income Summary account, the balance of

Illustration 4–4

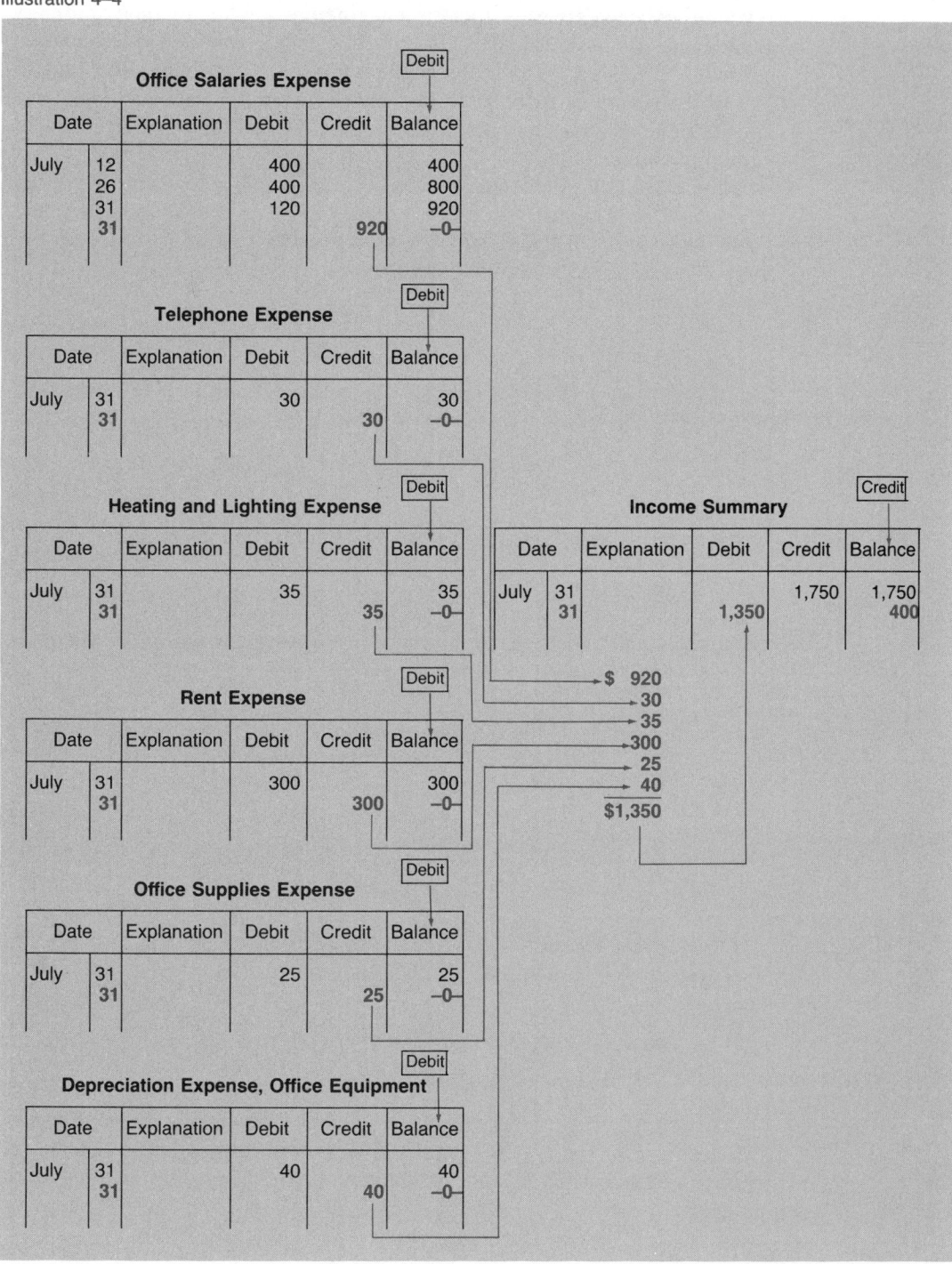

the Income Summary account is equal to the net income or loss. When revenues exceed expenses, there is a net income and the Income Summary account has a credit balance. On the other hand, when expenses exceed revenues, there is a loss and the account has a debit balance. But, regardless of the nature of its balance, the Income Summary account is cleared and its balance, the amount of net income or loss, is transferred to the capital account.

The Owen law practice earned $400 during July. Consequently, after its revenue and expense accounts are cleared, its Income Summary account has a $400 credit balance. This balance is transferred to the Larry Owen, Capital account with an entry like this:

July	31	Income Summary	400.00	
		Larry Owen, Capital		400.00
		To clear and close the Income Summary account.		

Posting this entry has the following effect on the accounts:

Income Summary

			Credit

Date	Explanation	Debit	Credit	Balance
July 31			1,750	1,750
31		1,350		400
31		400		–0–

Larry Owen, Capital

			Credit

Date	Explanation	Debit	Credit	Balance
July 1			5,000	5,000
31			400	5,400

Observe that the entry clears the Income Summary account, transferring its balance, the amount of the net income in this case to the capital account.

Closing the Withdrawals Account

At the end of an accounting period, the withdrawals account shows the decrease in the owner's equity due to withdrawals. The account is closed, and its debit balance is transferred to the capital account with an entry like this:

July	31	Larry Owen, Capital		200.00	
		Larry Owen, Withdrawals			200.00
		To close and clear the withdrawals account.			

Posting the entry has this effect on the accounts:

Larry Owen, Withdrawals [Debit] **Larry Owen, Capital** [Credit]

Date	Explanation	Debit	Credit	Balance		Date	Explanation	Debit	Credit	Balance
July 26		200		200		July 1			5,000	5,000
31			200	–0–		31			400	5,400
						31		200		5,200

After the entry closing the withdrawals account is posted, observe that the two reasons for making closing entries are accomplished: (1) All revenue and expense accounts have zero balances. (2) The net effect of the period's revenue, expense, and withdrawal transactions on the owner's equity is shown in the capital account.

Temporary Accounts

Revenue and expense accounts plus the Income Summary and withdrawals accounts are often called *temporary accounts* because in a sense the items recorded in these accounts are only temporarily recorded therein. At the end of each accounting period, through closing entries, their debit and credit effects are transferred out and on to other accounts.

SOURCES OF CLOSING ENTRY INFORMATION

Information for closing entries may be taken from the individual revenue and expense accounts. However, the work sheet provides this information in a more convenient form. Look at the work sheet on page 146. Every account having a balance in its Income Statement debit column has a debit balance in the ledger and must be credited in closing. Compare the amounts in the work sheet's Income Statement debit column with the credits in the compound closing entry on page 152. If the work sheet is used as the information source for the entry, it is not even necessary to add the entry's credits to learn the amount of the debit. The entry's debit to Income Summary is the column total.

The work sheet's Income Statement credit column is a convenient information source for the entry to close the revenue account.

THE ACCOUNTS AFTER CLOSING

At this stage, after both adjusting and closing entries have been posted, the Owen law practice accounts appear as in Illustration 4–5. Observe in the illustration that the asset, liability, and the owner's capital accounts show their end-of-period balances. Observe also that the revenue and expense accounts have zero balances and are ready for recording the new accounting period's revenues and expenses.

THE POST-CLOSING TRIAL BALANCE

It is easy to make errors in adjusting and closing the accounts. Consequently, after all adjusting and closing entries are posted, a new trial balance is prepared to retest the equality of the accounts. This new, after-closing trial balance is called a *post-closing trial balance,* and for Owen's law practice appears as in Illustration 4–6.

Illustration 4–5

\ DATE	EXPLANATION	PR	DEBIT	CREDIT	BALANCE
					Cash ACCOUNT NO. 111
198A July 1		G1	5,000 00		5,000 00
1		G1		900 00	4,100 00
3		G1		3,700 00	400 00
12		G1	500 00		900 00
12		G1		400 00	500 00
15		G1	450 00		950 00
26		G2		400 00	550 00
26		G2		200 00	350 00
29		G2	1,000 00		1,350 00
30		G2		100 00	1,250 00
31		G2		30 00	1,220 00
31		G2		35 00	1,185 00

Illustration 4–5 *(continued)*

Accounts Receivable   **ACCOUNT NO. 114**

DATE		EXPLANATION	PR	DEBIT	CREDIT	BALANCE
198A July	19		G2	1,000 00		1,000 00
	29		G2		1,000 00	–0–
	31		G3	100 00		100 00

Prepaid Rent   **ACCOUNT NO. 115**

DATE		EXPLANATION	PR	DEBIT	CREDIT	BALANCE
198A July	1		G1	900 00		900 00
	31		G3		300 00	600 00

Office Supplies   **ACCOUNT NO. 116**

DATE		EXPLANATION	PR	DEBIT	CREDIT	BALANCE
198A July	5		G1	60 00		60 00
	31		G3		25 00	35 00

Office Equipment   **ACCOUNT NO. 131**

DATE		EXPLANATION	PR	DEBIT	CREDIT	BALANCE
198A July	3		G1	3,700 00		3,700 00
	5		G1	300 00		4,000 00

Accumulated Depreciation, Office Equipment **ACCOUNT NO. 132**

DATE		EXPLANATION	PR	DEBIT	CREDIT	BALANCE
198A July	31		G3		40 00	40 00

Illustration 4–5 *(continued)*

Accounts Payable ACCOUNT NO. 212

DATE		EXPLANATION	PR	DEBIT	CREDIT	BALANCE
198A July	5		G1		360 00	360 00
	30		G2	100 00		260 00

Salaries Payable ACCOUNT NO. 213

DATE		EXPLANATION	PR	DEBIT	CREDIT	BALANCE
198A July	31		G3		120 00	120 00

Unearned Legal Fees ACCOUNT NO. 214

DATE		EXPLANATION	PR	DEBIT	CREDIT	BALANCE
198A July	15		G1		450 00	450 00
	31		G3	150 00		300 00

Larry Owen, Capital ACCOUNT NO. 311

DATE		EXPLANATION	PR	DEBIT	CREDIT	BALANCE
198A July	1		G1		5,000 00	5,000 00
	31		G3		400 00	5,400 00
	31		G3	200 00		5,200 00

Larry Owen, Withdrawals ACCOUNT NO. 312

DATE		EXPLANATION	PR	DEBIT	CREDIT	BALANCE
198A July	26		G2	200 00		200 00
	31		G3		200 00	–0–

Illustration 4–5 *(continued)*

Income Summary — ACCOUNT NO. 313

DATE		EXPLANATION	PR	DEBIT	CREDIT	BALANCE
198A July	31		G3		1,750 00	1,750 00
	31		G3	1,350 00		400 00
	31		G3	400 00		—0—

Legal Fees Earned — ACCOUNT NO. 411

DATE		EXPLANATION	PR	DEBIT	CREDIT	BALANCE
198A July	12		G1		500 00	500 00
	19		G2		1,000 00	1,500 00
	31		G3		250 00	1,750 00
	31		G3	1,750 00		—0—

Office Salaries Expense — ACCOUNT NO. 511

DATE		EXPLANATION	PR	DEBIT	CREDIT	BALANCE
198A July	12		G1	400 00		400 00
	26		G2	400 00		800 00
	31		G3	120 00		920 00
	31		G3		920 00	—0—

Telephone Expense — ACCOUNT NO. 512

DATE		EXPLANATION	PR	DEBIT	CREDIT	BALANCE
198A July	31		G2	30 00		30 00
	31		G3		30 00	—0—

Illustration 4–5 *(concluded)*

Heating and Lighting Expense · ACCOUNT NO. 513

DATE		EXPLANATION	PR	DEBIT	CREDIT	BALANCE
198A July	31		G2	35 00		35 00
	31		G3		35 00	–0–

Rent Expense · ACCOUNT NO. 514

DATE		EXPLANATION	PR	DEBIT	CREDIT	BALANCE
198A July	31		G3	300 00		300 00
	31		G3		300 00	–0–

Office Supplies Expense · ACCOUNT NO. 516

DATE		EXPLANATION	PR	DEBIT	CREDIT	BALANCE
198A July	31		G3	25 00		25 00
	31		G3		25 00	–0–

Depreciation Expense, Office Equipment · ACCOUNT NO. 517

DATE		EXPLANATION	PR	DEBIT	CREDIT	BALANCE
198A July	31		G3	40 00		40 00
	31		G3		40 00	–0–

Compare Illustration 4–6 with the accounts having balances in Illustration 4–5. Note that only asset, liability, and the owner's capital accounts have balances in Illustration 4–5. Note also that these are the only accounts that appear on the post-closing trial balance. The revenue and expense accounts have been cleared and have zero balances at this stage.

Illustration 4–6

LARRY OWEN, LAWYER **Post-Closing Trial Balance** **July 31, 19—**		
Cash	$1,185	
Accounts receivable	100	
Prepaid rent	600	
Office supplies	35	
Office equipment	4,000	
Accumulated depreciation, office equipment		$ 40
Accounts payable		260
Salaries payable		120
Unearned legal fees		300
Larry Owen, capital		5,200
Totals	$5,920	$5,920

ACCOUNTING FOR PARTNERSHIPS AND CORPORATIONS

Partnership Accounting

Accounting for a partnership is like accounting for a single proprietorship except for transactions directly affecting the partners' capital and withdrawal accounts. For these transactions, there must be a capital account and a withdrawals account for each partner. Also, the Income Summary account is closed with a compound entry that allocates to each partner his or her share of the income or loss.

Corporation Accounting

A corporation's accounting also differs from that of a single proprietorship for transactions affecting the accounts that show the equity of the corporation's shareholders in the assets of the corporation. The difference results because accounting principles require a corporation to distinguish between shareholders' equity resulting from amounts invested in the corporation by its shareholders, called ***contributed capital,*** and shareholders' equity resulting from earnings. This distinction is important because in most jurisdictions a corporation cannot pay a legal dividend unless it has shareholders' equity resulting from earnings. In making the distinction, two kinds of shareholders' equity accounts are kept: (1) contributed capital accounts and (2) retained earnings accounts. Amounts invested in a corporation (contributed) by its shareholders are shown in a contributed capital account such as the Common Stock account. Shareholders' equity resulting from earnings is shown in a retained earnings account.

To demonstrate corporation accounting, assume that five persons secured approved articles of incorporation for a new corporation. Each invested $10,000 in the corporation by buying 1,000 shares of its common stock. The corporation's entry to record their investments is:

Jan.	5	Cash	50,000.00	
		Common Stock		50,000.00
		Sold and issued 5,000 shares of common stock.		

If during its first year the corporation earned $8,000, the entry to close its Income Summary account is:

Dec.	31	Income Summary	8,000.00	
		Retained Earnings		8,000.00
		To close the Income Summary account.		

If these were the only entries affecting the Common Stock and Retained Earnings accounts during the first year, the corporation's year-end balance sheet will show the shareholders' equity as follows:

Shareholders' Equity

Common stock, 5,000 shares outstanding	$50,000	
Retained earnings	8,000	
Total shareholders' equity		$58,000

Since a corporation is a separate legal entity, the names of its shareholders are of little or no interest to a balance sheet reader and are not shown in the equity section. However, in this case, the section does show that the corporation's shareholders have a $58,000 equity in its assets, $50,000 of which resulted from their purchase of the corporation's stock and $8,000 from earnings. As to the equity from earnings, $8,000 more assets flowed into the corporation from revenues than flowed out for expenses. This not only increased the assets but also increased the shareholders' equity in the assets by $8,000.

Many beginning students have difficulty understanding the nature of the retained earnings item in the equity section of a corporation balance sheet. They would perhaps have less difficulty if the item were labeled "Shareholders' equity resulting from earnings." However, the retained earnings caption is common. Therefore, upon seeing it, a student must recognize that it represents nothing more than shareholders' equity resulting from earnings. Furthermore, it does not represent a specific amount of cash or any other asset, since these are shown in the asset section of the balance sheet.

To continue, assume that on January 10 of the corporation's second year its board of directors met and by vote declared a $1 per share dividend payable on February 1 to the January 25 *shareholders of record* (shareholder according to the corporation's records). The entries to record the declaration and payment are as follows:

Jan.	10	Retained Earnings	5,000.00	
		Common Dividend Payable		5,000.00
		Declared a $1 per share dividend.		
Feb.	1	Common Dividend Payable	5,000.00	
		Cash		5,000.00
		Paid the dividend declared on January 10.		

Note in the two entries that the dividend declaration and payment together reduced corporation assets and shareholders' equity just as a withdrawal of cash by the owner of a single proprietorship reduces assets and the owner's equity.

A cash dividend is normally paid by mailing cheques to the shareholders. Also, as in this case, three dates are normally involved in a dividend declaration and payment: (1) the *date of declaration,* (2) the *date of record,* and (3) the *date of payment.* Since shareholders may sell their stock to new investors at will, the three dates give new shareholders an opportunity to have their ownership entered in the corporation's records in time to receive the dividend. Otherwise it would go to the old shareholders.

A dividend must be formally voted by a corporation's board of directors. Furthermore, courts have generally held that the board is the final judge of when if at all a dividend should be paid. Consequently, shareholders have no right to a dividend until declared. However, as soon as a cash dividend is declared, it becomes a liability of the corporation, normally a current liability, and must be paid. Furthermore, shareholders have the right to sue and force payment of a cash dividend once it is declared.

If during its second year the corporation of this illustration suffered a $7,000 net loss, the entry to close its Income Summary account is:

Dec.	31	Retained Earnings	7,000.00	
		Income Summary		7,000.00
		To close the Income Summary account.		

Posting the entry has the effect shown on the last line of the following Retained Earnings account.

Retained Earnings

Date			Explanation	Post. Ref.	Debit	Credit	Balance
198A Dec.	31		Net income	G4		8,000.00	8,000.00
198B Jan.	10		Dividend declaration	G5	5,000.00		3,000.00
Dec.	31		Net loss	G9	7,000.00		**4,000.00**

After the entry was posted, due to the dividend and the net loss, the Retained Earnings account has a $4,000 debit balance. A debit balance in a Retained Earnings account indicates a negative amount of retained earnings, and a corporation with a negative amount of retained earnings is said to have a *deficit*. A deficit may be shown on a corporation's balance sheet as follows:

Shareholders' Equity

Common stock, 5,000 shares outstanding	$50,000
Deduct retained earnings deficit	(4,000)
Total shareholders' equity	$46,000

In most jurisdictions, it is illegal for a corporation with a deficit to pay a cash dividend. Such dividends are made illegal because as a separate legal entity a corporation is responsible for its own debts. Consequently, if its creditors are to be paid, they must be paid from the corporation's assets. Therefore, making a dividend illegal when there is a deficit helps prevent a corporation in financial difficulties from paying out all of its assets in dividends and leaving nothing for payment of its creditors.

THE ACCOUNTING CYCLE

Each accounting period in the life of a business is a recurring *accounting cycle,* beginning with transactions recorded in a journal and ending with a post-closing trial balance. All steps in the cycle have now been discussed. A knowledge of accounting requires that each step be understood and its relation to the others seen. The steps in the order of their occurrence are as follows:

1. **Journalizing** .... Analyzing and recording transactions in a journal.
2. **Posting** .... Copying the debits and credits of journal entries into the ledger accounts.
3. **Preparing a trial balance** .... Summarizing the ledger accounts and testing the recording accuracy.
4. **Preparing a work sheet** .... Gaining the effects of the adjustments before entering the adjustments in the accounts. Then sorting the account balances into the Balance Sheet and Income Statement columns and finally determining and proving the income or loss.
5. **Preparing the statements** .... Rearranging the work sheet information into a balance sheet and an income statement.
6. **Adjusting the ledger accounts** .... Preparing adjusting journal entries from information in the Adjustments columns of the work sheet and posting the entries in order to bring the account balances up to date.
7. **Closing the temporary accounts** .... Preparing and posting entries to close the temporary accounts and transfer the net income or loss to the capital account or accounts in a single proprietorship or partnership and to the Retained Earnings account in a corporation.
8. **Preparing a post-closing trial balance** .... Proving the accuracy of the adjusting and closing procedures.

GLOSSARY

Accounting cycle.   The accounting steps that recur each accounting period in the life of a business and that begin with the recording of transactions and proceed through posting the recorded amounts, preparing a trial balance, preparing a work sheet, preparing the financial statements, preparing and posting adjusting and closing entries, and preparing a post-closing trial balance.

Closing entries.   Entries made to close and clear the revenue and expense accounts and to transfer the amount of the net income or loss to a capital account or accounts or to the Retained Earnings account.

Closing procedures.   The preparation and posting of closing entries and the preparation of the post-closing trial balance.

Contributed capital.   Shareholders' equity in a corporation resulting among other ways from amounts invested in the corporation by its shareholders.

Date of declaration.   Date on which a dividend is declared.

Date of payment.   Date for the payment of a dividend.

Date of record.   Date on which the shareholders who are to receive a dividend is determined.

Deficit.   A negative amount of retained earnings.

Income Summary account. The account used in the closing procedures to summarize the amounts of revenues and expenses, and from which the amount of the net income or loss is transferred to the owner's capital account in a single proprietorship, the partners' capital accounts in a partnership, or the Retained Earnings account in a corporation.

Post-closing trial balance. A trial balance prepared after closing entries are posted.

Shareholders of record. A corporation's shareholders according to its records.

Temporary accounts. The revenue, expense, Income Summary, and withdrawals accounts.

Working papers. The memoranda, analyses, and other informal papers prepared by accountants and used as a basis for the more formal reports given to clients.

Work sheet. A working paper used by an accountant to bring together in an orderly manner the information used in preparing the financial statements and the adjusting and closing entries.

QUESTIONS FOR CLASS DISCUSSION

1. A work sheet is a tool accountants use to accomplish three tasks. What are these tasks?

2. Is it possible to complete the statements and adjust and close the accounts without preparing a work sheet? What is gained by preparing a work sheet?

3. At what stage in the accounting process is a work sheet prepared?

4. From where are the amounts that are entered in the Trial Balance columns of a work sheet obtained?

5. Why are the adjustments in the Adjustments columns of a work sheet keyed together with letters?

6. What is the result of combining the amounts in the Trial Balance columns with the amounts in the Adjustments columns of a work sheet?

7. Why must care be exercised in sorting the items in the Adjusted Trial Balance columns to the proper Income Statement or Balance Sheet columns?

8. In extending the items in the Adjusted Trial Balance columns of a work sheet, what would be the effect on the net income of extending (a) an expense into the Balance Sheet debit column, (b) a liability into the Income Statement credit column, and (c) a revenue into the Balance Sheet debit column? Would each of these errors be automatically detected on the work sheet? Which would be automatically detected? Why?

9. Why are revenue and expense accounts called temporary accounts?

10. What two purposes are accomplished by recording closing entries?

11. What accounts are affected by closing entries? What accounts are not affected?

12. Explain the difference between adjusting and closing entries.

13. What is the purpose of the Income Summary account?

14. Why is a post-closing trial balance prepared?

15. An accounting student listed the item, "Depreciation expense, building, $1,800," on a post-closing trial balance. What did this indicate?

16. What two kinds of accounts are used in accounting for shareholders' equity in a corporation?

17. Explain how the retained earnings item found on corporation balance sheets arises.

18. What three dates are normally involved in the declaration and payment of a cash dividend?

19. Explain why the payment of a cash dividend by a corporation with a deficit is made illegal.

MULTIPLE CHOICE

1. An error is indicated if the following account has a balance appearing on the post-closing trial balance:
    a. Office equipment.
    b. Accumulated depreciation, office equipment.
    c. Depreciation expense, office equipment.
    d. Ted Nash, capital.
    e. Salaries payable.

2. If the Balance Sheet columns of a work sheet fail to balance when the amount of the net income is added to the Balance Sheet credit column, the cause could be:
    a. An expense amount entered in the Balance Sheet debit column.
    b. A revenue amount entered in the Balance Sheet credit column.
    c. An asset amount entered in the Income Statement debit column.
    d. Any of the foregoing.
    e. None of the foregoing.

3. Throughout an accounting period the fees for legal services paid in advance by clients are recorded in an account called unearned legal fees. If the accountant fails to make the end-of-the-period adjusting entry to record the portion of these fees that has been earned, an effect will be:
    a. An overstatement of owner's equity.
    b. An understatement of owner's equity.
    c. An understatement of assets.
    d. An understatement of liabilities.
    e. None of the foregoing.

4. If the accountant fails to make an adjusting entry at the end of the period to record depreciation for the period, the omission will cause:
   a. An understatement of expenses.
   b. An overstatement of revenues.
   c. An understatement of assets.
   d. An overstatement of liabilities.
   e. None of the foregoing.

5. Over several accounting periods the accrual basis of accounting tends to:
   a. Increase reported assets.
   b. Decrease reported liabilities.
   c. Decrease reported net income.
   d. Increase reported net income.
   e. Have no effect on total income reported.

6. If the accountant failed to make the end-of-the-period adjustment to remove the amount of management fees earned from the unearned management fees account, the omission would cause:
   a. An overstatement of net income.
   b. An overstatement of assets.
   c. An overstatement of liabilities.
   d. An overstatement of owner's equity.
   e. None of these.

7. If in preparing a work sheet an adjusted trial balance amount is sorted to the wrong work sheet column, the Balance Sheet columns will balance on completing the work sheet, but with the wrong net income. This happens when the amount sorted in error is:
   a. An expense amount placed in the Balance Sheet credit column.
   b. A revenue amount placed in the Balance Sheet debit column.
   c. A liability amount placed in the Income Statement credit column.
   d. An asset amount placed in the Balance Sheet credit column.
   e. A liability amount placed in the Balance Sheet debit column.

8. Which of the following is the final step in the accounting cycle?
   a. Journalizing.
   b. Preparing a trial balance.
   c. Preparing a post-closing trial balance.
   d. Preparing the statements.
   e. Preparing a work sheet.

9. The post-closing trial balance of Jakes Realty contains several errors. Which one of the following items on that trial balance indicates an error?
   a. Broker's fees earned is listed with a credit balance of $8,000.
   b. Jakes, withdrawals, is listed with a debit balance of $5,000.
   c. Supplies expense is listed with a debit balance of $400.
   d. Income summary is listed with a $450 credit balance.
   e. All of the above indicate errors.

MINI DISCUSSION

Case 4–1
In the ''heyday'' of exploration and the quest for finding alternate routes to sources of spices, group-financed individual ventures were the order of the day. A venture lasted for two, three, or more years and once completed involved a windup. Financial statements were prepared with precision without the need for adjusting entries. Closing entries were, however, required to close out the profit on the venture and the capital accounts to complete the windup.

Required:

Discuss the similarities and differences between venture accounting of yesteryear and present-day accounting for similar ventures that would be required under GAAP.

CLASS EXERCISES

Exercise 4–1
The balances of the following alphabetically arranged accounts appeared in the Adjusted Trial Balance columns of a work sheet. Copy the account numbers in a column on a sheet of note paper and beside each number indicate by letter the income statement or balance sheet column to which the account's balance would be sorted in completing the work sheet. Use the letter *a* to indicate the Income Statement debit column, *b* to indicate the Income Statement credit column, *c* to indicate the Balance Sheet debit column, and *d* to indicate the Balance Sheet credit column.

1. Accounts Payable.
2. Accounts Receivable.
3. Accumulated Depreciation, Repair Equipment.
4. Advertising Expense.
5. Cash.
6. Ed Lee, Capital.
7. Ed Lee, Withdrawals.
8. Prepaid Insurance.
9. Rent Expense.
10. Repair Equipment.
11. Repair Supplies.
12. Revenue from Repairs.
13. Wages Expense.

Exercise 4–2
The following item amounts are from the Adjustments columns of a work sheet. From the information prepare adjusting journal entries. Use December 31 as the date.

	Adjustments	
	Debit	Credit
Prepaid insurance.....................................		(a) 850
Office supplies		(b) 215
Accumulated depreciation, office equipment		(c) 540
Accumulated depreciation, shop equipment		(d) 3,345
Office salaries expense	(e) 50	
Shop wages expense	(e) 280	
Insurance expense, office equipment	(a) 85	
Insurance expense, shop equipment	(a) 765	
Office supplies expense...............................	(b) 215	
Depreciation expense, office equipment	(c) 540	
Depreciation expense, shop equipment	(d) 3,345	
Salaries and wages payable		(e) 330
Totals	5,280	5,280

Exercise 4–3   Copy the following T-accounts and their end-of-period balances on a sheet of note paper. Below the accounts prepare entries to close the accounts. Post to the T-accounts.

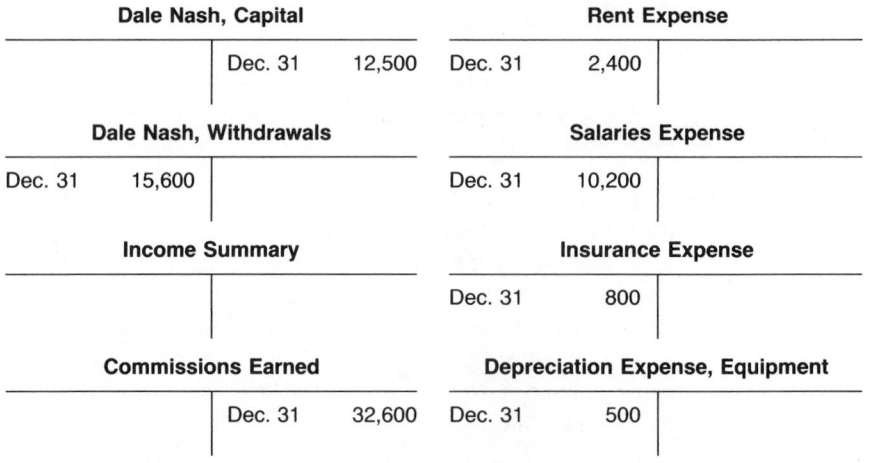

Dale Nash, Capital	
	Dec. 31 12,500

Rent Expense	
Dec. 31 2,400	

Dale Nash, Withdrawals	
Dec. 31 15,600	

Salaries Expense	
Dec. 31 10,200	

Income Summary	

Insurance Expense	
Dec. 31 800	

Commissions Earned	
	Dec. 31 32,600

Depreciation Expense, Equipment	
Dec. 31 500	

Exercise 4–4   The items that follow appeared in the Income Statement columns of a December 31 work sheet prepared for Walter Dole, a lawyer. Under the assumption that Mr. Dole withdrew $24,000 from his law practice during the year, prepare entries to close the revenue, expense, Income Summary, and withdrawals accounts.

	Income statement	
	Debit	Credit
Legal fees earned.....................		54,000
Office salaries expense	13,000	
Rent expense	6,000	
Insurance expense	1,200	
Office supplies expense...............	300	
Depreciation expense, office equipment ...	2,400	
	22,900	54,000
Net income	31,100	
	54,000	54,000

Exercise 4–5

On a sheet of note paper, open the following T-accounts for a corporation that does repair work for other companies. Below the T-accounts prepare entries to close the accounts. Post to the T-accounts.

Common Stock			**Rent Expense**		
	Dec. 31	50,000	Dec. 31	6,000	

Retained Earnings			**Salaries Expense**		
	Dec. 31	7,000	Dec. 31	25,000	

Income Summary		**Insurance Expense**		
		Dec. 31	1,000	

Revenue from Repairs			**Depreciation Expense, Equipment**		
	Dec. 31	50,000	Dec. 31	4,000	

Exercise 4–6

The following items appeared in the Income Statement columns of a December 31 work sheet prepared for a corporation that performs services for other concerns. Prepare closing journal entries for the corporation.

	Income statement	
	Debit	Credit
Revenue from services		88,600
Office salaries expense	27,000	
Rent expense	12,000	
Insurance expense	1,800	
Office supplies expense...............	400	
Depreciation expense, office equipment ...	5,200	
	46,400	88,600
Net income	42,200	
	88,600	88,600

Exercise 4–7

1. On a sheet of note paper open the following T-accounts: Cash, Accounts Receivable, Equipment, Notes Payable, Common Stock, Retained Earnings, Income Summary, Revenue from Services, and Operating Expenses.

2. Record directly in the T-accounts these transactions of a corporation:

    a. Sold and issued $10,000 of common stock for cash.
    b. Purchased $9,000 of equipment for cash.
    c. Sold and delivered $25,000 of services on credit.
    d. Collected $22,000 of accounts receivable.
    e. Paid $20,000 of operating expenses.
    f. Purchased $5,000 of additional equipment, giving $3,000 in cash and a $2,000 promissory note.
    g. Closed the Revenue from Services, Operating Expenses, and Income Summary accounts.

3. Answer these questions:
    a. Does the corporation have retained earnings?
    b. Does it have any cash?
    c. If the corporation has retained earnings, why does it not also have cash?
    d. Can the corporation declare a legal cash dividend?
    e. Can it pay the dividend?
    f. In terms of assets, what does the balance of the Notes Payable account represent?
    g. In terms of assets, what does the balance of the Common Stock account represent?
    h. In terms of assets, what does the balance of the Retained Earnings account represent?

Exercise 4–8

A list of trial balance accounts and their balances follows. All are normal balances. To save your time, the balances are in one- and two-digit numbers. However, to increase your skill in sorting adjusted trial balance amounts to the proper work sheet columns, the accounts are listed in alphabetical order.

Trial Balance Accounts and Balances

Accounts payable	$2	Rent expense	$ 2
Accounts receivable	3	Revenue from repairs	18
Accumulated depreciation,		Robert Ross, capital	11
shop equipment	2	Robert Ross, withdrawals	2
Cash	5	Shop equipment	7
Notes payable	1	Shop supplies	4
Prepaid insurance	3	Wages expense	8

Required:

1. Prepare a work sheet form on notebook paper and enter the trial balance accounts and amounts on the work sheet in their alphabetical order.
2. Complete the work sheet using the following information:
    a. Estimated depreciation of shop equipment, $1.
    b. Expired insurance, $1
    c. Unused shop supplies per inventory, $1.
    d. Earned but unpaid wages, $2.

Exercise 4–9   The following trial balance of Small Company, Inc. as of the end of its annual accounting period is:

SMALL COMPANY, INC.
Trial Balance
December 31, 19—

Cash	$ 3,800	
Prepaid insurance	1,200	
Repair supplies	2,000	
Repair equipment	15,000	
Accumulated depreciation, repair equipment		$ 1,000
Common stock		10,000
Retained earnings		1,500
Revenue from repairs		40,000
Salaries expense	21,500	
Rent expense	9,000	
Totals	$52,500	$52,500

Required:

1. Prepare a work sheet form on note paper and enter the trial balance.
2. Complete the work using the information that follows:
    a. Expired insurance, $800.
    b. Unused repair supplies per inventory, $300.
    c. Estimated depreciation of repair equipment, $2,100.
    d. Earned but unpaid salaries, $500.

Exercise 4–10   Prepare adjusting and closing journal entries for the corporation given in Exercise 4–9.

PROBLEMS

Problem 4–1   At the end of its annual accounting period a trial balance of the ledger Tim's Repair Service carried the items that follow.

TIM'S REPAIR SERVICE
Trial Balance
December 31, 19—

Cash	$ 1,215	
Prepaid insurance	865	
Repair supplies	2,925	
Repair equipment	5,240	
Accumulated depreciation, repair equipment		$ 1,280
Accounts payable		195
Tim Hill, capital		4,125
Tim Hill, withdrawals	18,800	
Revenue from repairs		37,230
Wages expense	10,140	
Rent expense	3,000	
Utilities expense	645	
Totals	$42,830	$42,830

Required:

1. Enter the trial balance on a work sheet form and complete the work sheet using the information that follows:
   a. Expired insurance, $535.
   b. A repair supplies inventory showed $775 of unused supplies on hand.
   c. Estimated depreciation on repair equipment, $660.
   d. Wages earned by the one employee but unpaid and unrecorded, $80.
2. From the work sheet prepare an income statement and a classified balance sheet.
3. Prepare adjusting journal entries and compound closing entries.

Problem 4–2   (Covers two accounting cycles)

Sue Gage opened a real estate office she called Sue Gage Realty, and during May she completed these transactions:

May 2 Invested $2,000 in cash and an automobile having a $12,000 fair value in the real estate agency.
   2 Rented furnished office space and paid one month's rent, $500.
   2 Purchased office supplies for cash, $150.
   10 Paid the premium on a one-year insurance policy, $720.
   14 Paid the biweekly salary of the office secretary, $400.
   17 Sold a house and collected a $5,340 commission.
   28 Paid the biweekly salary of the office secretary, $400.
   31 Paid the May telephone bill, $50.
   31 Paid for gas and oil used in the agency car during May, $60.

Required work for May:

1. Open these accounts: Cash; Prepaid Insurance; Office Supplies; Automobile; Accumulated Depreciation, Automobile; Salaries Payable; Sue Gage, Capital; Sue Gage, Withdrawals; Income Summary; Commissions Earned; Rent Expense; Salaries Expense; Gas, Oil, and Repairs Expense; Telephone Expense; Insurance Expense; Office Supplies Expense; and Depreciation Expense, Automobile.
2. Prepare and post journal entries to record the transactions.
3. Prepare a trial balance in the Trial Balance columns of a work sheet form and complete the work sheet using the following information.
   a. Two thirds of a month's insurance has expired.
   b. An inventory shows $125 of unused office supplies remaining.
   c. Estimated depreciation on the automobile, $165.
   d. Earned but unpaid salary of the office secretary, $80
4. Prepare a May income statement and a May 31 classified balance sheet.
5. Prepare and post adjusting and closing entries.
6. Prepare a post-closing trial balance.

During June, Sue Gage completed these transactions:

June 1 Paid the June rent on the office space, $500.
   5 Purchased additional office supplies for cash, $30.
   11 Paid the biweekly salary of the office secretary, $400.
   14 Sue Gage withdrew $2,000 cash from the business for personal uses.
   17 Sold a building lot and collected a $1,500 commission.
   25 Paid the biweekly salary of the office secretary, $400.

30   Paid for gas and oil used in the agency car during June, $55.
30   Paid the June telephone bill, $45.

Required work for June:

1.   Prepare and post journal entries to record the transactions.
2.   Prepare a trial balance in the Trial Balance columns of a work sheet form and complete the work sheet using the following information:
     a. . One month's insurance has expired.
     b.   An office supplies inventory shows $125 of unused supplies.
     c.   Estimated depreciation on the automobile, $165.
     d.   Earned but unpaid secretary's salary, $160.
3.   Prepare a June income statement and a June 30 classified balance sheet.
4.   Prepare and post adjusting and closing entries.
5.   Prepare a post-closing trial balance.

Problem 4–3   The accounts of Leisure Alleys, showing balances as of the end of its annual accounting period, appear in the booklet of working papers that accompanies this text, and a trial balance of its ledger is reproduced on a work sheet form provided there. The trial balance has the items that follow.

Required:

1.   If the working papers are being used, complete the work sheet provided there for the solution of this problem, using the information that follows. If the working papers are not being used, enter the trial balance on a work sheet form and complete the work sheet.
     a.   Bowling supplies inventory, $210.
     b.   Expired insurance, $1,120.
     c.   Estimated depreciation on bowling equipment, $4,750.
     d.   The December hydro bill for the bowling alley arrived in the mail after the trial balance was prepared. Its $220 amount was unrecorded.
     e.   Wages earned but unpaid and unrecorded, $280.

LEISURE ALLEYS
Trial Balance
December 31, 19—

Cash	$ 775	
Bowling supplies	1,420	
Prepaid insurance	1,335	
Bowling equipment	49,565	
Accumulated depreciation, bowling equipment		$ 7,640
Accounts payable		135
Mortgage payable		10,000
Gary Berg, capital		21,200
Gary Berg, withdrawals	15,650	
Bowling revenue		54,500
Wages expense	16,255	
Equipment repairs expense	420	
Rent expense	4,800	
Utilities expense	2,135	
Business taxes expense	520	
Interest expense	600	
Totals	$93,475	$93,475

f. The lease contract on the building calls for an annual rental equal to 10% of the annual bowling revenue, with $400 payable each month on the first day of the month. The $400 was paid each month and debited to the Rent Expense account.

g. Business taxes amounting to $190 have accrued but are unrecorded and unpaid.

h. The mortgage debt was incurred on September 1, and interest on the debt is at a 12% annual rate or $100 per month. The mortgage contract calls for the payment of $300 interest each three months in advance. Interest payments were made on September 1 and December 1. A $1,000 payment on the mortgage principal is due next September 1.

2. Prepare an income statement and a classified balance sheet.

3. Prepare adjusting and closing entries.

4. Post the adjusting and closing entries and prepare a post-closing trial balance. (Omit this requirement if the working papers are not being used.)

Problem 4–4   The accounts of Ed's Delivery Service, showing balances as of the end of its annual accounting period, appear in the booklet of working papers that accompanies this text, and a trial balance of the accounts is reproduced on a work sheet form there. The trial balance has the items that follow.

Required:

1. If the working papers are being used, complete the work sheet provided there for the solution of this problem, using the information that follows. If the working papers are not being used, enter the trial balance on a work sheet form and complete the work sheet.

   a. Insurance expired on the office equipment, $100, and on the delivery equipment, $1,890.

ED'S DELIVERY SERVICE
Trial Balance
December 31, 19—

Cash	$ 525	
Accounts receivable	670	
Prepaid insurance	2,275	
Office supplies	245	
Prepaid rent	250	
Office equipment	2,460	
Accumulated depreciation, office equipment		$ 570
Delivery equipment	14,790	
Accumulated depreciation, delivery equipment		3,150
Accounts payable		890
Unearned delivery service revenue		550
Edward Deal, capital		22,905
Edward Deal, withdrawals	12,000	
Delivery service revenue		41,555
Rent expense	2,500	
Telephone expense	345	
Office salaries expense	10,060	
Delivery wages expense	20,320	
Gas, oil, and repairs expense	3,180	
Totals	$69,620	$69,620

b. An inventory showed $110 of unused office supplies on hand.

c. Estimated depreciation on the office equipment, $300, and *(d)* on the delivery equipment, $2,415.

e. At the beginning of the year one month's rent was prepaid on the garage and office space occupied by the delivery service as shown by the balance of the Prepaid Rent account. Rents for February through November were paid each month and debited to the Rent Expense account. As of the trial balance date, the December rent had not been paid.

f. Three stores signed contracts with the delivery service in which they agreed to pay a fixed fee for the delivery of packages. Two of the stores made advance payments on their contracts, and the amounts paid were credited to the Unearned Delivery Service Revenue account. An examination of their contracts shows $280 of the $550 paid was earned by the accounting period end. The third store's contract provides for a $200 monthly fee to be paid at the end of each month's service. It was signed on December 15, and one half of a month's revenue has accrued but is unrecorded.

g. A $35 December telephone bill and a $60 bill for repairs to a motorcycle used in the business arrived in the mail on December 31. Neither bill was paid or recorded before the trial balance was prepared.

h. Office salaries, $80, and delivery wages, $175, have accrued but are unpaid and unrecorded.

2. Prepare an income statement and a classified balance sheet.
3. Prepare adjusting and closing entries.
4. Post the adjusting and closing entries to the accounts and prepare a post-closing trial balance. (If the working papers are not being used, omit this requirement.)

Problem 4–5 Dale Hall, John Nash, and Joel Teel began a business on January 5, 198A, in which each man invested $30,000. During 198A, the business lost $7,500; and during 198B, it earned $33,000. On January 3, 198C, the three men agreed to pay out to themselves $18,000 of the accumulated earnings of the business; and on January 8, the $18,000 was paid out.

Required:

1. Under the assumption that the business is a partnership in which the partners share losses and gains equally, give the entries to record the investments and to close the Income Summary account at the end of 198A and again at the end of 198B. Under the further assumption that the partners shared equally in the $18,000 of earnings paid out, give the entry to record the withdrawals.

2. Under the assumption that the business is organized as a corporation and that each man invested in it by buying 3,000 shares of its common stock at $10 per share, give the entry to record the investments. Also, give the entries to close the Income Summary account at the end of 198A and

again at the end of 198B and to record the declaration and payment of the $2 per share dividend. (Ignore corporation income taxes.)

ALTERNATE PROBLEMS

Problem 4–1A   A trial balance of the ledger of Mr. Clean Janitorial Service at the end of its annual accounting period carried the items that follow.

MR. CLEAN JANITORIAL SERVICE
Trial Balance
December 31, 19—

Cash	$ 1,065	
Accounts receivable	215	
Prepaid insurance	1,320	
Cleaning supplies	815	
Prepaid rent	300	
Cleaning equipment	2,610	
Accumulated depreciation, cleaning equipment		$ 1,140
Trucks	16,560	
Accumulated depreciation, trucks		3,820
Accounts payable		645
Unearned janitorial revenue		400
Tom Reed, capital		11,745
Tom Reed, withdrawals	15,450	
Janitorial revenue earned		34,610
Wages expense	12,440	
Rent expense	800	
Gas, oil, and repairs expense	785	
Totals	$52,360	$52,360

Required:

1. Enter the trial balance on a work sheet form and complete the work sheet using the information that follows:
    a. Expired insurance, $950.
    b. An inventory of cleaning supplies showed $125 of unused supplies on hand.
    c. The cleaning service rents garage and equipment storage space. At the beginning of the year, three months' rent was prepaid as shown by the debit balance of the Prepaid Rent account. Rents for April through November were paid on the first day of each month and debited to the Rent Expense account. The December rent was unpaid on the trial balance date.
    d. Estimated depreciation on the cleaning equipment, $365, and *(e)* on the trucks, $2,170.
    f. On November 15, the janitorial service contracted and began cleaning the office of Tops Realty for $200 per month. The realty company paid for two months' service in advance, and the amount paid was credited to the Unearned Janitorial Revenue account. The janitorial service also entered into a contract and began cleaning the office of

Kona Insurance Agency on December 15. By the month's end, a half month's revenue, $120, had been earned on this contract but was unrecorded.

g. Employee's wages amounting to $180 had accrued but were unrecorded on the trial balance date.

2. Prepare an income statement and a classified balance sheet for the business.
3. Prepare adjusting and closing entries.

Problem 4–2A   (Covers two accounting cycles)

Sue Gage began a business she called Sue Gage Realty, and during May she completed the transactions that follow:

May 1   Invested $2,500 in cash and an automobile having a $10,000 fair value in a real estate agency.
1   Rented furnished office space and paid one month's rent, $400.
1   Paid the premium on an insurance policy giving one year's protection, $660.
2   Purchased office supplies for cash, $140.
13   Paid the biweekly salary of the office secretary, $450.
18   Sold a building lot and collected a $1,600 commission on the sale.
27   Paid the biweekly salary of the office secretary, $450.
31   Paid the May telephone bill, $45.
31   Paid for gas and oil used in the agency car during May, $60.

Required work for May:

1. Open these accounts: Cash; Prepaid Insurance; Office Supplies; Automobile; Accumulated Depreciation, Automobile; Salaries Payable; Sue Gage, Capital; Sue Gage, Withdrawals; Income Summary; Commissions Earned; Rent Expense; Salaries Expense; Gas, Oil, and Repairs Expense; Telephone Expense; Insurance Expense; Office Supplies Expense; and Depreciation Expense, Automobile.
2. Prepare and post journal entries to record the transactions.
3. Prepare a trial balance in the Trial Balance columns of a work sheet form and complete the work sheet using the information that follows:
   a. One month's insurance has expired.
   b. An inventory shows $110 of unused office supplies remaining.
   c. Estimated depreciation on the automobile, $160.
   d. Earned but unpaid wages of the secretary, $135.
4. Prepare a May income statement and a May 31 classified balance sheet.
5. Prepare and post adjusting and closing entries.
6. Prepare a post-closing trial balance.

These transactions were completed by Sue Gage during June:

June 1   Paid the June rent on the office space, $400.
6   Sold a house and collected a $4,850 commission.
8   Sue Gage withdrew $1,500 from the business to pay personal expenses.
9   Paid the biweekly salary of the office secretary, $450.
20   Purchased additional office supplies for cash, $35.
23   Paid the biweekly salary of the office secretary, $450.
30   Paid the June telephone bill, $40.
30   Paid for gas and oil used in the agency car, $50.

Required work for June:

1. Prepare and post journal entries to record the transactions.
2. Prepare a trial balance in the Trial Balance columns of a work sheet form and complete the work sheet using the information that follows:
    a. One month's insurance has expired.
    b. An office supplies inventory shows $120 of unused office supplies.
    c. Estimated depreciation on the automobile, $160.
    d. Earned but unrecorded salary of the secretary, $225.
3. Prepare a June income statement and a June 30 classified balance sheet.
4. Prepare and post adjusting and closing entries.
5. Prepare a post-closing trial balance.

Problem 4–3A   The accounts of Leisure Alleys showing the end of its annual accounting period balances appear in the booklet of working papers that accompanies this text, and a trial balance of the accounts is reproduced on a work sheet form provided there. The trial balance has the items that follow.

Required:

1. If the working papers are being used, complete the work sheet provided there for the solution of this problem, using the information that follows. If the working papers are not being used, enter the trial balance on a work sheet form and complete the work sheet.
    a. Bowling supplies inventory, $180.
    b. Expired insurance, $1,195.
    c. Estimated depreciation on the bowling equipment, $4,715.

LEISURE ALLEYS
Trial Balance
December 31, 19—

Cash	$ 775	
Bowling supplies	1,420	
Prepaid insurance	1,335	
Bowling equipment	49,565	
Accumulated depreciation, bowling equipment		$ 7,640
Accounts payable		135
Mortgage payable		10,000
Gary Berg, capital		21,200
Gary Berg, withdrawals	15,650	
Bowling revenue		54,500
Wages expense	16,255	
Equipment repairs expense	420	
Rent expense	4,800	
Utilities expense	2,135	
Business taxes expense	520	
Interest expense	600	
Totals	$93,475	$93,475

d. A $165 bill for equipment repairs arrived in the mail after the trial balance was prepared. It is unrecorded and unpaid.
e. Wages earned but unpaid and unrecorded, $225.
f. The lease contract on the bowling alley space calls for an annual

rental equal to 11% of the annual bowling revenue, with $400 payable each month on the first day of the month. The $400 was paid each month and debited to the Rent Expense account.

g. Business taxes amounting to $215 have accrued but are unrecorded and unpaid.

h. The mortgage debt was incurred on August 1. The interest on the debt is at a 12% annual rate or $100 per month. The mortgage contract requires the payment of $300 interest each three months in advance. Interest was paid on August 1 and November 1. A $2,000 payment on the mortgage principal is due next August 1.

2. Prepare an income statement and a classified balance sheet.
3. Prepare adjusting and closing entries.
4. Post the adjusting and closing entries and prepare a post-closing trial balance. (Omit this requirement if the working papers are not being used.)

Problem 4–4A   The accounts of Ed's Delivery Service showing balances as of the end of its annual accounting period appear in the booklet of working papers that accompanies this text, and a trial balance of the accounts is reproduced on a work sheet form there. The trial balance has the items that follow.

Required:

1. If the working papers are being used, complete the work sheet provided there for the solution of this problem, using the information that follows. If the working papers are not being used, enter the trial balance on a work sheet form and complete the work sheet.

a. Expired insurance on the office equipment, $110, and on the delivery equipment, $1,775.

ED'S DELIVERY SERVICE
Trial Balance
December 31, 19—

Cash	$ 525	
Accounts receivable	670	
Prepaid insurance	2,275	
Office supplies	245	
Prepaid rent	250	
Office equipment	2,460	
Accumulated depreciation, office equipment		$ 570
Delivery equipment	14,790	
Accumulated depreciation, delivery equipment		3,150
Accounts payable		890
Unearned delivery service revenue		550
Edward Deal, capital		22,905
Edward Deal, withdrawals	12,000	
Delivery service revenue		41,555
Rent expense	2,500	
Telephone expense	345	
Office salaries expense	10,060	
Delivery wages expense	20,320	
Gas, oil, and repairs expense	3,180	
Totals	$69,620	$69,620

b. An inventory showed $120 of unused office supplies on hand.

c. Estimated depreciation on the office equipment, $290, and (d) on the delivery equipment, $2,330.

e. At the beginning of the current year, one month's rent was prepaid on the garage and office space occupied by the delivery service as shown by the debit balance in the Prepaid Rent account. Rents for February through November were paid each month and debited to the Rent Expense account. As of the trial balance date the December rent had not been paid.

f. The delivery service has contracts with three stores for the delivery of packages on a fixed-fee basis. Two of the stores made advance payments on their contracts, and the amounts paid were credited to the Unearned Delivery Service Revenue account. An examination of the contracts shows that $320 of the $550 paid was earned by the accounting period end. The third store's contract provides for a $250 monthly fee to be paid at the end of each month's service. One half of a month's revenue has accrued on this contract but it is unrecorded.

g. An $85 bill for repairs to a delivery truck during December arrived in the mail after the trial balance was prepared. It is unpaid and unrecorded.

h. Office salaries, $40, and delivery wages, $95, have accrued but are unpaid and unrecorded.

2. Prepare an income statement and a classified balance sheet.

3. Prepare adjusting and closing entries.

4. Post the adjusting and closing entries to the accounts and prepare a post-closing trial balance. (If the working papers are not being used, omit this requirement.)

Problem 4–5A   On January 3, 198A, Ted Hill, Jane Lee, and Carl Nye began a business in which Ted Hill invested $10,000, Jane Lee invested $20,000, and Carl Nye invested $30,000. During 198A, the business lost $3,000; and during 198B, it earned $18,000. On January 3, 198C, the three business owners agreed to pay out to themselves $12,000 of the accumulated earnings of the business; and on January 15, the $12,000 was paid out.

Required:

1. Under the assumption that the business is a partnership in which the partners share losses and gains in proportion to their investments, give the entries to record the investments and to close the Income Summary account at the end of 198A and again at the end of 198B. Under the further assumption that the partners paid out the accumulated earnings in proportion to their investments, give the entry to record the withdrawals.

2. Under the assumption that the business is organized as a corporation and that the owners invested in the corporation by buying its common stock at $10 per share, with Ted Hill buying 1,000 shares, Jane Lee buying

2,000 shares, and Carl Nye buying 3,000 shares, give the entry to record the investments. Also give the entries to close the Income Summary account at the end of 198A and again at the end of 198B. Then give the entries to record the declaration and payment of the $2 per share dividend. (Ignore corporation income taxes.)

PROVOCATIVE PROBLEMS

Provocative
Problem 4–1
Countrywide
Moving
Service

During his second year in the university, Dale West, as the only heir, inherited Countrywide Moving Service upon the death of his father. He immediately dropped out of school and took over management of the business. At the time he took over, Dale recognized he knew little about accounting. However, he reasoned that, since the business performed its services strictly for cash, if the cash of the business increased, the business was doing OK. Therefore, he was pleased as he watched the concern's cash balance grow from $1,250 when he took over to $11,975 at the year-end. Furthermore, at the year-end, he reasoned that, since he had withdrawn $25,000 from the business to buy a new car and to pay personal expenses, the business must have earned $35,725 during the year. He arrived at the $35,725 by adding the $10,725 increase in cash to the $25,000 he had withdrawn from the business. Consequently, he was shocked when he received the income statement that follows and learned that the business had earned less than the amounts withdrawn.

COUNTRYWIDE MOVING SERVICE
Income Statement
For Year Ended December 31, 19—

Revenue from moving services		$80,375
Operating expenses:		
Salaries and wages expense	$36,550	
Gas, oil, and repairs expense	3,225	
Telephone expense	350	
Taxes expense	2,475	
Insurance expense	2,325	
Office supplies expense	250	
Depreciation expense, office equipment ...	400	
Depreciation expense, trucks	6,250	
Depreciation expense, building	5,000	
Total operating expenses		56,825
Net income		$23,550

After mulling the statement over for several days, Dale has asked you to explain how, in a year in which the cash increased $10,725 and he had withdrawn $25,000, the business could have earned only $23,550. In examining the accounts of the business, you note that accrued salaries and wages payable at the beginning of the year were $125 but increased to $375 at the year's end. Likewise, the accrued taxes payable were $450 at the beginning of the year but had increased to $475 at the year-end. Also, the balance of the Prepaid Insurance account was $200 less and the balance of the Office Supplies account was $50 less at the end of the year than at the beginning. However, except for the changes in these accounts, the change in cash, and the changes in the balances of the accumulated depreciation accounts, there were no other changes in the balances of the concern's asset and liability accounts between the beginning of the year and the end. Back your explanation with a calculation accounting for the increase in the concern's cash.

Provocative
Problem 4–2,
Jane Otto,
Lawyer

During the first year-end closing of the accounts of Jane Otto's law practice, the office secretary became seriously ill and is in the hospital unable to have visitors. Ms. Otto is certain the secretary prepared a work sheet, income statement, and balance sheet, but she has only the income statement and cannot find either the work sheet or balance sheet. She does have a trial balance of the accounts of the law practice, and she wants you to prepare adjusting and closing entries from the following trial balance and income statement. She also wants you to prepare a classified balance sheet. She says the $1,200 of unearned legal fees on the trial balance represents a retainer fee paid by Security Bank. The bank retained Jane Otto on November 1 to do its legal work, agreeing to pay her $400 per month for her services. She says she has also entered into an agreement with Westside Realty to do its legal work on a fixed-fee basis. The agreement calls for a $300 monthly fee payable at the end of each three months. The agreement was signed on December 1, and one month's fee has accrued but has not been recorded.

JANE OTTO, LAWYER
Trial Balance
December 31, 19—

Cash	$ 1,225	
Legal fees receivable	1,500	
Office supplies	325	
Prepaid insurance	900	
Furniture and equipment	12,500	
Notes payable		$ 5,000
Accounts payable		350
Unearned legal fees		1,200
Jane Otto, capital		7,500
Jane Otto, withdrawals	18,000	
Legal fees earned		37,325
Salaries expense	11,750	
Rent expense	4,800	
Telephone expense	375	
Totals	$51,375	$51,375

JANE OTTO, LAWYER
Income Statement
For Year Ended December 31, 19—

Revenue:		
Legal fees earned		$38,425
Operating expenses:		
Salaries expense	$12,000	
Rent expense	4,800	
Telephone expense	375	
Office supplies expense	200	
Insurance expense	750	
Depreciation expense, furniture and equipment ...	1,200	
Interest expense	600	
Total operating expenses		19,925
Net income		$18,500

Provocative
Problem 4–3,
Hillside Realty

The balance sheet that follows was prepared for Hillside Realty at the end of its annual accounting period.

HILLSIDE REALTY
Balance Sheet
December 31, 19—

Assets

Current assets:			
Cash...		$ 1,525	
Prepaid insurance		500	
Office supplies		110	
Total current assets			$ 2,135
Plant and equipment:			
Office equipment	$ 5,240		
Less accumulated depreciation	1,010	$ 4,230	
Automobile	$12,400		
Less accumulated depreciation	2,700	9,700	
Total plant and equipment			13,930
Total assets			$16,065

Liabilities

Current liabilities:			
Accounts payable		$ 210	
Unearned property management fees		250	
Salaries payable		180	
Total liabilities			$ 640

Owner's Equity

Mary Hall, capital, January 1, 19—		$10,565	
Net income for the year	$28,860		
Less withdrawals	24,000		
Excess of income over withdrawals		4,860	
Mary Hall, capital, December 31, 19—			15,425
Total liabilities and owner's equity			$16,065

After completing the balance sheet, Hillside Realty's accountant prepared and posted the following adjusting and closing entries for the concern.

Dec. 31	Insurance Expense	1,150.00	
	Prepaid Insurance		1,150.00
31	Office Supplies Expense	210.00	
	Office Supplies		210.00
31	Depreciation Expense, Office Equipment	640.00	
	Accumulated Depreciation, Office Equipment		640.00
31	Depreciation Expense, Automobile	2,100.00	
	Accumulated Depreciation, Automobile		2,100.00
31	Unearned Property Management Fees	500.00	
	Property Management Fees Earned		500.00
31	Salaries Expense	180.00	
	Salaries Payable		180.00
31	Commissions Earned	49,600.00	
	Property Management Fees Earned	1,760.00	
	Income Summary		51,360.00
31	Income Summary	22,500.00	
	Salaries Expense		11,000.00
	Rent Expense		6,000.00
	Telephone Expense		460.00
	Gas, Oil, and Repairs Expense		940.00
	Insurance Expenses		1,150.00
	Office Supplies Expense		210.00
	Depreciation Expense, Office Equipment		640.00
	Depreciation Expense, Automobile		2,100.00
31	Income Summary	28,860.00	
	Mary Hall, Capital		28,860.00
31	Mary Hall, Capital	24,000.00	
	Mary Hall, Withdrawals		24,000.00

Enter the relevant information from the balance sheet and the adjusting and closing entries on a work sheet form and complete the work sheet by working backward to the items that appeared in its Trial Balance columns.

ANALYTICAL AND REVIEW PROBLEMS

Problem 4–1 A&R   The owner of Miracle Stores has come to you for assistance because his bookkeeper has just moved to another city. The following is the only information his bookkeeper left him.

(1)   Balance sheets as at December 31, 198A and 198B.

	198A	198B
Assets	$50,000	$40,000
Liabilities	$15,000	$10,000
Capital	35,000	30,000
	$50,000	$40,000

(2)   The owner withdrew $25,000 in 198B for his personal use.
(3)   The business incurred total expenses of $40,000 for 198B, of which $30,000 was for wages and $10,000 for advertising.

Required:

1.   Compute the total revenue and net income for 198B.
2.   Prepare closing or clearing entries for 198B (omit narratives).

Problem 4–2
A&R

JANE TURNER DELIVERY
Work Sheet for Year Ended December 31, 198A

Account Titles	Trial Balance Debit	Trial Balance Credit	Adjustments Debit	Adjustments Credit	Adjusted Trial Balance Debit	Adjusted Trial Balance Credit	Income Statement Debit	Income Statement Credit	Balance Sheet Debit	Balance Sheet Credit
Cash	5,650				560				560	
Accounts receivable	30,200				31,000				31,000	
Supplies on hand	1,400			800	600				600	
Prepaid insurance	2,400			1,200	1,200				1,200	
Prepaid rent	1,200			900	300				300	
Delivery trucks	40,000				40,000				4,000	
Accounts payable		3,130				3,130				3,130
Unearned delivery fees		5,200	2,000			3,000		3,000		3,000
Jane Turner, capital, 12/1/8A		50,000				50,000				50,000
Jane Turner, drawing	8,000				8,000				8,000	
Delivery service revenue		46,300		3,000		49,300		49,300		
Advertising expense	350				350		330			
Gas and oil expense	1,680				1,680		1,680			
Salaries expense	13,600		1,180		14,780		14,780			
Utilities expense	150				150		150			
	104,630	104,630								
Insurance expense			1,200		1,200		1,200			
Rent expense			900		900		900			
Supplies expense			800		800		800			
Depreciation expense—delivery trucks			2,750		2,750		2,750			
Accumulated depreciation—delivery trucks				2,750		2,750				2,750
Accrued salaries payable				1,180		1,180				1,180
			9,830	9,830	109,360	109,360	22,610	52,300	86,750	57,060
Net income							29,690			29,690
							52,300	52,300	86,750	86,750

Required:

1. Complete the work sheet.
2. Journalize the closing entries.

Problem 4–3
A&R

Your examination of the books of Dr. Milton Vacon, a local general practitioner, revealed that his nurse/secretary followed the cash basis of accounting in all matters with the exception of equipment. The equipment, which cost $62,000 at the time Dr. Vacon started practice (January 2, 1985), was set up as an asset and to date not depreciated. The equipment had an estimated useful life of 10 years at which time it would be sold for an estimated $2,000. Upon further examination you were able to identify the relevant data as follows:

	1985	1986	1987
Reported income	$71,000	$76,000	$69,000
Supplies on hand at year-end	600	300	1,200
Wages not paid at year-end	700	900	400
Billings to the Provincial Hospital Insurance during December for which a cheque has not been received	8,000	3,000	10,000
Miscellaneous expenses owing at year-end	800	900	200

Required:

Compute the correct net income for each year using the accrual basis of accounting (show all supporting calculations).

Problem 4–4
A&R

Your examination of the books of Carzin Company revealed that the company followed the cash basis of accounting with respect to certain items. Further examination revealed the following matters had not been taken into account in computing net income of $10,000 for 1985 a net loss of $5,000 for 1986 and net income of $8,000 for 1987:

	1985	1986	1987
Office supplies on hand at year-end	$400	$600	$200
Wages expense incurred during the year but neither paid nor recorded at year-end	500	400	700
Advances from customers recorded as revenues but unearned at year-end	650	700	500
Revenues earned during the year but not billed and not recorded at year-end	500	400	350

Required:

Compute the correct net income or net loss for each year using the accrual basis of accounting. (Show all supporting calculations.)

Accounting for a Merchandising Concern

5

After studying Chapter 5, you should be able to:

Explain the nature of each item entering into the calculation of cost of goods sold and be able to calculate cost of goods sold and gross profit from sales.

Prepare a work sheet and the financial statements, by using a periodic inventory system, for a merchandising business that is organized as either a corporation or a single proprietorship.

Prepare adjusting and closing entries for a merchandising business organized as either a corporation or a single proprietorship.

Define or explain the words and phrases listed in the chapter Glossary.

The accounting records and reports of the Owen law practice, as described in previous chapters, are those of a service enterprise. Other examples of service enterprises are laundries, taxicab companies, barber and beauty shops, theatres, and golf courses. Each performs a service for a commission or fee, and the net income of each is the difference between fees or commissions earned and operating expenses.

A merchandising company, on the other hand, whether a wholesaler or retailer, earns revenue by selling goods or merchandise. In such a company, a net income results when revenue from sales exceeds the cost of the goods sold plus operating expenses, as illustrated below:

XYZ STORE
Condensed Income Statement

Revenue from sales	$100,000
Less cost of goods sold	60,000
Gross profit from sales	$ 40,000
Less operating expenses	25,000
Net income	$ 15,000

The store of the illustrated income statement sold goods that cost $60,000 for $100,000. It thereby earned a $40,000 gross profit from sales. It subtracted from this $25,000 of operating expenses to show a $15,000 net income.

Gross profit from sales, [1] as shown on the illustrated income statement, is the "profit" before operating expenses are deducted. Accounting for the factors that enter into its calculation differentiates the accounting of a merchandising company from that of a service enterprise.

Gross profit from sales is determined by subtracting cost of goods sold from the revenue from sales. However, before the subtraction can be made, both revenue from sales and cost of goods sold must be determined.

REVENUE FROM SALES

Revenue from sales consists of gross proceeds from merchandise sales less returns, allowances, and discounts. It may be reported on an income statement as follows:

---

[1] Other names for gross profit are gross margin or margin on sales.

KONA SALES, INCORPORATED
Income Statement
For Year Ended December 31, 198B

Revenue from sales:		
Gross sales		$306,200
Less: Sales returns and allowances	$1,900	
Sales discounts	4,300	6,200
Net sales...........................		$300,000

Gross Sales

The gross sales item on the partial income statement is the total cash and credit sales made by the company during the year. Cash sales were "rung up" on the cash register as each sale was completed. At the end of each day, the register total showed the amount of that day's cash sales. This amount was recorded with an entry like this:

Nov.	3	Cash	1,205.00	
		Sales		1,205.00
		To record the day's cash sales.		

In addition, an entry like this was used to record credit sales:

Nov.	3	Accounts Receivable	45.00	
		Sales		45.00
		Sold merchandise on credit.		

Sales Returns and Allowances

In most stores, a customer is permitted to return any unsatisfactory merchandise purchased. Or the customer is sometimes allowed to keep the unsatisfactory goods and is given an allowance or an amount off its sales price. Either way, returns and allowances result from dissatisfied customers. Consequently, it is important for management to know the amount of such returns and allowances and their relation to sales. This information is supplied by the Sales Returns and Allowances account when each return or allowance is recorded as follows:

Nov.	4	Sales Returns and Allowances	20.00	
		Accounts Receivable (or Cash)		20.00
		Customer returned unsatisfactory merchandise.		

Sales Discounts

When goods are sold on credit, the terms of payment are always made definite so there will be no misunderstanding as to the amount and time of payment. The *credit terms* normally appear on the invoice or sales ticket and are part of the sales agreement. Exact terms granted usually depend upon the custom of the trade. In some trades, it is customary for invoices to become due and payable 10 days after the end of the month *(EOM)* in which the sale occurred. Invoices in these trades carry terms, ''n/10 EOM.'' In other trades, invoices become due and payable 30 days after the invoice date and carry terms of ''n/30.'' This means that the net amount of the invoice is due 30 days after the invoice date.

When credit periods are long, creditors commonly grant discounts, called *cash discounts,* for early payments. This reduces the amount invested in accounts receivable and thus the amount of money needed in carrying on the business operations. When discounts for early payment are granted, they are made part of the credit terms and appear on the invoice as, for example, ''Terms: 2/10, n/60.'' Terms of 2/10, n/60 mean that the *credit period* is 60 days but that the debtor may deduct 2% from the invoice amount if payment is made within 10 days after the invoice date. The 10-day period is known as the *discount period.*

Since at the time of a sale it is not known if the customer will pay within the discount period and take advantage of a cash discount, normally sales discounts are not recorded until the customer pays. For example, on November 12, Kona Sales, Incorporated, sold $100 of merchandise to a customer on credit, terms 2/10, n/60, and recorded the sale as follows:

Nov.	12	Accounts Receivable	100.00	
		Sales		100.00
		Sold merchandise, terms 2/10, n/60.		

At the time of the sale, the customer could choose either to receive credit for paying the full $100 by paying $98 any time on or before

November 22. Or the customer could wait 60 days, until January 11, and pay the full $100. If the customer elected to pay by November 22 and take advantage of the cash discount, Kona Sales, Incorporated, would record the receipt of the $98 as follows:

Nov.	22	Cash	98.00	
		Sales Discounts	2.00	
		Accounts Receivable		100.00
		Received payment for the November 12 sale less the discount.		

Sales discounts are accumulated in the Sales Discounts account until the end of an accounting period. Their total is then deducted from gross sales in determining revenue from sales. This is logical. A sales discount is an "amount off" the regular price of goods that is granted for early payment. As a result, it reduces revenue from sales.

COST OF GOODS SOLD

Automobile dealers and appliance stores make a limited number of sales each day. Consequently, they can easily refer to their records at the time of each sale and record the cost of the car or appliance sold. A drugstore, on the other hand, would find this difficult. For instance, if a drugstore sells a customer a tube of toothpaste, a box of aspirin, and a magazine, it can easily record with a cash register the sale of these items at marked selling prices. However, it would be difficult to maintain records that would enable it to also "look up" and record as "cost of goods sold" the costs of the items sold. As a result, stores such as drug, grocery, and others selling a volume of low-priced items make no effort to record the cost of the goods sold at the time of each sale. Rather, they wait until the end of an accounting period, take a physical inventory, and from the inventory and their accounting records determine at that time the cost of all goods sold during the period.

The end-of-period inventories taken by drug, grocery, or like stores in order to learn the cost of the goods they have sold are called periodic inventories. Also, the system used by such stores in accounting for cost of goods sold is known as a *periodic inventory system.* Such a system is described and discussed in this chapter. The system used by a car or appliance dealer to record the cost of each car or appliance sold depends on a perpetual inventory record of cars or appliances in stock. As a result, it is known as a *perpetual inventory system* of accounting for goods on hand and sold. It is discussed in Chapter 9.

COST OF GOODS SOLD, PERIODIC INVENTORY SYSTEM

As previously said, a store using a periodic inventory system does not record the cost of items sold as they are sold. Rather, it waits until the end of an accounting period and determines at one time the cost of all the goods sold during the period. To do this, it must know (1) the cost of the merchandise it had on hand at the beginning of the period, (2) the cost of the merchandise purchased during the period, and (3) the cost of the unsold goods remaining at the period end. With this information a store can, for example, determine the cost of the goods it sold during a period as follows:

Cost of goods on hand at beginning of period	$ 19,000
Cost of goods purchased during the period	232,000
Goods available for sale during the period	$251,000
Less unsold goods on hand at the period end	21,000
Cost of goods sold during the period	$230,000

The store of the calculation had $19,000 of merchandise at the beginning of the accounting period. During the period, it purchased additional merchandise costing $232,000. Consequently, it had available and could have sold $251,000 of merchandise. However, $21,000 of this merchandise was on hand unsold at the period end. Therefore, the cost of the goods it sold during the period was $230,000.

The information needed in calculating cost of goods sold is accumulated as follows.

Merchandise Inventories

The merchandise on hand at the beginning of an accounting period is called the beginning inventory and the merchandise on hand at the end is the ending inventory. Furthermore, since accounting periods follow one after another, the ending inventory of one period always becomes the beginning inventory of the next.

When a periodic inventory system is in use, the dollar amount of the ending inventory is determined by (1) counting the unsold items on the shelves in the store and in the stockroom, (2) multiplying the count for each kind of goods by its cost, and (3) adding the costs of the different kinds.

After the dollar cost of the ending inventory is determined in this manner, it is subtracted from the cost of the goods available for sale to determine cost of goods sold. Also, by means of a journal entry, the ending inventory amount is posted to an account called *Merchandise Inventory*. It remains there throughout the succeeding accounting period as a record of the inventory at the end of the period ended and the beginning of the succeeding period.

It should be emphasized that, other than to correct errors, entries are made in the Merchandise Inventory account only at the end of each accounting period. Furthermore, since some goods are soon sold and other goods purchased, the account does not long show the dollar amount of merchandise on hand. As soon as goods are sold or purchased, the account's balance becomes a historical record of the dollar amount of goods that were on hand at the end of the last period and the beginning of the current period.

Cost of Merchandise Purchased

Cost of merchandise purchased is determined by subtracting from purchases any discounts, returns, and allowances and then adding any freight or other transportation charges on the goods purchased. However, before examining this calculation it is best to see how the amounts involved are accumulated (the method of recording purchases illustrated in this chapter is referred to as the *gross method of recording purchases*. The ''net method'' is discussed in Chapter 7).

Under a periodic inventory system, when merchandise is bought for resale, its cost is debited to an account called Purchases, as follows:

Nov.	5	Purchases	1,000.00	
		Accounts Payable		1,000.00
		Purchased merchandise on credit, invoice dated November 2, terms 2/10, n/30.		

The Purchases account's sole purpose is the accumulation of the cost of all merchandise bought for resale during an accounting period. The account does not at any time show whether the merchandise is on hand or has been disposed of through sale or other means.

If a credit purchase is subject to a cash discount, payment within the discount period results in a credit to Purchases Discounts, as in the following entry:

Nov.	12	Accounts Payable	1,000.00	
		Purchases Discounts		20.00
		Cash		980.00
		Paid for the purchase of November 5 less the discount.		

When *purchases discounts* are involved, it is important that every invoice that has a discount be paid within the discount period, so that no discounts are lost. On the other hand, good cash management requires that no invoice be paid until the last day of its discount period. Consequently, to accomplish these objectives, every invoice must be filed in such a way that it automatically comes to the attention of the person responsible for its payment on the last day of its discount period. A simple way to do this is to provide a file with 31 folders, one for each day in a month. Then, after an invoice is recorded, it is placed in the file folder of the last day of its discount period. For example, if the last day of an invoice's discount period is November 12, it is filed in folder number 12. Then, on November 12, this invoice, together with any other invoices in the same folder, are removed and paid or refiled for payment without a discount on a later date.

Sometimes merchandise received from suppliers is not acceptable and must be returned, or, if kept, it is kept only because the supplier grants an allowance or reduction in its price. When merchandise is returned, the purchaser "gets its money back"; but from a managerial point of view more is involved. Buying merchandise, receiving and inspecting it, deciding that the merchandise is unsatisfactory, and returning it is a costly procedure that should be held to a minimum. The first step in holding it to a minimum is to know the amount of returns and allowances. To make this information available, returns and allowances on purchases are commonly recorded in an account called Purchases Returns and Allowances, as follows:

Nov.	14	Accounts Payable............................	65.00	
		Purchases Returns and Allowances		65.00
		Return defective merchandise.		

When an invoice is subject to a cash discount and a portion of its goods is returned before the invoice is paid, the discount applies to just the goods kept. For example, if $500 of merchandise is purchased and $100 of the goods are returned before the invoice is paid, any discount applies only to the $400 of goods kept.

Sometimes a manufacturer or wholesaler pays transportation costs on merchandise it sells. The total cost of the goods to the purchaser then is the amount paid the manufacturer or wholesaler. Other times the purchaser must pay transportation costs. When this occurs, such charges are a proper addition to the cost of the goods purchased and may be recorded with a debit to the Purchases account. However, more complete information is obtained if such costs are debited to an account called *Transportation-In,* as follows:

Nov.	24	Transportation-In	22.00	
		Cash		22.00
		Paid express charges on merchandise purchased.		

When transportation charges are involved, it is important that the buyer and seller understand which party is responsible for the charges. Normally, in quoting a price, the seller makes this clear by quoting a price of, say, $300, *FOB* factory. FOB factory means free on board or loaded on the means of transportation at the factory free of loading charges. The buyer then pays transportation costs from there. Likewise, FOB destination means the seller will pay transportation costs to the destination of the goods.

Sometimes, when terms are FOB factory, the seller will prepay the transportation costs as a service to the buyer, adding the amount onto the invoice. In such a case, if a cash discount is involved, the discount does not apply to the transportation charges.

When a classified income statement is prepared, the balances of the Purchases, Purchases Returns and Allowances, Purchases Discounts, and Transportation-In accounts are combined on it as follows to show the cost of the merchandise purchased during the period:

Purchases			$235,800
Less: Purchases returns and allowances ...	$1,200		
Purchases discounts	4,100		5,300
Net purchases			$230,500
Add transportation-in			1,500
Cost of goods purchased			$232,000

Cost of Goods Sold

The last item in the foregoing calculation is the cost of the merchandise purchased during the accounting period. It is combined with the beginning and ending inventories to arrive at cost of goods sold as follows:

Cost of goods sold:			
Merchandise inventory, January 1, 198B			$ 19,000
Purchases		$235,800	
Less: Purchases returns and allowances	$1,200		
Purchases discounts	4,100	5,300	
Net purchases		$230,500	
Add transportation-in		1,500	
Cost of goods purchased			232,000
Goods available for sale			$251,000
Merchandise inventory, December 31, 198B			21,000
Cost of goods sold			$230,000

Inventory Losses

Under a periodic inventory system, the cost of any merchandise lost through shrinkage, spoilage, or shoplifting is automatically included in cost of goods sold. For example, assume a store lost $500 of merchandise to shoplifters during a year. This caused its year-end inventory to be $500 less than it otherwise would have been, since these goods were not available for inclusion in the year-end count. Therefore, since the year-end inventory was $500 smaller because of the loss, the cost of the goods the store sold was $500 greater.

Many stores are troubled with shoplifting. Although under a periodic inventory system such losses are automatically included in cost of goods sold, it is often important to know their extent. Consequently, a way to estimate shoplifting losses is described in Chapter 9.

INCOME STATEMENT OF A MERCHANDISING CONCERN

A classified income statement for a merchandising concern has (1) a revenue section, (2) a cost of goods sold section, and (3) an operating expenses section. The first two sections have been discussed, but note in Illustration 5–1 how they are brought together to show gross profit from sales.

Observe also in Illustration 5–1 how operating expenses are classified as either "Selling expenses" or "General and administrative expenses." *Selling expenses* include expenses of storing and preparing goods for sale, promoting sales, actually making sales, and delivering goods to customers. *General and administrative expenses* include the general office, accounting, personnel, and credit and collection expenses.

Sometimes an expenditure should be divided or prorated part to selling expenses and part to general and administrative expenses. Kona Sales, Incorporated, divided the rent on its store building in this manner, as an examination of Illustration 5–1 will reveal. However, it did not prorate

Illustration 5–1

KONA SALES, INCORPORATED
Income Statement
For Year Ended December 31, 198B

Revenue from sales:			
Gross sales			$306,200
Less: Sales returns and allowances		$ 1,900	
Sales discounts		4,300	6,200
Net sales			$300,000
Cost of goods sold:			
Merchandise inventory, January 1, 198B		$ 19,000	
Purchases	$235,800		
Less: Purchases returns and allowances	$1,200		
Purchases discounts	4,100	5,300	
Net purchases		$230,500	
Add transportation-in		1,500	
Cost of goods purchased		232,000	
Goods available for sale		$251,000	
Merchandise inventory, December 31, 198B		21,000	
Cost of goods sold			230,000
Gross profit from sales			$ 70,000
Operating expenses:			
Selling expenses:			
Sales salaries expense	$ 18,500		
Rent expense, selling space	8,100		
Advertising expense	700		
Store supplies expense	400		
Depreciation expense, store equipment	3,000		
Total selling expenses		$ 30,700	
General and administrative expenses:			
Office salaries expense	$ 25,800		
Rent expense, office space	900		
Insurance expense	600		
Office supplies expense	200		
Depreciation expense, office equipment	700		
Total general and administrative expenses		28,200	
Total operating expenses			58,900
Income from operations			$ 11,100
Less income taxes expense			1,700
Net income			$ 9,400

its insurance expense because the amount involved was so small, the company felt the extra exactness did not warrant the extra work.

The last item subtracted in Illustration 5–1 is income taxes expense. This income statement was prepared for Kona Sales, Incorporated, a corporation. Of the three kinds of business organizations, corporations alone are subject to the payment of income taxes. Often on a corporation income statement, as in Illustration 5–1, the operating expenses are subtracted from gross profit from sales to arrive at income from operations; then income taxes are deducted to arrive at net income.

WORK SHEET OF A MERCHANDISING CONCERN

Like a service-type company, a concern selling merchandise uses a work sheet to bring together the end-of-period information needed to prepare its financial statements, and adjusting and closing entries. Kona Sales, Incorporated's work sheet is shown in Illustration 5–2.

Illustration 5–2 differs from the work sheet in the previous chapter in several ways, the first of which is that it was prepared for a corporation. This is indicated by the word Incorporated in the company name. It is also indicated by the appearance on the work sheet of the Common Stock and Retained Earnings accounts. Note on lines 13 and 14 how the balances of these two accounts are carried unchanged from the Trial Balance credit column into the Balance Sheet credit column.

Illustration 5–2 also differs in that it does not have any Adjusted Trial Balance columns. The experienced accountant commonly omits these columns from a work sheet in order to reduce the time and effort required in its preparation. He or she enters the adjustments in the Adjustments columns, combines the adjustments with the trial balance amounts, and sorts the combined amounts directly to the proper Income Statement or Balance Sheet columns in a single operation. In other words, the experienced accountant simply omits the adjusted trial balance in preparing a work sheet.

The remaining similarities and differences of Illustration 5–2 are best described column by column.

Account Titles Column

Several accounts that do not have trial balance amounts are listed in the Account Titles column. Each account is listed in the order of its appearance on the financial statements. These accounts receive debits and credits in making the adjustments. Entering their names on the work sheet in statement order at the time the work sheet is begun makes later preparation of the statements easier. If required account names are anticipated and listed without balances, as in Illustration 5–2, but later it is discovered that a name not listed is needed, it may be entered below the trial balance totals as was done in Chapter 4.

Trial Balance Columns

The amounts in the Trial Balance columns of Illustration 5–2 are the unadjusted account balances of Kona Sales, Incorporated, as of the end of its annual accounting period. They were taken from the company's ledger after all transactions were recorded but before any end-of-period adjustments were made.

Note the $19,000 inventory amount appearing in the Trial Balance debit column on line 3. This is the amount of inventory the company had on January 1, at the beginning of the accounting period. The $19,000 was debited to the Merchandise Inventory account at the end of the previous period and remained in the account as its balance throughout the current accounting period.

Adjustments Columns

Of the adjustments appearing on the illustrated work sheet, only the adjustment for income taxes is new. A business organized as a corporation is subject to the payment of income taxes. At the beginning of each year a corporation must estimate the amount of income it expects to earn during the year. It must then pay in advance in installments an estimated tax on this income. The advance payments are debited to the Income Taxes Expense account as each installment is paid. Consequently, a corporation that expects to earn a profit normally reaches the end of the year with a debit balance in its Income Taxes Expense account. However, since the balance is an estimate that is usually less than the full amount of the tax, an adjustment like that on lines 12 and 32 normally must be made to reflect the additional tax owed.

COMBINING AND SORTING THE ITEMS.   After all adjustments are entered on a work sheet like that of Illustration 5–2 and totaled, the amounts in the Trial Balance and Adjustments columns are combined and are sorted to the proper Income Statement and Balance Sheet columns. In sorting each item, answers to two questions are required. (1) Is the amount a debit or a credit and (2) on which statements does it appear? As to the first question, debit amounts must be sorted to a debit column and credit amounts must go into a credit column. As to the second question, asset, liability, and shareholders' (owners') equity items go on the balance sheet and are sorted to the Balance Sheet columns. Revenue, cost of goods sold, and expense items go on the income statement and are sorted to the Income Statement columns.

Income Statement Columns

Observe in Illustration 5–2 that revenue, cost of goods sold, and expense items maintain their debit and credit positions when sorted to the Income Statement columns. Note that sales returns and sales discounts in the debit column are in effect subtracted from sales in the credit column when the columns are totaled and the net income is determined.

Look at the beginning inventory amount on line 3. Note that the $19,000 trial balance amount is sorted to the Income Statement debit

Illustration 5–2

KONA SALES, INCORPORATED
Work Sheet for Year Ended December 31, 198B

	Account Titles	Trial Balance Dr.	Trial Balance Cr.	Adjustments Dr.	Adjustments Cr.	Income Statement Dr.	Income Statement Cr.	Balance Sheet Dr.	Balance Sheet Cr.
1	Cash	8,200 00						8,200 00	
2	Accounts receivable	11,200 00						11,200 00	
3	Merchandise inventory	19,000 00				19,000 00	21,000 00	21,000 00	
4	Prepaid insurance	900 00			(a) 600 00			300 00	
5	Store supplies	600 00			(b) 400 00			200 00	
6	Office supplies	300 00			(c) 200 00			100 00	
7	Store equipment	29,100 00						29,100 00	
8	Accumulated depreciation, store equipment		2,500 00		(d) 3,000 00				5,500 00
9	Office equipment	4,400 00						4,400 00	
10	Accumulated depreciation, office equipment		600 00		(e) 700 00				1,300 00
11	Accounts payable		3,600 00						3,600 00
12	Income taxes payable				(f) 100 00				100 00
13	Common stock		50,000 00						50,000 00
14	Retained earnings		4,600 00						4,600 00
15	Sales		306,200 00				306,200 00		
16	Sales returns and allowances	1,900 00				1,900 00			
17	Sales discounts	4,300 00				4,300 00			
18	Purchases	235,800 00				235,800 00			
19	Purchases returns and allowances		1,200 00				1,200 00		
20	Purchases discounts		4,100 00				4,100 00		
21	Transportation-In	1,500 00				1,500 00			
22	Sales salaries expense	18,500 00				18,500 00			

	Trial Balance Dr	Trial Balance Cr	Adjustments Dr	Adjustments Cr	Income Statement Dr	Income Statement Cr	Balance Sheet Dr	Balance Sheet Cr
23 Rent expense, selling space	8,100 00				8,100 00			
24 Advertising expense	700 00				700 00			
25 Store supplies expense			(b) 400 00		400 00			
26 Depreciation expense, store equipment			(d) 3,000 00		3,000 00			
27 Office salaries expense	25,800 00				25,800 00			
28 Rent expense, office space	900 00				900 00			
29 Insurance expense			(a) 600 00		600 00			
30 Office supplies expense			(c) 200 00		200 00			
31 Depreciation expense, office equipment			(e) 700 00		700 00			
32 Income taxes expense	1,600 00		(f) 100 00		1,700 00			
33	372,800 00	372,800 00	5,000 00	5,000 00	323,100 00	332,500 00	74,500 00	65,100 00
34 Net income					9,400 00			9,400 00
35					332,500 00	332,500 00	74,500 00	74,500 00
36								
37								
38								
39								
40								
41								
42								
43								
44								
45								
46								
47								

column. It is put in the Income Statement debt column because it is a debit amount and because it enters into the calculation of cost of goods sold and net income.

ENTERING THE ENDING INVENTORY ON THE WORK SHEET. Before beginning its work sheet, the company of Illustration 5–2 determined that it had a $21,000 ending inventory. The inventory amount was determined by counting the items of unsold merchandise and multiplying the count of each kind by its cost.

In preparing a work sheet like Illustration 5–2, after all items are sorted to the proper columns, the ending inventory amount is simply inserted or "plugged" into the Income Statement credit column and the Balance Sheet debit column. Observe the $21,000 ending inventory amounts that are "plugged" into these columns on line 3 of the work sheet.

In accounting, when an amount is "plugged" into a column of figures, it is simply put in the column to accomplish an objective. In this case, the ending inventory amount is "plugged" into the Income Statement credit column so that the difference between the two Income Statement columns will equal the net income. It is put in the Balance Sheet debit column because it is the amount of an end-of-period asset that must be added to the other asset amounts in completing the work sheet. (How the ending inventory amount gets into the accounts is explained later.)

COST OF GOODS SOLD ON THE WORK SHEET

The item amounts that enter into the calculation of cost of goods sold are shown in color in the Income Statement columns of Illustration 5–2. The beginning inventory, purchases, and transportation-in amounts appear in the debit column. The amounts of the ending inventory, purchases returns and allowances, and purchases discounts appear in the credit column. Note in the following calculations that the sum of the three debit items minus the sum of the three credit items equals the $230,000 cost of goods sold shown in the income statement of Illustration 5–1.

Beginning inventory	$ 19,000		Ending inventory	$21,000
Purchases	235,800		Purchases returns	1,200
Transportation-in	1,500		Purchases discounts	4,100
Total debits	$256,300		Total credits	$26,300
Less total credits	(26,300)			
Cost of goods sold	$230,000			

Therefore, the net effect of putting the six cost of goods sold amounts in the Income Statement columns is to put the $230,000 cost of the goods sold into the columns.

COMPLETING THE WORK SHEET

After all items are sorted to the proper columns and the ending inventory amount is "plugged" in, a work sheet like Illustration 5–2 is completed by adding the columns and determining and adding in the net income or loss, as was explained in the previous chapter.

PREPARING THE STATEMENTS

After the work sheet is completed, the items in its Income Statement columns are arranged into a formal income statement. The items in its Balance Sheet columns are then arranged into a formal balance sheet. A classified income statement prepared from information in the Income Statement columns of Illustration 5–2 is shown in Illustration 5–1. The balance sheet appears in Illustration 5–3. Observe that since none of

Illustration 5–3

KONA SALES, INCORPORATED
Balance Sheet
December 31, 198B

Assets

Current assets:		
Cash	$ 8,200	
Accounts receivable	11,200	
Merchandise inventory	21,000	
Prepaid expenses	600	
Total current assets		$41,000
Plant and equipment:		
Store equipment	$29,100	
Less accumulated depreciation	5,500	$23,600
Office equipment	$ 4,400	
Less accumulated depreciation	1,300	3,100
Total plant and equipment		26,700
Total assets		$67,700

Liabilities

Current liabilities:		
Accounts payable	$ 3,600	
Income taxes payable	100	
Total current liabilities		$ 3,700

Shareholders' Equity

Common stock, 10,000 shares outstanding	$50,000	
Retained earnings	14,000	
Total shareholders' equity		64,000
Total liabilities and shareholders' equity		$67,700

the company's prepaid items are material in amount, they are totaled and shown as a single item on the balance sheet. The $14,000 retained earnings amount on the balance sheet is the sum of the $4,600 of retained earnings appearing on line 14 of the work sheet plus the company's $9,400 net income.

RETAINED EARNINGS STATEMENT

In addition to an income statement and a balance sheet, a third financial statement called a *retained earnings statement* is commonly prepared for a corporation. It reports the changes that have occurred in the corporation's retained earnings during the period and accounts for the difference between the retained earnings reported on balance sheets of successive accounting periods.

The retained earnings statement of Kona Sales, Incorporated, appears in Illustration 5–4. It shows that the company began the year with $8,600 of retained earnings, which is also the amount of retained earnings it reported on its previous year-end balance sheet. Its retained earnings were reduced by the declaration of $4,000 of dividends and increased by the $9,400 net income to the $14,000 reported on its current year-end balance sheet. Information as to the beginning retained earnings and the dividends declared were taken from the company's Retained Earnings account.

RETAINED EARNINGS ACCOUNT

Illustration 5–5 shows the Retained Earnings account of Kona Sales, Incorporated. Compare the information in the account with the company's retained earnings statement. The account shows that the company began 198B with $8,600 of retained earnings. It declared and paid a $4,000

Illustration 5–4

KONA SALES, INCORPORATED
Retained Earnings Statement
For Year Ended December 31, 198B

Retained earnings, January 1, 198B	$ 8,600
Add 198B net income	9,400
Total	$18,000
Deduct dividends declared	4,000
Retained earnings, December 31, 198B ...	$14,000

Illustration 5–5

Retained Earnings				Account No. 312	
Date	Explanation	Post. Ref.	Debit	Credit	Balance
198A Dec. 31	198A net income	G10		8,600	8,600
198B Oct. 15	Dividend declared	G20	4,000		4,600
Dec. 31	198B net income	G23		9,400	14,000

dividend in October, and it earned a $9,400 net income. The items are identified in the Explanation column of the account, but they need not be. The $9,400 net income reached the account when the closing entries, which are discussed in the next section, were posted.

ADJUSTING AND CLOSING ENTRIES

After the work sheet and statements are completed, adjusting and closing entries must be prepared and posted. The entries for Kona Sales, Incorporated, are shown in Illustration 5–6. They differ from previously illustrated adjusting and closing entries in that an explanation for each entry is not given. Individual explanations may be given, but are unnecessary. The words **Adjusting entries** before the first adjusting entry and **Closing entries** before the first closing entry are sufficient to explain the entries.

As previously explained, the Adjustments columns of its work sheet provide the information needed in preparing a concern's adjusting entries. Each adjustment in the Adjustments columns requires an adjusting entry that is journalized and posted. Compare the adjusting entries in Illustration 5–6 with the adjustments on the work sheet of Illustration 5–2.

When a work sheet like Illustration 5–2 is prepared, its Income Statement columns are a source of the information needed in preparing closing entries. Look at the first closing entry of Illustration 5–6 and the items in the Income Statement debit column of Illustration 5–2. Note that Income Summary is debited for the column total and each account having an amount in the column is credited. This entry removes the $19,000 beginning inventory amount from the Merchandise Inventory account. It also clears and closes all the revenue, cost of goods sold, and expense accounts that have debit balances.

Compare the second closing entry with the items in the Income State-

Illustration 5–6

Date		Account Titles and Explanation	PR	Debit		Credit	
198B		Adjusting Entries:					
Dec.	31	Insurance Expense	653	600	00		
		Prepaid Insurance	115			600	00
	31	Store Supplies Expense	614	400	00		
		Store Supplies	116			400	00
	31	Office Supplies Expense	651	200	00		
		Office Supplies	117			200	00
	31	Depreciation Expense, Store Equipment	615	3,000	00		
		Accumulated Depr., Store Equip.	132			3,000	00
	31	Depreciation Expense, Office Equipment	655	700	00		
		Accumulated Depr., Office Equip.	134			700	00
	31	Income Taxes Expense	711	100	00		
		Income Taxes Payable	213			100	00
		Closing Entries:					
	31	Income Summary	313	323,100	00		
		Merchandise Inventory	113			19,000	00
		Sales Returns and Allowances	412			1,900	00
		Sales Discounts	413			4,300	00
		Purchases	511			235,800	00
		Transportation-In	514			1,500	00
		Sales Salaries Expense	611			18,500	00
		Rent Expense, Selling Space	612			8,100	00
		Advertising Expense	613			700	00
		Store Supplies Expense	614			400	00
		Depr. Expense, Store Equip.	615			3,000	00
		Office Salaries Expense	651			25,800	00
		Rent Expense, Office Space	652			900	00
		Insurance Expense	653			600	00
		Office Supplies Expense	654			200	00
		Depr. Expense, Office Equip.	655			700	00
		Income Taxes Expense	711			1,700	00
	31	Merchandise Inventory	113	21,000	00		
		Sales	411	306,200	00		
		Purchases Returns and Allowances	512	1,200	00		
		Purchase Discounts	513	4,100	00		
		Income Summary	313			332,500	00
	31	Income Summary	313	9,400	00		
		Retained Earnings	312			9,400	00

ment credit column of Illustration 5–2. Note that each account having an amount in the column is debited and the Income Summary account is credited for the column total. This entry clears and closes the revenue and cost of goods sold accounts having credit balances. It also enters the $21,000 ending inventory amount in the Merchandise Inventory account.

CLOSING ENTRIES AND THE INVENTORIES

There is nothing essentially new about the closing entries of a merchandising company. However, their effect on the Merchandise Inventory account should be understood.

Before its closing entries are posted, the Merchandise Inventory account of Kona Sales, Incorporated, shows in its $19,000 debit balance the amount of the company's beginning-of-period inventory as follows:

Merchandise Inventory					Account No. 113
Date	Explanation	Post. Ref.	Debit	Credit	Balance
198A Dec. 31		G10	19,000		19,000

Then when the first closing entry is posted, its $19,000 credit to Merchandise Inventory clears the beginning inventory amount from the inventory account as follows:

Merchandise Inventory					Account No. 113
Date	Explanation	Post. Ref.	Debit	Credit	Balance
198A Dec. 31		G10	19,000		19,000
198B Dec. 31		G23		19,000	–0–

When the second closing entry is posted, its $21,000 debit to Merchandise Inventory puts the amount of the ending inventory into the inventory account, as follows:

Merchandise Inventory					Account No. 113	
Date	Explanation	Post. Ref.	Debit	Credit	Balance	
198A Dec. 31		G10	19,000		19,000	
198B Dec. 31		G23		19,000	–0–	
31		G23	21,000		21,000	

The $21,000 remains throughout the succeeding year as the debit balance of the inventory account and as a historical record of the amount of inventory at the end of 198B and the beginning of 198C.

OTHER INVENTORY METHODS

There are several ways to handle the inventories in the end-of-period procedures. However, all have the same objectives. They are (1) to remove the beginning inventory amount from the inventory account and to charge (debit) it to Income Summary and (2) to enter the ending inventory amount in the inventory account and credit it to Income Summary. These objectives may be achieved with closing entries as explained in this chapter. Or, for example, adjusting entries to accomplish the same objectives may be used. Either method is satisfactory. However, most accountants prefer to use closing entries because less work is required than when adjusting entries are used.

INCOME STATEMENT FORMS

The income statement in Illustration 5–1 is called a classified income statement because its items are classified into significant groups. It is also a *multiple-step income statement* because cost of goods sold and the expenses are subtracted in steps to arrive at net income. Another income statement form, the *single-step form,* is shown in Illustration 5–7. This form is commonly used for published statements. Also, although it need not be, its information is commonly condensed as shown. Note how cost of goods sold and the expenses are added together in the illustration and are subtracted in "one step" from net sales to arrive at net income, thus the name of the form.

Illustration 5–7

KONA SALES, INCORPORATED
Income Statement
For Year Ended December 31, 198B

Revenue from sales		$300,000
Expenses:		
Cost of goods sold	$230,000	
Selling expenses	30,700	
General and administrative expenses . . .	28,200	
Income taxes expense	1,700	
Total expenses		290,600
Net income		$ 9,400

COMBINED INCOME AND RETAINED EARNINGS STATEMENT

Many companies combine their income and retained earnings statements into a single statement. Such a statement may be prepared in either single-step or multiple-step form. A single-step statement is shown in Illustration 5–8.

Illustration 5–8

KONA SALES, INCORPORATED
Statement of Income and Retained Earnings
For Year Ended December 31, 198B

Revenue from sales		$300,000
Expenses:		
Cost of goods sold	$230,000	
Selling expenses	30,700	
General and administrative expenses	28,200	
Income taxes expense	1,700	
Total expenses		290,600
Net income		$ 9,400
Add retained earnings, January 1, 198B . . .		8,600
Total		$ 18,000
Deduct dividends declared		4,000
Retained earnings, December 31, 198B		$ 14,000

STATEMENT OF CHANGES IN FINANCIAL POSITION

In addition to the retained earnings statement, another very important financial statement commonly prepared for a corporation is the *statement of changes in financial position.* It shows where the concern secured cash and where it applied or used the cash, such as in the purchase of plant assets or the payment of dividends. A discussion of this statement is deferred until Chapter 18, after further discussion of corporation accounting.

DEBIT AND CREDIT MEMORANDA

Merchandise purchased that does not meet specifications, goods received that were not ordered, goods received short of the amount ordered and billed, and invoice errors are matters for adjustment between the buyer and seller. In some cases, the buyer can make the adjustment, for example, when there is an invoice error. If the buyer makes the adjustment, it must notify the seller of its action. It commonly does this by sending a *debit memorandum* or a *credit memorandum.*

A debit memorandum is a business form on which are spaces for the name and address of the concern to which it is directed and the printed words, "WE DEBIT YOUR ACCOUNT," followed by space for typing in the reason for the debit. A credit memorandum carries the words, "WE CREDIT YOUR ACCOUNT." To illustrate the use of a debit memorandum, assume a buyer discovers an invoice error that reduces the invoice total by $10. For such an error, the buyer notifies the seller with a debit memorandum reading: "WE DEBIT YOUR ACCOUNT to correct a $10 error on your November 17 invoice." A debit memorandum is sent because the correction reduces an account payable of the buyer, and to reduce an account payable requires a debit. In recording the purchase, the buyer normally marks the correction on the invoice and attaches a copy of the debit memorandum to show that the seller was notified. The buyer then debits Purchases and credits Accounts Payable for the corrected amount.

An adjustment, such as merchandise that does not meet specifications, normally requires negotiations between the buyer and the seller. In such a case, the buyer may debit Purchases for the full invoice amount and enter into negotiations with the seller for a return or a price adjustment. If the seller agrees to the return or adjustment, the seller notifies the buyer with a credit memorandum. A credit memorandum is used because the return or adjustment reduces an account receivable on the books of the seller, and to reduce an account receivable requires a credit. Upon receipt of the credit memorandum, the buyer records it by debiting Accounts Payable and crediting Purchases Returns and Allowances, if the purchase was originally recorded at the full invoice price.

From this discussion it can be seen that a debit or a credit memorandum may originate with either party to a transaction. The memorandum gets its name from the action of the originator. If the originator debits, the originator sends a debit memorandum. If the originator credits, a credit memorandum is sent.

TRADE DISCOUNTS

A *trade discount* is a deduction (often as much as 40% or more) from a *list price* (or catalogue price) that is used in determining the actual price of the goods to which it applies. Trade discounts are commonly used by manufacturers and wholesalers to avoid republication of catalogues when selling prices change. If selling prices change, catalogue prices can be adjusted by merely issuing a new list of discounts to be applied to the catalogue prices. Such discounts are discussed here primarily to distinguish them from the cash discounts described earlier in this chapter.

Trade discounts are not entered in the accounts by either party to a sale. For example, if a manufacturer sells on credit an item listed in its catalogue at $100, less a 40% trade discount, it will record the sale as follows:

Dec.	10	Accounts Receivable	60.00	
		Sales		60.00
		Sold merchandise on credit.		

The buyer will also enter the purchase in its records at $60. Also, if a cash discount is involved, it applies only to the amount of the purchase, $60.

SUPPLEMENT 5–A

REVIEW OF ACCOUNTING CONCEPTS AND PRINCIPLES

Accounting is practiced within a conceptual framework. To implement that framework, the accounting profession has identified and defined certain guidelines. These guidelines involve *(a)* concepts, *(b)* principles, and *(c)* implementation constraints.

In Chapter 1, the four broad concepts were introduced; they significantly affect the recording, measuring, and accounting information. In Chapter 1 and subsequent chapters, accounting principles were introduced to facilitate and form the basis for recording financial transactions. Not all of the principles have been introduced through Chapter 5. Thus, some of the principles discussed below will be applied to situations arising in subsequent chapters. This supplement concludes with a discussion of implementation constraints.

ACCOUNTING CONCEPTS

An understanding of accounting principles begins with the recognition of four broad concepts as to the nature of the economic setting in which accounting operates.

The Business Entity Concept

Every business unit or enterprise is treated in accounting as a separate entity, with the affairs of the business and those of the owner or owners being kept entirely separate.

The Going-Concern Concept

Unless there is strong evidence to the contrary, it is assumed that a business will continue to operate as a going concern, earning a reasonable profit for a period longer than the life expectancy of any of its assets.

The Stable-Dollar Concept

Under this concept it is held that the function of accounting is not to account for value; rather it is (1) to record ''dollars invested'' and ''dollars borrowed,'' (2) to trace the various commitments of these ''dollars of capital'' as they are invested and reinvested in the business activities, and finally (3) to measure out of gross ''dollars of revenue'' the recapture of ''dollars of capital'' with any excess being designated as ''dollars of income.''

It is conceded that value can only subjectively be measured. It is also recognized that the ''value'' (purchasing power) of the accountant's unit of measure, the dollar, is itself constantly changing. Therefore, it is recognized that a balance sheet prepared under this concept simply shows the number of dollars received from all sources and shows where these dollars are committed. A reader cannot interpret the dollar amounts of the various assets as the values of these assets.

The Time-Period Concept

The environment in which accounting operates—the business community and the government—requires that the life of a business be divided into relatively short periods and that changes be measured over these short periods. Yet, it is generally agreed that earnings cannot be measured precisely over a short period and that it is impossible to learn the exact earnings of a business until it has completed its last transaction and converted all its assets to cash.

ACCOUNTING PRINCIPLES

Cost Principle

The cost principle specifies that cash-equivalent cost is the most useful basis for the initial accounting of the elements that are recorded in the accounts and reported on the financial statements. It is important to note that the cost principle applies to the initial recording of transactions and events.

The cost principle is supported by the fact that at the time of a completed arm's-length business transaction, the market value of the resources given up in the transaction provides reliable evidence of the valuation of the item acquired in the transaction.

When a noncash consideration is involved, cost is measured as the market value of the resources given, or the market value of the item received, whichever is more reliably determinable. For example, an asset may be acquired with a debt given as settlement. Cost in this instance is the present value of the amount of cash to be paid in the future, as specified by the terms of the debt. The cost principle applies to all of the elements of financial statements, including liabilities.

The cost principle provides guidance at the original recognition date. However, the original cost of some items acquired is subject to depreciation, depletion, amortization, and write-down in conformity with the matching principle and the conservatism constraint (discussed in the sections that follow).

Realization or Revenue Principle

The realization or revenue principle specifies when revenue should be recognized in the accounts and reported in the financial statements. Revenue is measured as the market value of the resources received or the product or service given, whichever is the more reliably determinable. The realization or revenue principle requires that all discounts be viewed as adjustments of the amount of revenue earned. For example, in determining the net cash exchange value of sales subject to a discount, sales discounts should be subtracted from gross sales revenue in measuring the net amount of sales revenue.

Under the realization or revenue principle, revenue from the sale of goods is recognized according to the sales method (i.e., at the time of sale) because the earning process usually is complete at the time of sale. At that time, the relevant information about the asset inflows to the seller would be known with reliability.

The conditions for completion of the earning process are *(a)* collection from the buyer is reasonably assured and *(b)* the expenses of making the sale can be determined reliably. Condition *(a)*—reasonable assurance of collection—provides the basis for the conclusion that the transaction provided a "probable future economic benefit" (i.e., an asset) to the seller. Without this condition, the principle of revenue realization would be altogether lacking in substantive economic content. Condition *(b)*—reliable determination of related expenses—provides the basis for measurement of the net economic benefit of the transaction. Without this condition, measurement of the effect of the revenue would ignore the related expenses. It would therefore be partial at best. Condition *(b)* is closely related to the matching principle, which is discussed below.

Under the realization or revenue principle, revenue from the sale of services is recognized on the basis of performance because performance determines the extent to which the earning process is complete.

The realization or revenue principle requires accrual basis accounting rather than cash basis accounting for revenues. For example, completed transactions for the sale of goods or services on credit usually are recognized as revenue in the period in which the sale or service occurred rather than in the period in which the cash is eventually collected.

Other types of revenue transactions posing problems of revenue recognition are installment sales, long-term construction contracts, sales of land with minimal down payments, and sales of franchises that require a certain level of performance on the part of the purchaser. In these and many other cases, both determination of when the earning process is complete and measurement of the amount of revenue are difficult tasks, and consideration of them is beyond the scope of this textbook.

Matching Principle

A major objective of accounting is the determination of periodic net income by matching appropriate costs against revenues. The principle recognizes that streams of revenues continually flow into a business, and it requires: (1) that there be a precise "cutoff" in these streams at the end of an accounting period, (2) that the inflows of the period be measured, (3) that the costs incurred in securing the inflows be determined, and (4) that the sum of the costs be deducted from the sum of the inflows to determine the period's net income.

The pattern of expense recognition varies. Some expenses reflect a direct cause-and-effect relationship with revenues. That is, the revenue and expense occur simultaneously. Examples are cost of goods sold, sales commission expense, and delivery expense. Other expenses are recognized on a time basis because their asset counterparts expire over time rather than reflecting direct cause-and-effect relationships with revenues. Examples are depreciation expense of the home office, interest expense, and property tax expense. For other expenses, there is no direct relationship with either revenue or time. Therefore, these expenses must be allocated to reporting periods on some subjective basis. Examples are expenditures for advertising, research and development, and charitable contributions. A common system of allocation is to recognize such costs as expense in full in the period in which they are incurred.

The Objectivity Principle

The objectivity principle holds that changes in account balances should be supported to the fullest extent possible by objective evidence.

Bargained transactions supported by verifiable business documents originating outside the business are the best objective evidence obtainable; and whenever possible, accounting data should be supported by such documents.

Full-Disclosure Principle

The full-disclosure principle requires that the financial statements of a business clearly report all of the relevant information about the economic affairs of the enterprise. This principle rests upon the primary characteristic of relevance. Full disclosure requires *(a)* reporting of all information that can make a difference in a decision and *(b)* that the accounting information reported must be understandable (i.e., not susceptible to misleading inferences). Full disclosure also requires that the major accounting policies and any special accounting policies used by the company be explained in the notes to the financial statements.

The Consistency Principle

In many cases two or more methods or procedures have been derived in accounting practice to accomplish a particular accounting objective. While recognizing the validity of different methods under varying circumstances, it is still necessary in order to insure a high degree of comparability in any concern's accounting data to insist on a consistent application in the company of any given accounting method, period after period. It is also necessary to insist that any departures from this doctrine of consistency be fully disclosed in the financial statements and the effects thereof on the statements be fully described.

The Principle of Conservatism

The principle of conservatism holds that the accountant should be conservative in his/her estimates and opinions and in the selection of procedures, choosing those that neither unduly understate nor overstate the situation.

Balance sheet conservatism was once considered the ''first'' principle of accounting, the objective being to place every item on the balance sheet at a conservative figure. This in itself was commendable; but it commonly resulted in overconservatism, which in turn resulted in (1) an understatement of asset and equity amounts, (2) an overstatement of costs in the year the assets were first understated, and (3) an understatement of costs on each income statement thereafter throughout the lives of the understated assets. Today, accountants recognize that balance sheet conservatism is not desirable when it misrepresents true situations; and they recognize that full, fair, and free from bias disclosure is a more important accounting objective.

The Principle of Materiality

A strict adherence to accounting principles is not required for items of little significance. Consequently, the accountant must always weigh the costs of complying with an accounting principle against the extra accuracy gained thereby; and in those situations where the cost is relatively great and the lack of compliance will have no material effect on the financial statements, compliance is not necessary.

There is no clear-cut distinction between material and immaterial items. Each situation must be individually judged, and an item is material or immaterial as it relates to other items. As a guide, the amount of an item is material if its omission, in the light of the surrounding circumstances, makes it probable that the judgment of a reasonable person would have been changed or influenced.

Implementation Constraints

Two of the principles listed, materiality and conservatism, are different from the other principles. In fact, some regard these as constraints which exert a modifying influence on financial accounting and reporting. The two other constraints are cost-benefit and industry peculiarities.

The cost of preparing and reporting accounting information should not exceed the value or usefulness of such information. Accounting focuses on usefulness and substance over form. Thus, peculiarities and practices of an industry may warrant selective exceptions to accounting principles and practices. These exceptions are permitted for specific items where there is a clear precedent in the industry based on uniqueness and usefulness.

Departure from the strict application of accounting principles and concepts must be fully disclosed whether it be on the basis of *(a)* materiality, *(b)* conservatism, *(c)* cost-benefit, or *(d)* industry peculiarity.

This review and summary of accounting concepts and principles and the constraints in their application provides an opportunity for reflection on the five chapters already covered and a frame of reference for study of subsequent chapters.

GLOSSARY

Cash discount. A deduction from the invoice price of goods allowed if payment is made within a specified period of time.

Credit memorandum. A memorandum sent to notify its recipient that the business sending the memorandum has in its records credited the account of the recipient.

Credit period. The agreed period of time for which credit is granted and at the end of which payment is expected.

Credit terms. The agreed terms upon which credit is granted in the sale of goods or services.

Debit memorandum. A memorandum sent to notify its recipient that the business sending the memorandum has in its records debited the account of the recipient.

Discount period. The period of time in which a cash discount may be taken.

EOM. An abbreviation meaning "end-of-month."

FOB. The abbreviation for "free on board," which is used to denote that goods purchased are placed on board the means of transportation at a specified geographic point free of any loading and transportation charges to that point.

General and administrative expenses. The general office, accounting, personnel, and credit and collection expenses.

Gross method of recording purchases. A method of recording purchases by which offered cash discounts are not deducted from the invoice price in determining the amount to be recorded.

Gross profit from sales. Net sales minus cost of goods sold.

List price. The catalogue or other listed price from which a trade discount is deducted in arriving at the invoice price for goods.

Merchandise inventory. The unsold merchandise on hand at a given time.

Multiple-step income statement. An income statement on which cost of goods sold and the expenses are subtracted in steps to arrive at net income.

Periodic inventory system. An inventory system in which periodically, at the end of each accounting period, the cost of the unsold goods on hand is determined by counting units of each product on hand, multiplying the count for each product by its cost, and adding costs of the various products.

Perpetual inventory system. An inventory system in which an individual record is kept for each product of the units on hand at the beginning, the units purchased, the units sold, and the new balance after each purchase or sale.

Purchases discounts. Discounts taken on merchandise purchased for resale.

Retained earnings statement. A statement which reports changes in a corporation's retained earnings that occurred during an accounting period.

Sales discounts. Discounts given on sales of merchandise.

Selling expenses. The expenses of preparing and storing goods for sale, promoting sales, making sales, and if a separate delivery department is not maintained, the expenses of delivering goods to customers.

Single-step income statement. An income statement on which cost of goods sold and the expenses are added together and subtracted in one step from revenue to arrive at net income.

Statement of changes in financial position. A statement that reports the effects on cash, or cash and cash equivalents, resulting from operations, financing, and investing activities.

Trade discount. The discount that may be deducted from a catalogue list price to determine the invoice price of goods.

Transportation-in. Freight, express, or other transportation costs on merchandise purchased for resale.

QUESTIONS FOR CLASS DISCUSSION

1. What is gross profit from sales?

2. May a concern earn a gross profit on its sales and still suffer a loss? How?

3. Why should a concern be interested in the amount of its sales returns and allowances?

4. Since sales returns and allowances are subtracted from sales on the income statement, why not save the effort of this subtraction by debiting all such returns and allowances directly to the Sales account?

5. What is a cash discount? If terms are 2/10, n/60, what is the length of the credit period? What is the length of the discount period?

6. How and when is cost of goods sold determined in a store using a periodic inventory system?

7. Which of the following are debited to the Purchases account of a grocery store: (a) the purchase of a cash register, (b) the purchase of a refrigerated display case, (c) the purchase of advertising space in a newspaper, and (d) the purchase of a case of tomato soup?

8. If a concern may return for full credit all unsatisfactory merchandise purchased, why should it be interested in controlling the amount of its returns?

9. When applied to transportation terms, what do the letters FOB mean? What does FOB destination mean?

10. At the end of an accounting period, which inventory, the beginning inventory or the ending, appears on the trial balance?

11. What is shown on a retained earnings statement? What is the purpose of the statement?

12. How does a single-step income statement differ from a multiple-step income statement?

13. During the year, a company purchased merchandise costing $220,000. What was the company's cost of goods sold if there were *(a)* no beginning or ending inventories? *(b)* a beginning inventory of $28,000 and no ending inventory? *(c)* a $25,000 beginning inventory and a $30,000 ending inventory? and *(d)* no beginning inventory and a $15,000 ending inventory?

14. In counting the merchandise on hand at the end of an accounting period, a clerk failed to count, and consequently omitted from the inventory, all the merchandise on one shelf. If the cost of the merchandise on the shelf was $100, what was the effect of the omission on *(a)* the balance sheet and *(b)* the income statement?

15. Suppose that the omission of the $100 from the inventory (Question 14) was not discovered. What would be the effect on the balance sheet and income statement prepared at the end of the next accounting period?

16. Distinguish between cash discounts and trade discounts. Is the amount of a trade discount on merchandise purchased credited to the Purchases Discounts account?

17. When a debit memorandum is issued, who debits, the originator of the memorandum or the company receiving it?

MULTIPLE CHOICE

1. The beginning inventory adjustment on the work sheet requires:
   a. A debit to merchandise inventory and a credit to income summary.
   b. A debit to merchandise inventory and a credit to ending inventory.
   c. A credit to merchandise inventory and a debit to income summary.
   d. A credit to merchandise inventory and a debit to ending inventory.
   e. A credit to merchandise inventory and a debit to retained earnings.

2. The Omega Company's beginning inventory for 198A was $16,000. During 198A Omega made purchases of $12,360 and returned $200 of merchandise. Their purchase discounts totaled $1,800. If Omega's ending inventory was $15,000 for 198A, what was cost of goods sold?
   a. $9,360.
   b. $10,360.
   c. $11,360.
   d. $13,160.
   e. $13,360.

3. If a concern's income statement showed cost of goods sold at $78,000, purchases of $80,000, freight-in at $300, purchases returns of $500, and end-of-the-period inventory at $11,900, its beginning-of-the-period inventory must have been:
   a. $10,400.
   b. $10,100.
   c. $9,900.
   d. $9,200.
   e. None of these amounts.

4. An inventory system in which periodically, at the end of each accounting period, the cost of the unsold goods on hand is determined by counting units of each product on hand, multiplying the count for each product by its cost, and adding costs of the various products, is called a:
   a. Professional inventory system.
   b. Perpetual inventory system.
   c. Periodic inventory system.
   d. Planned inventory system.
   e. Posting inventory system.

5. Using the periodic inventory method, the merchandise inventory amount appearing in the preadjusted trial balance columns of a year-end work sheet is the amount of:
   a. Merchandise purchased during the year.
   b. Merchandise available for sale during the year.
   c. Merchandise sold during the year.
   d. Merchandise on hand at the year-end.
   e. Merchandise available at the beginning of the year.

6. The merchandise inventory amount appearing in the Balance Sheet debit column of a completed year-end work sheet is the amount of:
   a. Merchandise purchased during the year.
   b. Merchandise available for sale during the year.
   c. Merchandise sold during the year.
   d. Merchandise on hand at the year-end.
   e. Merchandise at the beginning of the year.

7. With a periodic inventory system, an undiscovered error that overstates the 1987 year-end inventory will cause:
   a. An overstatement of 1987 net income and an understatement of 1988 net income.
   b. An understatement of assets on the 1987 balance sheet.
   c. An overstatement of 1987 cost of goods sold.
   d. An overstatement of 1987 net income and no effect on 1988 net income.
   e. None of the foregoing.

8. If a bookkeeper recorded a cash sale with a debit to cash and a credit to purchases, the error would:
   a. Have no effect on reported net income. –
   b. Cause an overstatement of net income.
   c. Cause an overstatement of cost of goods sold.
   d. Cause an understatement of gross profit.
   e. Cause an overstatement of net sales.

MINI DISCUSSION CASES

Case 5–1   The Case of Unrecorded Invoices

Part 1.   One month after purchasing a profitable wholesale plumbing distribution company, Mr. Gerald Innocente realized he had a nightmare on his hands. The head accountant resigned after only two weeks with the new owner, and Gerald was getting calls from suppliers with regard to overdue accounts. He could not understand why because he had instructed the staff to pay all accounts as they became due.

Part 2.   Gerald's wife, Jennifer, offered to help. She had been the accountant for a family owned firm, which had been sold about 15 years previously. With the aid of the assistant accountant, Jennifer found a folder of unpaid and unrecorded invoices all dated prior to the purchase date. Further investigation and discussion with the former head accountant's secretary revealed that Jennifer's discovery was nothing new. The secretary told the Innocentes that her former boss told her that he delayed the recording of invoices in order to make the statements look good. He told her that no one was hurt, the goods went into inventory as they arrived, the invoices were eventually recorded, and the suppliers paid. She also informed them that the amount of $90,000 of the current unrecorded invoices was about $40,000 more than at the last year-end.

Required:

If Mr. Innocente could turn the clock back one month, what do you believe he would have done with regard to accounts payable prior to finalizing the purchase of the business?

Case 5–2   Consider Part 2 of Case 5–1.

Required:

Discuss which statements were affected and how they were affected.

CLASS EXERCISES

Exercise 5–1

A store purchased merchandise having a $5,000 invoice price, terms 2/10, n/60, from a manufacturer and paid for the merchandise within the discount period. *(a)* Give without dates the journal entries made by the store to record the purchase and payment. *(b)* Give without dates the entries made by the manufacturer to record the sale and collection. *(c)* If the store borrowed sufficient money at a 12% annual rate of interest on the last day of the discount period to pay the invoice, how much did the store save by borrowing to take advantage of the discount?

Exercise 5–2

The following items, with the expenses condensed to conserve space, appeared in the Income Statement columns of a work sheet prepared for The Shop, a single proprietorship business, as of December 31, 198B, the end of its annual accounting period. From the information, prepare a 198B multiple-step income statement for The Shop.

	Income statement	
	Debit	Credit
Merchandise inventory	36,000	40,000
Sales		200,000
Sales returns and allowances	1,000	
Sales discounts	1,500	
Purchases	120,000	
Purchases returns and allowances		600
Purchases discounts		2,400
Transportation-in	500	
Selling expenses	30,000	
General and administrative expenses ...	20,000	
	209,000	243,000
Net income	34,000	
	243,000	243,000

Exercise 5–3

Part 1. Assume that The Shop of Exercise 5–2 is owned by June Ellis and prepare entries to close the shop's revenue, expense, and Income Summary accounts.

Part 2. Rule a balance column Merchandise Inventory account on note paper; and under a December 31, 198A, date, enter the $36,000 beginning inventory of Exercise 5–2 as its balance. Then post to the account the portions of the shop's closing entries that affect the account. Post first the credit that removes the beginning inventory from the account.

Exercise 5–4

The following items, with expenses condensed to conserve space, appeared in the Income Statement columns of a work sheet prepared for Little Store, Incorporated, as of December 31, 198B, the end of its annual accounting period. From the information, prepare a 198B multiple-step income statement for the corporation.

	Income statement	
	Debit	Credit
Merchandise inventory	40,000	50,000
Sales		300,000
Sales returns and allowances	1,500	
Sales discounts	3,000	
Purchases	180,000	
Purchases returns and allowances		1,000
Purchases discounts		2,500
Transportation-in	500	
Selling expenses	45,000	
General and administrative expenses . . .	35,500	
Income taxes expense	8,000	
	313,500	353,500
Net income	40,000	
	353,500	353,500

Exercise 5–5

Part 1. Prepare entries to close the revenue, expense, and Income Summary accounts of Little Store, Incorporated (Exercise 5–4).

Part 2. Rule a balance column Merchandise Inventory account on note paper, and under a December 31, 198A, date, enter the $40,000 beginning inventory of Exercise 5–4 as its balance. Then post to the account the portions of the store's closing entries that affect the account. Post first the credit that removes the beginning inventory from the account.

Exercise 5–6

The information that follows was taken from an income statement.

Sales	$150,000	Purchases returns	$ 500
Sales returns	1,000	Purchases discounts	1,500
Sales discounts	2,000	Transportation-in	3,000
Beginning inventory	40,000	Gross profit from sales	47,000
Purchases	95,000	Net loss	4,000

Required:

Prepare calculations to determine *(a)* total operating expenses, *(b)* cost of goods sold, and *(c)* ending inventory.

Exercise 5–7

The trial balance that follows was taken from the ledger of Beta, Incorporated, at the end of its annual accounting period. (To simplify the problem and to save time, the account balances are in one- and two-digit numbers.)

BETA, INCORPORATED
Trial Balance
December 31, 19—

Cash	$ 1	
Accounts receivable	2	
Merchandise inventory	5	
Store supplies	3	
Store equipment	9	
Accumulated depreciation, store equipment ...		$ 2
Accounts payable		2
Salaries payable	—	—
Common stock, 10 shares		10
Retained earnings		3
Sales		40
Sales returns and allowances	1	
Purchases	18	
Purchases discounts		1
Transportation-in	1	
Salaries expense	10	
Rent expense	6	
Advertising expense	2	
Depreciation expense, store equipment	—	—
Store supplies expense	—	—
Totals	$58	$58

Required:

Prepare a work sheet form having no Adjusted Trial Balance columns on note paper, and copy the trial balance onto the work sheet. Then complete the work sheet using the information that follows:

a.   Ending store supplies inventory $1.
b.   Estimated depreciation on the store equipment, $3.
c.   Accrued salaries payable, $1.
d.   Ending merchandise inventory, $6.

Exercise 5–8   Copy the following tabulation and fill in the missing amounts. Indicate a loss by placing parentheses around the amount. Each horizontal row of figures is a separate problem situation.

Sales	Beginning inventory	Purchases	Ending inventory	Cost of goods sold	Gross profit	Expenses	Net income or loss
$110,000	$ 80,000	$ 70,000	$?	$ 95,000	$?	$50,000	$?
185,000	65,000	?	75,000	80,000	?	55,000	50,000
150,000	50,000	?	30,000	?	85,000	45,000	40,000
?	75,000	110,000	60,000	?	100,000	40,000	?
160,000	60,000	95,000	?	105,000	?	70,000	?
50,000	15,000	?	25,000	30,000	?	?	5,000
?	115,000	220,000	130,000	?	140,000	?	50,000
80,000	?	50,000	35,000	?	30,000	?	10,000

Exercise 5–9   On January 6, 198A, X Company received $5,000 of merchandise and an invoice dated January 5, terms 2/10, n/30, FOB Y Company's factory. On the day the goods were received, X Company paid Fast Freight Company $150 of shipping charges on the merchandise purchased. The next day X Company

returned to Y Company $400 of the goods that were defective and on January 15 it mailed Y Company a cheque for the amount owed. Prepare general journal entries to record the foregoing transactions *(a)* on the books of X Company and *(b)* on the books of Y Company. Assume that Y Company recorded the return and the cheque the next day after each was sent.

Exercise 5–10   The following two closing entries (with expenses combined to shorten the exercise) were made by Southwest Sales, a single proprietorship, at the end of its 198B annual accounting period.

Dec. 31	Income Summary	264,000.00	
	Merchandise Inventory		35,000.00
	Sales Returns and Allowances		2,000.00
	Sales Discounts		3,000.00
	Purchases		150,000.00
	Transportation-In		4,000.00
	Selling Expenses		40,000.00
	General and Administrative Expenses		30,000.00
31	Merchandise Inventory	46,000.00	
	Sales	250,000.00	
	Purchases Returns and Allowances	1,000.00	
	Purchases Discounts	2,000.00	
	Income Summary		299,000.00

Required:

From the information in the closing entries prepare an income statement for Southwest Sales.

PROBLEMS

Problem 5–1   Prepare general journal entries to record the following transactions:

Dec. 1 Purchased merchandise priced at $2,400 on credit, terms 1/15, n/30.

2 A new computer for office use was purchased on credit for $6,000.

2 Sold merchandise on credit, terms 2/10, 1/30, n/60, $1,200.

3 Paid $75 cash for freight charges on the merchandise shipment of the December 1 transaction.

8 Sold merchandise for cash, $240.

9 Purchased merchandise on credit, terms 2/15, n/30, $1,000.

11 Received a $200 credit memorandum for merchandise purchased on December 9 and returned for credit.

18 Sold merchandise on credit, terms 2/10, n/30, $900.

19 Issued a $150 credit memorandum to the customer of December 18 who returned a portion of the merchandise purchased.

22 Purchased office supplies on credit, $125.

23 Received a credit memorandum for unsatisfactory office supplies purchased on December 22 and returned for credit, $40.

24 Paid for the merchandise purchased on December 9, less the return and the discount.

27 The customer who purchased merchandise on December 2 paid for the purchase of that date less the applicable discount.

28 Received payment for the merchandise sold on December 18, less the return and applicable discount.

31 Paid for the merchandise purchased on December 1.

Problem 5–2   A December 31, 198B, year-end trial balance from the ledger of The Handy Store, a single proprietorship business follows.

THE HANDY STORE
Trial Balance
December 31, 198B

Cash	$ 1,335	
Merchandise inventory	33,975	
Store supplies	785	
Office supplies	245	
Prepaid insurance	1,820	
Store equipment...........................	21,210	
Accumulated depreciation, store equipment ...		$ 8,540
Office equipment	5,915	
Accumulated depreciation, office equipment ...		2,130
Accounts payable		4,870
Ned Handy, capital		40,300
Ned Handy, withdrawals	18,000	
Sales		190,430
Sales returns and allowances	1,165	
Sales discounts	2,120	
Purchases	114,250	
Purchases returns and allowances		740
Purchases discounts		2,940
Transportation-in	645	
Sales salaries expense	21,280	
Rent expense, selling space	12,900	
Advertising expense	385	
Store supplies expense	–0–	
Depreciation expense, store equipment	–0–	
Office salaries expense	12,420	
Rent expense, office space	1,500	
Office supplies expense	–0–	
Insurance expense	–0–	
Depreciation expense, office equipment	–0–	
Totals...............................	$249,950	$249,950

Required:

1. Copy the trial balance on an eight-column work sheet form and complete the work sheet using the information that follows:
   a. Store supplies inventory, $135.
   b. Office supplies inventory, $85.
   c. Expired insurance, $1,490.
   d. Estimated depreciation of store equipment, $2,120.
   e. Estimated depreciation of office equipment, $385.
   f. Ending merchandise inventory, $34,880.
2. Prepare a multiple-step classified income statement showing the expenses and the items entering into cost of goods sold in detail.
3. Prepare compound closing entries for the store.
4. Open a balance-column Merchandise Inventory account and enter the beginning inventory under a December 31, 198A, date as its balance. Then post those portions of the closing entries that affect the account. Post first the entry that removes the beginning inventory from the account.

Problem 5–3   At the 198B year-end, the Income Statement columns of Phoenix Sales work sheet carried the items that follow. (Phoenix Sales is owned by J. Fee).

	Income statement	
	Debit	Credit
Merchandise inventory	22,510	23,860
Sales		220,340
Sales returns and allowances	1,315	
Purchases	144,510	
Purchases returns and allowances		520
Purchases discounts		2,170
Transportation-in	935	
Sales salaries expense	24,840	
Rent expense, selling space	10,800	
Advertising expense	790	
Store supplies expense	550	
Depreciation expense, store equipment . . .	2,115	
Office salaries expense	11,350	
Rent expense, office space	1,200	
Telephone expense	570	
Office supplies expense	215	
Insurance expense	1,440	
Depreciation expense, office equipment . . .	530	
	223,670	246,890
Net income	23,220	
	246,890	246,890

Required:

1. Prepare a 198B, classified, multiple-step income statement for Phoenix Sales showing the expenses and the items entering into cost of goods sold in detail.
2. Prepare compound closing entries for the company.
3. Open a Merchandise Inventory account and enter the $22,510 beginning inventory under a December 31, 198A, date as its balance. Then post the portions of the closing entries that affect the account. Post first the credit that clears the beginning inventory from the account.

Problem 5–4   *(If the working papers that accompany this text are not being used, omit this problem.)*

The unfinished work sheet of Western Store, Inc., is reproduced in the booklet of working papers. All adjustments have been made on the work sheet except for $550 of additional income taxes expense.

Required:

1. Enter the income tax adjustment, sort the items to the proper work sheet columns, plug in the $23,430 ending inventory, and complete the work sheet.
2. Prepare a classified multiple-step income statement showing the details of cost of goods sold and the expenses.
3. Prepare a balance-column Merchandise Inventory account and enter the $25,220 beginning inventory under a December 31, 198A, date as its balance.

Then prepare compound closing entries for Western Store, Inc., and post those portions of the entries that affect the account. Post first the entry that clears the beginning inventory from the account.

4. Prepare for the corporation a combined statement of income and retained earnings with the items condensed as in published statements. Western Store, Inc., began 198B with $12,160 of retained earnings, and it declared and paid $10,000 of dividends during the year.

Problem 5–5

The December 31, 198B, end of the annual accounting period trial balance of the ledger of Hobby Shop, Incorporated, follows.

Required:

1. Copy the trial balance on an eight-column work sheet form and complete the work sheet using the information that follows.

   a. Ending store supplies inventory, $165; and *(b)* ending office supplies inventory, $125.

   c. Expired insurance, $1,645.

   d. Estimated depreciation on the store equipment, $3,610; and *(e)* on the office equipment, $990.

   f. Accrued sales salaries payable, $225; and accrued office salaries payable, $160.

   g. Additional income taxes expense, $425.

   h. Ending merchandise inventory, $33,160.

2. Prepare a multiple-step classified income statement showing the expenses and the items entering into cost of goods sold in detail.

3. Prepare a retained earnings statement. Hobby Shop, Incorporated, began 198B with $14,550 of retained earnings, and it declared and paid $10,000 of dividends during the year.

4. Prepare compound closing entries for the corporation.

5. In addition to the foregoing, prepare a single-step statement of income and retained earnings with the items condensed as is commonly done in published statements.

HOBBY SHOP, INCORPORATED
Trial Balance
December 31, 198B

Cash	$ 3,650	
Merchandise inventory	34,875	
Store supplies	615	
Office supplies	315	
Prepaid insurance	2,110	
Store equipment	37,195	
Accumulated depreciation, store equipment		$ 3,540
Office equipment	8,440	
Accumulated depreciation, office equipment		925
Accounts payable		795
Salaries payable		–0–
Income taxes payable		–0–
Common stock, 4,000 shares		40,000
Retained earnings		4,550
Sales		274,820
Sales returns and allowances	1,860	
Purchases	167,810	
Purchases returns and allowances		745
Purchases discounts		2,925
Transportation-in	2,185	
Sales salaries expense	24,650	
Rent expense, selling space	10,500	
Advertising expense	3,435	
Store supplies expense	–0–	
Depreciation expense, store equipment	–0–	
Office salaries expense	25,160	
Rent expense, office space	1,500	
Insurance expense	–0–	
Office supplies expense	–0–	
Depreciation expense, office equipment	–0–	
Income taxes expense	4,000	
Totals	$328,300	$328,300

Problem 5–6   The December 31, 198B, end of the annual accounting period trial balance of the ledger of Universal Sales, Inc., follows.

Required:

1. Copy the trial balance on an eight-column work sheet form and complete the work sheet using the information that follows:
   a. Ending store supplies inventory, $295; and *(b)* ending office supplies inventory, $150.
   c. Expired insurance, $1,870.
   d. Estimated depreciation on the store equipment, $3,610; and *(e)* on the office equipment, $990.
   f. Accrued sales salaries payable, $295; and accrued office salaries payable, $140.
   g. Additional income taxes expense, $450.
   h. Ending merchandise inventory, $36,245.
2. Prepare a multiple-step income statement showing the expenses and cost of goods sold items in detail.

UNIVERSAL SALES, INC.
Trial Balance
December 31, 198B

Cash	$ 6,850	
Accounts receivable	15,110	
Merchandise inventory	34,565	
Store supplies	1,610	
Office supplies	515	
Prepaid insurance	2,170	
Store equipment	41,320	
Accumulated depreciation, store equipment		$ 7,220
Office equipment	8,340	
Accumulated depreciation, office equipment		1,885
Accounts payable		5,540
Salaries payable		–0–
Income taxes payable		–0–
Common stock, 10,000 shares		50,000
Retained earnings		10,675
Sales		374,760
Sales returns and allowances	3,380	
Purchases	256,725	
Purchases returns and allowances		1,215
Purchases discounts		3,140
Transportation-in	3,415	
Sales salaries expense	28,815	
Rent expense, selling space	13,500	
Store supplies expense	–0–	
Depreciation expense, store equipment	–0–	
Office salaries expense	32,220	
Rent expense, office space	1,500	
Office supplies expense	–0–	
Insurance expense	–0–	
Depreciation expense, office equipment	–0–	
Income taxes expense	4,400	
Totals	$454,435	$454,435

3. Prepare a year-end classified balance sheet with the prepaid expenses combined.

4. Prepare a retained earnings statement. Universal Sales, Inc., began 198B with $20,675 of retained earnings, and it declared and paid $10,000 of dividends during the year.

5. Prepare adjusting and compound closing entries.

6. Also prepare a single-step statement of income and retained earnings with the items condensed as is common in published statements.

ALTERNATE PROBLEMS

Problem 5–1A   Prepare general journal entries to record the following transactions:

Oct. 1 Purchased merchandise on credit, terms 2/10, n/30, $4,800.
    2 Sold merchandise for cash, $500.
    6 Purchased merchandise on credit, terms 2/10, n/30, $3,500.
    6 Paid $150 cash for freight charges on the merchandise shipment of the previous transaction.
    7 Purchased delivery equipment on credit, $8,000.

Oct. 13 Sold merchandise on credit, terms 2/15, 1/30, n/60, $2,000.
14 Received a $500 credit memorandum for merchandise purchased on October 6 and returned for credit.
14 Purchased office supplies on credit, $160.
16 Sold merchandise on credit, terms 2/10, 1/30, n/60, $1,400.
16 Paid for the merchandise purchased on October 6, less the return and the discount.
17 Received a credit memorandum for unsatisfactory office supplies purchased on October 14 and returned, $40.
20 Issued a $140 credit memorandum to the customer who purchased merchandise on October 16 and returned a portion for credit.
26 Received payment for the merchandise sold on October 16, less the return and applicable discount.
28 The customer of October 13 paid for the purchase of that date, less the applicable discount.
31 Paid for the merchandise purchased on October 1.

Problem 5–2A

The Corner Store, a single proprietorship business, had the items that follow in the Income Statement columns of its 198B year-end work sheet:

	Income statement	
	Debit	Credit
Merchandise inventory	28,210	27,770
Sales		319,255
Sales returns and allowances	2,820	
Sales discounts	1,460	
Purchases	219,915	
Purchases returns and allowances		1,045
Purchases discounts		2,950
Transportation-in	3,125	
Sales salaries expense	27,135	
Rent expense, selling space	13,500	
Advertising expense	1,940	
Store supplies expense	715	
Depreciation expense, store equipment . . .	2,950	
Office salaries expense	14,880	
Rent expense, office space	1,500	
Telephone expense	635	
Office supplies expense	210	
Insurance expense	1,890	
Depreciation expense, office equipment . . .	765	
	321,650	351,020
Net income	29,370	
	351,020	351,020

Required:

1. Prepare a classified, multiple-step, 198B income statement for the store showing the expenses and cost of goods sold items in detail.
2. Under the assumption that Walter Evans, the owner of The Corner Store, withdrew $21,000 to pay personal expenses during 198B, prepare compound closing entries for the store.
3. Open a balance column Merchandise Inventory account and enter the store's $28,210 beginning inventory under a December 31, 198A, date as its balance. Then post the portions of the closing entries that affect this account. Post first the credit that removes the beginning inventory from the account.

Problem 5–3A   The December 31, 198B, year-end trial balance of the ledger of Westgate Store, a single proprietorship business, follows.

WESTGATE STORE
Trial Balance
December 31, 198B

Cash	$ 4,870	
Merchandise inventory	31,335	
Store supplies	1,145	
Office supplies	430	
Prepaid insurance	2,560	
Store equipment..........................	38,490	
Accumulated depreciation, store equipment ...		$ 6,385
Office equipment	9,420	
Accumulated depreciation, office equipment ...		2,450
Accounts payable		3,120
Ned Handy, capital		62,390
Ned Handy, withdrawals	21,000	
Sales		319,235
Sales returns and allowances	2,125	
Sales discounts	3,460	
Purchases	220,875	
Purchases returns and allowances		1,230
Purchases discounts		3,150
Transportation-in	1,875	
Sales salaries expense	23,140	
Rent expense, selling space	16,000	
Advertising expense	815	
Store supplies expense	–0–	
Depreciation expense, store equipment	–0–	
Office salaries expense	18,420	
Rent expense, office space	2,000	
Office supplies expense	–0–	
Insurance expense	–0–	
Depreciation expense, office equipment	–0–	
Totals	$397,960	$397,960

Required:

1. Copy the trial balance on an eight-column work sheet form and complete the work sheet using the information that follows:
   a. Store supplies inventory, $225; and *(b)* office supplies inventory, $120.
   c. Expired insurance, $1,845.
   d. Estimated depreciation on the store equipment, $3,910; and *(e)* on the office equipment, $1,170.
   f. Ending merchandise inventory, $32,655.
2. Prepare a multiple-step classified income statement showing the expenses and cost of goods sold items in detail.
3. Prepare compound closing entries for the store.
4. Open a balance column Merchandise Inventory account and enter the $31,335 beginning inventory under a December 31, 198A, date as its balance. Then post those portions of the closing entries that affect the account. Post first the credit that removes the beginning inventory from the account.

Problem 5–4A   The December 31, 198B, end of the annual accounting period trial balance of the ledger of York Sales, Inc., carried the items that follow:

YORK SALES, INC.
Trial Balance
December 31, 198B

Cash	$ 5,890	
Merchandise inventory	44,540	
Store supplies	975	
Office supplies	440	
Prepaid insurance	2,895	
Store equipment	43,380	
Accumulated depreciation, store equipment		$ 6,235
Office equipment	9,670	
Accumulated depreciation, office equipment		1,525
Accounts payable		2,250
Salaries payable		–0–
Income taxes payable		–0–
Common stock, 5,000 shares		50,000
Retained earnings		4,305
Sales		356,540
Sales returns and allowances	2,120	
Purchases	234,895	
Purchases returns and allowances		1,445
Purchases discounts		3,280
Transportation-in	2,215	
Sales salaries expense	28,095	
Rent expense, selling space	13,000	
Advertising expense	3,665	
Store supplies expense	–0–	
Depreciation expense, store equipment	–0–	
Office salaries expense	26,200	
Rent expense, office space	2,000	
Insurance expense	–0–	
Office supplies expense	–0–	
Depreciation expense, office equipment	–0–	
Income taxes expense	5,600	
Totals	$425,580	$425,580

Required:

1. Copy the trial balance on an eight-column work sheet form and complete the work sheet using the information that follows.
   a. Ending store supplies inventory, $265; and (b) ending office supplies inventory, $125.
   c. Expired insurance, $2,475.
   d. Estimated depreciation on the store equipment, $4,260; and (e) on the office equipment, $1,145.
   f. Accrued sales salaries payable, $345; and accrued office salaries payable, $85.
   g. Additional income taxes expense, $525.
   h. Ending merchandise inventory, $42,870.
2. Prepare a multiple-step classified income statement showing the expenses and cost of goods sold items in detail.
3. Prepare a retained earnings statement. York Sales, Inc., began 198B with $9,305 of retained earnings, and it declared and paid $5,000 of dividends during the year.
4. Prepare compound closing entries for the corporation.

5. In addition to the foregoing, prepare a single-step statement of income and retained earnings with the items condensed as is commonly done in published statements.

Problem 5–5A   The December 31, 198B, end of the annual accounting period trial balance of the ledger of Monroe Sales, Inc., follows.

MONROE SALES, INC.
Trial Balance
December 31, 198B

Cash	$ 6,780	
Accounts receivable	15,945	
Merchandise inventory	34,570	
Store supplies	1,485	
Office supplies	560	
Prepaid insurance	2,380	
Store equipment	37,520	
Accumulated depreciation, store equipment		$ 6,115
Office equipment	7,925	
Accumulated depreciation, office equipment		1,835
Accounts payable		2,560
Salaries payable		–0–
Income taxes payable		–0–
Common stock, 10,000 shares		50,000
Retained earnings		8,560
Sales		367,840
Sales returns and allowances	2,990	
Purchases	254,680	
Purchases returns and allowances		1,280
Purchases discounts		2,875
Transportation-in	2,950	
Sales salaries expense	26,350	
Rent expense, selling space	13,500	
Store supplies expense	–0–	
Depreciation expense, store equipment	–0–	
Office salaries expense	27,930	
Rent expense, office space	1,500	
Office supplies expense	–0–	
Insurance expense	–0–	
Depreciation expense, office equipment	–0–	
Income taxes expense	4,000	
Totals	$441,065	$441,065

Required:

1. Copy the trial balance on an eight-column work sheet form and complete the work sheet using the information that follows.
    a. Ending store supplies inventory, $345; and *(b)* ending office supplies inventory, $185.
    c. Expired insurance, $1,970.
    d. Estimated depreciation on the store equipment, $3,310; and *(e)* on the office equipment, $945.
    f. Accrued sales salaries payable, $325; and accrued office salaries payable, $185.
    g. Additional income taxes expense, $450.
    h. Ending merchandise inventory, $35,890.

2. Prepare a multiple-step classified income statement showing the cost of goods sold and expense items in detail.
3. Prepare a year-end classified balance sheet with the prepaid expenses combined.
4. Prepare a retained earnings statement. Monroe Sales, Inc., began 198B with $18,560 of retained earnings, and it declared and paid $10,000 of dividends during the year.
5. Prepare adjusting and compound closing entries.
6. Also prepare a single-step statement of income and retained earnings with the items condensed as is common in published statements.

Problem 5–6A   Dockside Sales, Inc., began 198B with $34,310 of retained earnings, and during the year it declared and paid $15,000 of dividends on its outstanding common stock. At the year-end, the Income Statement columns of its work sheet carried the items that follow.

	Income statement	
	Debit	Credit
Merchandise inventory	46,220	44,365
Sales		642,480
Sales returns and allowances	3,810	
Sales discounts	9,720	
Purchases	434,490	
Purchases returns and allowances		1,820
Purchases discounts		5,980
Transportation-in	6,135	
Sales salaries expense	46,720	
Rent expense, selling space	22,000	
Store supplies expense	1,080	
Depreciation expense, store equipment . . .	5,940	
Office salaries expense	37,880	
Rent expense, office space	2,000	
Office supplies expense	490	
Insurance expense	2,260	
Depreciation expense, office equipment . . .	1,840	
Income taxes expense	12,750	
	633,335	694,645
Net income	61,310	
	694,645	694,645

Required:

Prepare (1) a 198B classified income statement and (2) the closing entries.

PROVOCATIVE PROBLEMS

Provocative Problem 5–1, Jed's Nursery   Jed Larkin and Sam Reed were partners in a nursery. They disagreed, closed the business, and ended their partnership. In settlement for his partnership interest, Jed Larkin received an inventory of trees, plants, and garden supplies having a $15,000 cost. Since there was nothing practical he could do with the inventory, except to open a new nursery, he did so by investing the inventory and $12,000 in cash. He used $10,000 of the cash to buy equipment, and he opened for business on March 1. During the succeeding 10 months, he paid out $42,500 to creditors for additional trees, plants, and garden supplies and $14,000 in operating expenses. He also withdrew $12,000 for personal expenses, and at the year-end, he prepared the balance sheet that follows.

JED'S NURSERY
Balance Sheet
December 31, 19—

Cash	$ 3,700	Accounts payable (all for		
Merchandise inventory	17,700	merchandise)	$ 2,200	
Equipment $10,000		Jed Larkin, capital	28,400	
Less depreciation ... 800	9,200			
		Total liabilities and		
Total assets	$30,600	owner's equity	$30,600	

Based on the information given, prepare calculations to determine the net income earned by the business, the cost of goods sold, and the amount of its sales. Then prepare an income statement showing the result of the nursery's operations during its first 10 months.

Provocative Problem 5–2, Southgate Store

The 198B financial statements of Southgate Store were completed just before closing time yesterday. Ted Allen, the store's owner, took the statements home last night to examine but was unable to do so because of unexpected guests. This morning, he inadvertently left the 198B income statement at home when he came to work. However, he has the store's 198A and 198B balance sheets, which show the following in condensed form:

	December 31	
	198A	198B
Cash	$ 2,500	$ 8,100
Accounts receivable	6,200	7,300
Merchandise inventory	30,400	28,500
Equipment (net after depreciation) ...	24,800	20,600
Total assets	$63,900	$64,500
Accounts payable	$ 9,300	$ 8,200
Accrued wages payable	300	500
Ted Allen, capital	54,300	55,800
Total liabilities and owner's equity ...	$63,900	$64,500

He also has the store's record of cash receipts and disbursements which shows:

Collection of accounts receivable ...	$268,400
Payments for:	
Accounts payable	$166,200
Employees' wages	48,100
Other operating expenses	18,500
Ted Allen, withdrawals	30,000

Under the assumption that the store makes all purchases and sales on credit, prepare calculations to determine the 198B amounts of its accrual basis sales, purchases, and wages expense. Then prepare a 198B accrual basis income statement for the store.

Provocative Problem 5–3, Elmer's Paints

Elmer Wells worked in the bank in Hidden Valley for 20 years, until his aunt died, leaving him a comfortable estate. After sitting around for a year, doing little except being bored and watching his bank balance dwindle, he decided to open a retail paint store. At the time he began business, Hidden Valley had no such store, and it appeared to Elmer that such a business would be successful.

He began by depositing $35,000 in a bank account opened in the name of the business, Elmer's Paints. He then bought store equipment costing $8,000, for which he paid cash. He expected the equipment to last 10 years, after which it would be valueless. He also bought a stock of merchandise costing $25,000, which he paid for with cash, and he paid the rent on the store space for six months in advance, $2,400.

He estimated that like stores in neighboring communities marked their goods for sale at prices averaging 35% above cost. In other words, an item that cost $10 was marked for sale at $13.50. In order to get his store off to a good start, he decided to mark his merchandise for sale at 30% above cost. Since his overhead would be low, he thought this would still leave a net income equal to 10% of sales.

Today, December 1, six months after opening his store, Elmer has come to you for advice. He thinks business has been good. He has replaced his inventory three times during the six months. He has paid his suppliers for all purchases when due and owes only for purchases, $7,900, made during the past 30 days and for which payment is not due. An income statement he has prepared for the six months ended November 30 shows a $22,500 gross profit and a $10,300 net income. However, you note that he has not charged any depreciation on his equipment. He says he has a full stock of merchandise that cost $25,000 and customers owe him $19,400. He explained that, since Hidden Valley is a small community and he personally knew all of his customers, he was generous in granting credit. In addition to the rent paid in advance, he has paid all his other expenses, $9,800, with cash.

Nevertheless, Elmer doubts the validity of his gross profit and net income figures, since he started business with $35,000 in cash, now has only $800 left, and owes $7,900 for merchandise purchased on credit.

Prepare an income statement for the business covering the six-month period ended November 30, a November 30 balance sheet, and a statement of cash receipts and disbursements accounting for the $800 ending cash balance of the business. (Hint: Begin by determining the various statement items. Then put the statements together.)

ANALYTICAL AND REVIEW PROBLEMS

Problem 5–1
A&R

The partially completed work sheet of Incomplete Data Company appears below. Complete the work sheet using the following additional data:

a. Inventory December 31, 1987, $12.
b. Balance of Samuel Smith's Capital account as of December 31, 1987, $36.

Account Titles	Trial Balance		Adjustments		Income Statement		Balance Sheet	
	Dr.	Cr.	Dr.	Cr.	Dr.	Cr.	Dr.	Cr.
Cash	6.00							
Accounts receivable								
Store equipment	18.00							
Accumulated depreciation, store equipment		4.00						6.00
Inventory					10.00			
Supplies	10.00						4.00	
Prepaid rent	12.00						4.00	
Accounts payable		4.00						
Samuel Smith, capital		38.00						
Samuel Smith, withdrawals	8.00							
Purchases								
Purchase returns		2.00						
Transportation-in	2.00							
Salaries expense	8.00				12.00			
Advertising expense	4.00				4.00			
Sales		62.00						
Sales returns	2.00							
		110.00						

Problem 5–2
A&R

The following selected data are related to Mystic Company:

1. Balance sheets

	December 31	
	1987	1986
Assets		
Cash	$ 1,000	$ 2,000
Accounts receivable	3,000	2,000
Inventories	60,000	46,000
Land	10,000	10,000
	$74,000	$60,000
Liabilities and Owner's Equity		
Accounts payable	$14,000	$16,000
Mortgage payable	20,000	18,000
Michael McDonald, capital	40,000	26,000
	$74,000	$60,000

2. Closing entries for sales, expenses, and withdrawals

Sales	160,000	
Sales Returns and Allowances		10,000
Income Summary		150,000
Purchases Returns and Allowances	400	
Purchases Discounts	600	
Income Summary		1,000
Income Summary	40,000	
Transportation-In		1,000
Sales Salaries Expense		20,000
Rent Expense		8,000
Delivery Expense		2,000
Advertising Expense		9,000
Michael McDonald, Capital	11,000	
Michael McDonald, Withdrawal		11,000

Required:

1. Compute the net income for 1987.
2. Compute the cost of goods sold and the amount of purchases for 1987.
3. Prepare the missing closing entry or entries.

**Problem 5–3
A&R**

The following are the selected data for Sunvalley Sales Company for the year 1987:

1. Selected closing entries

Income Summary	148,000	
Purchases Returns and Allowances	1,500	
Purchases Discounts	500	
Purchases		100,000
Transportation-In		2,000
Sales Salaries Expense		20,000
Advertising Expense		10,000
Rent Expense, Office Space		8,000
Delivery Expense		2,500
Office Salaries Expense		6,000
Depreciation—Office Equipment		1,000
Miscellaneous Expense		500
To close Expense and other nominal accounts.		
David Collinge, Capital	26,000	
David Collinge, Withdrawals		26,000
To close the Withdrawals account.		

2. David Collinge follows the practice of withdrawing half of the annual net income from the business.
3. There were no sales returns and allowances for the year. However, sales discounts amounted to $1,000.
4. Inventories—December 31, 1986 20,000
                    December 31, 1987 25,000

Required:

1. Compute the amount of net income for 1987.
2. Compute the amount of sales for 1987.
3. Prepare a classified income statement for 1987.

Problem 5–4
A&R

JOHN STONE
Balance Sheet
April 30, 1987

Assets			**Liabilities and Owner's Equity**		
Current assets:			Current liabilities:		
Cash		$ 20	Accounts payable		$ 10
Accounts receivable		30	Advance from customers		15
Merchandise inventory		25	Total liabilities		$ 25
Prepaid insurance		16			
Total current assets		$ 91	Owner equity:		
			John Stone, capital		156
Fixed assets:					
Equipment	$96				
Accumulated de-					
preciation—					
Equipment	6	90			
			Total liabilities and		
Total assets		$181	owner's equity		$181

May transactions:

Sales on account	$100
Purchases on account	55
Collection of accounts receivable	95
Payment of accounts payable	40
Withdrawals by owner	20
Sales returns	2
Purchases returns and allowances	1
Payment of wages during May	10
Payment of other expenses	8

Data for adjustment:

a.   Accrued unpaid wages on May 31 amounted to $1.

b.   A one-year insurance policy was purchased on January 1, 1987.

c.   Equipment has an estimated service life of four years.

d.   The necessary deliveries were made to all customers that had paid in advance.

e.   A physical count of inventory was made on May 31, 1987 and its cost was determined as $20.

Required:

1.   Journalize the May transactions.
2.   Post to appropriate general ledger accounts. (T-accounts are acceptable.)
3.   Take a trial balance (first two columns of work sheet).
4.   Complete work sheet.
5.   Prepare in good form the balance sheet and the income statement. (The fiscal period is May 1 to May 31) i.e., a monthly fiscal period.
6.   Journalize the adjusting and closing entries.
7.   Post the adjusting and closing journal entries.   (CGA adapted)

Accounting Systems

After studying Chapter 6, you should be able to:

Explain how columnar journals save posting labour.

State what type of transaction is recorded in each columnar journal described in the chapter.

Explain how a controlling account and its subsidiary ledger operate and give the rule for posting to a subsidiary ledger and its controlling account.

Record transactions in and post from the columnar journals described.

Explain how the accuracy of the account balances in the Accounts Receivable and Accounts Payable Ledgers is proved and be able to make such a proof.

Describe how data is processed in a large business.

Define or explain the words and phrases listed in the chapter Glossary.

An *accounting system* consists of the business papers, records, reports, and procedures that are used by a business in recording transactions and reporting their effects. Operation of an accounting system includes three important steps: (1) the quantities, dollar amounts, and other important data relating to business transactions must be captured on business papers or source documents; (2) the data contained in the source documents must be classified and recorded in the accounting records; and (3) the resulting information must be summarized in timely reports to management and other interested parties.

Even in relatively small businesses, the quantity of data that is processed through the accounting system is very large. As a result, the accounting system must be designed in a manner that allows the data to be processed efficiently.

The focus of Chapter 6 is to introduce some general procedures and techniques that are used in accounting systems to process data efficiently. The chapter begins with a discussion of techniques that are used primarily in manual, or pen-and-ink, accounting systems. Students should understand that the basic concepts introduced in this discussion are generally applicable to both manual and computerized accounting systems. Later in the chapter, the discussion turns specifically to electronic and computerized accounting systems.

REDUCING WRITING AND POSTING LABOUR

The General Journal used thus far is a flexible journal in which it is possible to record any transaction. However, each debit and credit entered in such a journal must be individually posted. Consequently, using a General Journal to record all the transactions of a business results in too much writing and too much labour in posting the individual debits and credits.

One way to reduce the writing and the posting labour is to divide the transactions of a business into groups of similar transactions and to provide a separate *special journal* for recording the transactions in each group. For example, if the transactions of a merchandising business are examined, the majority fall into four groups. They are sales on credit, purchases on credit, cash receipts, and cash disbursements. If a special journal is provided for each group, the journals are:

1. A Sales Journal for recording credit sales.
2. A Purchases Journal for recording credit purchases.
3. A Cash Receipts Journal for recording cash receipts.
4. A Cash Disbursements Journal for recording cash payments.

In addition, a General Journal must be provided for the few miscellaneous transactions that cannot be recorded in the special journals and also for adjusting, closing, and correcting entries.

Special journals require less writing in recording transactions than does a General Journal, as the following illustrations will show. In addition, they save posting labour by providing special columns for accumulating the debits and credits of similar transactions. The amounts entered in the special columns are then posted as column totals rather than as individual amounts. For example, if credit sales for a month are recorded in a Sales Journal like the one at the top of Illustration 6–1, posting labour is saved by waiting until the end of the month, totaling the sales recorded in the journal, and debiting Accounts Receivable and crediting Sales for the total.

Only seven sales are recorded in the illustrated journal. However, if the seven sales are assumed to represent 700 sales, a better appreciation is gained of the posting labour saved by the one debit to Accounts Receivable and the one credit to Sales, rather than 700 debits and 700 credits.

The special journal of Illustration 6–1 is also called a *columnar journal* because it has columns for recording the date, the customer's name, the invoice number, and the amount of each charge sale. Only charge sales can be recorded in it, and they are recorded daily with the information about each sale being placed on a separate line. Normally, the information is taken from a copy of the sales ticket or invoice prepared at the time of the sale. However, before discussing the journal further, the subject of *subsidiary ledgers* must be introduced.

SUBSIDIARY LEDGERS

The Accounts Receivable account used thus far does not readily tell how much each customer bought and paid for or how much each customer owes. As a result, a business selling on credit must maintain additional accounts receivable, one for each customer, to provide this information. One possible means of keeping a separate account receivable for each customer would be to replace the single Accounts Receivable account with many accounts. However, this usually is not done. Instead, an account for each customer is maintained in a supplemental record called a *subsidiary ledger.* This collection of customer accounts may exist on tape or disk storage in a computerized system. In a manual system, the *Accounts Receivable Ledger* (subsidiary ledger) may take the form of a book or tray containing the customer accounts. In either case, the customer accounts in the subsidiary ledger are kept separate from the Accounts Receivable account, which appears in the financial statement.

Illustration 6–1

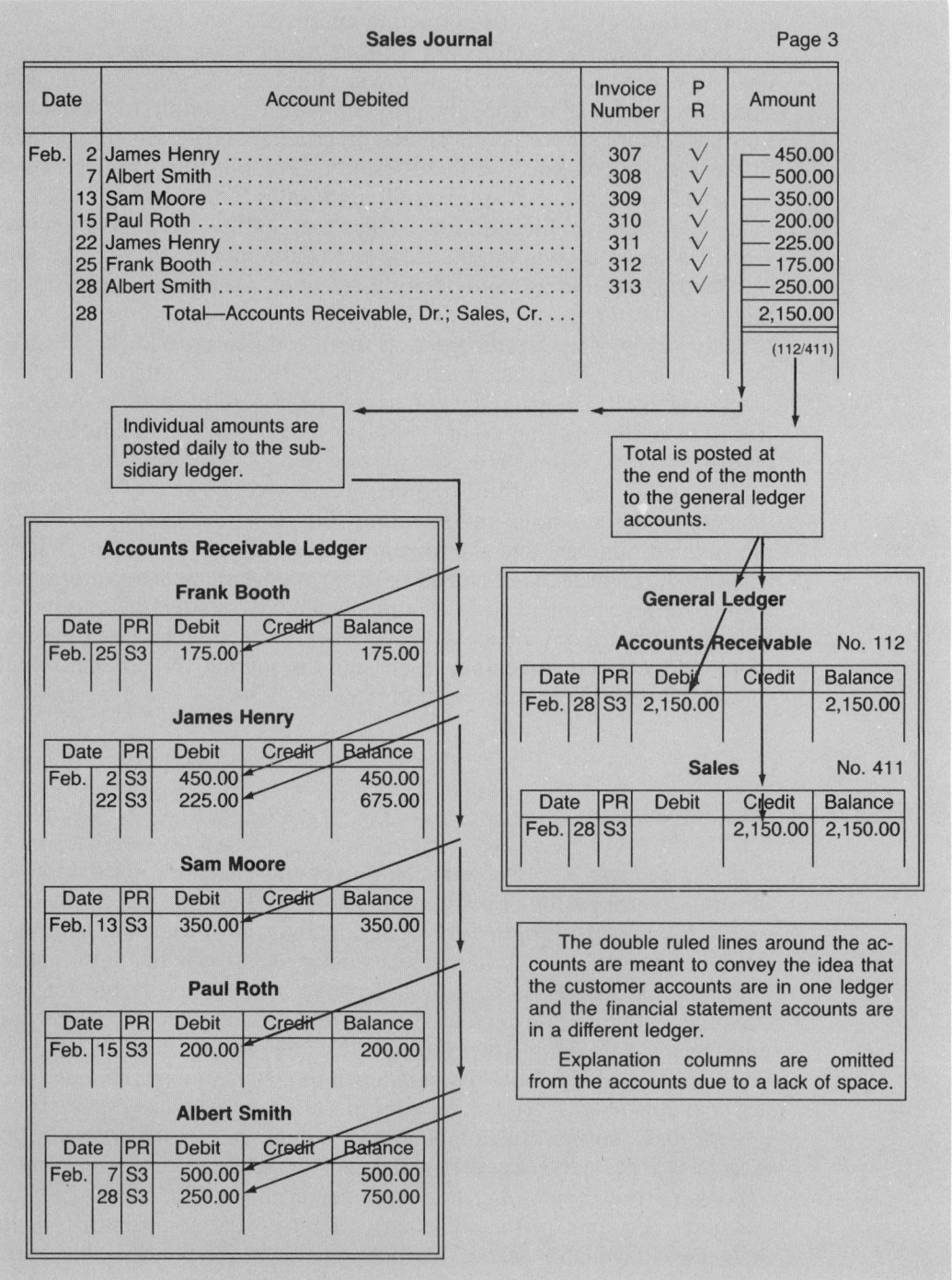

The collection of financial statement accounts are maintained in a separate record called the *General Ledger.*

POSTING THE SALES JOURNAL

When customer accounts are placed in a subsidiary ledger, a Sales Journal is posted as in Illustration 6–1. The individual sales recorded in the Sales Journal are posted each day to the proper customer accounts in the Accounts Receivable Ledger. These daily postings keep the customer accounts up to date. This is important in granting credit because the person responsible for granting credit should know in each case the amount currently owed by the credit-seeking customer. The source of this information is the customer's account. If the account is not up to date, an incorrect decision may be made.

Note the check marks in the Sales Journal's Posting Reference column. They indicate that the sales recorded in the journal were individually posted to the customer accounts in the Accounts Receivable Ledger. Check marks rather than account numbers are used because customer accounts may not be numbered. To help locate individual accounts, they may be alphabetically arranged in the Accounts Receivable Ledger, with new accounts added in their proper alphabetical positions as required.

In addition to the daily postings to customer accounts, at the end of the month, the Sales Journal's Amount column is totaled and the total is debited to Accounts Receivable and credited to Sales. The credit records the month's revenue from charge sales. The debit records the resulting increase in accounts receivable.

Before going on, note again in Illustration 6–1 that the individual customer accounts in the subsidiary Accounts Receivable Ledger do not replace the Accounts Receivable account described in previous chapters but are in addition to it. The Accounts Receivable account must still be maintained in the General Ledger where it serves three functions: (1) It shows the total amount owed by all customers. (2) It allows the General Ledger to be a balancing ledger in which debits equal credits. (3) It offers a proof of the accuracy of the customer accounts in the subsidiary Accounts Receivable Ledger.

IDENTIFYING POSTED AMOUNTS

When several journals are posted to ledger accounts, it is necessary to indicate in the Posting Reference column before each posted amount the journal as well as the page number of the journal from which the amount was posted. The journal is indicated by using its initial. Thus, items posted from the Cash Disbursements Journal carry the initial "D" before their journal page numbers in the Posting Reference columns.

Likewise, items from the Cash Receipts Journal carry the letter "R." Those from the Sales Journal carry the initial "S." Items from the Purchases Journal carry the initial "P," and from the General Journal, the letter "G."

CONTROLLING ACCOUNTS

When a company maintains an Accounts Receivable account in its General Ledger and puts its customer accounts in a subsidiary ledger, the Accounts Receivable account is said to control the subsidiary ledger and is called a *controlling account*. The extent of the control is that after all posting is completed, if no errors were made, the sum of the customer account balances in the subsidiary ledger will equal the balance of the controlling account in the General Ledger. This equality is also a proof of the total of the customer account balances.

CASH RECEIPTS JOURNAL

A Cash Receipts Journal designed to save labour through posting column totals must be a multicolumn journal. A multicolumn journal is necessary because cash receipts differ as to sources and, consequently, as to the accounts credited when cash is received from different sources. For example, if the cash receipts of a store are classified as to sources, they normally fall into three groups: (1) cash from charge customers in payment of their accounts, (2) cash from cash sales, and (3) cash from miscellaneous sources. Note in Illustration 6–2 (on the next page) how a special column is provided for the credits resulting when cash is received from each of these sources.

Cash from Charge Customers

When a Cash Receipts Journal such as Illustration 6–2 is used in recording cash received from a customer in payment of the customer's account, the customer's name is entered in the journal's Account Credited column. The amount credited to the customer's account is entered in the Accounts Receivable Credit column, and the debits to Sales Discounts and Cash are entered in the journal's last two columns.

Give close attention to the Accounts Receivable credit column. Observe that (1) only credits to customer accounts are entered in this column. (2) The individual credits are posted daily to the customer accounts in the subsidiary Accounts Receivable Ledger. (3) The column total is posted at the month-end to the credit of the Accounts Receivable controlling account. This is the normal recording and posting procedure when controlling accounts and subsidiary ledgers are used. When such accounts

Illustration 6–2

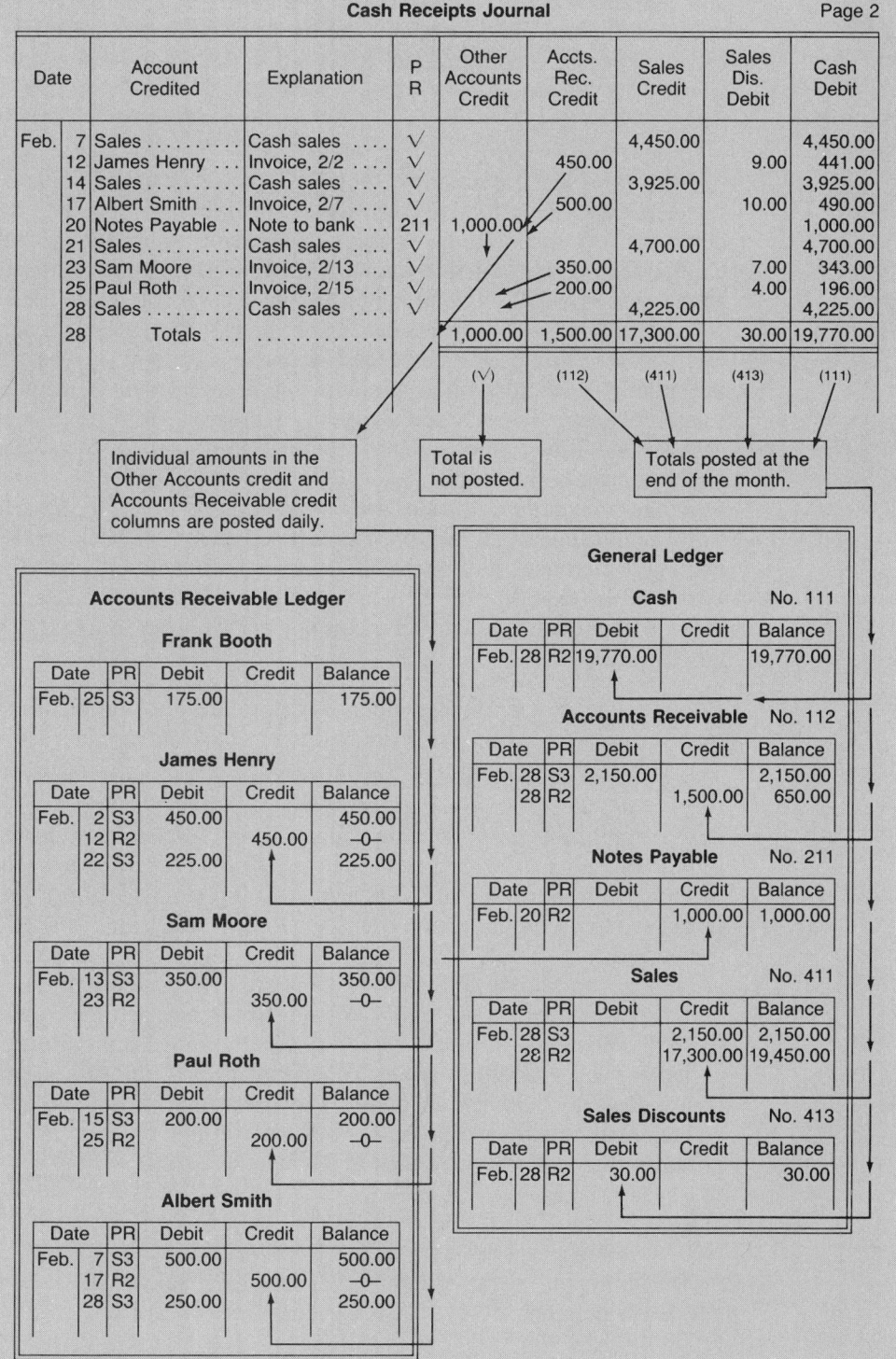

and ledgers are used, transactions are normally entered in a journal column. The individual amounts are then posted to the subsidiary ledger accounts, and the column total is posted to the controlling account.

Cash Sales

Cash sales are commonly ''rung up'' each day on one or more cash registers, and their total is recorded each day with an entry having a debit to Cash and a credit to Sales. When such sales are recorded in a Cash Receipts Journal like that of Illustration 6–2, the debits to Cash are entered in the Cash debit column and a special column headed ''Sales credit'' is provided for the credits to Sales. By entering each day's cash sales in this column, the cash sales of a month may be posted at the month's end in a single amount, the column total. (Although cash sales are normally recorded daily from the cash register reading, the cash sales of Illustration 6–2 are recorded only once each week in order to shorten the illustration.)

At the time daily cash sales are recorded in the Cash Receipts Journal, some bookkeepers, as in Illustration 6–2, place a check mark in the Posting Reference column to indicate that no amount is individually posted from that line of the journal. Other bookkeepers use a double check ($\sqrt{\!\!\sqrt{}}$) to distinguish amounts not posted from amounts posted to customer accounts.

Miscellaneous Receipts of Cash

Most cash receipts are from collections of accounts receivable and from cash sales. However, other sources of cash include less frequent transactions such as borrowing money from a bank in exchange for a promissory note or selling unneeded assets for cash. For miscellaneous receipts such as these, the Other Accounts credit column is provided. In an average company, the items entered in this column are few and are posted to a variety of general ledger accounts. As a result, postings are less apt to be omitted if these items are also posted daily.

The Cash Receipts Journal's Posting Reference column is used only for daily postings from the Other Accounts and Accounts Receivable columns. The account numbers appearing in the column indicate items posted to general ledger accounts. The check marks indicate either that an item like a day's cash sales was not posted or that an item was posted to the subsidiary Accounts Receivable Ledger.

Month-End Postings

The amounts in the Accounts Receivable, Sales, Sales Discounts, and Cash columns of the Cash Receipts Journal are posted as column totals at the end of the month. However, the transactions recorded in any journal must result in equal debits and credits to general ledger accounts. Consequently, debit and credit equality in a columnar journal such as the Cash Receipts Journal is proved by *crossfooting* or cross adding the column totals before they are posted. To *foot* a column of numbers is to add it. To crossfoot the Cash Receipts Journal, the debit column totals are added together, the credit column totals are added together, and the two sums are compared for equality. For Illustration 6–2, the two sums appear as follows:

Debit columns		Credit columns	
Sales discounts debit	$ 30	Other accounts credit	$ 1,000
Cash debit	19,770	Accounts receivable credit ...	1,500
		Sales credit	17,300
Total	$19,800	Total	$19,800

And since the sums are equal, the debits in the journal are assumed to equal the credits.

After the debit and credit equality is proved by crossfooting, the totals of the last four columns are posted as indicated in each column heading. As for the Other Accounts column, since the individual items in this column are posted daily, the column total is not posted. Note in Illustration 6–2 the check mark below the Other Accounts column. The check mark indicates that the column total was not posted. The account numbers of the accounts to which the remaining column totals were posted are indicated in parentheses below each column.

Posting items daily from the Other Accounts column with a delayed posting of the offsetting items in the Cash column (total) causes the General Ledger to be out of balance throughout the month. However, this is of no consequence because before the trial balance is prepared, the offsetting amounts reach the General Ledger in posting the Cash column total.

POSTING RULE

Posting to a subsidiary ledger and its controlling account from two journals has been demonstrated, and a rule to cover all such postings can now be given. The rule is: *In posting to a subsidiary ledger and its controlling account, the controlling account must be debited periodically for an amount or amounts equal to the sum of the debits to the subsidiary ledger and it must be credited periodically for an amount or amounts equal to the sum of the credits to the subsidiary ledger.*

CREDITOR ACCOUNTS

As with accounts receivable, the Accounts Payable account used thus far does not show how much is owed each creditor. As a result, to secure this information, an individual account, one for each creditor, must be maintained. These creditor accounts are commonly kept in an *Accounts Payable Ledger* that is controlled by an Accounts Payable controlling account in the General Ledger. Also, the controlling account, subsidiary ledger, and columnar journal techniques demonstrated thus far with accounts receivable apply to the creditor accounts. The only difference is that a Purchases Journal and a Cash Disbursements Journal are used in recording most of the transactions affecting these accounts.

PURCHASES JOURNAL

A Purchases Journal having one money column may be used to record purchases of merchandise on credit. However, a multicolumn journal in which purchases of both merchandise and supplies can be recorded is commonly preferred. Such a journal may have the columns shown in Illustration 6–3. In the illustrated journal, the invoice date and terms together indicate the date on which payment for each purchase is due. The Accounts Payable credit column is used to record the amounts credited to each creditor's account. These amounts are posted daily to the individual creditor accounts in the Accounts Payable Ledger. The column total is posted to the Accounts Payable controlling account at the month-end. The items purchased are recorded in the debit columns and are posted in the column totals.

THE CASH DISBURSEMENTS JOURNAL AND ITS POSTING

The Cash Disbursements Journal, like the Cash Receipts Journal, has columns that make it possible to post repetitive debits and credits in column totals. The repetitive debits and credits of cash payments are debits to the Accounts Payable controlling account and credits to both Purchases Discounts and Cash. In most companies, the purchase of merchandise for cash is not common; therefore, a Purchases column is not needed and a cash purchase is recorded as on line 2 of Illustration 6–4.

Observe that the illustrated journal has a column headed "Cheque Number" (Ch. No.). In order to gain control over cash disbursements, all such disbursements, except petty cash disbursements, should be made by cheque. (Petty cash disbursements are discussed in the next chapter.) The cheques should be prenumbered by the printer and should be entered in the journal in numerical order with each cheque's number in the

Illustration 6–3

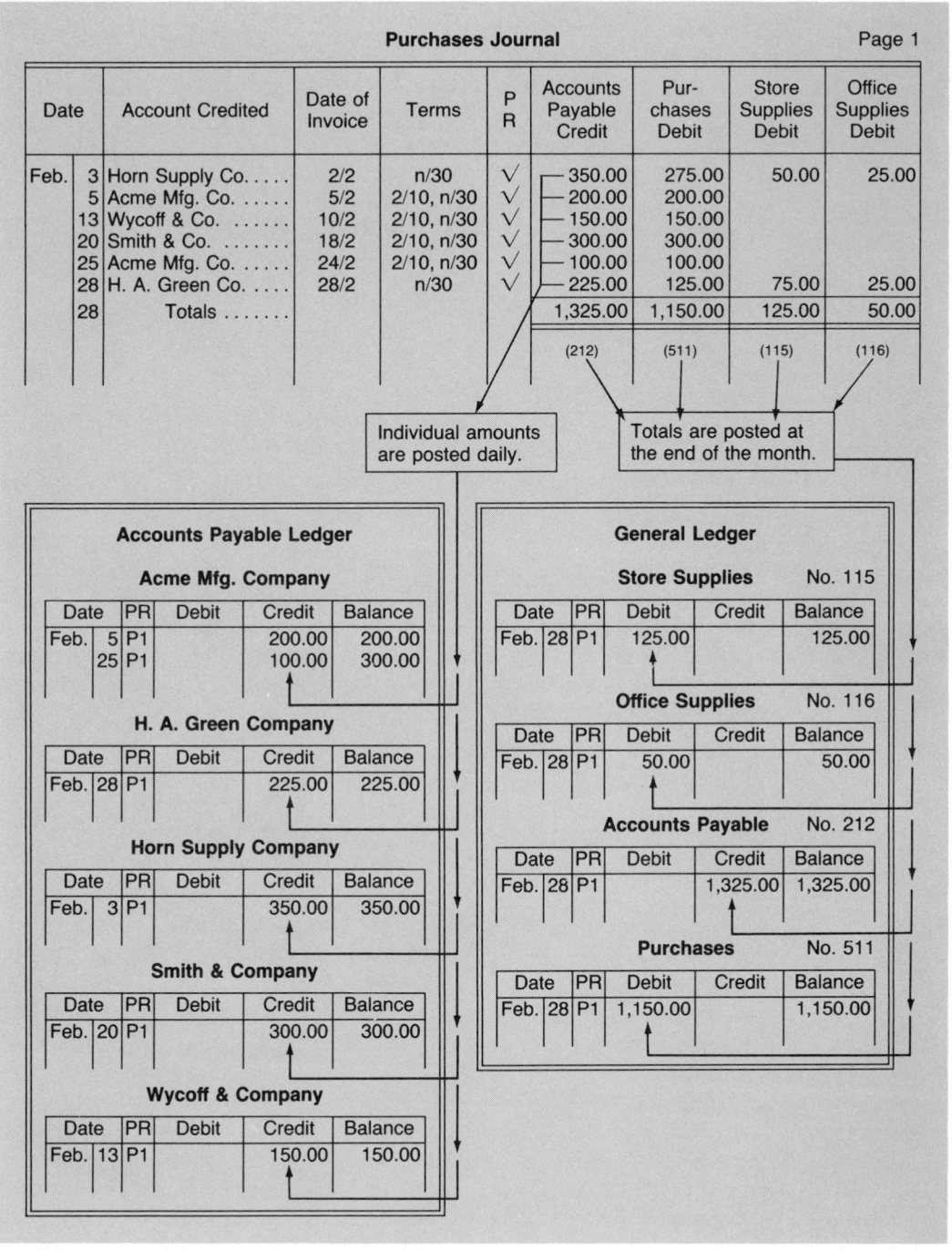

Purchases Journal   Page 1

Date	Account Credited	Date of Invoice	Terms	PR	Accounts Payable Credit	Purchases Debit	Store Supplies Debit	Office Supplies Debit
Feb. 3	Horn Supply Co.	2/2	n/30	√	350.00	275.00	50.00	25.00
5	Acme Mfg. Co.	5/2	2/10, n/30	√	200.00	200.00		
13	Wycoff & Co.	10/2	2/10, n/30	√	150.00	150.00		
20	Smith & Co.	18/2	2/10, n/30	√	300.00	300.00		
25	Acme Mfg. Co.	24/2	2/10, n/30	√	100.00	100.00		
28	H. A. Green Co.	28/2	n/30	√	225.00	125.00	75.00	25.00
28	Totals				1,325.00	1,150.00	125.00	50.00
					(212)	(511)	(115)	(116)

Individual amounts are posted daily.

Totals are posted at the end of the month.

Accounts Payable Ledger

Acme Mfg. Company

Date	PR	Debit	Credit	Balance
Feb. 5	P1		200.00	200.00
25	P1		100.00	300.00

H. A. Green Company

Date	PR	Debit	Credit	Balance
Feb. 28	P1		225.00	225.00

Horn Supply Company

Date	PR	Debit	Credit	Balance
Feb. 3	P1		350.00	350.00

Smith & Company

Date	PR	Debit	Credit	Balance
Feb. 20	P1		300.00	300.00

Wycoff & Company

Date	PR	Debit	Credit	Balance
Feb. 13	P1		150.00	150.00

General Ledger

Store Supplies   No. 115

Date	PR	Debit	Credit	Balance
Feb. 28	P1	125.00		125.00

Office Supplies   No. 116

Date	PR	Debit	Credit	Balance
Feb. 28	P1	50.00		50.00

Accounts Payable   No. 212

Date	PR	Debit	Credit	Balance
Feb. 28	P1		1,325.00	1,325.00

Purchases   No. 511

Date	PR	Debit	Credit	Balance
Feb. 28	P1	1,150.00		1,150.00

Illustration 6–4

Cash Disbursements Journal   Page 2

Date	Ch. No.	Payee	Account Debited	P R	Other Accounts Debit	Accts. Pay. Debit	Pur. Disc. Credit	Cash Credit
Feb. 3	105	L. & N. Railroad ..	Transportation-In .	514	15.00			15.00
12	106	East Sales Co....	Purchases	511	25.00			25.00
15	107	Acme Mfg. Co....	Acme Mfg. Co....	√		200.00	4.00	196.00
15	108	Jerry Hale	Salaries Expense	611	250.00			250.00
20	109	Wycoff & Co.	Wycoff & Co.	√		150.00	3.00	147.00
28	110	Smith & Co.	Smith & Co.	√		300.00	6.00	294.00
28		Totals			290.00	650.00	13.00	927.00
					(√)	(212)	(513)	(111)

Individual amounts in the Other Accounts debit column and Accounts Payable debit column are posted daily.

Totals posted at the end of the month.

Accounts Payable Ledger

Acme Mfg. Company

Date	PR	Debit	Credit	Balance
Feb. 5	P1		200.00	200.00
15	D2	200.00		–0–
25	P1		100.00	100.00

H. A. Green Company

Date	PR	Debit	Credit	Balance
Feb. 28	P1		225.00	225.00

Horn Supply Company

Date	PR	Debit	Credit	Balance
Feb. 3	P1		350.00	350.00

Smith & Company

Date	PR	Debit	Credit	Balance
Feb. 20	P1		300.00	300.00
28	D2	300.00		–0–

Wycoff & Company

Date	PR	Debit	Credit	Balance
Feb. 13	P1		150.00	150.00
20	D2	150.00		–0–

General Ledger

Cash   No. 111

Date	PR	Debit	Credit	Balance
Feb. 28	R2	19,770.00		19,770.00
28	D2		927.00	18,843.00

Accounts Payable   No. 212

Date	PR	Debit	Credit	Balance
Feb. 28	P1		1,325.00	1,325.00
28	D2	650.00		675.00

Purchases   No. 511

Date	PR	Debit	Credit	Balance
Feb. 12	D2	25.00		25.00
28	P1	1,150.00		1,175.00

Purchases Discounts   No. 513

Date	PR	Debit	Credit	Balance
Feb. 28	D2		13.00	13.00

Transportation-In   No. 514

Date	PR	Debit	Credit	Balance
Feb. 3	D2	15.00		15.00

Salaries Expense   No. 611

Date	PR	Debit	Credit	Balance
Feb. 15	D2	250.00		250.00

column headed "Ch. No." This makes it possible to scan the numbers in the column for omitted cheques. When a Cash Disbursements Journal has a column for cheque numbers, it is often called a *Cheque Register*.

A Cash Disbursements Journal or Cheque Register like Illustration 6–4 is posted as follows. The individual amounts in the Other Accounts column are posted daily to the debit of the general ledger accounts named. The individual amounts in the Accounts Payable column are posted daily to the subsidiary Accounts Payable Ledger to the debit of the creditors named. At the end of the month, after the column totals are crossfooted to prove their equality, the Accounts Payable column total is posted to the debit of the Accounts Payable controlling account. The Purchases Discounts column total is credited to the Purchases Discounts account, and the Cash column total is credited to the Cash account. Since the items in the Other Accounts column are posted individually, the column total is not posted.

PROVING THE LEDGERS

Periodically, after all posting is completed, the General Ledger and the subsidiary ledgers are proved. The General Ledger is normally proved first by preparing a trial balance. If the trial balance balances, the accounts in the General Ledger, including the controlling accounts, are assumed to be correct. The subsidiary ledgers are then proved, commonly by preparing schedules of accounts receivable and accounts payable. A *schedule of accounts payable,* for example, is prepared by listing with their balances the accounts in the Accounts Payable Ledger having balances. The balances are totaled; and if the total is equal to the balance of the Accounts Payable controlling account, the accounts in the Accounts Payable Ledger are assumed to be correct. Illustration 6–5 shows a schedule of the creditor accounts having balances in the Accounts Payable Ledger of Illustration 6–4. Note that the schedule total is equal to the balance of the Accounts Payable controlling account in the General Ledger of

Illustration 6–5

HAWAIIAN SALES COMPANY
Schedule of Accounts Payable,
December 31, 19—

Acme Mfg. Company	$100
H. A. Green Company	225
Horn Supply Company	350
Total accounts payable	$675

Illustration 6–4. A *schedule of accounts receivable* is prepared in the same way as a schedule of accounts payable. Also, if its total is equal to the balance of the Accounts Receivable controlling account, the accounts in the Accounts Receivable Ledger are assumed to be correct.

Instead of a formal schedule to prove the accounts in a subsidiary ledger, an adding machine list may be used. For example, the balances of the accounts in the Accounts Payable Ledger may be proved by listing on an adding machine the balance of each account in the ledger, totaling the list, and comparing the total with the balance of the Accounts Payable controlling account. A similar list may be used to prove the accounts in the Accounts Receivable Ledger.

SALES TAXES

Most provinces require retailers to collect sales taxes from their customers and periodically remit these taxes to the provincial treasurer. When a columnar Sales Journal is used, a record of taxes collected can be obtained by adding special columns in the journal as shown in Illustration 6–6.

In posting the journal, the individual amounts in the Accounts Receivable column are posted daily to customer accounts in the Accounts Receivable Ledger and the column total is posted at the end of the month to the Accounts Receivable controlling account. The individual amounts in the Sales Taxes Payable and Sales columns are not posted. However, at the end of the month the total of the Sales Taxes Payable column is credited to the Sales Taxes Payable account and the total of the Sales column is credited to Sales.

A concern making cash sales upon which sales taxes are collected may add a special Sales Taxes Payable column in its Cash Receipts Journal.

Illustration 6–6

Sales Journal

Date	Account Debited	Invoice Number	P R	Accounts Receivable Debit	Sales Taxes Payable Credit	Sales Credit
Dec. 1	D. R. Horn	7-1698		108.00	8.00	100.00

SALES INVOICES AS A SALES JOURNAL

To save labour, many companies do not enter charge sales in a Sales Journal. These companies post each sales invoice total directly to the customer's account in a subsidiary Accounts Receivable Ledger. Copies of the invoices are then bound in numerical order in a binder. At the end of the month, all the invoices of that month are totaled and a general journal entry is made debiting Accounts Receivable and crediting Sales for the total. In effect, the bound invoice copies act as a Sales Journal. Such a procedure is known as direct posting of sales invoices.

SALES RETURNS

A company having only a few sales returns may record them in a General Journal with an entry like the following:

Oct.	17	Sales Returns and Allowances	412	17.50	
		Accounts Receivable—George Ball ..	112/√		17.50
		Customer returned merchandise.			

The debit of the entry is posted to the Sales Returns and Allowances account. The credit is posted to both the Accounts Receivable controlling account and to the customer's account. Note the account number and the check, 112/√, in the Posting Reference column on the credit line. This indicates that both the Accounts Receivable controlling account in the General Ledger and the George Ball account in the Accounts Receivable Ledger were credited for $17.50. Both were credited because the balance of the controlling account in the General Ledger will not equal the sum of the customer account balances in the subsidiary ledger unless both are credited.

Companies having sufficient sales returns can save posting labour by recording them in a special Sales Returns and Allowances Journal like that of Illustration 6–7. Note that this is in keeping with the generally recognized idea that a company can design and use a special journal for any group of like transactions in which there are within the group sufficient transactions to warrant the journal. When a Sales Returns and Allowances Journal is used to record returns, the amounts entered in the journal are posted daily to the credit of each affected customer account. At the end of the month, the journal total is debited to Sales Returns and Allowances and credited to Accounts Receivable.

Illustration 6–7

Sales Returns and Allowances Journal

Date		Account Credited	Explanation	Credit Memo No.	P R	Amount
Oct.	7	Robert Moore	Defective mdse	203	√	10.00
	14	James Warren	Defective mdse	204	√	12.00
	18	T. M. Jones	Not ordered	205	√	6.00
	23	Sam Smith	Defective mdse	206	√	18.00
	31	Sales Returns and	Allow., Dr.; Accounts	Rec., Cr.		46.00
						412/112

GENERAL JOURNAL ENTRIES

When columnar journals like the ones described are used, a General Journal must be provided for adjusting, closing, and correcting entries and for a few transactions that cannot be recorded in the special journals. Among these transactions, if a Sales Returns and Allowances Journal is not provided, are sales returns, purchases returns, and purchases of plant assets. Illustrative entries for the last two kinds of transactions follow:

Oct.	8	Accounts Payable—Medford Company . . .	212/√	32.00	
		Purchases Returns and Allowances . .	512		32.00
		Returned defective merchandise.			
	11	Office Equipment	133	685.00	
		Accounts Payable—ABC Supply Co. . .	212/√		685.00
		Purchased a typewriter.			

MACHINE METHODS

Manual accounting systems such as the ones described thus far are used only by small businesses, and an increasing number of these businesses are switching to computerized accounting systems. However, even before computers became widely available, many businesses began to use electronic bookkeeping machines. While these machines are also being replaced by computers, a number of companies continue to use electronic bookkeeping machines.

An electronic bookkeeping machine usually has a typewriter-like keyboard and the keyboard of a 10-key calculator. It also has "function" keys that direct the machine's operation, instructing it to calculate, tabulate, and/or print out stored data. A bookkeeping machine can handle accounting for sales, cash receipts, purchases, cash payments, payroll, and other transactions, as well as posting to the General Ledger.

No attempt will be made here to describe a bookkeeping machine's operation in each of these applications. However, when used in accounting for credit sales, for example, the current page of the Sales Journal is placed in the machine. Then, for each charge sale, the operator puts the customer's account and month-end statement in the machine and depresses the proper keys to enter the information about the sale. The machine makes the entry in the Sales Journal, posts to the customer's account, updates the account balance, enters the sale on the customer's month-end statement, and updates the statement. At the same time, it accumulates the Sales Journal total for the month-end debit to Accounts Receivable and credit to Sales. Furthermore, it does all of this in one operation from one entry into the machine of the proper data. And, it is equally efficient in handling other kinds of transactions.

Bookkeeping machines speed the processing of accounting data. They also reduce transposition errors by printing the same information on several different records in one operation. However, the speed of operation and the amount of work such a machine can do efficiently are limited. Consequently, many businesses are turning to computerized data processing.

COMPUTERIZED DATA PROCESSING

Computerized data processing involves the processing of data without human intervention through the use of a machine, a *computer,* that is far more powerful and complex than a bookkeeping machine. A computer is capable of—

1. Inputting and storing data.
2. Performing arithmetic calculations on the data.
3. Comparing units of the data to find which are larger or smaller.
4. Sorting or rearranging data.
5. Printing reports from the data stored in the machine.

Computers vary in size and in the speed with which they process data. They range from small desktop microcomputers to machines that with their peripheral equipment occupy a large room. Peripheral equipment includes devices to input or output data and to store data on reels of magnetic tapes or on magnetic disks.

Data may be entered into a computer by means of a computer terminal, a device that commonly has a typewriter-like keyboard, a 10-key numerical keyboard, and a TV-like screen. Data may also be entered with previously prepared punched cards, reels of magnetic tape, magnetic disks, and in other ways. For example, another means of entry uses a laser light that reads a bar code such as is found on many consumer products. Inside the computer each alphabetical letter or numerical digit of data becomes a combination of electrical or magnetic states that a computer can manipulate at very high rates of speed. Consequently, if of sufficient size, a computer can do 1 million or more additions, subtractions, multiplications, and divisions per second, all without error in a predetermined sequence according to instructions stored in the machine.

A computer can do nothing without a previously prepared set of instructions, called a **program,** that is entered and stored in the computer. However, with a properly prepared program, a computer will accept data, store and process the data, and produce the processed results, perhaps in the form of a report displayed on a TV-like screen, or typed out on an electric typewriter at the rate of approximately 10 characters per second, or printed by a line printer at upwards to 2,000 lines per minute.

The Program

A *computer program* is a set of instructions written in a language the computer "understands." Some of the widely used languages are COBOL, BASIC, RPG, and FORTRAN. The instructions specify each operation a computer is to perform and are entered into the computer before the data to be processed. The program may contain only a few or several thousand detailed instructions. For example, the following shows the steps that must be programmed to have a computer process customers' orders for merchandise.

Instructions to Be Programmed for Processing Customers' Orders

1. For the first item on the customer's order, compare the quantity ordered with the quantity on hand as shown by inventory data stored in the computer.
    a. If the quantity ordered is not on hand:
       (1) Prepare a back order notifying the customer that the goods are not available but will be shipped as soon as a new supply is received.
       (2) Go to the next item on the customer's order.
    b. If the quantity on hand is greater than the amount ordered:
       (1) Deduct the amount ordered from the amount on hand.
       (2) Prepare instructions to ship the goods.
       (3) Compare the amount of the item remaining after filling the customer's order with the reorder point for the item.
          (i) If the amount remaining is greater than the reorder point:
             (a) Go to the next item on the customer's order.

(ii)   If the amount remaining is less than the reorder point:
  (a)   Compute the amount to be purchased and prepare documents for the purchase.
  (b)   Go to the next item on the customer's order.

In addition to these instructions, a program for processing customer orders would have instructions for preparing invoices, recording sales, and updating customer accounts.

Designing the Program

Computers have the ability to compare two numbers and decide which is larger. This ability makes it possible for the computer to process data one way or another, depending on the result of the comparison. Note that this ability to compare numbers is essential if the computer is to follow instructions such as those for processing customer orders.

If a computer is to process data correctly, a person (the programmer) must first design a program for the computer to follow. In designing the program, the programmer determines in advance the alternative sets of calculations or processing steps to be made. Then, the programmer must devise the appropriate comparisons that will identify the circumstances under which each particular set of processing steps should be performed. Finally, the programmer must write specific instructions telling the computer how to process the data. A computer can follow through the program's maze of decisions and alternate instructions rapidly and accurately. However, if it encounters an exception not anticipated in the program, it is helpless and can only process the exception incorrectly or stop.

The ability to store a program and data and then to race through the maze of decisions and alternate instructions is what distinguishes a computer from an electronic bookkeeping machine. Some electronic bookkeeping machines can do an addition, a multiplication, or a division at the speed of a computer. Yet with all this speed, their operating rates are relatively slow, since they must depend on a person to push their function keys to tell them what to do.

Modes of Operation

Computers operate in one of two modes: either *batch processing* or *online processing*. In the batch mode, the program and data to be processed are inputted to the computer, processed, and then removed from the computer before another batch is begun. Then, the program for a new job and a new set of data are entered and the new job is processed. Batch processing may result in customers' orders being processed daily, the payroll being run each week, financial statements being prepared monthly, and the processing of other jobs on a periodic basis. Because transactions are processed in groups or batches, this mode of operation may require less computer capacity, is usually less expensive than online operation, and is used when an immediate processing or an immediate computer response is not required.

In online processing, the program is kept in the computer along with any required data. As new data are entered, they are instantly processed by the computer. For example, in some department stores, the cash registers are connected directly into the store's computer. In addition to cash sales, the registers are used as follows in recording charge sales. After the customer selects merchandise for purchase, the salesperson uses the customer's plastic credit card to print the customer's name on a blank sales ticket. The sales ticket is then placed in the Forms Printer of the cash register and the sale is recorded. The register prints all pertinent information on the sales ticket and totals it. In order to finalize the sale, controls within the register require that the salesperson depress the proper register keys to record the customer's account number. This, in effect, posts the sale to the customer's account. The salesperson does not actually post to the account. Rather, the data entered with the cash register's keys cause the store's computer to update the customer's account. The computer will also produce the customer's month-end statement, ready for mailing.

Another example of online operation is found in supermarkets, where each item of merchandise is imprinted with a machine-readable price tag similar to Illustration 6–8. At one of the store's checkout stands, each item of merchandise selected by a customer is passed over an optical scanner in the countertop or an optical scanner in a wand is passed over each item's price tag. This actuates the cash register and eliminates the need for manually keying information into the register. It also transmits the sales information to a computer that updates the store's inventory records and prepares orders to a central warehouse to restock any item in low supply. At closing time, the computer prints out detailed summaries of the day's sales and item inventories. It thus provides management with up-to-the-minute information that could not otherwise be obtained.

Illustration 6–8

Other examples of online operations are found in banks, airlines, and factories. However, all have the same results: they reduce human labour, create more accurate records, and provide management with both better and more up-to-date reports. Furthermore, when there are sufficient transactions, they do the work at less cost per transaction.

Time Sharing

Computer service companies provide computer service to many concerns on a time-sharing basis, using computers that are capable of working on many jobs simultaneously. In providing such service, the computer service company installs an input-output device on the premises of a subscriber to its service. The input-output device is connected to the service company's computer through wires leased from the phone company. The subscriber uses the input-output device to input data into the service company's computer. It is held in storage there until processing time is available, usually within a few seconds. The computer then processes the data and transmits the results to the subscriber. For this service the subscriber pays a monthly fee plus a charge for the computer time used.

Through *time sharing,* a growing number of concerns are using computers, even very small businesses. For example, a dentist or a physician practicing alone is a small business. Yet a significant number of such dentists and physicians have their accounts receivable and customer billing done by computer service companies.

Microcomputers

Another important factor leading to the expanded use of computers is the development of microcomputers. These small computers have become less expensive in recent years and are now affordable by very small businesses and individuals. More and more people are becoming proficient in using these machines and manual accounting systems are being replaced by computerized systems.

RECORDING ACTUAL TRANSACTIONS

Transactions may be recorded in a pen-and-ink journal or with a bookkeeping machine or on a computer terminal, depending on the accounting system of the business completing the transactions. Nevertheless, in the remainder of this book, general journal entries will be used to illustrate the recording of most transactions. The general journal entries are intended to show the items increased and decreased by the transactions. The student should recognize that the entries actually would be made in a General Journal, or a columnar special journal, or with a bookkeeping machine or a computer terminal.

GLOSSARY

Accounting system. The business papers, records, reports, and procedures used by a business in recording transactions and reporting their effects.

Accounts Payable Ledger. A subsidiary ledger having an account for each creditor.

Accounts Receivable Ledger. A subsidiary ledger having an account for each customer.

Batch processing. A mode of computer operation in which a program and data are entered in the computer, processed, and removed from the computer before the next program and data are entered.

Cheque Register. A book of original entry for recording cash payments by cheque.

Columnar journal. A book of original entry having columns, each of which is designated as the place for entering specific data about each transaction of a group of similar transactions.

Computer. A complex electronic machine that has the capacity to store a program of instructions and data, process the data rapidly according to the instructions, and prepare reports showing the results of the processing operation.

Computer program. A set of instructions that are entered in a computer and that specify the operations the computer is to perform.

Controlling account. A General Ledger account the balance of which (after posting) equals the sum of the balances of the accounts in a related subsidiary ledger, thereby proving the sum of those subsidiary account balances.

Crossfoot. To add the debit column totals of a journal, add the credit column totals, and then compare the sums to prove that total debits equal total credits.

Foot. To add a column of numbers.

General Ledger. The ledger containing the financial statement accounts of a business.

Online processing. A mode of computer operation in which the program and required data are maintained in the computer so that as new data are entered, they are processed instantly.

Schedule of accounts payable. A list of the balances of all the accounts in the Accounts Payable Ledger that is summed to show the total amount of accounts payable outstanding.

Schedule of accounts receivable. A list of the balances of all the accounts in the Accounts Receivable Ledger that is summed to show the total amount of accounts receivable outstanding.

Special journal. A book of original entry that is designed and used for recording only a specified type of transaction.

Subsidiary ledger. A group of accounts other than General Ledger accounts which shows the details underlying the balance of a controlling account in the General Ledger.

Time sharing. A process by which several users of a computer, each having an input-output device, can input data into a single computer and, as processing time becomes available, have their data processed and transmitted back to their output device.

QUESTIONS FOR CLASS DISCUSSION

1. What are three steps in the operation of an accounting system?
2. How does a columnar journal save posting labor?
3. Most transactions of a merchandising business fall into four groups. What are these four groups?
4. Why should sales to and receipts of cash from charge customers be recorded and posted daily?
5. What functions are served by the Accounts Receivable controlling account?
6. Both credits to customer accounts and credits to miscellaneous accounts are individually posted from a Cash Receipts Journal like that of Illustration 6–2. Why not put both kinds of credits in the same column and thus save journal space?
7. How is a multicolumn journal crossfooted? Why is such a journal cross-footed?
8. How is the equality of a controlling account and its subsidiary ledger accounts maintained?
9. Describe how copies of a company's sales invoices may be used as a Sales Journal.
10. When a general journal entry is used to record a returned charge sale, the credit of the entry must be posted twice. Does this cause the trial balance to be out of balance? Why or why not?
11. How does one tell from which journal a particular amount in a ledger account was posted?
12. How is a schedule of accounts payable prepared? How is it used to prove the balances of the creditor accounts in the Accounts Payable Ledger? What may be substituted for a formal schedule?
13. After all posting is completed, the balance of the Accounts Receivable controlling account does not agree with the sum of the balances in the Accounts Receivable Ledger. If the trial balance is in balance, where is the error apt to be?
14. Are computerized accounting systems used by small businesses?
15. What are some of the ways data can be entered into a computer?

MULTIPLE CHOICE

1. The bookkeeper of a company using a one-column Purchases Journal made an error in totaling the journal's column. The existence of this error is most apt to be discovered:

    a. When the Purchases Journal is posted to the General Ledger.
    b. When the trial balance is prepared.
    c. When the total of the schedule of accounts payable is compared with the balance of the Accounts Payable account.
    d. When the creditors receive their payments.
    e. At none of these times.

2. The bookkeeper of a company using a one-column Sales Journal recorded a $10 credit sale as a $100 credit sale. The existence of this error is most apt to be discovered:

    a. When the Sales Journal is crossfooted.
    b. When the trial balance is prepared.
    c. When the total of the schedule of accounts receivable is compared with the balance of the Accounts Receivable account.
    d. When the customers receive their month-end statements.
    e. At none of these times.

3. If a bookkeeper correctly recorded a $25 sale in a Sales Journal but posted it to the customer's account as a $250 sale, the error is most apt to be discovered:

    a. When the customer receives his month-end statement.
    b. When the trial balance is prepared.
    c. When the schedule of accounts receivable is prepared.
    d. When the Sales Journal is crossfooted.
    e. At some other time.

4. If the bookkeeper correctly posted a sales return recorded in the General Journal to the Accounts Receivable controlling account and to the customer's account but failed to post to the Sales Returns and Allowances account, the error is most apt to be discovered:

    a. When the balance of the Sales Returns and Allowances account is determined.
    b. When the trial balance is prepared.
    c. When the schedule of accounts receivable is prepared.
    d. When the customer receives his month-end statement.
    e. At some other time.

5. If a bookkeeper recorded an $80 sale in the Sales Journal as an $800 sale, the error is most apt to be discovered:

    a. When the Sales Journal is crossfooted.
    b. When the trial balance is prepared.
    c. When the schedule of accounts receivable is prepared.

    d.   When the customer receives his month-end statement.

    e.   At some other time.

6. The use of an Accounts Payable controlling account:

    a.   Reduces the number of accounts in the subsidiary ledger.

    b.   Reduces the total number of accounts maintained.

    c.   Reduces the number of columns in the journals.

    d.   Reduces the number of accounts in the General Ledger.

    e.   Does none of these things.

7. The Accounts Receivable controlling account in the General Ledger:

    a.   Shows the total amount owed by all customers when posting is complete.

    b.   Helps keep the General Ledger a balancing ledger in which debits equal credits.

    c.   Offers a means of proving the accuracy of the customer account balances.

    d.   Does all of the foregoing.

    e.   Does none of the foregoing.

8. A set of computer instructions for processing data is a:

    a.   Working paper.

    b.   Peripheral unit.

    c.   Computer model.

    d.   Computer program.

    e.   None of the above.

9. The processing of data without human intervention is known as:

    a.   General accounting processing.

    b.   Objectivity processing.

    c.   Automated data processing.

    d.   Internal auditing.

    e.   Intangible data processing.

MINI DISCUSSION CASE

Case 6–1   Two students were discussing the similarities and dissimilarities of manual and computerized accounting systems. Their discussion focused on the following:

a.   Recording of data—use of specialized journals, etc.

b.   Processing of data—posting, etc.

c.   Necessity and function of trial balance.

d.   Problems of tracing entries in connection with verification and tracing of errors.

Required:

Present your comparison of the two systems focusing on the four areas given in the case.

CLASS EXERCISES

Exercise 6–1   A company that uses a Sales Journal, a Purchases Journal, a Cash Receipts Journal, a Cash Disbursements Journal, and a General Journal such as the ones described in this chapter completed the following transactions. List the transactions by letter and opposite each letter give the name of the journal in which the transaction should be recorded.

a.   A customer returned the merchandise sold for cash; a cheque was issued.
b.   Paid a creditor.
c.   Sold merchandise for cash.
d.   Sold merchandise on credit.
e.   Purchased merchandise on credit.
f.   Purchased office supplies on credit.
g.   Gave a customer credit for merchandise purchased on credit and returned.
h.   A customer paid for merchandise previously purchased on credit.
i.   Purchased office equipment on credit.
j.   Returned merchandise purchased on credit.
k.   Recorded adjusting and closing entries.

Exercise 6–2   A company uses a Sales Journal, a Purchases Journal, a Cash Receipts Journal, a Cash Disbursements Journal, and a General Journal. The following transactions occurred during the month of May.

May 1   Purchased merchandise for $12 on credit from B Company.
      6   Sold merchandise to I. May for $25 cash, invoice number 11.
      8   Sold merchandise to J. Clay for $90, terms 2/15, n/60 invoice number 12.
     10   Borrowed $15 from the bank by giving a note to the bank.
     13   Sold merchandise to Z. Smith for $60, terms n/30, invoice number 13.
     21   Sold used store equipment to F Company for $100.
     23   Received $88.20 from J. Clay to pay for the purchase of May 8.
     30   Sold merchandise to W. Barley for $75, terms n/30, invoice number 14.

Required:

On a sheet of notebook paper, draw a Sales Journal like the one that appears in Illustration 6–1. Journalize the transactions during May that should be recorded in the Sales Journal.

Exercise 6–3   A company uses a Sales Journal, a Purchases Journal, a Cash Receipts Journal, a Cash Disbursements Journal, and a General Journal. The following transactions occurred during the month of May.

May 1   J. Lay, the owner of the business, invested $20 in the business.
      5   Purchased merchandise for $12 on credit from B Company.
      8   Sold merchandise on credit to R. Dee for $8, subject to a $1 sales discount if paid by the end of the month.
     10   Borrowed $15 from the bank by giving a note to the bank.
     14   Sold merchandise to T. Barnes for $6 cash.
     28   Paid B Company $12 for the merchandise purchased on May 5.
     29   Received $7 from R. Dee to pay for the purchase of May 8.
     31   Paid salaries of $5.

Required:

1. On a sheet of notebook paper, draw a multicolumn Cash Receipts Journal like the one that appears in Illustration 6–2. (Dollar amounts in this exercise are small so that you may use narrow columns.)
2. Journalize the transactions during May that should be recorded in the Cash Receipts Journal.

Exercise 6–4

A company uses a Sales Journal, a Purchases Journal, a Cash Receipts Journal, a Cash Disbursements Journal, and a General Journal. The following transactions occurred during the month of May.

May 1 N. Blake, the owner of the business, invested $30 in the business.
  2 Purchased merchandise for $14 on credit from M Company, terms n/30.
  7 Purchased store supplies from O Company for $3 cash.
  9 Sold merchandise on credit to S. Dye for $10, subject to a $1 sales discount if paid by the end of the month.
  12 Purchased on credit from C Company office supplies for $4 and store supplies for $7, terms n/30.
  19 Sold merchandise to R. Tag for $16 cash.
  30 Paid M Company $14 for the merchandise purchased on May 2.

Required:

1. On a sheet of notebook paper, draw a multicolumn Purchases Journal like the one that appears in Illustration 6–3. (Dollar amounts in this exercise are small so that you may use narrow columns.)
2. Journalize the transactions during May that should be recorded in the Purchases Journal.

Exercise 6–5

A company uses a Sales Journal, a Purchases Journal, a Cash Receipts Journal, a Cash Disbursements Journal, and a General Journal. The following transactions occurred during the month of May.

May 1 Purchased merchandise for $40 on credit from G Company, terms 2/10, n/30.
  3 Purchased merchandise for $50 on credit from K Company, terms 2/15, n/60.
  6 Issued cheque number 4 to A Company to buy store supplies for $10.
  14 Sold merchandise on credit to H. Fine for $80, terms n/30.
  17 Issued cheque number 5 for $35 to repay a note payable to First Bank.
  18 Issued cheque number 6 to K Company to pay the amount due for the purchase of May 3, less the discount.
  31 Issued cheque number 7 to G Company to pay the amount due for the purchase of May 1.
  31 Paid salary of $20 to J. Doaks by issuing cheque number 8.

Required:

1. On a sheet of notebook paper, draw a multicolumn Cash Disbursements Journal like the one that appears in Illustration 6–4. (Dollar amounts in this exercise are small so that you may use narrow columns.)
2. Journalize the transactions during May that should be recorded in the Cash Disbursements Journal.

Exercise 6–6

A company uses a Sales Journal, a Purchases Journal, a Cash Receipts Journal, a Cash Disbursements Journal, and a General Journal. The following transactions occurred during the month of May.

May 1 F. Nifty, the owner of the business, invested $100 in the business.
     7 Purchased merchandise for $85 on credit from G Company, terms 2/10, n/30.
    10 Nifty contributed an automobile worth $500 to the business.
    12 Issued cheque number 4 to A Company to buy store supplies for $10.
    14 Sold merchandise on credit to H. Fine for $80, terms n/30.
    15 Returned $25 of defective merchandise to G Company from the purchase on
        May 7.
    18 Issued cheque number 6 to K Company to pay the $150 due for a purchase of
        April 19.
    25 H. Fine returned $30 of merchandise originally purchased on May 15.
    31 Accrued salaries payable of $20.

Required:

Journalize the transactions during May that should be recorded in the General Journal.

Exercise 6–7   A company uses the following journals: Sales Journal, Purchases Journal, Cash Receipts Journal, Cash Disbursements Journal, and General Journal. On January 12, the company purchased merchandise priced at $10,000, subject to credit terms of 2/10, n/30. On January 22, the company paid the net amount due. However, in journalizing the payment, the bookkeeper debited the net amount to Accounts Payable and failed to record the cash discount. In what journals would the January 12 and the January 22 transactions have been recorded? What procedure is likely to disclose the error in journalizing the January 22 transaction?

Exercise 6–8   At the end of January, the Sales Journal of Comcraft Company appeared as follows:

Sales Journal

Date		Account Debited	Invoice Number	PR	Amount
Jan.	3	Jane Wilkins	253	√	410.00
	8	Rafer Thomas	254	√	680.00
	14	Nancy Hall	255	√	570.00
	23	Jane Wilkins	256	√	190.00
	31	Total			1,850.00

The company had also recorded the return of merchandise with the following entry:

Jan. 20 Sales Returns and Allowances 100.00
             Accounts Receivable—Nancy Hall 100.00
         Customer returned merchandise.

Required:

1. On a sheet of notebook paper open a subsidiary Accounts Receivable Ledger having a T-account for each customer listed in the Sales Journal. Post to the customer accounts the entries of the Sales Journal and also the portion of the general journal entry that affects a customer's account.

2. Open a General Ledger having T-accounts for Accounts Receivable, Sales, and Sales Returns and Allowances. Post the Sales Journal and the portions of the general journal entry that affect these accounts.
3. Prove the subsidiary ledger accounts with a schedule of accounts receivable.

Exercise 6–9

Drafter Company, a company that posts its sales invoices directly and then binds the invoices to make them into a Sales Journal, had the following sales during August:

Aug.	2	Jill Frantz	$ 4,800
	7	Gil Blanken	6,600
	15	James Easton	9,600
	19	Gil Blanken	13,200
	23	James Easton	4,200
	29	George Dahl	9,000
		Total	$47,400

Required:

1. On a sheet of notebook paper open a subsidiary Accounts Receivable Ledger having a T-account for each customer listed above. Post the invoices to the subsidiary ledger.
2. Give the general journal entry to record the end-of-month total of the Sales Journal.
3. Open an Accounts Receivable controlling account and a Sales account and post the general journal entry.
4. Prove the subsidiary Accounts Receivable Ledger with a schedule of accounts receivable.

Exercise 6–10

A company that records credit sales in a Sales Journal and records sales returns in its General Journal made the following errors. List each error by letter, and opposite each letter tell when the error should be discovered:

a. Posted a sales return recorded in the General Journal to the Sales Returns and Allowances account and to the Accounts Receivable account but did not post to the customer's account.
b. Made an addition error in determining the balance of a customer's account.
c. Made an addition error in totaling the Amount column of the Sales Journal.
d. Posted a sales return to the Accounts Receivable account and to the customer's account but did not post to the Sales Returns and Allowances account.
e. Correctly recorded a $200 sale in the Sales Journal but posted it to the customer's account as a $2,000 sale.

Exercise 6–11

Following are the condensed journals of a merchandising concern. The journal column headings are incomplete in that they do not indicate whether the columns are debit or credit columns.

Required:

1. Prepare T-accounts on a sheet of ordinary notebook paper for the following general ledger and subsidiary ledger accounts. Separate the accounts of each ledger group as follows:

General ledger accounts	Accounts receivable ledger accounts
Cash	Customer A
Accounts Receivable	Customer B
Prepaid Insurance	Customer C
Store Equipment	
Notes Payable	Accounts payable ledger accounts
Accounts Payable	Company One
Sales	Company Two
Sales Returns	Company Three
Sales Discounts	
Purchases	
Purchases Returns	
Purchases Discounts	

2. Without referring to any of the illustrations showing complete column headings for the journals, post the following journals to the proper T-accounts.

Sales Journal

Account	Amount
Customer A	3,500
Customer B	5,250
Customer C	7,000
Total	15,750

Purchases Journal

Account	Amount
Company One	4,200
Company Two	4,900
Company Three	5,600
Total	14,700

General Journal

....	Sales Returns	700.00	
	Accounts Receivable—Customer C		700.00
...	Accounts Payable—Company Three	1,050.00	
	Purchases Returns		1,050.00

Cash Receipts Journal

Account	Other Accounts	Accounts Receivable	Sales	Sales Discounts	Cash
Customer A...	...	3,500	...	70	3,430
Cash Sales	...	...	5,075	...	5,075
Notes Payable	7,000	...	...	...	7,000
Cash Sales	...	...	5,775	...	5,775
Customer B...	...	5,250	...	105	5,145
Store Equipment	525	...	...	...	525
	7,525	8,750	10,850	175	26,950

Cash Disbursements Journal

Accounts	Other Accounts	Accounts Payable	Purchases Discounts	Cash
Prepaid Insurance	350	...	...	350
Company Two...	...	4,900	98	4,802
Company Three	...	4,550	91	4,459
Store Equipment...	1,750	...	...	1,750
	2,100	9,450	189	11,361

PROBLEMS

Problem 6–1   Garfield Company completed these transactions during February of the current year:

Feb. 1 Purchased merchandise on credit from Burnaby Company, invoice dated January 31, terms 2/10, n/60, $3,600.
       1 Issued Cheque No. 770 to *The County Reporter* for advertising expense, $385.
       2 Sold merchandise on credit to James Asner, Invoice No. 476, $6,450. (The terms of all credit sales are 2/10, n/60.)
       3 Purchased on credit from Mason Company merchandise, $5,200; store supplies, $250; and office supplies, $200. Invoice dated February 2, terms n/10 EOM.
       5 Received a $50 credit memorandum from Mason Company for unsatisfactory store supplies received on February 3 and returned for credit.
       7 Sold merchandise on credit to Sharon Gable, Invoice No. 477, $5,850.
       8 Purchased store equipment on credit from Casner Company, invoice dated February 8, terms n/10 EOM, $8,800.
      10 Issued Cheque No. 771 to Burnaby Company in payment of its January 31 invoice, less the discount.
      11 Sold merchandise on credit to Darla Tilman, Invoice No. 478, $2,300.
      12 Received payment from James Asner for the February 2 sale, less the discount.
      13 Sold merchandise on credit to James Asner, Invoice No. 479, $3,200.
      15 Issued Cheque No. 772, payable to payroll, in payment of the sales salaries for the first half of the month, $2,230. Cashed the cheque and paid the employees.
      15 Cash sales for the first half of the month, $14,870. (Cash sales are usually recorded daily from the cash register readings. However, they are recorded only twice in this problem to reduce the repetitive transactions.)
      17 Received payment from Sharon Gable for the February 7 sale, less the discount.
      18 Purchased merchandise on credit from Lang Company, invoice dated February 17, terms 2/10, n/60, $3,450.
      19 Borrowed $12,000 from Dodge City Bank by giving a note payable.
      20 Received payment from Darla Tilman for the February 11 sale, less the discount.
      22 Purchased on credit from Casner Company merchandise, $1,400; store supplies, $180; and office supplies, $120. Invoice dated February 21, terms n/10 EOM.
      23 Received payment from James Asner for the February 13 sale, less the discount.
      23 Purchased merchandise on credit from Burnaby Company, invoice dated February 22, terms 2/10, n/60, $2,100.
      24 Received a $250 credit memorandum from Lang Company for defective merchandise received on February 18 and returned.
      27 Issued Cheque No. 773 to Lang Company in payment of its February 17 invoice, less the return and the discount.
      27 Sold merchandise on credit to Sharon Gable, Invoice No. 480, $2,840.
      28 Sold merchandise on credit to Darla Tilman, Invoice No. 481, $1,650.
      28 Issued Cheque No. 774, payable to Payroll, in payment of the sales salaries for the last half of the month, $2,230.
      28 Cash sales for the last half of the month were $15,920.

Required:

1. Open the following general ledger accounts: Cash, Accounts Receivable, Notes Payable, Sales, and Sales Discounts. Also open subsidiary accounts receivable ledger accounts for James Asner, Sharon Gable, and Darla Tilman.
2. Prepare a Sales Journal and a Cash Receipts Journal similar to the ones illustrated in this chapter.
3. Review the transactions of Garfield Company and enter those transactions that should be journalized in the Sales Journal and those that should be journalized in the Cash Receipts Journal. Ignore any transactions that should

be journalized in a Purchases Journal, a Cash Disbursements Journal, or a General Journal.

4. Foot and crossfoot the journals and make the month-end postings.
5. Prepare a trial balance of the General Ledger and prove the subsidiary ledger by preparing a schedule of accounts receivable.

Problem 6–2

On January 31, Garfield Company had a cash balance of $50,000 and a Notes Payable balance of $50,000. The February transactions of Garfield Company included those listed in Problem 6–1.

Required:

1. Open the following general ledger accounts: Cash, Store Supplies, Office Supplies, Store Equipment, Notes Payable, Accounts Payable, Purchases, Purchases Returns and Allowances, Purchases Discounts, Advertising Expense, and Sales Salaries Expense. Enter the January 31 balances of Cash and Notes Payable ($50,000 each).
2. Open subsidiary accounts payable ledger accounts for Casner Company, Lang Company, Mason Company, and Burnaby Company.
3. Prepare a General Journal, a Purchases Journal, and a Cash Disbursements Journal similar to the ones illustrated in this chapter.
4. Review the February transactions of Garfield Company and enter those transactions that should be journalized in the General Journal, the Purchases Journal, or the Cash Disbursements Journal. Ignore any transactions that should be journalized in a Sales Journal or Cash Receipts Journal.
5. Foot and crossfoot the journals and make the month-end postings.
6. Prepare a trial balance and a schedule of accounts payable.

Problem 6–3

(If the working papers that accompany this text are not being used, omit this problem.)

It is July 20 and you have just taken over the accounting work of Nevada Company, a concern operating with annual accounting periods that end each June 30. The company's previous accountant journalized its transactions through July 19 and posted all items that required posting as individual amounts, as an examination of the journals and ledgers in the booklet of working papers will show.

The company completed these transactions beginning on July 20:

July 20 Purchased on credit from Taft Suppliers merchandise, $1,635; store supplies, $240; and office supplies, $165. Invoice dated July 20, terms n/10 EOM.
21 Received a $255 credit memorandum from Norton Company for merchandise received on July 16 and returned for credit.
22 Received a $60 credit memorandum from Taft Suppliers for office supplies received on July 20 and returned for credit.
23 Sold merchandise on credit to Sheila Barnes, Invoice No. 556, $1,845. (Terms of all credit sales are 2/10, n/60.)
24 Issued a credit memorandum to Jack Short for defective merchandise sold on July 19 and returned for credit, $195.
25 Purchased store equipment on credit from Taft Suppliers, invoice dated July 25, terms n/10 EOM, $2,205.

July 26 Issued Cheque No. 815 to Norton Company in payment of its July 16 invoice less the return and the discount.

26 Received payment from Sheila Barnes for the July 16 sale less the discount.

27 Issued Cheque No. 816 to Able Company in payment of its July 17 invoice less a 2% discount.

28 Sold merchandise on credit to Roger Nesland, Invoice No. 557, $2,475.

28 Sold a neighboring merchant a roll of wrapping paper (store supplies) for cash at cost, $90.

29 Received payment from Jack Short for the July 19 sale less the return and the discount.

30 Received merchandise and an invoice dated July 28, terms 2/10, n/60, from Able Company, $2,835.

30 Sally Fowler, the owner of Nevada Company, used Cheque No. 817 to withdraw $3,000 cash from the business for personal use.

31 Issued Cheque No. 818 to David Malone, the company's only sales employee, in payment of his salary for the last half of July, $960.

31 Issued Cheque No. 819 to City Power Company in payment of the July hydro bill, $555.

31 Cash sales for the last half of the month, $29,985. (Cash sales are usually recorded daily but are recorded only twice in this problem in order to reduce the repetitive transactions.)

Required:

1. Record the transactions in the journals provided.

2. Foot and crossfoot the journals and make the month-end postings.

3. Prepare a July 31 trial balance and prove the subsidiary ledgers by preparing schedules of accounts receivable and payable.

Problem 6–4   Motorcraft Company completed these transactions during March of the current year:

Mar. 1 Received merchandise and an invoice dated February 28, terms 2/10, n/60, from Slater Company, $5,250.

2 Sold merchandise on credit to Harry Ost, Invoice No. 425, $2,400. (Terms of all credit sales are 2/10, n/60.)

3 Purchased on credit from Nagle Company merchandise, $5,565; store supplies, $225; and office supplies, $105. Invoice dated March 1, terms n/10 EOM.

5 Sold merchandise on credit to Shirley Tucker, Invoice No. 426, $3,750.

7 Borrowed $15,000 by giving Tempest National Bank a promissory note payable.

8 Purchased office equipment on credit from Intelcomp Company, invoice dated March 7, terms n/10 EOM, $1,875.

9 Sent Slater Company Cheque No. 341 in payment of its February 28 invoice less the discount.

11 Sold merchandise on credit to Kevin Stone, Invoice No. 427, $4,950.

12 Received payment from Harry Ost for the March 2 sale less the discount.

15 Received payment from Shirley Tucker for the March 5 sale less the discount.

15 Received merchandise and an invoice dated March 14, terms 2/10, n/60, from Newland Company, $5,955.

15 Issued Cheque No. 342, payable to Payroll, in payment of sales salaries for the first half of the month, $2,565. Cashed the cheque and paid the employees.

15 Cash sales for the first half of the month, $55,380. (Normally, cash sales are recorded daily; however, they are recorded only twice in this problem to reduce the number of repetitive entries.)

17 Purchased on credit from Nagle Company merchandise, $1,230; store supplies, $135; and office supplies, $90. Invoice dated March 16, terms n/10 EOM.

17 Received a credit memorandum from Newland Company for unsatisfactory merchandise received on March 15 and returned for credit, $255.

18 Received a credit memorandum from Intelcomp Company for office equipment received on March 8 and returned for credit, $390.

Mar. 21 Received payment from Kevin Stone for the sale of March 11 less the discount.
 23 Issued Cheque No. 343 to Newland Company in payment of its invoice of March 14 less the return and the discount.
 24 Sold merchandise on credit to Kevin Stone, Invoice No. 428, $2,505.
 27 Sold merchandise on credit to Shirley Tucker, Invoice No. 429, $2,325.
 29 Issued Cheque No. 344, payable to Payroll, in payment of sales salaries for the last half of the month, $2,565. Cashed the cheque and paid the employees.
 29 Cash sales for the last half of the month, $60,645.
 29 *Foot and crossfoot the journals and make the month-end postings.*

Required:

1. Open the following general ledger accounts: Cash, Accounts Receivable, Store Supplies, Office Supplies, Office Equipment, Notes Payable, Accounts Payable, Sales, Sales Discounts, Purchases, Purchases Returns and Allowances, Purchases Discounts, and Sales Salaries Expense.

2. Open the following accounts receivable ledger accounts: Harry Ost, Kevin Stone, and Shirley Tucker.

3. Open the following accounts payable ledger accounts: Intelcomp Company, Nagle Company, Newland Company, and Slater Company.

4. Enter the transactions in a Sales Journal, a Purchases Journal, a Cash Receipts Journal, a Cash Disbursements Journal, and a General Journal similar to the ones illustrated in this chapter. Post when appropriate and when instructed.

5. Prepare a trial balance and prove the subsidiary ledgers by preparing schedules of accounts receivable and payable.

Problem 6–5   Eagle Grove Company completed these transactions during October of the current year:

Oct. 2 Received merchandise and an invoice dated September 29, terms 2/10, n/60, from Allen Company, $12,600.
 2 Purchased store equipment on credit from Humboldt Company, invoice dated October 1, terms n/10 EOM, $4,700.
 5 Sold merchandise on credit to Charles Beckwith, Invoice No. 388, $5,500. (Terms of all credit sales are 2/10, n/60.)
 6 Sold merchandise on credit to Janis Shoop, Invoice No. 389, $7,100.
 8 Cash sales for the week ended October 8, $14,800.
 8 Issued Cheque No. 490 to The Pink Sheets for advertising, $400.
 9 Sold merchandise on credit to Bob Hodges, Invoice No. 390, $3,200.
 9 Issued Cheque No. 491 to Allen Company in payment of its September 29 invoice less the discount.
 11 Purchased on credit from Transfer Company merchandise, $3,900; store supplies, $370; and office supplies, $260. Invoice dated October 10, terms n/10 EOM.
 13 Sold unneeded store equipment at cost for cash, $340.
 15 Cash sales for the week ended October 15, $11,500.
 15 Received payment from Charles Beckwith for the sale of October 5 less the discount.
 15 Issued Cheque No. 492, payable to Payroll, in payment of the sales salaries for the first half of the month, $2,600. Cashed the cheque and paid the employees.
 16 Received payment from Janis Shoop for the sale of October 6 less the discount.
 17 Sold merchandise on credit to Bob Hodges, Invoice No. 391, $4,350.
 19 Sold merchandise on credit to Charles Beckwith, Invoice No. 392, $2,500.
 19 Received merchandise and an invoice dated October 18, terms 2/10, n/60, from Lockhart Company, $6,300.
 19 Received payment from Bob Hodges for the sale of October 9 less the discount.

Oct. 20 Issued a credit memorandum to Bob Hodges for defective merchandise sold on October 17 and returned for credit, $450.
22 Cash sales for the week ended October 22, $13,800.
23 Received a $200 credit memorandum from Lockhart Company for defective merchandise received on October 19 and returned for credit.
24 Purchased on credit from Transfer Company merchandise, $2,700; store supplies, $300; and office supplies, $150. Invoice dated October 23, terms n/10 EOM.
25 Received merchandise and an invoice dated October 23, terms 2/10, n/60, from Allen Company, $5,700.
26 Received payment from Bob Hodges for the October 17 sale less the return and the discount.
27 Sold merchandise on credit to Janis Shoop, Invoice No. 393, $1,850.
27 Issued Cheque No. 493 to Lockhart Company in payment of its October 18 invoice, less the return and the discount.
29 Issued Cheque No. 494, payable to Payroll, in payment of the sales salaries for the last half of the month, $2,600.
29 Cash sales for the week ended October 29 were $12,750.
31 *Foot and crossfoot the journals and make the month-end postings.*

Required:

1. Open the following general ledger accounts: Cash, Accounts Receivable, Store Supplies, Office Supplies, Store Equipment, Accounts Payable, Sales, Sales Returns and Allowances, Sales Discounts, Purchases, Purchases Returns and Allowances, Purchases Discounts, Sales Salaries Expense, and Advertising Expense.

2. Open the subsidiary accounts receivable ledger accounts: Charles Beckwith, Bob Hodges, and Janis Shoop.

3. Open these subsidiary accounts payable ledger accounts: Allen Company, Humboldt Company, Lockhart Company, and Transfer Company.

4. Prepare a Sales Journal, a Purchases Journal, a Cash Receipts Journal, a Cash Disbursements Journal, and a General Journal like the ones illustrated in this chapter. Enter the transactions in the journals and post when appropriate and when instructed to do so.

5. Prepare a trial balance and prove the subsidiary ledgers with schedules of accounts receivable and payable.

ALTERNATE PROBLEMS

Problem 6–1A   Hamilton Company completed these transactions during February of the current year:

Mar. 1 Issued Cheque No. 610 to *The Daily Review* for advertising expense, $720.
2 Purchased merchandise on credit from Roch Company, invoice dated March 1, terms 2/10, n/60, $4,350.
3 Sold merchandise on credit to Vickie Bedford, Invoice 570, $7,100. (The terms of all credit sales are 2/10, n/60.)
4 Purchased on credit from Nabors Company merchandise, $4,700; store supplies, $330; and office supplies, $170. Invoice dated March 4, terms n/10 EOM.
6 Sold merchandise on credit to Jerry Ingle, Invoice No. 571, $8,200.
7 Received a $350 credit memorandum from Nabors Company for unsatisfactory store supplies received on March 4 and returned for credit.
9 Purchased store equipment on credit from Bruhl Company, invoice dated March 9, terms n/10 EOM, $11,600.

Mar. 10 Issued Cheque No. 611 to Roch Company in payment of its March 1 invoice, less the discount.
   11 Sold merchandise on credit to Paul Tolo, Invoice No. 572, $3,100.
   13 Received payment from Vickie Bedford for the March 3 sale, less the discount.
   15 Issued Cheque No. 612, payable to payroll, in payment of the sales salaries for the first half of the month, $3,250. Cashed the cheque and paid the employees.
   15 Sold merchandise on credit to Vickie Bedford, Invoice No. 573, $4,900.
   15 Cash sales for the first half of the month, $9,890. (Cash sales are usually recorded daily from the cash register readings. However, they are recorded only twice in this problem to reduce the repetitive transactions.)
   16 Received payment from Jerry Ingle for the February 6 sale, less the discount.
   17 Purchased merchandise on credit from Liggett Company, invoice dated March 16, terms 2/10, n/60, $5,500.
   19 Borrowed $10,000 from First State Bank by giving a note payable.
   21 Received payment from Paul Tolo for the March 11 sale, less the discount.
   22 Received a $200 credit memorandum from Liggett Company for defective merchandise received on March 17 and returned.
   24 Purchased on credit from Bruhl Company merchandise, $2,940; store supplies, $230; and office supplies, $130. Invoice dated March 23, terms n/10 EOM.
   25 Received payment from Vickie Bedford for the March 15 sale, less the discount.
   26 Purchased merchandise on credit from Roch Company, invoice dated March 25, terms 2/10, n/60, $2,600.
   26 Issued Cheque No. 613 to Liggett Company in payment of its March 16 invoice, less the return and the discount.
   28 Sold merchandise on credit to Jerry Ingle, Invoice No. 574, $3,390.
   30 Sold merchandise on credit to Paul Tolo, Invoice No. 575, $2,330.
   31 Issued Cheque No. 614 payable to Payroll, in payment of the sales salaries for the last half of the month, $3,250.
   31 Cash sales for the last half of the month were $13,880.

Required:

1. Open the following general ledger accounts: Cash, Accounts Receivable, Notes Payable, Sales, and Sales Discounts. Also open subsidiary accounts receivable ledger accounts for Vickie Bedford, Jerry Ingle, and Paul Tolo.
2. Prepare a Sales Journal and a Cash Receipts Journal like the ones illustrated in this chapter.
3. Review the transactions of Hamilton Company and enter those transactions that should be journalized in the Sales Journal and those that should be journalized in the Cash Receipts Journal. Ignore any transactions that should be journalized in a Purchases Journal, a Cash Disbursements Journal, or a General Journal.
4. Foot and crossfoot the journals and make the month-end postings.
5. Prepare a trial balance of the General Ledger and prove the subsidiary ledger by preparing a schedule of accounts receivable.

Problem 6–2A   On February 28, Hamilton Company had a cash balance of $20,000 and a Notes Payable balance of $20,000. The March transactions of Hamilton Company included those listed in Problem 6–1A.

Required:

1. Open the following general ledger accounts: Cash, Store Supplies, Office Supplies, Store Equipment, Notes Payable, Accounts Payable, Purchases,

Purchases Returns and Allowances, Purchases Discounts, Advertising Expense, and Sales Salaries Expense. Enter the February 28 balances of Cash and Notes Payable ($20,000 each).

2. Open subsidiary accounts payable ledger accounts for Bruhl Company, Liggett Company, Nabors Company, and Roch Company.

3. Prepare a General Journal, a Purchases Journal, and a Cash Disbursements Journal like the ones illustrated in this chapter.

4. Review the March transactions of Hamilton Company and enter those transactions that should be journalized in the General Journal, the Purchases Journal, or the Cash Disbursements Journal. Ignore any transactions that should be journalized in a Sales Journal or Cash Receipts Journal.

5. Post when appropriate the items that should be posted as individual amounts from the journals.

6. Foot and crossfoot the journals and make the month-end postings.

7. Prepare a trial balance and a schedule of accounts payable.

Problem 6–3A   *(If the working papers that accompany this text are not being used, omit this problem.)*

It is July 20 and you have just taken over the accounting work of Branch Company, a concern operating with annual accounting periods that end each June 30. The company's former accountant journalized its transactions through July 19 and posted all items that required posting as individual amounts, as an examination of the journals and ledgers in the booklet of working papers will show.

The company completed these transactions beginning on July 20:

July 20 Sold merchandise on credit to Sheila Barnes, Invoice No. 556, $5,535. (Terms of all credit sales are 2/10, n/60.)

21 Received a $455 credit memorandum from Norton Company for merchandise received on July 16 and returned for credit.

21 Purchased on credit from Taft Suppliers merchandise, $4,905; store supplies, $720; and office supplies, $495. Invoice dated July 20, terms n/10 EOM.

23 Issued a credit memorandum to Jack Short for defective merchandise sold on July 19 and returned for credit, $295.

24 Received a $180 credit memorandum from Taft Suppliers for office supplies received on July 21 and returned for credit.

24 Purchased store equipment on credit from Taft Suppliers, invoice dated July 23, terms n/10 EOM, $6,615.

25 Sold merchandise on credit to Roger Nesland, Invoice No. 557, $7,425.

26 Issued Cheque No. 815 to Norton Company in payment of its July 16 invoice less the return and the discount.

26 Received payment from Sheila Barnes for the July 16 sale less the discount.

27 Issued Cheque No. 816 to Able Company in payment of its July 17 invoice less a 2% discount.

29 Received merchandise and an invoice dated July 29, terms 2/10, n/60, from Able Company, $8,505.

29 Received payment from Jack Short for the July 19 sale less the return and the discount.

30 Sold a neighboring merchant a carton of computer ribbons (store supplies) for cash at cost, $270.

31 Issued Cheque No. 817 to City Power Company in payment of the July hydro bill, $1,665.

July 31 Issued Cheque No. 818 to Lisa Dow, the company's only sales employee, in payment of her salary for the last half of July, $960.

31 Cash sales for the last half of the month, $34,650. (Cash sales are usually recorded daily but are recorded only twice in this problem in order to reduce the repetitive transactions.)

31 Sally Fowler, the owner of Branch Company, used Cheque No. 819 to withdraw $5,000 cash from the business for personal use.

Required:

1. Record the transactions in the journals provided.
2. Post when appropriate to the customer and creditor accounts and also post any amounts that should be posted as individual amounts to the general ledger accounts.
3. Foot and crossfoot the journals and make the month-end postings.
4. Prepare a July 31 trial balance and prove the subsidiary ledgers by preparing schedules of accounts receivable and payable.

Problem 6–4A   Ottawa Company completed these transactions during December of the current year:

Dec. 1 Borrowed $24,000 by giving World National Bank a promissory note payable.

2 Received merchandise and an invoice dated November 30, terms 2/10, n/60, from Slater Company, $8,400.

3 Purchased on credit from Nagle Company merchandise, $7,300; store supplies, $300; and office supplies, $150. Invoice dated December 2, terms n/10 EOM.

4 Sold merchandise on credit to Harry Ost, Invoice No. 723, $6,200. (Terms of all credit sales are 2/10, n/60.)

6 Purchased office equipment on credit from Intelcomp Company, invoice dated March 5, terms n/10 EOM, $9,700.

8 Sold merchandise on credit to Shirley Tucker, Invoice No. 724, $5,900.

10 Sent Slater Company Cheque No. 580 in payment of its November 30 invoice less the discount.

13 Received merchandise and an invoice dated December 12, terms 2/10, n/60, from Newland Company, $8,600.

14 Received payment from Harry Ost for the December 4 sale less the discount.

15 Issued Cheque No. 581, payable to Payroll, in payment of sales salaries for the first half of the month, $4,800. Cashed the cheque and paid the employees.

15 Cash sales for the first half of the month, $29,800. (Normally, cash sales are recorded daily; however, they are recorded only twice in this problem to reduce the number of repetitive entries.)

16 Sold merchandise on credit to Kevin Stone, Invoice No. 725, $7,250.

17 Purchased on credit from Nagle Company merchandise, $3,650; store supplies, $350; and office supplies, $280. Invoice dated March 16, terms n/10 EOM.

18 Received payment from Shirley Tucker for the December 8 sale less the discount.

20 Received a credit memorandum from Newland Company for unsatisfactory merchandise received on December 13 and returned for credit, $800.

21 Issued Cheque No. 582 to Newland Company in payment of its invoice of December 12 less the return and the discount.

24 Sold merchandise on credit to Kevin Stone, Invoice No. 726, $4,700.

26 Received payment from Kevin Stone for the sale of December 16 less the discount.

26 Received a credit memorandum from Intelcomp Company for office equipment received on December 6 and returned for credit, $500.

27 Sold merchandise on credit to Shirley Tucker, Invoice No. 727, $4,100.

31 Issued Cheque No. 583, payable to Payroll, in payment of sales salaries for the last half of the month, $4,800. Cashed the cheque and paid the employees.

31 Cash sales for the last half of the month, $33,700.

31 Foot and crossfoot the journals and make the month-end postings.

Required:

1. Open the following general ledger accounts: Cash, Accounts Receivable, Store Supplies, Office Supplies, Office Equipment, Notes Payable, Accounts Payable, Sales, Sales Discounts, Purchases, Purchases Returns and Allowances, Purchases Discounts, and Sales Salaries Expense.

2. Open the following accounts receivable ledger accounts: Harry Ost, Kevin Stone, and Shirley Tucker.

3. Open the following accounts payable ledger accounts: Intelcomp Company, Nagle Company, Newland Company, and Slater Company.

4. Enter the transactions in a Sales Journal, a Purchases Journal, a Cash Receipts Journal, a Cash Disbursements Journal, and a General Journal similar to the ones illustrated in this chapter. Post when appropriate and when instructed to do so.

5. Prepare a trial balance and prove the subsidiary ledgers by preparing schedules of accounts receivable and payable.

Problem 6–5A   Dubuque Company completed these transactions during August of the current year:

Aug. 3 Received merchandise and an invoice dated August 2, terms 2/10, n/60, from Allen Company, $17,900.

4 Sold merchandise on credit to Charles Beckwith, Invoice No. 476, $8,100. (Terms of all credit sales are 2/10, n/60.)

5 Issued Cheque No. 520 to *The Daily Times* for advertising, $1,560.

7 Purchased store equipment on credit from Humboldt Company, invoice dated August 5, terms n/10 EOM, $24,200.

7 Sold merchandise on credit to Janis Shoop, Invoice No. 477, $9,300.

8 Cash sales for the week ended August 8, $16,400.

10 Sold merchandise on credit to Bob Hodges, Invoice No. 478, $5,950.

11 Received a credit memorandum from Humboldt Company for the return of defective equipment originally purchased on August 7, $700.

12 Issued Cheque No. 521 to Allen Company in payment of its August 2 invoice less the discount.

12 Sold unneeded store equipment at cost for cash, $480.

14 Received payment from Charles Beckwith for the sale of August 4 less the discount.

15 Cash sales for the week ended August 15, $15,300.

15 Issued Cheque No. 522, payable to Payroll, in payment of the sales salaries for the first half of the month, $3,300. Cashed the cheque and paid the employees.

16 Purchased on credit from Transfer Company merchandise, $7,500; store supplies, $620; and office supplies, $380. Invoice dated August 15, terms n/10 EOM.

17 Received payment from Janis Shoop for the sale of August 7 less the discount.

18 Received merchandise and an invoice dated August 18, terms 2/10, n/60, from Lockhart Company, $11,100.

18 Sold merchandise on credit to Bob Hodges, Invoice No. 479, $8,900.

19 Sold merchandise on credit to Charles Beckwith, Invoice No. 480, $7,850.

20 Received payment from Bob Hodges for the sale of October 10 less the discount.

21 Issued a credit memorandum to Bob Hodges for defective merchandise sold on August 18 and returned for credit, $100.

22 Cash sales for the week ended August 22, $18,300.

23 Received a $300 credit memorandum from Lockhart Company for defective merchandise received on August 18 and returned for credit.

24 Purchased on credit from Transfer Company merchandise, $6,800; store supplies, $220; and office supplies, $280. Invoice dated August 23, terms n/10 EOM.

25 Received merchandise and an invoice dated August 24, terms 2/10, n/60, from Allen Company, $10,200.

Aug. 27   Received payment from Bob Hodges for the August 18 sale less the return and the discount.

      27   Issued Cheque No. 523 to Lockhart Company in payment of its August 18 invoice, less the return and the discount.

      28   Sold merchandise on credit to Janis Shoop, Invoice No. 481, $5,950.

      29   Issued Cheque No. 524, payable to Payroll, in payment of the sales salaries for the last half of the month, $3,300.

      29   Cash sales for the week ended August 29 were $9,750.

      31   *Foot and crossfoot the journals and make the month-end postings.*

Required:

1. Open the following general ledger accounts: Cash, Accounts Receivable, Store Supplies, Office Supplies, Store Equipment, Accounts Payable, Sales, Sales Returns and Allowances, Sales Discounts, Purchases, Purchases Returns and Allowances, Purchases Discounts, Sales Salaries Expense and Advertising Expense.

2. Open the subsidiary accounts receivable ledger accounts: Charles Beckwith, Bob Hodges, and Janis Shoop.

3. Open these subsidiary accounts payable ledger accounts: Allen Company, Humboldt Company, Lockhart Company, and Transfer Company.

4. Prepare a Sales Journal, a Purchases Journal, a Cash Receipts Journal, a Cash Disbursements Journal, and a General Journal like the ones illustrated in this chapter. Enter the transactions in the journals and post when appropriate and when instructed to do so.

5. Prepare a trial balance and prove the subsidiary ledgers with schedules of accounts receivable and payable.

ANALYTICAL AND REVIEW PROBLEMS

Problem 6–1
A&R

     The following problem is designed to test your ability in the use of special journals and subsidiary ledgers. The special journals of E. T. Notea Department Store are reproduced below, followed by a number of representative transactions which occurred during the period. The money columns in the journals are numbered to minimize clerical work in recording each transaction.

Debit	Credit
1	2

Accounts Receivable Debit	Sales Credit						Sales Tax Credit
	Men's Clothing	Women's Clothing	Appliances	Furniture	Bargain Basement	Other Departments	
3	4	5	6	7	8	9	10

Cash Debit	Sales Discounts Debit	Sales Credit						Accounts Receivable Credit	Other Accounts Credit	Sales Tax Credit
		Men's Clothing	Women's Clothing	Appli-ances	Furni-ture	Bargain Basement	Other Departments			
11	12	13	14	15	16	17	18	19	20	21

Purchases Debit						Accounts Payable Credit
Men's Clothing	Women's Clothing	Appliances	Furniture	Bargain Basement	Other Departments	
22	23	24	25	26	27	28

Accounts Payable Debit	Supplies Expense Debit	Other Accounts Debit	Cash Credit
29	30	31	32

Transactions (*Note:* All sales are subject to sales tax of 7%):

	Debit	Credit
a. Purchases of $8,200 on account of Appliances from E. G. Inc.		
b. Sale on account $1,400 of Furniture to Gates Brown.		
c. Sale for cash $1,000 less 5% discount—Appliances.		
d. Collection of account receivable from Cec Oak, $600.		
e. Payment of account payable to J. T. Inglis, $4,200.		
f. Borrowed $25,000 from Great Northern Bank on note payable.		
g. Sale on account $300 to J. C. Snead—Men's Clothing.		
h. Sale for cash of baked goods—$10.		
i. Purchases of $7,500 on account of goods—Bargain basement from C. L. Co.		
j. J. C. Snead returned for credit a shirt that had a flaw—$40.		

Required:

1. Identify each of the journals.
2. Journalize by indicating the column number in the spaces provided after each transaction. For example: Purchase for cash of supplies (immediately expensed.)

Debit	Credit
31	32

3. Indicate how the data in the special journals are posted to various accounts by filling in the spaces provided with the following posting possibilities.
   a. Posted as a *debit* to some general ledger account.
   b. Posted as a *debit* to some subsidiary ledger account.
   c. Posted as a *credit* to some general ledger account.
   d. Posted as a *credit* to some subsidiary ledger account.
   e. Not posted.

Note: The numbers in parenthesis are the identification numbers for the money columns of the special journals. For example: (31) money column.

		Posted as
(00) Total of column (31) Example		a
a.	Total of column (1).	
b.	Detail items of column (3).	
c.	Detail items of column (8).	
d.	Total of column (9).	
e.	Detail items of column (17).	
f.	Total of column (20).	
g.	Total of column (26).	
h.	Detail items of column (27).	
i.	Detail items of column (32).	
j.	Detail items of column (1).	
k.	Total of column (19).	
l.	Detail items of column (18).	
m.	Total of column (29).	
n.	Total of column (5).	
o.	Detail items of column (10).	

PRACTICE SET

BRAVO COMPANY

(If the working papers that accompany this text are not being used, omit this minipractice set.)

Assume it is Monday, June 3, the first business day of the month, and you have just been hired as accountant by Bravo Company, a company that operates with monthly accounting periods. All of the company's accounting work has been completed through the end of May, its ledgers show May 31 balances, and you are ready to begin work by recording the following transactions:

June 3 Purchased on credit from Easton Suppliers merchandise, $3,670; store supplies, $320; and office supplies, $110. Invoice dated June 3, terms n/10 EOM.

4 Sold merchandise on credit to Tisdale Company, Invoice No. 672, $3,700. (The terms of all credit sales are 2/10, n/60.)

4 Issued Cheque No. 812 to Commercial Realty in payment of the June rent, $1,950. (Use two lines to record the transaction. Charge 80% of the rent to Rent Expense, Selling Space, and the balance to Rent Expense, Office Space.)

5 Received a $260 credit memorandum from Goodman Products for merchandise received on May 30 and returned for credit.

5 Issued a $150 credit memorandum to Berry Company for defective merchandise sold on May 31 and returned for credit.

6 Purchased office equipment on credit from Easton Suppliers, invoice dated June 5, terms n/10 EOM, $3,925.

7 Sold store supplies to the merchant next door at cost for cash, $25.

7 Issued Cheque No. 813 to Goodman Products to pay for the $2,360 of merchandise received on May 30 less the return and a 2% discount.

10 Received payment from Berry Company for the sale of May 31 less the return and the discount.

12 Received merchandise and an invoice dated June 11, terms 2/10, n/60, from Settle Brothers, $4,300.

13 Received a $175 credit memorandum from Easton Suppliers for defective office equipment received on June 6 and returned for credit.

14 Received payment from Tisdale Company for the June 4 sale less the discount.

15 Issued Cheque No. 814, payable to Payroll, in payment of sales salaries, $875, and office salaries, $750. Cashed the cheque and paid the employees.

15 Cash sales for the first half of the month, $14,290. (Such sales are normally recorded daily. They are recorded only twice in this problem in order to reduce the number of repetitive transactions.)

17 Received merchandise and an invoice dated June 17, terms 2/10, n/60, from Ulrich Materials, $5,300.

17 Sold merchandise on credit to Nate's Repairs, Invoice No. 673, $2,750.

19 Issued Cheque No. 815 to Settle Brothers in payment of its June 11 invoice less the discount.

19 Sold merchandise on credit to Berry Company, Invoice No. 674, $2,200.

21 Purchased on credit from Easton Suppliers merchandise, $3,330; store supplies, $110; and office supplies, $160. Invoice dated June 20, terms n/10 EOM.

24 Sold merchandise on credit to Mayfield Constructors, Invoice No. 675, $4,165.

25 Issued Cheque No. 816 to Ulrich Materials in payment of its June 17 invoice less the discount.

26 Received merchandise and an invoice dated June 26, terms 2/10, n/60, from Settle Brothers, $2,780.

June 27   Received payment from Nate's Repairs for the June 17 sale less the discount.
     27   Ralph Weber, the owner of Bravo Company, used Cheque No. 817 to withdraw $1,800 from the business for personal use.
     29   Issued Cheque No. 818, payable to Payroll, in payment of sales salaries, $875, and office salaries, $750. Cashed the cheque and paid the employees.
     29   Issued Cheque No. 819 to City Utility in payment of the June hydro bill, $495.
     29   Cash sales for the last half of the month were $15,610.
     29   Foot and crossfoot the journals and make the month-end postings.

Required:

1. Enter the transactions in the journals and post when appropriate and when instructed to do so.
2. Prepare a trial balance in the Trial Balance columns of the work sheet form provided and complete the work sheet using the following information:
    a.   Ending merchandise inventory, $32,440.
    b.   Expired insurance, $340.
    c.   Ending store supplies inventory, $305; and office supplies inventory, $160.
    d.   Estimated depreciation of store equipment, $300; and of office equipment, $200.
3. Prepare a multiple-step classified June income statement and a June 30 classified balance sheet.
4. Prepare and post adjusting and closing entries.
5. Prepare a post-closing trial balance and prove the subsidiary ledgers with schedules of accounts payable and accounts receivable.

Accounting for Assets

PART THREE

Accounting for Cash

7

After studying Chapter 7, you should be able to:

Explain why internal control procedures are needed in a large concern and state the broad principles of internal control.

Describe internal control procedures to protect cash received from cash sales, cash received through the mail, and cash disbursements.

Explain the operation of a petty cash fund and be able to make entries to establish and reimburse a petty cash fund.

Explain why the bank balance and the book balance of cash are reconciled and be able to prepare such a reconciliation.

Tell how recording invoices at net amounts helps gain control over cash discounts taken and be able to account for invoices recorded at net amounts.

Define or explain the words and phrases listed in the chapter Glossary.

Cash has universal usefulness, small bulk for high value, and no convenient identification marks by which ownership may be established. Consequently, in accounting for cash, the procedures for protecting it from fraud and theft are very important. They are called **internal control procedures** and apply to all assets owned by a business and to all phases of its operations.

INTERNAL CONTROL

In a small business, the owner-manager commonly controls the entire operation through personal supervision and direct participation in the activities of the business. For example, he or she commonly buys all the assets, goods, and services to be used in the business. Such a manager also hires and closely supervises all employees, negotiates all contracts, and signs all cheques. As a result, in signing cheques, for example, the manager knows from personal contact and observation that the assets, goods, and services for which the cheques are in payment were received by the business. However, as a business grows, it becomes increasingly difficult to maintain this personal contact. Therefore, at some point it becomes necessary for the manager to delegate responsibilities and rely on internal control procedures rather than personal contact in controlling the operations of the business. A properly designed *internal control system* encourages adherence to prescribed managerial policies. It also promotes operational efficiencies; protects the business assets from waste, fraud, and theft; and ensures accurate and reliable accounting data.

Internal control procedures vary from company to company, depending on such factors as the nature of the business and its size. However, the same broad principles of internal control apply to all companies. These broad principles are described in the following paragraphs.

Responsibilities Should Be Clearly Established

Good internal control necessitates that responsibilities be clearly established and that one person be made responsible for each task. When responsibility is shared and something goes wrong, it is difficult to determine who is at fault. For example, when two salesclerks share the same cash drawer and there is a shortage, it is normally impossible to tell which clerk is at fault. Each will tend to blame the other. Neither can prove that he or she is not responsible. In such a situation, each clerk should be assigned a separate cash drawer or one of the clerks should be given responsibility for making all change.

Adequate Records Should Be Maintained

Good records are an important means of protecting assets and assuring that employees follow prescribed procedures. They also give management reliable information to use in monitoring the operations of the business. For example, if detailed subsidiary records of manufacturing equipment and tools are not maintained, items may disappear without any discrepancy being noticed. And if a comprehensive chart of accounts is not documented carefully and followed precisely, some expenses may be debited to the wrong accounts. As a result, management may never discover that some expenses are excessive.

Numerous forms and internal business papers must be designed and properly used to maintain good internal control. For example, if sales slips are properly designed, sales personnel can record the proper information efficiently and without irritating delays to customers. And if all sales slips are prenumbered and controlled, each salesperson can be held responsible for the sales slips under his or her control. Thus, a salesperson is not apt to make a sale, destroy the sales slip, and pocket the cash.

Assets Should Be Insured and Employees Bonded

Assets should be covered by adequate casualty insurance, and employees who handle cash and negotiable assets should be bonded. Bonding provides a means for recovery if a loss occurs. It also tends to prevent losses, since a bonded employee is less apt to take assets if the employee knows a bonding company must be dealt with when the shortage is revealed.

Record-keeping and Custody Should Be Separated

A fundamental principle of internal control requires that the person who has access to or is responsible for an asset should not maintain the accounting record for that asset. When this principle is observed, the custodian of an asset, knowing that a record of the asset is being kept by another person, is not apt to either misappropriate the asset or waste it; and the record-keeper, who does not have access to the asset, has no reason to falsify the record. Furthermore, if the asset is to be misappropriated and the theft concealed in the records, collusion is necessary.

Responsibility for Related Transactions Should Be Divided

Responsibility for a divisible transaction or a series of related transactions should be divided between individuals or departments in such a manner that the work of one acts as a check on that of another. This does not mean there should be duplication of work. Each employee or department should perform an unduplicated portion. For example, responsibility for placing orders, receiving the merchandise, and paying the vendors should not be given to one individual or department. To do so is to invite laxity in checking the quality and quantity of goods received, and carelessness in verifying the validity and accuracy of invoices. It also invites the purchase of goods for an employee's personal use and the payment of fictitious invoices.

Mechanical Devices Should Be Used Whenever Practicable

Cash registers, cheque protectors, time clocks, and mechanical counters are examples of control devices that should be used whenever practicable. A cash register with a locked-in tape makes a record of each cash sale. A cheque protector, by perforating the amount of a cheque into its face, makes it very difficult to change the amount. A time clock registers the exact time an employee arrived on the job and when the employee departed.

Regular and Independent Reviews

Regardless of how well-designed the internal control system may be, there is a tendency for it to deteriorate over time. Changes in personnel and the stress of time pressures tend to bring about short cuts and omissions. Regular reviews of internal control procedures are necessary to be sure that the procedures are in fact being followed. These reviews should be performed by internal auditors who are not directly involved in operations. From this independent perspective, internal auditors can evaluate the overall efficiency of operations as well as the effectiveness of the internal control system.

Many companies also have audits by external public accountants. After testing the company's financial records, the public accountants give an opinion as to whether the company's financial statements are presented fairly in accordance with *Generally Accepted Accounting Principles* (GAAP). However, before public accountants can decide on how much testing must be done, they first must evaluate the effectiveness of the internal control system.

COMPUTERS AND INTERNAL CONTROL

The broad principles of internal control should be followed whether the accounting system is manual or computerized. However, computers have several important effects on internal control. Perhaps the most obvious is that computers provide much more rapid access to large quantities of information. As a result, management's ability to monitor and control business operations is greatly improved.

Computers Reduce Processing Errors

Computers reduce the number of errors in processing information. Once the data have been entered correctly, the human tendency to make mechanical and mathematical errors is largely eliminated. On the other hand, data entry errors may occur because the process of entering data sometimes appears less logical in a computerized system. Also, the lack of human involvement in later processing may cause data entry errors to go undiscovered.

Computers Allow More Extensive Testing of Records

The regular review and audit of records can include more extensive testing if a computerized system is used. To reduce the cost of testing when manual methods are used, only small samples of data might be tested. But when computers are used to process data, large samples or even complete data files can be reviewed and analyzed.

Computerized Systems May Limit Hard Evidence of Processing Steps

Because many data processing steps are performed by the computer, less hard evidence in the form of written forms and analyses may be available for review. Therefore, internal control may depend more on reviews of the design and operation of the computerized processing system and less on reviews of the documents left behind by the system.

Separation of Duties Must Be Maintained

A common risk with computerized systems is that the separation of critical responsibilities is not maintained. Companies that use computers must have employees with special skills to program and operate the computers. The duties of these employees must be carefully controlled to avoid the risk of fraud. The person who designs and programs the system generally should not also serve as the operator. Control over cash receipts and disbursements should be separated. And cheque-writing should not be controlled by the computer operator. This problem is particularly difficult in small companies.

INTERNAL CONTROL FOR CASH

A good system of internal control for cash should provide adequate procedures for protecting both cash receipts and cash disbursements. In the procedures, three basic principles should always be observed. First, there should be a separation of duties so that the people responsible for handling cash and for its custody are not the same people who keep the cash records. Second, all cash receipts should be deposited in the bank, intact, each day. Third, all payments should be made by cheque. The one exception to the last principle is that small disbursements may be made in cash from a petty cash fund. Petty cash funds are discussed later in this chapter.

The reason for the first principle is that a division of duties necessitates collusion between two or more people if cash is to be embezzled and the theft concealed in the accounting records. The second, requiring that all receipts be deposited intact each day, prevents an employee from making personal use of the money for a few days before depositing it. And if all receipts are deposited intact and all payments made by cheque, the bank records provide a separate and external record of all cash transactions. These bank records are useful in proving the company's own records.

The exact procedures used to achieve control over cash vary from company to company. They depend upon such things as company size, number of employees, cash sources, and so on. Consequently, the following procedures are only illustrative of some that are in use.

Cash from Cash Sales

Cash sales should be rung up on a cash register at the time of each sale. To help ensure that correct amounts are rung up, each register should be placed so that customers can see the amounts rung up. Also, the clerks should be required to ring up each sale before wrapping the merchandise. Finally, each cash register should be designed to provide a permanent, locked-in record of each transaction. In some cases, this is accomplished by a direct connection between the register and a computer. The computer is programmed to accept cash register transactions and enter them in the accounting records. In other cases, the register prints a record of each transaction on a paper tape that is locked inside the register.

Good cash control, as previously stated, requires that custody over cash be separated from record-keeping for cash. For cash sales, this separation begins with the cash register. The salesclerk who has access to the cash in the register should not have access to its locked-in record. At the end of each day, the salesclerk is usually required to count the cash in the register and to turn the cash and its count over to an employee in the cashier's office. The employee in the cashier's office, like the salesclerk, has access to the cash and should not have access to the computerized accounting records (or the register tape if one is used). A third employee, usually from the accounting department, examines the computerized record of register transactions (or the register tape) and compares its daily total with the total cash receipts reported by the cashier's office. If a register tape is used, it becomes the basis for the entry recording cash sales. The accounting department employee has access to the records for cash but does not have access to the actual cash. The salesclerk and the employee from the cashier's office do not have access to the accounting records and cannot take any cash without the shortage being revealed.

Cash Received through the Mail

Control of cash coming in through the mail begins with the person who opens the mail. Preferably, two people should be present when the mail is opened. One of them should make a list in triplicate of the money received. The list should give each sender's name, the purpose for which the money was sent, and the amount. One copy of the list is sent to the cashier with the money. The second copy goes to the bookkeeper. The third copy is kept by the mail clerk. The cashier deposits the money in the bank, and the bookkeeper records the amounts received in the accounting records. Then, if the bank balance is reconciled (discussed later) by a fourth person, errors or fraud by the mail clerk, the cashier, or bookkeeper will be detected. They will be detected because the cash deposited and the records of three people must agree. Furthermore, fraud is impossible, unless there is collusion. The mail clerk must report all receipts or customers will question their account balances. The cashier must deposit all receipts because the bank balance must agree with the bookkeeper's cash balance. The bookkeeper and the person reconciling the bank balance do not have access to cash and, therefore, have no opportunity to withhold any.

Cash Disbursements

It is important to gain control over cash from sales and cash received through the mail. However, most large embezzlements have not involved cash receipts but have been accomplished through the payment of fictitious invoices. Consequently, procedures for controlling cash disbursements are equally as important and sometimes more important than those for cash receipts.

To gain control over cash disbursements, all disbursements should be made by cheque, excepting those from petty cash. If authority to sign cheques is delegated to some person other than the business owner, that person should not have access to the accounting records. This helps prevent a fraudulent disbursement being made and concealed in the accounting records.

In a small business, the owner-manager usually signs cheques and normally knows from personal contact that the items to be paid for were received by the business. However, this is impossible in a large business. In a large business, internal control procedures must be substituted for personal contact. The procedures tell the person who signs cheques that the obligations for which the cheques were written are proper obligations, properly incurred, and should be paid. Often these procedures take the form of a *voucher system.*

THE VOUCHER SYSTEM AND CONTROL

A voucher system helps gain control over cash disbursements as follows: (1) It permits only authorized individuals to incur obligations that will result in cash disbursements. (2) It establishes procedures for incurring such obligations and for their verification, approval, and recording. (3) It permits cheques to be issued only in payment of properly verified, approved, and recorded obligations. Finally (4), it requires that every obligation be recorded at the time it is incurred and every purchase be treated as an independent transaction, complete in itself. It requires this even though a number of purchases may be made from the same company during a month or other billing period.

When a voucher system is in use, control over cash disbursements begins with the incurrence of obligations that will result in cash disbursements. Only specified departments and individuals are authorized to incur such obligations, and the kind each may incur is limited. For example, in a large store, only the purchasing department may incur obligations by purchasing merchandise. However, to gain control, the purchasing-receiving-and-paying procedures are divided among several departments. They are the departments requesting that merchandise be purchased, the purchasing department, the receiving department, and the accounting department. To coordinate and control the responsibilities of these departments, business papers are used. A list of the papers follows, and an explanation of each will show how a large concern may gain control over cash disbursements resulting from the purchase of merchandise.

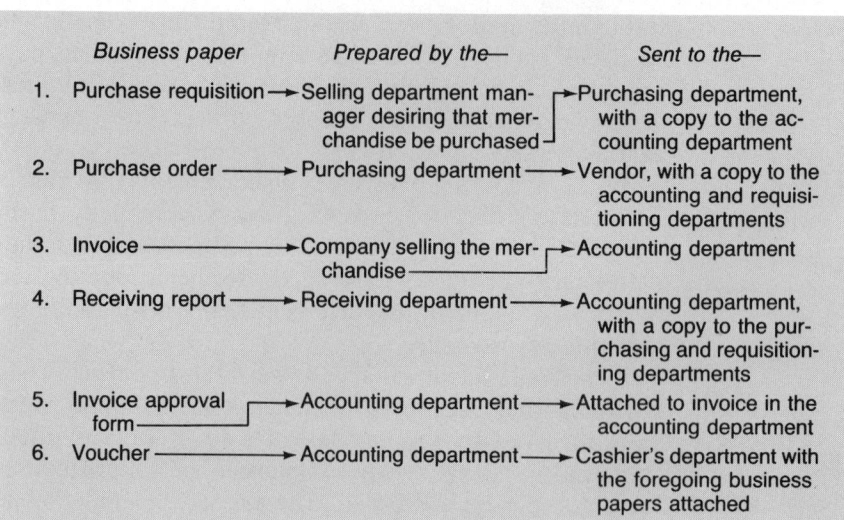

Purchase Requisition

The department managers in a large store cannot be permitted to place orders directly with supply sources. If each manager were permitted to deal directly with wholesalers and manufacturers, the amount of merchandise purchased and the resulting liabilities could not be controlled. Therefore, to gain control over purchases and resulting liabilities, department managers are commonly required to place all orders through the purchasing department. In such cases, the function of the several department managers in the purchasing procedure is to inform the purchasing department of their needs. Each manager performs this function by preparing in triplicate and signing a business paper called a *purchase requisition*. On the requisition, the manager lists the merchandise needs of his or her department. The original and a duplicate copy of the purchase requisition are sent to the purchasing department. The third copy is retained by the requisitioning department as a check on the purchasing department.

Purchase Order

A *purchase order* is a business form used by the purchasing department in placing an order with a manufacturer or wholesaler. It authorizes the supplier to ship the merchandise ordered and takes the place of a typewritten letter placing the order. On receipt of a purchase requisition from a selling department, the purchasing department prepares four or more copies of the purchase order. The copies are distributed as follows:

Copy 1, the original copy, is sent to the supplier as a request to purchase and as authority to ship the merchandise listed.

Copy 2, with a copy of the purchase requisition attached, is sent to the accounting department where it will ultimately be used in approving the invoice of the purchase for payment.

Copy 3 is sent to the department issuing the requisition to acknowledge the requisition and tell the action taken.

Copy 4 is retained on file by the purchasing department.

Invoice

An *invoice* is an itemized statement of goods bought and sold. It is prepared by the seller or *vendor,* and to the seller it is a sales invoice. However, when the same invoice is received by the buyer or *vendee,* it becomes a purchase invoice to the buyer. Upon receipt of a purchase order, the manufacturer or wholesaler receiving the order ships the ordered merchandise to the buyer and mails a copy of the invoice covering the shipment. The goods are delivered to the buyer's receiving department. The invoice is sent directly to the buyer's accounting department.

Receiving Report

Most large companies maintain a special department assigned the duty of receiving all merchandise or other assets purchased. As each shipment is received, counted, and checked, the receiving department prepares four or more copies of a *receiving report.* On this report are listed the quantity, description, and condition of the items received. The original copy is sent to the accounting department. The second copy is sent to the department that requisitioned the merchandise. The third copy is sent to the purchasing department. The fourth copy is retained on file in the receiving department. The copies sent to the purchasing and requisitioning departments act as notification of the arrival of the goods.

Invoice Approval Form

When the receiving report arrives in the accounting department, it has in its possession copies of the—

1. Requisition listing the items that were to be ordered.
2. Purchase order that lists the merchandise actually ordered.
3. Invoice showing quantity, description, unit price, and total of the goods shipped by the seller.
4. Receiving report that lists quantity and condition of the items received.

With the information of these papers, the accounting department is in a position to approve the invoice for entry on the books and ultimate payment. In approving the invoice, the accounting department checks and compares the information on all the papers. To facilitate the checking procedure and to ensure that no step is omitted, an *invoice approval form* is commonly used. This may be a separate business paper that is attached to the invoice, or the information shown in Illustration 7–1, may be stamped directly on the invoice with a rubber stamp.

As each step in the checking procedure is completed, the clerk making the check initials the invoice approval form. Initials in each space on the form indicate:

1. Requisition check . . . . The items on the invoice agree with the requisition and were requisitioned.
2. Purchase order check . . . . The items on the invoice agree with the purchase order and were ordered.
3. Receiving report check . . . . The items on the invoice agree with the receiving report and were received.
4. Invoice check:
   Price approval . . . . The invoice prices are the agreed prices.
   Calculations . . . . The invoice has no mathematical errors.
   Terms . . . . The terms are the agreed terms.

Illustration 7–1

INVOICE APPROVAL FORM

Purchase order number _____

Requisition check _____

Purchase order check _____

Receiving report check _____

Invoice check:

  Price approval _____

  Calculations_____

  Terms_____

Approved for payment:

_____

The Voucher

When a voucher system is in use, after the invoice is checked and approved, a *voucher* is prepared. A voucher is a business paper on which a transaction is summarized, its correctness certified, and its recording and payment approved. Vouchers vary somewhat from company to company. However, in general, they are so designed that the invoice, bill, or other documents from which they are prepared are attached to and folded inside the voucher. This makes for ease in filing. The inside of a voucher is shown in Illustration 7–2, and the outside in Illustration 7–3. The preparation of a voucher is a simple task requiring only that a clerk enter the required information in the proper blank spaces on a voucher form. The information is taken from the invoice and its supporting documents. After the voucher is completed, the invoice and its supporting documents are attached to and folded inside the voucher. The voucher is then sent to the desk of the chief clerk or auditor who makes an additional check, approves the accounting distribution (the accounts to be debited), and approves the voucher for recording.

After being approved and recorded, a voucher is filed until its due date, when it is sent to the office of the company cashier or other disbursing officer for payment. Here the person responsible for issuing cheques depends upon the approved voucher and its signed supporting documents to verify that the obligation is a proper obligation, properly incurred, and should be paid. For example, the purchase requisition and purchase order attached to the voucher confirm that the purchase was authorized. The receiving report shows that the items were received, and the invoice

Illustration 7–2   Inside of a Voucher

Voucher No. _767_

VALLEY SUPPLY COMPANY
Halifax, Nova Scotia

Date ___Oct. 1, 19--___
Pay to ___A.B. Seay Wholesale Company___
City ___Digby___   Province ___Nova Scotia___

For the following: (attach all invoices and supporting papers)

Date of Invoice	Terms	Invoice Number and Other Details	Amount
Sept. 30, 19--	2/10, n/60	Invoice No. C-11756	800.00
		Less Discount	16.00
		Net Amount Payable	784.00

Payment Approved

9. O. Neal
Auditor

approval form verifies that the invoice was checked for errors. As a result, there is little chance for fraud, unless all the documents were stolen and the signatures forged, or there was collusion.

THE VOUCHER SYSTEM AND EXPENSES

Under a voucher system, to gain control over disbursements, every obligation that will result in a cash disbursement must be approved for payment and recorded as a liability at the time it is incurred. This includes all expenses. As a result, for example, when the monthly telephone bill is received, it is verified and any long-distance calls are approved. A voucher is then prepared, and the telephone bill is attached to and folded inside the voucher. The voucher is then recorded, and a cheque is issued in its payment, or the voucher is filed for payment at a later date.

Illustration 7–3   Outside of a Voucher

ACCOUNTING DISTRIBUTION		
Account Debited	Amount	
Purchases	800.00	
Transportation-In		
Store Supplies		
Office Supplies		
Sales Salaries		

Voucher No. _767_

Due date _____ _October 6, 19--_

Pay to __A. B. Seay Wholesale Co.__
City __Digby__
Province __Nova Scotia__

Total Vouch. Pay.Cr.	800.00

Summary of charges:
  Total charges _____ 800.00
  Discount _____ 16.00
  Net payment _____ 784.00

Record of payment:
  Paid _____
  Cheque No. _____

Requiring that an expense be approved for payment and recorded as an expense and a liability at the time it is incurred helps ensure that every expense payment is approved when information for its approval is available. Often invoices, bills, and statements for such things as equipment repairs are received weeks after the work is done. If no record of the repairs exists, it is difficult at that time to determine whether the invoice or bill is a correct statement of the amount owed. Also, if no records exist, it is possible for a dishonest employee to arrange with an outsider for more than one payment of an obligation, for payment of excessive amounts, and for payment for goods and services not received, all with kickbacks to the dishonest employee.

RECORDING VOUCHERS

Normally, a company large enough to use a voucher system will use a computer in recording its transactions. Consequently, for this reason and also because the primary purpose of this discussion is to describe the control techniques of a voucher system, a pen-and-ink system of recording vouchers is not described here. However, such a system is described in the Appendix at the end of this chapter.

THE PETTY CASH FUND

A basic principle in controlling cash disbursements is that all such disbursements be made by cheque. However, an exception to this rule is made for petty cash disbursements. Every business must make many small payments for items such as postage, express charges, telegrams, and small items of supplies. If each such payment is made by cheque, many cheques for immaterial amounts are written. This is both time consuming and expensive. Therefore, to avoid writing cheques for small amounts, a petty cash fund is established, and such payments are made from this fund.

When a petty cash fund is established, an estimate is made of the total small payments likely to be disbursed during a short period, usually not more than a month. A cheque is drawn and debited to the Petty Cash account for an amount slightly in excess of this estimate. The cheque is cashed, and the money is turned over to a member of the office staff who is designated **petty cashier** and who is responsible for the petty cash and for making payments therefrom.

The petty cashier usually keeps the petty cash in a locked box in the office safe. As each disbursement is made, a **petty cash receipt,** Illustration 7–4, is signed by the person receiving payment and is placed with the

Illustration 7–4

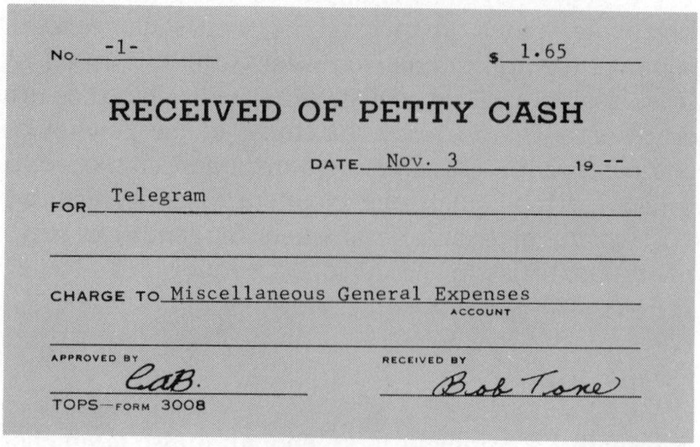

No. -1- $ 1.65

RECEIVED OF PETTY CASH

DATE Nov. 3   19 --

FOR Telegram

CHARGE TO Miscellaneous General Expenses
                              ACCOUNT

APPROVED BY   RECEIVED BY
CaB.   Bob Tone
TOPS—FORM 3008

Courtesy Tops Business Forms

remaining money in the petty cashbox. Under this system, the petty cashbox should always contain paid petty cash receipts and money equal to the amount of the fund.

Each disbursement reduces the money and increases the sum of the receipts in the petty cashbox. When the money is nearly exhausted, the fund is reimbursed. To reimburse the fund, the petty cashier presents the receipts for petty cash payments to the company cashier. The company cashier stamps each receipt ''paid'' so that it may not be reused, retains the receipts, and gives the petty cashier a cheque for their sum. When this cheque is cashed and the proceeds returned to the petty cashbox, the money in the box is restored to its original amount and the fund is ready to begin anew the cycle of its operations.

In making petty cash payments, some companies have the petty cashier enter each payment in a Petty Cash Record. This is a book in which the various petty cash payments are entered in columns according to the expense or other accounts to be debited when the fund is reimbursed. The columns have such headings as Postage, Transportation-In, Miscellaneous General Expenses, Office Supplies, and so forth. The Petty Cash Record is not a book of original entry. It is only a supplementary record, the column totals of which provide information as to the amounts to be debited to the various accounts when the petty cash fund is reimbursed.

Although some companies use a Petty Cash Record, many companies are of the opinion that such a record is unnecessary. In the latter companies, when the petty cash fund is to be reimbursed, the petty cashier sorts the paid petty cash receipts into groups according to the expense or other accounts to be debited in recording payments from the fund. Each group is then totaled, and the totals are used in making the reimbursing entry. This method is assumed in the illustration that follows.

PETTY CASH FUND ILLUSTRATED

To avoid writing numerous cheques for small amounts, a company established a petty cash fund on November 1, designating one of its office clerks, Ned Fox, petty cashier. A $75 cheque was drawn, cashed, and the proceeds turned over to the clerk. The entry to record the cheque is shown in Illustration 7–5. The effect of the entry was to transfer $75 from the regular Cash account to the Petty Cash account.

Observe that the entry transfers $75 from the regular Cash account to the Petty Cash account. Also remember that the Petty Cash account is debited when the fund is established but is not debited or credited again unless the size of the fund is changed. If the fund is exhausted and reimbursements occur too often, the fund should be increased. This results in an additional debit to the Petty Cash account and a credit to the regular Cash account for the amount of the increase. If the fund is too large, part of its cash should be returned to general cash.

Illustration 7–5

		Cash Disbursements Journal				
Date	Ch. No.	Payee	Account Debited	P R	Other Accts. Debit	Cash Credit
Nov. 1	58	Ned Fox, Petty Cashier	Petty Cash		75.00	75.00

During November, the petty cashier of this illustration made several payments from the petty cash fund, each time taking a receipt from the person receiving payment. Then on November 27, the petty cashier made a $26.50 payment for repairs to an office typewriter and realized there was not sufficient cash in the fund for another payment. Consequently, the petty cash receipts were summarized and totaled as shown in Illustration 7–6. The summary and the petty cash receipts were then given to the company cashier in exchange for a $71.30 cheque to reimburse the fund. The petty cashier cashed the cheque, put the $71.30 proceeds in the petty cash box, and was ready to begin again to make payments from the fund.

The reimbursing cheque was recorded in the Cash Disbursements Journal with the second entry of Illustration 7–7. Information for this entry came from the petty cashier's payments summary. Note that its debits record the petty cash payments. Such an entry is necessary to get the debits into the accounts. Consequently, petty cash must be reimbursed at the end of each accounting period, as well as at any time the money in the fund is low. If the fund is not reimbursed at the end of

Illustration 7–6 Summary of Petty Cash Payments

Miscellaneous general expense:		
Nov. 2, washing windows	$10.00	
Nov. 17, washing windows	10.00	
Nov. 27, typewriter repairs	26.50	$46.50
Transportation-in:		
Nov. 5, delivery of merchandise purchased	$ 6.75	
Nov. 20, delivery of merchandise purchased	8.30	15.05
Delivery expense:		
Customer's package delivered		5.00
Office supplies:		
Nov. 15, purchased paper clips		4.75
Total		$71.30

Illustration 7–7

Cash Disbursements Journal

Date	Ch. No.	Payee	Account Debited	P R	Other Accts. Debit	Cash Credit
Nov. 1	58	Ned Fox, Petty Cashier	Petty Cash		75.00	75.00
Nov. 27	106	Ned Fox, Petty Cashier	Transportation-In ..... Misc. Gen. Expense .. Office Supplies .... Delivery Expense		15.05 46.50 4.75 5.00	71.30

each accounting period, the asset petty cash is overstated and the expenses and assets of the petty cash payments are understated on the financial statements.

Occasionally, at the time of a petty cash expenditure, a petty cashier will forget to secure a receipt, and by the time the fund is reimbursed, will have forgotten the expenditure. This causes the fund to be short. If for whatever reason the petty cash fund is short at reimbursement time, the shortage is recorded as an expense in the reimbursing entry with a debit to the *Cash Over and Short Account* discussed in the next section.

CASH OVER AND SHORT

Regardless of care exercised in making change, customers are sometimes given too much change or are shortchanged. As a result, at the end of a day, the actual cash from a cash register is commonly not equal to the cash sales "rung up" on the register. For example, if actual cash as counted is $557 but the register shows cash sales of $556, the entry in general journal form to record sales and the overage is:

Nov.	23	Cash	557.00	
		Cash Over and Short		1.00
		Sales		556.00
		Day's cash sales and overage.		

If, on the other hand, cash is short, the entry in general journal form to record sales and the shortage would look like the following:

Nov.	24	Cash	621.00	
		Cash Over and Short	4.00	
		Sales		625.00
		Day's cash sales and shortage.		

Over a period of time, cash overages should about equal cash shortages. However, customers are more prone to report instances in which they are given too little change. Therefore, amounts of cash short are apt to be greater than amounts of cash over. Consequently, the Cash Over and Short account normally reaches the end of the accounting period with a debit balance. When it does so, the balance represents an expense. The expense may appear on the income statement as a separate item in the general and administrative expense section. Or if the amount is small, it may be combined with other miscellaneous expenses and appear as part of the item, miscellaneous expenses. When Cash Over and Short reaches the end of the period with a credit balance, the balance represents revenue and normally appears on the income statement as part of the item, miscellaneous revenues.

[handwritten margin notes:]
1) Acc is Dr. bal
Its an Expense
2) Acc is Cr bal.
go under
misc. revenue

RECONCILING THE BANK BALANCE

Once every month banks provide each commercial depositor with a bank statement showing the activity in the depositor's account during the month. Different banks use a variety of different formats for their bank statements. However, all of them include in one place or another: (1) the balance of the depositor's account at the beginning of the month, (2) deposits and any other amounts added to the account, (3) cheques and any other amounts deducted from the account, and (4) the account balance at the end of the month, according to the records of the bank. A typical bank statement is shown in Illustration 7–8.

Note that the changes in the account are summarized in part A of Illustration 7–8. Specific debits and credits to the account (other than canceled cheques) are listed in part B. All canceled cheques are listed in numerical order in part C. And the daily account balances are shown in part D.

Banks usually mail the bank statement to the depositor each month. Included in the envelope with the statement are the depositor's *canceled cheques* and any debit or credit memoranda that have affected the account. The cheques returned are the ones that bank has paid during the month.

Illustration 7–8

First National Bank   VICTORIA, BRITISH COLUMBIA

	ACCOUNT NUMBER	DATE OF THIS STATEMENT	DATE OF LAST STATEMENT	PAGE NO.
01	494 504 2	31/10/--	30/9/--	1

First National Bank
VICTORIA,
BRITISH COLUMBIA

VALLEY COMPANY
1300 FALCON LEDGE
VICTORIA, B.C.

```
        BALANCE OF PREVIOUS STATEMENT ON 30/9/-- .......      1,609.58
            5 DEPOSITS AND OTHER CREDITS TOTALING .....       1,155.00
           10 CHEQUES AND OTHER DEBITS TOTALING .......         723.00
              SERVICE CHARGE AMOUNT ...................            .00
              INTEREST AMOUNT AT 5.2500% .............            8.42
   A    CURRENT BALANCE AS OF THIS STATEMENT ..........       2,050.00

        AVERAGE BALANCE AS OF THIS STATEMENT ..........       1,924.95
        TOTAL INTEREST PAID YEAR TO DATE .............          124.00
```

```
        CHEQUING ACCOUNT TRANSACTIONS °°°°°°°°°°°°°°°°°°°°°°°°°°°°°°°°°°°
        .DATE............AMOUNT.....TRANSACTION DESCRIPTION...........
          2/10         240.00+      DEPOSIT
          9/10         180.00+      DEPOSIT
         12/10          23.00-      CHARGE FOR PRINTING NEW CHEQUES
   B     15/10         100.00+      DEPOSIT
         16/10         150.00+      DEPOSIT
         23/10         485.00+      NOTE COLLECTION LESS FEE
         25/10          30.00-      NSF CHEQUE AND NSF CHARGE
         31/10           8.42+      INTEREST PAID
```

```
        .DATE.. CHEQUE NO........AMOUNT..DATE.. CHEQUE NO.........AMOUNT
          3/10   119              55.00 16/10   123               25.00
         19/10   120             200.00 23/10   125*              10.00
   C     10/10   121             120.00 26/10   127*              50.00
         14/10   122              75.00 29/10   128              135.00
        *INDICATES A SKIP IN CHEQUE NUMBER SEQUENCE
```

```
        DAILY BALANCE SUMMARY °°°°°°°°°°°°°°°°°°°°°°°°°°°°°°°°°°°°°°°°°°°°°
        .DATE.......BALANCE .DATE........BALANCE .DATE.......BALANCE
          1/10      1,609.58  12/10      1,831.58  23/10     2,256.58
          2/10      1,849.58  14/10      1,756.58  25/10     2,226.58
   D      3/10      1,794.58  15/10      1,856.58  26/10     2,176.58
          9/10      1,974.58  16/10      1,981.58  29/10     2,041.58
         10/10      1,854.58  19/10      1,781.58  31/10     2,050.00
```

They are called canceled cheques because they have been stamped or punched to show that they have been paid. Other deductions that may appear on the bank statement include withdrawals through automatic teller machines (ATM withdrawals) and periodic payments arranged in advance by the depositor. In addition, the bank may deduct from the depositor's account amounts for service charges and fees, items deposited that are uncollectible, and amounts to correct previous errors. The bank notifies the depositor of each such deduction with a debit memorandum. A copy of each memorandum is included with the monthly statement.

In addition to deposits made by the depositor, the bank may add amounts to the depositor's account. Examples of additions would be amounts the bank has collected for the depositor and corrections of previous errors. A credit memorandum is used to notify the depositor of any such additions.

Another addition might be for interest the depositor has earned. Some chequing accounts pay the depositor interest based on the average cash balance maintained in the account. The bank calculates the amount of interest earned and credits it to the depositor's account each month. Note in Illustration 7–8 that the bank has credited $8.42 of interest to the account of Valley Company. The methods used to calculate interest are discussed in the next chapter.

If all receipts are deposited intact and all payments, other than petty cash payments, are drawn from the chequing account, the bank statement becomes a device for proving the depositor's cash records. The proof normally begins with the preparation of a *reconciliation of the bank balance*.

Need for Reconciling the Bank Balance

Normally, when the bank statement arrives, the balance of cash as shown by the statement does not agree with the balance in the depositor's accounting records. Consequently, in order to prove the accuracy of both the depositor's records and those of the bank, it is necessary to *reconcile* and account for any differences between the two balances.

Numerous things may cause the bank statement balance to differ from the depositor's book balance of cash. Some are:

1. *Outstanding cheques.* These are cheques that have been drawn by the depositor and deducted on the depositor's records but have not reached the bank for payment and deduction.
2. *Unrecorded deposits.* Businesses often make deposits at the end of each business day, after the bank has closed. These deposits are made in the bank's night depository and are not recorded by the bank until the next business day. Consequently, if a deposit is placed in the night depository the last day of the month, it does not appear on the bank statement for that month.

3. *Charges for uncollectible items and for service.* Sometimes, a company deposits a customer's cheque that is found to be uncollectible. Usually, the problem is nonsufficient funds in the customer's account to cover the amount of the cheque. Thus, the cheque is called a nonsufficient funds (NSF) cheque. The bank first credits the depositor's account for the full amount of the deposit. Then, when the bank learns that the cheque is uncollectible, it debits the depositor's account for the amount of the cheque. Also, the bank may charge the depositor a fee for processing the NSF cheque. The bank notifies the depositor of each such deduction with a debit memorandum. If the item is material in amount, the memorandum is mailed to the depositor on the day of the deduction. Although each deduction should be recorded on the day the memorandum is received, sometimes an entry is not made until the bank reconciliation is prepared. Also, memoranda for small amounts may not be sent to the depositor until the bank statement is mailed.

Banks charge a depositor's account for other services such as the printing of new cheques. And a monthly service charge may be made for general processing of chequing account activity.

4. *Credits for collections and for interest.* Banks often act as collection agents for their depositors, collecting for a small fee promissory notes and other items. When an item such as a promissory note is collected, the bank usually deducts its fee and adds the net proceeds to the depositor's account. It then sends a credit memorandum as notification of the transaction. As soon as the memorandum is received, it should be recorded. Occasionally, these items remain unrecorded until the time of the bank reconciliation.

Some bank accounts earn interest on the average cash balance in the account during the month. If an account earns interest, the bank statement will include a credit for the amount earned during the past month.

5. *Errors.* Regardless of care and systems of internal control for automatic error detection, both the bank and the depositor make errors that affect the bank balance. Occasionally, these errors are not discovered until the balance is reconciled. Also, the depositor may make errors in the accounting records. Such errors often are not discovered until the balance is reconciled.

Steps in Reconciling the Bank Balance

The steps in reconciling the bank balance are as follow:

1. Compare deposits listed on the bank statement with deposits shown in the accounting records. Note any discrepancies and discover which record is correct. List any errors or unrecorded items.

2. Examine all other credits to the account shown on the bank statement and determine whether each one has been recorded in the books. These items include collections by the bank, corrections of previous bank statement errors, and interest earned by the depositor. List any unrecorded items.

3. Compare the list of canceled cheques on the bank statement with the actual cheques returned with the statement. For each cheque, make sure that the correct amount was deducted by the bank and that the returned cheque was properly charged to the company's account. Note any discrepancies or errors.

4. Compare the *outstanding cheques* listed on the previous month's bank reconciliation with the canceled cheques listed on the bank statement. Prepare a list of any cheques that remain outstanding at the end of the current month.

5. Compare the canceled cheques listed on the bank statement with the cheques recorded in the books since the last reconciliation. To make this process easier, the bank statement normally lists canceled cheques in the same numerical order as the cheques are numbered. List any outstanding cheques. Although companies with reasonable internal controls would rarely if ever write a cheque without recording it, an individual may occasionally write a cheque and fail to record it in the books. List any canceled cheques that are unrecorded in the books.

6. Examine all other debits to the account as shown on the bank statement and determine whether each one has been recorded in the books. These include bank charges for newly printed cheques, NSF cheques, stop payment orders, and monthly service charges.

7. Prepare a reconciliation of the bank statement balance with the book balance of cash. Such a reconciliation is shown in Illustration 7–9.

8. Determine if any debits or credits appearing on the bank statement are unrecorded in the books of account. Make journal entries to record them.

ILLUSTRATION OF A BANK RECONCILIATION

To illustrate a bank reconciliation, assume that Valley Company found the following when it attempted to reconcile its bank balance of October 31. The bank balance as shown by the bank statement was $2,050, and the cash balance according to the accounting records was $1,404.58. A $145 deposit, placed in the bank's night depository after banking hours on October 31, was unrecorded by the bank at the time the bank statement was mailed. Included with the bank statement was a credit memorandum showing the bank had collected a note receivable for the company on October 23. The note's proceeds of $500 less a $15 collection

Illustration 7–9

VALLEY COMPANY
Bank Reconciliation
October 31, 19—

Book balance of cash		$1,404.58	Bank statement balance		$2,050.00
Add:			Add:		
Proceeds of note less collection fee	$485.00		Deposit of 31/10		145.00
Interest earned	8.42	493.42			
		$1,898.00			$2,195.00
Deduct:			Deduct:		
NSF cheque plus service charge	$ 30.00		Outstanding cheques: No. 124	$150.00	
Cheque printing charge	23.00	53.00	No. 126	200.00	350.00
		$1,845.00			$1,845.00

fee were credited to the company's account. The bank statement also showed a credit of $8.42 for interest earned on the average cash balance in the account. Neither the collection of the note nor the interest had been recorded on the company books.

A comparison of canceled cheques with the company's books showed that two cheques were outstanding. Cheque No. 124 for $150 and Cheque No. 126 for $200 were outstanding and unpaid by the bank. Other debits on the bank statement that had not been recorded on the books included: (1) a $23 debit memorandum for cheques printed by the bank; and (2) an NSF (not sufficient funds) cheque for $20 plus related processing fee of $10. The NSF cheque had been received from a customer, Frank Jones, on October 16, and had been included in that day's deposit.

The bank reconciliation that reflects the above items is shown in Illustration 7–9.

A bank reconciliation helps locate any errors made by either the bank or the depositor. It discloses any items which have been entered on the company books but have not come to the bank's attention. Also, it discloses items that should be recorded on the company books but are unrecorded on the date of the reconciliation. For example, in the reconciliation illustrated, the reconciled cash balance, $1,845, is the true cash balance. However, at the time the reconciliation is completed, Valley Company's accounting records show a $1,404.58 book balance. Consequently, entries must be made to adjust the book balance, increasing it to the true cash balance. This requires four entries. The first in general journal form is:

Nov.	2	Cash	485.00	
		Collection Expense	15.00	
		Notes Receivable		500.00
		To record the proceeds and collection fee of a note collected by the bank.		

This entry is self-explanatory. The bank collected a note receivable, deducted a collection fee, and deposited the difference to the Valley Company account. The entry increases the amount of cash on the books, records the collection expense, and reduces notes receivable.

The second entry records the interest credited to Valley Company's account by the bank. Interest earned is a revenue and the entry recognizes both the revenue and the related increase in Cash. As mentioned earlier, interest calculations are discussed in the next chapter. The entry is:

Nov.	2	Cash	8.42	
		Interest Earned		8.42
		To record interest earned on the average cash balance maintained in the chequing account.		

The third entry is:

Nov.	2	Accounts Receivable—Frank Jones	30.00	
		Cash		30.00
		To charge Frank Jones's account for his NSF cheque and for the bank's fee.		

This entry records the NSF cheque returned as uncollectible. The $20 cheque was received from Jones in payment of his account and was deposited as cash. The bank, unable to collect the cheque, charged $10 for handling the NSF cheque and deducted $30 from the Valley Company account. This made it necessary for the company to reverse the entry made when the cheque was received and also to record the $10 processing fee. Valley Company charged the $10 fee to Jones's account and will attempt to collect the entire $30 from Jones.

The fourth entry debits the cheque printing charge to Miscellaneous General Expenses and in general journal form is:

Nov.	2	Miscellaneous General Expense	23.00	
		Cash		23.00
		Cheque printing charge.		

OTHER INTERNAL CONTROL PROCEDURES

Internal control procedures apply to every phase of a company's operations from purchases through sales, cash receipts, cash disbursements, and the control of plant assets. Many of these procedures are discussed in later chapters. However, the way in which a company can gain control over purchases discounts is discussed here and the technique is illustrated below.

Recall that thus far the following entries in general journal form have been used in recording the receipt and payment of an invoice for merchandise purchased.

Oct.	2	Purchases	1,000.00	
		Accounts Payable		1,000.00
		Purchased merchandise, terms 2/10, n/60.		
	12	Accounts Payable	1,000.00	
		Purchases Discounts		20.00
		Cash		980.00
		Paid the invoice of October 2.		

The invoice of these entries was recorded at its **gross,** $1,000, amount. This is the way in which invoices are recorded in many companies. However, well-managed companies follow the practice of taking all offered cash discounts. In many of these companies, invoices are recorded at their **net** (after discount) amounts. To illustrate, a company that records invoices at net amounts purchased merchandise having a $1,000 invoice price, terms 2/10, n/60. On receipt of the goods, it deducted the offered $20 discount from the gross invoice amount and recorded the purchase with this debit and credit:

Oct.	2	Purchases	980.00	
		Accounts Payable		980.00
		Purchased merchandise on credit.		

If the invoice for this purchase is paid within the discount period, the cash disbursements entry to record the payment has a debit to Accounts Payable and a credit to Cash for $980. However, if payment is not made within the discount period and the discount is **lost,** an entry like the following must be made in the General Journal either before or when the invoice is paid:

Dec.	1	Discounts Lost	20.00	
		Accounts Payable		20.00
		To record the discount lost.		

A cheque for the full $1,000 invoice amount is then drawn, recorded, and mailed to the creditor.

Advantage of the Net Method

When invoices are recorded at gross amounts, the amount of discounts taken is deducted from the balance of the Purchases account on the income statement to arrive at the cost of merchandise purchased. However, when invoices are recorded at gross amounts, if through oversight or carelessness discounts are lost, the amount of discounts lost does not appear in any account or on the income statement and may not come to the attention of management. On the other hand, when purchases are recorded at net amounts, the amount of discounts taken does not appear on the income statement. However, the amount of *discounts lost* is called to management's attention through the appearance on the income statement of the expense account, Discounts Lost, as in the condensed income statement of Illustration 7–10.

Illustration 7–10

XYZ COMPANY
Income Statement
For Year Ended December 31, 19—

Sales	$100,000
Cost of goods sold	60,000
Gross profit from sales	$ 40,000
Operating expenses	28,000
Income from operations	$ 12,000
Other revenues and expenses:	
Discounts lost	(150)
Net income	$ 11,850

Of the two methods, recording invoices at their net amounts probably supplies management with the more valuable information, the amount of discounts lost through oversight, carelessness, or other cause. It also gives management better control over the work of the people responsible for taking cash discounts. If discounts are lost, someone must explain why. As a result, few discounts are lost through carelessness. The *net method of recording purchases* is also consistent with the cost principle.

APPENDIX

RECORDING VOUCHERS, PEN-AND-INK SYSTEM

When a voucher system is in use, an account called Vouchers Payable replaces the Accounts Payable account described in previous chapters. And, for every transaction that will result in a cash disbursement, a voucher is prepared and credited to this account. For example, when merchandise is purchased, the voucher covering the transaction is recorded with a debit to Purchases and a credit to Vouchers Payable. Likewise, when a plant asset is purchased or an expense is incurred, the voucher of the transaction is recorded with a debit to the proper plant asset or expense account and a credit to Vouchers Payable.

In a pen-and-ink system, vouchers are recorded in a *Voucher Register* similar to Illustration 7A–1. Such a register has a Vouchers Payable credit column and a number of debit columns. The exact debit columns vary from company to company, but merchandising concerns always provide a Purchases debit column. Also, as long as space is available, special debit columns are provided for transactions that occur frequently. In addition, an Other Accounts debit column is provided for transactions that do not occur often.

In recording vouchers in a register like that of Illustration 7A–1, all information about each voucher, other than information about its payment, is entered as soon as the voucher is approved for recording. The information as to payment date and the number of the paying cheque is entered later as each voucher is paid.

In posting a Voucher Register like that in Illustration 7A–1, the columns are first totaled and crossfooted to prove their equality. The Vouchers Payable column total is then credited to the Vouchers Payable account. The totals of the Purchases, Transportation-In, Sales Salaries Expense, Advertising Expense, Delivery Expense, and Office Salaries Expense are debited to these accounts. None of the individual amounts in these columns are posted. However, the individual amounts in the Other Accounts column are posted as individual amounts and the column total is not posted.

Illustration 7A–1

Page 32							Voucher
Date 19—	Voucher No.	Payee	When and How Paid		Vouchers Payable Credit	Purchases Debit	Transportation-In Debit
			Date	Cheque No.			
Oct. 1	767	A. B. Seay Co.	6/10	733	800.00	800.00		1
1	768	Daily Sentinel	9/10	744	53.00			2
2	769	Seaboard Supply Co.	12/10	747	235.00	155.00	10.00	3
6	770	George Smith	6/10	734	85.00			4
6	771	Frank Jones	6/10	735	95.00			5
6	772	George Roth	6/10	736	95.00			6
30	998	First National Bank	30/10	972	505.00			33
								34
30	999	Pacific Telephone Co.	30/10	973	18.00			35
31	1000	Tarbell Wholesale Co.			235.00	235.00		36
31	1001	Office Equipment Co.	31/10	974	195.00			37
31		Totals			5,079.00	2,435.00	156.00	38
					(213)	(511)	(514)	39
								40
								41

THE UNPAID VOUCHERS FILE

When a voucher system is in use, some vouchers are paid as soon as they are recorded. Others must be filed until payment is due. As an aid in taking cash discounts, vouchers for which payment is not due are generally filed in an unpaid vouchers file under the dates on which they are to be paid.

The file of unpaid vouchers takes the place of a subsidiary Accounts Payable Ledger. Actually, the file is a subsidiary ledger of amounts owed creditors. Likewise, the Vouchers Payable account is in effect a controlling account controlling the unpaid vouchers file. Consequently, after posting is completed at the end of a month, the balance of the Vouchers Payable account should equal the sum of the unpaid vouchers in the unpaid vouchers file. This is verified each month by preparing a schedule or an adding machine list of the unpaid vouchers in the file and comparing its total with the balance of the Vouchers Payable account. In addition, the unpaid vouchers in the file are compared with the unpaid vouchers shown in the Voucher Register's record of payments column.

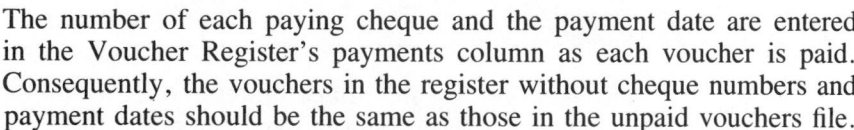

	Sales Salaries Expense Debit	Adver- tising Expense Debit	Delivery Expense Debit	Office Salaries Expense Debit	Other Accounts Debit		
					Account Name	Post. Ref.	Amount Debit
1							
2		53.00					
3					Store Supplies	117	70.00
4				85.00			
5	95.00						
6	95.00						
33					Notes Payable	211	500.00
34					Interest Expense	721	5.00
35					Telephone Expense	655	18.00
36							
37					Office Equipment	134	195.00
38	740.00	115.00	358.00	340.00			935.00
39	(611)	(612)	(615)	(651)			(√)
40							
41							

Register — Page 32

The number of each paying cheque and the payment date are entered in the Voucher Register's payments column as each voucher is paid. Consequently, the vouchers in the register without cheque numbers and payment dates should be the same as those in the unpaid vouchers file.

THE VOUCHER SYSTEM CHEQUE REGISTER

In a voucher system, the Cash Disbursements Journal is replaced by a simpler Cheque Register. All cheques drawn in payment of vouchers are recorded in the Cheque Register. No obligation is paid until a voucher covering the payment is prepared and recorded in the Voucher Register. Likewise, no cheque is drawn except in payment of a specific voucher. Consequently, all cheques drawn result in debits to Vouchers Payable and credits to Cash, unless a discount must be recorded. Then, there are credits to both Purchases Discounts and to Cash. A Cheque Register is shown in Illustration 7A–2. Note that it has columns for debits to Vouchers Payable and credits to Purchases Discounts and to Cash. In

Illustration 7A–2

Cheque Register

Date 19—		Payee	Voucher No.	Cheque No.	Vouchers Payable Debit	Purchases Discounts Credit	Cash Credit
Oct.	1	C. B. & Y. RR. Co.	765	728	14.00		14.00
	3	Frank Mills	766	729	73.00		73.00
	3	Ajax Wholesale Co.	753	730	250.00	5.00	245.00
	4	Normal Supply Co.	747	731	100.00	2.00	98.00
	5	Office Supply Co.	763	732	43.00		43.00
	6	A. B. Seay Co.	767	733	800.00	16.00	784.00
	6	George Smith	770	734	85.00		85.00
	6	Frank Jones	771	735	95.00		95.00
	30	First National Bank	998	972	505.00		505.00
	30	Pacific Telephone Co.	999	973	18.00		18.00
	31	Office Equipment Co.	1001	974	195.00		195.00
	31	Totals			6,468.00	28.00	6,440.00
					(213)	(512)	(111)

posting, all amounts entered in these columns are posted in the column totals.

PURCHASES RETURNS

Occasionally, an item must be returned after the voucher recording its purchase has been prepared and entered in the Voucher Register. In such cases, the return may be recorded with a general journal entry similar to the following:

Nov.	5	Vouchers Payable	15.00	
		Purchases Returns and Allowances		15.00
		Returned defective merchandise.		

In addition to the entry, the amount of the return is deducted on the voucher and the credit memorandum and other documents verifying the return are attached to the voucher. Then, when the voucher is paid, a cheque is drawn for its corrected amount.

GLOSSARY

Bank reconciliation. An analysis explaining the difference between an enterprise's book balance of cash and its bank statement balance.

Canceled cheques. Cheques that have been punched or stamped by the bank to show they have been paid.

Cash Over and Short account. An income statement account in which are recorded cash overages and cash shortages arising from making change.

Discounts lost. Cash discounts offered but not taken.

GAAP. Generally Accepted Accounting Principles.

Internal control system. The procedures adopted by a business to encourage adherence to prescribed managerial policies, to protect its assets from waste, fraud, and theft, and to ensure accurate and reliable accounting data.

Invoice. A document, prepared by a vendor, on which are listed the items sold, the sales prices, the customer's name, and the terms of sale.

Invoice approval form. A document on which the accounting department notes that it has performed each step in the process of checking an invoice and approving it for recording and payment.

Net method of recording purchases. A method of recording purchases by which offered cash discounts are deducted from the invoice price in determining the amount to be recorded.

Outstanding cheques. Cheques that have been written, recorded, and sent or given to payees but have not been received, paid, and canceled by the bank.

Purchase order. A business form used in placing an order for the purchase of goods from a vendor.

Purchase requisition. A business form used within a business to ask the purchasing department of the business to buy needed items.

Receiving report. A form used within a business to notify the proper persons of the receipt of goods ordered and of the quantities and condition of the goods.

Reconcile. To account for the difference between two amounts.

Vendee. The purchaser of something.

Vendor. The individual or enterprise selling something.

Voucher. A business paper used in summarizing a transaction and approving it for recording and payment.

Voucher Register. A book of original entry in which approved vouchers are recorded.

Voucher system. An accounting system used to control the incurrence and payment of obligations requiring the disbursement of cash.

QUESTIONS FOR CLASS DISCUSSION

1. Name some of the broad principles of internal control.

2. Why should the person who keeps the record of an asset be a different person from the one responsible for custody of the asset?

3. Internal control procedures are important in every business, but at what stage in the development of a business do they become critical?

4. Why should responsibility for a sequence of related transactions be divided among different departments or individuals?

5. In a small business, it is sometimes impossible to separate the functions of record-keeping and asset custody, and it is sometimes impossible to divide responsibilities for related transactions. What should be substituted for these control procedures?

6. Are the principles of internal control for computerized accounting systems different from the principles of internal control for manual accounting systems?

7. What are some of the effects of computers on internal control?

8. What is meant by the phrase *all receipts should be deposited intact?* Why should all receipts be deposited intact on the day of receipt?

9. Why should a company's bookkeeper not be given responsibility for receiving cash for the company or the responsibility for signing cheques or making cash disbursements in any other way?

10. In purchasing merchandise in a large store, why are the department managers not permitted to deal directly with the sources of supply?

11. What are the duties of the selling department managers in the purchasing procedures of a large store?

12. Tell *(a)* who prepares, *(b)* who receives, and *(c)* the purpose of each of the following business papers:

    a. Purchase requisition.   *d.* Receiving report.
    b. Purchase order.   *e.* Invoice approval form.
    c. Invoice.   *f.* Voucher.

13. Do all companies need a voucher system? At what approximate point in a company's growth would you recommend the installation of such a system?

14. When a disbursing officer issues a cheque in a large business, he or she usually cannot know from personal contact that the assets, goods, or services for which the cheque pays were received by the business or that the purchase was properly authorized. However, if the company has an internal control system, the officer can depend on the system. Exactly what documents does the officer depend on to tell that the purchase was authorized and properly made and the goods were actually received?

15. Why are some cash payments made from a petty cash fund? Why are not all payments made by cheque?

16. What is a petty cash receipt? When a petty cash receipt is prepared, who signs it?

17. Explain how a petty cash fund operates.

18. Why must a petty cash fund be reimbursed at the end of each accounting period?

19. What are two results of reimbursing the petty cash fund?

20. What is a bank statement? What kind of information appears on a bank statement?

21. What is the meaning of the phrase *to reconcile a bank balance?*

22. Why are the bank statement balance of cash and the depositor's book balance of cash reconciled?

23. What valuable information becomes readily available to management when invoices are recorded at net amounts? Is this information readily available when invoices are recorded at gross amounts?

MULTIPLE CHOICE

1. Petty cash was originally established for $50. In the petty cash fund you find the following items:

   Receipts
   Postage $12.75
   Misc. office expenses 16.45
   Office equipment repair 10.15
   Cash 9.60

   What entry should be prepared to replenish the petty cash fund?

   a. Petty Cash 40.40
        Cash 40.40
   b. Petty Cash 50.00
        Cash 50.00
   c. Postage Expense 12.75
      Misc. Office Expenses 16.45
      Office Equipment Repair Expense 10.15
        Cash 39.35
   d. Postage Expense 12.75
      Misc. Office Expenses 16.45
      Office Equipment Repair Expense 10.15
      Cash Short and Over 1.05
        Cash 40.40
   e. Postage Expense 12.75
      Misc. Office Expense 16.45
      Office Equipment Repair Expense 10.15
      Cash Short and Over 1.05
        Petty Cash 40.40

2. A good system of internal control:
   a. Encourages adherence to prescribed managerial policies.
   b. Promotes operational efficiencies.

c.   Helps ensure accurate accounting data.

d.   Does all the foregoing.

e.   Does none of the foregoing.

3.   When a petty cash fund is in use:

   a.   Expense accounts are apt to be debited when the fund is replenished.

   b.   Most small payments are made from cash receipts before they are deposited.

   c.   The Cash account is not affected when the fund is replenished.

   d.   Petty cash is debited when the fund is replenished.

   e.   Petty cash is credited when the fund is replenished.

4.   In reimbursing the petty cash fund:

   a.   Cash is debited.

   b.   Petty cash is debited.

   c.   Petty cash is credited.

   d.   Expense accounts usually are debited.

   e.   None of the foregoing.

5.   A cheque that was outstanding on last month's bank reconciliation was not among the canceled cheques returned by the bank this month. As a result, in preparing this month's reconciliation, the amount of this cheque should be:

   a.   Added to the book balance of cash.

   b.   Deducted from the book balance of cash.

   c.   Added to the bank statement balance.

   d.   Deducted from the bank statement balance.

   e.   Ignored.

6.   The Skipper Company purchased $1,650 worth of merchandise on terms 2/10, N/30. If Skipper uses the net method of recording purchases, which entry should be made to record the purchase?

a.	Purchases	1,650	
	Accounts Payable		1,650
b.	Purchases	1,650	
	Accounts Payable		1,617
	Purchases Discounts		33
c.	Purchases	1,617	
	Discounts Lost	33	
	Accounts Payable		1,650
d.	Purchases	1,617	
	Accounts Payable		1,617
e.	None of the above.		

7.   The Bevo Company had a cash balance of $962 on August 31. This included a bank deposit of $87 that was in transit on the 31st. The August 31 bank statement contained the following information:

Bank statement balance	$1,089
NSF cheque	16
Bank service charge	7
Collection of notes receivable (net)	68

Bevo also had cheques outstanding of $169. What is Bevo's reconciled balance?

    a. $920.
    b. $962.
    c. $1,007.
    d. $1,089.
    e. $1,176.

8. In reconciling the bank balance, a cheque outstanding on the previous month's reconciliation but returned with this month's canceled cheques should be:

    a. Ignored.
    b. Added to the book balance of cash.
    c. Deducted from the book balance of cash.
    d. Added to the bank statement balance of cash.
    e. Deducted from the bank statement balance of cash.

9. In a company that records invoices at net amounts, an invoice for goods purchased from Able Company was filed in error and the discount was lost. The entry to record the lost discount is:

    a. Debit Accounts Payable—Able Company and credit Cash.
    b. Debit Discounts Lost and credit Accounts payable—Able Company.
    c. Debit Purchases Discounts and credit Accounts Payable—Able Company.
    d. Credit Discounts Lost and debit Cash.
    e. Some other entry.

MINI DISCUSSION CASES

Case 7–1
To add to Innocente's problems (Mini Discussion Case 5–1), auditors hired by him (after the purchase was completed) discovered that the purchased accounts receivable were substantially overstated. Reconstruction of events prior to the purchase by Gerald Innocente revealed that all cash sales made during the period January 1 to August 15 (date of the purchase of business) were recorded as sales on account; the cash was "pocketed" and fictitious accounts receivable created. Cash sales during the period recorded as credit sales totaled $40,000.

Required:

1. Discuss the effect on the financial statements of the manner in which cash sales were handled.
2. Discuss the safeguards or internal control that was lacking in the situation.

Case 7–2
Refer to Case 7–1.

Required:

Discuss procedures that should have been followed prior to the purchase of the business to ensure the accuracy of accounts receivable.

CLASS EXERCISES

Exercise 7–1

A company established a $100 petty cash fund on March 15. Two weeks later, on March 29, there was $6.75 in cash in the fund and receipts for these expenditures: postage, $22.75; transportation-in, $18.25; miscellaneous general expenses, $28; and office supplies, $24.25.

a.   Give in general journal form the entry to establish the fund.

b.   Give the entry to reimburse it on March 29.

c.   Assume that since the fund was exhausted so quickly, it was not only reimbursed on March 29 but also increased in size to $150. Give the entry to reimburse and increase the fund to $150.

Exercise 7–2

A company established a $125 petty cash fund on August 10. On August 31, there was $34.50 in cash in the fund and receipts for these expenditures: transportation-in, $14.75; miscellaneous general expenses, $27.50; and office supplies, $46.25. The petty cashier could not account for the $2 shortage in the fund. Give in general journal form *(a)* the entry to establish the fund and *(b)* the August 31 entry to reimburse the fund and reduce it to $100.

Exercise 7–3

Some of Trace Company's cash receipts from customers are sent to the company in the mail. Trace Company's bookkeeper opens the letters and deposits the cash received each day. What internal control problems are inherent in this arrangement? What changes would you recommend?

Exercise 7–4

Eastside Store deposits all receipts intact on the day received and makes all payments by cheque; and on December 31, after all posting was completed, its Cash account showed a $3,775 debit balance; but its December 31 bank statement showed only $3,256.50 on deposit in the bank on that day. Prepare a bank reconciliation for the store, using the following information:

a.   Outstanding cheques, $500.

b.   Included with the December canceled cheques returned by the bank was a $10 debit memorandum for bank services.

c.   Cheque No. 642, returned with the canceled cheques, was correctly drawn for $28 in payment of the telephone bill and was paid by the bank on December 8, but it had been recorded with a debit to Telephone Expense and a credit to Cash as though it were for $82.

d.   The December 31 cash receipts, $1,062.50 were placed in the bank's night depository after banking hours on that date and were unrecorded by the bank at the time the December bank statement was prepared.

Exercise 7–5

Give in general journal form any entries that Eastside Store should make as a result of having prepared the bank reconciliation of the previous exercise.

Exercise 7–6   Barr Company incurred $28,000 of operating expenses in July, a month in which its sales were $100,000. The company began July with a $52,000 merchandise inventory and ended the month with a $56,000 inventory. During the month, it purchased merchandise having a $64,000 invoice price, all of which was subject to a 2% discount for prompt payment. The company took advantage of the discounts on $44,000 of the purchases, but through an error in filing it did not earn and could not take the discount on a $20,000 invoice paid on July 31.

Required:

1. Prepare a July income statement for the company under the assumption that it records invoices at gross amounts.
2. Prepare a second income statement for the company under the assumption that it records invoices at net amounts.

Exercise 7–7   Complete the following bank reconciliation by filling in the missing amounts.

EATON COMPANY
Bank Reconciliation
May 31, 19—

Book balance of cash	$?		Bank statement balance	$3,634
Add: Collection of note	400		Add: Deposit of May 31	?
Interest earned	12		Bank error	20
	$3,912			$?
Deduct: Service charge	?		Deduct: Outstanding	
NSF cheque	200		cheques	750
Reconciled balance	$?		Reconciled balance	$3,704

PROBLEMS

Problem 7–1   A concern completed the following petty cash transactions during January of the current year:

Jan. 1 Drew a $100 cheque, cashed it, and gave the proceeds and the petty cash box to Tom Gray, an office clerk who was to act as petty cashier.

5 Purchased computer paper with petty cash, $22.50.

7 Paid $7.75 COD delivery charges on merchandise purchased for resale.

10 Paid $6.25 parcel post charges on merchandise sold to a customer and delivered by mail.

12 Gave Mr. Bruce Hanson, husband of the business owner, $15 from petty cash for cab fare and other personal expenses.

19 Paid $7.50 COD delivery charges on merchandise purchased for resale.

23 Paid a service station attendant $6.50 for washing the personal car of Kay Hanson, the business owner.

24 Paid Speedy Delivery Service $5.50 from petty cash to deliver merchandise sold to a customer.

26 Paid $25.50 for minor repairs to an office typewriter.

29 Tom Gray sorted the petty cash receipts by accounts affected and exchanged them for a cheque to reimburse the fund for expenditures and, since there was only $1.50 in cash in the fund, for the shortage for which he could not account.

Required:

1. Prepare a general journal entry to record the cheque establishing the petty cash fund.
2. Prepare a summary of petty cash payments that has these categories: Office Supplies, Transportation-in, Delivery Expense, Withdrawals, and Miscellaneous Expenses. Sort the payments into the appropriate categories, total the expenses in each category, and prepare the general journal entry to reimburse the fund.

Problem 7–2   A business completed these transactions:

May 20 Drew a $75 cheque to establish a petty cash fund, cashed it, and delivered the proceeds and the petty cash box to James Taft, an office secretary who was to act as petty cashier.
22 Paid Cy's Delivery Service $10 to deliver merchandise sold to a customer.
26 Purchased office supplies with petty cash, $17.75.
29 Paid $25 from petty cash to have the office windows washed.
31 Jay Speck, the owner of the business, signed a petty cash receipt and took $10 from petty cash for lunch money.
June 3 Paid $9.50 COD delivery charges on merchandise purchased for resale.
4 James Taft noted that there was only $2.75 cash remaining in the fund. Thus, he sorted the paid petty cash receipts by accounts affected and exchanged them for a cheque to reimburse the fund. However, since the fund had been so rapidly exhausted, the cheque was made for an amount sufficiently large enough to increase the size of the fund to $150.
6 Paid Cy's Delivery Service $9.50 to deliver merchandise to a customer.
10 Paid the Westside Cleaner's delivery person $17.50 upon the delivery to the office of clothes Mr. Speck had dropped off at the cleaners.
12 Paid $21.50 COD delivery charges on merchandise purchased for resale.
18 Gave Mrs. Speck, the wife of the business owner, $25 from petty cash for cab fare and other personal expenditures.
21 Paid $38 for minor repairs to an office typewriter.
25 Purchased office supplies with petty cash, $8.50.
28 Paid $7.75 COD delivery charges on merchandise purchased for resale.
30 James Taft sorted the petty cash receipts by accounts affected and exchanged them for a cheque to reimburse the fund for expenditures and, since there was only $12.50 in cash in the fund, for the shortage which he could not explain.

Required:

1. Prepare a general journal entry to record the cheque establishing the petty cash fund.
2. Prepare a summary of petty cash payments prior to June 4 that has these categories: Office Supplies, Transportation-in, Delivery Expense, Withdrawals, and Miscellaneous Expenses. Sort the expenditures into the appropriate categories and total the expenses in each category. Prepare a similar summary of petty cash payments after June 4.
3. Prepare entries to reimburse the fund and increase its size on June 4 and to reimburse the fund on June 30.

Problem 7–3   The George Company has only one journal in its accounting system and records all transactions in that general journal. However, the company recently set up a petty cash fund to facilitate payments of small items. The following transactions involving the petty cash fund were noted by the petty cashier as occurring during March (the last month of the company's fiscal year).

Mar. 1   Received a company cheque for $150 to establish the petty cash fund.
     11   Received a company cheque to replenish the fund for the following expenditures made since March 1 and to increase the fund to $450.
        a.   Payment of $28.50 to Ace Trucking for freight on merchandise delivered to George Company.
        b.   Purchased postage stamps for $35.
        c.   Gave Katherine Jones, owner of the business, $25 for personal use.
        d.   Paid $42.75 to Appliance Company for repairs of office equipment.
        e.   Discovered that only $17.25 remained in the petty cash box.
     31   Having decided that the March 11 increase in the fund was too large, received a company cheque to replenish the fund for the following expenditures made since March 11 but allowing the fund to be reduced in size to $350.
        a.   Payment of $67.50 for emergency repairs to the company's office computer printer.
        b.   Payment of $45 for janitorial service.
        c.   Purchased office supplies for $56.75.
        d.   Payment of $72.30 to Black Advertising for a space advertisement in a weekly newsletter.

Required:

1. Prepare general journal entries to record the establishment of the fund on March 1 and its replenishments on March 11 and on March 31.
2. If George Company had failed to replenish the petty cash fund on March 31, what would have been the effect on net income for the fiscal year ended March 31 and on total assets on March 31? Explain your answer.

Problem 7–4   The following information was available to reconcile Prince Company's book balance of cash with its bank statement balance as of December 31:

a. The December 31 cash balance according to the accounting records was $8,340, and the bank statement balance for that date was $7,959.
b. Two cheques, No. 722 for $309 and No. 726 for $279, were outstanding on November 30 when the book and bank statement balances were last reconciled. Cheque No. 726 was returned with the December canceled cheques but Cheque No. 722 was not.
c. Cheque No. 803 for $237 and Cheque No. 805 for $219, both written and entered in the accounting records in December, were not among the canceled cheques returned.
d. When the December cheques were compared with entries in the accounting records, it was found that Cheque No. 751 had been correctly drawn for $514 in payment for store supplies but was entered in the accounting records in error as though it were drawn for $415.
e. Two debit memoranda and a credit memorandum were included with the returned cheques and were unrecorded at the time of the reconciliation. The credit memorandum indicated that the bank had collected a $1,500 note receivable for the company, deducted a $12 collection fee, and credited the balance to the company's account. One of the debit memoranda was for $132 and had attached to it an NSF cheque in that amount that had been received from a customer, Lee Branch, in payment of his account. The second debit memorandum was for a special printing of cheques and was for $36.
f. The December 31 cash receipts, $2,367, had been placed in the bank's night depository after banking hours on that date and did not appear on the bank statement.

Required:

Prepare a December 31 bank reconciliation for the company and the entries in general journal form required to bring the company's book balance of cash into conformity with the reconciled balance.

Problem 7–5   Bacon Company reconciled its book and bank statement balances of cash on October 31 and showed two cheques outstanding at that time, No. 713 for $825 and No. 716 for $426. The following information was available for the November 30 reconciliation:

From the November 30 bank statement:

BALANCE OF PREVIOUS STATEMENT ON 31/10/—	5,736.00
5 DEPOSITS AND OTHER CREDITS TOTALING	8,526.00
9 CHEQUES AND OTHER DEBITS TOTALING	7,227.00
SERVICE CHARGE AMOUNT	9.00
CURRENT BALANCE AS OF THIS STATEMENT	7,026.00

CHEQUING ACCOUNT TRANSACTIONS°°°

. DATE .... AMOUNT		TRANSACTION DESCRIPTION ....
3/11	936.00+	Deposit
14/11	1,653.00+	Deposit
21/11	1,536.00+	Deposit
28/11	1,416.00+	Deposit
29/11	129.00−	NSF cheque
30/11	9.00−	Service charge
30/11	2,985.00+	Credit memorandum

. DATE	... CHEQUE NO ...	... AMOUNT ...	. DATE .	... CHEQUE NO ...	... AMOUNT
2/11	713	825.00	9/11	721	2,211.00
3/11	718*	654.00	12/11	722	396.00
5/11	719	906.00	18/11	724*	852.00
12/11	720	225.00	28/11	725	1,029.00

* Indicates a skip in cheque sequence

From Bacon Company's accounting records:

Cash Receipts Deposited			**Cash Disbursements**		
Date		Cash Debit	Cheque No.		Cash Credit
Nov. 3		936.00	718		654.00
14		1,653.00	719		960.00
21		1,536.00	720		225.00
28		1,416.00	721		2,211.00
30		741.00	722		396.00
		6,282.00	723		408.00
			724		852.00
			725		1,029.00
			726		159.00
					6,894.00

Cash

Date		Explanation	PR	Debit	Credit	Balance
Oct.	31	Balance	√			4,485.00
Nov.	30	Total receipts	R-8	6,282.00		10,767.00
	30	Total disbursements	D-9		6,894.00	3,873.00

Cheque No. 719 was correctly drawn for $906 in payment for office equipment; however, the bookkeeper misread the amount and entered it in the accounting records with a debit to Office Equipment and a credit to Cash as though it were for $960.

The NSF cheque was received from a customer, Bob Burns, in payment of his account. Its return is unrecorded. The credit memorandum resulted from a $3,000 note collected for Bacon Company by the bank. The bank had deducted a $15 collection fee. The collection fee is not recorded.

Required:

1. Prepare a November 30 bank reconciliation for the company.
2. Prepare in general journal form the entries needed to adjust the book balance of cash to the reconciled balance.

Problem 7–6   The March 31 credit balance in the Sales account of Austin Sales showed it had sold $97,000 of merchandise during the month. The concern began August with a $109,200 merchandise inventory and ended the month with a $90,200 inventory. It had incurred $33,000 of operating expenses during the month, and it had also recorded the following transactions:

Mar. 1   Received merchandise purchased at a $10,000 invoice price, invoice dated February 28, terms 2/10, n/30.
     5   Received a $1,000 credit memorandum (invoice price) for merchandise received on March 1 and returned for credit.
   11   Received merchandise purchased at a $16,000 invoice price, invoice dated March 9, terms 2/10, n/30.
   15   Received merchandise purchased at a $15,000 invoice price, invoice dated March 12, terms 2/10, n/30.
   19   Paid for the merchandise received on March 11, less the discount.
   22   Paid for the merchandise received on March 15, less the discount.
   27   The invoice received on March 1 had been refiled in error, after the credit memorandum was attached, for payment on this the last day of its credit period, causing the discount to be lost. Paid the invoice.

Required:

1. Assume the concern records invoices at gross amounts:
    a. Prepare general journal entries to record the transactions.
    b. Prepare a March income statement for the concern.
2. Assume the concern records invoices at net amounts:
    a. Prepare general journal entries to record the transactions.
    b. Prepare a second income statement for the concern under this assumption.

Problem 7–7   *(This problem is based on information in the Appendix to this chapter.)* Marney Company completed these transactions involving vouchers payable:

Mar. 3   Recorded Voucher No. 452 payable to Frost Company for merchandise having a $2,850 invoice price, invoice dated February 28, terms FOB factory, 2/10, n/30. The vendor had prepaid the freight, $135, adding the amount to the invoice and bringing its total to $2,985.
     5   Recorded Voucher No. 453 payable to *The Globe* for advertising expense, $330. Issued Cheque No. 838 in payment of the voucher.
     6   Received a credit memorandum for merchandise having a $450 invoice price. The merchandise had been received from Frost Company on March 3, recorded on Voucher No. 452, and later returned for credit.
     8   Recorded Voucher No. 454 payable to Central Realty for one month's rent on the space occupied by the store, $1,500. Issued Cheque No. 839 in payment of the voucher.

Mar. 10   Recorded Voucher No. 455 payable to Over Supply Company for store supplies, $195, terms n/10 EOM.

12   Recorded Voucher No. 456 payable to San Marcos Company for merchandise having a $3,750 invoice price, invoice dated March 10, terms FOB factory, 2/10, n/60. The vendor had prepaid the freight charges, $150, adding the amount to the invoice and bringing its total to $3,900.

14   Recorded Voucher No. 457 payable to Payroll for sales salaries, $1,500, and office salaries, $1,125. Issued Cheque No. 840 in payment of the voucher. Cashed the cheque and paid the employees.

17   Recorded Voucher No. 458 payable to Bong Company for merchandise having a $2,250 invoice price, invoice dated March 15, terms 2/10, n/60, FOB factory. The vendor had prepaid the freight charges, $105, adding the amount to the invoice and bringing its total to $2,355.

20   Issued Cheque No. 841 in payment of Voucher No. 456.

24   Recorded Voucher No. 459 payable to San Marcos Company for merchandise having a $4,500 invoice price, invoice dated March 22, terms FOB factory, 2/10, n/60. The vendor had prepaid the freight charges, $210, adding the amount to the invoice and bringing its total to $4,710.

28   Discovered that Voucher No. 452 had been filed in error for payment on the last day of its credit period rather than on the last day of its discount period, causing the discount to be lost. Issued Cheque No. 842 in payment of the voucher, less the return.

31   Recorded Voucher No. 460 payable to Payroll for sales salaries, $1,500, and office salaries, $1,125. Issued Cheque No. 843 in payment of the voucher. Cashed the cheque and paid the employees.

Required:

1. Assume that Marney Company records vouchers at gross amounts. Prepare a Voucher Register, a Cheque Register, and a General Journal, and record the transactions.

2. Prepare a Vouchers Payable account and post those entry portions that affect the account.

3. Prove the balance of the Vouchers Payable account by preparing a schedule of vouchers payable.

ALTERNATE PROBLEMS

Problem 7–1A   A concern completed the following petty cash transactions:

Apr. 1   Drew a $200 cheque, cashed it, and turned the proceeds and the petty cash box over to Frank Smith, an office clerk who was to act as petty cashier.

4   Paid $13.25 parcel post charges on merchandise sold to a customer and delivered by mail.

7   Purchased office supplies with petty cash, $33.60.

9   Paid $53.20 from petty cash for repairs to an office copier.

11   Paid $14 COD delivery charges on merchandise purchased for resale.

16   Paid Fastest Delivery service $12.50 to deliver merchandise sold to a customer.

20   Gave Fred Strayer, the owner of the business, $25 from petty cash for personal use.

22   Paid $15.75 COD delivery charges on merchandise purchased for resale.

26   Fred Strayer, owner of the business, signed a petty cash receipt and took $10 from petty cash for lunch money.

29   Frank Smith exchanged his paid petty cash receipts for a cheque reimbursing the fund for expenditures and a shortage of cash in the fund that he could not account for. He reported a cash balance of $12.70 in the fund.

Required:

1. Prepare a general journal entry to record the cheque establishing the petty cash fund.
2. Prepare a summary of petty cash payments that has these categories: Office Supplies, Transportation-in, Delivery Expense, Withdrawals, and Miscellaneous Expenses. Sort the payments into the appropriate categories, total the expenses in each category, and prepare the general journal entry to reimburse the fund.

Problem 7–2A

A concern completed these petty cash transactions:

Feb. 2 Drew a $50 cheque to establish a petty cash fund, cashed it, and turned the proceeds and the petty cash box over to June Eaton, an office worker who was appointed petty cashier.

4 Paid $7.25 parcel post charges on merchandise sold to a customer and delivered by mail.

8 Paid $12 to have the office windows washed.

10 Purchased office supplies with petty cash, $14.50.

12 Carol Rash, owner of the business, signed a petty cash receipt and took $5 from petty cash for coffee money.

13 Paid $9.75 COD delivery charges on merchandise purchased for resale.

15 June Eaton noted that only $1.50 remained in the petty cash box. Thus, she sorted the petty cash receipts in terms of the accounts affected and exchanged the receipts for a cheque to reimburse the fund. However, since the fund had been exhausted so quickly, the cheque was made sufficiently large enough to increase the size of the fund to $100.

16 Paid $22 from petty cash for minor repairs to an office machine.

19 Paid $7.50 COD delivery charges on merchandise purchased for resale.

21 Paid City Delivery Service $5 to deliver merchandise sold to a customer.

25 Purchased office supplies with petty cash, $10.50.

27 Carol Rash, owner of the business, signed a petty cash receipt and took $10 from petty cash for lunch money.

Mar. 2 Paid $14.50 COD delivery charges on merchandise purchased for resale.

6 Purchased paper clips and pencils with petty cash, $9.75.

11 Paid $16.75 COD delivery charges on merchandise purchased for resale.

12 June Eaton sorted the petty cash receipts and exchanged them for a cheque to replenish the fund for expenditures and, since there was only $1 in cash in the fund, for the unexplained shortage.

Required:

1. Prepare a general journal entry to record the cheque establishing the petty cash fund.
2. Prepare a summary of petty cash payments prior to February 15 that has these categories: Delivery Expense, Office Supplies, Miscellaneous Expenses, Withdrawals, and Transportation-in. Sort the payments into the appropriate categories and total the expenses in each category. Prepare a similar summary of petty cash payments after February 15.
3. Prepare entries to reimburse the fund and increase its size on February 15 and to reimburse the fund on March 12.

Problem 7–3A

The accounting system used by the Crawford Company requires that all entries be journalized in a general journal. To facilitate payments of small items Crawford Company recently established a petty cash fund. The following transactions involving the petty cash fund occurred during April (the last month of the company's fiscal year).

Apr. 1 A company cheque for $100 was drawn and made payable to the petty cashier to establish the petty cash fund.

12 A company cheque was drawn to replenish the fund for the following expenditures made since April 1 and to increase the fund to $250.
   a. Purchased postage stamps for $25.
   b. Payment of $38.25 to Smith Trucking for delivery of merchandise to customers.
   c. Gave Roger Banes, owner of the business, $20 for personal use.
   d. Paid $12.75 to Appliance Company for repairs of office equipment.
   e. Discovered that only $1.00 remained in the petty cash box.

30 The petty cashier noted that $2.55 remained in the fund. Having decided that the April 12 increase in the fund was not large enough, a company cheque was drawn to replenish the fund for the following expenditures made since April 12 and to increase it to $350.
   a. Payment of $89.50 for office supplies to support the company's computer.
   b. Payment of $34.25 for items classified as miscellaneous general expense.
   c. Payment of $46 for janitorial service.
   d. Payment of $77.70 to Specialty Advertising Company for a space advertisement in a weekly newsletter.

Required:

1. Prepare general journal entries to record the establishment of the fund on April 1 and its replenishments on April 12 and on April 30.

2. If Crawford Company had failed to replenish the petty cash fund on April 30, what would have been the effect on net income for the fiscal year ended April 30 and on total assets on April 30? Explain your answer. (Hint: The amount of Office Supplies to appear on a balance sheet is determined by a physical count of the supplies on hand.)

Problem 7–4A   The following information was available to reconcile Tango Company's book balance of cash with its bank statement balance as of July 31:

a. After all posting was completed on July 31, the Company's Cash account had a $5,983 debit balance, but its bank statement showed a $7,845 balance.

b. Cheques, No. 721 for $306 and No. 726 for $591 were outstanding on the June 30 bank reconciliation. Cheque No. 726 was returned with the July canceled cheques, but Cheque No. 721 was not.

c. In comparing the canceled cheques returned with the bank statement with the entries in the accounting records, it was found that Cheque No. 801 for the purchase of office equipment was correctly drawn for $619 but was entered in the accounting records as though it were for $691. It was also found that Cheque No. 835 for $375 and Cheque No. 837 for $150, both drawn in July, were not among the canceled cheques returned with the statement.

d. A credit memorandum enclosed with the bank statement indicated that the bank had collected a $3,000 noninterest-bearing note for the concern, deducted a $30 collection fee, and had credited the remainder to the concern's account.

e. A debit memorandum for $370 listed a $360 NSF cheque plus a $10 NSF charge. The cheque had been received from a customer, Joe Schultz, and was among the canceled cheques returned.

f. Also among the canceled cheques was a $15 debit memorandum for bank services. None of the memoranda had been recorded.

g. The July 31 cash receipts, $1,626, were placed in the bank's night depository after banking hours on that date and their amount did not appear on the bank statement.

Required:

1. Prepare a bank reconciliation for the company.
2. Prepare entries in general journal form to bring the company's book balance of cash into conformity with the reconciled balance.

Problem 7–5A   Medusa Company reconciled its bank balance on May 31 and showed two cheques outstanding at that time, No. 808 for $524 and No. 813 for $186. The following information is available for the June 30 reconciliation:

From the June 30 bank statement:

```
BALANCE OF PREVIOUS STATEMENT ON 31/5/—...................   3,668.00
     5 DEPOSITS AND OTHER CREDITS TOTALING..................   6,120.00
     8 CHEQUES AND OTHER DEBITS TOTALING ...................   4,736.00
          SERVICE CHARGE AMOUNT ..............................     6.00
CURRENT BALANCE AS OF THIS STATEMENT ......................   5,046.00
```

CHEQUING ACCOUNT TRANSACTIONS °

. DATE	.... AMOUNT	TRANSACTION DESCRIPTION ....
3/6	446.00+	Deposit
12/6	1,890.00+	Deposit
22/6	1,298.00+	Deposit
28/6	1,496.00+	Deposit
29/6	480.00−	NSF cheque
30/6	6.00−	Service charge
30/6	990.00+	Credit memorandum

. DATE	... CHEQUE NO ...	... AMOUNT ...	. DATE .	... CHEQUE NO ...	.... AMOUNT
25/5	808	524.00	15/6	817	102.00
5/6	814*	612.00	15/6	818	234.00
3/6	815	450.00	28/6	819	642.00
6/6	816	1,692.00			

* Indicates a skip in cheque sequence

From Medusa Company's accounting records:

Cash Receipts Deposited

Date		Cash Debit
June	3	446.00
	12	1,890.00
	22	1,298.00
	28	1,496.00
	30	638.00
		5,768.00

Cash Disbursements

Cheque No.		Cash Credit
814		612.00
815		450.00
816		1,692.00
817		102.00
818		234.00
819		624.00
820		258.00
821		326.00
		4,298.00

Cash

Date		Explanation	PR	Debit	Credit	Balance
May	31	Balance				2,958.00
June	30	Total receipts	R-8	5,768.00		8,726.00
	30	Total disbursements	D-9		4,298.00	4,428.00

Cheque No. 819 was correctly drawn for $642 in payment for store equipment; however, the bookkeeper misread the amount and entered it in the accounting records with a debit to Store Equipment and a credit to Cash as though it were for $624. The bank paid and deducted the correct amount.

The NSF cheque was received from a customer, John Higgan, in payment of his account. Its return was unrecorded. The credit memorandum resulted from a $1,000 note which the bank had collected for the company, deducted a $10 collection fee, and deposited the balance in the company's account. The collection fee was not recorded.

Required:

1. Prepare a bank reconciliation for Medusa Company.
2. Prepare in general journal form the entries needed to bring the company's book balance of cash into agreement with the reconciled balance.

Problem 7–6A

The August 31 credit balance in the Sales account of Bailey Sales showed it had sold $262,000 of merchandise during the month. The concern began in August with a $229,000 merchandise inventory and ended the month with a $181,000 inventory. It had incurred $87,500 of operating expenses during the month, and it had also recorded the following transactions:

Aug. 3 Received merchandise purchased at a $30,000 invoice price, invoice dated July 30, terms 2/10, n/30.
  7 Received a $5,000 credit memorandum (invoice price) for merchandise received on August 3 and returned for credit.
  10 Received. merchandise purchased at an $45,000 invoice price, invoice dated August 8, terms 2/10, n/30.
  14 Received merchandise purchased at a $42,500 invoice price, invoice dated August 12, terms 2/10, n/30.
  18 Paid for the merchandise received on August 10, less the discount.
  22 Paid for the merchandise received on August 14, less the discount.
  30 Discovered that the invoice received on August 3 had been refiled in error, after the credit memorandum was attached, for payment on this the last day of its credit period, causing the discount to be lost. Paid the invoice.

Required:

1. Assume the concern records invoices at gross amounts:
   a. Prepare general journal entries to record the transactions.
   b. Prepare an August income statement for the concern.
2. Assume the concern records invoices at net amounts:
   a. Prepare general journal entries to record the transactions.
   b. Prepare a second income statement for the concern under this assumption.

Problem 7–7A

(This problem is based on information in the Appendix to this chapter.) Neff Company completed these transactions involving vouchers payable:

June 1 Recorded Voucher No. 511 payable to Daggett Company for merchandise having a $1,500 invoice price, invoice dated May 28, terms FOB destination, 2/10, n/30.

June 5 Recorded Voucher No. 512 payable to Hanson Company for merchandise having a $2,300 invoice price, invoice dated June 3, terms FOB factory, 2/10, n/60. The vendor had prepaid the freight charges, $100, adding the amount to the invoice and bringing its total to $2,400.

6 Received a credit memorandum for merchandise having a $500 invoice price. The merchandise was received on June 1, Voucher No. 511, and returned for credit.

13 Issued Cheque No. 710 in payment of Voucher No. 512.

15 Recorded Voucher No. 513 payable to Payroll for sales salaries, $800, and office salaries, $600. Issued Cheque No. 711 in payment of the voucher. Cashed the cheque and paid the employees.

18 Recorded Voucher No. 514 payable to Office Designers for the purchase of office equipment having a $600 invoice price, terms n/10 EOM.

22 Recorded Voucher No. 515 payable to *The Chronicle* for advertising expense, $250. Issued Cheque No. 712 in payment of the voucher.

25 Recorded Voucher No. 516 payable to Gong Company for merchandise having an $1,700 invoice price, invoice dated June 22, terms FOB factory, 2/10, n/60. The vendor had prepaid the freight charges, $60, adding the amount to the invoice and bringing its total to $1,760.

27 Discovered that Voucher No. 511 had been filed in error for payment on the last day of its credit period rather than on the last day of its discount period, causing the discount to be lost. Issued Cheque No. 713 in payment of the voucher, less the return.

30 Recorded Voucher No. 517 payable to Payroll for sales salaries, $800, and office salaries, $600. Issued Cheque No. 714 in payment of the voucher. Cashed the cheque and paid the employees.

Required:

Assume that Neff Company records vouchers at gross amounts.

a. Prepare a Voucher Register, a Cheque Register, and a General Journal and record the transactions.

b. Prepare a Vouchers Payable account and post those portions of the journal and register entries that affect the account.

c. Prove the balance of the Vouchers Payable account by preparing a schedule of unpaid vouchers.

PROVOCATIVE PROBLEMS

Provocative Problem 7–1, Magic Products Company

The Magic Products Company has enjoyed rapid growth since its beginning several years ago. Last year its sales were in excess of $10,000,000. However, its purchasing procedures may not have kept pace with its growth. When a plant supervisor or department head needs raw materials, plant assets, or supplies, he or she telephones a request to the purchasing department manager. The purchasing department manager prepares a purchase order in duplicate, sends one copy to the company selling the goods, and keeps the other copy in the files. When the seller's invoice is received, it is sent directly to the purchasing department. When the goods arrive, receiving department personnel count and inspect the items and prepare one copy of a receiving report which is sent to the purchasing department. The purchasing department manager attaches the receiving report and the retained copy of the purchase order to the invoice. If all is in order, the invoice is stamped "approved for payment" and signed by the purchasing department manager. The invoice and its supporting documents are then sent to the accounting department to be recorded and filed until due. On its due date, the invoice and its supporting documents are sent to the office of the company treasurer where a cheque is prepared and mailed. The number of the paying cheque is entered on the invoice and the invoice is sent to the accounting department for an entry to record its payment.

Do the procedures of Magic Products Company make it fairly easy for someone in the company to institute the payment of fictitious invoices by the company? If so, who is most likely to commit the fraud and what would that person have to do to receive payment of a fictitious invoice? What changes should be made in the company's purchasing procedures, and why should each change be made?

Provocative Problem 7–2, The Long-Term Employee

The bookkeeper at Old Time Company will retire next week after more than 40 years of service, having been hired by the father of the store's present owner. The bookkeeper has always been a very dependable employee, and as a result has been given more and more responsibilities over the years. Actually, for the past 15 years, he has "run" the store's office, keeping books, verifying invoices, and issuing cheques in their payment, which in the absence of the store's owner, Jay Jones, he could sign. In addition, at the end of each day, the store's salesclerks turn over their daily cash receipts to the bookkeeper. After counting the money and comparing the amounts with the cash register tapes, which he is responsible for removing from the cash registers, he makes the journal entry to record cash sales and then deposits the money in the bank. He also reconciles the bank balance with the book balance of cash each month.

Mr. Jones realizes he cannot expect a new bookkeeper to accomplish as much in a day as the old bookkeeper. And since the store is not large enough to warrant more than one office employee, he recognizes he must take over some of the old bookkeeper's duties when he retires. Mr. Jones already places all orders for merchandise and supplies and closely supervises all employees and does not want to add more to his duties than necessary.

Name the internal control principle violated here and tell which of the old bookkeeper's tasks should be taken over by Mr. Jones in order to improve the store's internal control over cash.

ANALYTICAL AND REVIEW PROBLEMS

Problem 7–1 A&R

Your assistant prepared the following bank reconciliation statement. Obviously the statement is unacceptable and the task of preparing a proper reconciliation falls upon you.

J. EVANS COMPANY
Bank Reconciliation
October 31, 198A

Balance per books October 31		$9,000
Add:		
Note collected	$1,500	
Interest on note	165	
Deposit in transit	5,800	7,465
		1,535
Deduct:		
Bank charges	25	
NSF cheque	375	
Outstanding cheques	1,090	
Error in Cheque No. 78 issued for $872 and		
recorded in the books as $827	45	1,535
True bank balance*		–0–

* Balance per bank statement is $5,510.

Required:

1. Prepare a proper bank reconciliation showing the true cash balance.
2. Prepare the necessary journal entries.

Problem 7–2
A&R

The bank statement for October arrived in Friday's mail. You were especially anxious to receive the statement as one of your assignments was to prepare a bank reconciliation for the Saturday meeting. You got around to preparing the reconciliation rather late in the afternoon and found all the necessary data with the exception of the bank balance. The bottom portion of the bank statement was smudged, and several figures, including the balance, were obliterated. A telephone call to the bank was answered by a recording with the information that the bank was closed until 10 A.M. Monday. Since the reconciliation had to be prepared you decided to plug-in the bank balance.

In preparation you assembled the necessary material as follows:

a. Cash balance per books was $7,200.
b. From the canceled cheques returned by the bank you determined that six cheques remained outstanding. The total of these cheques was $3,300.
c. In checking the canceled cheques you noted that Cheque No. 274 was properly made for $672 but was recorded in the cash disbursement journal as $627. The cheque was in payment of an account.
d. Included with the bank statement were two memoranda; the credit memorandum was for collection of a note for $1,500 and $90 of interest thereon and the debit memorandum was for $15 of bank charges.
e. While you were sorting the canceled cheques, one of the cheques caught your attention. You were astounded by the similarity of name with that of your company and the similarity of the cheques. The cheque was for $510 and was obviously in error charged to your company's account.
f. From the deposit book you determined that a $3,400 deposit was made after hours on October 31.

Required:

1. Prepare a bank reconciliation statement as of October 31 (plug-in the indicated bank balance).
2. Prepare the necessary journal entries.

Problem 7–3 A&R

The newly hired junior accountant of John Yu Company prepared the November 30 bank reconciliation statement as follows:

JOHN YU COMPANY
Bank Reconciliation
November 30, 198A

Balance per books		$ 6,800
Add:		
Collection of note by bank	$3,000	
Interest thereon	240	
Error re John Yee Company cheque	600	
Error re Cheque No. 282	54	3,894
		10,694
Deduct:		
Bank charges		24
True cash balance		10,670
Balance per bank		$ 9,400
Add:		
Deposit in transit	3,600	
NSF cheque	650	4,250
		13,650
Deduct:		
Outstanding cheques		2,980
True cash balance		$10,670

The controller took one glance at the reconciliation statement prepared by the junior accountant and screamed, "Where did we get him?" Therefore, the task of preparing a correct bank reconciliation fell upon you.

You determined the following:

a. All amounts in the reconciliation prepared by the junior accountant were correct.
b. The $600 John Yee Company cheque was erroneously credited by the bank to the John Yu Company account.
c. John Yu Company's Cheque No. 282 was properly drawn for $539 but was entered in the cash disbursement journal as $593. The cheque was in payment of an account.
d. The NSF cheque returned by the bank was from one of John Yu Company's customers.

Required:

1. Prepare a proper bank reconciliation statement, indicating the true cash balance.
2. Prepare the required journal entries.

Problem 7–4
A&R

Doug Langs acquired a sports equipment distribution business with a staff of six salespersons and two clerks. Because of the trust that Doug had in his employees—after all, they were all his friends and just like members of his family—he believed that an honour system with regard to the operation of the petty cash fund was adequate. Consequently, Doug placed $100 in a coffee jar, which, for convenience, was kept in a cupboard in the common room. All employees had access to the petty cash fund and withdrew amounts as required. No vouchers were required for withdrawals. As required, additional funds were placed in the coffee jar and the amount of the replenishment was charged to "miscellaneous selling expense."

Required:

1. From the internal control point of view, discuss the weaknesses of the petty cash fund operation and suggest steps necessary for improvement.
2. Does the petty cash fund operation as described above violate any of the generally accepted accounting principles? If yes, which and how is/are the principle(s) violated?

Credit Sales and Accounts Receivable

8

After studying Chapter 8, you should be able to:

Prepare entries to account for credit card sales.

Prepare entries accounting for bad debts both by the allowance method and the direct write-off method.

Explain the materiality principle and the full-disclosure principle.

Calculate the interest on promissory notes and the discount on notes receivable discounted.

Prepare entries to record the receipt of promissory notes and their payment or dishonour.

Prepare entries to record the discounting of notes receivable and if dishonoured, their dishonour.

Prepare reversing entries and explain the reasons for their use.

Define or explain the words and phrases listed in the chapter Glossary.

Several issues arise when accounting for transactions with customers, especially when sales are on credit. This chapter begins with a discussion of the procedures used to record credit card sales. It then focuses on accounting for the bad debts resulting from granting credit to customers and on accounting for notes receivable. Finally, the example of notes receivable is used to introduce the bookkeeping convenience of reversing entries.

CREDIT CARD SALES

Many customers use credit cards such as VISA, MasterCard, or American Express, to charge purchases from various businesses. This practice gives customers the ability to make purchases without carrying cash or writing cheques. In addition, the customer usually obtains credit for a period of time and can defer payment to the credit card company. Having established credit with the credit card company, the customer also avoids having to establish credit with each store and having to make several monthly payments to a variety of creditors.

There are also good reasons why many businesses allow customers to use credit cards. First, the business does not have to evaluate the credit standing of each customer and make decisions about who should get credit and how much. Second, the business avoids the risk of extending credit to customers who cannot pay. Third, the business often receives cash from the credit card company quicker than it would if customers were granted credit.

With some credit cards, usually those issued by banks, the business deposits a copy of each credit card receipt in its bank account just as it would deposit a customer's cheque. Thus, the business receives a cash credit immediately upon deposit. In the case of other credit cards, the business sends the appropriate copy of each receipt to the credit card company and then is paid by the company. Until payment is received, the business has an account receivable from the credit card company. In return for the services provided to the business, credit card companies charge a fee ranging from 2 to 5% of credit card sales. This charge is deducted from the cash payment to the business.

Accounting for credit card sales depends on whether cash is received immediately upon deposit or is delayed until paid by the credit card company. If cash is received immediately, the entry (in general journal form) to record credit card sales would be as follows:

Jan.	25	Cash	96.00	
		Credit Card Expense	4.00	
		Sales		100.00
		To record credit card sales less a 4% credit card expense.		

If the business must send the receipts to the credit card company and wait for payment, the entry to record credit card sales would be:

Jan.	25	Accounts Receivable, Credit Card Co.	100.00	
		Sales		100.00
		To record credit card sales.		

When cash is received from the credit card company, the entry to record the receipt would be:

Feb.	10	Cash	96.00	
		Credit Card Expense	4.00	
		Accounts Receivable, Credit Card Co.		100.00
		To record cash receipt less 4% credit card expense.		

Observe in the above entries that the credit card expense was not recorded until cash was received from the credit card company. This is a matter of convenience. By following this procedure, the business avoids having to calculate the credit card expense each time a sale is recorded. Instead, the expense related to many sales can be calculated once and recorded when cash is received. However, the **matching principle** requires that credit card expense be reported in the same period as the sale. If the sales and the cash receipt occur in different periods, credit card expense should be accrued and reported in the period of sale.

 Credit card expense is sometimes disclosed in the income statement as a type of discount that is deducted from sales to obtain net sales. Other companies classify it as a selling expense or even as an administrative expense. Arguments can be made for all three alternatives.

BAD DEBTS

When a company grants credit to its customers, there are almost always a few customers who do not pay. The accounts of such customers are called *bad debts* and are an expense of selling on credit.

It might be asked: Why do merchants sell on credit if bad debts result? The answer is, of course, that they sell on credit in order to increase sales and profits. They are willing to take a reasonable loss from bad debts in order to increase sales and profits. Therefore, bad debt losses are an expense of selling on credit, an expense incurred in order to increase sales. Consequently, if the requirements of the **matching**

principle are met, bad debt losses must be matched against the sales they helped produce.

MATCHING BAD DEBT LOSSES WITH SALES

Credit sales that result in bad debt losses are made in one accounting period, but final recognition that the customers will not pay commonly does not occur until a later period. Final recognition waits until every means of collecting has been exhausted, which may take a year or more. Therefore, if bad debt losses are matched with the sales they helped to produce, they must be matched on an estimated basis. The *allowance method of accounting for bad debts* does just that.

ALLOWANCE METHOD OF ACCOUNTING FOR BAD DEBTS

Under the allowance method of accounting for bad debts, an estimate is made at the end of each accounting period of the total bad debts that are expected to result from the period's sales. An allowance is then provided for the loss. This has two advantages: (1) the estimated loss is charged to the period in which the revenue is recognized; and (2) the accounts receivable appear on the balance sheet at their estimated realizable value, a more informative balance sheet amount.

Recording the Estimated Bad Debts Expense

Under the allowance method of accounting for bad debts, the estimated bad debts expense is recorded at the end of each accounting period with a work sheet adjustment and an adjusting entry. For example, assume that Alpha Company had charge sales of $300,000 during the first year of its operations. At the end of the year, $20,000 remains uncollected in accounts receivable. Based on these facts, Alpha Company estimates that $1,500 of accounts receivable will prove to be uncollectible. This estimated expense is recorded with an adjusting entry such as the following:

Dec.	31	Bad Debts Expense	1,500.00	
		Allowance for Doubtful Accounts		1,500.00
		To record the estimated bad debts.		

The debit of this entry causes the estimated bad debts expense to appear on the income statement of the year in which the sales were made. As a result, the estimated $1,500 expense of selling on credit is matched with the $300,000 of revenue it helped to produce.

Note that the credit of the entry is to the contra account, Allowance for Doubtful Accounts. It is necessary to credit the contra account because at the time of the adjusting entry it is not known for certain which customers will fail to pay. (The total loss from bad debts can be estimated from past experience. However, the exact customers who will not pay cannot be known until every means of collecting from each has been exhausted.) Consequently, since the bad accounts are not identifiable at the time of the adjusting entry, they cannot be removed from the subsidiary Accounts Receivable Ledger. As a result, the Allowance for Doubtful Accounts account must be credited instead of the controlling account. The allowance account must be credited because to credit the controlling account without removing the bad accounts from the subsidiary ledger would cause the controlling account balance to differ from the sum of the balances in the subsidiary ledger.

Bad Debts in the Accounts and on the Balance Sheet

Bad debts expense normally appears on the income statement as an administrative expense rather than as a selling expense because granting credit is usually not a responsibility of the sales department. Therefore, since the sales department is not responsible for granting credit, it should not be held responsible for bad debts expenses. The sales department is usually not given responsibility for granting credit because it may at times be swayed in its judgment of a credit risk by its desire to increase sales.

Recall the assumption that Alpha Company has $20,000 of outstanding accounts receivable at the end of its first year of operations. Thus, after the bad debts adjusting entry is posted, the company's Accounts Receivable and Allowance for Doubtful Accounts accounts will show these balances:

Accounts Receivable		Allowance for Doubtful Accounts	
Dec. 31 20,000			Dec. 31 1,500

The $1,500 credit balance in Allowance for Doubtful Accounts has the effect of reducing accounts receivable (net of the allowance) to their estimated *realizable value*. Realizable value is the amount of cash that should be received as the assets are converted into cash in the ordinary course of business. Although $20,000 is legally owed to Alpha Company, only $18,500 is likely to be realized in cash.

When the balance sheet is prepared, the *allowance for doubtful accounts* is subtracted thereon from the accounts receivable to show the amount that is expected to be realized from the accounts, as follows:

Current assets:
Cash $11,300
Accounts receivable $20,000
Less allowance for doubtful accounts ... (1,500)   18,500
Merchandise inventory 67,200
Prepaid expenses 1,100
Total current assets $98,100

Writing off a Bad Debt

When an allowance for doubtful accounts is provided, accounts deemed uncollectible are written off against this allowance. For example, after spending a year trying to collect, Alpha Company finally concluded the $100 account of George Vale was uncollectible and made the following entry to write it off:

Jan.	23	Allowance for Doubtful Accounts	100.00	
		Accounts Receivable—George Vale		100.00
		To write off an uncollectible account.		

Posting the credit of the entry to the Accounts Receivable account removes the amount of the bad debt from the controlling account. Posting it to the George Vale account removes the amount of the bad debt from the subsidiary ledger. Posting the entry has this effect on the general ledger accounts:

Accounts Receivable				**Allowance for Doubtful Accounts**			
Dec. 31	20,000	Jan. 23	100	Jan. 23	100	Dec. 31	1,500

Two points should be observed in the entry and accounts. First, although bad debts are an expense of selling on credit, the allowance account rather than an expense account is debited in the write-off. The allowance account is debited because the expense was recorded at the end of the period in which the sale occurred. At that time, the loss was foreseen, and the expense was recorded in the estimated bad debts adjusting entry.

Second, although the write-off removed the amount of the account receivable from the ledgers, it did not affect the estimated realizable amount of Alpha Company's accounts receivable, as the following tabulation shows:

	Before write-off	After write-off
Accounts receivable	$20,000	$19,900
Less allowance for doubtful accounts	1,500	1,400
Estimated realizable accounts receivable	$18,500	$18,500

BAD DEBT RECOVERIES

Frequently, an error in judgment is made and accounts written off as uncollectible are later sometimes collected in full or in part. If an account is written off as uncollectible and later the customer pays part or all of the amount previously written off, the payment should be shown in the customer's account for future credit action. It should be shown because when a customer fails to pay and his or her account is written off, the customer's credit standing is impaired. Later when the customer pays, the payment helps restore the credit standing. When an account previously written off as a bad debt is collected, two entries are made. The first reinstates the customer's account and has the effect of reversing the original write-off. The second entry records the collection of the reinstated account.

For example, assume that George Vale, whose account was previously written off, pays in full on August 15. The entries in general journal form to record the bad debt recovery are:

Aug.	15	Accounts Receivable—George Vale	100.00	
		Allowance for Doubtful Accounts		100.00
		To reinstate the account of George Vale written off on January 23.		
	15	Cash	100.00	
		Accounts Receivable—George Vale		100.00
		In full of account.		

In this case, George Vale paid the entire amount previously written off. Sometimes after an account is written off the customer will pay a portion of the amount owed. The question then arises, should the entire balance of the account be returned to accounts receivable or just the amount paid? The answer is a matter of judgment. If it is thought the customer will pay in full, the entire amount owed should be returned.

However, only the amount paid should be returned if it is thought that no more will be collected.

ESTIMATING THE AMOUNT OF BAD DEBTS EXPENSE

As previously discussed, the allowance method of accounting for doubtful accounts requires an adjusting entry at the end of each accounting period to estimate the bad debts expense for the period. That entry takes the following form:

Dec.	31	Bad Debts Expense	????	
		Allowance for Doubtful Accounts		????

What is the process by which a company estimates the amount to be recorded in this entry? There are two broad alternatives. One is to focus on the income statement relationship between bad debts expense and sales. The other is to focus on the balance sheet relationship between accounts receivable and allowance for doubtful accounts. Both alternatives involve a careful analysis of past experience.

Estimating Bad Debts by Focusing on the Income Statement

The income statement approach to estimating bad debts is based on the idea that some particular percentage of a company's credit sales will prove to be uncollectible. Hence, in the income statement the amount of bad debts expense should be the same as the percentage of credit sales. Suppose, for example, that Baker Company's credit sales in 198A amounted to $400,000. Also suppose that according to past experience and knowledge of similar companies, 0.6% of credit sales are typically uncollectible. Using this information, Baker Company can expect $2,400 of bad debts expense to result from the year's sales ($400,000 × 0.006 = $2,400). Therefore, the adjusting entry to record bad debts expense would be as follows:

Dec.	31	Bad Debts Expense	2,400.00	
		Allowance for Doubtful Accounts		2,400.00

Importantly, this entry **does not** mean the December 31, 198A, balance in Allowance for Doubtful Accounts will be $2,400. It will probably be some other amount. There are three reasons why this is true:

1. The bad debts percentage (0.6%) was only an estimate. The actual amount of accounts receivable that becomes uncollectible will likely be somewhat larger or smaller than this.
2. Some of the accounts arising from 198A credit sales may have been written off prior to December 31, 198A. If so, the entries to write them off involved debits to Allowance for Doubtful Accounts. Thus, the December 31 balance would be $2,400 less the amounts previously written off.
3. There probably was a credit balance in the account at the beginning of the year. In each past year, bad debts were estimated at year-end, and accounts that became uncollectible were written off. The balance in Allowance for Doubtful Accounts reflects these events from past years as well as those in the current year.

Often when the addition to the Allowance for Doubtful Accounts account is based on a percentage of sales, the passage of several accounting periods often is required before it becomes apparent that the percentage is either too large or too small. In such cases, when it becomes apparent the percentage is incorrect, a change in the percentage to be used in future periods should be made.

Estimating Bad Debts by Focusing on the Balance Sheet

The balance sheet approach to estimating bad debts is based on the idea that some portion of the outstanding accounts receivable as shown in the balance sheet will become uncollectible. Hence, after the bad debts adjusting entry is posted, the balance in Allowance for Doubtful Accounts should equal the portion of outstanding accounts receivable estimated to be uncollectible. The amount to be debited to Bad Debts Expense and credited to Allowance for Doubtful Accounts is whatever is necessary to result in the correct balance in Allowance for Doubtful Accounts. The balance sheet approach may take two forms: (1) a simplified approach, and (2) aging of accounts receivable.

A SIMPLIFIED BALANCE SHEET APPROACH.   Using the simplified balance sheet approach, a company observes the amount of outstanding accounts receivable at year-end. Based on past experience, some percentage of outstanding receivables is estimated to become uncollectible. This percentage is multiplied by the amount of outstanding receivables to determine the required ending balance in Allowance for Doubtful Accounts. Whatever balance exists in the account prior to the adjustment is then compared to the required balance to determine the amount of the adjustment.

For example, assume that Baker Company of the previous illustration has $50,000 of outstanding accounts receivable on December 31, 198A. Past experience indicates that 5% of outstanding receivables will become uncollectible. Thus, after the adjusting entry is posted, Allowance for Doubtful Accounts should have a $2,500 credit balance. Assume that before making the necessary adjustment, the account appears as follows:

Allowance for Doubtful Accounts

		Dec. 31 bal.	2,000
Feb. 6	800		
July 10	600		
Nov. 20	400		

Understand that the $2,000 beginning balance appeared on last year's balance sheet. Then, during 198A, accounts of specific customers were written off on February 6, July 10, and November 20. Consequently, the account has a $200 credit balance prior to the December 31, 198A, adjustment. The adjusting entry to give the account the required $2,500 balance is:

Dec.	31	Bad Debts Expense	2,300.00	
		Allowance for Doubtful Accounts		2,300.00

AGING ACCOUNTS RECEIVABLE. Both the income statement approach and the simplified balance sheet approach use the knowledge gained from past experience to estimate bad debts expense. However, neither method of analysis is as refined as is the balance sheet approach involving *aging of accounts receivable.*

Aging of accounts receivable requires that each outstanding account at the end of the period be classified in terms of how long it has been outstanding. In some cases, executives of the sales and credit departments may examine each account listed and by judgment decide which are probably uncollectible. More often, they use past experience to estimate a percentage of each category that will become uncollectible. This is done with a schedule like the one for Baker Company shown in Illustration 8–1.

The analysis of Illustration 8–1 indicates that the adjusted balance in Baker Company's Allowance for Doubtful Accounts should be $2,290 ($740 + $325 + $350 + $475 + $400 = $2,290). Since the account was previously assumed to have a preadjusted credit balance of $200,

Illustration 8–1

BAKER COMPANY Schedule of Accounts Receivable by Age					
Customer's Name	Not Due	1 to 30 Days Past Due	31 to 60 Days Past Due	61 to 90 Days Past Due	Over 90 Days Past Due
Charles Abbot	450.00				
Frank Allen	710.00				
George Arden		200.00	300.00		
Paul Baum					640.00
Totals	37,000.00 × 2%	6,500.00 × 5%	3,500.00 × 10%	1,900.00 × 25%	1,000.00 × 40%
Est. uncollectible accounts	740.00	325.00	350.00	475.00	400.00

the aging of accounts receivable approach would require the following adjusting entry:

Dec.	31	Bad Debts Expense	2,090.00	
		Allowance for Doubtful Accounts		2,090.00

Recall from page 350 that when the income statement approach was used, bad debts expense was estimated to be $2,400. When the simplified balance sheet approach was used (page 351), the estimate was $2,300. And when aging of accounts receivable was used, the estimate was $2,090. It should not be surprising that the amounts are different. After all, each approach is only an estimate. However, the aging of accounts receivable allows a more detailed examination of outstanding accounts and is usually most reliable.

DIRECT WRITE-OFF OF BAD DEBTS

The allowance method of accounting for bad debts is designed to satisfy the requirements of the *matching principle*. Consequently, it is the method that should be used in most cases. However, under certain circumstances another method, called the *direct write-off method,* may be acceptable. Under this method, when it is decided that an account is uncollectible, it is written off directly to Bad Debts Expense with an entry like this:

Nov.	23	Bad Debts Expense	52.50	
		Accounts Receivable—Dale Hall		52.50
		To write off the uncollectible account.		

The debit of the entry charges the bad debt loss directly to the current year's Bad Debts Expense account. The credit removes the balance of the account from the subsidiary ledger and controlling account.

If an account previously written off directly to Bad Debts Expense is later collected in full, the following entries are used to record the recovery:

Mar.	11	Accounts Receivable—Dale Hall	52.50	
		Bad Debts Expense		52.50
		To reinstate the account of Dale Hall previously written off.		
	11	Cash	52.50	
		Accounts Receivable—Dale Hall		52.50
		In full of account.		

Sometimes a bad debt previously written off directly to the Bad Debts Expense account is recovered in the year following the write-off. If at that time the Bad Debts Expense account has no balance from other write-offs and no write-offs are expected, the credit of the entry recording the recovery can be to a revenue account called Bad Debt Recoveries.

DIRECT WRITE-OFF MISMATCHES REVENUE AND EXPENSES. The direct write-off method commonly mismatches revenues and expenses. The mismatch results because the revenue from a bad debt sale appears on the income statement of one year while the expense of the loss may be deducted on the income statement of the following or a later year. Nevertheless, it may still be used in situations where its use does not materially affect reported net income. For example, it may be used in a concern where bad debt losses are immaterial in relation to total sales and net income. In such a concern, the use of direct write-off comes under the accounting *principle of materiality*.

The Principle of Materiality

Under the *principle of materiality,* it is held that a strict adherence to any accounting principle, in this case the *matching principle,* is not required when the lack of adherence does not materially affect the financial statements. Or in other words, failure to adhere is permissible when the failure does not produce an error or misstatement sufficiently large as to influence a financial statement reader's judgment of a given situation.

INSTALLMENT ACCOUNTS AND NOTES RECEIVABLE

Many companies grant credit to customers and allow them to make periodic payments over several months. When this is done, the selling company's asset may be in the form of an installment account receivable or a note receivable. *Installment accounts receivable,* like any other accounts receivable, are typically evidenced by sales slips or invoices describing each sales transaction. A note receivable, on the other hand, is a written document promising payment and signed by the customer. In either case, when payments are to be made over several months or if the credit period is long, the customer is typically charged interest. Although the credit period of installment accounts and notes receivable often may be more than one year, they are normally classified as current assets if the company regularly offers customers such terms.

Notes receivable are generally preferred over accounts receivable when the credit period is long and the receivable relates to a single sale of fairly large amount. Notes are also used to replace accounts receivable when customers ask for additional time in which to pay their past-due accounts. In these situations, creditors prefer notes to accounts receivable because the notes may be converted into cash before becoming due by discounting (selling) them to a bank. Likewise, notes are preferred for legal reasons. If a lawsuit is needed to collect, a note represents written acknowledgment by the debtor of both the debt and its amount.

PROMISSORY NOTES

A promissory note is an unconditional promise in writing to pay on demand or at a fixed or determinable future date a definite sum of money. In the note shown in Illustration 8–2, Hugo Brown promises to pay Frank Black or his order a definite sum of money at a fixed future date. Hugo Brown is the *maker* of the note. Frank Black is the *payee.* To Hugo Brown, the illustrated note is a **note payable,** a liability. To Frank Black, the same note is a **note receivable,** an asset.

The illustrated Hugo Brown note bears interest at 14%. Interest is a charge for the use of money. To a borrower, interest is an expense. To

Illustration 8–2

$ 1,000.00	Windsor, Ontario	March 9, 19--

Sixty days _____ after date _____ I _____ promise to pay to

the order of _____ Frank Black

One thousand and no/100--dollars

for value received with interest at ____14%

payable at ____First National Bank, Windsor, Ontario

Hugo Brown

a lender, it is a revenue. A note may be interest bearing or it may be noninterest bearing. If a note bears interest, the rate or the amount of interest must be stated on the note.

LEGAL DUE DATES

All notes, except notes payable on demand, are due and payable three days (called days of grace) after the time indicated in each note. The time of a note may be indicated in different ways. For example:

1. A note may read: "I promise to pay $500 on December 18." To determine the legal due date of this note, three days of grace are added to December 18 and the note is due on December 21.
2. A note dated June 10 may read: "Ninety days after date I promise to pay $1,000." In such a case exact days, not including the day of the note's date but including the day of its legal due date, are counted and this note is due on September 11, calculated as follows:

Number of days in June	30
Minus the date of the note, June 10	10
Gives the number of days the note runs in June	20
Adds the number of days in July	31
Add the number of days in August	31
Total through August 31	82
Days needed in September to equal the time stated in the note plus 3 days of grace, a total of 93 days, and also the legal due date of the note, September 11	11
Total time the note runs in days	93

3. A note dated June 15 may read: "Four months after date I promise to pay $800." In such a case four months and three days (of grace) are added to June 15 and this note is due on October 18.

4. A note dated August 9, 1984, may read: "Four years after date I promise to pay $5,000." Such a note is due on August 12, 1988, which is four years and three days after its date.

Some notes are payable on demand and read: "On demand, I promise to pay $1,500." Such a note is due on the day the payee demands payment and no days of grace are allowed.

Notes often fall due on a legal holiday or nonjudicial day, and such notes are due on the first business day thereafter. Saturdays, Sundays, New Year's Day, Good Friday, Easter Monday, Victoria Day, Dominion Day, Labour Day, Remembrance Day, Thanksgiving Day, Christmas Day, and the birthday of the reigning sovereign are legal holidays or nonjudicial days throughout Canada. The Epiphany, Ascension Day, All Saints Day, and Conception Day are also legal holidays in Quebec. In addition, legal holidays that are observed only in that province or city may be proclaimed by the Lieutenant Governor or by a resolution of the municipal authority.

CALCULATING INTEREST

Unless otherwise stated, the rate of interest on a note is the rate charged for the use of the principal for one year or 365 days (366 days in a leap year). The formula for calculating interest is:

$$\frac{\text{Principal of}}{\text{the note}} \times \frac{\text{Rate of}}{\text{interest}} \times \frac{\text{Time of}}{\text{the note}} = \text{Interest}$$

The time of a note always includes the days of grace, and exact days are used in calculating interest. For example, the interest on a $1,000, 8%, one-year note is calculated as follows:

$$\$1,000 \times 0.08 \times \frac{368}{365} = \$80.66$$

And the interest on a $5,000, 7%, 90-day note is calculated:

$$\$5,000 \times 0.07 \times \frac{93}{365} = \$89.18$$

Also, interest on a note dated June 5 that reads "Three months after date I promise to pay $1,000 with interest at 12%" is calculated:

1. First the legal due date of the note, September 8, is determined by adding three months plus three days of grace to June 5.

2. Next the time of the note is calculated as follows:

Number of days in June	30
Minus the date of the note, June 5	5
Days the note runs in June	25
Days in July	31
Days in August	31
Days the note runs in September	8
Total time the note runs in days	95

3. Then the interest on the note is calculated:

$$\$1,000 \times 0.12 \times \frac{95}{365} = \$31.23$$

RECORDING THE RECEIPT OF A NOTE

Notes receivable are recorded in a single Notes Receivable account. Each note may be identified in the account by writing the name of the maker in the Explanation column on the line of the entry recording its receipt or payment. Only one account is needed because the individual notes are on hand. Consequently, the maker, rate of interest, due date, and other information may be learned by examining each note.

A note received at the time of a sale is recorded as follows:

Dec.	5	Notes Receivable	650.00	
		Sales		650.00
		Sold merchandise, terms six-month, 9% note.		

When a note is taken in granting a time extension on a past-due account receivable, the creditor usually attempts to collect part of the past-due account in cash. This reduces the debt and requires the acceptance of a note for a smaller amount. For example, Symplex Company agrees to accept $232 in cash and a $500, 60-day, 14% note from Joseph Cook in settlement of his $732 past-due account. When Symplex receives the cash and note, the following entry in general journal form is made:

Oct.	5	Cash	232.00	
		Notes Receivable	500.00	
		Accounts Receivable—Joseph Cook		732.00
		Received cash and a note in settlement of an account.		

Observe that this entry changes the form of $500 of the debt from an account receivable to a note receivable.

When Cook pays the note, this entry in general journal form is made:

Dec.	7	Cash	512.08	
		Notes Receivable		500.00
		Interest Earned		12.08
		Collected the Joseph Cook note.		

Look again at the last two entries. If Symplex Company uses columnar journals, the entry of December 7 would be recorded in its Cash Receipts Journal. Two lines would be required, one for the credit to Interest Earned and a second for the credit to Notes Receivable. Likewise, the October 5 transaction would be recorded with two entries, one in the Cash Receipts Journal for the money received and a second entry in the General Journal for the note. Nevertheless, to simplify the illustrations, general journal entries are shown here and will be used through the remainder of this text. However, the student should realize that the entries would be made in a Cash Receipts Journal or other appropriate journal.

DISHONOURED NOTES RECEIVABLE

Occasionally, the maker of a note either cannot or will not pay the note at maturity. When a note's maker refuses to pay at maturity, the note is said to be *dishonoured*. Dishonour does not relieve the maker of the obligation to pay. Furthermore, every legal means should be made to collect. However, collection may require lengthy legal proceedings.

The balance of the Notes Receivable account should show only the amount of notes that have not matured. Consequently, when a note is dishonoured, its amount should be removed from the Notes Receivable account and charged back to the account of its maker. To illustrate, Simplex Company holds an $800, 12%, 60-day note of George Jones. At maturity, Jones dishonours the note. To remove the dishonoured note from its Notes Receivable account, the company makes the following entry:

Oct.	14	Accounts Receivable—George Jones	816.57	
		Interest Earned		16.57
		Notes Receivable		800.00
		To charge the account of George Jones for his dishonoured note.		

Charging a dishonoured note back to the account of its maker serves two purposes. It removes the amount of the note from the Notes Receivable account, leaving in the account only notes that have not matured. It also records the dishonoured note in the maker's account. The second purpose is important. If in the future the maker of the dishonoured note again applies for credit, his or her account will show all past dealings, including the dishonoured note.

Observe in the entry that the Interest Earned account is credited for interest earned even though it was not collected. The reason for this is that Jones owes both the principal and the interest. Consequently, his account should reflect the full amount owed on the date of the entry.

DISCOUNTING NOTES RECEIVABLE

As previously stated, a note receivable is preferred to an account receivable because the note can be turned into cash before maturity by discounting (selling) it to a bank. In *discounting a note receivable* the owner endorses and delivers the note to the bank in exchange for cash. The bank holds the note to maturity and then collects its maturity value from the maker. To illustrate, assume that on May 28 Symplex Company received a $1,200, 60-day, 12% note dated May 27 from John Owen. It held the note until June 2 and then discounted it at its bank at 15%. Since the *maturity date* of this note is July 29, the bank must wait 57 days after discounting the note to collect from Owen. These 57 days are called the *discount period* and are calculated as follows:

Time of the note in days		63
Less time held by Symplex Company:		
Number of days in May	31	
Less the date of the note	27	
Days held in May	4	
Days held in June	2	
Total days held		6
Discount period in days		57

At the end of the discount period the bank expects to collect the *maturity value* of this note from Owen. Therefore, as is customary, it bases its discount on the maturity value of the note, which is calculated as follows:

Principal of the note	$1,200.00
Interest on $1,200 for 63 days at 12% . . .	24.85
Maturity value	$1,224.85

In this case the bank's discount rate, or the rate of interest it charges for lending money, is 15%. Consequently, in discounting the note, it will deduct 57 days' interest at 15% from the note's maturity value and will give Symplex Company the remainder. The remainder is called the *proceeds of the note.* The amount of interest deducted is known as *bank discount.* The bank discount and the proceeds are calculated as follows:

Maturity value of the note	$1,224.85
Less: Interest on $1,224.85 for 57 days at 15% ...	28.69
Proceeds	$1,196.16

Observe in this case that the proceeds, $1,196.16, are $3.84 less than the $1,200 principal amount of the note. Consequently, Symplex will make this entry in recording the discount transaction:

June	2	Cash	1,196.16	
		Interest Expense	3.84	
		Notes Receivable		1,200.00
		Discounted the John Owen note for 57 days at 15%.		

In recording the transaction, Symplex in effect offsets the $24.85 interest it would have earned by holding the note to maturity against the $28.69 discount charged by the bank and records only the difference, the $3.84 excess of expense.

In the situation just described the principal of the discounted note exceeded the proceeds. However, in many cases the proceeds exceed the principal. When this happens, the difference is credited to Interest Earned. For example, suppose that instead of discounting the John Owen note on June 2, Symplex held the note and discounted it on June 29. If the note is discounted on June 29 at 15%, the discount period is 30 days, the discount is $15.10, and the proceeds of the note are $1,209.75, calculated as follows:

Maturity value of the note	$1,224.85
Less: Interest on $1,224.85 for 30 days at 15% ...	15.10
Proceeds	$1,209.75

And since the proceeds exceed the principal, the transaction is recorded as follows:

June	29	Cash	1,209.75	
		Interest Earned		9.75
		Notes Receivable		1,200.00
		Discounted the John Owen note for 30 days at 15%.		

Contingent Liability

A person or company discounting a note is ordinarily required to endorse the note because an endorsement, unless it is qualified, makes the endorser contingently liable for payment of the note.[1] The *contingent liability* depends upon the note's dishonour by its maker. If the maker pays, the endorser has no liability. However, if the maker defaults, the endorser's contingent liability becomes an actual liability, and the endorser must pay the note for the maker.

A contingent liability, since it can become an actual liability, may affect the credit standing of the person or concern contingently liable. Consequently, a discounted note should be shown as such in the Notes Receivable account. Also, if a balance sheet is prepared before the discounted note's maturity date, the contingent liability should be indicated on the balance sheet. For example, if in addition to the John Owen note, Symplex Company holds $500 of other notes receivable, the record of the discounted John Owen note may appear in its Notes Receivable account as follows:

Notes Receivable						
Date		Explanation	Post Ref.	Debit	Credit	Balance
May	28	John Owen note	G6	1,200.00		1,200.00
June	7	Earl Hill note	G6	500.00		1,700.00
	26	Discounted the J. Owen note	G7		1,200.00	500.00

The contingent liability resulting from discounted notes receivable is commonly shown on a balance sheet by means of a footnote. If Symplex Company follows this practice, it will show the $500 of notes it has not discounted and the contingent liability resulting from discounting the John Owen note on its June 30 balance sheet, as follows:

---

[1] A qualified endorsement is one in which the endorser states in writing that he or she will not be liable for payment.

Current assets:
Cash .... $ 5,315
Notes receivable (Footnote 2) 500
Accounts receivable 21,475

Footnote 2: Symplex Company is contingently liable for $1,200 of notes receivable discounted.

Full-Disclosure Principle

The balance sheet disclosure of contingent liabilities is required under the *full-disclosure principle*. Under this principle, it is held that financial statements and their accompanying footnotes should disclose fully and completely all relevant data of a material nature relating to the financial position of the company for which they are prepared. This does not necessarily mean that the information should be detailed, for details can at times obscure. It simply means that all information necessary to an appreciation of the company's position be reported in a readily understandable manner and that nothing of a significant nature be withheld. For example, any of the following would be considered relevant and should be disclosed.

CONTINGENT LIABILITIES. In addition to discounted notes, a company that is contingently liable due to possible additional tax assessments, pending lawsuits, or product guarantees should disclose this on its statements.

LONG-TERM COMMITMENTS UNDER A CONTRACT. If the company has signed a long-term lease requiring a material annual payment, this should be disclosed even though the liability does not appear in the accounts. Also, if the company has pledged certain of its assets as security for a loan, this should be revealed.

ACCOUNTING METHODS USED. Whenever there are several acceptable accounting methods that may be followed, a company should report in each case the method used, especially when a choice of methods can materially affect reported net income. For example, a company should report by means of footnotes accompanying its statements the inventory method or methods used, depreciation methods, method of recognizing revenue under long-term construction contracts, and the like.[2]

---

[2] *CICA Handbook* (Toronto: The Canadian Institute of Chartered Accountants), par. 1505.09.

DISHONOUR OF A DISCOUNTED NOTE

A bank always tries to collect a discounted note directly from the maker. If it is able to do so, the one who discounted it will not hear from the bank and will need to do nothing more in regard to the note. However, according to law, if a discounted note is dishonoured, the bank must before the end of the next business day notify each endorser of the note if it is to hold the endorsers liable on the note. To notify the endorsers, the bank will normally protest the dishonoured note. To protest a note, the bank prepares and mails before the end of the next business day a *notice of protest* to each endorser. A notice of protest is a statement, usually attested by a notary public, that says the note was duly presented to the maker for payment and payment was refused. The cost of protesting a note is called a *protest fee,* and the bank will look to the one who discounted the note for payment of both the note's maturity value and the protest fee.

For example, suppose that instead of paying the $1,200 note previously illustrated, John Owen dishonoured it. In such a situation, the bank would notify Symplex Company immediately of the dishonour by mailing a notice of protest and a letter asking payment of the note's maturity value plus the protest fee. If the protest fee is, say, $5, Symplex must pay the bank $1,229.85; and in recording the payment, Symplex will charge the $1,229.85 to the account of John Owen, as follows:

July	30	Accounts Receivable—John Owen	1,229.85	
		Cash		1,229.85
		To charge the account of Owen for the maturity value of his dishonoured note plus the protest fee.		

Of course, upon receipt of the $1,229.85, the bank will deliver to Symplex the dishonoured note. Symplex Company will then make every legal effort to collect from Owen not only the maturity value of the note and protest fee but also interest on both from the date of dishonour until the date of final settlement. However, it may not be able to collect, and after exhausting every legal means to do so, it may have to write the account off as a bad debt. Normally in such cases no additional interest is taken onto the books before the write-off.

Although dishonoured notes commonly have to be written off as bad debts, some are also eventually paid by their makers. For example, if 30 days after dishonour, John Owen pays the maturity value of his dishonoured note, the protest fee, and interest at 12% on both for 30 days beyond maturity, he will pay the following:

Maturity value	$1,224.85	
Protest fee	5.00	
Interest on $1,229.85 for 30 days at 12%	12.13	
Total	$1,241.98	

And Symplex will record receipt of his money as follows:

Aug.	28	Cash	1,241.98	
		Interest Earned		12.13
		Accounts Receivable—John Owen		1,229.85
		Dishonoured note and protest fee collected with interest.		

END-OF-PERIOD ADJUSTMENTS

If any notes receivable are outstanding at the accounting period end, their accrued interest should be calculated and recorded. For example, on December 16 a company accepted a $3,000, 60-day, 12% note from a customer in granting an extension on a past-due account. If the company's accounting period ends on December 31, by then $14.79 interest has accrued on this note and should be recorded with this adjusting entry:

Dec.	31	Interest Receivable	14.79	
		Interest Earned		14.79
		To record accrued interest on a note receivable.		

The adjusting entry causes the interest earned to appear on the income statement of the period in which it was earned. It also causes the interest receivable to appear on the balance sheet as a current asset.

Collecting Interest Previously Accrued

When the note is collected, the transaction may be recorded as follows:

Feb.	17	Cash	3,062.14	
		Interest Earned		47.35
		Interest Receivable......................		14.79
		Notes Receivable		3,000.00
		Received payment of a note and its interest.		

The entry's credit to Interest Receivable records collection of the interest accrued at the end of the previous period.

REVERSING ENTRIES

To correctly record a transaction like that of the February 17 entry just shown, a bookkeeper must remember the accrued interest recorded at the end of the previous year and divide the amount of interest received between the Interest Earned and Interest Receivable accounts. Many bookkeepers find this difficult, and they avoid "the need to remember" by preparing and posting entries to reverse any end-of-the-period adjustments of accrual items. These *reversing entries* are made after the adjusting and closing entries are posted and are normally dated the first day of the new accounting period.

To demonstrate reversing entries, assume that a company accepted a $3,000, 12%, 60-day note dated December 19, 12 days before the end of its annual accounting period; 63 days' interest on this note is $62.14, and by December 31, $11.84 of the $62.14 has been earned. Consequently, the company's bookkeeper should make the following adjusting and closing entries to record the accrued interest on the note and to close the Interest Earned account.

Dec.	31	Interest Receivable	11.84	
		Interest Earned		11.84
		To record the accrued interest.		
	31	Interest Earned	11.84	
		Income Summary		11.84
		To close the Interest Earned account.		

In addition to the adjusting and closing entries, if the bookkeeper chooses to make reversing entries, he or she will make the following entry to reverse the accrued interest adjusting entry:

Jan.	1	Interest Earned	11.84	
		Interest Receivable		11.84
		To reverse the accrued interest adjusting entry.		

Observe that the reversing entry is debit for credit and credit for debit— the reverse of the adjusting entry it reverses. After the adjusting, closing, and reversing entries are posted, the Interest Receivable and Interest Earned accounts appear as follows:

	Interest Receivable						**Interest Earned**			
Date		Explanation	Dr.	Cr.	Bal.	Date		Explanation	Dr.	Cr.	Bal.

Date		Explanation	Dr.	Cr.	Bal.	Date		Explanation	Dr.	Cr.	Bal.
Dec.	31	Adjusting	11.84		11.84	Dec.	31	Adjusting		11.84	11.84
Jan.	1	Reversing		11.84	–0–		31	Closing	11.84		–0–
						Jan.	1	Reversing	11.84		(11.84)

Notice that the reversing entry cancels the $11.84 of interest appearing in the Interest Receivable account. It also causes the accrued interest to appear in the Interest Earned account as a $11.84 debit. (Remember that an encircled balance means a balance opposite from normal.) Consequently, due to the reversing entry, when the note and interest are paid on February 20, the bookkeeper can record the transaction with this entry:

Feb.	20	Cash	3,062.14	
		Interest Earned		62.14
		Notes Receivable		3,000.00
		Received payment of a note and interest.		

The entry's $62.14 credit to Interest Earned includes both the $11.84 of interest earned during the previous period and the $50.30 of interest earned during the current period. However, when the entry is posted, because of the previously posted reversing entry, the balance of the Interest Earned account shows only the $50.30 of interest applicable to the current period, as follows:

Interest Earned

Date		Explanation	Dr.	Cr.	Bal.
Dec.	31	Adjusting		11.84	11.84
	31	Closing	11.84		–0–
Jan.	1	Reversing	11.84		11.84
Feb.	20	Payment		62.14	50.30

Reversing entries are applicable to all accrued items, such as accrued interest earned, accrued interest expense, accrued taxes, and accrued salaries and wages. Nevertheless, they are not required but are a matter of convenience that enable a bookkeeper to forget an accrued item once its adjusting entry has been reversed.

ALTERNATIVE METHOD OF INTEREST CALCULATION

In calculating interest in the foregoing examples, the "exact," or proper, method was used. For classroom purposes, however, instructors may prefer to use a less accurate simplified method of interest calculation in order to focus on comprehension rather than on lengthy procedural calculation. To simplify interest calculations, the following assumptions are made:

1. Treat a year as having 360 days divided into 12 months of 30 days each.
2. Use the exact days of the note; that is, do not give consideration to the days of grace.

Thus, interest on a 90-day, 12%, $1,500 note is calculated as:

$$\$1,500 \times \frac{12}{100} \times \frac{90}{360} = \$45$$

Because of the ready access to calculators, homework assignments should be solved using the exact method unless otherwise directed.

GLOSSARY

Aging of accounts receivable.   A process of classifying accounts receivable in terms of how long they have been outstanding.

Allowance for doubtful accounts.   The estimated amount of accounts receivable that will prove uncollectible.

Allowance method of accounting for bad debts.   An accounting procedure that (1) estimates the bad debts arising from credit sales and reports bad debt expense during the period of the sales, and (2) reports accounts receivable in the balance sheet net of estimated uncollectibles, which is their estimated realizable value.

Bad debt.   An uncollectible account receivable.

Bank discount.   The amount of interest charged by a bank when the interest is deducted in advance from money loaned.

Contingent liability.   A potential liability that will become an actual liability if, and only if, certain events occur.

Direct write-off method of accounting for bad debts.   The accounting procedure whereby uncollectible accounts are not estimated in advance and are not charged to expense until they prove to be uncollectible.

Discount period of a note.   The number of days following the date on which a note is discounted at the bank until the maturity date of the note.

Discounting a note receivable.   Selling a note receivable to a bank or other concern.

Dishonouring a note.   Refusal of a promissory note's maker to pay the amount due upon maturity of the note.

Full-disclosure principle.   The accounting requirement that financial statements and their accompanying notes disclose all information of a material nature relating to the financial position and operating results of the company for which they were prepared.

Installment accounts receivable.   Accounts receivable that allow the customer to make periodic payments over several months and which typically earn interest.

Maker of a note.   One who signs a note and promises to pay it at maturity.

Materiality principle.   The accounting rule that strict adherence to any accounting principle is not required if lack of adherence will not produce an error sufficiently large as to influence the judgment of financial statement readers.

Maturity date of a note.   The date on which a note and any interest are due and payable.

Maturity value of a note.   Principal of the note plus any interest due on the note's maturity date.

Notes receivable discounted.   Notes receivable that have been discounted or sold by the payee and for which the payee is contingently liable.

Notice of protest.   A document informing each endorser of a promissory note that the note was presented for payment on its due date and payment was refused.

Payee of a note.   The one to whom a promissory note is made payable.

Proceeds of a discounted note.   The maturity value of a note minus any interest deducted because of its being discounted before maturity.

Protest fee.   The fee charged for preparing and issuing a notice of protest.

Realizable value. The amount of cash that should be received from the conversion of an asset into cash in the ordinary course of business.

Reversing entry. An entry, made as a bookkeeping convenience at the beginning of an accounting period, the debit and credit of which are opposite to an adjusting entry for an accrual that was made at the end of the previous period. As a result of the reversing entry, the subsequent receipt or payment of cash can be debited (or credited) entirely to the expense (or revenue) account.

QUESTIONS FOR CLASS DISCUSSION

1. Why do customers often prefer to charge their purchases to credit cards?
2. How do businesses benefit from allowing their customers to use credit cards?
3. Where is credit card expense disclosed on a classified income statement?
4. In meeting the requirements of the matching principle, why must bad debt expenses be matched with sales on an estimated basis?
5. What term describes the balance sheet valuation of accounts receivable less allowance for doubtful accounts?
6. What is a contra account? Why is estimated bad debt expense credited to a contra account rather than to the Accounts Receivable controlling account?
7. When bad debts are estimated by the income statement approach, what relationship is the focus of attention?
8. A company had $560,000 of charge sales in a year. How many dollars of bad debts expense may the company expect to experience from these sales if its past debts expense has averaged one fourth of 1% of charge sales?
9. Classify the following accounts:
   a. Accounts Receivable.
   b. Allowance for Doubtful Accounts.
   c. Bad Debts Expense.
10. Explain why writing off a bad debt against the allowance account does not reduce the estimated realizable value of a company's accounts receivable.
11. What are three reasons why Bad Debts Expense usually does not have the same adjusted balance as Allowance for Doubtful Accounts?
12. When bad debts are estimated by the simplified balance sheet approach, what relationship is the focus of attention?
13. Why does the direct write-off method of accounting for bad debts commonly fail in matching revenues and expenses?
14. What is the essence of the accounting principle of materiality?

15. Why might a business prefer a note receivable to an account receivable?
16. Define:
    a. Promissory note.   f. Discount period of a note.
    b. Payee of a note.   g. Maker of a note.
    c. Maturity date.   h. Principal of a note.
    d. Dishonoured note.   i. Maturity value.
    e. Notice of protest.   j. Contingent liability.
17. What are the due dates of the following notes:
    a. A 90-day note dated July 10.
    b. A 60-day note dated April 14.
    c. A 90-day note dated November 12?
18. Distinguish between bank discount and cash discount.
19. What does the full-disclosure principle require in a company's accounting statements?

MULTIPLE CHOICE

1. Beta Company ages its Accounts Receivables to determine their Allowance for Doubtful Accounts. At the end of 198A, management estimated that $14,750 of the accounts receivable balances would be uncollectible. The Allowance for Doubtful Accounts account had a debit balance of $175. What entry should Beta make on December 31, 198A, to estimate bad debts expense?

a.	Bad Debts Expense	14,750	
	Allowance for Doubtful Accounts		14,750
b.	Bad Debts Expense	14,575	
	Allowance for Doubtful Accounts		14,575
c.	Bad Debts Expense	14,925	
	Allowance for Doubtful Accounts		14,925
d.	Accounts Receivable	14,750	
	Bad Debts Expense	175	
	Allowance for Doubtful Accounts		14,925
e.	Accounts Receivable	14,925	
	Allowance for Doubtful Accounts		14,925

2. The balance of the Allowance for Doubtful Accounts account represents:
    a. Money set aside to take care of any bad debts.
    b. The amount of bad debts incurred in the previous periods.
    c. The amount of bad debts incurred in the current period.
    d. The amount of bad debts incurred in the current and previous periods.
    e. None of the foregoing.

3. The accounting procedure whereby an estimate is made at the end of each accounting period of the portion of the period's credit sales that will prove uncollectible, and an entry is made to charge this estimated amount to an

expense account and to an allowance account against which actual uncollectible accounts can be written off, is the:

    a. Allowance method of accounting for bad debts.

    b. Aging of accounts receivable.

    c. Adjustment method for uncollectible debts.

    d. Direct write-off method of accounting for bad debts.

    e. Cash basis method of accounting for bad debts.

4. The amount of interest a bank deducts in advance when lending money is a(n):

    a. Retained earning.

    b. Unearned revenue.

    c. Purchase discount.

    d. Sales discount.

    e. Bank discount.

5. A potential liability that may become an actual liability if certain events occur is a(n):

    a. Unearned liability.

    b. Accrued liability.

    c. Contingent liability.

    d. Temporary liability.

    e. Contra liability.

6. The accounting procedure whereby uncollectible accounts are written off directly to an expense account is the:

    a. Allowance method of accounting for bad debts.

    b. Aging accounts receivable method.

    c. Estimated method of accounting for bad debts.

    d. Direct write-off method of accounting for bad debts.

    e. None of the above.

7. Under the allowance method, the entry to write off the uncollectible account of Hank Reeves is:

    a. Debit Bad Debts Expense and credit Accounts Receivable—Hank Reeves.

    b. Debit Bad Debts Expense and credit Allowance for Doubtful Accounts.

    c. Debit Allowance for Doubtful Accounts and credit Accounts Receivable—Hank Reeves.

    d. Debit Allowance for Doubtful Accounts and credit Bad Debts Expense.

    e. Some other entry.

8. The amount of interest deducted when a note receivable is discounted is calculated as a percentage of:

    a. The proceeds of the note.

    b. The principal of the note.

c. The face amount of the note.
d. The maturity value of the note.
e. The market value of the note.

9. The accounting rule requiring that financial statements and their accompanying notes disclose all information of a material nature relating to the financial position and operating results of the company for which the statements are prepared is the:
    a. Realization principle.
    b. Full-disclosure principle.
    c. Cost principle.
    d. Materiality principle.
    e. Objectivity principle.

MINI DISCUSSION CASES

Case 8–1   In addition to recording cash sales as indicated in Mini Discussion Case 7–1, there were also a number of fictitious sales recorded as receivables. Inventory represented by the fictitious sales was removed by the seller to another location. Interviews with employees in the stockroom also indicated that there was some substitution of inventory by the previous owner. That is, he removed the newest lines in inventory to his other place of business and brought in older and slow-moving items.

The auditor's report indicated $120,000 of fictitious sales and the corresponding cost of goods sold of $80,000.

The auditors were not able to fully document the amount of inventory substitution.

Required:

1. Discuss the effect on the financial statements of the fictitious sales.
2. Discuss the safeguards or internal control that was lacking in the situation.

Case 8–2   John Crane could not understand the discounting procedure followed with regard to customers' notes receivable. Specifically, he could not understand why the discount was based on the maturity value of the note and not on the face value or the face value plus accrued interest to the discount date.

Required:

Explain to John Crane why the maturity value of the note receivable is discounted.

CLASS EXERCISES

Exercise 8–1   Ackers Company allows customers to use two alternative credit cards in charging purchases. With the Northern Bank Card Ackers receives an immediate credit upon depositing sales receipts in its chequing account. Northern Bank makes a 3.5% service charge for credit card sales. The second credit card Ackers accepts is Western Card. Ackers sends the accumulated Western Card receipts to the Western Company on a weekly basis and is paid by Western Company approximately 10 days later. Western charges 3% of sales for using its card. Prepare entries in general journal form to record the following credit card transactions of Ackers Company:

Mar. 1 Sold merchandise for $2,300 on this day, accepting the customers' Northern Bank Card. At the end of the day, the Northern Bank Card receipts were deposited in the company's account at the bank.
2 Sold merchandise for $150, accepting the customer's Western Card.
6 Mailed $4,000 of credit card receipts to Western Company, requesting payment.
18 Received Western Company's cheque for the March 6 billing, less the normal service charge.

Exercise 8–2

On December 31, at the end of its annual accounting period, a company estimated it would lose as bad debts an amount equal to one half of 1% of its $450,000 of charge sales made during the year, and it made an addition to its Allowance for Doubtful Accounts equal to that amount. On the following April 7, it decided the $340 account of Ron Koplen was uncollectible and wrote it off as a bad debt. Two months later, on June 7, Mr. Koplen unexpectedly paid the amount previously written off. Give the required entries in general journal form to record these transactions.

Exercise 8–3

At the end of each year, a company uses the simplified balance sheet approach to estimate bad debts. On December 31, 198B, it has outstanding accounts receivable of $48,000 and estimates that 4% will prove to become uncollectible.

a. Give the entry to record bad debts expense for 198B under the assumption that Allowance for Doubtful Accounts had a $250 credit balance before the adjustment.
b. Give the entry under the assumption that Allowance for Doubtful Accounts has a $300 debit balance before the adjustment.

Exercise 8–4

Prepare general journal entries to record these transactions:

May 3 Accepted a $900, 60-day, 12% note dated this day from Ellen Doene in granting a time extension on her past-due account.
July 5 Ellen Doene dishonoured her note when presented for payment.
Dec. 31 After exhausting all legal means of collecting, wrote off the account of Ellen Doene against the allowance for doubtful accounts.

Exercise 8–5

Prepare general journal entries to record these transactions:

Mar. 10 Sold merchandise to Jerry Dow, $1,800, terms 2/10, n/60.
May 10 Received $600 in cash and a $1,200, 90-day, 10% note dated May 9 in granting a time extension on the amount due from Jerry Dow.
June 8 Discounted the Jerry Dow note at the bank at 12%.
Aug. 10 Since notice protesting the Jerry Dow note had not been received, assumed that it had been paid.

Exercise 8–6

Prepare general journal entries to record these transactions:

June 5 Accepted a $3,000, 60-day, 12% note dated June 3 from Donald Tucker granting a time extension on his past-due account.

8 Discounted the Donald Tucker note at the bank at 14%.

Aug. 7 Received notice protesting the Donald Tucker note. Paid the bank the maturity value of the note plus a $20 protest fee.

20 Received payment from Donald Tucker of the maturity value of his dishonoured note, the protest fee, and interest at 12% on both for 15 days beyond maturity.

Exercise 8–7

On April 9, Mid-City Sales sold Larry Jones merchandise having a $4,500 catalogue list price, less a 20% trade discount, 2/10, n/60. Jones was unable to pay and was granted a time extension on receipt of his 60-day, 11% note for the amount of the debt, dated June 8. Mid-City Sales held the note until June 23, when it discounted the note at its bank at 14%. The note was not protested. Answer these questions:

a. How many dollars of trade discount were granted on the sale?

b. How many dollars of cash discount could Todd have earned?

c. What was the maturity date of the note?

d. How many days were in the discount period?

e. How much bank discount was deducted by the bank?

f. What were the proceeds of the discounted note?

Exercise 8–8

Bradford Company accepted a $13,500, 12%, 60-day note dated December 16, 15 days before the end of its annual accounting period, in granting a time extension on the past-due account of Frank Worst.

Required:

1. Present general journal entries for Bradford Company:

a. To record receipt of the note on December 16.

b. To record the accrued interest on the note of December 31.

c. To close the Income Summary account.

d. To reverse the accrued interest adjusting entry.

e. To record payment of the note and interest on February 17.

2. Open balance column accounts for Interest Receivable and Interest Earned and post the portions of the foregoing entries that affect these accounts.

PROBLEMS

Problem 8–1

Barrington Company allows a few customers to make sales on credit. Other customers may use either of two credit cards. The First Northern Bank makes a 4% service charge for sales on its credit card but immediately credits the chequing account of its commercial customers when credit card receipts are deposited. Barrington deposits the First Northern Bank credit card receipts at the close of each business day.

When customers use the National Credit Card, Barrington Company accumulates the receipts for two or three days and then submits them to the National

Credit Company for payment. National makes a 3% service charge and usually pays within one week of being billed.

Barrington Company completed the following transactions:

Nov. 2 Sold merchandise on credit to Tom Hall for $975. (Terms of all credit sales are 2/10, n/60.)

3 Sold merchandise for $2,700 to customers who used their First Northern Bank credit cards. Sold merchandise for $2,000 to customers who used their National credit cards.

4 Sold merchandise for $1,500 to customers who used their National credit cards.

5 Wrote off the account of J. Marsh against the allowance for doubtful accounts. The $350 balance in Marsh's account stemmed from a credit sale in December of last year.

5 The National Credit Card receipts accumulated since November 2 were submitted to the National Credit Company for payment.

12 Received Tom Hall's cheque paying for the purchase of November 2.

14 Received amount due from National Credit Company.

Required:

Prepare general journal entries to record the above transactions.

Problem 8–2   On December 31, 198A, Conroe Company's unadjusted trial balance included the following items:

	Dr.	Cr.
Cash sales		126,100
Credit sales		257,000
Accounts receivable	111,200	
Allowance for doubtful accounts	1,150	

Required:

1. Prepare the adjusting entry on the books of Conroe Company to estimate bad debts under each of the following independent assumptions:

 a. Bad debts are estimated to be 2% of total sales.

 b. Bad debts are estimated to be 3.5% of credit sales.

 c. An analysis suggests that 5% of outstanding accounts receivable on December 31, 198A, will become uncollectible.

2. Show how Accounts Receivable and Allowance for Doubtful accounts would appear on the December 31, 198A, balance sheet given the facts in (1*b*) above.

3. Show how Accounts Receivable and Allowance for Doubtful Accounts would appear on the December 31, 198A, balance sheet given the facts in (1*c*) above.

Problem 8–3   Brandon Corporation had credit sales of $3,500,000 in 198A. On December 31, 198A, the company's Allowance for Doubtful Accounts had a credit balance of $4,000. The accountant for Brandon Corporation has prepared a schedule of the December 31, 198A, accounts receivable by age and on the basis of past experience has estimated the percentage of the receivables in each age category that will become uncollectible. This information is summarized as follows:

December 31, 198A accounts receivable	Age of accounts receivable	Uncollectible % expected
$350,000	Not due (under 30 days)	2
180,000	1 to 30 days past due	3
55,000	31 to 60 days past due	15
35,000	61 to 90 days past due	40
20,000	over 90 days past due	80

Required:

1. Calculate the amount that should appear in the December 31, 198A, balance sheet as allowance for doubtful accounts.
2. Prepare the general journal entry to record bad debts expense for 198A.
3. On March 3, 198B, Brandon Corporation concluded that a customer's $6,500 accounts receivable was uncollectible and that the account should be written off. What effect will this action have on Brandon Corporation's 198B net income? Explain your answer.

Problem 8–4   Prepare entries in general journal form to record these transactions:

Jan.   3   Accepted a $3,825, 60-day, 12% note dated this day in granting a time extension on the past-due account of Gary White.
Mar.   7   Gary White paid the maturity value of his $3,825 note.
      10   Accepted a $1,500, 60-day, 10% note dated this day in granting a time extension on the past-due account of Bobbie Blaine.
May   12   Bobbie Blaine dishonoured her note when presented for payment.
      13   Accepted a $2,500, 90-day, 14% note dated May 9 in granting a time extension on the past-due account of Jack Hobby.
      17   Discounted the Jack Hobby note at the bank at 16%.
Aug. 14   Since notice protesting the Jack Hobby note had not been received, assumed that it had been paid.
      15   Accepted a $2,000, 60-day, 12% note dated August 11 in granting a time extension on the past-due account of Bill Dame.
Sept. 7   Discounted the Bill Dame note at the bank at 14%.
Oct. 14   Received notice protesting the Bill Dame note. Paid the bank the maturity value of the note plus a $20 protest fee.
      15   Received a $3,000, 60-day, 11% note dated this day from Kay Whelan in granting a time extension on her past-due account.
Nov. 14   Discounted the Kay Whelan note at the bank at 14%.
Dec. 18   Received notice protesting the Kay Whelan note. Paid the bank the maturity value of the note plus a $20 protest fee.
      26   Received payment from Kay Whelan for the maturity value of her dishonoured note, the protest fee, and interest on both for 12 days beyond maturity at 11%.
      31   Wrote off the accounts of Bobbie Blaine and Bill Dame against Allowance for Doubtful Accounts.

Problem 8–5   Prepare general journal entries to record these transactions:

Dec. 19   Accepted a $2,500, 60-day, 12% note dated this day in granting Dan Boggs a time extension on his past-due account.
      31   Made an adjusting entry to record the accrued interest on the Dan Boggs note.
      31   Closed the Interest Earned account.
Jan. 18   Discounted the Dan Boggs note at the bank at 14%.
Feb. 21   Received notice protesting the Dan Boggs note. Paid the bank the maturity value of the note plus a $20 protest fee.
Mar.   6   Accepted a $1,800 11%, 60-day note dated this day in granting a time extension on the past-due account of Wallace Rogers.
      30   Discounted the Wallace Rogers note at the bank at 14%.

May 11 Since notice protesting the Wallace Rogers note had not been received, assumed that it had been paid.

June 8 Accepted a $2,000, 60-day, 10% note dated this day in granting a time extension on the past-due account of Mark Mangum.

Aug. 10 Received payment in full of the maturity value of the Mark Mangum note.

Aug. 13 Accepted an $1,500, 60-day, 10% note dated this day in granting Amy Searcy a time extension on her past-due account.

Sept. 2 Discounted the Amy Searcy note at the bank at 13%.

Oct. 17 Received notice protesting the Amy Searcy note. Paid the bank the maturity value of the note plus a $20 protest fee.

Nov. 11 Received payment from Amy Searcy for the maturity value of her dishonoured note, the protest fee, and interest on both for 30 days beyond maturity at 10%.

Dec. 27 Wrote off the Dan Boggs account against Allowance for Doubtful Accounts.

Problem 8–6   A concern completed these transactions:

Dec. 16 Received $650 cash as partial payment of Jud Arrington's account and accepted a $2,200, 60-day, 12% note dated this day in granting a time extension on the remaining past-due balance.

31 Aged the accounts receivable and estimated that $3,450 would prove uncollectible. Examined the Allowance for Doubtful Accounts account and determined that it had a $220 debit balance. Made adjusting entries to provide for the estimated bad debts and to record interest earned.

31 Closed the Bad Debts Expense and Interest Earned accounts.

Feb. 17 Received payment of the maturity value of the Jud Arrington note.

18 Learned of the bankruptcy of Mike Stewart and recorded a claim on his receiver in bankruptcy for the $975 owed by Mr. Stewart for merchandise purchased on credit.

Mar. 10 Learned that Glenn Reeves had gone out of business, leaving no assets to attach. Wrote off his $450 account as a bad debt.

Apr. 17 Accepted $300 in cash and a $1,200, 60-day, 12% note dated this day in granting a time extension on the past-due account of Bill Polkinghorn.

23 Discounted the Bill Polkinghorn note at the bank at 14%.

June 22 Received notice protesting the Bill Polkinghorn note. Paid the bank the maturity value of the note plus a $15 protest fee.

July 7 Glenn Reeves paid $150 of the amount written off on March 10. In the letter accompanying the payment, he stated that his finances had improved and he expected to pay the balance owed within a short time.

Aug. 8 Received $150 from the receiver in bankruptcy of Mike Stewart. A letter accompanying the payment said that no more would be paid. Recorded the receipt of the $150 and wrote off the balance owed as a bad debt.

Oct. 4 Decided that the Bill Polkinghorn account was uncollectible and wrote it off as a bad debt.

Dec. 24 Made a compound entry to write off the accounts of H. C. Carnes, $595, and Frank Doan, $415.

31 Aged the accounts receivable and determined that $2,900 would probably prove uncollectible. Made the adjusting entry to provide for them.

31 Closed the Bad Debts Expense and Interest Earned accounts.

Required:

1. Open Interest Receivable, Allowance for Doubtful Accounts, Interest Earned, and Bad Debts Expense accounts. Enter the $220 debit balance in the Allowance for Doubtful Accounts account.

2. Prepare general journal entries to record the transactions and post those portions of the entries that affect the accounts opened.

ALTERNATE PROBLEMS

Problem 8–1A   A few of Bradford Company's customers are granted credit by the company. Other customers may use either of two credit cards. The Hilltop Bank makes a 4% service charge for sales on its credit card but immediately credits the chequing account of its commercial customers when credit card receipts are deposited. Bradford deposits the Hilltop Bank credit card receipts at the close of each business day.

When customers use the World Credit Card, Bradford Company accumulates the receipts for two or three days and then submits them to the World Credit Company for payment. World makes a 3.2% service charge and usually pays within one week of being billed.

Bradford Company completed the following transactions:

Mar. 12   Sold merchandise on credit to Terry Bray for $650. (Terms of all credit sales are 2/10, n/60.)
   13   Sold merchandise for $2,250 to customers who used their Hilltop Bank credit cards. Sold merchandise for $2,500 to customers who used their World credit cards.
   14   Sold merchandise for $1,800 to customers who used their World credit cards.
   15   Wrote off the account of K. Britt against the allowance for doubtful accounts. The $475 balance in Britt's account stemmed from a credit sale in December of last year.
   15   The World Credit Card receipts accumulated since March 12 were submitted to the World Credit Company for payment.
   22   Received Terry Bray's cheque paying for the purchase of March 12.
   24   Received amount due from World Credit Company.

Required:

Prepare general journal entries to record the above transactions.

Problem 8–2A   On December 31, 198A, Bazley Corporation's unadjusted trial balance included the following items:

	Dr.	Cr.
Cash sales		302,000
Credit sales		488,000
Accounts receivable	175,000	
Allowance for doubtful accounts		1,400

Required:

1. Prepare the adjusting entry on the books of Bazley Corporation to estimate bad debts under each of the following independent assumptions:
   a.   Bad debts are estimated to be 1.5% of total sales.
   b.   Bad debts are estimated to be 3% of credit sales.
   c.   An analysis suggests that 7% of outstanding accounts receivable on December 31, 198A, will become uncollectible.
2. Show how Accounts Receivable and Allowance for Doubtful Accounts would appear on the December 31, 198A, balance sheet given the facts in (1*b*) above.

3. Show how Accounts Receivable and Allowance for Doubtful Accounts would appear on the December 31, 198A, balance sheet given the facts in (1c) above.

Problem 8–3A   Diskette Corporation had credit sales of $5,600,000 in 198A. On December 31, 198A, the company's Allowance for Doubtful Accounts had a debit balance of $6,200. The accountant for Diskette Corporation has prepared a schedule of the December 31, 198A, accounts receivable by age and on the basis of past experience has estimated the percentage of the receivables in each age category that will become uncollectible. This information is summarized as follows:

December 31, 198A accounts receivable	Age of accounts receivable	Uncollectible % expected
$500,000	Not due (under 30 days)	1.75
200,000	1 to 30 days past due	3.25
60,000	31 to 60 days past due	18.00
30,000	61 to 90 days past due	45.00
24,000	over 90 days past due	75.00

Required:

1. Calculate the amount that should appear in the December 31, 198A, balance sheet as allowance for doubtful accounts.
2. Prepare the general journal entry to record bad debts expense for 198A.
3. On April 7, 198B, Diskette Corporation concluded that a customer's $7,800 accounts receivable was uncollectible and that the account should be written off. What effect will this action have on Diskette Corporation's 198B net income? Explain your answer.

Problem 8–4A   Prepare entries in general journal form to record these transactions:

Jan. 14   Accepted a $2,500, 60-day, 10% note dated this day in granting a time extension on the past-due account of Hank Williams.

Mar. 18   Hank Williams dishonoured his note when presented for payment.

    21   Accepted a $1,700, 90-day, 11% note dated this day in granting a time extension on the past-due account of Jane Rubin.

    27   Discounted the Jane Rubin note at the bank at 14%.

June 28   Since notice protesting the Jane Rubin note had not been received, assumed the note had been paid.

    29   Accepted $600 in cash and a $1,000, 60-day, 12% note dated June 26 in granting a time extension on the past-due account of Frank Dipprey.

July 21   Discounted the Frank Dipprey note at the bank at 15%.

Aug. 28   Received notice protesting the Frank Dipprey note. Paid the bank the maturity value of the note plus a $20 protest fee.

Sept. 6   Accepted a $1,300, 60-day, 13% note dated this day in granting a time extension on the past-due account of Barbara Gibb.

Oct. 12   Discounted the Barbara Gibb note at the bank at 16%.

Nov. 11   Received notice protesting the Barbara Gibb note. Paid the bank the maturity value of the note plus a $20 protest fee.

Dec. 8   Received payment from Barbara Gibb of the maturity value of her dishonoured note, the protest fee, and interest at 13% on both for 30 days beyond maturity.

    27   Decided the accounts of Hank Williams and Frank Dipprey were uncollectible and wrote them off against Allowance for Doubtful Accounts.

Problem 8–5A   Prepare general journal entries to record these transactions:

Dec. 11   Accepted a $2,800, 60-day, 12% note dated this day in granting a time extension on the past-due account of Lane Thompson.
    31   Made an adjusting entry to record the accrued interest on the Lane Thompson note.
    31   Closed the Interest Earned account.
Jan. 10   Discounted the Lane Thompson note at the bank at 15%.
Feb. 15   Since notice protesting the Lane Thompson note had not been received, assumed that it had been paid.
Mar. 1   Accepted a $1,600, 90-day, 11% note dated this day in granting a time extension on the past-due account of Jane Riddles.
     7   Discounted the Jane Riddles note at the bank at 14%.
June 3   Received notice protesting the Jane Riddles note. Paid the bank the maturity value of the note plus a $25 protest fee.
    30   Received payment from Jane Riddles of the maturity value of her dishonoured note, the protest fee, and interest on both for 30 days beyond maturity at 11%.
July 2   Accepted a $1,250, 60-day, 11% note dated June 28 in granting a time extension on the past-due account of Gay Jackson.
Aug. 30   Gay Jackson dishonoured her note when presented for payment.
    31   Accepted $500 in cash and a $1,000, 60-day, 10% note dated August 28 in granting a time extension on the past-due account of Tom Nixon.
Oct. 6   Discounted the Tom Nixon note at the bank at 13%.
    31   Received notice protesting the Tom Nixon note. Paid the bank its maturity value plus a $25 protest fee.
Dec. 27   Decided the Gay Jackson and Tom Nixon accounts were uncollectible and wrote them off against Allowance for Doubtful Accounts.

Problem 8–6A   A company completed these transactions:

Dec. 1   Accepted $400 in cash and a $1,200, 60-day, 12% note dated November 28 from Lanny Mingle in granting a time extension on his past-due account.
    31   Made an adjusting entry to record the accrued interest on the Lanny Mingle note.
    31   Examined the Allowance for Doubtful Accounts account and determined that it had a $380 credit balance. Made an adjusting entry to provide an addition to the allowance equal to one half of 1% of the $315,000 charge sales for the year.
    31   Closed the Interest Earned and Bad Debts Expense accounts.
Jan. 30   Received payment of the maturity value of the Lanny Mingle note.
Feb. 3   Learned of the bankruptcy of Grant Hester and made a claim on his receiver in bankruptcy for the $670 owed by Mr. Hester for merchandise purchased on credit.
Mar. 12   After making effort to collect, decided the $550 account of Candice Voth was uncollectible and wrote it off as a bad debt.
June 15   Received a letter from Candice Voth enclosing a $150 payment on the account written off on March 12. She stated in her letter that her finances had improved and that she expected to pay the balance owed within a short time.
Nov. 3   Received $195 from Grant Hester's receiver in bankruptcy. A letter accompanying the payment stated that no more would be paid. Made an entry to record the cash received and to write off the balance of Hester's account.
Dec. 22   Made a compound entry to write off the accounts of Ed Parsons, $840; Frank Daniels, $440; and Nancy Wilson, $1,365.
    31   Provided an addition to the allowance for doubtful accounts equal to one half of 1% of the $650,000 charge sales for the year.
    31   Closed the Interest Earned and Bad Debts Expense accounts.

Required:

1.   Open these accounts: Interest Receivable, Allowance for Doubtful Accounts, Interest Earned, and Bad Debts Expense. Enter the $380 credit balance in

the Allowance for Doubtful Accounts account. Prepare general journal entries to record the transactions and post those portions affecting the accounts opened.

2. Prepare an alternate bad debts adjusting entry for the second December 31 of the problem under the assumption that rather than providing an addition to the allowance account equal to one half of 1% of charge sales, the company aged its accounts receivable and estimated that $2,400 of accounts were probably uncollectible.

PROVOCATIVE PROBLEMS

Provocative
Problem 8–1,
An Internal
Control Failure

When his auditor arrived early in January to begin the annual audit, Greg Smith, the owner of Advanced Sales, asked that careful attention be given to accounts receivable. Two things caused this request: (1) During the previous week, Mr. Smith had met Jan Burr, a former customer, on the street and had asked about her account which had recently been written off as uncollectible. Ms. Burr had indignantly replied that her $310 account had been paid in full. She later produced canceled cheques endorsed by Advanced Sales to prove it. (2) The income statement prepared for the quarter ended the previous December 31 showed an unusually large volume of sales returns. The bookkeeper who had prepared the statement was a new employee, having begun work on October 1, after being hired on the basis of out-of-town letters of reference. In addition to doing all the record-keeping, the bookkeeper also acts as cashier, receiving and depositing the cash from both cash sales and those received through the mail.

In the process of performing the audit, the auditor prepared from the company's records the following analysis of the accounts receivable for the period October 1 through December 31:

	Ashe	Burr	Cote	Duke	Eloe	Fout	Gage
Balance, Oct. 1	$ 420	$250	$ 690	$500	$ 260	$1,090	$ 820
Sales	1,390	260	1,060		1,320	840	1,150
Total	$1,810	$510	$1,750	$500	$1,580	$1,930	$1,970
Collections	(1,020)		(790)		(820)	(980)	(1,230)
Returns	(170)	(90)	(80)		(160)	(120)	(50)
Bad debts written off		(420)		(500)			
Balance, December 31 ...	$ 620	–0–	$ 880	–0–	$ 600	$ 830	$ 690

The auditor communicated with all charge customers and learned that although their account balances as of December 31 agreed with the amounts shown in the company's records, the individual transactions did not. The customers reported credit purchases totaling $6,870 during the three-month period and $170 of returns for which credit had been granted. Correspondence with Mr. Duke, the customer whose $500 account had been written off, revealed that he had become bankrupt and his creditors' claims had been settled by his receiver in bankruptcy at $0.22 on the dollar. The cheques had been mailed by his receiver on October 30, and all had been paid and returned by the bank, properly endorsed by the recipients.

Under the assumption that the bookkeeper has embezzled cash from the company, determine the total amount he has taken and attempted to conceal with false accounts receivable entries. Account for the deficiency by listing the concealment methods used and the amount he attempted to conceal with each method. Also outline an internal control system that will help protect the company's cash from future embezzlement. Assume the company will hire a new bookkeeper, but that it is small and can have only one office employee who must do all the bookkeeping.

Provocative Problem 8–2, All-Parts Store

Kevin Barrows has operated All-Parts Store for five years. Three years ago he liberalized the store's credit policy in an effort to increase credit sales. Credit sales have increased, but now Kevin is concerned with the effects of the more liberalized credit policy. Bad debts written off (the store uses the direct write-off method) have increased materially in the last three years, and now Kevin wonders if the increase justifies the substantial bad debt losses which he is certain have resulted from the more liberal credit policy.

An examination of the shop's credit sales records, bad debt losses, and accounts receivable for the five years' operations reveal:

	1st year	2d year	3d year	4th year	5th year
Credit sales ..... _Sales_ ..	$150,000	$165,000	$225,000	$270,000	$300,000
Cost of goods sold	90,000	99,300	134,850	162,450	180,150
Gross profit from credit sales	$ 60,000	$ 65,700	$ 90,150	$107,550	$119,850
Expenses other than bad debts	45,000	49,350	67,800	80,700	90,000
Income before bad debts .... _7.I.A.._ ...	$ 15,000	$ 16,350	$ 22,350	$ 26,850	$ 29,850
Bad debts written off	150 ,	660	1,125	3,510	3,600
Income from credit sales	$ 14,850	$ 15,690	$ 21,225	$ 23,340	$ 26,250
Bad debts by year of sales	$ 600	$ 495	$ 2,925	$ 3,240 .	$ 4,200

The last line in the tabulation results from reclassifying bad debt losses by the years in which the sales that resulted in the losses were made. Consequently, the $4,200 of fifth-year losses includes $2,415 of estimated bad debts that are still in the accounts receivable.

Prepare a schedule showing in columns by years: income from credit sales before bad debt losses, bad debts incurred, and the resulting income from credit sales. Then below the income figures show for each year bad debts written off as a percentage of sales followed on the next line by bad debts incurred as percentage of sales. Also prepare a report for Mr. Barrows answering his concern about the new credit policy and recommending any changes you consider desirable in his accounting for bad debts.

ANALYTICAL AND REVIEW PROBLEMS

**Problem 8–1
A&R**

The Tor-Mont Company has been in business three years and has applied for a significant bank loan. Prior to considering the applications, the bank asks you to conduct an audit for the last three years. Concerning accounts receivable, you find that the company has been charging off receivables as they finally proved uncollectible and treating them as expenses at the time of write-off.

Your investigation indicates that receivable losses have approximated (and can be expected to approximate) 1% of net sales. Until this first audit, the company's sales and direct receivable write-off experience was:

Year of sales	Amount of sales	Accounts written off in		
		1985	1986	1987
1985	$300,000	$750	$2,000	$ 200
1986	400,000	—	1,000	2,400
1987	500,000	—	—	1,500

Required:

1. Indicate the amount by which net income was understated or overstated each year because the company used the direct write-off method rather than the more acceptable allowance method.
2. Prepare all the entries for each of the three years that would have been made if Tor-Mont had used the allowance method from the start of the business.
3. Which of the entries in (2) are year-end adjusting entries?

(CGA Adapted)

**Problem 8–2
A&R**

The following information pertains to the accounts receivable and related accounts of Appollo Company for the current year.

1.
Sales	$1,088,600
Sales returns and allowances	6,000
Sales discounts	80,000

2. Accounts receivable aging schedule

Number of day outstanding	Amount	Probability of collecting
1–30	$ 50,000	100%
31–60	30,000	80%
61–90	20,000	60%
91 and over	6,000	50%
Total accounts receivable balance	$106,000	

3. Allowance for doubtful accounts:

Allowance for Doubtful Accounts

March 31	660	Opening balance	8210
June 30	810	Sept. 30	260
		Ending balance	17,000

4. A recent study shows that the industry's bad debts expense over the past few years is approximately 1% of its total net sales. Appollo is considered as one of the most representative companies in the industry.

Required:

1. What method of estimating bad debt losses is employed by the company? Explain.
2. What is the amount of bad debts expense for the year?
3. Prepare an adjusting entry to record the bad debts expense for the year.
4. Would the entry be different from (3) above if an equally acceptable alternative method for estimating bad debt losses is used? What is the ending balance of the allowance account?

Problem 8–3
A&R

On July 7, 1987 when X Ltd.'s accounts receivable and allowance for doubtful accounts stood at $104,600 and $5,600, respectively, it wrote off one of its customer's accounts, Y Company, having a $600 balance.

A few months later, when X Ltd.'s accounts receivable and allowance for doubtful accounts stood at $160,000 and $4,600, respectively, Y Company paid its account in full.

Required:

1. Prepare the journal entries for the write-off and the subsequent collection of Y Company's account.
2. Compute the estimated realizable value of X Ltd.'s accounts receivable immediately prior to the write-off of the Y Company account.
3. Compute the estimated realizable value of X Ltd.'s accounts receivable immediately after the write-off of the Y Company account.
4. Compute the estimated realizable value of X Ltd.'s accounts receivable immediately after the collection of the Y Company account.

Problem 8–4
A&R

The All Credit Sales Company recognizes revenues at the time of delivery. Uncollectible Accounts Receivable are expected to average 1% of sales. The information below is for the year ending December 31, 1987.

Accounts Receivable, Jan. 1, 1987	$250,000
Allowance for doubtful accounts, Jan. 1, 1987	12,500
Collection of accounts receivable during the year	800,000
Write-offs of uncollectible accounts	9,000
Accounts receivable, Dec. 31, 1987	270,000
Bad debt recoveries during the year	600

Required:

Prepare the adjusting entry as of December 31, 1987, to the Allowance for Doubtful Accounts account.

Problem 8–5 A&R

The following pertains to the dealings of York Company and one of its customers, James Clark.

Dec. 1 Received a 12%, 60-day note from James Clark in full settlement of his account.
  31 Recorded the necessary adjusting entry pertaining to the Clark note, this being the end of the company's fiscal year.
Jan. 5 Discounted at 10% the Clark note at the bank.
Feb. 3 Received notification from the bank that the Clark note was dishonoured, when due, and the bank charged the company's account with the maturity value of the note and the standard $10 protest fee.
Mar. 4 Received from James Clark a certified cheque for the amount owing, including interest for the 30 days since the maturity of the note.

Required:

1. Prepare the balance of the necessary entries without amounts in connection with the James Clark note payable on the basis of the additional information provided above (the December 1, entry has already been prepared).
2. Indicate how the following are determined:
   a. Cash proceeds from the Clark note on January 5.
   b. Interest on January 5.
   c. The amount of cash charged the York account by the bank when the Clark note was dishonoured.
   d. Amount of cash received from Clark on March 4.
3. Calculate the amounts referred to in (2) on the assumption that the Clark note was for $1,000.

Dec.	1	Notes Receivable	XXX	
		Accounts Receivable—James Clark		XXX

Problem 8–6 A&R

Risky Company required a loan of $2,400 and was offered two alternatives by the Security Bank. The alternatives are:
a. Risky would give the bank a one-year $2,400 note payable, dated December, 1, 1987, with interest at 25%.*
b. Risky would give the bank a one-year $3,000 noninterest-bearing note payable, dated December 1, 1987. The bank would precalculate and deduct interest at 20%.*

Required:

1. Prepare *all* the necessary entries (including repayment on November 30, 1988) with regard to alternative *(a)*. Assume that Risky Company's fiscal year ends December 31.
2. Repeat the journal entries for alternative *(b)*.

---

* Interest to be calculated on monthly basis and no days of grace.

Inventories and Cost of Goods Sold

9

After studying Chapter 9, you should be able to:

Calculate the cost of an inventory based on *(a)* specific invoice prices, *(b)* weighted-average cost, *(c)* FIFO, and *(d)* LIFO.

Relate what is required by the accounting principle of consistency and why the application of this principle is important.

Relate what is required of a concern when it changes its accounting procedures.

Relate what is required by the accounting principle of conservatism.

Explain the effect of an inventory error on the income statements of the current and succeeding years.

Relate how a perpetual inventory system operates.

Estimate an inventory by the retail method and by the gross profit method.

Define or explain the words and phrases listed in the chapter Glossary.

A merchandising business earns revenue by selling merchandise. For such a concern the phrase **merchandise inventory** is used to describe the aggregate of the items of tangible personal property it holds for sale. As a rule the items are sold within a year or one cycle. Consequently, the inventory is a current asset, usually the largest current asset on a merchandising concern's balance sheet.

MATCHING MERCHANDISE COSTS WITH REVENUES

In accounting for inventories, the Canadian Institute of Chartered Accountants has said: The method of determining cost should be one which results in the fairest matching of costs against revenues regardless of whether or not the method corresponds to the physical flow of goods.[1] The matching process referred to is one with which the student is already somewhat familiar. For inventories, it consists of determining how much of the cost of the goods that were available for sale during a period should be deducted from the period's revenue from sales and how much should be carried forward as inventory to be matched against a future period's revenue.

The cost of the goods that were available for sale during an accounting period may be determined from the accounting records by adding to the cost of the beginning inventory the cost of goods purchased during the period. But since most firms do not keep a record of the cost of the goods sold during a period, normally cost of goods sold cannot be determined from accounting records but must be ascertained by separating cost of goods for sale into cost of goods sold and cost of goods unsold.

In separating goods available for sale into its components of goods sold and goods not sold, the key problem is that of assigning a cost to the goods not sold or to the ending inventory. However, it should be constantly borne in mind that the procedures for assigning a cost to the ending inventory are also the means of determining cost of goods sold, because whatever portion of the cost of goods for sale is assigned to the ending inventory, the remainder goes into cost of goods sold.

TAKING AN ENDING INVENTORY

As previously stated, when a periodic inventory system is in use, the dollar amount of the ending inventory is determined by counting the items of unsold merchandise remaining in the store, multiplying the count for each kind by its cost, and adding the costs for all the kinds. In making the count, items are less apt to be counted twice or

---

[1] *CICA handbook* (Toronto: The Canadian Institute of Chartered Accountants), par. 3030.09.

Illustration 9–1

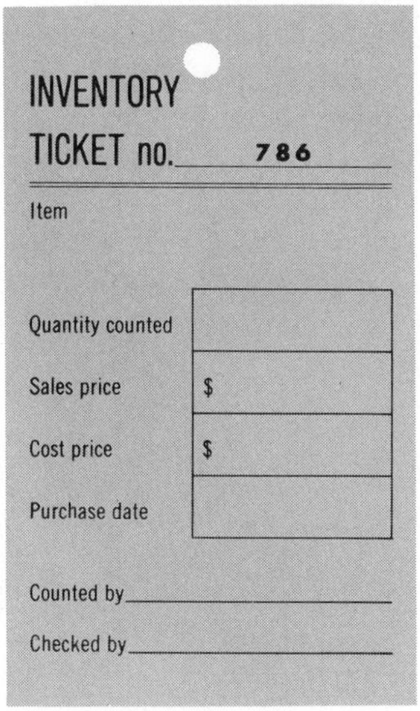

```
INVENTORY
TICKET no.      786

Item

Quantity counted

Sales price      $

Cost price       $

Purchase date

Counted by_____

Checked by_____
```

omitted from the count if prenumbered **inventory tickets** like the one in Illustration 9–1 are used. Before beginning the inventory, a sufficient number of the tickets, at least one for each kind of product on hand, is issued to each department in the store. Next a clerk counts the quantity of each product and from the count and the price tag attached to the merchandise fills in the information on the inventory ticket and attaches it to the counted items. After the count is completed, each department is examined for uncounted items. At this stage, inventory tickets are attached to all counted items. Consequently, any products without tickets attached are uncounted. After all items are counted and tickets attached, the tickets are removed and sent to the accounting department for completion of the inventory. To ensure that no ticket is lost or left attached to merchandise, all the prenumbered tickets issued are accounted for when the tickets arrive in the accounting department.

In the accounting department, the information on the tickets is copied on inventory summary sheets. The sheets are then completed by multiplying the number of units of each product by its cost. This gives the dollar amount of each product in the inventory, and the total for all the products is the dollar total of the inventory.

ASSIGNING COSTS TO INVENTORY ITEMS

In completing an inventory it is necessary to assign costs to the inventory items. This offers no problem when costs remain fixed. However, when identical items were purchased during a period at different costs, a problem arises as to which costs apply to the ending inventory and which apply to the goods sold. There are four commonly used ways of assigning costs to goods in the ending inventory and to goods sold. They are (1) specific invoice prices; (2) weighted-average cost; (3) first-in, first-out; and (4) last-in; first-out. Each is a generally accepted accounting procedure.

To illustrate the four, assume that a company has on hand at the end of an accounting period 12 units of Article X. Also, assume that the company began the year and purchased Article X during the year as follows:

Jan.	1	Beginning inventory	10 units at $100 =	$1,000
Mar.	13	Purchased	15 units at $108 =	1,620
Aug.	17	Purchased	20 units at $120 =	2,400
Nov.	10	Purchased	10 units at $125 =	1,250
		Total	55 units	$6,270

Specific Invoice Prices

When it is possible to identify each item in an inventory with a specific purchase and its invoice, *specific invoice prices* may be used to assign costs. For example, assume that 6 of the 12 unsold units of Article X were from the November purchase and 6 were from the August purchase. Under this assumption, costs are assigned to the inventory and goods sold by means of specific invoice prices as follows:

Total cost of 55 units available for sale		$6,270
Less ending inventory priced by means of specific invoices:		
6 units from the November purchase at $125 each	$750	
6 units from the August purchase at $120 each	720	
12 units in ending inventory		1,470
Cost of goods sold		$4,800

Weighted Average

Under this method prices for the units in the beginning inventory and in each purchase are weighted by the number of units in the beginning inventory and in each purchase and are averaged to find the *weighted-average cost* per unit as follows:

```
10 units at $100 = $1,000
15 units at $108 =  1,620
20 units at $120 =  2,400
10 units at $125 =  1,250
55                 $6,270

$6,270 ÷ 55 = $114, weighted-average cost per unit
```

After the weighted-average cost per unit is determined, this average is used to assign costs to the inventory and the units sold as follows:

```
Total cost of 55 units available for sale ................  $6,270
   Less: Ending inventory priced on a weighted-average
      cost basis (12 units at $114 each) ................   1,368
Cost of goods sold ...................................  $4,902
```

First-In, First-Out

In this method it is assumed that the oldest merchandise is sold first. Consequently, we assume that merchandise tends to flow out on a first-in, first-out basis. When first-in, first-out is applied in pricing an inventory, it is assumed that costs follow this pattern. As a result, the costs of the last items received are assigned to the ending inventory and the remaining costs are assigned to goods sold. When first-in, first-out, or *FIFO* as it is often called from its first letters, is used, costs are assigned to the inventory and goods sold as follows:

```
Total cost of 55 units available for sale ....................    $6,270
   Less ending inventory priced on a basis of FIFO:
      10 units from the November purchase at $125 each ......  $1,250
       2 units from the August purchase at $120 each .........    240
      12 units in the ending inventory ........................            1,490
Cost of goods sold ........................................            $4,780
```

Last-In, First-Out

Under this method of inventory pricing, commonly called *LIFO,* the costs of the last goods received are matched with revenue from sales. The theoretical justification for this is that a going concern must at all times keep a certain amount of goods in stock. Consequently, when goods are sold, replacements are purchased. Thus it is a sale that causes the replacement of goods. If costs and revenues are then matched, the latest costs should be matched with the sales that induced the acquisitions.

Under LIFO, costs are assigned to the 12 remaining units of Article X and to the goods sold as follows:

Total cost of 55 units available for sale		$6,270
Less ending inventory priced on a basis of LIFO:		
10 units in the beginning inventory at $100 each	$1,000	
2 units from the first purchase at $108 each	216	
12 units in the ending inventory		1,216
Cost of goods sold		$5,054

Notice that this method of matching costs and revenue results in the final inventory being priced at the cost of the oldest 12 units.

Comparison of Methods

In a stable market where prices remain unchanged, the inventory pricing method is of little importance. For when prices are unchanged over a period of time, all methods give the same cost figures. However, in a changing market where prices are rising or falling, each method may give a different result. This may be seen by comparing the costs of the units in the ending inventory and the units of Article X sold as calculated by the several methods discussed. These costs are as follows:

	Ending inventory	Cost of units sold
Based on specific invoice prices	$1,470	$4,800
Based on weighted average	1,368	4,902
Based on FIFO	1,490	4,780
Based on LIFO	1,216	5,054

Each of the four pricing methods is recognized as a generally accepted accounting procedure, and arguments can be advanced for the use of each. Specific invoice prices exactly match costs and revenues. However, this method is of practical use only for relatively high-priced items of which only a few units are kept in stock and sold. Weighted-average costs tend to smooth out price fluctuations. FIFO causes the last costs incurred to be assigned to the ending inventory. It thus provides an inventory valuation for the balance sheet that most closely approximates current replacement cost. LIFO causes last costs incurred to be assigned to cost of goods sold. Therefore, it results in a better matching of current costs with revenues. However, the method used commonly affects the amounts of reported ending inventory, cost of goods sold, and net income. Consequently, the *full-disclosure principle* requires that a company show in its statements by means of footnotes or other manner the pricing method used.[2]

THE PRINCIPLE OF CONSISTENCY

Look again at the table of costs for Article X. Note that a company can change its reported net income for an accounting period simply by changing its inventory pricing method. However, the change would violate the accounting *principle of consistency*. Furthermore, it would make a comparison of the company's inventory and income with previous periods more or less meaningless.

As with inventory pricing, more than one generally accepted method or procedure has been derived in accounting practice to account for an item or an activity. In each case one method may be considered better for one enterprise, while another may be considered more satisfactory for a concern operating under different circumstances. Nevertheless, the *principle of consistency* requires a persistent application by a company of any selected accounting method or procedure, period after period. As a result, a reader of a company's financial statements may assume that in keeping its records and in preparing its statements the company used the same procedures used in previous years. Only on the basis of this assumption can meaningful comparisons be made of the data in a company's statements year after year.

CHANGING ACCOUNTING PROCEDURES

In achieving comparability, the *principle of consistency* does not require that a method or procedure once chosen can never be changed. Rather, if a company decides that a different acceptable method of procedure from the one in use will better serve its needs, a change may be made. However, when such a change is made, the *full-disclosure principle* requires that the nature of the change, justification for the change, and the effect of the change on net income be disclosed in notes accompanying the statements.[3]

ITEMS INCLUDED ON AN INVENTORY

A concern's inventory should include all goods owned by the business and held for sale, regardless of where the goods may be located at the

---

[2] Ibid., par. 3030.10.

[3] Ibid., sec. 1506.

time of the inventory. In the application of this rule, there are generally no problems with respect to most items. For most items all that is required is to see that they are counted, that nothing is omitted, and that nothing is counted more than once. However, goods in transit, goods sold but not delivered, goods on consignment, and obsolete and damaged goods do require special attention.

When goods are in transit on the inventory date, the purchase should be recorded and the goods should appear on the purchaser's inventory if ownership has passed to the purchaser. Generally, if the buyer is responsible for paying the freight charges, ownership passes as soon as the goods are loaded aboard the means of transportation. Likewise, if the seller is to pay the freight charges, ownership passes when the goods arrive at their destination.

Goods on consignment are goods shipped by their owner (known as the *consignor*) to another person or firm (called the *consignee*) who is to sell the goods for the owner. Consigned goods belong to the consignor and should appear on the consignor's inventory.

Damaged goods and goods that have deteriorated or become obsolete should not be placed on the inventory if they are not salable. If such goods are salable but at a reduced price, they should be placed on the inventory at a conservative estimate of their realizable value (sale price less the cost of making the sale). This causes the accounting period in which the goods were damaged, deteriorated, or became obsolete to suffer the resultant loss.

Elements of Inventory Cost

The Canadian Institute of Chartered Accountants has said: "In the case of inventories of merchandise purchased for resale or of raw materials, cost should be the laid-down cost."[4] Therefore, the cost of an inventory item includes the invoice price, less the discount, plus any additional incidental costs necessary to put the goods into place and condition for sale. The additional incidental costs include import duties, transportation, storage, insurance, and any other applicable costs, such as those incurred during an aging process.

If incurred, any of the foregoing enter into the cost of an inventory. However, in pricing an inventory, most concerns do not take into consideration the incidental costs of acquiring merchandise. They price the inventory on the basis of invoice prices only, and treat all incidental costs as expenses of the period in which they are incurred.

Although not correct in theory, treating incidental costs as expenses of the period in which they are incurred is commonly permissible. In theory a share of each incidental cost should be assigned to every unit purchased. This causes a portion of each to be carried forward in the

---

[4] Ibid., par. 3030.06.

inventory to be matched against the revenue of the period in which the inventory is sold. However, the expense of computing costs on such a precise basis usually outweighs any benefit from the extra accuracy. Consequently, when possible, most concerns take advantage of the *principle of materiality* and treat such costs as expenses of the period in which incurred. *(incidental costs)* .

THE LOWER OF COST AND MARKET

Over the years the traditional rule for pricing inventory items has been *the lower of cost or market*. ''Cost'' is the price that was paid for an item when it was purchased. While ''market'' is **normally** interpreted as the price that would have to be paid to purchase or replace the item on the inventory date, its application has varied with differences in results. Consequently, the *CICA Handbook* has recommended that:

> In view of the lack of precision in meaning, it is desirable that the term ''market'' not be used in describing the basis of valuation. A term more descriptive of the method of determining market, such as ''replacement cost,'' ''net realizable value'' or ''net realizable value less normal profit margin'' would be preferable.[5]

Throughout this textbook, ''replacement'' is used in place of market.

The argument advanced to support the use of lower of cost or replacement was that if the replacement cost of an inventory item had declined, then its selling price would probably have to be reduced. Since this might result in a loss, the loss should be anticipated and taken in the year of the price decline. It was a good argument. However, selling prices do not always follow cost prices exactly or quickly. As a result, the application of the rule often resulted in misstating net income in the year of a price decline and again in the succeeding year. For example, suppose that a firm purchased merchandise costing $1,000, marked it up to a $1,500 selling price, and sold one half of the goods. The gross profit on the goods sold would be calculated as follows:

Sales	$750
Cost of goods sold	500
Gross profit on sales	$250

However, if the $500 replacement cost of the unsold goods declined to $450 by the inventory date, an income statement based upon the traditional application of cost or market would show the following:

---

[5] Ibid., par. 3030.11.

Sales		$750
Cost of goods sold:		
Purchases	$1,000	
Less: Ending inventory	450	550
Gross profit on sales		$200

The $450 would be a conservative balance sheet figure for the unsold goods. However, if these goods were sold at their full price early in the following year, the $450 inventory figure would have the erroneous effect of deferring $50 of income to the second year's income statement as follows:

Sales	$750
Cost of goods sold:	
Beginning inventory	450
Gross profit on sales	$300

Merchants are prone to be slow in marking down goods; they normally try to sell merchandise at its full price if possible. Consequently, the illustrated situation is not uncommon. For this reason the lower-of-cost-or-replacement rule has been modified as follows for situations in which replacement costs are below actual costs.[6]

1. Goods should be placed on an inventory at cost, even though replacement cost is lower, if there has not been and there is not expected to be a decline in selling price.

2. Goods should at times be placed on an inventory at a price below cost but above replacement cost. For example, suppose the cost of an item that is normally bought for $20 and sold for $30 declines from $20 to $16, and its selling price declines from $30 to $27. The normal profit margin on this item is one third of its selling price. If this normal margin is applied to $27, the item should be placed on the inventory at two thirds of $27, or at $18. This is below cost but above replacement cost.

3. At times, goods should be placed on an inventory at a price below replacement cost. For example, assume that the goods described in the preceding paragraph can only be sold for $18.50 and that the disposal costs are estimated at $3. In this case the goods should be placed on the inventory at $15.50, a price below their replacement cost of $16.

---

[6] Ibid., par. 3030.11.

PRINCIPLE OF CONSERVATISM

Decisions based on estimates and opinions as to future events affect financial statements. Financial statements are also affected by the selection of accounting procedures. The *principle of conservatism* holds that accountants should be conservative in their estimates and opinions and in the selection of procedures, choosing those that neither unduly understate nor overstate the situation.

Something called balance sheet conservatism was once considered the "first" principle of accounting. Its objective was to place every item on the balance sheet at a conservative figure. This in itself was commendable. However, it was often carried too far, and it resulted not only in the misstatement of asset values but also in unconservative income statements. For example, when prices are falling, the blind application of the lower of cost or market to inventories may result in a conservative balance sheet figure for inventories. It may also result in an improper deferring of net income and in inaccurate income statements. Consequently, accountants recognize that balance sheet conservatism does not outweigh other factors. They favour practices that result in a fair statement of net income period after period.

INVENTORY ERRORS

An error in determining the end-of-the-period inventory will cause misstatements in cost of goods sold, gross profit, net income, current assets, and owner's equity. Also, the ending inventory of one period is the beginning inventory of the next. Therefore, the error will carry forward and cause misstatements in the succeeding period's cost of goods sold, gross profit, and net income. Furthermore, since the amount involved in an inventory is often large, the misstatements can be material without being readily apparent.

To illustrate the effects of an inventory error, assume that in each of the years 19A, 19B, and 19C a company had $100,000 in sales. If the company maintained a $20,000 inventory throughout the period and made $60,000 in purchases in each of the years, its cost of goods sold each year was $60,000 and its annual gross profits were $40,000. However, assume the company incorrectly calculated its December 31, 19A, inventory at $18,000 rather than $20,000. The error would have the effects shown in Illustration 9–2.

Observe in Illustration 9–2 that the $2,000 understatement of the December 31, 19A, inventory caused a $2,000 overstatement in 19A cost of goods sold and a $2,000 understatement in gross profit and net income. Also, since the ending inventory of 19A became the beginning inventory of 19B, the error caused an understatement in the 19B cost

Illustration 9–2

	19A		19B		19C	
Sales		$100,000		$100,000		$100,000
Cost of goods sold:						
Beginning inventory	$20,000		$18,000*		$20,000	
Purchases	60,000		60,000		60,000	
Goods for sale	80,000		78,000		80,000	
Ending inventory	18,000*		20,000		20,000	
Total cost of goods sold		62,000		58,000		60,000
Gross profit		$ 38,000		$ 42,000		$ 40,000

  * Should have been $20,000.

of goods sold and a $2,000 overstatement in gross profit and net income. However, by 19C the error had no effect.

In Illustration 9–2 the December 31, 19A, inventory is understated. Had it been overstated, it would have caused opposite results—the 19A net income would have been overstated and the 19B income understated.

It has been argued that an inventory mistake is not too serious, since the error it causes in reported net income the first year is exactly offset by an opposite error in the second. However, such reasoning is unsound. It fails to consider that management, creditors, and owners base many important decisions on fluctuations in reported net income. Consequently, such mistakes should be avoided.

PERPETUAL INVENTORIES

Concerns selling a limited number of products of relatively high value often keep perpetual, or book, inventories. Also, concerns that use computers in processing their accounting data commonly keep such records. Furthermore, the essential information provided is the same whether accumulated by computer or with pen and ink.

A perpetual or book inventory based on pen and ink makes use of a subsidiary record card for each product in stock. On these individual cards, the number of units received is recorded as units are received and the number of units sold is recorded as units are sold. Then, after each receipt or sale, the balance remaining is recorded. (An inventory record card for Product Z is shown in Illustration 9–3.) At any time, each perpetual inventory card tells the balance on hand of any one product; and the total of all cards is the amount of the inventory.

The January 10 sale on the card of Illustration 9–3 indicates that the inventory of this card is kept on a first-in, first-out basis, since the sale

Illustration 9–3

Item Product Z					Location in stock room Bin 8				
Maximum 25					Minimum 5				

Date	Received			Sold			Balance		
	Units	Cost	Total	Units	Cost	Total	Units	Cost	Balance
1/1							10	10.00	100.00
5/1				5	10.00	50.00	5	10.00	50.00
8/1	20	10.50	210.00				5	10.00	
							20	10.50	260.00
10/1				3	10.00	30.00	2	10.00	
							20	10.50	230.00

is recorded as being from the oldest units in stock. Perpetual inventories may also be kept on a last-in, first-out basis. When this is done, each sale is recorded as being from the last units received, until these are exhausted, then sales are from the next to last, and so on.

When a concern keeps perpetual inventory records, it normally also makes a once-a-year physical count of each kind of goods in stock in order to check the accuracy of its book inventory records.

Perpetual inventories not only tell the amount of inventory on hand at any time but they also aid in controlling the total amount invested in inventory. Each perpetual inventory card may have on it the maximum and minimum amounts of that item that should be kept in stock. By keeping the amount of each item within these limits, an oversupply or an undersupply of inventory is avoided.

PERPETUAL INVENTORY SYSTEMS

Under a *perpetual inventory system,* cost of goods sold during a period, as well as the ending inventory, may be determined from the accounting records. Under such a system an account called Merchandise is used in the place of the Purchases and Merchandise Inventory accounts. It is a controlling account that controls the numerous perpetual inventory cards described in previous paragraphs.

When merchandise is purchased by a concern using a perpetual inventory system, the acquisition is recorded as follows:

```
Jan.   8 Merchandise ..............................    210.00
           Accounts Payable—Blue Company ........              210.00
         Purchased merchandise on credit.
```

In addition to the entry debiting the purchase to the Merchandise account, entries are also made on the proper perpetual inventory cards in the Received columns to show the kinds of merchandise bought. (See Illustration 9–3.)

When a sale is made, since the inventory cards show the cost of each item sold, it is possible to record both the sale and the cost of the goods sold. For example, if goods that, according to the inventory cards, cost $30 are sold for $50, cost of goods sold and the sale may be recorded as follows:

```
Jan.  10 Accounts Receivable—George Black ..........    50.00
         Cost of Goods Sold ........................    30.00
           Sales ................................              50.00
           Merchandise .........................               30.00
         Sold merchandise on credit.
```

In addition to the credit in this entry to the Merchandise account for the cost of the goods sold, the costs of the items sold are also deducted in the Sold columns of the proper inventory cards.

Note the debit to the Cost of Goods Sold account in the entry just given. If this account is debited at the time of each sale for the cost of the goods sold, the debit balance of the account will show at the end of the accounting period the cost of all goods sold during the period.

Note also the debit and the credit to the Merchandise account as they appear in the two entries just given. If this account is debited for the cost of merchandise purchased and credited for the cost of merchandise sold, at the end of an accounting period its debit balance will show the cost of the unsold goods on hand, the ending inventory.

ESTIMATED INVENTORIES

Retail Method

Good management requires that income statements be prepared more often than once each year, and inventory information is necessary in their preparation. However, taking a physical inventory in a retail store is both time-consuming and expensive. Consequently, many retailers use the so-called *retail inventory method* to estimate inventories for monthly or quarterly statements. These monthly or quarterly statements are called *interim statements,* since they are prepared in between the regular year-end statements.

ESTIMATING AN ENDING INVENTORY BY THE RETAIL METHOD. When the retail method is used to estimate an inventory, a store's records must show the amount of inventory it had at the beginning of the period both **at cost** and **at retail.** At cost for an inventory means just that, while "at retail" means the dollar amount of the inventory at the marked selling prices of the inventory items.

In addition to the beginning inventory, the records must also show the amount of goods purchased during the period both at cost and at retail plus the net sales at retail. The last item is easy; it is the balance of the Sales account, less returns and discounts. Then, with this information the interim inventory is estimated as follows: (Step 1) The amount of goods that were for sale during the period both at cost and at retail is first computed. Next (Step 2), "at cost" is divided by "at retail" to obtain the *inventory cost ratio.* Then (Step 3), sales (at retail) are deducted from goods for sale (at retail) to arrive at the ending inventory (at retail). And finally (Step 4), the ending inventory at retail is multiplied by the cost ratio to reduce it to a cost basis. These calculations are shown in Illustration 9–4.

This is the essence of Illustration 9–4: (1) The store had $100,000 of goods (at marked selling prices) for sale during the period. (2) These goods cost 60% of the $100,000 total amount at which they were marked for sale. (3) The store's records (its Sales account) showed that $70,000 of these goods were sold, leaving $30,000 of merchandise unsold and presumably in the ending inventory. Therefore, (4) since cost in this store is 60% of retail, the estimated cost of this ending inventory is $18,000.

An ending inventory calculated as in Illustration 9–4 is an estimate

---

Illustration 9–4

		At cost	At retail
(Step 1)	Goods available for sale:		
	Beginning inventory	$20,500	$ 34,500
	Net purchases	39,500	65,500
	Total goods available for sale	$60,000	100,000
(Step 2)	Cost ratio: $60,000 ÷ $100,000 = 60%		
(Step 3)	Deduct sales at retail		70,000
	Ending inventory at retail		$ 30,000
(Step 4)	Ending inventory at cost ($30,000 × 60%)	$18,000	

arrived at by deducting sales (goods sold) from goods for sale. Inventories estimated in this manner are satisfactory for interim statements, but for year-end statements, or at least once each year, a store should take a physical inventory.

USING THE RETAIL METHOD TO REDUCE A PHYSICAL INVENTORY TO COST.   Items for sale in a store normally have price tickets attached that show selling prices. Consequently, when a store takes a physical inventory, it commonly takes the inventory at the marked selling prices of the inventoried items. It then reduces the dollar total of this inventory to a cost basis by applying its cost ratio. It does this because the selling prices are readily available and the application of the cost ratio eliminates the need to look up the invoice price of each inventoried item.

For example, assume that the store of Illustration 9–4, in addition to estimating its inventory by the retail method, also takes a physical inventory at the marked selling prices of the inventoried goods. Assume further that the total of this physical inventory is $29,600. Under these assumptions the store may arrive at a cost basis for this inventory, without having to look up the cost of each inventoried item, simply by applying its cost ratio to the $29,600 inventory total as follows:

$$\$29,600 \times 60\% = \$17,760$$

The $17,760 cost figure for this store's ending physical inventory is a satisfactory figure for year-end statement purposes.

INVENTORY SHORTAGE.   An inventory determined as in Illustration 9–4 is an estimate of the amount of goods that should be on hand. However, since it is arrived at by deducting sales from goods for sale, it does not reveal any actual shortages due to breakage, loss, or theft. Nevertheless, the amount of such shortages may be determined by first estimating an inventory as in Illustration 9–4 and then taking a physical inventory at marked selling prices.

For example, by means of the Illustration 9–4 calculations, it was estimated the store of this discussion had a $30,000 ending inventory at retail. However, in the previous section it was assumed that this same store took a physical inventory and had only $29,600 of merchandise on hand. Therefore, if this store should have had $30,000 of goods in its ending inventory as determined in Illustration 9–4, but had only $29,600 when it took a physical inventory, it must have had a $400 inventory shortage at retail or a $240 shortage at cost ($400 × 60% = $240).

MARKUPS AND MARKDOWNS.   The calculation of a cost ratio is often not as simple as that shown in Illustration 9–4. It is not simple because many stores not only have a *normal markup* (often called a *markon*) that they apply to items purchased for sale but also make additional *markups* and *markdowns.* A normal markup, or markon, is the normal amount or percentage that is applied to the cost of an item to arrive at its selling price. For example, if a store's normal markup is 50% on cost and it applies this markup to an item that cost $10, it will mark the item for sale at $15. Normal markups appear in the calculation of a store's cost ratio as the difference between net purchases at cost and at retail.

"Additional markups" are markups made in addition to normal markups. Stores commonly give goods of outstanding style or quality such additional markups because they can get a higher than normal price for such goods. They also commonly mark down for a clearance sale any slow-moving merchandise.

When a store using the retail inventory method makes additional markups and markdowns, it must keep a record of them. It then uses the information in calculating its cost ratio and in estimating an interim inventory as in Illustration 9–5.

Illustration 9–5

	At cost	At retail
Goods available for sale:		
Beginning inventory	$18,000	$27,800
Net purchases	34,000	50,700
Additional markups		1,500
Total goods available for sale	$52,000	80,000
Cost ratio: $52,000 ÷ $80,000 = 65%		
Sales and markdowns:		
Sales at retail		54,000
Markdowns		2,000
Total sales and markdowns		56,000
Ending inventory at retail ($80,000 − $56,000)		$24,000
Ending inventory at cost ($24,000 × 65%)	$15,600	

Observe in Illustration 9–5 that the store's $80,000 of goods for sale at retail were reduced $54,000 by sales and $2,000 by markdowns, a total of $56,000. (To understand markdowns, visualize this effect. The store had an item for sale during the period at $25. The item did not sell, and to move it the manager marked its price down from $25 to $20. By this act the amount of goods for sale in the store at retail was reduced by $5. Likewise, by a number of such markdowns during the year goods for sale at retail in the store of Illustration 9–5 were reduced $2,000.) Now back to the calculations of Illustration 9–5. The store's $80,000 of goods for sale were reduced $54,000 by sales and $2,000 by markdowns, leaving an estimated $24,000 ending inventory at retail. Therefore, since cost is 65% of retail, the ending inventory at cost is $15,600.

In Illustration 9–5 markups enter into the calculation of the cost ratio but markdowns do not. It has long been customary in using the retail inventory method to add additional markups but to ignore markdowns in computing the percentage relation between goods for sale at cost and at retail. The justification for this was and is that a more conservative figure for the ending inventory results, a figure that approaches "cost of replacement, the lower." A further discussion of this phase of the retail inventory method is reserved for a more advanced text.

Gross Profit Method

Often retail price information about beginning inventory, purchases, and markups is not kept. In such cases the retail inventory method cannot be used. However, if a company knows its normal gross profit margin or rate; has information at cost in regard to its beginning inventory, net purchases, and transportation-in; and knows the amount of its sales and sales returns, the company can estimate its ending inventory by the *gross profit method*.

For example, on March 27, the inventory of a company was totally destroyed by a fire. The company's average gross profit rate during the past five years has been 30% of net sales. And on the date of the fire the company's accounts showed the following balances:

Sales	$31,500
Sales returns	1,500
Inventory, January 1, 19—	12,000
Net purchases	20,000
Transportation-in	500

With this information the gross profit method may be used to estimate the company's inventory loss for insurance purposes. The first step in applying the method is to recognize that whatever portion of each dollar of net sales was gross profit, the remaining portion was cost of goods sold. Consequently, if the company's gross profit rate averaged 30%, then 30% of each dollar of net sales was gross profit and 70% was cost of goods sold. The 70% is used in estimating the inventory and inventory loss as in Illustration 9–6.

To understand Illustration 9–6, recall that in a normal situation an ending inventory is subtracted from goods for sale to determine cost of goods sold. Then observe in Illustration 9–6 that the opposite subtraction is made. Estimated cost of goods sold is subtracted from goods for sale to arrive at the estimated ending inventory.

In addition to its use in insurance cases, as in this illustration, the gross profit method is also commonly used by accountants in checking on the probable accuracy of a physical inventory taken and priced in the normal way.

Illustration 9–6

Goods available for sale:		
Inventory, January 1, 19—		$12,000
Net purchases	$20,000	
Add: Transportation-in	500	20,500
Total goods available for sale		32,500
Less estimated cost of goods sold:		
Sales	31,500	
Less sales returns	(1,500)	
Net sales	$30,000	
Estimated cost of goods sold (70% × $30,000) . .		(21,000)
Estimated March 27 inventory and inventory loss . .		$11,500

GLOSSARY

Conservatism principle. The rule that accountants should be conservative in their estimates and opinions and in their selection of procedures.

Consignee. One to whom something is consigned, or shipped.

Consignor. One who consigns, or ships, something to another person or enterprise.

Consistency principle. The accounting rule requiring a persistent application of a selected accounting method or procedure, period after period.

FIFO inventory pricing. The pricing of an inventory under the assumption that the first items received were the first items sold.

Gross profit inventory method. A procedure for estimating an ending inventory in which an estimated cost of goods sold based on past gross profit rates is subtracted from the cost of goods available for sale to arrive at an estimated ending inventory.

Interim statements. Financial statements prepared in between the regular annual statements.

Inventory cost ratio. The ratio of goods available for sale at cost to goods available for sale at retail prices.

LIFO inventory pricing. The pricing of an inventory under the assumption that the last items received were the first items sold.

Lower-of-cost-or-replacement pricing of an inventory. The pricing of inventory at the lower of what each item actually cost or what it would cost to replace each item on the inventory date.

Markdown. A reduction in the marked selling price of an item.

Markon. The normal percentage of its cost that is added to the cost of an item to arrive at its selling price.

Markup. An addition to the normal markon given to an item.

Normal markup. A phrase meaning the same as markon.

Periodic inventory system. An inventory system in which inventories and cost of goods sold are based on periodic physical inventories.

Perpetual inventory system. An inventory system in which inventories and cost of goods sold are based on book inventory records.

Retail inventory method. A method for estimating an ending inventory based on the ratio of the cost of goods for sale at cost and cost of goods for sale at marked selling prices.

Specific invoice inventory pricing. The pricing of an inventory where each inventory item can be associated with a specific invoice and be priced accordingly.

Weighted-average cost inventory pricing. An inventory pricing system in which the units in the beginning inventory of a product and in each purchase of the product are weighted by the number of units in the beginning inventory and in each purchase to determine a weighted-average cost per unit of the product, and after which this weighted-average cost is used to price the ending inventory of the product.

QUESTIONS FOR CLASS DISCUSSION

1. It has been said that cost of goods sold and ending inventory are opposite sides of the same coin. What is meant by this?

2. Give the meanings of the following when applied to inventory: *(a)* first-in, first-out, *(b)* FIFO, *(c)* last-in, first-out, *(d)* LIFO, *(e)* cost, *(f)* market, *(g)* the lower of cost and replacement, *(h)* perpetual inventory, *(i)* physical inventory, *(j)* book inventory.

3. If prices are rising, will the LIFO or the FIFO method of inventory valuation result in the higher gross profit?

4. May a company change its inventory pricing method at will?

5. What is required by the accounting principle of consistency?

6. If a company changes one of its accounting procedures, what is required of it under the full-disclosure principle?

7. Of what does the cost of an inventory item consist?

8. Why are incidental costs commonly ignored in pricing an inventory? Under what accounting principle is this permitted?

9. What is meant when it is said that inventory errors ''correct themselves''?

10. If inventory errors ''correct themselves,'' why be concerned when such errors are made?

11. What is required of an accountant under the principle of conservatism?

12. Give the meanings of the following when applied in the retail method of estimating an inventory: *(a)* at cost, *(b)* at retail, *(c)* cost ratio, *(d)* normal markup, *(e)* markon, *(f)* additional markup, and *(g)* markdown.

MULTIPLE CHOICE

1. During a period of steadily rising prices the inventory pricing method that results in reporting the lowest net income is:
   - *a.* Specific invoice pricing.
   - *b.* Average cost.
   - *c.* Weighted-average cost.
   - *d.* FIFO.
   - *e.* LIFO.

2. With a periodic inventory system, an undiscovered error that overstates the 1987 year-end inventory will cause:
   - *a.* An overstatement of 1987 net income and an understatement of 1988 net income.
   - *b.* An understatement of assets on the 1987 balance sheet.
   - *c.* An overstatement of 1987 cost of goods sold.
   - *d.* An overstatement of 1987 net income and no effect on 1988 net income.
   - *e.* None of the foregoing.

3. Alpha Company had the following purchases during 19A:

   Jan. 1   10 units at $120
   Feb. 1   20 units at $130
   May 1   15 units at $140
   Sept. 1   12 units at $150
   Nov. 1   10 units at $160

   On December 31, 19A, there were 26 units in ending inventory. These 26 units consisted of 2 from the January 1 shipment, 4 from the February 1 shipment, 6 from the May 1 shipment, 4 from the September 1 shipment, and 10 from the November 1 shipment. Using specific invoice prices, what is the cost of the ending inventory?
   - *a.* $3,520.
   - *b.* $3,800.
   - *c.* $3,960.
   - *d.* $3,280.
   - *e.* $3,640.

4. X Company was destroyed completely by fire on May 31, 19A. The following information was the only record that could be salvaged:

Inventory, January 1, 19A	$28,000
Purchases......................	16,000
Transportation-in	1,000
Sales	55,000
Sales returns	700

X Company's average gross profit was 35%. What was the estimated value of the May 31, 19A inventory that was lost?

    a. $9,705.

    b. $25,995.

    c. $29,250.

    d. $44,000.

    e. $45,000.

5. The Beta Corporation made the following purchases of Product X during 19A:

Jan. 1 200 units at $ 6.50
Mar. 1 175 units at $ 8.00
Aug. 1 225 units at $12.00
Nov. 1 150 units at $14.00

There was no beginning inventory, but ending inventory consisted of 225 units. If Beta uses the FIFO inventory method, what would be the cost of their ending inventory?

    a. $1,500.

    b. $2,250.

    c. $3,000.

    d. $4,500.

    e. $6,000.

6. A company began an accounting period and purchased item XOX as follows:

Jan. 1	Beginning inventory	100 units at $10 =	$ 1,000
Mar. 9	Purchased	500 units at 11 =	5,500
July 6	Purchased	300 units at 13 =	3,900
Dec. 5	Purchased	100 units at 14 =	1,400
	Total	1,000	$11,800

If the ending inventory of item XOX consists of 110 units, the cost of these units based on LIFO is:

    a. $1,540.

    b. $1,530.

    c. $1,298.

    d. $1,110.

    e.   Some other amount.

7. A company began an accounting period and purchased an item as follows:

Jan. 1	Beginning inventory	200 units at $1.10 =	$ 220
Feb. 12	Purchased	300 units at 1.00 =	300
June 7	Purchased	200 units at 1.15 =	230
Oct. 16	Purchased	200 units at 1.25 =	250
Dec. 12	Purchased	100 units at 1.30 =	130
	Total	1,000	$1,130

If the ending inventory consists of 300 units, the cost of these units based on weighted-average cost is

   a. $380.
   b. $348.
   c. $339.
   d. $320.
   e.   Some other amount.

MINI DISCUSSION CASES

Case 9–1

Your friend is the controller of Waterloo Manufacturing Company and has come to you for some advice about the valuation of the finished goods inventory. The inventory is currently listed on the books of the company at its cost of $62,500. The controller has recently learned that the goods could have been purchased from an overseas supplier for $56,500. The controller is unsure as to whether she should price the inventory on the year-end financial statements, which are to be prepared in two weeks, at the higher or lower value. She says that if she prices them at the lower value, she will violate both the cost and the consistency principles.

Required:

Advise your friend and give the reasons behind your advice.

Case 9–2

In November of 19B the accountant for the PQ Company discovered that the December 31, 19A inventory had been misstated in the 19A financial statements. The inventory should have been $46,000 but had been entered on the statements as $64,000. His assistant indicated that the company would have to correct and restate the 19A statements when preparing the statements for the 19B year-end. The accountant said that no corrections will be necessary since the error will have corrected itself by the end of 19B and that the Retained Earnings figure will be correct as of December 31, 19B.

Required:

Comment on the positions taken by the accountant and his assistant. What do you propose should be done in preparing the financial statements for 19B? Why?

CLASS EXERCISES

Exercise 9–1

A concern began a year and purchased Product Z as follows:

Jan. 1	Beginning inventory	10 units at $ 9.20 =	$ 92
Feb. 5	Purchased	40 units at $10.00 =	400
June 8	Purchased	20 units at $10.60 =	212
Aug. 3	Purchased	30 units at $11.20 =	336
Dec. 9	Purchased	20 units at $11.00 =	220
	Total	120 units	$1,260

Required:

Under the assumption the ending inventory consisted of 30 units, 10 from each of the last three purchases, determine the share of the $1,260 cost of the units for sale that should be assigned to the ending inventory and to goods sold under each of the following assumptions: *(a)* costs are assigned on the basis of specific invoice prices, *(b)* costs are assigned on a weighted average cost basis, *(c)* costs are assigned on the basis of FIFO, and *(d)* costs are assigned on the basis of LIFO.

Exercise 9–2

A company had $80,000 of sales during each of three consecutive years, and it purchased merchandise costing $50,000 during each of the years. It also maintained a $10,000 inventory from the beginning to the end of the three-year period. However, it made an error that caused its December 31, end-of-year-one, inventory to appear on its statements at $11,000, rather than the correct $10,000.

Required:

1. State the actual amount of the company's gross profit in each of the years.
2. Prepare a comparative income statement like the one illustrated in this chapter to show the effect of this error on the company's cost of goods sold and gross profit for each of Year 1, Year 2, and Year 3.

Exercise 9–3

During an accounting period a company sold $78,000 of merchandise at marked retail prices. At the period end the following information was available from its records:

	At cost	At retail
Beginning inventory	$15,000	$21,000
Net purchases	55,000	74,000
Additional markups.....		5,000
Markdowns		2,000

Use the retail method to estimate the store's ending inventory at cost.

Exercise 9–4

Assume that in addition to estimating its ending inventory by the retail method, the store of Exercise 9–3 also took a physical inventory at the marked selling prices of the inventory items. Assume further that the total of this physical inventory at marked selling prices was $19,500. Then *(a)* determine the amount of this inventory at cost and *(b)* determine the store's inventory shrinkage from breakage, theft, or other cause at retail and at cost.

Exercise 9–5

On January 1 a company had a $17,000 inventory at cost. During the first quarter of the year it purchased $65,000 of merchandise, returned $500, and paid freight charges on merchandise purchased totaling $3,500. During the past several years the company's gross profit on sales has averaged 35%. Under the assumption the company had $100,000 of sales during the first quarter of the year, use the gross profit method to estimate its end of the first quarter inventory.

PROBLEMS

Problem 9–1
A company began the year with 20 units of a product that cost $60 each, and it made successive purchases of the product as follows:

Jan. 15   60 units at $75 each.
May 10   50 units at $80 each.
Aug. 17   30 units at $90 each.
Nov. 30   40 units at $85 each.

Required:

1. Prepare a calculation showing the number and total cost of the units for sale during the year.
2. Under the assumption the company had 50 of the units in its December 31, end-of-the-year inventory, prepare calculations showing the portions of the total cost of the units for sale during the year that should be assigned to the ending inventory and to the units sold *(a)* first on a FIFO basis, *(b)* then on a LIFO basis, and *(c)* finally on a weighted-average cost basis.

Problem 9–2
Alpha Company incurred $50,000 of operating expenses last year in selling 850 units of its Product X at $200 per unit. It began the year and purchased the product as follows:

January 1 inventory . . . .   100 units at $121 each
Purchases:
    January 28 . . . .   300 units at $120 each
    April 29 . . . .   200 units at $125 each
    July 27 . . . .   300 units at $129 each
    December 2 . . . .   100 units at $132 each

Required:

Prepare a comparative income statement for the company showing in adjacent columns the net incomes earned from the sale of the product under the assumptions the company priced its ending inventory on the basis of *(a)* FIFO, *(b)* LIFO, and *(c)* weighted-average cost.

Problem 9–3
The inventory record for Item ABC showed the following transactions:

Jan. 1   Balance 5 units costing $5 each.
     2   Received 10 units costing $5.40 each.
     6   Sold 3 units.
    10   Sold 8 units.
    14   Received 8 units costing $6 each.
    18   Sold 3 units.
    28   Sold 4 units.

Required:

1. Assume the perpetual inventory record card for Item ABC is kept on a FIFO basis and enter the beginning balance and transactions on the card.
2. Assume the perpetual inventory record for Item ABC is kept on a LIFO basis and enter the beginning balance and transactions on a second card.
3. Assume the four units sold on January 28 were sold on credit at $8 each

to Glen Eads and give the entry to record the sale and the cost of goods sold on a LIFO basis.

Problem 9–4   Ski Shop takes a year-end physical inventory at marked selling prices and by the retail inventory method reduces the total to a cost basis for statement purposes. It also estimates its year-end inventory by the retail method and by a comparison determines the amount of any inventory shortage. At the end of last year the following information from the store's records and from its physical inventory was available:

	At cost	At retail
January 1 beginning inventory	$ 18,500	$ 28,450
Purchases	143,880	217,180
Purchases returns	1,180	1,820
Additional markups		4,190
Markdowns		2,110
Sales		220,120
Sales returns		1,830
December 31 physical inventory		27,200

Required:

1. Prepare an estimate of the store's year-end inventory at cost.
2. Use the store's cost ratio to reduce the amount of its year-end physical inventory to a cost basis.
3. Prepare a schedule showing the amount of the inventory shortage at cost and at retail.

Problem 9–5   The Clothes Tree suffered a disastrous fire during the night of April 27, and everything except its accounting records, which were in a fireproof vault, was destroyed. As an insurance adjuster, you have been called upon to determine the store's inventory loss. The following information is available from its accounting records for the period January 1 through April 27:

Merchandise inventory, January 1, at cost	$23,400
Purchases	63,520
Purchases returns	1,260
Freight-in	660
Sales	94,730
Sales returns	2,230

The accounting records also show that the store's gross profit rate has averaged 34% over the past four years.

Required:

Use the gross profit method to prepare an estimate of the store's inventory loss.

Problem 9–6   Able Company's records provide the following information for the year ended last December 31:

	At cost	At retail
Year's sales		$221,560
Sales returns		2,345
January 1 inventory	$ 21,540	32,950
Purchases	146,490	219,735
Purchases returns	980	1,470
Additional markups		5,785
Markdowns		1,285

Required:

Use the retail method to prepare a calculation estimating Able Company's December 31, year-end inventory.

Problem 9–7

Best Company wants an estimate of its June 30 inventory. The following information is available from its accounting records:

January 1 inventory at cost	$ 42,850
Purchases	123,900
Purchases returns	1,200
Freight-in	2,680
Sales	189,900
Sales returns	3,400
Average gross profit rate	32%

The gross profit rate is an average for the past five years. The remaining figures are for the six-month period, January 1 through June 30.

Required:

Use the gross profit method and prepare a calculation estimating Best Company's June 30 inventory.

Problem 9–8

Mesa Sales sold 1,000 units of its Product 2XY in each of three successive years at the following weighted-average prices:

Year 1, 1,000 units at $115 per unit $115,000
Year 2, 1,000 units at $133 per unit 133,000
Year 3, 1,000 units at $138 per unit 138,000

It began the three-year period with 200 units of the product, costing $50 each, in its inventory; and it ended each of the years with 200 units in the inventory. Also, it made successive purchases of the product as follows:

Year One		Year Three	
200 units at $55	$11,000	200 units at $70	$14,000
200 units at $50	10,000	400 units at $65	26,000
300 units at $60	18,000	200 units at $65	13,000
300 units at $65	19,500	200 units at $75	15,000
1,000	$58,500	1,000	$68,000

Year Two	
500 units at $60	$30,000
300 units at $70	21,000
200 units at $70	14,000
1,000	$65,000

Required:

1. Set up three comparative income statements for the company, one for each year, on four-column paper. (If the working papers that accompany this text are in use, these statements are already set up there.)

2. In the first two columns of each statement show sales, cost of goods sold, and gross profit under the assumption the company priced its inventories on a FIFO basis, and in the second two columns show sales, cost of goods sold, and gross profit under the assumption the company priced its inventories on a LIFO basis.

3. Answer these questions: *(a)* Which inventory pricing method results in the smaller annual incomes for the company? *(b)* Which better synchronizes costs and revenues?

ALTERNATE PROBLEMS

Problem 9–1A   A concern began a year with 300 units of Product A in its inventory that cost $50 each, and it made successive purchases of the product as follows:

Mar. 1   400 units at $60 each.
June 10   500 units at $70 each.
Aug. 29   400 units at $80 each.
Nov. 15   400 units at $60 each.

Required:

1. Prepare a calculation showing the number and total cost of the units that were for sale during the year.

2. Assume the concern had 500 of the units in its December 31, year-end inventory and prepare calculations showing the portions of the total costs of the units for sale during the year that should be assigned to the ending inventory and to cost of goods sold *(a)* first on a FIFO basis, *(b)* then on a LIFO basis, and finally *(c)* on a weighted-average cost basis.

Problem 9–2A   Last year Omega Company sold 8,500 units of its product at $10 per unit. It incurred marketing costs of $2 per unit in selling the 8,500 units, and it began the year and made successive purchases of the product as follows:

January 1 beginning inventory .... 1,000 units costing $5.60 per unit
Purchases:
    January 29 .... 1,000 units costing $6.00 per unit
    March 15 .... 3,000 units costing $6.20 per unit
    July 12 .... 4,000 units costing $6.50 per unit
    November 3 .... 1,000 units costing $7.00 per unit

Required:

Prepare a comparative income statement for the company showing in adjacent columns the net incomes earned from the sale of the product under the assumptions the company priced its ending inventory on the basis of: *(a)* FIFO, *(b)* LIFO, and *(c)* weighted-average cost.

Problem 9–3A The perpetual inventory record card for Article XYZ showed the following beginning balance and transactions during January of this year:

Jan. 1 Balance 12 units costing $6 each.
     4 Received 20 units costing $7 each.
     9 Sold 10 units.
    15 Sold 15 units.
    19 Received 20 units costing $8 each.
    24 Sold 5 units.
    29 Sold 16 units.

Required:

1. Under the assumption that the concern keeps its records on a FIFO basis, enter the beginning balance and the transactions on a perpetual inventory record card like the one illustrated in this chapter.
2. Under the assumption that the concern keeps its inventory records on a LIFO basis, enter the beginning inventory and the transactions on a second inventory record card.
3. Assume that the 16 units sold on January 29 were sold on credit to Glen Eads at $12.50 each, and prepare a general journal entry to record the sale and cost of goods sold on a LIFO basis.

Problem 9–4A Hobby Shop takes a year-end physical inventory at marked selling prices and uses the retail method to reduce the inventory total to a cost basis for statement purposes. It also uses the retail method to estimate the amount of inventory it should have at the end of a year, and by comparison determines any inventory shortage due to shoplifting or other cause. At the end of last year its physical inventory at marked selling prices totaled $20,950, and the following information was available from its records:

	At cost	At retail
January 1 inventory	$12,210	$ 18,100
Purchases	83,385	119,900
Purchases returns	1,415	1,950
Additional markups		2,450
Markdowns		1,530
Sales		117,340
Sales returns		1,870

Required:

1. Use the retail method to estimate the shop's year-end inventory at cost.
2. Use the retail method to reduce the shop's year-end physical inventory to a cost basis.
3. Prepare a schedule showing the inventory shortage at cost and at retail.

Problem 9–5A On Monday morning, June 14, the manager of Smart Shop unlocked the store to learn that thieves had broken in over the weekend and stolen the store's entire inventory. The following information for the period, January 1 through June 13, was available to establish the amount of loss:

January 1 merchandise inventory at cost	$ 32,500
Purchases	92,310
Purchases returns	415
Freight-in	560
Sales	139,875
Sales returns	1,375

Required:

Under the assumption that the store had earned an average 32% gross profit on sales during the past five years, prepare a statement showing the estimated loss.

Problem 9–6A   Charles Company's records provided the following information for the year ended December 31:

	At cost	At retail
January 1 beginning inventory	$ 23,830	$ 31,350
Purchases	162,116	229,590
Purchases returns	2,210	3,160
Additional markups		4,700
Markdowns		1,170
Sales		228,240
Sales returns		2,880

Required:

Prepare an estimate of the concern's December 31 inventory by the retail method.

Problem 9–7A   David Company wants an estimate of its March 31, end-of-the-first quarter inventory. Its January 1 beginning inventory at cost was $38,750. During the last five years its gross profit rate has averaged 34%, and the following information as to purchases and sales for the first quarter is available from its accounting records:

Purchases	$ 91,400
Purchases returns	850
Freight-in	1,130
Sales	144,640
Sales returns	2,140

Required:

Use the gross profit method to prepare an estimate of the company's March 31 inventory.

PROVOCATIVE PROBLEMS

Provocative Problem 9–1, The In Sole   The In Sole Centre suffered extensive smoke and water damage and a small amount of fire damage on October 3. The store carried adequate insurance, and the insurance company's claims adjuster appeared the same day to inspect the damage. After completing his survey, the adjuster agreed with Al Berg, the store's owner, that the inventory could be sold to a company specializing in fire sales for about one fifth of its cost. The adjuster offered Mr. Berg $20,000 in full settlement for the damage to the inventory. He suggested that the offer be accepted and said he had authority to deliver at once a cheque for that amount. He also pointed out that a prompt settlement would provide funds to replace the inventory in time for the store to participate in the Christmas shopping season.

Mr. Berg felt the loss might exceed $20,000, but he recognized that a time-consuming count and inspection of each item in the inventory would be required to establish the loss more precisely; and he was reluctant to take the time for the inventory, since he was anxious to get back into business before the Christmas rush, the season making the largest contribution to his annual net income. Yet he was also unwilling to take a substantial loss on the insurance settlement; so he asked for and received a one-day period in which to consider the insurance company offer, and he immediately went to his records for the following information:

		At cost	At retail
a.	January 1 inventory	$ 29,150	$ 46,800
	Purchases, January 1 through October 3	172,350	277,900
	Net sales, January 1 through October 3		280,100

b. On March 1 the remaining inventory of winter footwear was marked down from $12,000 to $9,000, and placed on sale in the annual end-of-winter sale. Two thirds of the shoes were sold; the markdown on the remaining sale shoes was canceled. (A markdown cancellation is subtracted from a markdown, and a markup cancellation is subtracted from a markup.)

c. In May a special line of imported shoes proved popular, and 84 high-styled pairs were marked up from their normal $30 retail price to $35 per pair. Sixty pairs were sold at this higher price, and on July 15 the markup on the remaining 24 pairs was canceled and they were returned to their regular $30 per pair price.

d. Between January 1 and October 3 markdowns totaling $1,400 were taken on several odd lots of shoes.

Recommend whether or not you think Mr. Berg should take the insurance company's offer. Back your recommendation with figures.

Provocative
Problem 9–2,
Budget
Furniture Store

Budget Furniture Store has been in operation for six years, during which it has earned a 34% average gross profit on sales. However, night before last, June 2, it suffered a disastrous fire that destroyed its entire inventory; and Fred Arne, the store's owner, has filed a $49,600 inventory loss claim with the store's insurance company. When asked on what he based his claim, he replied that during the day before the fire he had marked every item in the store down 20% in preparation for the annual summer clearance sale, and during the marking down process he had taken an inventory of the merchandise in the store. Furthermore, he said, "It's a big loss, but every cloud has a silver lining, because I am giving you fellows (the insurance company) the benefit of the 20% markdown in filing this claim.''

When it was explained to Mr. Arne that he had to back his loss claim with more than his word as to the amount of the loss, he produced the following information from his pre-sale inventory and accounting records, which fortunately were in a fireproof vault and were not destroyed in the fire.

1. The store's accounts were closed on December 31, of last year.
2. After posting was completed, the accounts showed the following June 2 balances:

Merchandise inventory, January 1 balance	$ 43,250
Purchases	116,400
Purchases returns	1,225
Freight-in	2,940
Sales	186,710
Sales returns	4,210

3. Mr. Arne's pre-fire inventory totaled $62,000 at pre-markdown prices.

From the information given, present figures to show the amount of loss suffered by Mr. Arne. Also, show how he arrived at the amount of his loss claim. Can his pre-sale inventory be used to substantiate the actual amount of his loss? If so, use the pre-sale inventory figure to substantiate the actual loss.

ANALYTICAL AND REVIEW PROBLEMS

Problem 9–1 A&R   The LIFO versus FIFO controversy has spanned a number of decades. Proponents of each of the inventory procedures attribute certain merits to each.

Required:

Identify the inventory procedure to which the following merits are attributed by writing either "LIFO" or "FIFO" opposite each of the letters (a) to (n).

Inventory Procedure

a.	_____Matches actual physical flow of goods.
b.	_____Matches old costs with new prices.
c.	_____Costs inventory at approximate replacement cost.
d.	_____Matches new cost with new prices.
e.	_____Emphasizes balance sheet.
f.	_____Emphasizes income statement.
g.	_____Opens door for "profit manipulation."
h.	_____Understates the current ratio in a period of inflation.
i.	_____Overstates inventory turnover in a period of inflation.
j.	_____Gives higher profits in a period of inflation.
k.	_____Matches current costs with current revenues.
l.	_____More accurately reflects net income available to owners.
m.	_____Gives lower profits in a period of deflation.
n.	_____Results in a procession of costs in the same order as incurred.

Problem 9–2
A&R

The following information is taken from the records of Nitram Company for four consecutive operating periods:

	Periods			
	1	2	3	4
Beginning inventory	$12,000	$18,000	$13,000	$16,000
Ending inventory	18,000	13,000	16,000	7,000
Net income	10,000	12,000	14,000	18,000

Assuming that the company made the errors below:

Period	Error in ending inventory	
1	Overstated	$4,000
2	Understated	3,000
3	Overstated	2,000

Required:

1. Compute the revised net income for each of the four periods..
2. Assuming that the company's ending inventory for period 4 is correct, · how would these errors affect the total net income for the four periods combined? Explain.

Problem 9–3
A&R

The records of Philips Company as of December 31, 19A, show the following:

	Net purchases	Net income	Accounts payable	Inventory
Balance per company's books	$186,000	$15,500	$19,500	$3,000
(a)				
(b)				
(c)				
(d)				
(e)				
Correct balances				

The accountant of Philips Company discovers in the first week of January 19B that the following errors were made by his staff.

a. Goods costing $2,000 were in transit (FOB shipping point) and were not included in the ending inventory. The invoice had been received and the purchase recorded.

b. Damaged goods (cost $2,000) which were being held for return to the supplier were included in inventory. The goods had been recorded as a purchase and the entry for the return of these goods had also been made.

c. Inventory items costing $1,000 were incorrectly excluded from the final inventory. These goods had not been recorded as a purchase and had not been paid for by the company.

d. Goods which were shipped FOB destination had not yet arrived and were not included in inventory. However, the invoice had arrived on December 30, 19A, and the purchase for $1,800 was recorded.

e. Goods which cost $1,400 were segregated and not included in inventory because a customer expressed an intention to buy the goods. The sale of the goods for $2,100 had been recorded in December, 19A.

Required:

Using the format provided above, show the correct amount for net purchases, net income, accounts payable, and inventory for Philips Company as at December 31, 19A.

Problem 9–4 A&R

The Southern Pacific Company accounts for Product Y using LIFO and periodic procedures. Data relative to this product for the year ended December 31, 19A, are: Inventory January 1, 19A, 4,500 units at $9.

Purchases	Sales
1st quarter 9,000 units at $11	6,000 units at $17
2d quarter 20,000 units at $12	16,000 units at $18
3d quarter 16,000 units at $15	18,000 units at $20
4th quarter 8,000 units at $18	12,000 units at $23

Required:

1. Compute the gross margin on sales of Product X for 19A.
2. Repeat part (1) assuming that 4,000 rather than 8,000 units were purchased in the 4th quarter.
3. Repeat part (1) assuming that 12,000 rather than 8,000 units were purchased in the 4th quarter.
4. Solve parts (1), (2), and (3) on the assumption that Southern Pacific used the FIFO rather than LIFO inventory method.
5. Which method permits the manipulation of net income?
6. Which method emphasizes the balance sheet?
7. Which method emphasizes the income statement?
8. Which method matches current costs with current revenues?
9. Which method results in a processing of costs in the same order as incurred?
10. Which method costs inventory at approximately replacement cost?

Problem 9–5 A&R

For each of the statements **enter** agree or disagree and state why you agree or disagree.

a. An improper valuation of inventory affects the income statement but does not affect the balance sheet.
b. Under perpetual inventory system, an income statement may be prepared without taking a physical inventory.
c. In general, the inventory policy should be to select an assumed flow of goods that matches the physical flow of the goods.
d. The cost principle is the justification for the lower of cost or replacement rule.
e. Under the periodic inventory method, cost of goods sold is computed as a residual.
f. Under the perpetual inventory method, a physical inventory count is never taken.
g. Damaged or obsolete inventory is valued at cost for balance sheet purposes until such time as sold.

h. The LIFO inventory costing method lends itself most to manipulation of reported net incomes between periods.

i. The specific inventory cost method of inventory flow is more likely to be employed by a jewelry store than a groceteria.

j. The LIFO inventory costing method emphasizes the income statement rather than the balance sheet.

Plant and Equipment

10

After studying Chapter 10, you should be able to:

Relate what is included in the cost of a plant asset.

Allocate the cost of lump-sum purchases to the separate assets being purchased.

Describe the causes of depreciation and the reasons for depreciation accounting.

Calculate depreciation by the (a) straight-line, (b) units-of-production, (c) declining-balance, and (d) sum-of-the-years'-digits methods.

Explain how the original cost of a plant asset is recovered through the sale of the asset's product or service.

Define or explain the words and phrases listed in the chapter Glossary.

Tangible assets that are used in the production or sale of other assets or services and that have a useful life longer than one accounting period are called **plant and equipment** or **plant assets.** The phrase "fixed assets" was used for many years. However, it is rapidly disappearing from published balance sheets. The more descriptive "plant and equipment" or "property, plant, and equipment" is now used more often.

Use in the production or sale of other assets or services is the characteristic that distinguishes a plant asset from an item of merchandise or an investment. An office or factory machine held for sale by a dealer is merchandise to the dealer. Likewise, land purchased and held for future expansion but presently unused is classified as a long-term investment. Only when the asset is put to use in the production or sale of other assets or services should it be classified as plant and equipment. However, standby equipment for use in case of a breakdown or for use during peak periods of production is a plant asset. When equipment is removed from service and held for sale, it ceases to be a plant asset.

A productive or service life longer than one accounting period distinguishes an item of plant and equipment from an item of supplies. An item of supplies may be consumed in a single accounting period. If consumed, its cost is charged to the period of consumption. The productive life of a plant asset, on the other hand, is longer than one period. It contributes to production for several periods. Therefore, as a result of the *matching principle,* its cost must be allocated to these periods in a systematic and rational manner.

COST OF A PLANT ASSET

Cost is the basis for recording the acquisition of a plant asset. The cost of a plant asset includes all normal and reasonable expenditures necessary to get the asset in place and ready to use. For example, the cost of a factory machine includes its invoice price, less any discount for cash, plus freight, unpacking, and assembling costs. Cost also includes any special concrete base or foundation, electrical or power connections, and adjustments needed to place the machine in operation. In short, the cost of a plant asset includes all normal, necessary, and reasonable costs incurred in getting the asset in place and ready to produce.

A cost must be normal and reasonable as well as necessary if it is to be properly included in the cost of a plant asset. For example, if a machine is damaged by being dropped in unpacking, repairs should not be added to its cost. They should be charged to an expense account. Likewise, a fine paid for moving a heavy machine on city streets without proper permits is not part of the cost of the machine. However, if the permits were secured, the cost of the permits would be charged to the cost of the machine.

After being purchased but before being put to use, a plant asset must sometimes be repaired or remodeled to meet the needs of the purchaser. In such a case the repairing or remodeling expenditures are part of its cost and should be charged to the asset account. Furthermore, depreciation charges should not begin until the asset is put in use.

When a plant asset is constructed by a concern for its own use, cost includes material and labour costs plus a reasonable amount of overhead or indirect expenses such as heat, lights, power, and depreciation on the machinery used in constructing the asset. Cost also includes architectural and design fees, building permits, and insurance during construction. Needless to say, insurance on the same asset after it has been placed in production is an expense.

When land is purchased for a building site, its cost includes the amount paid for the land plus any real estate commissions. It also includes escrow and legal fees, fees for examining and insuring the title, and any accrued property taxes paid by the purchaser, as well as expenditures for surveying, clearing, grading, draining, and landscaping. All are part of the cost of the land. Furthermore, any assessments incurred at the time of purchase or later for such things as the installation of streets, sewers, and sidewalks should be debited to the Land account since they add a more or less permanent value to the land.

Land purchased as a building site sometimes has an old building that must be removed. In such cases the entire purchase price, including the amount paid for the to-be-removed building, should be charged to the Land account. Also, the cost of removing the old building, less any amounts recovered through the sale of salvaged materials, should be charged to this account.

Since land has an unlimited life, it is not subject to depreciation. However, *land improvements* such as parking lot surfaces, fences, and lighting systems have limited useful lives. Such costs improve the value or usefulness of land but must be charged to separate Land Improvement accounts and subjected to depreciation. Finally, a separate Building account must be charged for the cost of purchasing or constructing a building to be used as a plant asset.

Often land, land improvements, and buildings are purchased together for one lump sum. When this occurs, the purchase price must be apportioned among the assets on some fair basis, since some of the assets depreciate and some do not. A fair basis may be tax-assessed values or appraised values. For example, assume that land independently appraised at $30,000, land improvements appraised at $10,000, and a building appraised at $60,000 are purchased together for $90,000. The cost may be apportioned on the basis of appraised values as follows:

	Appraised value	Per cent of total	Apportioned cost
Land	$ 30,000	30	$27,000
Land improvements	10,000	10	9,000
Building	60,000	60	54,000
Totals	$100,000	100	$90,000

NATURE OF DEPRECIATION

When a plant asset is purchased, in effect a quantity of usefulness that will contribute to production throughout the service life of the asset is acquired. However, since the life of any plant asset (other than land) is limited, this quantity of usefulness will in effect be consumed by the end of the asset's service life. Consequently, depreciation, as the term is used in accounting, is nothing more than the expiration of a plant asset's quantity of usefulness, and the recording of depreciation is a process of allocating and charging the cost of this usefulness to the accounting periods that benefit from the asset's use.

For example, when a company purchases an automobile to be used in the business, it in effect purchases a quantity of usefulness, a quantity of transportation. The cost of this quantity of usefulness is the cost of the car less whatever will be received for it when sold or traded in at the end of its service life. Recording depreciation on the car is a process of allocating the cost of this usefulness to the accounting periods that benefit from the car's use. Note that it is not the recording of physical deterioration nor the recording of the decline in the car's market value. Depreciation is a process of allocating cost.

The foregoing is in line with the pronouncements of the Canadian Institute of Chartered Accountants which described depreciation accounting as follows:

> An accounting procedure in which the cost or other recorded value of a fixed asset less estimated salvage (if any) is distributed over its estimated useful life in a systematic and rational manner. It is a process of allocation, not valuation.[1]

SERVICE LIFE OF A PLANT ASSET

The *service life* of a plant asset is the period of time it will be used in producing or selling other assets or services. This may not be the same as the asset's potential life. For example, typewriters have a potential

---

[1] *Terminology for Accountants, 3d ed.* (Toronto: The Canadian Institute of Chartered Accountants, 1983), p. 52.

six- or eight-year life. However, if a company finds that it is economically wise to trade its old typewriters on new ones every three years, in this company typewriters have a three-year service life. Furthermore, in this business the cost of new typewriters less their trade-in value should be charged to depreciation expense over this three-year period.

Predicting a plant asset's service life is sometimes difficult because several factors are often involved. Wear and tear determine the useful life of some assets. However, two additional factors, *inadequacy* and *obsolescence,* often need to be considered. When a business acquires plant assets, it should acquire assets of a size and capacity to take care of its foreseeable needs. However, a business often grows more rapidly than anticipated. In such cases the capacity of the plant assets may become too small for the productive demands of the business long before they wear out. When this happens, inadequacy is said to have taken place. Inadequacy cannot easily be predicted. Obsolescence, like inadequacy, is also difficult to foresee because the exact occurrence of new inventions and improvements normally cannot be predicted. Yet, new inventions and improvements often cause an asset to become obsolete and make it wise to discard the obsolete asset long before it wears out.

A company that has previously used a particular type of asset may estimate the service life of a new asset of like kind from past experience. A company without previous experience with a particular asset must depend upon the experience of others or upon engineering studies and judgement. There are associations that publish information giving estimated service lives for hundreds of new assets. Many business executives refer to this information in estimating the life of a new asset.

SALVAGE VALUE

The total amount of depreciation that should be taken over an asset's service life is the asset's cost minus its *salvage value.* The salvage value of a plant asset is the portion of its cost that is recovered at the end of its service life. Some assets such as typewriters, trucks, and automobiles are traded in on similar new assets at the end of their service lives. The salvage values of such assets are their trade-in values. Other assets may have no trade-in value and little or no salvage value. For example, at the end of its service life, some machinery can be sold only as scrap metal.

When the disposal of a plant asset involves certain costs, as in the wrecking of a building, the salvage value is the net amount realized from the sale of the asset. The net amount realized is the amount received for the asset less its disposal cost. In the case of a machine, the cost to remove the machine often will equal the amount that can be realized from its sale. In such a case the machine has no salvage value.

ALLOCATING DEPRECIATION

Many methods of allocating a plant asset's total depreciation to the several accounting periods in its service life have been suggested and are used. Four of the more common are the *straight-line method,* the *units-of-production method,* the *declining-balance method,* and the *sum-of-the-years'-digits method.* Each is acceptable and falls within the realm of *generally accepted accounting principles (GAAP).*

Straight-Line Method

When the straight-line method is used, the cost of the asset minus its estimated salvage value is divided by the estimated number of accounting periods in the asset's service life. The result is the amount of depreciation to be taken each period. For example, if a machine costs $550, has an estimated service life of five years, and has an estimated $50 salvage value, its depreciation per year by the straight-line method is $100 and is calculated as follows:

$$\frac{\text{Cost} - \text{Salvage}}{\substack{\text{Service life} \\ \text{in years}}} = \frac{\$550 - \$50}{5} = \$100$$

Note that the straight-line method allocates an equal share of an asset's total depreciation to each accounting period in its life.

Units-of-Production Method

The purpose of recording depreciation is to charge each accounting period in which an asset is used with a fair share of its cost. The straight-line method charges an equal share to each period; and when plant assets are used about the same amount in each accounting period, this method fairly allocates total depreciation. However, in some lines of business the use of certain plant assets varies greatly from accounting period to accounting period. For example, a contractor may use a particular piece of construction equipment for a month and then not use it again for many months. For such an asset, since use and contribution to revenue may not be uniform from period to period, it is argued that the **units-of-production method** better meets the requirements of the *matching principle,* than does the straight-line method.

When the units-of-production method is used in allocating depreciation, the cost of an asset minus its estimated salvage value is divided by the estimated units it will produce during its entire service life. This calculation gives depreciation per unit of production. Then, the amount the asset is depreciated in any one accounting period is determined by multiplying the units produced in that period by the depreciation per unit. Units of production may be expressed as units of product or in any other unit of measure such as hours of use or kilometers (kms.) driven. For example, a truck costing $15,000 is estimated to have a $3,000 salvage value, If it is also estimated that during the truck's service life it will be driven 80,000 kms., the depreciation per kilometer, or the depreciation per unit of production, is $0.15 and is calculated as follows:

$$\frac{\text{Cost} - \text{Salvage value}}{\text{Estimated units of production}} = \frac{\text{Depreciation per}}{\text{unit of production}}$$

or

$$\frac{\$15,000 - \$3,000}{80,000 \text{ kms.}} = \$0.15 \text{ per km.}$$

If these estimates are used and the truck is driven 20,000 kms. during its first year, depreciation for the first year is $3,000. This is 20,000 kms. at $0.15 per km. If the truck is driven 15,000 kms. in the second year, depreciation for the second year is 15,000 times $0.15 or $2,250.

Declining-Balance Method

Some depreciation methods result in larger depreciation charges during the early years of an asset's life and smaller charges in the later years. These methods are called *accelerated depreciation*. The diminishing, or declining-balance, method is one of these. Under this method, depreciation of usually twice the straight-line rate, without considering salvage value, is applied each year to the declining book value of a new plant asset. If this method is followed and twice the straight-line rate is used, depreciation on an asset is determined as follows: (1) calculate a straight-line depreciation rate for the asset; (2) double this rate; and (3) at the end of each year in the asset's life, apply this doubled rate to the asset's remaining *book value*. (The book value of a plant asset is its cost less accumulated depreciation; it is the net amount shown for the asset on the books.)

If this method is used to charge depreciation on a $10,000 new asset that has an estimated five-year life and no salvage value, these steps are followed: (Step 1) A straight-line depreciation rate is calculated by dividing 100% by five (years) to determine the straight-line annual depreciation rate of 20%, (Step 2) this rate is doubled, and (Step 3) annual depreciation charges are calculated as in the following table:

Year	Annual depreciation calculation	Annual depreciation expense	Remaining book value
1st year	40% of $10,000	$4,000.00	$6,000.00
2d year	40% of 6,000	2,400.00	3,600.00
3d year	40% of 3,600	1,440.00	2,160.00
4th year	40% of 2,160	864.00	1,296.00
5th year	40% of 1,296	518.40	777.60

Under the declining-balance method the book value of a plant asset never reaches zero. Consequently, when the asset is sold, exchanged, or scrapped, any remaining book value is used in determining the gain or loss on the disposal. However, if an asset has a salvage value, the asset may not be depreciated beyond its salvage value. For example, if, instead of no salvage value, the foregoing $10,000 asset has an estimated $1,000 salvage value, depreciation for its fifth year is limited to $296. This is the amount required to reduce the asset's book value to its salvage value.

Sum-of-the-Years'-Digits Method

Another method of accelerated depreciation is called **sum-of-the-years' digits.** Under the sum-of-the-years'-digits method, the years in an asset's service life are added. Their sum becomes the denominator of a series of fractions used in allocating total depreciation to the periods in the asset's service life. The numerators of the fractions are the years in the asset's life in their reverse order. For example, assume a machine is purchased that costs $7,000, has an estimated five-year life and has an estimated $1,000 salvage value. The sum-of-the-years' digits in the asset's life are:

$$1 + 2 + 3 + 4 + 5 = 15$$

and annual depreciation charges are calculated as follows:

Year	Annual depreciation calculation	Annual depreciation expense
1st year	$5/15$ of $6,000	$2,000
2d year	$4/15$ of 6,000	1,600
3d year	$3/15$ of 6,000	1,200
4th year....................	$2/15$ of 6,000	800
5th year....................	$1/15$ of 6,000	400
Total depreciation		$6,000

When a plant asset has a long life, the sum-of-the-years' digits in its life may be calculated by using the formula: $SYD = n[(n + 1)/2]$. For example, sum-of-the-years' digits for a five-year life is:

$$5\left(\frac{5+1}{2}\right) = 15.$$

Accelerated depreciation methods are advocated by many accountants who claim that their use results in a more equitable "use charge" for long-lived plant assets than other methods. These accountants point out, for example, that as assets grow older, repairs and maintenance increase. Therefore, smaller amounts of depreciation are added to increasing repair costs, resulting in a more equitable total expense charge to match against revenue. Also, they point out that as an asset grows older, in some instances its ability to produce revenue is reduced. For example, rentals from an apartment building may be higher in the earlier years of its life but then decline as the building becomes less attractive. In such cases many accountants argue that the requirements of the *matching principle* are better met with heavier depreciation charges in the earlier years and lighter charges in the later years of the asset's life.

DEPRECIATION FOR PARTIAL YEARS

Plant assets may be purchased or disposed of any time during the year. When an asset is purchased (or disposed of) at some time other than the beginning (or end) of an accounting period, depreciation must be recorded for part of a year. Otherwise, the year of purchase or the year of disposal is not charged with its share of the asset's depreciation. For example, assume a machine costing $4,600 and having an estimated five-year service life and a $600 salvage value is purchased on October 8 and the annual accounting period ends on December 31. Three months' depreciation on the machine must be recorded on the latter date. Three months are $3/12$ of a year. Consequently, if straight-line depreciation is used, the three months' depreciation is calculated as follows:

$$\frac{\$4,600 - \$600}{5} \times \frac{3}{12} = \$200$$

Note that depreciation was calculated for a full three months, even though the asset was purchased on October 8. Depreciation is an estimate; therefore, calculation to the nearest full month is usually sufficiently accurate. This means that depreciation is usually calculated for a full month on assets purchased before the 15th of the month. Likewise, depreciation for the month of purchase is normally disregarded if the asset is purchased after the middle of the month.

The entry to record depreciation for three months on the machine purchased on October 8 is:

Dec.	31	Depreciation Expense, Machinery	200.00	
		Accumulated Depreciation, Machinery		200.00
		To record depreciation for three months.		

On December 31, 19B, and at the end of each of the following three years, a journal entry to record a full year's depreciation on this machine is required. The entry is:

Dec.	31	Depreciation Expense, Machinery	800.00	
		Accumulated Depreciation, Machinery		800.00
		To record depreciation for one year.		

After the December 31, 19E, depreciation entry is recorded, the accounts showing the history of this machine appear as follows:

Machinery		Accumulated Depreciation, Machinery	
Oct. 8, 19A 4,600		Dec. 31, 19A	200
		Dec. 31, 19B	800
		Dec. 31, 19C	800
		Dec. 31, 19D	800
		Dec. 31, 19E	800

If this machine is disposed of during 19F, two entries must be made to record the disposal. The first records 19F depreciation to the date of disposal, and the second records the actual disposal. For example, assume that the machine is sold for $800 on June 24, 19F. To record the disposal, depreciation for six months (depreciation to the nearest full month) must first be recorded. The entry for this is:

June	24	Depreciation Expense, Machinery	400.00	
		Accumulated Depreciation, Machinery		400.00
		To record depreciation for one-half year.		

After making the entry to record depreciation to the date of sale, a second entry to record the actual sale is made. This entry is:

```
June  24  Cash ...................................     800.00
          Accumulated Depreciation, Machinery ........   3,800.00
              Machinery .............................              4,600.00
          To record the sale of a machine at book value.
```

In this instance the machine was sold for its book value. Plant assets are commonly sold for either more or less than book value, and cases illustrating this are described in the next chapter.

APPORTIONING ACCELERATED DEPRECIATION

When accelerated depreciation is used and accounting periods do not coincide with the years in an asset's life, depreciation must be apportioned between periods if it is to be properly charged. In the case of declining balance, depreciation for a partial year is calculated for the first period (partial year). Subsequent accounting periods coincide with the years in the asset's service life, and depreciation is calculated on the remaining book value. For example, if a machine was purchased on October 1, 19A, for $10,000 and depreciated at a 40% declining balance rate, depreciation for 19A would be one fourth (40% of $10,000), or $1,000. Depreciation for a full year 19B would be 40% of $9,000, or $3,600. In the case of sum-of-the-years'-digits, for an asset with an expected service life of five years and acquired on April 1, 19A, depreciation for the year of acquisition would be three fourths of depreciation for a full first year. In 19B, depreciation would be the remaining one fourth from the first year plus three fourths of the amount for a full second year. Similar calculations should be used for the remaining periods in the asset's life.

DEPRECIATION ON THE BALANCE SHEET

In presenting information about the plant assets of a business, the *full-disclosure principle* requires that both the cost of such assets and their accumulated depreciation be shown by major classes in the statements or in related footnotes. Also, a general description of the depreciation method or methods used must be given in a balance sheet footnote or other manner.[2] To comply, the plant assets of a concern may be shown on its balance sheet or in a schedule accompanying the balance sheet as follows:

---

[2] *CICA Handbook* (Toronto: The Canadian Institute of Chartered Accountants), par. 3060.05.

	Cost	Accumulated depreciation	Book value
Plant assets:			
Store equipment	$ 12,400	$1,500	$10,900
Office equipment	3,600	450	3,150
Building	72,300	7,800	64,500
Land	15,000		15,000
Totals	$103,300	$9,750	$93,550

When plant assets are thus shown and the depreciation methods described, a much better understanding can be gained by a balance sheet reader than if only information as to undepreciated cost is given. For example, $50,000 of assets with $40,000 of accumulated depreciation are quite different from $10,000 of new assets. Yet, the net undepreciated cost is the same in both cases. Likewise, the picture is different if the $40,000 of accumulated depreciation resulted from accelerated depreciation rather than straight-line depreciation.

BALANCE SHEET PLANT ASSET VALUES

From the discussion thus far, students should recognize that the recording of depreciation is not a valuing process. Rather it is a process of allocating the costs of plant assets to the several accounting periods that benefit from their use. Because the recording of depreciation is a cost allocation process rather than a valuing process, plant assets are reported in balance sheets at their remaining (undepreciated) costs, not at market values.

The fact that balance sheets show undepreciated costs rather than market values seems to disturb many beginning accounting students. It should not. Normally, a company has no intention of selling its plant assets. Consequently, the market values of these assets may be of little significance to financial statement readers. Students should recognize that a balance sheet is prepared under the assumption the company is a going concern. This means the company is expected to continue in business long enough to recover the original costs of its plant assets through the sale of its products.

The assumption that a company will continue in business long enough to recover its plant asset costs through the sale of its products is known in accounting as the *continuing- or going-concern concept.* It provides the justification for carrying plant assets on the balance sheet at cost less accumulated depreciation, in other words, at the share of their cost applicable to future periods. It is also the justification for carrying at cost such things as stationery imprinted with the company name, though salable only as scrap paper. In all such instances the intention is to use the assets in carrying on the business operations. They are not for sale, so it is pointless to place them on the balance sheet at market or realizable values, whether these values are greater or less than book values.

Uninformed financial statement readers sometimes mistakenly think that the accumulated depreciation shown on a balance sheet represents funds accumulated to buy new assets when present assets must be replaced. However, an informed reader recognizes that accumulated depreciation represents the portion of an asset's cost that has been charged off to depreciation expense during its life. Accumulated depreciation accounts are contra accounts having credit balances that cannot be used to buy anything. Furthermore, an informed reader knows that if a concern has cash with which to buy assets, it is shown on the balance sheet as a current asset, "Cash."

RECOVERING THE COSTS OF PLANT ASSETS

A company that earns a profit or breaks even (neither earns a profit nor suffers a loss) eventually recovers the original cost of its plant assets through the sale of its products. This is best explained with a condensed income statement like that of Illustration 10–1 which shows that Even Steven Company broke even during the year of the illustrated income statement. However, in breaking even it also recovered $5,000 of the cost of its plant assets through the sale of its products. It recovered the $5,000 because $100,000 flowed into the company from sales and only $95,000 flowed out to pay for goods sold, rent, and salaries. No funds flowed out for depreciation expense. As a result, the company recovered this $5,000 portion of the cost of its plant assets through the sale of its products. Furthermore, if the company remains in business for the life of its plant assets, either breaking even or earning a profit, it will recover their entire cost in this manner.

At this point students commonly ask, "Where is the recovered $5,000?" The answer is that the company may have the $5,000 in the

Illustration 10–1

EVEN STEVEN COMPANY Income Statement For Year Ended December 31, 19—		
Sales		$100,000
Cost of goods sold	$60,000	
Rent expense	10,000	
Salaries expense	25,000	
Depreciation expense	5,000	
Total		100,000
Net income		$ 0

bank. However, the funds may also have been spent to increase merchandise inventory, to buy additional equipment, or to pay off a debt, or they may have been withdrawn by the business owner. In short, the funds may still be in the bank or they may have been used for any purpose for which a business uses funds, and only an examination of its balance sheets as of the beginning and end of the year will show this.

REASONS FOR USING ACCELERATED DEPRECIATION

The reducing charge methods (both the declining-balance and the sum-of-the-years'-digits method) are advocated by many accountants who claim that their use results in a more equitable "use charge" for long-lived plant assets than other methods. These accountants point out, for example, that as assets grow older, repairs and maintenance increase. Therefore, smaller amounts of depreciation computed by a reducing charge method are added to increasing repair costs; this results in a more equitable total expense charge to match against revenue. Also, they point out that as an asset grows older, in some instances its ability to produce revenue is reduced. For example, rentals from an apartment building are normally higher in the earlier years of its life but will decline as the building becomes less attractive and less modern. Certainly in such cases the requirements of the *matching principle* are better met with heavier depreciation charges in the earlier years and lighter charges in the later years of the asset's life.

The foregoing are sound reasons for the use under applicable conditions of reducing charge or accelerated depreciation. However, a tax reason rather than sound accounting theory is probably more responsible for the increase in their popularity. The tax reason is that accelerated depreciation normally results in deferring income taxes from the early years of a plant asset's life until its later years. Taxes are deferred because accelerated depreciation causes larger amounts of depreciation to be charged to the early years, which results in smaller amounts of income and income taxes in these years. However, the taxes are only deferred because offsetting smaller amounts of depreciation are charged in later years, which results in larger amounts of income and taxes in these years. Nevertheless, through accelerated depreciation a company does have the "interest-free" use of the deferred tax dollars until the later years of a plant asset's life.

Since 1949 the Income Tax Act requires the use of the declining-balance method for tax purposes. Depreciable assets are grouped into classes and depreciation (described in the Act as capital cost allowance) may be taken at rates prescribed by the income tax legislation. A taxpayer may take the maximum depreciation allowed or any part for tax purposes in any fiscal year. The amount of depreciation taken for tax purposes does not depend in any way on the amount of depreciation shown in the books or on the financial statements. Thus a taxpayer may record ⚡ depreciation on his books using the straight-line method and claim, for tax purposes, depreciation based on the declining-balance method.

Special problems in measuring net income may occur when a company uses one depreciation method for financial accounting purposes and another for tax purposes. These problems are discussed in Chapter 28.

CONTROL OF PLANT ASSETS

Good internal control for plant assets requires specific identification of each plant asset and formal records. It also requires periodic inventories in which each plant asset carried in the records is identified and its continued existence and use are verified. For identification purposes, each plant asset is commonly assigned a serial number at the time it is acquired. The serial number is stamped, etched, or affixed to the asset with a small decal not easily removed or altered. The exact kind of records kept depends upon the size of the business and the number of its plant assets. They range from handwritten records to punched cards and computer tapes. However, regardless of their nature, all provide the same basic information contained in the handwritten records which follow.

In keeping plant asset records, concerns normally divide their plant assets into functional groups and provide in their General Ledger separate asset and accumulated depreciation accounts for each group. For example, a store will normally provide an Office Equipment account and an Accumulated Depreciation, Office Equipment account. It will also provide a Store Equipment account and an Accumulated Depreciation, Store Equipment account. In short, the store will normally provide in its General Ledger a separate plant asset account and a separate accumulated depreciation account for each functional group of plant assets it owns. Furthermore, each plant asset account and its related accumulated depreciation account is normally a controlling account that controls detailed subsidiary records. For example, the Office Equipment account and the Accumulated Depreciation, Office Equipment account control a subsidiary ledger having a separate record for each individual item of office equipment. Likewise, the Store Equipment account and its related Accumulated Depreciation, Store Equipment account become controlling accounts over a subsidiary store equipment ledger. In a handwritten system these subsidiary records are kept on plant asset record cards.

To illustrate handwritten plant asset records, assume that a concern's office equipment consists of just one desk and a chair. The general ledger record of these assets is maintained in the Office Equipment controlling account and the Accumulated Depreciation, Office Equipment controlling account. Since in this case there are only two assets, only two subsidiary record cards are needed. The general ledger and subsidiary ledger record of these assets appear as in Illustration 10–2.

Observe at the top of the cards the plant asset numbers assigned to these two items of office equipment. In each case the assigned number consists of the number of the Office Equipment account, 132, followed by the asset's number. As previously stated, these numbers are stenciled on or otherwise attached to the items of office equipment as a means of identification and to increase control over the items. The remaining information on the record cards is more or less self-evident. Note how the balance of the general ledger account, Office Equipment, is equal to the sum of the balances in the asset record section of the two subsidiary ledger cards. The general ledger account controls this section of the subsidiary ledger. Observe also how the Accumulated Depreciation, Office Equipment account controls the depreciation record section of the cards. The disposition section at the bottom of the card is used to record the final disposal of the asset. When the asset is discarded, sold, or exchanged, a notation telling of the final disposition is entered here. The card is then removed from the subsidiary ledger and filed for future reference.

Illustration 10–2

Plant Asset
No. *132-1*

SUBSIDIARY PLANT ASSET AND DEPRECIATION RECORD

Item *Office chair*   General Ledger
                                            Account *Office Equipment*
Description *Office chair*

Mfg. Serial No.   Purchased
                                            from *Office Equipment Co.*
Where Located *Office*
Person Responsible for the Asset *Office Manager*
Estimated Life *12 years* Estimated Salvage Value *$4.00*
Depreciation per Year *$6.00* per Month *$0.50*

Date	Explanation	P R	Asset Record			Depreciation Record		
			Dr.	Cr.	Bal.	Dr.	Cr.	Bal.
July 2, 198A		G1	76.00		76.00			
Dec. 31, 198A		G23					3.00	3.00
Dec. 31, 198B		G42					6.00	9.00
Dec. 31, 198C		G65					6.00	15.00

Final Disposition of the Asset

Illustration 10–2 *(concluded)*

Plant Asset
No. *132-2*

SUBSIDIARY PLANT ASSET AND DEPRECIATION RECORD

General Ledger

Item *Desk*   Account *Office Equipment*

Description *Office desk*

Purchased

Mfg. Serial No. _____ from *Office Equipment Co.*

Where Located *Office*

Person Responsible for the Asset *Office Manager*

Estimated Life *12 years* Estimated Salvage Value *$25.00*

Depreciation per Year *$36.00* per Month *$3.00*

Date	Explanation	P R	Asset Record Dr.	Asset Record Cr.	Asset Record Bal.	Depreciation Record Dr.	Depreciation Record Cr.	Depreciation Record Bal.
July 2, 198A		G1	457.00		457.00			
Dec. 31, 198A		G23					18.00	18.00
Dec. 31, 198B		G42					36.00	54.00
Dec. 31, 198C		G65					36.00	90.00

Final Disposition of the Asset _____

Office Equipment　　　　　　　　　　　**Account No. 132**

Date		Explanation	Fo-lio	Debit		Credit		Balance	
19A July	2	Desk and chair	G1	533	00			533	00

Accumulated Depreciation, Office Equipment　　　**Account No. 132A**

Date		Explanation	Fo-lio	Debit		Credit		Balance	
19A Dec.	31		G23			21	00	21	00
19B Dec	31		G42			42	00	63	00
19C Dec.	31		G65			42	00	105	00

PLANT ASSETS OF LOW COST

Individual plant asset records are expensive to keep. Consequently, many concerns establish a minimum, say $50 or $100, and do not keep such records for assets costing less than the minimum. Rather, they charge the cost of such assets directly to an expense account at the time of purchase. Furthermore, if about the same amount is expended for such assets each year, this is acceptable under the *materiality principle*.

GLOSSARY

Accelerated depreciation.   Any depreciation method resulting in greater amounts of depreciation expense in the early years of a plant asset's life and lesser amounts in later years.

Book value.   The carrying amount for an item in the accounting records. When applied to a plant asset, it is the cost of the asset minus its accumulated depreciation.

Declining-balance depreciation.   A depreciation method in which normally twice the straight-line rate of depreciation, without considering salvage value, is applied to the remaining book value of a plant asset to arrive at the asset's annual depreciation charge.

Diminishing-balance depreciation.   Another name for declining-balance depreciation.

Fixed asset.   A plant asset.

Inadequacy.   The situation where a plant asset does not produce enough product to meet current needs.

Land improvements.   Assets that improve or increase the value or usefulness of land but which have a limited useful life and are subject to depreciation.

Obsolescence.   The situation where because of new inventions and improvements, an old plant asset can no longer produce its product on a competitive basis.

Office Equipment Ledger.   A subsidiary ledger having a record card for each item of office equipment owned.

Plant and equipment.   Assets which have a useful life of longer than one accounting period and which are used in the production and/or sale of other assets.

Plant assets.   See plant and equipment.

Salvage value.   The share of a plant asset's cost recovered at the end of its service life through a sale or as a trade-in allowance on a new asset.

Service life.   The period of time a plant asset is used in the production and sale of other assets or services.

Store Equipment Ledger. A subsidiary ledger having a record card for each item of store equipment owned.

Straight-line depreciation. A depreciation method that allocates an equal share of the total estimated amount a plant asset will be depreciated during its service life to each accounting period in that life.

Sum-of-the-years'-digits depreciation. A depreciation method that allocates depreciation to each year in a plant asset's life on a fractional basis. The denominator of the fractions used is the sum-of-the-years' digits in the estimated service life of the asset, and the numerators are the years' digits in reverse order.

Units-of-production depreciation. A depreciation method that allocates depreciation on a plant asset based on the relation of the units of product produced by the asset during a given period to the total units the asset is expected to produce during its entire life.

QUESTIONS FOR CLASS DISCUSSION

1. What are the characteristics of assets classified as plant and equipment?
2. What is the balance sheet classification of land held for future expansion? Why is such land not classified as a plant asset?
3. What is the difference between land and land improvements?
4. What in general is included in the cost of a plant asset?
5. A company asked for bids from several machine shops for the construction of a special machine. The lowest bid was $12,500. The company decided to build the machine itself and did so at a total cash outlay of $10,000. It then recorded the machine's construction with a debit to machinery for $12,500, a credit to Cash for $10,000, and a credit to Gain on the Construction of Machinery for $2,500. Was this a proper entry? Discuss.
6. As used in accounting, what is the meaning of the term *depreciation?*
7. Is it possible to keep a plant asset in such an excellent state of repair that recording depreciation is unnecessary?
8. A company has just purchased a machine that has a potential life of 15 years. However, the company's management believes that the development of a more efficient machine will make it necessary to replace the machine in eight years. What period of useful life should be used in calculating depreciation on this machine?
9. A building estimated to have a useful life of 30 years was completed at a cost of $85,000. It was estimated that at the end of the building's life it would be wrecked at a cost of $1,000 and that materials salvaged from the wrecking operation would be sold for $2,000. How much straight-line depreciation should be charged on the building each year?
10. Define the following terms as used in accounting for plant assets:
    a. Trade-in value.   *c.* Book value.   *e.* Inadequacy.
    b. Market value.   *d.* Salvage value.   *f.* Obsolescence.

11. When straight-line depreciation is used, an equal share of the total amount that a plant asset is to be depreciated during its life is assigned to each accounting period in that life. Describe a situation in which this may not be a fair basis of allocation. Name a more fair basis for the situation described.

12. What is the sum-of-the-years' digits in the life of a plant asset that will be used for 12 years?

13. Does the recording of depreciation cause a plant asset to appear on the balance sheet at market value? What is accomplished by recording depreciation?

14. What is the essence of the going-concern concept of a business?

15. Explain how a concern that breaks even recovers the cost of its plant assets through the sale of its products. Where are the funds thus recovered?

16. Does the balance of the account, Accumulated Depreciation, Machinery represent funds accumulated to replace the machinery as it wears out? Tell in your own words what the balance of such an account represents.

MULTIPLE CHOICE

1. A company purchased a machine which it estimated would produce 24,000 units of product during its four-year life. The machine cost $15,600 and was estimated to have a $1,200 salvage value. If the machine produced 5,800 units of product during its first year, depreciation for the year calculated by the units-of-production method is:
   a. $3,480.
   b. $3,600.
   c. $3,770.
   d. $3,900.
   e. Some other amount.

2. A company purchased a machine which it estimated would produce 24,000 units of product during its four-year life. The machine cost $15,600 and was estimated to have a $1,200 salvage value. If depreciation on the machine is calculated by the declining-balance method at twice the straight-line rate, depreciation for the first year is:
   a. $5,760.
   b. $6,240.
   c. $7,200.
   d. $7,800.
   e. Some other amount.

3. Cream Company bought an automobile on September 1, 19A. The automobile cost $9,000, had a salvage value of $600 and a useful life of five years. How much depreciation expense should Cream Company record in 19A using the straight-line method?

   a. $420.
   b. $560.
   c. $600.
   d. $1,680.
   e. $1,800.

4. A business purchased a cash register on April 1, 19A, for $4,800. The cash register had a useful life of eight years and a salvage value of $300. What should be the depreciation expense for 19B using a sum-of-the-years'-digits method?

   a. $875.00.
   b. $906.25.
   c. $966.67.
   d. $1,000.00.
   e. $1,033.33.

5. Alpha Corporation purchased a plot of land upon which to build a new building. The tract of land cost $150,000. Additional costs incurred were:

Real estate commissions	$15,000
Legal fees of purchasing the real estate	800
Expense of clearing land	2,000
Expense to raze old house	1,000
Salvage proceeds from old house	400

  What portion of the above costs should be charged to land and what portion should be charged to the new building?

   a. $150,000 to land; $18,400 to new building.
   b. $152,600 to land; $15,800 to new building.
   c. $165,800 to land; $ 2,400 to new building.
   d. $168,400 to land; $ –0– to new building.
   e. $169,200 to land; $ –0– to new building.

MINI DISCUSSION CASES

Case 10–1   The Kitchener Company and the Waterloo Company have each purchased similar properties consisting of land and a small commercial building. The two properties each cost approximately $850,000 and are used for rental purposes.

  Management of the Kitchener Company wishes to allocate a large portion of the purchase price to the building because of the company's excellent overall profitability. They argue that a large depreciation expense will reduce income taxes, alleviate shareholders' demands for dividends, and allow the company to retain cash for future investment. In contrast, the Waterloo Company, which has been much less profitable, wishes to allocate a large portion of the purchase price to the land in order to show lower depreciation expense and thus enhance their profits.

Required:

a. Evaluate the approaches taken by each of the companies.
b. Indicate, with reasons, how the allocation of the purchase price between the land and building should be conducted for each company.

Case 10–2   Your friend, who has had no experience with accounting, says that there are a couple of items on the balance sheet that she does not understand. For example, she knows that the building, shown at $45,000 could be sold for almost twice that amount. She also wonders where all the cash has gone; accumulated depreciation is $17,650 but the cash account only shows $3,825.

Required:

Explain what is wrong with your friend's reasoning about accounting.

CLASS EXERCISES

Exercise 10–1   A machine was purchased for $2,000, terms 2/10, n/60, FOB shipping point. The manufacturer prepaid the freight charges, $110, adding the amount to the invoice and bringing its total to $2,110. The machine required a special concrete base and power connections costing $285, and $270 was paid a millwright to assemble the machine and get it into operation. In moving the machine onto its concrete base, it was dropped and damaged. The damages cost $70 to repair, and after being repaired, $30 of raw materials were consumed in adjusting the machine so it would produce a satisfactory product. The adjustments were normal for this type of machine and were not the result of its having been damaged. The product produced while the adjustments were being made was not salable. Prepare a calculation to show the cost of this machine for accounting purposes.

Exercise 10–2   Three machines were purchased for $8,400 at an auction sale of a bankrupt company's machinery. The purchaser paid $400 to transport the machines to his factory. Machine No. 1 was twice as big and weighed twice as much as Machine No. 2. Machines 2 and 3 were approximately equal in size and weight. The machines had the following appraised values and installation costs:

	Machine No. 1	Machine No. 2	Machine No. 3
Appraised values	$5,000	$4,000	$3,000
Installation costs	300	200	150

Determine the cost of each machine for accounting purposes.

Exercise 10–3   A machine was installed in a factory at a $15,800 cost. Its useful life was estimated at five years or 50,000 units of product with an $800 trade-in value. During its second year the machine produced 12,000 units of product. Determine the machine's second-year depreciation with depreciation calculated in each of the following ways: *(a)* straight-line basis, *(b)* units-of-production basis, *(c)* declining-balance basis at twice the straight-line rate, and *(d)* sum-of-the-years'-digits basis.

Exercise 10–4   A company purchased real estate for $120,000 plus $4,000 in closing costs. The real estate included land appraised at $46,000; land improvements at $12,200; and a building at $72,000. The company plans to use the building as a warehouse. Prepare a journal entry to record the purchase.

Exercise 10–5   A machine cost $2,000 installed and was estimated to have a four-year life and a $200 trade-in value. Use declining-balance depreciation at twice the straight-line rate to determine the amount of depreciation to be charged against the machine in each of the four years of its life.

Exercise 10–6   A machine was installed on January 4, 19B, at a total cost of $6,000. A full year's depreciation on a straight-line basis was charged against the machine on December 31, at the end of each of the first four years in its life under the assumption it would have a five-year life and no salvage value. The machine was disposed of on March 31, during its fifth year. *(a)* Give the entry to record the partial year's depreciation on March 31, and give the entry to record the disposal under each of the following unrelated assumptions; *(b)* the machine was sold for $1,000; *(c)* it was sold for $850; and *(d)* the machine was totally destroyed in a fire and the insurance company settled the insurance claim for $750.

PROBLEMS

Problem 10–1   A machine costing $5,200, having a four-year life, and an estimated $400 salvage value was installed in a factory. The factory management estimated the machine would produce 60,000 units of product during its life. It actually produced the following numbers of units: Year 1—11,000; Year 2—18,000; Year 3—16,000; and Year 4—15,000.

Required:

1. Prepare a calculation showing the number of dollars of this machine's cost that should be charged to depreciation over its four-year life.
2. Prepare a form with the following column headings:

Year	Straight Line	Units of Production	Declining Balance	Sum-of-the-Years' Digits

Then show the depreciation for each year and the total depreciation for the machine under each depreciation method. Use twice the straight-line rate for the declining-balance method.

Problem 10–2

A secondhand machine was purchased for $2,280 on January 2. The next day it was repaired and repainted at a cost of $270 and was installed on a new concrete base that cost $210. It was estimated the machine would be used for three years and would then have a $360 salvage value. Depreciation was to be charged on a straight-line basis. A full year's depreciation was charged on December 31, at the end of the first year of the machine's use; and on July 2, in its second year of use, the machine was retired from service.

Required:

1. Prepare general journal entries to record the purchase of the machine, the cost of repairing and repainting it, and its installation. Assume cash was paid in each case.
2. Prepare entries to record depreciation on the machine on December 31 and on July 2.
3. Prepare entries to record the retirement of the machine under each of the following unrelated assumptions: *(a)* the machine was sold for $1,600; *(b)* it was sold for $1,500; and *(c)* it was destroyed in a fire and the insurance company paid $1,250 in full settlement of the loss claim.

Problem 10–3

A concern purchased four machines during 19A and 19B. Machine No. 1 was placed in use on June 27, 19A. It cost $25,750 installed, had an estimated six-year life and a $1,750 salvage value, and was depreciated on a straight-line basis. Machine No. 2 was placed in use on August 10, 19A, and was depreciated on a units-of-production basis. It cost $17,500 installed, and it was estimated it would produce 80,000 units of product during its ten-year life, after which it would have an estimated $1,500 salvage value. It produced 2,800 units during 19A, 8,200 during 19B, and 7,800 during 19C. Machines 3 and 4 were purchased from a bankrupt firm for $42,000 on August 30, 19B, and were placed in use on the following October 3. Machine No. 3 was depreciated on a declining-balance basis at twice the straight-line rate, and sum-of-the-years'-digits depreciation was used for Machine No. 4. Additional information about these machines follows:

Machine number	Appraised value	Salvage value	Estimated life	Installation cost
3	$30,000	$600	8 years	$800
4	45,000	900	6 years	900

Required:

1. Prepare a form with the following columnar headings:

Machine Number	Amount to Be Charged to Depreciation	19A Depreciation	19B Depreciation	19C Depreciation

Enter the machine numbers in the first column and complete the information opposite each machine's number. Total the columns.

2. Prepare entries to record the purchase of Machines 3 and 4 and their installation. Assume cash was paid for the installation charges on the day the machines were placed in use.

3. Prepare an entry to record the 19C depreciation on the four machines.

Problem 10–4   On August 3, 19J, a company made a lump-sum purchase of two machines at a bankruptcy sale. The machines cost $27,300 and were placed in use on August 30, 19J. This additional information about the machines is available:

Machine number	Appraised value	Salvage value	Estimated life	Installation cost	Depreciation method
1	$15,000	$ 500	4 years	$ 800	Sum-of-the-years' digits
2	20,000	1,500	4 years	1,200	Declining balance

The machines were depreciated at the ends of 19J, 19K, and 19L. Machine No. 2's depreciation was calculated at twice the straight-line rate. During the first week in January 19M, the company decided to replace the machines, and on January 10 it sold them in separate sales for cash, Machine No. 1 for $3,000, and Machine No. 2 for $3,700.

Required:

1. Prepare a form with the following headings:

Machine Number	19J Depreciation	19K Depreciation	19L Depreciation	19M Depreciation	19N Depreciation

Fill in the machine numbers in the first column and the amounts of depreciation in the remaining columns.

2. Prepare general journal entries to record the purchase of the machines, their installation, the depreciation for each year they were in use, and their sale. Assume that cash was paid and received in all transactions and that the installation charges were paid for on the day the machines were put in use.

Problem 10–5   Store A and Store B are identical in almost all respects. Both opened their doors for business on January 2 of last year with equipment costing $30,000, having a 10-year life, and $5,000 salvage value; neither added to its equipment during the year; and both purchased merchandise as follows:

Jan. 2 .... 100 units at $100 each
Mar. 15 .... 200 units at $ 96 each
July 7 .... 300 units at $110 each
Oct. 12 .... 200 units at $116 each
Dec. 15 .... 100 units at $120 each

At the year-end, before recording depreciation, their records showed the following revenues and expenses:

	Store A	Store B
Sales	$135,000	$135,000
Salaries expense	18,000	18,000
Rent expense	9,000	9,000
Other expenses	1,000	1,000

However, Store A used declining-balance depreciation at twice the straight-line rate, while Store B chose straight-line depreciation. Also, Store A priced its 150-unit ending inventory on a LIFO basis, while Store B used FIFO for its 150-unit inventory.

Required:

1. Prepare an income statement for each store showing last year's results.
2. Prepare a schedule accounting for the difference in their net incomes.

Problem 10–6   Bargain Mart completed these transactions involving plant assets:

19A
Jan. 3 Purchased on credit from Store Equipment Company an Econ Scale priced at $265. The serial number of the scale was B–23452, its service life was estimated at 10 years with a trade-in value of $25, and it was assigned plant asset No. 132–1.

Apr. 7 Purchased on credit from Store Equipment Company a Regal cash register priced at $323. The serial number of the register was 3–32564, its service life was estimated at eight years with a trade-in value of $35, and it was assigned plant asset No. 132–2.

Dec. 31 Recorded the 19A depreciation on the store equipment.

19B
Oct. 28 Sold the Regal cash register to Ted Beal for $250 cash.
     28 Purchased a new Accurate cash register on credit from Beta Equipment Company for $360. The serial number of the register was XXX–12345, its service life was estimated at 10 years with a trade-in value of $48, and it was assigned plant asset No. 132–3.

Dec. 31 Recorded the 19B depreciation on the store equipment.

Required:

1. Open general ledger accounts for Store Equipment and for Accumulated Depreciation, Store Equipment. Prepare a subsidiary plant asset record card for each item of equipment purchased.
2. Prepare general journal entries to record the transactions and post to the proper general ledger and subsidiary ledger accounts.
3. Prove the December 31, 19B, balances of the Store Equipment and Accumulated Depreciation, Store Equipment accounts by preparing a list showing the cost and accumulated depreciation on each item of store equipment owned by Bargain Mart on that date.

Problem 10–7   Eaton Company was organized early in January of the current year; and in making your audit of the company's records at the end of the year, you discover that the company's bookkeeper has debited an account called "Land, Buildings, and Equipment" for what he thought was the cost of the company's new factory. The account has a $821,950 debit balance made up of the following items:

Cost of land and an old building on the land purchased as the site of the company's new factory (appraised value of the land, $80,000, and of the old building, $10,000)	$ 84,600
Lawyer's fees resulting from land purchase	500
Escrow fees connected with the land purchase	300
Cost of removing old building from plant site	1,800
Surveying and grading plant site	2,800
Cost of retaining wall and the placing of tile to drain the site	1,200
Cost of new building (The contract price was $381,900; however, the contractor accepted $79,400 in cash and 30 bonds having a $300,000 par value. The company had purchased the bonds as a temporary investment at the start of construction for $300,000. The market value of the bonds on the day they were given to the contractor was $302,500.)	379,400
Architect's fee for planning building	23,100
Cost of paving parking lot	8,600
Lights for parking lot	400
Landscaping	2,700
Machinery (including the $800 cost of a machine dropped and made useless while being unloaded from a freight car)	312,500
Fine and permit to haul heavy machinery on city streets. The company was cited for hauling machinery without a permit. It then secured the permit (fine, $200; cost of permit, $50)	250
Cost of hauling machinery on city streets	3,000
Cost of replacing damaged machine	800
Total	$821,950

In auditing the company's other accounts it was discovered that the bookkeeper had credited the $300 proceeds from the sale of materials salvaged from the old building removed from the plant site to an account called "Miscellaneous Revenues." He had also credited this account for $50 from the sale of the wrecked machine.

An examination of the payroll records showed that an account called "Superintendence" had been debited for the plant superintendent's $15,000 salary for the ten-month period, March 1 through December 31. From March 1 through August 31 the superintendent had supervised construction of the factory building. During September, October, and November he had supervised installation of the factory machinery. The factory began manufacturing operations on December 1.

Required:

1. Prepare a form having the following four column headings: Land, Land Improvements, Buildings, and Machinery. List the items and sort their amounts to the proper columns. Show a negative amount in parentheses. Total the columns.

2. Under the assumption that the company's accounts had not been closed, prepare an entry to remove the foregoing item amounts from the accounts in which they were incorrectly entered and record them in the proper accounts.

3. The company closes its books annually on December 31. Prepare the entry to record the partial year's depreciation on the plant assets. Assume the building and land improvements are estimated to have 30-year lives and no salvage values and that the machinery is estimated to have a 12-year life and a salvage value equal to 10% of its cost.

ALTERNATE PROBLEMS

Problem 10–1A

A machine costing $7,200 was installed in a factory. Its useful life was estimated at four years, after which it would have a $600 salvage value; and it was estimated the machine would produce 132,000 units of product during its life. It actually produced the following numbers of units: Year 1, 30,000; Year 2, 35,000; Year 3, 34,000; and Year 4, 33,000.

Required:

1. Prepare a calculation to show the total number of dollars of this machine's cost that should be charged to depreciation during its four-year life.
2. Prepare a form with the following column headings:

Year	Straight-Line	Units-of-Production	Declining-Balance	Sum-of-the-Years'-Digits

Then enter on the form the depreciation for each year and the total depreciation on the machine under each depreciation method. Use twice the straight-line rate for declining-balance depreciation.

Problem 10–2A

A secondhand delivery truck was purchased for $8,795 in cash on March 18, 19A. The next day $350 was paid for special racks and shelves in the truck, and $695 was paid to Service Garage for minor repairs to the truck's motor and for a new set of tires. The repairs were priced at $120, and the tires at $650. However, a $75 trade-in allowance was received on the truck's old tires.

At the time of its purchase it was estimated the truck would be driven 60,000 kilometers after which it would have a $1,200 trade-in value. The truck was driven 28,000 kilometers during the remaining months of 19A; and between January 1 and July 12, 19B, the truck was driven an additional 19,000 kilometers. On the latter date it was retired from service.

Required:

Prepare general journal entries to record the purchase of the truck, payment for racks and shelves, payment for the new tires and motor repairs, and the depreciation expense for 19A and 19B. Also, give the entries to record the truck's retirement under each of the following unrelated assumptions: *(a)* the truck was sold on July 12, 19A, for $3,250; *(b)* the truck was totally destroyed in a wreck, and the insurance company paid $2,650 in full settlement of the loss claim.

Problem 10–3A

A company purchased four machines during 19M and 19N and has used four ways to allocate depreciation on the machines. Information about the machines follows:

Machine number	Placed in use on—	Cost	Estimated life	Salvage value	Depreciation method
1	Oct. 5, 19M	$ 6,150	8 years	$ 550	Straight-line
2	July 2, 19M	19,500	8 years	1,500	Sum-of-the-years'-digits
3	Mar. 29, 19N	35,000	60,000 units	2,000	Units-of-production
4	June 28,19N	?	10 years	2,000	Declining balance at twice the straight-line rate

Machine No. 3 produced 7,000 units of product in 19N and 9,300 in 19O. Machine No. 4 had an invoice price of $29,500, 2/10, n/60, FOB point of shipment. The invoice was paid on the last day of the discount period June 29, but the company had to borrow $15,000 on a 60-day, 8% note in order to do so. The loan was repaid on August 31. Freight charges on Machine No. 4 were $215, and the machine was placed on a special concrete base that cost $460. It was assembled and installed by the company's own employees. Their wages during the installation period were $415. Payments for the freight charges, the concrete base, and the employees' wages were made on June 30.

Required:

1. Prepare a form with the following columnar headings:

Machine Number	Amount to Be Charged to Depreciation	19M Depreciation	19N Depreciation	19O Depreciation

Enter the machine numbers in the first column and complete the information opposite each machine's number. Total the columns.
2. Prepare entries to record all transactions involving the purchase of Machine No. 4, including the note transactions.
3. Prepare an entry to record the December 31, 19O, depreciation.

Problem 10–4A

On March 16, 19Q, a company made a lump-sum purchase of two machines from another company that was going out of business. The machines cost $48,600 and were placed in use on April 4, 19Q. This additional information about the machines is available:

Machine number	Appraised value	Salvage value	Estimated life	Installation cost	Depreciation method
1	$24,000	$1,200	4 years	$ 600	Sum-of-the-years' digits
2	30,000	2,000	4 years	1,000	Declining balance at twice the straight-line rate

The machines were depreciated at the ends of 19Q, 19R, and 19S; and during the first week in January 19T, the company decided to sell and replace them. Consequently, on January 12, 19T, it sold Machine No. 1 for $4,000 and on January 14 it sold Machine No. 2 for $4,500.

Required:

1. Prepare a form with the following columnar headings:

Machine Number	19Q Depre- ciation	19R Depre- ciation	19S Depre- ciation	19T Depre- ciation	19U Depre- ciation

Enter the machine numbers in the first column and the amounts of depreciation in the remaining columns.

2. Prepare general journal entries to record the purchase of the machines, their installation, the depreciation for each year they were in use, and their sale. Assume cash was paid and received in all transactions and the installation charges were paid for on the day the machines were put in use.

Problem 10–5A

Stores X and Y are identical in almost all respects. Both began business one year ago, on January 2, with equipment that cost $25,000 each, and which has an estimated 10-year life and a $5,000 salvage value. Neither store added to its equipment during the year and each purchased merchandise as follows:

Jan. 2   100 units at $150 each.
Feb. 27   100 units at $160 each.
Apr. 5   300 units at $164 each.
Aug. 25   200 units at $176 each.
Nov. 17   100 units at $180 each.

At the year-end, on December 31, before recording depreciation, their records showed the following revenues and expenses:

	Store X	Store Y
Sales	$175,000	$175,000
Salaries expense	20,000	20,000
Rent expense	12,000	12,000
Other expenses	4,000	4,000

However, Store X used declining-balance depreciation at twice the straight-line rate, while Store Y chose straight-line depreciation. Also, Store X priced its 110-unit ending inventory on a LIFO basis, while Store Y used FIFO for its 110-unit inventory.

Required:

1. Prepare an income statement for each store showing last year's results.
2. Prepare a schedule accounting for the difference in their net incomes.

Problem 10–6A

Monroe Company completed the following plant asset transactions:

19A
Jan. 7   Purchased on credit from Quicko, Ltd., a Quicko calculator, $550. The serial number of the machine was X2X345. Its service life was estimated at eight years with a $70 trade-in value. It was assigned plant asset number 132–1.
       9   Purchased on credit from Office Outfitters an Accurate typewriter for $380. The machine's serial number was MMM-0156, and it was assigned plant asset number 132–2. Its service life was estimated at four years with a $44 trade-in value.
Dec. 31   Recorded the 19A depreciation on the office equipment.

19B

June 3 Sold the Accurate typewriter for $200 cash.

4 Purchased on credit for $415 from Speedy Typewriter Company a Speedy typewriter. The machine's serial number was MO7781, and it was assigned plant asset number 132–3. Its service life was estimated at four years with a $55 trade-in value.

Dec. 31 Recorded the 19B depreciation on the office equipment.

Required:

1. Open an Office Equipment account and an Accumulated Depreciation, Office Equipment account plus subsidiary plant asset record cards as needed.
2. Prepare general journal entries to record the transactions. Post to the general ledger accounts and subsidiary record cards.
3. Prove the December 31, 19B, balances of the Office Equipment and Accumulated Depreciation, Office Equipment accounts by preparing a schedule showing the cost and accumulated depreciation of each plant asset owned by the company on that date.

PROVOCATIVE PROBLEMS

Provocative Problem 10–1, Echo Company

Echo Company earns more than a half million dollars each year, and it has just invested $88,000 in new machinery that will increase its earnings $45,000 per year before depreciation on the new machinery and income taxes on the extra earnings. The new machinery is expected to have a four-year life and an $8,000 salvage value. Explain whether the straight-line or the declining-balance at double the straight-line depreciation method is best from a net income point of view for the company to use. Back your answer with calculations to show the number of extra dollars the company will earn by using the "best method." In making your calculations, assume that income taxes take one half of the company's before-tax earnings and that it can invest any deferred tax dollars to earn a 5% after-tax return, compounded annually. Also, to simplify the problem, assume that income taxes must be paid on the first day of January following the year of incurrence.

Provocative Problem 10–2, first audit

Last week you went to work for a local accounting firm and today you are working on your first audit, a company that has been organized just one year; and in examining the company's plant asset accounts, you find the following debits and credits in an account called Land and Buildings:

Debits

Jan.	3	Cost of land and buildings acquired for new plant site	$ 50,000
	10	Lawyer's fee for title search	500
	27	Cost of wrecking old building on plant site	5,000
Feb.	1	Six months' liability and fire insurance on new building	1,500
June	30	Payment to building contractor on completion of building	225,250
July	1	Architect's fee for new building	13,500
	3	City assessment for street improvements	3,500
	14	Cost of landscaping new plant site	2,000
			$301,250

Credits

Jan. 25	Proceeds from sale of salvaged materials from old building	$ 1,000
July 3	Refund of one month's insurance premium	250
Dec. 31	Depreciation at 2½% per year	3,750
31	Balance	296,250
		$301,250

In consultation with the senior accountant in charge of the audit, you learn that 40 years is a reasonable life expectancy for a building of the type involved and that it is reasonable to assume that there will be no salvage value at the end of the building's life. He also tells you to prepare a schedule with columns headed Date, Description, Total Amount, Land, Buildings, and Other Accounts and to enter the items found in the Land and Buildings account on the schedule, distributing the amounts to the proper columns. He suggests that you show credits on your schedule by enclosing the amounts in parentheses; and finally he suggests that since the accounts have not been closed, you draft any required correcting entry or entries. Assume that an account called Depreciation Expense, Land and Buildings was debited in recording the $3,750 of depreciation.

ANALYTICAL AND REVIEW PROBLEMS

Problem 10–1
A&R

At the last meeting of the executive committee of F. W. White, Ltd., Michael Gross, controller, was severely criticized by both President White and Vince Edmonds, vice president of production. The subject of criticism was in the recognition of periodic depreciation. President White was unhappy with the fact that what he referred to as "a fictitious item" was deducted, resulting in depressed net income. In his words, "Depreciation is a fiction when the assets being depreciated are worth far more than we paid for them. What the controller is doing is unduly understating our net income. This in turn is detrimental to our shareholders because it results in the undervaluation of our shares on the market."

Vice President Edmonds was equally adamant about the periodic depreciation charges, however, he came on from another side. He said, "Our maintenance people tell me that the level of maintenance is such that our plant and equipment will virtually last forever." He further stated that charging depreciation on top of maintenance expenses is double-counting—it seems reasonable to either charge maintenance or depreciation but not both.

The time taken by other pressing matters did not permit Gross to answer; instead the controller was asked to prepare a report to the executive committee to deal with the issues raised by the president and vice president.

Required:

The controller asks you, his assistant, to prepare the required report.

Problem 10–2
A&R

The vice president of finance of Rockie, Ltd., presented you with the following contentious accounting issue facing the company:

Rockie has not in the past recorded depreciation on its fixed assets. The president noted this fact in last year's report to the shareholders as follows: "Our fixed assets are increasing, not decreasing in value. The recording of a fictitious expense (depreciation) will make our statements misleading." The Board of Directors share in the president's opinion, however, they agreed to have depreciation recorded this year in order to obtain an unqualified opinion.

Required:

Evaluate the president's statement in the light of applicable GAAP.

**Problem 10–3
A&R**

The following amounts would be charged in the second year of the asset's service life by three different methods:

	Method		
Year	a	b	c
1			
2	$30,000	$36,000	$40,000
3			
4			
5			

Required:

1. Identify the three methods used and complete the table showing depreciation expense by each method for each year. Assume a five-year service life with no salvage value.
2. Assuming that income before depreciation is $150,000 for each of the five years, show the amount of income after depreciation for the period covered by the assets. Briefly explain the impact which the depreciation method may have on reported net income for a business.

**Problem 10–4
A&R**

The Bob Trucking Company purchased a large earth-mover four years ago at a cost of $66,000. At that time it was estimated that the economic life of the equipment would be 12 years and that its ultimate salvage value would be $6,000.

Assuming the company uses straight-line depreciation, state whether each of the following events requires a revision of the original depreciation rate, with reasons for your answer:

a. Due to the persistent inflation, the present replacement cost of the same type of equipment is $92,000.
b. Because of the higher replacement cost (as described in [a] above) the ultimate salvage value is now estimated at $10,000.
c. The company, in connection with having its line of credit increased, was required by the bank to have the assets appraised. The earth-mover was estimated to have a current value of $55,000.
d. At the time the appraisal was made in (c) above, it was determined that technological change was progressing more slowly than originally estimated

and that the earth-mover would probably remain in service for 15 years with the ultimate salvage value as originally estimated at the end of 12 years.

Problem 10–5
A&R

Two companies, MN Ltd., and XY Ltd., purchased identical assets costing $400,000 at the beginning of 19A. MN Ltd. depreciated its assets on a straight-line basis assuming a $20,000 salvage value and a useful life of 10 years. XY Ltd. decided to use the declining-balance method also assuming a useful life of 10 years.

Required:

1. Which method (the one used by MN or by XY) is correct and should be used?
2. What will be the difference, if any, in the reported incomes of the two companies in each of years 19A, 19B, and 19C assuming that their net incomes, before depreciation, are identical?
3. Prepare the balance sheet figures with respect to the assets purchased, for MN Ltd. and XY Ltd. as at the end of 19C.

Plant and Equipment; Intangible Assets

11

After studying Chapter 11, you should be able to:

Prepare entries to record the purchase and sale or discarding of a plant asset.

Prepare entries to record the exchange of plant assets.

Make the calculations and prepare the entries to account for revisions in depreciation rates.

Make the calculations and prepare the entries to account for plant asset repairs and betterments.

Prepare entries to account for wasting assets and for intangible assets.

Define or explain the words and phrases listed in the chapter Glossary.

Some of the problems met in accounting for property, plant, and equipment were discussed in the previous chapter. Additional problems involving plant assets and some of the accounting problems encountered with intangible assets are examined in this chapter.

PLANT ASSET DISPOSALS

Sooner or later a plant asset wears out, becomes obsolete, or becomes inadequate. When this occurs, the asset is discarded, sold, or traded in on a new asset. The entry to record the disposal depends on which action is taken.

Discarding a Plant Asset

When an asset's accumulated depreciation is equal to its cost, the asset is said to be fully depreciated; and if a fully depreciated asset is discarded, the entry to record the disposal is:

Jan.	7	Accumulated Depreciation, Machinery	1,500.00	
		Machinery		1,500.00
		Discarded a fully depreciated machine.		

Although often discarded, sometimes a fully depreciated asset is kept in use. In such situations the asset's cost and accumulated depreciation should not be removed from the accounts; they should remain on the books until the asset is sold, traded, or discarded. Otherwise, the accounts do not show its continued existence. However, no additional depreciation should be recorded, since the reason for recording depreciation is to charge an asset's cost to depreciation expense. In no case should the expense exceed the asset's cost.

Sometimes an asset is discarded before being fully depreciated. For example, suppose an error was made in estimating the service life of a $1,000 machine and it becomes worthless and is discarded after having only $800 of depreciation recorded against it. In such a situation there is a loss, and the entry to record the disposal is:

Jan.	10	Loss on Disposal of Machinery	200.00	
		Accumulated Depreciation, Machinery	800.00	
		Machinery		1,000.00
		Discarded a worthless machine.		

Discarding a Damaged Plant Asset

Occasionally, before the end of its service life, a plant asset is wrecked in an accident or destroyed by fire. For example, a machine that cost $900 and which had been depreciated $400 was totally destroyed in a fire. If the loss was partially covered by insurance and the insurance company paid $350 to settle the loss claim, the entry to record the machine's destruction is:

Jan.	12	Cash	350.00	
		Loss from Fire	150.00	
		Accumulated Depreciation, Machinery	400.00	
		Machinery		900.00
		To record the destruction of machinery and the receipt of insurance compensation.		

If the machine was uninsured, the entry to record its destruction would not have a debit to Cash and the loss from fire would be $500.

Selling a Plant Asset

When a plant asset is sold, if the selling price exceeds the asset's book value, there is a gain. If the price is less than book value, there is a loss. For example, assume that a machine which cost $5,000 and had been depreciated $4,000 is sold for a price in excess of its book value, say for $1,200. In this case, there is a gain and the entry to record the sale is:

Jan.	4	Cash	1,200.00	
		Accumulated Depreciation, Machinery	4,000.00	
		Machinery		5,000.00
		Gain on the Sale of Plant Assets		200.00
		Sold a machine at a price in excess of book value.		

However, if the machine is sold for $750, there is a $250 loss and the entry to record the sale is:

Jan.	4	Cash	750.00	
		Loss on the Sale of Plant Assets	250.00	
		Accumulated Depreciation, Machinery	4,000.00	
		Machinery		5,000.00
		Sold a machine at a price below book value.		

EXCHANGING PLANT ASSETS

Some plant assets are sold at the end of their useful lives. Others, such as machinery, automobiles, and office equipment, are commonly exchanged for new, up-to-date assets of like purpose. In such exchanges a trade-in allowance is normally received on the old asset, with the balance being paid in cash. In recording the exchanges, material book losses and gains should be recognized in the accounts. A book loss is experienced when the trade-in allowance is less than the book value of the traded asset. A book gain results from a trade-in allowance that exceeds the book value of the traded asset.

Recognizing a Material Book Loss

To illustrate recognition of a material book loss on an exchange of plant assets, assume that a machine, which cost $18,000 and had been depreciated $15,000, was traded in on a new machine having a $21,000 cash price. A $1,000 trade-in allowance was received, and the $20,000 balance was paid in cash. Under these assumptions the book value of the old machine is $3,000, calculated as follows:

Cost of old machine	$18,000
Less: Accumulated depreciation ...	15,000
Book value	$ 3,000

And since the $1,000 trade-in allowance resulted in a $2,000 loss on the exchange, the transaction should be recorded as follows:

Jan.	5	Machinery	21,000.00	
		Loss on Exchange of Machinery	2,000.00	
		Accumulated Depreciation, Machinery	15,000.00	
		Machinery		18,000.00
		Cash		20,000.00
		Exchanged old machine and cash for a new machine.		

The $21,000 debit to Machinery puts the new machine in the accounts at its cash price. The debit to Loss on Exchange of Machinery records the loss. The old machine is removed from the accounts with the $15,000 debit to accumulated depreciation and the $18,000 credit to Machinery.

Recognizing a Material Book Gain

To illustrate recognition of a material book gain on an exchange of plant assets, assume that in acquiring the $21,000 machine of the previous section a $4,500 trade-in allowance, rather than a $1,000 trade-in allowance, was received, and a $16,500 balance was paid in cash. A $4,500 trade-in allowance would result in a $1,500 gain on exchange. The transaction is recorded as follows:

Jan.	5	Machinery	21,000.00	
		Accumulated Depreciation, Machinery	15,000.00	
		Machinery		18,000.00
		Cash		16,500.00
		Gain on Exchange of Machinery		1,500.00
		Exchanged old machine and cash for a new machine.		

Nonrecognition of a Book Loss or Gain

In the previous two sections, recognition of book loss and book gain was discussed and illustrated. Such accounting procedure is dictated by adherence to the cost principle; that is, recording the new plant asset at the cash equivalent amount, the price that would be paid without a trade-in. In the illustrations above, $21,000 was given as the new machine's cash price. There are times when the cash price of the new machine may not be readily available, however, the old machine may have a ready market at an easily determinable amount. In such cases the cash equivalent amount of the new machine would be the sum of cash paid and the fair value of the trade-in. Once the cash equivalent amount of the new machine is determined, the recording of the trade-in transaction is the same as illustrated in the previous sections.

Notwithstanding the above discussion, departure from the outlined procedure is permitted under the *principle of materiality*. Under this principle, the loss or gain if considered immaterial in amount is not recognized. The new asset is then recorded at an amount equal to the sum of the book value of the trade-in plus the cash paid. For example, an old typewriter that cost $500 was traded in at $50 on a new $600 typewriter, with the $550 difference being paid in cash. Depreciation on the old typewriter in the amount of $420 had been taken. In this case the old typewriter's book value is $80; and with the trade-in of $50, there was a $30 book loss on the exchange. However, the $30 loss is an immaterial amount, and the following method may be used in recording the exchange.

Jan.	7	Office Equipment	630.00	
		Accumulated Depreciation, Office Equipment ...	420.00	
		Office Equipment		500.00
		Cash..................................		550.00
		Traded an old typewriter and cash for a new typewriter.		

The $630 at which the new typewriter is taken into the accounts is calculated as follows:

Book value of old typewriter ($500 less $420)	$ 80
Cash paid ($600 less the $50 trade-in allowance)	550
Cost basis of the new typewriter	$630

When there is an immaterial loss on an exchange, as in this case, the violation of the cost principle is permissible under the *principle of materiality*. Under this principle an adherence to any accounting principle is not required when the cost to adhere is proportionally great and the lack of adherence does not materially affect reported periodic net income. In this case, failing to record the $30 loss on the exchange would not materially affect the average company's statements.

REVISING DEPRECIATION RATES

An occasional error in estimating the useful life of a plant asset is to be expected. Furthermore, when such an error is discovered, it is corrected by spreading the remaining amount the asset is to be depreciated over its remaining useful life.[1] For example, seven years ago a machine was purchased at a cost of $10,500. At that time the machine was estimated to have a 10-year life with a $500 salvage value. Therefore, it was depreciated at the rate of $1,000 per year [($10,500 − $500) ÷ 10 = $1,000]; and it began its eighth year with a $3,500 book value, calculated as follows:

Cost	$10,500
Less: 7 years' accumulated depreciation	7,000
Book value	$ 3,500

---

[1] *CICA Handbook* (Toronto: The Canadian Institute of Chartered Accountants), par. 3480.11–.12 and 3600.03.

Assume that at the beginning of its eighth year the estimated number of years remaining in this machine's useful life is changed from three to five years with no change in salvage value. Under this assumption, depreciation for each of the machine's remaining years should be calculated as follows:

$$\frac{\text{Book value} - \text{Salvage value}}{\text{Remaining useful life}} = \frac{\$3,500 - \$500}{5 \text{ years}} = \$600 \text{ per year}$$

And $600 of depreciation should be recorded on the machine at the end of the eighth and each succeeding year in its life.

If depreciation is charged at the rate of $1,000 per year for the first seven years of this machine's life and $600 per year for the next five, depreciation expense is overstated during the first seven years and understated during the next five. However, if an enterprise has many plant assets, the lives of some will be underestimated and the lives of others will be overestimated at the time of purchase. Consequently, such errors will tend to cancel each other out with little or no effect on the income statement.

ORDINARY AND EXTRAORDINARY REPAIRS

Repairs made to keep an asset in its normal good state of repair are classified as *ordinary repairs*. A building must be repainted and its roof repaired. A machine must be cleaned, oiled, adjusted, and have any worn small parts replaced. Such repairs and maintenance are necessary, and their costs should appear on the current income statement as an expense.

Extraordinary repairs are major repairs made not to keep an asset in its normal good state of repair but to extend its service life beyond that originally estimated. As a rule, the cost of such repairs should be debited to the repaired asset's accumulated depreciation account under the assumption they make good past depreciation, add to the asset's useful life, and benefit future periods. For example, a machine was purchased for $8,000 and depreciated under the assumption it would last eight years and have no salvage value. As a result, at the end of the machine's sixth year its book value is $2,000, calculated as follows:

Cost of machine	$8,000
Less: 6 years' accumulated depreciation	6,000
Book value	$2,000

If at the beginning of the machine's seventh year a major overhaul extends its estimated useful life three years beyond the eight originally estimated, the $2,100 cost should be recorded as follows:

Jan.	12	Accumulated Depreciation, Machinery	2,100.00	
		Cash (or Accounts Payable)		2,100.00
		To record extraordinary repairs.		

In addition, depreciation for each of the five years remaining in the machine's life should be calculated as follows:

Book value before extraordinary repairs	$2,000
Extraordinary repairs	2,100
Total	$4,100
Annual depreciation expense for remaining years ($4,100 ÷ 5 years)	$ 820

And, if the machine remains in use for five years after the major overhaul, the five annual $820 depreciation charges will exactly write off its new book value, including the cost of the extraordinary repairs.

BETTERMENTS

A *betterment* involves modifying an existing plant asset to make it more efficient, usually by replacing part of the asset with an improved or superior part. The result of a betterment is a more efficient or more productive asset but not necessarily one having a longer life. For example, if the manual controls on a machine are replaced with automatic controls, the cost of labour may be reduced. When a betterment is made, its cost should be debited to the improved asset's account, say the Machinery account, and depreciated over the remaining service life of the asset. Also, the cost and applicable depreciation of the replaced asset portion should be removed from the accounts.

CAPITAL AND REVENUE EXPENDITURES

A *revenue expenditure* is one that should appear on the current income statement as an expense that is deducted from the period's revenues. Expenditures for ordinary repairs, rent, and salaries are examples. Expenditures for betterments and for extraordinary repairs, on the other hand, are examples of what are called *capital expenditures* or *balance sheet expenditures*. They should appear on the balance sheet as asset increases.

Obviously, care must be exercised to distinguish between capital and revenue expenditures when transactions are recorded. For if errors are made, such errors often affect a number of accounting periods. For instance, an expenditure for a betterment initially recorded in error as an expense overstates expenses in the year of the error and understates net income. Also, since the cost of a betterment should be depreciated over the remaining useful life of the bettered asset, depreciation expense of future periods is understated and net income is overstated.

NATURAL RESOURCES

Natural resources such as standing timber, mineral deposits, and oil reserves are known as wasting assets. In their natural state they represent inventories that will be converted into a product by cutting, mining, or pumping. However, until cut, mined, or pumped they are noncurrent assets and commonly appear on a balance sheet under such captions as "Timberlands," "Mineral deposits," or "Oil reserves."

Natural resources are accounted for at cost and appear on the balance sheet at cost less accumulated *depletion.* The amount such assets are depleted each year by cutting, mining, or pumping is commonly calculated on a "units-of-production" basis. For example, if a mineral deposit having an estimated 500,000 tons of available ore is purchased for $500,000, the depletion charge per ton or ore mined is $1. Furthermore, if 85,000 tons are mined during the first year, the depletion charge for the year is $85,000 and is recorded as follows:

Dec.	31	Depletion of Mineral Deposit	85,000.00	
		Accumulated Depletion, Mineral Deposit ...		85,000.00
		To record depletion of the mineral deposit.		

On the balance sheet prepared at the end of the first year, the mineral deposit should appear at its $500,000 cost less $85,000 accumulated depletion. If the 85,000 tons of ore are sold by the end of the first year, the entire $85,000 depletion charge reaches the income statement as the depletion cost of the ore mined and sold. However, if a portion remains unsold at the year-end, the depletion cost of the unsold ore is carried forward on the balance sheet as part of the cost of the unsold ore inventory, a current asset.

Often, machinery must be installed or a building constructed in order to exploit a natural resource. The costs of such assets should be depreciated over the life of the natural resource with annual depreciation charges that are in proportion to the annual depletion charges. For example, if a machine is installed in a mine and one eighth of the mine's ore is removed during a year, one eighth of the amount the machine is to be depreciated should be recorded as a cost of the ore mined.

INTANGIBLE ASSETS

Intangible assets have no physical existence; rather, they represent certain legal rights and economic relationships which are beneficial to the owner. Patents, copyrights, leaseholds, goodwill, trademarks, and organization costs are examples. Notes and accounts receivable are also intangible in nature. However, these appear on the balance sheet as current assets rather than under the intangible assets classification.

Intangible assets are accounted for at cost and should appear on the balance sheet in the intangible asset section at cost or at that portion of cost not previously written off. Normally, the intangible asset section follows on the balance sheet immediately after the plant and equipment section. Intangibles should be systematically amortized or written off to expense accounts over their estimated useful lives, which in most cases should not exceed 40 years. Amortization is a process similar to the recording of depreciation. However, amortizing of intangibles is usually limited to the straight-line method.[2]

Patents

Patents are granted by the federal government to protect the inventors of new machines and mechanical devices. A *patent* gives its owner the exclusive right to manufacture and sell a patented machine or device for a period of 17 years. When patent rights are purchased, all costs of acquiring the rights may be debited to an account called Patents. Also, the costs of a successful lawsuit in defense of a patent may be debited to this account.

A patent gives its owner exclusive rights to the patented device for 17 years. However, its cost should be *amortized,* or written off, over a shorter period if its useful or economic life is estimated to be less than 17 years. For example, if a patent costing $25,000 has an estimated useful life of only 10 years, the following adjusting entry is made at the end of each year in the patent's life to write off one tenth of its cost.

Dec.	31	Amortization of Patents	2,500.00	
		Patents		2,500.00
		To write off one tenth of patent costs.		

The entry's debit causes $2,500 of patent costs to appear on the annual income statement as one of the costs of the patented product

---

[2] Ibid., par. 1580.58.

manufactured. The credit directly reduces the balance of the Patents account. Normally, patents are written off directly to the Patents account as in this entry.

Copyrights

A *copyright* is granted by the federal government and in most cases gives its owner the exclusive right to publish and sell a musical, literary, or artistic work during the life of the composer, author, or artist and for 50 years thereafter. Many copyrights have value for a much shorter time, and their costs should be amortized over the shorter period. Often the only cost of a copyright is the fee paid to the government. If this fee is not material, it may be charged directly to an expense account. Otherwise, the copyright costs should be capitalized and a copyright should be charged to Amortization Expense, Copyrights.

Leaseholds

Property is rented under a contract called a *lease*. The person or company owning the property and granting the lease is called the *lessor*. The person or company securing the right to possess and use the property is called the *lessee*. The rights granted the lessee under the lease are called a *leasehold*.

Some leases require no advance payment from the lessee but do require monthly rent payments. In such cases a Leasehold account is not needed and the monthly payments are debited to a Rent Expense account. Sometimes a long-term lease is so drawn that the last year's rent must be paid in advance at the time the lease is signed. When this occurs, the last year's advance payment is debited to the Leasehold account. It remains there until the last year of the lease, at which time it is transferred to Rent Expense.

Often, a long-term lease, one running 20 or 25 years, becomes very valuable after a few years because its required rent payments are much less than current rentals for identical property. In such cases the increase in value of the lease should not be entered on the books since no extra cost was incurred in acquiring it. However, if the property is subleased and a cash payment is made for the rights under the old lease, the new tenant should debit the payment to a Leasehold account and write it off as additional rent expense over the remaining life of the lease.

Leasehold Improvements

Long-term leases often require the lessee to pay for any alterations or improvements to the leased property, such as new partitions and store fronts. Normally, the costs of *leasehold improvements* are debited to an account called Leasehold Improvements. Also, since the improvements become part of the property and revert to the lessor at the end of the lease, their cost should be amortized over the life of the lease or the life of the improvements, whichever is shorter. The amortization entry commonly debits Rent Expense and credits Leasehold Improvements.

Goodwill

The term *goodwill* has a special meaning in accounting. In accounting, *a business is said to have goodwill when its rate of expected future earnings is greater than the rate of earnings normally realized in its industry.* Above-average earnings and the existence of goodwill may be demonstrated as follows with Companies A and B, both of which are in the same industry:

	Company A	Company B
Net assets (other than goodwill)	$100,000	$100,000
Normal rate of return in this industry	10%	10%
Normal return on net assets	10,000	10,000
Expected net income	10,000	15,000
Expected earnings above average	$ 0	$ 5,000

Company B is expected to have an above-average earnings rate compared to its industry and is said to have goodwill. This goodwill may be the result of excellent customer relations, the location of the business, monopolistic privileges, superior management, or a combination of factors. Furthermore, a prospective investor would normally be willing to pay more for Company B than for Company A if the investor agreed the extra earnings rate should be expected. Thus, goodwill is an asset having value, and it can be sold.

Accountants are in agreement that goodwill should not be recorded unless it is bought or sold. This normally occurs only when a business is purchased and sold in its entirety. When this occurs, the goodwill of the business may be valued in several ways. Examples of three follow:

1. The buyer and seller may place an arbitrary value on the goodwill of a business being sold. For instance, a seller may be willing to sell a business having an above-average earnings rate for $115,000, and a buyer may be willing to pay that amount. If they both agree that the net assets of the business other than its goodwill have a $100,000 value, they are arbitrarily valuing the goodwill at $15,000.

2. Goodwill may be valued at some multiple of that portion of expected earnings which is above average. For example, if a company is expected to have $5,000 each year in above-average earnings, its goodwill may be valued at, say, four times that portion of its earnings

which are above average or at $20,000. In this case it may also be said that the goodwill is valued at four years' above-average earnings. However, regardless of how it is said, this too is placing an arbitrary value on the goodwill.

3. The portion of a concern's earnings which is above average may be capitalized in order to place a value on its goodwill. For example, if a business is expected to continue to have $5,000 each year in earnings that are above average and the normal rate of return on invested capital in its industry is 10%, the excess earnings may be capitalized at 10% and a $50,000 value may be placed on its goodwill ($5,000 ÷ 10% = $50,000). Note that this values the goodwill at the amount that must be invested at the normal rate of return in order to earn the extra $5,000 each year ($50,000 × 10% = $5,000). It is a satisfactory method if the extra earnings are expected to continue indefinitely. However, this may not happen. Consequently, extra earnings are often capitalized at a rate higher than the normal rate of the industry, say in this case at twice the normal rate or at 20%. If the extra earnings are capitalized at 20%, the goodwill is valued at $25,000 ($5,000 ÷ 20% = $25,000).

There are other ways to value goodwill. Nevertheless, in the final analysis goodwill is always valued at the price a seller is willing to accept and a buyer is willing to pay.

Trademarks and Trade Names

Proof of prior use of a trademark or trade name is sufficient under common law to prove ownership and right of use. However, both may be registered at the Patent Office at a nominal cost for the same purpose. The cost of maintaining or enhancing the value of a trademark or trade name, perhaps through advertising, should be charged to an expense account in the period or periods incurred. However, if a trademark or trade name is purchased, its cost should be amortized as explained in the next section.

Research and Development Costs

Business concerns spend millions of dollars each year on research and new product development, and these expenditures are vital to our country's economic growth. However, the accounting treatment for such expenditures in the years prior to 1978 was not uniform. Some companies charged all research and development costs to expense accounts in the year incurred. Others treated such costs as an intangible asset to be amortized over the lives of successful new products developed. Consequently, as a result of the lack of uniformity, the CICA identified the elements of cost that can be attributed to research and those that can be identified with development activities and recommended that (1) research costs be expensed as incurred and (2) development costs be expensed as incurred except when specific criteria for deferment are met and the development costs can reasonably be regarded as assured of recovery through related future revenues, in which case deferral is required.[3]

Amortization of Intangibles

Some intangibles, such as patents, copyrights, and leaseholds, have determinable lives based on a law, contract, or the nature of the asset. The costs of such assets should be amortized over the shorter of their legal existence or the period expected to be benefited by their use. Other intangibles, such as goodwill, trademarks, and trade names, have indeterminable lives. However, since the value of any intangible will eventually disappear; that a reasonable estimate of the period of usefulness of such assets should be made; and that their costs should be amortized by systematic charges to income over the periods estimated to be benefited by their use, which should not exceed 40 years. The CICA designated the use of straight-line amortization method.[4]

GLOSSARY

Amortize.   To periodically write off as an expense a share of the cost of an asset, usually an intangible asset.

Balance sheet expenditure.   See capital expenditure.

Betterment.   A modification of an existing plant asset to make it more efficient, usually by replacing part of the asset with an improved or superior part.

Capital expenditure.   An expenditure that increases net assets.

Copyright.   An exclusive right granted by the federal government to publish and sell a musical, literary, or artistic work for a period of years.

Depletion.   The amount that a wasting asset (e.g., timber, mineral deposits, oil reserves) is depleted through cutting, mining, or pumping.

Extraordinary repairs.   Major repairs that extend the service life of a plant asset beyond the number of years originally estimated.

Goodwill.   That portion of the value of a business due to its expected ability to earn a rate of return greater than the average in its industry.

Intangible asset.   An asset having no physical existence but having value due to the rights resulting from its ownership and possession.

---

[3] Ibid., sec. 3450.

[4] Ibid., par. 1580.58.

Lease. A contract that grants the right to possess and use property.

Leasehold. The rights granted to a lessee under the terms of a lease contract.

Leasehold improvements. Improvements to leased property made by the lessee.

Lessee. An individual granted possession of property under the terms of a lease contract.

Lessor. The individual or enterprise that has granted possession and use of property under the terms of a lease contract.

Ordinary repairs. Repairs made to keep a plant asset in its normal good operating condition.

Patent. An exclusive right granted by the federal government to manufacture and sell a given machine or mechanical device for a period of years.

Revenue expenditure. An expenditure that should be deducted from current revenue on the income statement.

QUESTIONS FOR CLASS DISCUSSION

1. When should a loss on the exchange of a plant asset be recorded? When is it permissible to absorb a loss into the cost basis of the new plant asset? Should a gain on a plant asset exchange be recorded as such?

2. When plant assets are exchanged, what determines the cost basis of the newly acquired asset?

3. How should an immaterial loss or gain on exchange of plant assets be treated?

4. How should a material loss or gain on exchange of plant assets be treated?

5. What is the essence of the accounting principle of materiality?

6. If at the end of four years it is discovered that a machine that was expected to have a five-year life will actually have an eight-year life, how is the error corrected?

7. Distinguish between ordinary repairs and replacements and extraordinary repairs and replacements.

8. How should ordinary repairs to a machine be recorded? How should extraordinary repairs be recorded?

9. What is a betterment? How should a betterment to a machine be recorded?

10. Distinguish between revenue expenditures and capital expenditures.

11. What are the characteristics of an intangible asset?

12. In general, how are intangible assets accounted for?

13. Define (a) lease, (b) lessor, (c) leasehold, and (d) leasehold improvement.

14. In accounting, when is a business said to have goodwill?

MULTIPLE CHOICE

1. If major repairs to a machine have the effect of extending the machine's service life beyond the original estimate, the cost of the repairs should be debited to:
   a. Machinery.
   b. Ordinary repairs expense.
   c. Accumulated depreciation, machinery.
   d. Extraordinary repairs expense.
   e. Depreciation expense.

2. X-Ray Company sold for $6,000 an X-ray machine that originally cost $10,000. The accumulated depreciation on this machine was $4,000. X-Ray Company's gain (loss) on this sale is:
   a. $0.
   b. $2,000.
   c. $4,000.
   d. $6,000.
   e. $10,000.

3. Cherokee Company's bulldozer was destroyed by fire. The bulldozer originally cost $16,000, but insurance paid only $14,200. Accumulated depreciation on this bulldozer was $2,000. The gain (loss) from the fire is:
   a. $0.
   b. $200.
   c. $(200).
   d. $(14,000).
   e. $(16,000).

4. A company purchased mineral land estimated to contain 200,000 tons of recoverable ore. It installed machinery costing $120,000, having a 12-year life and no salvage value, and capable of exhausting the mine in 10 years. If during the first full year's operation the company mined 25,000 tons of ore, it should record depreciation on the machinery for this year in the amount of:
   a. $10,000.
   b. $12,000.
   c. $15,000.
   d. $20,000.
   e. Some other amount.

5. A machine was purchased for $8,800 and depreciated for six years on a straight-line basis under the assumption it would have an eight-year life and an $800 salvage value. At the beginning of the machine's seventh year it was recognized that the machine had four years of life instead of two, and that at the end of the four years its salvage value would be $400. As a result, each of the machine's remaining years should be charged depreciation on the machine at the annual rate of:

      a. $1,000.
      b. $700.
      c. $600.
      d. $500.
      e. Some other amount.

6. The Red Company exchanged its used copy machine for a newer model. The old machine had cost $900 and had been depreciated $700. The new copier had a cash price of $1,200, but Red Company was given a $350 trade-in allowance. What amount of gain or loss should Red Company show on the exchange?
      a. $0.
      b. $150 gain.
      c. $200 gain.
      d. $200 loss.
      e. $350 gain.

MINI DISCUSSION CASES

Case 11–1   You have just been appointed auditor of the Conestoga Company. During your first examination of the records you discover that the company charges all of its repairs and maintenance costs to their respective asset accounts. Management indicates that regular maintenance increases the life of an asset; therefore, the maintenance costs, instead of being charged to expense as incurred, will be reflected in the <u>increased</u> depreciation charges as the asset is being used.

Required:

Evaluate Conestoga's policy with respect to GAAP. Why is their policy (in)correct?

Case 11–2   Two of your classmates are having a discussion about accounting for intangible assets. Classmate 1 says that all intangible assets should be written off immediately since they have no physical substance. Classmate 2 argues that intangible assets should be written off over their legal lifetime as is provided by law.

Required:

Mediate between your classmates explaining, with reasons, the proper accounting treatment for intangible assets.

CLASS EXERCISES

Exercise 11–1   A machine that cost $4,500 and had $3,200 of accumulated depreciation recorded against it was traded in on a new machine having a $5,000 cash price. A $1,000 trade-in allowance was received, and the balance was paid in cash. Determine *(a)* the book value of the old machine, *(b)* the cash given in the exchange, *(c)* the book loss on the exchange, *(d)* the cost basis of the new machine, and *(e)* the annual straight-line depreciation on the new machine under the assumption it will have an estimated six-year life and an $800 salvage value.

Exercise 11–2   A machine that cost $4,000 and which had been depreciated $2,500 was disposed of on January 4. Give without explanations the entries to record the disposal under each of the following unrelated assumptions:

a.   The machine was sold for $1,750 cash.
b.   The machine was sold for $600 cash.
c.   The machine was traded in on a new machine having a $4,500 cash price. A $1,600 trade-in allowance was received, and the balance was paid in cash. The loss or gain was considered immaterial in amount.
d.   A $600 trade-in allowance was received for the machine on a new machine of like purpose having a $4,500 cash price. The balance was paid in cash, and the loss was considered material.

Exercise 11–3   On January 1, 19A, a company exchanged a $5,000, two-year, noninterest-bearing note payable for a machine having a cash price that was not readily determinable. Under the assumption that the market rate for interest on the day of the exchange was 6%, prepare *(a)* the entry to record the exchange and *(b)* the December 31, 19A, entry to amortize a portion of the discount on the note payable. *(c)* Show how the note should appear on the December 31, 19A, balance sheet. Prepare entries to record *(d)* the December 31, 19B, amortization of the remainder of the discount and *(e)* the January 1, 19C, entry to pay the note.

Exercise 11–4   A machine that cost $12,000 was depreciated on a straight-line basis for six years under the assumption it would have an eight-year life and a $2,000 trade-in value. At that point it was recognized that the machine had four years of remaining useful life, after which it would have an estimated $1,500 trade-in value. *(a)* Determine the machine's book value at the end of its sixth year. *(b)* Determine the amount of depreciation to be charged against the machine during each of the remaining years in its life.

Exercise 11–5   A company owns a building that appeared on its balance sheet at the end of last year at its original $246,000 cost less $205,000 accumulated depreciation. The building has been depreciated on a straight-line basis under the assumption it would have a 30-year life and no salvage value. During the first week in January of the current year, major structural repairs were completed on the building at a $64,000 cost. The repairs did not improve the building's usefulness, but they did extend its expected life for 10 years beyond the 30 years originally estimated. *(a)* Determine the building's age on last year's balance sheet date. *(b)* Give the entry to record the cost of the repairs. *(c)* Determine the book value of the building after its repairs were recorded. *(d)* Give the entry to record the current year's depreciation.

Exercise 11–6   Six years ago a company purchased for $1,000,000 the mineral rights to an ore body containing 1,000,000 tons of ore. The company invested an additional $1,000,000 in mining machinery designed to exhaust the mine in 10 years. During the first five years the mine produced 500,000 tons of ore that were sold at a profit. During the sixth year 100,000 tons of ore were mined; but due to technological changes in the manufacturing processes of the customers to whom the ore was normally sold, there was little demand for the ore and it was sold at a $1 per ton loss.

Required:

Under the assumption that the remaining 400,000 tons of ore can be mined and sold at a $1 per ton loss during the next four years and there is no prospect of ever doing better, recommend whether the mine should be closed and the loss stopped or it should be continued in operation at a loss. Cite figures to back your recommendation.

Exercise 11–7   On January 1, 19A, a company paid $90,000 for the copyright to a new cookbook. The copyright legally protects the owner for 40 more years. However, management believes that the book will be out-of-date and will require revision in five years.

Required:

Prepare journal entries to record *(a)* the purchase of the copyright and *(b)* annual amortization for the first two years.

PROBLEMS

Problem 11–1   A company completed the following transactions involving the purchase and operation of delivery trucks.

19Q
July 7 Paid cash for a new truck, $5,700 plus $285 state and city sales taxes. The truck was estimated to have a four-year life and a $1,500 salvage value.
     10 Paid $315 for special racks and shelves installed in the truck. The racks and shelves did not increase the truck's estimated trade-in value.
Dec. 31 Recorded straight-line depreciation on the truck.

19R
June 26 Paid $410 to install an air conditioning unit in the truck. The unit increased the truck's estimated trade-in value $50.
Dec. 31 Recorded straight-line depreciation on the truck.

19S
May 29 Paid $55 for repairs to the truck's rear bumper damaged when the driver backed into a loading dock.
Dec. 31 Recorded straight-line depreciation on the truck.

19T
Aug. 26 Traded the old truck and $3,885 in cash for a new truck. The new truck was estimated to have a three-year life and a $1,600 trade-in value, and the invoice for the exchange showed the following items:

Price of the truck	$6,200
Trade-in allowance granted . . .	(2,500)
Balance	$3,700
Sales taxes	185
Balance paid in cash	$3,885

The loss on the exchange was considered immaterial.
Aug. 29   Paid $465 for special shelves and racks installed in the truck.
Dec. 31   Recorded straight-line depreciation on the new truck.

Required:

Prepare general journal entries to record the transactions.

Problem 11–2   A company completed the following transactions involving machinery:

Machine No. 133–5 was purchased on May 2, 19A, at an installed cost of $3,500. Its useful life was estimated at five years with a $500 trade-in value. Straight-line depreciation was recorded on the machine at the ends of 19A and 19B; and on January 5, 19C, it was traded in on Machine No. 133–23. A $2,000 trade-in allowance was received, and the loss was considered immaterial.

Machine No. 133–23 was purchased on January 5, 19C, at an installed cost of $4,300, less the trade-in allowance received for Machine No. 133–5. Its life was estimated at five years with a $600 trade-in value. Sum-of-the-years'-digits depreciation was recorded on the machine on each December 31 of its life, and it was sold on October 7, 19G, for $800.

Machine No. 133–25 was purchased on January 9, 19C, at an installed cost of $6,400. Its useful life was estimated at four years, after which it would have a $400 salvage value. Declining-balance depreciation at twice the straight-line rate was recorded on the machine on each December 31 of its life, and it was traded in on Machine No. 133–30 on January 4, 19G. A $400 trade-in allowance was received.

Machine No. 133–30 was purchased on January 4, 19G, at an installed cost of $6,500 less the trade-in allowance received on Machine No. 133–25. It was estimated the new machine would produce 12,000 units of product during its life, after which it would have a $500 trade-in value. It produced 2,500 units of product in 1980 and 500 additional units in 19H before its sale for $4,000 on June 3, 19H.

Required:

Prepare general journal entries to record (1) the purchase of each machine, (2) the depreciation recorded on the first December 31 of each machine's life, and (3) the disposal of each machine. (Treat the entries for the first two machines as one series of transactions and those of the next two machines as an unrelated second series. Only one entry is needed to record the exchange of one machine for another.)

Problem 11–3   Prepare general journal entries to record the following transactions. Use straight-line depreciation.

19X1

Jan. 10   Purchased and placed in operations Machine No. 133–8 at an $18,000 installed cost. The machine's useful life was estimated at six years with no salvage value.

Dec. 31   Recorded depreciation on the machine.

19X2

Mar. 14   After a little over 14 months of satisfactory use, Machine No. 133–8 was cleaned, inspected, oiled, and adjusted by a factory representative at a cost of $215.

Dec. 31   Recorded depreciation on Machine No. 133–8.

19X3

June 28   Added a new device to Machine No. 133–8 at a $700 cost. The device did not change the machine's expected life nor change its zero salvage value, but it did increase its output by one fourth.

Dec. 31   Recorded depreciation on the machine.

19X4

Dec. 31   Recorded depreciation on the machine.

19X5

Jan. 9   Repaired and completely overhauled Machine No. 133–8 at a $4,000 cost, consisting of $400 for ordinary repairs and $3,600 for extraordinary repairs. The extraordinary repairs were expected to extend the machine's expected useful life for two years beyond the six years originally expected but were not expected to change its zero salvage value.

Dec. 31   Recorded depreciation on the machine.

19X6

July 9   Machine No. 133–8 was destroyed in a fire. The insurance company settled the loss claim for $5,000.

Problem 11–4

Part 1. Five years ago Parkway Opticians leased space in a building for a period of 15 years. The lease contract calls for $7,200 annual rental payments on each January 1 throughout the life of the lease, and also provides that the lessee must pay for all additions and improvements to the leased property. The recent construction of a shopping center across the street has made the location more valuable, and on December 20 Parkway Opticians subleased the space to The Optical Shop for the remaining 10 years of the lease, beginning on the next January 1. The Optical Shop paid $30,000 for the privilege of subleasing the property and in addition agreed to assume and pay the building owner the $7,200 annual rental charges. During the first 10 days after taking possession of the leased space, The Optical Shop remodeled the shop front of the leased space at a $10,000 cost. The remodeled shop front is estimated to have a life equal to the remaining life of the building, 20 years, and was paid for on January 12.

Required:

Prepare entries in general journal form to record *(a)* the Optical Shop's payment to sublease the shop space, *(b)* its payment of the annual rental charge to the building owner, and *(c)* payment for the new shop front. Also, prepare the adjusting entries required at the end of the first year of the sublease to amortize *(d)* a proper share of the $30,000 cost of the sublease and *(e)* a proper share of the shop front cost.

Part 2. On March 12 of the current year Hardrock Mine paid $800,000 for mineral land estimated to contain 4,000,000 tons of recoverable ore. It installed machinery costing $120,000, having a 12-year life and no salvage value, and capable of exhausting the mine in 10 years. The machinery was paid for on July 5, three days after mining operations began. During the first six months' operations the company mined 165,000 tons of ore.

Required:

Prepare entries to record *(a)* the purchase of the mineral land, *(b)* the installation of the machinery, *(c)* the first six months' depletion under the assumption that the land will be valueless after the ore is mined, and *(d)* the first six months' depreciation on the machinery.

Problem 11–5

Thomas Nye wishes to buy an established business and is considering Companies A and B, both of which have been in business for exactly five years, during which time Company A has reported an average annual net income of $11,835 and Company B has reported an average of $14,250. However, the incomes are not comparable, since the companies have not used the same accounting procedures. Current balance sheets of the companies show the following items:

	Company A	Company B
Assets		
Cash	$ 6,700	$ 8,200
Accounts receivable	51,600	58,500
Allowance for doubtful accounts	(3,200)	–0–
Merchandise inventory	71,300	86,100
Store equipment	28,800	25,600
Accumulated depreciation, store equipment	(24,000)	(16,000)
Total Assets	$131,200	$162,400
Liabilities and Owners' Equity		
Current liabilities	$ 62,400	$ 68,900
Owners' equity	68,800	93,500
Total Liabilities and Owners' Equity	$131,200	$162,400

Company A has used the allowance method in accounting for bad debts and has added to its allowance each year an amount equal to 1% of sales. However, this seems excessive, since an examination shows only $1,500 of its accounts that are probably uncollectible. Company B, on the other hand, has used the direct write-off method but has been slow to write off bad debts, and an examination of its accounts shows $3,000 of accounts that are probably uncollectible.

During the past five years Company A has priced its inventories on a LIFO basis with the result that its current inventory appears on its balance sheet at an amount that is $12,000 below replacement cost. Company B has used FIFO, and its ending inventory appears at approximately its replacement cost.

Both companies have assumed eight-year lives and no salvage value in depreciating equipment; however, Company A has used sum-of-the-years'- digits depreciation, while Company B has used straight line. Mr. Nye is of the opinion that straight-line depreciation has resulted in Company B's equipment appearing on its balance sheet at approximately its fair market value and that it would have had the same result for Company A.

Mr. Nye is willing to pay what he considers fair market value for the assets of either business, not including cash, but including goodwill measured at four times average annual earnings in excess of 15% on the fair market value of the net tangible assets. He defines net tangible assets as all assets other than goodwill, including accounts receivable, minus liabilities. He will also assume the liabilities of the purchased business, paying its owner the difference between total assets purchased and the liabilities assumed.

Required:

Prepare the following schedules: *(a)* a schedule showing the net tangible assets of each company at their fair market values according to Mr. Nye, *(b)* a schedule showing the revised net incomes of the companies based on FIFO inventories and straight-line depreciation, *(c)* a schedule showing the calculation of each company's goodwill, and *(d)* a schedule showing the amount Mr. Nye would pay for each business.

ALTERNATE PROBLEMS

Problem 11–1A

Prepare general journal entries to record these transactions involving the purchase and operation of a secondhand truck:

19X1

Jan. 8   Purchased for $3,850 cash a secondhand delivery truck having an estimated three years of remaining useful life and an $800 trade-in value.

      9   Paid Service Garage for the following:

Minor repairs to the truck's motor ...	$ 46
New tires for the truck	193
Gas and oil	15
Total	$254

Dec. 31   Recorded straight-line depreciation on the truck.

19X2

Jan. 4   Paid $550 to install a hydraulic loader on the truck. The loader increased the truck's trade-in value to $850.

June 27   Paid Service Garage for the following:

Minor repairs to the truck's motor ...	$ 78
New battery for the truck	65
Gas and oil	12
Total	$155

Nov. 3   Paid $55 for repairs to the hydraulic loader damaged when the driver backed into a loading dock.

Dec. 31   Recorded straight-line depreciation on the truck.

19X3

Jan. 11   Paid Service Garage $350 to overhaul the truck's motor, replacing its bearings and rings and extending the truck's life one year beyond the original three years planned. However, it was also estimated that the extra year's operation would reduce the truck's trade-in value to $650.

Dec. 31 Recorded straight-line depreciation on the truck.

19X4

July 7 Traded the old truck on a new one having a $5,600 cash price. Received a $1,200 trade-in allowance, and paid the balance in cash. The loss on trade-in was considered immaterial.

Problem 11–2A

A company completed the following transactions involving machinery:

Machine No. 133–51 was purchased on April 1, 19A1, at an installed cost of $5,400. Its useful life was estimated at four years with a $600 trade-in value. Straight-line depreciation was recorded on the machine at the ends of 19A1 and 19A2, and on July 2, 19A3, it was traded on Machine No. 133–85. A $2,700 trade-in allowance was received, and the balance was paid in cash.

Machine No. 133–85 was purchased on July 2, 19A3, at an installed cost of $6,700, less the trade-in allowance received on Machine 133–51. The new machine's life was estimated at five years with a $700 trade-in value. Sum-of-the-years'-digits depreciation was recorded on each December 31 of its life, and on January 4, 19A8, it was sold for $1,000.

Machine No. 133–72 was purchased on January 5, 19A3, at an installed cost of $5,000. Its useful life was estimated at five years, after which it would have a $500 trade-in value. Declining-balance depreciation at twice the straight-line rate was recorded on the machine at the ends of 19A3, 19A4, 19A5, and 19A6; and on September 26, 19A7, it was traded on Machine No. 133–99. A $400 trade-in allowance was received, the balance was paid in cash, and the loss was considered immaterial.

Machine No. 133–99 was purchased on September 26, 19A7, at a $5,900 installed cost, less the trade-in allowance received on Machine No. 133–72. It was estimated the new machine would produce 90,000 units of product during its useful life, after which it would have a $600 trade-in value. Units-of-production depreciation was recorded on the machine for the last three months of 19A7, a period in which it produced 6,000 units of product. Between January 1 and October 12, 19A8, the machine produced 16,000 more units, and on the latter date it was sold for $4,000.

Required:

Prepare general journal entries to record *(a)* the purchase of each machine, *(b)* the depreciation recorded on the first December 31 of each machine's life, and *(c)* the disposal of each machine. Treat the entries for the first two machines as one series of transactions and those of the next two machines as an unrelated second series. Only one entry is needed to record the exchange of one machine for another.

Problem 11–3A

Part 1. On January 7, 19X1, a company purchased and placed in operation a machine estimated to have a 10-year life and no salvage value. The machine cost $15,000 and was depreciated on a straight-line basis. On January 3, 19X5, a $600 device that increased its output by one fourth was added to the machine. The device did not change the machine's estimated life nor its zero salvage value. During the first week of January 19X8, the machine was completely overhauled at a $4,500 cost (paid for on January 9). The overhaul added three additional years to the machine's estimated life but did not change its zero salvage value. On June 27, 19X9, the machine was destroyed in a fire and the insurance company settled the loss claim for $5,000.

Required:

Prepare general journal entries to record *(a)* the purchase of the machine, *(b)* the 19X1 depreciation, *(c)* the addition of the new device, *(d)* the 19X5 depreciation, *(e)* the machine's overhaul, *(f)* the 19X8 depreciation, and *(g)* the insurance settlement.

Part 2. A company purchased Machine A at a $12,400 installed cost on January 5, 19X3, and depreciated it on a straight-line basis at the ends of 19X3, 19X4, 19X5, and 19X6 under the assumption it would have a 10-year life and a $2,400 salvage value. After more experience and before recording 19X7 depreciation, the company revised its estimate of the machine's remaining years downward from six years to four and revised the estimate of its salvage value downward to $2,000. On April 2, 19X9, after recording 19X7, 19X8, and part of a year's depreciation for 19X9, the company traded in Machine A on Machine B, receiving a $4,000 trade-in allowance. Machine B cost $15,300, less the trade-in allowance, the loss was considered immaterial, and the balance was paid in cash. Machine B was depreciated on a straight-line basis on December 31, 19X9, under the assumption it would have a six-year life and $2,300 salvage value.

Required:

Prepare entries to record *(a)* the purchase of Machine A, *(b)* its 19X3 depreciation, *(c)* its 19X7 depreciation, *(d)* the exchange of the machines, and *(e)* the 19X9 depreciation on Machine B.

Problem 11–4A

Part 1. Eight years ago A. Merchant leased a store building for a 20-year period. The lease contract requires a $9,000 annual rental payment on each January 1 throughout the life of the lease, and it requires the lessee to pay for all improvements to the leased property. Due to traffic pattern changes the lease has become more valuable, and on December 19 Mr. Merchant subleased the property for the remaining 12 years of the lease, beginning on January 1, to Allied Shops. Allied Shops paid Mr. Merchant $24,000 for his rights under the lease, and it also agreed to pay the annual rental charges directly to the building owner. In addition, during the first two weeks of January it remodeled the store front on the leased building at a $9,600 total cost, paying the contractor on January 14. The remodeled store front was estimated to have a life equal to the remaining life of the building, 24 years.

Required:

Prepare general journal entries to record Allied Shops payments for the sublease, the annual rental charge, and the new store front. Also, prepare the end-of-the-year adjusting entries to amortize portions of the sublease cost and the cost of the store front.

Part 2. On March 2, 19—, Redimix Company paid $200,000 for land containing an estimated 1,000,000 cubic metres of gravel suitable for preparing concrete. The gravel was to be removed by stripping, and the company estimated that it would cost $20,000 to return the land to a condition that would meet governmental safety and ecological standards, after which the land could be sold for its rehabilitation cost. The company installed machinery costing $160,000 (paid for on June 27), having a 10-year life and no salvage value, and capable of exhausting the site in eight years. During the first six months of operations, ending December 31, the company removed 60,000 metres of gravel.

Required:

Prepare general journal entries to record *(a)* the purchase of the land, *(b)* the installation of the machinery, *(c)* the first six months' depreciation, and *(d)* the first six months' depletion.

PROVOCATIVE PROBLEMS

Provocative
Problem 11–1,
Junior
Accountant

In helping to verify the records of a concern being audited by the public accounting firm for which you work as a junior accountant, you find the following entries:

19X5		Cash	8,500.00	
Oct.	20	Loss from Fire	3,500.00	
		Accumulated Depreciation, Machinery	9,000.00	
		Machinery		21,000.00
		Received payment of fire loss claim.		
Nov.	15	Cash	24,000.00	
		Factory Land		24,000.00
		Sold unneeded factory land.		

An investigation revealed that the first entry resulted from recording an $8,500 cheque from an insurance company in full settlement of a loss claim resulting from the destruction of a machine in a small plant fire on September 29, 19X5. The machine had originally cost $18,000, was put in operation on January 5, 19X1, and had been depreciated on a straight-line basis at the ends of each of the first four years in its life under the assumption it would have an eight-year life and no salvage value. During the first week of January 19X5, the machine had been overhauled at a $3,000 cost. The overhaul did not increase the machine's capacity nor change its zero salvage value. However, it was expected that the overhaul would lengthen the machine's service life two years beyond the eight years originally expected.

The second entry resulted from recording a cheque received from selling a portion of a tract of land. The tract was adjacent to the company's plant and had been purchased the year before. It cost $32,000, and $3,000 was paid for clearing and grading it. Both amounts had been debited to the Factory Land account. The land was to be used for storing raw materials; but after the grading was completed, it was obvious the company did not need the entire tract, and it was pleased when it received an offer from a purchaser who was willing to pay $18,000 for the east half or $24,000 for the west half. The company decided to sell the west half, and it recorded receipt of the purchaser's cheque with the entry previously given.

Were any errors made in recording the transactions described here? If so, describe the errors and in each case give an entry or entries that will correct the account balances under the assumption the 19X5 revenue and expense accounts have not been closed.

Provocative Problem 11–2, Jane Holt

Jane Holt plans to buy an established business, and she has narrowed her list to three choices, Companies A, B, and C. All three have been in business for exactly four years and have reported average annual net incomes as follows: Company A, $13,125; Company B, $11,912; and Company C, $20,970. However, since they have used different accounting methods, their reported incomes are not comparable, nor are their current balance sheets which show these items:

	Company A	Company B	Company C
Assets			
Cash	$ 9,800	$ 12,500	$ 19,400
Accounts receivable	82,500	93,400	97,600
Allowance for doubtful accounts	(6,500)	(1,800)	–0–
Merchandise inventory	94,700	75,600	92,100
Equipment	27,500	30,000	26,000
Accumulated depreciation, equipment	(17,000)	(17,712)	(10,400)
Building	110,000	98,000	105,000
Accumulated depreciation, building	(11,000)	(9,800)	–0–
Land	20,000	20,000	20,000
Goodwill			2,500
Total Assets	$310,000	$300,188	$352,200
Liabilities and Owners' Equity			
Current liabilities	$ 80,000	$ 95,000	$ 85,000
Mortgage payable	85,000	80,000	90,000
Owners' equity	145,000	125,188	177,200
Total Liabilities and Owners' Equity	$310,000	$300,188	$352,200

Company A has added an amount to its allowance for doubtful accounts each year equal to one half of 1% of sales. These amounts seem to have been excessive, since an analysis shows just $2,000 of the company's accounts receivable that are probably uncollectible. Company B has been more conservative, and its allowance is approximately equal to its uncollectible accounts. Company C has used the direct write-off method in accounting for bad debts; but it has always been slow to recognize a bad debt, and an examination shows accounts totaling $8,500 that are probably uncollectible.

Company B has accounted for its inventories on a LIFO basis; and as a result its current inventory appears on its books as an amount that is $15,000 below replacement cost. Companies A and C have used FIFO, and their inventories are stated at amounts near replacement costs.

The three companies have not added to their plant assets since beginning operations, and all three have assumed 10-year lives and no salvage values in recording depreciation on equipment. However, Company A has used sum-of-the-years'-digits depreciation, Company B has used declining balance at twice the straight-line rate, and Company C has used straight line.

The buildings of the companies are of concrete construction and are comparable in most respects. Companies A and B have recorded straight-line depreciation on their buildings, assuming 40-year lives and no salvage values. However, since its building is of concrete construction and "will last forever," Company C has taken no depreciation on its building.

Ms. Holt is of the opinion that if all three companies had used straight-line depreciation for both buildings and equipment, the resulting book values would approximate market values.

The goodwill on Company C's balance sheet resulted from capitalizing advertising costs during the company's first year in business.

In purchasing a business, Ms. Holt will buy its tangible assets, including the accounts receivable but not including cash; and she will pay what she thinks is fair market value. She will assume the liabilities of the business and will pay for goodwill measured at four times average annual earnings in excess of a 10% return on net tangible assets, based on first-in, first-out inventories and straight-line depreciation.

Prepare schedules showing (a) the net tangible assets of each company based on first-in, first-out inventories and straight-line depreciation; (b) corrected average net incomes based on first-in, first-out inventories and straight-line depreciation; (c) the calculation of each company's goodwill; and (d) the price Ms. Holt will pay for each company.

ANALYTICAL AND REVIEW PROBLEMS

Problem 11–1 A&R   Susan's Saddlery traded in an old stitching machine for a new heavy-duty automated model. The following data are available:

Old machine—cost $4,200*
Accumulated depreciation 2,800
List price of new model 7,900
Amount paid with trade-in 6,900
Expected life of 10 years with a $600 residual value. Susan's uses straight-line depreciation.

   * Market value at time of trade-in = $800

Required:

1. Prepare the journal entry to record the purchase of the new machine.
2. Using the data above, explain why it is important to current and future

periods to determine the proper "cost" for assets subject to depreciation particularly when trade-ins are involved.

Problem 11–2
A&R

The Machinery and the Accumulated Depreciation accounts in the ledger of Seneca Stamping Company contain the following entries:

Machinery account:

Debits

Prior to December 31, 19A, Machines No. 1, 2, 3, and 4 at $6,000	$72,000
May 3, 19B, Machine No. 5	24,000
August 30, 19B, Machine No. 6	30,000

Credits

August 31, Machine No. 2	10,800
September 30, Machine No. 4	9,600

Accumulated Depreciation-Machinery account:

Debits

No entries

Credits

Prior to December 31, 19A	$30,600
May 3, 19B	1,125
August 30, 19B	3,000
September 30, 19B	3,375

The following events took place during 19B:

a. Machine No. 5 replaced Machine No. 1 which became obsolete and was removed from the premises at no cost to the company. Accumulated depreciation on Machine No. 1 on December 31, 19A, amounted to $8,400. Machine No. 5 was purchased for $24,000 cash.

b. Machine No. 2 was traded in on Machine No. 6 costing $30,000. The fair market value of Machine No. 2, on August 30, was $3,600 and the accumulated depreciation on December 31, 19A, amounted to $3,600.

c. Machine No. 4 was totally destroyed by fire on September 30. Accumulated depreciation on this machine on December 31, 19A, amounted to $6,000. The machine was insured and Seneca received $9,600 from the insurance company.

The company uses straight-line depreciation, four-year service life with no salvage value and computes depreciation to the nearest month.

Required:

1. Give the probable entries that were made by Seneca's accountant.
2. Give the entries that you would make (assume that all gains and losses are material).

Problem 11–3
A&R

The following data are taken from the financial statements of Superior Company, Limited:

	198A	198B	198C	198D
Total assets, December 31	$420,000	$440,000	$450,000	$550,000
Total liabilities, December 31	60,000	80,000	70,000	105,000
Net income	48,000	53,000	57,000	62,000

Additional information indicates that $100,000 was spent on a new plant completed in November of 198D and currently undergoing pre-production testing.

You have been asked by a client to determine the value of the business. Your investigation indicates that the asset values reflected in the statements are sound values and that the normal rate of earnings for the industry is 12%.

Required:

Determine the value of the business on the assumption that excess earnings are to be capitalized at 25%.

**Problem 11–4
A&R**

Part 1. Thorne has been depreciating equipment over a 20-year life on a straight-line basis. The equipment cost $68,000 and has an estimated residual value of $8,000. On the basis of experience, since acquisition on January 2, five years ago, management has decided that a total life of 14 years instead of 20 years is more appropriate, with no change in residual value. The change is to be effective January 1 of the fifth year.

Required:

Prepare the December 31 adjusting entry to recognize depreciation expense for the fifth year. Show calculations.

Part 2. Thorne discovered during the year that the cost of an operational asset purchased on January 3, three years before January of the current year, was debited to operating expenses. The asset cost $25,000 and was estimated to have a five-year service life with no residual value. The company uses the diminishing-balance method of depreciation at twice the straight-line rate for assets of this nature.

Required:

Compute the understatement/overstatement of net income for each of the three years as a result of the error.

**Problem 11–5
A&R**

Interprovincial Oil Company drilled 10 oil wells at an average cost of $5,000,000 each. Four of the oil wells were found to be "producers," with estimated total reserves of 10,000,000 barrels, while the remaining six were "dry." Interprovincial's experience was representative of the industry. The same year 1,000,000 barrels of crude were pumped.

Accountant A argues that the following entries are proper for the recording of the above:

Oil wells	50,000,000	
Cash (or Payables)		50,000,000
Depletion expense	5,000,000	
Accumulated depletion—oil wells		5,000,000

Accountant B argues that the entries should be:

Oil wells	20,000,000	
Loss on drilling of dry wells	30,000,000	
Cash (Payables)		50,000,000
Depletion expense	2,000,000	
Accumulated depletion—oil wells		2,000,000

Required:

You have been asked to arbitrate the case. Present your supported views.

Accounting for Equities: Liabilities and Partners' Equities

PART FOUR

Current and Long-Term Liabilities

12

After studying Chapter 12, you should be able to:

Explain the difference between current and long-term liabilities.

Explain the meaning of definite and estimated liabilities.

Explain the difference between liabilities and contingent liabilities.

Record transactions involving liabilities such as property taxes payable, product warranties, and short-term notes payable.

Calculate the present value of a sum of money to be received a number of periods in the future or to be received periodically.

Account for long-term noninterest-bearing notes payable and for capital and operating leases.

Define or explain the words and phrases listed in the chapter Glossary.

Liabilities have been introduced in previous chapters as one of the three elements of the accounting equation (Assets = Liabilities + Owners' Equity). Examples of liabilities that have been discussed include accounts payable, notes payable, wages payable, and unearned revenues.

Liabilities are examined more closely in this chapter, which explains how liabilities are defined, classified, and measured. Several types of liabilities are considered. They include property taxes payable, product warranties, single-payment notes payable, and leases. Contingent liabilities are also discussed. An important topic in this chapter is present value, which is a concept that is used in measuring many liabilities. Payroll liabilities are examined in Chapter 13, and in Chapter 17 installment notes payable and bonds payable are discussed.

THE DEFINITION AND CLASSIFICATION OF LIABILITIES

Liabilities are obligations that require the future payment of assets or performance of services. Not every expected future payment is a liability. To qualify as a liability, the obligation to make a future payment must have resulted from past transactions. Because liabilities result from past transactions, they normally are enforceable as legal claims against the enterprise.

Current and Long-Term Liabilities

CURRENT LIABILITIES.　A business typically has several kinds of liabilities, which are classified as either current or long-term liabilities. **Current liabilities** are debts or other obligations the liquidation of which is expected to require the use of existing current assets or the creation of other current liabilities.[1] Current liabilities are due within one year of the balance sheet date or the operating cycle of the business, whichever is longer. Accounts payable, short-term notes payable, wages payable, dividends payable, product warranty liabilities, payroll and other taxes payable, and unearned revenues are common examples of current liabilities.

PROPERTY TAXES PAYABLE

A variety of governmental authorities such as cities and school districts levy taxes on property. However, the exact amount of the tax may not become known until the year is partially over. For example, the 198A tax to be paid on each item of property may not be fixed in amount

---

[1] *CICA Handbook* (Toronto: The Canadian Institute of Chartered Accountants), par. 1510.03.

until September 198A. And the tax may not be due perhaps until October 198A. Thus, if financial statements are prepared monthly, the tax expense must be estimated when statements are prepared for January through August.

For example, throughout 198B, a company owns property that has been assessed by the city as having a valuation of $400,000 for property tax purposes. The tax on the property during the previous year (198A) was $11,400. In preparing monthly financial statements during 198B, before the actual tax is known, the company estimates a monthly tax expense of $11,400/12 = $950. Until the 198B tax becomes definite, the company will make monthly adjusting entries as follows:

198B Jan.	31	Property Taxes Expense	950.00	
		Estimated Property Taxes Payable		950.00
		To record estimated property taxes for the month of January.		

In September 198B, the city announces that the tax levy for 198B will be $3.00 per $100 of assessed valuation. Now, the company calculates the actual 198B tax as (400,000/$100) × $3.00 = $12,000, which is $1,000 per month. For the first eight months (January through August), the estimated tax was less than the actual tax by $50 × 8 = $400. This may be recorded at the end of September along with the $1,000 monthly tax, as follows:

Sept.	31	Property Taxes Expense	1,400.00	
		Estimated Property Taxes Payable		1,400.00
		To record property taxes for the month of September and to correct for $50 estimate error during first eight months.		

LONG-TERM LIABILITIES. Obligations that will not require the use of existing current assets because they do not mature within one year (or one operating cycle, whichever is longer) are classified as *long-term liabilities*. Examples of long-term liabilities include leases, long-term notes payable, product warranty liabilities, and bonds payable. Note that many liabilities may be either current or long-term. The critical difference is the question of whether or not payment is to be made within one year or the current operating cycle of the business, whichever is longer.

Definite versus Estimated Liabilities

Three important questions concerning liabilities are: Who is to be paid? When is payment due? How much is to be paid? In many situations, the answers to these three questions are immediately determined at the time the liability is incurred. For example, an account payable may be for precisely $100, payable to J. J. Dow, and due on August 15, 1988. This type of liability is definite with respect to all three questions.

WHEN THE IDENTITY OF THE CREDITOR IS UNCERTAIN. Other types of liabilities may be indefinite with respect to one or more of the three questions. For example, in the case of dividends payable, the amount to be paid and the due date are definite. The question of who is to be paid, however, is not answerable until after the date of record. Even though the identity of the creditor may be uncertain, there is no doubt that the obligation is real and a liability should be recognized.

WHEN THE DUE DATE IS UNCERTAIN. An example of a liability with an uncertain due date is unearned legal fees that a lawyer accepts in return for the obligation to provide services to a client upon call. In this case, the amount of the liability is known. And the client for whom services are to be provided is also known. However, the question of when the services are to be performed is not definite. Usually, such arrangements are short-term and are classified as current liabilities.

WHEN THE AMOUNT TO BE PAID IS UNCERTAIN. When an obligation definitely exists but the amount to be paid is uncertain, the obligation is called an *estimated liability*. Two important examples of estimated liabilities are property taxes and product warranties.

When the annual tax is paid at the end of October 198B, the entry to record the payment is:

Oct.	31	Property Taxes Expense (Oct.)	1,000.00	
		Prepaid Property Taxes (Nov. and Dec.)	2,000.00	
		Estimated Property Taxes Payable	9,000.00	
		Cash		12,000.00
		To pay property tax for 198B.		

PRODUCT WARRANTY LIABILITIES

Another example of an estimated liability is product warranty liability. Most companies provide warranties or guarantees for their products. A *product warranty* is a promise to the customer; the promise obligates the seller or manufacturer for a limited period of time to pay for items such as replacement parts or repair costs if the product breaks or fails to perform. For example, an automobile may be sold with a warranty that covers the mechanical parts for a period of one year or 12,000 kilometres, whichever comes first. The warranty may also include labour costs to install replacement parts.

When a product with a warranty is sold, the *matching principle* requires that all expenses to produce the sale be recorded in the same period as the sale. Therefore, the expense of the warranty must be recognized at the time of the sale. Since the exact amount of expense is not known at the time of the sale, the amount must be estimated based on past experience.

Consider the example of a used auto that is sold with a one-year or 12,000-kilometre warranty. The warranty covers mechanical parts, but the customer must pay for labour charges. Suppose the auto was sold on September 1, 198A, at a price of $16,000. Past experience shows that warranty expense runs 2% of the sales price. The entry to record the expense is:

Sept.	1	Warranty Expense	320.00	
		Estimated Warranty Liability		320.00
		$16,000 × 0.02 = $320.		

Now suppose the customer has a problem with the car and returns it for warranty repairs on January 9, 198B. The auto dealer performs the warranty work by replacing parts that cost $90 and charging the customer $110 for labour. The entry to record the warranty work and the customer's payment are as follows:

Jan.	9	Cash	110.00	
		Estimated Warranty Liability	90.00	
		Auto Parts Inventory		90.00
		Service Revenue		110.00
		To record warranty work and service revenue.		

What happens if the total warranty costs actually turn out to be different than the estimated $320 amount? On any given sale, some difference is very likely. Over the longer term, management must monitor warranty costs to be sure that 2% is the best estimate. When continued experience shows that warranty costs have changed, the percentage should be modified.

CONTINGENT LIABILITIES

Contingent liabilities were discussed in Chapter 8 when discounted notes receivable were presented as an example of contingent liabilities. Contingent liabilities are not existing obligations and, therefore, are not recorded in the books as liabilities. However, the *full disclosure principle* requires that contingent liabilities be disclosed in the financial statements or in footnotes.

What Distinguishes Liabilities from Contingent Liabilities?

Contingent liabilities become real liabilities only if some uncertain event takes place. For example, discounted notes receivable are contingent liabilities that become real liabilities only if the original signers of the notes fail to pay them.

Are product warranties a liability or contingent liability? A product warranty requires service or payment only if the product fails. That sounds like a contingent liability. However, if a contingency is probable and if the liability can be reasonably estimated, it should be recorded in the books as a liability. Most product warranties are real liabilities because the failure of some percentage of the products sold is probable and past experience allows a reasonable estimate of the amount of the liability.

What Are Other Examples of Contingent Liabilities?

POTENTIAL LEGAL CLAIMS. In today's legal environment, many companies may find themselves being sued for damages for a variety of reasons. Until such lawsuits are settled, the potential claims of the plaintiffs are contingent liabilities of the defendant.

DEBT GUARANTIES. Sometimes a company will guarantee the payment of a supplier, customer, or other company's debt, usually by cosigning the note payable of the other company. When this is done, the guarantor is contingently liable for the debt of the other company.

SHORT-TERM NOTES PAYABLE

Another current liability that requires further attention is short-term notes payable. Short-term notes payable sometimes arise in gaining an extension of time in which to pay an account payable. They frequently arise in borrowing from a bank.

Note Given to Secure a Time Extension on an Account

A note payable may be given to secure an extension of time in which to pay an account payable. For example, Brock Company cannot pay its past-due, $600 account with Ajax Company, and Ajax Company has agreed to accept Brock Company's 60-day, 12%, $600 note in granting an extension on the due date of the debt. Brock Company will record the issuance of the note as follows:

Aug.	23	Accounts Payable—Ajax Company	600.00	
		Notes Payable		600.00
		Give a 60-day, 12% note to extend the due date on the amount owed.		

Observe that the note does not pay the debt. It merely changes it from an account payable to a note payable. Ajax Company should prefer the note to the account because in case of default and a lawsuit to collect, the note is written evidence of the debt and its amount.

When the note becomes due, Brock Company will give Ajax Company a cheque for $612.43 and record the payment of the note and its interest with an entry like this:

Oct.	25	Notes Payable	600.00	
		Interest Expense	12.43	
		Cash		612.43
		Paid our note with interest.		

Borrowing from a Bank

In lending money, banks distinguish between **loans** and **discounts.** In case of a loan, the bank collects interest when the loan is repaid. In a **discount,** it deducts the precalculated interest at the time the loan is made. In recent years the practice of discounting noninterest-bearing notes has returned. Some banks, however, refer to the practice as "deducting the precalculated interest from the face value of the note." Whatever the term used, the effect and accounting is the same. To illustrate loans and discounts, assume that H. A. Green wishes to borrow approximately $2,000 for 60 days at the prevailing 15% rate of interest.

A LOAN. In a loan transaction, the bank will lend Green $2,000 in exchange for a signed promissory note. The note will read: "Sixty days after date I promise to pay $2,000 with interest at 15%." Green will record the transaction as follows:

Sept.	10	Cash	2,000.00	
		Notes Payable...........................		2,000.00
		Gave the bank a 60-day, 15% note.		

When the note and interest are paid, Green makes this entry:

Nov.	12	Notes Payable	2,000.00	
		Interest Expense	51.78	
		Cash...................................		2,051.78
		Paid our 60-day, 15% note.		

Observe that in a loan transaction, the interest is paid at the time the loan is repaid.

A DISCOUNT.   If it is the practice of Green's bank to deduct interest at the time a loan is made, the bank will discount Green's $2,000 note. If it discounts the note at 15% for 63 days, it will deduct from the face amount of the note 63 days' interest at 15%, which is $51.78, and will give Green the difference, $1,948.22. The $51.78 of deducted interest is called *bank discount,* and the $1,948.22 are the **proceeds** of the discounted note. Green will record the transaction as follows:

Sept.	10	Cash	1,948.22	
		Interest Expense	51.78	
		Notes Payable...........................		2,000.00
		Discounted our $2,000 note payable at 15%.		

When the note matures, Green is required to pay the bank just the face amount of the note, $2,000, and Green will record the transaction like this:

Nov.	12	Notes Payable	2,000.00	
		Cash...................................		2,000.00
		Paid our discounted note payable.		

Since the precalculated interest is deducted in a discount transaction at the time the loan is made, the note used in such a transaction must state that only the principal amount is to be repaid at maturity. Such a note may read: "Sixty days after date I promise to pay $2,000 with no interest," and is commonly called a noninterest-bearing note. However, banks are not in business to lend money interest free. Interest is paid in a discount transaction. However, since it is deducted at the time the loan is made, the note must state that no additional interest is to be collected at maturity. Nevertheless, interest is collected in a discount transaction and at a rate slightly higher than in a loan transaction at the same stated interest rate. For example, in this instance, Green paid $51.78 for the use of $1,948.22 for 63 days, which was at an effective interest rate just a little in excess of 15% on the $1,948.22 received.

END-OF-PERIOD ADJUSTMENTS

Accrued Interest Expense

Interest accrues daily on all interest-bearing notes. Consequently, if any notes payable are outstanding at the end of an accounting period, the accrued interest should be recorded. For example, a company gave its bank a $4,000, 60-day, 13.5% note on December 16 to borrow that amount of money. If the company's accounting period ends on December 31, by then 15 days' or $22.19 interest has accrued on this note. It may be recorded with this adjusting entry:

Dec.	31	Interest Expense	22.19	
		Interest Payable		22.19
		To record accrued interest on a note payable.		

The adjusting entry causes the $22.19 accrued interest to appear on the income statement as an expense of the period benefiting from 15 days' use of the money. It also causes the interest payable to appear on the balance sheet as a current liability.

When the note matures in the next accounting period, its payment may be recorded as follows:

Feb.	17	Notes Payable	4,000.00	
		Interest Payable	22.19	
		Interest Expense	71.02	
		Cash..................................		4,093.21
		Paid a $4,000 note and its interest.		

Interest on this note for 63 days is $93.21. In the illustrated entry, the $93.21 is divided between the interest accrued at the end of the previous period, $22.19, and interest applicable to the current period, $71.02. Some accountants avoid the necessity of making this division by reversing the accrued interest adjusting entry as a last step in their end-of-period work.

Discount on Notes Payable

When a note payable is discounted at a bank, interest based on the principal of the note is deducted and the interest is normally recorded as interest expense. Furthermore, since most such notes run for 30, 60, or 90 days, the interest is usually an expense of the period in which it is deducted. However, when the time of a note extends beyond a single accounting period, the precalculated interest deducted from the principal of the note should be debited to a Discount on Notes Payable account and an adjusting entry is required at year-end. For example, on December 11, 198A, a company discounted at 15% its own $6,000, 60-day, noninterest-bearing note payable. It recorded the transaction as follows:

198A			
Dec.	11	Cash	5,844.66	
		Discount on Notes Payable	155.34	
		Notes Payable...........................		6,000.00
		Discounted our noninterest-bearing, 60-day note at 15%.		

If this company operates with accounting periods that end each December 31, 20 days' interest on this note, or $49.31 of the $155.34 discount, is an expense of the 198A accounting period and 43 days' interest or $106.03 is an expense of 198B. Consequently, if revenues and expenses are matched, the company must make the following December 31, 198A, adjusting entry:

198A			
Dec.	31	Interest Expense	49.31	
		Discount on Notes Payable...............		49.31
		To record interest expense applicable to 198B.		

The adjusting entry removes from the Discount on Notes Payable account the $49.31 of interest that is applicable to 198A. It leaves in the account the $106.03 that is applicable to 198B. The $49.31 then appears on the 198A income statement as an expense, and the $106.03 appears on the December 31, 198A, balance sheet. If this is the only note the company has outstanding, the $106.03 is deducted on the balance sheet as follows:

Current liabilities:		
Notes payable	$6,000.00	
Less discount on notes payable ...	106.03	$5,893.97

When the adjusted discount on notes payable is subtracted as a contra liability, the net liability on the balance sheet shows the amount received in discounting the note plus the accrued interest on the note to the balance sheet date. In this example, $5,844.66 was received in discounting the note and accrued interest on the note is $49.31. Together they total $5,893.97, which is the net liability to the bank on December 31.

THE CONCEPT OF PRESENT VALUE

The concept of present value enters into many financing and investing decisions and any resulting liabilities. Consequently, an understanding of present value is important for all students of business. The concept is based on the idea that the right to receive, say, $1 a year from today is worth somewhat less than $1 today. Or stated another way, $1 to be received a year hence has a *present value* of somewhat less than $1. How much less depends on how much can be earned on invested funds. If, say, a 10% annual return can be earned, the expectation of receiving $1 a year hence has a present value of $0.9091. This can be verified as follows: $0.9091 invested today to earn 10% annually will earn $0.09091 in one year, and when the $0.09091 earned is added to the $0.9091 invested—

Investment	$0.9091
Earnings	0.09091
Total	$1.00001

the investment plus the earnings equal $1.00001, which rounds to the $1 expected.

Likewise, the present value of $1 to be received two years hence is $0.8265 if a 10% compound annual return is expected. This also can be verified as follows: $0.8265 invested to earn 10% compounded annually will earn $0.08265 the first year it is invested, and when the $0.08265 earned is added to the $0.8265 invested—

Investment	$0.8265
First year earnings	0.08265
End-of-year-one amount	$0.90915

the investment plus the first year's earnings total $0.90915. And during the second year, this $0.90915 will earn $0.090915, which when added to the end-of-first-year amount—

End-of-year-one amount	$0.90915
Second-year earnings	0.090915
End-of-year-two amount	$1.000065

equals $1.000065, which rounds to the $1 expected at the end of the second year.

Present Value Tables

The **present value** of $1 to be received any number of years in the future can be calculated by using the formula, $1/(1 + i)^n$. The i is the interest rate, and n is the number of years to the expected receipt. However, the formula need not be used, since tables showing present values computed with the formula at various interest rates are readily available. Table 12–1, with its amounts rounded to four decimal places, is such a table. (Four decimal places would not be sufficiently accurate for some uses but will suffice here.)

Observe in Table 12–1 that the first amount in the 10% column is the 0.9091 used in the previous section to introduce the concept of present value. The 0.9091 in the 10% column means that the expectation of receiving $1 a year hence when discounted for one period, in this case one year, at 10%, has a present value of $0.9091. Then, note that the second amount in the 10% column is the 0.8265 previously used, which means that the expectation of receiving $1 two years hence, discounted at 10%, has a present value of $0.8265.

Using a Present Value Table

To demonstrate the use of the *present value table*, Table 12–1, assume that a company has an opportunity to invest $55,000 in a project, the risks of which it feels justify a 12% compound return. The investment will return $20,000 at the end of the first year, $25,000 at the end of

Table 12–1   Present Value of $1 at Compound Interest

Periods hence	4½%	5%	6%	7%	8%	9%	10%	12%	14%	16%
1	0.9569	0.9524	0.9434	0.9346	0.9259	0.9174	0.9091	0.8929	0.8772	0.8621
2	0.9157	0.9070	0.8900	0.8734	0.8573	0.8417	0.8265	0.7972	0.7695	0.7432
3	0.8763	0.8638	0.8396	0.8163	0.7938	0.7722	0.7513	0.7118	0.6750	0.6407
4	0.8386	0.8227	0.7921	0.7629	0.7350	0.7084	0.6830	0.6355	0.5921	0.5523
5	0.8025	0.7835	0.7473	0.7130	0.6806	0.6499	0.6209	0.5674	0.5194	0.4761
6	0.7679	0.7462	0.7050	0.6663	0.6302	0.5963	0.5645	0.5066	0.4556	0.4104
7	0.7348	0.7107	0.6651	0.6228	0.5835	0.5470	0.5132	0.4524	0.3996	0.3538
8	0.7032	0.6768	0.6274	0.5820	0.5403	0.5019	0.4665	0.4039	0.3506	0.3050
9	0.6729	0.6446	0.5919	0.5439	0.5003	0.4604	0.4241	0.3606	0.3075	0.2630
10	0.6439	0.6139	0.5584	0.5084	0.4632	0.4224	0.3855	0.3220	0.2697	0.2267
11	0.6162	0.5847	0.5268	0.4751	0.4289	0.3875	0.3505	0.2875	0.2366	0.1954
12	0.5897	0.5568	0.4970	0.4440	0.3971	0.3555	0.3186	0.2567	0.2076	0.1685
13	0.5643	0.5303	0.4688	0.4150	0.3677	0.3262	0.2897	0.2292	0.1821	0.1452
14	0.5400	0.5051	0.4423	0.3878	0.3405	0.2993	0.2633	0.2046	0.1597	0.1252
15	0.5167	0.4810	0.4173	0.3625	0.3152	0.2745	0.2394	0.1827	0.1401	0.1079
16	0.4945	0.4581	0.3937	0.3387	0.2919	0.2519	0.2176	0.1631	0.1229	0.0930
17	0.4732	0.4363	0.3714	0.3166	0.2703	0.2311	0.1978	0.1456	0.1078	0.0802
18	0.4528	0.4155	0.3503	0.2959	0.2503	0.2120	0.1799	0.1300	0.0946	0.0691
19	0.4333	0.3957	0.3305	0.2765	0.2317	0.1945	0.1635	0.1161	0.0830	0.0596
20	0.4146	0.3769	0.3118	0.2584	0.2146	0.1784	0.1486	0.1037	0.0728	0.0514

the second year, $30,000 at the end of the third year, and nothing thereafter. Will the project return the original investment plus the 12% demanded? The calculations of Illustration 12–1, which use the first three amounts in the 12% column of Table 12–1, indicate that it will. In Illustration 12–1, the expected returns in the second column are multiplied by the present value amounts in the third column to determine the present values in the last column. Since the total of the present values exceeds the

Illustration 12–1

Years hence	Expected returns	Present value of $1 at 12%	Present value of expected returns
1........	$20,000	0.8929	$17,858
2........	$25,000	0.7972	19,930
3........	$30,000	0.7118	21,354
Total present value of the returns			$59,142
Less investment required			55,000
Excess over 12% demanded			$ 4,142

required investment by $4,142, the project will return the $55,000 investment, plus a 12% return thereon, and $4,142 extra.

In Illustration 12–1, the present value of each year's return was separately calculated, after which the present values were added to determine
their total. Separately calculating the present value of each of several
returns from an investment is necessary when the returns are unequal,
as in this example. However, in cases where the periodic returns are
equal, there are shorter ways of calculating the sum of their present
values. For instance, suppose a $17,500 investment will return $5,000
at the end of each year in its five-year life and an investor wants to
know the present value of these returns, discounted at 12%. In this
case, the periodic returns are equal, and a short way to determine their
total present value at 12% is to add the present values of $1 at 12%
for periods one through five (from Table 12–1) as follows—

0.8929
0.7972
0.7118
0.6355
0.5674
3.6048

and then to multiply $5,000 by the total. The $18,024 result ($5,000
× 3.6048 = $18,024) is the same as would be obtained by calculating
the present value of each year's return and adding the present values.
However, although the result is the same either way, the method demonstrated here requires four fewer multiplications.

Present Value of $1 Received Periodically for a Number of Periods

Table 12–2 is based on the idea demonstrated in the previous paragraph.
To summarize, the present value of a series of equal returns to be received
at periodic intervals is nothing more than the sum of the present values
of the individual returns. Note the amount on the table's fifth line in
the 12% column. It is the same 3.6048 amount arrived at in the previous
section by adding the first five present values of $1 at 12%. All the
amounts shown in Table 12–2 could be arrived at by adding amounts
found in Table 12–1. However, there would be some slight variations
due to rounding.

When available, Table 12–2 is used to determine the present value
of a series of equal amounts to be received at periodic intervals. For
example, what is the present value of a series of 10 $1,000 amounts,
with one $1,000 amount to be received at the end of each of 10 successive
years, discounted at 8%? To determine the answer, go down the 8%
column to the amount opposite 10 periods (years in this case). It is

Table 12–2   Present Value of $1 Received Periodically for a Number of Periods

Periods hence	4½%	5%	6%	7%	8%	9%	10%	12%	14%	16%
1	0.9569	0.9524	0.9434	0.9346	0.9259	0.9174	0.9091	0.8929	0.8772	0.8621
2	1.8727	1.8594	1.8334	1.8080	1.7833	1.7591	1.7355	1.6901	1.6467	1.6052
3	2.7490	2.7232	2.6730	2.6243	2.5771	2.5313	2.4869	2.4018	2.3216	2.2459
4	3.5875	3.5460	3.4651	3.3872	3.3121	3.2397	3.1699	3.0374	2.9137	2.7982
5	4.3900	4.3295	4.2124	4.1002	3.9927	3.8897	3.7908	3.6048	3.4331	3.2743
6	5.1579	5.0757	4.9173	4.7665	4.6229	4.4859	4.3553	4.1114	3.8887	3.6847
7	5.8927	5.7864	5.5824	5.3893	5.2064	5.0330	4.8684	4.5638	4.2883	4.0386
8	6.5959	6.4632	6.2098	5.9713	5.7466	5.5348	5.3349	4.9676	4.6389	4.3436
9	7.2688	7.1078	6.8017	6.5152	6.2469	5.9953	5.7590	5.3283	4.9464	4.6065
10	7.9127	7.7217	7.3601	7.0236	6.7101	6.4177	6.1446	5.6502	5.2161	4.8332
11	8.5289	8.3064	7.8869	7.4987	7.1390	6.8052	6.4951	5.9377	5.4527	5.0286
12	9.1186	8.8633	8.3838	7.9427	7.5361	7.1607	6.8137	6.1944	5.6603	5.1971
13	9.6829	9.3936	8.8527	8.3577	7.9038	7.4869	7.1034	6.4236	5.8424	5.3423
14	10.2228	9.8986	9.2950	8.7455	8.2442	7.7862	7.3667	6.6282	6.0021	5.4675
15	10.7395	10.3797	9.7123	9.1079	8.5595	8.0607	7.6061	6.8109	6.1422	5.5755
16	11.2340	10.8378	10.1059	9.4467	8.8514	8.3126	7.8237	6.9740	6.2651	5.6685
17	11.7072	11.2741	10.4773	9.7632	9.1216	8.5436	8.0216	7.1196	6.3729	5.7487
18	12.1600	11.6896	10.8276	10.0591	9.3719	8.7556	8.2014	7.2497	6.4674	5.8179
19	12.5933	12.0853	11.1581	10.3356	9.6036	8.9501	8.3649	7.3658	6.5504	5.8775
20	13.0079	12.4622	11.4699	10.5940	9.8182	9.1286	8.5136	7.4694	6.6231	5.9288

6.7101, and $6.7101 is the present value of $1 to be received annually at the end of each of 10 years, discounted at 8%. Therefore, the present value of the 10 $1,000 amounts is 1,000 times $6.7101, or $6710.10.

Discount Periods Less than a Year in Length

In the examples thus far, the discount periods have been measured in intervals one year in length. Often discount periods are based on intervals shorter than a year. For instance, although interest rates on corporation bonds are usually quoted on an annual basis, the interest on such bonds is normally paid semiannually. As a result, the present value of the interest to be received on such bonds must be based on interest periods six months in length.

To illustrate a calculation based on six-month interest periods, assume an investor wants to know the present value of the interest that will be received over a period of five years on some corporation bonds. The bonds have a $10,000 par value, and interest is paid on them every six months at a 14% annual rate. Although the interest rate is stated as an annual rate of 14%, it is actually a rate of 7% per six-month interest period. Consequently, the investor will receive $10,000 times 7% or $700 in interest on these bonds at the end of each six-month interest period. In five years, there are 10 such periods. Therefore, if these 10 receipts of $700 each are to be discounted at the interest rate of the bonds, to determine their present value, go down the 7% column of Table 12–2 to the amount opposite 10 periods. It is 7.0236, and the present value of the 10 $700 semiannual receipts is 7.0236 times $700, or $4,916.52.

Students who want a more complete exposure to discounting should turn to Supplement 12–A at the end of this chapter. Supplement 12–A expands the discussion of how present value tables are developed and explains the development of future value tables. Large present value and future value tables are included with numerous exercises related to discounting.

EXCHANGING A NOTE FOR A PLANT ASSET

When a relatively high-cost plant asset is purchased, particularly if the credit period is long, a note is sometimes given in exchange for the purchased asset. If the amount of the note is approximately equal to the cash price for the asset and the interest on the note is at approximately the prevailing rate, the transaction is recorded as follows:

Feb.	12	Store Equipment	4,500.00	
		Notes Payable		4,500.00
		Exchanged a $4,500, three-year, 16% note payable for a refrigerated display case.		

A note given in exchange for a plant asset has two elements, which may or may not be stipulated in the note. They are (1) a dollar amount equivalent to the bargained cash price of the asset and (2) an interest factor to compensate the supplier for the use of the funds that otherwise would have been received in a cash sale. Consequently, when a note is exchanged for a plant asset and the face amount of the note approximately equals the cash price of the asset and the note's interest rate is at or near the prevailing rate, the asset may be recorded at the face amount of the note as in the previous illustration.

Notes That Have an Unreasonable or No Stated Interest Rate

Sometimes no interest rate is stated on a note, or the interest rate is unreasonable, or the face amount of the note materially differs from the cash price for the asset. In such cases, the asset should be recorded at its cash price or at the present value of the note, whichever is more clearly determinable. In such a situation, to record the asset at the face amount of the note would cause the asset, the liability, and interest expense to be misstated. Furthermore, the misstatements could be material in the case of a long-term note.

To illustrate a situation in which a note having no interest rate stated is exchanged for a plant asset, assume that on January 2, 198A, a noninterest-bearing, five-year, $10,000 note payable is exchanged for a factory machine, the cash price of which is not readily determinable. If the prevailing rate for interest on the day of the exchange is 14%, the present value of the note on that day is $5,194 [based on the fifth amount in the 14% column of Table 12–1 ($10,000 × 0.5194 = $5,194)], and the exchange should be recorded as follows:

198A				
Jan.	2	Factory Machinery	5,194.00	
		Discount on Notes Payable	4,806.00	
		Long-Term Notes Payable		10,000.00
		Exchanged a five-year, noninterest-bearing note for a machine.		

The $5,194 debit amount in the entry is the present value of the note on the day of the exchange. It is also the cost of the machine and is the amount to be used in calculating depreciation and any future loss or gain on the machine's sale or exchange. The entry's notes payable and discount amounts together measure the liability resulting from the transaction. They should appear on a balance sheet prepared immediately after the exchange as follows:

Long-term liabilities:
    Long-term notes payable $10,000
        Less unamortized discount based on the 14% interest
          rate prevailing on the date of issue 4,806 $5,194

Amortizing the Discount on a Note Payable

The $4,806 discount is a contra liability and also the interest element of the transaction. Column 3 of Illustration 12–2 shows the portions of the $4,806 that should be amortized and charged to Interest Expense at the end of each of the five years in the life of the note.

The first year's amortization entry is:

198A			
Dec.	31	Interest Expense	727.00	
		Discount on Notes Payable		727.00
		To amortize a portion of the discount on our long-term note.		

The $727 amortized is interest at 14% on the note's $5,194 value on the day it was exchanged for the machine. [The $727 is rounded to the nearest full dollar, as are all the Column 3 amounts ($5,194 × 14% = $727.16).]

Posting the amortization entry causes the note to appear on the December 31, 198A, balance sheet as follows:

Long-term liabilities:
    Long-term notes payable $10,000
    Less unamortized discount based on the 14% interest
        rate prevailing on the date of issue 4,079 $5,921

Compare the net amount at which the note is carried on the December 31, 198A, balance sheet with the net amount shown for the note on the balance sheet prepared on its date of issue. Observe that the *carrying amount of the note* increased $727 between the two dates. The $727 is the amount of discount amortized and charged to Interest Expense at the end of 198A.

At the end of 198B and each succeeding year, the remaining amounts of discount shown in Column 3 of Illustration 12–2 should be amortized and charged to Interest Expense. This will cause the carrying amount of the note to increase each year by the amount of discount amortized

Illustration 12–2

Year	Beginning-of-year carrying amount	Discount to be amortized each year	Unamortized discount at the end of year	End-of-year carrying amount
198A	$5,194	$ 727	$4,079	$ 5,921
198B	5,921	929	3,250	6,750
198C	6,750	945	2,305	7,695
198D	7,695	1,077	1,228	8,772
198E	8,772	1,228	–0–	10,000

that year and to reach $10,000, the note's maturity value, at the end of the fifth year. Payment of the note may then be recorded as follows:

```
198F
Jan.   2  Long-Term Notes Payable .................  10,000.00
              Cash .................................              10,000.00
          Paid our long-term noninterest-bearing note.
```

Now return to Illustration 12–2. Each end-of-year carrying amount in the last column is determined by subtracting the end-of-year unamortized discount from the $10,000 face amount of the note. For example, $10,000 − $4,079 = $5,921. Each beginning-of-year carrying amount is the same as the previous year's end-of-year amount. The amount of discount to be amortized each year is determined by multiplying the beginning-of-year carrying amount by the 14% interest rate prevailing at the time of the exchange. For example, $5,921 × 14% = $829 (rounded). Each end-of-year amount of unamortized discount is the discount remaining after subtracting the discount amortized that year. For example, $4,806 − $727 = $4,079.

In the balance sheet at the end of each year, the carrying amount of a note payable must be divided into two parts. The portion to be paid during the next year must be shown as a current liability, with the remaining portion shown as a long-term liability.

LIABILITIES FROM LEASING

How to Classify Leases

The leasing of plant assets, rather than purchasing them, has increased tremendously in recent years, primarily because leasing does not require a large cash outflow at the time the assets are acquired. Leasing has been called off-balance sheet financing because assets leased under certain conditions do not appear on the balance sheet of the lessee. However, some leases have essentially the same economic consequences as if the lessee secured a loan and purchased the leased asset. Such leases are called *capital leases* or *financing leases.* The *CICA Handbook* recommends that a lease meeting any one of the following criteria is a capital lease.[2]

1. Ownership of the leased asset is transferred to the lessee at the end of the lease period.
2. The lease gives the lessee the option of purchasing the leased asset

---

[2] Ibid., par. 3065.06.

at less than fair value at some point during or at the end of the lease period.

3. The period of the lease is 75% or more of the estimated service life of the leased asset.

4. The present value of the minimum lease payments is 90% or more of the fair value of the leased asset.

A lease that does not meet any one of the four criteria is classified as an *operating lease.*

To illustrate accounting for leases, assume that Alpha Company plans to produce a product requiring the use of a new machine costing approximately $35,000 and having an estimated 10-year life and no salvage value. Alpha Company does not have $35,000 in available cash and is planning to lease the machine as of December 31, 198A. It will lease the machine under one of the following contracts, each of which requires Alpha Company to pay maintenance, taxes, and insurance on the machine: (1) Lease the machine for five years, annual payments of $7,500 payable at the end of each of the five years, the machine to be returned to the lessor at the end of the lease period; (2) Lease the machine for five years, annual payments of $10,000 payable at the end of each of the five years, the machine to become the property of Alpha Company at the end of the lease period.

Accounting for an Operating Lease

If the interest rate available to Alpha Company is 16%, the first lease contract does not meet any of the four criteria stated above. Therefore, it is an operating lease. If Alpha Company chooses this contract, it should make no entry to record the lease contract. However, each annual rental payment should be recorded as follows:

198B				
Dec.	31	Machinery Rentals Expense	7,500.00	
		Cash		7,500.00
		Paid the annual rent on a leased machine.		

Alpha Company should also charge to expense all payments for taxes, insurance, and any repairs to the machine. But since the leased machine was not recorded as an asset, depreciation expense is not recorded. Alpha should also append a footnote to its income statement giving a general description of the leasing arrangements.

Accounting for a Capital Lease

The second lease contract meets the first and fourth criteria of the *CICA Handbook* and is a capital lease. It is in effect a purchase transaction with the lessor company financing the purchase of the machine for Alpha Company. To charge each of the $10,000 lease payments to an expense account would overstate expenses during the first five years of the machine's life and understate expenses during the last five. It would also understate the company's assets and liabilities. Consequently, the *CICA Handbook* recommends that such a lease should be treated as a purchase transaction and be recorded on the lease date at the present value of the lease payments.

RECORDING THE LEASE LIABILITY. If Alpha Company chooses the second lease contract and the interest rate available to Alpha on such contracts is 16% annually, it should (based on the fifth amount in the 16% column of Table 12–2) multiply $10,000 by 3.2743 to arrive at a $32,743 present value for the five lease payments. It should then make this entry:

198A				
Dec.	31	Machinery	32,743.00	
		Discount on Lease Financing	17,257.00	
		Long-Term Lease Liability		50,000.00
		Purchased a machine through a long-term lease contract.		

The $32,743 is the cost of the machine. As with any plant asset, it should be charged off to depreciation expense over the machine's expected service life. Note, however, that the expected service life of a leased asset may be limited to the term of the lease. If the lessee does not have the right to ownership at the end of the lease, and the lease period is less than the asset's expected life, the lease period becomes the useful life of the asset.

REPORTING A LONG-TERM LEASE LIABILITY ON THE BALANCE SHEET. The $17,257 discount is the interest factor in the transaction. The long-term lease liability less the amount of the discount measures the net liability resulting from the purchase. The two items should appear on a balance sheet prepared immediately after the transaction as follows:

Long-term liabilities:		
Long-term lease liability[3]	$50,000	
Less unamortized discount based on the 16% interest rate available on the date of the contract	17,257	$32,743

---

[3] To simplify the illustration, the fact that the first installment on the lease should probably be classified as a current liability is ignored here and should be ignored in the problems at the end of the chapter.

ENTRIES TO RECORD DEPRECIATION, LEASE PAYMENTS, AND INTEREST. If Alpha Company plans to depreciate the machine on a straight-line basis over its 10-year life, it should make the following entries at the end of the first year in the life of the lease:

198B			
Dec.	31	Depreciation Expense, Machinery	3,274.30	
		Accumulated Depreciation, Machinery		3,274.30
		To record depreciation on the machine.		
	31	Long-Term Lease Liability	10,000.00	
		Cash		10,000.00
		Made the annual payment on the lease.		
	31	Interest Expense	5,239.00	
		Discount on Lease Financing		5,239.00
		Amortized a portion of the discount on the lease financing.		

The first two entries need no comment. The $5,239 amortized in the third entry is interest at 16% for one year on the $32,743 beginning-of-year carrying amount of the lease liability ($32,743 × 16% = $5,239). The $5,239 is rounded to the nearest full dollar, as are all amounts in Column 5 of Illustration 12–3.

Posting the entries recording the $10,000 payment and the amortization of the discount causes the *carrying amount of the lease* to appear on the December 31, 198B, balance sheet as follows:

Long-term liabilities:		
Long-term lease liability	$40,000	
Less unamortized discount based on the 16% interest rate prevailing on the date of the contract	12,018	$27,982

Illustration 12–3

Year	Beginning-of-year lease liability	Beginning-of-year unamortized discount	Beginning-of-year carrying amount	Discount to be amortized	Unamortized discount at end of year	End-of-year lease liability	End-of-year carrying amount
198B	$50,000	$17,257	$32,743	$5,239	$12,018	$40,000	$27,982
198C	40,000	12,018	27,982	4,477	7,541	30,000	22,459
198D	30,000	7,541	22,459	3,593	3,948	20,000	16,052
198E	20,000	3,948	16,052	2,568	1,380	10,000	8,620
198F	10,000	1,380	8,620	1,380*	–0–	–0–	–0–

* Adjusted for rounding.

At the end of 198C and each succeeding year thereafter, the remaining amounts in Column 5 of Illustration 12–3 should be amortized. This, together with $10,000 annual payments, will reduce the carrying amount of the lease liability to zero by the end of the fifth year.

Return again to Illustration 12–3, Column 5. Each year's amount of discount to be amortized is determined by multiplying the beginning-of-year carrying amount of the lease liability by 16%. For example, the 198C amount to be amortized is $4,477 ($27,982 × 16% = $4,477 rounded). Likewise, each end-of-year carrying amount is determined by subtracting the end-of-year unamortized discount from the remaining end-of-year lease liability. For example, the December 31, 198C, carrying amount is $30,000 − $7,541 = $22,459.

SUPPLEMENT 12–A

PRESENT AND FUTURE VALUES

AN EXPANSION

The concept of present values was introduced in this chapter and was applied to accounting problems in the chapter. This presentation is designed to supplement the treatment of present values with additional discussion, more complete tables, and additional homework exercises. The appendix also includes the concept of future values.

Present Value of a Single Amount

The present value of a single amount to be received or paid at some future date may be expressed as:

$$p = \frac{f}{(1 + i)^n} \tag{1}$$

where p = present value.
f = future value.
i = rate of interest per period.
n = number of periods.

For example, assume $2.20 is to be received one period from now. This amount will be received because a smaller amount ($2.00) was invested now for one period, at an interest rate of 10%. Using the formula:

$$p = \frac{f}{(1 + i)^n} = \frac{\$2.20}{(1 + .10)^1} = \$2.00$$

Alternatively, assume the present investment of $2.00 is to remain invested for two periods at 10% and the future amount to be received is $2.42. Using the formula:

$$p = \frac{f}{(1 + i)^n} = \frac{\$2.42}{(1 + .10)^2} = \$2.00$$

Note that n (the number of periods) need not be expressed in years. Any period of time such as a day, a month, a quarter, or a year may be used. However, whatever period is used, i (the interest rate) must be for the same period. Thus, if a problem requires that n be expressed in months, then an i of 1% means 1% per month. This means that each month, 1% of the invested amount at the beginning of the month is earned and added to the investment. Another way of expressing this is to say that interest is compounded monthly.

A present value table is designed to show present values for a variety of is (interest rates) and a variety of ns (number of periods). Throughout the table, each present value is based on the assumption that f (the future value) is 1.00. Since the future value is assumed to be 1 (in other words, $f = 1$), the formula to construct a table of present values of a single future amount is as follows:

Since $f = 1$,

$$p = \frac{f}{(1 + i)^n} = \frac{1}{(1 + i)^n}$$

A table of present values of a single future amount often is called a *present value of 1* table. Table 12A–1 on page 520 is such a table.

Future Value of a Single Amount

The formula for the present value of a single amount may be manipulated to solve for the future value of a single amount. Thus, the formula presented above as (1) may be manipulated as follows:

$$p = \frac{f}{(1 + i)^n} \tag{1}$$

multiply both sides of the equation by $(1 + i)^n$,

$$(1 + i)^n \times p = (1 + i)^n \times \frac{f}{(1 + i)^n}$$

cancel the common terms in the numerator and denominator,

$$(1 + i)^n \times p = \cancel{(1 + i)^n} \times \frac{f}{\cancel{(1 + i)^n}}$$

and the result is,

$$(1 + i)^n \times p = f$$

or

$$f = p \times (1 + i)^n \tag{2}$$

For example, assume that \$2.00 is to be invested for one period at an interest rate of 10%. The \$2.00 amount will increase to a future value of \$2.20. Using the formula:

$$f = p \times (1 + i)^n = \$2.00 \times (1 + .10)^1 = \$2.20$$

Alternatively, assume the present investment of \$2.00 is to remain invested for three periods at 10%. The amount to be received three periods hence is \$2.662, and is calculated with the formula as follows:

$$f = p \times (1 + i)^n = \$2.00 \times (1 + .10)^3 = \$2.662$$

A future value table is designed to show future values for a variety of is (interest rates) and a variety of ns (number of periods). Throughout the table, each future value is based on the assumption that p (the present value) is 1.00. Since the present value is assumed to be 1 (in other words, $p = 1$), the formula to construct a table of future values of a single amount is as follows:

Since $p = 1$,

$$f = p(1 + i)^n = (1 + i)^n$$

A table of future values of a single amount is often called a *future value of 1* table. Table 12A–2 on page 521 is such a table.

In Table 12A–2, look at the row where $n = 0$ and observe that regardless of the interest rate, the future value is 1. When $n = 0$, the period of time over which interest is earned is zero. Hence, no interest is earned. The future value is calculated as of the date of the investment. Since the table assumes that the investment is 1, the "future value" on that date is also 1.

Students should also observe that a table showing the present values of 1 and a table showing the future values of 1 contain exactly the same information. Both tables are based on the same equation. That is,

$$p = \frac{f}{(1 + i)^n}$$

is nothing more than a reformulation of $f = p(1 + i)^n$. Both tables reflect the same four variables, p, f, i, and n. Therefore, any problem that can be solved using one of the two tables can also be solved using the other table.

For example, suppose a person invests \$100 for five years and expects to earn 12% per year. How much should the person receive five years hence?

To solve the problem using Table 12A–2, look in the table to find the future value of 1, five periods hence, compounded at 12%. In the table, $f = 1.7623$. Thus,

$$\$100 \times 1.7623 = \$176.23$$

To solve the problem using Table 12A–1, look in the table to find the present value of 1, five periods hence, discounted at 12%. In the table, where $n = 5$, and $i = 12\%$, $p = 0.5674$. Recall that $f = 1$ in the table. This relationship between present value and future value may be expressed as:

$$\frac{p}{f} = \frac{0.5674}{1}$$

This relationship between p and f is the same as in the problem where $100 is to be invested for five years. Thus,

$$\frac{0.5674}{1} \text{ is the same as } \frac{\$100}{f}$$

$$\frac{0.5674}{1} = \frac{\$100}{f}$$

$$0.5674 \times f = \$100 \times 1$$

$$f = \frac{\$100}{0.5674} = \$176.24$$

The $0.01 difference between the two answers ($176.23 and $176.24) occurs only because the numbers in the tables were rounded.

Present Value of an Annuity

A series of equal payments is called an annuity. For example, if a person offers to make three annual payments of $100 each, the person is offering an annuity. The present value of an annuity is defined as the value of the payments one period prior to the first payment. Graphically, this may be presented as follows:

$$\qquad \$100 \qquad\qquad \$100 \qquad\qquad \$100$$

p

To calculate the present value of this annuity, one might calculate the present value of each payment and add them together. For example, assuming an interest rate of 18%, the calculation would be:

$$p = \frac{\$100}{(1 + .18)^1} + \frac{\$100}{(1 + .18)^2} + \frac{\$100}{(1 + .18)^3} = \$217.43$$

Another way of calculating the present value of the annuity is to use Table 12A–1. The calculation appears as follows:

First payment: $p = \$100 \times 0.8475 = \$\ 84.75$
Second payment: $p = \$100 \times 0.7182 = \ \ \ 71.82$
Third payment: $p = \$100 \times 0.6086 = \ \ \ \underline{60.86}$
            Total: $p = \underline{\underline{\$217.43}}$

Another way of using Table 12A–1 to solve the problem is to add the present values of three payments of 1 and multiply the answer times $100. Thus:

From Table 12A–1

$i = 18\%, n = 1, p = \ \ 0.8475$
$i = 18\%, n = 2, p = \ \ 0.7182$
$i = 18\%, n = 3, p = \ \ \underline{0.6086}$
                       2.1743

$2.1743 \times \$100 = \underline{\underline{\$217.43}}$

The easiest way to solve the problem is to use a table that shows the present values of a series of payments. That type of table often is called a **present value of an annuity of 1** table. Table 12A–3 on page 522 is such a table. Look in Table 12A–3 on the row where $n = 3$ and $i = 18\%$ and observe that the present value is 2.1743. Stated in other words, an annuity of 1 for 3 periods, discounted at 18%, is 2.1743.

Although a formula is used to construct a table showing the present values of an annuity,[4] students should understand that the table can be constructed simply by adding together the amounts in a present value of 1 table (such as Table 12A–1). To check your understanding of this, examine Tables 12A–1 and 12A–3 to confirm that the following numbers were drawn from those tables.

From Table 12A–1		*From Table 12A–3*	
$i = 8\%, n = 1$	0.9259	$i = 8\%, n = 1$	0.9259
$i = 8\%, n = 2$	0.8573		
$i = 8\%, n = 3$	0.7938		
$i = 8\%, n = 4$	0.7350		
Total	3.3120	$i = 8\%, n = 4$	3.3121

---

[4] The formula for a table showing the present values of an annuity of 1 is:

$$p = \frac{1 - \dfrac{1}{(1 + i)^n}}{i}$$

The minor difference in the results (3.3120 and 3.3121) occurs only because the numbers in the tables have been rounded.

Future Value of an Annuity

An annuity was previously defined as any series of equal payments. Just as the present value of an annuity may be calculated, so may be the future value of an annuity. The future value of an annuity is defined as the value of the annuity on the date of the final payment. Consider the earlier example of a person who offers to make three annual payments of $100 each. Graphically, the points in time at which the present value and the future value are calculated may be shown as follows:

$100 $100 $100

p   *f*

To calculate the future value of this annuity, one might calculate the future value of each payment and add them together. Assuming an interest rate of 18%, the calculation would be:

$$f = \$100(1 + .18)^2 + \$100(1 + .18)^1 + \$100(1 + .18)^0 = \$357.24$$

Another way of calculating the future value of the annuity is to use Table 12A–2. The calculation appears as follows:

First payment: $f = \$100 \times 1.3924 = \$139.24$
Second payment: $f = \$100 \times 1.1800 = 118.00$
Third payment: $f = \$100 \times 1.0000 = 100.00$
     Total: $f = \$357.24$

In the calculations and the graph above, note that the first payment is made two periods prior to the point at which future value is determined. Therefore, for the first payment, $n = 2$. For the second payment, $n = 1$. Since the third payment occurs on the future value date, $n = 0$.

Instead of adding the future value of each payment, another approach is to add the future values of three payments of 1 and multiply the answer times $100. This approach appears as follows:

From Table 12A–2

$i = 18\%, n = 2, f = 1.3924$
$i = 18\%, n = 1, f = 1.1800$
$i = 18\%, n = 0, f = 1.0000$
                           3.5724

$3.5724 \times \$100 = \$357.24$

The easiest way to solve the problem is to use a table that shows the future values of a series of payments. That type of table often is called a **future value of an annuity of 1** table. Table 12A–4 on page 523 is such a table. Note in Table 12A–4 that when $n = 1$, the future values are equal to $1(f = 1)$ for all rates of interest. When $n = 1$, the "annuity" consists of only one payment and the future value is determined on the date of the payment. Hence, the future value equals the payment.

Although a formula[5] is used to construct a table showing the future values of an annuity of 1, students should understand that the table can be constructed simply by adding together the amount in a future value of 1 table (such as Table 12A–2). To check your understanding of this, examine Tables 12A–2 and 12A–4 to confirm that the following numbers were drawn from those tables.

From Table 12A–2		From Table 12A–4	
$i = 8\%, n = 0$	1.0000	$i = 8\%, n = 1$	1.0000
$i = 8\%, n = 1$	1.0800		
$i = 8\%, n = 2$	1.1664		
$i = 8\%, n = 3$	1.2597		
Total	4.5061	$i = 8\%, n = 4$	4.5061

Minor differences in the results may sometimes occur but only because the numbers in the tables have been rounded.

Observe that in Table 12A–2, the future value is 1.0000 when $n = 0$. However, in Table 12A–4, the future value is 1.000 when $n = 1$. Why is this true?

When $n = 0$ in Table 12A–2, the future value is determined on the same date as the single payment of 1 is made. The investment period over which interest is earned is zero ($n = 0$). However, Table 12A–4 is designed so that one payment is made each period. When $n = 2$, two payments are assumed, or when $n = 1$, one payment is assumed. And since future value is calculated as of the date of the last payment, future value = 1 when $n = 1$.

---

[5] The formula for a table showing the future values of an annuity of 1 is:

$$f = \frac{(1 + i)^n - 1}{i}$$

Table 12A–1 Present Value of 1 Due in *n* Periods

Periods	1.0%	1.5%	3.0%	4.0%	8.0%	10.0%	12.0%	14.0%	16.0%	18.0%	20.0%
1	0.9901	0.9852	0.9709	0.9615	0.9259	0.9091	0.8929	0.8772	0.8621	0.8475	0.8333
2	0.9803	0.9707	0.9426	0.9246	0.8573	0.8264	0.7972	0.7695	0.7432	0.7182	0.6944
3	0.9706	0.9563	0.9151	0.8890	0.7938	0.7513	0.7118	0.6750	0.6407	0.6086	0.5787
4	0.9610	0.9422	0.8885	0.8548	0.7350	0.6830	0.6355	0.5921	0.5523	0.5158	0.4823
5	0.9515	0.9283	0.8626	0.8219	0.6806	0.6209	0.5674	0.5194	0.4761	0.4371	0.4019
6	0.9420	0.9145	0.8375	0.7903	0.6302	0.5645	0.5066	0.4556	0.4104	0.3704	0.3349
7	0.9327	0.9010	0.8131	0.7599	0.5835	0.5132	0.4523	0.3996	0.3538	0.3139	0.2791
8	0.9235	0.8877	0.7894	0.7307	0.5403	0.4665	0.4039	0.3506	0.3050	0.2660	0.2326
9	0.9143	0.8746	0.7664	0.7026	0.5002	0.4241	0.3606	0.3075	0.2630	0.2255	0.1938
10	0.9053	0.8617	0.7441	0.6756	0.4632	0.3855	0.3220	0.2697	0.2267	0.1911	0.1615
11	0.8963	0.8489	0.7224	0.6496	0.4289	0.3505	0.2875	0.2366	0.1954	0.1619	0.1346
12	0.8874	0.8364	0.7014	0.6246	0.3971	0.3186	0.2567	0.2076	0.1685	0.1372	0.1122
13	0.8787	0.8240	0.6810	0.6006	0.3677	0.2897	0.2292	0.1821	0.1452	0.1163	0.0935
14	0.8700	0.8118	0.6611	0.5775	0.3405	0.2633	0.2046	0.1597	0.1252	0.0985	0.0779
15	0.8613	0.7999	0.6419	0.5553	0.3152	0.2394	0.1827	0.1401	0.1079	0.0835	0.0649
16	0.8528	0.7880	0.6232	0.5339	0.2919	0.2176	0.1631	0.1229	0.0930	0.0708	0.0541
17	0.8444	0.7764	0.6050	0.5134	0.2703	0.1978	0.1456	0.1078	0.0802	0.0600	0.0451
18	0.8360	0.7649	0.5874	0.4936	0.2502	0.1799	0.1300	0.0946	0.0691	0.0508	0.0376
19	0.8277	0.7536	0.5703	0.4746	0.2317	0.1635	0.1161	0.0829	0.0596	0.0431	0.0313
20	0.8195	0.7425	0.5537	0.4564	0.2145	0.1486	0.1037	0.0728	0.0514	0.0365	0.0261
21	0.8114	0.7315	0.5375	0.4388	0.1987	0.1351	0.0926	0.0638	0.0443	0.0309	0.0217
22	0.8034	0.7207	0.5219	0.4220	0.1839	0.1228	0.0826	0.0560	0.0382	0.0262	0.0181
23	0.7954	0.7100	0.5067	0.4057	0.1703	0.1117	0.0738	0.0491	0.0329	0.0222	0.0151
24	0.7876	0.6995	0.4919	0.3901	0.1577	0.1015	0.0659	0.0431	0.0284	0.0188	0.0126
25	0.7798	0.6892	0.4776	0.3751	0.1460	0.0923	0.0588	0.0378	0.0245	0.0160	0.0105
26	0.7720	0.6790	0.4637	0.3607	0.1352	0.0839	0.0525	0.0331	0.0211	0.0135	0.0087
27	0.7644	0.6690	0.4502	0.3468	0.1252	0.0763	0.0469	0.0291	0.0182	0.0115	0.0073
28	0.7568	0.6591	0.4371	0.3335	0.1159	0.0693	0.0419	0.0255	0.0157	0.0097	0.0061
29	0.7493	0.6494	0.4243	0.3207	0.1073	0.0630	0.0374	0.0224	0.0135	0.0082	0.0051
30	0.7419	0.6398	0.4120	0.3083	0.0994	0.0573	0.0334	0.0196	0.0116	0.0070	0.0042
31	0.7346	0.6303	0.4000	0.2965	0.0920	0.0521	0.0298	0.0172	0.0100	0.0059	0.0035
32	0.7273	0.6210	0.3883	0.2851	0.0852	0.0474	0.0266	0.0151	0.0087	0.0050	0.0029
33	0.7201	0.6118	0.3770	0.2741	0.0789	0.0431	0.0238	0.0132	0.0075	0.0042	0.0024
34	0.7130	0.6028	0.3660	0.2636	0.0730	0.0391	0.0212	0.0116	0.0064	0.0036	0.0020
35	0.7059	0.5939	0.3554	0.2534	0.0676	0.0356	0.0189	0.0102	0.0055	0.0030	0.0017
36	0.6989	0.5851	0.3450	0.2437	0.0626	0.0323	0.0169	0.0089	0.0048	0.0026	0.0014
37	0.6920	0.5764	0.3350	0.2343	0.0580	0.0294	0.0151	0.0078	0.0041	0.0022	0.0012
38	0.6852	0.5679	0.3252	0.2253	0.0537	0.0267	0.0135	0.0069	0.0036	0.0019	0.0010
39	0.6784	0.5595	0.3158	0.2166	0.0497	0.0243	0.0120	0.0060	0.0031	0.0016	0.0008
40	0.6717	0.5513	0.3066	0.2083	0.0460	0.0221	0.0107	0.0053	0.0026	0.0013	0.0007
41	0.6650	0.5431	0.2976	0.2003	0.0426	0.0201	0.0096	0.0046	0.0023	0.0011	0.0006
42	0.6584	0.5351	0.2890	0.1926	0.0395	0.0183	0.0086	0.0041	0.0020	0.0010	0.0005
43	0.6519	0.5272	0.2805	0.1852	0.0365	0.0166	0.0076	0.0036	0.0017	0.0008	0.0004
44	0.6454	0.5194	0.2724	0.1780	0.0338	0.0151	0.0068	0.0031	0.0015	0.0007	0.0003
45	0.6391	0.5117	0.2644	0.1712	0.0313	0.0137	0.0061	0.0027	0.0013	0.0006	0.0003
46	0.6327	0.5042	0.2567	0.1646	0.0290	0.0125	0.0054	0.0024	0.0011	0.0005	0.0002
47	0.6265	0.4967	0.2493	0.1583	0.0269	0.0113	0.0049	0.0021	0.0009	0.0004	0.0002
48	0.6203	0.4894	0.2420	0.1522	0.0249	0.0103	0.0043	0.0019	0.0008	0.0004	0.0002
49	0.6141	0.4821	0.2350	0.1463	0.0230	0.0094	0.0039	0.0016	0.0007	0.0003	0.0001
50	0.6080	0.4750	0.2281	0.1407	0.0213	0.0085	0.0035	0.0014	0.0006	0.0003	0.0001

Table 12A–2   Future Value of 1 Due in *n* Periods

Periods	1.0%	1.5%	3.0%	4.0%	8.0%	10.0%	12.0%	14.0%	16.0%	18.0%	20.0%
0	1.0000	1.0000	1.0000	1.0000	1.0000	1.0000	1.0000	1.0000	1.0000	1.0000	1.0000
1	1.0100	1.0150	1.0300	1.0400	1.0800	1.1000	1.1200	1.1400	1.1600	1.1800	1.2000
2	1.0201	1.0302	1.0609	1.0816	1.1664	1.2100	1.2544	1.2996	1.3456	1.3924	1.4400
3	1.0303	1.0457	1.0927	1.1249	1.2597	1.3310	1.4049	1.4815	1.5609	1.6430	1.7280
4	1.0406	1.0614	1.1255	1.1699	1.3605	1.4641	1.5735	1.6890	1.8106	1.9388	2.0736
5	1.0510	1.0773	1.1593	1.2167	1.4693	1.6105	1.7623	1.9254	2.1003	2.2878	2.4883
6	1.0615	1.0934	1.1941	1.2653	1.5869	1.7716	1.9738	2.1950	2.4364	2.6996	2.9860
7	1.0721	1.1098	1.2299	1.3159	1.7138	1.9487	2.2107	2.5023	2.8262	3.1855	3.5832
8	1.0829	1.1265	1.2668	1.3686	1.8509	2.1436	2.4760	2.8526	3.2784	3.7589	4.2998
9	1.0937	1.1434	1.3048	1.4233	1.9990	2.3579	2.7731	3.2519	3.8030	4.4355	5.1598
10	1.1046	1.1605	1.3439	1.4802	2.1589	2.5937	3.1058	3.7072	4.4114	5.2338	6.1917
11	1.1157	1.1779	1.3842	1.5395	2.3316	2.8531	3.4785	4.2262	5.1173	6.1759	7.4301
12	1.1268	1.1956	1.4258	1.6010	2.5182	3.1384	3.8960	4.8179	5.9360	7.2876	8.9161
13	1.1381	1.2136	1.4685	1.6651	2.7196	3.4523	4.3635	5.4924	6.8858	8.5994	10.6993
14	1.1495	1.2318	1.5126	1.7317	2.9372	3.7975	4.8871	6.2613	7.9875	10.1472	12.8392
15	1.1610	1.2502	1.5580	1.8009	3.1722	4.1772	5.4736	7.1379	9.2655	11.9737	15.4070
16	1.1726	1.2690	1.6047	1.8730	3.4259	4.5950	6.1304	8.1372	10.7480	14.1290	18.4884
17	1.1843	1.2880	1.6528	1.9479	3.7000	5.0545	6.8660	9.2765	12.4677	16.6722	22.1861
18	1.1961	1.3073	1.7024	2.0258	3.9960	5.5599	7.6900	10.5752	14.4625	19.6733	26.6233
19	1.2081	1.3270	1.7535	2.1068	4.3157	6.1159	8.6128	12.0557	16.7765	23.2144	31.9480
20	1.2202	1.3469	1.8061	2.1911	4.6610	6.7275	9.6463	13.7435	19.4608	27.3930	38.3376
21	1.2324	1.3671	1.8603	2.2788	5.0338	7.4002	10.8038	15.6676	22.5745	32.3238	46.0051
22	1.2447	1.3876	1.9161	2.3699	5.4365	8.1403	12.1003	17.8610	26.1864	38.1421	55.2061
23	1.2572	1.4084	1.9736	2.4647	5.8715	8.9543	13.5523	20.3616	30.3762	45.0076	66.2474
24	1.2697	1.4295	2.0328	2.5633	6.3412	9.8497	15.1786	23.2122	35.2364	53.1090	79.4968
25	1.2824	1.4509	2.0938	2.6658	6.8485	10.8347	17.0001	26.4619	40.8742	62.6686	95.3962
26	1.2953	1.4727	2.1566	2.7725	7.3964	11.9182	19.0401	30.1666	47.4141	73.9490	114.4755
27	1.3082	1.4948	2.2213	2.8834	7.9881	13.1100	21.3249	34.3899	55.0004	87.2598	137.3706
28	1.3213	1.5172	2.2879	2.9987	8.6271	14.4210	23.8839	39.2045	63.8004	102.9666	164.8447
29	1.3345	1.5400	2.3566	3.1187	9.3173	15.8631	26.7499	44.6931	74.0085	121.5005	197.8136
30	1.3478	1.5631	2.4273	3.2434	10.0627	17.4494	29.9599	50.9502	85.8499	143.3706	237.3763
31	1.3613	1.5865	2.5001	3.3731	10.8677	19.1943	33.5551	58.0832	99.5859	169.1774	284.8516
32	1.3749	1.6103	2.5751	3.5081	11.7371	21.1138	37.5817	66.2148	115.5196	199.6293	341.8219
33	1.3887	1.6345	2.6523	3.6484	12.6760	23.2252	42.0915	75.4849	134.0027	235.5625	410.1863
34	1.4026	1.6590	2.7319	3.7943	13.6901	25.5477	47.1425	86.0528	155.4432	277.9638	492.2235
35	1.4166	1.6839	2.8139	3.9461	14.7853	28.1024	52.7996	98.1002	180.3141	327.9973	590.6682
36	1.4308	1.7091	2.8983	4.1039	15.9682	30.9127	59.1356	111.8342	209.1643	387.0368	708.8019
37	1.4451	1.7348	2.9852	4.2681	17.2456	34.0039	66.2318	127.4910	242.6306	456.7034	850.5622
38	1.4595	1.7608	3.0748	4.4388	18.6253	37.4043	74.1797	145.3397	281.4515	538.9100	1020.6747
39	1.4741	1.7872	3.1670	4.6164	20.1153	41.1448	83.0812	165.6873	326.4838	635.9139	1224.8096
40	1.4889	1.8140	3.2620	4.8010	21.7245	45.2593	93.0510	188.8835	378.7212	750.3783	1469.7716
41	1.5038	1.8412	3.3599	4.9931	23.4625	49.7852	104.2171	215.3272	439.3165	885.4464	1763.7259
42	1.5188	1.8688	·3.4607	5.1928	25.3395	54.7637	116.7231	245.4730	509.6072	1044.8268	2116.4711
43	1.5340	1.8969	3.5645	5.4005	27.3666	60.2401	130.7299	279.8392	591.1443	1232.8956	2539.7653
44	1.5493	1.9253	3.6715	5.6165	29.5560	66.2641	146.4175	319.0167	685.7274	1454.8168	3047.7183
45	1.5648	1.9542	3.7816	5.8412	31.9204	72.8905	163.9876	363.6791	795.4438	1716.6839	3657.2620
46	1.5805	1.9835	3.8950	6.0748	34.4741	80.1795	183.6661	414.5941	922.7148	2025.6870	4388.7144
47	1.5963	2.0133	4.0119	6.3178	37.2320	88.1975	205.7061	472.6373	1070.3492	2390.3106	5266.4573
48	1.6122	2.0435	4.1323	6.5705	40.2106	97.0172	230.3908	538.8065	1241.6051	2820.5665	6319.7487
49	1.6283	2.0741	4.2562	6.8333	43.4274	106.7190	258.0377	614.2395	1440.2619	3328.2685	7583.6985
50	1.6446	2.1052	4.3839	7.1067	46.9016	117.3909	289.0022	700.2330	1670.7038	3927.3569	9100.4382

Table 12A–3   Present Value of an Annuity of 1 per Period

Periods	1.0%	1.5%	3.0%	4.0%	8.0%	10.0%	12.0%	14.0%	16.0%	18.0%	20.0%
1	0.9901	0.9852	0.9709	0.9615	0.9259	0.9091	0.8929	0.8772	0.8621	0.8475	0.8333
2	1.9704	1.9559	1.9135	1.8861	1.7833	1.7355	1.6901	1.6467	1.6052	1.5656	1.5278
3	2.9410	2.9122	2.8286	2.7751	2.5771	2.4869	2.4018	2.3216	2.2459	2.1743	2.1065
4	3.9020	3.8544	3.7171	3.6299	3.3121	3.1699	3.0373	2.9137	2.7982	2.6901	2.5887
5	4.8534	4.7826	4.5797	4.4518	3.9927	3.7908	3.6048	3.4331	3.2743	3.1272	2.9906
6	5.7955	5.6972	5.4172	5.2421	4.6229	4.3553	4.1114	3.8887	3.6847	3.4976	3.3255
7	6.7282	6.5982	6.2303	6.0021	5.2064	4.8684	4.5638	4.2883	4.0386	3.8115	3.6046
8	7.6517	7.4859	7.0197	6.7327	5.7466	5.3349	4.9676	4.6389	4.3436	4.0776	3.8372
9	8.5660	8.3605	7.7861	7.4353	6.2469	5.7590	5.3282	4.9464	4.6065	4.3030	4.0310
10	9.4713	9.2222	8.5302	8.1109	6.7101	6.1446	5.6502	5.2161	4.8332	4.4941	4.1925
11	10.3676	10.0711	9.2526	8.7605	7.1390	6.4951	5.9377	5.4527	5.0286	4.6560	4.3271
12	11.2551	10.9075	9.9540	9.3851	7.5361	6.8137	6.1944	5.6603	5.1971	4.7932	4.4392
13	12.1337	11.7315	10.6350	9.9856	7.9038	7.1034	6.4235	5.8424	5.3423	4.9095	4.5327
14	13.0037	12.5434	11.2961	10.5631	8.2442	7.3667	6.6282	6.0021	5.4675	5.0081	4.6106
15	13.8651	13.3432	11.9379	11.1184	8.5595	7.6061	6.8109	6.1422	5.5755	5.0916	4.6755
16	14.7179	14.1313	12.5611	11.6523	8.8514	7.8237	6.9740	6.2651	5.6685	5.1624	4.7296
17	15.5623	14.9076	13.1661	12.1657	9.1216	8.0216	7.1196	6.3729	5.7487	5.2223	4.7746
18	16.3983	15.6726	13.7535	12.6593	9.3719	8.2014	7.2497	6.4674	5.8178	5.2732	4.8122
19	17.2260	16.4262	14.3238	13.1339	9.6036	8.3649	7.3658	6.5504	5.8775	5.3162	4.8435
20	18.0456	17.1686	14.8775	13.5903	9.8181	8.5136	7.4694	6.6231	5.9288	5.3527	4.8696
21	18.8570	17.9001	15.4150	14.0292	10.0168	8.6487	7.5620	6.6870	5.9731	5.3837	4.8913
22	19.6604	18.6208	15.9369	14.4511	10.2007	8.7715	7.6446	6.7429	6.0113	5.4099	4.9094
23	20.4558	19.3309	16.4436	14.8568	10.3711	8.8832	7.7184	6.7921	6.0442	5.4321	4.9245
24	21.2434	20.0304	16.9355	15.2470	10.5288	8.9847	7.7843	6.8351	6.0726	5.4509	4.9371
25	22.0232	20.7196	17.4131	15.6221	10.6748	9.0770	7.8431	6.8729	6.0971	5.4669	4.9476
26	22.7952	21.3986	17.8768	15.9828	10.8100	9.1609	7.8957	6.9061	6.1182	5.4804	4.9563
27	23.5596	22.0676	18.3270	16.3296	10.9352	9.2372	7.9426	6.9352	6.1364	5.4919	4.9636
28	24.3164	22.7267	18.7641	16.6631	11.0511	9.3066	7.9844	6.9607	6.1520	5.5016	4.9697
29	25.0658	23.3761	19.1885	16.9837	11.1584	9.3696	8.0218	6.9830	6.1656	5.5098	4.9747
30	25.8077	24.0158	19.6004	17.2920	11.2578	9.4269	8.0552	7.0027	6.1772	5.5168	4.9789
31	26.5423	24.6461	20.0004	17.5885	11.3498	9.4790	8.0850	7.0199	6.1872	5.5227	4.9824
32	27.2696	25.2671	20.3888	17.8736	11.4350	9.5264	8.1116	7.0350	6.1959	5.5277	4.9854
33	27.9897	25.8790	20.7658	18.1476	11.5139	9.5694	8.1354	7.0482	6.2034	5.5320	4.9878
34	28.7027	26.4817	21.1318	18.4112	11.5869	9.6086	8.1566	7.0599	6.2098	5.5356	4.9898
35	29.4086	27.0756	21.4872	18.6646	11.6546	9.6442	8.1755	7.0700	6.2153	5.5386	4.9915
36	30.1075	27.6607	21.8323	18.9083	11.7172	9.6765	8.1924	7.0790	6.2201	5.5412	4.9929
37	30.7995	28.2371	22.1672	19.1426	11.7752	9.7059	8.2075	7.0868	6.2242	5.5434	4.9941
38	31.4847	28.8051	22.4925	19.3679	11.8289	9.7327	8.2210	7.0937	6.2278	5.5452	4.9951
39	32.1630	29.3646	22.8082	19.5845	11.8786	9.7570	8.2330	7.0997	6.2309	5.5468	4.9959
40	32.8347	29.9158	23.1148	19.7928	11.9246	9.7791	8.2438	7.1050	6.2335	5.5482	4.9966
41	33.4997	30.4590	23.4124	19.9931	11.9672	9.7991	8.2534	7.1097	6.2358	5.5493	4.9972
42	34.1581	30.9941	23.7014	20.1856	12.0067	9.8174	8.2619	7.1138	6.2377	5.5502	4.9976
43	34.8100	31.5212	23.9819	20.3708	12.0432	9.8340	8.2696	7.1173	6.2394	5.5510	4.9980
44	35.4555	32.0406	24.2543	20.5488	12.0771	9.8491	8.2764	7.1205	6.2409	5.5517	4.9984
45	36.0945	32.5523	24.5187	20.7200	12.1084	9.8628	8.2825	7.1232	6.2421	5.5523	4.9986
46	36.7272	33.0565	24.7754	20.8847	12.1374	9.8753	8.2880	7.1256	6.2432	5.5528	4.9989
47	37.3537	33.5532	25.0247	21.0429	12.1643	9.8866	8.2928	7.1277	6.2442	5.5532	4.9991
48	37.9740	34.0426	25.2667	21.1951	12.1891	9.8969	8.2972	7.1296	6.2450	5.5536	4.9992
49	38.5881	34.5247	25.5017	21.3415	12.2122	9.9063	8.3010	7.1312	6.2457	5.5539	4.9993
50	39.1961	34.9997	25.7298	21.4822	12.2335	9.9148	8.3045	7.1327	6.2463	5.5541	4.9995

Table 12A–4   Future Value of an Annuity of 1 per Period

Periods	1.0%	1.5%	3.0%	4.0%	8.0%	10.0%	12.0%	14.0%	16.0%	18.0%	20.0%
1	1.0000	1.0000	1.0000	1.0000	1.0000	1.0000	1.0000	1.0000	1.0000	1.0000	1.0000
2	2.0100	2.0150	2.0300	2.0400	2.0800	2.1000	2.1200	2.1400	2.1600	2.1800	2.2000
3	3.0301	3.0452	3.0909	3.1216	3.2464	3.3100	3.3744	3.4396	3.5056	3.5724	3.6400
4	4.0604	4.0909	4.1836	4.2465	4.5061	4.6410	4.7793	4.9211	5.0665	5.2154	5.3680
5	5.1010	5.1523	5.3091	5.4163	5.8666	6.1051	6.3528	6.6101	6.8771	7.1542	7.4416
6	6.1520	6.2296	6.4684	6.6330	7.3359	7.7156	8.1152	8.5355	8.9775	9.4420	9.9299
7	7.2135	7.3230	7.6625	7.8983	8.9228	9.4872	10.0890	10.7305	11.4139	12.1415	12.9159
8	8.2857	8.4328	8.8923	9.2142	10.6366	11.4359	12.2997	13.2328	14.2401	15.3270	16.4991
9	9.3685	9.5593	10.1591	10.5828	12.4876	13.5795	14.7757	16.0853	17.5185	19.0859	20.7989
10	10.4622	10.7027	11.4639	12.0061	14.4866	15.9374	17.5487	19.3373	21.3215	23.5213	25.9587
11	11.5668	11.8633	12.8078	13.4864	16.6455	18.5312	20.6546	23.0445	25.7329	28.7551	32.1504
12	12.6825	13.0412	14.1920	15.0258	18.9771	21.3843	24.1331	27.2707	30.8502	34.9311	39.5805
13	13.8093	14.2368	15.6178	16.6268	21.4953	24.5227	28.0291	32.0887	36.7862	42.2187	48.4966
14	14.9474	15.4504	17.0863	18.2919	24.2149	27.9750	32.3926	37.5811	43.6720	50.8180	59.1959
15	16.0969	16.6821	18.5989	20.0236	27.1521	31.7725	37.2797	43.8424	51.6595	60.9653	72.0351
16	17.2579	17.9324	20.1569	21.8245	30.3243	35.9497	42.7533	50.9804	60.9250	72.9390	87.4421
17	18.4304	19.2014	21.7616	23.6975	33.7502	40.5447	48.8837	59.1176	71.6730	87.0680	105.9306
18	19.6147	20.4894	23.4144	25.6454	37.4502	45.5992	55.7497	68.3941	84.1407	103.7403	128.1167
19	20.8109	21.7967	25.1169	27.6712	41.4463	51.1591	63.4397	78.9692	98.6032	123.4135	154.7400
20	22.0190	23.1237	26.8704	29.7781	45.7620	57.2750	72.0524	91.0249	115.3797	146.6280	186.6880
21	23.2392	24.4705	28.6765	31.9692	50.4229	64.0025	81.6987	104.7684	134.8405	174.0210	225.0256
22	24.4716	25.8376	30.5368	34.2480	55.4568	71.4027	92.5026	120.4360	157.4150	206.3448	271.0307
23	25.7163	27.2251	32.4529	36.6179	60.8933	79.5430	104.6029	138.2970	183.6014	244.4868	326.2369
24	26.9735	28.6335	34.4265	39.0826	66.7648	88.4973	118.1552	158.6586	213.9776	289.4945	392.4842
25	28.2432	30.0630	36.4593	41.6459	73.1059	98.3471	133.3339	181.8708	249.2140	342.6035	471.9811
26	29.5256	31.5140	38.5530	44.3117	79.9544	109.1818	150.3339	208.3327	290.0883	405.2721	567.3773
27	30.8209	32.9867	40.7096	47.0842	87.3508	121.0999	169.3740	238.4993	337.5024	479.2211	681.8528
28	32.1291	34.4815	42.9309	49.9676	95.3388	134.2099	190.6989	272.8892	392.5028	566.4809	819.2233
29	33.4504	35.9987	45.2189	52.9663	103.9659	148.6309	214.5828	312.0937	456.3032	669.4475	984.0680
30	34.7849	37.5387	47.5754	56.0849	113.2832	164.4940	241.3327	356.7868	530.3117	790.9480	1181.8816
31	36.1327	39.1018	50.0027	59.3283	123.3459	181.9434	271.2926	407.7370	616.1616	934.3186	1419.2579
32	37.4941	40.6883	52.5028	62.7015	134.2135	201.1378	304.8477	465.8202	715.7475	1103.4960	1704.1095
33	38.8690	42.2986	55.0778	66.2095	145.9506	222.2515	342.4294	532.0350	831.2671	1303.1253	2045.9314
34	40.2577	43.9331	57.7302	69.8579	158.6267	245.4767	384.5210	607.5199	965.2698	1538.6878	2456.1176
35	41.6603	45.5921	60.4621	73.6522	172.3168	271.0244	431.6635	693.5727	1120.7130	1816.6516	2948.3411
36	43.0769	47.2760	63.2759	77.5983	187.1021	299.1268	484.4631	791.6729	1301.0270	2144.6489	3539.0094
37	44.5076	48.9851	66.1742	81.7022	203.0703	330.0395	543.5987	903.5071	1510.1914	2531.6857	4247.8112
38	45.9527	50.7199	69.1594	85.9703	220.3159	364.0434	609.8305	1030.9981	1752.8220	2988.3891	5098.3735
39	47.4123	52.4807	72.2342	90.4091	238.9412	401.4478	684.0102	1176.3378	2034.2735	3527.2992	6119.0482
40	48.8864	54.2679	75.4013	95.0255	259.0565	442.5926	767.0914	1342.0251	2360.7572	4163.2130	7343.8578
41	50.3752	56.0819	78.6633	99.8265	280.7810	487.8518	860.1424	1530.9086	2739.4784	4913.5914	8813.6294
42	51.8790	57.9231	82.0232	104.8196	304.2435	537.6370	964.3595	1746.2358	3178.7949	5799.0378	10577.3553
43	53.3978	59.7920	85.4839	110.0124	329.5830	592.4007	1081.0826	1991.7088	3688.4021	6843.8646	12693.8263
44	54.9318	61.6889	89.0484	115.4129	356.9496	652.6408	1211.8125	2271.5481	4279.5465	8076.7603	15233.5916
45	56.4811	63.6142	92.7199	121.0294	386.5056	718.9048	1358.2300	2590.5648	4965.2739	9531.5771	18281.3099
46	58.0459	65.5684	96.5015	126.8706	418.4261	791.7953	1522.2176	2954.2439	5760.7177	11248.2610	21938.5719
47	59.6263	67.5519	100.3965	132.9454	452.9002	871.9749	1705.8838	3368.8380	6683.4326	13273.9480	26327.2863
48	61.2226	69.5652	104.4084	139.2632	490.1322	960.1723	1911.5898	3841.4753	7753.7818	15664.2586	31593.7436
49	62.8348	71.6087	108.5406	145.8337	530.3427	1057.1896	2141.9806	4380.2819	8995.3869	18484.8251	37913.4923
50	64.4632	73.6828	112.7969	152.6671	573.7702	1163.9085	2400.0182	4994.5213	10435.6488	21813.0937	45497.1908

GLOSSARY

Bank discount. Precalculated interest charged and deducted by a bank at the time a loan is made.

Capital lease. A lease having essentially the same economic consequences as if the lessee had secured a loan and purchased the leased asset.

Carrying amount of a note. The face amount of a note minus the unamortized discount on the note.

Carrying amount of a lease. The remaining lease liability minus the unamortized discount on the lease financing.

Estimated liability. An obligation that definitely exists but for which the amount to be paid is uncertain.

Financing lease. Another name for a capital lease.

Long-term liabilities. Debts or obligations that will not require the use of existing current assets in their liquidation because they do not mature within one year or one operating cycle, whichever is longer.

Operating lease. A lease not meeting any one of the criteria of the *CICA Handbook* that would make it a capital lease.

Present value. The estimated worth today of an amount of money to be received at a future date.

Present value table. A table showing the present values of one amount to be received at various future dates when discounted at various interest rates.

Product warranty. A promise to a customer that obligates the seller or manufacturer for a limited period of time to pay for items such as replacement parts or repair costs if the product breaks or fails to perform.

QUESTIONS FOR CLASS DISCUSSION

1. What is a liability?
2. Are all expected future payments liabilities?
3. Define (a) a current liability and (b) a long-term liability.
4. There are three important questions about which a liability may or may not be definite. What are those questions?
5. What is the nature of an estimated liability?
6. If a property tax liability is estimated at the end of Year 1 and the actual payment of the liability in Year 2 turns out to be more than the amount that was estimated, how is the excess accounted for in Year 2?
7. Why are product warranties often recorded as liabilities instead of being disclosed as contingent liabilities?
8. The legal position of a company may be improved by its acceptance of

a promissory note in exchange for granting a time extension on the due date of a customer's debt. Why?

9. What distinction do banks make between loans and discounts?

10. Which is to the advantage of a bank: *(a)* making a loan to a customer in exchange for the customer's $1,000, 60-day, 9% note, or *(b)* making a loan to the customer by discounting the customer's $1,000 noninterest-bearing note for 60 days at 9%? Why?

11. Distinguish between bank discount and cash discount.

12. What determines the present value of $1,000 to be received at some future date?

13. If a $5,000 noninterest-bearing, five-year note is exchanged for a machine, the face amount of the note equals the sum of two different economic costs. What are these two costs?

14. If the Machinery account is debited for $5,000 and Notes Payable is credited for $5,000 in recording the machine of Question 13, what effects will this have on the financial statements?

15. What is the advantage of leasing a plant asset instead of purchasing it?

16. Distinguish between a capital lease and an operating lease. Which causes an asset and a liability to appear on the balance sheet?

17. At what amount is a machine acquired through a capital lease recorded?

MULTIPLE CHOICE

1. The Alpha Company discounted its own $5,000, 90-day, note payable at the bank and agreed to a discount rate of 10%. Which of the following journal entries should Alpha use to record the note?

a.	Cash	4,872.60	
	Interest Expense	127.40	
	Notes Payable		5,000.00
b.	Cash	5,000.00	
	Notes Payable		5,000.00
c.	Cash	4,872.60	
	Notes Payable		4,872.60
d.	Cash	4,500.00	
	Interest Expense	500.00	
	Notes Payable		5,000.00
e.	Cash	5,000.00	
	Accounts Payable		5,000.00

2. Franklin Company discounted its own $1,000 note at the bank for one year at an interest rate of 12%. The cash proceeds to Franklin Company were:

   a. $1,120.
   b. $1,000.

  c. $980.

  d. $880.

  e. Some other amount.

3. A corporation issued a three-year, $18,000 note in exchange for a truck. There was no interest rate recorded on the note, but the prevailing interest rate on the day of the exchange was 12%. The present value of $1 received three periods hence, discounted at 12%, is 0.712. At what amount should the truck be recorded?

  a. $20,160.

  b. $18,000.

  c. $12,816.

  d. $11,520.

  e. Some other amount.

4. A corporation issued a 10-year, $25,000 note in exchange for a piece of land. There was no interest rate recorded on the note, but the prevailing interest rate on the day of the exchange was 10%. The present value of the note is $9,650. What is the amount of the first year's discount amortization?

  a. $965.

  b. $1,535.

  c. $2,500.

  d. $5,000.

  e. None of the above.

5. Acme Company entered into a lease contract for five years to acquire a delivery truck. After the term of the lease expires, Acme will own the truck. The annual payments are $6,000, and the prevailing rate of interest for this type of contract is 8%. The present value of $1 received periodically for five periods, discounted at 8%, is 3.993. Which entry would Acme use to record the lease?

  a. No entry would be made until the first lease payment is made.

b.	Equipment, Truck	30,000	
	Long-Term Lease Liability		30,000
c.	Equipment, Truck	23,958	
	Interest Expense	6,042	
	Long-Term Lease Liability		30,000
d.	Equipment, Truck	23,958	
	Discount on Lease Financing	6,042	
	Long-Term Lease Liability		30,000
e.	Equipment, Truck	6,000	
	Cash		6,000

6. The present value of $1 received periodically for a number of periods is:

Periods hence	6%	12%
1	0.943	0.893
2	1.833	1.690
3	2.673	2.402
4	3.465	3.037

If an investment paid $1,000 each six months for two years, beginning six months from now, and the investor required a 12% annual rate of return, how much would the investor be willing to pay for the investment?

- *a.* $3,465.
- *b.* $3,380.
- *c.* $3,037.
- *d.* $4,000.
- *e.* $3,666.

7. The present value of $1 received periodically for a number of periods is:

Periods hence	6%	12%
1	0.943	0.893
2	1.833	1.690
3	2.673	2.402
4	3.465	3.037

Hasty Company is planning to purchase a truck and has been offered credit terms whereby it must make four annual payments of $4,000 each, with the first payment coming one year from today. Hasty Company has determined that similar credit terms could be obtained from a bank at an annual interest rate of 12%. What is the present value (price) of the machine?

- *a.* $4,000 × 0.893.
- *b.* $4,000 × 0.943.
- *c.* $4,000 × 2.402.
- *d.* $4,000 × 3.037.
- *e.* $4,000 × 3.465.

8.

Periods hence	Present value of $1 at compound interest at 8%	Present value of $1 received periodically for a number of periods at 8%
1	0.926	0.926
2	0.857	1.783
3	0.794	2.577
4	0.735	3.312

What amount should be deposited in a bank today if it is to earn 8% per year and grow to $1,000 three years from today?

- *a.* $1,000 divided by 0.794.
- *b.* $1,000 divided by 0.926 × 3.
- *c.* ($1,000 × 0.926) + ($1,000 × 0.857) + ($1,000 × 0.794).
- *d.* $1,000 × 0.794.
- *e.* $1,000 × 2.577.

MINI DISCUSSION CASE

Case 12–1   John Longball, star centrefielder with the Puce River Mudsharks, is negotiating for renewal of his contract. Prior to making an offer to Longball, Gordon Golvest—president of the club—asks you to check out the three alternatives he intends to present to the centrefielder. The three alternatives are for a five-year period and are as follows:

a. $200,000 per year payable at the end of each year for 10 years.
b. $300,000 per year payable at the end of each year for five years.
c. $1,100,000 payable on signing of the five-year contract.

Required:

1.   Identify the accounting issues raised in the case.
2.   Discuss the resolution of the issues in light of GAAP.

CLASS EXERCISES

Exercise 12–1   Throughout 198B, X Company owned property that was subject to county property taxes and had an assessed valuation for tax purposes of $600,000. The 198A tax levy was $0.50 per $100 of assessed valuation and the company expected the 198B rate to remain unchanged. In early July, the county announced that the 198B tax levy would be $0.55 per $100 and that taxes would be due August 31, 198B. Prepare entries to record property tax expense for the months of June, July, and August (including the payment of the annual tax on August 31).

Exercise 12–2   A company manufactures one product for $8 per unit and sells it for $15 per unit. In November, the company sold 100,000 units subject to a one-year warranty. According to the warranty, customers must pay a $1.50 service charge to return a broken unit and have it replaced by a new unit. When a unit under warranty fails, the company simply discards the broken unit and replaces it with a new one. Past experience suggests a 1.5% failure rate of new products sold, and customers actually returned 1,200 broken units during the month of November. Prepare summary entries for the month of November to record product warranty expense and to record the replacement of 1,200 broken units.

Exercise 12–3   On December 1, 198A, a company borrowed $100,000 by giving a 90-day, 12% note payable. The company has an annual, calendar-year accounting period and uses reversing entries. Prepare general journal entries to record: *(a)* the issuance of the note, *(b)* the required year-end adjusting entry, *(c)* the reversing entry on January 1, 198B, and *(d)* the entry to pay the note.

Exercise 12–4   On December 1, 198A, a company discounted its own $100,000, 90-day note payable at the bank. The discount rate was 12%. Prepare general journal entries to record: *(a)* the issuance of the note, *(b)* the required year-end adjusting entry, and *(c)* the entry to pay the note. (The company uses an annual, calendar-year accounting period.)

Exercise 12–5   Present calculations to show the following: *(a)* the present value of $20,000 to be received eight years hence, discounted at 14%, *(b)* the total present value of three payments consisting of $25,000 to be received one year hence, $30,000 to be received two years hence, and $40,000 to be received three years hence, all discounted at 12%, *(c)* the present value of seven payments of $6,000 each, with a payment to be received at the end of each of the next seven years, discounted at 9%.

Exercise 12–6   A company is offered a contract whereby it will be paid $8,000 every six months for the next 10 years. The first payment would be received six months from today. What will the company be willing to pay for this contract if it expects a 16% annual return on the investment? What if it expects an annual return of only 9%?

Exercise 12–7   A company is offered a contract whereby it will be paid $16,000 annually for the next 10 years. The first payment would be received one year from today. What will the company be willing to pay for this contract if it expects a 16% return on the investment? What if it expects an annual return of only 9%?

Exercise 12–8   An individual has offered to sell a machine for $9,000. A potential buyer has agreed to purchase the machine for the stated price but, as an alternative, has given the seller the option of receiving 10 annual payments of $1,500 each, the first payment to be one year from now. Assuming the seller expects an annual return of at least 8%, which of the two alternatives should the seller accept?

Exercise 12–9   Equipment was purchased on January 1 of the current year, with the terms of purchase including $14,000 cash plus a $25,000, noninterest-bearing, five-year note. The available interest rate on this date was 12%.

Required:

a. Prepare the entry to record the purchase of the machine.
b. Show how the liability will appear on a balance sheet prepared on the day of the purchase.
c. Prepare the entry to amortize a portion of the discount on the note at the end of the first year.

Exercise 12–10   On January 1, 198A, a day when the available interest rate was 14%, a company leased a machine for five years under a contract calling for a $30,000 annual lease payment at the end of each of the next five years, with the machine becoming the property of the lessee at the end of that period. The company decided to lease the machine. Prepare entries to record: *(a)* the leasing of the machine, *(b)* the amortization of the discount of the lease financing at the end of the first year, and *(c)* the first annual payment under the lease.

EXERCISES BASED ON SUPPLEMENT 12–A (EXERCISES 12–11 TO 12–28)

Exercise 12–11

X Company is considering an investment which, if paid for immediately, is expected to return $80,000, seven years hence. If X Company demands a 16% return, how much will X Company be willing to pay for this investment?

Exercise 12–12

Y Company invested $20,000 in a project that is expected to earn a 14% rate of return. The earnings will be reinvested in the project each year until the entire investment is liquidated 15 years hence. What will be the cash proceeds when the project is liquidated?

Exercise 12–13

Z Company is considering a contract that will return $10,000 annually at the end of each year for 18 years. If Z Company demands an annual return of 20% and pays for the investment immediately, how much should it be willing to pay?

Exercise 12–14

James Smith is planning to begin an individual retirement program in which he will invest $2,000 annually at the end of each year. Mr. Smith plans to retire after making 45 annual investments in a program that earns a return of 8%. What will be the value of the program on the date of the last investment?

Exercise 12–15

Mr. Blue has been offered the possibility of investing $0.1486 for 20 years, after which he will be paid $1. What annual rate of interest will Mr. Blue earn? (Use Table 12A–1 to find the answer.)

Exercise 12–16

Mr. White has been offered the possibility of investing $0.0245. The investment will earn 16% per year and will at the end of the investment return Mr. White $1. How many years must Mr. White wait to receive the $1? (Use Table 12A–1 to find the answer.)

Exercise 12–17

Ms. North expects to invest $1 at 12% and, at the end of the investment, receive $15.1786. How many years will elapse before Ms. North receives the payment? (Use Table 12A–2 to find the answer.)

Exercise 12–18

Ms. West expects to invest $1 for 15 years, after which she will receive $7.1379. What rate of interest will Ms. West earn? (Use Table 12A–2 to find the answer.)

Exercise 12–19

Mr. Blue expects an immediate investment of $5.8775 to return $1 annually for 19 years, the first payment to be received in 1 year. What rate of interest will Mr. Black earn? (Use Table 12A–3 to find the answer.)

Exercise
12–20

Ms. Brown expects an investment of $7.3667 to return $1 annually for several years. If Ms. Brown is to earn a return of 10%, how many annual payments must she receive? (Use Table 12A–3 to find the answer.)

Exercise
12–21

Mr. Dame expects to invest $1 annually for 30 years and have an accumulated value of $113.2832 on the date of the last investment. If this occurs, what rate of interest will Mr. Dame earn? (Use Table 12A–4 to find the answer.)

Exercise
12–22

Ms. Jain expects to invest $1 annually in a fund that will earn 18%. How many annual investments must Ms. Jain make to accumulate $50.818 on the date of the last investment? (Use Table 12A–4 to find the answer.)

Exercise
12–23

Kay Long financed a new automobile by paying $2,500 cash and agreeing to make 24 monthly payments of $400 each, the first payment to be made one month after the purchase. The loan was said to bear interest at an annual rate of 12%. What was the cost of the automobile?

Exercise
12–24

Frank Thomas deposited $5,000 in a savings account that earns interest at an annual rate of 16%, compounded quarterly. The $5,000 plus earned interest must remain in the account three years before it can be withdrawn. How much money will be in the account at the end of three years?

Exercise
12–25

Joan Johnson plans to have $100 withdrawn from her monthly pay and deposited in a savings account that earns 12% annually, compounded monthly. If Joan continues with her plan for two and one-half years, how much will be accumulated in the account on the date of the last deposit?

Exercise
12–26

Fry Company has decided to establish a fund that will be used five years hence to replace an aging productive facility. The company makes an initial contribution of $100,000 to the fund and plans to make quarterly contributions of $25,000 beginning in three months. The fund is expected to earn 12%, compounded quarterly. What will be the value of the fund five years hence?

Exercise
12–27

Jets Company expects to earn 14% on an investment that will return $100,000, 12 years hence. Use Table 12A–2 to calculate the present value of the investment.

Exercise
12–28

Barth Company invests $100,000 at 16% for 10 years. Use Table 12A–1 to calculate the future value of the investment, 10 years hence.

PROBLEMS

Problem 12–1

Part 1. Baffle Company sells a single product subject to a six-month warranty that covers replacement parts but not labour. The company uses a periodic inventory system to account for merchandise. Prepare journal entries to record the following transactions completed by the company during the month of May.

May 1 Purchased 1,000 units of merchandise for $22 per unit, paying cash.

      4 Purchased $2,600 of spare parts for making repairs to merchandise that is expected to be returned for warranty work.

      7 Sold 400 units of merchandise for $50 per unit, receiving cash.

    10 Repaired 20 units of merchandise that customers returned under the warranty. Replacement parts cost $344 and the customers paid $265 for labour.

    17 Sold 500 units of merchandise for $55 per unit.

    20 Repaired 14 units of merchandise under the product warranty. Replacement parts cost $210 and the customers paid $190 for labour.

    29 Recorded warranty expense for May. Past experience shows that 4.0% of the units sold require warranty work and the average cost of replacement parts is $16 per unit returned. Average labour charges are $12.50.

Part 2. Superior Company expects to accrue 198B property taxes at the end of each month using recent experience as a means of estimating the tax. In January 198A, Superior's property was appraised at $800,000. The 198A tax levy was $1.50 per $100. In January 198B, Superior's property was reappraised at $880,000. (The reappraisal was not expected to affect the tax levy of $1.50 per $100.) Early in June 198B, the annual tax levy was set at $1.80 per $100. On November 30, 198B, Superior paid the 198B tax. Complete financial statements are prepared by the company on a monthly basis and the company does not use reversing entries.

Required:

Prepare entries at the end of January, June, November, and December 198B, to record property tax expense for each of those months and to record the annual tax payment.

Problem 12–2   Prepare general journal entries to record these transactions:

Jan. 9 Purchased merchandise on credit from Foster Company, invoice dated January 8, terms 2/10, n/60, $10,400.

Feb. 6 Borrowed money at First City Bank by discounting our own $15,000 note payable for 60 days at 14%.

Mar. 9 Gave Foster Company $1,400 cash and a $9,000, 60-day, 14% note to secure an extension on our account that was due.

Apr. 10 Paid the note discounted at First City Bank on February 6.

May 11 Paid the note given Foster Company on March 9.

Nov. 1 Borrowed money at First City Bank by discounting our own $20,000 note payable for 90 days at 15%.

Dec.16 Borrowed money at InterSecond Bank by giving a $15,000, 60-day, 15% note payable.

    31 Made an adjusting entry to recognize the interest expense applicable to the current year on the note discounted at First City Bank on November 1.

    31 Made an adjusting entry to record the accrued interest on the note given InterSecond Bank on December 16.

Feb. 2 Paid the note discounted at First City Bank on November 1.

    17 Paid the note given InterSecond Bank on December 16.

Problem 12–3   South Seas Adventures is negotiating with a naval architect and shipyard in planning the construction of a 70-foot, trimaran that South Seas expects to acquire and place in charter service. The yacht will be completed and ready for service four years hence. If Jordan pays for the yacht upon completion (Payment Plan A), it will cost $337,500. However, two alternative payment plans are available. Plan B would require an immediate payment of $243,750. Plan C would require four annual payments of $71,250, the first of which would be made one year hence. In evaluating the three alternatives, the management of South Seas has decided to assume an interest rate of 10%.

Required:

Calculate the present value of each payment and indicate which plan South Seas should follow.

Problem 12–4   On January 2, 198A, a company gave its own $100,000 noninterest-bearing, five-year note payable in exchange for a machine, the cash price of which was not readily determinable. The market rate for interest on such notes on the day of the exchange was 9% annually.

Required:

(Round all amounts in your answers to the nearest whole dollar.)

1. Prepare a form with the following column headings. Calculate and fill in the required amounts for the five years the note is outstanding.

Year	Beginning-of-Year Carrying Amount	Discount to Be Amortized Each Year	Unamortized Discount at End of Year	End-of-Year Carrying Amount

2. Prepare general journal entries to record: *(a)* the acquisition of the machine, *(b)* the discount amortized at the end of each year, and *(c)* the payment of the note on January 2, 198F.
3. Show how the note should appear on the December 31, 198C, balance sheet.

Problem 12–5   Hyden Production Company leased a machine on January 1, 198A, under a contract calling for annual payments of $32,000 on December 31 at the end of each of five years, with the machine becoming the property of the lessee company after one fifth $32,000 payment. The machine was estimated to have an eight-year life and no salvage value, and the interest rate available to Hyden for equipment loans on the day the lease was signed was 12%. The machine was delivered on January 4, 198A, and was immediately placed in operation. At the beginning of the eighth year in the machine's life, it was overhauled at a $2,040 total cost. The overhaul was paid for on January 10, and it did not increase the machine's efficiency but it did add an additional year to its expected service life. On March 31, during the ninth year in the machine's life, it was traded in on a new machine having a $96,000 cash price. An $8,000 trade-in allowance was received and the balance was paid in cash. The gain or loss on the exchange was not material in amount.

Required:

(Round all amounts in your answers to the nearest whole dollar.)

1. Prepare a schedule with the columnar headings of Illustration 12–3. Enter the years 198A through 198E in the first column and complete the schedule by filling in the proper amounts.
2. Prepare the entry to record the leasing of the machine.
3. Prepare December 31, 198B, entries to record annual depreciation on a straight-line basis, to record the lease payment, and to amortize the discount in the life of the lease. Also show how the machine and the lease liability should appear on the December 31, 198B, balance sheet.
4. Prepare the entries to record the machine's overhaul and the depreciation on the machine at the end of its eighth year.
5. Prepare the March 31, 198I, entries to record the exchange of the machines.

Problem 12–6   The Bigtime Freight Company needs two new trucks, each of which has an estimated service life of nine years. The trucks could be purchased for $90,000 each, but Bigtime does not have enough cash to pay for them. Instead, Bigtime agrees to lease Truck 1 for six years, after which the truck remains the property of the lessor. In addition, Bigtime agrees to lease Truck 2 for eight years, after which the truck remains the property of the lessor. According to the lease contracts, Bigtime must pay $18,750 annually for each truck ($37,500 for two trucks), with the payments to be made at the end of each lease year. Both leases were signed on December 31, 198A, at which time the prevailing interest rate available to Bigtime for equipment loans was 12%.

Required:

(Round all amounts in your answers to the nearest whole dollar.)

1. Prepare any required entries to record the lease of *(a)* Truck 1 and *(b)* Truck 2.
2. Prepare the required entries as of the end of the first year in *(a)* the life of Truck 1 and *(b)* the life of Truck 2. Use straight-line depreciation. (Hint: If the length of a capital lease is less than the asset's estimated service life and the asset remains the property of the lessor, depreciation must be taken over the length of the lease.)
3. Truck 1 was returned to the lessor on December 31, 198G, the end of the sixth year. Prepare the required entries as of the end of the sixth year in *(a)* the life of Truck 1 and *(b)* the life of Truck 2.
4. Show how Truck 2 and the lease liability for the truck should appear on the balance sheet as of the end of the sixth year in the life of the lease (after the year-end lease payment).

ALTERNATE PROBLEMS

Problem 12–1A   *Part 1.*   Terry Company sells a single product subject to a one-year warranty that covers replacement parts but not labour. The company uses a periodic inventory system to account for merchandise. Prepare journal entries to record the following transactions completed by the company during the month of August.

Aug. 1   Purchased 3,500 units of merchandise for $77 per unit, paying cash.
     3   Purchased $31,850 of spare parts for making repairs to merchandise that is expected to be returned for warranty work.
     6   Sold 1,400 units of merchandise for $175 per unit, receiving cash.
   12   Repaired 70 units of merchandise that customers returned under the warranty. Replacement parts cost $4,214 and the customers paid $3,246 for labour.
   19   Sold 1,750 units of merchandise for $193 per unit.
   24   Repaired 49 units of merchandise under the product warranty. Replacement parts cost $2,570 and the customers paid $2,328 for labour.
   30   Recorded warranty expense for August. Past experience shows that 4.0% of the units sold require warranty work and the average cost of replacement parts is $56 per unit returned. Average labour charges are $44.

Part 2. Wimberley Company accrues property taxes at the end of each month and uses recent experience as a means of estimating the tax. In early 198A, Wimberley's property was appraised at $600,000. The 198A tax levy was $1.40 per $100. In January 198B, Wimberley's property was reappraised at $644,000. (The reappraisal was not expected to affect the tax levy of $1.40 per $100.) Early in July 198B, the annual tax levy was set at $1.65 per $100. On October 31, 198B, Wimberley paid the 198B tax. Complete financial statements are prepared by the company on a monthly basis and the company does not use reversing entries.

Required:

Prepare entries at the end of January, July, October, and November 198B, to record property tax expense for each of those months and to record the annual tax payment.

Problem 12–2A

Prepare general journal entries to record these transactions:

Jan. 28   Purchased merchandise on credit from Gaffey Company, invoice dated January 8, terms 2/10, n/60, $37,440.
Feb. 20   Borrowed money at Capital City Bank by discounting our own $54,000 note payable for 60 days at 10%.
Apr. 5   Gave Gaffey Company $2,440 cash and a $35,000, 60-day, 12% note to secure an extension on our past-due account.
   24   Paid the note discounted at Capital City Bank on February 20.
June 7   Paid the note given Gaffey Company on April 5.
Nov. 16   Borrowed money at Capital City Bank by discounting our own $70,000 note payable for 90 days at 13%.
Dec. 1   Borrowed money at Farmers' First Bank by giving a $50,000, 60-day, 14% note payable.
   31   Made an adjusting entry to recognize interest expense applicable to the current year on the note discounted at Capital City Bank on November 16.
   31   Made an adjusting entry to record the accrued interest on the note given Farmers' First Bank on December 1.
Feb. 2   Paid the note given Farmers' First Bank on December 1.
   17   Paid the note discounted at Capital City Bank on November 16.

Problem 12–3A

High Sky Airways is negotiating with an airframe outfitter in planning the interior finishings of a nine-passenger turboprop that High Sky Airways expects to acquire and place in charter service. The airplane will be completed and ready for service four years hence. If High Sky pays for the airplane upon completion (Payment Plan A), it will cost $1,687,500. However, two alternative payment plans are available. Plan B would require an immediate payment of $1,218,750. Plan C would require four annual payments of $356,250, the first of which would be made one year hence. In evaluating the three alternatives, the management of High Sky has decided to assume an interest rate of 9%.

Required:

Calculate the present value of each payment and indicate which plan High Sky should follow.

Problem 12–4A

On January 1, 198A, Infomart Company gave its own $300,000 noninterest-bearing, six-year note payable in exchange for a machine, the cash price of which was not readily determinable. The market rate for interest on such notes on the day of the exchange was 8% annually.

Required:

(Round all amounts in your answers to the nearest whole dollar.)

1. Prepare a form with the following columnar headings and calculate and fill in the required amounts for the six years the note is outstanding.

Year	Beginning-of-Year Carrying Amount	Discount to Be Amortized Each Year	Unamortized Discount at End of Year	End-of-Year Carrying Amount

2. Prepare general journal entries to record: *(a)* the acquisition of the machine, *(b)* the discount amortized at the end of each of the first three years, and *(c)* the payment of the note on January 1, 198G.
3. Show how the note should appear on the December 31, 198C, balance sheet.

Problem 12–5A

Jetstar Production Company leased a machine on January 1, 198A, under a contract calling for annual payments of $57,600 on December 31 at the end of each of five years, with the machine becoming the property of the lessee company after the fifth $57,600 payment. The machine was estimated to have a six-year life and no salvage value, and the interest rate available to Jetstar for equipment loans on the day the lease was signed was 14%. The machine was delivered on January 3, 198A, and was immediately placed in operation. At the beginning of the sixth year in the machine's life, it was overhauled at a $6,800 total cost. The overhaul was paid for on January 6, and it did not increase the machine's efficiency but it did add an additional two years to its expected service life. On April 30, during the eighth year in the machine's life, it was traded in on a new machine having a $172,000 cash price. A $12,000 trade-in allowance was received and the balance was paid in cash. The gain or loss on the exchange was not material in amount.

Required:

(Round all amounts in your answers to the nearest whole dollar.)

1. Prepare a schedule with the columnar headings of Illustration 12–3. Enter the years 198A through 198E in the first column and complete the schedule by filling in the proper amounts.
2. Prepare the entry to record the leasing of the machine.
3. Prepare December 31, 198B, entries to record annual depreciation on a straight-line basis, to record the lease payment, and to amortize the discount in the life of the lease. Also show how the machine and the lease liability should appear on the December 31, 198B, balance sheet.
4. Prepare the entries to record the machine's overhaul and the depreciation on the machine at the end of its sixth year.
5. Prepare the April 30, 198H, entries to record the exchange of the machines.

Problem 12–6A

The Northwest News Company leased two new printing presses. Each of the presses has an estimated service life of seven years. Press 1 was leased for five years. Press 2 was leased for six years. Each lease agreement calls for $20,000 annual lease payments at the end of the year ($40,000 for both presses). When the period of each lease expires, each press will be returned to the lessor. Both leases were signed on December 31, 198A, at which time the prevailing interest rate available to Northwest News for equipment loans was 10%. Each of the presses could have been purchased for $90,000 cash.

Required:

(Round all amounts in your answers to the nearest whole dollar.)

1. Prepare any required entries to record the lease of *(a)* Press 1 and *(b)* Press 2.
2. Prepare the required entries as of the end of the first year in *(a)* the life of Press 1 and *(b)* the life of Press 2. Use straight-line depreciation. (Hint: If the length of a capital lease is less than the asset's estimated service life and the asset remains the property of the lessor, depreciation must be taken over the length of the lease.)
3. Press 1 was returned to the lessor on December 31, 198F, the end of the fifth year. Prepare the required entries as of the end of the fifth year in *(a)* the life of Press 1 and *(b)* the life of Press 2.
4. Show how Press 2 and the lease liability for the press should appear on the balance sheet as of the end of the fifth year in the life of the lease (after the year-end lease payment).

PROVOCATIVE PROBLEMS

Provocative Problem 12–1, Yellow Bird Coach Industries, Inc.

Yellow Bird Coach Industries, Inc., is a manufacturing company with operations in both Canada and the United States. The footnotes to the company's 1985 financial statements included the following comments:

In April 1985, the Arrow Corporation filed suit against the Company for $25 million in compensatory damages plus punitive damages for an equal amount. The suit alleges that at the time of the sale by the Company of a transit bus business to Arrow Corporation in January 1980, the Company materially misrepresented and concealed material facts relative to the development and testing of the Model 870 bus. The Company has engaged counsel, filed an answer to the complaint totally denying the allegations, and has commenced pretrial, discovery proceedings. The Company intends to vigorously defend this matter. It believes that it has numerous and substantial defenses, that it will ultimately prevail in the lawsuit, and that the resolution of this matter will not have a material adverse financial impact upon the Company.

Comment on the reasons why the management of Yellow Bird Coach Industries, Inc., decided to include the above statements among the footnotes to the company's financial statements. Based on the description in the footnote, would you expect to find a loss reported in Yellow Bird's 1985 income statement? Support your answer with reasons.

Provocative Problem 12–2, Financing Beckwith Corporation's New Equipment

Beckwith Corporation is planning to acquire some new equipment from Nelson Company and has asked you to assist in analyzing the situation. The equipment may be purchased for $275,000 and then will be leased by Beckwith under a 10-year lease contract to a customer for $50,000 payable at the end of each year. After the lease expires, Beckwith expects to sell the equipment for $75,000.

1. Suppose Beckwith has $275,000 cash available to buy the equipment and requires a 14% rate of return on its investments. Should the company buy the equipment and lease it to the customer?

2. As an alternative to paying cash, Beckwith can invest the $275,000 in other operations for five years and earn 14% annually on its investment. If this is done, the equipment may be purchased by signing a $500,000, five-year, noninterest-bearing note payable to Nelson Company. Should Beckwith pay $275,000 now or sign the $500,000 note?

3. Now suppose Beckwith does not have the option of signing a $500,000, five-year, noninterest-bearing note. Instead, the company may either pay $275,000 cash or lease the equipment from Nelson Company for eight years, after which the equipment would become the property of Beckwith. The lease contract would require $62,500 payments at the end of each year. If Beckwith leases the equipment, it will invest the $275,000 available cash in other operations and earn 14% on the investment. Should Beckwith pay cash or lease the equipment from Nelson?

ANALYTICAL AND REVIEW PROBLEMS

Problem 12–1 A&R

Refer to Mini Discussion Case 12–1 and prepare journal entries for each of the alternatives as of the date of signing the contract and at the end of the first year. Also indicate balance sheet presentation as of the end of the first year. Assume:

1. The going rate of interest is 12%.
2. The company amortizes and/or depreciates assets on a straight-line basis.
3. Use interest method to recognize interest expense.

Problem 12–2 A&R

On September 1, 1987, Wong Company acquired a machine by paying $10,000 cash and signing a two-year note that carried a face amount of $40,000 due at the end of the two-year period; the note did not specify interest. Assume the going rate of interest for this company for this type of loan is 12%. The accounting period ends December 31.

Required:

Give the entry to record the purchase of the machine and complete a tabulation as follows (round amounts to nearest dollar):

	Straight-line method	Interest method
1. Cash to be paid at maturity	$_____	$_____
2. Total interest expense	$_____	$_____
3. Interest expense on income statement for 1987	$_____	$_____
4. Amount of the liability reported on balance sheet at end of 1987	$_____	$_____
5. Depreciation expense for 1987 (assume straight-line, partial year, no residual value and useful life of five years)	$_____	$_____

Problem 12–3 A&R

For the purpose of stimulating sales, Aroma Coffee Company places a coupon in each can of coffee sold; the coupons are redeemable in dishes. Each premium cost the company $1.00 (the cost of printing is negligible). Ten coupons must be presented by the customers to receive one premium. The following data are available:

Year	Cans of coffee sold	Premiums purchased	Coupons redeemed
198A	1,000,000	65,000	500,000
198B	1,200,000	100,000	1,100,000
198C	900,000	70,000	600,000

It is estimated that only 80% of the coupons will be presented for redemption.

Required:

a. Compute the amount of the premium inventory, liability for premiums outstanding and the expenses applicable to each year.
b. Give all the necessary entries for each year.

Payroll Accounting

13

After studying Chapter 13, you should be able to:

List the taxes that are withheld from employees' wages and the payroll taxes that are levied on employers.

Calculate an employee's gross pay and the various deductions from the pay.

Prepare a Payroll Register and make the entries to record its information and to pay the employees.

Explain the operation of a payroll bank account.

Calculate and prepare the entries to record the payroll taxes levied on an employer and to record employee fringe benefit costs.

Define or explain the words and phrases listed in the chapter Glossary.

An understanding of payroll accounting and the design and use of payroll records require some knowledge of the laws and programs that affect payrolls. Consequently, the more pertinent of these are discussed in the first portion of this chapter before the subject of payroll records is introduced.

UNEMPLOYMENT INSURANCE

To alleviate hardships caused by interruptions in earnings through unemployment, the federal government, with the concurrence of all provincial governments, implemented an employee-employer financed unemployment insurance plan in 1940. The 1940 Unemployment Insurance Act created a federal agency, the Unemployment Commission, which was charged with the administration of the Act. Under the Act, all employment in Canada was subjected to compulsory insurance unless specifically exempt by the legislation. Exempted classifications included employment as (1) a member of the Canadian Forces; (2) a private duty nurse; (3) a teacher; (4) a farmer; (5) a hunter or trapper; (6) a domestic; (7) a permanent civil servant; (8) employee of husband, wife, etc.; (9) a commission salesperson of insurance, real estate, and securities; and (10) employment where annual remuneration was in excess of $7,800. In 1971 the then existing legislation was rescinded and the Unemployment Insurance Act, 1971, was passed. Under this Act, compulsory *unemployment insurance* coverage was extended to all Canadian workers who are not self-employed. As of January 1, 1984, over 12 million employees, including teachers, hospital workers, and top-level executives were covered by the insurance plan.

The purpose of an unemployment insurance program is usually twofold:

1. To pay unemployment compensation for limited periods to unemployed individuals eligible for benefits.
2. To establish and operate employment facilities that assist unemployed individuals in finding suitable employment and assist employers in finding employees.

Such was the purpose of the original Unemployment Insurance Act from its passage to April 1, 1966. On that date the employment function was transferred to the Department of Manpower and Immigration. The Unemployment Commission continued the compensation function with responsibility for (1) revenue collection and control and (2) administration of claims and benefits. On July 1, 1971, the collection function was assumed by Revenue Canada, Taxation Division.

The unemployment insurance fund from which benefits are paid is jointly financed by employees and their employers. Under the original act, equal contributions were made by each group. Under the current act, in 1986, an employer is required to deduct from his/her employees' wages 2.35% of insured earnings, to add his/her contribution of 1.4 times the amount deducted from employees' wages, and to remit both amounts to the Receiver General of Canada. Insured earnings refer to average weekly *gross pay* in the range of $99 to $495. Employees paid in whole or in part on a time-worked or fixed-salary basis must be employed at least 15 hours in a weekly pay period or earn 20% of the maximum weekly insurable earnings ($460 in 1986) in order to be insurable. The maximum amount deductible per year is $604.90 (in 1986). This amount is adjusted for weekly or monthly pay periods by dividing by the appropriate number; that is, 52, 12, and so on.

The Unemployment Insurance Act, in addition to setting rates, requires that an employer:

1. Withhold from the wages of each employee each payday an amount of unemployment insurance tax calculated at the current rate.
2. Pay an unemployment insurance tax equal to 1.4 times the amount withheld from the wages of all employees.
3. Periodically remit both the amounts withheld from employees' wages and the employer's tax to the Receiver General of Canada. (Remittance is discussed later in this chapter.)
4. To complete a "Record of Employment" form for employees who experience an "interruption of earnings" because of termination of employment, illness, injury, or pregnancy.
5. Keep a record for each employee that shows among other things wages subject to unemployment insurance and taxes withheld. (The law does not specify the exact form of the record, but most employers keep individual employee earnings records similar to the one shown later in this chapter.)

WEEKLY UNEMPLOYMENT BENEFITS

The amount of weekly benefits received by an unemployed individual who qualifies is based on his/her average insurable weekly earnings. The federal government has varied the benefit period from region to region on the basis of percentage and duration of unemployment in the region.

WITHHOLDING EMPLOYEES' INCOME TAX

With few exceptions, employers are required to calculate, collect, and remit to the Receiver General of Canada the income taxes of their employees. Historically, although the first federal income tax law became effective in 1917, it applied to only a few individuals having high earnings, and it was not until World War II that income taxes were levied on substantially all wage earners. At that time Parliament recognized that many individual wage earners could not be expected to save sufficient money with which to pay their income taxes once each year. Consequently, Parliament instituted a system of pay-as-you-go, withholding of taxes each payday at their source. This pay-as-you-go withholding of employee income taxes requires an employer to act as a tax collecting agent of the federal government.

The amount of income tax to be withheld from an employee's wages is determined by his wages and the amount of his exemptions. Each individual is entitled, in 1986, to the following exemptions (as applicable) at a minimum:

1.	Basic exemption for a single person	$4,180
2.	Married or equivalent exemption, an additional . . .	3,660
3.	Exemption for each dependent child:	
	Under 18 years of age	710
	Over 18 years of age	1,420

With maximum earnings by dependent stipulated

The $4,180 basic exemption, or withholding allowance, of a single person exempts the first $4,180 of an employee's annual wages from income tax; and if entitled, an employee may claim the additional exemptions listed. Also, an employee may claim other exemptions, such as for a dependent parent, grandparent, or relative, or for seasonal or part-time employment.

Employers are responsible for determining and withholding each payday the required amount from each of their employee's pay for income taxes. However, to do so an employer must know the exemptions claimed by each of his employees. Consequently, every employee is required to file with his employer an Employee's Tax Deduction Return, Form TD1, on which he claims the exemption to which he is entitled, and he must file a revised Form TD1 each time his exemptions change during a year.

In determining the amounts of income taxes to be withheld from the wages of employees, employers normally use tax withholding tables provided by Revenue Canada, Taxation. The tables indicate the tax to be withheld from any amount of wages and with any number of exemptions. The to-be-withheld amounts include both federal and provincial income taxes except for the province of Quebec. The province of Quebec levies and collects its own income tax and its own pension plan contributions. Employers in that province remit separately, to the respective authority, federal and provincial tax deductions.

In addition to determining and withholding income taxes from each employee's wages every payday, employers are required to:

1. Remit the withheld taxes to the Receiver General of Canada.
2. On or before the last day of February following each year, give each employee a T-4 statement which tells the employee:
   a. Total wages for the preceding year.
   b. Taxable benefits received from the employer.
   c. Income taxes withheld.
   d. Deductions for registered pension plan.
   e. Canada Pension Plan contributions.
   f. Unemployment insurance deductions.
3. On or before the last day of February following each year, forward to the District Taxation office copies of the employees' T-4 statements plus a T-4 A form on which is summarized the information contained on the employees' T-4 statements.

THE CANADA PENSION PLAN

The *Canada Pension Plan* applies, with few exceptions, to everyone who is working. Every employee and the self-employed between the ages of 18 and 70 must make contributions in required amounts to the Canada Pension Plan. Self-employed individuals are required to remit periodically appropriate amounts to the Receiver General of Canada. Employee contributions are deducted by the employer from salary, wages, or other remuneration paid to the employee. Furthermore, each employer is required to contribute an amount equal to that deducted from his employees' earnings.

Contributions are based on earnings with the first $2,500 of each employee's annual earnings being exempt. On earnings above that amount, and up to the 1986 ceiling of $23,300 a year, the employee contributes at the rate of 1.8%. Thus, the total contribution from both employee and employer is 3.6% of earnings subject to the Canada Pension Plan tax. The ceiling on pensionable earnings has been raised in stages from the $5,400 in 1971 to $23,300 in 1986.

Employers are responsible for making the proper deductions from their employees' earnings. The employer remits these deductions each month, together with his own contributions, to the Receiver General of Canada.

Self-employed individuals pay the combined rate for employees and employers, or 3.6% on annual earnings between $2,500 and the tax-exempt ceiling of $23,300.

Most employers use *wage bracket withholding tables* similar to the one for 1986 shown in Illustration 13–1 in determining Canada Pension Plan and Unemployment Insurance to be withheld from employee's gross earnings. The illustrated table is for a weekly pay period; different tables are provided for different pay periods. Somewhat similar tables are available for determining income tax withholdings.

Illustration 13–1

UNEMPLOYMENT INSURANCE PREMIUMS   **PRIMES D'ASSURANCE-CHÔMAGE**

For minimum and maximum insurable earnings amounts for various pay periods see Schedule II. For the maximum premium deduction for various pay periods see bottom of this page.

Les montants minimum et maximum des gains assurables pour diverses périodes de paie figurent en annexe II. La déduction maximale de primes pour diverses périodes de paie figure au bas de la présente page.

Remuneration / Rémunération		U.I. Premium Prime	Remuneration / Rémunération		U.I. Premium Prime	Remuneration / Rémunération		U.I. Premium Prime	Remuneration / Rémunération		U.I. Premium Prime
From-de	To-à	d'a.-c.	From-de	To-à	d'a.-c.	From-de	To-à	d'a.-c.	From-de	To-à	d'a.-c.
245.32	245.74	5.77	275.96	276.38	6.49	306.60	307.02	7.21	337.24	337.65	7.93
245.75	246.17	5.78	276.39	276.80	6.50	307.03	307.44	7.22	337.66	338.08	7.94
246.18	246.59	5.79	276.81	277.23	6.51	307.45	307.87	7.23	338.09	338.51	7.95
246.60	247.02	5.80	277.24	277.65	6.52	307.88	308.29	7.24	338.52	338.93	7.96
247.03	247.44	5.81	277.66	278.08	6.53	308.30	308.72	7.25	338.94	339.36	7.97
247.45	247.87	5.82	278.09	278.51	6.54	308.73	309.14	7.26	339.37	- .78	7.98
247.88	248.29	5.83	278.52	278.93	6.55	309.15	309.57	7.27		.21	7.99
248.30	248.72	5.84	278.94	279.36	6.56	309.58	309.99			.63	8.00
248.73	249.14	5.85	279.37	279.78	6.57	310.00	310.			.06	8.01
249.15	249.57	5.86	279.79	280.21	6.58					.8	8.02
249.58	249.99	5.87	280.22	280.63						.1	8.03
250.00	250.42	5.88	280.64								8.04
250.43	250.85		281.								8.05
250.86	251.27	5.90									8.06
251.28	251.70										8.07
251.71	-										8.08
											8.09
											8.10
											8.11
											8.12
											8.13
											8.14
											8.15

COTISATIONS AU RÉGIME DE PENSIONS DU CANADA

CANADA PENSION PLAN CONTRIBUTIONS

WEEKLY PAY PERIOD — PÉRIODE HEBDOMADAIRE DE PAIE

207.80 — 367.79

Remuneration / Rémunération		C.P.P. R.P.C.	Remuneration / Rémunération		C.P.P. R.P.C.	Remuneration / Rémunération		C.P.P. R.P.C.	Remuneration / Rémunération		C.P.P. R.P.C.
From-de	To-à		From-de	To-à		From-de	To-à		From-de	To-à	
207.80	208.34	2.88	247.80	248.34	3.60	287.80	288.34	4.32	327.80	328.34	5.04
208.35	208.90	2.89	248.35	249.45	3.61	288.35	289.45	4.33	328.35	329.45	5.05
208.91	209.45	2.91	248.91	250.01	3.62	288.91	290.01	4.35	328.91	330.01	5.07
209.46	210.56	2.92	249.46	250.56	3.64	289.46	290.56	4.36	329.46	330.01	5.08
210.02	211.12	2.93	250.02	251.12	3.65	290.02	291.12	4.37	330.02	331.12	5.10
210.57	211.68	2.94	250.57	251.68	3.66	290.57	291.68	4.38	330.57	331.58	5.11
211.13	212.23	2.95	251.13	252.23	3.67	291.13	292.23	4.40	331.13	332.23	5.12
211.69	212.79		251.69	252.79	3.68	291.69	292.79		331.69	332.79	
212.24			252.24			292.24					5.13
212.80	213.74	2.97	252.80	253.34	3.69	292.80	293.74	4.41	332.80	333.34	5.14
213.35	213.90	2.98	253.35	253.90	3.70	293.35	293.90	4.42	333.35	333.90	5.15
213.91	214.45	2.99	253.91	254.45	3.71	293.91	294.45	4.43	333.91	334.45	5.17
214.46	215.01	3.00	254.46	255.01	3.72	294.46	295.01	4.45	334.46	335.01	5.18
215.02	215.56	3.01	255.02	256.12	3.73	295.02	296.12	4.46	335.02	335.56	5.19
215.57	216.68	3.02	255.57	256.68	3.74	295.57	296.68	4.47	335.57	336.13	5.20
216.13	217.23	3.03	256.13	257.23	3.75	296.13	297.23	4.48	336.13	337.23	5.22
216.69	217.79	3.04	256.69	257.79	3.76	296.69	297.79		336.69	337.23	5.23
217.24		3.05	257.24		3.77	297.24			337.24		5.24
217.80	218.34	3.06	257.80	258.34	3.78	297.80	298.34	4.50	337.80	338.34	5.25
218.35	218.90	3.07	258.35	258.90	3.79	298.35	298.90	4.52	338.35	339.45	5.26
218.91	219.45	3.08	258.91	260.01	3.80	298.91	300.01	4.53	338.91	340.01	5.27
219.46	220.01	3.09	259.46	260.56	3.81	299.46	300.56	4.54	339.46	340.01	5.28
220.02	220.56	3.10	260.02	261.12	3.82	300.02	301.12	4.55	340.02	341.12	5.29
220.57	221.12	3.11	260.57	261.68	3.83	300.57	301.68	4.56	340.57	341.68	5.30
221.13	221.69	3.12	261.13	262.23	3.84	301.13	302.23	4.57	341.13	342.23	
221.69	222.23	3.13	261.69	262.79	3.85	301.69	302.79		341.65	342.79	5.31
222.24	222.79	3.14	262.24		3.86	302.24			342.24		5.32
222.80	223.34	3.15	262.80	263.34	3.87	302.80	303.34	4.58	342.80	343.34	5.33
223.35	223.90	3.16	263.35	263.90	3.88				343.35	343.90	
223.91	224.45		263.91	264.45	3.89				343.91		

Determining the amount of withholdings from an employee's gross wages is quite easy when withholding tables are used. First, the employee's wage bracket is located in the first two columns. Then the amounts to be withheld for Canada Pension Plan and Unemployment Insurance are found on the line of the wage bracket in the appropriate columns.

WORKERS' COMPENSATION

Legislation is in effect in all provinces for payments to employees for an injury or disability arising out of or in the course of their employment. Under the provincial workers' compensation acts, employers are in effect required to "insure" their employees against injury or disability that may arise as a result of employment. Premiums are normally based on: (1) accident experience of the industrial classification to which each business is assigned and (2) the total payroll.

Procedures for payment are as follows:

1. At the beginning of each year every covered employer is required to submit to the Workers' Compensation Board an estimate of his/her expected payroll for the ensuing year.
2. Provisional premiums are then established by the board by relating estimated requirements for disability payments to estimated payroll. Provisional premium notices are then sent to all employers.
3. Provisional premiums are normally payable in from three to six installments during the year.
4. At the end of each year actual payrolls are submitted to the board and final assessments are made based on actual payrolls and actual payments. Premiums are normally between 1% and 3% of payrolls and are borne by the employer.

WAGES, HOURS, AND UNION CONTRACTS

All provinces have laws establishing maximum hours of work and minimum pay rates; and while the details vary with each province, generally, employers are required to pay an employee for hours worked in excess of 40 in any one week at the employee's regular pay rate plus an overtime premium of at least one half of his or her regular rate. This gives an employee an overtime rate of at least $1\frac{1}{2}$ times his or her regular hourly rate for hours in excess of 40 in any one week. In addition, employers commonly operate under contracts with their employees' union that provide even better terms. For example, union contracts often provide for time and a half for work in excess of eight hours in any one day, time and a half for work on Saturdays, and double time for Sundays and holidays. When an employer is under such a union contract, since the contract terms are better than those provided for by law, the contract terms take precedence over the law.

In addition to specifying working hours and wage rates, union contracts often provide for the collection of employees' union dues by the employer. Such a requirement commonly provides that the employer shall deduct dues from the wages of each employee and remit the amounts deducted to the union. The employer is usually required to remit once each month and to report the name and amount deducted from each employee's pay.

OTHER PAYROLL DEDUCTIONS

In addition to the payroll deductions discussed thus far, employees may individually authorize additional deductions. Some examples of these might be:

1. Deductions to accumulate funds for the purchase of Government of Canada bonds.
2. Deductions to pay health, accident, hospital, or life insurance premiums.
3. Deductions to repay loans from the employer or the employees' credit union.
4. Deductions to pay for merchandise purchased from the company.
5. Deductions for donations to charitable organizations such as Boy Scouts, Girl Scouts, United Way Fund, or Red Cross.

TIMEKEEPING

Compiling a record of the time worked by each employee is called *timekeeping.* In an individual company the method of compiling such a record depends upon the nature of the business and the number of its employees. In a very small business timekeeping may consist of no more than pencil notations of each employee's working time made in a memorandum book by the manager or owner. On the other hand, in larger companies a time clock or several time clocks are often used to record on *clock cards* each employee's time of arrival and departure. When time clocks are used, they are usually placed near entrances to the office, store, or factory. At the beginning of each payroll period a clock card for each employee similar to Illustration 13–2 is placed in a rack for use by the employee. Upon arriving at work, an employee takes his or her card from the rack and places it in a slot in the time clock. This actuates the clock to stamp the date and arrival time on the card. The employee then returns the card to the rack and proceeds to his or her place of work. Upon leaving the plant, store, or office for lunch or at the end of the day, the procedure is repeated. The employee takes the card from the rack and places it in the clock, and the time of departure is automatically stamped. As a result, at the end of each pay period the card shows the hours the employee was at work.

THE PAYROLL REGISTER

Each pay period the total hours worked as compiled on clock cards or otherwise is summarized in a Payroll Register. A typical example of such a register is shown in Illustration 13–3. The illustrated register is for a weekly pay period and shows the payroll data for each employee on a separate line. The column headings and the data recorded in the columns are, for the most part, self-explanatory.

The columns under the heading "Daily Time" show the hours worked each day by each employee. The total of each employee's hours is

Illustration 13–2

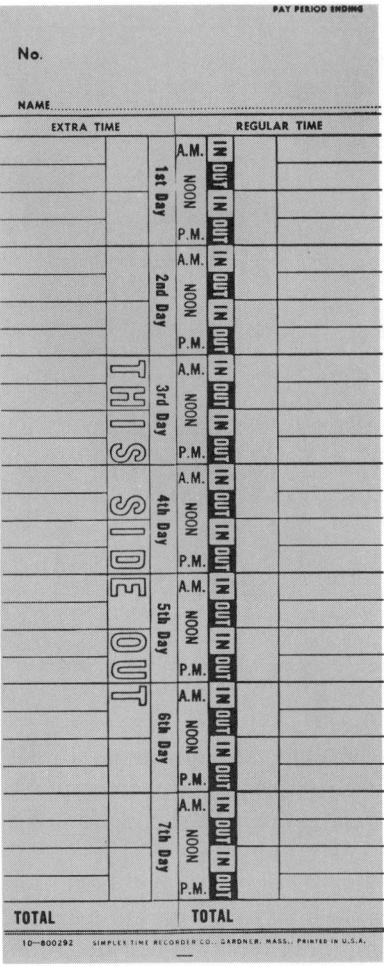

Courtesy Simplex Time Recorder Co.

entered in the column headed "Total Hours." If hours worked include overtime hours, these are entered in the column headed "O.T. Hours."

The column headed "Reg. Pay Rate" is for the hourly pay rate of each employee. Total hours worked multiplied by the regular pay rate equals regular pay. Overtime hours multiplied by the overtime premium rate equals overtime premium pay. And, regular pay plus overtime premium pay is the gross pay of each employee.

Under the heading "Deductions," the amounts withheld from each employee's gross pay for unemployment insurance premiums are shown

Illustration 13–3

Payroll
Week ended

Employees	Clock Card No.	Daily Time							Total Hours	O.T. Hours	Earnings			
		M	T	W	T	F	S	S			Reg. Pay Rate	Reg-ular Pay	O.T. Pre-mium Pay	Gross Pay
Robert Austin	114	8	8	8	8	8			40		10.00	400.00		400.00
Judy Cross	102	8	8	8	8	8			40		15.00	600.00		600.00
John Cruz	108	0	8	8	8	8	8		40		12.00	480.00		480.00
Kay Keife	109	8	8	8	8	8	8		48	8	12.00	576.00	48.00	624.00
Lee Miller	112	8	8	8	8	0			32		12.00	384.00		384.00
Dale Sears	103	8	8	8	8	8	4		44	4	15.00	660.00	30.00	690.00
Totals												3100.00	78.00	3178.00

in the column marked "Unemployment Insurance." The amounts were determined by multiplying the gross pay of each employee, by the 2.35% unemployment insurance rate. Maximum deduction of $11.63 per week is reached at gross weekly earnings of $495 (1986).

As previously stated, the income tax withheld from the wages of each employee depends upon his gross pay and exemptions and is commonly determined by using a tax table. When determined, it is entered in the column headed "Income Taxes."

Deductions from employees' wages for Canada Pension Plan (C.P.P.) are entered in the column carrying that heading. In determining the amounts to be withheld, employers commonly use a tax table. Recall that the first $2,500 of an employee's earnings are exempt from pension plan deductions. Likewise, earnings above a $23,300 ceiling in 1986 are also exempt. The table spreads the $2,500 exemption over the entire year for an employee having annual earnings less than $23,300; and if it is a weekly table, it allocates 1/52d of the $2,500, or $48.08 to each week. As a result of the allocation the pension plan deduction of the first employee of the Illustration 13–2 payroll is $400 gross pay, minus $48.08 multiplied by 1.8% or $6.33.

The column headed "Hosp. Ins." shows the amounts withheld from employees' wages to pay hospital insurance premiums for the employees and their families. The total withheld from all employees is a current

Register
March 26, 19—

U.I. Premium	Income Taxes	Hosp. Ins.	C.P.P.	Total Deductions	Net Pay	Cheque No.	Sales Salaries	Office Salaries
9.40	74.95	8.00	6.33	98.68	301.32	893		400.00
11.63	138.40	8.00	9.97	168.00	432.00	894	600.00	
11.28	96.15	15.00	7.77	130.20	349.80	895	480.00	
11.63	145.90	8.00	10.33	175.86	448.14	896	624.00	
9.02	65.05	8.00	6.05	88.12	295.88	897	384.00	
11.63	172.15	15.00	11.59	210.37	479.63	898		690.00
64.59	692.60	62.00	52.04	871.23	2,306.77		2,088,00	1,090.00

(Column group headers: **Deductions** spans U.I. Premium through Total Deductions; **Payment** spans Net Pay and Cheque No.; **Distribution** spans Sales Salaries and Office Salaries.)

liability of the employer until paid to a provincial agency or an insurance company.

Additional columns may be added to the Payroll Register for deductions that occur sufficiently often to warrant special columns. For example, a company that regularly deducts amounts from its employees' pay for Government of Canada bonds may add a special column for this deduction.

An employee's gross pay less his or her total deductions is his or her *net pay* and is entered in the column headed "Net Pay." The total of this column is the amount to be paid the employees. The numbers of the cheques in paying the employees are entered in the column headed "Cheque No."

The two columns under the heading "Distribution" are for sorting the various salaries into kinds of salary expense. Here each employee's gross salary is entered in the proper column according to the type of work performed. The column totals then indicate the amounts to be debited to the salary expense accounts.

RECORDING THE PAYROLL

Generally a Payroll Register such as the one shown is a supplementary memorandum record. As such, its information is not posted directly to the accounts but is first recorded with a general journal entry, which is then posted. The entry to record the payroll shown in Illustration 13–3 is:

March	26	Sales Salaries Expense	2,088.00	
		Office Salaries Expense	1,090.00	
		Unemployment Insurance Payable		64.59
		Employees' Income Taxes Payable		692.60
		Canada Pension Plan Payable		52.04
		Employees' Hospital Insurance Payable		62.00
		Accrued Payroll Payable		2,306.77
		To record the March 26 payroll.		

The debits of this entry are taken from the Payroll Register's distribution column totals, and they charge the employees' gross earnings to the proper salary expense accounts. The credits to Unemployment Insurance Taxes Payable, Employees' Income Taxes Payable, Canada Pension Plan Taxes Payable, and Employees' Hospital Insurance Payable record these amounts as current liabilities. The credit to Accrued Payroll Payable records as a liability the net amount to be paid the employees.

PAYING THE EMPLOYEES

Almost every business pays its employees by cheque. In a company having but few employees these cheques are often drawn on the regular bank account. When this is done, each cheque is recorded in either a Cheque Register or a Cash Disbursements Journal. Since each cheque results in a debit to the Accrued Payroll Payable account, posting labour may be saved by adding an Accrued Payroll Payable debit column to the Cheque Register or Cash Disbursements Journal. For example, assume that a firm uses a Cheque Disbursements Journal like that described in Chapter 6, before the introduction of the voucher system. If a firm uses such a register and adds an Accrued Payroll debit column, the entries to pay the employees of the Illustration 13–3 payroll will appear somewhat like those in Illustration 13–4.

Although not required by law, most employers furnish each employee an earnings statement each payday. The objective of such a statement is to inform the employee and give him a record of hours worked, gross pay, deductions, and net pay that may be retained. The statement usually takes the form of a detachable pay cheque portion that is removed before the cheque is cashed. A pay cheque with a detachable portion showing deductions is reproduced in Illustration 13–5.

Illustration 13–4

Cash Disbursements Journal

Date	Ch. No.	Payee	Account Debited	PR	Other Accounts Debit	Accts. Pay. Debit	Accr. Payroll Pay. Debit	Pur. Dis. Credit	Cash Credit
Mar. 26	893	Robert Austin	Accrued Payroll				301.32		301.32
26	894	Judy Cross	"				432.00		432.00
26	895	John Cruz	"				349.80		349.80
26	896	Kay Keife	"				448.14		448.14
26	897	Lee Miller	"				295.88		295.88
26	898	Dale Sears	"				479.63		479.63

Illustration 13–5

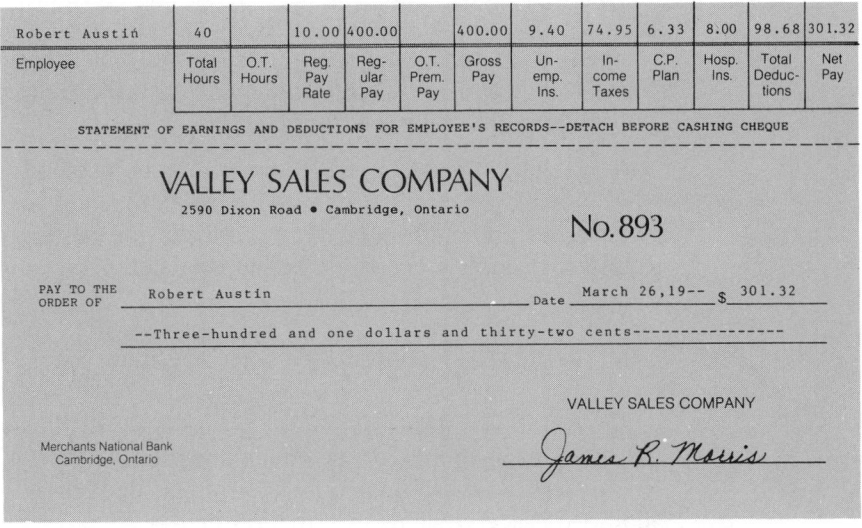

Robert Austin	40		10.00	400.00		400.00	9.40	74.95	6.33	8.00	98.68	301.32
Employee	Total Hours	O.T. Hours	Reg. Pay Rate	Regular Pay	O.T. Prem. Pay	Gross Pay	Un-emp. Ins.	In-come Taxes	C.P. Plan	Hosp. Ins.	Total Deduc-tions	Net Pay

STATEMENT OF EARNINGS AND DEDUCTIONS FOR EMPLOYEE'S RECORDS--DETACH BEFORE CASHING CHEQUE

- -

VALLEY SALES COMPANY
2590 Dixon Road • Cambridge, Ontario

No. 893

PAY TO THE ORDER OF   Robert Austin   Date March 26,19-- $ 301.32

--Three-hundred and one dollars and thirty-two cents----------------

VALLEY SALES COMPANY

James R. Morris

Merchants National Bank
Cambridge, Ontario

PAYROLL BANK ACCOUNT

A business with many employees normally makes use of a special *payroll bank account* in paying its employees. When such an account is used, one cheque for the amount of the payroll is drawn on the regular bank account and deposited in the special payroll bank account. Individual payroll cheques are then drawn on this special payroll account. Because only one cheque for the payroll is drawn on the regular bank account each payday, a special payroll bank account simplifies reconciliation of the regular bank account. It may be reconciled without considering the payroll cheques outstanding, and there may be many of these. Likewise, when the payroll bank account is separately reconciled, only the outstanding payroll cheques need be considered.

A company using a special payroll bank account completes the following steps in paying its employees:

1. First, it records the information shown on its Payroll Register in the usual manner with a general journal entry similar to the one previously illustrated. This entry causes the sum of the employees' net pay to be credited to the liability account Accrued Payroll Payable.
2. Next, a single cheque payable to Payroll Bank Account for the amount of the payroll is drawn and entered in the Cheque Register. This results in a debit to Accrued Payroll Payable and a credit to Cash.
3. Then this cheque is endorsed and deposited in the payroll bank account. This transfers cash equal to the payroll from the regular bank account to the special payroll bank account.
4. Last, individual payroll cheques are drawn on the special payroll bank account and delivered to the employees. These pay the employees and, as soon as all employees cash their cheques, exhaust the funds in the special account.

A special Payroll Cheque Register may be used in connection with a payroll bank account. However, most companies do not use such a register but prefer to enter the payroll cheque numbers in their Payroll Register, making it act as a Cheque Register.

EMPLOYEE'S INDIVIDUAL EARNINGS RECORD

An *Employee's Individual Earnings Record,* Illustration 13–6, provides for each employee in one record a full year's summary of the employee's working time, gross earnings, deductions, and net pay. In addition, it accumulates information that—

1. Serves as a basis for the employer's payroll tax returns.
2. Tells when an employee's earnings have reached the tax-exempt points for Canada Pension Plan and unemployment insurance taxes.
3. Supplies data for the Statement of Remuneration, Form T-4, which must be given to the employee at the end of the year.

The payroll information on an Employee's Individual Earnings Record is taken from the Payroll Register. The information as to earnings, deductions, and net pay is first recorded on a single line in the Payroll Register, from where it is posted each pay period to the earnings record.

Illustration 13–6

EMPLOYEE'S INDIVIDUAL EARNINGS RECORD

Employee's Name ___Robert Austin___   Soc. Ins. No. ___307-032-195___   Employee No. ___114___

Home Address ___111 South Greenwood___   Notify in Case of Emergency ___Margaret Austin___   Phone No. ___964-9834___

Employed ___June 7,1980___   Date of Termination _____   Reason _____

Date of Birth ___June 6, 1962___   Date Becomes 65 ___June 6, 2027___   Male (X) Female ( )   Married (X) Single ( )   Number of Exemptions ___1___   Pay Rate ___$10.00___

Occupation ___Clerk___   Place ___Office___

Date		Time Lost		Time Wk.		Reg. Pay	O.T. Prem. Pay	Gross Pay	U.I.	Income Taxes	Hosp. Ins.	C.P.P.	Total Deductions	Net Pay	Ch. No.	Cumulative Pay
Per. Ends	Paid	Hrs.	Reason	Total	O.T. Hours											
8/1	8/1			40		400.00		400.00	9.40	74.95	8.00	6.33	98.68	301.32	173	400.00
15/1	15/1			40		400.00		400.00	9.40	74.95	8.00	6.33	98.68	301.32	201	800.00
22/1	22/1			40		400.00		400.00	9.40	74.95	8.00	6.33	98.68	301.32	243	1,200.00
29/1	29/1			40		400.00		400.00	9.40	74.95	8.00	6.33	98.68	301.32	295	1,600.00
5/2	5/2			40		400.00		400.00	9.40	74.95	8.00	6.33	98.68	301.32	339	2,000.00
12/2	12/2			40		400.00		400.00	9.40	74.95	8.00	6.33	98.68	301.32	354	2,400.00
19/2	19/2			40		400.00		400.00	9.40	74.95	8.00	6.33	98.68	301.32	397	2,800.00
26/2	26/2			40		400.00		400.00	9.40	74.95	8.00	6.33	98.68	301.32	446	3,200.00
26/3	26/3			40		400.00		400.00	9.40	74.95	8.00	6.33	98.68	301.32	608	4,800.00

PAYROLL DEDUCTIONS REQUIRED BY THE EMPLOYER

Under the previous discussion of the Canada Pension Plan, it was pointed out that pension deductions are required in like amounts on both employed workers and their employers. A covered employer is required by law to deduct from the employees' pay the amounts of their Canada Pension Plan, but in addition, he must himself pay an amount equal to the sum of his employees' Canada pension. Commonly, the amount deducted by the employer is recorded at the same time the payroll to which it relates is recorded. Also, since both the employees' and employer's shares are reported on the same form and are paid in one amount, the liability for both is normally recorded in the same liability account, the Canada Pension Plan Payable account.

In addition to the Canada Pension Plan, an employer is required to pay unemployment insurance that is 1.4 times the sum of his employees' unemployment insurance deductions. Most employers record both of these payroll deductions with a general journal entry that is made at the time the payroll to which they relate is recorded. For example, the entry to record the employer's amounts on the payroll of Illustration 12–3 is:

Mar.	26	Payroll Expense	142.47	
		Unemployment Insurance Payable		90.43
		Canada Pension Plan Payable		52.04
		To record the employer's payroll taxes.		

The debit of the entry records as an expense the payroll taxes levied on the employer, and the credits record the liabilities for the taxes. The $90.43 credit to Unemployment Insurance Payable is 1.4 times the sum of the amounts deducted for this tax from the pay of the employees whose wages are recorded in the Payroll Register of Illustration 12–3, and the credit to Canada Pension Plan Payable is equal to the total of the employees' pension plan deductions.

In the illustration it was assumed that Hospital Insurance was shared equally by the employee and employer. A journal entry is, therefore, required to record the employer's portion of Hospital Insurance as follows:

Mar.	26	Hospital Insurance Expense	62.00	
		Employees' Hospital Insurance Payable		62.00
		To record the employer's hospital insurance expense.		

PAYING THE PAYROLL DEDUCTIONS

Income Tax, Unemployment Insurance, and Canada Pension Plan amounts withheld each payday from the employees' pay plus the employer's portion of Unemployment Insurance and Canada Pension Plan are current liabilities until paid to the Receiver General of Canada. The normal method of payment is to pay the amounts due at any chartered bank or remit directly to the Receiver General of Canada. Payment of these amounts must be made before the 15th of the month following the month that deductions were made from the earnings of the employees. Payment of these liabilities is recorded in the same manner as payment of any other liabilities.

ACCRUING EXPENSES BASED ON WAGES

Mandatory payroll deductions are based on wages actually paid; consequently, there is no legal liability for these on accrued wages. Nevertheless, if the requirements of the *matching principle* are to be met, both accrued wages and the accrued deductions on the wages should be recorded at the end of an accounting period. However, since there is no legal liability and these amounts vary little from one accounting period to the next, most employers apply the *materiality principle* and do not accrue payroll deductions.

EMPLOYEE (FRINGE) BENEFIT COSTS

In addition to the wages earned by employees and the related payroll deductions paid by the employer, many companies provide their employees with a variety of benefits. Since the costs of these benefits are paid by the employer and the benefits are in addition to the amount of wages earned, they are often called fringe benefits. For example, an employer may pay for part (or all) of the employees' health insurance, life insurance, and disability insurance. Another frequent employee benefit involves employer contributions to a retirement income plan.

The entries for employee benefit costs are similar to those used for payroll taxes. For example, assume the employer with the previously described $3,178 payroll has agreed to match the employees' contributions for hospital insurance and also to contribute 10% of employees' salaries to a retirement program. The entry to record these employee benefits is:

Employees' Benefits Expense	379.80	
Employees' Hospital Insurance Payable		62.00
Employees' Retirement Program Payable ...		317.80

Payroll deductions and employee benefits costs are often a major category of expense incurred by a company. They may amount to well over 25% of the salaries earned by employees.

COMPUTERIZED PAYROLL SYSTEMS

Manually prepared records like the ones described in this chapter are found in many small concerns and very satisfactorily meet their needs. However, concerns having many employees commonly use computers to process their payroll. The computer programs are designed to take advantage of the fact that the same calculations are performed each pay period and that much of the same information must be entered for each employee in the Payroll Register, on the employee's earnings record, and on the employee's pay cheque. The computers simultaneously store or print the information in all three places.

GLOSSARY

Canada Pension Plan.   A national contributory retirement pension scheme.

Clock card.   A card used by an employee to record the time of his or her arrival at his or her place of work and the time of departure.

Gross pay.   The amount of an employee's pay before any deductions.

Individual earnings record.   A record of an employee's hours worked, gross pay, deductions, net pay, and certain personal information about the employee.

Net pay.   Gross pay minus deductions.

Payroll bank account.   A special bank account into which at the end of each pay period the total amount of an employer's payroll is deposited and on which the employees' payroll cheques are drawn.

Payroll deduction.   An amount deducted usually based on the amount of an employee's gross pay.

Timekeeping.   Making a record of the time each employee is at his or her place of work.

Unemployment insurance.   An employee-employer financed unemployment insurance plan.

Withholding allowance.   An amount of an employee's annual earnings not subject to income tax.

Wage bracket withholding table.   A table showing the amounts to be withheld from employees' wages at various levels of earnings.

QUESTIONS FOR CLASS DISCUSSION

1.   Who pays under the Canada Pension Plan?

2.   Who pays premiums under the workers' compensation laws?

3.   What benefits are paid to unemployed workers from funds raised by the Federal Unemployment Insurance Act?

4.   Who pays federal unemployment insurance? What is the rate?

5.   What are the objectives of unemployment insurance laws?

6.   To whom and when are payroll deductions remitted?

7.   What determines the amount that must be deducted from an employee's wages for income taxes?

8.   What is a tax withholding table?

9.   What is the Canada Pension Plan deduction rate for self-employed individuals?

10. How is a clock card used in recording the time an employee is on the job?

11. How is a special payroll bank account used in paying the wages of employees?

12. At the end of an accounting period a firm's special payroll bank account has a $562.35 balance because the payroll cheques of two employees have not cleared the bank. Should this $562.35 appear on the firm's balance sheet? If so, where?

13. What information is accumulated on an employee's individual earnings record? Why must this information be accumulated? For what purposes is the information used?

14. What payroll charges are levied on the employer? What amounts are deducted from the wages of an employee?

15. What are employee fringe benefits? Name some examples.

MULTIPLE CHOICE

1. Net pay is:
   a. The amount of an employee's pay due in income tax.
   b. Gross pay minus deductions.
   c. The amount of an employee's pay before any deductions.
   d. Gross pay plus employer's tax.
   e. None of the above.

2. The weekly payroll register shows:
   a. The number of hours worked by each employee each day during the week.
   b. The regular pay rate of each employee.
   c. The earnings of each employee.
   d. The deductions for each employee to determine the net pay.
   e. All of the above.

3. A card used by an employee to record his or her time of arrival and departure to and from work is a(n):
   a. Accounting card.
   b. Clock card.
   c. I.D. card.
   d. Charge card.
   e. Payroll card.

4. A special bank account into which at the end of each pay period the total amount of an employer's payroll is deposited and on which the employee's payroll checks are drawn is known as a(n):
   a. Employees' bank account.
   b. Employers' bank account.

      c. Payroll bank account.

      d. Contra bank account.

      e. Drawing bank account.

5. Making a record of the time each employee is at his or her place of work is:

      a. Auditing.

      b. Budgeting.

      c. Timekeeping.

      d. Bookkeeping.

      e. Spying.

6. If the payroll bank account has a $210 balance because an employee's payroll check has not cleared, the $210 should appear:

      a. On the balance sheet as a current asset.

      b. On the balance sheet as a current liability.

      c. On the income statement as an expense.

      d. On the balance sheet as a current asset and on the income statement as an expense.

      e. On none of the foregoing.

MINI DISCUSSION CASE

Case 13–1   You are the accountant for a high-tech company most of whose employees have an annual salary in excess of $30,000 per year. In discussing the cost of salary increases for the coming year, senior management has asked you to outline what additional costs are involved. After all, they reason, there are caps on the amounts deducted for both Unemployment Insurance and Canada Pension Plan. Therefore, these would not add to the company's cost since the employees are already over the maximum amounts.

Required:

Respond to senior management.

CLASS EXERCISES

Exercise 13–1   William Smith, an employee of Crown Derby Company , received his notice of employment termination on May 19, 1986. The reason for dismissal was lack of work. Smith worked for the company for nearly a year and his rate of pay in 1986 was $10.50 per hour. During 1986 Smith did not miss a day of work and worked full eight-hour shifts, five days per week.

Required:

a. Calculate Smith's total contribution to the Unemployment Insurance Fund during 1986.

b. Calculate the company's related amount for the same period.

c. Calculate Smith's weekly Canada Pension Plan contribution.

Exercise 13–2

On January 9, at the end of its first weekly pay period in the year, the column totals of a company's Payroll Register showed that its sales employees had earned $1,200 and its office employees had earned $600. Withholdings from employees were as follows: income taxes, $319.58; unemployment insurance, $42.30; union dues, $45; hospital insurance, $48; and Canada Pension Plan of $28.07.

Required:

Give the general journal entry to record the Payroll Register.

Exercise 13–3

Give the general journal entry to record the employer's payroll expenses resulting from the Exercise 13–2 payroll.

Exercise 13–4

The following information as to earnings and deductions for the pay period ended November 22 was taken from a company's payroll records:

Employees' Names	Gross Pay	Earnings to End of Previous Week	Income Taxes	Hospital Insurance Deductions
James Abbott	$ 450	$18,900	$ 78.72	$ 8.00
Jane Cotton................	460	19,320	78.48	8.00
George Green	580	24,360	120.12	8.00
Jerry Hall	700	29,400	168.48	8.00
	$2,190		$445.80	$32.00

Required:

1. Calculate the employees' unemployment insurance withholdings.
2. Which employees have reached the tax-exempt point for Canada Pension Plan deduction?
3. Prepare a general journal entry to record the payroll information.
4. Prepare a general journal entry to record the employer's payroll taxes resulting from the payroll.

PROBLEMS

Problem 13–1

The column totals of a company's Payroll Register indicated its sales employees had earned $6,000 and its office employees $1,200 during the pay period ended January 9, and no employee had earned more than $425 or less than $80 during the period. Unemployment insurance had been withheld from each employee's pay; and in addition, $80 of Canada Pension Plan, $1,050 of income taxes, $210 of group insurance, and $150 of union dues had been withheld from the pay of all employees.

Required:

1. Calculate the total of the Unemployment Insurance column in the Payroll Register.
2. Prepare a general journal entry to record the payroll register information.
3. Prepare a general journal entry to record the employer's payroll taxes resulting from the payroll.
4. Under the assumption the company uses special payroll cheques and a payroll bank account in paying its employees, give the cheque register entry (Cheque No. 815) to transfer funds equal to the payroll from the regular bank account to the payroll bank account.
5. After the cheque register entry is made and posted, are additional debit and credit entries required to record the payroll cheques and pay the employees? Why?

Problem 13–2   The following information was taken from a company's payroll records for the weekly pay period ended December 14:

Employees' Names	Clock Card No.	Daily Time							Pay Rate	Income Taxes	Medical Insurance	Earnings to End of Previous Week
		M	T	W	T	F	S	S				
Roy Andrews ...	11	8	8	8	8	8	0	0	9.50	131.50	8.00	18,650
Jerry Dale	12	8	8	8	8	8	0	0	9.50	133.45	8.00	19,175
Ray Lewis	13	8	8	8	8	8	4	0	12.50	181.55	8.00	24,825
Walter Mohr	14	8	8	8	8	8	0	0	13.50	141.25	8.00	21,950
Mary Page	15	8	8	8	8	8	4	0	10.00	151.05	8.00	15,910

Required:

1. Enter the relevant information in the proper columns of a Payroll Register. The company pays time and one half for the hours over 40 in any one week. Calculate and enter the employees' unemployment insurance tax deductions (use 1986 rates). Calculate and enter pension plan deductions for the employees whose wages have not reached the tax-exempt ceiling. (To do this subtract $48.08 from each employee's gross pay and multiply the remainder by the 1.8% rate.) Complete the register under the assumption the first two employees are salespersons, the third drives the delivery truck, and the last two work in the office.
2. Prepare a general journal entry to record the payroll register information.
3. Make the cheque register entry (Cheque No. 234) to transfer funds equal to the payroll from the regular bank account to the payroll bank account under the assumption that the company uses special payroll cheques and a payroll bank account in paying its employees. Assume the first payroll cheque is numbered 668 and enter the payroll cheque numbers in the Payroll Register.
4. Prepare a general journal entry to record the employer's payroll expenses resulting from the payroll.

Problem 13–3 A company that pays time and a half for hours in excess of 40 per week accumulated the following payroll information for the weekly pay period ended December 15:

Employees' Names	Clock Card No.	Daily Time							Pay Rate	Income Taxes	Canada Pension Plan	Medical Insur- ance
		M	T	W	T	F	S	S				
Paul Baer......	22	8	8	8	8	8	0	0	9.90	54.00	6.26	6.00
Frank Clift	23	8	8	8	8	8	0	0	8.90	31.25	5.54	6.00
Dale Duff	24	0	0	8	8	8	0	0	8.50	25.60	2.81	6.00
June Nash	25	8	8	8	8	9	3	0	9.25	55.40	6.79	6.00
Lee Ross	26	8	8	8	9	9	0	0	10.50	50.45	7.26	6.00

Required:

1. Enter the relevant information in the proper columns of a Payroll Register. Calculate and enter the employees' unemployment insurance deductions. Complete the register. Assume the first two employees are salespeople, the second two work in the office, and the last drives the delivery truck.
2. Prepare a general journal entry to record the payroll register information.
3. Make the cheque register entry to transfer funds equal to the payroll from the regular bank account to the payroll bank account (Cheque No. 567) under the assumption that the company uses special payroll cheques and a payroll bank account in paying its employees. Assume the first payroll cheque is numbered 444 and enter the payroll cheque numbers in the Payroll Register.
4. Prepare a general journal entry to record the employer's payroll expenses resulting from the payroll.

Problem 13–4 The All-salary Company computes its payroll on a monthly basis and gives its employees an advance on the 15th of the month for approximately one half of the net pay. On June 30 (after all entries pertaining to the June payroll were posted) the following account balances appeared in the company's ledger:

a. Unemployment Insurance Payable, $128.
b. Canada Pension Payable, $133.80.
c. Employees' Income Taxes Payable, $584.
d. Employees' Group Insurance Payable, $160.
e. Accrued Payroll Payable, $1,982. (The mid-month advance of $1,960 was debited to this account.)

Required:

1. General journal entry made by the company to record the payroll register information.
2. General journal entry made by the company to record the employer's payroll related expenses.

3. Under the assumption the company uses a payroll bank account and special payroll cheques in paying its employees, give the cheque register entry (Cheque No. 747) to transfer funds equal to the balance of the payroll from the regular bank account to the payroll bank account.

4. Record the issuance of Cheque No. 812 to the Receiver General of Canada for the amount due on July 15, resulting from the June payroll.

ALTERNATE PROBLEMS

Problem
13–1A

On January 9, at the end of the first weekly pay period of the year, the column totals of a company's Payroll Register indicated its sales employees had earned $13,250, its office employees had earned $6,250, and its delivery employees $1,500. Unemployment insurance had been withheld from each employee's wages, and no employee had earned more than $425 or less than $80 during the period. In addition, $278 of Canada Pension Plan, $2,100 of income taxes, $320 of hospital insurance, and $225 of union dues had been withheld from the pay of all employees.

Required:

1. Calculate the total of the Unemployment Insurance Taxes Payable column in the Payroll Register, and prepare a general journal entry to record the register information.

2. Prepare a general journal entry to record the employer's payroll deductions resulting from the payroll.

3. Under the assumption the company uses a payroll bank account and special payroll cheques in paying its employees, give the cheque register entry (Cheque No. 745) to transfer funds equal to the payroll from the regular bank account to the payroll bank account.

4. After the cheque register entry is made and posted, are additional debit and credit entries required to record the payroll cheque and pay the employees? Why?

Problem
13–2A

A company's payroll records provided the following information for the weekly pay period ended December 20:

Employees' Names	Clock Card No.	Daily Time							Pay Rate	Income Taxes	Medical Insurance	Earnings to End of Previous Week
		M	T	W	T	F	S	S				
Dale Agnew	14	8	8	8	8	8	0	0	14.50	120.45	8.00	18,920
Mary Hall	15	8	8	8	8	8	4	0	16.00	143.75	8.00	22,000
John Koop	16	8	8	8	8	8	0	0	15.50	128.30	8.00	15,710
Carl Lee	17	8	8	8	8	8	0	0	15.50	131.50	8.00	15,325
Roy Page	18	8	8	8	8	8	2	0	18.00	170.90	8.00	25,610

Required:

1. Enter the relevant information in the proper columns of a Payroll Register. The company pays time and one half for hours in excess of 40 in any one week. Calculate and enter the employees' unemployment insurance deductions (use 1986 rates). Calculate and enter pension plan deductions for the employees whose wages have not reached the tax-exempt ceiling. (To do this subtract $48.08 from each employee's gross pay and multiply the remainder by the 1.8% tax rate.) Complete the register under the assumption that the first two employees work in the office, the next two are salespeople, and the last drives the delivery truck.
2. Prepare a general journal entry to record the payroll register information.
3. Assume the company uses special payroll cheques drawn on a payroll bank account in paying its employees, and make the cheque register entry (Cheque No. 202) to transfer funds equal to the payroll from the regular bank account to the payroll bank account. Also assume the first payroll cheque is No. 653 and enter the payroll cheque numbers in the Payroll Register.
4. Prepare a general journal entry to record the employer's payroll taxes resulting from the payroll.

Problem 13–3A

The following information for the weekly pay period ended December 17 was taken from the records of a company that pays time and one half for hours worked in excess of 40 per week:

Employees' Names	Clock Card No.	Daily Time							Pay Rate	Income Taxes	Canada Pension Plan	Union Dues
		M	T	W	T	F	S	S				
Mary Alt.........	21	8	8	8	8	8	0	0	14.50	119.00	9.57	–0–
Harry Bray	22	8	8	8	8	8	2	0	14.50	124.20	–0–	–0–
Jerry Hamm	23	8	8	8	8	8	0	0	15.80	132.70	–0–	8.50
Alex Hunt	24	8	8	8	8	8	0	0	15.80	136.25	10.51	8.50
Gary Sage	25	8	8	8	8	8	4	0	18.00	172.80	–0–	8.50

Required:

1. Enter the relevant information in the proper columns of a Payroll Register. Calculate and enter the employees' unemployment insurance deductions. Complete the register. Assume the first two employees work in the office, the next two are salespeople, and the last drives the delivery truck.
2. Prepare a general journal entry to record the payroll register information.
3. Make the cheque register entry (Cheque No. 789) to transfer funds equal to the payroll from the regular bank account to the payroll bank account. Assume the first payroll cheque is numbered 901 and enter the payroll cheque numbers in the Payroll Register.
4. Prepare a general journal entry to record the employer's payroll taxes resulting from the payroll. The company has a fully paid Hospital Insurance Plan. The company pays $9 per week for each employee.

Problem
13–4A

The Yukon Company computes its payroll on a monthly basis and gives its employees a mid-month advance for approximately one half of the monthly net pay. On June 30 (after all entries pertaining to the June payroll were posted) the following account balances appeared in the company's ledger:

a. Unemployment Insurance Payable, $187.92.
b. Canada Pension Payable, $284.20.
c. Employees' Income Taxes Payable, $1,062.
d. Employees' Group Insurance Payable, $140.
e. Accrued Payroll, $2,920. (The mid-month advance of $2,900 was debited to this month's account.)

Required:

1. General journal entry made by the company to record the payroll register information.
2. General journal entry made by the company to record the employer's payroll taxes.
3. Under the assumption the company uses a payroll bank account and special payroll cheques in paying its employees, give the cheque register entry (Cheque No. 642) to transfer funds equal to the balance of the payroll from the regular bank account to the payroll bank account.
4. Record the issuance of Cheque No. 706 to the Receiver General of Canada for amount due on July 15 resulting from the June payroll.

PROVOCATIVE PROBLEM

Provocative
Problem 13–1,
Joy Toy
Company

Joy Toy Company manufactures a number of products from plastics. It has 200 full-time employees, all earning $8,000 or more per year.

Recently the company secured an order for Christmas toys from a large chain of department stores. The order should be very profitable and will probably be repeated each year. In filling the order Joy Toy Company can stamp out the parts for the toys with its present machines and employees. However, it will have to add 40 employees to its work force for 40 hours per week for 10 weeks to assemble the toys and pack them for shipment.

The company can hire these workers and add them to its own payroll, or it can secure their services through Extra Hands, Ltd., a company in the business of supplying temporary help. If the temporary help is secured through Extra Hands, Ltd., Joy Toy Company will pay Extra Hands, Ltd., $13.25 per hour for each hour worked by each person supplied. The people supplied will be employees of Extra Hands, Ltd., and it will pay their wages and all taxes on the wages. On the other hand, if Joy Toy Company employs the workers and places them on its payroll, it will pay them $9.75 per hour and will pay the usual payroll taxes and an estimated 90 cents per hour in addition to the regular rate for such things as the company's portion of medical insurance, workers' compensation, vacation pay, and so forth. If the company secures the temporary help through Extra Hands, Ltd., it will save an estimated $1,400 in "want-ads" and in interviewing and selection costs. Also, it will not incur an estimated $425 per week in additional office expenses required to process the payroll, and so forth.

Should Joy Toy Company place the temporary help on its own payroll or should it secure their services through Extra Hands, Ltd.? Justify your answer.

ANALYTICAL AND REVIEW PROBLEMS

Problem 13–1 A&R

Using current year's withholding tables for Canada Pension Plan, Unemployment Insurance, and Income Tax, update the Payroll Register of Illustration 13–3. In computing income tax withholdings, state *your* assumption as to each employee's personal deductions. Assume that Hospital Insurance deductions continue at the same amounts as in Illustration 13–3.

Problem 13–2 A&R

The following data were taken from the Payroll Register of Laurentian Company:

```
Gross salary ....................... XXX
Employees' income tax deductions ..... XXX
UI deductions ...................... XXX
CPP deductions ..................... XXX
Hospital insurance deductions ......... XXX
Union dues deductions .............. XXX
```

Laurentian contributes an equal amount to the hospital insurance plan, in addition to the statutory payroll taxes, and 6% of gross salaries to a pension program.

Required:

Record in general journal form the payroll, payment of the employees, and remittance to the appropriate authority amounts owing in connection with the payroll. (Note: All amounts are to be indicated as XXX.)

Problem 13–3 A&R

Computer Services Company employs a highly skilled systems specialist at an annual salary of $54,000. The company pays $65 per month for disability insurance and matches the employee's life insurance premium of $54 per month. Effective July 1, the company agreed to contribute 8% of the employee's gross pay to a retirement program. The maximum Unemployment Insurance deduction on a monthly salary is $50.41.

What was the total monthly cost of employing the specialist in January, March, August, and December? Assuming the employee works 170 hours each month, what is the cost per hour in January? If the annual gross salary is increased by $5,000, what will be the increase in the total annual costs of employing the specialist?

Partnership Accounting

After studying Chapter 14, you should be able to:

List the characteristics of a partnership and explain the importance of mutual agency and unlimited liability to a person about to become a partner.

Allocate partnership earnings to partners (a) on a stated fractional basis, (b) in the partners' capital ratio, and (c) through the use of salary and interest allowances.

Prepare entries for (a) the sale of a partnership interest, (b) the admission of a new partner by investment, and (c) the retirement of a partner by the withdrawal of partnership assets.

Prepare entries required in the liquidation of a partnership.

Define or explain the words and phrases listed in the chapter Glossary.

A partnership is a voluntary association of individuals which is based on a partnership agreement or contract. The provincial Partnership Acts and the Civil Code, with minor variation, defined a *partnership* as: "Partnership is the relation which subsists between persons carrying on a business in common with a view of profit; but the relationship between members of any company or association incorporated under the provisions of any Act of the legislature is not a partnership within the meaning of the Act." A partnership has been further defined as "an association of two or more competent persons under a contract to combine some or all their property, labour, and skills in the operation of a business." And although both of these definitions tell something of its legal nature, a better understanding of a partnership as a form of business organization may be gained by examining some of its characteristics.

CHARACTERISTICS OF A PARTNERSHIP

A Voluntary Association

A partnership is a voluntary association into which a person cannot be forced against his or her will. This is because a partner is responsible for the business acts of his or her partners when the acts are within the scope of the partnership. Also, a partner is personally liable for all of the debts of his or her partnership. Consequently, partnership law recognizes it is only fair that a person be permitted to select the people he or she wishes to join in a partnership. Normally, a person will select only financially responsible people who have good judgment.

Based on a Contract

One advantage of a partnership as a form of business organization is the ease with which it may be begun. All that is required is that two or more legally competent people agree to be partners. Their agreement becomes a *partnership contract*. It should be in writing, with all anticipated points of future disagreement covered. However, it is binding if only orally expressed.

Limited Life

The life of a partnership is always limited. Death, **bankruptcy,** or anything that takes away the ability of one of the partners to contract automatically ends a partnership. In addition, since a partnership is based on a contract, if the contract is for a definite period, the partnership ends when that period expires. If the contract does not specify a time period, the partnership ends when the business for which it was created is completed. Or, if no time is stated and the business cannot be completed but goes on indefinitely, the partnership may be terminated at will by any one of the partners.

Mutual Agency

Normally, there is *mutual agency* in a partnership. This means that under normal circumstances, every partner is an agent of the partnership and can enter into and bind it to any contract within the apparent scope of its business. For example, a partner in a merchandising business can bind the partnership to contracts to buy merchandise, lease a store building, borrow money, or hire employees. These are all within the scope of a merchandising firm. On the other hand, a partner in a law firm, acting alone, cannot bind his or her partners to a contract to buy merchandise for resale or rent a store building. These are not within the normal scope of a law firm's business.

Partners among themselves may agree to limit the right of any one or more of the partners to negotiate certain contracts for the partnership. Such an agreement is binding on the partners and on outsiders who know of the agreement. However, it is not binding on outsiders who are unaware of its existence. Outsiders who are unaware of anything to the contrary have a right to assume that each partner has the normal agency rights of a partner.

Mutual agency offers an important reason for care in the selection of partners. Good partners benefit all; but a poor partner can do great damage. Mutual agency plus unlimited liability are the reasons most partnerships have only a few members.

Unlimited Liability

When a partnership business is unable to pay its debts, the creditors may satisfy their claims from the personal assets of the partners. Furthermore, if the property of a partner is insufficient to meet his or her share, the creditors may turn to the assets of the remaining partners who are able to pay. Thus, a partner may be called on to pay all the debts of his or her partnership and is said to have *unlimited liability* for its debts.

Unlimited liability may be illustrated as follows. Ned Albert and Carol Bates each invested $5,000 in a store to be operated as a partnership, under an agreement to share losses and gains equally. Albert has no property other than his $5,000 investment. Bates owns her own home, a farm, and has sizable savings in addition to her investment. The partners rented store space and bought merchandise and fixtures costing $30,000. They paid $10,000 in cash and promised to pay the balance at a later date. However, the night before the store opened the building in which it was located burned and the merchandise and fixtures were totally destroyed. There was no insurance, all the partnership assets were lost, and Albert has no other assets. Consequently, the partnership creditors may collect the full $20,000 of their claims from Bates. However, Bates may look to Albert for payment of one half at a later date, if Albert ever becomes able to pay.

Limited Partnerships

In the business associations described thus far as partnerships, all of the partners have unlimited liability. Sometimes, however, a group of individuals want to invest in a partnership but are unwilling to accept the risk of unlimited liability. This can be accomplished by using a unique form of business called a *limited partnership.* A limited partnership has two classes of partners, general partners and limited partners. At least one of the partners, the *general partner(s),* must assume unlimited liability for the debts of the partnership. However, the remaining partners, the *limited partners,* have no personal liability beyond the amounts they invest in the business. Usually, a limited partnership is managed by the general partner(s). The limited partners have no active role except for certain major decisions as specified in the partnership agreement. To distinguish limited partnerships from others, partnerships in which all of the partners have unlimited liability are often called *general partnerships.*

ADVANTAGES AND DISADVANTAGES OF A PARTNERSHIP

Limited life, mutual agency, and unlimited liability are disadvantages of a partnership. Yet, a partnership has advantages over both the single proprietorship and corporation forms of organization. A partnership has the advantage of being able to bring together more money and skills than a single proprietorship. It is much easier to organize than a corporation. It does not have the corporation's governmental supervision nor its extra burden of taxation. And, partners may act freely and without the necessity of shareholders' and directors' meetings, as is required in a corporation.

PARTNERSHIP ACCOUNTING

Partnership accounting is exactly like that of a single proprietorship except for transactions that directly affect the partners' equities. Because ownership rights in a partnership are divided between two or more partners, there must be (1) a capital account for each partner, (2) a withdrawals account for each partner, and (3) an accurate measurement and division of earnings.

Each partner's capital account is credited, and asset accounts showing the nature of the assets invested are debited in recording the investment of each partner. A partner's withdrawals are debited to his or her withdrawals account. And, in the end-of-period closing procedure, the capital account is credited for a partner's share of the net income. Obviously, these closing procedures are like those used for a single proprietorship. The only difference is that separate capital and withdrawals accounts are maintained for each partner. Thus, the closing procedures for a partnership require no further consideration. However, the matter of dividing earnings among partners requires additional discussion.

NATURE OF PARTNERSHIP EARNINGS

Law and custom recognize that partners cannot enter into an employer-employee contractural relationship with themselves. Hence, partners cannot legally hire themselves and pay themselves a salary. Furthermore, law and custom recognize that a partner works for partnership profits and not a salary. Also, law and custom recognize that a partner invests in a partnership for earnings and not for interest. However, it should be recognized that partnership earnings may include a return for services, even though the return is contained within the earnings and is not a salary in a legal sense. Likewise, partnership earnings may include a return on invested capital, although the return is not interest in the legal sense of the term. Furthermore, if partnership earnings are to be fairly shared, it is often necessary to recognize this. For example, if one partner contributes five times as much capital as another, it is only fair that this be taken into consideration in the method of sharing. Likewise, if the services of one partner are much more valuable than those of another, some provision should be made for the unequal service contributions.

DIVISION OF EARNINGS

The law provides that in the absence of a contrary agreement, partnership income or loss is shared equally by the partners. However, partners may agree to any method of sharing. If they agree to a method of sharing income but say nothing of losses, losses are shared in the same way as income.

Several methods of sharing partnership earnings may be employed. All attempt in one way or another to recognize differences in service contributions or in investments, when such differences exist. Three frequently used methods to share earnings are: (1) on a stated fractional basis, (2) based on the ratio of capital investments, or (3) based on salary and interest allowances and the remainder in a fixed ratio.

EARNINGS ALLOCATED ON A STATED FRACTIONAL BASIS

The easiest way to divide partnership earnings is to give each partner a stated fraction of the total. A division on a fractional basis may provide for an equal sharing if service and capital contributions are equal. An equal sharing may also be provided when the greater capital contribution of one partner is offset by a greater service contribution of another. Or, if the service and capital contributions are unequal, a fixed ratio may easily provide for an unequal sharing. All that is necessary in any case is for the partners to agree as to the fractional share to be given each.

For example, the partnership agreement of Morse and North may provide that each partner is to receive half the earnings. Or the agreement may provide for two thirds to Morse and one third to North. Or it may provide for three fourths to Morse and one fourth to North. Any fractional basis may be agreed upon as long as the partners feel earnings are fairly shared. For example, assume the agreement of Morse and North provides for a two-thirds and one-third sharing, and net income for a year is $30,000. After all revenue and expense accounts are closed, if net income is $30,000, the partnership Income Summary account has a $30,000 credit balance. It is closed, and the earnings are allocated to the partners with the following entry:

Dec.	31	Income Summary	30,000.00	
		A. P. Morse, Capital		20,000.00
		R. G. North, Capital		10,000.00
		To close the Income Summary account and allocate the earnings.		

DIVISION OF EARNINGS BASED ON THE RATIO OF CAPITAL INVESTMENTS

If the business of a partnership is of a nature that earnings are closely related to money invested, a division of earnings based on the ratio of partners' investments offers a fair sharing method. To illustrate this method, assume that Chase, Davis, and Fall have agreed to share earnings in the ratio of their investments. If these are Chase, $50,000, Davis, $30,000, and Fall, $40,000, and if net income for the year is $48,000, the respective shares of the partners are calculated as follows:

Step 1:	Chase, capital	$ 50,000
	Davis, capital	30,000
	Fall, capital	40,000
	Total invested	$120,000

Step 2:   Share of earnings to Chase $\dfrac{\$50,000}{\$120,000} \times \$48,000 = \$20,000$

Share of earnings to Davis $\dfrac{\$30,000}{\$120,000} \times \$48,000 = \$12,000$

Share of earnings to Fall $\dfrac{\$40,000}{\$120,000} \times \$48,000 = \$16,000$

The entry to allocate the earnings to the partners is then:

Dec.	31	Income Summary	48,000.00	
		T. S. Chase, Capital.....................		20,000.00
		S. A. Davis, Capital		12,000.00
		R. R. Fall, Capital		16,000.00
		To close the Income Summary account and allocate the earnings.		

SALARIES AND INTEREST AS AIDS IN SHARING

Sometimes partners' capital contributions are unequal. Also, the service contributions of the partners may not be equal. Even in partnerships in which all partners work full-time, the services of one partner may be more valuable than the services of another. When these situations occur and, for example, the capital contributions are unequal, the partners may allocate a portion of their net income to themselves in the form of interest, so as to compensate for the unequal investments. Or, when service contributions are unequal, they may use salary allowances as a means of compensating for unequal service contributions. Or, when investment and service contributions are both unequal, they may use a combination of interest and salary allowances in an effort to share earnings fairly.

For example, Hill and Dale began a partnership business of a kind in which Hill has had experience and could command a $36,000 annual salary working for another firm of like nature. Dale is new to the business and could expect to earn not more than $24,000 working elsewhere. Furthermore, Hill invested $30,000 in the business and Dale invested $10,000. Consequently, the partners agreed that in order to compensate for the unequal service and capital contributions, they will share income or losses as follows:

1. A share of the profits equal to interest at 10% is to be allowed on the partners' initial investments.
2. Annual salary allowances of $36,000 per year to Hill and $24,000 per year to Dale are to be allowed.
3. The remaining balance of income or loss is to be shared equally.

Under this agreement, a first year $69,000 net income would be shared as in Illustration 14–1.

After the shares in the net income are determined, the following entry is used to close the Income Summary account. Observe in the entry that the credit amounts may be taken from the first two column totals of the computation of Illustration 14–1.

Dec.	31	Income Summary	69,000.00	
		Hill, Capital		41,500.00
		Dale, Capital		27,500.00
		To close the Income Summary account and allocate the earnings.		

In a legal sense, partners do not work for salaries, nor do they invest in a partnership to earn interest. They invest and work for earnings. Consequently, when a partnership agreement provides for salaries and interest, the partners should understand that the salaries and interest are not really expenses of the partnership. They are only a means of sharing income or losses.

In the illustration just completed, the $69,000 net income exceeded the salary and interest allowances of the partners. However, the partners would use the same method to share a net income smaller than their

Illustration 14–1   Sharing Income When Income Exceeds Interest and Salary Allowances

	Share to Hill	Share to Dale	Income allocated
Total net income			$69,000
Allocated as interest:			
Hill (10% on $30,000)	$ 3,000		
Dale (10% on $10,000)		$ 1,000	
Total allocated as interest			4,000
Balance of income after interest allowances			$65,000
Allocated as salary allowances:			
Hill	36,000		
Dale		24,000	
Total allocated as salary allowances ...			60,000
Balance of income after interest and salary allowances			$ 5,000
Balance allocated equally:			
Hill	2,500		
Dale		2,500	
Total allocated equally			5,000
Balance of income			–0–
Shares of the partners	$41,500	$27,500	

Illustration 14–2 Sharing Income When Interest and Salary Allowances Exceed Income

	Share to Hill	Share to Dale	Income allocated
Total net income			$ 45,000
Allocated as interest:			
Hill (10% on $30,000)	$ 3,000		
Dale (10% on $10,000)		$ 1,000	
Total allocated as interest			4,000
Balance of income after interest allowances			$ 41,000
Allocated as salary allowances:			
Hill	36,000		
Dale		24,000	
Total allocated as salary allowances ...			60,000
Balance of income after interest and salary allowances (a negative amount)			$(19,000)
Balance allocated equally:			
Hill	(9,500)		
Dale		(9,500)	
Total allocated equally			(19,000)
Balance of income			–0–
Shares of the partners	$29,500	$15,500	

salary and interest allowances, or to share a loss. For example, assume that Hill and Dale earned only $45,000 in a year. A $45,000 net income would be shared by the partners as in Illustration 14–2.

A net loss would be shared by Hill and Dale in the same manner as the foregoing $45,000 net income. The only difference being that the income-and-loss-sharing procedure would begin with a negative amount of income, in other words, a net loss. The amount allocated equally would then be a larger negative amount.

PARTNERSHIP FINANCIAL STATEMENTS

In most respects, partnership financial statements are like those of a single proprietorship. However, one common difference is that the income allocation is often shown on the income statement following the reported net income. For example, an income statement prepared for Hill and Dale might show the allocation of the $45,000 net income of Illustration 14–2 as in Illustration 14–3.

ADDITION OR WITHDRAWAL OF A PARTNER

A partnership is based on a contract between specific individuals. Consequently, an existing partnership is ended when a partner withdraws

Illustration 14–3

HILL AND DALE
Income Statement
For Year Ended December 31, 19—

Sales		$332,400
Net income		$ 45,000
Allocation of net income to the partners:		
To Hill:		
Interest at 10% on investment	$ 3,000	
Salary allowance	36,000	
Total	$39,000	
Less one half the remaining deficit	(9,500)	
Share of the net income		$ 29,500
To Dale:		
Interest at 10% on investment	$ 1,000	
Salary allowance	24,000	
Total	$25,000	
Less one half the remaining deficit	(9,500)	
Share of the net income		15,500
Net income allocated		$ 45,000

or a new partner is added. A partner may sell his or her partnership interest and withdraw from a partnership. Also, a partner may withdraw his or her equity, taking partnership cash or other assets. Likewise, a new partner may join an existing partnership by purchasing an interest from one or more of its partners or by investing cash or other assets in the business.

Sale of a Partnership Interest

Assume that Abbott, Burns, and Camp are partners in a partnership that has no liabilities and the following assets and owners' equity:

Assets		Owners' Equity	
Cash	$ 3,000	Abbott, capital	$ 5,000
Other assets	12,000	Burns, capital	5,000
		Camp, capital	5,000
Total assets	$15,000	Total owners' equity	$15,000

Camp's equity in this partnership is $5,000. If Camp sells this equity to Davis for $7,000, Camp is selling a $5,000 interest in the partnership assets. The entry on the partnership books to transfer the equity is:

Feb.	4	Camp, Capital	5,000.00	
		Davis, Capital		5,000.00
		To transfer Camp's equity in the partner-ship assets to Davis.		

After this entry is posted, the assets and owners' equity of the new partnership are:

Assets		Owners' Equity	
Cash	$ 3,000	Abbott, capital	$ 5,000
Other assets	12,000	Burns, capital	5,000
		Davis, capital	5,000
Total assets	$15,000	Total owners' uity	$15,000

Two points should be noted in regard to this transaction. First, the $7,000 Davis paid Camp is not recorded in the partnership books. Camp sold and transferred a $5,000 equity in the partnership assets to Davis. The entry that records the transfer is a debit to Camp, Capital and a credit to Davis, Capital for $5,000. Furthermore, the entry is the same whether Davis pays Camp $7,000, or $70,000. The amount is paid directly to Camp. It is a side transaction between Camp and Davis and does not affect partnership assets.

The second point to be noted is that Abbott and Burns must agree to the sale and transfer if Davis is to become a partner. Abbott and Burns cannot prevent Camp from selling the interest to Davis. On the other hand, Camp cannot force Abbott and Burns to accept Davis as a partner. If Abbott and Burns agree to accept Davis, a new partnership is formed and a new contract with a new income-and-loss-sharing ratio must be drawn. If Camp sells to Davis and either Abbott or Burns refuses to accept Davis as a partner, under the Uniform Partnership Act Davis gets Camp's share of partnership gains and losses and Camp's share of partnership assets if the firm is liquidated. However, Davis gets no voice in the management of the firm until admitted as a partner.

Investing in an Existing Partnership

Instead of purchasing the equity of an existing partner, an individual may gain an equity by investing assets in the business, with the invested assets becoming the property of the partnership. For example, assume that the partnership of Evans and Gage has assets and owners' equity as follows:

Assets		Owners' Equity	
Cash	$ 3,000	Evans, capital	$20,000
Other assets	37,000	Gage, capital	20,000
Total assets	$40,000	Total owners' equity	$40,000

Also, assume that Evans and Gage have agreed to accept Hart as a partner with a one-half interest in the business upon his investment of $40,000. The entry to record Hart's investment is:

Mar.	2	Cash	40,000.00	
		Hart, Capital		40,000.00
		To record the investment of Hart.		

After the entry is posted, the assets and owners' equity of the new partnership appear as follows:

Assets		Owners' Equity	
Cash	$43,000	Evans, capital	$20,000
Other assets	37,000	Gage, capital	20,000
		Hart, capital	40,000
Total assets	$80,000	Total owners' equity	$80,000

In this case, Hart has a 50% equity in the assets of the business. However, he does not necessarily have a right to one half of its net income. The sharing of income and losses is a separate matter on which the partners must agree. Furthermore, the agreed method may bear no relation to their capital ratio.

A Bonus to the Old Partners

Sometimes, when the equity of a partnership is worth more than the amounts of equity recorded in the accounting records, its partners may require an incoming partner to give a bonus for the privilege of joining the firm. For example, Judd and Kirk operate a partnership business, sharing its earnings equally. The partnership's accounting records show that Judd has a $38,000 equity in the business, and Kirk has a $32,000 equity. They have agreed to allow Lee a one-third equity and a one-third share of the partnership's earnings upon the investment of $50,000. Lee's equity is determined with a calculation like this:

Equities of the existing partners ($38,000 + $32,000) .	$ 70,000
Investment of the new partner	50,000
Total equities in the new partnership	$120,000
Equity of Lee (⅓ of total)........................	$ 40,000

And the entry to record Lee's investment is:

May	15	Cash	50,000.00	
		Lee, Capital		40,000.00
		Judd, Capital		5,000.00
		Kirk, Capital		5,000.00
		To record the investment of Lee.		

The $10,000 difference between the $50,000 invested by Lee and the $40,000 credited to his capital account is a bonus that is shared by Judd and Kirk in their income-and-loss-sharing ratio. Such a bonus is always shared by the old partners in their income-and-loss-sharing ratio. This is fair because the bonus compensates the old partners for increases in the worth of the partnership that have not yet been recorded as income.

RECORDING GOODWILL.   Instead of allowing bonuses to the old partners, goodwill may be recorded in the admission of a new partner, with the amount of the goodwill being used to increase the equities of the old partners. This can be justified only if the old partnership has a sustained earnings rate in excess of the average for its industry. However, in practice, goodwill is seldom recognized upon the admission of a new partner. Instead, the bonus method is used.

Bonus to the New Partner

Sometimes the members of an existing partnership may be very anxious to bring a new partner into their firm. The business may need additional cash or the new partner may have exceptional abilities or business contacts that will increase profits. In such a situation, the old partners may be willing to give the new partner a larger equity in the business than the amount of his or her investment. For example, Moss and Owen are partners with capital account balances of $30,000 and $18,000, respectively, and sharing income and losses in a 2 to 1 ratio. The partners are anxious to have Pitt join their partnership and will allow him a one-fourth equity in the firm if he will invest $12,000. If Pitt accepts, his equity in the new firm is calculated as follows:

Equities of the existing partners ($30,000 + $18,000) ..	$48,000
Investment of the new partner......................	12,000
Total equities in the new partnership	$60,000
Equity of Pitt (¼ of total)	$15,000

And the entry to record Pitt's investment is:

June	1	Cash	12,000.00	
		Moss, Capital	2,000.00	
		Owen, Capital	1,000.00	
		Pitt, Capital		15,000.00
		To record the investment of Pitt.		

Note that Pitt's bonus is contributed by the old partners in their income-and-loss-sharing ratio. Also remember that Pitt's one-fourth equity does not necessarily entitle him to one fourth of the earnings of the business, since the sharing of income and losses is a separate matter for agreement by the partners.

Withdrawal of a Partner

The best practice in regard to a partner's withdrawal from a partnership is for the partners to provide in advance in their partnership contract the procedures to be followed. Such procedures commonly provide for an audit of the accounting records and a revaluation of the partnership assets. The revaluation is very desirable since it places the assets on the books at current values. It also causes the retiring partner's capital account to reflect the current value of the partner's equity. Often in such cases the agreement also provides that the retiring partner is to withdraw assets equal to the book amount of the revalued equity.

For example, assume that Blue is retiring from the partnership of Smith, Blue, and Short. The partners have always shared income and losses in the ratio of Smith, one half; Blue, one fourth; and Short, one fourth. Their partnership agreement provides for an audit and asset revaluation upon the retirement of a partner. Just prior to the audit and revaluation, their balance sheet shows the following assets and equities:

Assets			Owners' Equity	
Cash		$11,000	Smith, capital	$22,000
Merchandise inventory		16,000	Blue, capital	10,000
Equipment	$20,000		Short, capital	10,000
Less accum. depr. .	5,000	15,000		
Total assets		$42,000	Total owners' equity	$42,000

The audit and appraisal indicate the merchandise inventory is over-valued by $4,000. Also, due to market changes, the partnership equipment should be valued at $25,000 with accumulated depreciation of $8,000. The entries to record these revaluations are:

Oct.	31	Smith, Capital	2,000.00	
		Blue, Capital	1,000.00	
		Short, Capital	1,000.00	
		Merchandise Inventory		4,000.00
		To revalue the inventory.		
	31	Equipment	5,000.00	
		Accumulated Depreciation, Equipment		3,000.00
		Smith, Capital		1,000.00
		Blue, Capital		500.00
		Short, Capital		500.00
		To revalue the equipment.		

Note in the illustrated entries that income and losses are shared in the partners' income-and-loss-sharing ratio. Income and losses from asset revaluations are always so shared. The fairness of this is easy to see when it is remembered that if the partnership did not terminate, such gains and losses would sooner or later be reflected on the income statement.

After the entries revaluing the partnership assets are recorded, a balance sheet will show these revalued assets and equities for Smith, Blue, and Short:

Assets			**Owners' Equity**	
Cash		$11,000	Smith, capital	$21,000
Merchandise inventory		12,000	Blue, capital	9,500
Equipment	$25,000		Short, capital	9,500
Less accum. depr. .	8,000	17,000		
Total assets		$40,000	Total owners' equity	$40,000

After the revaluation, if Blue withdraws, taking assets equal to his revalued equity, the entry to record the withdrawal is:

Oct.	31	Blue, Capital	9,500.00	
		Cash		9,500.00
		To record the withdrawal of Blue.		

In withdrawing, Blue does not have to take cash in settlement of his equity. He may take any combination of assets to which the partners agree, or he may take the new partnership's promissory note. Also, the withdrawal of Blue generally creates a new partnership. Consequently, a new partnership contract and a new income-and-loss-sharing agreement may be required.

Partner Withdraws Taking Assets of Less Value than His Book Equity

Sometimes when a partner retires, the remaining partners may not wish to have the assets revalued and the new values recorded. In such cases, the partners may agree, for example, that the assets are overvalued. And, due to the overvalued assets, the retiring partner should in settlement of his equity take assets of less value than the book value of his equity. Sometimes, too, when assets are not overvalued, the retiring partner may be so anxious to retire that he is willing to take less than the current value of his equity just to get out of the partnership.

When a partner retires taking assets of less value than his equity, he is in effect leaving a portion of his book equity in the business. In such cases, the remaining partners share the unwithdrawn equity portion in their income-and-loss-sharing ratio. For example, assume that Black, Brown, and Green are partners sharing income and losses in a 2:2:1 ratio. Their assets and equities are:

Assets		Owners' Equity	
Cash	$ 5,000	Black, capital	$ 6,000
Merchandise	9,000	Brown, capital	6,000
Store equipment	4,000	Green, capital	6,000
Total assets	$18,000	Total owners' equity	$18,000

Brown is so anxious to withdraw from the partnership that he is willing to retire if permitted to take $4,500 in cash in settlement for his equity. Black and Green agree to the $4,500 withdrawal, and Brown retires. The entry to record the retirement is:

Mar.	4	Brown, Capital	6,000.00	
		Cash		4,500.00
		Black, Capital		1,000.00
		Green, Capital		500.00
		To record the withdrawal of Brown.		

In retiring, Brown did not withdraw $1,500 of his book equity. This is divided between Black and Green in their income-and-loss-sharing ratio. The income-and-loss-sharing ratio of the original partnership was Black, 2; Brown, 2; and Green, 1. Therefore in the original partnership, Black and Green shared in a 2 to 1 ratio. Consequently, the unwithdrawn book equity of Brown is shared by Black and Green in this ratio.

Partner Withdraws Taking Assets of Greater Value than His Book Equity

There are two common reasons for a partner receiving upon retirement assets of greater value than his book equity. First, certain of the partnership assets may be undervalued. Or, the partners continuing the business may be so anxious for the retiring partner to withdraw that they are willing to give him assets of greater value than his book equity.

When assets are undervalued and the partners do not wish to change the recorded values, the partners may agree to permit a retiring member to withdraw assets of greater value than his book equity. In such cases, the retiring partner is, in effect, withdrawing his own book equity and a portion of his partners' equities. For example, assume that Jones, Thomas, and Finch are partners sharing income and losses in a 3:2:1 ratio. Their assets and equities are:

Assets		Owners' Equity	
Cash	$ 5,000	Jones, capital	$ 9,000
Merchandise	10,000	Thomas, capital	6,000
Equipment	3,000	Finch, capital	3,000
Total assets	$18,000	Total owners' equity	$18,000

Finch wishes to withdraw from the partnership. Jones and Thomas plan to continue the business. The partners agree that certain of their assets are undervalued, but they do not wish to increase the recorded values. They further agree that if current values were recorded, the asset total would be increased $6,000 and the equity of Finch would be increased $1,000. Therefore, the partners agree that $4,000 is the proper value for Finch's equity and that he may withdraw that amount in cash. The entry to record the withdrawal is:

May	7	Finch, Capital	3,000.00	
		Jones, Capital	600.00	
		Thomas, Capital	400.00	
		Cash		4,000.00
		To record the withdrawal of Finch.		

DEATH OF A PARTNER

A partner's death automatically dissolves and ends a partnership, and the deceased partner's estate is entitled to receive the amount of his or her equity. The partnership contract should contain provisions for settlement in case a partner dies. Included should be provisions for *(a)* an immediate closing of the books to determine earnings since the end of the previous accounting period and *(b)* a method for determining and recording current values for the assets. After earnings are shared and the current value of the deceased partner's equity is determined, the remaining partners and the deceased partner's estate must agree to a disposition of the equity. They may agree to its sale to the remaining partners or to an outsider, or they may agree to the withdrawal of assets in settlement. Entries for both of these procedures have already been discussed.

LIQUIDATIONS

When a partnership is liquidated, its business is ended. The assets are converted into cash, and the creditors are paid. The remaining cash is then distributed to the partners, and the partnership is dissolved. Although many combinations of circumstances occur in liquidations, only three are discussed here.

All Assets Realized before a Distribution; Assets Are Sold at a Profit

A partnership liquidation under this assumption may be illustrated with the following example. Ottis, Skinner, and Parr have operated a partnership for a number of years, sharing incomes and losses in a 3:2:1 ratio. Due to several unsatisfactory conditions, the partners decide to liquidate as of December 31. On that date, the books are closed, the income from operations is transferred to the partners' capital accounts, and the following balance sheet is prepared:

Assets		Liabilities and Owners' Equity	
Cash	$10,000	Accounts payable	$ 5,000
Merchandise inventory	15,000	Ottis, capital	15,000
Other assets	25,000	Skinner, capital	15,000
		Parr, capital	15,000
		Total liabilities and	
Total assets	$50,000	owners' equity	$50,000

In a *liquidation,* either a gain or a loss normally results from the sale of each group of assets. These losses and gains are called ''losses and gains from realization.'' They are shared by the partners in their income-and-loss-sharing ratio. If Ottis, Skinner, and Parr sell their inventory for $12,000 and their other assets for $34,000, the sales and the net gain allocation are recorded as follows:

Jan.	12	Cash	12,000.00	
		Loss or Gain from Realization	3,000.00	
		Merchandise Inventory..................		15,000.00
		Sold the inventory at a loss.		
	15	Cash	34,000.00	
		Other Assets		25,000.00
		Loss or Gain from Realization		9,000.00
		Sold the other assets at a profit.		
	15	Loss or Gain from Realization	6,000.00	
		Otis, Capital		3,000.00
		Skinner, Capital		2,000.00
		Parr, Capital		1,000.00
		To allocate the net gain from realization to the partners in their 3:2:1 income-and-loss-sharing ratio.		

Careful attention should be given to the last journal entry. In a partnership termination, when assets are sold at a loss or gain, the loss or gain is allocated to the partners in their income-and-loss-sharing ratio. In solving liquidation problems, students sometimes attempt to allocate the assets to the partners in their income-and-loss-sharing ratio. Obviously this is not correct. It is not assets but gains and losses that are shared in the income-and-loss-sharing ratio.

After the merchandise and other assets of Ottis, Skinner, and Parr are sold and the net gain is allocated, a new balance sheet shows the following:

Assets		Liabilities and Owners' Equity	
Cash	$56,000	Accounts payable	$ 5,000
		Ottis, capital	18,000
		Skinner, capital	17,000
		Parr, capital	16,000
		Total liabilities and	
Total assets	$56,000	owners' equity	$56,000

Observe that the one asset, cash, $56,000, exactly equals the sum of the liabilities and the equities of the partners.

After partnership assets are realized and the gain or loss shared, entries are made to distribute the realized cash to the proper parties. Since creditors have first claim, they are paid first. After the creditors are paid, the remaining cash is divided among the partners. Each partner has the right to cash equal to his equity or, in other words, cash equal to the balance of his capital account. The entries to distribute the cash of Ottis, Skinner, and Parr are:

Jan.	15	Accounts Payable............................	5,000.00	
		Cash....................................		5,000.00
		To pay the claims of the creditors.		
	15	Ottis, Capital	18,000.00	
		Skinner, Capital	17,000.00	
		Parr, Capital	16,000.00	
		Cash....................................		51,000.00
		To distribute the remaining cash to the partners according to their capital account balances.		

Notice that after the net gain is shared and the creditors are paid, each partner receives liquidation cash equal to the balance remaining in his capital account. The partners receive these amounts because a partner's capital account balance shows his equity in the one partnership asset, cash.

All Assets Realized before a Distribution; Assets Sold at a Loss; Each Partner's Capital Account Is Sufficient to Absorb His Share of the Loss

In a partnership liquidation, the assets are sometimes sold at a net loss. For example, if contrary to the previous assumptions the inventory of Ottis, Skinner, and Parr is sold for $9,000 and the other assets for $13,000, the entries to record the sales and loss allocation are:

Jan.	12	Cash	9,000.00	
		Loss or Gain from Realization	6,000.00	
		Merchandise Inventory....................		15,000.00
		Sold the inventory at a loss.		
	15	Cash	13,000.00	
		Loss or Gain from Realization	12,000.00	
		Other Assets		25,000.00
		Sold the other assets at a loss.		
	15	Ottis, Capital	9,000.00	
		Skinner, Capital	6,000.00	
		Parr, Capital	3,000.00	
		Loss or Gain from Realization		18,000.00
		To allocate the loss from realization to the partners in their income-and-loss-sharing ratio.		

After the entries are posted, a balance sheet shows that the partnership cash exactly equals the liabilities and the equities of the partners, as follows:

Assets		Liabilities and Owners' Equity	
Cash	$32,000	Accounts payable	$ 5,000
		Ottis, capital	6,000
		Skinner, capital	9,000
		Parr, capital	12,000
		Total liabilities and	
Total assets	$32,000	owners' equity	$32,000

The following entries are required to distribute the cash to the proper parties:

Jan.	15	Accounts Payable.........................	5,000.00	
		Cash..................................		5,000.00
		To pay the partnership creditors.		
	15	Ottis, Capital	6,000.00	
		Skinner, Capital	9,000.00	
		Parr, Capital	12,000.00	
		Cash..................................		27,000.00
		To distribute the remaining cash to the partners according to the balances of their capital accounts.		

Notice again that after losses are shared and creditors are paid, each partner receives cash equal to his capital account balance.

All Assets Realized before a Distribution; Assets Sold at a Loss; a Partner's Capital Account Is Not Sufficient to Cover His or Her Share of the Loss

Sometimes, a partner's share of realization losses is greater than the balance of his or her capital account. In such cases, the partner must, if he or she can, cover the deficit by paying cash into the partnership. For example, assume contrary to the previous illustrations that Ottis, Skinner, and Parr sell their merchandise for $3,000 and the other assets for $4,000. The entries to record the sales and the loss allocation are:

Jan.	12	Cash	3,000.00	
		Loss or Gain from Realization	12,000.00	
		Merchandise Inventory		15,000.00
		Sold the inventory at a loss.		
	15	Cash	4,000.00	
		Loss or Gain from Realization	21,000.00	
		Other Assets		25,000.00
		Sold the other assets at a loss.		
	15	Ottis, Capital	16,500.00	
		Skinner, Capital	11,000.00	
		Parr, Capital	5,500.00	
		Loss or Gain from Realization		33,000.00
		To record the allocation of the loss from realiza-tion to the partners in their income-and-loss-sharing ratio.		

After the entry allocating the realization loss is posted, the capital account of Ottis has a $1,500 debit balance and appears as follows:

Ottis, Capital

Date		Explanation	Debit	Credit	Balance
Dec.	31	Balance			15,000.00
Jan.	15	Share of loss from realization	16,500.00		1,500.00

The partnership agreement provides that Ottis is allocated one half the losses or gains. Consequently, since his capital account balance is not large enough to absorb his loss share in this case, he must, if he can, pay $1,500 into the partnership to cover the *deficit*. If he is able to pay, the following entry is made:

Jan.	15	Cash	1,500.00	
		Ottis, Capital		1,500.00
		To record the additional investment of Ottis to cover his share of realization losses.		

After the $1,500 is received, the partnership has $18,500 in cash. The following entries are then made to distribute the cash to the proper parties:

Jan.	15	Accounts Payable.........................	5,000.00	
		Cash.................................		5,000.00
		To pay the partnership creditors.		
	15	Skinner, Capital	4,000.00	
		Parr, Capital	9,500.00	
		Cash.................................		13,500.00
		To distribute the remaining cash to the partners according to the balances of their capital accounts.		

When a partner's share of partnership losses exceeds his capital account balance, he may be unable to make up the deficit. In such cases, since each partner has unlimited liability, the deficit must be borne by the remaining partner or partners. For example, assume that Ottis is unable to pay in the $1,500 necessary to cover the deficit in his capital account. If Ottis is unable to pay, his deficit must be shared by Skinner and Parr in their income-and-loss-sharing ratio. The partners share income and losses in the ratio of Ottis, 3; Skinner, 2; and Parr, 1. Therefore, Skinner and Parr share in a 2 to 1 ratio. Consequently, the $1,500 by which Ottis's share of the losses exceeded his capital account balance is apportioned between them in this ratio. Normally, the defaulting partner's deficit is transferred to the capital accounts of the remaining partners. This is accomplished for Ottis, Skinner, and Parr with the following entry:

Jan.	15	Skinner, Capital	1,000.00	
		Parr, Capital	500.00	
		Ottis, Capital		1,500.00
		To transfer the deficit of Ottis to the capital accounts of Skinner and Parr.		

After the deficit is transferred, the capital accounts of the partners appear as in Illustration 14–4.

After the deficit is transferred, the $17,000 of liquidation cash is distributed with the following entries:

Illustration 14–4

Ottis, Capital

Date		Explanation	Debit	Credit	Balance
Dec.	31	Balance			15,000.00
Jan.	15	Share of loss from realization	16,500.00		1,500.00
	15	Deficit to Skinner and Parr		1,500.00	–0–

Skinner, Capital

Date		Explanation	Debit	Credit	Balance
Dec.	31	Balance			15,000.00
Jan.	15	Share of loss from realization	11,000.00		4,000.00
	15	Share of Ottis's deficit	1,000.00		3,000.00

Parr, Capital

Date		Explanation	Debit	Credit	Balance
Dec.	31	Balance			15,000.00
Jan.	15	Share of loss from realization	5,500.00		9,500.00
	15	Share of Ottis's deficit	500.00		9,000.00

Jan.	15	Accounts Payable..........................		5,000.00	
		Cash...................................			5,000.00
		To pay the partnership creditors.			
	15	Skinner, Capital		3,000.00	
		Parr, Capital		9,000.00	
		Cash...................................			12,000.00
		To distribute the remaining cash to the partners according to their capital account balances.			

It should be understood that the inability of Ottis to meet his loss share at this time does not relieve him of liability. If he becomes able to pay at some future time, Skinner and Parr may collect from him the full $1,500. Skinner may collect $1,000, and Parr, $500.

The sharing of an insolvent partner's deficit by the remaining partners in their original income-and-loss-sharing is generally regarded as equitable. In England, however, in the case of *Garner* v. *Murray,* Judge Joyce ruled that the debit balance of the insolvent partner's Capital account is a personal debt due to the other partners and to be borne by them in the ratio of their Capital account balances immediately prior to liquidation.

While the *Garner* v. *Murray* decision still appears to be good law, it is considered by most to be inequitable. The decision applies only when the partnership agreement does not cover this situation and, although rendered in 1904, has not been applied in Canada. It is common practice to provide in the partnership agreement for the sharing of a partner's debit balance by the remaining partners in their income-and-loss-sharing ratio.

GLOSSARY

Deficit.   A negative balance in an account.

General partner.   A partner who assumes unlimited liability for the debts of the partnership.

General partnership.   A partnership in which all partners have unlimited liability for partnership debts.

Limited partners.   Partners who have no personal liability for debts of the limited partnership beyond the amounts they have invested in the partnership.

Limited partnership.   A partnership that has two classes of partners, limited partners and one or more general partners.

Liquidation.   The process of ending a business by converting its assets to cash and distributing the cash to the proper parties.

Mutual agency.   The legal characteristic of a partnership whereby each partner is an agent of the partnership and is able to bind the partnership to contracts within the normal scope of the partnership business.

Partnership.   An association of two or more persons to carry on a business as co-owners for profit.

Partnership contract.   The document setting forth the agreed terms under which the members of a partnership will conduct the partnership business.

Unlimited liability of partners.   The legal characteristic of a partnership that makes each partner responsible for paying all the debts of the partnership if his or her partners are unable to pay their shares.

QUESTIONS FOR CLASS DISCUSSION

1.   Hill and Dale are partners. Hill dies, and his son claims the right to take his father's place in the partnership. Does he have this right? Why?

2.   If Ted Hall cannot legally enter into a contract, can he become a partner?

3.   If a partnership contract does not state the period of time the partnership is to exist, when does the partnership end?

4.   What is the meaning of the term *mutual agency* as applied to a partnership?

5.   Karen and Frank are partners in the operation of a store. Without consulting Karen, Frank enters into a contract for the purchase of merchandise for

resale by the store. Karen contends that she did not authorize the order and refuses to take delivery. The vendor sues the partners for the contract price of the merchandise. Will the firm have to pay? Why?

6. Would your answer to Question 2 differ if Karen and Frank were partners in a public accounting firm?

7. May partners limit the right of a member of their firm to bind their partnership to contracts? Is such an agreement binding *(a)* on the partners and *(b)* on outsiders?

8. What is the meaning of the term *unlimited liability* when it is applied to members of a partnership?

9. Jones organized a limited partnership and is the only general partner. Craven invested $10,000 in the partnership and was admitted as a limited partner with the understanding that he would receive 5% of the profits. After two unprofitable years, the partnership ceased doing business. At that point, partnership liabilities were $75,000 larger than partnership assets. How much money can the crediters of the partnership obtain from Craven in satisfaction of the unpaid partnership debts?

10. How does a limited partnership differ from a general partnership?

11. Brown, Dyckman, and Granger have been partners for three years. The partnership is dissolving. Brown is leaving the firm while Dyckman and Granger are planning to carry on the business. In the final settlement, Brown places a $60,000 salary claim against the partnership. His contention is that since he devoted all of his time for three years to the affairs of the partnership, he has a claim for a salary of $20,000 for each year. Is his claim valid? Why?

12. The partnership agreement of Aimes and Bartlett provides for a two-thirds, one-third sharing of income but says nothing of losses. The first year of partnership operations resulted in a loss and Aimes argues that the loss should be shared equally since the partnership agreement said nothing of sharing losses. Do you agree?

13. A, B, and C are partners with capital account balances of $6,000 each. D gives A $7,500 for his one-third interest in the partnership. The bookkeeper debits A, Capital and credits D, Capital for $6,000. D objects. He wants his capital account to show a $7,500 balance, the amount he paid for his interest. Explain why D's capital account is credited for $6,000.

14. After all partnership assets are converted to cash and all liabilities have been paid, the remaining cash should equal the sum of the balances of the partners' capital accounts. Why?

15. Jim, Kathy, and Larry are partners. In a liquidation, Jim's share of partnership losses exceeds his capital account balance. He is unable to meet the deficit from his personal assets, and the excess losses are shared by his partners. Does this relieve Jim of liability?

16. A partner withdraws from a partnership and receives assets of greater

value than the book value of his equity. Should the remaining partners share the resulting reduction in their equities in the ratio of their relative capital balances or in their income-and-loss-sharing ratio?

MULTIPLE CHOICE

1. Brown, Jones and Smith formed a partnership in which Brown contributed $60,000, Jones contributed $50,000 and Smith contributed $40,000. Their partnership agreement called for earnings division to be based on the ratio of capital investments. If the partnership had earnings of $74,000 for its first year of operation, what amount of earnings would be credited to Smith's capital account?
    a. $19,733.
    b. $24,666.
    c. $29,600.
    d. $40,000.
    e. $74,000.

2. If a partnership contract provides for interest at 10% annually on each partner's investment, the interest:
    a. Is ignored when earnings are not sufficient to pay interest.
    b. Provides for the sharing of a portion of the partnership earnings in the capital ratio.
    c. Is an expense of the business.
    d. Must be paid because the partnership contract provides for it.
    e. Is interest in the legal sense of the term.

3. If Rayfield and Simms are partners sharing profits and losses equally and possessing capital balances of $60,000 and $40,000, respectively, and Jones pays $50,000 for a one-third interest in profits, losses, and capital, the entry of Jones should be recorded:
    a. In a manner that recognizes goodwill and allocates the goodwill to the old partners.
    b. In a manner that provides a bonus to Jones.
    c. In a manner that provides a bonus to the old partners.
    d. In a manner that does not involve a bonus and does not involve goodwill.
    e. With a credit of $33,000 to the capital account of Jones.

4. Black and White formed a partnership with capital contributions of $40,000 and $80,000, respectively. The partnership agreement calls for earnings or losses to be divided as follows: (1) $12,000 salary to Black, (2) 8% return on capital contribution, and (3) the remainder to be divided equally. If the earnings for the year were $16,000, Black's share would be:
    a. $12,000.
    b. $12,400.

c. $15,200.

d. $18,000.

e. Some other amount.

5. Jones and Smith are partners with capital balances of $14,000 each. Brown is admitted as a partner by investing $23,000 in the partnership and giving a bonus to the old partners. Brown is to have a one-third interest in the partnership equity and earnings. The entry to establish Brown's capital account is:

a. Cash   23,000
    Jones, Capital   3,000
    Smith, Capital   3,000
    Brown, Capital   17,000

b. Cash   23,000
    Brown, Capital   23,000

c. Cash   23,000
  Goodwill   6,000
    Brown, Capital   23,000
    Jones, Capital   3,000
    Smith, Capital   3,000

d. Cash   23,000
    Jones, Capital   7,666
    Smith, Capital   7,666
    Brown, Capital   7,667

e. None of the above.

6. The partnership of Mo and Curly has the following capital balances: Mo, $16,000; and Curly, $8,000. Curly sells his share of partnership equity to Shemp for $12,000. Mo agrees to this, so the entry to record this transaction is as follows:

a. Cash   12,000
    Shemp, Capital   12,000

b. Cash   4,000
  Curly, Capital   8,000
    Shemp, Capital   12,000

c. Cash   12,000
  Curly, Capital   8,000
    Shemp, Capital   12,000
    Mo, Capital   8,000

d. Curly, Capital   8,000
    Shemp, Capital   8,000

e. Curly, Capital   8,000
  Mo, Capital   4,000
    Shemp, Capital   12,000

7. Jack invested $5,000 and Jill invested $10,000 in a partnership in which they agreed to share profits and losses by allowing a $9,000 per year

salary allowance to Jack and a $12,000 per year salary allowance to Jill, interest on the partners' investments at 10% and the balance equally. Under this agreement the shares of the partners in a $21,000 net income are:

    a. $10,500 to Jack and $10,500 to Jill.

    b. $7,000 to Jack and $14,000 to Jill.

    c. $9,000 to Jack and $12,000 to Jill.

    d. $8,750 to Jack and $12,250 to Jill.

    e. Some other amounts.

8.   Lee and Kardash are partners sharing income and losses in a 2 to 1 ratio, and they decided to liquidate their partnership. On the date of their decision they had $45,000 of liabilities and capital account balances of $270,000 and $180,000, respectively. If their cash accounts has a $225,000 balance after all noncash assets are sold and all liabilities are paid, Kardash's share of the liquidation losses is:

    a. $60,000.

    b. $75,000.

    c. $90,000.

    d. $112,500.

    e. Some other amount.

MINI DISCUSSION CASES

Case 14–1   Two students were overheard discussing the virtues and pitfalls of the partnership form of business organization. Their conclusion was that the disadvantages far outweighed the advantages. The partnership form had many pitfalls and should be entered into as a last resort. Entry should be made with extreme caution and with as many protective features as can be negotiated.

Required:

The above conclusion seems to be extreme. You are asked to critically evaluate the conclusion of the two students.

Case 14–2   There are certain types of businesses that cannot incorporate and must be operated as sole proprietorships or partnerships.

Required:

1.   List types of businesses that cannot be incorporated.
2.   Discuss why the businesses you listed must be organized as sole proprietorships or partnerships but not as corporations.

CLASS EXERCISES

Exercise 14–1   On January 20, 198A, Freetag and Williamson formed a partnership in which Freetag contributed $50,000 and Williamson contributed land valued at $30,000 and a building valued at $70,000. They agreed to share profits as follows: Freetag is to receive an annual salary of $25,000, each partner is to receive 10% of his or her original capital investment, and any remaining profit or loss is to be shared equally. On November 12, 198A, Freetag withdrew cash of $20,000 and Williamson withdrew $10,000. Present general journal entries to record the initial capital investments of the partners, the cash withdrawals of the partners, the December 31 closing of the withdrawals accounts and the Income Summary account, which had a credit balance of $48,000.

Exercise 14–2   Maybrey and Nickles began a partnership by investing $44,000 and $66,000, respectively; and during its first year, the partnership earned $168,000.

Required:

Prepare calculations showing how the income should be allocated to the partners under each of the following plans for sharing income:

a.   The partners failed to agree on a method of sharing income.
b.   The partners had agreed to share income in their investment ratio.
c.   The partners had agreed to share income by allowing 10% interest on investments, a $72,000 per year salary allowance to Maybrey, a $56,000 per year salary allowance to Nickles, and the balance equally.

Exercise 14–3   Assume the partners of Exercise 14–2 agreed to share losses and gains by allowing 10% interest on their investments, yearly salary allowances of $72,000 to Maybrey and $56,000 to Nickles, and the balance equally. *(a)* Determine the shares of Maybrey and Nickles in a $131,200 first-year net income. *(b)* Determine the partners' shares in a first-year $20,800 net loss.

Exercise 14–4   The partners in Triple Y Partnership have agreed that partner Tavenor may sell his $60,000 equity in the partnership to Olsen, for which Olsen will pay Tavenor $45,000. Present the partnership's journal entry to record the sale on August 30.

Exercise 14–5   The Schnurr-Higgins Partnership has total partners' equity of $280,000, which is made up of Schnurr, Capital, $210,000, and Higgins, Capital, $70,000. The partners share gains and losses in a ratio of 75% to Schnurr and 25% to Higgins. On January 1, Geer is admitted to the partnership and given a 20% interest in equity and in gains and losses. Prepare the journal entry to record the entry of Geer under each of the following unrelated assumptions. Geer invests cash of *(a)* $70,000; *(b)* $105,000; and *(c)* $42,000.

Exercise 14–6   Kent, Morris, and Nathan have been partners sharing income and losses in a 3:5:2 ratio. On November 30, the date Nathan retires from the partnership, the equities of the partners are Kent, $120,000; Morris, $180,000; and Nathan, $20,000.

Required:

Present general journal entries to record Nathan's retirement under each of the following unrelated assumptions:

a. Nathan is paid $20,000 in partnership cash for his equity.
b. Nathan is paid $25,000 in partnership cash for his equity.
c. Nathan is paid $16,000 in partnership cash for his equity.

Exercise 14–7

The Bing, Bang, and Bong partnership was begun with investments by the partners as follows: Bing, $87,500; Bang, $52,500; and Bong, $70,000. The first year of operations did not go well, and the partners finally decided to liquidate the partnership, sharing all losses equally. On December 31, after all assets were converted to cash and all creditors were paid, only $21,000 in partnership cash remained.

Required:

1. Calculate the capital account balances of the partners after the liquidation of assets and payment of creditors.
2. Assume that any partner with a deficit pays cash to the partnership to cover the deficit. Then, present the general journal entries on December 31 to record the cash receipt from the deficient partner(s) and the final disbursement of cash to the partners.
3. Now make the contrary assumption that any partner with a deficit is not able to reimburse the partnership. Present journal entries *(a)* to transfer the deficit of any deficient partners to the other partners and *(b)* to record the final disbursement of cash to the partners.

Exercise 14–8

Crosby, Davis, and Hill are partners sharing incomes and losses in a 1:3:4 ratio. After lengthy disagreements among the partners and several unprofitable periods, the partners decided to liquidate the partnership. Before the liquidation, the partnership balance sheet showed total assets, $150,000; liabilities, $120,000; Crosby, Capital, $6,000; Davis, Capital, $9,000; and Hill, Capital, $15,000. The cash proceeds from selling the assets were sufficient to repay all of the creditors except $25,000. Calculate the loss from selling the assets, allocate the loss to the partners, and determine how much of the remaining liability should be paid by each partner.

Exercise 14–9

Assume that the Crosby, Davis, and Hill partnership of Exercise 14–8 is a limited partnership. Crosby and Davis are general partners and Hill is a limited partner. How much of the remaining $25,000 liability should be paid by each partner?

PROBLEMS

Problem 14–1

Bruce Brown, Kay Craig, and Randal Gilpin invested $52,500, $42,000, and $31,500, respectively, in a partnership. During its first year, the firm earned $142,800.

Required:

Prepare entries to close the firm's Income Summary account as of December 31 and to allocate the net income to the partners under each of the assumptions below. (Round your answers to the nearest whole dollar.)

a.   The partners could not agree as to the method of sharing earnings.
b.   The partners had agreed to share earnings in the ratio of their beginning investments.
c.   The partners had agreed to share income by allowing a share of the income equal to 10% interest on the partners' investments; allowing annual salary allowances of $42,000 to Brown, $49,000 to Craig, and $35,000 to Gilpin; and sharing the remainder equally.

Problem 14–2   Barry Pingle and Shannon Hill are in the process of forming a partnership to which Pingle will devote one-third time and Hill will devote full time. They have discussed the following plans for sharing income and losses.

a.   In the ratio of their investments which they have agreed to maintain at $25,000 for Pingle and $37,500 for Hill.
b.   In proportion to the time devoted to the business.
c.   A salary allowance of $2,500 per month to Hill and the balance in their investment ratio.
d.   A $2,500 per month salary allowance to Hill, 10% interest on their investments, and the balance equally.

The partners expect the business to generate income as follows: Year 1, $15,000 net loss; Year 2, $45,000 net income; and Year 3, $90,000 net income.

Required:

1.   Prepare three schedules with the following columnar headings:

Income-Sharing Plan	Year _____		
	Calculations	Pingle	Hill

2.   Complete a schedule for each of the first three years by showing how the partnership income for each year would be allocated to the partners under each of the four plans being considered. (Round your answers to the nearest whole dollar.)

Problem 14–3   Tom Boyd, Mike DeMoss, and Shirley Tucker formed the BDT Partnership by making capital contributions of $86,400, $96,000, and $105,600, respectively. They anticipate annual net incomes of $150,000 and are considering the following alternative plans of sharing income and losses: *(a)* equally; *(b)* in the ratio of their initial investments; or *(c)* interest allowances of 10% on initial investments, salary allowances of $32,000 to Boyd, $17,000 to DeMoss, and $38,000 to Tucker, with any remaining balance shared equally.

Required:

1. Prepare a schedule with the following column headings:

Income-Sharing Plan	Calculations	Share to Boyd	Share to DeMoss	Share to Tucker	Income Allo-cated

Use the schedule to show how a net income of $150,000 would be distributed under each of the alternative plans being considered.

2. Prepare the section of the partner's first year income statement showing the allocation of income to the partners' assuming they agree to use alternative *(c)* and the net income actually earned is $72,000.

3. Prepare the December 31 journal entry to close the Income Summary account assuming they agree to use alternative *(c)* and the net income is $72,000.

Problem 14–4

Part 1. Linder, Perry, and Wisner are partners with capital balances as follows: Linder, $122,500; Perry, $87,500; and Wisner, $210,000. The partners share income and losses in a 1:2:3 ratio. Prepare general journal entries to record the April 1 withdrawal of Perry from the partnership under each of the following unrelated assumptions:

a. Perry sells his interest to Reed for $112,000 after Linder and Wisner approve the entry of Reed as a partner.

b. Perry gives his interest to a son-in-law, Bob McMeans. Linder and Wisner accept McMeans as a partner.

c. Perry is paid $87,500 in partnership cash for his equity.

d. Perry is paid $129,500 in partnership cash for his equity.

e. Perry is paid $17,500 in partnership cash plus delivery equipment recorded on the partnership books at $77,000 less accumulated depreciation of $42,000.

Part 2. Assume that Perry does not retire from the partnership described in Part 1. Instead, Baker is to be admitted to the partnership on April 1 and is to have a 25% equity. Prepare general journal entries to record the entry of Baker into the partnership under each of the following unrelated assumptions:

a. Baker invests $140,000.

b. Baker invests $105,000.

c. Baker invests $175,000.

Problem 14–5

Gilles, Halter, and Reeves plan to liquidate their partnership. They have always shared income and losses in a 1:4:5 ratio, and on the day of the liquidation their balance sheet appeared as follows:

GILLES, HALTER, AND REEVES
Balance Sheet
May 31, 19—

Assets		**Liabilities and Owners' Equity**	
Cash	$ 12,250	Accounts payable	$ 47,250
Other assets	157,500	Don Gilles, capital	17,500
		Eve Halter, capital	70,000
		Paula Reeves, capital	35,000
		Total liabilities and	
Total assets	$169,750	owners' equity	$169,750

Required:

Prepare general journal entries to record the sale of the other assets and the distribution of the cash to the proper parties under each of the following unrelated assumptions:

a. The other assets are sold for $176,750.
b. The other assets are sold for $105,000.
c. The other assets are sold for $77,000, and any partners with resulting deficits can and do pay in the amount of their deficits.
d. The other assets are sold for $70,000, and the partners have no assets other than those invested in the business.

Problem 14–6

Until June 17 of the current year, Fleck, Ham, and Moore were partners sharing incomes and losses in the ratio of their capital account balances (before closing their withdrawal accounts). On that date, Ham suffered a heart attack and died. Fleck and Moore immediately ended the business operations and prepared the following adjusted trial balance.

FLECK, HAM, AND MOORE
Adjusted Trial Balance
June 17, 19—

Cash	$ 15,750	
Accounts receivable	36,750	
Allowance for doubtful accounts		$ 1,750
Supplies inventory	80,500	
Equipment	47,250	
Accumulated depreciation, equipment		12,250
Land	15,750	
Building	175,000	
Accumulated depreciation, building		33,250
Accounts payable		10,500
Mortgage payable		35,000
Tom Fleck, capital		105,000
Donna Ham, capital		105,000
Ray Moore, capital		52,500
Tom Fleck, withdrawals	3,500	
Donna Ham, withdrawals	3,500	
Ray Moore, withdrawals	3,500	
Revenues		136,500
Expenses	110,250	
Totals	$491,750	$491,750

Required:

1. Prepare June 17 entries to close the revenue, expense, income summary, and withdrawals accounts of the partnership.
2. Assume the estate of Ham agreed to accept the land and building and assume the mortgage thereon in settlement of its claim against the partnership assets, and that Fleck and Moore planned to continue the business and rent the building from the estate. Give the June 29 entry to transfer the land, building, and mortgage and to settle with the estate.
3. Assume that in the place of the foregoing the estate of Ham demanded a cash settlement and the business had to be sold to a competitor who gave $238,000 for the noncash assets and assumed the mortgage but not the accounts payable. Give the June 29 entry to transfer the noncash assets and mortgage to the competitor, and give the entries to allocate the loss to the partners and to distribute the partnership cash to the proper parties.

ALTERNATE PROBLEMS

Problem 14–1A

Joan Crown, Bob Fogg, and Jan Hempel invested $78,750, $63,000, and $47,250, respectively, in a partnership. During its first year, the firm earned $214,200.

Required:

Prepare entries to close the firm's Income Summary account as of December 31 and to allocate the net income to the partners under each of the assumptions below. (Round your answers to the nearest whole dollar.)

a. The partners could not agree as to the method of sharing earnings.
b. The partners had agreed to share earnings in the ratio of their beginning investments.
c. The partners had agreed to share income by allowing a share of the income equal to 10% interest on the partners' investments; allowing annual salary allowances of $63,000 to Crown, $73,500 to Fogg, and $52,500 to Hempel; and sharing the remainder equally.

Problem 14–2A

Katherine Shell and Henry Dock are in the process of forming a partnership to which Shell will devote one-fourth time and Dock will devote full time. They have discussed the following plans for sharing gains and losses.

a. In the ratio of their investments which they have agreed to maintain at $42,500 for Shell and $63,750 for Dock.
b. In proportion to the time devoted to the business.
c. A salary allowance of $4,250 per month to Dock and the balance in their investment ratio.
d. A $4,250 per month salary allowance to Dock, 10% interest on their investments, and the balance equally.

The partners expect the business to generate income as follows: Year 1, $25,500 net loss; Year 2, $76,500 net income; and Year 3, $153,000 net income.

Required:

1. Prepare three schedules with the following columnar headings:

Income-Sharing Plan	Year ———————————		
	Calculations	Shell	Dock

2. Complete a schedule for each of the first three years by showing how the partnership income for each year would be allocated to the partners under each of the four plans being considered. Round your answers to the nearest whole dollar.

Problem 14–3A

Karen Bell, Dan Flint, and Joe Hallis formed the BFH Partnership by making capital contributions of $175,000, $200,000, and $125,000, respectively. They anticipate annual net incomes of $300,000 and are considering the following alternative plans of sharing incomes and losses: *(a)* equally; *(b)* in the ratio of their initial investments; or *(c)* interest allowances of 12% on initial investments, salary allowances of $75,000 to Bell, $25,000 to Flint, and $50,000 to Hallis, with any remaining balance shared equally.

Required:

1. Prepare a schedule with the following column headings:

Income-Sharing Plan	Calculations	Share to Bell	Share to Flint	Share to Hallis	Income Allocated

Use the schedule to show how a net income of $300,000 would be distributed under each of the alternative plans being considered.

2. Prepare the section of the partner's first-year income statement showing the allocation of income to the partners' assuming they agree to use alternative *(c)* and the net income actually earned is $75,000.

3. Prepare the December 31 journal entry to close the Income Summary account assuming they agree to use alternative *(c)* and the net income is $75,000.

Problem 14–4A

Part 1. Burns, Jacobs, and Kruse are partners with capital balances as follows: Burns, $127,500; Jacobs, $42,500; and Kruse, $85,000. The partners share incomes and losses in a 2:4:2 ratio. Prepare general journal entries to record the October 31 withdrawal of Kruse from the partnership under each of the following unrelated assumptions:

a. Kruse sells his interest to Legg for $35,700 after Burns and Jacobs approve the entry of Legg as a partner.

b. Kruse gives his interest to a son-in-law, S. Platt. Burns and Jacobs accept Platt as a partner.

c. Kruse is paid $85,000 in partnership cash for his equity.

d. Kruse is paid $49,000 in partnership cash for his equity.

e. Kruse is paid $39,000 in partnership cash plus delivery equipment recorded on the partnership books at $56,000 less accumulated depreciation of $37,000.

Part 2. Assume that Kruse does not retire from the partnership described in Part 1. Instead, Quick is to be admitted to the partnership on October 31 and is to have a 20% equity. Prepare general journal entries to record the entry of Quick under each of the following unrelated assumptions:

a. Quick invests $63,750.

b. Quick invests $45,000.

c. Quick invests $102,000.

Problem 14–5A

Forbes, Hofman, and Kasper, who have always shared incomes and losses in a 3:1:1 ratio, plan to liquidate their partnership. Just prior to the liquidation their balance sheet appeared as follows:

FORBES, HOFMAN, AND KASPER
Balance Sheet
July 15, 19—

Assets		Liabilities and Owners' Equity	
Cash	$ 11,250	Accounts payable	$ 47,250
Other assets	198,000	T. Forbes, capital	76,000
		J. Hofman, capital	50,000
		R. Kasper, capital	36,000
		Total liabilities and	
Total assets	$209,250	owners' equity	$209,250

Required:

Under the assumption the other assets are sold and the cash is distributed to the proper parties on July 15 give the entries for the sales, the loss or gain allocations, and the distributions if—

a. The other assets are sold for $225,000.

b. The other assets are sold for $141,750.

c. The other assets are sold for $60,500, and any partners with resulting deficits can and do pay in the amount of their deficits.

d. The other assets are sold for $46,000, and the partners have no assets other than those invested in the business.

Problem 14–6A

Marcus, Newfeld, and Price are partners. Marcus devotes full time to partnership affairs; Newfeld and Price devote very little time; and as a result, they share incomes and losses in a 4:1:1 ratio. Of late, the business has not been too profitable, and the partners have decided to liquidate. Just prior to the first realization sale, a partnership balance sheet appeared as follows:

MARCUS, NEWFELD, AND PRICE
Balance Sheet
August 10, 19—

Assets			Liabilities and Owners' Equity	
Cash		$ 3,750	Accounts payable	$10,500
Accounts receivable		14,250	Marcus, capital	9,000
Merchandise inventory		24,000	Newfeld, capital	18,000
Equipment	$18,000		Price, capital	18,000
Less accumulated				
depreciation	4,500	13,500		
			Total liabilities and	
Total assets		$55,500	owners' equity	$55,500

The assets were sold, the creditors were paid, and the remaining cash was distributed to the partners on the following dates:

Aug. 11 The accounts receivable were sold for $9,750.
    12 The merchandise inventory was sold for $16,500.
    14 The equipment was sold for $7,500.
    15 The creditors were paid.
    17 The remaining cash was distributed to the partners.

Required:

1. Prepare general journal entries to record the asset sales, the allocation of the realization loss, and the payment of the creditors.
2. Under the assumption that any partners with capital deficits can and do pay in the amount of their deficits on July 17, give the entry to record the receipt of the cash and the distribution of partnership cash to the remaining partners.
3. Under the assumption that any partners with capital deficits cannot pay, give the entry to allocate the deficits to the remaining partners. Then give the entry to distribute the partnership cash to the remaining partners.

PROVOCATIVE PROBLEMS

Provocative Problem 14–1, Which Partner Gets the Profits?

    Haire and Kardash are partners who have agreed to share the annual profits or losses of their business as follows. If the partnership earns a net income, the first $40,000 is allocated 25% to Haire and 75% to Kardash so as to reflect the time devoted to the business by each partner. Gains in excess of $40,000 are shared equally. However, if business operations result in a loss for the year, the partners have agreed to share the loss equally.

Required:

1. Prepare a schedule showing how the 198A net income of $48,000 should be allocated to the partners.

2. Immediately after the closing entries for 198A were posted on December 31, 198A, the partners discovered unrecorded accounts payable amounting to $60,000. The accounts payable related to expenses incurred by the business. Kardash suggests that the $60,000 should be allocated equally between the partners as a loss. Haire disagrees and argues that an entry should be made to record the accounts payable and correct the capital accounts to reflect a $12,000 net loss for 198A. *(a)* Present the January 1, 198B, journal entry to record the accounts payable and allocate the loss to the partners according to Kardash's suggestion. *(b)* Now give the January 1, 198B, journal entry to record the accounts payable and correct the capital accounts according to Haire's argument. Show how you calculated the amounts in the entry.

3. Which partner do you think is right? Why?

Provocative Problem 14–2, Good Sounds

Janis Stern and Sally Tharp are partners that own and operate Good Sounds, a phonographic records and tapes store. Stern has a $63,000 equity in the business, and Tharp has a $38,250 equity. They share incomes and losses by allowing annual salary allowances of $22,500 to Stern and $18,000 to Tharp, with any remaining balance being shared 60% to Stern and 40% to Tharp.

Karen Stern, Janis Stern's daughter, has been working in the store on a salary basis. Prior to working in the store, Karen was a successful disk jockey and is well known among record and tape buyers in the community. As a result, Karen attracts a great deal of business to the store. The partners believe that at least one third of the past three years' sales can be traced directly to Karen's association with the store, and it is reasonable to assume she was instrumental in attracting even more.

Karen is paid $1,500 per month, but feels this is not sufficient to induce her to remain with the firm as an employee. However, she likes her work and would like to remain in the records and tapes business. What she really wants is to become a partner in the business.

Her mother is anxious for her to remain in the business and proposes the following:

a. That Karen be admitted to the partnership with a 20% equity in the partnership assets.

b. That she, Janis Stern, transfer from her capital account to that of Karen's one half the 20% interest; that Karen contribute to the firm's assets a noninterest-bearing note for the other half; and that she, Janis Stern, will guarantee payment of the note.

c. That incomes and losses be shared by continuing the $22,500 and $18,000 salary allowances of the original partners and that Karen be given an $18,000 annual salary allowance, after which any remaining income or loss would be shared 40% to Janis Stern, 40% to Sally Tharp, and 20% to Karen Stern.

Prepare a report to Ms. Tharp on the advisability of accepting Janis Stern's proposal. Under the assumption that net incomes for the past three years have been $55,500, $61,500, and $64,500, respectively, prepare schedules showing: *(a)* how net income was allocated during the past three years, *(b)* how it would have been allocated had the proposed new agreement been in effect, and *(c)* prepare a schedule showing the partners' capital interests as they would be immediately after the admission of Karen.

Provocative Problem 14–3, Withdrawal of a Partner

The balance sheet of the Oldtime Partnership on December 31, 198A, is as follows:

Assets		Liabilities and Owners' Equity	
Cash	$30,000	Franks, capital	$15,000
Other assets	37,500	Maynard, capital	22,500
Land	22,500	Stone, capital	52,500
		Total liabilities and	
Total assets	$90,000	owners' equity	$90,000

The income-and-loss-sharing percentages are: Franks, 20%; Maynard, 30%; and Stone, 50%. Franks wishes to withdraw from the partnership, and the partners finally agree that the land owned by the partnership should be transferred to Franks in full payment for his equity. In reaching this decision, they recognize that the land has appreciated since it was purchased and is now worth $40,000. If Franks retires on January 1, 198B, what journal entries should be made on that date?

ANALYTICAL AND REVIEW PROBLEMS

Problem 14–1 A&R

Kay and Mart entered into a partnership to carry on a business under the firm name of Kay-Mart Sportsland. Prior to the final signing of the agreement Kay asks you to evaluate the "income/loss distribution clause" contained in the agreement.

Your examination revealed that the agreement called for the following: Equal sharing of net income and losses after an initial allocation of $50,000 to Kay and $12,500 to Mart in order to reflect the difference in time and expertise devoted to the business by each partner. The initial allocation would be made regardless of the level of net income/loss. √

Required:

Prepare a report to Kay on the particular clause of the agreement. Your report should show the consequence on each partner of operating results as follows: *(a)* net income of $100,000; *(b)* net income of $25,000; *(c)* operation at break-even, that is, no net income nor loss; *(d)* loss of $25,000; *(e)* loss of $100,000.

Problem 14–2 A&R

The summarized balance sheet of Bell, Trunk and Field showed:

Assets		Equities	
Cash	$ 20,000	Liabilities	$ 50,000
Other assets	280,000	Bell, capital	80,000
		Trunk, capital	120,000
		Field, capital	50,000
Total assets	$300,000	Total equities	$300,000

The partnership has operated successfully for nearly 25 years, and Field because of his age and health is pushing for sale of the business. In fact, he has found Spector, a buyer who is willing to pay cash $300,000 and take over the liabilities. Both Bell and Trunk are not anxious to sell to what they refer to as our "little gold mine."

Field is adamant about getting out and has proposed the following:

1. Either sell to Spector, or Bell and Trunk (a new partnership) should buy out Field at an amount Field would receive if the business was sold to Spector.
2. Admit Spector to partnership upon the purchase of Field's share for an amount Field and Spector will negotiate.

The present partnership agreement calls for a distribution of net income/loss on a 3:5:2 basis. If Spector is admitted to partnership the ratio would not change, he would be entitled to Field's 20% share of net income/loss. If Bell and Trunk buy out for an amount based on the Spector offer, Bell and Trunk would continue to share net income/loss on the same relative basis. They would (the new partnership of Bell and Trunk) have to borrow sufficient funds from the bank to retain a minimum cash balance of $8,000.

Required:

1. Prepare the general journal entry for admission of Spector to the partnership upon his purchase of Field's interest for an undisclosed amount.
2. Prepare the necessary entries to record Field's withdrawal from the partnership. The amount paid to Field is equal to the amount he would have received if the partnership was sold to Spector.

Problem 14–3
A&R

After closing the revenue and expense accounts a partial list of account balances of the CMS Partnership appears below:

Cash	20,000	
Accounts payable		10,000
Income summary		48,000
C. Capital		50,000
M. Capital		60,000
S. Capital		70,000
C. Withdrawals	15,000	
M. Withdrawals	12,000	
S. Withdrawals	20,000	

The partnership agreement reads as follows: "In distributing any profits or losses, an initial allocation will be made to recognize the expertise and time spent by each of the partners, the balance after the initial distribution is to be allocated equally. The initial distribution shall be: $30,000 to C, $20,000 to M, and $10,000 to S.''

Required:

Prepare the balance of the closing journal entries for the CMS Partnership.

Problem 14–4 A&R

Assume that in Problem 14–3 A&R, the ''Income Summary'' account had a debit balance of $15,000 instead of the $48,000 credit balance and all the other account balances were the same.

Required:

Prepare the balance of the closing entries for the CMS Partnership.

Problem 14–5 A&R

Y, F, and D were partners sharing income and losses equally. The business was considered very successful until the last two or three years. Changes in technology and additional competition from abroad led the partners to conclude that they should sell. As Y stated, ''We had many good years with each of us withdrawing various amounts, nearly $5 million in total. Why wait for rigor mortis to set in? Let's get out while we still can.'' These sentiments were shared by both F and D.

Both Y and D were taking their wives on a round-the-world cruise to celebrate their 40th and 50th anniversaries. Consequently, F was authorized to negotiate the sale of the business.

Upon Y's and D's return, F informed them that he had disposed of the business for a price that both Y and D agreed was excellent. Consequently, D demanded an accounting when informed that he owed Y and F $2,000 each.

The partnership balance sheet at the time of the sale of the business was as follows:

Y, F, D
Balance Sheet
June 15, 1985

Assets

Cash	$ 2,000	
Accounts receivable (net of $200 allowance)	80,000	
Inventory	120,000	
Prepayments	18,000	
Total current assets		$220,000
Goodwill, patents and other intangibles	.	60,000
Plant and equipment (net of $620,000 accumulated depreciation)		80,000
Total assets		$360,000

Liabilities

Accounts payable	50,000	
Notes payable	150,000	
Total liabilities		$200,000

Partners' Equity

Y, capital	70,000	
F, capital	70,000	
D, capital	20,000	
Total partners' equity		160,000
Liabilities and partners' equity		$360,000

Required:

1. What value was placed on the assets? (The book value of liabilities was agreed upon.)
2. Show the computations F made to arrive at the amount owed by D to Y and F.
3. How much did Y and F receive prior to settlement with D?
4. Present the general journal entries to record the sale of the partnership and the closing of the partnership books.

Problem 14–6 A&R

Repeat the requirements of Problem 14–5 A&R on the assumption that F gave D a cheque for $30,000 as his share of the cash available to the partners upon the sale of the business.

Corporation Accounting

PART FIVE

Organization and Operation
of Corporations

15

After studying Chapter 15, you should be able to:

State the advantages and disadvantages of the corporate form of business organization and explain how a corporation is organized and managed.

Describe the differences in accounting for the owners' equity in a partnership and the shareholders' equity in a corporation.

Record the issuance of no-par stock.

Record the issuance of par value stock at par or at a premium.

Record transactions involving stock subscriptions and explain the effects of subscribed stock on corporation assets and shareholders' equity.

State the differences between common and preferred stocks and explain why preferred stock is issued.

Describe the meaning and significance of par, book, market, and redemption values of corporate stock.

Define or explain the words and phrases listed in the chapter Glossary.

The three common types of business organizations are single proprietorships, partnerships, and corporations. Of the three, corporations are fewer in number. In dollar volume, however, they transact more business than do the other two combined. In terms of their economic impact, corporations are clearly the most important form of business organization. Almost every student will at some time either work for or own an interest in a corporation. For these reasons, an understanding of corporations and corporation accounting is important to all students of business.

ADVANTAGES OF THE CORPORATE FORM

Corporations have become the dominant type of business in our country because of the advantages offered by this form of business organization. Among the advantages are the following:

Separate Legal Entity

A corporation is a separate legal entity, separate and distinct from its shareholders who are its owners. Because it is a separate legal entity, a corporation, through its agents, may conduct its affairs with the same rights, duties, and responsibilities as a person.

Lack of Shareholders' Liability

As a separate legal entity a corporation is responsible for its own acts and its own debts, and its shareholders have no liability for either. From the viewpoint of an investor, this is perhaps the most important advantage of the corporate form.

Ease of Transferring Ownership Rights

Ownership rights in a corporation are represented by shares of stock that generally can be transferred and disposed of any time the owner wishes. Furthermore, the transfer has no effect on the corporation and its operations.

Continuity of Life

A successful corporation is said to have a perpetual life. In cases where a corporation's life is stated in its articles of incorporation or charter or is restricted by the jurisdiction of its incorporation, extension of time is normally a mere formality.

No Mutual Agency

Mutual agency does not exist in a corporation. A corporation shareholder, acting as a shareholder, has no power to bind the corporation to contracts. Shareholders' participation in the affairs of the corporation is limited to the right to vote in the shareholders' meetings. Consequently, shareholders need not exercise the care partners must use in selecting people with whom they associate themselves in the ownership of a corporation.

Ease of Capital Assembly

Lack of shareholders' liability, lack of mutual agency, and the ease with which an ownership interest may be transferred make it possible for a corporation to assemble large amounts of capital from the combined investments of many shareholders. Actually, a corporation's capital-raising ability is as a rule limited only by the profitableness with which it can employ the funds. This is very different from a partnership. In a partnership, capital-raising ability is always limited by the number of partners and their individual wealth. The number of partners is in turn usually limited because of mutual agency and unlimited liability.

DISADVANTAGES OF THE CORPORATE FORM

Governmental Regulation

Corporations are created by fulfilling the requirements of federal or provincial corporation laws, and the laws subject a corporation to considerable regulation and control. Single proprietorships and partnerships escape this regulation as well as the filing of many governmental reports required of corporations.

Taxation

Corporations as business units are subject to the same taxes as single proprietorships and partnerships. In addition, corporations are subject to several taxes not levied on either of the other two. The most burdensome of these are federal and provincial income taxes which together may take 50% of a corporation's pretax income. However, for the shareholders of a corporation, the burden does not end there. The income of a corporation is taxed twice, first as corporation income and again as personal income when distributed to the shareholders as dividends. This differs from single proprietorships and partnerships, which as business units are not subject to income taxes. Their income is normally taxed only as the personal income of their owners.

While the tax characteristics of a corporation are generally viewed as a disadvantage, in some instances they may work to the advantage of shareholders. If the shareholders have very large personal incomes and pay taxes at rates that exceed the corporate rate, the corporation may choose to avoid paying dividends. By not paying dividends, the income of the corporation is, at least temporarily, taxed only once at the lower corporate rate. Additionally, the dividend tax credit gives some relief from the effects of double taxation.

ORGANIZING A CORPORATION

A corporation is created by securing a certificate of incorporation or a charter from the federal or provincial government. Under the Canada Business Corporations Act, 1975, incorporation is a matter of right. One person, over 18, of sound mind, and not bankrupt may incorporate by submitting completed articles of incorporation and other required documentation to the Director, Corporations Branch, Department of Consumer and Corporate Affairs. Once the documentation is in order, the Director issues a certificate of incorporation and a corporation comes into existence. This new procedure replaces the previous letters patent system which viewed incorporation as a privilege. In provinces where incorporation is by *letters patent*, a corporation is created when a charter is issued to the incorporators.

Corporations intending to operate in several provinces may find it convenient and advantageous to incorporate under federal legislation, since such incorporation carries the right to operate in any province. However, a company incorporated in one of the provinces may normally (through registration) carry on its business activities in other provinces.

As indicated above, requirements for incorporation vary somewhat in each jurisdiction, but in general the same type of information is required in the articles of incorporation (federal) as in a provincial application. The articles of incorporation must include the following information:

1. The proposed corporate name, the last word of which shall be Limited, Incorporated, or Corporation, including their French equivalents or the abbreviation thereof.
2. The place within Canada where the registered office is to be situated.
3. The classes and any maximum number of shares that the corporation is authorized to issue, and *(a)* if there will be two or more classes of shares, the rights, privileges, restrictions, and conditions attaching to each class of shares; and *(b)* if a class of shares may be issued in series, the authority given to the directors to fix the number of shares in, and to determine the designation of, and the rights, privileges, restrictions, and conditions attaching to the shares of, each series.

4. If the right to transfer shares of the corporation is to be restricted, a statement that the right to transfer shares is restricted and the nature of such restrictions.
5. The number of directors.
6. Any restrictions on the business of the corporation. The articles *may* also include any matter to be set out in *(a)* the bylaws of the corporation or *(b)* a unanimous shareholder agreement.

Most corporations are incorporated through the procedure discussed above. Certain other corporations such as crown corporations (publicly owned, e.g., Canadian National Railways, Canadian Broadcasting Corporation, Eldorado Nuclear, and Air Canada) or those engaged in railroading, banking, insurance, and telegraphy, and which seek powers of a different kind from those granted to ordinary business corporations, are incorporated under special acts of the Canadian parliament or provincial legislatures.

After a corporation comes into existence, at the first meeting its directors usually—

a. Make bylaws (effective until confirmed by the shareholders).
b. Adopt forms of security certificates and corporate records.
c. Authorize the issue of securities.
d. Appoint officers.
e. Appoint an auditor to hold office until the first annual meeting of the shareholders.
f. Transact any other business.

ORGANIZATION COSTS

The costs of organizing a corporation, such as legal fees, promoters' fees, and amounts paid the provincial or federal government to secure approval of articles of incorporation, are called *organization costs* and are debited on incurrence to the account, Organization Costs. Theoretically, the sum of these costs represents an intangible asset from which the corporation will benefit throughout its life. However, the life of a corporation is always indeterminable; consequently, the period over which it will benefit from being organized is indeterminable. Nevertheless, a corporation should make a reasonable estimate of the benefit period, which, in line with the CICA recommendations, should not exceed 40 years, and write off its organization costs over this period. Although not necessarily related to the benefit period, income tax rules permit a corporation to write off 50% of the post-1972 organization costs as a tax-deductible expense at an annual 10% rate on a diminishing balance basis. Consequently, some corporations adopt the tax period over which to write off such costs. There is no theoretical justification for this, but it is generally accepted in practice because organization costs are usually immaterial in amount, and under the *materiality principle* the writeoff eliminates an unnecessary balance sheet item.

MANAGEMENT OF A CORPORATION

Although ultimate control of a corporation rests with its shareholders, this control is exercised indirectly through the election of the board of directors. The individual shareholder's right to participate in management begins and ends with a vote in the shareholders' meeting, where each shareholder has one vote for each share of stock owned.

Normally a corporation's shareholders meet once each year to elect directors and transact such other business as is provided in the corporation's bylaws. Theoretically, shareholders owning or controlling the votes of 50% plus one share of a corporation's stock can elect the board and control the corporation. Actually, because many shareholders do not attend the annual meeting, a much smaller percentage is frequently sufficient for control. Commonly, shareholders who do not attend the annual meeting delegate to an agent their voting rights. This is done by signing a legal document called a *proxy,* which gives the agent the right to vote the stock.

A corporation's board of directors is responsible and has final authority for the direction of corporation affairs. However, it may act only as a collective body. An individual director, as a director, has no power to transact corporation business. And as a rule, although it has final authority, a board will limit itself to establishing policy. It will then delegate the day-by-day direction of corporation business to the corporation's administrative officers whom it selects and elects.

A corporation's administrative officers are commonly headed by a president who is directly responsible to the board for supervising the corporation's business. To aid the president, many corporations have one or more vice presidents who are vested with specific managerial powers and duties. In addition, the corporation secretary keeps the minutes of the meetings of the shareholders and directors. In a small corporation, the secretary may also be responsible for keeping a record of the shareholders and the changing amounts of their stock interest.

STOCK CERTIFICATES AND THE TRANSFER OF STOCK

When a person invests in a corporation by buying its stock, the person receives a stock certificate as evidence of the shares purchased. Usually, in a small corporation, only one certificate is issued for each block of stock purchased. The one certificate may be for any number of shares. For example, the certificate of Illustration 15–1 is for 50 shares. Large corporations commonly use preprinted 100-share denomination certifi-

Illustration 15–1

cates in addition to blank certificates that may be made out for any number of shares.

An owner of stock may transfer at will either part or all of the shares represented by a stock certificate. To do so, the owner completes and signs the transfer endorsement on the reverse side of the certificate and sends the certificate to the corporation secretary in a small corporation or to the corporation's transfer agent in a large one. The old certificate is canceled and retained, and a new certificate is issued to the new shareholder.

Transfer Agent and Registrar

A large corporation whose stock is sold on a major stock exchange must have a registrar and a transfer agent who are assigned the responsibilities of transferring the corporation's stock. Also, the registrar is assigned the duty of keeping shareholder records and preparing official lists of shareholders for shareholders' meetings and for payment of dividends. Usually, registrars and transfer agents are large banks or trust companies.

When the owner of stock in a corporation having a registrar and a transfer agent wishes to transfer the stock to a new owner, he or she completes the transfer endorsement on the back of the stock certificate and, usually through a stockbroker, sends the certificate to the transfer agent. The transfer agent cancels the old certificate and issues one or more new certificates which the agent sends to the registrar. The registrar enters the transfer in the shareholder records and sends the new certificate or certificates to the proper owners.

CORPORATION ACCOUNTING

Corporation accounting was initially discussed in Chapter 4. In that discussion, entries were shown to record several basic transactions. An issue of common stock for cash was recorded. A net income (credit balance) was closed from Income Summary to Retained Earnings. The declaration and later payment of cash dividends were recorded. And, a net loss was closed from Income Summary to Retained Earnings. **At this point, students should review the discussion in Chapter 4 on pages 161 through 163, which explains these entries.** After completing that review, keep in mind that the shareholders' equity accounts of a corporation are divided into (1) contributed capital accounts and (2) retained earnings accounts. Also, remember that when a corporation's board of directors declares a cash dividend on the **date of declaration,** a legal liability of the corporation is incurred. The board of directors declares that on a specific future date—the **date of record**—the shareholders, according to the corporation's records, will be designated as those to receive the dividend. Finally, on the **date of payment,** the liability for the declared cash dividend is paid by the corporation.

The financial statements of a corporation were first illustrated in Chapter 5. The income statement was shown in Illustration 5–1, the balance sheet was shown in Illustration 5–3, and the retained earnings statement was shown in Illustration 5–4. Reviewing these illustrations, students should note that income taxes were deducted on the income statement as an expense. Recall that a business which is organized as a corporation must pay income taxes, while a proprietorship or partnership does not pay income taxes. Also, cash dividends to shareholders are not an expense of the corporation; they are not deducted on the income statement. Instead, dividends are a **distribution of** net income and are subtracted on the retained earnings statement. Finally, notice that the shareholders' equity in Illustration 5–3 is divided into common stock and retained earnings.

SHAREHOLDERS' EQUITY ACCOUNTS COMPARED TO PARTNERSHIP ACCOUNTS

To demonstrate the use of separate accounts for contributed capital and retained earnings as found in corporation accounting and to contrast their use with the accounts used in partnership accounting, assume the following. On January 5, 198A, a partnership involving two equal partners and a corporation having five shareholders were formed. Assume further that $25,000 was invested in each. In the partnership J. Olm invested $10,000 and A. Baker invested $15,000; in the corporation, each of the five shareholders bought 500 shares of its common stock at $10 per share. Without dates and explanations, general journal entries to record the investments are:

Partnership		Corporation	
Cash 10,000		Cash 25,000	
J. Olm, Capital	10,000	Common Stock	25,000
Cash 15,000			
A. Baker, Capital	15,000		

After the entries were posted, the owners' equity accounts of the two concerns appeared as follows:

Partnership
J. Olm, Capital

Date	Dr.	Cr.	Bal.
Jan. 5, 198A		10,000	10,000

A. Baker, Capital

Date	Dr.	Cr.	Bal.
Jan. 5, 198A		15,000	15,000

Corporation
Common stock

Date	Dr.	Cr.	Bal.
Jan. 5, 198A		25,000	25,000

To continue the illustration, assume that during 198A, each concern earned a net income of $8,000 and also distributed $5,000 to its owners. The partners share income equally, and the cash distribution was also divided equally. The corporation declared the dividends on December 20, 198A, and both concerns made the cash payments to owners on December 25, 198A. The entries to record the distribution of cash to partners and the declaration and payment of dividends to shareholders are as follows:

Partnership		
J. Olm, Withdrawals	2,500	
A. Baker, Withdrawals	2,500	
Cash		5,000

Corporation		
Retained Earnings	5,000	
Dividends Payable		5,000
Dividends Payable	5,000	
Cash		5,000

At the end of the year, the entries to close the Income Summary accounts are as follows:

Partnership		
Income Summary	8,000	
J. Olm, Capital		4,000
A. Baker, Capital		4,000

Corporation		
Income Summary	8,000	
Retained Earnings		8,000

Finally, the entry to close the Withdrawals accounts is:

Partnership		
J. Olm, Capital	2,500	
A. Baker, Capital	2,500	
J. Olm, Withdrawals		2,500
A. Baker, Withdrawals ...		2,500

Corporation

After posting the above entries, the owners' equity accounts of the two concerns are as follows:

Partnership
J. Olm, Capital

Date	Dr.	Cr.	Bal.
Jan. 5, 198A		10,000	10,000
Dec. 31, 198A		4,000	14,000
Dec. 31, 198A	2,500		11,500

Corporation
Common Stock

Date	Dr.	Cr.	Bal.
Jan. 5, 198A		25,000	25,000

A. Baker, Capital

Date	Dr.	Cr.	Bal.
Jan. 5, 198A		15,000	15,000
Dec. 31, 198A		4,000	19,000
Dec. 31, 198A	2,500		16,500

Retained Earnings

Date	Dr.	Cr.	Bal.
Dec. 20,198A	5,000		(5,000)
Dec. 31,198A		8,000	3,000

Partnership
J. Olm, Withdrawals

Date	Dr.	Cr.	Bal.
Dec. 25, 198A	2,500		2,500
Dec. 31, 198A		2,500	–0–

A. Baker, Withdrawals

Date	Dr.	Cr.	Bal.
Dec. 25, 198A	2,500		2,500
Dec. 31, 198A		2,500	–0–

Observe that in the partnership, after all entries have been posted, the $28,000 equity of the owners appears in the capital accounts of the partners:

```
J. Olm, capital  . . . . . . . . . . . . .   $11,500
A. Baker, capital  . . . . . . . . . . .     16,500
    Total owners' equity  . . . . .         $28,000
```

By comparison, the shareholders' equity of the corporation is divided between the contributed capital account and the Retained Earnings account, as follows:

```
Common stock . . . . . . . . . . . . . . . . . .   $25,000
Retained earnings . . . . . . . . . . . . . . .      3,000
    Total shareholders' equity . . . . . .         $28,000
```

AUTHORIZATION AND ISSUANCE OF STOCK

The Canada Business Corporations Act and the more recently passed provincial acts abandoned the *authorized capital concept*. Under these acts, corporations may or may not have a limit on the number of shares they may issue. If a corporation chooses to place a limitation on the number of shares it may issue, such a limitation must be stated in the articles, not in the bylaws.

In provincial jurisdictions where authorized capital is a requirement, corporations may issue no more shares than the amount authorized unless the authorization is increased. In order to increase the authorization, corporations must follow a procedure that parallels that of incorporation.

Sale of Stock for Cash

When stock is sold for cash and immediately issued, an entry in general journal form like the following may be used to record the sale and issuance:

June	5	Cash	300,000.00	
		Common Stock		300,000.00
		Sold and issued 30,000 at $10 per share.		

Exchanging Stock for Noncash Assets

A corporation may accept assets other than cash in exchange for its stock. When it does so, the transaction may be recorded like this:

Apr.	3	Machinery	10,000.00	
		Buildings	25,000.00	
		Land	5,000.00	
		Common Stock		40,000.00
		Exchanged 4,000 shares of common stock for machinery, buildings, and land.		

A corporation may also give shares of its stock to its promoters in exchange for their services in organizing the corporation. In such a case the corporation receives the intangible asset of being organized in exchange for its stock. The transaction is recorded as follows:

Apr.	5	Organization Costs	5,000.00	
		Common Stock		5,000.00
		Gave the promoters 500 shares of common stock in exchange for their services in organizing the corporation.		

SALE OF STOCK THROUGH SUBSCRIPTIONS

Often stock is sold for cash and immediately issued. Often, too, especially in organizing a new corporation, stock is sold by means of *subscrip-*

tions. In the latter instance, a person wishing to become a shareholder signs a subscription blank or a subscription list, agreeing to buy a certain number of the shares at a specific price. When the subscription is accepted by the corporation, it becomes a contract; and the corporation acquires an asset, the right to receive payment from the subscriber. At the same time, the subscriber gains an equity in the corporation equal to the amount the subscriber agrees to pay. Payment may be in one amount or in installments.

To illustrate the sale of stock through subscriptions, assume that on June 6 Northgate Corporation accepted subscriptions to 5,000 shares of its common stock at $12 per share. The subscription contracts called for a 10% down payment to accompany the subscriptions and the balance in two equal installments due in 30 and 60 days.

The subscriptions are recorded with the following entry:

June	6	Subscriptions Receivable, Common	60,000	
		Common Stock Subscribed..............		60,000
		Accepted subscriptions for 5,000 common shares at $12 per share.		

The subscriptions receivable and *common stock subscribed* accounts are of temporary nature. The subscriptions receivable will be turned into cash when the subscribers pay for their stock. Likewise, when payment is completed, the subscribed stock will be issued and will become outstanding stock. Normally, subscribed stock is not issued until completely paid for.

Receipt of the down payments and the two installment payments may be recorded with these entries.

June	6	Cash	6,000.00	
		Subscriptions Receivable, Common Stock ..		6,000.00
		Collected 10% down payments on the common stock subscribed.		
July	6	Cash	27,000.00	
		Subscriptions Receivable, Common Stock ..		27,000.00
		Collected the first installment payments on the common stock subscribed.		
Aug.	5	Cash	27,000.00	
		Subscriptions Receivable, Common Stock ..		27,000.00
		Collected the second installment payments on the common stock subscribed.		

In this case, the down payments accompanied the subscriptions. Consequently, the entry to record the receipt of the subscriptions and the entry to record the down payments may be combined.

When stock is sold through subscriptions, the stock is usually not issued until the subscriptions are paid in full. However, as soon as the subscriptions are paid, the stock is issued. The entry to record the issuance of the Northgate common stock appears as follows:

Aug.	5	Common Stock Subscribed	60,000.00	
		Common Stock		60,000.00
		Issued 5,000 shares of common stock sold through subscriptions.		

Most subscriptions are collected in full, although not always. Sometimes a subscriber fails to pay. If this happens, the subscription contract must be canceled. In such a case, if the subscriber has made a partial payment on the contract, the amount paid may be returned. Or, a smaller amount of stock than that subscribed, an amount equal to the partial payment, may be issued. Or, in some jurisdictions the subscriber's partial payment may be kept by the corporation to compensate for any damages suffered.

Subscriptions Receivable and Stock Subscribed on the Balance Sheet

Subscriptions receivable are normally to be collected within a relatively short time. Consequently, they appear on the balance sheet as a current asset. If a corporation prepares a balance sheet after accepting subscriptions to its stock but before the stock is issued, it should show both its issued stock and its subscribed stock on the balance sheet as follows:

Common stock 20,000 shares issued	$200,000
Unissued common stock subscribed, 5,000 shares	60,000
Total common stock issued and subscribed	$260,000

RIGHTS OF COMMON SHAREHOLDERS

When investors buy a corporation's *common stock,* they acquire all the specific rights granted by the corporation's charter to its common shareholders. They also acquire the general rights granted shareholders by the laws of the jurisdiction in which the company is incorporated. The laws vary, but common shareholders generally have the following rights:

1. The right to vote in the shareholders' meetings.
2. The right to sell or otherwise dispose of their stock.
3. The right to share pro rata with other common shareholders in any dividends declared.
4. The right to share in any assets remaining after creditors are paid if the corporation is liquidated.

In addition, if desired, the articles of incorporation may provide additional rights. For example, the articles may specifically provide for the *preemptive right*. This right holds that no shares of a class shall be issued unless the shares have first been offered to the shareholders holding shares of that class, and that those shareholders have a first opportunity to acquire the offered shares in proportion to their holdings of the shares of that class, at such a price and on such terms as those shares are to be offered to others.

PAR AND NO-PAR VALUE

The Canada Business Corporations Act, 1975, as well as the more recently passed provincial counterparts, require that all shares be of *no-par* or nominal value. These acts also require the total consideration received by the corporation for each share issued must be added to the stated capital account maintained for the shares of that class or series. Some provinces still permit the issuance of par value shares. *Par value* is an arbitrary value a corporation places on a share of its stock.

When a corporation issues par value stock, the par is printed on each certificate and is used in accounting for the stock. If the stock is issued at par, the entry to record the issue is the same as if the stock was no-par value. If, however, the stock is issued at a price above the stock's par value, the stock is said to be issued at a *premium*. For example, if a corporation sells and issues its $10 par value common stock at $12 per share, the stock is sold at a $2 per share premium. Although a premium is an amount in excess of par paid by purchasers of newly issued stock, it is not considered a profit to the issuing corporation. Rather a premium is part of the investment of shareholders who pay more than the par for the stock.

In accounting for stock sold at a premium, the premium is recorded separately from the par value of the stock to which it applies. For example, if a corporation sells and issues 10,000 shares of its $10 par value common stock for cash at $12 per share, the sale is recorded as follows:

Dec.	1	Cash	120,000.00	
		Common Stock		100,000.00
		Premium on Common Stock		20,000.00
		Sold and issued 10,000 shares of $10 par value common stock at $12 per share.		

When a balance sheet is prepared, stock premium is disclosed under "Other contributed capital."

CLASSES OF SHARES

The Canada Business Corporations Act allows corporations to issue registered no-par-value shares by class and by series of the class, so long as there exists one "residual" class of shares that may vote at all meetings of shareholders (except for meetings of specified classes of shareholders) and that may receive the remaining assets of a corporation upon dissolution. The act does not use the adjectives "common" and "preferred" but simply refers to shares in general. Classes of shares may continue to be called common, preferred, Class A, Class B, and so on; however, the act does require the articles to set out the rights, privileges, restrictions, and conditions attaching to each class and series of shares. Because of their widespread usage the terms *common* and *preferred* are used throughout this book.

Preferred Stock

Preferred stock is so called because of the preferences granted its owners. These commonly include a preference as to payment of dividends and may include a preference in the distribution of assets in a liquidation.

A preference as to *dividends* does not grant an absolute right to dividends. Rather if dividends are declared, it gives the preferred shareholders the right to receive their preferred dividend before the common shareholders are paid a dividend. In other words, if dividends are declared, a dividend must be paid the preferred shareholders before a dividend may be paid to the common shareholders. However, if the directors are of the opinion that no dividends should be paid, then neither the preferred nor the common shareholders receive a dividend.

Dividends on the majority of preferred stocks are limited to a fixed maximum amount. For example, a $6 dividend rate, nonparticipating preferred stock has a preference each year to a dividend equal to $6 per share; but the dividend is limited to that amount.

Although dividends on the majority of preferred stocks are limited in amount, dividends on a corporation's common stock are unlimited, except by the earning power of the corporation and the judgment of its board of directors.

While dividends on most preferred stocks are limited to a fixed basic amount, or percentage in the case of par value shares, some preferred stocks have the right under certain circumstances to dividends in excess of a fixed basic percentage or amount. Such preferred stocks are called *participating preferred stock*.[1] Participating preferred stock may be fully participating, or participation may be limited to a fixed amount, depending in each case on the exact terms set forth in the corporation's articles or charter. For example, if a corporation issues fully participating, 6%, $100 par value, preferred stock and $50 par value common stock, the owners of the preferred stock have a preference to a 6% or $6 per share dividend each year. Then, each year, after the common shareholders have received a 6% or $3 per share dividend, the preferred shareholders have a right to participate with the common shareholders in any additional dividends declared. The participation is usually on the basis of the same additional per cent-on-par-value-per-share dividend to each kind of stock. For instance, if in this case the common shareholders are paid an additional 2% or $1 per share dividend, the preferred shareholders should receive an additional 2% or $2 per share dividend.

In the case of no-par value shares, the preferred dividend is stated as an amount per share. Consequently, the participation feature must also be stated as an amount per share relative to the common per share dividend. For example, the provision may be that after the $7.60 preferred and a $3 common per share dividends are paid, additional amounts paid shall be distributed in the ratio of 2 to 1 per share. Thus, in this case, if common shareholders are paid an additional $1 per share dividend, the preferred shareholders should receive an additional $2 per share dividend.

Often when preferred stock is participating, participation is limited. For example, the right of the preferred to participate may be limited to a percentage of par value or an amount per share. Once the limit is reached, participation rights end.

In addition to being participating or nonparticipating, preferred stocks are either **cumulative** or **noncumulative.** A *cumulative preferred stock* is one on which any undeclared dividends accumulate each year until paid. A *noncumulative preferred stock* is one on which the right to receive dividends is forfeited in any year in which dividends are not declared.

The accumulation of dividends on cumulative preferred stocks does not guarantee their payment. Dividends cannot be guaranteed because earnings from which they are paid cannot be guaranteed. However, when

---

[1] Although participating preferred shares are rare, as far as listed corporations are concerned, these types of shares or similarly designed financing arrangements are commonplace in the case of the small newly formed businesses.

a corporation issues cumulative preferred stock, it does agree to pay its cumulative preferred shareholders both their current dividends and any unpaid back dividends, called *dividends in arrears,* before it pays a dividend to its common shareholders.

In addition to the preferences it receives, preferred stock carries with it all the rights of common stock, unless such rights are specifically denied in the articles of incorporation or the corporation charter. Preferred stock often is denied the right to vote in the shareholders' meetings.

Convertible Preferred Stock

To make an issue more attractive, preferred shareholders may be given the right to exchange their preferred shares for a fixed number of shares of the issuing company's common stock. Such preferred shares are known as **convertible shares.** Convertible preferred shares offer investors certain advantages; for example, priority in distribution of dividends. If the issuing company prospers and the market value of its stock goes up, investors are given an opportunity to share in the prosperity by converting the preferred shares into common shares. Conversion is always at the preferred shareholders' option and is not exercised except when doing so is to their advantage.

The convertible provision is fairly common. It is designed to make the issue more attractive to investors and thus help the corporation acquire capital at possibly more advantageous terms.

When convertible preferred stock is converted into common stock, the preferred shareholders' rights are transformed into common shareholders' rights. The generally accepted rule for measuring the contribution for the new issue of common shares is the carrying amount of the converted preferred shares.

Preferred Dividends in Arrears on the Balance Sheet Date

A liability for a dividend does not come into existence until the dividend is declared by the board of directors; and unlike interest, dividends do not accrue. Consequently, if on the dividend date a corporation's board of directors fails to declare a dividend on its cumulative preferred stock, the dividend in arrears is not a liability and does not appear on the balance sheet as such. However, if there are preferred dividends in arrears, the *full-disclosure principle* requires that this information appear on the balance sheet. Normally, such information is given in a balance sheet footnote. When a balance sheet does not carry such a footnote, a balance sheet reader has the right to assume that there are no dividends in arrears.

WHY PREFERRED STOCK IS ISSUED

Two common reasons why preferred stock is issued can best be shown by an example. Suppose that three persons with a total of $100,000 to invest wish to organize a corporation requiring $200,000 capital. If they sell and issue $200,000 of common stock, they will have to share control with other shareholders. However, if they sell and issue $100,000 of common stock to themselves and sell to outsiders $100,000 of 8%, cumulative preferred stock having no voting right, they can retain control of the corporation for themselves.

Also, suppose the three promoters expect their new corporation to earn an annual after-tax return of $24,000. If they sell and issue $200,000 of common stock, this will mean a 12% return. However, if they sell and issue $100,000 of each kind of stock, retaining the common for themselves, they can increase their own return to 16%, as follows:

Net after-tax income	$24,000
Less: Preferred dividends at 8%	(8,000)
Balance to common shareholders (equal to 16% on their $100,000 investment)	$16,000

In this case the common shareholders earn 16% because the dividends on the preferred stock are less than the amount that is earned on the preferred shareholders' investment.

STOCK VALUES

In addition to a par value, stocks may have a redemption value, a market value, and a book value.

Redemption Value

Redemption values apply to preferred stocks. Corporations that issue preferred stock often reserve the right to redeem or retire the stock by paying a specified amount to the preferred shareholders. The amount a corporation agrees to pay to redeem a share of its preferred stock is set at the time the stock is issued and is called the redemption value of the stock. To this amount must be added any dividends in arrears.

Market Value

The **market value** of a share of stock is the price at which a share can be bought or sold. Market values are influenced by earnings, dividends, future prospects, and general market conditions.

Book Value

The *book value of a share of stock* measures the equity of the owner of one share of the stock in the net assets of the issuing corporation. If a corporation has issued only common stock, its book value per share is determined by dividing total shareholders' equity by the number of shares outstanding. For example, if total shareholders' equity is $285,000 and there are 10,000 shares outstanding, the book value per share is $28.50 ($285,000 ÷ 10,000 = $28.50).

To compute book values when both common and preferred stock are outstanding, the preferred stock is assigned a portion of the total shareholders' equity equal to its redemption value (or par value if there is no redemption value) plus any cumulative dividends in arrears. The remaining shareholders' equity is then assigned to the common shares outstanding. After this, the book value of each class is determined by dividing its share of shareholders' equity by the number of shares of that class outstanding. For instance, assume a corporation has the shareholders' equity shown in Illustration 15–2. If the preferred stock is redeemable at $103 per share and two years of cumulative preferred dividends are in arrears, the book values of the corporation's shares are calculated as follows:

Total shareholders' equity		$ 447,000
Less equity applicable to preferred shares:		
Redemption value	$103,000	
Cumulative dividends in arrears	14,000	(117,000)
Equity applicable to common shares		$330,000
Book value of preferred shares ($117,000 ÷ 1,000)		$117
Book value of common shares ($330,000 ÷ 10,000)		33

Corporations in their annual reports to their shareholders often highlight the increase that has occurred in the book value of the corporation's shares during a year. Book value may also be of significance in a contract. For example, a shareholder may enter into a contract to sell shares at

Illustration 15–2

Shareholders' Equity

Share capital:	
Preferred stock, $9.50 cumulative and nonparticipating,	
1,000 shares issued and outstanding	$105,000
Common stock, 10,000 shares issued and outstanding	260,000
Total contributed capital	365,000
Retained earnings	82,000
Total shareholders' equity..........................	$447,000

their book value at some future date. However, book value should not be confused with **liquidation value** because if a corporation is liquidated, its assets will probably sell at prices quite different from the amounts at which they are carried on the books. Also, book value generally has little bearing upon the market value of stock. Dividends, earning capacity, and future prospects are usually of much more importance. For instance, a common stock having an $11 book value may sell for $25 per share if its earnings, dividends, and prospects are good. However, it may sell for $5 per share if these factors are unfavorable.

GLOSSARY

Book value of a share of stock.   The equity represented by one share of stock in the issuing corporation's net assets.

Common stock.   Stock of a corporation that has only one class of stock; if there is more than one class, the class that has no preferences relative to the corporation's other classes of stock.

Common stock subscribed.   Unissued common stock for which the issuing corporation has a subscription contract to issue.

Cumulative preferred stock.   Preferred stock on which undeclared dividends accumulate annually until paid.

Dividend.   A distribution made by a corporation to its shareholders of cash, other assets, or additional shares of the corporation's own stock.

Dividends in arrears.   Unpaid prior-period dividends are paid to common shareholders.

Market value.   The price at which a share of stock can be bought or sold.

Noncumulative preferred stock.   A preferred stock for which the right to receive dividends is forfeited in any year in which dividends are not declared.

No-par stock.   A class of stock having no par value.

Organization costs.   Costs of bringing a corporation into existence, such as legal fees, promoters' fees, and amounts paid to secure a certificate of incorporation.

Participating preferred stock.   Preferred stock that has the right to share in dividends above the fixed amount or percentage which is preferred.

Par value.   An arbitrary value placed on a share of stock at the time the corporation seeks authorization of the stock.

Preemptive right.   The right of a common shareholder to have the first opportunity to purchase additional shares of common stock issued by the corporation.

Preferred stock.   Stock of which the owners are granted certain preferences over common shareholders such as a preference to payment of dividends or in the distribution of assets in a liquidation.

Premium on stock. The amount of capital contributed by shareholders above the stock's par value.

Proxy. A legal document which gives an agent of a shareholder the right to vote the shareholder's shares.

Redemption value of stock. The amount a corporation must pay for the return of a share of preferred stock previously issued by the corporation.

Stated value of no-par stock. The aggregate consideration received by a corporation on the issue of each class of share capital.

Stock subscription. A contractual commitment to purchase unissued shares of stock and become a shareholder.

QUESTIONS FOR CLASS DISCUSSION

1. What are the advantages and disadvantages of the corporate form of business organization?

2. Why is the income of a corporation said to be taxed twice?

3. Who is responsible for directing the affairs of a corporation?

4. What is a proxy?

5. What are organization costs? List several.

6. How are organization costs classified on the balance sheet?

7. What are the duties and responsibilities of a corporation's registrar and transfer agent?

8. Why is a corporation the stock of which is sold on a stock exchange required to have a registrar and transfer agent? Why is such a corporation required to have both a registrar and a transfer agent?

9. List the general rights of common shareholders.

10. What is the preemptive right of common shareholders?

11. Laws place no limit on the amounts partners may withdraw from a partnership. On the other hand, laws regulating corporations place definite limits on the amounts shareholders may withdraw from a corporation in dividends. Why is there a difference?

12. What is a stock premium?

13. Does a corporation earn a profit by selling its stock at a premium?

14. What is the main advantage of no-par stock?

15. What are the meanings of the following when applied to preferred stock: (a) preferred, (b) participating, (c) nonparticipating, (d) cumulative, and (e) noncumulative?

16. What are the balance sheet classifications of the accounts: (a) Subscriptions Receivable, Common Stock and (b) Common Stock Subscribed?

17. What are the meanings of the following terms when applied to a share of stock: (a) par value, (b) book value, (c) market value, and (d) redemption value?

MULTIPLE CHOICE

1. A contractual commitment to purchase unissued shares of stock and become a shareholder is a:
    - *a.* Proxy.
    - *b.* Preemptive right.
    - *c.* Stock subscription.
    - *d.* Preferred stock.
    - *e.* Promissory note.

2. The receipt of cash from a subscriber in payment of a subscription to common stock results in a credit to:
    - *a.* Common stock.
    - *b.* Common stock subscribed.
    - *c.* Subscriptions receivable, common stock.
    - *d.* Cash.
    - *e.* Some other account.

3. Most preferred stocks are cumulative because:
    - *a.* Laws generally require it.
    - *b.* It provides protection to the creditors.
    - *c.* If the corporation is very successful, the preferred shareholders can share the increasing dividends that would otherwise go entirely to common shareholders.
    - *d.* It makes the stock more attractive to investors.
    - *e.* Of some other reason.

4. A preferred stock for which the right to receive dividends is forfeited in any one year in which dividends are not declared is:
    - *a.* Nonparticipating preferred stock.
    - *b.* Participating preferred stock.
    - *c.* Cumulative preferred stock.
    - *d.* Common stock subscribed.
    - *e.* Noncumulative preferred stock.

5. The amount a corporation must pay for the return of a share of preferred stock previously issued by the corporation is the:
    - *a.* Premium on stock.
    - *b.* Minimum capital.
    - *c.* Contributed capital.
    - *d.* Redemption value of stock.
    - *e.* Stated value of stock.

6. X Corporation has outstanding 1,000 shares of $10, preferred stock, and 6,000 shares of common stock. X Corporation paid out dividends for the last four years as follows: 198A, $9,000; 198B, $10,000; 198C, $17,000; 198D, $33,000. If the preferred stock is noncumulative and nonparticipating, the allocation of 198B dividends between preferred and common stock is:

a. $1,428 preferred, $8,572 common.
b. $8,333 preferred, $1,667 common.
c. $10,000 preferred, $0 common.
d. $0 preferred, $10,000 common.
e. None of the above

7. X Corporation has outstanding 1,000 shares of $10, preferred stock, and 6,000 shares of common stock. X Corporation paid out dividends for the last four years as follows: 198A, $9,000; 198B, $10,000; 198C, $17,000; 198D, $33,000. If the preferred stock is cumulative and nonparticipating, the allocation of 198C dividends between preferred and common stock is:

a. $14,166 preferred, $2,834 common.
b. $10,000 preferred, $7,000 common.
c. $2,828 preferred, $14,172 common.
d. $11,000 preferred, $6,000 common.
e. None of the above

8. X Corporation has outstanding 1,000 shares of $10, preferred stock issued at $100 per share and 6,000 shares of common stock issued at $20 per share. X Corporation paid out dividends for the last four years as follows: 198A, $9,000; 198B, $10,000; 198C, $17,000; 198D, $33,000. If the preferred stock is cumulative and fully participating based on percentage of stated capital, the allocation of 198B dividends between preferred and common stock is:

a. $0 preferred, $10,000 common.
b. $1,429 preferred, $7,571 common.
c. $4,545 preferred, $4,455 common.
d. $10,000 preferred, $0 common.
e. None of the above.

9. Mark Company's shareholders' equity section of its year-end balance sheet is as follows:

Preferred stock, $7, cumulative and nonparticipating, 2,000 shares outstanding	$212,000
Common stock, 50,000 shares outstanding	$530,000
Total contributed capital	$742,000
Retained earnings	$200,000
Total shareholders' equity	$942,000

The preferred stock has one year of dividends in arrears and a redemption value of $105. The book value per common share is:

a. $14.32.
b. $14.60.
c. $14.36.
d. $10.60.
e. Some other amount.

MINI DISCUSSION CASE

Case 15–1   James Service operated the Dawson Inn Motel and Restaurant as a sole proprietorship for five years. The business was successful and he had two modest expansions since starting.

Service had reached a level of operation that required a major decision of sell or expand. After much deliberation and consultation with a close friend, Service decided to undertake a major expansion. Prior to proceeding with the expansion, he incorporated the business.

Carrying the plans for the expansion under his arm, he set out to keep an appointment with his banker. Service was somewhat annoyed with the banker's apparent lack of interest in the plans. It appeared to Service that the banker was more interested in obtaining Service's and his wife's personal guarantees for the required loan than in his plans. On returning home he remarked to his wife that he couldn't understand the banker's attitude—in prior borrowings the banker had never asked for any sort of guarantees.

Required:

Discuss the banker's attitude.

CLASS EXERCISES

Exercise 15–1   Prepare general journal entries on October 10 to record the following issuances of stock by various corporations:

1. Fifty shares of no-par value common stock are issued for $800 cash.
2. One hundred shares of no-par common stock are issued to promoters in exchange for their efforts in organizing the corporation. The promoters' efforts are estimated to be worth $15,000.
3. Assume the same facts as in (2) above, except that the stock has a $10 par value.

Exercise 15–2   Barry Dow and Jane Harwood begin a new business on January 5 by investing $75,000 each in the company. Assume that on December 25, it is decided that $12,000 of the company's cash will be distributed equally between the owners. Cheques for $6,000 are prepared and given to the owners on December 30. On December 31, the company reports a $21,000 net income. Prepare journal entries to record the investments by the owners, the distribution of cash to the owners, and the closing of the Income Summary account assuming: *(a)* the business is a partnership and *(b)* the business is a corporation that issued 1,000 shares of no-par value common stock to each owner.

Exercise 15–3   A corporation sold and issued 5,000 shares of its common stock for $157,500 on May 25. *(a)* Give the entry to record the sale under the assumption the stock is no-par stock. *(b)* Give the entry to record the sale under the assumption the stock is $10 par stock.

Exercise 15–4   On June 23, Expando Corporation accepted subscriptions to 20,000 shares of its no-par value common stock at $12.50 per share. The subscription contracts called for one fourth of the subscription price to accompany each contract as a down payment and the balance to be paid on August 15. Give the entries to record: *(a)* the subscriptions, *(b)* the down payments, *(c)* receipt of the remaining amounts due on the subscriptions, and *(d)* issuance of the stock.

Exercise 15–5   A corporation has outstanding 10,000 shares of $8, cumulative and nonparticipating preferred stock and 45,000 shares of no-par value common stock. During the first four years of its life, the corporation paid out the following amounts in dividends: first year, $0; the second year, $95,000; third year, $200,000; and fourth year $125,000. Determine the total dividends paid to each class of shareholders each year.

Exercise 15–6   Determine the total dividends paid each class of shareholders of the previous exercise under the assumption that rather than being cumulative and nonparticipating, the preferred stock is noncumulative and nonparticipating.

Exercise 15–7   A corporation has outstanding 10,000 shares of $9, preferred stock cumulative and fully participating on the basis of stated capital issued at $100 per share, and 60,000 shares of no-par value common stock issued at $10 per share. It has regularly paid all dividends on the preferred stock. This year the board of directors voted to pay out a total of $200,000 in dividends to the two classes of shareholders. Determine the per cent of stated value to be paid each class of shareholders and the dividend per share to be paid each class.

Exercise 15–8   Three individuals have agreed to begin a new business that will require a total investment of $1,000,000. Each of the three will contribute $150,000; and the remaining $550,000 will be raised from other investors. Two alternative plans for raising the money are being considered: (1) issue at $100 per share no-par, common stock to all investors; or (2) issue common stock at $100 per share to the three founders and $9, preferred stock at $100 per share to the remaining investors. If the business is expected to earn an after-tax net income of $120,000, which of the two plans will provide the highest return to the three founders? What rate of return will the founders earn under each alternative?

Exercise 15–9   What would be your answer to Exercise 15–8 if the business is expected to earn an annual, after-tax net income of only $80,000?

Exercise 15–10   The shareholders' equity section from a corporation's balance sheet appeared as follows:

Shareholders' Equity

Preferred stock, $10, cumulative and nonparticipating, $108 redemption value, 4,000 shares issued and outstanding	$ 400,000
Common stock, 80,000 shares issued and outstanding	800,000
Retained earnings	300,000
Total shareholders' equity	$1,500,000

Required:

1. Determine the book value per share of the preferred stock and of the common stock under the assumption there are no dividends in arrears on the preferred stock.
2. Determine the book value per share for each kind of stock under the assumption that two years' dividends are in arrears on the preferred stock.

PROBLEMS

Problem 15–1   When Airride Corporation was organized, it was authorized to issue 10,000 shares of no-par value, $9, cumulative and nonparticipating, preferred stock and an unlimited number of no-par value common shares. It completed the following transactions:

June 3   Accepted subscriptions to 75,000 shares of common stock at $18 per share. Down payments equal to 20% of the subscription price accompanied each subscription.

14   Gave the corporation's promoters 2,000 shares of common stock for their services in getting the corporation organized. The board valued the services at $35,000.

July 5   Accepted subscriptions to 5,000 shares of preferred stock at $120 per share. The subscriptions were accompanied by 50% down payments.

20   Collected the balance due on the June 3 common stock subscriptions and issued the stock.

31   Accepted subscriptions to 2,500 shares of preferred stock at $110 per share. The subscriptions were accompanied by 50% down payments.

Aug. 5   Collected the balance due on the July 5 preferred stock subscriptions and issued the stock.

Required:

1. Prepare general journal entries to record the transactions.
2. Prepare the shareholders' equity section of the corporation's balance sheet as of the close of business on August 5.

Problem 15–2   Polansky Corporation was authorized to issue an unlimited number of common shares and 30,000 shares of $6, cumulative and nonparticipating, preferred stock. The company completed the following transactions:

198A

Apr. 7   Issued 135,000 shares of common stock at $1 per share for cash.

30   Gave the corporation's promoters 90,000 shares of common stock for their services in getting the corporation organized. The directors valued the services at $150,000.

May 2   Exchanged 300,000 shares of common stock for the following assets at fair market values: land, $75,000; buildings, $300,000; and machinery, $375,000.

Dec. 31   Closed the Income Summary account. A $75,000 loss was incurred.

198B

Jan. 12   Issued 3,000 shares of preferred stock at $50 per share.

Mar. 15   Accepted subscriptions to 30,000 shares of common stock at $1.80 per share. Down payments of 25% accompanied the subscription contracts.

Dec. 31   Closed the Income Summary account. A $207,000 net income was earned.

198C

Jan. 18   The board of directors declared a $6 dividend to preferred shares and $0.10 per share to outstanding common shares, payable on February 8 to the January 26 shareholders of record.

Feb. 8   Paid the previously declared dividends.

Mar. 10   Polansky Corporation has outstanding bonds payable that are convertible into common stock at the rate of 700 shares per $1,000 bond. On this date, $30,000 par value of bonds with a carrying value of $31,500 were converted into common stock.

Dec. 31   Closed the Income Summary account. A $240,000 net income was earned.

Required:

1.   Prepare general journal entries to record the transactions.
2.   Prepare the shareholders' equity section of a balance sheet as of the close of business on December 31, 198C.

Problem 15–3   *Part 1.*   The balance sheet of Exotic Boat Charters Corporation includes the following information:

Shareholders' Equity

Preferred stock, $9, cumulative and nonparticipating,
    authorized and issued 1,500 shares $150,000
Common stock, no-par value, 60,000 shares issued   600,000
Retained earnings   90,000
    Total shareholders' equity $840,000

Required:

Assume that the preferred stock has a redemption value of $105 plus any dividends in arrears. Calculate the book value per share of the preferred and common stocks under each of the following assumptions:

a.   There are no dividends in arrears on the preferred stock.
b.   One year's dividends are in arrears on the preferred stock.
c.   Three years' dividends are in arrears on the preferred stock.

Part 2.   Since its organization, Singleton Corporation has had outstanding 3,000 shares of $11, preferred stock and 45,000 shares of common stock. No dividends have been paid this year, and two prior years' dividends are in arrears on the preferred stock. However, the company has recently prospered and the board of directors wants to know how much cash will be required for dividends if a $1.60 per share dividend is paid on the common stock. Preferred shares were issued at $100 per share and the common at $10 per share.

Required:

Prepare a schedule showing the amounts of cash required for dividends to each class of shareholders under each of the following assumptions:
a. The preferred stock is noncumulative and nonparticipating.
b. The preferred stock is cumulative and nonparticipating.
c. The preferred stock is cumulative and fully participating based on percentage of stated value.
d. The preferred stock is cumulative and participating to 14% based on percentage of stated value.

Problem 15–4   Wide Ranch Corporation has outstanding 1,200 shares of 10%, preferred stock issued at $100 per share and 25,000 shares of common stock issued at $10 per share. During a seven-year period, the company paid out the following amounts in dividends: 198A, nothing; 198B, $35,000; 198C, $0; 198D, $20,000; 198E, $26,000; 198F, $32,000; and 198G, $74,000.

Required:

1. Prepare three schedules with columnar headings as follows:

Year	Calculations	Preferred Dividend per Share	Common Dividend per Share

2. Complete a schedule under each of the following assumptions. There were no dividends in arrears for the years prior to 198A.
a. The preferred stock is noncumulative and nonparticipating.
b. The preferred stock is cumulative and nonparticipating.
c. The preferred stock is cumulative and fully participating based on percentage of stated value.

Problem 15–5   Crenshaw Corporation's common stock is selling on a stock exchange today at $21.75 per share, and a just-published balance sheet shows the shareholders' equity in the corporation as follows:

Shareholders' Equity

Preferred stock, 9.5% cumulative and nonparticipating, $100 par value 3,000 shares authorized and outstanding	$ 300,000
Common stock, no par value 75,000 shares authorized and outstanding	750,000
Retained earnings	252,000
Total shareholders' equity	$1,302,000

Required:

Answer these questions: (1) What is the market value of the corporation's common stock? (2) What are the par values of its *(a)* preferred stock and *(b)* common stock? (3) If there are no dividends in arrears, what are the book values of the *(a)* preferred stock and *(b)* common stock? (4) If two years' dividends are in arrears on the preferred stock, what are the book values of the *(a)* preferred stock and the *(b)* common stock? (Assume the corporation does not have the right to redeem the preferred stock, which therefore has no redemption value.)

ALTERNATE PROBLEMS

Problem 15–1A

Overdrive Corporation is authorized to issue 18,000 shares of $10, cumulative and nonparticipating, preferred stock and an unlimited number of common shares. It then completed the following transactions:

Sept. 7 Accepted subscriptions to 135,000 shares of common stock at $16 per share. Down payments equal to 30% of the subscription price accompanied each subscription.

16 Gave the corporation's promoters 3,600 shares of common stock for their services in getting the corporation organized. The board valued the services at $63,000.

Oct. 3 Accepted subscriptions to 9,000 shares of preferred stock at $115 per share. The subscriptions were accompanied by 40% down payments.

7 Collected the balance due on the September 7 common stock subscriptions and issued the stock.

31 Accepted subscriptions to 4,500 shares of preferred stock at $109 per share. The subscriptions were accompanied by 40% down payments.

Nov. 10 Collected the balance due on the October 3 preferred stock subscriptions and issued the stock.

Required:

1. Prepare general journal entries to record the transactions.
2. Prepare the shareholders' equity section of the corporation's balance sheet as of the close of business on November 10.

Problem 15–2A

Rathgaber Corporation is authorized to issue 500,000 shares of no-par value common stock and 25,000 shares of $11, cumulative and nonparticipating, no-par value preferred stock. The company completed the following transactions:

198A
May 8 Issued 26,000 shares of common stock at $10 per share for cash.

27 Gave the corporation's promoters 1,800 shares of common stock for their services in getting the corporation organized. The directors valued the services at $20,000.

June 6 Exchanged 80,000 shares of common stock for the following assets at fair market values: land, $185,000; buildings, $380,000; and machinery, $270,000.

Dec. 31 Closed the Income Summary account. A $47,000 loss was incurred.

198B
Jan. 26 Issued 2,000 shares of preferred stock at $100 per share.

Feb. 22 Accepted subscriptions to 6,000 shares of common stock at $12.50 per share. Down payments of 30% accompanied the subscription contracts.

Dec. 31 Closed the Income Summary account. A $166,000 net income was earned.

198C

Mar. 14 The board of directors declared an $11 dividend to preferred shares and $0.50 per share to outstanding common shares, payable on April 2 to the March 23 shareholders of record.

Apr. 2 Paid the previously declared dividends.

May 19 Rathgaber Corporation has outstanding bonds payable that are convertible into common stock at the rate of 85 shares per $1,000 bond. On this date, $100,000 par value of bonds with a carrying value of $95,900 were converted into common stock.

Dec. 31 Closed the Income Summary account. A $198,000 net income was earned.

Required:

1. Prepare general journal entries to record the transactions.
2. Prepare the shareholders' equity section of a balance sheet as of the close of business on December 31, 198C.

Problem 15–3A

Part 1. The balance sheet of Crumley Services Corporation includes the following information:

Shareholders' Equity

Preferred stock, $10, cumulative and nonparticipating, preferred stock, issued 1,000 shares	$100,000
Common stock, no-par value, 40,000 shares issued ..	400,000
Retained earnings	60,000
Total shareholders' equity	$560,000

Required:

Assume that the preferred stock has a redemption value of $106 plus any dividends in arrears. Calculate the book value per share of the preferred and common stocks under each of the following assumptions:

a. There are no dividends in arrears on the preferred stock.
b. One year's dividends are in arrears on the preferred stock.
c. Three years' dividends are in arrears on the preferred stock.

Part 2. Since its organization, Triple Corporation has had outstanding 4,000 shares of $12, preferred stock and 60,000 shares of common stock. No dividends have been paid this year, and two prior years' dividends are in arrears on the preferred stock. However, the company has recently prospered and the board of directors wants to know how much cash will be required for dividends if a $1.75 per share dividend is paid on the common stock. Preferred and common shares were issued at $100 and $10 respectively.

Required:

Prepare a schedule showing the amounts of cash required for dividends to each class of shareholders under each of the following assumptions:

a. The preferred stock is noncumulative and nonparticipating.
b. The preferred stock is cumulative and nonparticipating.
c. The preferred stock is cumulative and fully participating based on percentage of stated capital.
d. The preferred stock is cumulative and participating to 14% of stated capital.

Problem
15–4A

Farm Finance Corporation has outstanding 2,000 shares of $11, preferred stock issued at $100 per share and 60,000 shares of common stock issued at $10 per share. During a seven-year period, the company paid out the following amounts in dividends: 198A, nothing; 198B, $46,000; 198C, $0; 198D, $25,000; 198E, $52,000; 198F, $60,000; and 198G, $140,000.

Required:

1. Prepare three schedules with columnar headings as follows:

Year	Calculations	Preferred Dividend per Share	Common Dividend per Share

2. Complete a schedule under each of the following assumptions. Round your calculations of dividends per share to the nearest penny. There were no dividends in arrears for the years prior to 198A.

a. The preferred stock is noncumulative and nonparticipating.
b. The preferred stock is cumulative and nonparticipating.
c. The preferred stock is cumulative and fully participating based on percentage of stated capital.

Problem
15–5A

Daley Corporation's common stock is selling on a stock exchange today at $26.25 per share, and a just-published balance sheet shows the shareholders' equity in the corporation as follows:

Shareholders' Equity

Preferred stock, 8.8% cumulative and nonparticipating, $100 par value, 2,100 shares outstanding	$ 210,000
Common stock, no-par value 9,200 shares outstanding	920,000
Retained earnings	336,000
Total shareholders' equity	$1,466,000

Required:

Answer these questions: (1) What is the market value of the corporation's common stock? (2) What are the par values of its *(a)* preferred stock and *(b)* common stock? (3) If there are no dividends in arrears, what are the book values of the *(a)* preferred stock and *(b)* common stock? (4) If two years' dividends are in arrears on the preferred stock, what are the book values of the *(a)* preferred stock and *(b)* common stock? (Assume the corporation does not have the right to redeem the preferred stock, which therefore has no redemption value.)

PROVOCATIVE PROBLEMS

Provocative
Problem 15–1,
MEL'S Sports,
Inc.

Mark Mangum and Mike Linder have operated a sports equipment company, M & M's Sports, for a number of years as partners sharing losses and gains in a 3:2 ratio. Because the business is growing, the two partners entered into an agreement with Tim Ewing to reorganize their firm into a corporation. The new corporation, MEL's Sports, Inc., is authorized to issue 50,000 shares of no-par value common stock. On the date of the reorganization, November 13 of the current year, a trial balance of the partnership ledger appears as follows:

M & M's SPORTS
Trial Balance
November 13, 19—

Cash	$ 25,500	
Accounts receivable	46,500	
Allowance for doubtful accounts		$ 1,750
Merchandise inventory	211,250	
Store equipment	49,000	
Accumulated depreciation, store equipment		10,500
Buildings	250,000	
Accumulated depreciation, buildings		50,000
Land	62,500	
Accounts payable		27,750
Mortgage payable		175,000
Mark Mangum, capital		226,250
Mike Linder, capital		153,500
Totals	$644,750	$644,750

The agreement between the partners and Ewing carries these provisions:

1. The partnership assets are to be revalued as follows:
   a. The $1,500 account receivable of Lost Cagers is known to be uncollectible and is to be written off as a bad debt.
   b. After (a) the allowance for doubtful accounts is to be increased to 5% of the remaining accounts receivable.
   c. The merchandise inventory is to be written down to $190,000 to allow for damaged and shopworn goods.
   d. Insufficient depreciation has been taken on the store equipment; consequently, its book value is to be decreased to $32,500 by increasing the balance of the accumulated depreciation account.
   e. The building is to be written up to its replacement cost, $325,000, and the balance of the accumulated depreciation account is to be increased to show the building to be one-fifth depreciated.
2. After the partnership assets are revalued, the assets and liabilities are to be transferred to the corporation in exchange for its stock, with each partner accepting stock at $10 per share for his equity in the partnership.
3. Tim Ewing is to buy any remaining stock for cash at $10 per share.

After reaching the agreement outlined, the three men hired you as accountant for the new corporation. Your first task is to determine the amount of stock each person should receive, and to prepare entries on the corporation's books to record the issuance of stock in exchange for the partnership assets and liabilities and the issuance of stock to Ewing for cash. In addition, prepare a balance sheet for the corporation as it should appear after all its stock is issued.

Provocative Problem 15–2, Harkins Company

The management of Harkins Company is considering the expansion of its business operations to a new and exciting line of business in which newly invested assets can be expected to earn 15% per year. At the present time Harkins Company has only 16,000 shares of common stock outstanding originally issued at $50 per share, no other contributed capital accounts, and retained earnings of $160,000. Existing operations consistently earn approximately $120,000 each year. To finance the new expansion, management is considering three alternatives: (a) Issuing 4,000 shares of $10 cumulative, nonparticipating, nonvoting, preferred stock. Investment advisors of the company have concluded that these shares could be issued at $100. (b) Issuing 2,000 shares of $10, cumulative, fully participating on a per share basis, nonvoting, preferred stock. The investment advisers conclude that these shares could be sold for $200 per share. (c) Issuing 5,000 shares of common stock at $80 per share.

In evaluating these three alternatives, Harkins Company management has asked you to calculate the dividends that would be distributed to each class of shareholder based on the assumption that each year the board of directors will declare dividends equal to the total net income earned by the corporation. Your calculations should show the distribution of dividends to preferred and common shareholders under each of the three alternative financing plans. You should also calculate dividends per share of preferred and dividends per share of common.

As a second part of your analysis assume that you own 1,000 of the common shares outstanding prior to the expansion and that you will not acquire or purchase any of the newly issued shares. Based on your whole analysis, would you prefer that the proposed expansion in operations be rejected? If not, comment on the relative merits of each alternative from your point of view as a common shareholder.

Provocative Problem 15–3, A Comparison of Alternative Investments

Having recently inherited $50,000, Ross Barnett is thinking about investing the money in one of two securities. They are: Barnhold Corporation common stock or the preferred stock issued by Blazertype Company Ltd. The companies manufacture and sell competing products, and both have been in business about the same length of time—four years in the case of Barnhold Corporation and five years for Blazertype Company. Also, the two companies have about the same amount of shareholders' equity, as the following equity sections from their latest balance sheets show:

BARNHOLD CORPORATION

Common stock, no-par value, unlimited number of shares authorized, 2,000,000 shares issued	$2,000,000
Retained earnings	1,000,000
Total shareholders' equity	$3,000,000

BLAZERTYPE COMPANY LIMITED

Preferred stock, no-par value, $7 cumulative and nonparticipating, 10,000 shares authorized and issued	$1,000,000*
Common stock, no-par value, 200,000 shares authorized and issued	2,000,000
Retained earnings	75,000
Total shareholders' equity	$3,075,000

* The current and one prior year's dividends are in arrears on the preferred stock.

Barnhold Corporation did not pay a dividend on its common stock during its first year's operations; however, since then, for the past three years, it has paid a $0.10 per share annual dividend on the stock. The stock is currently selling for $1.59 per share. The preferred stock of Blazertype Company, on the other hand, is selling for $92 per share. Mr. Barnett favours this stock as an investment. He feels the stock is a real bargain since it is not only selling below the average issue price but also $22 below book value, and as he says, "Since it is a preferred stock, the dividends are guaranteed." Too, he feels the common stock of Barnhold Corporation, selling at 6% above book value and 59% above the average issue price while paying only a $0.10 per share dividend, is overpriced.

Required:

a. Is the preferred stock of Blazertype Company selling at a price $22 below its book value, and is the common stock of Barnhold Corporation selling at a price 6% above book value and 59% above the average issue price?
b. From an analysis of the shareholders' equity sections, express your opinion of the two stocks as investments and describe some of the factors Mr. Barnett should consider in choosing between the two securities.

ANALYTICAL AND REVIEW PROBLEMS

Problem 15–1
A&R

Incorporation of AB Partnership; XYZ Corporation *uses old books* with appropriate adjustments.

Balance sheet of AB Partnership prior to incorporation is as follows:

Debit

Cash	$ 2,000
Accounts receivable	10,000
Allowance for doubtful accounts ...	(1,000)
Inventory	21,000
Operational assets	40,000
Accumulated depreciation	(15,000)
	$57,000

Credit

Accounts payable .... $ 5,000
Note payable 2,000
A, capital 32,000
B, capital 18,000
$57,000

Note: Partners A and B had divided profits and losses: 60% for A and 40% for B.

Incorporation terms and related facts:

a. XYZ Corporation is formed with unlimited shares of common stock authorized; 10,000 of the shares are issued in exchange for the assets; the liabilities are assumed by the corporation.

b. It was agreed that the inventory should be written down to $16,000 and that the accumulated depreciation should be $14,000. The book value of the remaining assets represented market value at the time of transfer to XYZ Corporation.

c. The 10,000 shares are to be divided between A and B according to their capital balances after the above adjustments and after recognition of goodwill based on the sale to "outsiders" of 10,000 shares at $6 per share. (Hint: Goodwill is based on the $6 per share value established by the sale to outsiders.)

Required:

Prepare all the necessary entries to change the books from a partnership to a corporation including the issuance of the 20,000 shares.

Problem 15–2 A&R

Repeat Problem 15–1 A&R on the assumption that the partnership books are closed and new books are opened by the corporation.

Problem 15–3 A&R

After 10 years in the Navy, Gerald Labonte decided not to reenlist. He located in Windsor, Ontario, and began looking for opportunities. By accident he discovered that an unfilled demand by farmers existed for prepackaged variety of standard-sized nuts and bolts. After an initial market testing in various parts of Essex and Kent Counties, Mr. Labonte was convinced he had found his niche. He incorporated Continental Bolt Corporation, and recruited a cadre of commission salespersons throughout the country. The business proved to be an instant success.

However, the more the sales increased and, of course, profit, the more was Mr. Labonte's need for cash. It got to the point of Mr. Labonte remarking, "I am going broke while making a profit." He was so desperate for cash that he sold to Mr. Kozimack a 10% interest for the equivalent of $\frac{1}{20}$ of the then annual net income. One year later he could not stand Mr. Kozimack questioning his policies. Consequently, he offered and Mr. Kozimack accepted a sum five times what Mr. Kozimack originally paid for his shares. The company continued to prosper, at least on paper. Mr. Labonte hocked everything he could lay his hands on and then some. He even pledged his house for a bank loan to the company.

A year after Mr. Labonte started the Canadian company, he incorporated one in the United States. Sales were growing at a 25% annual rate, and the relationship of net income to sales continued at 10%. These rates of growth and profitability were expected to continue over the next few years. All earnings were reinvested in the business.

In the midst of this success, bankers and suppliers were growing more and more uneasy. It was taking Mr. Labonte longer and longer to pay supplier accounts and interest on outstanding bank loans was being paid out of proceeds of new loans. Mr. Labonte realized that he was nearing the end of his juggling act and that he had to get long-term financing. The condensed financial statements are presented below:

CONTINENTAL BOLT CORPORATION
Condensed Balance Sheet
December 31, 198A

Cash	$ 300
Accounts receivable (net)	126,000
Inventory	126,000
Other assets	30,300
	$282,600
Accounts payable	$ 31,800
Bank loans (demand) payable	139,200
Share capital 1,000 shares	8,400
Retained earnings	103,200
	$282,600

CONTINENTAL BOLT CORPORATION
Condensed Income Statement
For the Year Ended December 31, 198A

Sales	$504,000
Cost of sales	252,000
	252,000
Expenses, including income taxes	201,600
Net income	$ 50,400

Required:

Focus on Mr. Labonte's remark: "I am going broke while making a profit." Using the financial statements given in the case, discuss the basis for support or prove Mr. Labonte's remark to be erroneous. Your answer should be supported by projected balance sheets and income statements through at least December 31, 198D. In preparing the projected statements assume that *(a)* sales will increase at 25% per annum and net income will remain constant as a percentage of sales (10%), *(b)* receivables, inventory, and payables will grow at the same rate as sales (25% per annum), *(c)* the amount of other assets are expected to increase at a 50% annual rate, *(d)* no dividends will be declared, *(e)* the bank will not permit the loan to exceed $144,000, and *(f)* the amount of cash (could be negative) is the variable necessary to balance; if negative, additional borrowing required to have at least a zero balance in the cash account.

Problem 15–4 A&R

This problem continues the case of Continental Bolt Corporation. As best as Mr. Labonte could figure out, in the next two years he needed to raise $240,000 to substantially eliminate the bank loan and provide an adequate cash balance. To provide for growth for the following five-year period (total of seven years from now) and the anticipated more rapid growth of the U.S. market, Mr. Labonte decided to aim at raising $600,000. The amount would replace the bank loan and provide for the necessary working capital.

What appears to be excess cash in the earlier years would in fact be required to partially finance the expanded operations and accommodate purchasing arrangements with new suppliers. It was intended that large lots of product would be purchased principally from Japanese suppliers at a substantial saving. The "catch" was that payment had to be made at the time shipment was made, and shipping time was three to five months. Consequently, inventory turnover would be reduced from the current twice a year to once a year.

Once he had this plan formulated, he approached Michael Finn, professor of business administration, at the University of Southwestern Ontario, with an invitation to serve on the board of directors. Dr. Finn accepted, and the two started to set out alternatives to raise the necessary capital. At first they thought of approaching Eric Denham, a wealthy manufacturer, who was just "itching" to get back into the swing of things. He was forced to retire at age 55 as chairman of the board of DKS, Limited, an auto parts manufacturer, in which he held a 38% interest. Two alternatives that would be presented to him were as follows:

1. A straight loan of $600,000 for 10 years at 15% (the same rate the bank charged on the current loan).
2. A loan of $240,000 for 10 years at 15% and $360,000 for 40% interest in Continental Bolt common stock (class B).

The price for the common shares in the second alternative had been determined using what Dr. Finn and Mr. Labonte considered to be a conservative price/ earnings multiple based on the projected income for the first year after the financing.

Another proposal was to approach underwriters to arrange for an issue of $240,000 of 12% nonvoting preferred stock (class A) and $360,000 of common stock (class B). The common stock issue would represent 40% of the total common stock outstanding after the issue. In making calculations of the implications of these proposals, Brown prepared the following pro forma partial income statement:

CONTINENTAL BOLT CORPORATION
Pro Forma Income Statement
For the First Year after Financing

Sales	$960,000
Cost of sales	432,000
	528,000
Expenses, excluding interest charges	
and income taxes*	264,000
	$264,000

* Income tax rate is expected to average 40%.

Assume that Retained Earnings at the beginning of the year covered by the pro forma income statement were estimated at $200,000 and the bank loan was fully repaid out of the proceeds of new financing.

Required:

1. For each of the proposals, calculate the return on the ending common (class B) shareholders' equity and indicate, giving your reasons, which proposal you would recommend to Mr. Labonte.
2. Which of the two alternatives is Eric Denham likely to prefer, if either? Explain your thinking.
3. Discuss some of the problems that you think might be encountered in attempting to locate a willing underwriter for the latter proposal given the size and nature of the issue.

Additional Corporation Transactions and Stock Investments

16

After studying Chapter 16, you should be able to:

Record stock dividends and compare them with stock splits.

Record purchases and retirement of a corporation's own stock.

Record purchases and sales of treasury stock and describe their effects on shareholders' equity.

Describe restrictions and appropriations of retained earnings and the disclosure of such items in the financial statements.

State the criteria for classifying stock investments as current assets or as long-term investments.

Describe the circumstances under which the cost method of accounting for stock investments is used and the circumstances under which the equity method is used.

Record and maintain the accounts for stock investments according to the cost method and the equity method.

Prepare consolidated financial statements that include such matters as excess of investment cost over book value and minority interests.

Define or explain the words and phrases listed in the chapter Glossary.

When a corporation earns a net income, more assets flow into the business from revenues than flow out for expenses. As a result, a net income increases both assets and shareholders' equity. The increase in shareholders' equity appears on the corporation's balance sheet as retained earnings. Once retained earnings were commonly called *earned surplus*. However, since the word **surplus** is subject to misinterpretation, it has all but disappeared from published balance sheets. The 14th Edition of *Financial Reporting in Canada* shows that in 1980, "earned surplus" was not used by any of the 325 companies in the survey.

RETAINED EARNINGS AND DIVIDENDS

In most jurisdictions, a corporation must have retained earnings in order to pay a cash dividend. However, the payment of a cash dividend reduces in equal amounts both cash and shareholders' equity. Consequently, in order to pay a cash dividend, a corporation must have not only a credit balance in its Retained Earnings account but also cash with which to pay the dividend. If cash or assets that will shortly become cash are not available, a board of directors may think it wise to forgo the declaration of a dividend, even though retained earnings exist. Often, the directors of a corporation with a large retained earnings balance will not declare a dividend because all current assets will be needed in the operation of the business.

In considering the wisdom of a dividend, a board of directors must recognize that earnings are a source of assets. Perhaps some assets from earnings should be paid out in dividends and some should be retained for emergencies and to pay dividends in years when earnings are not sufficient to pay normal dividends. Also, if a corporation is to expand, management may wish to finance the expansion by using assets acquired through earnings rather than by borrowing or selling equity.

As was noted in Chapter 15, shareholders enjoy limited liability, consequently corporation laws provide for the protection of creditors and others dependent on the continuity of the corporation. To this end, the more recently passed corporations acts include a solvency test. For example, the Canada Business Corporation Act 1975 provides in section 40 that:

A corporation shall not declare or pay a dividend if there are responsible grounds for believing that
(*a*) the corporation is, or would after the payment be, unable to pay its liabilities as they become due; or
(*b*) the realizable value of the corporation's assets would thereby be less than the aggregate of its liabilities and stated capital of all classes.

Entries for the declaration and distribution of a cash dividend were presented on page 163 and need not be repeated here.

STOCK DIVIDENDS

A *stock dividend* is a distribution by a corporation of shares of its own common stock to its common shareholders without any consideration being given in return therefor. A clear distinction should be made between a cash dividend and a stock dividend. A cash dividend reduces both assets and shareholders' equity. A stock dividend differs in that shares of the corporation's own stock rather than cash are distributed; and such a dividend has no effect on assets, total capital, or the amount of shareholders' equity.

A stock dividend has no effect on corporation assets, total capital, and the amount of shareholders' equity because such a dividend involves nothing more than a transfer of retained earnings to contributed capital. To illustrate this, assume that Northwest Corporation has the following capital stock and retained earnings:

Capital Stock and Retained Earnings	
Common stock, no-par value, issued and outstanding 10,000 shares	$108,000
Retained earnings	35,000
Total contributed capital and retained earnings	$143,000

Assume further that on December 28 the directors of Northwest Corporation declared a 10% or 1,000-share stock dividend distributable on January 20 to the January 15 shareholders of record.

If the fair market value of Northwest Corporation's stock on December 28 is $15 per share, the following entries may be made to record the dividend declaration and distribution:

Dec.	28	Retained Earnings	15,000.00	
		Common Stock Dividend Distributable		15,000.00
		To record the declaration of a 1,000-share common stock dividend.		
Jan.	20	Common Stock Dividend Distributable	15,000.00	
		Common Stock		15,000.00
		To record the distribution of a 1,000-share common stock dividend.		

Note that the entries change $15,000 of the shareholders' equity from retained earnings to contributed capital, or as it is commonly said, $15,000 of retained earnings are **capitalized.** Note also that the retained earnings capitalized are equal to the fair market value of the 1,000 shares issued ($15 × 1,000 = $15,000).[1]

As previously pointed out, a stock dividend does not distribute funds from retained earnings to the shareholders, nor does it affect in any way the corporation assets. Likewise, it has no effect on total capital and on the individual equities of the shareholders. To illustrate these last points, assume that Johnson owned 100 shares of Northwest Corporation's stock prior to the dividend. The corporation's total contributed and retained capital before the dividend and the book value of Johnson's 100 shares were as follows:

```
Common stock (10,000 shares) ....................... $108,000
Retained earnings ...................................    35,000
      Total contributed and retained capital ..............  $143,000

$143,000 ÷ 10,000 shares outstanding = $14.30 per share book value.
$14.30 × 100 = $1,430 for the book value of Johnson's 100 shares.
```

A 10% stock dividend gives a shareholder one new share for each 10 shares previously held. Consequently, Johnson received 10 new shares; and after the dividend, the contributed and retained capital of the corporation and the book value of Johnson's holdings are as follows:

```
Common stock (11,000 shares) .................... $123,000
Retained earnings ................................    20,000
      Total contributed and retained capital ............  $143,000

$143,000 ÷ 11,000 shares outstanding = $13 per share book value.
$13 × 110 = $1,430 for the book value of Johnson's 110 shares.
```

Before the stock dividend, Johnson owned 100/10,000 or 1/100 of the Northwest Corporation stock and his holdings had a $1,430 book value. After the dividend, he owned 110/1,000 or 1/100 of the corporation and his holdings still had a $1,430 book value. In other words, there was no effect on his equity other than that it was prepackaged from 100 units into 110. Likewise, the only effect on corporation capital was a permanent transfer to contributed capital of $15,000 from retained earnings. Consequently, insofar as both the corporation and Johnson are concerned, there was no shift in equities or corporation assets.

---

[1] The Canada Business Corporations Act requires that the value of the stock dividend be added to the stated capital account. In other jurisdictions, for example, Ontario, the amount to be capitalized is left to the board of directors.

Why Stock Dividends Are Distributed

If a stock dividend has no effect on corporation assets and shareholders' equities other than to repackage the equities into more units, why are such dividends declared and distributed? One of the reasons for the declaration of stock dividends is directly related to the market price of a corporation's common stock. For example, if a profitable corporation grows by retaining earnings, the price of its common stock also tends to grow. Eventually, the price of a share may become high enough to prevent some investors from considering a purchase of the stock. Thus, the corporation may declare stock dividends to keep the price of its shares from growing too high. For this reason, some corporations declare small stock dividends each year.

Shareholders may benefit from a stock dividend in another way. Often, corporations declaring stock dividends continue to pay the same cash dividend per share after a stock dividend as before, with the result that shareholders receive more cash each time dividends are declared.

Stock Dividends on the Balance Sheet

Since a stock dividend is "payable" in stock rather than in assets, it is not a liability of its issuing corporation. Therefore, if a balance sheet is prepared between the declaration and distribution dates of a stock dividend, the amount of the dividend distributable should appear on the balance sheet in the shareholders' equity section as follows:

Common stock, no-par value, 20,000 shares issued ...	$200,000
Common stock subscribed, 5,000 shares	50,000
Common stock dividend distributable, 1,900 shares ...	19,000
Total common stock issued and to be issued	$269,000

STOCK SPLITS

Sometimes, when a corporation's stock is selling at a high price, the corporation will call it in and issue two, three, four, five, or more new shares in the place of each old share previously outstanding. For example, a corporation having outstanding stock selling for $375 a share may call in the old shares and issue to the shareholders 2 shares, 4 shares, 10 shares, or any number of shares of stock in exchange for each share formerly held. In the case of par value shares, par value is split proportionately. For example, 4 shares of $25 par, or 10 shares of $10 par, or any number of no-par shares replace 1 share of $100 par value. This is known as a *stock split* or a *stock split-up,* and its usual purpose is to cause a reduction in the market price of the stock and, consequently facilitate trading in the stock. Less frequently than a stock split, a corporation may have a **reverse stock split.** In that case a corporation calls in the old shares and issues 1 new share for each 2 shares, 3 shares, 10 shares, or any number of shares previously held. The usual purpose of a reverse stock split is to reduce the number of shares outstanding and to cause an increase in the per share market value.

A stock split (or reverse stock split) has no effect on total shareholders' equity, the equities of the individual shareholders, or on the balances of any of the contributed or retained capital accounts. Consequently, all that is required in recording a stock split or a reverse stock split is a memorandum entry in the stock account reciting the facts of the split. For example, such a memorandum might read, "Issued 10 new shares common stock for each old share previously outstanding." There would also be a change in the number of shares outstanding on the balance sheet.

RETIREMENT OF STOCK

Under the Canada Business Corporations Act, as well as under the more recently passed provincial acts, for example, Ontario, a corporation may purchase for cancellation shares of its own outstanding stock if it can satisfy a solvency test as follows:

1. The corporation would after the payment be able to pay its liabilities as they become due.
2. The realizable value of the corporation's assets would, after the payment, be greater than the aggregate of its liabilities and stated capital of all classes.

When stock is purchased for cancellation, the debit to the stated capital account is the product of the number of shares acquired multiplied by the weighted average per share invested by the shareholders. If the shares are purchased for less than the weighted average per share invested by the shareholders, the difference is credited to an account such as Contributed Capital from Retirement of Stock. On the other hand, if the shares are purchased for more than the weighted average per share invested by the shareholders, the difference is debited to contributed capital from previous stock retirement transactions to the extent of its balance with any remainder debited to Retained Earnings.

For example, assume a corporation which has outstanding 100,000 common shares and stated capital—common of $2,500,000, and no contributed capital from previous stock retirement transactions, reacquires for cancellation 1,000 of the shares at $22 per share. The entry to record the retirement is:

Apr.	12	Common Stock	25,000.00	
		Contributed Capital from Retirement		
		of Common Stock		3,000.00
		Cash		22,000.00

If the shares were reacquired at $30 per share, the entry is:

Apr.	12	Common Stock	25,000.00	
		Retained Earnings	5,000.00	
		Cash		30,000.00

In jurisdictions which have par values when such shares are reacquired for cancellation, all capital items related to the shares being retired are removed from the accounts and the difference between the purchase price and the weighted average per share invested by the shareholders is treated in a like manner to that illustrated above for no-par-value shares.

TREASURY STOCK

Under the Canada Business Corporations Act, a corporation may purchase for cancellation shares of its own outstanding stock. However, in some jurisdictions a corporation may reacquire shares of its own outstanding stock and reissue these shares at a future date. Such reacquired shares are known as *treasury stock.*

PURCHASE OF TREASURY STOCK[2]

When a corporation purchases its own stock, it reduces in equal amounts both its assets and its shareholders' equity. To illustrate this, assume that on May 1 of the current year the condensed balance sheet of Curry Corporation appears as in Illustration 16–1.

---

[2] There are alternate ways of accounting for treasury stock transactions. This text will discuss the so-called cost basis or single transaction method. This method is recommended by the CICA.

Illustration 16–1

CURRY CORPORATION
Balance Sheet
May 1, 19—

Assets		Capital	
Cash	$ 30,000	Common stock, no par	
Other assets	95,000	value, authorized and	
		issued 10,000 shares ...	$100,000
		Retained earnings	25,000
Total assets	$125,000	Total capital	$125,000

If on May 1, Curry Corporation purchases 1,000 shares of its outstanding stock at $11.50 per share, the transaction is recorded as follows:

May	1	Treasury Stock, Common	11,500.00	
		Cash		11,500.00
		Purchased 1,000 shares of treasury stock at $11.50 per share.		

The debit of the entry records a reduction in the equity of the shareholders. The credit records a reduction in assets. Both are equal to the cost of the treasury stock. After the entry is posted, a new balance sheet will show the reductions as in Illustration 16–2.

Illustration 16–2

CURRY CORPORATION
Balance Sheet
May 1, 19—

Assets		Capital	
Cash	$ 18,500	Common stock, no par	
Other assets	95,000	value, authorized and	
		issued 10,000 shares of	
		which 1,000 are in the	
		treasury	$100,000
		Retained earnings of which	
		$11,500 is restricted by the	
		purchase of treasury	
		stock	25,000
		Total................	125,000
		Less: Cost of treasury	
		stock	11,500
Total assets	$113,500	Total capital	$113,500

Notice in the second balance sheet that the cost of the treasury stock appears in the shareholders' equity section as a deduction from common stock and retained earnings. In comparing the two balance sheets, notice that the treasury stock purchase reduces both assets and shareholders' equity by the $11,500 cost of the stock. Also, observe that the dollar amount of issued stock remains at $100,000 and is unchanged from the first balance sheet. The amount of **issued stock** is not changed by the purchase of treasury stock. However, the purchase does reduce **outstanding stock.** In Curry Corporation, the purchase reduced the outstanding stock from 10,000 to 9,000 shares.

There is a distinction between issued stock and outstanding stock. Issued stock may or may not be outstanding. Outstanding stock has been issued and remains currently outstanding. Only outstanding stock is effective stock, receives cash dividends, and is given a vote in the meetings of shareholders.

Restricting Retained Earnings by the Purchase of Treasury Stock

The purchase of treasury stock by a corporation has the same effect on its assets and shareholders' equity as the payment of a cash dividend. Both transfer corporation assets to shareholders and thereby reduce assets and shareholders' equity. Consequently, in jurisdictions that sanction treasury stock a corporation may purchase its stock or it may pay cash dividends, but the sum of both cannot exceed the amount of its retained earnings available for dividends.

Unlike the payment of a cash dividend, the purchase of treasury stock does not reduce the balance of the Retained Earnings account. However, the purchase does place a restriction on the amount of retained earnings available for dividends. Note how the restriction is shown in Illustration 16–2. It is also commonly shown by means of a balance sheet footnote.

The *restriction of retained earnings* because of treasury stock purchases is a matter of law. Other types of legal restrictions on retained earnings may be imposed by law or by contract.

REISSUING TREASURY STOCK

When treasury stock is reissued, it may be reissued at cost, above cost, or below cost. If reissued at cost, the entry to record the transaction is the reverse of the entry used to record the purchase.

Although treasury stock may be sold at cost, it is commonly sold at a price either above or below cost. When sold above cost, the amount received in excess of cost is credited to a contributed capital account called Contributed Capital, Treasury Stock Transactions. For example, if Curry Corporation sells for $12 per share 500 of the treasury shares purchased at $11.50 per share, the entry to record the transaction appears as follows:

June	3	Cash	6,000.00	
		Contributed Capital, Treasury Stock		
		Transactions		250.00
		Treasury Stock		5,750.00
		Sold at $12 per share 500 treasury shares that cost $11.50 per share.		

When treasury stock is reissued at a price below cost, the entry to record the sale depends upon whether or not there is contributed capital from previous treasury stock transactions. If there is no such contributed capital, the "loss" is debited to Retained Earnings. However, if there is such contributed capital, the "loss" is debited to the account of this contributed capital to the extent of its balance. Any remainder is then debited to Retained Earnings. For example, if Curry Corporation sells its remaining 500 shares of treasury stock at $10 per share, the entry to record the sale is:

July	10	Cash	5,000.00	
		Contributed Capital, Treasury Stock		
		Transactions	250.00	
		Retained Earnings	500.00	
		Treasury Stock		5,750.00
		Sold at $10 per share 500 treasury shares that cost $11.50 per share.		

APPROPRIATIONS OF RETAINED EARNINGS

A corporation may *appropriate retained earnings* for some special purpose or purposes and show the amounts appropriated as separate items in the equity section of its balance sheet. In contrast to retained earnings **restrictions** which are binding by law or by contract, appropriations of retained earnings are voluntarily made by the board of directors. Such appropriations may be recorded by transferring portions of retained earnings from the Retained Earnings account to accounts such as Retained Earnings Appropriated for Contingencies.

The appropriations do not reduce total retained earnings. Rather, their purpose is to inform balance sheet readers that portions of retained earnings are not available for the declaration of cash dividends. When the contingency or other reason for an appropriation has passed, the appropriation account is eliminated by returning its balance to the Retained Earnings account.

Appropriations of retained earnings were once common, but such appropriations are seldom seen on balance sheets today. Today the same information is conveyed with less chance of misunderstanding by means of footnotes accompanying the financial statements.

NET INCOME AND RETAINED EARNINGS— ADDITIONAL FACTORS

Determination of net income and of retained earnings has been based, to this point, on consideration of the normal or the usual items. On occasion, however, there are items that fall outside the normal or usual classification. These items are described as *(a)* extraordinary items, *(b)* prior period adjustments, and *(c)* accounting changes.

Extraordinary items *(CICA Handbook,* Section 3480, paragraphs 5 through 11) are material gains and losses and provisions for losses which, by their nature, are not typical of the normal business activities of the enterprise. Examples are gains or losses from *(a)* sale or abandonment of a plant or major segment of the business, *(b)* sale of an investment not acquired for resale, *(c)* write-off of goodwill due to unusual events or developments within the period, and *(d)* property condemnation or expropriation. Items that do not qualify as extraordinary include *(a)* write-downs of receivables and inventories regardless of amount, *(b)* adjustments of accrued contract prices, and *(c)* gains or losses from foreign exchange translation. These latter three items are considered as ordinary gains or losses.

With respect to extraordinary items, the income statement should distinguish:

Income before extraordinary item(s).

Extraordinary item(s), including the applicable income tax.

Prior period adjustments are accounted for and reported as direct charges (or credits, including disclosure of the applicable income tax) to Retained Earnings; they cause the opening balance of retained earnings to be restated. To qualify as prior period adjustments, items must be rare in occurrence and must meet the specific criteria set out in paragraphs 3600.02–.03 of the *CICA Handbook.*

Accounting changes (Section 1506 of the *CICA Handbook*) include *(a)* accounting errors, *(b)* changes in accounting policy, and *(c)* changes in estimates. The first two types of items—accounting errors arising in prior periods and changes in accounting policy necessitated by a change in circumstances or the development of new accounting principles—

receive parallel treatment to that described for prior period adjustments. That is, they are applied retroactively with a restatement of the opening retained earnings. The latter, change in estimate, is accorded prospective treatment. As a company gains more experience in such areas as estimating bad debts, warranty costs, and useful lives of depreciable assets, there is often a sound basis for revising previous estimates. Such changes affect only the present and future statements. A detailed discussion and comparative statement presentation of the above items is left to a more advanced textbook.

STOCKS AS INVESTMENTS

The stock transactions illustrated thus far have been transactions in which a corporation sold and issued its own stock. Such transactions represent only a small portion of the daily transactions in stocks. Most stock sales involve transactions between investors that are arranged through brokers who charge a commission for their services.

Brokers, acting as agents for their customers, buy and sell stocks and bonds on exchanges such as the Toronto Stock Exchange. Some securities are not listed or traded on an organized stock exchange, and brokers act for their customers to buy and sell such securities in the "over-the-counter" market. Each security in this market is handled by one or more brokers who receive offers from other brokers to buy or sell the security at specific "bid" or "ask" prices. Stock prices are quoted on the basis of dollars and ⅛ dollars per share. For example, a stock quoted at 46⅛ means $46.125 per share, and a stock quoted at 25½ means $25.50 per share.

CLASSIFYING INTERESTS

Equity securities generally include common and preferred stocks. Many equity securities are actively traded, so that "sales prices or bid and ask prices are currently available on a national securities exchange or in the over-the-counter market." Such securities are called *marketable equity securities*. If, in addition to being marketable, a stock investment is held as "an investment of cash available for current operations," it is classified as Temporary Investment, a current asset.[3]

Investments that are not intended as a ready source of cash in case of need are classified as *long-term investments*. They include funds earmarked for a special purpose, such as bond sinking funds, as well as land or other assets owned but not employed in the regular operations

---

[3] *CICA Handbook* (Toronto: The Canadian Institute of Chartered Accountants), sec. 3010.

of the business. They also include investments in stocks which are not marketable or which, although marketable, are not intended to serve as a ready source of cash. Long-term investments appear on the balance sheet in a classification of their own titled "Long-term investments."

ACCOUNTING FOR INVESTMENTS IN STOCK

Most investments in a corporation's stock represent a small percentage of the total amount of stock outstanding. As a consequence, the investor does not exercise a significant influence over the financial affairs of the corporation. However, in some cases, an investor will buy a large share of the outstanding stock of a corporation in order to influence or control its operations. For example, corporations frequently buy a large share of another corporation's stock in order to influence its activities as well as to receive part of its income.

The method of accounting for stock investments on the books of the investor depends upon whether the investor has the ability to significantly influence the activities of the corporation. If the investor can exercise a significant financial influence, the accounting method used is called the *equity method*, and if the investor does not have a significant financial influence, the accounting method used is called the *cost method*. The CICA holds that

> the ability to exercise significant influence may be indicated by, for example, representation on the board of directors, participation in policy-making processes, material intercompany transactions, interchange of managerial personnel or provision of technical information. If the investor holds less than 20% of the voting interest in the investee, it should be presumed that the investor does not have the ability to exercise significant influence, unless such influence is clearly demonstrated. On the other hand, the holding of 20% or more of the voting interest in the investee does not in itself confirm the ability to exercise significant influence.[4]

In order to simplify discussion in this chapter, it is assumed that ownership of 20% or more of the voting stock is indicative of the presence of other elements for the exercise of significant influence (such as those named above). Thus, such investments are accounted for according to the equity method while investments of less than 20%, referred to as **portfolio investments,** are accounted for according to the cost method.

The Cost Method of Accounting for Stock Investments

When stock is purchased as either a temporary- or long-term investment, the purchase is recorded at total cost, which includes any commis-

---

[4] Ibid., par. 3050.19.

sion paid to the broker. For example, 1,000 (10%) of Dot Corporation's 10,000 outstanding common shares were purchased as an investment at 23¼ plus a $300 broker's commission. The entry to record the transaction is:

Sept.	10	Investment in Dot Corporation Stock	23,550.00	
		Cash		23,550.00
		Purchased 1,000 shares of stock for $23,250 plus a $300 broker's commission.		

When the cost method is used to account for either a temporary or long-term investment and a dividend is received on the stock, an entry similar to the following is made:

Oct.	5	Cash	1,000.00	
		Dividends Earned		1,000.00
		Received a $1 per share dividend on the stock.		

Dividends on stocks do not accrue; consequently, an end-of-period entry to record accrued dividends is never made. However, if a balance sheet is prepared after a dividend is declared but before it is paid, an entry debiting Dividends Receivable and crediting Dividends Earned would be appropriate.

A dividend in shares of stock is not income, and a debit and credit entry recording it should not be made. However, a memorandum entry or a notation as to the additional shares should be made in the investment account. Also, receipt of a stock dividend does affect the per share cost of the old shares. For example, if a 20-share dividend is received on 100 shares originally purchased for $1,500 or at $15 per share, the cost of all 120 shares is $1,500 and the cost per share is $12.50 ($1,500 ÷ 120 shares = $12.50 per share).

Under the cost method, when an investment in stock is sold and the proceeds net of any sales commission differ from cost, a gain or loss must be recorded. For example, consider the 1,000 shares of Dot Corporation common stock that were purchased at a cost of $23,550. If these shares are sold at 25¾ less a sales commission of $315, there is a $1,885 gain, and the transaction is recorded:

Jan.	7	Cash	25,435.00	
		Investment in Dot Corporation Stock		23,550.00
		Gain on Sale of Investments		1,885.00
		Sold 1,000 shares of stock for $25,750		
		less a $315 commission.		

If the net annual received for these shares had been less than their $23,550 cost, there would have been a loss on the transaction.

Lower of Cost or Market

For balance sheet presentation, investments in marketable equity securities are divided (on basis of intent of management) into two portfolios: (1) those to be shown as current assets and (2) those to be shown as long-term investments. When the market value of the temporary (current) investments has declined below the carrying value, they should be carried at market value.[5] In the case of long-term investments, they are shown at cost with market value disclosed even if cost is below market value, so long as the decline in value is temporary. However, when there has been a loss in value other than a temporary decline, the investment should be written down to recognize the loss. The write-down (loss) would be included in determining net income. When the investment has been written down to recognize a loss, the new carrying value is deemed to be the new cost basis for subsequent accounting purposes. A subsequent increase in value would be recognized only when realized. For purposes of calculating a gain or loss on the sale of investments, the cost of the investments sold should be calculated on the basis of the average carrying value.[6]

The Equity Method of Accounting for Common Stock Investments

If a common stock investor has a significant influence over or controls the investee, the equity method of accounting for the investment must be used. When the stock is acquired, the purchase is recorded at cost just as it is under the cost method. For example, on January 1, 198A, James, Inc., purchased 3,000 shares (30%) of RMS, Inc., common stock for a total cost of $70,650. The entry to record the purchase on the books of James, Inc., is as follows:

---

[5] *CICA Handbook,* par. 3010.06.

[6] Ibid., par. 3010.27–.35.

Jan.	1	Investment in RMS, Inc.	70,650.00	
		Cash		70,650.00
		Purchased 3,000 shares of common stock.		

Under the equity method, it is recognized that the earnings of the investee corporation not only increase the net assets of the investee corporation but also increase the investor's equity in the assets. Consequently, when the investee closes its books and reports the amount of its earnings, the investor takes up its share of those earnings in its investment account. For example, RMS, Inc., reported net income of $20,000. James, Inc.'s entry to record its share of these earnings is:

Dec.	31	Investment in RMS, Inc.	6,000.00	
		Earnings from Investment in RMS, Inc.		6,000.00
		To record 30% equity in investee's earnings of $20,000.		

The debit records the increase in James, Inc.'s equity in RMS, Inc. The credit causes 30% of RMS, Inc.'s net income to appear on James, Inc.'s income statement as earnings from the investment, and James, Inc., closes the earnings to its Income Summary account and on to its Retained Earnings account just as it would close earnings from any investment.

If, instead of a net income, the investee corporation incurs a loss, the investor debits the loss to an account called Loss from Investment and credits and reduces its Investment in Stock account. It then transfers the loss to its Income Summary account and on to its Retained Earnings account.

Dividends paid by an investee corporation decrease the investee's assets and retained earnings, and also decrease the investor's equity in the investee. Since, under the equity method, the investor records its equity in the full amount of earnings reported by an investee, the receipt of dividends does not constitute income; instead, dividend receipts from the investee represent a decrease in the equity. For example, RMS, Inc., declared and paid $10,000 in dividends on its common stock. The entry to record James, Inc.'s share of these dividends, which it received on January 9, 198B, is:

```
Jan.   9 Cash  ......................................    3,000.00
          Investment in RMS, Inc.  .................              3,000.00
          To record receipt of 30% of the $10,000
          dividend paid by RMS, Inc.
```

Notice that the carrying value of a common stock investment, accounted for by the equity method, changes in reflection of the investor's equity in the undistributed earnings of the investee. For example, after the above transactions have been recorded on the books of James, Inc., the investment account would appear as follows:

Investment in RMS, Inc.

Date		Explanation	Debit	Credit	Balance
198A					
Jan.	1	Investment	70,650.00		70,650.00
Dec.	31	Share of earnings	6,000.00		76,650.00
198B					
Jan.	9	Share of dividend		3,000.00	73,650.00

When common stock, accounted for by the equity method, is sold, the gain or loss on the sale is determined by comparing the proceeds from the sale with the carrying value of the stock on the date of sale. For example, on January 10, 198B, James, Inc., sold its RMS, Inc., stock for $80,000. The entry to record the sale is as follows:

```
Jan.  10 Cash  ......................................   80,000.00
          Investment in RMS, Inc.  .................             73,650.00
          Gain on Sale of Investments  ............              6,350.00
          Sold 3,000 shares of stock for $80,000.
```

PARENT AND SUBSIDIARY CORPORATIONS

Corporations commonly own stock in and may even control other corporations. For example, if Corporation A owns more than 50% of the voting stock of Corporation B, Corporation A can elect Corporation B's board of directors and thus control its activities and resources. In such a situation, the controlling corporation, Corporation A, is known as the *parent company* and Corporation B is called a *subsidiary*.

When a corporation owns all the outstanding stock of a subsidiary, it can take over the subsidiary's assets, cancel its stock, and fuse the subsidiary into the parent company. However, instead of operating the business as a single corporation, there are often financial, legal, and tax advantages if a large business is operated as a parent company that controls one or more subsidiaries. Actually, most large companies are parent corporations owning one or more subsidiaries.

When a business is operated as a parent company with subsidiaries, separate accounting records are kept for each corporation. Also, from a legal viewpoint, the parent and each subsidiary are separate entities with all the rights, duties, and responsibilities of a separate corporation. However, investors in the parent company depend on the parent to present a set of **consolidated statements** which show the results of all operations under the parent's control, including those of any subsidiaries. In these statements, the assets and liabilities of all affiliated companies are combined on a single balance sheet and their revenues and expenses are combined on a single income statement, as though the business were in fact a single company.

CONSOLIDATED BALANCE SHEETS

When parent and subsidiary balance sheets are consolidated, duplications in items are eliminated so that the combined figures do not show more assets and equities than actually exist. For example, a parent's investment in a subsidiary is evidenced by shares of stock which are carried as an asset in the parent company's records. However, these shares actually represent an equity in the subsidiary's assets. Consequently, if the parent's investment in a subsidiary and the subsidiary's assets were both shown on the consolidated balance sheet, the same resources would be counted twice. To prevent this, the parent's investment and the subsidiary's capital accounts are offset and eliminated in preparing a consolidated balance sheet.

Likewise, a single enterprise cannot owe a debt to itself. This would be analogous to a student borrowing $20 for a date from funds saved for next semester's expenses and then preparing a balance sheet showing the $20 as both a receivable from himself and a payable to himself. To prevent such a double counting, intercompany debts and receivables are also eliminated in preparing a consolidated balance sheet.

Balance Sheets Consolidated at Time of Acquisition

When a parent's and a subsidiary's assets are combined in the preparation of a consolidated balance sheet, a work sheet is normally used to effect the consolidation. Illustration 16–3 shows such a work sheet. It was prepared to consolidate the accounts of Parent Company and its subsidiary, called Subsidiary Company, on January 1, 198A, the day Parent Company acquired Subsidiary Company through the cash purchase of all 10,000 shares of its outstanding common stock. The stock had a book value of $115,000, or $11.50 per share, which in this first illustration is the amount Parent Company is assumed to have paid for it. Explanation of the work sheet's two eliminating entries follow.

ENTRY (a). On the day it acquired Subsidiary Company, Parent Company lent Subsidiary Company $10,000 for use in the subsidiary's operations. It took the subsidiary's note as evidence of the transaction. This intercompany debt was in reality a transfer of funds within the organization. Consequently, since it did not increase the total assets and total liabilities of the affiliated companies, it is eliminated by means of entry *(a)*. To understand this entry, recall that the subsidiary's promissory note is represented by a $10,000 debit in Parent Company's Notes Receivable account. Then observe that the first credit in the Eliminations column exactly offsets and eliminates this item. Next, recall that the subsidiary's note appears as a credit in its Notes Payable account. Then observe that the $10,000 debit in the Eliminations column completes the elimination of this intercompany debt.

Illustration 16–3

PARENT COMPANY AND SUBSIDIARY COMPANY
Work Sheet for a Consolidated Balance Sheet
January 1, 198A

	Parent Company	Subsidiary Company	Eliminations		Consolidated Amounts
			Debit	Credit	
Assets					
Cash	5,000	15,000			20,000
Notes receivable	10,000			(a) 10,000	
Investment in Subsidiary Company	115,000			(b) 115,000	
Other assets	190,000	117,000			307,000
	320,000	132,000			327,000
Liabilities and Equities					
Accounts payable	15,000	7,000			22,000
Notes payable		10,000	(a) 10,000		
Common stock	250,000	100,000	(b) 100,000		250,000
Retained earnings	55,000	15,000	(b) 15,000		55,000
	320,000	132,000	125,000	125,000	327,000

ENTRY (b).   When a parent company buys a subsidiary's stock, the investment appears on the parent's balance sheet as an asset, Investment in Subsidiary. The investment represents an equity in the subsidiary's net assets. Consequently, to show both the subsidiary's (net) assets and the parent company's investment in the subsidiary on a consolidated balance sheet would be to double count those resources. As a result, on the work sheet the amount of the parent's investment (an equity in the subsidiary's assets) is offset against the subsidiary's shareholder equity accounts, which also represent an equity in the assets, and both are eliminated.

After the intercompany items are eliminated on a work sheet like Illustration 16–3, the assets of the parent and the subsidiary and the remaining equities in these assets are combined and carried into the work sheet's last column. The combined amounts are then used to prepare a consolidated balance sheet showing all the assets and equities of the parent and its subsidiary.

Parent Company Does Not Buy All of Subsidiary's Stock and Does Not Pay Book Value

In the situation just described, Parent Company purchased all of its subsidiary's stock, paying book value for it. Often, a parent company purchases less than 100% of a subsidiary's stock, and commonly pays a price either above or below book value. To illustrate such a situation, assume Parent Company purchased for cash only 80% of its subsidiary's stock rather than 100%, and that it paid $13 per share, a price $1.50 above the stock's book value.

These new assumptions result in a more complicated work sheet entry to eliminate the parent's investment and the subsidiary's shareholders' equity accounts. The entry is complicated by (1) the minority interest in the subsidiary and (2) the excess over book value paid by the parent company for the subsidiary's stock.

MINORITY INTEREST.   When a parent buys a controlling interest in a subsidiary, the parent company is the subsidiary's majority shareholder. However, when the parent owns less than 100% of the subsidiary's stock, the subsidiary has other shareholders who own a *minority interest* in its assets and share its earnings. Consequently, when there is a minority interest, the minority interest must be set out as on the last line of Illustration 16–4 in making the work sheet entry to eliminate the shareholders' equity accounts of the subsidiary. In this case, the minority stockholders have a 20% interest in the subsidiary. Consequently, 20% of the subsidiary's common stock and retained earnings accounts [($100,000 + $15,000) × 20% = $23,000] is set out on the work sheet as the minority interest.

Illustration 16–4

PARENT COMPANY AND SUBSIDIARY COMPANY
Work Sheet for a Consolidated Balance Sheet
January 1, 198A

	Parent Company	Subsidiary Company	Eliminations		Consolidated Amounts
			Debit	Credit	
Assets					
Cash	16,000	15,000			31,000
Notes receivable	10,000			(a) 10,000	
Investment in Subsidiary Company	104,000			(b) 104,000	
Other assets	190,000	117,000			307,000
Excess of cost over book value			(b) 12,000		12,000
	320,000	132,000			350,000
Liabilities and Equities					
Accounts payable	15,000	7,000			22,000
Notes payable		10,000	(a) 10,000		
Common stock	250,000	100,000	(b) 100,000		250,000
Retained earnings	55,000	15,000	(b) 15,000		55,000
Minority interest				(b) 23,000	23,000
	320,000	132,000	137,000	137,000	350,000

EXCESS OF INVESTMENT COST OVER BOOK VALUE. Parent Company paid $13 per share for its 8,000 shares of Subsidiary Company's stock. Consequently, the cost of these shares exceeded their book value by $12,000, calculated as follows:

Cost of stock (8,000 shares at $13 per share)	$104,000
Book value (8,000 shares at $11.50 per share) ...	92,000
Excess of cost over book value	$ 12,000

Now observe how this excess of cost over book value is set out on the work sheet in eliminating the parent's investment in the subsidiary. Then it is carried into the Consolidated Amounts column as an asset.

After the work sheet of Illustration 16–4 was completed, the consolidated amounts in the last column were used to prepare the consolidated balance sheet of Illustration 16–5. Note the treatment of the minority interest in the balance sheet. The minority shareholders have a $23,000 equity in the consolidated assets of the affiliated companies. Many have argued that this item should be disclosed in the shareholders' equity section. Others believe it should be shown in the long-term liabilities section. However, a more common alternative is to disclose the minority interest as a separate item between the liabilities and shareholders' equity sections, as is shown in Illustration 16–5.

Next, observe that the $12,000 excess over book value paid by the parent company for the subsidiary's stock appears on the consolidated balance sheet as the asset described as "Goodwill from consolidation." When a parent company purchases an interest in a subsidiary, it may pay more than book value for its equity because (1) certain of the subsidiary's assets are carried on the subsidiary's books at less than fair value, (2) certain of the subsidiary's liabilities are carried at book values which are greater than fair values, or (3) the subsidiary's earnings prospects are good enough to justify paying more than the net fair (market) value of its assets and liabilities. In this illustration, it is assumed that the book values of Subsidiary Company's assets and liabilities are their fair values. However, Subsidiary Company's expected earnings justified paying $104,000 for an 80% equity in the subsidiary's net assets (assets less liabilities).

Where a company pays more than book value because the subsidiary's assets are undervalued or its liabilities are overvalued, the cost in excess of book value should be allocated to those assets and liabilities so that they are restated at fair values. After the subsidiary's assets and liabilities have been restated to reflect fair values, any remaining cost in excess

Illustration 16–5

PARENT COMPANY AND SUBSIDIARY
Consolidated Balance Sheet
January 1, 198A

Assets

Cash	$ 31,000	
Other assets	307,000	
Goodwill from consolidation	12,000	
Total assets		$350,000

Liabilities and Shareholders' Equity

Liabilities:		
Accounts payable		$ 22,000
Minority interest		23,000
Shareholders' equity:		
Common stock	$250,000	
Retained earnings	55,000	
Total shareholders' equity		305,000
Total liabilities and shareholders' equity		$350,000

of book value should be reported on the consolidated balance sheet as "Goodwill from consolidation."[7]

Occasionally, a parent company pays less than book value for its interest in a subsidiary. In such a case, since a "bargain" purchase is very unlikely, the logical reason for a price below book value is that certain of the subsidiary's assets are carried on its books at amounts in excess of fair value. In such a situation, the amounts at which the over-valued assets are placed on the consolidated balance sheet should be reduced accordingly.

EARNINGS AND DIVIDENDS OF A SUBSIDIARY

As previously discussed, a parent accounts for its investment in a subsidiary according to the equity method. As a consequence, the parent's recorded net income and Retained Earnings account include the parent's equity in the net income earned by the subsidiary since the date of acquisition. Also, the balance of the parent's Investment in Subsidiary account increases (or decreases) each year by an amount equal to the parent's equity in the subsidiary's earnings (or loss) less the parent's share of any dividends paid by the subsidiary.

For example, assume that Subsidiary Company of this illustration earned $12,500 during its first year as a subsidiary and at year-end paid out $7,500 in dividends. Parent company recorded its 80% equity in these earnings and dividends as follows:

Dec.	31	Investment in Subsidiary Company	10,000.00	
		Earnings from Investment in Subsidiary		10,000.00
		To record 80% of the net income reported by Subsidiary Company.		
Dec.	31	Cash	6,000.00	
		Investment in Subsidiary Company		6,000.00
		To record the receipt of 80% of the $7,500 dividend paid by Subsidiary Company.		

CONSOLIDATED BALANCE SHEETS AT A DATE AFTER ACQUISITION

Illustration 16–6 shows the December 31, 198B, work sheet to consolidate the balance sheets of Parent Company and Subsidiary Company. To simplify the illustration, it is assumed that Parent Company had no

[7] *CICA Handbook*, par. 1580.44.

transactions during the year other than to record its equity in Subsidiary Company's earnings and dividends. Also, the other assets and liabilities of Subsidiary Company did not change, and the subsidiary has not paid the note given Parent Company.

Compare Illustration 16–6 with 16–4 and note the changes in Parent Company's balance sheet (the first column). Parent Company's Cash increased from $16,000 to $22,000 as a result of the dividends received from the subsidiary. The Investment in Subsidiary Company account increased from $104,000 to $108,000 as a result of the equity method entries during the year. Finally, Parent Company's Retained Earnings increased by $10,000, which was the parent's equity in the subsidiary's earnings.

In the second column of Illustration 16–6, note only two changes: (1) Subsidiary Company's Cash balance increased by $5,000, which is the difference between its $12,500 net income and $7,500 payment of dividends; (2) Retained Earnings also increased from $15,000 to $20,000, which is the amount eliminated on the work sheet.

Two additional items in Illustration 16–6 require explanation. First, the minority interest set out on the year-end work sheet is greater than

Illustration 16–6

PARENT COMPANY AND SUBSIDIARY COMPANY
Work Sheet for a Consolidated Balance Sheet
December 31, 198B

	Parent Company	Subsidiary Company	Eliminations Debit	Eliminations Credit	Consolidated Amounts
Assets					
Cash	22,000	20,000			42,000
Notes receivable	10,000			(a) 10,000	
Investment in Subsidiary Company	108,000			(b) 108,000	
Other assets	190,000	117,000			307,000
Excess of cost over book value			(b) 12,000		12,000
	330,000	137,000			361,000
Liabilities and Equities					
Accounts payable	15,000	7,000			22,000
Notes payable		10,000	(a) 10,000		
Common stock	250,000	100,000	(b) 100,000		250,000
Retained earnings	65,000	20,000	(b) 20,000		65,000
Minority interest				(b) 24,000	24,000
	330,000	137,000	142,000	142,000	361,000

on the beginning-of-year work sheet (Illustration 16–4). The minority shareholders have a 20% equity in Subsidiary Company, and the $24,000 shown on the year-end work sheet is 20% of the year-end balances of the Subsidiary's Common Stock and Retained Earnings accounts. This $24,000 is $1,000 greater than the beginning-of-year minority interest because the subsidiary's retained earnings increased $5,000 during the year and the minority shareholder's share of this increase is 20% or $1,000. Second, the $12,000 amount set out as the excess cost of Parent Company's investment over its book value is, in this illustration, the same on the end-of-year work sheet as on the work sheet at the beginning. Such excess cost or ''goodwill'' should be amortized by systematic charges to income over the accounting periods estimated to be benefited.[8] An explanation of the amortization entries is left to a more advanced text.

OTHER CONSOLIDATED STATEMENTS

Consolidated income statements and consolidated retained earnings statements are also prepared for affiliated companies. However, a discussion of the procedures to prepare these statements is deferred to an advanced accounting course. Knowledge of the procedures is not necessary for a general understanding of such statements. At this point, the reader should recognize that all duplications in items and all profit arising from intercompany transactions are eliminated in their preparation. Also, the amounts of net income and retained earnings which are reported in consolidated statements are equal to the amounts recorded by the parent under the equity method.

THE CORPORATION BALANCE SHEET

A number of balance sheet sections have been illustrated in this and previous chapters. To bring together as much of the information from all these sections as space allows, the balance sheet of Betco Corporation is shown in Illustration 16–7.

Betco Corporation's balance sheet is a consolidated balance sheet, as indicated in the title and by the items ''Goodwill from consolidation'' and ''Minority interest.'' In preparing the balance sheet, Betco Corporation's investment in its subsidiary was eliminated. Consequently, the Toledo Corporation stock shown on the consolidated balance sheet represents an investment in an unconsolidated (outside) company that is not a subsidiary of either Betco or Betco's subsidiary.

---

[8] *CICA Handbook,* par. 1580.58.

Illustration 16–7

BETCO CORPORATION
Consolidated Balance Sheet
December 31, 198A

Assets

Current assets:

Cash		$ 15,000
Marketable securities		5,000
Accounts receivable	$ 50,000	
Less: Allowance for doubtful accounts	1,000	49,000
Merchandise inventory		115,000
Subscriptions receivable, common stock		15,000
Prepaid expenses		1,000
Total current assets		$200,000

Long-term investments:

Bond sinking fund		15,000
Toledo Corporation common stock		5,000
Total long-term investments		20,000

Plant assets:

Land		50,000
Buildings	285,000	
Less: Accumulated depreciation	30,000	255,000
Store equipment	85,000	
Less: Accumulated depreciation	20,000	65,000
Total plant assets		370,000

Intangible assets:

Goodwill from consolidation		10,000
Total assets		$600,000

Liabilities

Current liabilities:

Notes payable	$ 10,000	
Accounts payable	14,000	
Income taxes payable	16,000	
Total current liabilities		$ 40,000

Long-term liabilities:

First 8% real estate mortgage bonds, due in 199E	100,000	
Less: Unamortized discount based on the 8¼% market rate for bond interest prevailing on the date of issue	2,000	98,000
Total liabilities		$138,000
Minority interest		15,000

Shareholders' Equity

Contributed capital:

Common stock, no par value, issued 30,000 shares of which 1,000 are in the treasury		333,000
Unissued common stock subscribed, 2,500 shares		25,000
Total contributed capital		358,000
Retained earnings (Note 1)		105,000
Total contributed and retained capital		463,000
Less: Cost of treasury stock		16,000
Total shareholders' equity		447,000
Total liabilities and shareholders' equity		$600,000

Note 1: Retained earnings in the amount of $31,000 is restricted under an agreement with the corporation's bondholders and because of the purchase of treasury stock, leaving $74,000 of retained earnings not so restricted.

GLOSSARY

Appropriated retained earnings. Retained earnings voluntarily earmarked for a special use as a means of informing shareholders that assets from earnings equal to the appropriations are unavailable for dividends.

Cost method of accounting for stock investments. The investment is recorded at total cost and maintained at that amount; subsequent investee earnings and dividends do not affect the investment account.

Earned surplus. A synonym for retained earnings, no longer in use.

Equity method of accounting for stock investments. The investment is recorded at total cost, investor's equity in subsequent earnings of the investee increases the investment account, and subsequent dividends of the investee reduce the investment account.

Long-term investments. Investments, not intended as a ready source of cash in case of need, such as bond sinking funds, land, and marketable securities that are not held as a temporary investment of cash.

Marketable equity securities. Common and preferred stocks that are actively traded so that sales prices or bid and ask prices are currently available on a national securities exchange or in the over-the-counter market.

Minority interest. Shareholders' equity in a subsidiary not owned by the parent corporation.

Parent company. A corporation that owns a controlling interest (more than 50% of the voting stock is required) in another corporation.

Restricted retained earnings. Retained earnings that are unavailable for dividends as a result of law or binding contract.

Stock dividend. A distribution by a corporation of shares of its own common stock to its common shareholders without any consideration being received in return therefor.

Stock split. The act of a corporation of calling in its stock and issuing more than one new share in exchange for each share previously outstanding. Also known as stock split-up.

Subsidiary. A corporation that is controlled by another (parent) corporation because the parent owns more than 50% of the subsidiary's voting stock.

Treasury stock. Issued stock that has been reacquired by the issuing corporation.

QUESTIONS FOR CLASS DISCUSSION

1. What effect does the declaration of a cash dividend have on the assets, liabilities, and shareholders' equity of the corporation that declares the dividend? What is the effect of the subsequent payment of the cash dividend?

2. What effect does the declaration of a stock dividend have on the assets, liabilities, and total shareholders' equity of the corporation that declares the dividend? What is the effect of the subsequent distribution of the stock dividend?

3. What amount of retained earnings should be capitalized in accounting for a stock dividend?

4. What is the difference between a stock dividend and a stock split?

5. If a balance sheet is prepared between the date of declaration and the date of payment (or distribution) of a dividend, how should the dividend be shown if it is *(a)* a cash dividend, or *(b)* a stock dividend?

6. What is treasury stock? How is it like unissued stock? How does it differ from unissued stock? What is the legal significance of this difference?

7. Western Products Corporation bought 10,000 shares of National Iron Corporation stock and turned it over to the treasurer of Western Products for safekeeping. Is this treasury stock? Why or why not?

8. What effect does the purchase of treasury stock have on assets and total shareholders' equity?

9. Distinguish between issued stock and outstanding stock.

10. Why do laws place limitations on the purchase of treasury stock?

11. What is meant by *marketable securities?*

12. Under what conditions should a stock investment be classified as a current asset?

13. In accounting for common stock investments, when should the cost method be used? When should the equity method be used?

14. When a parent corporation uses the equity method to account for its investment in a subsidiary, what recognition is given by the parent corporation to the income or loss reported by the subsidiary? What recognition is given to dividends declared by the subsidiary?

15. What are consolidated financial statements?

16. What account balances must be eliminated in preparing a consolidated balance sheet? Why are they eliminated?

17. Why would a parent corporation pay more than book value for the stock of a subsidiary?

18. When a parent pays more than book value for the stock of a subsidiary, how should this additional cost be reported in the consolidated balance sheet?

19. What is meant by *minority interest?* Where is this item disclosed on a consolidated balance sheet?

MULTIPLE CHOICE

1. Dividends become a liability of a corporation:
   - *a.* If not declared on cumulative preferred stock.
   - *b.* When they are in arrears.
   - *c.* When declared by the board of directors.
   - *d.* On the record date.
   - *e.* On the payment date.

2. Issued stock that has been reacquired and canceled by the issuing corporation is:
   - *a.* Capital stock.
   - *b.* Treasury stock.
   - *c.* Retired stock.
   - *d.* Preferred stock.
   - *e.* All of the above.

3. X Company paid $45,000 for 500 shares of Y Company's common stock, of which there are 10,000 shares outstanding. In the first year after the purchase, Y Company reported net income of $100,000, paid total cash dividends of $60,000 to common shares, and declared a common stock dividend of 1,000 shares. After these events, X Company's balance in its investment in Y Company common stock account should be:
   - *a.* $45,000.
   - *b.* $47,000.
   - *c.* $50,000.
   - *d.* $55,000.
   - *e.* $57,000.

4. The investment is recorded at total cost; investor's equity in subsequent earnings of the investee increases the investment account; and subsequent dividends of the investee reduce the investment account in the:
   - *a.* Gross method of accounting for stock investments.
   - *b.* Purchase method of accounting for stock investments.
   - *c.* Equity method of accounting for stock investments.
   - *d.* Cost method of accounting for stock investments.
   - *e.* Net method of accounting for stock investments.

5. Which one of the following items is likely to be affected by a stock split?
   - *a.* Total assets.
   - *b.* Market value per share of stock.
   - *c.* Total shareholders' equity.
   - *d.* Total book value of the shares held by an individual shareholder.
   - *e.* All of the above.

6. Failure to record the declaration and distribution of a dividend in stock would:

    a.   Cause the balance sheet to be out of balance.
    b.   Cause the outstanding stock to exceed the shareholders' equity.
    c.   Cause an understatement of shareholders' equity.
    d.   Cause an overstatement of shareholders' equity.
    e.   Have no effect on total shareholders' equity.

7.   When a subsidiary pays a cash dividend, the parent company records receipt of its share with:

    a.   A credit to its investment in the Subsidiary Company account.
    b.   A credit to its Retained Earnings account.
    c.   A credit to its earnings from investment in the Subsidiary Company account.
    d.   A debit to its investment in the Subsidiary Company account.
    e.   None of these.

8.   On January 1, 198A, P Company purchased 90% of S Company's outstanding stock for $57,000. On that date, P Company's shareholders' equity included common stock of $100,000 and retained earnings of $50,000; S Company's shareholders' equity included common stock of $50,000 and retained earnings of $10,000. During 198A, P Company earned a net income of $10,000 and paid dividends of $5,000; S Company earned $7,000 and paid dividends of $1,000. What amount of minority interest should be disclosed on the December 31, 198A, consolidated balance sheet?

    a. $6,900.
    b. $6,600.
    c. $6,500.
    d. $6,300.
    e. $6,000.

9.   In regard to consolidated statements, which one of the following statements is true:

    a.   Minority interest is a current liability on the consolidated balance sheet.
    b.   Goodwill from consolidation arises when the cost of the parent's investment in the subsidiary is more than the fair value of the subsidiary's net assets (assets less liabilities).
    c.   If the parent clearly has a significant financial influence over the subsidiary, consolidated financial statements should be prepared even though the parent may own less than 50% of the subsidiary's outstanding stock.
    d.   Consolidated financial statements are the primary source of information used by minority interests in evaluating the activities of a subsidiary.
    e.   None of the above is true.

MINI DISCUSSION CASE

Case 16–1   The acquisition of previously issued shares, whether for retirement or for subsequent reissue, continues to be a controversial matter. There are people who argue that there is something unsavory about a corporation "trafficking" in its own shares. On the other hand, there are people who hold that a corporation should have a wide latitude in adjusting its capital structure.

Required:

Discuss the pros and cons of a corporation's right to reacquire its own shares for:
a.   Retirement.
b.   For reissue at a future date.

CLASS EXERCISES

Exercise 16–1   Shareholders' equity in a corporation (incorporated under federal laws) appeared as follows on May 15:

Common stock, no-par value, 200,000 shares	
authorized, 36,000 shares issued	$388,800
Retained earnings	50,000
Total shareholders' equity	$438,800

On May 15, when the stock was selling at $12.50 per share, the corporation's directors voted a 5% stock dividend distributable on June 10 to the May 25 shareholders of record. The stock was selling at $12.00 per share at the close of business on June 11.

Required:

1. Prepare general journal entries to record the declaration and distribution of the dividend.
2. Under the assumption that Patricia Kelley owned 900 of the shares on May 15 and received her dividend shares on June 10, prepare a schedule showing the numbers of shares she held on May 15 and June 11, with their total book values and total market values. Assume no change in total shareholders' equity from May 15 to June 11.

Exercise 16–2   On June 30, 198A, the stock of a corporation was selling for $150 per share and the shareholders' equity section of the corporation's balance sheet appeared as follows:

Common stock, no-par value, unlimited number of shares
   authorized, 5,000 shares issued $300,000
Retained earnings 400,000
     Total shareholders' equity $700,000

Required:

1. Assume that the corporation declares and immediately issues a 100% stock dividend and capitalizes an amount per share equal to the average stated capital of retained earnings. Answer the following questions about the shareholders' equity of the corporation after the new shares are issued:

    a. What will be the retained earnings balance?
    b. What will be the total amount of shareholders' equity?
    c. How many shares will be outstanding?

2. Assume that instead of declaring a 100% stock dividend, the corporation split its stock 2 for 1. Answer the following questions about the shareholders' equity of the corporation after the stock split takes place:

    a. What will be the retained earnings balance?
    b. What will be the total amount of shareholders' equity?
    c. How many shares will be outstanding?

Exercise 16–3   The shareholders' equity section of Kratovil Company's December 31, 198A, balance sheet is as follows:

Common stock, no-par value, 150,000 shares
   authorized, 60,000 shares issued $480,000
Retained earnings 120,000
     Total shareholders' equity $600,000

On the date of the balance sheet, the company purchased and retired 1,000 shares of its common stock. Prepare general journal entries to record the purchase and retirement under each of the following independent assumptions: *(a)* the stock was purchased for $6 per share, *(b)* the stock was purchased for $8 per share, *(c)* the stock was purchased for $12 per share.

Exercise 16–4   On April 30, the shareholders' equity section of a corporation's balance sheet appeared as follows:

Shareholders' Equity

Common stock, no-par value, 17,500 shares
   authorized and issued $437,500
Retained earnings 148,750
     Total shareholders' equity $586,250

On April 30, the corporation purchased 500 shares of treasury stock at $40 per share. Give the entry to record the purchase and prepare a shareholders' equity section as it would appear immediately after the purchase.

Exercise 16–5

On May 29, the corporation of Exercise 16–3 sold at $44 per share 200 of the treasury shares purchased on April 30, and on October 12, it sold the remaining treasury shares at $34 per share. Prepare general journal entries to record the sales.

Exercise 16–6

Prepare general journal entries to record the following events on the books of X Company:

198A
Jan. 3   Purchased 5,000 shares of Y Company's common stock for $62,500 plus broker's fee of $1,750. Y Company has 100,000 shares of common stock outstanding, and X Company does not have a significant influence on Y Company policies.
May 11   Y Company declared and paid a cash dividend of $0.60 per share.
Dec. 31   Y Company announced that net income for the year amounted to $75,000.

198B
May 20   Y Company declared and paid a cash dividend of $0.30 per share.
Aug. 18   Y Company declared and issued a stock dividend of one additional share for each 10 shares already outstanding. The board of directors decided that $10 per share of retained earnings is to be capitalized.
Dec. 29   X Company sold 2,750 shares of Y Company for $35,000.
      31   Y Company announced that net income for the year amounted to $40,000.

Exercise 16–7

Prepare general journal entries to record the following events on the books of Echo Company:

198A
Jan. 2   Purchased 5,000 shares of Hotel Company for $62,500 plus a broker's fee of $1,750. Hotel Company has 25,000 shares of common stock outstanding and has acknowledged the fact that its policies will be significantly influenced by Echo Company.
May 16   Hotel Company declared and paid a cash dividend of $0.60 per share.
Dec. 31   Hotel Company announced that net income for the year amounted to $64,000.

198B
May 28   Hotel Company declared and paid a cash dividend of $1.20 per share.
Aug. 21   Hotel Company declared and issued a stock dividend of one additional share for each 10 shares already outstanding. The board of directors decided that $10 per share of retained earnings is to be capitalized.
Dec. 31   Hotel Company announced that net income for the year amounted to $44,000.
      31   Echo Company sold 2,750 shares of Hotel Company for $35,000.

Exercise 16–8

On December 31, 198A, X Company and Y Company each purchased 6,000 shares of N Company stock at a cost of $15 per share. On that date, the shareholders' equity of N Company appeared as follows:

Common stock (30,000 shares) ...	$300,000
Retained earnings	150,000
Total	$450,000

Because of certain legal agreements, Y Company does not have a significant influence over N Company. However, X Company is presumed to have a significant influence over N Company.

During 198B and 198C, N Company earned an annual net income of $50,000 and paid cash dividends of $20,000 each year. On December 31, 198C, calculate the carrying value of (a) X Company's investment in N Company, and (b) Y Company's investment in N Company.

Exercise 16–9

On December 31, S Company had the following shareholders' equity:

Common stock, 75,000 shares issued and outstanding ...	$ 75,000
Total earnings	45,000
Total shareholders' equity	$120,000

On the same day (December 31), P Company purchased 50,000 of S Company's outstanding shares, paying $2 per share, and a work sheet to consolidate the balance sheets of the two companies was prepared. In general journal form, give the entry made on this work sheet to eliminate P Company's investment and the related shareholders' equity accounts of S Company.

Exercise 16–10

During the year following its acquisition by P Company (see Exercise 16–9), S Company earned $15,000, paid out $9,000 in dividends, and retained the balance for use in its operations. In general journal form, give the entry to eliminate P Company's investment and S Company's shareholders' equity account balances as of the end of the year.

PROBLEMS

Problem 16–1

Riviera Corporation's shareholders' equity (incorporated under federal laws) at the beginning of the current year consisted of the following:

Common stock, no-par value, unlimited number of shares authorized, 9,600 shares issued	$276,000
Retained earnings	92,000
Total shareholders' equity	$368,000

During the year, the company completed these transactions:

Apr.	9	Purchased 800 shares of treasury stock at $38 per share.
	29	The directors voted a $0.40 per share cash dividend payable on May 28 to the May 14 shareholders of record.
May	28	Paid the dividend declared on Apr. 29.
July	18	Sold 400 of the treasury shares at $43 per share.
Oct.	11	Sold 400 of the treasury shares at $35 per share.
Dec.	20	The directors voted a $0.40 per share cash dividend payable on January 27 to the January 15 shareholders of record, and they voted a 2% stock dividend distributable on February 16 to the February 1 shareholders of record. The market value of the stock was $39 per share.
	31	Closed the Income Summary account and carried the company's $24,500 net income to Retained Earnings.

Required:

1. Prepare general journal entries to record the transactions.
2. Prepare a retained earnings statement for the year and the shareholders' equity section of the company's year-end balance sheet.

Problem 16–2   Last September 30, Tortolla Corporation had a $540,000 credit balance in its retained earnings account. On that date, the corporation's contributed capital consisted of 50,000 authorized shares of common stock, of which 6,000 shares had been issued at $110 and were outstanding. It then completed the following transactions:

Oct. 1 The board of directors declared a $24 per share dividend on the common stock, payable on November 3 to the October 20 shareholders of record.

Nov. 3 Paid the dividend declared on October 1.
    10 The board declared a 10% stock dividend, distributable on December 5 to the November 24 shareholders of record. The stock was selling at $120 per share, and the directors voted to use this amount in recording the dividend.

Dec. 5 Distributed the stock dividend declared on November 10.
    31 On this day the company earned $165,000, and then closed the Income Summary account.

Jan. 9 The board of directors voted to split the corporation's stock 5 for 1. The shareholders voted approval of the split. All legal requirements were met, and the split was completed on February 8.

Required.

1. Prepare general journal entries to record these transactions and to close the Income Summary account at year-end. (No entry is required for the split; however, a memorandum reciting the facts would be entered in the Common Stock account.)
2. Under the assumption Jay Evans owned 500 shares on September 30 and neither bought nor sold any shares during the period of the transactions, prepare a schedule with columns for the date, supporting calculations, book value per share, and book value of Evans's shares. Then complete the schedule by calculating the book value per share of the corporation's stock and the book value of Evans's shares at the close of business on September 30, October 1, November 3, December 5, December 31, and February 8.
3. Prepare three shareholders' equity sections for the corporation, the first showing the shareholders' equity on September 30, the second on December 31, and the third on February 8. Assume that the only income earned by the company during these periods was the $165,000 earned and closed on December 31.

Problem 16–3   The equity sections from the 198A and 198B balance sheets of Moran Industries, Inc., appeared as follows:

**Shareholders' Equity
(As of December 31, 198A**

Common stock, no-par value, unlimited number of shares authorized, 60,000 shares issued .	$ 720,000
Retained earnings	585,480
Total shareholders' equity	$1,305,480

Shareholders' Equity
(As of December 31, 198B)

Common stock, no-par value, unlimited number of shares authorized, 65,940 shares issued of which 600 are in the treasury	$ 862,560
Retained earnings	471,180
Total	$1,333,740
Less: Cost of treasury stock	12,600
Total shareholders' equity	$1,321,140

On March 9, June 3, August 27, and again on November 14, 198B, the board of directors declared $0.30 per share dividends on the outstanding stock. The treasury stock was purchased on June 26. On August 27, while the stock was selling for $24 per share, the corporation declared a 10% stock dividend on the outstanding shares. The board of directors used the market price of the shares to record the stock dividend. The new shares were issued on September 18.

Required:

Under the assumption that there were no transactions affecting retained earnings other than the ones given, determine the 198B net income of Moran Industries, Inc. Show your calculations.

Problem 16–4   Holder Company was organized on January 1, 198A, for the purpose of investing in the shares of other companies. Holder Company immediately issued 30,000 shares of common stock for which it received $150,000 cash. On January 6, 198A, Holder Company purchased 8,000 shares (20%) of Tarton Company's outstanding stock at a cost of $150,000. The following transactions and events subsequently occurred:

198A
May   31   Tarton Company declared and paid a cash dividend of $1.50 per share.
Dec. 31   Tarton Company announced that its net income for the year was $90,000.
198B
July   14   Tarton Company declared and issued a stock dividend of one share for each two shares already outstanding.
Sept. 9   Tarton Company declared and paid a cash dividend of $1.00 per share.
Dec. 31   Tarton Company announced that its net income for the year was $75,000.
198C
Jan.   2   Holder Company sold all of its investment in Tarton Company for $168,000 cash.

Part 1.   Because Holder Company owns 20% of Tarton Company's outstanding stock and participates in policy-making processes, Holder Company is presumed to have a significant influence over Tarton Company.

Required:

1. Give the entries on the books of Holder Company to record the above events regarding its investment in Tarton Company.
2. Calculate the cost per share of Holder Company's investment, as reflected in the investment account on January 1, 198C.

3. Calculate Holder Company's retained earnings balance on January 3, 198C, after a closing of the books.

Part 2. Although Holder Company owns 20% of Tarton Company's outstanding stock, a thorough investigation of the surrounding circumstances indicates that Holder Company does not have a significant influence over Tarton Company, and the cost method is the appropriate method of accounting for the investment.

Required:

1. Give the entries on the books of Holder Company to record the above events regarding its investment in Tarton Company.
2. Calculate the cost per share of Holder Company's investment, as reflected in the investment account on January 1, 198C.
3. Calculate Holder Company's retained earnings balance on January 3, 198C, after a closing of the books.

Problem 16–5   *Part 1.* On January 1, 198A, Brownwood Company Inc., purchased 80% of Mondak Company's outstanding stock at $32 per share. On that date, Brownwood Company had retained earnings of $345,000. Mondak Company Inc. had retained earnings of $90,000, and had outstanding 15,000 shares of common stock originally issued at $10 per share.

Required:

1. Give the elimination entry to be used on a work sheet for a consolidated balance sheet dated January 1, 198A.
2. Determine the amount of consolidated retained earnings that should be shown on a consolidated balance sheet dated January 1, 198A.

Part 2. During the year ended December 31, 198A, Brownwood Company Inc., paid cash dividends of $45,000 and earned a net income of $85,000 excluding earnings from its investment in Mondak Company Inc. Mondak Company Inc., earned net income of $42,000 and paid dividends of $20,000. Except for Brownwood Company's Retained Earnings account and the Investment in Mondak Company account, the balance sheet accounts for the two companies on December 31, 198A, are as follows:

	Brownwood Company Inc.	Mondak Company Inc.
Cash	$105,200	$ 82,800
Notes receivable	36,000	
Merchandise	244,800	118,800
Building (net)	232,000	144,000
Land	140,000	126,000
Investment in Mondak Company Inc.	?	
Total assets	$?	$471,600
Accounts payable	$293,000	$173,600
Note payable		36,000
Common stock	448,000	150,000
Retained earnings	?	112,000
Total liabilities and shareholders' equity	$?	$471,600

Brownwood Company Inc., loaned $36,000 to Mondak Company Inc., during 198A, for which Mondak Company Inc., signed a note. On December 31, 198A, the note had not been repaid.

Required:

1. Calculate the December 31, 198A, balances in Brownwood Company's Investment in Mondak Company account and Retained Earnings account.
2. Complete a work sheet to consolidate the balance sheets of the two companies.

Problem 16–6   The following items appeared in the first two columns of a work sheet prepared to consolidate the balance sheets of Parent Corporation and Subsidiary Corporation on the day Parent Corporation gained control of Subsidiary Corporation by purchasing 21,250 shares of its common stock at $13 per share. Subsidiary Corporation had 25,000 common shares outstanding.

	Parent Corporation	Subsidiary Corporation
Assets		
Cash	$ 18,750	$ 27,500
Note receivable, Subsidiary Corporation	25,000	
Accounts receivable, net	70,000	60,000
Inventories	105,000	87,500
Investment in Subsidiary Corporation	276,250	
Equipment, net	200,000	175,000
Buildings, net	212,500	
Land	50,000	
Total assets	$957,500	$350,000
Liabilities and Shareholders' Equity		
Accounts payable	$ 52,500	$ 25,000
Note payable, Parent Corporation		25,000
Common stock	625,000	250,000
Retained earnings	280,000	50,000
Total liabilities and shareholders' equity	$957,500	$350,000

At the time Parent Corporation acquired control of Subsidiary Corporation, it took Subsidiary Corporation's note in exchange for $25,000 in cash, and it sold and delivered $5,000 of equipment at cost to Subsidiary Corporation on open account (account receivable). Both transactions are reflected in the foregoing accounts.

Required:

1. Prepare a work sheet to consolidate the balance sheets of the two companies and prepare a consolidated balance sheet.
2. Under the assumption that Subsidiary Corporation earned $25,000 during the first year after it was acquired by Parent Corporation, paid out $15,000 in dividends, and retained the balance of its earnings in its operations, give the entry to eliminate Parent Corporation's investment in the subsidiary and Subsidiary Corporation's shareholders' equity accounts at the year's end.

ALTERNATE PROBLEMS

Problem 16–1A

Dapper Corporation's shareholders' equity at the beginning of the current year consisted of the following:

Common stock, 800,000 shares authorized, 408,000 shares issued	$469,200
Retained earnings	156,400
Total shareholders' equity	$625,600

During the year, the company completed these transactions:

Feb. 12 Purchased 20,000 shares of treasury stock at $1.20 per share.
Mar. 26 The directors voted a $0.05 per share cash dividend payable on April 21 to the April 10 shareholders of record.
Apr. 21 Paid the dividend declared on Mar. 26.
June 9 Sold 8,000 of the treasury shares at $1.40 per share.
Nov. 6 Sold 12,000 of the treasury shares at $0.90 per share.
Dec. 22 The directors voted a $0.05 per share cash dividend payable on January 14 to the January 1 shareholders of record, and they voted a 3% stock dividend distributable on February 1 to the January 15 shareholders of record. The market value of $1.10 per share was used to record the stock dividend.
31 Closed the Income Summary account and carried the company's $56,000 net income to Retained Earnings.

Required:

1. Prepare general journal entries to record the transactions.
2. Prepare a retained earnings statement for the year and the shareholders' equity section of the company's year-end balance sheet.

Problem 16–2A

Last March 31, St. Thomas Corporation, a federal corporation, had a $2.5 million credit balance in its Retained Earnings account. On that date, the corporation's contributed capital consisted of an unlimited number of shares of common stock of which 100,000 shares had been issued at $15 and were outstanding. It then completed the following transactions:

Apr. 1 The board of directors declared a $4 per share dividend on the common stock, payable on May 5 to the April 18 shareholders of record.
May 5 Paid the dividend declared on April 1.
10 The board declared a 20% stock dividend, distributable on June 12 to the May 26 shareholders of record. The stock was selling at $45 per share, and the directors voted to use this amount in recording the dividend.
June 12 Distributed the stock dividend declared on May 10.
30 On this day, the corporation earned $600,000 which was closed from Income Summary to Retained Earnings.
July 15 The board of directors voted to split the corporation's stock 5 for 1. The shareholders voted approval of the split. All legal requirements were met, and the split was completed on August 4.

Required:

1. Prepare general journal entries to record these transactions and to close the Income Summary account at year-end. (No entry is required for the split; however, a memorandum reciting the facts would be entered in the Common Stock account.)

2. Under the assumption Karen Froh owned 2,500 of the shares on March 31 and neither bought nor sold any shares during the period of the transactions, prepare a schedule with columns for the date, supporting calculations, book value per share, and book value of Froh's shares. Then complete the schedule by calculating the book value per share of the corporation's stock and the book value of Froh's shares at the close of business on March 31, April 1, May 5, June 12, June 30, and July 15.

3. Prepare three shareholders' equity sections for the corporation, the first showing the shareholders' equity on March 31, the second on June 30, and the third on July 15. Assume that the only income earned by the company during these periods was the $600,000 earned and closed on June 30.

Problem 16–3A

The equity sections from the 198A and 198B balance sheets of Berry Island Corporation appeared as follows:

Shareholders' Equity
(As of December 31, 198A)

Common stock, 400,000 shares authorized,
 75,000 shares issued . . . . $ 900,000
Retained earnings   731,850
  Total shareholders' equity $1,631,850

Shareholders' Equity
(As of December 31, 198B)

Common stock, 400,000 shares authorized,
 78,650 shares issued of which 2,000
 are in the treasury $1,009,500
Retained earnings   588,975
  Total $1,598,475
Less: Cost of treasury stock   44,000
  Total shareholders' equity $1,554,475

On March 1, May 28, August 30, and again on November 20, 198B, the board of directors declared $0.40 per share dividends on the outstanding stock. The treasury stock was purchased on June 15. On August 30, while the stock was selling for $30 per share, the corporation declared a 5% stock dividend on the outstanding shares. The new shares were issued on September 27. The market value of the shares was used to record the dividend.

Required:

Under the assumption that there were no transactions affecting retained earnings other than the ones given, determine the 198B net income of Berry Island Corporation. Show your calculations.

Problem 16–4A

Buyer Company was organized on January 1, 198A, for the purpose of investing in the shares of other companies. Buyer Company immediately issued 36,000 shares of common stock for which it received $180,000 cash. On January 6, 198A, Buyer Company purchased 16,000 shares (20%) of Hunter Company's outstanding stock at a cost of $180,000. The following transactions and events subsequently occurred:

198A
Apr. 30 Hunter Company declared and paid a cash dividend of $0.80 per share.
Dec. 31 Hunter Company announced that its net income for the year was $130,000.
198B
July 1 Hunter Company declared and issued a stock dividend of one share for each four shares already outstanding.
Oct. 15 Hunter Company declared and paid a cash dividend of $0.75 per share.
Dec. 31 Hunter Company announced that its net income for the year was $140,000.
198C
Jan. 3 Buyer Company sold all of its investment in Hunter Company for $200,000 cash.

Part 1.   Because Buyer Company owns 20% of Hunter Company's outstanding stock and participates in policy-making processes, Buyer Company is presumed to have a significant influence over Hunter Company.

Required:

1. Give the entries on the books of Buyer Company to record the above events regarding its investment in Hunter Company.
2. Calculate the cost per share of Buyer Company's investment, as reflected in the investment account on January 2, 198C.
3. Calculate Buyer Company's retained earnings balance on January 4, 198C, after a closing of the books.

Part 2.   Although Buyer Company owns 20% of Hunter Company's outstanding stock, a thorough investigation of the surrounding circumstances indicates that Buyer Company does not have a significant influence over Hunter Company, and the cost method is the appropriate method of accounting for the investment.

Required:

1. Give the entries on the books of Buyer Company to record the above events regarding its investment in Hunter Company.
2. Calculate the cost per share of Buyer Company's investment, as reflected in the investment account on January 2, 198C.
3. Calculate Buyer Company's retained earnings balance on January 4, 198C, after a closing of the books.

Problem 16–5A

Part 1.   On January 1, 198A, Bigtime Corporation purchased 90% of Littletime Corporation's outstanding stock at $48 per share. On that date, Bigtime had retained earnings of $517,500. Littletime had retained earnings of $210,000, and had outstanding 15,000 shares of common stock, originally issued at $10 per share.

Required:

1. Give the elimination entry to be used on a work sheet for a consolidated balance sheet dated January 1, 198A.
2. Determine the amount of consolidated retained earnings that should be shown on a consolidated balance sheet dated January 1, 198A.

Part 2. During the year ended December 31, 198A, Bigtime paid cash dividends of $67,500 and earned net income of $127,500 excluding earnings from its investment in Littletime. Littletime earned net income of $63,000 and paid dividends of $30,000. Except for Bigtime's Retained Earnings account and the Investment in Littletime Corporation account, the balance sheet accounts for the two companies on December 31, 198A, are as follows:

	Bigtime Corporation	Littletime Corporation
Cash	$160,800	$124,200
Notes receivable	54,000	
Merchandise	295,200	178,200
Building (net)	348,000	216,000
Land	210,000	189,000
Investment in Littletime Corporation	?	
Total assets	$?	$707,400
Accounts payable	$439,500	$260,400
Note payable		54,000
Common stock	672,000	150,000
Retained earnings	?	243,000
Total liabilities and shareholders' equity	$?	$707,400

Bigtime loaned $54,000 to Littletime during 198A, for which Littletime signed a note. On December 31, 198A, the note had not been repaid.

Required:

1. Calculate the December 31, 198A, balances in Bigtime Corporation's Investment in Littletime Corporation account and Retained Earnings account.
2. Complete a work sheet to consolidate the balance sheets of the two companies.

Problem 16–6A

The following items appeared in the first two columns of a work sheet prepared to consolidate the balance sheets of Top Corporation and Bottom Corporation on the day Top gained control of Bottom by purchasing 12,750 shares of its common stock at $65 per share. Bottom had outstanding 15,000 common shares.

At the time Top acquired control of Bottom, it took Bottom's note in exchange for $64,000 in cash, and it sold and delivered $25,000 of equipment at cost to

	Top Corporation	Bottom Corporation
Assets		
Cash	$ 67,250	$ 82,500
Note receivable, Bottom Corporation	64,000	
Accounts receivable, net	210,000	180,000
Inventories	315,000	262,500
Investment in Bottom Corporation	828,750	
Equipment, net	600,000	525,000
Buildings, net	637,500	
Land	150,000	
Total assets	$2,872,500	$1,050,000

Liabilities and Shareholders' Equity

Accounts payable	$ 157,500	$ 86,000
Note payable, Top Corporation		64,000
Common stock	1,875,000	750,000
Retained earnings	840,000	150,000
Total liabilities and shareholders' equity	$2,872,500	$1,050,000

Bottom on open account (Account Receivable). Both transactions are reflected in the foregoing accounts.

Required:

1. Prepare a work sheet to consolidate the balance sheets of the two companies and prepare a consolidated balance sheet.
2. Under the assumption that Bottom earned $75,000 during the first year after it was acquired by Top, paid out $45,000 in dividends, and retained the balance of its earnings in its operations, give the entry to eliminate Top Corporation's investment in the subsidiary and Bottom Corporation's shareholders equity accounts at the year's end.

PROVOCATIVE PROBLEMS

Provocative
Problem 16–1,
Farmtree
Corporation

On January 1, 198A, Bob Algoe purchased 500 shares of Farmtree Corporation stock at $37.50 per share. On that date, the corporation had the following shareholders' equity:

Common stock, 400,000 shares authorized, 200,000 shares issued and outstanding	$5,625,000
Retained earnings	1,400,000
Total shareholders' equity	$7,025,000

Since purchasing the 500 shares, Mr. Algoe has neither purchased nor sold any additional shares of the company's stock; and on December 31 of each year, he has received dividends on the shares held as follows: 198A, $825; 198B, $1,031.25; and 198C, $1,375.

On May 15, 198A, at a time when its stock was selling for $43.75 per share, Farmtree Corporation declared a 10% stock dividend which was distributed one month later. On September 22, 198B, the corporation split its stock 2 for 1; and on April 7, 198C, it purchased 10,000 shares of treasury stock at $22.50 per share. The shares were still in its treasury at year-end.

Required:

Under the assumption that Farmtree Corporation's stock had a book value of $33.75 per share on December 31, 198A, a book value of $18.00 per share on December 31, 198B, and a book value of $19.25 on December 31, 198C, do the following:

1. Prepare statements showing the nature of the shareholders' equity in the corporation at the end of 198A, 198B, and 198C.

2. Prepare a schedule showing the amount of the corporation's net income for each of 198A, 198B, and 198C, under the assumption that the changes in the company's retained earnings during the three-year period resulted solely from earnings and dividends.

Provocative Problem 16–2, MoCity Company

MoCity Company's shareholders' equity on October 15 consisted of the following amounts:

Common stock, 300,000 shares authorized, 70,000 shares issued and outstanding . . .	$4,025,000
Retained earnings	2,275,000
Total shareholders' equity	$6,300,000

On October 15, when the stock was selling at $100 per share, the corporation's directors voted a 20% stock dividend, distributable on November 5 to the October 22 shareholders of record. The directors also voted a $4.25 per share annual cash dividend, payable on December 25 to the December 12 shareholders of record. The amount of the latter dividend was a disappointment to some shareholders, since the company had for a number of years paid a $5.00 per share annual cash dividend.

Julie Stewart owned 1,000 shares of MoCity Company stock on October 22, which she had purchased a number of years ago, and as a result she received her dividend shares. She continued to hold all of her shares until after she received the December 25 cash dividend. However, she did note that her stock had a $100 per share market value on October 15, a market value it held until the close of business on October 22, when the market value declined to $87.50 per share.

Give the entries to record the declaration and payment of the dividends involved here, and answer these questions:

a. What was the book value of Stewart's total shares on October 15, and what was the book value on November 5, after she received the dividend shares?

b. What fraction of the corporation did Stewart own on October 15, and what fraction did she own on November 5?

c. What was the market value of Stewart's total shares on October 15, and what was the market value at the close of business on October 22?

d. What did Stewart gain from the stock dividend?

Provocative Problem 16–3, Questions from Shareholders

When corporations have their annual meetings with shareholders, the managements often have to deal with difficult questions from shareholders. For example, at the recent shareholders' meeting of Tekcon, Inc., one of the shareholders made the following statement:

I have owned shares of Tekcon for several years, but am now questioning whether management is telling the truth in the annual financial statements. At the end of 1983, you announced that Tekcon had just acquired a 30% interest in the outstanding stock of Fibercrete Corporation. You also stated that the 112,000 shares had cost Tekcon about $11,200,000. In the financial statements for 1984, you told us that the investments of Tekcon were proving to be very profitable, and reported that earnings from all investments had amounted to more than $3.22 million. In the financial statements for 1985, you explained that Tekcon had sold the Fibercrete shares during the first week of the year, receiving $12,740,000 cash proceeds from the sale. Nevertheless, the income statement for 1985 reports only a $280,000 gain on the sale (before taxes). I realize that Fibercrete did not pay any dividends during 1984, but it was very profitable. As I recall, it reported net income of $4,200,000 for 1984. Personally, I do not think you should have sold the shares. But, much more importantly, you reported to us that our company gained only $280,000 from the sale. How can that be true if the shares were purchased for $11,200,000 and were sold for $12,740,000?

Explain to this shareholder why the $280,000 gain is correctly reported.

Provocative Problem 16–4, American Motor Inns, Incorporated

American Motor Inns, Inc. (AMI), is engaged in the business of operating hotels and restaurants. In 1983, the company operated hotels in nine states and in St. Thomas in the U.S. Virgin Islands. The 1983 annual report of AMI included the following footnote to its financial statements:

(7) MINORITY INTEREST IN SUBSIDIARY
In December 1980, the Company's previously wholly owned subsidiary, Universal Communication Systems, Inc., sold 750,000 shares of its common stock to the public resulting in net proceeds of $8,725,000. This reduced the Company's holding in that subsidiary to approximately 84% of the outstanding common stock.

Given this information, would you expect American Motor Inns' 1980 (and years thereafter) consolidated financial statements to reflect its investment in Universal Communication Systems according to the equity method? Why or why not? Also, assume that American Motor Inns, Inc., prepared a consolidated balance sheet immediately after the subsidiary's sale of stock to the public. Did the sale of stock have any effects on that balance sheet? If so, explain the effects.

ANALYTICAL AND REVIEW PROBLEMS

Problem 16–1 A&R

Part 1. The more recent business corporations acts restrict the directors by the "solvency" test in the matter of declaration and payment of dividends in money or property and in the case of retirement of a corporation's own stock. A similar restriction is not, however, imposed in the case of a stock dividend.

Required:

Discuss why a restriction is deemed necessary in the former but not in the latter situation.

Part 2. In the case of stock dividends, the Canada Business Corporations Act prescribes that the amount of retained earnings to be capitalized is the product of the number of shares issued as a stock dividend multiplied by the market value of each share. The revised Ontario Business Corporations Act does not stipulate the amount to be capitalized, simply stating that the amount to be added to the stated capital account is the amount declared by the directors.

Required:

Can a case be made for either of the positions? Support your answer.

Problem 16–2, A&R

Note 5 and a portion of the Shareholders' Equity section of Total Petroleum (North America) Ltd. and Subsidiaries are reproduced from the company's 1985 *Annual Report.*

TOTAL PETROLEUM (NORTH AMERICA) LTD. AND SUBSIDIARIES
Consolidated Balance Sheet
As of December 31, 1985
(in thousands)

	1985	*1984*
Shareholders' Equity		
Capital stock:		
Preferred shares	**116,599**	116,599
Common shares	**93,574**	91,823

Note 5: **Capital Stock.** The company's authorized capital at December 31, 1985, consists of 12,800,000 preferred shares and 10,000,000 second preferred shares without nominal or par value, issuable in series, and an unlimited number of common shares without nominal or par value.

At December 31, 1985, 2,800,000 of the authorized and issued preferred shares were designated as $2.88 cumulative redeemable convertible preferred shares (convertible preferred shares) with 2,798,590 shares outstanding. The holders of the convertible preferred shares are entitled to receive fixed cumulative preferential cash dividends, if and when declared by the board of directors, at an annual rate of (Can.) $2.88 per share payable quarterly. The convertible preferred shares are convertible into common shares at any time at the option of the holder at a conversion rate of 1.43 common shares for each convertible preferred share. These shares may be redeemed by the company for approximately (Can.) $50.00 per share.

Required:

1. What was the per share issue price of the preferred shares?
2. Prepare the necessary journal entry to record an assumed conversion in 1987 of 200,000 of the preferred shares.

3. What problems, if any, do you envision in recording a redemption of 100,000 of the preferred shares? Explain.
4. Record the purchase and retirement of 200,000 preferred shares purchased through the Toronto Stock Exchange on May 21, 1986 at the U.S. dollar equivalent of $35 per share.

Problem 16–3 A&R

The Consolidated Statement of Retained Earnings and Note 14 are reproduced from Northern Telecom Limited Annual Report for 1985.

Consolidated Statement of Retained Earnings
Year ended December 31
($ millions)

	1985	1984	1983
Balance at beginning of year	$ 933.0	$ 667.4	$443.7
Net earnings	411.4	333.9	268.4
	1,344.4	1,001.3	712.1
Dividends—preferred shares	(34.6)	(16.4)	—
—common shares	(58.0)	(46.0)	(44.7)
Expenses of issue of preferred shares, net of related income taxes	(1.8)	(5.9)	—
Balance at end of year	$1,250.0	$ 933.0	$667.4

	1985		1984	
	Number of shares	Stated capital ($ million)	Number of shares	Stated capital ($ million)
January 1	115,560,532	$797.8	114,607,222	$755.7
Issued during the year ...	1,001,935	46.4	953,310	42.1
December 31	116,562,467	$844.2	115,560,532	$797.8

14. Common shares
NTL is authorized to issue an unlimited number of common shares without nominal or par value.
   Outstanding common shares and stated capital at December 31: At December 31, 1985, Bell Canada Enterprises Inc. (BCE) owned 52.0 percent of the outstanding common shares.

Required:

1. Prepare the necessary journal entry on the books of Bell Canada Enterprises Inc. (BCE) to record *(a)* its share of Northern Telecom's net income for 1985 and *(b)* to record its share of the dividends paid by Northern Telecom.
2. Would BCE's consolidated statements include Northern Telecom? Explain.

Problem 16–4 A&R

The following is an excerpt from the notes to the 1985 financial statements of CDC Life Sciences Inc.:

CDC Life holds a 35.4% interest in Montreal-based Nordic Laboratories which develops, manufactures and markets pharmaceutical products solely in the Canadian market. CDC Life accounts for its investment in Nordic by the equity method. During 1985, Nordic had a strong year, with revenues increasing 79.6% while net income more than doubled to $6.3 million. CDC Life's share of this net income was. . . .

Required:

1. Is CDC Life using the cost or equity method to account for its investment in Nordic Laboratories? Support your answer.
2. Prepare the journal entry to record CDC Life's share of Nordic's net income.
3. If Nordic paid out 50% of its 1985 net income as dividends, what entry would CDC Life make to record the receipt of cash?

Installment Notes Payable and Bonds

17

After studying Chapter 17, you should be able to:

Calculate and record the payments on an installment note.

Explain the differences between an installment note payable, a bond, and a share of stock.

Describe the advantages and disadvantages of securing capital by issuing bonds.

Explain how bond interest rates are established.

Use present value tables to calculate the premium or the discount on a bond issue.

Prepare entries to account for bonds issued between interest dates at par.

Prepare entries to account for bonds sold at par, at a discount, or at a premium.

Explain the purpose and operation of a bond sinking fund and prepare entries for its operation.

Describe the procedures used to account for investments in bonds.

Define or explain the words and phrases listed in the chapter Glossary.

When a business borrows money by signing a promissory note, the terms of the note may require a single lump-sum payment of the amount borrowed plus interest. Notes that require a single payment of the amount due were discussed in the previous chapter. Many notes, however, require a series of payments that consist of interest plus a portion of the original amount borrowed. Notes payable of this type are called *installment notes*. This chapter begins with a discussion of installment notes payable. The discussion then turns to bonds payable. By issuing bonds, a company may be able to borrow money from a large number of investors.

INSTALLMENT NOTES PAYABLE

When an installment note is used to borrow money, the borrower records the note in the same manner as any other note. For example, suppose a company borrows $60,000 by signing a 12% installment note that is to be repaid with six annual payments. The entry to record the loan is as follows:

198A					
Dec.	31	Cash	60,000.00	
		Notes Payable.........................		60,000.00
		Borrowed by signing a 12% note.		

An installment note payable requires the borrower to pay back the debt in a series of periodic payments. Usually, each payment includes all of the interest that has accrued to the date of the payment plus some portion of the original amount that was borrowed. The terms of installment notes commonly call for one of two alternative payment patterns.

Installment Payments of Accrued Interest plus Equal Amounts of Principal

Some installment notes require payments that consist of accrued interest to date plus equal amounts of principal. Since each periodic payment reduces the amount borrowed, the next period's interest is reduced and the total amount of each payment becomes smaller period after period. For example, suppose that the $60,000, 12% note recorded above requires that $10,000 of principal plus accrued interest be paid at the end of each year. The entries to record the first and the second annual payments are as follows:

198B					
Dec.	31	Notes Payable ($60,000/6)	10,000.00		
		Interest Expense ($60,000 × 0.12)	7,200.00		
		Cash			17,200.00
		To record first installment payment.			
198C					
Dec.	31	Notes Payable ($60,000/6)	10,000.00		
		Interest Expense ($50,000 × 0.12)	6,000.00		
		Cash			16,000.00
		To record second installment payment.			

Note that the balance of the debt at the beginning of each interest period is used to calculate the interest expense for the period. As a result, each payment is smaller than the previous payment.

Installment Payments that Are Equal in Total Amount

At this point students who are not sure of their understanding of the concept of present value should turn back to Chapter 12 and review this concept before going further into this chapter. For additional study of discounting, an expanded analysis of present and future values is presented in Supplement 12–A at the end of Chapter 12.

Many installment notes require a series of equal payments. In other words, the payments are equal in total amount and consist of changing amounts of interest and principal. For example, assume that the $60,000, 12% note does not require six principal payments of $10,000 each plus accrued interest. Instead, assume that the note simply requires a series of six equal payments to be made at the end of each year. Each payment is to be $14,594.

ALLOCATING EACH PAYMENT BETWEEN INTEREST AND PRINCIPAL. Each payment of $14,594 includes both principal and interest. To determine the amounts of interest and principal that are included in each payment, understand that $60,000 is the present value of $14,594 to be paid annually for six years, discounted at 12%. (In this chapter, all dollar amounts are rounded to the nearest whole dollar.) The allocation of each payment between interest and principal is shown in Illustration 17–1.

In Illustration 17–1, observe that interest expense is calculated each period as 12% multiplied by the beginning-of-period principal balance. Then, the interest expense is subtracted from the periodic payment to determine the portion of the payment that is a repayment of principal. Each number in the table has been rounded to the nearest whole dollar.

Illustration 17–1

Period ending	(a) Beginning-of-period principal balance	(b) Periodic payment	(c) Interest expense for the period (a) × 12%	(d) Portion of payment that is principal (b) − (c)	(e) End-of-period principal balance (a) − (d)
31/12/8B	$60,000	$14,594	$7,200	$ 7,394	$52,606
31/12/8C	52,606	14,594	6,313	8,281	44,325
31/12/8D	44,325	14,594	5,319	9,275	35,050
31/12/8E	35,050	14,594	4,206	10,388	24,662
31/12/8F	24,662	14,594	2,959	11,635	13,027
31/12/8G	13,027	14,590*	1,563	13,027	–0–

* Note that the final payment is $4 smaller than the first five payments due to rounding. Although the note called for equal payments, a minor adjustment to the final payment is commonly necessary to repay the exact amount of debt.

The journal entry to record the first periodic payment is:

198B				
Dec.	31	Notes Payable	7,394.00	
		Interest Expense	7,200.00	
		Cash		14,594.00
		To record first installment payment.		

Similar entries are used to record each of the remaining payments.

HOW TO CALCULATE THE PERIODIC PAYMENTS. In the example, the $60,000, 12% loan required six annual payments of $14,594. Illustration 17–1 proves that these payments are just what is necessary to repay the loan. But, how was the $14,594 calculated?

The correct amount of the periodic payments may be calculated with the help of a table for the present value of $1 received (or paid) periodically for a number of periods. (See Table 12–2). In Table 12–2, the present value of $1 paid at the end of each year for six years, discounted at 12%, is $4.1114. This relationship between the periodic payments of $1 and the present value of $4.1114 may be expressed as a ratio, as follows:

$$\frac{\textbf{Periodic payment}}{\textbf{Present value}} = \frac{\$1}{\$4.1114}$$

This ratio of periodic payments to present value is the same for all situations in which six payments ($n = 6$) are discounted at an interest rate of 12% ($i = 12\%$). In other words, when the present value is $60,000, the periodic payments can be calculated as follows:

$$\frac{\text{Periodic payment}}{\$60,000.00} = \frac{1}{4.1114}$$

$$\text{Periodic payment} = \frac{\$60,000 \times 1}{4.1114} = \$14,593.57, \text{ or } \$14,594$$

BORROWING BY ISSUING BONDS

Business corporations often borrow money by issuing *bonds.*[1] Like notes payable, bonds involve a written promise to pay interest and principal or *par value.* The par value, also called the *face amount,* is printed on the bond. The interest rate stated on the bond is applied to the par value in determining the annual interest to be paid. Also, the par value is the amount that is repaid when the bond matures. Bonds usually require that interest be paid semiannually, and that the par value be repaid at a fixed future date (the maturity date).

Difference between Notes Payable and Bonds

When a business (or an individual) borrows money by signing a note payable, the money is generally borrowed from a single creditor such as a bank. In contrast to a note payable, a bond issue typically includes a large number of bonds, usually in denominations of $1,000, that are sold to many different lenders. After they are originally issued, bonds are frequently bought and sold by investors and may be owned by a number of people before they mature.

Difference between Stocks and Bonds

The phrase **stocks and bonds** commonly appears on the financial pages of newspapers and is often heard in conversations. However, the difference between stocks and bonds should be clearly understood. A share of stock represents an equity or ownership right in a corporation. For example, if a person owns 1,000 of the 10,000 shares of common stock a corporation has outstanding, the person has an equity in the corporation measured at one tenth of the corporation's total shareholders' equity and has an equity in one tenth of the corporation's earnings. On the other hand, if a person owns a $1,000, 11%, 20-year bond issued by a corporation, the bond represents a debt or a liability of the corporation.

---

[1] The federal government and other governmental units such as cities and provinces also issue bonds. However, the examples and discussion of this chapter are limited to the bonds of business corporations.

Its owner has two rights: (1) the right to receive 11% or $110 interest each year the bond is outstanding, and (2) the right to be paid $1,000 when the bond matures 20 years after its date of issue.

WHY ISSUE BONDS INSTEAD OF STOCK?

A corporation in need of long-term funds may consider issuing additional shares of stock or issuing bonds. Each has its advantages and disadvantages. Since shareholders are owners, additional stock spreads ownership, control of management, and earnings over more shares. Bondholders, on the other hand, are creditors and do not share in either management or earnings. However, bond interest must be paid whether there are any earnings or not.

The issuance of bonds instead of stock often results in increased earnings for the common shareholders of the issuing corporation. For example, assume a corporation with 200,000 shares of common stock outstanding needs $1,000,000 to expand its operations. Management estimates that after the expansion, the company can earn $900,000 annually before bond interest, if any, and before corporation income taxes. Two plans for securing the needed funds are proposed. Plan A calls for issuing 100,000 additional shares of the corporation's common stock at $10 per share. This will increase the total outstanding shares to 300,000. Plan B calls for the sale at par of $1,000,000 of 10% bonds. Illustration 17–2 shows how the plans will affect the corporation's earnings.

Corporations are subject to provincial and federal income taxes, which together may take as much as 50% of the corporation's before-tax income. However, interest expense is a deductible expense in arriving at income subject to taxes. Consequently, when the combined provincial and federal tax rate is 50%, as in Illustration 17–2, the tax reduction from issuing bonds equals one half the annual interest on the bonds. In other words, the tax savings in effect pays one half the interest cost of the bonds.

Illustration 17–2

	Plan A	Plan B
Earnings before bond interest and income taxes......	$ 900,000	$ 900,000
Deduct bond interest expense		(100,000)
Income before corporation income taxes	$ 900,000	$ 800,000
Deduct income taxes (assumed 50% rate)	(450,000)	(400,000)
Net income	$ 450,000	$ 400,000
Plan A income per share (300,000 shares)	$1.50	
Plan B income per share (200,000 shares)		$2.00

CHARACTERISTICS OF BONDS

Over the years, corporation lawyers and financiers have created a wide variety of bonds, each with different combinations of characteristics. Some of the more common characteristics of different bond issues are discussed in the following paragraphs.

Serial Bonds

Some bond issues include bonds that mature at different points in time so that the entire bond issue is repaid gradually over a period of years. Bonds of this type are called *serial bonds*. For example, a $1,000,000 issue of serial bonds may include $100,000 of bonds that mature each year from year 6 through year 15.

Sinking Fund Bonds

In contrast to serial bonds, *sinking fund bonds* all mature on the same date and are paid in one lump sum from a separate pool of assets (a sinking fund) that was established specifically for that purpose. Sinking funds are discussed later in this chapter.

Registered Bonds and Bearer Bonds

Most bonds are registered. The name and address of the owner of a *registered bond* are recorded with the issuing corporation. This offers some protection from loss or theft. If bonds are not registered, they are made payable to bearer and are called *bearer bonds*.

Coupon Bonds

Interest payments on registered bonds are usually made by cheques mailed to the registered owners. If interest is not paid in this manner, the bonds are called *coupon bonds*. Coupon bonds obtain their name from the interest coupons attached to each bond. Each coupon calls for payment on the interest payment date of the interest due on the bond. The coupons are detached as they become due and are deposited with a bank for collection.

Secured Bonds and Debentures

When bonds are secured, specific assets of the issuing corporation are pledged or mortgaged to be used, if necessary, to repay the bonds. Mortgages are discussed later in this chapter. Unsecured bonds that depend upon the general credit standing of the issuing corporation for security are called *debentures*. A company generally must be financially strong if it is to successfully issue unsecured bonds.

THE PROCESS OF ISSUING BONDS

When a corporation issues bonds, it normally sells the bonds to an investment firm, known as the **underwriter.** The underwriter in turn resells the bonds to the public. The legal document that states the rights and obligations of the company and the bondholders is called the *bond indenture*. In other words, the bond indenture is the written, legal contract between the issuing company and the bondholders. Each bondholder receives a **bond certificate** which is evidence of the corporation's debt to the bondholder.

Since there may be many bondholders, they are represented by a **trustee.** The trustee has the responsibility of monitoring the corporation's actions to be sure that it fulfills its obligations as stated in the bond indenture. In most cases, the trustee is a large bank or trust company that is selected by the issuing company.

Accounting for the Issuance of Bonds

When a corporation issues bonds, the bond certificates are printed and the indenture is drawn and deposited with the trustee of the bondholders. At that point, a memorandum describing the bond issue is commonly entered in the Bonds Payable account. Such a memorandum might read, "Authorized to issue $8,000,000 of 9%, 20-year bonds dated January 1, 19—, and with interest payable semiannually on each July 1 and January 1." As in this case, bond interest is usually payable semiannually.

After the bond indenture is deposited with the trustee of the bondholders, all or a portion of the bonds may be sold. If all are sold at their par value, an entry like the following is made to record the sale:

Jan.	1	Cash	8,000,000.00	
		Bonds Payable		8,000,000.00
		Sold 9%, 20-year bonds at par on their interest date.		

When the semiannual interest is paid on these bonds, the transaction is recorded as follows:

July	1	Bond Interest Expense	360,000.00	
		Cash		360,000.00
		Paid the semiannual interest on the books.		

And when the bonds are paid at maturity, an entry like the following is made:

Jan.	1	Bonds Payable	8,000,000.00	
		Cash		8,000,000.00
		Paid bonds at maturity.		

BONDS SOLD BETWEEN INTEREST DATES

Sometimes bonds are sold on their date of issue, which is also their interest date, as in the previous illustration. More often they are sold after their date of issue and between interest dates. In such cases, it is customary to charge and collect from the purchasers the interest that has accrued on the bonds since the previous interest payment and to return this accrued interest to the purchasers on the next interest date. For example, assume that on March 1, a corporation sold at par $100,000 of 9% bonds on which interest is payable semiannually on each January 1 and July 1. (Small dollar amounts are used to conserve space.) The entry to record the sale between interest dates is:

Mar.	1	Cash	101,500.00	
		Bond Interest Expense		1,500.00
		Bonds Payable		100,000.00
		Sold $100,000 of 9%, 20-year bonds on which two months' interest has accrued.		

At the end of four months, on the July 1 semiannual interest date, the purchasers of these bonds are paid a full six months' interest. This payment includes four months' interest earned by the bondholders after March 1 and the two months' accrued interest collected from them at the time the bonds were sold. The entry to record the payment is:

July	1	Bond Interest Expense	4,500.00	
		Cash		4,500.00
		Paid the semiannual interest on the bonds.		

After both of these entries are posted, the Bond Interest Expense account has a $3,000 debit balance and appears as follows:

Bond Interest Expense

July 1 (Payment)	4,500.00	Mar. 1 (Accrued interest)	1,500.00

The $3,000 debit balance represents the interest on the $100,000 of bonds at 9% for the four months from March 1 to July 1.

It may seem strange to charge bond purchasers for accrued interest when bonds are sold between interest dates, and to return this accrued interest in the next interest payment. However, this is the custom. All bond transactions are "plus accrued interest," and there is a good reason for the practice. For instance, if a corporation sells portions of a bond issue on different dates during an interest period without collecting the accrued interest, it must keep records of the purchasers and the dates on which they bought bonds. Otherwise, it cannot pay the correct amount of interest to each. However, if it charges each buyer for accrued interest at the time of the purchase, it need not keep records of the purchasers and their purchase dates. It can pay a full period's interest to all purchasers for the period in which they bought their bonds; each receives the interest earned and gets back the accrued interest paid at the time of the purchase.

BOND INTEREST RATES

A corporation issuing bonds specifies in the bond indenture and on each bond certificate the interest rate it will pay. This rate is called the *contract rate*. It is usually stated on an annual basis, although bond interest is normally paid semiannually. Also, it is applied to the par value of the bonds to determine the dollars of interest the corporation will pay. For example, if a corporation issues a $1,000, 8% bond on which interest is paid semiannually, $80 will be paid each year in two semiannual installments of $40 each.

Although the contract rate establishes the interest a corporation will pay, it is not necessarily the interest the corporation will incur in issuing bonds. The interest it will incur depends upon what lenders consider their risks to be in lending to the corporation and upon the current *market rate for bond interest*. The market rate for bond interest is the rate borrowers are willing to pay and lenders are willing to take for the use of money at the level of risk involved. It fluctuates from day to day as the supply and demand for loanable funds fluctuate. It goes up when the demand for bond money increases and the supply decreases, and it goes down when the supply increases and the demand decreases.

Also, note that on any single day, the market rate for bond interest is not the same for all corporations. The rate for a specific corporation's bonds depends on the level of risk investors attach to those bonds. As the perceived level of risk increases, the rate increases.

A corporation issuing bonds usually offers a contract rate of interest equal to what it estimates the market will demand on the day the bonds are to be issued. If its estimate is correct, and the contract rate and market rate coincide on the day the bonds are issued, the bonds will sell at par, their face amount. However, when bonds are sold, their contract rate seldom coincides with the market rate. As a result, bonds usually sell either at a premium or at a discount.

BONDS SOLD AT A DISCOUNT

When a corporation offers to sell bonds carrying a contract rate below the prevailing market rate, the bonds will sell at a *discount.* Given the level of risk, investors can get the market rate of interest elsewhere for the use of their money, so they will buy the bonds only at a price that will yield the prevailing market rate on the investment. What price will they pay and how is it determined? The price they will pay is the **present value** of the expected returns from the investment. It is determined by discounting the returns at the current market rate for bond interest.

To illustrate how bond prices are determined, assume that on a day when the market rate for bond interest is 9%, a corporation offers to sell and issue bonds having a $100,000 par value, a 10-year life, and on which interest is to be paid semiannually at an 8% annual rate.[2] In exchange for current dollars, the buyers of these bonds will gain two monetary rights:

1. The right to receive $100,000 at the end of the bond issue's 10-year life.
2. The right to receive $4,000 in interest at the end of each 6-month interest period throughout the 10-year life of the bonds.

Since both are rights to receive money in the future, to determine their present value, the amounts to be received are discounted at the market rate of interest. If the market rate is 9% annually, it is 4½% semiannually; and in 10 years, there are 20 semiannual periods. Consequently, using the last number in the 4½% column of Table 12–1, to discount the first amount and the last number in the 4½% column of Table 12–2, to discount the series of $4,000 amounts, the present value of the rights and the price informed buyers will offer for the bonds is:

Present value of $100,000 to be received 20 periods hence, dis-
  counted at 4½% per period ($100,000 × 0.4146) $41,460
Present value of $4,000 to be received periodically for 20 periods,
  discounted at 4½% ($4,000 × 13.0079) 52,032
Present value of the bonds $93,492

---

[2] The spread between the contract rate and the market rate of interest on a new bond issue is seldom more than a fraction of a per cent. However, a spread of a full per cent is used here to simplify the illustrations.

If the corporation accepts the $93,492 offered for its bonds and sells them on their date of issue, the sale will be recorded with an entry like this:

Jan.	1	Cash	93,492.00	
		Discount on Bonds Payable	6,508.00	
		Bonds Payable		100,000.00
		Sold 8%, 10-year bonds at a discount on their date of issue.		

If the corporation prepares a balance sheet on the day the bonds are sold, it may show the bonds in the long-term liability section as follows:

Long-term liabilities:
First-mortgage, 8% bonds payable, due January 1,
199A $100,000
Less unamortized discount based on the 9%
market rate for bond interest prevailing on the
date of issue 6,508 $93,492

On a balance sheet, any unamortized discount on a bond issue is deducted from the par value of the bonds to show the amount at which the bonds are carried on the books, called the *carrying amount.*

Amortizing the Discount

The corporation of this discussion received $93,492 for its bonds, but in 10 years it must pay the bondholders $100,000. The difference, the $6,508 discount, is a cost of using the $93,492 that is incurred because the contract rate of interest on the bonds was below the prevailing market rate. It is a cost that must be paid when the bonds mature. However, each semiannual interest period in the life of the bond issue benefits from the use of the $93,492. Consequently, it is only fair that each should bear a fair share of this cost.

STRAIGHT-LINE METHOD. The procedure for dividing a discount and charging a share to each period in the life of the applicable bond issue is called **amortizing** a discount. A simple method of amortizing a discount is the **straight-line method,** a method in which an equal portion of the discount is amortized each interest period. If this method is used to amortize the $6,508 discount of this discussion, the $6,508 is divided by 20, the number of interest periods in the life of the bond issue, and $325 ($6,508 ÷ 20 = $325.40, or $325)[3] of the discount is amortized at the end of each interest period with an entry like this:

---

[3] In this chapter and in the problems at the end of the chapter, all calculations involving bonds have been rounded to the nearest whole dollar.

July	1	Bond Interest Expense		4,325.00	
		Discount on Bonds Payable			325.00
		Cash			4,000.00
		To record payment of six months' interest and amortization of one twentieth of the discount.			

Illustration 17–3, with amounts rounded to full dollars, shows the interest expense to be recorded, the discount to be amortized, and so forth, when the straight-line method of amortizing a discount is applied to the bonds in this discussion. In examining Illustration 17–3, note these points:

1. The bonds were sold at a $6,508 discount, which when subtracted from their face amount gives a beginning-of-Period-1 carrying amount of $93,492.
2. The semiannual $4,325 interest expense amounts equal $4,000 paid to bondholders plus $325 amortization of discount.
3. Interest to be paid bondholders each period is determined by multiplying the par value of the bonds by the contract rate of interest ($100,000 × 4% = $4,000).

Illustration 17–3

Period	Beginning-of-period carrying amount	Interest expense to be recorded	Interest to be paid the bondholders	Discount to be amortized	Unamortized discount at end of period	End-of-period carrying amount
1	$93,492	$4,325	$4,000	$325	$6,183	$ 93,817
2	93,817	4,325	4,000	325	5,858	94,142
3	94,142	4,325	4,000	325	5,533	94,467
4	94,467	5,325	4,000	325	5,208	94,792
5	94,792	4,325	4,000	325	4,883	95,117
6	95,117	4,325	4,000	325	4,558	95,442
7	95,442	4,325	4,000	325	4,233	95,767
8	95,767	4,325	4,000	325	3,908	96,092
9	96,092	4,325	4,000	325	3,583	96,417
10	96,417	4,325	4,000	325	3,258	96,742
11	96,742	4,325	4,000	325	2,933	97,067
12	97,067	4,325	4,000	325	2,608	97,392
13	97,392	4,325	4,000	325	2,283	97,717
14	97,717	4,325	4,000	325	1,958	98,042
15	98,042	4,325	4,000	325	1,633	98,367
16	98,367	4,325	4,000	325	1,308	98,692
17	98,692	4,325	4,000	325	983	99,017
18	99,017	4,325	4,000	325	658	99,342
19	99,342	4,325	4,000	325	333	99,667
20	99,667	4,333*	4,000	333*	–0–	100,000

* Adjusted to compensate for accumulated rounding of amounts.

4. The discount to be amortized each period is $6,508 ÷ 20 = $325.40, or $325.

5. The unamortized discount at the end of each period is determined by subtracting the discount amortized that period from the unamortized discount at the beginning of the period.

6. The end-of-period carrying amount for the bonds is determined by subtracting the end-of-period amount of unamortized discount from the face amount of the bonds. For example, at the end of Period 1: $100,000 − $6,183 = $93,817.

Straight-line amortization once was commonly used. However, it should be used only in situations where the results do not materially differ from those obtained through use of the so-called interest method.

INTEREST METHOD. When the interest method is used, the interest expense to be recorded each period is determined by applying a constant rate of interest to the beginning-of-period carrying amount of the bonds. The constant rate applied is the market rate for the bonds at the time the bonds were issued. The discount amortized each period is then determined by subtracting the interest to be paid the bondholders from the interest expense to be recorded. Illustration 17–4 shows the interest expense to be recorded, the discount to be amortized, and so forth, when the interest method is applied to the bonds in this discussion.

Compare Illustration 17–4 with 17–3 and note these unique aspects of the interest method as shown in Illustration 17–4.

1. The interest expense amounts result from multiplying each beginning-of-period carrying amount by the 4½% semiannual market rate that prevailed when the bonds were issued. For example, $93,492 × 4½% = $4,207 and $93,699 × 4½% = $4,216.

2. The discount to be amortized each period is determined by subtracting the amount of interest to be paid the bondholders from the amount of interest expense.

When the interest method is used in amortizing a discount, the periodic amortizing entries are like the entries used with the straight-line method; only the dollar amounts are different. For example, the entry to pay the bondholders and amortize a portion of the discount at the end of the first semiannual interest period of the bond issue in Illustration 17–4 is:

July	1	Bond Interest Expense	4,207.00	
		Discount on Bonds Payable		207.00
		Cash		4,000.00
		To record payment to the bondholders and amortization of a portion of the discount.		

Illustration 17–4

Period	Beginning-of-period carrying amount	Interest expense to be recorded	Interest to be paid the bondholders	Discount to be amortized	Unamortized discount at end of period	End-of-period carrying amount
1	$93,492	$4,207	$4,000	$207	$6,301	$ 93,699
2	93,699	4,216	4,000	216	6,085	93,915
3	93,915	4,226	4,000	226	5,859	94,141
4	94,141	4,236	4,000	236	5,623	94,377
5	94,377	4,247	4,000	247	5,376	94,624
6	94,624	4,258	4,000	258	5,118	94,882
7	94,882	4,270	4,000	270	4,848	95,152
8	95,152	4,282	4,000	282	4,566	95,434
9	95,434	4,295	4,000	295	4,271	95,729
10	95,729	4,308	4,000	308	3,963	96,037
11	96,037	4,322	4,000	322	3,641	96,359
12	96,359	4,336	4,000	336	3,305	96,695
13	96,695	4,351	4,000	351	2,954	97,046
14	97,046	4,367	4,000	367	2,587	97,413
15	97,413	4,384	4,000	384	2,203	97,797
16	97,797	4,401	4,000	401	1,802	98,198
17	98,198	4,419	4,000	419	1,383	98,617
18	98,617	4,438	4,000	438	945	99,055
19	99,055	4,457	4,000	457	488	99,512
20	99,512	4,488*	4,000	488	–0–	100,000

* Adjusted to compensate for accumulated rounding of amounts.

Similar entries, differing only in the amount of interest expense recorded and discount amortized, are made at the end of each semiannual interest period in the life of the bond issue.

Consider the differences between the interest method of amortizing a discount and the straight-line method (previously discussed). The following table shows these financial statement differences:

	Interest-method amortization			Straight-line amortization		
Period	Beginning-of-period carrying amount	Interest expense to be recorded	Interest expense as a percent of carrying amount	Beginning-of-period carrying amount	Interest expense to be recorded	Interest expense as a percent of carrying amount
1	$93,492	$4,207	4.5	$93,492	$4,325	4.63
11	96,037	4,322	4.5	96,742	4,325	4.47
19	99,055	4,457	4.5	99,342	4,325	4.35

The table shows the beginning-of-period carrying amount of the bond liability and the interest expense for each of three six-month periods during the life of the bonds. The first three columns of the table show that in each and every six-month period, the interest method provides an interest expense amount that is 4.5% of the beginning-of-period carrying amount. The last three columns show the amounts that would result from using the straight-line method. Observe that when the straight-line method is used, the percentage changes each period. Recall that the bonds were issued at a price that reflected a discounting of cash flows at 4.5% per six-month period. The interest method is most consistent with this fact; and it is the preferred method.

Because the above example involves a bond discount, the straight-line method results in a declining percentage. When a premium is amortized, the straight-line method results in an increasing percentage. In either case, however, the straight-line method can be used only where the results do not differ materially from those obtained through use of the interest method.

BONDS SOLD AT A PREMIUM

When a corporation offers to sell bonds carrying a contract rate of interest above the prevailing market rate for the risks involved, the bonds will sell at a *premium*. Buyers will bid up the price of the bonds, going as high, but no higher, than a price that will return the current market rate of interest on the investment. What price will they pay? They will pay the present value of the expected returns from the investment, determined by discounting these returns at the market rate of interest for the bonds. For example, assume that on a given day a corporation offers to sell bonds having a $100,000 par value and a 10-year life with interest to be paid semiannually at an 11% annual rate. On that day, the market rate of interest for the corporation's bonds is 10%. Buyers of these bonds will discount the expectation of receiving $100,000 in 10 years and the expectation of receiving $5,500 semiannually for 20 periods at the current 10% market rate as follows:

Present value of $100,000 to be received 20 periods hence, discounted at 5% per period ($100,000 × 0.3769)	$ 37,690
Present value of $5,500 to be received periodically for 20 periods, discounted at 5% ($5,500 × 12.4622)	68,542
Present value of the bonds	$106,232

Investors will offer the corporation a total of $106,232 for its bonds. If the corporation accepts and sells the bonds on their date of issue, say, May 1, 198A, it will record the sale as follows:

198A					
May	1	Cash	106,232.00	
		Premium on Bonds Payable		6,232.00
		Bonds Payable		100,000.00
		Sold bonds at a premium on their date of issue.		

It may then show the bonds on a balance sheet prepared on the day of the sale as follows:

Long-term liabilities:		
First-mortgage, 11% bonds payable, due May 1, 199A . .	$100,000	
Add unamortized premium based on the 10% market rate for bond interest prevailing on the date of issue	6,232	$106,232

On a balance sheet, any unamortized premium on bonds payable is added to the par value of the bonds to show the carrying amount of the bonds, as illustrated.

Amortizing the Premium

Although the corporation discussed here received $106,232 for its bonds, it will have to repay only $100,000 to the bondholders at maturity. The difference, the $6,232 premium, represents a reduction in the cost of using the $106,232. It should be amortized over the life of the bond issue in such a manner as to lower the recorded bond interest expense. If the $6,232 premium is amortized by the interest method, Illustration 17–5 shows the amounts of interest expense to be recorded each period, the premium to be amortized, and so forth.

Observe in Illustration 17–5 that the premium to be amortized each period is determined by subtracting the interest to be recorded from the interest to be paid the bondholders.

Based on Illustration 17–5, the entry to record the first semiannual interest payment and premium amortization is:

198A					
Nov.	1	Bond Interest Expense	5,312.00	
		Premium on Bonds Payable	188.00	
		Cash		5,500.00
		To record payment of the bondholders and amortization of a portion of the premium.		

Illustration 17–5

Period	Beginning-of-period carrying amount	Interest expense to be recorded	Interest to be paid the bondholders	Premium to be amortized	Unamortized premium at end of period	End-of period carrying amount
1	$106,232	$5,312	$5,500	$188	$6,044	$106,044
2	106,044	5,302	5,500	198	5,846	105,846
3	105,846	5,292	5,500	208	5,638	105,638
4	105,638	5,282	5,500	218	5,420	105,420
5	105,420	5,271	5,500	229	5,191	105,191
6	105,191	5,260	5,500	240	4,951	104,951
7	104,951	5,248	5,500	252	4,699	104,699
8	104,699	5,235	5,500	265	4,434	104,434
9	104,434	5,222	5,500	278	4,156	104,156
10	104,156	5,208	5,500	292	3,864	103,864
11	103,864	5,193	5,500	307	3,557	103,557
12	103,557	5,178	5,500	322	3,235	103,235
13	103,235	5,162	5,500	338	2,897	102,897
14	102,897	5,145	5,500	355	2,542	102,542
15	102,542	5,127	5,500	373	2,169	102,169
16	102,169	5,108	5,500	392	1,777	101,777
17	101,777	5,089	5,500	411	1,366	101,366
18	101,366	5,068	5,500	432	934	100,934
19	100,934	5,047	5,500	453	481	100,481
20	100,481	5,019*	5,500	481	–0–	100,000

* Adjusted to compensate for accumulated rounding of amounts.

Note how the amortization of the premium results in a reduction in the amount of interest expense recorded. Similar entries having decreasing amounts of interest expense and increasing amounts of premium amortized are made at the ends of the remaining periods in the life of the bond issue.

ACCRUED BOND INTEREST EXPENSE

Often when bonds are sold, the bond interest periods do not coincide with the issuing company's accounting periods. In such cases, it is necessary at the end of each accounting period to make an adjustment for accrued interest. For example, it was assumed that the bonds of Illustration 17–5 were issued on May 1, 198A, and interest was paid on these bonds on November 1 of that year. If the accounting periods of the corporation end each December 31, on December 31, 198A, two months' interest has accrued on these bonds, and the following adjusting entry is required:

198A					
Dec.	31	Bond Interest Expense	1,767.00		
		Premium on Bonds Payable	66.00		
		Bond Interest Payable		1,833.00	
		To record two months' accrued interest and amortize one third of the premium applicable to the interest period.			

Two months are one third of a semiannual interest period. Consequently, the amounts in the entry are one third of the amounts applicable to the second interest period in the life of the bond issue. Similar entries will be made on each December 31 throughout the life of the issue. However, the amounts will differ, since in each case they will apply to a different interest period.

When the interest is paid on these bonds on May 1, 198B, an entry like this is required:

198B					
May	1	Bond Interest Expense	3,535.00		
		Bond Interest Payable	1,833.00		
		Premium on Bonds Payable	132.00		
		Cash		5,500.00	
		Paid the interest on the bonds, a portion of which was previously accrued, and amortized four months' premium.			

SALE OF BONDS BY INVESTORS

A purchaser of a bond may not hold it to maturity but may sell it after a period of months or years to another investor at a price determined by the market rate for bond interest on the day of the sale. The market rate for bond interest on the day of the sale determines the price because the new investor could get this current rate elsewhere. Therefore, the investor will discount the right to receive the bond's face amount at maturity and the right to receive its interest for the remaining periods of its life at the current market rate to determine the price to pay for the bond. As a result, since bond interest rates may vary greatly over a period of months or years, a bond that originally sold at a premium may later sell at a discount, and vice versa.

REDEMPTION OF BONDS

Bonds are commonly issued with the provision that they may be redeemed at the issuing corporation's option, usually upon the payment of a redemption premium. Such bonds are known as *callable bonds*. Corporations commonly insert redemption clauses in deeds of trust because if interest rates decline, it may be advantageous to call and redeem outstanding bonds and issue in their place new bonds paying a lower interest rate.

Not all bonds have a provision giving their issuing company the right to call. However, even though the right is not provided, a company may secure the same effect by purchasing its bonds on the open market and retiring them. Often such action is wise when a company has funds available and its bonds are selling at a price below their carrying amount. For example, assume that a company has outstanding on their interest date $1,000,000 of bonds on which there is $12,000 unamortized premium. The bonds are selling at 98½ (98½% of par value), and the company decides to buy and retire one tenth of the issue. The entry to record the purchase and retirement is:

Apr.	1	Bonds Payable	100,000.00	
		Premium on Bonds Payable	1,200.00	
		Gain on the Retirement of Bonds		2,700.00
		Cash		98,500.00
		To record the retirement of bonds.		

The retirement resulted in a $2,700 gain in this instance because the bonds were purchased at a price $2,700 below their carrying amount.

In the last paragraph, the statement was made that the bonds were selling at 98½. Bond quotations are commonly made in this manner. For example, a bond may be quoted for sale at 101¼. This means the bond is for sale at 101¼% of its par value, plus accrued interest, of course, if applicable.

BOND SINKING FUND

Bonds appeal to some investors because bonds usually provide greater security than stocks. Often a corporation will give additional security by agreeing in the bond indenture to create a *bond sinking fund*. This is a fund of assets accumulated during the life of the bonds to repay the bondholders at maturity.

When a corporation agrees to create a bond sinking fund, it normally agrees to create the fund by making periodic cash deposits with a sinking fund trustee. It is the duty of the trustee to safeguard the cash, to invest it in securities of reasonably low risk, and to add the interest or dividends earned to the sinking fund. Generally, when the bonds become due, it is also the duty of the sinking fund trustee to sell the sinking fund securities and to use the proceeds to pay the bondholders.

When a sinking fund is created, the amount that must be deposited periodically in order to provide enough money to retire a bond issue at maturity will depend upon the net rate of compound interest that can be earned on the invested funds. The rate is a compound rate because earnings are continually reinvested by the sinking fund trustee to earn an additional return. It is a net rate because the fee for the trustee's services commonly is deducted from the earnings.

To illustrate the operation of a sinking fund, assume a corporation issues $1,000,000 par value, 10-year bonds and agrees to deposit with a sinking fund trustee at the end of each year in the bond issue's life sufficient cash to create a fund large enough to retire the bonds at maturity. If the trustee is able to invest the funds in such a manner as to earn an 8% net return, $69,029[4] must be deposited each year, and the fund will grow to maturity (in rounded dollars) as shown in Illustration 17–6.

Illustration 17–6

End of year	Amount deposited	Interest earned on fund balance	Balance in fund after deposit and interest
1	$69,029	$ –0–	$ 69,029
2	69,029	5,522	143,580
3	69,029	11,486	224,095
4	69,029	17,928	311,052
5	69,029	24,884	404,965
6	69,029	32,397	506,391
7	69,029	40,511	615,931
8	69,029	49,274	734,234
9	69,029	58,739	862,002
10	69,029	68,969	1,000,000

When a sinking fund is created by periodic deposits, the entry to record the amount deposited each year appears as follows:

Dec.	31	Bond Sinking Fund............................	69,029.00	
		Cash....................................		69,029.00
		To record the annual sinking fund deposit.		

---

[4] An understanding of how this number is calculated may be gained by studying Appendix A at the end of the book.

Each year the sinking fund trustee invests the amount deposited, and each year it collects and reports the earnings on the investments. The earnings report results in an entry to record the sinking fund income. For example, if $69,029 is deposited at the end of the first year in the sinking fund, the accumulation of which is shown in Illustration 17–6, and 8% is earned, the entry to record the sinking fund earnings of the second year is:

Dec.	31	Bond Sinking Fund............................	5,522.00	
		Sinking Fund Earnings..................		5,522.00
		To record the sinking fund earnings.		

Sinking fund earnings appear on the income statement as financial revenue in a section titled "Other revenues and expenses." A sinking fund is the property of the company creating the fund and should appear on its balance sheet in the long-term investments section.

When bonds mature, it is usually the duty of the sinking fund trustee to convert the fund's investments into cash and pay the bondholders. Normally the sinking fund securities, when sold, produce either a little more or a little less cash than is needed to pay the bondholders. If more cash than needed is produced, the extra cash is returned to the corporation; and if less cash is produced than needed, the corporation must make up the deficiency. For example, if the securities in the sinking fund of a $1,000,000 bond issue produce $1,001,325 when converted to cash, the trustee will use $1,000,000 to pay the bondholders and will return the extra $1,325 to the corporation. The corporation will then record the payment of its bonds and the return of the extra cash with an entry like the following:

Jan.	3	Cash	1,325.00	
		Bonds Payable.........................	1,000,000.00	
		Bond Sinking Fund		1,001,325.00
		To record payment of our bonds and the return of extra cash from the sinking fund.		

RESTRICTION ON DIVIDENDS DUE TO OUTSTANDING BONDS

To protect a corporation's financial position and the interests of its bondholders, a bond indenture may restrict the dividends the corporation may pay while its bonds are outstanding. Commonly, the restriction provides that the corporation may pay dividends in any year only to the extent that the year's earnings exceed sinking fund requirements.

CONVERTING BONDS TO STOCK

To make a bond issue more attractive, bondholders may be given the right to exchange their bonds for a fixed number of shares of the issuing company's common stock. Such *convertible bonds* offer investors initial investment security, and if the issuing company prospers and its stock increases in price, an opportunity to share in the prosperity by converting their bonds to the more valuable stock. Conversion is always at the bondholders' option and therefore does not take place unless it is to their advantage.

When bonds are converted into stock, the conversion changes a liability into owners' equity. The generally accepted rule for measuring the contribution for the issued shares is that the carrying amount of the converted bonds becomes the book value of the capital contributed for the new shares. For example, assume the following: (1) A company has outstanding $1,000,000 of bonds upon which there is $8,000 unamortized discount. (2) The bonds are convertible at the rate of a $1,000 bond for 90 shares of the company's no-par value common stock. And (3) $100,000 in bonds have been presented on their interest date for conversion. The entry to record the conversion is:

May	1	Bonds Payable	100,000.00	
		Discount on Bonds Payable		800.00
		Common Stock		99,200.00
		To record the conversion of bonds.		

Note in this entry that the bonds' $99,200 carrying amount sets the accounting value for the capital contributed. Usually, when bonds have a conversion privilege, it is not exercised until the stock's market value and normal dividend payments are sufficiently high to make the conversion profitable to the bondholders.

INVESTMENTS IN BONDS

The discussion of bonds has thus far focused on the issuing corporation. Attention is now shifted to the purchasers of bonds. When bonds are purchased as an investment, they are recorded at cost, including any brokerage fees. If interest has accrued at the date of purchase, it is also paid for by the purchaser and is recorded with a debit to Bond Interest Receivable. The entry to record a bond purchase is as follows:

May	1	Investment in X Corporation Bonds	46,400.00	
		Bond Interest Receivable	1,500.00	
		Cash		47,900.00
		Purchased 50 $1,000, 9%, 10-year bonds dated December 31, 198A, at a price of 92 plus a $400 brokerage fee and accrued interest.		

Note that the $46,400 cost of the bonds was 92% × $50,000 par value plus the $400 brokerage fee, which leaves a discount of $3,600. Most companies do not record the discount (or premium) in a separate account. The investment account is simply debited for the net cost. The accrued interest on May 1 was 4/12 × 9% × $50,000, or $1,500.

Assuming interest is paid semiannually on June 30 and December 31, the entry to record the receipt of interest on June 30 would be as follows:

June	30	Cash	2,250.00	
		Bond Interest Receivable		1,500.00
		Bond Interest Earned		750.00

This entry correctly reflects the fact that the purchaser owned the bonds for two months during which time interest amounted to 2/12 × 9% × $50,000, or $750. However, recall that the bonds were purchased at a discount and observe that the June 30 entry does not include any amortization of the discount. This is acceptable only if the bonds are held as a temporary investment. Under these conditions, the bond investment is shown as a current asset at cost. The market value of the bonds on the date of the balance sheet should also be reported parenthetically, as follows:

Current assets:
    Investment in X Corp. bonds (market value is $xx,xxx) $46,400

When the bonds are sold, the gain or loss on the sale is calculated as the difference between the sale proceeds and cost.

What if the bonds are held as a long-term investment? In this case, one should expect the market value of the bonds to move generally toward par value as the maturity date approaches. Therefore, any discount (or premium) should be amortized so that each interest period includes some amortization in the calculation of interest earned. The procedures for amortizing discount or premium on bond investments parallel those that were discussed and applied previously to bonds payable. The only difference is that the amount of discount (premium) to be amortized is debited (credited) directly to the investment account. As a consequence, on the maturity date, the investment account balance will equal the par value on the bonds.

MORTGAGES AS SECURITY FOR NOTES PAYABLE AND BONDS

Earlier in this chapter, bonds were said to be either secured or unsecured. This is also true of notes payable. When bonds or notes are unsecured, the obligation to pay interest and par or principal is equal in standing with other unsecured liabilities of the issuing company. If the company becomes financially troubled and is unable to pay, none of the unsecured creditors is given preference over any other.

The ability of a company to borrow money by signing an unsecured note or issuing unsecured bonds depends on the company's general credit standing. In many cases, a company simply cannot obtain debt financing without providing security to the creditors. In other cases, the rate of interest that creditors would charge to provide unsecured debt is very high. As a result, many notes payable and bond issues are secured by a mortgage.

A *mortgage* is a legal agreement that helps protect a lender if a borrower fails to make the payments required by a note payable or bond indenture. A mortgage gives the lender the right to be paid from the cash proceeds from the sale of the borrower's mortgaged assets.

The terms of a mortgage are written in a separate legal document, the *mortgage contract*. The mortgage contract is given to the trustee of the bond issue or to the lender along with the note payable. A mortgage contract commonly requires the borrower to keep the mortgaged property in a good state of repair and adequately insured. In addition, it normally grants the mortgage holder (the lender) the right to foreclose if the borrower fails to pay. In a foreclosure, a court either sells the property or grants possession of the mortgaged property to the lender who sells it. When the property is sold, the proceeds go first to pay court costs and the claims of the mortgage holder. Any money remaining is then paid to the former owner of the property.

GLOSSARY

Bearer bond. A bond that is not registered and is made payable to whoever holds the bond (the bearer).

Bond. A long-term liability of a corporation or governmental unit, usually issued in denominations of $1,000, that requires periodic payments of interest and final payment of par value when it matures.

Bond discount. The difference between the par value of a bond and the price at which it is issued when issued at a price below par.

Bond indentures. The contract between the issuing corporation and the bondholders that states the rights and obligations of both parties.

Bond premium. The difference between the par value of a bond and the price at which it is issued when issued at a price above par.

Bond sinking fund. A fund of assets accumulated to repay a bond issue at maturity.

Callable bond. A bond that may be redeemed or repaid before its maturity date at the option of the issuing corporation.

Carrying amount of a bond issue. The par value of a bond issue less any unamortized discount or plus any unamortized premium.

Contract rate of bond interest. The rate of interest that is applied to the par value of bonds to determine the annual cash payment to the bondholders.

Convertible bond. A bond that may be exchanged for shares of its issuing corporation's stock at the option of the bondholder.

Coupon bond. A bond that has interest coupons attached to the bond certificate, which are detached and submitted to the issuing corporation for payment.

Debenture. An unsecured bond.

Face amount of a bond. The bond's par value.

Installment notes. Notes that require a series of payments consisting of interest plus a portion of the original amount borrowed.

Market rate for bond interest. The interest rate that a corporation is willing to pay and investors are willing to take for the use of their money to buy that corporation's bonds.

Mortgage. A legal agreement that helps protect a lender by giving the lender the right to be paid from the cash proceeds from the sale of the borrower's mortgaged assets.

Mortgage contract. A legal document setting forth the rights of the lender and the obligations of the borrower with respect to mortgaged assets.

Par value of a bond. The face amount of the bond, which is the amount the borrower agrees to repay at maturity and the amount on which interest payments are based.

Registered bond. A bond for which the name and address of the owner are recorded with the issuing corporation.

Serial bonds. An issue of bonds that mature at different points in time so that the entire bond issue is repaid gradually over a period of years.

Sinking fund bonds. Bonds that require the issuing corporation to accumulate a separate fund of assets during the life of the bonds for the purpose of repaying the bondholders at maturity.

QUESTIONS FOR CLASS DISCUSSION

1. What are two commonly used payment patterns on installment notes?
2. How is the interest portion of an installment note payment calculated?
3. What is the difference between a note payable and a bond issue?
4. What is the primary difference between a share of stock and a bond?
5. Why may bonds be preferred to stock as a means of long-term financing?
6. What is a bond indenture? What are some of the provisions commonly contained in an indenture?
7. What role is played by the underwriter when bonds are issued?
8. What is the function of the trustee on a bond issue?
9. Define or describe: *(a)* registered bonds, *(b)* coupon bonds, *(c)* serial bonds, *(d)* sinking fund bonds, *(e)* callable bonds, *(f)* convertible bonds, and *(g)* debenture bonds.
10. Why does a corporation that issues bonds between interest dates charge and collect accrued interest from the purchasers of the bonds?
11. As it relates to a bond issue, what is the meaning of "contract rate of interest"? What is the meaning of "market rate for bond interest"?
12. What determines bond interest rates?
13. When the straight-line method is used to amortize bond discount, how is the interest expense for each period calculated?
14. When the interest method is used to amortize bond discount or premium, how is the interest expense for each period calculated?
15. If a $1,000 bond is sold at 98¼, at what price is it sold? If a $1,000 bond is sold at 101½, at what price is it sold?
16. If the quoted price for a bond is 97¾, does this include accrued interest?
17. What purpose is served by creating a bond sinking fund?
18. How are bond sinking funds classified for balance sheet purposes?
19. Why are convertible bonds attractive to investors?
20. What two legal documents are involved when a company signs a note payable that is secured by a mortgage? What is the purpose of each?

MULTIPLE CHOICE

1. If bonds are issued initially at a discount and the straight-line method of amortization is used for the discount, interest expense in the earlier years will be:
   a. Greater than if the interest method were used.
   b. The same as if the interest method were used.
   c. Less than if the interest method were used.
   d. Less than the amount of the interest payments.
   e. None of the above.

2. When the interest payment dates of a bond are May 1 and November 1, and a bond investment is sold on June 1, the amount of cash received by the selling investor will be:
   a. Decreased by accrued interest from June 1 to November 1.
   b. Decreased by accrued interest from May 1 to June 1.
   c. Increased by accrued interest from June 1 to November 1.
   d. Increased by accrued interest from May 1 to June 1.
   e. None of the above.

3. On March 1, 1987, Rapaich Corporation sold at 103 plus accrued interest, 100 9%, $1,000 bonds issued by Allen Co. The bonds are dated January 1, 1987, and mature on January 1, 1997. Interest is payable semiannually on January 1 and July 1. Rapaich paid broker's fees of $5,000. Based on the information above, Papaich would realize cash receipts from the sale of:
   a. $98,000.
   b. $99,500.
   c. $103,000.
   d. $104,500.
   e. Some other amount.

4. The December 31, 1987, statement of financial position of Buddy Corporation includes the following items:

9% bonds payable due December 31, 1996	$400,000
Unamortized premium on bonds payable	10,800

   The bonds were issued on December 31, 1986, at 103, with interest payable on July 1 and December 31 of each year.

   On March 1, 1988 Buddy retired $200,000 of these bonds at 98 plus accrued interest. What should Buddy record as a gain on retirement of these bonds? (Assume straight-line amortization.)
   a. $5,300.
   b. $5,900.
   c. $9,300.
   d. $10,800.
   e. Some other amount.

5. A company has $100,000 of bonds outstanding. The unamortized discount on these bonds is $4,500. The company redeemed these bonds for 97% of par. What was its gain (loss) on the redemption?

   a. $1,500.
   b. $(1,500).
   c. $3,000.
   d. $(3,000).
   e. $(4,500).

6. On January 1, 198A, Y Corporation issued $100,000 par value of 10-year, 10% bonds payable, and received $88,550 cash proceeds from the issue. The bonds pay interest semiannually on July 1 and January 1, and the market rate of interest on the date of issue was 12%. Y Corporation's respective interest expense and actual cash payment to be recorded on July 1, 198A, using the straight-line method, will be:

   a. $5,000 interest expense; $5,000 cash payment.
   b. $5,313 interest expense; $5,313 cash payment.
   c. $5,572.50 interest expense; $5,572.50 cash payment.
   d. $5,313 interest expense; $5,000 cash payment.
   e. $5,572.50 interest expense; $5,000 cash payment.

7. On January 1, 198A, a corporation issued $100,000 of 10-year bonds that pay 8% annually. At the time of the issue, the bonds' investors were demanding only a 7% return on their investment, and the cash proceeds of the bond issue to the corporation were $106,992. If the corporation uses the interest method, the premium amortization to be recorded on December 31, 198A, is:

   a. $6,992.00.
   b. $699.20.
   c. $559.36.
   d. $510.56.
   e. Some other amount.

8. A corporation has $50,000 of convertible bonds outstanding. The unamortized discount on these bonds is $600, and the market value of the bonds is $45,000. If the bonds are converted, the sum of the credits to contributed capital accounts in the entry to record the conversion will be:

   a. $50,000.
   b. $600.
   c. $50,600.
   d. $49,400.
   e. $45,000.

9. On April 30, 19A1, Banister, Inc., purchased Curzon Corporation, 10-year, 9% bonds with a face value of $120,000 for $133,600, which included $3,600 accrued interest. The bonds mature on January 1, 19A8, and pay interest on January 1 and July 1. Banister uses the straight-line method of amortization. The amount of income Banister should report for the year

ended December 31, 19A1, as a result of this long-term bond investment, is:

    a. $6,200.
    b. $6,393.
    c. $6,533.
    d. $8,200.
    e.   Some other amount.

MINI DISCUSSION CASE

Case 17–1   The June 1986 issue of "Investment Research Overview" published by Richardson Greenshields of Canada Limited states:

    Strip bonds (or "zero-coupon" bonds, as they are called in the United States) began to sell in Canada in 1982. In the four years since that time an estimated $5 billion bonds have been "stripped" and sold by investment dealers in Canada. Harold B. Ehrlich, Chairman, Berstein Macaulay Money Management Ltd., is quoted as saying, "When the history books are written, I am convinced zero-coupon bonds will be one of the great financial inventions of the 1970s and 1980s.

Required:

    Differentiate coupon and zero-coupon bonds and critically evaluate the claim made by Harold B. Ehrlich.

CLASS EXERCISES

    (In solving the exercises and problems at the end of Chapter 17, round all dollar amounts to the nearest whole dollar.)

Exercise 17–1   On December 31, 198A, a company borrowed $75,000 by signing a five-year, 14% installment note. The note requires annual payments on December 31 of accrued interest plus equal amounts of principal. Prepare journal entries to record the first payment on December 31, 198B, and the last payment on December 31, 198F.

Exercise 17–2   On December 31, 198A, a company borrowed $75,000 by signing a five-year, 14% installment note. The note requires annual payments of $21,846 to be made on December 31. Prepare journal entries to record the first payment on December 31, 198B, and the second payment on December 31, 198C.

Exercise 17–3   A company borrowed $80,000 by signing an eight-year, 12% installment note. The terms of the note require eight annual payments of an equal amount, the first of which is due one year after the date of the note. Calculate the amount of the installment payments, based on the present values contained in Table 12–2.

Exercise 17–4

On May 31 of the current year, a corporation sold at par plus accrued interest $1,000,000 of its 10.2% bonds. The bonds were dated January 1 of the current year, with interest payable on each July 1 and January 1. *(a)* Give the entry to record the sale. *(b)* Give the entry to record the first interest payment. *(c)* Set up a T-account for Bond Interest Expense and post the portions of the entries that affect the account. Answer these questions: *(d)* How many months' interest were accrued on these bonds when they were sold? *(e)* How many months' interest were paid on July 1? *(f)* What is the balance of the Bond Interest Expense account after the entry recording the first interest payment is posted? *(g)* How many months' interest does this balance represent? *(h)* How many months' interest did the bondholders earn during the first interest period?

Exercise 17–5

On March 1 of the current year, a corporation sold $3,000,000 of its 10.8%, 20-year bonds. The bonds were dated March 1 of the current year, with interest payable on each September 1 and March 1. Give the entries to record the sale at 98¾ and the first semiannual interest payment under the assumption that the straight-line method is used to amortize the discount.

Exercise 17–6

On December 31 of the current year, a corporation sold $2,000,000 of its 9.8%, 10-year bonds at a price that reflected a 12% market rate for bond interest. Interest is payable each June 30 and December 31. Calculate the sales price of the bonds and prepare a general journal entry to record the sale of the bonds. (Use the present value tables, Tables 12–1 and 12–2).

Exercise 17–7

The corporation of Exercise 17–6 uses the interest method of amortizing bond discount or premium. Under the assumption the corporation of Exercise 17–6 sold its bonds for $1,747,650, prepare a schedule with the columnar headings of Illustration 17–4 and present the amounts in the schedule for the first two interest periods. Also, prepare general journal entries to record the first and second payments of interest to bondholders.

Exercise 17–8

A corporation sold $800,000 of its own 11%, eight-year bonds on November 1, 198A, at a price that reflected a 10% market rate of bond interest. The bonds pay interest each May 1 and November 1. *(a)* Calculate the price at which the bonds sold, and *(b)* prepare a general journal entry to record the sale. (Use the present value tables, Tables 12–1 and 12–2.)

Exercise 17–9

Assume that the bonds of Exercise 17–8 sold for $843,343 and that the corporation uses the interest method to amortize bond discount or premium. Prepare general journal entries to accrue interest on December 31, 198A, and to record the first payment of interest on May 1, 198B.

Exercise 17–10

A corporation sold $700,000 of its 9.2%, 20-year bonds at 95½ on their date of issue, January 1, 19—. Five years later, on January 1, after the bond interest for the period had been paid and 25% of the total discount on the issue had been amortized, the corporation purchased $100,000 par value of the bonds on the open market at 101¼ and retired them. Give the entry to record the retirement.

Exercise 17–11

On January 1, 198A, a corporation sold $1,500,000 of 15-year sinking fund bonds. The corporation expects to earn 8% on assets deposited with the sinking fund trustee and is required to deposit $55,244 with the trustee at the end of each year in the life of the bonds. (a) Prepare a general journal entry to record the first deposit of $55,244 with the trustee on January 1, 198B. (b) Prepare a general journal entry on December 31, 198B, to record the $4,380 earnings for 198B reported to the corporation by the trustee. (c) After the final payment to the trustee, the sinking fund had an accumulated balance of $1,506,780. Prepare the general journal entry to record the payment to the bondholders on January 1, 199F.

Exercise 17–12

A corporation has outstanding $10,000,000 of 8%, 20-year bonds on which there is $225,000 of unamortized bond premium. The bonds are convertible into the corporation's no-par value common stock at the rate of one $1,000 bond for 200 shares of the stock, and $500,000 of the bonds have been presented for conversion. Give the entry to record the conversion as of July 12.

Exercise 17–13

On October 1, 198B, Nickle Company purchased 50 $1,000 par value, 12%, 10-year Blanco Corporation bonds dated December 31, 198A. The bonds pay interest semiannually on June 30 and December 31. Nickle Company bought the bonds at 96 plus accrued interest and a $900 brokerage fee. Nickle intends to hold the bonds as a temporary investment. Prepare journal entries for Nickle Company to record the purchase and to record the receipt of interest on December 31, 198B.

PROBLEMS

(In solving the problems at the end of this chapter, round all dollar amounts to the nearest whole dollar.)

Problem 17–1

Kramer Company financed a major expansion of its production capacity by borrowing money and signing an installment note at the bank. The four-year, 14%, $300,000 note is dated June 30, 198A, and requires equal semiannual payments beginning December 31, 198A.

Required:

1. Calculate the amount of the installment payments. (Use Table 12–2.)
2. Prepare a table with column headings as shown in Illustration 17–1. Complete the table for the Kramer Company note.

3. Prepare general journal entries to record the first and the last payments on the note.

4. Assume that the note does not require equal payments. Instead, assume the note requires payments of accrued interest plus equal amounts of principal. Prepare general journal entries to record the first and the last payments on the note.

Problem 17–2
A corporation sold $1,000,000 of its own 9.3%, 10-year bonds on their date of issue, January 1, 198A. Interest was payable on the bonds on each June 30 and December 31, and they were sold at a price to yield the buyers a 10% annual return. The corporation uses the straight-line method of amortizing discount or premium.

Required:

1. Prepare a calculation to show the price at which the bonds were sold. (Use the present value tables, Tables 12–1 and 12–2.)
2. Prepare a form with the columnar headings of Illustration 17–3 and fill in the amounts for the first two interest periods of the bond issue. Round all amounts to the nearest whole dollar.
3. Prepare entries in general journal form to record the sale of the bonds and the first two payments of interest.

Problem 17–3
On January 1, 198A, a corporation sold $1,500,000 of its own 12.9%, 10-year bonds. The bonds were dated January 1, 198A, with interest payable on each June 30 and December 31, and were sold to yield the buyers a 12% annual return. The corporation uses the interest method of amortizing premium or discount.

Required:

1. Prepare a calculation to show the price at which the bonds were sold. (Use the present value tables, Tables 12–1 and 12–2.)
2. Prepare a form with the columnar headings of Illustration 17–5 and fill in the amounts for the first two interest periods of the bond issue. Round all amounts to the nearest whole dollar.
3. Prepare entries in general journal form to record the sale of the bonds and the first two payments of interest.

Problem 17–4
Prepare general journal entries to record the following transactions of Dazzle Corporation. Use the present value tables, Tables 12–1 and 12–2, as necessary, to calculate the amounts in your entries. (Remember to round all amounts to the nearest whole dollar.)

198A
Jan. 1 Sold $700,000 of its own 13.3%, 10-year bonds dated January 1, 198A, with interest payable on each June 30 and December 31. The bonds sold for a price that reflected a 14% market rate of bond interest.
June 30 Paid the semiannual interest on the bonds and amortized a portion of the discount calculated by the straight-line method.

Dec. 31 Paid the semiannual interest on the bonds and amortized a portion of the discount calculated by the straight-line method.

31 Deposited $43,925 with the sinking fund trustee to establish the sinking fund to repay the bonds.

198B
Dec. 30 Received the report of the sinking fund trustee that the sinking fund had earned $4,350.

199A
Jan. 1 Received a report from the sinking fund trustee which noted that the bondholders had been paid $700,000 on that day. Included was a $2,160 cheque for the extra cash accumulated in the sinking fund.

Problem 17–5   Prepare general journal entries to record the following bond transactions of McAdams Corporation.

198A
Oct. 1 Sold $5,000,000 par value of its own 9.7%, 10-year bonds at a price to yield the buyers a 9% annual return. The bonds were dated October 1, 198A, with interest payable on each April 1 and October 1.

Dec. 31 Made an adjusting entry to record the accrued interest on the bonds and to amortize the premium applicable to 198A. The interest method was used in calculating the premium amortized.

198B
Apr. 1 Paid the semiannual interest on the bonds and amortized the remainder of the premium applicable to the first interest period.

Oct. 1 Paid the semiannual interest on the bonds and amortized the premium applicable to the second interest period of the issue.

198C
Oct. 1 After recording the entry paying the semiannual interest on the bonds on this date and amortizing a portion of the premium, the carrying amount of the bonds on McAdams Corporation's books was $5,196,330. McAdams then purchased one tenth of the bonds at 101¼ and retired them. Record the purchase and retirement of the bonds.

Problem 17–6   On December 31, 198A, Wimberly Corporation sold $2,500,000 of 10-year, 9.3% bonds payable at a price that reflected a 10% market rate of bond interest. The bonds pay interest on June 30 and December 31. Use the present value tables, Tables 12–1 and 12–2, as necessary, in calculating the amounts in your answers.

Required:

1. Present a general journal entry to record the sale of the bonds.
2. Present general journal entries to record the first and second payments of interest on June 30, 198B, and on December 31, 198B, assuming straight-line amortization of premium or discount.
3. Present general journal entries to record the first and second payments of interest on June 30, 198B, and on December 31, 198B, assuming the use of the interest method to amortize premium or discount.
4. Prepare a schedule like the one on page 717 that has columns for the beginning-of-period carrying amount, interest expense to be recorded, and interest expense as a percentage of carrying amount, assuming use of the (1) interest method, and (2) straight-line method. In completing the schedule, present the amounts for Periods 1 and 2.

ALTERNATE PROBLEMS

(In solving the following alternate and provocative problems, round all dollar amounts to the nearest whole dollar.)

Problem 17–1A

On June 30, 198A, Mandel Company borrowed $180,000 at the bank by signing a five-year, 12% installment note. The terms of the note require equal semiannual payments beginning December 31, 198A.

Required:

1. Calculate the amount of the installment payments. (Use Table 12–2.)
2. Prepare a table with column headings as shown in Illustration 17–1. Complete the table for the Mandel Company note.
3. Prepare general journal entries to record the first and the last payments on the note.
4. Assume that the note does not require equal payments. Instead, assume the note requires payments of accrued interest plus equal amounts of principal. Prepare general journal entries to record the first and the last payments on the note.

Problem 17–2A

Armen Corporation sold $500,000 of its own 8.5%, 10-year bonds on their date of issue, January 1, 198A. Interest was payable on the bonds on each June 30 and December 31, and they were sold at a price to yield the buyers a 9% annual return. The corporation uses the straight-line method of amortizing discount or premium.

Required:

1. Prepare a calculation to show the price at which the bonds were sold. (Use the present value tables, Tables 12–1 and 12–2.)
2. Prepare a form with the columnar headings of Illustration 17–3 and fill in the amounts for the first two interest periods of the bond issue.
3. Prepare entries in general journal form to record the sale of the bonds and the first two payments of interest.

Problem 17–3A

Nifty Corporation sold $1,200,000 of its own 14.8%, 10-year bonds on January 1, 198A. The bonds were dated January 1, 198A, with interest payable on each June 30 and December 31, and were sold to yield the buyers a 14% annual return. The corporation uses the interest method of amortizing premium or discount.

Required:

1. Prepare a calculation to show the price at which the bonds were sold. (Use the present value tables, Tables 12–1 and 12–2.)
2. Prepare a form with the columnar headings of Illustration 17–5 and fill in the amounts for the first two interest periods of the bond issue.
3. Prepare entries in general journal form to record the sale of the bonds and the first two payments of interest.

**Problem
17–4A**

Prepare general journal entries to record the following transactions of Westlink Corporation. Use the present value tables, Tables 12–1 and 12–2, as necessary, to calculate the amounts in your entries. (Remember to round all amounts to the nearest whole dollar.)

198A
Jan. 1   Sold $1,600,000 of its own 11.1%, 10-year bonds dated January 1, 198A, with interest payable on each June 30 and December 31. The bonds sold for a price that reflected a 12% market rate of bond interest.

June 30   Paid the semiannual interest on the bonds and amortized a portion of the discount calculated by the straight-line method.

Dec. 31   Paid the semiannual interest on the bonds and amortized a portion of the discount calculated by the straight-line method.

31   Deposited $91,175 with the sinking fund trustee to establish the sinking fund to repay the bonds.

198B
Dec. 30   Received the report of the sinking fund trustee that the sinking fund had earned $10,950.

199A
Jan. 1   Received a report from the sinking fund trustee that noted that the bondholders had been paid $1,600,000 on that day. Included was a $4,780 cheque for the extra cash accumulated in the sinking fund.

**Problem
17–5A**

Prepare general journal entries to record the following bond transactions of Reister Corporation.

198A
Nov. 1   Sold $3,000,000 par value of its own 9.5%, 10-year bonds at a price to yield the buyers a 9% annual return. The bonds were dated November 1, 198A, with interest payable on each May 1 and November 1.

Dec. 31   Made an adjusting entry to record the accrued interest on the bonds and to amortize the premium applicable to 198A. The interest method was used in calculating the premium amortized.

198B
May 1   Paid the semiannual interest on the bonds and amortized the remainder of the premium applicable to the first interest period.

Nov. 1   Paid the semiannual interest on the bonds and amortized the premium applicable to the second interest period of the issue.

198C
Nov. 1   After recording the entry paying the semiannual interest on the bonds on this date and amortizing a portion of the premium, the carrying amount of the bonds on Reister Corporation's books was $3,076,663. Reister then purchased one tenth of the bonds at 100¾ and retired them. Record the purchase and retirement of the bonds.

**Problem
17–6A**

On December 31, 198A, Raindeer Corporation sold $2,400,000 of 10-year, 11.3% bonds payable at a price that reflected a 12% market rate of bond interest. The bonds pay interest on June 30 and December 31. Use the present value tables, Tables 12–1 and 12–2, as necessary, in calculating the amounts in your answers.

Required:

1.   Present a general journal entry to record the sale of the bonds.
2.   Present general journal entries to record the first and second payments of interest on June 30, 198B, and on December 31, 198B, assuming straight-line amortization of premium or discount.

3. Present general journal entries to record the first and second payments of interest on June 30, 198B, and on December 31, 198B, assuming the use of the interest method to amortize premium or discount.

4. Prepare a schedule like the one on page 715 that has columns for the beginning-of-period carrying amount, interest expense to be recorded, and interest expense as a percentage of carrying amount, assuming use of the (1) interest method, and (2) straight-line method. In completing the schedule, present the amounts for Period 1 and Period 2.

PROVOCATIVE PROBLEMS

Provocative Problem 17–1, A Comparison of Alternative Bond Issues

Ticket Sales Company is planning a major expansion of its operations and needs $1,000,000 to finance the expansion. The company has been presented with three alternative financing proposals. Each involves issuing bonds that pay interest semiannually. The alternatives are:

Plan A: Issue at par $1,000,000 of 10-year, 12% bonds.

Plan B: Issue $1,130,000 of 10-year, 10% bonds.

Plan C: Issue $897,000 of 10-year, 14% bonds.

Regardless of which plan is followed, the market rate of interest for the bonds is expected to be 12%.

For each bond issue, calculate the cash proceeds of the issue, the interest expense for the first six-month period, and the expected cash outflow each six-month period for interest. Use the interest method of amortizing bond premium or discount. Which plan has the smallest cash demands on the company prior to the final payment at maturity? Which requires the largest payment upon maturity?

Provocative Problem 17–2, Financing with Stock or Bonds

The shareholders' equity of Raider Corporation consists of 500,000 shares of outstanding common stock on which the corporation has earned an average of $0.45 per share during each of the last three years. In an effort to increase earnings, management is planning an expansion that will require the investment of an additional $2,500,000 in the business. The $2,500,000 is to be acquired either by selling an additional 250,000 shares of the company's common stock at $10 per share or selling at par $2,500,000 of 8%, 20-year bonds. Management estimates that the expansion will double the company's before-tax earnings the first year after it is completed and will increase before-tax earnings an additional 25% over that level in the years that follow.

Raider Corporation's management wants to finance the expansion in the manner that will serve the best interests of present shareholders and has asked you to evaluate the two alternatives from this perspective. In your report express an opinion as to the relative merits and disadvantages of each of the proposed ways of securing the funds needed for the expansion. Attach to your report a schedule showing expected earnings per share of the common shareholders under each method of financing. In preparing your schedule, assume that the company presently pays out in income taxes 50% of its before-tax earnings and that it will continue to pay out the same share after the expansion.

ANALYTICAL AND REVIEW PROBLEMS

Problem 17–1 A&R

The accounts of Clues Corporation showed the following balances as of December 31, 1987:

Bonds Payable $1,000,000
Bond Discount 20,600

The 9% 10-year bonds dated August 1, 1985, were issued on December 1, 1985, and the cash proceeds were $1,006,800. Interest is payable semiannually.

Required:

Reconstruct the entries pertaining to the bond issue that were made on the company's books. Assume that the company's fiscal year coincides with the calendar year.

Problem 17–2 A&R

On June 30, 198A, Yee Chan Corporation issued $100,000 par value 10%, 10-year bonds convertible at the rate of $1,000 bond for 50 common shares. The bonds were dated June 30, 198A and were sold at a price to yield investors 12%. Interest was payable annually.

Required:

a. Prepare entries on the following dates (Yee uses straight-line to amortize discounts or premiums):

June 30, 198A, December 31, 198A (year-end), June 30, 198B, and June 30, 198C to record conversion of 20 of the bonds.

b. On the assumption that Yee used the interest method for amortization of discounts and premiums prepare entries on the following dates:

December 31, 198A.

June 30, 198B.

June 30, 198C.

Problem 17–3 A&R

On May 1, 198A, John Jraige purchased as a long-term investment 10, $1,000 par value, 12% bonds, due 5½ years from date of purchase. Interest on the bonds is due and payable annually on November 1. Jraige does not use discount or premium accounts related to investments of this nature and uses straight-line amortization.

Required:

a. On the assumption that Jraige's *total* cash outlay for the bonds was $8,520 prepare entries on the following 198A dates:

May 1, 198A.

November 1, 198A.

December 31, 198A (year-end).

b. On the assumption that Jraige's total cash outlay for the bonds was $11,260 prepare the entries on the following dates:

May 1, 198A.

November 1, 198A.

December 31, 198A (year-end).

**Problem 17–4
A&R**

Visser Co., Limited, had excellent prospects, however, currently was experiencing a severe cash flow problem which was expected to persist for the next three or four years. Visser was able to arrange a sale of "low" coupon bonds which would: *(a)* relieve the immediate cash flow problem and *(b)* not require large interest cost outflow during the life of the bonds. The bond issue was for $1,000,000 par value, 2% annual, five-year bonds. The bonds were dated and issued April 1, 1987, to yield 12%. Visser's fiscal year ends December 31.

Required (round calculations to the nearest dollar):

1. Journalize the bond issue.
2. Prepare the December 31, 1987, adjusting journal entry assuming straight-line amortization.
3. Prepare the necessary April 1, 1988, journal entry (assume amortization of discount is also recorded at the time of interest payment).
4. Repeat entries of (3) and (4) assuming interest method amortization calculations to be based on annual compounding on April 1 balance.

**Problem 17–5
A&R**

Assume that C. Ainslie Inc., purchased, as long-term investment, $100,000 of the Visser Co., Limited, bonds (Problem 17–4 A&R) on the date of issue. Ainslie's fiscal period ends December 31.

Required (round calculations to nearest dollar):

1. Prepare the journal entry to record the investment in Visser Co. bonds.
2. Prepare the December 31, 1987, adjusting entry.
3. Prepare the April 1, 1988, entry.
4. Prepare the October 1, 1988, entry or entries to record the sale of one half of the Visser Co. bonds at a gain of $5,000.
5. Prepare the December 31, 1988, adjusting entry.

**Problem 17–6
A&R**

DeLano Corporation issued $1,000,000 par value, 12% annual, 10-year bonds. The bonds were dated April 1, 1987; however, because of market conditions they were not sold until August 1, 1987. All of the bonds were sold on August 1 at *total* proceeds of $1,051,600.

DeLano's fiscal period ends December 31 and the company intends to use straight-line amortization of premium.

Required:

Prepare the necessary journal entries as of: *(a)* August 1, 1987, *(b)* December 31, 1987, *(c)* April 1, 1988, and *(d)* December 31, 1988.

Financial Statements,
Interpretation and
Modifications

PART SIX

Cash Flow Information: Statement of Changes in Financial Position (SCFP)

18

After studying Chapter 18, you should be able to:

Explain why an adequate amount of cash is important in the operation of a business.

List a number of sources and uses of cash.

Explain why the net income reported on an income statement is not the amount of cash generated by operations.

Describe the adjustments that must be made to the reported net income figure in order to determine the amount of cash generated by operations.

Describe the three methods used as tools of analysis in the preparation of a statement of changes in financial position.

Prepare a statement of changes in financial position on a cash basis.

Define or explain the words and phrases listed in the chapter Glossary.

When financial statements are prepared for a business, the balance sheet reports the financial position at a specific point of time; that is, at the year-end balance sheet date. When the beginning-of-year and the end-of-year balance sheets are compared, the amounts normally differ. The balance sheet is a static statement and does not explain why certain year-end balances differ from their beginning-of-year balances. In contrast, the income statement is a change statement; it helps to explain the change in retained earnings due to operations during the year. The income statement reports in detail the specific items that result in net income or loss. Similarly, the statement of retained earnings is an action statement and reports on changes in retained earnings caused by items other than operation results. The income statement and statement of retained earnings do not, however, show the effects of all the events which affected the company's ability to meet its cash obligations on time, nor do these statements report the causes of the changes in assets, liabilities, and stated capital.

To overcome these deficiencies or to supplement the accrual basis statements, a *statement of changes in financial position* (SCFP) is prepared. The SCFP is a change statement that reports the cumulative cash inflows and outflows of the business.

OBJECTIVE OF THE SCFP

The *CICA Handbook,* Section 1540 states:

> The objective of the statement of changes in financial position is to provide information about the operating, financing and investing activities of an enterprise and the effects of those activities on cash resources. The statement of changes in financial position assists users of financial statements in evaluating the liquidity and solvency of an enterprise, and in assessing its ability to generate cash from internal sources, to repay debt obligations, to reinvest and to make distributions to owners. This information is not provided or is only indirectly provided in the balance sheet, income statement and statement of retained earnings. Thus, the statement of changes in financial position complements, and presents information different from that provided in, the other financial statements.

Cash resources may be interpreted as cash only or *cash equivalents.* The latter would normally include cash and temporary investments net of short-term borrowing.

The phrase in the title of the SCFP, ''changes in financial position'' is descriptive. It is the changes in assets, liabilities, and owners' equity that cause the inflows and outflows of cash. The SCFP focuses on reporting these changes in financial position. The SCFP reports the total of all sources of cash, classified by each major source. It also shows the total of all uses of cash, classified by each major use.

SCFP NONCASH FINANCING AND INVESTING ACTIVITIES

The *CICA Handbook* (paragraph 1540.20) recommends that all resources be embraced in the SCFP. That is, the reporting entity should disclose all important aspects of its financing and investing activities regardless of whether cash is directly affected. Thus, the SCFP would report all direct exchanges of noncash items. This includes those transactions that involve the exchange of assets, liabilities, or capital stock even when there is no direct inflow or outflow of cash. For example, if a business acquires an asset (e.g., property) and "pays" for it in full by issuing its own capital stock to the vendor, there has been no inflow or outflow of cash. Nevertheless, this transaction would be reported as if there were: *(a)* an inflow of cash (from the issuance of the stock) and *(b)* an outflow of cash (for the acquisition of the asset-property). Transactions of this type are part of the financing and investing activities of the reporting entity; they affect its capital and asset structure and therefore need to be disclosed. The financing and investing aspects of such transactions would be disclosed separately in a manner that indicates the nature of their relationship.

Transactions such as stock dividends, stock splits, and appropriation of retained earnings do not affect the resources of the reporting entity, nor can they be regarded as financing and investing activities. Therefore, these transactions would not be disclosed in the SCFP.

DISCLOSURE OF THE SCFP

For various reasons such as industry peculiarities, capital structure, and others, the individual items disclosed in an SCFP will vary among reporting entities and from period to period. However, information relating to the operating, financing, and investing activities is common to all enterprises, and the resulting cash flows from these activities is of significance to users of financial statements of all enterprises.

Thus, a minimum required disclosure was set by the CICA Accounting Standards Committee. Paragraph 1540.12 of the *CICA Handbook* recommends that:

The statement of changes in financial position should disclose at least the following items:

(a) cash from operations: the amount of cash from operations should be reconciled to the income statement or the components of cash from operations should be disclosed;

(b) cash flows resulting from extraordinary items;

(c) outlays for acquisition and proceeds on disposal of assets, by major category, not included in *(a)* or *(b)* above;

(d)   the issue, assumption, redemption and repayment of debt not included in *(a)* or *(b)* above;

(e)   the issue, redemption and acquisition of share capital; and

(f)   the payment of dividends, identifying separately dividends paid by subsidiaries to minority interests.

FORMAT OF THE SCFP

Although there may be variations in the format of the SCFP, the minimum disclosure recommendation, as set out above (paragraph 1540.12) limits the variations in presentation. However, the three components of the statement—operations, financing, and investing activities— are broad categories that allow one to choose the items that are to be included under each heading. For example, are dividends that are regularly paid by the reporting entity to be included as part of normal operating activities or should they be regarded as a financing activity? The authors believe that disclosure and consistency must dictate where some contentious items are to be placed in the SCFP. Thus, the format is as follows:

1.   Cash flows from operating activities:
     Cash flows from operations as translated from the income statement (to include changes in the current assets and current liabilities (except for cash). Items *(a)* and *(b)* of paragraph 15.40.12.
2.   Cash flows from financing activities:
     Cash flows that result in changes in the size and composition of the capital structure (both debt and equity). Items *(d)* and *(e)* of paragraph 1540.12.
3.   Cash flows from investing activities:
     Cash flows from noncurrent asset transactions. Item *(c)* of paragraph 1540.12.
4.   Dividends. Item *(f)* of paragraph 1540.12.

A format similar to that set out is used by CDC Life Sciences Inc., and is reproduced as Illustration 18–1.

PREPARATION OF THE SCFP, CASH BASIS

To identify the various sources and uses of cash, three approaches will be illustrated. These are *(a)* the direct approach, *(b)* the working paper approach and *(c)* the T-account approach.

DIRECT APPROACH

The direct approach uses *(a)* comparative balance sheets (in which beginning-of-the-year and end-of-the-year amounts are compared), (b)

Illustration 18–1

CDC LIFE SCIENCES INC.
Consolidated Statement of Changes in Financial Position
Year ended December 31 (in thousands)

	1985	1984
Cash provided by operations:		
Income before extraordinary item	$12,527	$ 8,331
Adjusted for items not affecting cash		
Depreciation	3,562	3,599
Equity in income of other companies	(2,196)	(1,070)
Deferred income taxes	(1,610)	4,539
Minority interest	1,783	1,619
Loss on disposition of a subsidiary	466	—
	14,532	17,018
Less dividends—Class A preferred	374	408
—paid to minority interest	1,070	1,396
Free cash flow	13,088	15,214
Cash provided by extraordinary item	—	6,800
(Increase) decrease in net current assets other than cash:		
(Increase) decrease in:		
Accounts receivable	(7,229)	(4,825)
Inventories	560	4,958
(Decrease) increase in:		
Accounts payable and accrued liabilities	17,019	4,342
Income taxes payable	57	213
	10,407	4,688
Cash provided by operations	23,495	26,702
Cash used in investment activities		
Fixed asset additions	(11,811)	(7,651)
Additions to other assets	(801)	(4,855)
Cash used in investment activities	(12,612)	(12,506)
Cash provided by (used in) financing activities		
Reduction of minority interest (Note 6)	(3,000)	(3,007)
Decrease in total debt	(139)	(18,228)
Issue of common shares	—	30,000
Redemption of preference shares	—	(7,000)
Cash provided by (used in) financing activities	(3,139)	1,765
Increase in cash during the year	7,744	15,961
Cash balance—beginning of year	19,263	3,302
Cash balance—end of year	$27,007	$19,263

the current income statement, and *(c)* supplementary data to clarify certain transactions. To illustrate the direct approach, consider data given in Illustration 18–2. The related SCFP, cash basis, is shown in Illustration 18–3. Notice that the last column in Illustration 18–3 headed Increase/Decrease is helpful in the analysis. The comparative balance sheets show that cash increased by $2,700 during 198B. Therefore, $2,700 must be

Illustration 18–2

DELTA CORPORATION
Comparative Balance Sheet
December 31, 198B, and December 31, 198A

	198B	198A	Increase (decrease)	
Assets				
Current assets:				
Cash	$ 7,500	$ 4,800	$ 2,700	
Accounts receivable, net	8,000	9,500	(1,500)	
Merchandise inventory	31,500	32,000	(500)	
Prepaid expenses	1,000	1,200	(200)	
Total current assets	$ 48,000	$ 47,500		$ 500
Plant and equipment:				
Office equipment	$ 3,500	$ 3,000	500	
Accumulated depreciation, office equipment	(900)	(600)	(300)	
Store equipment	26,200	21,000	5,200	
Accumulated depreciation, store equipment	(5,200)	(4,200)	(1,000)	
Buildings	95,000	80,000	15,000	
Accumulated depreciations, buildings	(10,600)	(8,200)	(2,400)	
Land	25,000	25,000		
Total plant and equipment	$133,000	$116,000		17,000
Total assets	$181,000	$163,500		$17,500
Liabilities				
Current liabilities:				
Notes payable	$ 2,500	$ 1,500	$ 1,000	
Accounts payable	16,700	19,600	(2,900)	
Dividends payable	1,000	700	300	
Total current liabilities	$ 20,200	$ 21,800	($ 1,600)	
Long-term liabilities:				
Mortgage payable	$ 17,500	$ 20,000	($ 2,500)	
Total liabilities	$ 37,700	$ 41,800		($ 4,100)
Shareholders' Equity				
Common stock	$123,500	$105,000	18,500	
Retained earnings	19,800	16,700	3,100	
Total shareholders' equity	$143,300	$121,700		21,600
Total liabilities and shareholders' equity	$181,000	$163,500		$17,500

Income statement and supplementary data:
  a. Purchased office equipment costing $500 during the year.
  b. Purchased store equipment that cost $6,000.
  c. Discarded and junked fully depreciated store equipment that cost $800 when new.
  d. Added a new addition to the building that cost $15,000.
  e. Earned a $12,200 net income during the year.
  f. Delta Company deducted on its 198B income statement $300 of depreciation on office equipment,
     (g) $1,800 on its store equipment, and (h) $2,400 on its building.
  i. Made a $2,500 payment on the mortgage.
  j. Declared and issued a 5% (500 shares) stock dividend at a time when the company's stock was
     selling for $12 per share.
  k. Sold and issued 1,000 shares of common stock at $12.50 per share.
  l. Declared cash dividends totaling $3,100 during the year.

Illustration 18–3

DELTA CORPORATION
Statement of Changes in Financial Position (Cash Basis)
For Year Ended December 31, 198B

Cash from (used by) operations:
Current operations:
Net income $12,200
Add expenses not requiring cash outlays
in the current period:
Depreciation of buildings and equipment 4,500
Accounts receivable decrease 1,500
Merchandise inventory decrease 500
Prepaid expenses decrease 200
Notes payable increase 1,000
Accounts payable decrease .... (2,900)
Dividends payable increase 300
  Cash provided by operations $17,300

Cash from (used by) financing activities:
Issuance of common stock......................... $12,500
Payment of mortgage .... (2,500)
  Cash provided by financing activities 10,000

Cash from (used by) investing activities:
Purchase of office equipment .... $ (500)
Purchase of store equipment .... (6,000)
Addition to building .... (15,000)
  Cash used by investing activities.................. (21,500)
Dividends declared .... (3,100)
  Increase in cash .... $ 2,700

the amount of the bottom line of the SCFP (Illustration 18–3). This change in cash during 198B is explained by identifying each source and use of cash.

Analysis of Sources and Uses of Cash

In Illustration 18–3 the $17,300 of cash from operations consists of the following three elements: (a) reported net income (from income statement), (b) expenses not requiring cash outlay in the current period (from income statement), and (c) increases and decreases in current assets and current liabilities *except cash* (from comparative balance sheets). The amounts are

a. $12,200
b.   4,500
c.   600
    $17,300

The $10,000 source of cash from financing activities consists of two elements: (a) proceeds from the issuance of common stock, and (b) the use of cash to pay a portion of the mortgage. Both of these items are given in the supplementary data and can be derived from the comparative balance sheets. Mortgage payable reflects the $2,500 decrease between the comparative balance sheets. The Common Stock account shows an increase of $18,500. The $18,500 amount is made up of $6,000 of capitalized retained earnings from the 500-share stock dividend and the $12,500 in proceeds from the issue of 1,000 shares.

Investing activities used $21,500 of cash. The purchase of office equipment for $500 and the construction of an addition to the building for $15,000 are shown in the supplementary data and can also be derived from the comparative balance sheets. These amounts represent increases in the respective accounts from the December 31, 198A and 198B balance sheets. The use of $6,000 to purchase store equipment, although given in the supplementary data, can be derived from the comparative balance sheets. The comparative balance sheets indicate that store equipment increased by $5,200 between December 31, 198A and December 31, 198B. Nevertheless, this increase was after a write-off of $800 during 198B because of the discarding of fully depreciated equipment. Thus, the increase is $6,000.

The amount of cash dividends totaling $3,100 was also given in the supplementary data and can be derived by comparing the retained earnings account balances on the comparative balance sheets. The $16,700 retained earnings at December 31, 198A were increased by $12,200 of net income for 198B and decreased by $6,000 as a result of the 500-share stock dividend. The difference between $22,900 ($16,700 + $12,200 − $6,000) and $19,800 (balance at December 31, 198B) of $3,100 represents the amount of cash dividends declared during 198B. The stock dividend is a book entry only and represents only a transfer (capitalization of retained earnings) from the retained earnings account to the capital stock account. This transaction does not affect the cash and is, therefore, not reflected on the SCFP.

Though the direct approach technique is adequate in most cases, a more formal method may be used. This is the working paper approach as illustrated and discussed below.

WORKING PAPER APPROACH

Delta Corporation's sources and uses of cash resulted from simple transactions, and the SCFP could be prepared without a working paper as illustrated in the direct-approach method. However, using a working paper helps to organize the information needed for the statement and also offers a proof of the accuracy of the work.

The working paper for Delta Corporation's SCFP is shown in Illustration 18–4. Such a working paper is prepared as follows:

Illustration 18–4

DELTA CORPORATION
Working Paper for Statement of Changes in Financial Position
(Cash Basis)
For Year Ended December 31, 198B

	Account Balances 31/12/8A	Analyzing Entries Debit	Analyzing Entries Credit	Account Balances 31/12/8B
Debits				
Cash	4,800			7,500
Accounts receivable, net	9,500		(m) 1,500	8,000
Merchandise inventory	32,000		(n) 500	31,500
Prepaid expenses	1,200		(o) 200	1,000
Office equipment	3,000	(a) 500		3,500
Store equipment	21,000	(b) 6,000	(c) 800	26,200
Buildings	80,000	(d) 15,000		95,000
Land	25,000			25,000
Totals	176,500			197,700
Credits				
Notes payable	1,500		(p) 1,000	2,500
Accounts payable	19,600	(q) 2,900		16,700
Dividends payable	700		(r) 300	1,000
Accumulated depreciation, office equipment	600		(f) 300	900
Accumulated depreciation, store equipment	4,200	(c) 800	(g) 1,800	5,200
Accumulated depreciation, buildings	8,200		(h) 2,400	10,600
Mortgage payable	20,000	(i) 2,500		17,500
Common stock	105,000		(j) 6,000 (k) 12,500	123,500
Retained earnings	16,700	(j) 6,000 (l) 3,100	(e) 12,200	19,800
Totals	176,500			197,700
Sources of cash:				
Current operations:				
Net income		(e) 12,200		
Depreciation of office equipment		(f) 300		
Depreciation of store equipment		(g) 1,800		
Depreciation of buildings		(h) 2,400		
Notes payable		(p) 1,000		
Accounts payable			(q) 2,900	
Accounts receivable		(m) 1,500		
Inventory		(n) 500		
Prepaid expenses		(o) 200		
Financing activities:				
Sale of stock		(k) 12,500		
Reduction of mortgage			(i) 2,500	
Investment activities:				
Purchase of office equipment			(a) 500	
Purchase of store equipment			(b) 6,000	
Addition to building			(d) 15,000	
Payment of dividends		(r) 300	(l) 3,100	
Totals		69,500	69,500	

1. First, the balance sheet account balances as of the beginning of the year are entered in the first column and the end-of-year balances are entered in the fourth column. Note that the account balance listings are grouped as debits and credits.

2. Next analyzing entries are entered in the second and third money columns. These entries do two things: (1) they account for or explain the amount of change in each account; and (2) they show the sources and uses of cash. (The analyzing entries on the illustrated working paper are discussed later in this chapter.)

3. After the last analyzing entry is entered, the working paper is completed by adding the Analyzing Entries columns to determine their equality. The information as to sources and uses of cash is then used to prepare the formal SCFP as shown in Illustration 18–3.

It should be noted that the working paper is prepared solely for the purpose of gathering information on the sources and uses of cash. Its analyzing entries are never entered in the accounts.

Analyzing Entries

As previously stated, in addition to setting out sources and uses of cash, the analyzing entries on the working paper also account for or explain the amount of change in each account. The change in each account is explained with one or more analyzing entries because every transaction that caused an increase or decrease in cash also increased or decreased another account. Consequently, when all increases and decreases in accounts are explained by means of analyzing entries, all sources and uses of cash are set out on the working paper.

The analyzing entries on the working paper of Illustration 18–4 account for the changes in Delta Corporation's accounts and set out its sources and uses of cash. Explanations of the entries follow:

a. During the year, Delta Corporation purchased new office equipment that cost $500. This required the use of cash and also caused a $500 increase in the balance of its Office Equipment account. Consequently, the analyzing entry (a) has a $500 debit to Office Equipment and a like credit to "Uses of cash: Purchase of office equipment." The debit accounts for the change in the Office Equipment account, and the credit sets out the use of cash.

b. Delta purchased $6,000 of new store equipment during the period. This required the use of $6,000 of cash, and its use is shown in the analyzing entry (b). However, the $6,000 debit of the entry does not fully account for the change in the balance of the Store Equipment account. Analyzing entry (c) is also needed.

c. During the period under review, Delta discarded and junked fully depreciated store equipment. The equipment originally had cost $800, and the entry made to record the disposal decreased the company's Store Equipment and related accumulated depreciation accounts by

$800. However, the disposal had no effect on the company's cash. Nevertheless, analyzing entry *(c)* must be made to account for the changes in the accounts. Otherwise all changes in the company's noncurrent accounts will not be explained. Unless all changes are explained, the person preparing the working paper cannot be certain that all sources and uses of cash have been set out on the working paper.

d. Delta used $15,000 to increase the size of its building. The cost of the addition was debited to the Buildings account, and analyzing entry *(d)* sets out this use of cash.

e. Delta reported a $12,200 net income for 198B, and the income was a source of cash. In the end-of-year closing procedures, the amount of this net income was transferred from the company's Income Summary account to its Retained Earnings account. It helped change the balance of the latter account from $16,700 at the beginning of the year to $19,800 at the year-end. Observe the analyzing entry that sets out this source of cash. The entry's debit shows the net income as a source of cash, and the credit helps explain the change in the Retained Earnings account.

f. *(g),* and *(h).* On its 198B income statement, Delta deducted $300 of depreciation expense on its office equipment, $1,800 on its store equipment, and $2,400 on its building. As previously explained, although depreciation is a rightful deduction from revenues in arriving at net income, any depreciation so deducted must be added to net income in determining cash from operations. The debits of entries *(f),* *(g),* and *(h)* show the depreciation taken by the company as part of the cash generated by operations. The credits of the entries either account for or help account for the changes in the accumulated depreciation accounts.

i. On June 10, Delta made a $2,500 payment on the mortgage on its plant and equipment. The payment required the use of cash, and it reduced the balance of the Mortgage Payable account by $2,500. Entry *(i)* sets out this use of cash and accounts for the change in the Mortgage Payable account.

j. At the September board meeting, the directors of the company declared a 500-share stock dividend on a day the company's stock was selling at $12 per share. The declaration and later-distribution of this dividend had no effect on the company's cash. However, it did decrease Retained Earnings by $6,000 and increase the Common Stock account by $6,000. Entry *(j)* accounts for the changes in the accounts resulting from the dividend.

k. In October, the company sold and issued 1,000 shares of its common stock for cash at $12.50 per share. The sale was a source of cash that increased the balance of the company's Common Stock account by $12,500. Entry *(k)* sets out this source of cash and completes the explanation of the changes in the stock account.

l. At the end of each of the first three quarters in the year, the company declared a $700 quarterly cash dividend. Then, on December 22, it declared a $1,000 dividend, payable on the following January 15. The fourth dividend brought the total cash dividends declared during the year to $3,100. Each declaration required the use of cash, and each reduced the balance of the Retained Earnings account. On the working paper, the four dividends are combined and one analyzing entry is made for the $3,100 use of cash. The entry's debit helps account for the change in the balance of the Retained Earnings account, and its credit sets out the use of working capital.

After the last analyzing entry is entered on the working paper, an examination is made to be certain that all changes in the accounts listed on the paper have been explained with analyzing entries. To make this examination, the debits and credits in the Analyzing Entries columns opposite each beginning account balance are added to or subtracted from the beginning balance. The result must equal the ending balance. For example, the $3,000 beginning debit balance of office equipment plus the $500 debit of analyzing entry (a) equals the $3,500 ending amount of office equipment. Likewise, the $21,000 beginning balance of store equipment plus the $6,000 debit and minus the $800 credit equals the $26,200 ending balance for this asset, and so on down the working paper until all changes are accounted for. Then, if in every case the debits and credits opposite each beginning balance explain or change in the balance, all sources and uses of cash have been set out on the working paper, and the working paper is completed by adding the amounts in its Analyzing Entries columns.

Preparing the SCFP from the Working Paper

After the working paper is completed, the sources and uses of cash set out on the bottom of the paper are used to prepare the formal statement of changes in financial position. This is a simple task that requires little more than a relisting of the sources and uses of cash on the formal statement, properly classified as in Illustration 18–3.

A Net Loss on the Working Paper

When a business incurs a net loss, the amount of the loss is debited to its Retained Earnings account in the end-of-period closing procedures. Then, when the working paper for the statement of changes in financial position is prepared, the words **Net loss** are substituted for **Net income** in its sources of cash section. The amount of the loss is then debited to Retained Earnings and credited to ''Net loss'' on the working paper. After this, the loss is placed on the formal statement of changes in financial position as the first monetary item and the expenses not requiring outlays of working capital are deducted therefrom. If the net loss is less than these expenses, the resulting amount is cash provided by operations. If the net loss exceeds these expenses, the result is cash used in operations.

T-ACCOUNT APPROACH

There are three basic approaches to the analysis of data necessary for the preparation of an SCFP. These are: (1) the direct approach, (2) the working paper approach, (both discussed up to this point) and (3) the T-account approach. All three approaches require an analysis of all of the balance sheet items. The net increase or decrease in each of these accounts, between the two consecutive balance sheets, must be analyzed to identify the inflow or outflow of cash during the period. For the more complex situations the work sheet approach is recommended because it assimilates all relevant data (including the statement format) on one working paper page. The T-account, however, is preferred by some for instructional purposes.

The T-account approach is illustrated below using the same data that was used for both the direct approach and working paper approaches; that is, the comparative balance sheets of Delta Corporation.

Accounts Receivable				Merchandise Inventory			
198A	9,500	(m)	1,500	198A	32,000	(n)	500
198B	8,000			198B	31,500		

Prepaid Expenses				Notes Payable			
198A	1,200	(o)	200			198A	1,500
						(p)	1,000
						198B	2,500
198B	1,000						

Accounts Payable				Dividends Payable			
(q)	2,900	198A	19,600			198A	700
						(r)	300
						198B	1,000
		198B	16,700				

Office Equipment				Store Equipment			
198A	3,000			198A	21,000		
(a)	500			(b)	6,000	(c)	800
198B	3,500			198B	26,200		

Buildings			Land		
198A	80,000		198A	25,000	
(d)	15,000				
198B	95,000		198B	25,000	

Accumulated Depreciation—Office Equipment			Accumulated Depreciation—Store Equipment		
		198A	600		
		(f)	300	(c)	800
		198B	900		

Accumulated Depreciation—Store Equipment

	198A	4,200	
(c) 800	(g)	1,800	
	198B	5,200	

Accumulated Depreciation—Buildings			Mortgage Payable		
		198A	8,200		
			2,400	(i)	2,500
		198B	10,600		

Mortgage Payable

	198A	20,000	
(i) 2,500			
	198B	17,500	

Common Stock			Retained Earnings		
		198A	105,000	(j)	6,000
		(j)	6,000	(l)	3,100
		(k)	12,500		
		198B	123,500		

Retained Earnings

(j) 6,000	198A	16,700	
(l) 3,100	(e)	12,200	
	198B	19,800	

Cash

Sources		Uses	
(e) Net income	12,200	(a) Purchase of equipment (office)	500
(f) (g) (h) Expense not requiring funds depreciation	4,500	(b) Purchase of equipment (store)	6,000
(k) Sale of common stock	12,500	(d) Addition to building	15,000
(m) Accounts receivable	1,500	(i) Payment on mortgage	2,500
(n) Merchandise inventory	500	(l) Dividends (cash)	3,100
(o) Prepaid expenses	200	(q) Accounts payable	2,900
(p) Notes payable	1,000	Increase in cash	2,700
(r) Dividends payable	300		
	32,700		32,700

USING A CASH PLUS TEMPORARY INVESTMENTS BASIS

If an SCFP is designed to explain the change in cash plus temporary investments, only minor modifications to the statement and working paper are necessary. The cash and temporary investment balances are added and treated as a single item. All other items are listed separately on the working paper and analyzed in exactly the same manner as if a cash basis were being used.

Similarly, if the statement is designed to explain the change in *working capital* (current assets − current liabilities), working capital is treated as a single item. All noncurrent accounts are listed separately on the working paper and analyzed in exactly the same manner shown for the cash basis (see Illustration 18–5). The analysis of entries would be in

Illustration 18–5

DELTA CORPORATION
Working Paper for Statement of Changes in Financial Position
Working Capital Basis
For Year Ended December 31, 198B

	Account Balances 31/12/8A	Analyzing Entries Debit	Analyzing Entries Credit	Account Balances 31/12/8B
Debits				
Working capital	25,700			27,800
Office equipment	3,000	(a) 500		3,500
Store equipment	21,000	(b) 6,000	(c) 800	26,200
Buildings	80,000	(d) 15,000		95,000
Land	25,000			25,000
Totals	154,700			177,500
Credits				
Accumulated depreciation, office equipment	600		(f) 300	900
Accumulated depreciation, store equipment	4,200	(c) 800	(g) 1,800	5,200
Accumulated depreciation, buildings	8,200		(h) 2,400	10,600
Mortgage payable	20,000	(i) 2,500		17,500
Common stock	105,000		(j) 6,000 (k) 12,500	123,500
Retained earnings	16,700	(j) 6,000 (l) 3,100	(e) 12,200	19,800
Totals	154,700			177,500
Sources of working capital:				
Current operations:				
Net income		(e) 12,200		
Depreciation of office equipment		(f) 300		
Depreciation of store equipment		(g) 1,800		
Depreciation of buildings		(h) 2,400		
Other sources:				
Sale of stock		(k) 12,500		
Uses of working capital:				
Purchases of office equipment			(a) 500	
Purchase of store equipment			(b) 6,000	
Addition to building			(d) 15,000	
Reduction of mortgage			(i) 2,500	
Declaration of dividends			(l) 3,100	
Totals		63,100	63,100	

terms of effect on working capital, and the explanation of the changes in the noncurrent accounts would be the same as given for these items in Illustration 18–3 except for the substitution of working capital for cash.

Prior to 1985, most companies prepared their SCFP to reflect the change in working capital, however the trend toward using a cash basis was accelerating. The 1985 revision of section 1540 of the *CICA Handbook* recommendation that the SCFP be prepared to reflect a change in cash or in cash and cash equivalents may be regarded as a revision of the *Handbook* to reflect the trend. Thus, the recommendation is really a mandate to prepare statements of changes in financial position on a cash basis.

Summary

The objective of comparative balance sheets is to report on the financial position of a concern at specific points of time. The objective of an income statement is to report the operations on the accrual basis. Thus, an income statement only partially explains the change in financial position between those specific points in time. To compliment the balance sheet, the income statement, and the statement of retained earnings—a statement of changes in financial position is prepared. The SCFP is designed to show how the company obtained and used cash during a period that corresponds to the period covered by the income statement. Thus, the SCFP explains in terms of cash the causes of financial changes that occurred between balance sheet dates.

This chapter presented three approaches towards preparing a statement of changes in financial position from income statement and balance sheet information. It is essential to consider not only the information provided by the SCFP but the relationship of the SCFP to the other financial statements.

GLOSSARY

Cash equivalents. The liquid financial resources readily available to the enterprise. Normally included are cash, net of short-term borrowings, temporary investments, and other elements of working capital when they are readily convertible into cash at their carrying value.

Statement of changes in financial position. A statement that reports the operating, financing, and investing activities of a business during a period, generally indicating their effects on cash, or on cash and cash equivalents.

Working capital. The excess of a company's current assets over its current liabilities.

QUESTIONS FOR CLASS DISCUSSION

1. List several sources of cash and several uses of cash.

2. Explain why expenses such as depreciation, amortization of patents, and amortization of bond discount are added to net income in order to determine cash provided by operations.

3. Some people speak of depreciation as a source of cash. Is depreciation a source of cash?

4. On June 3, a company borrowed $50,000 by giving its bank a 60-day, interest-bearing note. Was this transaction a source of cash? Was it a source of working capital?

5. A company had $70,000 of merchandise inventory at the beginning of a period and $40,000 of merchandise inventory at the end of the same period. Was the decrease in inventory a source of cash? Explain.

6. What information is shown on a statement of changes in financial position?

7. Why are the accounts other than cash examined to discover changes in cash?

8. When a working paper for the preparation of a statement of changes in financial position is prepared, all changes in balance sheet accounts, except cash, are accounted for on the working paper. Why?

9. A company discarded and wrote off fully depreciated store equipment. What account balances appearing on the statement of changes in financial position working paper were affected by the write-off? What analyzing entry was made on the working paper to account for the write-off? If the write-off did not affect cash, why was the analyzing entry made on the working paper?

10. Explain why a decrease in a current liability represents a decrease in cash.

11. How should (a) declarations of dividends and (b) payments of dividends be disclosed on the statement of changes in financial position?

12. A temporary investment was purchased for $10,000 in Year 1 and sold for $10,000 in Year 2. Under what conditions would the sale appear on a statement of changes in financial position for Year 2?

13. Under what conditions would a purchase of inventory for cash be shown as a "use" on a statement of changes in financial position?

14. If a company reports a large net loss for the year, is it possible for the company to show that cash was provided by operations? Why or why not?

15. A company amortized $5,000 of premium on bonds payable during a year. How should this amortization of bond premium be treated in calculating cash provided by operations?

16. A company purchased $100,000 of land by signing a long-term note payable

for the entire amount. Should this item be disclosed on a cash basis statement of changes in financial position? If so, how should it be shown?

MULTIPLE CHOICE

1. On December 31, 198A, the balance in the Salary Expense account was $13,800. The Salaries Payable account had a January 1, 198A, balance of $1,000, and a December 31, 198A, balance of $2,200. How much cash was paid for salaries in 198A?

    a. $17,000.
    b. $15,000.
    c. $13,800.
    d. $12,600.
    e. $11,600.

2. The following information concerns the Omega Corporation for 198A:

Cash balance, January 1, 198A	$41,000
Cash generated by operations	43,000
Cash dividends paid by Omega	24,000
Depreciation expense for 198A	12,000
Sale of warehouse	42,000
Purchase of marketable equity securities ...	40,000

    What is Omega's December 31, 198A, cash balance?

    a. $50,000.
    b. $62,000.
    c. $74,000.
    d. $86,000.
    e. $126,000.

3. A company's operations included the following activities:

Net income	$22,400
Depreciation expense, buildings	2,300
Depletion expense, oil wells	5,000
Amortization of bond discount	500
Payment of dividends declared last year ...	3,200
Cost of treasury stock purchased	5,000
Proceeds from sale of equipment	2,200
Increase in current assets (except cash) ...	800
Increase in current liabilities	600

    Given the above information, what is the amount of cash from operations?

    a. $34,800.
    b. $31,400.
    c. $31,900.
    d. $32,400.
    e. $35,600.

4. The 198A income statement for the Acme Company follows:

Sales		$92,000
Cost of goods sold		45,000
Gross profit on sales		$47,000
Operating expenses:		
Wage expense	$14,000	
Rent expense	13,000	
Depreciation expense	6,000	33,000
Net income		$14,000

Additional information is as follows:

1. Acme received $82,500 cash from customers during 198A.
2. Acme paid $40,200 for merchandise.
3. Employees of Acme were paid $13,600 in 198A.
4. Rent payments amounted to $14,000.

Acme's cash generated by operations for 198A was:
   a. $8,700.
   b. $14,700.
   c. $20,700.
   d. $42,300.
   e. $82,500.

5. X Company has supplied you with the following information

	December 31, 198A	December 31, 198B
Current assets	$46,000	$47,500
Current liabilities	32,500	36,250

What is X Company's net increase (decrease) in working capital?
   a. $2,250.
   b. $(2,250).
   c. $3,750.
   d. $1,500.
   e. $(1,500).

6. Proper accounting for the acquisition of a building in exchange for a mortgage requires:

   a. No disclosure in the statement of changes in financial position.
   b. Disclosure in the statement of changes in financial position of only the building acquisition and not the mortgage issuance.
   c. Disclosure in the statement of changes in financial position of only the mortgage issuance and not the building acquisition.
   d. Disclosure in the statement of changes in financial position of both the building acquisition and mortgage issuance.
   e. None of the above.

MINI DISCUSSION CASES

Case 18–1

Sandy Berlasty, sole owner and chief executive of Berlasty Widget Company, operated from the basement of her home. She made carved widgets at a cost of $7 each and sold them for $10. The cost of selling the widgets was $1 each. She had no other expenses and therefore Berlasty Widget Company's income was $2 each.

All production costs were paid in cash, as the custom in this so-called "cottage industry" was not to provide credit to customers. Berlasty kept her inventory at the end of each month equal to the number of widgets sold during that month. All sales were made on 30-day credit and the terms were strictly enforced. The operation was steady with sales of 1,000 widgets per month since the business was started two years ago. The balance sheet on May 31, 1987 was as follows:

Cash	$ 3,000	Liabilities	–0–
Accounts receivable	10,000		
Inventory	7,000	Sandy Berlasty, capital.........	20,000
	$20,000		$20,000

During Rotary's Art in the Park display, at which Berlasty had a showing of her widgets, sales took off. In June she sold 1,250 widgets, and in July 1,500. By the middle of July it appeared that sales would continue to increase at 250 widgets a month.

The established policy of the company was to maintain an end-of-month inventory equal to the sales of the month. For example, at the end of May, inventory was 1,000 widgets and at the end of June 1,250 widgets.

The sales picture was so good that Sandy decided to go on vacation the third week of July. Three days after she left, she received a telephone call from home to return immediately. The bank was "bouncing" her cheques and her suppliers were irate. She asked about the company's production, sales, and collections and was told they were all on schedule. She was heard to remark, "How can I be going broke while making such a good profit?"

Puzzled by the situation, Sandy Berlasty turns to you to solve the apparent mystery.

Case 18–2

During the Gulf Canada Corp., takeover of Hiram Walker Resources, in the spring of 1986, much was written by financial analysts on the reasons for the takeover. The most common reason was that Gulf was primarily interested in the cash generating portions of Walker Resources. Gulf Canada was a cash "user" company and needed a cash-generating unit.

Required:

Discuss the characteristics of a company that *(a)* makes it a cash-generating company and *(b)* one that is a cash user company.

CLASS EXERCISE

Exercise 18–1

Examine each of the following items to determine how the item should be disclosed on a statement of changes in financial position that is designed to explain the change in cash. Prepare a table for your answers and record your answers with checks in the appropriate columns.

	Source	Use	Not disclosed
a. A six-month note receivable was accepted in exchange for a building that had been used in operations.	___	___	___
b. A cash dividend that had been declared in a previous period was paid.	___	___	___
c. Surplus merchandise inventory was sold, resulting in a material reduction in the ending inventory as compared to the beginning inventory.	___	___	___
d. A cash dividend was declared but is not to be paid in the current period.	___	___	___
e. Retired long-term bonds payable by issuing common stock.	___	___	___
f. Borrowed cash from the bank by signing a six-month note payable.	___	___	___

Exercise 18–2

Given the following condensed income statement, and a partial list of account balances, calculate the cash provided by operations:

COPPERFIELD COMPANY
Income Statement
For Year Ended December 31, 19B

Sales		$225,000
Cost of goods sold		130,000
Gross profit from sales		$ 95,000
Operating expenses:		
Salaries and wages (includes $250 accrued on December 31) . .	$31,250	
Depreciation expense	3,750	
Rent expense	9,000	
Amortization of patents	750	
Bad debts expense (allowance method)	1,000	45,750
Operating income		$ 49,250
Bond interest expense (includes $375 of bond discount		
amortized and $1,500 accrued on December 31)		3,375
Net income		$ 45,875

Copperfield Company's partial list of Comparative Account balances as of December 31, 19A and 19B.

	19A	19B
Cash	$ 2,200	$ 2,600
Accounts receivable (net) . . .	21,800	23,200
Inventory	19,300	17,900
Prepaid expenses	1,400	1,200
Accounts payable (trade) . . .	12,100	11,400
Salaries and wages		
payable	650	250
Interest payable	750	1,500

Exercise 18–3   Indicate how each transaction of Mankato Freight Corporation would be disclosed (under what classification) in an SCFP—cash basis.

a.   Mankato Freight earned $325,000 net income during 198B.
b.   Issued a four-year note payable in the amount of $390,000 and paid $104,000 in cash for new delivery trucks.
c.   Declared cash dividends totaling $32,500 during the year.
d.   Depreciation totaled $182,000 on all depreciable assets.
e.   Purchased 10 advanced microcomputers costing $97,500.
f.   Purchased miscellaneous equipment totaling $109,200.
g.   Made mortgage payments of $176,800.
h.   Sold and issued 10,000 shares of common stock at $14.69 per share.

Exercise 18–4   Use the information provided in Exercise 18–3 plus the following information on Mankato Freight Company's current asset and liability accounts to prepare a statement of changes in financial position designed to explain the change in cash.

	December 31, 198B	December 31, 198A
Cash	$ 76,700	$30,200
Accounts receivable, net	150,000	97,500
Prepaid expenses	15,600	9,100
Accounts payable	45,500	66,300
Dividends payable	–0–	7,800

Exercise 18–5   The 198B and 198A trial balances of Maynard, Inc., follow. Use the information in the trial balances to prepare an SCFP—cash basis. (Assume that no equipment was disposed or retired and no dividends declared during 19B.)

	19A	19A	19B	19B
Cash	$ 16,000		$ 24,000	
Notes receivable	8,000		4,800	
Accounts receivable, net	40,000		48,000	
Merchandise inventory	88,000		80,000	
Prepaid expenses	3,200		1,600	
Equipment	174,400		400,000	
Accumulated depreciation, equipment		$ 40,000		$ 32,000
Notes payable		16,000		12,800
Accounts payable		28,800		32,000
Taxes payable		6,400		8,000
Wages payable		3,200		1,600
Mortgage payable (due 199C)		40,000		40,000
Common stock		160,000		160,000
Retained earnings		35,200		272,000
Totals	$329,600	$329,600	$558,400	$558,400

Exercise 18–6   Ft. Dodge Corporation's 198B and 198A balance sheets carried the following items:

	December 31	
	198B	198A
Debits		
Cash	$ 63,000	$ 24,000
Accounts receivable, net	48,000	54,000
Merchandise inventory	126,000	108,000
Equipment	108,000	90,000
Totals	$345,000	$276,000
Credits		
Accumulated depreciation equipment	$ 24,000	$ 18,000
Accounts payable	42,000	30,000
Taxes payable	6,000	12,000
Dividends payable	9,000	–0–
Common stock	198,000	180,000
Retained earnings	66,000	36,000
Totals	$345,000	$276,000

Required:

Prepare a statement of changes in financial position—cash basis. Use the following information from the company's 198B income statement and accounts:

a. The company earned $60,000 during 198B.
b. Its equipment depreciated $9,000 in 198B.
c. Equipment costing $21,000 was purchased.
d. Fully depreciated equipment that cost $3,000 was discarded, and its cost and accumulated depreciation were removed from the accounts.
e. Fifteen hundred shares of stock were sold and issued at $12 per share.
f. The company declared $30,000 of cash dividends during the year and paid $21,000.

Exercise 18–7   Use the information provided in Exercise 18–6 to prepare a working paper for a statement of changes in financial position that is designed to explain the change in cash.

PROBLEMS

Problem 18–1   Grouper Corporation's 198B and 198A balance sheets carried these items:

	December 31	
	198B	198A
Debits		
Cash	$ 50,400	$ 25,800
Accounts receivable, net	48,000	60,000
Merchandise inventory	189,000	192,000
Prepaid expenses	6,000	7,200
Equipment	180,600	144,000
Totals	$474,000	$429,000

	December 31	
	198B	*198A*
Credits		
Accumulated depreciation, equipment ...	$ 36,600	$ 28,800
Accounts payable	85,800	107,400
Notes payable (short-term)	15,000	9,000
Long-term note payable	36,000	60,000
Common stock	195,000	150,000
Retained earnings	105,600	73,800
Totals	$474,000	$429,000

Required:

Prepare a statement of changes in financial position—cash basis. Use the following additional information from the company's 198B income statement and accounting records:

a. Net income for the year, $49,800.
b. The equipment depreciated $12,600 during the year.
c. Fully depreciated equipment that cost $4,800 was discarded, and its cost and accumulated depreciation were removed from the accounts.
d. Equipment costing $41,400 was purchased.
e. The long-term note payable was reduced by a $24,000 payment.
f. Five hundred shares of common stock were issued at $90 per share.
g. Cash dividends totaling $18,000 were declared and paid.

Problem 18–2 Bluebonnet, Inc.'s 198B and 198A balance sheets carried these items:

	December 31	
	198B	*198A*
Debits		
Cash	$ 38,100	$ 35,400
Accounts receivable, net	104,700	100,200
Merchandise inventory	257,700	260,100
Other current assets	6,000	5,400
Office equipment	16,200	18,300
Store equipment	95,100	83,400
Totals	$517,800	$502,800
Credits		
Accumulated depreciation, office equip. ...	$ 7,500	$ 7,200
Accumulated depreciation, store equip.	22,200	19,500
Accounts payable	58,500	71,100
Notes payable (short-term)	13,500	–0–
Federal income taxes payable	10,500	6,900
Dividends payable.....................	–0–	7,500
Common stock	370,500	316,500
Retained earnings	35,100	74,100
Totals	$517,800	$502,800

An examination of the company's statements and accounts showed:

a. A $45,000 net income was earned in 198B.

b. Depreciation charged on office equipment, $1,800; and on store equipment, $4,500.

c. Office equipment that had cost $2,100 and had been depreciated $1,500 was sold for its book value.

d. Store equipment costing $13,500 was purchased.

e. Fully depreciated store equipment that cost $1,800 was discarded, and its cost and accumulated depreciation were removed from the accounts.

f. Cash dividends totaling $30,000 were declared during the year.

g. A 3,000-share stock dividend was declared and distributed during the year at a time the company's stock was selling at $18 per share.

Required:

Prepare a statement of changes in financial position—cash basis.

Problem 18–3 Refer to the information in Problem 18–2 and prepare a working paper for a statement of changes in financial position—cash basis.

Problem 18–4 Jane Harwood operates the Harwood Art Gallery as a single proprietorship. Balance sheets for the business at the end of 198B and 198A included the following information:

	December 31	
	198B	198A
Debits		
Cash	$ 32,980	$ 21,760
Accounts receivable, net	57,120	58,480
Merchandise inventory	123,760	114,580
Other current assets	1,700	2,720
Store equipment	44,540	28,560
Totals	$260,100	$226,100
Credits		
Accumulated depreciation, store equipment	$ 6,120	$ 10,880
Accounts payable	48,280	57,120
Jane Harwood, capital	205,700	158,100
Totals	$260,100	$226,100

The 198B statement showing changes in the proprietor's Capital account carried the following information:

Jane Harwood, capital, January 1, 198B		$158,100
Add additional investment		17,000
Total investment		$175,100
Net income per income statement	$51,000	
Less withdrawals	20,400	
Excess of income over withdrawals		30,600
Jane Harwood, capital, December 31, 198B		$205,700

The store equipment accounts showed: (1) $4,080 depreciation expense on store equipment recorded in 198B; (2) store equipment costing $16,320 was purchased; (3) equipment carried on the books on the day of its exchange at its $9,520 cost, less $8,160 accumulated depreciation, was traded on new equipment having a $9,860 cash price, and a $1,360 trade-in allowance was received; and (4) fully depreciated equipment that cost $680 was junked and its cost and accumulated depreciation were removed from the accounts.

Required:

Prepare a statement of changes in financial position—cash basis.

Problem 18–5   The information contained in Pauley Corporation's December 31, 198B, and 198A balance sheets is listed below. Also, the company's noncurrent accounts are provided.

	December 31	
	198B	*198A*
Debits		
Cash	$ 35,820	$ 41,220
Accounts receivable, net	54,720	57,780
Merchandise inventory	99,180	101,520
Prepaid expenses	3,420	3,060
Store equipment	72,720	59,040
Land	54,000	54,000
Building	325,800	202,500
Totals	$645,660	$519,120
Credits		
Accumulated depreciation, store equip. ...	$ 29,160	$ 24,660
Accumulated depreciation, building	42,480	36,360
Accounts payable	46,260	44,280
Wages payable	3,780	3,240
Income taxes payable	7,380	7,560
Interest payable	1,800	–0–
Cash dividends payable	9,000	13,500
Long-term note payable	90,000	–0–
Common stock	297,000	297,000
Stock dividend distributable	18,900	–0–
Retained earnings	99,900	92,520
Totals	$645,660	$519,120

Store Equipment

Date	Explanation	Debit	Credit	Balance
198B				
Jan. 1	Balance			59,040
Mar. 25	Purchased new equipment	15,660		74,700
Apr. 19	Discarded equipment		1,980	72,720

Accumulated Depreciation, Store Equipment

Date	Explanation	Debit	Credit	Balance
198B				
Jan. 1	Balance			24,660
Apr. 19	Discarded equipment	1,980		22,680
Dec. 31	Year's depreciation		6,480	29,160

Land

Date	Explanation	Debit	Credit	Balance
198B				
Jan. 1	Balance			54,000

Building

Date	Explanation	Debit	Credit	Balance
198B				
Jan. 1	Balance			202,500
Mar. 26	Building addition	123,300		325,800

Accumulated Depreciation, Building

Date	Explanation	Debit	Credit	Balance
198B				
Jan. 1	Balance			36,360
Dec. 31	Year's depreciation		6,120	42,480

Long-term Note Payable

Date	Explanation	Debit	Credit	Balance
198B				
Mar. 21	Issued long-term note secured by mortgage		90,000	90,000

Common Stock

Date	Explanation	Debit	Credit	Balance
198B				
Jan. 1	Balance			297,000

Stock Dividend Distributable

Date	Explanation	Debit	Credit	Balance
198B				
Dec. 17	Stock dividend		18,900	18,900

Retained Earnings

Date	Explanation	Debit	Credit	Balance
198B				
Jan. 1	Balance			92,520
Dec. 17	Stock dividend	18,900		73,620
17	Cash dividend	9,000		64,620
31	Net income		35,280	99,900

Required:

Prepare a statement of changes in financial position—cash basis.

ALTERNATE PROBLEMS

Problem 18–1A

Winslow Company's 198B and 198A balance sheets carried these items:

	December 31	
	198B	*198A*
Assets		
Cash	$ 31,500	$ 21,600
Accounts receivable, net	38,250	42,750
Merchandise inventory	141,750	144,000
Prepaid expenses	4,500	5,400
Equipment	135,450	108,000
Accumulated depreciation, equipment	(27,450)	(21,600)
Totals	$324,000	$300,150
Liabilities and Shareholders' Equity		
Accounts payable	$ 64,350	$ 80,550
Notes payable (short-term)	11,250	6,750
Long-term note payable	27,000	45,000
Common stock	146,250	112,500
Retained earnings	75,150	55,350
Totals	$324,000	$300,150

Required:

Prepare a statement of changes in financial position—cash basis. Use the following additional information from the company's 198B income statement and accounting records:

a. Net income for the year, $33,300.
b. The equipment depreciated $9,450 during the year.
c. Fully depreciated equipment that cost $3,600 was discarded, and its cost and accumulated depreciation were removed from the accounts.
d. Equipment costing $31,050 was purchased.
e. The long-term note was reduced by an $18,000 payment.

f. Three thousand shares of common stock were issued at $11.25 per share.

g. Cash dividends totaling $13,500 were declared and paid.

Problem 18–2A

Paintbrush, Inc.'s 198B and 198A balance sheets carried these items:

	December 31	
	198B	*198A*
Debits		
Cash	$ 29,160	$ 22,680
Accounts receivable, net	52,380	59,220
Merchandise inventory	153,360	155,520
Prepaid expenses	2,700	3,240
Office equipment	9,000	10,080
Store equipment	53,640	50,940
Totals	$300,240	$301,680
Credits		
Accumulated depreciation, office equipment	$ 4,680	$ 4,320
Accumulated depreciation, store equipment	13,500	11,700
Accounts payable	33,120	37,980
Notes payable (short-term)	18,000	9,000
Dividends payable	7,200	4,320
Common stock	209,700	189,900
Retained earnings	14,040	44,460
Totals	$300,240	$301,680

An examination of the company's statements and accounts showed:

a. The company suffered a $3,420 net loss during 198B.

b. Depreciation charged on office equipment, $900; and on store equipment, $3,060.

c. Office equipment that had cost $1,080 and had been depreciated $540 was sold for its book value.

d. Store equipment costing $3,960 was purchased.

e. Fully depreciated store equipment that cost $1,260 was discarded, and its cost and accumulated depreciation were removed from the accounts.

f. Cash dividends totaling $7,200 were declared during the year.

g. A 1,800-share stock dividend was declared and distributed during the year at a time when the company's stock was selling at $11 per share.

Required:

Prepare a statement of changes in financial position—cash basis.

Problem 18–3A

Refer to the information in Problem 18–2A and prepare a working paper for a statement of changes in financial position—cash basis.

Problem 18–4A

Brian Tucker operates Tucker Engineering, Inc. Balance sheets for the business at the end of 198B and 198A included the following information:

	December 31	
	198B	198A
Debits		
Cash	$ 28,980	$ 40,140
Accounts receivable, net	29,160	28,080
Merchandise inventory	90,360	92,520
Prepaid expenses	2,340	1,980
Store equipment	46,800	43,740
Office equipment	7,920	7,560
Land ·.....................................	36,000	–0–
Building	180,000	–0–
Totals	$421,560	$214,020
Credits		
Accumulated depreciation, store equipment	$ 9,360	$ 6,480
Accumulated depreciation, office equipment	2,520	2,340
Accumulated depreciation, building	2,160	–0–
Accounts payable	31,140	33,660
Taxes payable	7,920	7,380
Long-term note payable	144,000	–0–
Common stock	187,200	144,000
Retained earnings	37,260	20,160
Totals	$421,560	$214,020

An examination of the company's 198B income statement and accounting records showed:

a. A $27,900 net income for the year.
b. Depreciation on store equipment, $4,320; on office equipment, $720; and on the building, $2,160.
c. Store equipment that cost $4,500 was purchased during the year.
d. Fully depreciated store equipment that cost $1,440 was discarded and its cost and accumulated depreciation were removed from the accounts.
e. Office equipment that cost $900 and had been depreciated $540 was traded in on new office equipment priced at $1,260. A $360 trade-in allowance was received.
f. During the year, the company purchased the land and building it occupied and had previously rented, paying $72,000 in cash and giving a 20-year note payable for the balance.
g. Three thousand six hundred shares of common stock were issued at $12 per share.
h. Cash dividends totaling $10,800 were declared during the year.

Required:

Prepare a statement of changes in financial position—cash basis.

Problem 18–5A   An investigation of Tarsus Corporation's December 31, 198B, and 198A balance sheets and noncurrent accounts reveals the following information:

	December 31	
	198B	*198A*
Debits		
Cash......................................	$ 53,820	$ 46,980
Accounts receivable, net	102,960	83,700
Merchandise inventory.......................	128,520	159,840
Prepaid expenses...........................	11,700	16,380
Store equipment	67,860	63,360
Land	90,000	90,000
Building	288,000	226,800
Totals	$742,860	$687,060
Credits		
Accumulated depreciation, store equipment	$ 23,760	$ 27,900
Accumulated depreciation, building	97,200	75,600
Accounts payable	74,880	84,060
Wages payable	7,920	11,880
Income taxes payable	23,040	17,100
Interest payable	2,160	–0–
Cash dividends payable	12,600	7,200
Long-term note payable	27,000	–0–
Common stock	172,800	172,800
Stock dividend distributable	21,600	–0–
Retained earnings	279,900	290,520
Totals	$742,860	$687,060

Changes in noncurrent accounts during 198B show the following information:

Store Equipment:
Beginning balance	$ 63,360
Purchase of new equipment	15,300
Discarded equipment	(10,800)
Ending balance	$ 67,860

Accumulated Depreciation, Store Equipment:
Beginning balance	$ 27,900
Discarded equipment	(10,800)
Depreciation for 198B	6,660
Ending balance	$ 23,760

Land:
Beginning and ending balance	$ 90,000

Building:
Beginning balance	$226,800
Building addition	61,200
Ending balance	$288,000

Accumulated Depreciation, Building:
Beginning balance	$ 75,600
Depreciation for 198B	21,600
Ending balance	$ 97,200

Long-term Note Payable:
Beginning balance	$ –0–
Loan to finance building	27,000
Ending balance	$ 27,000

Common Stock:
Beginning and ending balance $172,800

Stock Dividend Distributable:
Beginning balance . . . . $ –0–
Stock dividend . . . . *   21,600
Ending balance . . . . $ 21,600

Retained Earnings:
Beginning balance $290,520
Stock dividend . . . .   (21,600)
Cash dividend . . . .   (50,400)
Net income   61,380
Ending balance $279,900

Required:

Prepare a statement of changes in financial position—cash basis.

Problem 18–6A

Refer to the information in Problem 18–5A and prepare a working paper for a statement of changes in financial position—cash basis.

PROVOCATIVE PROBLEMS

Provocative Problem 18–1, Reporting the Change in Noncash Working Capital Items

Data Watch Corporation designs its statement of changes in financial position to explain the change in cash. On the 198B statement, a decrease in noncash working capital items was added to net income in calculating cash provided by operations. A director of the company criticized this format and argued that the statement appeared to overstate the amount of cash provided by operations. Instead, the director proposed that the decrease in noncash working capital items should be shown as an "Other source of cash."

The chief financial officer of the company does not believe that the method of reporting the decrease in noncash working capital items is particularly important. On the other hand, the officer wants to assure the board of directors that the method used was appropriate. To illustrate why the decrease in noncash working capital items is part of "Cash provided by operations," the officer asks you to recast the income statement from an accrual basis to a cash basis. In other words, the cash basis income statement should show the cash received from sales, the cash paid for merchandise, and the cash paid for each operating expense, and so forth. Then compare the net income on a cash basis with the calculation of cash provided by operations as it appeared on the statement of changes in financial position.

Data Watch Corporation's 198B income statement (accrual basis) was as follows:

Sales $180,000
Cost of goods sold   74,000
Gross profit $106,000
Salaries expense $37,000
Insurance expense   13,500
Utilities expense   14,700
Depreciation expense   11,600
Income tax expense   14,200   91,000
    Net income . . . . $ 15,000

The company's current assets and current liabilities were:

	December 31	
	198B	*198A*
Current assets:		
Cash	$19,700	$13,500
Accounts receivable	49,900	43,500
Merchandise inventory	28,500	32,400
Prepaid insurance	6,400	18,000
Current liabilities:		
Accounts payable (used for merchandise		
purchases only)	17,200	14,300
Salaries payable	–0–	6,600
Accrued utilities payable	5,900	4,100

Provocative Problem 18–2, Algoma Steel Corporation, Limited

Algoma's comparative statements of financial position are reproduced below from the company's *1985 Annual Report.*

THE ALGOMA STEEL CORPORATION, LIMITED
Consolidated Financial Statements
Changes in Financial Position
For the Years Ended December 31
(In thousands)

	1985	*1984*
Cash Provided from (Used for)		
Operations:		
Earnings from operations	$ 52,102	$ 14,865
Items included in earnings not		
resulting in an outlay of cash	84,032	68,388
Decrease (increase) in operating working capital	(33,727)	(9,702)
	102,407	73,551
Investment Activities:		
Fixed assets—manufacturing plants	(128,782)	(12,006)
—raw material properties	(14,401)	(12,407)
	(143,183)	(24,413)
Long-term investments	(14,910)	(6,482)
Dividends from associated company	—	14,909
Interest and other income	1,737	2,692
	(156,356)	(13,294)
Dividends	16,854)	(16,772)
Financing Activities:		
Interest on debt	(54,119)	(67,056)
Reduction of long-term debt	(9,016)	(22,296)
Preference shares purchased for cancellation	(1,125)	(3,117)
Other	(465)	3,764
Additional financing		
Funds received for seamless tube mill construction	55,081	—
Proceeds from long-term loans	76,547	36,438
	66,903	(52,267)
Cash (Loan) Position:		
Decrease during year	(3,900)	(8,782)
Balance at beginning of year	832	9,614
Balance at end of year	$ (3,068)	$ 832

THE ALGOMA STEEL CORPORATION, LIMITED (concluded)

	1985	1984
Changes in Operating Working Capital:		
Decrease (increase) in accounts receivable	$ (23,117)	$(24,656)
Decrease (increase) in inventories	(29,431)	(5,860)
Decrease (increase) in prepaid expenses	1,362	894
Increase (decrease) in accounts payable		
and accrued liabilities	13,284	20,997
Increase (decrease) in taxes payable.....................	4,175	(1,077)
Decrease (increase) in operating working capital	$ (33,727)	$ (9,702)

Note: See summary of significant accounting policies and notes to consolidated financial statements.

Required:

1. Recast Algoma's 1985 SCFP using the format suggested in the chapter.
2. Which format do you prefer? Why?

Provocative
Problem 18–3,
Hawkeye
Equipment   At the end of 198B, the accountant of Hawkeye Equipment prepared the following analysis of changes in working capital accounts, statement of changes in financial position, and income statements for the company's owner, Marcia Cantu:

Analysis of Changes in Working Capital Items
For Year Ended December 31, 198B

	December 31, 198B	December 31, 198A	Working Capital	
			Increases	Decreases
Current assets:				
Cash	$ 5,400	$ 27,900		$22,500
Accounts receivable	68,400	57,600	$10,800	
Merchandise inventory	63,000	45,000	18,000	
Prepaid expenses	1,800	900	900	
Total current assets	$138,600	$131,400		
Current liabilities:				
Notes payable	$ 9,000	$ –0–		9,000
Accounts payable	37,800	45,000	7,200	
Salaries and wages payable ...	1,800	3,600	1,800	
Total current liabilities	$ 48,600	$ 48,600		
Working capital	$ 90,000	$ 82,800		
			$38,700	$31,500
Increase in working capital				7,200
			$38,700	$38,700

Statement of Changes in Financial Position
For Year Ended December 31, 198B

Sources of working capital:
Current operations:
Net income $54,000
Add depreciation of plant assets 21,600
Total sources of working capital ... $75,600

Working capital was used for:

Purchases of new plant assets	$36,000	
Reduction of long-term note	10,800	
Personal withdrawals of proprietor	21,600	
Total uses of working capital		68,400
Increase in working capital		$ 7,200

Comparative Income Statements
For Years Ended December 31, 198B and 198A

	198B		198A	
Sales		$540,000		$450,000
Cost of goods sold:				
Inventory, January 1	$ 45,000		$ 54,000	
Purchases	342,000		270,000	
Goods for sale	$387,000		$324,000	
Inventory, December 31	63,000		45,000	
Cost of goods sold		324,000		279,000
Gross profit from sales		$216,000		$171,000
Operating expenses:				
Salaries and wages	$136,800		$124,200	
Depreciation of plant assets ...	21,600		17,100	
Insurance and supplies	3,600		2,700	
Total operating expenses		162,000		144,000
Net income		$ 54,000		$ 27,000

When Ms. Cantu saw the income statement, she was amazed to learn that net income had doubled in 198B, and she could not understand how this could happen in a year in which cash had declined to the point that she had found it necessary in late December to secure a $9,000 short-term bank loan in order to meet current expenses. Her accountant pointed to the statement of changes in financial position by way of explanation, but this statement only confused Ms. Cantu further. She could not understand how depreciation could be a source of working capital, while a bank loan was not, and she could not understand how working capital could increase $7,200 at a time when cash decreased $22,500.

Explain the points Ms. Cantu finds confusing. Attach to your explanation a statement of changes in financial position that explains the change in cash.

Provocative Problem 18–4, Berrymoore's Charts and Maps

Susan Berry and Frank Moore own Berrymore's Charts and Maps. During 198B, they remodeled and replaced $45,000 of the store's fully depreciated equipment with new equipment costing $56,250. By year-end, they were having trouble meeting the store's current expenses and had to secure a $13,500 short-term bank loan. To meet cash needs, Frank had to make an additional investment of $11,250 in the business. At year-end, Susan, who manages the business, asked the Berrymore accountant to prepare a report that summarizes the financing and investing activities of the business. As a result, the accountant prepared the following statement:

BERRYMOORE'S CHARTS AND MAPS
Statement of Changes in Financial Position
For Year Ended December 31, 198B

Sources of working capital:		
Income from operations	$39,825	
Depreciation on store equipment	11,250	
Additional investment by Moore	11,250	
New long-term note to purchase equipment . . .	28,125	$90,450
Uses of working capital:		
Purchase of new equipment (financed in		
part by long-term note)	$56,250	
Personal withdrawals of partners	27,000	83,250
Net increase in working capital		$ 7,200

On reading the report, Frank was confused by the $7,200 increase in working capital in a year he knew the store's bank balance had decreased by $18,000. Also, he could not understand how depreciation was a source of working capital but the $13,500 bank loan was not. What should Susan say by way of explaining these points to Frank? Also, can you reconcile the difference between the $7,200 increase in working capital and the $18,000 decrease in cash? Finally, present a statement of changes in financial position that explains the change in cash.

The following post-closing trial balances were used by the accountant in preparing the store's statement of changes in financial position:

BERRYMOORE'S CHARTS AND MAPS
Post-Closing Trial Balances
198B and 198A

	December 31, 198B		December 31, 198A	
Cash	$ 5,625		$ 23,625	
Accounts receivable	39,600		32,175	
Allowance for doubtful accounts		$ 1,125		$ 675
Merchandise inventory	66,600		39,150	
Prepaid expenses	1,800		1,125	
Store equipment	101,250		90,000	
Accumulated depreciation, store equipment		24,750		58,500
Notes payable		13,500		
Accounts payable		22,500		25,875
Accrued payables		1,350		1,575
Long-term note payable (due 198F–8H)		28,125		–0–
Susan Berry, capital		75,525		60,750
Frank Moore, capital		48,000		38,700
Totals	$214,875	$214,875	$186,075	$186,075

ANALYTICAL AND REVIEW PROBLEMS

Problem 18–1
A&R

Adjustments to Derive Cash Flow from Operations

	Adjust by	
Income element	*Adding*	*Subtracting*
1. Changes in current assets		
a. Increases	_____	_____
b. Decreases	_____	_____

		Adjust by	
Income element		Adding	Subtracting
2. Changes in current liabilities			
a. Increases		_____	_____
b. Decreases		_____	_____
3. Depreciation of plant assets		_____	_____
4. Amortization of intangible assets		_____	_____
5. Interest expense			
a. Premium amortized		_____	_____
b. Discount amortized		_____	_____
6. Sale of noncurrent asset			
a. Gain		_____	_____
b. Loss		_____	_____

Required:

Indicate by an x in the appropriate column whether an item is added or subtracted to derive cash flow from operations.

**Problem 18–2
A&R**

Abbott Corporation earned $42,000 net income during 19X4. Machinery was sold for $58,000, and a $12,000 loss on the sale was recorded. Machinery purchases totaled $165,000 including a July purchase for which a $40,000 promissory note was issued. Bonds were retired at their face value, and the issuance of new common shares produced an infusion of cash.

Abbott's comparative balance sheets were as follows (in thousands):

	December 31	
	19X3	19X4
Cash	$ 42	$ 58
Receivables	111	98
Inventory	155	162
Machinery	630	675
Accumulated depreciation	(105)	(95)
Total assets	$ 833	$898
Accounts payable	$ 143	$119
Notes payable	105	136
Dividends payable	10	16
Bonds payable	160	120
Common stock	280	350
Retained earnings	135	157
Total liabilities and shareholders' equity	$ 833	$898

a. What was Abbott's depreciation expense in 19X4?
b. What was the amount of cash flow from operations?
c. What was the amount of cash flow from investing activities?
d. What was the amount of the cash dividend declared? Paid?
e. By what amount would you expect the total sources of cash to differ from the total uses of cash?
f. What was the amount of cash flow from financing activities?

The data below refers to the activities of Stienman Corporation.

Required:

For each item, identify both the dollar amount and its classification—that is, whether it would appear as a positive or a negative adjustment to net income in the measurement of cash flow from operations or as some other source or use of cash.

1. Declared a $10,000 cash dividend; paid $8,000 during the year.
2. Sold for $24,000 cash land that had cost $27,000 two years earlier.
3. Sold for cash 2,000 shares for $6 a share.
4. Bought machinery for $8,500 in exchange for a note due in eight months.
5. Bought a computer which had fair value of $10,000 by giving in exchange real estate that had cost $8,000 in an earlier period.
6. Equipment depreciation, $2,200.
7. Issued for cash on December 31, 19X1, 10-year 10% $250,000 par-value bonds at $15,000 premium.
8. Bought its own stock for $4,000 and immediately canceled it.
9. Paid a lawyer $2,400 for services performed, billed, and recorded correctly in 19X1.
10. Reported net income of $38,000 net income for the year ended December 31, 19X2.

Accounting for Price-Level Changes

19

After studying Chapter 19 you should be able to:

Describe the effects of inflation on historical financial statements.

Explain how price-level changes are measured.

Tell how to construct both general and specific price-level indexes.

Describe the use of price indexes in constant-dollar accounting.

Restate unit-of-money financial statements for general price-level changes.

Explain how purchasing power gains and losses arise and how they are computed and integrated into constant-dollar financial statements.

State the differences between general price-level-adjusted costs and current values such as exit prices and current costs.

Explain what current costs measure and the use of recoverable amounts in current cost accounting.

Describe the reporting recommendations of the *CICA Handbook.*

Define or explain the words and phrases listed in the chapter Glossary.

Perhaps all accountants agree that conventional financial statements provide useful information for making economic decisions. However, many accountants also agree that conventional financial statements fail to adequately account for the impact of price-level changes. Usually, this means a failure to adequately account for the impact of inflation. Indeed, this failure of conventional financial statements may sometimes even make the statements misleading. That is, the statements may imply certain facts that are inconsistent with the real state of affairs. As a result, decision makers may be inclined to make decisions that are inconsistent with their objectives.

In what ways do conventional financial statements fail to account for inflation? The general problem is that transactions are recorded in terms of the historical number of dollars received or paid. These amounts are not adjusted even though subsequent price changes may dramatically change the purchasing power of the dollars received or paid. For example, Old Company purchased 10 acres of land for $25,000. At the end of each accounting period thereafter, Old Company presented a balance sheet showing "Land, $25,000." Six years later, after inflation of 97%, New Company purchased 10 acres of land that was adjacent and nearly identical to Old Company's land. New Company paid $49,250 for the land. In comparing the conventional balance sheets of the two companies, which own identical pieces of property, the following balances are observed:

Balance Sheets

	Old Company	New Company
Land	$25,000	$49,250

Without knowing the details that underlie these balances, a statement reader is likely to conclude that New Company either has more land than does Old Company or that New Company's land is more valuable. But both companies own 10 acres that are identical in value. The entire difference between the prices paid by the two companies is explained by the 97% inflation between the two purchase dates. That is, $25,000 × 1.97 = $49,250.

The failure of conventional financial statements to adequately account for inflation also shows up in the income statement. For example, assume that in the previous example, machinery was purchased instead of land. Also, assume that the machinery of Old Company and New Company is identical except for age; it is being depreciated on a straight-line basis over a 10-year period, with no salvage value. As a result, the annual income statements of the two companies show the following:

Income Statements		
	Old Company	New Company
Depreciation expense, machinery	$2,500	$4,925

Although assets of equal value are being depreciated, the income statements show that New Company's depreciation expense is 97% higher than is Old Company's. And if all other revenue and expense items are the same, Old Company will appear more profitable than New Company. This is inconsistent with the fact that both companies own the same machines that are subject to the same depreciation factors. Furthermore, although Old Company will appear more profitable, it must pay more income taxes due to the apparent extra profits. Old Company also may not recover the full replacement cost of its machinery through the sale of its product.

Some of the procedures used in conventional accounting tend to reduce the impact of price-level changes on the income statement. LIFO inventory pricing and accelerated depreciation are examples. However, these are only partial solutions, since they do not offset the impact on both the income statement and the balance sheet.

Because of these deficiencies in conventional accounting practices, accountants have devoted increasing attention to alternatives that make comprehensive adjustments for the effects of price-level changes. This chapter discusses the two that have received the greatest attention. The first alternative involves adjusting conventional financial statements for changes in the general level of prices. This is called *constant-dollar accounting,* or *general price-level-adjusted accounting.* Later, consideration is given to another alternative, *current cost accounting.* This makes adjustments for changes in the specific prices of the specific assets owned by the company.

UNDERSTANDING PRICE-LEVEL CHANGES

In one way or another, all readers of this book have experienced the effects of inflation, such as a general increase in the prices paid for goods and services. Of course, the prices of specific items do not all change at the same rate. Even when most prices are rising, the prices of some goods or services may be falling. For example, consider the following prices of four different items:

Item	Price/unit in 1985	Price/unit in 1986	Percent change
A	$1.00	$1.30	+30
B	2.00	2.20	+10
C	1.50	1.80	+20
D	3.00	2.70	−10
Totals ...	$7.50	$8.00	

What can be said to describe these price changes? One possibility is to state the percentage change in the price per unit of each item (see above). This information is very useful for some purposes. But, it does not show the average effect or impact of the price changes that occurred. A better indication of the average effect would be to determine the average increase in the per unit prices of the four items. Thus: $8.00/$7.50 − 1.00 = 6.7% average increase in per unit prices.[1] However, even this average probably fails to show the impact of the price changes on most individuals or businesses. It is a good indicator only if the typical buyer purchased an equal number of units of each item. But what if these items are typically purchased in the following ratio? For each unit of A purchased, 2 units of B, 5 units of C, and 1 unit of D are purchased. With a different number of each item being purchased, the impact of changing prices must take into account the typical quantity of each item purchased. Hence, the average change in the price of the A, B, C, D "market basket" would be calculated as follows:

Item	Units purchased	1985 prices		Units purchased	1986 prices	
A	1 unit	× $1.00 =	$ 1.00	1 unit	× $1.30 =	$ 1.30
B	2 units	× $2.00 =	4.00	2 units	× $2.20 =	4.40
C	5 units	× $1.50 =	7.50	5 units	× $1.80 =	9.00
D	1 unit	× $3.00 =	3.00	1 unit	× $2.70 =	2.70
Totals			$15.50			$17.40

Weighted-average price change = $17.40/$15.50 − 1.00 = 12%

It may now be said that the annual rate of inflation in the prices of these four items was 12%. Of course, not every individual and business will purchase these four items in exactly the same proportion of 1 unit of A, 2 units of B, 5 units of C, and 1 unit of D. As a consequence, the stated 12% inflation rate is only an approximation of the impact of price changes on each buyer. But if these proportions represent the typical buying pattern, the stated 12% inflation rate fairly reflects the inflationary impact on the average buyer.

---

[1] Throughout this chapter amounts are rounded to the nearest 1/10 per cent or to the nearest full dollar.

CONSTRUCTION OF A PRICE INDEX

When the cost of purchasing a given market basket is determined for each of several periods, the results can be expressed as a *price index*. In constructing a price index, one year is arbitrarily selected as the ''base'' year. The cost of purchasing the market basket in that year is then assigned a value of 100. For example, suppose the cost of purchasing the A, B, C, D market basket in each year is:

1978	$ 9.00
1979	11.00
1980	10.25
1981	12.00
1982	13.00
1983	15.50
1984	17.40
1985	18.30

If 1981 is selected as the base year, then the $12 cost for 1981 is assigned a value of 100. The index number for each of the other years is then calculated and expressed as a per cent of the base year's cost. For example, the index number for 1980 is 85, or ($10.25/$12.00 × 100 = 85). The index numbers for the remaining years are calculated in the same way. The entire price index for the years 1978 through 1985 is presented in Illustration 19–1.

Having constructed a price index for the A, B, C, D market basket, it is possible to make comparative statements about the cost of purchasing these items in various years. For example, it may be said that the price level in 1985 was 53% (153/100) higher than it was in 1981; the price level in 1985 was 42% (153/108) higher than it was in 1982; 19% (153/129) higher than it was in 1983; and 6% (153/145) higher than it was in 1984. Stated another way, it may be said that $1 in 1985 would purchase the same amount of A, B, C, D as would $0.65 in 1981

Illustration 19–1

Year	Calculations of price level	Price index
1978	($9.00/$12.00) × 100 =	75
1979	($11.00/$12.00) × 100 =	92
1980	($10.25/$12.00) × 100 =	85
1981	($12.00/$12.00) × 100 =	100
1982	($13.00/$12.00) × 100 =	108
1983	($13.50/$12.00) × 100 =	129
1984	($17.40/$12.00) × 100 =	145
1985	($18.30/$12.00) × 100 =	153

(100/153 = 0.65). Also, $1 in 1985 would purchase the same amount of A, B, C, D as would $0.49 in 1978 (75/153 = 0.49).

USING PRICE INDEX NUMBERS

In accounting, the most important use of a price index is to restate dollar amounts of cost that were paid in earlier years into the current price level. In other words, a specific dollar amount of cost in a previous year can be restated in terms of the comparable number of dollars that would be incurred if the cost were paid with dollars of the current amount of purchasing power. For example, suppose that $1,000 were paid in 1980 to purchase items, A, B, C, D. Stated in terms of 1985 prices, that 1980 cost is $1,000 × (153/85) = $1,800. As another example, if $1,500 were paid for A, B, C, D in 1981, that 1981 cost, restated in terms of 1985 prices, is $1,500 × (153/100) = $2,295.

Note that the 1981 cost of $1,500 correctly states the number of monetary units (dollars) expended for items A, B, C, D in 1981. Also, the 1980 cost of $1,000 correctly states the units of money expended in 1980. These two costs can be added together to determine the cost for the two years, stated in terms of the historical number of monetary units (units of money) expended. However, in a very important way, the 1980 monetary units do not mean the same thing as do the 1981 monetary units. A dollar (one monetary unit) in 1980 represented a different amount of purchasing power than did a dollar in 1981. Both of these dollars represent different amounts of purchasing power than a dollar in 1985. If one intends to communicate the amount of purchasing power expended or incurred, the historical number of monetary units must be adjusted so that they are stated in terms of dollars with the same amount of purchasing power. For example, the total amount of cost incurred during 1980 and 1981 could be stated in terms of the purchasing power of 1981 dollars, or stated in terms of the purchasing power of 1985 dollars. These calculations are presented in Illustration 19–2.

Illustration 19–2

Year cost was incurred	Monetary units expended	Adjustment to 1981 dollars	Historical cost stated in 1981 dollars	Adjustment to 1985 dollars	Historical cost stated in 1985 dollars
1980	$1,000	1,000 × (100/85)	$1,176	1,176 × (153/100)	$1,800*
1981	1,500	—	1,500	1,500 × (153/100)	2,295
Total cost	$2,500		$2,676		$4,095

* Raised $1 to correct for rounding. An alternative calculation is $1,000 × (153/85) = $1,800.

SPECIFIC VERSUS GENERAL PRICE-LEVEL INDEXES

Price changes and price-level indexes can be calculated for narrow groups of commodities or services, such as housing construction material costs; or for broader groups of items, such as all construction costs; or for very broad groups of items, such as all items produced in the economy. A *specific price-level index,* as for housing construction materials, indicates the changing purchasing power of a dollar spent for items in that specific category, that is, to pay for housing construction materials. A *general price-level index,* as for all items produced in the economy, indicates the changing purchasing power of a dollar, in general. Two general indexes are the consumer price index (CPI) and the Gross National Expenditure Implicit Price Deflator prepared by Statistics Canada.

USING PRICE INDEXES IN ACCOUNTING

There are at least two important accounting systems that use price indexes to develop comprehensive financial statements. Both are major alternatives to the conventional accounting system in general use in Canada. One alternative, called current cost accounting, uses specific price-level indexes (along with appraisals and other means) to develop statements that report assets and expenses in terms of the current costs to acquire those assets or services. Additional consideration is given to this alternative later in this chapter.

The other alternative is called constant-dollar accounting. It uses general price-level indexes to restate the conventional, unit-of-money financial statements into dollar amounts that represent current, general purchasing power. The following sections of this chapter explain how a general price index, such as the CPI, is used to prepare constant-dollar financial statements.

CONSTANT-DOLLAR ACCOUNTING

Conventional financial statements disclose revenues, expenses, assets, liabilities, and owners' equity in terms of the historical monetary units exchanged when the transactions occurred. As such, they are sometimes referred to as *unit-of-money* or *nominal-dollar financial statements.* This is intended to emphasize the difference between conventional statements and constant-dollar statements. In the latter, the dollar amounts shown are adjusted for changes in the general purchasing power of the dollar.

Students should understand clearly that the same principles for determining depreciation expense, cost of goods sold, accruals of revenue, and so forth, apply to both unit-of-money statements and constant dollar statements. The same generally accepted accounting principles apply to both. The only difference between the two is that constant-dollar statements reflect adjustments for general price-level changes; unit-of-money statements do not. As a matter of fact, constant-dollar financial statements are prepared by adjusting the amounts appearing on the unit-of-money financial statements.

CONSTANT-DOLLAR ACCOUNTING FOR ASSETS

The effect of general price-level changes on investments in assets depends on the nature of the assets involved. Some assets, called *monetary assets,* represent money or claims to receive a fixed amount of money. The number of dollars owned or to be received does not change, regardless of changes that may occur in the purchasing power of the dollar. Examples of monetary assets are cash, accounts receivable, notes receivable, and investments in bonds.

Because the amount of money owned or to be received from a monetary asset does not change with price-level changes, the constant-dollar balance sheet amount of a monetary asset is not adjusted for general price-level changes. For example, if $200 in cash was owned at the end of 1984 and was held throughout 1985, during which time the general price-level index increased from 150 to 168,[2] the cash reported on both the December 31, 1984, and 1985, constant-dollar balance sheets is $200. However, although no balance sheet adjustment is made, it is important to note that an investment in monetary assets held during a period of inflation results in a loss of purchasing power. The $200 would buy less at the end of 1985 than it would have at the end of 1984. The reduction in purchasing power constitutes a loss. The amount of the loss is calculated as follows:

Monetary asset balance on December 31, 1984	$ 200
Adjustment to reflect an equal amount of purchasing power on December 31, 1985: $200 × 168/150	$ 224
Amount of monetary asset balance on December 31, 1985	(200)
General purchasing power loss	$ 24

Nonmonetary assets are defined as all assets other than monetary assets. The prices at which nonmonetary assets may be bought and sold

---

[2] Observe that these index numbers, and those used in the remaining sections of the chapter, are different from those that were calculated on page 786. Since the earlier calculations were based on only four items (A, B, C, D), that index would not be appropriate to illustrate a general price index, which must reflect the prices of many, many items.

tend to increase or decrease over time as the general price level increases or decreases. Consequently, as the general price level changes, investments in nonmonetary assets tend to retain the amounts of purchasing power originally invested. As a result, the reported amounts of nonmonetary assets on constant-dollar balance sheets are adjusted to reflect changes in the price level that have occurred since the nonmonetary assets were acquired.

For example, assume $200 was invested in land (a nonmonetary asset) at the end of 1984, and the investment was held throughout 1985. During this time, the general price index increased from 150 to 168. The constant-dollar balance sheets would disclose the following amounts:

Asset	December 31, 1984, constant-dollar balance sheet	Adjustment to December 31, 1985, price level	December 31, 1985, constant-dollar balance sheet
Land	$200	$200 × (168/150)	$224

The $224 shown as the investment in land at the end of 1985 has the same amount of general purchasing power as did $200 at the end of 1984. Thus, no change in general purchasing power was recognized from holding the land.

CONSTANT-DOLLAR ACCOUNTING FOR LIABILITIES AND SHAREHOLDERS' EQUITY

The effect of general price-level changes on liabilities depends on the nature of the liability. Most liabilities are monetary items, but shareholders' equity and a few liabilities are nonmonetary items.[3] *Monetary liabilities* represent fixed amounts that are owed. The number of dollars to be paid does not change regardless of changes in the general price level.

Since monetary liabilities are unchanged in amounts owed, and even when price levels change, monetary liabilities are not adjusted for price-level changes. However, a company with monetary liabilities outstanding during a period of general price-level change will experience a general purchasing power gain or loss. Assume, for example, that a note payable for $300 was outstanding on December 31, 1984, and remained outstanding throughout 1985. During that time, the general price index increased from 150 to 168. On the constant-dollar balance sheets for December

---

[3] Depending on its nature, preferred stock may be treated as a monetary item. If so, it is an exception to the general rule that shareholders' equity items are nonmonetary items.

31, 1984, and 1985, the note payable would be reported at $300. The general purchasing power gain or loss is calculated as follows:

Monetary liability balance on December 31, 1984	$ 300
Adjustment to reflect an equal amount of purchasing power on December 31, 1985: $300 × (168/150)	$ 336
Amount of monetary liability balance on December 31, 1985	(300)
General purchasing power gain	$ 36

The $336 at the end of 1985 has the same amount of general purchasing power as $300 had at the end of 1984. Since the company can pay the note with $300, the $36 difference is a gain in general purchasing power realized by the firm. Alternatively, if the general price index had decreased during 1985, the monetary liability would have resulted in a general purchasing power loss.

Nonmonetary liabilities are obligations that are not fixed in amount. They therefore tend to change with changes in the general price level. For example, product warranties may require that a manufacturer pay for repairs and replacements for a specified period of time after the product is sold. The amount of money required to make the repairs or replacements tends to change with changes in the general price level. Consequently, there is no purchasing power gain or loss associated with such warranties. Further, the balance sheet amount of such a nonmonetary liability must be adjusted to reflect changes in the general price index that occur after the liability comes into existence. Shareholders' equity items, with the possible exception of preferred stock, are also nonmonetary items. Hence, they also must be adjusted for changes in the general price index.

Illustration 19–3 summarizes the impact of general price-level changes

Illustration 19–3

Financial statement item	When the general price level rises (inflation)		When the general price level falls (deflation)	
	Balance sheet adjustment required	Income statement gain or loss	Balance sheet adjustment required	Income statement gain or loss
Monetary assets	No	Loss	No	Gain
Nonmonetary assets	Yes	None	Yes	None
Monetary liabilities	No	Gain	No	Loss
Nonmonetary equities and liabilities*	Yes	None	Yes	None

* However, a nonmonetary liability may require an additional adjustment to assure that the balance sheet shows the current estimated amount to satisfy the liability.

on monetary items and nonmonetary items. The illustration indicates what adjustments must be made in preparing a constant-dollar balance sheet and what purchasing power gains and losses must be recognized on a constant-dollar income statement.

PREPARING COMPREHENSIVE, CONSTANT-DOLLAR FINANCIAL STATEMENTS

The previous discussion of price indexes and of constant-dollar accounting for assets, liabilities, and shareholders' equity provides a basis for understanding the procedures used in preparing comprehensive constant-dollar financial statements. In the following discussion, examples of these procedures are based on the unit-of-money (nominal-dollar) financial statements for Delivery Service Company (Illustration 19–4).

Delivery Service Company was organized on January 1, 1984. Of the original $30,000 invested in the company, $25,000 was used to buy delivery trucks. The trucks are being depreciated over five years on a straight-line basis. They have a $5,000 salvage value. Since the company was organized, the general price index has changed as follows:

Date	Price index
December 1983	130
June 1984 (also average for 1984)	140
December 1984	150
Average for 1985	160
December 1985	168

Delivery Service Company's cash balance increased from $8,000 to $30,000 during 1985 and is explained as follows:

Beginning cash balance	$ 8,000
Revenues, earned uniformly throughout the year ..	100,000
Expenses, paid uniformly throughout the year	(78,000)
Ending cash balance	$ 30,000

Restatement of the Balance Sheet

In preparing a constant-dollar balance sheet, the account balances are first classified as being monetary items or nonmonetary items. Since monetary items do not change regardless of changes in the price level, each monetary item is placed on the constant-dollar balance sheet without adjustment. Each nonmonetary item, on the other hand, must be adjusted

Illustration 19–4

DELIVERY SERVICE COMPANY
Balance Sheets
For Years Ended December 31, 1984, and 1985

	1984	1985
Assets		
Cash	$ 8,000	$30,000
Land (acquired December 31, 1984)	12,000	12,000
Delivery equipment (acquired January 1, 1984)	25,000	25,000
Accumulated depreciation	(4,000)	(8,000)
Total assets	$41,000	$59,000
Liabilities and Shareholders' Equity		
Note payable (issued July 1, 1984)	$ 5,000	$ 5,000
Capital stock (issued January 1, 1984)	30,000	30,000
Retained earnings	6,000	24,000
Total liabilities and shareholders' equity	$41,000	$59,000

DELIVERY SERVICE COMPANY
Income Statement
For Year Ended December 31, 1985

Delivery revenues	$100,000
Depreciation expense	(4,000)
Other expenses	(78,000)
Net income	$ 18,000

for the price-level changes occurring since the original transactions that gave rise to the item.

The restatement of Delivery Service Company's balance sheet is presented in Illustration 19–5. Observe that the monetary items "Cash" and "Note payable" are transferred without adjustment from the unit-of-money column to the price-level-adjusted column. All of the remaining items are nonmonetary and are adjusted. The land was purchased on December 31, 1984, when the price level was 150.[4] Thus, the historical cost of the land is restated from December 1984 dollars to December 1985 dollars (price index 168) as follows: $12,000 \times (168/150) = $13,440. The delivery equipment was purchased on January 1, 1984, at the same time the capital stock was issued. Therefore, "Delivery equipment," "Accumulated depreciation," and "Capital stock" are restated

---

[4] Normally, price index numbers are determined for a period of time, such as one quarter or one month, and are not determined for a specific point in time, such as December 31. For example, the CPI is prepared for each month. Thus, the index number for December is used to approximate the price level on December 31.

Illustration 19–5

DELIVERY SERVICE COMPANY, LTD.
Restatement of Balance Sheet
December 31, 1985

	Unit-of-money balances	Restatement factor from price index	Price-level-adjusted amounts
Assets			
Cash	$30,000	—	$ 30,000
Land..........................	12,000	168/150	13,440
Delivery equipment	25,000	168/130	32,308
Less accumulated depreciation	(8,000)	168/130	(10,338)
Total assets	$59,000		$ 65,410
Liabilities and Shareholders' Equity			
Note payable	$ 5,000	—	$ 5,000
Capital stock	30,000	168/130	38,769
Retained earnings	24,000	(See discussion)	21,641
Total liabilities and shareholders' equity	$59,000		$ 65,410

from January 1984 prices (index number 130) to December 1985 prices by applying the restatement factor of 168/130.

The retained earnings balance of $24,000 cannot be adjusted in a single step because this balance resulted from more than one transaction. However, the correct, adjusted amount of retained earnings can be determined simply by "plugging" the necessary amount to make the balance sheet balance, as follows:

Total assets, adjusted..........		$ 65,410
Less: Note payable	$ 5,000	
Capital stock	38,769	(43,769)
Necessary retained earnings		$ 21,641

The process of confirming this restated retained earnings amount is explained later in the chapter.

Students should recognize that Delivery Service Company is a simplified illustration. Only two of its balance sheet amounts (cash and retained earnings) resulted from more than one transaction. In a more complex case, most account balances would reflect several past transactions that took place at different points in time. In such a situation, the adjustment procedures are more detailed. For example, suppose that the $12,000 balance in the Land account resulted from three different purchases of land, as follows:

January 1, 1984, purchased land	$ 3,000
July 1, 1984, purchased land	4,000
December 31, 1984, purchased land	5,000
Total	$12,000

Under this assumption, the following adjustments would be required to prepare the constant-dollar balance sheet as of December 31, 1985:

	Unit-of-money balances	Restatement factor from price index	Restated to December 31, 1985, general, price level
Land purchased on:			
January 1, 1984	$ 3,000	168/130	$ 3,877
July 1, 1984	4,000	168/140	4,800
December 31, 1984	5,000	168/150	5,600
Total	$12,000		$14,277

Restatement of the Income Statement

To prepare a constant-dollar income statement, every individual revenue and expense transaction must be restated from the price index level on the date of the transaction to the price index level at the end of the year. The restated amounts are then listed on the constant-dollar income statement along with the purchasing power gain or loss that resulted from holding or owing monetary items.

The calculations to restate the 1985 income statement of Delivery Service Company from units of money to the price-level-adjusted amounts are presented in Illustration 19–6.

As previously mentioned, Delivery Service Company's revenues were received and its other expenses were incurred in many transactions that occurred throughout the year. To be completely precise, each of these individual transactions would have to be separately restated. However, these revenues and expenses occurred in a nearly uniform pattern throughout the year. Restating the total revenue and the total other expenses from the average price level during the year (160) to the end-of-year price level (168) is therefore an acceptable approximation procedure.

The unit-of-money amount of depreciation expense on delivery trucks ($4,000) was determined by taking 20% of the $25,000 − $5,000 cost to be depreciated. Since this cost was incurred on January 1, 1984, the

Illustration 19–6

DELIVERY SERVICE COMPANY, LTD.
Restatement of Income Statement
For Year Ended December 31, 1985

	Unit-of-money amounts	Restatement factor from price index	Price-level-adjusted amounts
Delivery service revenues	$100,000	168/160	$105,000
Depreciation expense	(4,000)	168/130	(5,169)
Other expenses	(78,000)	168/160	(81,900)
	18,000		17,931
Purchasing power loss (from Illustration 19–7)			(1,460)
Net income	$ 18,000		$ 16,471

restatement of depreciation expense must be based on the price index for that date (130) and on the index number for the end of 1985 (168).

Purchasing Power Gain or Loss

As we explained, the purchasing power gain or loss experienced by Delivery Service Company (shown in Illustration 19–6) stems from the amount of monetary assets held and monetary liabilities owed by the company during the year. During 1985, cash was the only monetary asset held by the company; the only monetary liability was a $5,000 note payable. The purchasing power gain or loss for these items is calculated in Illustration 19–7.

Note in Illustration 19–7 that the purchasing power loss from holding cash must take into account the changes in the cash balance that occurred during the year. First, the beginning cash balance of $8,000 is restated as an equivalent amount of general purchasing power at the end of the year. Since the December 1985 price index was 168 and the December 1984 price index was 150, the balance is restated as follows: $8,000 × 168/150 = $8,960. Next, each cash change is adjusted from the price level at the time the change occurred to the price level at the end of the year. In the example, cash receipts from revenues occurred uniformly throughout the year. Therefore, the average price index number for the year (160) is used to approximate the price level in effect when the revenues were received. The $100,000 cash received from revenues during the year is restated to the equivalent general purchasing power at the year's end, as follows: $100,000 × 168/160 = $105,000. Cash payments for expenses were also made uniformly throughout the year, so they

Illustration 19–7

DELIVERY SERVICE COMPANY, LTD.
Calculation of Purchasing Power Gain or Loss
For Year Ended December 31, 1985

	Unit-of-money amounts	Restatement factor from price index	Restated to December 31, 1985	Gain or loss
Cash:				
Beginning balance	$ 8,000	168/150	$ 8,960	
Delivery revenue receipts	100,000	168/160	105,000	
Payments for expenses	(78,000)	168/160	(81,900)	
Ending balance, adjusted			32,060	
Ending balance, actual	$ 30,000		(30,000)	
Purchasing power loss				$2,060
Note payable: beginning				
balance	$ 5,000	168/150	5,600	
Ending balance, actual	$ 5,000		(5,000)	
Purchasing power gain				(600)
Net purchasing power loss				$1,460

are restated using the same index numbers. In other words, the $78,000 of cash expenses are restated as follows: $78,000 × 168/160 = $81,900. With the initial cash balance and the cash changes restated into end-of-year purchasing power, the adjusted end-of-year purchasing power for cash is $32,060. Since the actual ending cash balance is only $30,000, the $2,060 difference represents a loss of general purchasing power.

The $5,000 note payable was issued on July 1, 1984, when the price index was 140. Nevertheless, the purchasing power gain associated with this monetary liability is calculated by adjusting the $5,000 from the beginning-of-1985 price level (index number 168). Since the calculation is being made for the purpose of preparing a 1985 constant-dollar income statement, only the purchasing power gain arising from inflation during 1985 should be included. The gain associated with the price index change from 140 to 150 occurred during 1984 and would have been included in the constant-dollar income statement for 1984.

Adjusting the Retained Earnings Balance

The December 31, 1985, adjusted retained earnings balance was previously determined by "plugging" the amount necessary to make liabilities plus shareholders' equity equal to total assets (page 795). Alternatively, if a constant-dollar balance sheet for December 31, 1984, was available, the adjusted retained earnings balance on that date could be restated to the December 31, 1985, price level. Then the constant-dollar net income for 1985 could be added to determine constant-dollar retained earnings at December 31, 1985. For example, had constant-dollar financial statements been prepared for 1984, the $6,000 retained earnings balance in units of money (see Illustration 19–4) would have been adjusted to a December 31, 1984, general price-level-adjusted amount of $4,616.[5] With this additional information, the adjusted retained earnings balance for December 31, 1985, is calculated as follows:

	Restated to December 31, 1984, general price level	Factor from price index	Restated to December 31, 1985, general price level
Retained earnings, December 31, 1984	$4,616	168/150	$ 5,170
Constant dollar net income for 1985 (see Illustration 19–6)			16,471
Dividends declared during 1985			–0–
Retained earnings, December 31, 1985			$21,641

CONSTANT-DOLLAR ACCOUNTING AND CURRENT VALUES

Early in this chapter, the fact that prices do not all change at the same rate was discussed. Indeed, when the general price level is rising, some specific prices may be falling. If this were not so, if prices all changed at the same rate, then constant-dollar accounting would report current values on the financial statements. For example, suppose that a company purchased land for $50,000 on January 1, 1984, when the general price index was 130. Then the price level increased until December 1985, when the price index was 168. A constant-dollar balance sheet for this company on December 31, 1985, would report the land at $50,000 × 168/130 = $64,615. If all prices increased at the same rate during that period, the price of the land would have increased from $50,000 to $64,615, and the company's constant-dollar balance sheet would coincidentally disclose the land at its current value.

However, since all prices do not change at the same rate, the current value of the land may differ substantially from the constant-dollar amount of $64,615. For example, assume that the company obtained an appraisal of the land and determined that its current value on December 31, 1985, was $80,000. The difference between the original purchase price of $50,000 and the current value of $80,000 can be explained as follows:

---

[5] Notice that the $4,616 price-level-adjusted retained earnings on December 31, 1984, is smaller than the $6,000 units-of-money amount. This decrease was caused by the same factors that caused the adjusted net income for 1985 to be less than the unit-of-money net income (see Illustration 19–6).

Unrealized holding gain .... $80,000 − $64,615 = $15,385
Adjustment for general price-level
   increase .... $64,615 − $50,000 =   14,615
                                                    $30,000

In that case, the constant-dollar balance sheet would report land at $64,615, which is $15,385 ($80,000 − $64,615) less than its current value. This illustrates a very important fact concerning constant-dollar accounting; it is not a form of *current value accounting.* Rather, constant-dollar accounting restates original transaction prices into equivalent amounts of current, *general purchasing power.* Only if current, *specific* purchasing power were the basis of valuation would the balance sheet display current values.

CURRENT VALUE ACCOUNTING

Constant-dollar accounting often has been proposed as a way of improving accounting information. Proponents argue that conventional, unit-of-money financial statements have questionable relevance to decision makers. Conventional statements may even be misleading in a world of persistent, long-run inflation. Since constant-dollar accounting adjusts for general price-level changes, its proponents believe that constant-dollar financial statements provide a more meaningful portrayal of a company's past operations and financial position. And, they argue, constant-dollar accounting is sufficiently objective to allow its practical application without damaging the credibility of financial statements.

Other accountants argue that even constant-dollar accounting fails to communicate to statement readers the economic values of most relevance. They would design financial statements so that each item in the statements is measured in terms of current value.

Some arguments for current value accounting conclude that the current liquidation price, or "exit value," of an item is the most appropriate basis of valuation for financial statements. However, other arguments, which appear to be more widely supported, conclude that the price to replace an item, its *current cost,* is the best basis of financial statement valuation.

CURRENT COST ACCOUNTING

Current Costs on the Income Statement

In the current cost approach to accounting, the reported amount of each expense should be the number of dollars that would be required, at the time the expense is incurred, to acquire the resources consumed.

For example, assume that the annual sales of a company included an item that was sold in May for $1,500 and the item had been acquired on January 1 for $500. Also, suppose that in May, at the time of the sale, the cost to replace this item was $700. Then the annual current cost income statement would show sales of $1,500 less cost of goods sold of $700. To state this idea more generally, when an asset is acquired and then held for a time before it expires, the historical cost of the asset likely will differ from its current cost at the time it expires. Current cost accounting requires that the reported amount of expenses be measured at the time the asset expires.

The result of measuring expenses in terms of current costs is that revenue is matched with the current (at the time of the sale) cost of the resources that were used to earn the revenue. Thus, operating profit is not positive unless revenues are sufficient to replace all of the resources that were consumed in the process of producing those revenues. The operating profit figure is therefore thought to be an important (and improved) basis for evaluating the effectiveness of operating activities.

Current Costs on the Balance Sheet

On the balance sheet, current cost accounting requires that assets be reported at the amounts that would have to be paid to purchase them as of the balance sheet date. Similarly, liabilities should be reported at the amounts that would have to be paid to satisfy the liabilities as of the balance sheet date. Note that this valuation basis is similar to constant-dollar accounting in that a distinction exists between monetary and nonmonetary assets and liabilities. Monetary assets and liabilities are fixed in amount regardless of price-level changes. Therefore, monetary assets need not be adjusted in amount. But all of the nonmonetary items must be evaluated at each balance sheet date to determine the best approximation of current cost.

A little reflection on the variety of assets reported on balance sheets will confirm the presence of many difficulties in obtaining reliable estimates of current costs. In some cases, specific price indexes may provide the most reliable source of current cost information. In other cases, where an asset is not new and has been partially depreciated, its current cost may be estimated by determining the cost to acquire a new asset of like nature. Depreciation on the old asset is then based on the current cost of the new asset. Clearly, the accountant's professional judgement is an important factor in developing current cost data.

CICA HANDBOOK RECOMMENDATION— CURRENT COST INFORMATION

In December 1982 the standard titled *Reporting the Effects of Changing Prices,* was incorporated into the *CICA Handbook.* The standard calls for current cost reporting by Canada's major corporations, that is, updated, as opposed to historical, information on the cost of goods and services a corporation uses or produces. It also calls for financial reporting on the impact of price changes on corporate operations and profitability.

Some 400 of Canada's largest publicly traded corporations are directly affected by the new requirement of disclosure. The specific recommendation is that supplementary information about the effects of changing prices should be disclosed by enterprises whose debt or equity securities are traded in a public market and that have either (1) inventories and property, plant, and equipment (before deducting accumulated depreciation, depletion, and amortization) totaling $50 million or more or (2) total assets (after deducting accumulated depreciation, depletion, and amortization) of $350 million or more.

Traditional historical cost financial statements are retained in annual reports as the primary means of reporting. Current cost financial data are to be included in annual reports as a supplement to the historical cost statements and are not audited. The supplementary information is intended to assist users of financial data in their assessment of an enterprise in some or all of the following ways:

1. Enable the assessment of the extent to which revenues are sufficient to enable an enterprise to maintain its operating capability.
2. Enable a more accurate measurement of return generated on capital invested by common shareholders.
3. Provide a uniform basis for evaluating the relative performance of different enterprises and interperiod comparisons of the performance of an individual enterprise.
4. Enable the assessment of whether an enterprise has maintained the general purchasing power of its capital.
5. Facilitate the assessment of future prospects of an enterprise and hence the prospects of future cash flows to investors.

Under the CICA's standards, financial data show the effect of specific price changes and the impact of general inflation. An example of the recommended disclosure is presented in Illustration 19–8. Observe that the only restated income statement items are "Cost of goods sold" and "Depreciation and amortization expense." These are the only income statement items (plus depletion expense, if any) which must be restated to meet the CICA's recommendation. Net sales, other operating expense, interest expense, and provision for income taxes do not have to be restated. These latter items may well have been affected by inflation, however, the CICA does not require their adjustment.

Note that the general purchasing power gain or loss is called "gain from decline in purchasing power of net amounts owed." The CICA decided not to include this item in the calculation of income (loss); instead, it is shown separately.

Illustration 19–8

**Statement of Income
Adjusted for Changing Prices
(unaudited)
For the Year Ended December 31, 19E
($000)**

	As reported in the primary statements	Adjusted for changes in specific prices (current costs)
Net sales and other operating revenues	$253,000	$253,000
Cost of goods sold	197,000	205,408
Depreciation and amortization expense	10,000	19,500
Other operating expense	20,835	20,835
Interest expense	7,165	7,165
Provision for income taxes	9,000	9,000
	244,000	261,908
Income (loss)	$ 9,000	$ (8,908)
Gain from decline in purchasing power of net amounts owed		$ 7,729
Increase in specific prices (current cost) of inventories and property, plant, and equipment held during the year		$ 24,608
Effect of increase in general price level		18,959
Excess of increase in specific prices over increase in the general price level		$ 5,649
Financing adjustment		$ 6,152*

* The $6,152 financing adjustment is the increase in the current cost amounts of the portion of inventory and property, plant, and equipment financed through debt. It is calculated by multiplying the increase in current amounts—$24,608—by the company's debt/equity ratio, in this example it is assumed to be one fourth.

Supplementary information about the effects of changing prices should also disclose at least the following items.[6]

1. The amount of the changes during the reporting period in the current cost amounts of inventory and property, plant and equipment, identifying the reduction from current cost to lower recoverable amount.
2. The carrying value of (a) inventory and (b) property, plant, and equipment on a current cost basis at the end of the reporting period, identifying the reduction from current cost to lower recoverable amount.
3. Net assets after restating inventory and property, plant and equipment on a current cost basis at the end of the reporting period.

[6] *CICA Handbook,* par. 4510.18.

The presentation of current cost information has always been a controversial subject and has become more so in the current climate of low inflation. Of the 400 or so companies in Canada that meet the size criteria of the *CICA Handbook,* section 4510, ''Reporting the Effects of Changing Prices,'' less than 30% comply. One of the major arguments against presenting this information is that it would be confusing to the users of the financial statements. Both the CICA and the FASB are studying further the presentation and use of current value information in annual reports.

Using Recoverable Amounts that Are Lower than Current Cost

In general, ''current cost'' is the cost that would be required to currently acquire (or replace) an asset or service. Current cost accounting involves reporting assets and expenses in terms of their current costs. However, the CICA recognized an important exception to this general description of current cost accounting. That exception involves the use of recoverable amounts.

In the case of an asset about to be sold, the recoverable amount is its net realizable value. In other words, recoverable amount is the asset's expected sales price less related costs to sell. If an asset is to be used rather than sold, the recoverable amount is the present value of future cash flows expected from using the asset. A recoverable amount is reported instead of current cost whenever the recoverable amount appears to be materially and permanently lower than current cost. Both the asset and the expense associated with using it (or selling it) should be measured in terms of the recoverable amount.[7]

The reason for using recoverable amounts emphasizes the value of an asset to its owner. The idea is that an asset should not be reported at an amount that is larger than its value to its owner. If the recoverable amount of an asset is less than its current cost, a business is not likely to replace it. A business would not be willing to pay more for an asset than it could expect to recover from using or selling the asset. Hence, the value of the asset to the business can be no higher than the recoverable amount. When value to the business is less than current cost, it is believed that current cost is not relevant to an analysis of the business. Following this line of reasoning, Section 4510 calls for reporting current cost or recoverable amount, if lower.

THE MOMENTUM TOWARD MORE COMPREHENSIVE PRICE-LEVEL ACCOUNTING

The question of whether procedures of accounting for price-level changes should be implemented has been debated and discussed for

---

[7] Ibid., par. 4510.36–37.

many years. Granted, inflation and taxes have caused the expanded use of certain procedures, such as LIFO. But the first significant requirements to report inflation-adjusted information were not imposed until 1976. At that time, the U.S. Securities and Exchange Commission (SEC) began to require certain large companies to report supplemental information on a replacement cost basis.

The SEC's replacement cost disclosure requirements generated many complaints and public statements of opposition by corporate managements. Thus, when *FASB Statement No. 33* was issued in 1979, the SEC withdrew its 1976 requirements and supported those specified by the FASB.

The SEC's action was limited to large companies, and the required information was obviously much less than a complete set of financial statements prepared on a replacement cost basis. Nevertheless, the SEC action represented a major break with the tradition of relying totally on unit-of-money financial statements.

The CICA requirements constituted another major step toward improved accounting for price-level changes. While still limited to large companies and still substantially less than complete financial statements, they do involve current cost information, with important inclusions of income statement information. No doubt, conventional, unit-of-money financial statements will continue to represent the primary basis of Canadian and U.S. accounting in the near future. But a basic shift to one or the other inflation accounting alternatives is a distinct possibility. Both constant-dollar accounting and current cost accounting are being used in some countries. The strength of the calls for expanded usage of them in Canada and the United States will probably depend on how much future inflation as well as specific price changes undermine the perceived relevance of existing reporting methods.

GLOSSARY

Constant-dollar accounting.   An accounting system that adjusts unit-of-money financial statements for changes in the general purchasing power of the dollar. Also called **general price-level-adjusted accounting.**

Current cost.   On the income statement, the numbers of dollars that would be required, at the time the expense is incurred, to acquire the resources consumed. On the balance sheet, the amounts that would have to be paid to replace the assets or satisfy the liabilities as of the balance sheet date.

Current cost accounting.   An accounting system that uses specific price-level indexes (and other means) to develop financial statements that report items such as assets and expenses in terms of the current costs to acquire or replace those assets or services.

Current value accounting.   An accounting system that provides financial statements in which current values are reported; different versions of current value are possible, for example, current replacement costs or current exit values.

General price-level-adjusted (GPLA) accounting.   Synonym for **constant-dollar accounting.**

General price-level index.   A measure of the changing purchasing power of a dollar in general; measures the price changes for a broad market basket that includes a large variety of goods and services, for example, the Gross National Expenditure Implicit Price Deflator or the consumer price index.

General purchasing power gain or loss.   The gain or loss that results from holding monetary assets and/or owing monetary liabilities during a period in which the general price-level changes.

Monetary assets.   Money or claims to receive a fixed amount of money with the number of dollars to be received not changing regardless of changes in the general price level.

Monetary liabilities.   Fixed amounts which are owed, with the number of dollars to be paid not changing regardless of changes in the general price level.

Nominal-dollar financial statements.   See **Unit-of-money.**

Nonmonetary assets.   All assets other than monetary assets.

Nonmonetary liabilities.   Liabilities which must be satisfied through the delivery of goods and/or services.

Price index.   A measure of the changes in prices of a particular market basket of goods and/or services.

Specific price-level index.   An indicator of the changing purchasing power of a dollar spent for items in a specific category; includes a much more narrow range of goods and services than does a general price index.

Unit-of-money financial statements.   Conventional financial statements which disclose revenues, expenses, assets, liabilities, and owners' equity in terms of the historical monetary units exchanged at the time the transactions occurred.

QUESTIONS FOR CLASS DISCUSSION

1. Some people argue that conventional financial statements fail to adequately account for inflation. What is the general problem with conventional financial statements that generates this argument?

2. Are there any procedures used in conventional accounting that offset the effects of inflation on financial statements? Give some examples.

3. What is the fundamental difference in the price-level adjustments made under current cost accounting and under constant-dollar accounting?

4. Explain the difference between an "average change in per unit prices" and a "weighted-average change in per unit prices."

5. What is the significance of the "base" year in constructing a price index? How is the base year chosen?

6. For accounting purposes, what is the most important use of a price index?

7. What is the difference between a specific price-level index and a general price-level index?

8. What is meant by "unit-of-money" financial statements?

9. Define *monetary assets*.

10. Explain the meaning of *nonmonetary assets*.

11. Define *monetary liabilities* and *nonmonetary liabilities*. Give examples.

12. If the monetary assets held by a firm exceed its monetary liabilities throughout a period in which prices are rising, which should be recorded on a constant-dollar income statement—a purchasing power gain or loss? What if monetary liabilities exceed monetary assets during a period in which prices are falling?

13. If accountants preferred to display current values in the financial statements, would they use constant-dollar accounting or current cost accounting? Are there any other alternatives?

14. Describe the meaning of *operating profit* under a current cost accounting system.

15. "The distinction between monetary assets and nonmonetary assets is just as important for current cost accounting as it is for general price-level-adjusted accounting." Is this statement true? Why?

16. Discuss the general disclosure recommendations of the *CICA Handbook*, section 4510.

MULTIPLE CHOICE

1. In preparing a GPLA balance sheet, which of the following categories must be adjusted from unit-of-money amounts to constant-dollar amounts?
    a. Monetary assets.
    b. Nonmonetary assets.
    c. Monetary liabilities.
    d. All assets.
    e. All liabilities and equities.

2. A nonmonetary asset was purchased for $20,000 in 198A, when the general price index was 85. At the end of 1984, when the general price index was 153, the amount that should be shown for the asset on a GPLA balance sheet is:
    a. $11,111.
    b. $20,000.
    c. $30,600.
    d. $36,000.
    e. $40,000.

3. If land was purchased in 198A for $10,000 and was restated for the 198G GPLA balance sheet to $16,400, the $16,400 would represent:
   a. The historical units-of-money cost of the land.
   b. The current value of the land in 198G.
   c. The current (198G) replacement cost of the land.
   d. The historical cost of the land restated for general price-level changes from 198A to 198G.
   e. The current (198G) exit price of the land.

4. X Company invested $125,000 in land in 198A. The general price-level index increased from 120 to 144 in 198B. What should X show as general purchasing power gain (loss) in 198B resulting from owning this asset?
   a. $ 0.
   b. $20,833.
   c. $(20,833).
   d. $25,000.
   e. $(25,000).

5. An individual purchased the following market basket in both 198A and 198B:

Item	Units purchased	198A prices	Units	198B prices
A	3	1.00	3	1.20
B	1	4.50	1	4.90
C	4	2.75	4	3.00
D	5	1.30	5	1.50

   The weighted-average price change of the market basket is:
   a. 11%.
   b. 12%.
   c. 13%.
   d. 14%.
   e. 15%.

6. A company acquired $150,000 of monetary assets in December 198A when the general price index was 100. The company held this same amount of monetary assets until December 31, 198D. The company incurred $175,000 of monetary liabilities in December 198B when the general price index was 112 and owed this same amount of monetary liabilities until December 31, 198D. If the general price index was 125 in December 198C and 140 in December 198D, what general purchasing power gain (or loss) should be shown on the constant-dollar income statement for 198D?
   a. $3,000 gain.
   b. $(3,000) loss.
   c. $(16,250) loss.
   d. $16,250 gain.
   e. Some other amount.

MINI DISCUSSION CASES

Case 19–1   A simple way to reflect the changing value of the monetary unit in financial statements is simply to adjust the price level of the figures. In this way the statements would be reflected in units of common value.

Required:

Discuss the advantages and disadvantages of price-level-adjusted financial statements.

Case 19–2   Several years ago, a "top-of-the-line" hand calculator could be purchased for about $300. Five years later, a similar model with even better features had a retail price of $250. Assume that inflation was a steady 8% per year over those five years.

Required:

If the calculator represented your company's machinery and equipment, what value would you use for machinery and equipment on (1) a price-level-adjusted balance sheet and (2) a current-value balance sheet. Why?

CLASS EXERCISE

Solutions to the following exercises and problems should be rounded to the nearest 1/10 percent and to the nearest full dollar.

Exercise 19–1   Market basket No. 1 consists of 3 units of A, 4 units of B, and 2 units of D. Market basket No. 2 consists of 2 units of B, 3 units of C, and 4 units of D. The per unit prices of each item during 19A and during 19B are as follows:

Item	19A Price per unit	19B Price per unit
A	$1.00	$0.60
B	3.00	3.10
C	5.00	4.80
D	1.00	1.80

Required:

Compute the annual rate of inflation for market basket No. 1 and for market basket No. 2.

Exercise 19–2   The following total prices of a specified market basket were calculated for each of the years 19A through 19E:

Year	Total price
19A	$24,000
19B	30,000
19C	38,000
19D	42,000
19E	48,000

Required:

1. Using 19C as the base year, prepare a price index for the five-year period.
2. Convert the index from a 19C base year to a 19E base year.

Exercise 19–3   A company's plant and equipment consisted of equipment purchased during 19A for $150,000, land purchased during 19C for $40,000, and a building purchased during 19E for $260,000. The general price index during these and later years was as follows:

19A	100
19B	110
19C	120
19D	130
19E	140
19F	150
19G	160

Required:

1. Assuming the above price index adequately represents end-of-year price levels, calculate the amount of each cost that would be shown on a GPLA balance sheet for *(a)* December 31, 19F, and *(b)* December 31, 19G. Ignore any accumulated depreciation.
2. Would the GPLA income statement for 19G disclose any purchasing power gain or loss as a consequence of holding the above assets? If so, how much?

Exercise 19–4   Determine whether the following items are monetary or nonmonetary items.

1. Trade accounts receivable.
2. Petty cash.
3. Notes receivable.
4. Goodwill.
5. Income taxes payable.
6. Retained earnings deficit.
7. Merchandise.
8. Product warranties liability.
9. Common stock subscribed.
10. Prepaid rent.
11. Furniture and fixtures.
12. Common stock.
13. Prepaid fire and casualty insurance.
14. Accounts payable.

Exercise 19–5   Calculate the general purchasing power gain or loss in 19B given the following information:

Time period	Price index
December 19A	120.0
Average during 19B	144.0
December 19B	180.0

a. The Cash balance on December 31, 19A, was $1,200. During 19B, cash sales occurred uniformly throughout the year and amounted to $18,400. Payments of expenses also occurred evenly throughout the year and amounted to $12,500. Accounts payable of $4,100 were paid in December.

b. Accounts payable amounted to $2,000 on December 31, 19A. Additional accounts payable amounting to $3,800 were recorded evenly throughout 19B. The only payment of accounts during the year was $4,100 in late December.

Exercise 19–6   Calculate the general purchasing power gain or loss in 19B given the following information:

Time period	Price index
December 19A	105
Average during 19B	120
December 19B	138

a. The Accounts Receivable balance on December 31, 19A, was $500. During 19B, sales on account occurred uniformly throughout the year and amounted to $1,500. Receipts also occurred evenly throughout the year and amounted to $600.

b. Accounts payable amounted to $200 on December 31, 19A. Additional accounts payable amounting to $800 were recorded evenly throughout 19B. None of the accounts were paid.

c. A note payable of $250 was issued during 19A and was repaid on December 30, 19B.

PROBLEMS

Problem 19–1   The costs of purchasing a common "market basket" in each of several years are as follows:

Year	Cost of market basket
19A	$30,000
19B	31,800
19C	34,000
19D	33,800
19E	40,000
19F	42,000
19G	41,200
19H	45,000

Required:

1. Construct a price index using 19E as the base year.
2. Using the index constructed in 1, what was the per cent increase in prices from 19F to 19H?
3. Using the index constructed in (1), how many dollars in 19H does it take to have the same purchasing power as $1 in 19B?

4. Using the index constructed in (1), if $14,000 were invested in land during 19A and $17,000 were invested in land during 19E, what would be reported as the total land investment on a GPLA balance sheet prepared in 19G? What would your answer be if the investments were in Government of Canada long-term bonds rather than in land?

Problem 19–2   The directors of Dew Company have expressed an interest in general price-level-adjusted financial statements and the concepts of purchasing power gains and losses. The price index in December 19A was 120, and in December 19B, it was 140. The average price index during 19B was 128.

The unit-of-money financial statements for Dew Company are presented below. The increase in notes payable during 19B occurred on July 15, at which time the reported price index was 125. The funds derived from the increase in notes payable were used to increase the cash balance. Dew Company purchased the equipment several years ago when the price index was 105.

DEW COMPANY, LTD.
Balance Sheets
December 31, 19A, and 19B

	19A	19B
Assets		
Cash	$120,000	$210,000
Accounts receivable	100,000	100,000
Equipment (net of depreciation)	80,000	75,000
Total assets	$300,000	$385,000
Liabilities and Shareholders' Equity		
Notes payable	$100,000	$140,000
Capital stock	100,000	100,000
Retained earnings	100,000	145,000
Total liabilities and shareholders' equity	$300,000	$385,000

DEW COMPANY, LTD.
Income Statement
For Year Ended December 31, 19B

Revenues		$200,000
Depreciation expense	$ 5,000	
Other expenses	150,000	155,000
Net income		$ 45,000

Required:

1. Calculate the purchasing power gain or loss incurred by Dew Company during 19B. You should assume that revenues were received in cash evenly throughout the year and that expenses other than depreciation were paid in cash evenly throughout the year.
2. Prepare a general price-level-adjusted income statement for 19B.

Problem 19–3   Dew Company, for which data were presented in Problem 19–2, was organized at a time when the price index was 105. All of the $100,000 capital stock was issued at that time.

Required:

1. Based on the above information and the data provided in Problem 19–2, prepare a GPLA balance sheet for Dew Company as of December 31, 19B. (The retained earnings balance may be determined simply by "plugging" in the amount that is necessary to make the balance sheet balance.)
2. On Dew Company's GPLA balance sheet on December 31, 19A, retained earnings was reported as $97,144. Assuming that GPLA net income for 19B was $23,332, present a calculation that confirms the retained earnings balance as it is reported on the GPLA balance sheet for December 31, 19B.

Problem 19–4   Martin Company purchased machinery for $576,000 on January 2, 19B. The equipment was expected to last nine years and have no salvage value; straight-line depreciation was to be used. The equipment was sold on December 31, 19E, for $425,000. End-of-year general price index numbers during this period of time were as follows:

19A	98.0
19B	127.4
19C	137.2
19D	156.8
19E	166.6

Required (round all answers to the nearest whole dollar):

1. What should be presented for the equipment and accumulated depreciation on a historical cost/constant-dollar balance sheet dated December 31, 19C? (Hint: Depreciation is the total amount of cost that has been allocated to expense. Therefore, the price index numbers that are used to adjust the nominal dollar cost of the asset should also be used to adjust the nominal dollar amount of depreciation.)
2. How much depreciation expense should be shown on the historical cost/constant-dollar income statement for 19D?
3. How much depreciation expense should be shown on the historical cost/constant-dollar income statement for 19E?
4. How much gain on the sale of equipment would be reported on the historical cost/nominal-dollar income statement for 19E?
5. After adjusting the equipment's cost and accumulated depreciation to the end-of-19E price level, how much gain in (loss of) general purchasing power was realized by the sale of the equipment?

Problem 19–5   Bancroft Express had three monetary items during 19B—cash, accounts receivable, and accounts payable. The changes in these accounts during the year were as follows:

Cash:
Beginning balance .... $ 8,000
Cash proceeds from sale of surplus equipment (in
mid-January 19B) 12,800
Cash receipts from customers (spread evenly
throughout the year 87,400
Payments of accounts payable (spread evenly
throughout the year) .... (49,200)
Payments of other cash expenses during March 19B ... (19,600)
Dividends declared and paid in mid-September 19B .... (15,000)
Ending balance .... $ 24,400

Accounts receivable:
Beginning balance .... $ 14,500
Sales to customers (spread evenly throughout
the year) 96,100
Cash receipts from customers (spread evenly
throughout the year) .... (87,400)
Ending balance .... $ 23,200

Accounts payable:
Beginning balance .... $ 16,900
Merchandise purchases (spread evenly
throughout the year) 38,500
Special purchase near end of December, 19B 11,000
Payments of accounts payable (spread evenly
throughout the year) .... (49,200)
Ending balance .... $ 17,200

General price index numbers at the end of 19A and during 19B are as follows:

December 19A 175.0
January 19B 178.0
March 19B 182.7
September 19B 189.7
December 19B 193.0
Average for 19B ... 186.0

Required:

Calculate the general purchasing power gain or loss experienced by Bancroft Express in 19B. (Round all amounts to the nearest whole dollar.)

ALTERNATE PROBLEMS

Problem
19–1A

The costs of purchasing a common "market basket" in each of several years are as follows:

Year	Cost of market basket
19A	$41,000
19B	44,000
19C	43,500
19D	48,000
19E	50,000
19F	54,000
19G	57,000
19H	56,000

Required:

1. Construct a price index using 19D as the base year.
2. Using the index constructed in (1), what was the per cent increase in prices from 19E to 19H?
3. Using the index constructed in (1), how many dollars in 19H does it take to have the same purchasing power as $1 in 19B?
4. Using the index constructed in (1), if $18,000 were invested in land during 19A and $24,000 were invested in land during 19E, what would be reported as the total land investment on a GPLA balance sheet prepared in 19G? What would your answer be if the investments were in corporate bonds rather than in land?

Problem 19–2A

The unit-of-money income statement for 19B and December 31, 19A, and 19B, balance sheets of Crafter Company are given below:

CRAFTER COMPANY, LTD.
Income Statement
For Year Ended December 31, 19B

Commissions revenue ...		$120,000
Depreciation expense ...	$15,000	
Other expenses	80,000	95,000
Net income		$ 25,000

CRAFTER COMPANY
Balance Sheets
December 31, 19A, and 19B

	19A	19B
Assets		
Cash	$ 70,000	$100,000
Accounts receivable	30,000	55,000
Equipment (net of depreciation)	90,000	75,000
Total assets	$190,000	$230,000
Liabilities and Shareholders' Equity		
Notes payable	$ 50,000	$ 65,000
Capital stock	130,000	130,000
Retained earnings	10,000	35,000
Total liabilities and shareholders' equity	$190,000	$230,000

Selected numbers from a general price-level index are as follows:

Price index

December 19A	80
Average during 19B	90
September 19B	95
December 19B	105

The increase in notes payable during 19B occurred on September 10, and the funds derived from the increase in notes payable were used to increase the cash balance. Crafter Company purchased the equipment at a time when the general price index was 62.

Required:

1. Calculate the purchasing power gain or loss incurred by Crafter Company during 19B. You should assume that all commissions were earned evenly throughout the year and were debited to Accounts Receivable. Cash receipts from receivables ($95,000) were also distributed evenly throughout the year, and expenses other than depreciation were paid in cash evenly throughout the year.
2. Prepare a general price-level-adjusted income statement for 19B.

Problem 19–3A

Assume the same facts as were presented in Problem 19–2A. In addition, Crafter Company was organized some time ago when the price index was 59. All of the capital stock ($130,000) was issued at that time.

Required:

1. Based on the above information and the data provided in Problem 19–2A, prepare a GPLA balance sheet for Crafter Company on December 31, 19B. (The retained earnings balance may be determined simply by "plugging" in the amount that is necessary to make the balance sheet balance.)
2. On Crafter Company's GPLA balance sheet on December 31, 19A, retained earnings was reported as a deficit of $10,142.48. Assuming that Crafter Company reported a GPLA net loss for 19B of $1,028, present a calculation that confirms the retained earnings balance as it is reported on the GPLA balance sheet for December 31, 19B.

Problem 19–4A

Senchak Corporation purchased machinery for $668,000 on December 30, 19A. The equipment was expected to last eight years and have no salvage value; straight-line depreciation was to be used. The equipment was sold on December 31, 19E, for $500,000. End-of-year general price index numbers during this period of time were as follows:

19A	197.0
19B	254.8
19C	274.4
19D	313.6
19E	333.2

Required (round all answers to the nearest whole dollar):

1. What should be presented for the equipment and accumulated depreciation on a historical cost/constant-dollar balance sheet dated December 31, 19C? (Hint: Depreciation is the total amount of cost that has been allocated to expense. Therefore, the price index numbers that are used to adjust the nominal dollar cost of the asset should also be used to adjust the nominal dollar amount of depreciation.)
2. How much depreciation expense should be shown on the historical cost/constant-dollar income statement for 19D?
3. How much depreciation expense should be shown on the historical cost/constant-dollar income statement for 19E?
4. How much gain on the sale of equipment would be reported on the historical cost/nominal-dollar income statement for 19E?

5. After adjusting the equipment's cost and accumulated depreciation to the end-of-19E price level, how much gain in (loss of) general purchasing power was realized by the sale of the equipment?

Problem 19–5A

Westlake Drafters had three monetary items during 19B, cash, accounts receivable, and accounts payable. The changes in these accounts during the year were as follows:

Cash:

Beginning balance	$ 19,200
Cash proceeds from sale of land (in mid-January 19B)	30,720
Cash receipts from customers (spread evenly throughout the year)	209,760
Payments of accounts payable (spread evenly throughout the year)	(118,080)
Dividends declared and paid during March 19B	(47,040)
Payments of other cash expenses in mid-September 19B ...	(36,000)
Ending balance	$ 58,560

Accounts receivable:

Beginning balance	$ 34,800
Sales to customers (spread evenly throughout the year)	230,640
Cash receipts from customers (spread evenly throughout the year)	(209,760)
Ending balance	$ 55,680

Accounts payable:

Beginning balance	$ 40,560
Merchandise purchases (spread evenly throughout the year)	92,400
Special purchase near end of December, 19B	26,400
Payments of accounts payable (spread evenly throughout the year)	(118,080)
Ending balance	$ 41,280

General price index numbers at the end of 19A and during 19B are as follows:

December 19A	105.0
January 19B	106.8
March 19B	109.6
September 19B	113.8
December 19B	115.8
Average for 19B ...	111.6

Required:

Calculate the general purchasing power gain or loss experienced by Westlake Drafters in 19B. (Round all amounts to the nearest whole dollar.)

PROVOCATIVE PROBLEMS

Provocative Problem 19–1, Diversified Enterprises

Diversified Enterprises purchased a plot of land in 19A when the general price index was 94. The land cost $200,000 and was zoned for heavy industrial use. In 19D, the general price index is 118. However, a specific price index for heavy industrial property in the general area of the land in question has risen from 80 in 19A to 140 in 19D.

Diversified Enterprises has no intention of building a plant on the property. It is being held only as an investment and will eventually be sold. Some of the employees of Diversified Enterprises have been arguing over the matter of how the land should be presented in the balance sheet at the close of 19D and also over the amount of real economic benefit the company will have obtained from the investment if the land were to be sold immediately. Prepare an analysis that recognizes the alternative balance sheet valuation possibilities and will help to resolve the dispute.

Provocative Problem 19–2, Helmsman Corporation

Although Helmsman Corporation is not required to present financial information adjusted for price changes, the company has often been willing to consider innovative ways of reporting to its stockholders. For example, it has presented supplemental historical cost/constant-dollar financial statements in its annual reports. The constant-dollar balance sheets of Helmsman Corporation for December 31, 19A, and 19B, are as follows:

HELMSMAN CORPORATION
Historical Cost/Constant-Dollar Balance Sheets

	As presented on December 31, 19B	As presented on December 31, 19A
Assets		
Cash	$ 35,000	$ 10,000
Accounts receivable	93,000	50,000
Notes receivable	20,000	—
Inventory	25,761	12,960
Equipment	198,545	171,818
Accumulated depreciation	(56,727)	(24,545)
Land	156,391	98,182
Total assets	$471,970	$318,415
Liabilities and Shareholders' Equity		
Accounts payable	$ 61,000	$ 11,000
Notes payable	43,000	13,000
Common stock	283,636	245,455
Retained earnings	84,334	48,960
Total liabilities and shareholders' equity	$471,970	$318,415

A new member of Helmsman Corporation's board of directors has expressed interest in the relationship between historical cost/constant-dollar statements and historical cost/nominal-dollar statements. The board member understands that constant-dollar statements are derived from nominal-dollar statements, but wonders if the process can be reversed. Specifically, you are asked to show how the historical cost/constant-dollar balance sheets for December 31, 19A, and 19B could be restated back into nominal-dollar statements.

Additional information:

1. The outstanding stock was issued in January 19A, and the company's equipment was purchased at that time. The equipment has no salvage value and is being depreciated over seven years.

2. The note receivable was acquired on June 30, 19B.
3. Notes payable consists of two notes, one for $13,000 (which was issued on January 1, 19A) and the other for $30,000 (which was issued on January 1, 19B).
4. The land account includes two parcels, one of which was acquired for $80,000 on January 1, 19A. The remaining parcel was acquired in June 19B.
5. Selected numbers from a general price-level index are:

January 19A 165.0
June 19A (also average for 19A) ... 187.5
December 19A 202.5
June 19B (also average for 19B) ... 218.0
December 19B 234.0

6. The inventory at the end of each year was acquired evenly throughout that
    year.
7. Hint: If all other accounts are properly adjusted from constant dollars back to nominal dollars, the correct retained earnings balance can be determined simply by "plugging" the amount necessary to make the balance sheet balance.

Provocative Problem 19–3, John Labatt Company   The John Labatt Company is an increasingly diversified business with its primary operations in the brewing industry. In its 1985 annual reports, the company included the following information concerning the effects of price changes:

JOHN LABATT
Summary of Results Adjusted for Effects
of Changing Prices (unaudited)
For the year ended April 30, 1985
(in millions except per share amounts)

	Historical cost dollars 1985	Current cost dollars 1985
Net sales	$2,426.5	$2,426.5
Operating costs:		
Cost of products sold	1,615.3	1,630.0
Selling and administrative expenses	586.2	586.2
Depreciation and amortization	52.0	86.5
Interest	40.3	40.3
	2,293.8	2,343.0
Operating income	132.7	83.5
Investment and sundry income	8.3	8.3
	141.0	91.8
Financing adjustment		17.1
Income before taxes	141.0	108.9
Income taxes	52.5	52.5
Earnings before share of net		
losses of partly owned businesses	88.5	56.4

JOHN LABATT

	Historical cost dollars 1985	Current cost dollars 1985
Share of net losses of partly owned businesses	6.8	7.6
Net earnings	$ 81.7	$ 48.8
Fully diluted earnings per common share	$ 2.35	$ 1.49
Assets and equity		
Inventory	$ 328.1	$ 328.1
Fixed assets (net)	637.9	990.0
Shareholders' equity	518.1	870.3
Return on average equity	16.9%	5.8%
Increase in current cost amounts of inventory and fixed assets		$ 79.2
Effect of general inflation		43.9
Increase in current cost over the effect of general inflation		$ 35.3
Gain in general purchasing power from having net monetary liabilities		$ 16.7

Required:

1. Given that 1985 was a year of inflation, were the monetary assets owned by the John Labatt Company more than or less than monetary liabilities owed?

2. Based on the information presented, did price changes appear to have positive or negative effects on the financial operations and position of the John Labatt Company? Explain the basis for your answer.

3. To what extent did price changes effect the importance of income taxes incurred by Labatts?

ANALYTICAL AND REVIEW PROBLEMS

Problem 19–1
A&R

The essence of the economists' concept of profit (net income) is:

Profit is the amount that can be distributed to the owners at the end of the period leaving the company as well off at the end as it was at the beginning of the period.

For 19A, the reported net income (accounting net income) was $31 billion for the 29 of the 30 companies of the Dow Jones Industrial Average. If the net incomes were adjusted using the current cost method, the reported net income would drop to $13.8 billion from the $31 billion.

Required:

Which of the amounts, the $31 billion or the $13.8 billion, approximates the economists' concept of income, and why?

Problem 19–2
A&R

Janet Bamford writing in the July 4, 1983, issue of *Forbes* makes the point that "A few years ago inflation accounting was a hot topic. Now (1983) nobody seems to be interested. That's a mistake."

Allen Seed, consultant with Arthur D. Little states, "Inflation accounting was a hot topic after World War I, then again after World War II, then in the late 60's."

Required:

1. Why do you think interest and disinterest in "inflation accounting" repeats in a predictable pattern?
2. Do you agree with Bamford's conclusion, "That's a mistake"? Why?

Problem 19–3
A&R

The 1985 reported net incomes (accounting net income) and adjusted net incomes using the current cost method for four selected companies are as follows:

Company	1985 net income ($ millions)	
	As reported (accounting net income)	As adjusted using the current cost method
Bell Canada Enterprises	1,009.0	799.8
Imperial Oil Limited	684.0	434.0
Texaco Canada Inc.	336.0	244.0
George Weston Limited	100.9	73.9

Required:

1. Why do you think there is such a significant difference in variation between the two net incomes for the last two compared to the first two companies?
2. Why do you think that in 1985, a year of abatement of inflation, there is, especially for the last two companies, such a significant difference between the two incomes?

Analyzing Financial Statements

After studying Chapter 20, you should be able to:

List the three broad objectives of financial reporting by business enterprises.

Describe comparative financial statements, how they are prepared, and the limitations associated with interpreting them.

Prepare common-size comparative statements and interpret them.

Explain the importance of working capital in the analysis of financial statements and list the typical ratios used to analyze working capital.

Calculate the common ratios used in analyzing the balance sheet and income statement and state what each ratio is intended to measure.

State the limitations associated with using financial statement ratios and the sources from which standards for comparison may be obtained.

Define or explain the words and phrases listed in the chapter Glossary.

A large variety of persons are interested in receiving and analyzing financial information about business firms. They range from managers, employees, directors, customers, suppliers, owners, lenders, and potential investors to brokers, regulatory authorities, lawyers, economists, labor unions, financial advisers, and the financial press. Some of these groups, such as managers and some regulatory agencies, have the ability to require a company to prepare specialized financial reports designed to meet their specific interests. Many other groups must rely on the *general-purpose financial statements* that are periodically published by the companies. General-purpose financial statements usually include the income statement, balance sheet, statement of retained earnings, and statement of changes in financial position. These statements are typically accompanied by a variety of additional financial information such as that contained in the footnotes to the financial statements. See, for example, the financial statements and related footnotes to Moore Corporation shown in the Appendix beginning on page 1201. Financial information about companies may also be obtained from a variety of news announcements issued from time to time by management.

The process of preparing and issuing financial information about a company is called *financial reporting*. While this is broader than just issuing general-purpose financial statements, the objectives of those statements are essentially the same as are the objectives of financial reporting.

OBJECTIVES OF FINANCIAL REPORTING

The people who use a business's financial information have different reasons for analyzing that information. Nevertheless, users of financial information are generally interested in information that enables them to make informed decisions on investments, credit, and other financial matters. A research study[1] issued in 1980 by the CICA lists 13 categories of user needs. These are:

1. *Assessment of performance:* Users are interested in assessing the performance of the company (which they may define to themselves in different ways) not only in absolute numerical terms but also by comparison with their own expectations formulated in the past, by comparison with past expectations expressed by management, and by comparison with the performance of other entities in the same or other industries.

2. *Assessment of management quality:* The quality of management cannot be measured merely in financial terms, but financial statements will nevertheless be helpful in providing indicators of management's

---

[1] *Corporate Reporting: Its Future Evolution,* (Toronto: The Canadian Institute of Chartered Accountants, 1980), pp. 50–51.

ability to maintain and improve profits, operate the enterprise efficiently, discharge its stewardship function effectively, etc.

3. *Estimating future prospects:* Different users will be interested in estimating different aspects of the company's future prospects. Some will be interested in the trend of profits, others in the trend of dividends and interest payments, in requirements for further capital trends in future capital investment, prospects for employment in the future, the likelihood that the company will continue to be a good customer or source of supply, and even the likelihood that it will be able to continue to support pension payments to past employees, and to fund those of present employees.

4. *Assessing financial strength and stability:* Many users will be concerned to make judgments about the company's stability, its possible vulnerability to and its ability to take advantage of, various changes in the economic climate.

5. *Assessing solvency:* A number of users will be concerned with this matter, especially if there is any doubt about the company's solvency, in deciding what decisions to take in the future regarding investments, purchases, supplies, extensions of credit to the company, and so forth.

6. *Assessing liquidity:* Many users will be interested in this, for example, in deciding whether and on what terms to extend credit to the company, or in assessing the likelihood of changes in dividend or interest payments.

7. *Assessing risk and uncertainty:* Financial statements can assist in this by indicating the extent of the variability of the company's past record; this will be used as a guide in estimating what may happen in the future.

8. *As an aid to resource allocation:* Various groups of users will allocate resources to companies, either by primary investment or through grants or other payments to the company. Similarly, investors operating in the secondary financial markets make decisions, based in part on reading published financial reports, that can directly or indirectly affect primary resource allocation decisions.

9. *In making comparisons:* Many groups of users are interested in comparing various aspects of a company's position or performance either with its own past record (thereby developing trends) or with other entities or groups of entities.

10. *In valuation decisions:* The figures contained in published financial statements may help debt and equity investors assess the value of their holdings or potential holdings in the company.

11. *In assessing adaptability:* Users may be interested in estimating the ability of a company to switch its areas of operations in response to possible changes in economic conditions. Financial statements may help them make such assessments.

12. *Determining compliance with the law or regulations:* Although

government departments such as the Income Tax Department may demand specific information for their own purposes, legal and regulatory bodies may find published audited financial statements useful in assessing compliance with the law or regulations. Similarly, other users may wish to assure themselves that there has been such compliance, and reading financial statements may help them do so.

13. *Assessing contribution to society, etc.:* Users may wish to know about the company's contribution to job creation, exports, national income, development of national resources, or about its efforts to eliminate pollution or improve the environment, and they may be assisted by reading published financial statements.

Although the user of financial information may have other reasons for analyzing financial statements, he or she should understand that the authoritative body for establishing accounting principles intends for financial reporting (and financial statements) to be focused on these basic needs. The primary idea is that financial reporting should help the information user predict the amounts, timing, and uncertainty of future net cash inflows to the business. The methods of analysis and techniques explained in this chapter should contribute to this process.

When the financial statements of a business are analyzed, individual statement items are in themselves generally not too significant. However, relationships between items and groups of items plus changes that have occurred are significant. As a result, financial statement analysis requires that relationships between items and groups of items, and changes in items and groups be described.

COMPARATIVE STATEMENTS

Changes in statement items can usually best be seen when item amounts for two or more successive accounting periods are placed side by side in columns on a single statement. Such a statement is called a *comparative statement.* Each of the financial statements, or portions thereof, may be presented in the form of a comparative statement.

In its most simple form, a comparative balance sheet consists of the item amounts from two or more of a company's successive balance sheets arranged side by side so that changes in amounts may be seen. However, such a statement can be improved by also showing, in both dollar amounts and in percentages, the changes that have occurred. When this is done, as in Illustration 20–1, large dollar and large percentage changes become more readily apparent.

A comparative income statement is prepared in the same manner as a comparative balance sheet. Income statement amounts for two or more successive periods are placed side by side, with dollar and percentage changes in additional columns. Such a statement is shown in Illustration 20–2.

Illustration 20–1

ANCHOR SUPPLY COMPANY, LTD.
Comparative Balance Sheet
December 31, 198B, and December 31, 198A

	Years ended December 31		Amount of increase or (decrease) during 198B	Per cent of increase or (decrease) during 198B
	198B	198A		
Assets				
Current assets:				
Cash	$ 18,000	$ 90,500	$ (72,500)	(80.1)%
Accounts receivable, net	68,000	64,000	4,000	6.3
Merchandise inventory	90,000	84,000	6,000	7.1
Prepaid expenses	5,800	6,000	(200)	(3.3)
Total current assets	181,800	244,500	(62,700)	(25.6)
Long-term investments:				
Real estate	–0–	30,000	(30,000)	(100.0)
Apex Company common stock	–0–	50,000	(50,000)	(100.0)
Total long-term investments	–0–	80,000	(80,000)	(100.0)
Plant and equipment:				
Office equipment, net	3,500	3,700	(200)	(5.4)
Store equipment, net	17,900	6,800	11,100	163.2
Buildings, net	176,800	28,000	148,800	531.4
Land	50,000	20,000	30,000	150.0
Total plant and equipment	248,200	58,500	189,700	324.3
Total assets	$430,000	$383,000	$ 47,000	12.3
Liabilities				
Current liabilities:				
Notes payable	$ 5,000	–0–	$ 5,000	
Accounts payable	43,600	$ 55,000	(11,400)	(20.7)
Taxes payable	4,800	5,000	(200)	(4.0)
Wages payable	800	1,200	(400)	(33.3)
Total current liabilities	54,200	61,200	(7,000)	(11.4)
Long-term liabilities:				
Mortgage payable	60,000	10,000	50,000	500.0
Total liabilities	114,200	71,200	43,000	60.4
Capital				
Common stock, 25,000 shares	250,000	250,000	–0–	–0–
Retained earnings	65,800	61,800	4,000	6.5
Total capital	315,800	311,800	4,000	1.3
Total liabilities and capital	$430,000	$383,000	$ 47,000	12.3

Illustration 20–2

ANCHOR SUPPLY COMPANY, LTD.
Comparative Income Statement
Years Ended December 31, 198B, and 198A

	Years Ended December 31		Amount of Increase or (Decrease) during 198B	Per Cent of Increase or (Decrease) during 198B
	198B	198A		
Gross sales	$973,500	$853,000	$120,500	14.1%
Sales returns and allowances	13,500	10,200	3,300	32.4
Net sales	960,000	842,800	117,200	13.9
Cost of goods sold	715,000	622,500	92,500	14.9
Gross profit from sales	245,000	220,300	24,700	11.2
Operating expenses:				
Selling expenses:				
Advertising expense	7,500	5,000	2,500	50.0
Sales salaries expense	113,500	98,000	15,500	15.8
Store supplies expense	3,200	2,800	400	14.3
Depreciation expense, store equipment ..	2,400	1,700	700	41.2
Delivery expense	14,800	14,000	800	5.7
Total selling expenses	141,400	121,500	19,900	16.4
General and administrative expenses:				
Office salaries expense	41,000	40,050	950	2.4
Office supplies expense	1,300	1,250	50	4.0
Insurance expense	1,600	1,200	400	33.3
Depreciation expense, office equipment ..	300	300	–0–	–0–
Depreciation expense, buildings	2,850	1,500	1,350	90.0
Bad debts expense	2,250	2,200	50	2.3
Total general and admin. expenses ...	49,300	46,500	2,800	6.0
Total operating expenses	190,700	168,000	22,700	13.5
Operating income	54,300	52,300	2,000	3.8
Less interest expense	2,300	1,000	1,300	130.0
Income subject to taxes	52,000	51,300	700	1.4
Income taxes	19,000	18,700	300	1.6
Net income	$ 33,000	$ 32,600	$ 400	1.2

Analyzing and Interpreting Comparative Statements

In analyzing and interpreting comparative data, it is necessary for the analyst to select for study any items showing significant dollar or percentage changes. The analyst then tries to determine the reasons for each change and if possible whether they are favourable or unfavourable. For example, in Illustration 20–1, the first item, "Cash," shows a large decrease. At first glance this appears unfavourable. However, when the decrease in "Cash" is considered with the decrease in "Investments" and the increases in "Store equipment," "Buildings," and "Land," plus the increase in "Mortgage payable," it becomes apparent the company has materially increased its plant assets between the two balance sheet dates. Further study reveals the company has apparently constructed a new building on land that was held as an investment until it was needed in this expansion. Also, it seems the company paid for its new plant assets by reducing cash, selling its Apex Company common stock, and issuing a $50,000 mortgage.

As an aid in controlling operations, a comparative income statement is usually more valuable than a comparative balance sheet. For example, in Illustration 20–2, "Gross sales" increased 14.1% and "Net sales" increased 13.9%. At the same time, "Sales returns" increased 32.4%, or at a rate more than twice that of gross sales. Returned sales represent wasted sales effort and indicate dissatisfied customers. Consequently, such an increase in returns should be investigated, and the reason for increase determined if at all possible. Also, in addition to the large increase in the "Sales returns," it is significant that the rate of increase in "Cost of goods sold" is greater than that of "Net sales." This is an unfavourable trend and should be remedied if at all possible.

In attempting to account for Anchor Supply Company's increase in sales, the increases in advertising and in plant assets merit attention. It is reasonable to expect an increase in advertising to increase sales. It is also reasonable to expect an increase in plant assets to result in a sales increase.

Calculating Percentage Increases and Decreases

When percentage increases and decreases are calculated for comparative statements, the increase or decrease in an item is divided by the amount shown for the item in the base year. No problems arise in these calculations when positive amounts are shown in the base year. However, when no amount is shown or a negative amount is shown in the base year, a percentage increase or decrease cannot be calculated. For example, in Illustration 20–1, there were no notes payable at the end of 198A, and a percentage change for this item cannot be calculated.

In this text, percentages and ratios are typically rounded to one or two decimal places. However, there is no uniform agreement on this matter. In general, percentages should be carried out to the point of assuring that meaningful information is conveyed. Nevertheless, they should not be carried so far that the significance of relationships tends to become "lost" in the length of the numbers.

Trend Percentages

Trend percentages or index numbers emphasize changes that have occurred from period to period and are useful in comparing data covering a number of years. Trend percentages are calculated as follows:

1. A base year is selected, and each item amount on the base year statement is assigned a weight of 100%.
2. Then, each item from the statements for the years after the base year, is expressed as a percentage of its base year amount. To determine these percentages, the item amounts in the years after the base year are divided by the amount of the item in the base year.

For example, if 198A is made the base year for the following data, the trend percentages for "Sales" are calculated by dividing by $210,000 the amount shown for "Sales" in each year after the first. The trend percentages for "Cost of goods sold" are found by dividing by $145,000 the amount shown for "Cost of goods sold" in each year after the first. And, the trend percentages for "Gross profit" are found by dividing the amounts shown for "Gross profit" by $65,000.

	198A	198B	198C	198D	198E	198F
Sales	$210,000	$204,000	$292,000	$284,000	$310,000	$324,000
Cost of goods sold	145,000	139,000	204,000	198,000	218,000	229,000
Gross profit	$ 65,000	$ 65,000	$ 88,000	$ 86,000	$ 92,000	$ 95,000

When these divisions are made, the trends for these three items appear as follows:

	198A	198B	198C	198D	198E	198F
Sales	100	97	139	135	148	154
Cost of goods sold	100	96	141	137	150	158
Gross profit	100	100	135	132	142	146

It is interesting to note in the illustrated trends that while after the second year the sales trend is upward, the cost of goods sold trend is upward at a slightly more rapid rate. This indicates a contracting gross profit rate and should receive attention.

It should be pointed out in a discussion of trends that the trend for a single balance sheet or income statement item is seldom informative. However, a comparison of trends for related items often tells the analyst a great deal. For example, a downward sales trend with an upward trend for merchandise inventory, accounts receivable, and losses on bad debts would generally indicate an unfavourable situation. On the other hand, an upward sales trend with a downward trend or a slower upward trend for accounts receivable, merchandise inventory, and selling expenses would indicate an increase in operating efficiency.

Illustration 20–3

ANCHOR SUPPLY COMPANY, LTD.
Common-Size Comparative Balance Sheet
December 31, 198B, and December 31, 198A

	Years Ended December 31		Common-Size Percentages	
	198B	198A	198B	198A
Assets				
Current assets:				
Cash	$ 18,000	$ 90,500	4.19%	23.63%
Accounts receivable, net	68,000	64,000	15.81	16.71
Merchandise inventory	90,000	84,000	20.93	21.93
Prepaid expenses	5,800	6,000	1.35	1.57
Total current assets	181,800	244,500	42.28	63.84
Long-term investments:				
Real estate	–0–	30,000		7.83
Apex Company common stock .	–0–	50,000		13.05
Total long-term investments ..	–0–	80,000		20.88
Plant and equipment:				
Office equipment, net	3,500	3,700	0.81	0.97
Store equipment, net	17,900	6,800	4.16	1.78
Buildings, net	176,800	28,000	41.12	7.31
Land	50,000	20,000	11.63	5.22
Total plant and equipment ...	248,200	58,500	57.72	15.28
Total assets	$430,000	$383,000	100.00%	100.00%
Liabilities				
Current liabilities:				
Notes payable	$ 5,000	–0–	1.16%	
Accounts payable	43,600	$ 55,000	10.14	14.36%
Taxes payable	4,800	5,000	1.12	1.31
Wages payable	800	1,200	0.19	0.31
Total current liabilities	54,200	61,200	12.61	15.98
Long-term liabilities:				
Mortgage payable	60,000	10,000	13.95	2.61
Total liabilities	114,200	71,200	26.56	18.59
Capital				
Common stock, 25,000 shares ...	250,000	250,000	58.14	65.27
Retained earnings	65,800	61,800	15.30	16.14
Total capital	315,800	311,800	73.44	81.44
Total liabilities and capital	$430,000	$383,000	100.00%	100.00%

Common-Size Comparative Statements

The comparative statements illustrated thus far do not show proportional changes in items except in a general way. Changes in proportions are often shown and emphasized by *common-size comparative statements.*

A common-size statement is so called because its items are shown in common-size figures, figures that are fractions of 100%. For example, on a common-size balance sheet (1) the asset total is assigned a value of 100%. (2) The total of the liabilities and owners' equity is also assigned a value of 100%. Then (3), each asset, liability, and owners' equity

Illustration 20–4

ANCHOR SUPPLY COMPANY, LTD.
Common-Size Comparative Income Statement
Years Ended December 31, 198B, and 198A

	Years Ended December 31		Common-Size Percentages	
	198B	198A	198B	198A
Gross sales	$973,500	$853,000	101.41%	101.21%
Sales returns and allowances	13,500	10,200	1.41	1.21
Net sales.......................................	960,000	842,800	100.00	100.00
Cost of goods sold	715,000	622,500	74.48	73.86
Gross profit from sales	245,000	220,300	25.52	26.14
Operating expenses:				
Selling expenses:				
Advertising expense...........................	7,500	5,000	0.78	0.59
Sales salaries expense	113,500	98,000	11.82	11.63
Store supplies expense	3,200	2,800	0.33	0.33
Depreciation expense, store equipment	2,400	1,700	0.25	0.20
Delivery expense	14,800	14,000	1.54	1.66
Total selling expenses	141,400	121,500	14.72	14.41
General and administrative expenses:				
Office salaries expense	41,000	40,050	4.27	4.75
Office supplies expense	1,300	1,250	0.14	0.15
Insurance expense	1,600	1,200	0.17	0.14
Depreciation expense, office equipment	300	300	0.03	0.04
Depreciation expense, buildings	2,850	1,500	0.30	0.18
Bad debts expense	2,250	2,200	0.23	0.26
Total general and administrative expenses	49,300	46,500	5.14	5.52
Total operating expenses	190,700	168,000	19.86	19.93
Operating income	54,300	52,300	5.66	6.21
Less: Interest expense	2,300	1,000	0.24	0.12
Income subject to taxes	52,000	51,300	5.42	6.09
Income taxes	19,000	18,700	1.98	2.22
Net income	$ 33,000	$ 32,600	3.44%	3.87%

item is shown as a percentage of total assets (or total equities). When a company's successive balance sheets are shown in this manner (see Illustration 20–3), proportional changes are emphasized.

A common-size income statement is prepared by assigning net sales a 100% value and then expressing each statement item as a per cent of net sales. Such a statement is an informative and useful tool. If the 100% sales amount on the statement is assumed to represent one sales dollar, then the remaining items show how each sales dollar was distributed to costs, expenses, and profit. For example, on the comparative income statement shown in Illustration 20–4, the 198A cost of goods sold consumed 73.86 cents of each sales dollar. In 198B, cost of goods sold consumed 74.48 cents of each sales dollar. Although this increase is small, had the proportion of cost of goods sold in 198B remained at the 198A level, almost $6,000 of additional gross profit would have been earned.

Common-size percentages point out efficiencies and inefficiencies that are otherwise difficult to see. For this reason, they are a valuable management tool. To illustrate, sales salaries of Anchor Supply Company took a higher percentage of each sales dollar in 198B than in 198A. On the other hand, office salaries took a smaller percentage. Furthermore, although the loss from bad debts is greater in 198B than in 198A, loss from bad debts took a smaller proportion of each sales dollar in 198B than in 198A.

While it is difficult to attribute cause and effect without further investigation, some possible conclusions may be considered. The higher sales in 198B may have resulted from a better motivated sales staff; the current office staff was likely capable of handling the increased sales activity; and one would expect that more sales would result in more bad debts, but not necessarily in the same proportion.

ANALYSIS OF WORKING CAPITAL

When balance sheets are analyzed, working capital always receives close attention because an adequate amount of working capital enables a company to meet current debts, carry sufficient inventories, and take advantage of cash discounts. However, the amount of working capital a company has is not a measure of these abilities. This may be demonstrated as follows with Companies A and B:

	Company A	Company B
Current assets	$100,000	$20,000
Current liabilities	90,000	10,000
Working capital	$ 10,000	$10,000

Companies A and B have the same amounts of working capital. However, Company A's current liabilities are nine times its working capital, while Company B's current liabilities and working capital are equal. As a result, if liabilities are to paid on time, Company A must experience much less shrinkage and delay in converting its current assets to cash than Company B. Thus, the amount of a company's working capital is not a measure of its working capital position. However, the relation of its current assets to its current liabilities is such a measure.

Current Ratio

The relation of a company's current assets to its current liabilities is known as its *current ratio*. A current ratio is calculated by dividing current assets by current liabilities. The current ratio of the foregoing Company B is calculated as follows:

$$\frac{\text{Current assets, \$20,000}}{\text{Current liabilities, \$10,000}} = 2$$

After the division is made, the relation can be described by saying that Company B's current assets are two times its current liabilities, or simply Company B's current ratio is 2 to 1.

The current ratio is the relation of current assets and current liabilities expressed mathematically. A high current ratio indicates a large proportion of current assets to current liabilities. The higher the ratio, the better is a company's current position, and normally the more capable of meeting its current obligations.

For years, bankers and other credit grantors measured a credit-seeking company's debt-paying ability by whether or not it had a 2-to-1 current ratio. Today, most credit grantors realize that the 2-to-1 rule of thumb is not an adequate test of debt-paying ability. They realize that whether or not a company's current ratio is good or bad depends upon at least three factors:

1. The nature of the company's business.
2. The composition of its current assets.
3. The turnover of certain of its assets.

The nature of a company's business has much to do with whether or not its current ratio is adequate. A public utility that has no inventories other than supplies and that grants little or no credit can operate on a current ratio of less than 1 to 1. On the other hand, because a misjudgment of style can make an inventory of goods for sale almost worthless, a company in which style is the important sales factor may find a current ratio of much more than 2 to 1 to be inadequate. Consequently, when the adequacy of working capital is studied, consideration must be given to the type of business under review.

Also, in an analysis of a company's working capital, the composition of its current assets should be considered. Normally, a company with a high proportion of cash to accounts receivable and merchandise is in a better position to meet quickly its current obligations than is a company with most of its current assets tied up in accounts receivable and merchandise. The company with cash can pay its current debts at once. The company with accounts receivable and merchandise must convert these items into cash before it can pay.

Acid-Test Ratio

An easily calculated check on current asset composition is the *acid-test ratio*, also called the *quick ratio* because it is the ratio of "quick assets" to current liabilities. **Quick assets** are cash, notes receivable, accounts receivable, and temporary investments in marketable securities. They are the current assets that can quickly be turned into cash. An acid-test ratio of 1 to 1 is normally considered satisfactory. However, this is a rule of thumb and should be applied with care. The acid-test ratio of Anchor Supply Company as of the end of 198B is calculated as follows:

Quick assets:		Current liabilities:	
Cash	$18,000	Notes payable	$ 5,000
Accounts receivable	68,000	Accounts payable	43,600
		Taxes payable	4,800
		Wages payable	800
Total	$86,000	Total	$54,200

Acid-test ratio is $86,000 ÷ $54,200 = 1.59 or is 1.6 to 1

Certain current asset turnovers affect working capital requirements. For example, assume Companies A and B sell the same amounts of merchandise on credit each month. However, Company A grants 30-day terms to its customers, while Company B grants 60 days. Both collect their accounts at the end of the credit periods granted. But as a result of the differences in terms, Company A turns over or collects its accounts twice as rapidly as does Company B. Also, as a result of the more rapid turnover, Company A requires only one half the investment in accounts receivable that is required of Company B and can operate with a smaller current ratio.

Accounts receivable turnover is calculated by dividing net sales for a year by the year-end accounts receivable. Anchor Supply Company's turnovers for 198B and 198A are calculated as follows:

		198B	198A
a.	Net sales for year	$960,000	$842,800
b.	Year-end accounts receivable	68,000	64,000
	Times accounts receivable were turned over $(a ÷ b)$	14.1	13.2

The turnover of 14.1 times in 198B in comparison to 13.2 in 198A indicates the company's accounts receivable were collected more rapidly in 198B.

The year-end amount of accounts receivable is commonly used in calculating accounts receivable turnover. However, if year-end accounts receivable are not representative, an average of the year's accounts receivable by months should be used. Also, credit sales should be used rather than the sum of cash and credit sales; and accounts receivable before subtracting the allowance for doubtful accounts should be used. However, information as to credit sales is seldom available in a published balance sheet. Likewise, many published balance sheets report accounts receivable at their net amount. Consequently, total sales and net accounts receivable must often be used.

Days' Sales Uncollected

Accounts receivable turnover is one indication of the speed with which a company collects its accounts. **Days' sales uncollected** is another indication of the same thing. To illustrate the calculation of days' sales uncollected, assume a company had charge sales during a year of $250,000, and that it has $25,000 of accounts receivable at the year-end. In other words, $\frac{1}{10}$ of its charge sales, or the charge sales made during $\frac{1}{10}$ of a year, or the charge sales of 36.5 days ($\frac{1}{10} \times$ 365 days in a year = 36.5 days) are uncollected. This calculation of days' sales uncollected in equation form appears as follows:

$$\frac{\text{Accounts receivable, \$25,000}}{\text{Charge sales, \$250,000}} \times 365 = 36.5 \text{ days' sales uncollected}$$

Days' sales uncollected takes on more meaning when credit terms are known. According to a rule of thumb, a company's days' sales uncollected should not exceed $1\frac{1}{3}$ times the days in its credit period when it does not offer discounts and $1\frac{1}{3}$ times the days in its discount period when it does. If the company, whose days' sales uncollected is calculated in the illustration just given, offers 30-day terms, then 36.5 days is within the rule-of-thumb amount. However, if its terms are 2/10, n/30, its days' sales uncollected seem excessive.

Turnover of Merchandise Inventory

A company's *merchandise turnover* is the number of times its average inventory is sold during an accounting period. A high turnover is considered an indication of good merchandising. Also, from a working capital point of view, a company with a high turnover requires a smaller investment in inventory than one producing the same sales with a low turnover. Merchandise turnover is calculated by dividing cost of goods sold by average inventory. Cost of goods sold is the amount of merchandise at cost that was sold during an accounting period. Average inventory is the average amount of merchandise at cost on hand during the period.

The 198B merchandise turnover of Anchor Supply Company is calculated as follows:

$$\frac{\text{Cost of goods sold, \$715,000}}{\text{Average merchandise inventory, \$87,000}}$$

$$= \text{Merchandise turnover of 8.2 times}$$

The cost of goods sold is taken from the company's 198B income statement. The average inventory is found by dividing by 2 the sum of the $84,000, January 1, 198B, inventory and the $90,000, December 31, 198B, inventory. In a company in which beginning and ending inventories are not representative of the inventory normally on hand, a more accurate turnover may be secured by using the average of all the 12 month-end inventories.

STANDARDS OF COMPARISON

When financial statements are analyzed by computing ratios and turnovers, the analyst must determine whether the ratios and turnovers obtained are good, bad, or just average. Furthermore, in making the decision, the analyst must have some basis for comparison. The following are available:

1. A trained analyst may compare the ratios and turnovers of the company under review with mental standards acquired from past experiences.
2. An analyst may calculate for purposes of comparison the ratios and turnovers of a selected group of competitive companies in the same industry as the one whose statements are under review.
3. Published ratios and turnovers such as those published by Dun & Bradstreet may be used for comparison.
4. Some local and national trade associations gather data from their members and publish standard or average ratios for their trade or industry. These offer the analyst a very good basis of comparison when available.
5. Rule-of-thumb standards may be used as a basis for comparison.

Of these five standards, the ratios and turnovers of a selected group of competitive companies normally offer the best basis for comparison. Rule-of-thumb standards must be applied with care to avoid erroneous conclusions.

OTHER BALANCE SHEET AND INCOME STATEMENT RELATIONS

Several balance sheet and income statement relationships, in addition to those dealing with working capital, are important to the analyst. Some of the more important are discussed below.

Capital Contributions of Owners and Creditors

The share of a company's assets contributed by its owners and the share contributed by creditors are always of interest to the analyst. The owners' and creditors' contributions of Anchor Supply Company are calculated as follows:

		198B	198A
a.	Total liabilities	$114,200	$ 71,200
b.	Total owners' equity	315,800	311,800
c.	Total liabilities and owners' equity	$430,000	$383,000
	Creditors' equity (a ÷ c)	26.6%	18.6%
	Owners' equity (b ÷ c)	73.4%	81.4%

Creditors like to see a high proportion of owners' equity because owners' equity acts as a cushion that absorbs losses. The greater the equity of the owners in relation to liabilities, the greater the losses that can be absorbed by the owners before the creditors begin to lose.

From the creditors' standpoint, a high percentage of owners' equity is desirable. However, if an enterprise can earn a return on borrowed capital that is in excess of the capital's cost, then a reasonable amount of creditors' equity is desirable from the owners' viewpoint.

Pledged Plant Assets to Long-Term Liabilities

Companies commonly borrow by issuing a note or bonds secured by a mortgage on certain of their plant assets. The ratio of pledged plant assets to long-term debt is often calculated to measure the security granted to mortgage or bondholders by the pledged assets. This ratio is calculated by dividing the pledged assets' book value by the liabilities for which the assets are pledged. It is calculated for Anchor Supply Company as of the end of 198B and 198A as follows:

		198B	198A
	Buildings, net	$176,800	$28,000
	Land	50,000	20,000
a.	Book value of pledged plant assets	$226,800	$48,000
b.	Mortgage payable	$ 60,000	$10,000
	Ratio of pledged assets to secured liabilities (a ÷ b)	3.8 to 1	4.8 to 1

The usual rule-of-thumb minimum for this ratio is 2 to 1. However, the ratio needs careful interpretation because it is based on the book value of the pledged assets. Book values often bear little or no relation to the amount that would be received for the assets in a foreclosure or a liquidation. As a result, estimated liquidation values or foreclosure values are normally a better measure of the protection offered bond or mortgage holders by pledged assets. Also, the long-term earning ability of the company whose assets are pledged is usually more important to long-term creditors than the pledged assets' book value.

Times Fixed Interest Charges Earned

The number of *times fixed interest charges* were earned is often calculated to measure the security of the return offered to bondholders or mortgage holders. The calculation is made by dividing income, before fixed interest charges and income taxes, by fixed interest charges. The result is the number of times fixed interest charges were earned. Often, fixed interest charges are considered secure if the company consistently earns its fixed interest charges two or more times each year. This indicates the ability of the company to pay fixed interest charges out of current income earned.

Rate of Return on Total Assets Employed

The return earned on total assets employed is a measure of management's performance. Assets are used to earn a profit, and management is responsible for the way in which they are used. Consequently, the *rate of return on total assets employed* is a measure of management's performance.

The return figure used in this calculation should be after-tax income plus interest expense. Interest expense is included because it is a return paid creditors for assets they have supplied. Likewise, if the amount of assets has fluctuated during the year, an average of the beginning- and end-of-year assets employed should be used.

The rates of return earned on the average total assets employed by Anchor Supply Company during 198B and 198A are calculated as follows:

		198B	198A
	Net income	$ 33,000	$ 32,600
	Add interest expense	2,300	1,000
a.	Net income plus interest plus expense ...	$ 35,300	$ 33,600
b.	Average total assets employed	$406,500	$380,000
	Rate of return on total assets employed *(a ÷ b)*	8.7%	8.8%

In the case of Anchor Supply Company, the change in the rates is not too significant. It is also impossible to tell whether the returns are good or bad without some basis of comparison. The best comparison would be the returns earned by similar-size companies engaged in the same kind of business. A comparison could also be made with the returns earned by this company in previous years. Neither of these is available in this case.

Rate of Return on Common Shareholders' Equity

A primary reason for the operation of a corporation is to earn a net income for its common shareholders. The *rate of return on common shareholders' equity* is a measure of the success achieved in this area. Usually an average of the beginning- and end-of-year equities is used in calculating the return. For Anchor Supply Company, the 198B and 198A calculations are as follows:

		198B	198A
a.	Net income	$ 33,000	$ 32,600
b.	Average shareholders' equity	313,800	309,000
	Rate of return on shareholders'		
	equity (a ÷ b)	10.5%	10.6%

Compare Anchor Supply Company's returns on shareholders' equity with its returns on total assets employed and note that the return on the shareholders' equity is greater in both years. The greater returns resulted from using borrowed money.

When there is preferred stock outstanding, the preferred dividend requirements must be subtracted from net income to arrive at the common shareholders' share of income to be used in this calculation.

Earnings per Common Share

Earnings per common share data are among the most commonly quoted figures on the financial pages of daily newspapers. Such data are used by investors in evaluating the past performance of a business, in projecting its future earnings, and in weighing investment opportunities. Because of the significance attached to earnings per share data by investors and others, the *CICA Handbook,* Section 3500 recommends disclosure of earnings per common share or net loss per common share.

For corporations having only common stock outstanding, the amount of earnings per share is determined by dividing net income by the number of common shares outstanding. For example, Anchor Supply Company of previous illustrations earned $33,000 in 198B and it had 25,000 common shares outstanding. Consequently, the amount of its earnings per common share is calculated:

$$\frac{\text{Net income, }\$33,000}{25,000 \text{ common shares}} = \$1.32 \text{ per share}$$

Where there are also preferred shares outstanding, the year's preferred dividend requirement must be deducted from net income before dividing by the number of outstanding common shares. Also, if the number of common shares changed during the year, a weighted-average number of shares (weighted by the length of time each number of shares was outstanding) is used in the calculation.

Many corporations, like Anchor Supply Company, have simple capital structures consisting only of common stock and, perhaps preferred stock that is not convertible into common stock. Other corporations have more complex capital structures that include preferred stocks and bonds that are convertible into common stock at the option of the owners. In the latter corporations, if conversion should occur, earnings per share would undoubtedly change due solely to the conversion. Recognizing this, the *CICA Handbook* provided specific requirements in Section 3500 for calculating and reporting earnings per share for corporations with complex capital structures. However, these requirements are lengthy and involved so that a discussion must be left to an advanced course.

Price-Earnings Ratio

Price-earnings ratios are commonly used in comparing investment opportunities. A price-earnings ratio is calculated by dividing market price per share by earnings per share. For example, if Anchor Supply Company's common stock sold at $12 per share at the end of 198B, the stock's end-of-year price-earnings ratio is calculated as:

$$\frac{\text{Market price per share, \$12}}{\text{Earnings per share, \$1.32}} = 9.09$$

After the calculation is made, it may be said that the stock had a 9.1 price-earnings ratio at the end of 198B, or it may be said that approximately $9.10 was required at that time to buy $1 of the company's 198B earnings.

In comparing price-earnings ratios, it must be remembered that such ratios vary from industry to industry. For example, in the steel industry, a price-earnings ratio of 8 to 10 is normal, while in a growth industry, such as microcomputers, a price-earnings ratio of 20 to 25 might be expected.

GLOSSARY

Accounts receivable turnover.   An indication of how long it takes a company to collect its accounts, calculated by dividing net sales or credit sales by ending or average accounts receivable.

Acid-test ratio.   The relation of quick assets, such as cash, notes receivable, accounts receivable, and temporary investments in marketable securities to current liabilities, calculated as quick assets divided by current liabilities.

Common-size comparative statements. Comparative financial statements in which each amount is expressed as a percentage of a base amount. In the balance sheet, total assets is usually selected as the base amount and is expressed as 100%. In the income statement, net sales is usually selected as the base amount.

Comparative statement. A financial statement with data for two or more successive accounting periods placed in columns side by side in order to better illustrate changes in the data.

Current ratio. The relation of a company's current assets to its current liabilities, that is, current assets divided by current liabilities.

Financial reporting. The process of preparing and issuing financial information about a company.

General-purpose financial statements. Financial statements (usually including the income statement, balance sheet, statement of retained earnings, and statement of changes in financial position) published by a company for use by persons who do not have the ability to obtain specialized financial reports designed to meet their interests.

Merchandise turnover. The number of times a company's average inventory is sold during an accounting period, calculated by dividing cost of goods sold by average merchandise inventory.

Price-earnings ratio. Market price per share of common stock divided by earnings per share.

Quick ratio. A synonym for **acid-test ratio.**

Rate of return on common shareholders' equity. Net income after dividends on preferred stock divided by average common shareholders' equity.

Rate of return on total assets employed. Net income plus interest expense, expressed as a percentage of total assets employed during the period.

Times fixed interest charges earned. An indicator of a company's ability to satisfy fixed interest charges, calculated as net income before fixed interest charges and income taxes divided by fixed interest charges.

QUESTIONS FOR CLASS DISCUSSION

1. What are the objectives of financial reporting?
2. Comparative balance sheets often have columns showing increases and decreases in both dollar amounts and percentages. Why is this so?
3. When trends are calculated and compared, what item trends should be compared with the trend of sales?
4. What is meant by *common-size* financial statements?
5. What items are assigned a value of 100% *(a)* on a common-size balance sheet and *(b)* on a common-size income statement?

6. Why is working capital given special attention in the process of analyzing balance sheets?

7. For the following transactions indicate which increase working capital, which decrease working capital, and which have no effect on working capital:
   a. Collected amounts receivable.
   b. Borrowed money by giving a 90-day interest-bearing note.
   c. Declared a cash dividend.
   d. Paid a cash dividend previously declared.
   e. Sold plant assets at their book value.
   f. Sold merchandise at a profit.

8. List several factors that have an effect on working capital requirements.

9. A company has a 2-to-1 current ratio. List several reasons why this ratio may not be adequate.

10. State the significance of each of the following ratios and turnovers and tell how each is calculated:
   a. Current ratio.
   b. Acid-test ratio.
   c. Turnover of accounts receivable.
   d. Turnover of merchandise inventory.
   e. Rate of return on common shareholders' equity.
   f. Ratio of pledged plant assets to long-term liabilities.

11. How are days' sales uncollected calculated? What is the significance of the number of days' sales uncollected?

12. Why do creditors like to see a high proportion of total assets being financed by owners' equity?

13. What is the ratio of pledged plant assets to long-term liabilities supposed to measure? Why must this ratio be interpreted with care?

14. What does the rate of return on assets employed tell about management?

15. How are earnings per share calculated in a corporation having outstanding only common stock and preferred stock that is not convertible into common stock?

16. How is a price-earnings ratio calculated?

MULTIPLE CHOICE

1. Y Company had a cost of goods sold for 198A of $460,000 and net sales of $620,000. Its beginning inventory was $39,000 and its ending inventory is $45,000. What was Y Company's merchandise turnover?
   a. 10.2.
   b. 11.0.
   c. 11.8.
   d. 13.8.
   e. 14.8.

2. The XYZ Company had earnings per share of $2.44, net income of $29,280 and 12,000 common shares outstanding throughout the year for 198A. On December 31, 198A, the stock of XYZ Company sold for $32. What is XYZ's price-earnings ratio?

   a. 2.44.
   b. 13.11.
   c. 375.00.
   d. 915.00.
   e. None of the above.

3. X Company's sales in 198A were $120,000. Sales in 198B were $147,600. Using 198A as the base year, the trend percentage for 198B is:

   a. 81.3%.
   b. 100.0%.
   c. 123.0%.
   d. 147.6%.
   e. None of the above.

4. The Texas Drill Company had income tax expense of $20,000 and net income after taxes of $30,000 for 198A. Its average common shareholders' equity was $250,000 and ending shareholders' equity was $300,000. What is Texas Drill Company's rate of return on the common shareholders' equity?

   a. 10%.
   b. 11%.
   c. 12%.
   d. 17%.
   e. 20%.

5. Selected facts for X Company's performance in 198A are:

Beginning-of-year accounts receivable ...	$ 21,000
End-of-year accounts receivable	22,500
Net sales	265,000
Charge sales	180,000

   X Company's days' sales uncollected is:

   a. 30.0 days.
   b. 31.0 days.
   c. 42.6 days.
   d. 44.1 days.
   e. 45.6 days.

6. The X Company has the following balance sheet for the year ended December 31, 198A:

Assets		Equities	
Cash	$ 10,000	Current liabilities	$ 23,250
Accounts receivable ...	21,000	Long-term liabilities ...	40,000
Inventory	14,000	Common stock	40,000
Plant assets	80,000	Retained earnings	21,750
Total assets	$125,000	Total equities	$125,000

X Company's acid-test ratio is:

a. .1.

b. .3.

c. .4.

d. 1.3.

e. 1.9.

MINI DISCUSSION CASES

Case 20–1   Analysts have often used working capital ratios to test for companies' financial health. Some years ago, however, there were several cases of companies with healthy working capital ratios which, shortly thereafter, were forced into bankruptcy apparently because they were not able to pay their debts as they became due.

Required:

Discuss the shortcomings of working capital analysis. What other kinds of analyses might be used which would overcome these deficiencies? Why?

Case 20–2   A friend comes to you excitedly urging you to take advantage of an investment opportunity. As support for her recommendation the friend shows you the company's Annual Report and says, "This company has Earnings per Share of $6.73." She says that she has just purchased 500 of the company's shares at $45.50 and urges you to do the same before the price goes up any further.

Required:

It is now 5:00 P.M. and the markets have closed for the day. Your friend has allowed you to borrow her copy of the Annual Report until tomorrow morning. What analyses are you going to use to evaluate this investment? What further information do you think you might require? Why?

CLASS EXERCISES

Exercise 20–1   Calculate trend percentages for the following items and tell whether the situation shown by the trends is favourable or unfavourable:

	19A	19B	19C	19D	19E
Sales	$200,000	$226,000	$238,000	$248,000	$260,000
Cost of goods sold	120,000	144,000	162,000	168,000	180,000
Accounts receivable	20,000	25,000	27,000	28,000	31,000

Exercise 20–2   Where possible calculate percentages of increase and decrease for the following unrelated items. The parentheses indicate deficit items.

	19B	19A
Equipment, net	$80,000	$60,000
Notes receivable	–0–	3,000
Notes payable	10,000	–0–
Retained earnings	(2,400)	12,000
Cash	10,000	(1,000)

Exercise 20–3   Express the following income statement information in common-size percentages and tell whether the situation shown is favourable or unfavourable.

HARRISON COMPANY
Comparative Income Statement
Years Ended December 31, 19A, and 19B

	19B	19A
Sales	$100,000	$90,000
Cost of goods sold	66,800	59,850
Gross profit from sales	$ 33,200	$30,150
Operating expenses	25,100	22,320
Net income	$ 8,100	$ 7,830

Exercise 20–4   The year-end statements of Great Abaco Company follow:

GREAT ABACO COMPANY, LTD.
Balance Sheet
December 31, 19—

Assets		Equities	
Cash	$ 6,000	Accounts payable	$ 20,000
Accounts receivable, net	24,000	Mortgage payable, secured by	
Merchandise inventory, net . . .	28,500	a lien on the plant assets . .	35,000
Prepaid expenses	1,500	Common stock, 10,000	
Plant assets, net	140,000	shares par value	100,000
Total assets	$200,000	Retained earnings	45,000
		Total equities	$200,000

GREAT ABACO COMPANY, LTD.
Income Statement
For Year Ended December 31, 19—

Sales		$365,000
Cost of goods sold:		
Merchandise inventory, January 1, 19—	$ 31,500	
Purchases	267,000	
Goods available for sale	$298,500	
Merchandise inventory, December 31, 19—	28,500	
Cost of goods sold		270,000
Gross profit on sales		$ 95,000
Operating expenses		74,000
Operating income		$ 21,000
Mortgage interest expense		2,100
Income before taxes		$ 18,900
Income taxes		4,900
Net income		$ 14,000

Required:

Calculate the following: *(a)* current ratio, *(b)* acid-test ratio, *(c)* days' sales uncollected, *(d)* merchandise turnover, *(e)* capital contribution of owners expressed as a per cent, *(f)* ratio of pledged plant assets to long-term debt, *(g)* times fixed interest charges earned, *(h)* return on shareholders' equity, and *(i)* earnings per share. (Assume all sales were on credit and the shareholders' equity was $135,000 on January 1.)

Exercise 20–5   Common-size and trend percentages for a company's sales, cost of goods sold, and expenses follow:

Common-size percentages				*Trend percentages*			
	19A	*19B*	*19C*		*19A*	*19B*	*19C*
Sales	100.0	100.0	100.0	Sales	100.0	95.0	90.0
Cost of goods sold ...	64.0	63.0	63.0	Cost of goods sold ...	100.0	93.5	88.6
Expenses	28.0	28.0	27.0	Expenses	100.0	95.0	86.8

Required:

Present statistics to prove whether the company's net income increased, decreased, or remained unchanged during the three-year period represented above.

PROBLEMS

Problem 20–1   The year-end statements of Spinaker Company follow:

SPINAKER COMPANY, INC.
Income Statement
For Year Ended December 31, 19—

Sales		$510,000
Cost of goods sold:		
Merchandise inventory, January 1, 19—	$ 37,800	
Purchases	320,400	
Goods available for sale	$358,200	
Merchandise inventory, December 31, 19—	34,200	
Cost of goods sold		324,000
Gross profit from sales		$186,000
Operating expenses		158,700
Operating income		$ 27,300
Mortgage interest expense		4,200
Income before taxes		$ 23,100
Income taxes		5,100
Net income		$ 18,000

SPINAKER COMPANY, INC.
Balance Sheet
December 31, 19—

Assets		Equities	
Cash	$ 8,600	Accounts payable	$ 23,800
Temporary investments	10,000	Accrued wages payable	1,100
Notes receivable	3,000	Income taxes payable	5,100
Accounts receivable, net	25,500	Mortgage payable, secured by	
Merchandise inventory	34,200	a lien on the plant assets ...	68,000
Prepaid expenses	1,200	Common stock, 20,000	
Plant assets, net	170,000	shares no par value	100,000
Total assets	$252,500	Retained earnings	54,500
		Total equities	$252,500

Required:

Calculate the following: *(a)* current ratio, *(b)* acid-test ratio, *(c)* days' sales uncollected, *(d)* merchandise turnover, *(e)* ratio of pledged plant assets to long-term debt, *(f)* times fixed interest charges earned, *(g)* return on total assets employed, *(h)* return on shareholders' equity, and *(i)* earnings per share. Assume all sales were on credit, the assets totaled $247,500 on January 1, and the shareholders' equity at the beginning of the year was $145,500.

Problem 20–2   The condensed statements of Fort Dodge Metals follow:

FORT DODGE METALS, LTD.
Comparative Income Statements
Years Ended December 31, 19A, 19B, and 19C
(in thousands)

	19A	19B	19C
Sales	$8,000	$9,000	$10,000
Cost of goods sold	5,688	6,480	7,150
Gross profit from sales	$2,312	$2,520	$ 2,850
Selling expenses	$1,216	$1,359	$ 1,500
Administrative expenses	784	855	940
Total expenses	$2,000	$2,214	$ 2,440
Income before taxes	$ 312	$ 306	$ 410
Income taxes	152	149	196
Net income	$ 160	$ 157	$ 214

FORT DODGE METALS, LTD.
Comparative Balance Sheets
December 31, 19A, 19B, and 19C
(in thousands)

	19A	19B	19C
Assets			
Current assets	$ 750	$ 615	$ 696
Long-term investments	50	5	–0–
Plant and equipment	2,400	2,676	2,664
Total assets	$3,200	$3,296	$3,360

	19A	19B	19C
Liabilities and Capital			
Current liabilities	$ 250	$ 280	$ 290
Common stock	2,000	2,100	2,100
Other contributed capital	50	61	61
Retained earnings	900	855	909
Total liabilities and capital ...	$3,200	$3,296	$3,360

Required:

1. Calculate each year's current ratio.
2. Express the income statement data in common-size percentages.
3. Express the balance sheet data in trend percentages.
4. Comment on any significant relationships revealed by the ratios and percentages.

Problem 20–3   Following are the condensed 19A and 19B statements of Weber Feeds:

WEBER FEEDS, LTD.
Comparative Income Statements
Years Ended December 31, 19A, and 19B

	19B	19A
Sales (all on credit)	$476,000	$451,000
Cost of goods sold:		
Merchandise inventory, January 1	$ 43,000	$ 41,000
Purchases	305,600	273,800
Goods for sale	$348,600	$314,800
Merchandise inventory, December 31	56,000	43,000
Cost of goods sold	$292,600	$271,800
Gross profit from sales	$183,400	$179,200
Operating expenses	163,400	156,600
Income before taxes	$ 20,000	$ 22,600

WEBER FEEDS, LTD.
Comparative Balance Sheets
December 31, 19A, and 19B

	19B	19A
Assets		
Cash	$ 14,000	$ 12,000
Accounts receivable	38,000	44,000
Merchandise inventory	56,000	43,000
Plant assets, net	104,000	102,000
Total assets	$212,000	$201,000
Liabilities and Shareholders' Equity		
Accounts payable	$ 26,000	$ 28,000
Notes payable	10,000	6,000
Mortgage payable (due in 1990)	40,000	40,000
Common stock	100,000	100,000
Retained earnings	36,000	27,000
Total liabilities and shareholders' equity	$212,000	$201,000

Required:

1. Calculate common-size percentages for sales, cost of goods sold, gross profit from sales, operating expenses, and income before taxes; and calculate the current ratio, acid-test ratio, merchandise turnover, and days' sales uncollected for each of the two years.
2. Comment on the situation shown by your calculations.

Problem 20–4   The condensed comparative statements of Belton Bolt Company follow:

BELTON BOLT COMPANY, LTD.
Comparative Income Statements
For Years Ended December 31, 19A–G
(in thousands)

	19A	19B	19C	19D	19E	19F	19G
Sales	$400	$500	$572	$680	$760	$840	$872
Cost of goods sold	250	310	360	430	515	585	604
Gross profit from sales	$150	$190	$212	$250	$245	$255	$268
Operating expenses	100	110	118	138	197	220	238
Income before taxes	$ 50	$ 80	$ 94	$112	$ 48	$ 35	$ 30

BELTON BOLT COMPANY, LTD.
Comparative Balance Sheets
December 31, 19A–G
(in thousands)

	19A	19B	19C	19D	19E	19F	19G
Assets							
Cash	$ 20	$ 14	$ 17	$ 15	$ 12	$ 10	$ 4
Accounts receivable, net	40	52	54	62	88	90	92
Merchandise inventory	100	118	141	165	204	218	226
Other current assets	2	4	4	6	2	4	2
Long-term investments	38	38	38	38	–0–	–0–	–0–
Plant and equipment, net	200	198	204	202	446	450	440
Total assets	$400	$424	$458	$488	$752	$772	$764
Liabilities and Capital							
Current liabilities	$ 50	$ 64	$ 82	$ 90	$140	$156	$159
Long-term liabilities	40	38	36	34	182	180	178
Common stock	250	250	250	250	310	310	310
Retained earnings	60	72	90	114	120	126	117
Total liabilities and capital	$400	$424	$458	$488	$752	$772	$764

Required:

1. Calculate trend percentages for the items of the statements.
2. Analyze and comment on any situations shown in the statements.

Problem 20–5   A company had $180,000 of current assets, a 3 to 1 current ratio, and a 1½ to 1 quick ratio. It then completed the following transactions:

a. Collected a $2,500 account receivable.
b. Wrote off a $1,000 bad debt against the allowance for doubtful accounts.
c. Borrowed $20,000 by giving its bank a 60-day, 6% note.

d. Bought $10,000 of merchandise on credit. The company uses a perpetual inventory system.

e. Declared a $0.50 per share cash dividend on its 20,000 shares of outstanding common stock.

f. Paid the dividend declared in (e) above.

g. Declared a 1,000-share stock dividend. The stock was selling at $15 per share on the day of the declaration.

h. Distributed the dividend stock of (g) above.

i. Sold for $10,000 merchandise that cost $5,000.

Required:

Prepare a schedule showing the company's current ratio, its acid-test ratio, and the amount of its working capital after each of the foregoing transactions. Round to two decimal places.

ALTERNATE PROBLEMS

Problem
20–1A

The year-end statements of Rayford Tarp Company follow:

RAYFORD TARP COMPANY, LTD.
Balance Sheet
For Year Ended 19—

Assets		Equities	
Cash	$ 12,000	Accounts payable	$ 19,800
Temporary investments	8,000	Accrued wages payable	550
Notes receivable	2,500	Income taxes payable	4,650
Accounts receivable, net	23,000	Mortgage payable, secured by	
Merchandise inventory	36,300	a lien on the plant assets	70,000
Prepaid expenses	1,200	Common stock, 10,000	
Plant assets, net	168,000	shares	100,000
Total assets	$251,000	Retained earnings	56,000
		Total equities	$251,000

RAYFORD TARP COMPANY, LTD.
Income Statement
For Year Ended December 31, 19—

Sales			$460,000
Cost of goods sold:			
Merchandise inventory, January 1, 19—		$ 33,700	
Purchases		300,100	
Goods available for sale		$333,800	
Merchandise inventory, December 31, 19—		36,300	
Cost of goods sold			297,500
Gross profit from sales			$162,500
Operating expenses			136,850
Operating income			$ 25,650
Mortgage interest expense			4,500
Income before taxes			$ 21,150
Income taxes			4,650
Net income			$ 16,500

Required:

Calculate the following: *(a)* current ratio, *(b)* acid-test ratio, *(c)* days' sales uncollected, *(d)* merchandise turnover, *(e)* ratio of pledged plant assets to long-term debt, *(f)* times fixed interest charges earned, *(g)* return on total assets employed, *(h)* return on shareholders' equity, and *(i)* earnings per share. Assume all sales were on credit, assets employed at the beginning of the year totaled $249,000, and shareholders' equity at the beginning of the year was $144,000.

Problem 20–2A

The condensed statements of Schwab Technics Company follow:

SCHWAB TECHNICS COMPANY, LTD.
Comparative Income Statements
Years Ended December 31, 19A, 19B, and 19C
(in thousands)

	19A	19B	19C
Sales	$5,000	$6,000	$6,500
Cost of goods sold	3,600	4,398	4,745
Gross margin on sales	$1,400	$1,602	$1,755
Selling expenses	$ 700	$ 810	$ 884
Administrative expenses	500	588	637
Total expenses	$1,200	$1,398	$1,521
Income before taxes	$ 200	$ 204	$ 234
Income taxes	90	92	105
Net income	$ 110	$ 112	$ 129

SCHWAB TECHNICS COMPANY, LTD
Comparative Balance Sheets
December 31, 19A, 19B, and 19C
(in thousands)

	19A	19B	19C
Assets			
Current assets	$ 400	$ 256	$ 240
Plant and equipment	1,200	1,380	1,440
Total assets	$1,600	$1,636	$1,680
Liabilities and Capital			
Current liabilities	$ 125	$ 131	$ 127
Common stock, 100 shares	1,000	1,000	1,000
Other contributed capital	175	175	175
Retained earnings	300	330	378
Total liabilities and capital	$1,600	$1,636	$1,680

Required:

1. Calculate each year's current ratio.
2. Express the income statement data in common-size percentages.
3. Express the balance sheet data in trend percentages.
4. Comment on any significant relationships revealed by the ratios and percentages.

**Problem
20–3A**

Following are data from the statements of two companies selling similar products:

Balance Sheet at Current Year-End

	Company X	Company Y
Assets		
Cash	$ 8,500	$ 12,500
Notes receivable	3,500	2,000
Accounts receivable	30,000	40,000
Merchandise inventory	44,000	54,800
Prepaid expenses	1,200	1,200
Plant and equipment, net	165,800	172,500
Total assets	$253,000	$283,000
Liabilities and Capital		
Current liabilities	$ 40,000	$ 50,000
Mortgage payable	50,000	50,000
Common stock, 10,000 shares	100,000	100,000
Retained earnings	63,000	83,000
Total liabilities and capital	$253,000	$283,000

Income Statement for Current Year

Sales	$480,000	$550,000
Cost of goods sold	377,200	437,400
Interest expense	3,000	3,500
Net income	16,695	18,060

Beginning-of-Year Data

Merchandise inventory	$ 38,000	$ 53,200
Total assets	247,000	277,000
Shareholders' equity	155,000	178,200

Required:

1. Calculate current ratios, acid-test ratios, merchandise turnovers, and days' sales uncollected for the two companies. Then state which company you think is the better short-term credit risk and why.
2. Calculate earnings per share, rate of return on total assets employed, and rate of return on shareholders' equity. Then under the assumption that each company's stock can be purchased at book value, state which company's stock you think is the better investment and why.

**Problem
20–4A**

PRICKLY CACTUS COMPANY LTD.
Comparative Income Statements
For Years Ending December 31, 19E–19A
(in thousands)

	19E	19D	19C	19B	19A
Sales	710	620	590	530	500
Cost of goods sold	560	500	485	405	390
Gross profit from sales	150	120	105	125	110
Operating expenses	27	25	24	21	20
Income subject to taxes	123	95	81	104	90

PRICKLY CACTUS COMPANY LTD.
Comparative Balance Sheets
December 31, 19E–19A
(in thousands)

	19E	19D	19C	19B	19A
Assets					
Cash	10	16	20	19	24
Accounts receivable, net	365	340	260	255	245
Merchandise inventory	430	410	365	340	275
Other current assets	3	2	4	3	5
Long-term investments	0	0	25	18	5
Plant assets, net	236	268	274	312	342
Total assets	1,044	1,036	948	947	896
Liabilities and Capital					
Current liabilities	265	262	245	198	200
Long-term liabilities	345	365	360	380	300
Common stock	75	75	75	75	75
Retained earnings	359	334	268	294	321
Total liabilities and capital	1,044	1,036	948	947	896

Required:

1. Calculate trend percentages for the items of the statements.
2. Assuming flexibility in the use of plant assets, analyze the situation and suggest reasons for the company's financial position.

Problem 20–5A

A company began the month of August with $200,000 of current assets, a 2½ to 1 current ratio, and a 1¼ to 1 acid-test ratio. During the month it completed the following transactions:

Aug. 1 Bought $20,000 of merchandise on account. (The company uses a perpetual inventory system.)
    5 Sold for $10,000 merchandise that cost $5,000.
    7 Collected a $2,500 account receivable.
    11 Paid a $10,000 account payable.
    15 Wrote off a $1,500 bad debt against the allowance for doubtful accounts.
    18 Declared a $1 per share cash dividend on the 10,000 shares of outstanding common stock.
    28 Paid the dividend declared on May 18.
    29 Borrowed $10,000 by giving the bank a 60-day, 6% note.
    30 Borrowed $25,000 by placing a 10-year mortgage on the plant.
    31 Used the $25,000 proceeds of the mortgage to buy additional machinery.

Required:

Prepare a schedule showing the company's current ratio, acid-test ratio, and working capital after each of the foregoing transactions. Round to two decimal places.

PROVOCATIVE PROBLEMS

Provocative Problem 20–1, Beaumont Retail Company

As controller of Beaumont Retail Company you have calculated the following ratios, turnovers, and percentages to enable you to answer questions the directors will ask at their next meeting.

	19C	19B	19A
Current ratio	2.91/1	2.47/1	2.09/1
Acid-test ratio	0.88/1	1.07/1	1.48/1
Merchandise turnover	9.5 times	10.1 times	10.5 times
Accounts receivable turnover	6.9 times	7.4 times	8.2 times
Return on shareholders' equity	6.11%	6.51%	6.89%
Return on total assets	6.20%	6.29%	6.52%
Sales to plant assets	4.70/1	4.50/1	4.20/1
Sales trend	124.00	114.00	100.00
Selling expenses to net sales	14.65%	14.85%	15.21%

Using the statistics given, answer each of the following questions and explain how you arrived at your answer.

a. Is it becoming easier for the company to meet its current debts on time and to take advantage of cash discounts?
b. Is the company collecting its accounts receivable more rapidly?
c. Is the company's investment in accounts receivable decreasing?
d. Are dollars invested in inventory increasing?
e. Is the company's investment in plant assets increasing?
f. Is the shareholders' investment becoming more profitable?
g. Is the company using debt leverage to the advantage of its shareholders?
h. Did the dollar amount of selling expenses decrease during the three-year period?

Provocative Problem 20–2, Ace Company and Fox Company

Ace Company and Fox Company are competitors; both were organized about 10 years ago; and both have seen their sales increase 10-fold during the 10-year period. However, the 10-fold increase is not as good as it sounds because the costs and selling prices of the items the companies sell have doubled during the same period. Nevertheless, the sales of the companies have continued to increase. Both offer the same credit terms; age their accounts receivable to allow for bad debts; and collect their accounts in about the same length of time. Actually about the only real difference in the accounting procedures of the two companies is that since its organization Ace Company has used LIFO in costing its goods sold and Fox Company has used FIFO.

The current ratios of the two companies for the past four years were as follows:

Current Ratios

	Ace Company	Fox Company
December 31, 19A	3.1 to 1	5.4 to 1
December 31, 19B	3.4 to 1	5.8 to 1
December 31, 19C	2.8 to 1	6.0 to 1
December 31, 19D	2.6 to 1	6.1 to 1

You are the loan officer of a bank and both companies have come to your bank for 90-day loans. In addition to the current ratios, you note that Ace Company turned its inventory twice as fast as Fox Company in each of 19A and 19B and three times as fast in each of the last two years. You also discover that for each $10,000 of current liabilities the companies have the following amounts of inventory:

	Ace Company	Fox Company
December 31, 19A	$19,000	$44,000
December 31, 19B	23,000	49,000
December 31, 19C	16,000	52,000
December 31, 19D	14,000	54,000

Which company do you think is the better short-term credit risk? Back your opinion with computations showing why. Are the inventory turnovers of the two companies comparable? Explain. Which company seems to have the better inventory turnover?

Provocative Problem 20–3, Adell Davis

Adell Davis has an opportunity to invest in either of two companies, both of which operate locally and in the same line of business. The stock of either company can be bought at its book value, and Adell is undecided which is the better managed company and which is the better investment. Following are data from the financial statements of the companies:

Balance Sheet at Current Year-End

	Eastgate Company	Westgate Company
Assets		
Cash	$ 26,000	$ 28,000
Accounts receivable, net	64,000	78,500
Merchandise inventory	85,000	102,500
Prepaid expenses	2,000	3,000
Plant and equipment, net	320,000	350,000
Total assets	$ 497,000	$ 562,000
Liabilities and Capital		
Current liabilities	$ 75,000	$ 98,000
Mortgage payable	106,000	110,000
Common stock, 20,000 shares	200,000	200,000
Retained earnings	116,000	154,000
Total liabilities and capital	$ 497,000	$ 562,000

Income Statement for Current Year

	Eastgate Company	Westgate Company
Sales	$1,220,000	$1,395,000
Cost of goods sold	860,500	993,000
Gross profit on sales	$ 359,500	$ 402,000
Operating expenses	280,000	336,000
Operating income	$ 79,500	$ 66,000
Interest expense	10,500	11,000
Income before taxes	$ 69,000	$ 55,000
Income taxes	26,600	19,900
Net income	$ 42,400	$ 35,100

	Eastgate Company	Westgate Company
Beginning-of-Year Data		
Merchandise inventory	$ 67,000	$ 87,500
Total assets	480,000	550,000
Shareholders' equity	310,000	360,000

Prepare a report to Adell Davis stating which company you think is the better managed and which company's stock you think is the better investment. Back your report with any ratios, turnovers, and other analyses you think pertinent.

ANALYTICAL AND REVIEW PROBLEMS

Problem 20–1
A&R

RATIO DATA COMPANY, LTD.
Balance Sheet
As at June 1, 1979

Cash	$_____	Current liabilities	$_____
Accounts receivable . . .	_____	Long-term debt at 10% . . .	_____
Inventory	_____	Shareholders' equity	_____
Fixed assets	_____		
	$_____		$_____

Required:

Using the format shown above complete the balance sheet for Ratio Data Company Ltd., from the following ratios (round items to the nearest thousand dollars).

Net income	$ 600,000
Sales	$7,500,000
Current ratio	2 to 1
Debt to total assets	50%
Inventory turnover	10 times
Average (collection period, based on 360 days)	100 days
Fixed asset turnover	5 times
Total asset turnover	1.5 times
Expenses (including income tax at 50%)	$1,900,000

Problem 20–2
A&R

On the basis of the information given, complete the balance sheet.

RATIO COMPANY LIMITED
Balance Sheet
December 31, 1979

Cash	$_____	Current liabilities	$_____
Accounts receivable . . .	_____	8% bonds payable	_____
Inventory	_____	Shareholders' equity . . .	_____
Fixed assets	_____		
	$_____		$_____

Sales (all credit) $40,000
Cost of goods sold 24,000
Expenses............. 8,000
Income taxes 4,000
Net income 4,000

Net income/shareholders' equity 25%
Bonds payable/shareholders' equity .... 1 to 2
Inventory turnover .... 4 times
Accounts receivable collection period (360-day year) ..... 72 days
Current ratio .... 2.5 to 1
Total asset turnover .... 1.25 times
Rate of return (after taxes) on total investment 12.5%

Problem 20–3
A&R

A company began the month of May with $200,000 of current assets, a 2½ to 1 current ratio, and a 1¼ to 1 acid-test (quick) ratio. During the month it completed the following transactions:

		Current ratio			Working capital		
		Inc.	Dcr.	No Change	Inc.	Dcr.	No Change
a.	Bought $20,000 of merchandise on account (The company uses a perpetual inventory system)						
b.	Sold for $18,000 merchandise that cost $13,000						
c.	Collected a $3,500 account receivable						
d.	Paid a $12,000 account payable						
e.	Wrote off a $1,000 bad debt against the allowance for doubtful accounts						
f.	Declared a $1 per share cash dividend on the 10,000 shares of outstanding common stock						
g.	Paid the dividend declared in (f)						
h.	Borrowed $12,000 by giving the bank a 60-day, 10% note						
i.	Borrowed $30,000 by placing a 10-year mortgage on the plant						
j.	Used the $30,000 proceeds of the mortgage to buy additional machinery						

Required:

1. Indicate the effect on *(a)* current ratio and *(b)* working capital of each transaction. Set up a chart in your answer similar to that shown above and use check marks to indicate your answers. (Working capital is defined as ''current assets minus current liabilities.'')

2. At the end of May the
   a. Current ratio was _____
   b. Acid-test ratio was _____
   c. Working capital was _____

Managerial Accounting for Costs

Manufacturing Accounting

21

After studying Chapter 21, you should be able to:

Describe the basic differences in the financial statements of manufacturing companies and merchandising companies.

Describe the procedures inherent in a general accounting system for a manufacturing company.

List the different accounts that appear on a manufacturing company's books and state what the accounts represent.

Explain the purpose of a manufacturing statement, how one is composed, and how the statement is integrated with the primary financial statements.

Prepare financial statements for a manufacturing company from a work sheet.

Prepare the adjusting and closing entries for a manufacturing company.

Explain the procedures for assigning costs to the different manufacturing inventories.

Define or explain the words and phrases listed in the chapter Glossary.

In previous chapters, consideration has been given to the accounting problems of service-type and merchandising companies. In this chapter, some problems of manufacturing enterprises are examined.

Manufacturing and merchandising companies are alike in that both depend upon the sale of one or more commodities or products for revenue. However, they differ in one important way. A merchandising company buys the goods it sells in the same condition in which they are sold. On the other hand, a manufacturing company buys raw materials that it manufactures into the finished product it sells. For example, a shoe store buys shoes and sells them in the same form in which they are purchased; but a manufacturer of shoes buys leather, cloth, glue, nails, and dye and turns these items into salable shoes.

BASIC DIFFERENCE IN ACCOUNTING

The basic difference in accounting for manufacturing and merchandising companies grows from the idea that a merchandising company buys the goods it sells in their finished ready-for-sale state. A manufacturer must create what it sells from raw materials. As a result, the merchandising company can easily determine the cost of the goods it has bought for sale by examining the debit balance of its Purchases account. In contrast, the manufacturer must combine the balances of a number of material, labour, and overhead accounts to determine the cost of the goods it has manufactured for sale.

To emphasize this difference, the cost of goods sold section from a merchandising company's income statement is condensed and presented below alongside the cost of goods sold section of a manufacturing company.

Merchandising company		*Manufacturing company*	
Cost of goods sold:		Costs of goods sold:	
Beginning merchandise inventory......................	$14,200	Beginning finished goods inventory	$ 11,200
Cost of goods purchased	34,150	Cost of goods manufactured (see Manufacturing Statement)	170,500
Goods available for sale	48,350	Goods available for sale	181,700
Ending merchandise inventory	12,100	Ending finished goods inventory ...	10,300
Cost of goods sold	$36,250	Cost of goods sold	$171,400

Notice in the cost of goods sold section from the manufacturing company's income statement that the inventories of goods for sale are called *finished goods inventories* rather than merchandise inventories. Notice too that the "Cost of goods purchased" element of the merchandising company becomes "Cost of goods manufactured" (see Manufacturing Statement) on the manufacturer's income statement. These differences exist because the merchandising company buys its goods ready for sale, while the manufacturer creates its salable products from raw materials.

The words **see** *Manufacturing Statement* refer the income statement reader to a separate schedule called a manufacturing statement (see page 870) which shows the costs of manufacturing the products produced by a manufacturing company. The records and techniques used in accounting for these costs are the distinguishing characteristics of manufacturing accounting.

SYSTEMS OF ACCOUNTING IN MANUFACTURING COMPANIES

The accounting system used by a manufacturing company may be either a so-called general accounting system like the one described in this chapter or a cost accounting system. A general accounting system uses periodic physical inventories of raw materials, goods in process, and finished goods; and it has as its goal the determination of the total cost of all goods manufactured during each accounting period. Cost accounting systems differ in that they use perpetual inventories and have as their goal the determination of the unit cost of manufacturing a product or performing a service. Such systems are discussed in Chapter 22.

ELEMENTS OF MANUFACTURING COSTS

A manufacturer takes *raw materials* and by applying *direct labour* and *factory overhead* converts these materials into finished products. Raw materials, direct labour, and factory overhead are the "elements of manufacturing costs."

Raw Materials

Raw materials are the commodities that enter into and become a part of a finished product. Such items as leather, dye, cloth, nails, and glue are raw materials used by shoe manufacturers. Raw materials are often called *direct materials.* Since direct materials physically become part of the finished product, the cost of direct materials is easily traced to units of product or batches of production, and the direct materials cost of production can be directly charged to units of product or batches of production without the use of arbitrary or highly judgmental cost allocation procedures.

Direct materials are distinguished from *indirect materials* or factory supplies, which are such items as grease and oil for machinery and cleaning fluids. Indirect materials are not easily traced to specific units or batches of production and are accounted for as factory overhead.

The materials of a manufacturer are called raw materials, even though they may not necessarily be in their natural raw state. For example, leather is manufactured from hides, nails from steel, and cloth from cotton. Nevertheless, leather, nails, and cloth are the raw materials of a shoe manufacturer, even though they are the finished products of previous manufacturers.

Direct Labour

Direct labour is often described as the labour of those people who work, either with machines or hand tools, specifically on the materials converted into finished products. The cost of direct labour can therefore be easily associated with and charged to the units or batches of production to which the labour was applied. In manufacturing, direct labour is distinguished from *indirect labour.* Indirect labour is the labour of superintendents, foremen, millwrights, engineers, janitors, and others who do not work specifically on the manufactured products but do aid in production. The labour provided by these workers often makes production possible but is not applied specifically to the finished product. Indirect labour is accounted for as a factory overhead cost.

In a general accounting system, an account called **Direct Labour** is debited each payday for the wages of those workers who work directly on the product. Likewise, each payday, the wages of indirect workers are debited to one or more indirect labour accounts. Also, at the end of each period, the amounts of accrued direct and indirect labour are recorded in the direct and indirect labour accounts by means of adjusting entries. From this it can be seen that a manufacturing company's payroll accounting is similar to that of a merchandising company. When a cost accounting system is not involved, no new techniques are required, and only the new direct and indirect labour accounts distinguish the payroll accounting of a manufacturer from that of a merchant.

Factory Overhead

Factory overhead, often called *manufacturing overhead* or *factory burden,* includes all manufacturing costs other than direct materials and direct labour costs. Factory overhead may include:

Indirect labour.	Heat, lights, and power.
Factory supplies.	Depreciation of plant and equipment.
Repairs to buildings and equipment.	Amortization of patents.
Insurance on plant and equipment.	Small tools written off.
Taxes on plant and equipment.	Workers' compensation insurance.

Insurance on raw materials and work in process.   Payroll taxes on the wages of the factory workers.

Factory overhead does not include selling and administrative expenses. Selling and administrative expenses are not factory overhead because they are not incurred in the manufacturing process. These costs could be called selling and administrative overhead, but not factory overhead.

All factory overhead costs are accumulated in overhead cost accounts that vary in number and description from company to company. The exact accounts used in each case depend upon the nature of the company and the information desired. For example, one account called Expired Insurance on Plant Equipment may be maintained, or separate expired insurance accounts for buildings and the different kinds of equipment may be used. Regardless of the accounts used, overhead costs are recorded in the same ways as are selling and administrative expenses. Some, such as indirect labour, and light and power, are recorded in registers or journals as they are paid and are then posted to the accounts. Other costs, such as depreciation and expired insurance, are recorded in the accounts through adjusting entries.

ACCOUNTS UNIQUE TO A MANUFACTURING COMPANY

Because of the nature of its operations, a manufacturing company's ledger normally contains more accounts that that of a merchandising company. However, some of the same accounts are found in the ledgers of both, for example, Cash, Accounts Receivable, Sales, and many selling and administrative expenses. Nevertheless, many accounts are unique to a manufacturing company. For instance, accounts such as Machinery and Equipment, Accumulated Depreciation of Machinery and Equipment, Factory Supplies, Factory Supplies Used, Raw Materials Inventory, Raw Material Purchases, Goods in Process Inventory, Finished Goods Inventory, and Manufacturing Summary are normally found only in the ledgers of manufacturing companies. Some of these accounts merit special attention.

Raw Material Purchases Account

When a general accounting system is in use, the cost of all raw materials purchases is debited to an account called Raw Material Purchases. Often a special column is provided in the Voucher Register or other special journal for the debits of the individual purchases. Thus, it is possible to periodically post these debits in one amount, the column total.

Raw Materials Inventory Account

When a general accounting system is in use, the raw materials on hand at the end of each accounting period are determined by a physical inventory count; and through a closing entry, the cost of this inventory is debited to Raw Materials Inventory. That account becomes a record of the materials on hand at the end of one period and the beginning of the next.

Goods in Process Inventory Account

Most manufacturing companies have on hand at all times partially processed products called *goods in process* or *work in process*. These are products in the process of being manufactured, products that have received a portion or all of their materials and have had some labour and overhead applied but that are not completed.

When a general manufacturing accounting system is used, the amount of goods in process at the end of each accounting period is determined by a physical inventory count; and through a closing entry, the cost of this inventory is debited to Goods in Process Inventory. This account then becomes a record of the goods in process at the end of one period and the beginning of the next.

Finished Goods Inventory Account

The **finished goods** of a manufacturer are the equivalent of a store's merchandise; they are products in their completed state ready for sale. Actually, the only difference is that a manufacturing company creates its finished goods from raw materials, while a store buys its merchandise in a finished, ready-for-sale state.

In a general accounting system, the amount of finished goods on hand at the end of each period is determined by a physical inventory; and through a closing entry, the cost of this inventory is debited to Finished Goods Inventory. That account provides a record of the finished goods at the end of one period and the beginning of the next.

The three inventories—raw materials, goods in process, and finished goods—are classified as current assets for balance sheet purposes. Factory supplies is also a current asset.

INCOME STATEMENT OF A MANUFACTURING COMPANY

The income statement of a manufacturing company is similar to that of a merchandising company. To see this, compare the income statement of Kona Sales Incorporated, Illustration 5–1, with that of Excel Manufacturing Company, Illustration 21–1. Notice that the revenue, selling, and

Illustration 21–1

THE EXCEL MANUFACTURING COMPANY, INC.
Income Statement
For Year Ended December 31, 198A

Revenue:		
Sales		$310,000
Cost of goods sold:		
Finished goods inventory, January 1, 198A	$ 11,200	
Cost of goods manufactured (see		
Manufacturing Statement)	170,500	
Goods available for sale	181,700	
Finished goods inventory, December 31,		
198A	10,300	
Cost of goods sold		171,400
Gross profit		138,600
Operating expenses:		
Selling expenses:		
Sales salaries expense	$18,000	
Advertising expense	5,500	
Delivery wages expense	12,000	
Shipping supplies expense	250	
Delivery equipment insurance expense	300	
Depreciation expense, delivery equipment	2,100	
Total selling expenses	38,150	
General and administrative expenses:		
Office salaries expense	15,700	
Miscellaneous general expense	200	
Bad debts expense	1,550	
Office supplies expense	100	
Depreciation expense, office equipment	200	
Total general and administrative		
expenses	17,750	
Total operating expenses		55,900
Operating income		82,700
Financial expense:		
Mortgage interest expense		4,000
Income before income taxes		78,700
Less: Income taxes		32,600
Net income		$ 46,100
Net income per common share (20,000 shares		
outstanding		$2.31

general and administrative expense sections are quite similar. However, when the cost of goods sold sections are compared, a difference is apparent. Here the item "Cost of goods manufactured" replaces the "Purchases" element, and finished goods inventories take the place of merchandise inventories.

Observe the cost of goods sold section of Excel Manufacturing Company's income statement. Only the **total** cost of goods manufactured is shown. It would be possible to expand this section to show the detailed costs of the materials, direct labour, and factory overhead entering into the cost of goods manufactured. However, this would make the income statement long and unwieldy. Consequently, the common practice is to show only the total cost of goods manufactured on the income statement and to attach a supporting schedule showing the details. This supporting schedule is called a *manufacturing statement* or a *schedule of the cost of goods manufactured*.

MANUFACTURING STATEMENT

The cost elements of manufacturing are raw materials, direct labour, and factory overhead; and a manufacturing statement is normally constructed in such a manner as to emphasize these elements. Notice in

Illustration 21–2

EXCEL MANUFACTURING COMPANY, INC.
Manufacturing Statement
For Year Ended December 31, 198A

1	Raw materials:		
	Raw materials inventory, January 1, 198A		$ 8,000
	Raw materials purchased	$85,000	
	Freight on raw materials purchased	1,500	
	Delivered cost of raw materials purchased		86,500
	Raw materials available for use		94,500
	Raw materials inventory, December 31, 198A . .		9,000
	Raw materials used		$ 85,500
2	Direct labour		60,000
3	Factory overhead costs:		
	Indirect labour	9,000	
	Supervision	6,000	
	Power	2,600	
	Repairs and maintenance	2,500	
	Factory taxes	1,900	
	Factory supplies used	500	
	Factory insurance expired	1,200	
	Small tools written off	200	
	Depreciation of machinery and equipment	3,500	
	Depreciation of building	1,800	
	Amortization of patents	800	
4	Total factory overhead costs		30,000
	Total manufacturing costs		175,500
	Add: Goods in process inventory,		
	January 1, 198A		2,500
	Total goods in process during the year . .		178,000
	Deduct: Goods in process inventory,		
	December 31, 198A		7,500
	Cost of goods manufactured		$170,500

Illustration 21–2 that the first section of the statement shows the cost of raw materials used. Also observe the manner of presentation is the same as that used on the income statement of a merchandising company to show cost of goods purchased and sold.

The second section shows the cost of direct labour used in production, and the third section shows factory overhead costs. If overhead accounts are not too numerous, the balance of each is often listed in this third section, as in Illustration 21–2. However, if overhead accounts are numerous, only the total of all may be shown. In such cases, the total is supported by a separate schedule showing each cost.

In the fourth section, the calculation of costs of goods manufactured is completed. Here the cost of the beginning goods in process inventory is added to the sum of the manufacturing costs to show the total cost of all goods in process during the period. From this total, the cost of the goods still in process at the end of the period is subtracted to show cost of the goods manufactured.

The manufacturing statement is prepared from the Manufacturing Statement columns of a work sheet. The items that appear on the statement are summarized in these columns, and all that is required in constructing the statement is a rearrangement of the items into the proper statement order. Illustration 21–3 shows the manufacturing work sheet.

WORK SHEET FOR A MANUFACTURING COMPANY

In examining Illustration 21–3, note first that there are no Adjusted Trial Balance columns. The experienced accountant commonly omits such columns to save time and effort. How a work sheet without Adjusted Trial Balance columns is prepared and how this saves time and effort were explained in Chapter 5.

To understand the work sheet of Illustration 21–3, recall that a work sheet is a tool with which the accountant—

1. Achieves the effect of adjusting the accounts before entering the adjustments in a journal and posting them to the accounts.
2. Sorts the adjusted account balances into columns according to the financial statement upon which they appear.
3. Calculates and confirms the mathematical accuracy of the net income.

With the foregoing in mind, a primary difference between the work sheet of a manufacturing company and that of a merchandising company is an additional set of columns. Insofar as the adjustments are concerned, they are made in the same way on both kinds of work sheets. Also, the mathematical accuracy of the net income is confirmed in the same way. However, since an additional accounting statement, the manufacturing statement, is prepared for a manufacturing company, the work sheet of such a company has an additional set of columns, the Manufacturing

Illustration 21–3

THE EXCEL MANUFACTURING COMPANY, INC.
Manufacturing Work Sheet
For Year Ended December 31, 198A

Account Titles	Trial Balance Dr.	Trial Balance Cr.	Adjustments Dr.	Adjustments Cr.	Mfg. Statement Dr.	Mfg. Statement Cr.	Income Statement Dr.	Income Statement Cr.	Balance Sheet Dr.	Balance Sheet Cr.
Cash	11,000								11,000	
Accounts receivable	32,000								32,000	
Allowance for doubtful accounts		300		(a) 1,550						1,850
Raw materials inventory	8,000				8,000	9,000			9,000	
Goods in process inventory	2,500				2,500	7,500			7,500	
Finished goods inventory	11,200						11,200	10,300	10,300	
Office supplies	150			(b) 100					50	
Shipping supplies	300			(c) 250					50	
Factory supplies	750			(d) 500					250	
Prepaid insurance	1,800			(e) 1,500					300	
Small tools	1,300			(f) 200					1,100	
Delivery equipment	9,000								9,000	
Accumulated depreciation of delivery equipment		1,900		(g) 2,100						4,000
Office equipment	1,700								1,700	
Accumulated depreciation of office equipment		200		(h) 200						400
Machinery and equipment	72,000								72,000	
Accumulation depreciation of machinery and equipment		3,000		(i) 3,500						6,500
Factory building	90,000								90,000	
Accumulated depreciation of factory building		1,500		(j) 1,800						3,300
Land	9,500								9,500	
Patents	12,000			(k) 800					11,200	
Accounts payable		14,000								14,000
Mortgage payable		50,000								50,000
Common stock, 20,000 shares		100,000								100,000
Retained earnings		3,660								3,660
Sales		310,000						310,000		
Raw material purchases	85,000				85,000					
Freight on raw materials	1,500				1,500					
Direct labour	59,600		(i) 400		60,000					
Indirect labour	8,940		(i) 60		9,000					

Account	Trial Balance Dr	Trial Balance Cr	Adjustments Dr	Adjustments Cr	Manufacturing Dr	Manufacturing Cr	Income Statement Dr	Income Statement Cr	Balance Sheet Dr	Balance Sheet Cr
Supervision	6,000				6,000					
Power expense	2,600				2,600					
Repairs and maintenance	2,500				2,500					
Factory taxes	1,900				1,900					
Sales salaries expense	18,000						18,000			
Advertising expense	5,500						5,500			
Delivery wages expense	11,920		(l) 80				12,000			
Office salaries expense	15,700						15,700			
Miscellaneous general expense	200						200			
Mortgage interest expense	2,000		(m) 2,000				4,000			
	484,560	484,560								
Bad debt expense			(a) 1,550				1,550			
Office supplies expense			(b) 100				100			
Shipping supplies expense			(c) 250				250			
Factory supplies used			(d) 500		500					
Factory insurance expired			(e) 1,200		1,200					
Delivery equipment insurance expense			(e) 300				300			
Small tools written off			(f) 200		200					
Depreciation expense, delivery equipment			(g) 2,100				2,100			
Depreciation expense, office equipment			(h) 200				200			
Depreciation of machinery and equipment			(i) 3,500		3,500					
Depreciation of building			(j) 1,800		1,800					
Amortization of patents			(k) 800		800					
Accrued wages payable				(l) 540						540
Mortgage interest payable				(m) 2,000						2,000
Income taxes expense			(n) 32,600				32,600			
Income taxes payable				(n) 32,600						32,600
			47,640	47,640						
Cost of goods manufactured to Income Statement columns					187,000	170,500	170,500		16,500	
						187,000				
					170,500	187,000	274,200	320,300	264,950	218,850
Net income							46,100			46,100
							320,300	320,300	264,950	264,950

Statement columns, into which are sorted the items appearing on the manufacturing statement.

PREPARING A MANUFACTURING COMPANY'S WORK SHEET

A manufacturing company's work sheet is prepared in the same manner as that of a merchandising company. First, a trial balance of the ledger is entered in the Trial Balance columns. Next, information for the adjustments is assembled, and the adjustments are entered in the Adjustments columns. The adjustments information for the work sheet shown in Illustration 21–3 is as follows:

a.   Estimated bad debt losses ½% of sales, or $1,550.
b.   Office supplies used, $100.
c.   Shipping supplies used, $250.
d.   Factory supplies used, $500.
e.   Expired insurance on factory, $1,200; and expired insurance on the delivery equipment, $300.
f.   The small tools inventory shows $1,100 of usable small tools on hand. As is frequently done, small hand tools are in this case accounted for in the same manner as are supplies.
g.   Depreciation of delivery equipment, $2,100.
h.   Depreciation of office equipment, $200.
i.   Depreciation of factory machinery and equipment, $3,500.
j.   Depreciation of factory building, $1,800.
k.   Yearly amortization of $1/17$ of the cost of patents, $800.
l.   Accrued wages: direct labour, $400; indirect labour, $60; delivery wages, $80. All other employees paid monthly on the last day of each month.
m.   One-half year's interest accrued on the mortgage, $2,000.
n.   Income taxes expense, $32,600.

After the adjustments are completed, the amounts in the Trial Balance columns are combined with the amounts in the Adjustments columns and are sorted to the proper Manufacturing Statement, Income Statement, or Balance Sheet columns, according to the statement on which they appear.

In the sorting process, just two decisions are required for each item: First, does the item have a debit balance or a credit balance; and second, on which statements does it appear? The first decision is necessary because a debit item must be sorted to a Debit column and a credit item to a Credit column. As for the second, a work sheet is a tool for sorting items according to their statement appearance. Asset, liability, and owners' equity items appear on the balance sheet and are sorted to the Balance Sheet columns. The finished goods inventory plus the revenue, selling, general and administrative, and financial expense items should appear on the income statement and are sorted to the Income Statement columns. And finally, the raw material, goods in process, direct labour, and factory overhead items appear on the manufacturing statement and are sorted to the Manufacturing Statement columns.

After the trial balance items with their adjustments are sorted to the proper statement columns, the ending inventory amounts are entered on the work sheet. The raw materials and goods in process inventories appear on the manufacturing statement. Therefore, the ending raw materials and goods in process inventory amounts are entered in the Manufacturing Statement Credit and Balance Sheet Debit columns. They must be entered in the Manufacturing Statement credit column in order to make the difference between the two columns equal cost of goods manufactured. Likewise, since these inventory amounts represent end-of-period assets, they must be entered in the balance Sheet Debit column with the other assets.

The ending finished goods inventory is the equivalent of an ending merchandise inventory and receives the same work sheet treatment. It is entered in the Income Statement Credit column and the Balance Sheet Debit column. It is entered in the Income Statement Credit column so that the net income may be determined; and since it is a current asset, it must also be entered in the Balance Sheet Debit column.

After the ending inventories are entered on the work sheet, the Manufacturing Statement columns are added and their difference determined. This difference is the cost of the goods manufactured; and after it is determined, it is entered in the Manufacturing Statement Credit column to make the two columns equal. Also, it is entered in the Income Statement Debit column, the same column in which the balance of the Purchases account of a merchant is entered. After this, the work sheet is completed in the usual manner.

PREPARING STATEMENTS

After completion, the manufacturing work sheet is used in preparing the statements and in making adjusting and closing entries. The manufacturing statement is prepared from the information in the work sheet's Manufacturing Statement columns, the income statement from the information in the Income Statement columns, and the balance sheet from information in the Balance Sheet columns. After this, the adjusting and closing entries are entered in the journal and posted.

ADJUSTING ENTRIES

The adjusting entries of a manufacturing company are prepared in the same way as those of a merchandising company. An adjusting entry is entered in the General Journal for each adjustment appearing in the work sheet Adjustments columns. No new techniques are required.

CLOSING ENTRIES

The account balances that enter into the calculation of cost of goods manufactured reflect the manufacturing costs for a particular accounting period and must be closed at the end of each period. Normally they are closed to a Manufacturing Summary account, which is in turn closed to the Income Summary account.

The entries to close the manufacturing accounts of Excel Manufacturing Company are as follows:

Dec.	31	Manufacturing Summary	187,000.00	
		Raw Materials Inventory		8,000.00
		Goods in Process Inventory		2,500.00
		Raw Material Purchases		85,000.00
		Freight on Raw Materials		1,500.00
		Direct Labour..........................		60,000.00
		Indirect Labour		9,000.00
		Supervision		6,000.00
		Power Expense........................		2,600.00
		Repairs and Maintenance		2,500.00
		Factory Taxes		1,900.00
		Factory Supplies Used.................		500.00
		Factory Insurance Expired		1,200.00
		Small Tools Written Off		200.00
		Depreciation of Machinery and Equipment ..		3,500.00
		Depreciation of Building................		1,800.00
		Amortization of Patents		800.00
		To close those manufacturing accounts having debit balances.		
	31	Raw materials	9,000.00	
		Goods in Process........................	7,500.00	
		Manufacturing Summary		16,500.00
		To set up the ending raw materials and goods in process inventories and to remove their balances from the Manufacturing Summary account.		

The entries are taken from the information in the Manufacturing Statement columns of the Illustration 21–3 work sheet. Compare the first entry with the information shown in the Manufacturing Statement Debit column. Note how the debit to the Manufacturing Summary account is taken from the column total, and how each account having a balance in the column is credited to close it. Also observe that the second entry has the effect of subtracting the ending raw materials and goods in process inventories from the manufacturing costs shown in the work sheet's Debit column.

The effect of the two entries is to cause the Manufacturing Summary account to have a debit balance equal to the $170,500 cost of goods manufactured. This $170,500 balance is closed to the Income Summary account along with the other cost and expense accounts having balances in the Income Statement Debit column. Observe the following entry which is used to close the accounts having balances in the Income Statement Debit column of the Illustration 21–3 work sheet and especially note its last credit.

Dec.	31	Income Summary	274,200.00	
		Finished Goods Inventory		11,200.00
		Sales Salaries Expense.................		18,000.00
		Advertising Expense		5,500.00
		Delivery Wages Expense		12,000.00
		Office Salaries Expense		15,700.00
		Miscellaneous General Expense		200.00
		Mortgage Interest Expense		4,000.00
		Bad Debts Expense		1,550.00
		Office Supplies Expense		100.00
		Shipping Supplies Expense		250.00
		Delivery Equipment Insurance Expense		300.00
		Depreciation Expense, Delivery Equipment ..		2,100.00
		Depreciation Expense, Office Equipment ...		200.00
		Income Taxes Expense		32,600.00
		Manufacturing Summary		170,500.00
		To close the income statement accounts having debit balances.		

After the foregoing entry, the remainder of the income statement accounts of Illustration 21–3 are closed as follows:

Dec.	31	Finished Goods Inventory	10,300.00	
		Sales	310,000.00	
		Income Summary		320.300.00
		To close the Sales account and to bring the ending finished goods inventory on the books.		
	31	Income Summary	46,100.00	
		Retained Earnings		46,100.00
		To close the Income Summary account.		

INVENTORY VALUATION PROBLEMS OF A MANUFACTURER

In a manufacturing company using a general accounting system, at the end of each period, an accounting value must be placed on the inventories of raw materials, goods in process, and finished goods. No particular problems are encountered in valuing raw materials because the items are in the same form in which they were purchased and a cost or market price may be applied. However, placing a valuation on goods in process and finished goods is generally not as easy. These goods consist of raw materials to which certain amounts of labour and overhead have been added. They are not in the same form in which they were purchased. Consequently, a price paid to a previous producer cannot be used to measure their inventory value. Instead, their inventory value must be built up by adding together estimates of the raw materials, direct labour, and overhead costs applicable to each item.

Estimating raw material costs applicable to a goods in process or finished goods item is usually not too difficult. Likewise, a responsible plant official normally can estimate an item's percentage of completion and then make a reasonably accurate estimate of the direct labour applicable to an item. However, estimating factory overhead costs presents more of a problem, which is often solved by assuming that factory overhead costs are closely related to direct labour costs. This is often a fair assumption. Frequently there is a close relation between direct labour costs and such indirect costs as supervision, power, repairs, and so forth. Furthermore, when this relation is used to apply overhead costs, it is assumed that the relation of overhead costs to the direct labour costs in each goods in process and finished goods item is the same as the relation between total factory overhead costs and total direct labour costs for the accounting period.

For example, an examination of the manufacturing statement in Illustration 21–2 shows that Excel Manufacturing Company's total direct labour costs were $60,000 and its overhead costs were $30,000. Or, in other words, during the year the company incurred in the production of all its products $2 of direct labour for each $1 of factory overhead costs; overhead costs were 50% of direct labour cost.

Overhead costs, $30,000 ÷ Direct labour, $60,000 = 50%

Consequently, in estimating the overhead applicable to a goods in process or finished goods item, Excel Manufacturing Company may assume that this 50% overhead rate is applicable. Since total overhead costs were 50% of total labour costs, it would appear reasonable to assume that this relationship applies to each goods in process and finished goods item.

If Excel Manufacturing Company makes this assumption and its goods in process inventory consists of 1,000 units of Item X with each unit containing $3.75 of raw material and having $2.50 of applicable direct labour, then the goods in process inventory is valued as shown in Illustration 21–4.

Excel Manufacturing Company may use the same procedure in placing an accounting value on the items of its finished goods inventory.

Illustration 21–4

Product	Estimated Raw Material Cost	Estimated Direct Labour Applicable	Overhead (50% of direct labour)	Estimated Total Unit Cost	No. of Units	Estimated Inventory Cost
Item X	$3.75	$2.50	$1.25	$7.50	1,000	$7,500.00

GLOSSARY

Direct labour. The labour of those people who work specifically on the conversion of new materials into finished products; in other words, labour that can be easily associated with units of product.

Direct materials. A synonym for raw materials.

Factory overhead. All manufacturing costs other than for direct materials and direct labour.

Finished goods. Products in their complete state, ready for sale; equivalent to a store's merchandise.

Goods in process. Products in the process of being manufactured that have received a portion or all of their materials and have had some labour and overhead applied but that are not completed. Also called work in process.

Indirect labour. The labour of superintendents, foremen, millwrights, engineers, janitors, and others that contribute to production but do not work specifically on the manufactured products, and whose labour therefore cannot be easily associated with specific units of product.

Indirect materials. Commodities that are used in production but that do not enter into and become a part of the finished product, for example, grease and oil for machinery, or cleaning fluid.

Manufacturing overhead. A synonym for factory overhead. Also called manufacturing or factory burden.

Manufacturing statement. A financial report showing the costs incurred to manufacture a product or products during a period. Also called schedule of the cost of goods manufactured.

Raw materials. Commodities that enter into and become a part of a finished product; therefore, commodities that are easily associated with specific units of product.

Work in process. Another name for goods in process.

QUESTIONS FOR CLASS DISCUSSION

1. Manufacturing costs consist of three elements What are they?

2. Explain how the income statement of a manufacturing company differs from the income statement of a merchandising company.

3. What are (a) direct labour, (b) indirect labour, (c) direct material, (d) indirect material, and (e) factory overhead costs?

4. Factory overhead costs include a variety of items. List several examples of factory overhead costs.

5. Name several accounts that are often found in the ledgers of both manufacturing and merchandising companies. Name several accounts that are found only in the ledgers of manufacturing companies.

6. What three new inventory accounts appear in the ledger of a manufacturing company?

7. How are the raw material inventories handled on the work sheet of a manufacturing company? How are the goods in process inventories handled? How are the finished goods inventories handled?

8. Which inventories of a manufacturing company receive the same work sheet treatment as the merchandise inventories of a merchandising company?

9. Which inventories of a manufacturing company appear on its manufacturing statement? Which appear on the income statement?

10. What accounts are summarized in the Manufacturing Summary account? What accounts are summarized in the Income Summary account?

11. What are the three manufacturing cost elements emphasized on the manufacturing statement?

12. What account balances are carried into the Manufacturing Statement columns of the manufacturing work sheet? What account balances are carried into the Income Statement columns? What account balances are carried into the Balance Sheet columns?

13. Why is the cost of goods manufactured entered in the Manufacturing Statement credit column of a work sheet and again in the Income Statement debit columns?

14. May prices paid a previous manufacturer for items of raw materials to be used to determine the balance sheet value of the items in the raw material inventory? Why? May such prices also be used to determine the balance sheet values of the goods in process and finished goods inventories? Why?

15. Standard Company used an overhead rate of 75% of direct labour cost to apply overhead to the items of its goods in process inventory. If the manufacturing statement of the company showed total overhead costs of $98,400, how much direct labour did it show?

MULTIPLE CHOICE

1. In Canoe Company's manufacturing accounting system, the relationship between overhead and direct labour costs is used to apply overhead to goods in process and finished goods inventories. Canoe Company's manufacturing costs for 198A were: direct labour $36,000, direct materials, $48,000, and factory overhead, $6,000. Their overhead application rate was:

   a. 12.5%.
   b. 16.7%.
   c. 52.0%.
   d. 75.0%.
   e. 87.5%.

2. The R Company manufactures razors. Costs for August were direct labour, $13,000; indirect labour, $6,500; direct materials, $15,000; taxes on raw materials and work in process, $800; heat, hydro, and power, $1,000; and insurance on plant and equipment, $200. R Company's factory overhead for August is:

   a. $2,000.
   b. $6,500.
   c. $8,500.
   d. $21,500.
   e. $36,500.

3. A Manufacturing Company has a beginning finished goods inventory of $13,600; a cost of goods manufactured of $29,400; and an ending finished goods inventory of $15,400. The cost of goods sold for this company is:

   a. $16,000.
   b. $27,600.
   c. $34,800.
   d. $43,000.
   e. Answer cannot be determined from the information given.

4. Given the following information, what is the cost of goods manufactured?

Beginning raw materials	$ 5,500
Ending raw materials	4,000
Direct labour	12,250
Raw material purchases	7,400
Depreciation on factory equipment	6,500
Factory repairs and maintenance	3,300
Beginning finished goods inventory	10,200
Ending finished goods inventory	8,900
Beginning goods in process inventory	5,700
Ending goods in process inventory	6,300

   a. $36,650.
   b. $30,950.
   c. $30,650.
   d. $30,350.
   e. $31,650.

5. If Product X used $2.50 of raw material and $3.00 of direct labour, sold for $8.00, and was assigned an overhead rate of 30% of labour costs, what would be the gross margin on this product?

    a. $8.00.

    b. $5.50.

    c. $2.50.

    d. $1.60.

    e. None of the above.

6. The following information appeared in the financial statements of A Manufacturing Company:

Goods in process inventory, beginning	$ 20,000
Cost of goods manufactured	$320,000
Cost of raw materials used	$160,000
Factory overhead, 50% of direct labour	$ 55,000

What was the goods in process inventory at the end of the year?

    a. $15,000.

    b. $25,000.

    c. $125,000.

    d. $135,000.

    e. Some other amount.

MINI DISCUSSION CASES

Case 21–1

A friend has been operating a manufacturing business for the last few months and has come to you for assistance. He says that he understands the idea of direct versus indirect labour but has problems in applying the ideas in his operations.

His machine operators work on as many as 10 different products or jobs during each day, sometimes looking after more than one machine at the same time. Therefore, it is very difficult to assign the labour costs amongst these jobs. Your friend asks you, "Just what is direct labour?"

Required:

Reply to your friend in the context of his problem. Should he treat his machine operators as indirect labour? Why or why not?

Case 21–2

The Greasy Wheel Manufacturing Company has a policy whereby it always assumes that its work in process inventories are 50% complete. The accountant says that this makes the preparation of the year-end financial statements much easier because no one has to estimate the actual degree of completion. All that is required is to take a count of the uncompleted units.

Required:

Evaluate the company's policy. Do you agree or disagree with this policy? Why?

CLASS EXERCISES

The following items appeared in the Manufacturing Statement and Income Statement columns of Donaldson Equipment Company's year-end work sheet:

	Manufacturing Statement		Income Statement	
	Debit	Credit	Debit	Credit
Raw materials inventory	13,000	14,000	......	......
Goods in process inventory	15,000	12,000	......	......
Finished goods inventory	......	......	16,000	17,000
Sales	......	......	......	210,000
Raw materials purchases	44,000	......	......	......
Direct labour	52,000	......	......	......
Indirect labour	12,000	......	......	......
Power..............................	5,000	......	......	......
Machinery repairs	2,000	......	......	......
Rent expense, factory building	6,000	......	......	......
Selling expenses, controlling	......	......	38,000	......
Administrative expenses, controlling			22,000	......
	149,000	26,000	......	......
Cost of goods manufactured		123,000	123,000	......
	149,000	149,000	199,000	227,000
Net income			28,000	
			227,000	227,000

Exercise 21–1   From the information just given, prepare a manufacturing statement for Donaldson Equipment Company.

Exercise 21–2   Prepare an income statement for Donaldson Equipment Company.

Exercise 21–3   Prepare compound closing entries for Donaldson Equipment, a corporation.

Exercise 21–4   A company that uses the relation between overhead and direct labour costs to apply overhead to its goods in process and finished goods inventories incurred the following costs during a year: materials, $95,000; direct labour, $80,000; and factory overhead costs, $160,000.

Required:

a.   Determine the company's overhead rate.
b.   Under the assumption the company's $12,500 goods in process inventory had $3,000 of direct labour costs, determine the inventory's material costs.
c.   Under the assumption the company's $17,000 finished goods inventory had $5,000 of material costs, determine the inventory's labour cost and overhead costs.

Exercise 21–5   An end-of-the-accounting period trial balance of Edwards Awning Company follows. To simplify the problem and to save time the trial balance is in numbers of not more than two integers.

EDWARDS AWNING COMPANY, LTD.
Trial Balance
December 31, 19—

Cash	$ 4	
Accounts receivable	5	
Allowance for doubtful accounts		$ 1
Raw materials inventory	2	
Goods in process inventory	4	
Finished goods inventory	3	
Factory supplies	3	
Prepaid factory insurance	4	
Factory machinery	23	
Accumulated depreciation, factory machinery		2
Common stock		20
Retained earnings		5
Sales		81
Raw material purchases	15	
Freight on raw materials	1	
Direct labour	12	
Indirect labour	3	
Power	5	
Machinery repairs	2	
Rent expense, factory	8	
Selling expenses, controlling	9	
Administrative expenses, controlling	6	
Totals	$109	$109

Required:

1. Prepare a manufacturing work sheet form on ordinary notebook paper.
2. Copy the trial balance on the work sheet form and complete the work sheet using the following information:
    a. Ending inventories:
    > Raw materials, $3.
    > Goods in process, $5.
    > Finished goods, $2.
    > Factory supplies, $1.
    b. Allowance for doubtful accounts, an additional $2.
    c. Expired factory insurance, $1.
    d. Depreciation of factory machinery, $3.
    e. Accrued payroll:
    > Direct labour, $4.
    > Indirect labour, $2.
    > Office salaries, $1. (Debit Administration Expenses, controlling account.)

PROBLEMS

Problem 21–1   Following are the items from the Manufacturing Statement columns of Lasater Manufacturing Company's work sheet prepared at the end of last year. The illustrated columns show the items as they appeared after all adjustments were completed but before the ending work in process inventory was calculated and entered and before the cost of goods manufactured was calculated.

Lasater Manufacturing Company makes a single product called NuBlock. On December 31, at the end of last year, the goods in process inventory consisted of 5,000 units of NuBlock with each unit containing an estimated $0.80 of raw materials and having had an estimated $2 of direct labour applied.

	Manufacturing Statement	
	Debit	Credit
Raw materials inventory	21,200	19,300
Goods in process inventory	17,800	?
Raw materials purchased	81,400	
Direct labour	100,000	
Indirect labour	16,900	
Factory supervision	12,000	
Heat, light, and power	8,600	
Machinery repairs	6,300	
Rent expense, factory	7,200	
Property taxes, machinery	1,900	
Factory insurance expired	3,300	
Factory supplies used	7,400	
Depreciation expense, factory machinery	16,900	
Small tools written off	500	
	301,400	?
Cost of goods manufactured		?
	301,400	301,400

Required:

1. Calculate the relation between direct labour and factory overhead costs and use this relation to determine the value of the ending goods in process inventory.
2. After placing a value on the ending goods in process inventory, determine the cost of goods manufactured.
3. Prepare a manufacturing statement for Lasater Manufacturing Company.
4. Prepare entries to close the manufacturing accounts and to summarize their balances in the Manufacturing Summary account.
5. Prepare an entry to close the Manufacturing Summary account.

Problem 21–2   The following items appeared in the Manufacturing Statement and Income Statement columns of a work sheet prepared for Ranger Airparts Company, Inc., on December 31, 19–, at the end of an annual accounting period:

	Manufacturing Statement		Income Statement	
	Debit	Credit	Debit	Credit
Raw materials inventory	12,600	12,100	......	......
Goods in process inventory	14,800	12,900	......	......
Finished goods inventory	......	......	16,100	18,800
Sales.....................................	......	......	......	361,500
Raw material purchases...................	59,000	......	......	......
Discounts on raw material purchases	......	800	......	......
Direct labour	90,000	......	......	......
Indirect labour	13,800	......	......	......
Factory supervision......................	12,000	......	......	......
Heat, light, and power	18,400	......	......	......
Machinery repairs	4,500	......	......	......
Rent expense, factory	7,200	......	......	......
Property taxes, machinery	1,700	......	......	......
Selling expenses, controlling	......	......	30,800	......
Administrative expenses, controlling..........	......	......	28,900	......
Expired factory insurance	2,400	......	......	......
Factory supplies used	6,100	......	......	......
Depreciation expense, factory machinery	10,500	......	......	......
Small tools written off	400	......	......	......
Patents written off	2,500	......	......	......
Income taxes expense	......	......	29,500	......
	255,900	25,800	......	......
Cost of goods manufactured	......	230,100	230,100	......
	255,900	255,900	335,400	380,300
Net income			44,900	......
			380,300	380,300

Required:

1. From the information given prepare an income statement and a manufacturing statement for the company.
2. Prepare compound closing entries for the company.

Problem 21-3   Cork Production Company began this year with the following inventories: raw materials, $9,200; goods in process, $10,300; and finished goods, $12,500. The company uses the relation between its overhead and direct labour costs to apply overhead to its inventories of goods in process and finished goods; and at the end of this year its inventories were assigned these costs:

	Raw materials	Goods in process	Finished goods
Material costs	$8,600	$2,800	$ 4,500
Direct labour costs	–0–	3,600	5,600
Overhead costs	–0–	?	7,000
Totals	$8,600	?	$17,100

And this additional information was available from the company's records:

Total factory overhead costs incurred during the year...... $ 82,500
Cost of all goods manufactured during the year 198,400

Required:

On the basis of the information given plus any data you can derive from it, prepare a manufacturing statement for Cork Production Company.

Problem 21–4   The December 31, 19–, trial balance of Hull Manufacturing Company's ledger carried the following items:

HULL MANUFACTURING COMPANY, LTD.
Trial Balance
December 31, 19—

Cash	$ 32,300	
Accounts receivable	36,200	
Allowance for doubtful accounts		$ 200
Raw materials inventory	37,100	
Goods in process inventory	34,400	
Finished goods inventory	48,700	
Prepaid factory insurance	4,100	
Factory supplies	13,100	
Machinery	227,500	
Accumulated depreciation, machinery		78,400
Accounts payable		25,300
Common stock		100,000
Retained earnings		94,900
Sales		692,500
Raw materials purchased	185,100	
Direct labour	159,500	
Indirect labour	36,600	
Heat, light, and power	13,600	
Machinery repairs	9,400	
Selling expenses, controlling	81,200	
Administrative expenses, controlling	72,500	
Totals	$991,300	$991,300

The following adjustments and inventory information was available at the year-end:

a. Allowance for doubtful accounts to be increased to $1,700. (Debit Administrative Expenses, controlling account.)
b. An examination of policies showed $3,100 of factory insurance expired.
c. An inventory of factory supplies showed $9,700 of factory supplies used.
d. Estimated depreciation of factory machinery, $31,300.
e. Accrued direct labour, $500; and accrued indirect labour, $300.
f. Accrued incomes taxes payable amount to $37,500.
g. Year-end inventories:
   (1) Raw materials, $36,700.
   (2) Goods in process consisted of 3,200 units of product with each unit containing an estimated $3.65 of materials and having had an estimated $4 of direct labour applied.
   (3) Finished goods inventory consisted of 3,000 units of product with each unit containing an estimated $7.50 of materials and having had an estimated $6 of direct labour applied.

Required:

1. Enter the trial balance on a work sheet form and make the adjustments from the information given. Then sort the items to the proper Manufacturing Statement, Income Statement, and Balance Sheet columns.
2. After the Direct Labour and factory overhead accounts have been adjusted and carried into the Manufacturing Statement columns, determine the relation between direct labour and overhead costs and use this relation to determine the overhead applicable to each unit of goods in process and finished goods. Next, calculate the balance sheet values for these inventories, enter the inventory amounts on the work sheet, and complete the work sheet.
3. From the work sheet prepare a manufacturing statement and an income statement.
4. Prepare compound closing entries.

Problem 21–5   A trial balance of Macro Pumps Company's ledger on December 31, 19—, the end of an annual accounting period, appeared as follows:

MACRO PUMPS COMPANY, LTD.
Trial Balance
December 31, 19—

Cash	$ 14,800	
Raw materials inventory	13,700	
Goods in process inventory	12,500	
Finished goods inventory	15,100	
Prepaid factory insurance	3,600	
Factory supplies	6,800	
Factory machinery	168,200	
Accumulated depreciation, factory machinery		$ 31,300
Small tools	4,100	
Patents	6,700	
Common stock		100,000
Retained earnings		16,700
Sales		370,000
Raw material purchases	62,000	
Discounts on raw material purchases		1,200
Direct labour	98,400	
Indirect labour	12,100	
Factory supervision	11,700	
Heat, light, and power	17,900	
Machinery repairs	4,200	
Rent expense, factory	6,000	
Property taxes, machinery	1,700	
Selling expenses, controlling	31,400	
Administrative expenses, controlling	28,300	
Totals	$519,200	$519,200

Additional information:

1. Expired factory insurance, $2,400.
2. Factory supplies used, $5,900.
3. Depreciation of factory machinery, $10,200.
4. Small tools written off, $500.
5. Patents written off, $1,400.

6. Accrued wages payable:
   a. Direct labour, $1,600.
   b. Indirect labour, $700.
   c. Factory supervision, $300.
7. Ending inventories:
   a. Raw materials, $13,200.
   b. Goods in process consisted of 2,500 units of product with each unit containing an estimated $1.10 of raw materials and having had an estimated $2 of direct labour applied.
   c. Finished goods consisted of 2,000 units of product with each unit containing an estimated $2.60 of raw materials and having had an estimated $3.60 of direct labour applied.
8. Estimated income taxes payable, $30,000.

Required:

1. Enter the trial balance on a work sheet form. Make the adjustments from the information given. Sort the items to the proper Manufacturing Statement, Income Statement, and Balance Sheet columns.
2. After the Direct Labour account and the factory overhead cost accounts have been adjusted and carried into the Manufacturing Statement columns, determine the relation between overhead costs and direct labour cost and use the relation to determine the amount of overhead applicable to each unit of goods in process and finished goods. After overhead applicable to each unit of goods in process and finished goods is determined, calculate the inventory values of the goods in process and finished goods inventories. Enter these inventory amounts on the work sheet and complete the work sheet.
3. From the work sheet prepare a manufacturing statement and an income statement.
4. Prepare closing entries.

ALTERNATE PROBLEMS

Problem
21–1A

A work sheet prepared by Zoom Lens Company at the end of last year had the following items in its Manufacturing Statement columns:

	Manufacturing Statement	
	Debit	Credit
Raw materials inventory	12,300	13,500
Goods in process inventory	14,700	?
Raw material purchases	54,300	
Direct labour	90,000	
Indirect labour	35,600	
Heat, light, and power	16,900	
Machinery repairs	5,200	
Rent expense, factory	12,000	
Property taxes, machinery	3,200	
Expired factory insurance	2,600	
Factory supplies used	6,100	
Depreciation expense, machinery	15,300	
Patents written off	2,100	
	270,300	?
Cost of goods manufactured		?
	270,300	270,300

Zoom Lens Company's work sheet does not show the amount of the ending goods in process inventory and cost of goods manufactured. However, the company makes a single product; and on December 31, at the end of last year, there were 3,000 units of goods in process with each unit containing an estimated $1.05 of materials and having had an estimated $1.50 of direct labour applied.

Required:

1. Calculate the relation between direct labour and factory overhead costs and use this relation to place an accounting value on the ending goods in process inventory.
2. After placing a value on the ending goods in process inventory, prepare a manufacturing statement for the company.
3. Prepare entries to close the manufacturing accounts and to summarize their balances in the Manufacturing Summary account.
4. Prepare an entry to close the Manufacturing Summary account.

Problem 21–2A The following alphabetically arranged items were taken from the Manufacturing Statement and Income Statement columns of Soccer Manufacturing Company's year-end work sheet:

Advertising	$ 1,200	Freight on raw materials	1,500
Depreciation, machinery	2,100	Heat and power, factory	2,000
Depreciation, office equipment	500	Indirect labour	3,500
Depreciation, selling equipment ...	600	Inventories:	
Direct labour	38,800	Raw materials, January 1	9,800
Factory supplies used	1,100	Raw materials, December 31 ...	10,100
Income taxes expense	8,100	Goods in process, January 31 ...	8,200

Goods in process, December 31	$ 7,500	Rent expense, office space	1,400
Finished goods, January 1	10,500	Rent expense, selling space	1,600
Finished goods December 31 ..	8,400	Repairs to machinery	1,800
Miscellaneous factory expenses ..	500	Sales	180,100
Office salaries	4,200	Sales discounts	3,400
Raw material purchases	51,500	Sales salaries	17,500
Rent expense, factory building ...	4,800	Superintendence, factory	7,200

Required:

Prepare an income statement and a manufacturing statement for the company.

Problem 21–3A

Fibre Products Company incurred a total of $217,200 of material, labour, and factory overhead costs in manufacturing its product last year; and of this amount, $93,600 represented factory overhead costs. The company began last year with the following inventories: raw materials, $8,400; goods in process, $14,500; and finished goods, $17,500. It applies overhead to its goods in process and finished goods inventories on the basis of the relation of overhead to direct labour costs; and at the end of last year it assigned the following cost to its inventories:

	Raw materials	Goods in process	Finished goods
Material costs	$9,200	$4,700	$ 5,750
Direct labour costs	–0–	4,800	5,800
Overhead costs	–0–	?	8,700
Totals	$9,200	$?	$20,250

Required:

On the basis of the information given plus any information you can derive from it, prepare a manufacturing statement for Fibre Products Company.

Problem 21–4A

The December 31, 198A, trial balance of Sapp Manufacturing Company's ledger carried the following items:

SAPP MANUFACTURING COMPANY, LTD.
Trial Balance
December 31, 198A

Cash	$ 15,500	
Accounts receivable	21,600	
Allowance for doubtful accounts		$ 400
Raw materials inventory	29,600	
Goods in process inventory	11,200	
Finished goods inventory	31,400	
Prepaid factory insurance	4,600	
Factory supplies	7,900	
Machinery	125,000	
Accumulated depreciation, machinery		38,700
Accounts payable		18,600
Common stock		40,000
Retained earnings		46,900
Sales		510,800
Raw materials purchases	125,900	
Direct labour	133,800	
Indirect labour	18,500	
Heat, light, and power	12,300	
Machinery repairs	4,100	
Selling expenses, controlling	53,900	
Administrative expenses, controlling	60,100	
Totals	$655,400	$655,400

The following adjustments and inventory information was available at year-end:

a. Allowance for doubtful accounts to be increased to $1,200. (Debit Administrative Expenses, controlling account.)
b. An examination of policies showed $3,600 of factory insurance expired.
c. An inventory of factory supplies showed $5,200 of factory supplies used.
d. Estimated depreciation of factory machinery, $19,500.
e. Accrued direct labour, $1,200; and accrued indirect labour, $400.
f. Accrued income taxes payable amount to $18,600.
g. Year-end inventories:
    (1) Raw materials, $24,800.
    (2) Goods in process consisted of 2,200 units of product with each unit containing an estimated $2.60 of materials and having had an estimated $3.75 of direct labour applied.
    (3) Finished goods inventory consisted of 3,600 units of product with each unit containing an estimated $5.90 of materials and having had an estimated $6.50 of direct labour applied.

Required:

1. Enter the trial balance on a work sheet form and make the adjustments from the information given. Then sort the items to the proper Manufacturing Statement, Income Statement, and Balance Sheet columns.
2. After the Direct Labour and factory overhead accounts have been adjusted and carried into the Manufacturing Statement columns, determine the relation between direct labour and overhead costs and use this relation to determine

the overhead applicable to each unit of goods in process and finished goods. Next, calculate the balance sheet values for these inventories (rounded to the nearest whole dollar). Enter the inventory amounts on the work sheet and complete the work sheet.

3. From the work sheet prepare a manufacturing statement and an income statement.
4. Prepare compound closing entries.

Problem 21–5A

Keel Manufacturing Company prepared the following trial balance at the end of its annual accounting period:

KEEL MANUFACTURING COMPANY, LTD.
Trial Balance
December 31, 198—

Cash	$ 17,500	
Raw materials inventory	13,300	
Goods in process inventory	15,300	
Finished goods inventory	16,600	
Prepaid factory insurance	4,200	
Factory supplies	6,400	
Factory machinery	175,500	
Accumulated depreciation, factory machinery		$ 28,800
Small tools	3,700	
Patents	4,500	
Common stock		100,000
Retained earnings		34,400
Sales		359,700
Raw material purchases	61,800	
Discounts on raw material purchases		1,000
Direct labour	89,100	
Indirect labour	13,300	
Factory supervision	11,800	
Heat, light, and power	17,900	
Machinery repairs	4,400	
Rent expense, factory	7,200	
Property taxes, machinery	800	
Selling expenses, controlling	31,400	
Administrative expenses, controlling	29,200	
Totals	$523,900	$523,900

Additional information:

1. Expired factory insurance, $2,200.
2. Factory supplies used, $6,300.
3. Depreciation of factory machinery, $9,900.
4. Small tools written off, $700.
5. Patents written off, $1,300.
6. Accrued wages payable: (a) direct labour, $900; (b) indirect labour, $500; and (c) factory supervision, $200.
7. Ending inventories: (a) raw materials, $12,800; (b) goods in process consisted of 4,000 units of product with each unit containing an estimated $1.40 of materials and having had an estimated $1 of direct labour applied; and (c) finished goods consisted of 3,000 units of product with each unit

containing an estimated $1.96 of raw materials and having an estimated $2.40 of direct labour applied.

8. Estimated income taxes expense, $29,000.

Required:

1. Enter the trial balance on a work sheet form and make the adjustments from the information given. Then sort the items to the proper Manufacturing Statement, Income Statement, and Balance Sheet columns.

2. After the Direct Labour and factory overhead cost accounts have been adjusted and carried into the Manufacturing Statement columns, determine the relation between direct labour and overhead costs and use this relation to determine the overhead applicable to each unit of goods in process and finished goods. After the amounts of overhead applicable to the units of goods in process and finished goods are determined, calculate the balance sheet values of these inventories, enter these inventory amounts on the work sheet, and complete the work sheet.

3. From the work sheet prepare a manufacturing statement and an income statement.

4. Prepare compound closing entries.

PROVOCATIVE PROBLEMS

Provocative Problem 21–1, Schwab Airconditioning

Schwab Airconditioning Company has been in operation for three years, manufacturing and selling a single product. Sales have increased during each of the three years, but profits have not, and the company president, Chuck Schwab, has asked you to analyze the situation and tell him why. Mr. Schwab is primarily a production man and knows nothing about accounting. The company bookkeeper knows a debit from a credit, is an excellent clerk, but has little accounting training.

The company's condensed income statements for the past three years show:

	19A	19B	19C
Sales	$250,000	$350,000	$400,000
Cost of goods sold:			
Finished goods inventory, January 1	$ 0	$ 15,000	$ 45,000
Cost of goods manufactured	165,000	256,000	280,000
Goods for sale	$165,000	$271,300	$325,500
Finished goods inventory, December 31	15,000	45,000	60,000
Cost of goods sold	$150,000	$226,000	$265,500
Gross profit from sales	$100,000	$124,000	$134,500
Selling and administrative expenses	75,000	98,000	108,000
Net income	$ 25,000	$ 26,000	$ 26,500

Investigation disclosed the following additional information:

a. The company sold 5,000 units of its product during 19A, 7,000 during 19B, and 8,000 during 19C. All sales were at $50 per unit, and no discounts were granted.

b. There were 500 units in the finished goods inventory at the end of 19A, 1,500 at the end of 19B, and 2,000 at the end of 19C.

c. The units in the finished goods inventory were priced each year at 60% of their selling price, or at $30 per unit.

Prepare a report to Mr. Schwab which shows (1) the number of units of product manufactured each year, (2) the cost each year to manufacture a unit of product, and (3) the selling and administrative expenses per unit of product sold each year. Also, (4) prepare an income statement showing the correct net income each year, using a first-in, first-out basis for pricing the finished goods inventory. And finally, (5) express an opinion as to why net income has not kept pace with the rising sales volume.

Provocative Problem 21–2, Patterson's Boat Yard

Several years ago Will Patterson took over the operation of his family's boat yard from his father. Once the shop specialized in manufacturing power boats, but of late years it has turned more and more to building sailboats to the specifications of its customers. However, this business is seasonal in nature, since few people order boats in October, November, December, and January. As a result, things are rather slow around the shop during these months.

Will has tried to increase business during the slow months. However, most prospective customers who come into the shop during these months are shoppers; and when Will quotes a price for a new boat, they commonly decide the price is too high and walk out. Will thinks the trouble arises from his application of a rule established by his father when he ran the shop. The rule is that in pricing a job to a customer, "always set the price so as to make a 10% profit over and above all costs, and be sure that all costs are included."

Will says that in pricing a job, the material and labour costs are easy to figure but that overhead is another thing. His overhead consists of depreciation of building and machinery, heat, light, power, taxes, and so on, which in total run to $600 per month whether he builds any boats or not. Furthermore, when he follows his father's rule, he has to charge more for a boat built during the slow months because the overhead is spread over fewer jobs. He readily admits that this seems to drive away business during the months he needs business most, but he finds it difficult to break his father's rule, for as he says, "Dad did all right in this business for many years."

Explain with assumed figures to illustrate your point why Will charges more for a boat made in December than for one built in May, a very busy month. Suggest how Will might solve his pricing problem and still follow his father's rule.

Provocative Problem 21–3, Digital Manufacturing Company, Limited

Digital Manufacturing Company, Limited, had outstanding 6,000 shares of common stock on January 1, 198A. The stock was issued at $12 per share. The assets and liabilities of the company on that date were as follows:

Cash $16,000
Accounts receivable 8,000
Raw materials inventory 10,000
Goods in process inventory 12,000
Finished goods inventory 14,000

Plant and equipment, net 34,000
Accounts payable 8,000

During 198A the company paid no dividends, although it earned a 198A net income (ignore income taxes) of $7,500. At the year-end the amounts of the company's accounts receivables, accounts payable, and common stock outstanding were the same as of the beginning of the year. However, its cash decreased $1,500, its raw materials inventory increased by 40%, its goods in process inventory increased by 25%, and its finished goods inventory increased by one half during the year. The net amount of its plant and equipment decreased $5,000 due to depreciation, chargeable four fifths to factory overhead costs and one fifth to general and administrative expenses. The year's direct labour costs were $20,000, and factory overhead costs excluding depreciation were 60% of that amount. Costs of finished goods sold was $50,000, and all sales were made at prices 50% above cost. Selling expenses were 10%, and general and administrative expenses excluding depreciation were 12% of sales.

Based on the information given and on amounts you can derive therefrom, prepare a manufacturing work sheet for the company.

ANALYTICAL AND REVIEW PROBLEMS

Problem 21–1
A&R

Depreciation of plant and equipment is normally considered as a cost attributable to a specific period of time. For example, the cost of plant is allocated over the service life of that plant with specific amounts charged to each period. In accounting for manufacturing companies depreciation calculated in a particular period may be carried forward to future period(s). Alternately, more than the calculated depreciation for the current period may be included in the current period's income statement.

Required:

Do you agree with the above statements? Using a numerical example, prove or disprove the above statements.

Problem 21–2
A&R

In manufacturing accounting, the inclusion of depreciation of plant and equipment as part of the overhead is, in fact, converting a fixed (long-term) asset into a current asset.

Required:

Does conversion of fixed assets into current assets, via the process of depreciation, take place in nonmanufacturing companies, for example, merchandising companies? Discuss and support your answer.

Cost Accounting, Job Order, and Process

22

After studying Chapter 22, you should be able to:

State the conditions under which job order cost accounting should be used and those under which process cost accounting should be used.

Describe how costs for individual jobs are accumulated on job cost sheets and how control accounts are charged with the total costs of all jobs.

Allocate overhead to jobs and distribute any over- or underapplied overhead.

Describe how costs are accumulated by departments under process costing.

Explain what an equivalent finished unit is and how equivalent finished units are used in calculating unit costs.

Prepare a process cost summary.

Define or explain the words and phrases listed in the chapter Glossary.

Where a company uses a general manufacturing accounting system such as that described in the previous chapter, physical counts of inventories are required at the end of each accounting period in order to determine cost of goods manufactured. Furthermore, cost of goods manufactured as determined under such a system is the cost of all goods that were manufactured during the period; usually, no effort is made to determine unit costs. In contrast to a general manufacturing accounting system; a *cost accounting system* is based on perpetual inventories, and it emphasizes unit costs and the control of costs.

There are two common types of cost accounting systems: (1) job order cost systems and (2) process cost systems. However, of the two there are an infinite number of variations and combinations. A job order system is described first.

JOB ORDER COST ACCOUNTING

In job order cost accounting a *job* is a turbine, machine, or other product manufactured especially for and to the specifications of a customer. A job may also be a single construction project of a contractor. A *job lot* is a quantity of identical items, such as 500 typewriters, manufactured in one lot as a job or single order; and a *job order cost system* is one in which costs are assembled in terms of jobs or job lots of product.

As previously stated, a job cost system differs from a general accounting system in that its primary objective is the determination of the cost of producing each job or job lot. A job cost system also differs in that all inventory accounts used in such a system are perpetual inventory accounts that control subsidiary ledgers. For example, in a job cost system the purchase and use of all materials are recorded in a perpetual inventory account called Materials. The Materials account controls a subsidiary ledger having a separate ledger card (Illustration 22–1) for each different kind of material used. Likewise, in a job cost system the Goods in Process and Finished Goods accounts are also perpetual inventory accounts controlling subsidiary ledgers.[1]

In addition to perpetual inventory controlling accounts, job cost accounting is also distinguished by the flow of manufacturing costs through the accounts. Costs flow from the Materials, Factory Payroll, and Overhead Costs accounts into and through the Goods in Process and Finished Goods accounts and on to the Cost of Goods Sold account. This flow is diagrammed in Illustration 22–2. An examination of the diagram will show that costs flow through the accounts in the same way materials, labour, and overhead are placed in production in the factory, are combined to become finished goods, and finally are sold.

---

[1] In a computerized system the ledger cards would be replaced by computer files. However, the basic system would be essentially the same.

Illustration 22–1

MATERIALS LEDGER CARD

Item _Whatsit clip_   Stock No. _C-347_   Location in Storeroom _Bin 137_

Maximum _400_   Minimum _150_   Number to Reorder _200_

	Received				Issued				Balance		
Date	Receiving Report No.	Units	Unit Price	Total Price	Requi-sition No.	Units	Unit Price	Total Price	Units	Unit Price	Total Price
1/3									180	1.00	180.00
5/3					4345	20	1.00	20.00	160	1.00	160.00
11/3					4416	10	·1.00	10.00	150	1.00	150.00
12/3	C-114	200	1.00	200.00					350	1.00	350.00
25/3					4713	21	1.00	21.00	329	1.00	329.00

Illustration 22–2 also shows the relationships between the controlling accounts and the subsidiary ledgers in a job cost system. In order to better understand the role played by each component of the system, students should refer back to Illustration 22–2 as they study the discussion of each component.

JOB COST SHEETS

The heart of a job cost system is a subsidiary ledger of *job cost sheets* called a *Job Cost Ledger.* The cost sheets are used to accumulate costs by jobs. A separate cost sheet is used for each job.

Observe in Illustration 22–3 that a job cost sheet is designed to accumulate costs. Although this accumulation is discussed in more detail later, it may be summarized as follows. When a job is begun, information regarding the customer, job number, and job description is recorded on a blank cost sheet or onto a computer file and the cost sheet is placed in the Job Cost Ledger. Identifying each job with a job number simplifies the process of charging materials, labour, and overhead to the job. As materials are required for the job, they are transferred from the materials storeroom and are used to complete the job. At the same time their cost is charged to the job in the Materials column of the job's cost sheet. Labour used directly on the job is likewise charged to the job in the Labour column; and when the job is finished, the amount of overhead applicable is entered in the Overhead Costs Applied column. After this, the cost totals are summarized, and the job's total cost is determined.

Illustration 22–2 Cost Flows and Subsidiary Ledgers for a Job Cost System

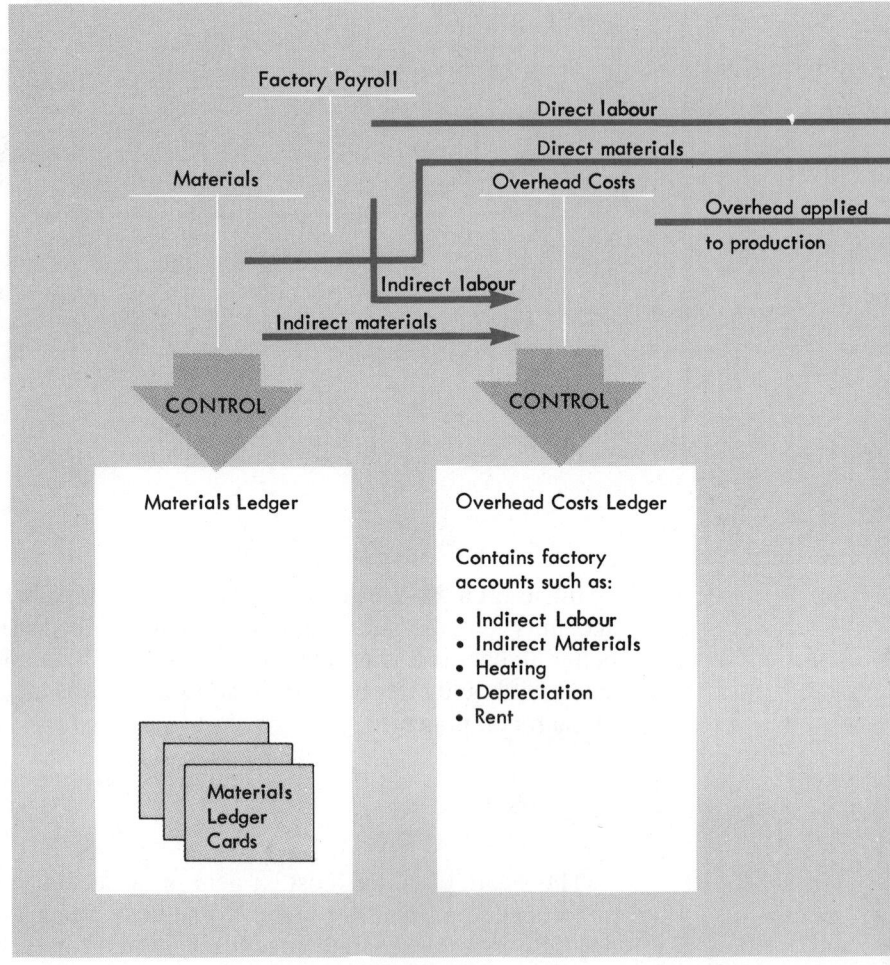

THE GOODS IN PROCESS ACCOUNT

The job cost sheets in the Job Cost Ledger are controlled by the Goods in Process account, which is kept in the General Ledger. And, the Goods in Process account and its subsidiary ledger of cost sheets operate in the usual manner of controlling accounts and subsidiary ledgers. The material, labour, and overhead costs debited to each individual job on its cost sheet must be debited to the Goods in Process account either as individual amounts or in totals. Likewise, all credits to jobs on their

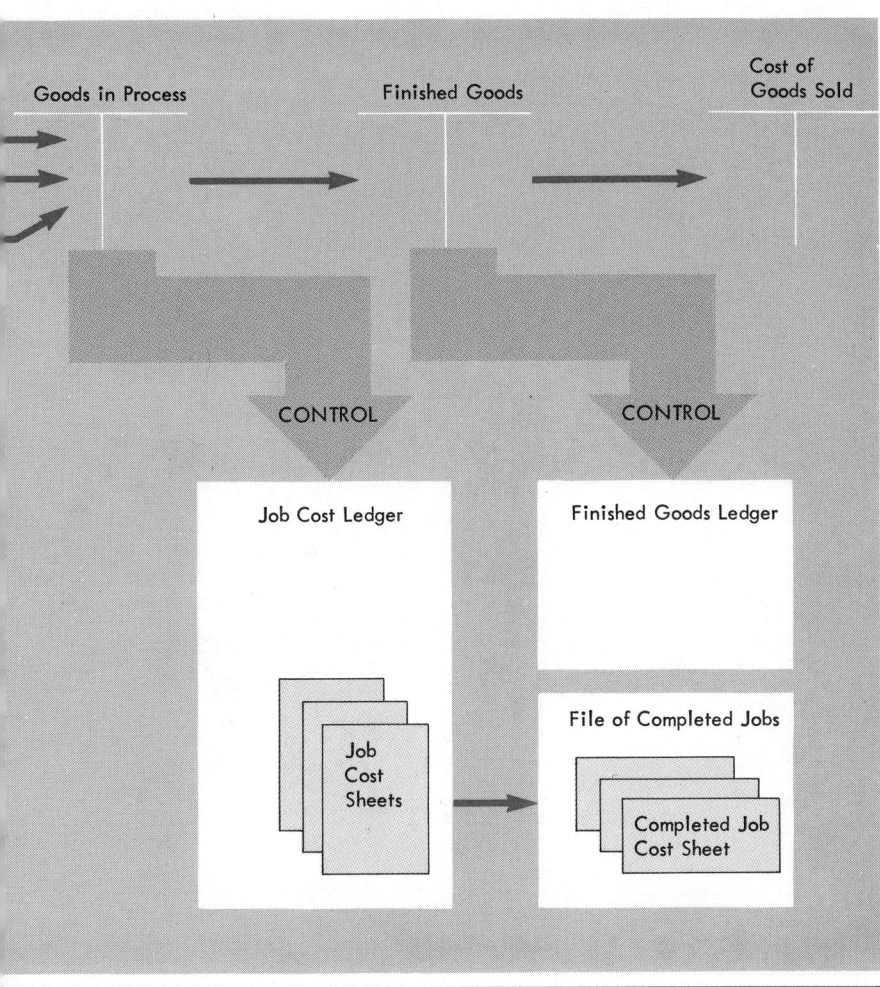

cost sheets must be credited individually or in totals to the Goods in Process account.

In addition to being a controlling account, the Goods in Process account is a perpetual inventory account. At the beginning of a cost period the cost of any unfinished jobs in process appears in the Goods in Process account as a debit balance. Throughout the cost period materials, labour, and overhead are placed in production, and periodically their costs are debited to the account (note the last three debits in the Goods in Process account that follows). Also, throughout the period the cost of each job

Illustration 22–3

JOB COST SHEET

Customer's Name ___Cone Lumber Company_____ Job No. _7452_
Address _Burnaby, B.C._____
Job Description _10 H.P. electric motor to customer's specifications_____

Date
Promised ___1/4_____

Date
Started __23 / 3_____

Date
Completed _29/3_____

| Date | Materials | | Labour | | Overhead Costs Applied | | |
	Requisition No.	Amount	Time Ticket No.	Amount	Date	Rate	Amount
19-- Mar. 23	4698	53.00	C-3422	12.00	29/3	150 per cent of the direct labour	$123.00
24			C-3478 C-3479	16.00 6.00			
25	4713	21.00	C-4002	16.00			
26			C-4015	10.00			
27			C-4032	12.00			
28			C-4044	10.00			
	Total	74.00	Total	82.00			

Summary of Costs

Materials_____ $ 74.00

Labour _____ 82.00

Overhead_____ 123.00

Total cost
of the job_____ 279.00

Remarks:
   Completed and shipped
   29/3

completed (the sum of the job's material, labour, and overhead costs) is credited to the account as each job is finished. As a result, the account functions as a perpetual inventory account. After all entries are posted, the debit balance shows the cost of the unfinished jobs still in process. This current balance is obtained and maintained without having to take a physical count of inventory, except as an occasional means of confirming the account balance. For example, the following Goods in Process account shows a $12,785 March 31 ending inventory of unfinished jobs in process.

Goods in Process				
Date	Explanation	Debit	Credit	Balance
Mar. 1	Balance, beginning inventory			2,850
10	Job 7449 completed		7,920	(5,070)
18	Job 7448 completed		9,655	(14,725)
24	Job 7450 completed		8,316	(23,041)
29	Job 7452 completed		279	(23,320)
29	Job 7451 completed		6,295	(29,615)
31	Materials used	17,150		(12,465)
31	Labour applied	10,100		(2,365)
31	Overhead applied	15,150		12,785

ACCOUNTING FOR MATERIALS UNDER A JOB COST SYSTEM

Under a job cost system all materials purchased are placed in a materials storeroom under the care of a storeroom keeper and are issued to the factory only in exchange for properly prepared material *requisitions* (Illustration 22–4). The storeroom provides physical control over materials. The requisitions enhance the control and also provide a means of charging material costs to jobs or, in the case of indirect materials, to factory overhead costs. The use of requisitions is described in the next paragraphs.

When a material is needed in the factory, a material requisition is prepared and signed by a superintendent or other responsible person. The requisition identifies the material and shows the job number or overhead account to which it is to be charged, and is given to the storeroom keeper in exchange for the material. The storeroom keeper collects the

Illustration 22–4

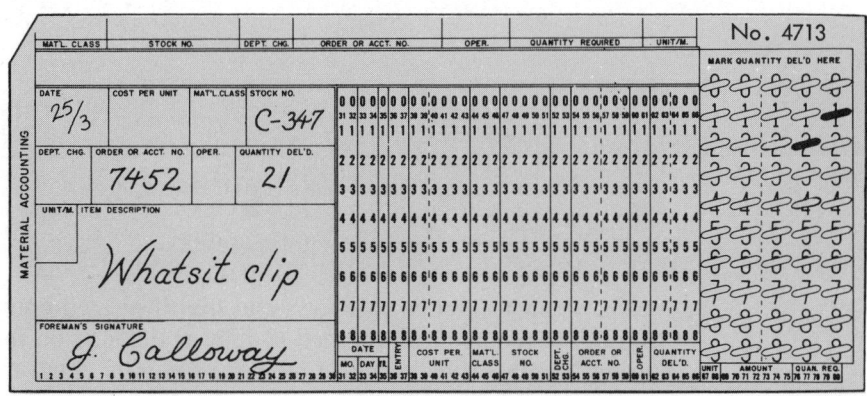

requisitions and then forwards them, in batches, to the accounting department.

Issuing units of material to the factory obviously reduces the amount of that particular material in the storeroom. Consequently, when a material requisition reaches the accounting department, it is first recorded in the Issued column of the materials ledger card of the material issued. This reduces the number of units of that material shown to be on hand. Note the last entry in Illustration 22–1, which records the requisition of Illustration 22–4.

Materials issued to the factory may be used on jobs or for some overhead task, such as machinery repairs. Consequently, after being entered in the Issued columns of the proper materials ledger cards, a batch of requisitions is coded for and charged to the proper jobs and overhead accounts. Materials used on jobs are charged to the jobs in the Materials columns of the job cost sheets. (Note the last entry in the Materials column on the cost sheet of Illustration 22–3 where the requisition of Illustration 22–4 is recorded). Materials used for overhead tasks are charged to the proper overhead accounts in the Overhead Costs ledger. A company using a job cost system commonly has an Overhead Costs, controlling account in its General Ledger which controls a subsidiary Overhead Costs Ledger having an account for each overhead cost, such as Heating and Lighting or Machinery Repairs. Consequently, a requisition for light bulbs, for example, is charged to the Heating and Lighting account in the subsidiary Overhead Costs Ledger.

Material ledger cards, job cost sheets, and overhead cost accounts are all subsidiary ledger accounts controlled by accounts in the General ledger. Consequently, in addition to the entries just described, entries must also be made in the controlling accounts. To make these entries, the requisitions charged to jobs and the requisitions charged to overhead accounts are accumulated until the end of a month or other cost period when they are separately totaled. If, for example, the requisitions charged to jobs during the month total $17,150 and those charged to overhead accounts total $320, an entry like the following is made:

Mar.	31	Goods in Process	17,150.00	
		Overhead Costs	320.00	
		Materials		17,470.00
		To record the materials used during March.		

The debit to Goods in Process in the illustrated entry is equal to the sum of the requisitions charged to jobs as detailed on the job cost sheets during March. The debit to Overhead Costs is equal to the sum of the requisitions charged to overhead accounts, and the credit to Materials is equal to the sum of all requisitions entered in the Issued columns of the material ledger cards during the month.

ACCOUNTING FOR LABOUR IN A JOB COST SYSTEM

Time clocks, clock cards, and a Payroll Register similar to those described in an earlier chapter are commonly used in factories to record the hours and cost of the direct and indirect labour provided by employees. Without the complications of payroll deductions, income taxes, and other items, the entry to pay the employees is as follows:

Mar.	7	Factory Payroll	2,900.00	
		Cash		2,900.00
		To record the factory payroll and pay the employees.		

This entry is repeated at the end of each pay period. Thus, at the end of a month or other cost period the Factory Payroll account has a series of debits (see Illustration 22–6) like the debit of this entry. The sum of these debits is the total amount paid to employees for the direct and indirect labour during the month.

The clock cards just mentioned are a record of hours worked each day by each employee, but they do not show how the employees spent their time or the specific jobs and overhead tasks on which they worked. Consequently, if the hours worked by each employee are to be charged to specific jobs and overhead accounts, another record called a *labour time ticket* must be prepared. Labour time tickets like the one shown in Illustration 22–5 describe how each employee's time was spent while at work.

The time ticket of Illustration 22–5 is a "pen-and-ink" ticket and is suitable for use in a plant in which only a small number of such tickets are prepared and recorded each day. In a plant in which many tickets are prepared, a time ticket that can be made into a punched card similar to Illustration 22–4 would be more suitable.

Labour time tickets serve as a basis for charging jobs and overhead accounts for an employee's wages. Throughout each day a labour time ticket is prepared each time an employee moves from one job or overhead task to another. The tickets may be prepared by the worker, the worker's supervisor, or a clerk called a timekeeper. If the employee works on only one job all day, only one ticket is prepared. If more than one job is worked on, a separate ticket is made for each. At the end of the day all the tickets prepared that day are sent to the accounting department.

Illustration 22–5 Labour Time Ticket

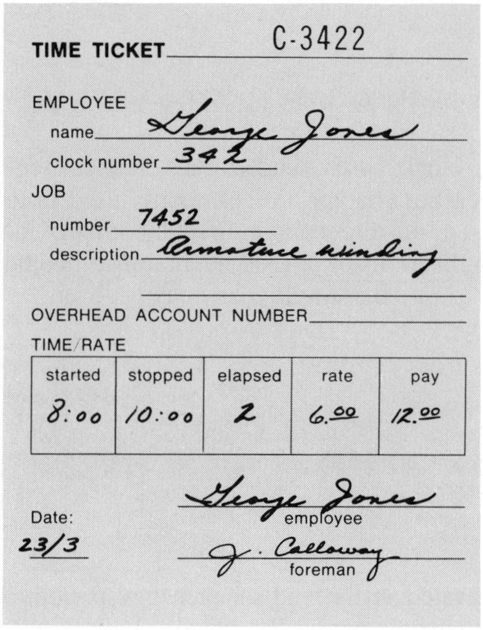

TIME TICKET C-3422

EMPLOYEE

name George Jones

clock number 342

JOB

number 7452

description Armature winding

OVERHEAD ACCOUNT NUMBER

TIME/RATE

started	stopped	elapsed	rate	pay
8:00	10:00	2	6.00	12.00

Date: 23/3

George Jones
employee

J. Calloway
foreman

In the accounting department the direct labour time tickets are charged to jobs on the job cost sheets (see the first entry in the Labour column of Illustration 22–3 where the ticket of Illustration 22–5 is recorded); and the indirect labour tickets are charged to overhead accounts in the Overhead Costs Ledger. The tickets are then accumulated until the end of the cost period when they are separately totaled. If, for example, the direct labour tickets total $10,100 and the indirect labour tickets total $2,500, the following entry is made:

Mar.	31	Goods in Process	10,100.00	
		Overhead Costs	2,500.00	
		Factory Payroll		12,600.00
		To record the March time tickets.		

The first debit in the illustrated entry is the sum of all direct labour time tickets charged to jobs on the job cost sheets, and the second debit is the sum of all tickets charged to overhead accounts. The credit is the total of the month's labour time tickets, both direct and indirect. Notice in Illustration 22–6 that after this credit is posted, the Factory Payroll account has a $605 credit balance. This $605 is the accrued factory payroll payable at the month's end, and it is also the dollar amount of time tickets prepared and recorded during the last three days of March.

Illustration 22–6

Factory Payroll				
Date	Explanation	Debit	Credit	Balance
Mar. 7	Weekly payroll payment	2,900		2,900
14	Weekly payroll payment	2,950		5,850
21	Weekly payroll payment	3,105		8,955
28	Weekly payroll payment	3,040		11,995
31	Labour cost summary		12,600	(605)

ACCOUNTING FOR OVERHEAD IN A JOB COST SYSTEM

In a job cost system, if the cost of each job is to be determined at the time it is finished, it is necessary to associate with each job the cost of its materials, labour, and overhead. Requisitions and time tickets make possible a direct association of material and labour costs with jobs. However, overhead costs are incurred for the benefit of all jobs and cannot be related directly to any one job. Consequently, to associate overhead with jobs it is necessary to relate overhead to another variable, such as direct labour costs, and to apply overhead to jobs by means of a *predetermined overhead application rate.*

A predetermined overhead application rate based on direct labour cost is established before a cost period begins by (1) estimating the total overhead that will be incurred during the period; (2) estimating the cost of the direct labour that will be incurred during the period; then (3) calculating the ratio, expressed as a percentage, of the estimated overhead to the estimated direct labour cost. For example, if a cost accountant estimates that a factory will incur $180,000 of overhead during the next year, and that $120,000 of direct labour will be applied to production during the year, these estimates are used to establish an overhead application rate of 150%, calculated as follows:

$$\frac{\text{Next year's estimated overhead costs, \$180,000}}{\text{Next year's estimated direct labour costs, \$120,000}} = 150\%$$

After a predetermined overhead application rate is estimated, it is used throughout the year to apply overhead to jobs as they are finished. Overhead is assigned to each job, and its cost is calculated as follows: (1) As each job is completed, the cost of its materials is determined by adding the amounts in the Materials column of its cost sheet. Then (2) the cost of its labour is determined by adding the amounts in the Labour column. Next (3) the applicable overhead cost is calculated by multiplying the job's total labor cost by the predetermined overhead application rate and is entered in the Overhead Costs Applied column. Finally (4) the job's material, labour, and overhead costs are entered in the summary section of the cost sheet and totaled to determine the total cost of the job.

The predetermined overhead application rate is also used to assign overhead to any jobs still in process at the cost period end. Then, the total overhead assigned to all jobs during the period is recorded in the accounts with an entry like this:

Mar.	31	Goods in Process	15,150.00	
		Overhead Costs		15,150.00
		To record the overhead applied to jobs during March.		

The illustrated entry assumes that the overhead applied to all jobs during March totaled $15,150. After it is posted, the Overhead Costs account appears as in Illustration 22–7.

In the Overhead Costs account of Illustration 22–7 the actual overhead costs incurred during March are represented by four debits. The first two need no explanation; the third represents the many payments for such things as water and telephone; the fourth represents such things as depreciation, expired insurance, and taxes.

When overhead is applied to jobs on the basis of a predetermined overhead rate based upon direct labour costs, it is assumed that the overhead applicable to a particular job bears the same relation to the job's direct labour cost as the total estimated overhead of the factory bears to the total estimated direct labor costs. This assumption may not be proper in every case. However, when the ratio of overhead to direct

Illustration 22–7

	Overhead Costs				
Date	Explanation	PR	Debit	Credit	Balance
Mar. 31	Indirect materials	G24	320		320
31	Indirect labour	G24	2,500		2,820
31	Miscellaneous payments	D89	3,306		6,126
31	Accrued and prepaid items	G24	9,056		15,182
31	Applied			15,150	32

labor cost is approximately the same for all jobs, an overhead rate based upon direct labour cost offers an easily calculated and fair basis for assigning overhead to jobs. In those cases in which the ratio of overhead to direct labour cost does not remain the same for all jobs, some other relationship must be used. Often overhead rates based upon the ratio of overhead to direct labour hours or overhead to machine-hours are used. However, a discussion of these alternate bases is reserved for a course in cost accounting.

OVERAPPLIED AND UNDERAPPLIED OVERHEAD

When overhead is applied to jobs by means of an overhead application rate based on estimates, the Overhead Costs account seldom, if ever, has a zero balance. At times actual overhead incurred exceeds overehead applied, and at other times overhead applied exceeds actual overhead incurred. When the account has a debit balance (overhead incurred in excess of overhead applied), the balance is known as *underapplied overhead* (see Illustration 22–7); and when it has a credit balance (overhead applied in excess of overhead incurred), the balance is called *overapplied overhead.* Usually the balance is small and fluctuates from debit to credit throughout a year. However, any remaining balance in the account at the end of each year must be disposed of before a new accounting period begins.

If the year-end balance of the Overhead Costs account is material in amount, it is reasonable that it be disposed of by apportioning it among the goods still in process, the finished goods inventory, and cost of goods sold. This has the effect of restating the inventories and goods sold at ''actual'' cost. For example, assume that at the end of an accounting period, (1) a company's Overhead Costs account has a $1,000 debit balance (underapplied overhead) and (2) the company had charged the following amounts of overhead to jobs during the period: jobs still in process, $10,000; jobs finished but unsold, $20,000; and jobs finished and sold, $70,000. In such a situation the following entry apportions the underapplied overhead fairly among the jobs worked on during the period:

Dec.	31	Goods in Process	100.00	
		Finished Goods	200.00	
		Cost of Goods Sold	700.00	
		Overhead Costs		1,000.00
		To clear the Overhead Costs account and charge the underapplied overhead to the work of the accounting period.		

When the amount of over- or underapplied overhead is immaterial, all of it is closed to Cost of Goods Sold under the assumption that the major share of these costs would be charged to this account anyway and any extra exactness gained from prorating would not be worth the extra record-keeping involved.

RECORDING THE COMPLETION OF A JOB

When a job is completed, its cost is transferred from the Goods in Process account to the Finished Goods account. For example, the following entry transfers the cost of the job the cost sheet of which appears on page 902.

Mar.	29	Finished Goods	279.00	
		Goods in Process		279.00
		To transfer the cost of Job No. 7452 to		
		Finished Goods.		

At the same time this entry is made, the completed job's cost sheet is removed from the Job Cost Ledger, marked "completed," and filed. This is in effect the equivalent of posting a credit to the Job Cost Ledger equal to the credit to the Goods in Process controlling account.

RECORDING COST OF GOODS SOLD

When a cost system is in use, the cost to manufacture a job or job lot of product is known as soon as the goods are finished. Consequently, when goods are sold, since their cost is known, the cost can be recorded at the time of sale. For example, if goods costing $279 are sold for $450 the cost of the goods sold may be recorded at the time of sale as follows:

Mar.	29	Accounts Receivable—Cone Lumber Co.	450.00	
		Cost of Goods Sold	279.00	
		Sales		450.00
		Finished Goods		279.00
		Sold for $450 goods costing $279.		

When cost of goods sold is recorded at the time of each sale, the balance of the Cost of Goods Sold account shows at the end of an accounting period the cost of goods sold during the period.

—————— PROCESS COST ACCOUNTING ——————

A *process* is a step in manufacturing a product, and a *process cost system* is one in which costs are assembled in terms of processes or manufacturing steps.

Process cost systems are found in companies producing cement, flour, or other products, the production of which is characterized by a large volume of standardized units manufactured on a more or less continuous basis. In such companies, responsibility for completing each step in the production of a product is assigned to a department. Costs are then assembled by departments, and the efficiency of each department is measured by comparing planned and actual processing costs incurred in processing the units of product that flow through the department.

ASSEMBLING COSTS BY DEPARTMENTS

When costs are assembled by departments in a process cost system, a separate goods in process account is used for the costs of each department. For example, assume a company makes a product from metal that is cut to size in a cutting department, then sent to a bending department to be bent into shape, and then to a painting department to be painted. Such a concern would collect costs in three goods in process accounts, one for each department, and costs would flow through the accounts as in Illustration 22–8.

Observe in Illustration 22–8 that each department's material, labour, and overhead costs are charged to the department's Goods in Process account. (It is assumed there were additional materials charged directly to the bending department.) Observe, too, how costs are transferred from department to department, just as the product is physically transferred in the manufacturing procedure. The cost to cut the product in the cutting department is transferred to the bending department; and the sum of the costs in the first two departments is transferred to the third department; and finally the sum of the processing costs in all three departments, which is the total cost to make the product, is transferred to Finished Goods.

CHARGING COSTS TO DEPARTMENTS

Since there are no jobs in a process cost system, accounting for material and labour costs in such a system is greatly simplified. Material requisitions may be used. However, a consumption report kept by the storeroom keeper and showing the materials issued to each department during a cost period is often substituted. Likewise, labour time tickets may be used; but since most employees spend all their working time in the same department, an end-of-the-period summary of the payroll records

Illustration 22–8

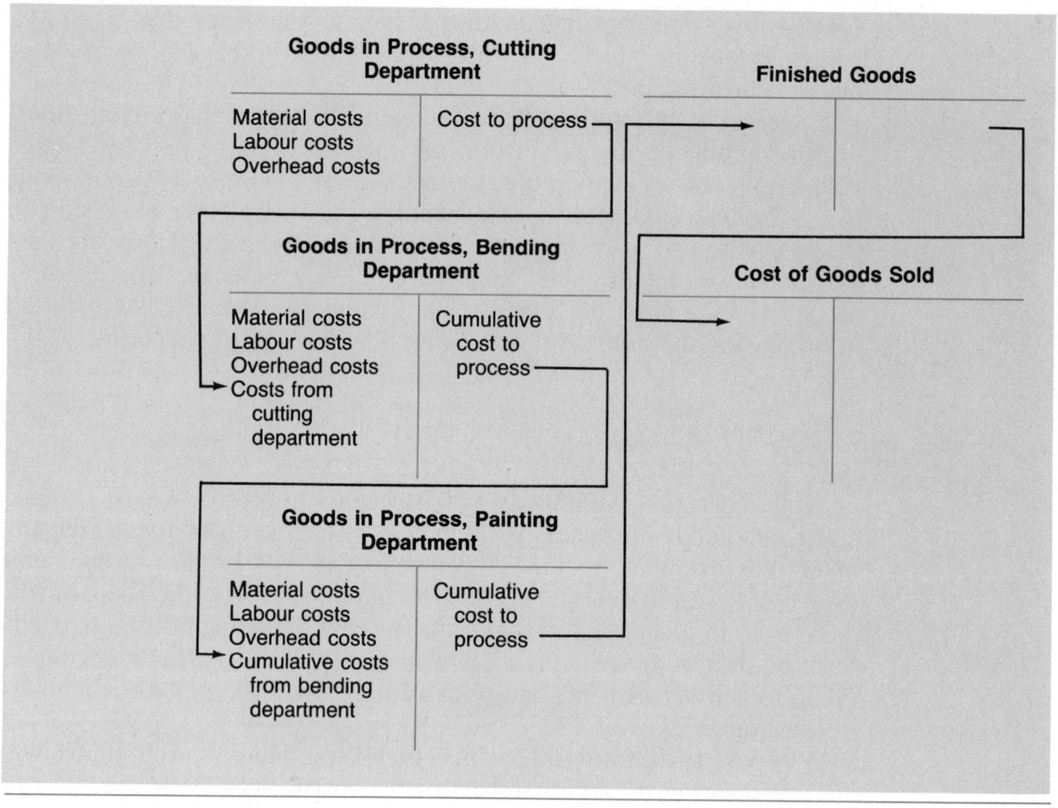

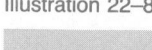

is usually all that is required in charging labour to the departments. And since there are no jobs, there is no need to distinguish between direct and indirect materials, and direct and indirect labour. All that is required is that material and labour costs, both direct and indirect, be charged to the proper departments.

The lack of jobs also simplifies accounting for overhead in a process cost system. Since there are no jobs to charge with overhead on completion, predetermined overhead application rates are not required and actual overhead incurred may be charged directly to the goods in process accounts of the departments.

EQUIVALENT FINISHED UNITS

A basic objective of a process cost system is the determination of unit processing costs for material, labour, and overhead in each processing department. This requires that (1) material, labour, and overhead costs be accumulated for each department for a cost period of, say, a month; (2) a record be kept of the number of units processed in each department during the period; and then (3) that costs be divided by units processed to determine unit costs. However, it should be observed that when a department begins and ends a cost period with partially processed units of product, the units completed in the department are not an accurate measure of the department's total production. When the production of the period includes completing units that were partially finished at the beginning of the period, and also includes working on units that remain partially finished at the end of the period, the following question arises: How many units did the department produce during the period? In other words, how many units would have been produced if all activity in the department had been concentrated on units that were started this period and finished this period? The answer is the number of *equivalent finished units* produced by the department during the period. Thus, when a department's beginning and ending inventories include partially finished units, the department's production for the period must be measured in terms of **equivalent finished units,** and unit costs become equivalent finished unit costs.

The idea of an equivalent finished unit is based on the assumption that it takes the same amount of labour, for instance, to finish one half of each two units of product as it takes to fully complete one, or it takes the same amount of labour to finish one third of each of three units as to complete one. Also, since a department may add materials to production at a different rate than it adds labour and overhead, separate measures of production are often required for materials, for labour, and for overhead. For example, a department may have added enough materials to produce 1,000 equivalent finished units, and during the same period, the department may have added enough labour and overhead to produce 900 equivalent finished units. The concept of equivalent finished units and the related calculations are discussed further in the Delta Processing Company illustration that follows.

PROCESS COST ACCOUNTING ILLUSTRATED

The process cost system of Delta Processing Company, a company manufacturing a patented home remedy called Noxall, is used to illustrate process cost accounting.

The procedure for manufacturing Noxall is as follows: Material A is finely ground in Delta Processing Company's grinding department. Then, it is transferred to the mixing department where Material B is added, and the two materials are thoroughly mixed. The mixing process results in the finished product, Noxall, which is transferred on completion to finished goods. All the Material A placed in process in the grinding department is placed in process at the beginning of the grinding process;

but the Material B added in the mixing department is added evenly throughout its process. In other words, a product one-third mixed in the latter department has received one third of its Material B and a product three-fourths mixed has received three fourths. Labour and overhead are applied evenly throughout each department's process.

At the end of the April cost period, after entries recording materials, labour, and overhead were posted, the company's two goods in process accounts appeared as follows:

Goods in Process, Grinding Department

Date		Explanation	Debit	Credit	Balance
Apr.	1	Beginning inventory			4,250
	30	Materials	9,900		14,150
	30	Labour	5,700		19,850
	30	Overhead	4,275		24,125

Goods in Process, Mixing Department

Date		Explanation	Debit	Credit	Balance
Apr.	1	Beginning inventory			3,785
	30	Materials	2,040		5,825
	30	Labour	3,570		9,395
	30	Overhead	1,020		10,415

The production reports prepared by the company's two department managers give the following information about inventories and goods started and finished in each department during the month:

	Grinding department	Mixing department
Units in the beginning inventories of goods in process...................	30,000	16,000
April 1 stage of completion of the beginning inventories of goods in process	1/3	1/4
Units started in process and finished during period	70,000	85,000
Total units finished and transferred to next department or to finished goods	100,000	101,000
Units in the ending inventories of goods in process	20,000	15,000
Stage of completion of ending inventories of goods in process	1/4	1/3

Process Cost Summary

After receiving the production reports, the company's cost accountant prepared a process cost summary, Illustration 22–9, for the grinding department. A process cost summary is a report unique to a processing

Illustration 22–9

DELTA PROCESSING COMPANY
Process Cost Summary, Grinding Department
For Month Ended April 30, 198A

COSTS CHARGED TO THE DEPARTMENT:

Material requisitioned	$ 9,900
Labour charged	5,700
Overhead costs incurred	4,275
Total processing costs	19,875
Goods in process at the beginning of the month	4,250
Total costs to be accounted for	$24,125

EQUIVALENT UNIT PROCESSING COSTS:

	Units involved	Fraction of a unit added	Equivalent units added
Material:			
Beginning inventory	30,000	–0–	–0–
Units started and finished	70,000	1	70,000
Ending inventory	20,000	1	20,000
Total equivalent units			90,000

Equivalent unit processing cost for material: $9,900 ÷ 90,000 = $0.11

	Units involved	Fraction of a unit added	Equivalent units added
Labour and overhead:			
Beginning inventory	30,000	⅔	20,000
Units started and finished	70,000	1	70,000
Ending inventory	20,000	¼	5,000
Total equivalent units			95,000

Equivalent unit processing cost for labour: $5,700 ÷ 95,000 = $0.06
Equivalent unit processing cost for overhead: $4,275 ÷ 95,000 = $0.045

ASSIGNMENT OF COSTS TO THE WORK OF THE DEPARTMENT:

Goods in process, one third processed at the beginning of April:

Costs charged to the beginning inventory of goods in process during previous month	$4,250	
Material added (all added during March)	–0–	
Labour applied (20,000 × $0.06)	1,200	
Overhead applied (20,000 × $0.045)	900	
Cost to process		$ 6,350

Goods started and finished in the department during April:

Material added (70,000 × $0.11)	7,700	
Labour applied (70,000 × $0.06)	4,200	
Overhead applied (70,000 × $0.045)	3,150	
Cost to process		15,050
Total cost of the goods processed in the department and transferred to the mixing department (100,000 units at $0.214 each)*		21,400

Goods in process, one fourth processed at the end of April:

Material added (20,000 × $0.11)	2,200	
Labour applied (5,000 × $0.06)	300	
Overhead applied (5,000 × $0.045)	225	
Cost to one-fourth process		2,725
Total costs accounted for		$24,125

* Note that the $0.214 is an average unit cost based on all 100,000 units finished. Other alternatives such as FIFO and LIFO are deferred to a more advanced course.

company. A separate report is prepared for each processing department and shows (1) the costs charged to the department, (2) the department's equivalent unit processing costs, and (3) the assignment of costs to the department's goods in process inventories and its goods started and finished.

COSTS CHARGED TO THE DEPARTMENT.   Observe in Illustration 22–9 that a process cost summary has three sections. In the first, headed Costs Charged to the Department, the costs charged to the department are summarized. Information for this section comes from the department's goods in process account. Compare the first section of Illustration 22–9 with the goods in process account of the grinding department shown on page 915.

EQUIVALENT UNIT PROCESSING COSTS.   The second section of a process cost summary shows the calculation of equivalent unit costs. The information for this section as to units involved and fractional units applicable to the inventories comes from the production report prepared by the department manager. Information as to material, labour, and overhead costs comes from the first section of the summary.

Notice in the second section of Illustration 22–9 that there are two separate equivalent unit calculations. Two calculations are required because material, labour, and overhead are not added in the same proportions or at the same stages in the processing procedure of this department. As previously stated, all material is added at the beginning of this department's process, and labour and overhead are added evenly throughout the process. Consequently, the number of equivalent units of material added is not the same as the number of equivalent units of labour and overhead added.

Observe in the calculation of equivalent finished units for materials that the beginning-of-the-month inventory is assigned no additional material. In the grinding department, all material placed in process is placed there at the beginning of the process. The 30,000 beginning inventory units were begun during March and were one third completed at the beginning of April. Consequently, these units received all their material during March when their processing was first begun.

Note also how the $9,900 cost of the material charged to the department in April is divided by 90,000 equivalent units of material to arrive at an $0.11 per equivalent unit cost for material consumed in this department.

Now move on to the calculation of equivalent finished units for labour and overhead and note that the beginning inventory units were each assigned two thirds of a unit of labour and overhead. If these units were one third completed on April 1, then two thirds of the work done on these units were done in April. Beginning students often have difficulty with this. Students commonly assign only an additional one-third unit of labour and overhead when two thirds are required.

Before going further, observe that the essence of the equivalent unit calculation for labour and overhead is that to do two thirds of the work on 30,000 units, all the work on 70,000 units, and one fourth the work on 20,000 units is the equivalent of completing all the work on 95,000 units. Consequently, the $5,700 of labour cost and $4,275 of overhead cost charged to the department are each divided by 95,000 to determine equivalent unit costs for labour and overhead.

ASSIGNMENT OF COSTS TO THE WORK OF THE DEPARTMENT. When a department begins and ends a cost period with partially processed units of product, it is necessary to apportion the department's costs between the units that were in process in the department at the beginning of the period, the units started and finished during the period, and the ending inventory units. This division is necessary to determine the cost of the units completed in the department during the period; and the division and assignment of costs are shown in the third section of the process cost summary.

Notice in the third section of Illustration 22–9 how costs are assigned to the beginning inventory. The first amount assigned is the $4,250 beginning inventory costs. This amount represents the material, labour, and overhead costs used to one-third complete the inventory during March, the previous cost period. Normally, the second charge to a beginning inventory is for additional material assigned to it. However, in the grinding department no additional material costs are assigned the beginning inventory because these units received all of their material when their processing was first begun during the previous month. The second charge to the beginning inventory is for labour. The $1,200 portion of applicable labour costs is calculated by multiplying the number of equivalent finished units of labour used to complete the beginning inventory by the cost of an equivalent finished unit of labour (20,000 equivalent finished units at $0.06 each). The third charge to the beginning inventory is for overhead. The applicable $900 portion is determined by multiplying the equivalent finished units of overhead used to complete the beginning inventory by the cost of an equivalent finished unit of overhead (20,000 × $0.45).

After costs are assigned to the beginning inventory, the procedures used in their assignment are repeated for the units started and finished. Then the cost of the units completed and transferred to finished goods, in this case the cost of the 30,000 beginning inventory units plus the cost of the 70,000 units started and finished, is determined by adding the costs assigned to the two groups. In this situation the total is $21,400, or $0.214 per unit ($21,400 ÷ 100,000 units = $0.214 per unit).

Before proceeding further, notice in the second section of the grinding department's process cost summary that the equivalent finished unit cost for materials is $0.11, for labour, is $0.06, and for overhead is $0.045, a total of $0.215. Notice, however, in the third section of the summary that the unit cost of the 100,000 units finished and transferred is $0.214, which is less than $0.215. It is less because costs were less in the department during the previous month and the 30,000 beginning units were one-third processed at these lower costs.

Transferring Costs from One Department to the Next

The grinding department's process cost summary is completed by assigning costs to the ending inventory, and after the summary was completed the accountant prepared the following entry to transfer from the grinding department to the mixing department the cost of the 100,000 units processed in the department and transferred during April. Information for the entry as to the cost of the units transferred was taken from the third section of Illustration 22–9.

Apr.	30	Goods in Process, Mixing Department	21,400.00	
		Goods in Process, Grinding Department . . .		21,400.00
		To transfer the cost of the 100,000 units of product transferred to the mixing department.		

Posting this entry had the effect on the accounts shown in Illustration 22–10. Observe that the effect is one of transferring and advancing costs from one department to the next just as the product is physically transferred and advanced in the manufacturing procedure.

Illustration 22–10

Goods in Process, Grinding Department

Date		Explanation	Debit	Credit	Balance
Apr.	1	Beginning inventory			4,250
	30	Materials	9,900		14,150
	30	Labour	5,700		19,850
	30	Overhead	4,275		24,125
	30	Units to mixing department		21,400	2,725

Goods in Process, Mixing Department

Date		Explanation	Debit	Credit	Balance
Apr.	1	Beginning inventory			3,785
	30	Materials	2,040		5,825
	30	Labour	3,570		9,395
	30	Overhead	1,020		10,415
	30	Units from grinding department	21,400		31,815

Process Cost Summary—Mixing Department

After posting the entry transferring to the mixing department the grinding department costs of the units transferred, the cost accountant prepared a process cost summary for the mixing department. Information required in its preparation was taken from the mixing department's goods in process account and production report. The summary appeared as in Illustration 22–11.

Two points in Illustration 22–11 require special attention. The first is the calculation of equivalent finished units. Since the materials, labour, and overhead added in the mixing department are all added evenly throughout the process of this department, only a single equivalent unit calculation is required. This differs from the grinding department where two equivalent unit calculations were required. Two were required because material was not placed in process at the same stage in the processing procedure as were labour and overhead.

The second point needing special attention in the mixing department cost summary is the method of handling the grinding department costs transferred to this department. During April, 100,000 units of product, with accumulated grinding department costs of $21,400, were transferred to the mixing department. Of these 100,000 units, 85,000 were started in process in the department, finished, and transferred to Finished Goods. The remaining 15,000 were still in process in the department at the end of the cost period.

Notice in the first section of Illustration 22–11 how the $21,400 of grinding department costs transferred to the mixing department are added to the other costs charged to the department. Compare the information in this first section with the mixing department's Goods in Process account as it is shown on page 914 and again in Illustration 22–10.

Notice again in the third section of the mixing department's process cost summary how the $21,400 of grinding department costs are apportioned between the 85,000 units started and finished and the 15,000 units still in process in the department. The 16,000 beginning goods in process units received none of this $21,400 charge because they were transferred from the grinding department during the previous month. Their grinding department costs are included in the $3,785 beginning inventory costs.

Apr.	30	Finished Goods	28,280.00	
		Goods in Process, Mixing Department		28,280.00
		To transfer the accumulated grinding department and mixing department costs of the 101,000 units transferred to Finished Goods.		

Illustration 22–11

DELTA PROCESSING COMPANY
Process Cost Summary, Mixing Department
For Month Ended April 30, 198A

COSTS CHARGED TO THE DEPARTMENT:
Materials requisitioned .... $ 2,040
Labour charged 3,570
Overhead costs incurred 1,020
    Total processing costs 6,630
Goods in process at the beginning of the month 3,785
Cost transferred from the grinding department (100,000 units at $0.214 each) 21,400
    Total costs to be accounted for $31,815

EQUIVALENT UNIT PROCESSING COSTS:

	Units involved	Fraction of a unit added	Equivalent units added
Materials, labour, and overhead:			
Beginning inventory	16,000	¾	12,000
Units started and finished	85,000	One	85,000
Ending inventory	15,000	⅓	5,000
Total equivalents units			102,000

Equivalent unit processing cost for materials: $2,040 ÷ 102,000 = $0.02
Equivalent unit processing cost for labour: $3,570 ÷ 102,000 = $0.035
Equivalent unit processing cost for overhead: $1,020 ÷ 102,000 = $0.01

ASSIGNMENT OF COSTS TO THE WORK OF THE DEPARTMENT:
Goods in process, one fourth completed at the beginning of April:
  Costs charged to the beginning inventory of goods in process during
    previous month .... $ 3,785
  Materials added (12,000 × $0.02) 240
  Labour applied (12,000 × $0.035) 420
  Overhead applied (12,000 × $0.01) 120
  Cost to process .... $ 4,565
Goods started and finished in the department during April:
  Costs in the grinding department (85,000 × $0.214) 18,190
  Materials added (85,000 × $0.02) 1,700
  Labour applied (85,000 × $0.035) 2,975
  Overhead applied (85,000 × $0.01) 850
  Cost to process 23,715
    Total accumulated cost of goods transferred to finished goods
      (101,000 units at $0.28) 28,280
Goods in process, one third processed at the end of April:
  Costs in the grinding department (15,000 × $0.214) 3,210
  Materials added (5,000 × $0.02) 100
  Labour applied (5,000 × $0.035) 175
  Overhead applied (5,000 × $0.01) 50
  Cost to one-third process 3,535
    Total costs accounted for $31,815

The third section of the mixing department's process cost summary shows that 101,000 units of product (16,000 beginning inventory units plus 85,000 started and finished) with accumulated costs of $28,280 were completed in the department during April and transferred to Finished Goods. The cost accountant used the entry below to transfer the accumulated cost of these 101,000 units from the mixing department's Goods in Process account to the Finished Goods account. Posting the entry had the effect shown in Illustration 22–12.

Illustration 22–12

Goods in Process, Mixing Department

Date		Explanation	Debit	Credit	Balance
Apr.	1	Beginning inventory			3,785
	30	Materials	2,040		5,825
	30	Labour	3,570		9,395
	30	Overhead	1,020		10,415
	30	Units from grinding department	21,400		31,815
	30	Units to finished goods		28,280	3,535

Finished Goods

Date		Explanation	Debit	Credit	Balance
Apr.	30	Units from mixing department	28,280		28,280

GLOSSARY

Cost accounting system. An accounting system based on perpetual inventory records that is designed to emphasize the determination of unit costs and the control of costs.

Equivalent finished units. A measure of production with respect to materials or labour, expressed as the number of units that could have been manufactured from start to finish during a period given the amount of materials or labour used during the period.

Job. A special production order to meet a customer's specifications.

Job Cost Ledger. A subsidiary ledger to the Goods in Process account in which are kept the job cost sheets of unfinished jobs.

Job cost sheet. A record of the costs incurred on a single job.

Job lot. A quantity of identical items manufactured in one lot or single order.

Job order cost system.   A cost accounting system in which costs are assembled in terms of jobs or job lots.

Labour time ticket.   A record of how an employee's time at work was used; the record serves as the basis for charging jobs and overhead accounts for the employee's wages.

Overapplied overhead.   The amount by which overhead applied on the basis of a predetermined overhead application rate exceeds overhead actually incurred.

Predetermined overhead application rate.   A rate that is used to charge overhead cost to production; calculated by relating estimated overhead cost for a period to another variable such as estimated direct labour cost.

Process.   A step in manufacturing a product.

Process cost system.   A cost accounting system in which costs are assembled in terms of steps in manufacturing a product.

Requisition.   A document that identifes the materials needed for a specific job and the account to which the materials cost should be charged, and that is given to a storeroom keeper in exchange for the materials.

Underapplied overhead.   The amount by which actual overhead incurred exceeds the overhead applied to production, based on a predetermined application rate and evidenced by a debit balance in the overhead account at the end of the period.

QUESTIONS FOR CLASS DISCUSSION

1. What are the two primary types of cost accounting systems? Indicate which of the two would best fit the needs of a manufacturer who:
    a.   Produces special-purpose machines designed to fit the particular needs of each customer.
    b.   Produces electric generators in lots of 10.
    c.   Manufactures copper tubing.

2. Define the following terms in the context of cost accounting:
    a.   Job order cost system.
    b.   Process cost system.
    c.   Job.
    d.   Job lot.
    e.   Job cost sheet.
    f.   Labour time ticket.
    g.   Materials requisition.
    h.   Process cost summary.

3. The Materials account and the Goods in Process account each serves as a control account for a subsidiary ledger. What subsidiary ledgers do these accounts control?

4. How is the inventory of goods in process determined in a general accounting system like that described in Chapter 21? How may this inventory be determined in a job cost system?

5. What is the purpose of a job cost sheet? What is the name of the ledger

containing the job cost sheets of the unfinished jobs in process? What account controls this ledger?

6. What business papers provide the information that is used to make the job cost sheet entries for:
   a. Materials?
   b. Labour?

7. Refer to the job cost sheet of Illustration 22–3. How was the amount of overhead costs charged to this job determined?

8. How is a predetermined overhead application rate established? Why is such a predetermined rate used to charge overhead to jobs?

9. Why does a company using a job cost system normally have either overapplied or underapplied overhead at the end of each accounting period?

10. At the end of a cost period the Overhead Costs controlling account has a debit balance. Does this represent overapplied or underapplied overhead?

11. What are the basic differences in the products and in the manufacturing procedures of a company to which a job cost system is applicable as opposed to a company to which a process cost system is applicable?

12. What is an equivalent finished unit of labour? Of materials?

13. What is the assumption on which the idea of an equivalent finished unit of, for instance, labour is based?

14. What is the production of a department measured in equivalent finished units if it began an accounting period with 8,000 units of product that were one-fourth completed at the beginning of the period, started and finished 50,000 units during the period, and ended the period with 6,000 units that were one-third processed at the period end?

15. The process cost summary of a department commonly has three sections. What is shown in each section?

MULTIPLE CHOICE

1. If a company applies overhead to production on the basis of a predetermined rate, a credit balance in the Overhead Costs account at the end of the period means that:
   a. The bookkeeper has made an error because the debits do not equal the credits.
   b. The balance will be carried forward to the next period as an overhead cost.
   c. Actual overhead was less than the amount charged to production.
   d. The overhead was underapplied for the period.
   e. Actual overhead was greater than the amount charged to production.

2. If the Goods in Process account of a manufacturing company that uses an overhead rate based on direct labour cost has a $4,400 debit balance after

all posting is completed, and the cost sheet of the one job still in process shows material charges of $2,000 and direct labour charges of $800, the company's overhead application rate is:

    a. 40%.

    b. 50%.

    c. 80%.

    d. 200%.

    e. Some other.

3.   In respect to direct labour costs, a company's beginning work in process inventory contained 20,000 units that were one-fifth complete. The next year's production included completion of these units, and another 90,000 units were started. Of those started, 60,000 were finished and the remaining 30,000 were left one-third complete. The equivalent finished units were:

    a. 60,000.

    b. 74,000.

    c. 76,000.

    d. 86,000.

    e. 96,000.

4.   The MAE Company's Overhead Costs account has a credit balance of $5,000 at year-end, which is a material amount. MAE also charged the following amounts of overhead to jobs during the period: $20,000 to jobs still in process, $60,000 to jobs completed but not sold, and $120,000 to jobs finished and sold. What entry should MAE make at year-end?

a. No entry.		
b. Overhead Costs	5,000	
Cost of Goods Sold		5,000
c. Overhead Costs	5,000	
Cost of Goods Sold		1,666
Goods in Process		1,667
Finished Goods		1,667
d. Overhead Costs	5,000	
Cost of Goods Sold		3,000
Goods in Process		500
Finished Goods		1,500
e. Cost of Goods Sold	3,000	
Goods in Process	500	
Finished Goods	1,500	
Overhead Costs		5,000

5.   Bee Bee Company, which uses a job cost system, incurred $80,000 of overhead and $100,000 of direct labour during the last period. Bee Bee estimates that its overhead next period will be $75,000. They also expect to incur $100,000 of direct labour. If Bee Bee bases their overhead applied on direct labour cost, their overhead application rate next period should be:

    a. 75%.

    b. 80%.

c. 107%.

d. 125%.

e. 133%.

6. X Company, which uses a job cost system, had accumulated labor time tickets totaling $24,600 for direct labour and $4,300 for indirect labour. These costs were charged to factory payroll as they were paid. Which entry should X make at the end of a cost period to dispose of the factory payroll balance?

a.	Payroll Expense	28,900	
	Cash		28,900
b.	Payroll Expense	24,600	
	Overhead Costs	4,300	
	Factory Payroll		28,900
c.	Goods in Process	24,600	
	Overhead Costs	4,300	
	Factory Payroll		28,900
d.	Goods in Process	24,600	
	Overhead Costs	4,300	
	Accrued Wages Payable		28,900
e.	Goods in Process	28,900	
	Factory Payroll		28,900

MINI DISCUSSION CASES

Case 22–1

Assume that the amount of underapplied overhead for the Able Company is material and that it is to be allocated to Cost of Goods Sold and the ending inventory. Also assume that the underapplied overhead was caused by inefficiencies in the manufacturing process.

Some accountants have said that by allocating these inefficiencies to the inventories, we are incorrectly increasing their balance sheet amount and misleading the readers of the financial statements.

Required:

Do you agree or disagree with the allocation of underapplied overheads to the inventory accounts? Why?

Case 22–2

The Small Boat Company manufactures nine-foot dinghies which are often used as tenders for larger yachts. The dinghies may be rowed or used as a small sailboat. The company manufactures only one type of fibreglass hull using a common mould for all of its boats. However, customers may order different kinds of fittings, colours, and trim, which essentially makes every dinghy unique.

The president of the company, George Small, has come to you to ask about the kind of cost accounting system he should use in his factory. He remembers seeing an article in a trade journal some time ago that described a "process job costing system."

Required:

a. Explain the two types of costing systems to Mr. Small.
b. Which costing system(s) would you recommend for the Small Boat Company? Why?

CLASS EXERCISES

Exercise 22–1   *Part 1.*   During December 198A, a cost accountant established his company's 198B overhead application rate based on direct labour cost. In setting the rate, he estimated the company would incur $200,000 of overhead costs during 198B and it would apply $160,000 of direct labour to the products that would be manufactured during 198B.

Required:

Determine the rate.

Part 2.   During February 198B, the company of Part 1 began and completed Job No. 619.

Required:

Determine the job's cost under the assumption that on its completeion the job's cost sheet showed the following materials and labour charged to it:

					JOB COST SHEET					
Customer's Name			Lowview Department				Job No.		619	
Job Description		24 Amp. Generator								

Date	Materials		Labour		Overhead Costs Applied		
	Requisition Number	Amount	Time Ticket Number	Amount	Date	Rate	Amount
Feb. 2	1524	68.00	2116	10.00			
3	1527	47.00	2117	20.00			
4	1531	10.00	2122	22.00			

Exercise 22–2   In December 198A, a cost accountant for Jason Company established the following overhead application rate for applying overhead to the jobs that would be completed during 198B:

$$\frac{\text{Estimated overhead costs, \$147,000}}{\text{Estimated direct labour costs, \$98,000}} = 150\%$$

At the end of 198B the company's accounting records showed that $149,000 of overhead costs had actually been incurred during 198B and $100,000 of direct labour, distributed as follows, had been applied to jobs during the year.

Direct labour on jobs completed and sold .... $ 85,000
Direct labour on jobs completed and in the finished goods
   inventory 10,000
Direct labour on jobs still in process 5,000
                                                                                $100,000

Required:

1. Set up an Overhead Costs T-account and enter on the proper sides the amounts of overhead costs incurred and applied. State whether overhead was overapplied or underapplied during the year.
2. Give the entry to close the Overhead Costs account and allocate its balance between jobs sold, jobs finished but unsold, and jobs in process.

Exercise 22–3

    Franklin Company uses a job cost system in which overhead is charged to jobs on the basis of direct labour cost. At the end of a year the company's Goods in Process account showed the following:

Goods in Process

Materials	85,000	To finished goods	205,500
Labour	60,000		
Overhead	75,000		

Required:

1. Determine the overhead application rate used by the company under the assumption that the labour and overhead costs actually incurred were the same as the amounts estimated.
2. Determine the cost of the labour and the cost of the overhead charged to the one job in process at the year-end under the assumption it had $5,500 of materials charged to it.

Exercise 22–4

    During a cost period a department finished and transferred 56,000 units of product to finished goods, of which 16,000 were in process in the department at the beginning of the cost period and 40,000 were begun and completed during the period. The 16,000 beginning inventory units were three-fourths completed when the period began. In addition to the 56,000 units completed, 12,000 more units were in process in the department, one-half completed when the period ended.

Required:

    Calculate the equivalent units of product completed in the department during the cost period.

Exercise 22–5

    Assume the department of Exercise 22–4 had $25,000 of labour charged to it during the cost period of the exercise and that labour is applied in the process of the department evenly throughout the process.

Required:

Calculate the cost of an equivalent unit of labour in the department and the portion of the department's $25,000 labour cost that should be assigned to each of its inventories and to the units started and finished.

Exercise 22–6   Forty-eight thousand units of product were completed in a department and transferred to finished goods during a cost period. Of these 48,000 units, 12,000 were in process and were one-third completed at the beginning of the period and 36,000 units were begun and completed during the period. In addition to the 48,000 units completed, 10,000 more units were in process in the department, three-fifths processed at the period end.

Required:

Calculate the equivalent units of material added to the product processed in the department during the period under each of the following unrelated assumptions: *(a)* All material added to the product of the department is added when the department's process is first begun. *(b)* The material added to the product of the department is added evenly throughout the department's process. *(c)* One half the material added in the department is added when the department's process is first begun and the other half is added when the process is three-fourths completed.

PROBLEMS

Problem 22–1   A cost accountant for Snell Company estimated before a year began that the company would incur during the year the direct labour cost of 10 persons working 2,000 hours each at an average rate of $13 per hour. The accountant also estimated that the following overhead costs would be incurred during the year:

Indirect labour	$ 25,750
Superintendence	22,000
Rent of factory building	28,800
Heat, light, and power	14,800
Insurance expense	6,600
Depreciation of machinery	24,200
Machinery repairs	3,000
Supplies expense	10,500
Miscellaneous factory expenses	7,350
Total	$143,000

At the end of the year for which the estimates were made the cost records showed the company had actually incurred $143,350 of overhead costs and had completed and sold five jobs which had direct labour costs as follows:

Job No. 603	$50,800
Job No. 604	46,400
Job No. 605	43,400
Job No. 606	45,600
Job No. 607	49,800

In addition Job No. 608 was in process at the period end and had had $22,500 of direct labour assigned.

Required:

Under the assumption the concern used a predetermined overhead application rate based on the foregoing overhead and direct labour estimates, determine:

1. The predetermined application rate used.
2. The total overhead applied to jobs during the year.
3. The over- or underapplied overhead at the year-end.
4. Under the further assumption that the company considered the amount of its over- or underapplied overhead to be material, give the entry to close the Overhead Costs account prorating it to the completed jobs and work in process.

Problem 22–2

A company completed the following internal and external transactions, among others, during a cost period:

a. Purchased materials on account, $16,000.
b. Paid factory wages, $12,400.
c. Paid miscellaneous factory overhead costs, $800.
d. Material requisitions were used during the cost period to charge materials to jobs. The requisitions were then accumulated until the end of the cost period when they were totaled and recorded with a general journal entry. (Instructions for this entry are given in Item *j.*) An abstract of the requisitions showed the following materials charged to jobs. (Charge the materials to the jobs by making entries directly in the job T-accounts in the subsidiary Job Cost Ledger.)

Job No. 1	$ 2,600
Job No. 2	1,300
Job No. 3	2,800
Job No. 4	3,000
Job No. 5	600
Total	$10,300

e. Labour time tickets were used to charge jobs with direct labour. The tickets were then accumulated until the end of the cost period when they were totaled and recorded with a general journal entry. (Instructions for the entry are given in Item *k.*) An abstract of the tickets showed the following labour charged to jobs. (Charge the labour to the jobs by making entries directly in the job T-accounts in the Job Cost Ledger.)

Job No. 1	$2,400
Job No. 2	1,400
Job No. 3	2,600
Job No. 4	2,800
Job No. 5	400
Total	$9,600

f.   Job Nos. 1, 3, and 4 were completed and transferred to finished goods. A predetermined overhead application rate, 150% of direct labour cost, was used to apply overhead to each job upon its completion. (Enter the overhead in the job T-accounts; mark the jobs "completed"; and make a general journal entry to transfer their costs to the Finished Goods account.)

g.   Job Nos. 1 and 3 were sold on account for a total of $24,000.

h.   At the end of the cost period charged overhead to the jobs in process at the rate of 150% of direct labour cost. (Enter the overhead in the job T-accounts.)

i.   At the end of the cost period made a general journal entry to record: depreciation, factory building, $2,300; depreciation, machinery, $4,100; expired factory insurance, $600; and accrued factory taxes payable, $1,200.

j.   Separated the material requisitions into direct material requisitions and indirect material requisitions, totaled each kind, and made a general journal entry to record them. The requisition totals were:

Direct materials	$10,300
Indirect materials	2,000
Total	$12,300

k.   Separated the labour time tickets into direct labour time tickets and indirect labour time tickets, totaled each kind, and made a general journal entry to record them. The time ticket totals were:

Direct labour	$ 9,600
Indirect labour	3,100
Total	$12,700

l.   Determined the total overhead assigned to all jobs and made a general journal entry to record it.

Required:

1.   Open the following general ledger T-accounts: Materials, Goods in Process, Finished Goods, Factory Payroll, Overhead Costs, and Cost of Goods Sold.

2.   Open an additional T-account for each of the five jobs. Assume that each job's T-account is a job cost sheet in a subsidiary Job Cost Ledger.

3.   Prepare general journal entries to record the applicable information of Items *a, b, c, f, g, i, j, k,* and *l.* Post the entry portions that affect the general ledger accounts opened.

4.   Enter the applicable information of Items *d, e, f,* and *h* directly in the T-accounts that represent job cost sheets.

5.   Present statistics to prove the balances of the Goods in Process and Finished Goods accounts.

6.   List the general ledger accounts and tell what is represented by the balance of each.

Problem 22–3   *If the working papers that accompany this text are not being used, omit this problem.*

Lakatos Company manufactures a machine called a dynatester to the special order of its customers. On January 1 the company had a $2,230 materials inventory but no inventories of goods in process and finished goods. However, on that date it began Job No. 1, a dynatester for Farsome Company, and Job No. 2, for Nearsome Company; and during the January cost period it completed the following summarized internal and external transactions:

a. Recorded invoices for the purchase of materials on credit. The invoices and receiving reports carried this information:
Receiving report No. 1, Material A, 200 units at $11 each.
Receiving report No. 2, Material B, 300 units at $5 each.
(Record the invoices with a single general journal entry and post to the general ledger T-accounts, using the transaction number to identify the amounts in the accounts. Enter the receiving report information on the proper materials ledger cards.)

b. Materials were requisitioned as follows:
Requisition No. 1, for Job No. 1, 100 units of Material A.
Requisition No. 2, for Job No. 1, 120 units of Material B.
Requisition No. 3, for Job No. 2, 80 units of Material A.
Requisition No. 4, for Job No. 2, 100 units of Material B.
Requisition No. 5, for 10 units of machinery lubricant.
(Enter the requisition amounts for direct materials on the materials ledger cards and on the job cost sheets. Enter the indirect material amount on the proper materials ledger card and debit it to the Indirect Materials account in the subsidiary Overhead Costs Ledger. Assume the requisitions are accumulated until the end of the month and will be recorded with a general journal entry. Instructions for this entry follow in the problem.)

c. Received the following labour time tickets from the timekeeping department:
Time tickets Nos. 1 through 60 for direct labour on Job No. 1, $1,000.
Time tickets Nos. 61 through 100 for direct labour on Job No. 2, $800.
Time tickets Nos. 101 through 120 for machinery repairs, $375.
(Charge the direct labour time tickets to the proper jobs and charge the indirect labour time tickets to the Indirect Labour account in the subsidiary Overhead Costs Ledger. Assume the time tickets are accumulated until the end of the month for recording with a general journal entry.)

d. Made the following cash disbursements during the month:
Paid the month's factory payroll, $2,100.
Paid for miscellaneous overhead items totaling $1,000.
(Record the payments with general journal entries and post the general ledger accounts. Enter the charge for miscellaneous overhead items in the subsidiary Overhead Costs Ledger.)

e. Finished Job No. 1 and transferred it to the finished goods warehouse.
(The company charges overhead to each job by means of a predetermined overhead application rate based on direct labour costs. The rate is 80%. (1) Enter the overhead charge on the cost sheet of Job No. 1. (2) Complete the cost summary section of the cost sheet. (3) Mark "Finished" on the cost sheet. (4) Prepare and post a general journal entry to record the job's completion and transfer to finished goods.)

f. Prepared and posted a general journal entry to record both the cost of goods sold and the sale of Job No. 1 to Farsome Company, sale price $5,000.

g. At the end of the cost period, charged overhead to Job No. 2 based on the amount of direct labour applied to the job thus far. *(Enter the applicable amount of overhead on the job's cost sheet.)*

h. Totaled the requisitions for direct materials, totaled the requisitions for indirect materials, and made and posted a general journal entry to record them.

i. Totaled the direct labour time tickets, totaled the indirect labour time tickets, and made and posted a general journal entry to record them.

j. Determined the amount of overhead applied to jobs, and made and posted a general journal entry to record it.

Required:

1. Record the transactions as instructed in the narrative.
2. Complete the statements in the book of working papers by filling in the blanks.

Problem 22–4

In the sanding department of a processing concern, labour is added to the department's product evenly throughout its processing. During a cost period 50,000 units of product were finished in this department and transferred to finished goods. Of these 50,000 units, 15,000 were in process at the beginning of the period and 35,000 were begun and completed during the period. The 15,000 beginning goods in process units were one-fifth completed when the period began. In addition to the foregoing units, 9,000 additional units were in process and were one-third completed at the period end.

Required:

Under the assumption that $13,800 of labour was charged to the sanding department during the period, determine (1) the equivalent units of labour applied to the department's product, (2) the cost of an equivalent unit of labour, and (3) the shares of the $13,800 that should be charged to the beginning inventory, the units started and finished, and the ending inventory.

Problem 22–5

The product of Rosewell Manufacturing Company is produced on a continuous basis in a single processing department in which material, labour, and overhead are added to the product evenly throughout the manufacturing process.

At the end of the current May cost period, after the material, labour, and overhead costs were charged to the Goods in Process account of the single processing department, the account appeared as follows:

Goods in Process

May	1	Balance	1,362	
	31	Materials	5,325	
	31	Labour	10,863	
	31	Overhead	15,194	
			32,744	

During the cost period the company finished and transferred to finished goods 72,000 units of the product, of which 9,000 were in process at the beginning of the period and 63,000 were begun and finished during the period. The 9,000 that were in process were one-third processed when the period began. In addition to the foregoing units, 8,000 additional units were in process and were one-fourth completed at the end of the cost period.

Required:

1. Prepare a process cost summary for the department.
2. Draft the general journal entry to transfer to Finished Goods the cost of the product finished in the department during the month.

Problem 22–6

Easytime Processing Company manufactures a simple product on a continuous basis in one department. All materials are added in the manufacturing process of this product when the process is first begun. Labour and overhead are added evenly throughout the process.

During the current April cost period the company completed and transferred to finished goods 43,000 units of the product. These consisted of 5,000 units that were in process at the beginning of the period and 38,000 units begun and finished during the period. The 5,000 beginning goods in process units were complete as to materials and four-fifths complete as to labor and overhead when the period began. In addition to the foregoing units, 6,000 additional units were in process at the end of the period, complete as to materials and one-half complete as to labour and overhead.

Since the company has only one processing department, it has only one Goods in Process account. At the end of the period, after entries recording material, labour, and overhead had been posted, the account appeared as follows:

Goods in Process

Apr. 1	Balance	5,333
30	Materials	27,060
30	Labour	9,744
30	Overhead	14,868
		57,005

Required:

Prepare a process cost summary and the entry to transfer to Finished Goods the cost of the product completed in the department during April.

ALTERNATE PROBLEMS

Problem
22–1A

Late in 19A a cost accountant for Breton Company established the 19B overhead application rate for the paint department by estimating that the company would assign three persons to direct labour tasks during 19B and that each person would work 2,000 hours at $10 per hour during the year. At the same time the accountant estimated that the department would incur the following amounts of overhead costs during 19B:

Indirect labour	$20,000
Factory building rent........................	12,000
Depreciation expense, machinery	15,000
Machinery repairs expense	3,000
Heat, light, and power	6,000
Factory supplies expense	1,000
Total	$57,000

At the end of 19B the accounting records showed the department had actually incurred $58,560 of overhead costs during the year while completing four jobs and beginning the fifth. The completed jobs were assigned overhead on completion, and the in-process job was assigned overhead at the year-end. The jobs had the following direct labour costs:

Job No. 1 (sold and delivered)	$12,800
Job No. 2 (sold and delivered)	13,000
Job No. 3 (sold and delivered)	14,200
Job No. 4 (in finished goods inventory)	14,000
Job No. 5 (in process, unfinished)	7,000
Total	$61,000

Required:

1. Determine the overhead application rate established by the cost accountant under the assumption that it was based on direct labour cost.
2. Determine the total overhead applied to jobs during the year and the amount of over- or underapplied overhead at the year-end.
3. Give the entry to dispose of the over- or underapplied overhead by prorating it between goods in process, the finished goods inventory, and cost of goods sold.

Problem 22–2A

During its first cost period a company completed the following internal and external transactions:

a. Purchased materials on account, $22,000.
b. Paid factory wages, $18,800.
c. Paid miscellaneous factory overhead costs, $3,000.
d. Material requisitions were used during the cost period to charge materials to jobs. The requisitions were then accumulated until the end of the cost period when they were totaled and recorded with a general journal entry. (Instructions for the entry are given in Item *j.*) An abstract of the requisitions showed the following materials charged to jobs. (Charge the materials to the jobs by making entries directly in the job T-accounts in the subsidiary Job Cost Ledger.)

Job No. 1	$ 4,000
Job No. 2	2,100
Job No. 3	3,900
Job No. 4	4,300
Job No. 5	800
Total..........	$15,100

e. Labour time tickets were used to charge jobs with direct labour. The tickets were then accumulated until the end of the cost period when they were totaled and recorded with a general journal entry. (Instructions for the entry are given as Item *k*.) An abstract of the tickets showed the following labour charged to jobs. (Charge the labour to the jobs by making entries directly in the job T-accounts in the Job Cost Ledger.)

Job No. 1	$ 3,800
Job No. 2	2,200
Job No. 3	4,000
Job No. 4	3,600
Job No. 5	400
Total	$14,000

f. Job Nos. 1, 3, and 4 were completed and transferred to finished goods. A predetermined overhead application rate, 200% of direct labour cost, was using the 200% of direct labour cost application rate. (Enter the overhead head in the job T-accounts; mark the jobs "completed"; and make a general journal entry to transfer their costs to the Finished Goods account.)

g. Job Nos. 1 and 4 were sold on account for a total of $40,000.

h. At the end of the cost period, charged overhead to the jobs in process, using the 200% of direct labour cost application rate. (Enter the overhead in the job T-accounts.)

i. Made a general journal entry at the end of the cost period to record depreciation on the factory building, $6,000; machinery depreciation, $6,700; expired factory insurance, $1,200; and accrued factory taxes payable, $2,000.

j. Separated the material requisitions into direct and indirect material requisitions, totaled each kind, and made a general journal entry to record them. The requisition totals were:

Direct materials	$15,100
Indirect materials	4,000
Total	$19,100

k. Separated the labour time tickets into direct and indirect labour time tickets, totaled each kind, and made a general journal entry to record them. The time ticket totals were:

Direct labour	$14,000
Indirect labour	5,000
Total	$19,000

l. Determined the total overhead assigned to all jobs and made a general journal entry to record it.

Required:

1. Open the following general ledger T-accounts: Materials, Goods in Process, Finished Goods, Factory Payroll, Overhead Costs, and Cost of Goods Sold.
2. Open an additional T-account for each of the five jobs. Assume that each job's T-account is a job cost sheet in a subsidiary Job Cost Ledger.
3. Prepare general journal entries to record the applicable information of Items

a, b, c, f, g, i, j, k, and *l.* Post the entry portions that affect the general ledger accounts opened.

4. Enter the applicable information of Items *d, e, f,* and *h* directly in the T-accounts that represent job cost sheets.

5. Present statistics to prove the balances of the Goods in Process and Finished Goods accounts.

6. List the general ledger accounts and tell what is represented by the balance of each.

Problem 22–3A

(If the working papers that accompany this text are not being used, omit this problem.)

Conestoga Company manufactures a machine called a formhose to the special order of its customers. On April 1 of the current year the company had a $5,320 materials inventory but no inventories of goods in process or finished goods. However, on that date it began Job No. 1, a formhose for Big Company, and Job No. 2, a formhose for Little Company; and during April it completed the following summarized internal and external transactions:

a. Recorded invoices for the purchase on credit of 420 units of Material R and 40 units of Material S. The invoices and receiving reports carried this information:

Receiving Report No. 1, Raw Material R 420 units at $7 each.
Receiving Report No. 2, Raw Material S 40 units at $12 each.

(Record the invoices with a single journal entry and post to the general ledger T-accounts, using the transaction numbers to identify the amounts in the accounts. Enter the receiving report information on the proper materials ledger cards.)

b. Requisitioned materials as follows:

Requisition No. 1, for Job No. 1 . . . .   200 units of Material R
Requisition No. 2, for Job No. 1 . . . .   55 units of Material S
Requisition No. 3, for Job No. 2 . . . .   165 units of material R
Requisition No. 4, for Job No. 2 . . . .   45 units of Material S
Requisition No. 5, for 20 units of machinery lubricant.

(Enter the requisition amounts for direct materials on the materials ledger cards and on the job cost sheets. Enter the indirect material amount on the proper materials ledger card and debit it to the Indirect Materials account in the subsidiary Overhead Costs Ledger. Assume that the requisitions are accumulated until the end of the month and will be recorded with a general journal entry. Instructions for this entry follow in the problem.)

c. Received time tickets from the timekeeping department as follows:
Time tickets Nos. 1 through 60 for direct labour on Job No. 1, $2,000.
Time tickets Nos. 61 through 100 for direct labour on Job No. 2, $1,600.
Time tickets Nos. 101 through 120 for machinery repairs, $350.

(Charge the direct labour tickets to the proper jobs and charge the indirect labour time tickets to the Indirect Labour account in the Subsidiary Overhead

Costs Ledger. Assume the time tickets are accumulated until the end of the month for recording with a general journal entry.)

d. Made the following cash disbursements during the month:

Paid factory payrolls totaling $4,000.

Paid for miscellaneous overhead items totaling $1,900.

(Record the payments with general journal entries and post to the general ledger accounts. Enter the charge for miscellaneous overhead items in the Subsidiary Overhead Costs Ledger.)

e. Finished Job No. 1 and transferred it to the finished goods warehouse. *(The company charges overhead to each job by means of a predetermined overhead application rate based on direct labour costs. The rate is 75%. (1) Enter the overhead charge on the cost sheet. (2) Complete the cost summary section of the cost sheet. (3) Mark "Finished" on the cost sheet. (4) Prepare and post a general journal entry to record completion of the job and its transfer to finished goods.)*

f. Prepared and posted a general journal entry to record both the cost of goods sold and the sale of Job No. 1 to Big Company for $6,200.

g. At the end of the cost period, charged overhead to Job No. 2 based on the amount of direct labour applied to the job thus far. *(Enter the applicable amount of overhead on the job's cost sheet.)*

h. Totaled the requisitions for direct materials, totaled the requisitions for indirect materials, and made and posted a general journal entry to record them.

i. Totaled the direct labour time tickets, totaled the indirect labour time tickets, and made and posted a general journal entry to record them.

j. Determined the amount of overhead applied to jobs and made and posted a general journal entry to record it.

Required:

1. Record the transactions as instructed in the italicized narrative.
2. Complete the statements in the book of working papes by filling in the blanks.

Problem
22–4A

The Harris Machine Shop is a one-department operation in which labour and overhead are added to the department's product evenly throughout the production process. In July, 42,000 units of product were transferred from the shop to finished goods inventory. Included in these 42,000 units were 16,000 units from the June 30 work in process inventory, at which time those units were one-fourth finished. In addition to the beginning inventory, 54,000 units were placed in process during July. On July 31, the units that remained in process were one-half complete. Total overhead costs of the shop incurred during July were $93,600.

Required:

Determine (1) the equivalent units of production in July to be used in applying overhead costs to the product of the shop, (2) the overhead cost of an equivalent unit of production, and (3) the portions of July overhead cost that should be charged to completing the units in beginning inventory, to units started and finished during July, and to the ending inventory.

Two operations, cutting and molding, and two departments are used in the manufacturing procedure of Gorge Manufacturing Company. The procedure is begun in the cutting department and completed in the molding department.

At the beginning of the May cost period there were 5,000 units of product in the cutting department that were three-fifths processed. These units were completed during the period and transferred to the molding department. The processing of 31,000 additional units was also begun in the cutting department during the period. Of these 31,000 units, 23,000 were finished and transferred to the molding department. The remaining 8,000 units were in the department in a one-half processed state at the end of the period.

It is assumed that the material, labour, and overhead in the cutting department are applied evenly throughout the process of the department.

At the end of the cost period, after entries recording materials, labour, and overhead were posted, the company's Goods in Process, Cutting Department account appeared as follows:

Goods in Process, Cutting Departmant

May 1	Balance	2,901
31	Materials	9,280
31	Labour	12,209
31	Overhead	6,090
		30,480

Required:

1. Prepare a process cost summary for the cutting department.
2. Prepare the journal entry to transfer to the molding department the cost of the goods completed in the cutting department and transferred.

The product of Meridian Company is manufactured in one continuous process in which all materials are entered into production at the beginning of the process. Labour and overhead are applied evenly throughout the process. Meridian Company's Goods in Process account reflects the following charges during the month of October:

Beginning balance.....................	$ 7,200
Materials added to production	42,294
Labour charged to production	33,948
Overhead charged to production	50,922

During October the company completed the manufacture of 15,000 units of product. These included 2,400 units that had entered production the previous month and on October 1 were complete as to materials and two-thirds complete as to labour and overhead. At the end of October 3,400 units remained in process, completed as to materials and one-half complete as to labour and overhead.

Required:

Prepare a process cost summary and the general journal entry to transfer to Finished Goods the cost of the product completed during October.

PROVOCATIVE PROBLEMS

Provocative
Problem 22–1,
Rayford
Processing

Rayford Processing Company uses a job order cost system in accounting for manufacturing costs, and following are a number of its general ledger accounts with the January 1 balances and some January postings shown. The postings are incomplete. Commonly only the debit or credit of a journal entry appears in the accounts, with the offsetting debits and credits being omitted. Also, the amounts shown represent total postings for the month and no date appears. However, this additional information is available: (1) the company charges jobs with overhead on the basis of direct labour cost, using a 150% overhead application rate. (2) The $17,000 debit in the Overhead Costs account represents the sum of all overhead costs for January other than indirect materials and indirect labour. (3) The accrued factory payroll on January 31 was $3,000.

Materials

Jan. 1 Bal.	11,000	12,000
	15,000	

Factory Payroll

19,000	Jan. 1 Bal.	2,000

Goods in Process

Jan. 1 Bal.	6,000	48,000
Materials	10,000	
Labour	16,000	

Cost of Goods Sold

Finished Goods

Jan. 1 Bal.	12,000	50,000

Factory Overhead Costs

17,000	

Copy the accounts on a sheet of paper, supply the missing debits and credits, and tie together the debits and credits of an entry with key letters. Answer these questions: (1) What was the January 31 balance of the Finished Goods account? (2) How many dollars of factory labour cost (direct plus indirect) were incurred during January? (3) What was the cost of the goods sold during January? (4) How much overhead was actually incurred during the month? (5) How much overhead was charged to jobs during the month? (6) Was overhead overapplied or underapplied during the month?

Provocative
Problem 22–2,
The Browning
Company

The production facility of the Browning Company was nearly destroyed on June 10, 19B, as a consequence of an explosion and fire in the plant. Assets lost in the blaze included all of the inventories. In addition, many of the accounting records were destroyed. In preparation for settlement with the insurance company, you are requested to estimate the amounts of raw materials, goods in process, and finished goods destroyed. Through your investigation, you determined that the company used a job order cost system, and also obtained the following additional information:

a. The company's December 31, 19A, balance sheet showed the following inventory amounts: materials, $15,000; goods in process, $21,000; and finished goods, $24,000. The balance sheet also showed a $3,000 liability for accrued factory wages payable.

b. The overhead application rate used by the company was 70% of direct labour cost.

c. Goods costing $81,000 were sold and delivered to customers between January 1 and June 10, 19B.

d. Materials purchased between January 1 and June 10 amounted to $31,000, and $27,000 of direct and indirect materials were issued to the factory during the same period.

e. Factory wages totaling $35,000 were paid between January 1 and June 10, and there were $1,000 of accrued factory wages payable on the latter date.

f. The debits to the Overhead Costs account during the period before the fire totaled $21,000 of which $3,000 was for indirect materials and $5,000 was for indirect labor.

g. The cost of goods finished and transferred to finished goods inventory during the January 1 to June 10 period amounted to $76,000.

h. It was decided that the June 10 balance of the Overhead Costs account should be apportioned between goods in process, finished goods, and cost of goods sold. Between January 1 and June 10 the company had charged the following amounts of overhead to jobs: to jobs sold, $12,740; to jobs finished but unsold, $3,920; and to jobs still in process on June 10, $2,940.

Determine the June 10 inventories of materials, goods in process, and finished goods. (T-accounts may be helpful in organizing the data.)

Provocative
Problem 22–3,
White
Company

The processing department of White Company began January 19A with 20,000 units in the Goods in Process inventory, each of which was 40 percent complete. During January, an additional 24,000 units were entered into the production process.

A total of 210,000 units were completed and transferred to finished goods.

Required:

If January's equivalent units of production amounted to 212,000 units, how many units remained in process at the end of the month, and what was their average stage of completion?

ANALYTICAL AND REVIEW PROBLEM

Problem 22–1
A&R

Handy Tool Company manufactures a single product, a tool that it sells to distributors who in turn sell it to hardware stores. The company uses a job cost system to accumulate costs on job lots of tools. During the past several years it has sold an average of 30,000 of the tools annually at $20 each, using about 80% of its production capacity. Next year's estimated costs for manufacturing the tool, assuming 30,000 units are produced, are $14 per unit and consist of the following:

Materials	$ 4.00
Direct labour	4.00
Manufacturing overhead (150% of direct labour cost)	6.00
Estimated cost per unit	$14.00

The company's overhead application rate was established at 150% two years ago by the accountant who set up its cost system. The same rate was used again last year and proved satisfactory, since sales volume and costs did not materially vary from the previous year. The company had planned to use the 150% rate again next year, and it had estimated next year's overhead costs at $180,000 and direct labour costs for 30,000 units at $120,000. However, although the company's volume and costs have been stable in the recent past, this morning it received an offer from a mail-order company to purchase 6,000 units of its tool at $12.50 each with the mail-order company's name attached. No changes in the tool are required to fit it to the mail-order company's specifications other than affixing the company's name, which will cost 25 cents per unit for additional materials.

The company president can see no point in accepting the order, for, as he says, "Why manufacture and sell something when you lose money on every unit sold?" The sales manager is not sure the new business should be rejected, and he has asked that a further study of costs be made before a final decision is reached.

You have been asked to make the cost study. In your investigation you find that next year's estimated manufacturing overhead consists of $150,000 of what is known as fixed overhead costs plus variable overhead costs of $1 per unit for 30,000 units, which together total $180,000. (Fixed overhead costs are such costs as depreciation of factory building, taxes, insurance, and the like. They receive their name from the fact that their total amounts do not change with a change in the number of units produced but remain fixed. Variable overhead costs are costs that vary with the number of units produced and are for such things as power and indirect materials.)

You also find that selling and administrative expenses consist of $100,000 of fixed expenses plus 50 cents per unit of variable selling and administrative expenses. Acceptance of the mail-order business will not affect fixed costs nor change present variable costs per unit, including material and direct labour costs per unit.

Attach to your report a condensed columnar income statement that shows the revenue, costs, and before-tax income from present business in its first two columns; the revenue, costs, and before-tax income from the new business in the second columns; and the combined results of present and the new business in the third set of columns. In preparing the statement, show as separate amounts the material, direct labour, fixed overhead, variable overhead, fixed selling and administrative, and variable selling and administrative costs for the present business, for the new business, and for the combined businesses.

Accounting for the Segments and Departments of a Business; Responsibility Accounting

23

After studying Chapter 23, you should be able to:

Describe the segmental information disclosed in the financial reports of large companies having operations in several lines of business.

List the four basic issues faced by accountants in developing segmental information.

State the reasons for departmentalization of business.

Describe the types of expenses that should be allocated among departments, the bases for allocating such expenses, and the procedures involved in the allocation process.

Explain the differences between reports designed to measure the profitability of a department and reports that are used to evaluate the performance of a department's margin.

Describe the problems associated with allocation of joint costs between departments.

Define or explain the words and phrases listed in the chapter Glossary.

In previous chapters, attention was focused on understanding financial statements and related accounting information for a **whole** business. This chapter shifts the attention to accounting for the parts, or subunits, of a business. This is normally called **segmental reporting** or **departmental accounting.** Information on the subunits of a business may be useful to (1) outsiders generally interested to an overall evaluation of the business and (2) internal managers responsible for planning and controlling the operations of the business.

The term *segmental reporting* is used most often in reference to published information for the use of outsiders; this information generally relates to a company's operations in different industries or geographical areas. Usually, the term *departmental accounting* relates to information on the subunits of a business that is prepared for the use of internal managers.

REPORTING ON BROAD BUSINESS SEGMENTS

When a company is large and has operations in more than one type of business, outsiders may gain a better understanding of the overall business by examining information on each segment. For example, Illustration 23–1 shows segmental information provided in the annual report of Denison Mines Limited.

SEGMENTAL INFORMATION TO BE DISCLOSED. In Illustration 23–1, observe that the activities of the business are grouped into three major segments: (1) Mining, (2) Oil and gas, and (3) Cement. The company also provides information on geographic grouping: Canada, Europe, and the rest of the world. Note that five different items of information are presented for each segment. They are as follows:

1. Revenues.
2. Operating profits (before interest and taxes).
3. Identifiable assets.
4. Capital expenditures.
5. Depreciation, depletion, and amortization expense.

Large firms that operate in more than one industry are required to disclose these items of information on each industrial segment of the business. In addition, they may be required to report (1) a geographical distribution of sales and (2) sales to major customers. Additional examples of reported segmental information are shown in the Appendix at the end of the book.

Four Basic Issues in Segmental Reporting

Companies face four basic problems in developing segmental information. Detailed guidelines for dealing with these problems are provided

Illustration 23–1

DENISON MINES LIMITED
Notes to Consolidated Financial Statements
For the Year Ended December 31, 1985

12. Segmented Information (in thousands)

Operations are in the following industries:

Mining—primarily involves mining, milling, and sale of uranium oxide, together with exploration and development of coal, potash, uranium, and other types of minerals.

Oil and Gas—exploration, development, production, and sale of oil, natural gas, condensates, and sulphue.

Cement—manufacture and sale of cement, ready-mix concrete, and concrete products

Industry data

	Mining		Oil & gas		Cement		Total	
	1985	1984	1985	1984	1985	1984	1985	1984
Revenue	$245,913	$ 246,285	$307,627	$308,700	$183,068	$147,797	$ 736,608	$ 702,782
Operating profit	63,236*	69,189*	135,201	109,935	26,836	16,635	225,273	195,759
Identifiable assets:								
Held for or under development	380,918†	299,756†	258,322	175,740	—	—	639,240	475,496
Producing assets	447,678	464,489	422,759	549,540	134,160	122,619	1,004,597	1,136,648
	828,596	764,245	681,081	725,280	134,160	122,619	1,643,837	1,612,144
Corporate assets‡							80,246	352,427
Total assets							$1,724,083	$1,964,571
Capital expenditures	110,301	99,044	106,726	43,572	8,856	4,794		
Depreciation, depletion and amortization	23,840	23,155	101,776	117,597	6,469	6,137		

Geographic data

	Canada		Europe		Rest of world		Total	
	1985	1984	1985	1984	1985	1984	1985	1984
Revenue	$416,869	$ 382,384	$275,048	$272,188	$ 44,691	$ 48,210	$ 736,608	$ 702,782
Operating profit (loss)	101,008	98,377	123,052	123,273	1,213	(25,891)	225,273	195,759
Identifiable assets	977,001	1,164,289	523,104	622,979	223,978	177,303	1,724,083	1,964,571
Export sales							176,795	182,839

* Includes profit on management fees from projects proportionately consolidated and management fees from projects and operations accounted for by the equity method referred to in note 11.

† Includes total assets of $246,060 (1984—$156,497) in connection with Denison-Potacan Potash Company.

‡ Includes investment in Quintette Coal Limited referred to in note 4(c).

by the *CICA Handbook*. While the study of these guidelines is too detailed for inclusion at this introductory level, students should be aware of each basic issue.

IDENTIFYING SIGNIFICANT SEGMENTS.   The operations of a business may not be neatly organized in terms of segments that are important to financial statement readers. For purposes of segmental reporting, the business must be divided into enough segments to show the basic industries in which the business operates. On the other hand, it should not be divided into so many segments that the information becomes confusing.

TRANSFER PRICING BETWEEN SEGMENTS.   Sometimes one or more segments of a business make sales of products or services to the other segments. These sales are eliminated when the overall statements for the business are prepared. However, sales between segments should not be eliminated when evaluating the performance of each segment. Sales between segments result in revenues to the selling segment and costs to the purchasing segment. The problem is to determine a fair price at which to report such sales, so that the profitability of both the selling segment and the purchasing segment are fairly measured.

MEASURING SEGMENTAL PROFITABILITY.   Even if each segment operates as a highly independent unit, some expenses of the business will benefit more than one segment. Some of these common expenses can be allocated to the segments on a reasonable basis. Others may defy meaningful allocation. The accountant must first decide which expenses are to be allocated and which are to be left unallocated when measuring the profitability of each segment. For those expenses to be allocated, the accountant must then determine the most reasonable basis for allocation.

IDENTIFYING SEGMENTAL ASSETS.   Many assets are easily identified with specific segments because they are used solely by one segment or another. Other assets are shared by more than one segment. The accountant must determine reasonable bases for allocating shared assets to the segments that benefit from the assets.

DEPARTMENTAL ACCOUNTING

The previous discussion of segmental reporting was concerned primarily with large businesses that have operations in more than one industry. However, students should not presume that accounting for the subunits of a business is limited to large companies with diverse operations. Businesses are divided into subunits or departments whenever they become too large to be effectively managed as a single unit. Accounting for the departments of a business is characterized by two primary goals. One goal is to provide information that management can use in evaluating the profitability or cost effectiveness of each department. The second goal is to assign costs and expenses to the particular managers who are responsible for controlling those costs and expenses. In this way, the performance of managers can be evaluated in terms of their responsibilities. Thus, departmental accounting is closely related to what is called *responsibility accounting*.

DEPARTMENTALIZING A BUSINESS

Most businesses are large and complex enough to require that they be divided into subunits or departments. When a business is departmentalized, a manager is usually placed in charge of each department. If the business grows even larger, each department may be further divided into smaller segments. Thus, a particular manager can be assigned responsibilities over the activities of a unit that is not too large for the manager to effectively oversee and control. Also, departments can be organized so that the specialized skills of each manager can be used most effectively.

BASIS FOR DEPARTMENTALIZATION

In a departmentalized business there are two basic kinds of departments, *productive departments* and *service departments*. In a factory, the productive departments are those engaged directly in manufacturing operations. In a store, they are the departments making sales. Departmental divisions in a factory are commonly based on manufacturing processes employed or products or components manufactured. The divisions in a store are usually based on kinds of goods sold, with each selling or productive department being assigned the sale of one or more kinds of merchandise. In either type of business, the service departments such as the general office, advertising, purchasing, payroll, and personnel departments assist or perform services for the productive departments.

INFORMATION TO EVALUATE DEPARTMENTS

When a business is divided into departments, management must be able to know how well each department is performing. Thus, it is necessary for the accounting system to supply information by departments as to resources expended and outputs achieved. This requires that revenue and expense information be measured and accumulated by departments. However, before going further it should be observed that such information is generally not made public, since it might be of considerable benefit to competitors. Rather, it is for the use of management in controlling operations, appraising performances, allocating resources, and in taking remedial actions. For example, if one of several departments is particularly profitable, perhaps it should be expanded. Or, if a department is showing poor results, information as to its revenues, costs, and expenses may point to a proper remedial action.

The information used to evaluate a department depends on whether the department is a *cost centre* or a *profit centre*. A cost centre is a unit of the business that incurs costs (or expenses) but does not directly generate revenues. The productive departments of a factory and such service departments as the general office, advertising, and purchasing departments are cost centres. A profit centre differs from a cost centre in that it not only incurs costs but also generates revenues. The selling departments of a store are profit centres. Managers of cost centres are judged on their ability to control costs and keep costs within a satisfactory range. Managers of profit centres, on the other hand, are judged on their ability to generate earnings, which are the excess of revenues over costs.

SECURING DEPARTMENTAL INFORMATION

Modern cash registers enable a merchandising concern to accumulate information relating to sales and sales returns of each department. Often the registers transfer the information directly into the store's computer. This kind of system is capable of much more than accumulating sales information by departments. The cash registers will print all pertinent information on the sales ticket given to the customer, total the ticket, and initiate entries to record credit sales in the customer's account. Also, if the type of goods sold is keyed into the registers by means of code numbers, the computer can daily print out detailed departmental summaries of goods sold and item inventories of unsold goods.

Cash registers also enable a small store to determine daily totals for sales and sales returns by departments. However, since the registers often are not connected to a computer, the totals must be accumulated by some other method. Two methods are commonly used. A small store may provide separate Sales and Sales Returns accounts in its ledger for each of its departments, or it may use analysis sheets. Either method may also be used to accumulate information as to purchases and purchases returns by departments.

If a store chooses to provide separate Sales, Sales Returns, Purchases, and Purchases Returns accounts in its ledger for each of its departments, it may also provide columns in its journals to record transactions by departments. Illustration 23–2 shows such a journal for recording sales by departments. The amounts to be debited to the customers' accounts are entered in the Accounts Receivable Debit column and are posted to these accounts each day. The column's total is debited to the Accounts Receivable controlling account at the end of the month. The departmental

Illustration 23–2

					Sales Journal			
						Department Sales		
Date		Account Debited	Invoice Number	P R	Accounts Receivable Debit	Dept. 1 Credit	Dept. 2 Credit	Dept. 3 Credit
Oct.	1	Walter Marshfield ...	737		145.00	90.00	55.00	.....
	1	Thomas Higgins	738		85.00	.....	40.00	45.00

sales are entered in the last three columns and are posted as column totals at the end of the month.

Separate departmental accounts are practical only for a store having a limited number of departments. In a store having more than a few departments, a more practical procedure is to use departmental sales analysis sheets.

When a store uses departmental sales analysis sheets, it provides only one undepartmentalized general ledger account for sales, another account for sales returns, another for purchases, and another for purchases returns; and it records its transactions and posts to these accounts as though it were not departmentalized. In addition to this, each day it also summarizes its transactions by departments and enters the summarized amounts on analysis sheets. For example, a concern using analysis sheets, in addition to recording sales in its usual manner, will total each day's sales by departments and enter the daily totals on a sales analysis sheet like Illustration 23–3. As a result, at the end of a month or other period,

Illustration 23–3

			Departmental Sales Analysis Sheet			
Date		Men's Wear Dept.	Boys' Wear Dept.	Shoe Dept.	Leather Goods Dept.	Women's Wear Dept.
May	1	$357.15	$175.06	$115.00	$ 75.25	$427.18
	2	298.55	136.27	145.80	110.20	387.27

the column totals of the analysis sheet show sales by departments, and the grand total of all the columns should equal the balance of the Sales account.

When a store uses departmental analysis sheets, it uses one analysis sheet to accumulate sales figures, another for sales returns, another for purchases, and still another for purchases returns. At the end of the period the several analysis sheets show the store's sales, sales returns, purchases, and purchases returns by departments. If the store then takes inventories by departments, it can calculate gross profits by departments.

Accumulating information and arriving at a gross profit figure for each selling department in a departmentalized business is not too difficult as the discussion thus far reveals. However, to go beyond this and arrive at useful departmental net income figures is not so easy. As a result, many concerns make no effort to calculate more than gross profits by departments.

ALLOCATING EXPENSES

If a business attempts to measure not only departmental gross profit but also departmental net income, special problems are confronted. They involve dividing the expenses of the business among the selling departments of the business. Some expenses, called *direct expenses,* are easily traced to specific departments. The direct expenses of a department are easily traced to the department because they are incurred for the sole benefit of that department. For example, the salary of an employee who works in only one department is a direct expense of that department.

The expenses of a business include both direct expenses and *indirect expenses.* Indirect expenses are incurred for the joint benefit of more than one department. For example, where two or more departments share a single building, the expenses of renting, heating, and lighting the building jointly benefit all of the departments in the building. Although such indirect expenses cannot be easily traced to a specific department, they must be allocated among the departments which benefited from the expenses. Each indirect expense should be allocated on a basis that fairly approximates the relative benefit received by each department. However, measuring the benefit each department receives from an indirect expense is often difficult. Even after a reasonable allocation basis is chosen, considerable doubt often exists regarding the proper share to be charged to each department.

To illustrate the allocation of an indirect expense, assume that a jewelry store purchases janitorial services from an outside firm. The jewelry store then allocates the cost among its three departments according to the floor space occupied. The cost of janitorial services for a short period is $280, and the amounts of floor space occupied are:

Jewelry department . . . . 250 sq.m.
Watch repair department 125
China and silver department 500
Total . . . . 875 sq.m.

The calculations to allocate janitorial expense to the departments are:

Jewelry department: $\dfrac{250}{875} \times \$280 = \$80$

Watch repair department: $\dfrac{125}{875} \times \$280 = \$40$

China and silver department: $\dfrac{500}{875} \times \$280 = \$160$

Students should note that the concepts of "direct" costs or expenses and "indirect" costs or expenses can be usefully applied in a variety of situations in addition to departmental accounting. In general, direct costs are easily traced to or associated with a "cost object." In this chapter, the cost object of significance is the department. However, other cost objects may also be of interest. For example, recall that the discussion of Chapters 21 and 22 dealt with manufacturing companies. In that context, the cost object was a unit or batch of product. Direct costs were recognized to be those that can be easily identified with a unit of product. Other costs which are essential to the manufacturing process but which cannot be easily traced to specific units of product were called indirect costs.

BASES FOR ALLOCATING EXPENSES

In the following paragraphs, bases for allocating some common indirect expenses are discussed. In the discussions, no hard-and-fast rules are given because several factors are often involved in an expense allocation and the relative importance of the factors varies from situation to situation. As previously stated, indirect expenses are, by definition, subject to doubt as to how they should be allocated between departments. Judgment rather than hard-and-fast rules is required, and different accountants may not agree on the proper basis for allocating an indirect expense.

Wages and Salaries

An employee's wages may be either a direct or an indirect expense. If an employee's time is spent all in one department, the employee's wages are a direct expense of the benefited department; but if an employee works in more than one department, the wages become an indirect expense to be allocated between or among the benefited departments. Normally, working time spent in each department is a fair basis for allocating wages.

A supervisory employee may supervise more than one department, and in such cases the time spent in each department is usually a fair basis for allocating his or her salary. However, since a supervisory employee is frequently on the move from department to department, the time spent in each is often difficult to measure. Consequently, some companies allocate the salary of such an employee to his or her departments on the basis of the number of employees in each department, while others make the allocation on the basis of the supervised departments' sales. When a supervisor's salary is allocated on the basis of employees, it is assumed that he or she is supervising people and the time spent in each department is related to the number of employees in each. When the salary is allocated on the basis of sales, it is assumed that the time devoted to each department is related to the department's production.

Rent or Depreciation and Related Expenses of Buildings

Rent expense is normally allocated to benefited departments on the basis of the amount and value of the floor space occupied by each. Furthermore, since all customers who enter a store must pass the departments by the entrance and only a fraction of these people go beyond the first floor, ground floor space is more valuable for retail purposes than is basement or upper floor space, and space near the entrance is more valuable than is space in an out-of-the-way corner. Yet, since there is no exact measure of floor space values, all such values and the allocations of rent based on such values must depend on judgment. Fair allocations depend on the use of good judgment, statistics as to customer traffic patterns, and the opinions of experts who are familiar with current rental values. When a building is owned instead of being rented, expenses such as depreciation, taxes, and insurance on the building are allocated like rent expense.

Advertising

When a store advertises a department's products, if the advertising is effective, people come into the store to buy the products. However, at the same time they also often buy other unadvertised products. Consequently, advertising benefits all departments, even those the products of which are not advertised. Thus, many stores treat advertising as an indirect expense and allocate it on the basis of sales. When advertising costs are allocated on a sales basis, a department producing $\frac{1}{10}$ of the total sales is charged with $\frac{1}{10}$ of the advertising cost; a department producing $\frac{1}{6}$ of the sales is charged with $\frac{1}{6}$.

Although in many stores advertising costs are allocated to departments on the basis of sales, this can often lead to problems because dollar sales volume can be misleading. For example, more effort is likely required to sell many low-value units than fewer high-value units. Yet, the latter would be allocated more of the advertising expense. A more equitable method would be to analyze each advertisement and to charge the cost of the column inches of newspaper space or minutes of TV or radio time devoted to the products of a department to that department.

Depreciation of Equipment

Depreciation on equipment used solely in one department is a direct expense of that department; and if detailed plant asset records are kept, the depreciation applicable to each department may be determined by examining the records. Where adequate records are not maintained, depreciation must be treated as an indirect expense and allocated to the departments on the basis of the value of the equipment in each. Where items of equipment are used by more than one department, the relative number of hours used is usually a fair basis of allocating depreciation costs by each department.

Heating and Lighting Expense

Heating and lighting expense is usually allocated on the basis of floor space or total volume occupied under the assumption that the amount of heat and the number of lights, their wattage, and the extent of their use are uniform throughout the store. Should there be a material variation in lighting, however, further analysis and a separate allocation may be advisable.

Service Departments

In order to manufacture products and make sales, the productive departments must have the services supplied by departments such as the general office, personnel, payroll, advertising, and purchasing departments. Such departments are called **service departments.** Since service departments do not produce revenues, they are evaluated as cost centres rather than as profit centres. Although each service department should be separately evaluated, the costs it incurs must also be allocated among the departments it services. Thus, the costs of service departments are, in effect, indirect expenses of the selling departments; and the allocation of service department costs to selling departments is required if net incomes of the selling departments are to be calculated. The following list shows commonly used bases for these allocations:

Departments	Expense allocation bases
General office department	Number of employees in each department or sales
Personnel department	Number of employees in each department
Payroll department	Number of employees in each department
Advertising department	Sales or amounts of advertising charged directly to each department
Purchasing department	Dollar amounts of purchases or number of purchase invoices processed
Cleaning and maintenance department	Square metres of floor space occupied

MECHANICS OF ALLOCATING EXPENSES

It would be difficult or impossible to analyse each indirect expense incurred and allocate and charge portions to several departmental expense accounts at the time of incurrence or payment. Consequently, expense amounts paid or incurred, both direct and indirect, are commonly accumulated in undepartmentalized expense accounts until the end of a period, when a **departmental expense allocation sheet** (see Illustration 23–4) is used to allocate and charge each expense to the benefited departments.

To prepare an expense allocation sheet, the names of the to-be-allocated expenses are entered in the sheet's first column along with the names of the service departments. Next, the bases of allocation are entered in the second column, and the expense amounts are entered in the third. Then, each expense is allocated according to the basis shown, and the allocated portions are entered in the departmental columns. After this the departmental columns are totaled and the service department column totals are allocated in turn to the selling departments. Upon completion, the amounts in the departmental columns are available for preparing income statements showing net income by departments, as in Illustration 23–5.

DEPARTMENTAL CONTRIBUTIONS TO OVERHEAD

Some people argue that departmental net incomes do not provide a fair basis for evaluating departmental performance. This is because the assumptions and somewhat arbitrary decisions involved in allocating the indirect expenses impact on the net income figures. The criticism

Illustration 23—4

BETA HARDWARE STORE
Departmental Expense Allocation Sheet
Year Ended December 31, 19—

Undepartmentalized Expense Accounts and Service Departments	Bases of Allocation	Expense Account Balance	Allocation of Expenses to Departments				
			General Office Dept.	Pur-chasing Dept.	Hard-ware Dept.	House-wares Dept.	Appli-ances Dept.
Salaries expense	Direct, payroll records	51,900	13,300	8,200	15,600	7,000	7,800
Rent expense	Amount and value of space	12,000	500	500	6,000	1,400	3,600
Heating and lighting	Floor space	2,000	100	100	1,000	200	600
Advertising expense	Sales	1,000	......	......	500	300	200
Depreciation, equipment	Direct, depreciation records	1,500	500	300	400	100	200
Supplies expense	Direct, requisitions	900	200	100	300	200	100
Insurance expense	Value of assets insured	2,500	400	200	900	600	400
Total expenses by departments		71,800	15,000	9,400	24,700	9,800	12,900
Allocation of service department expenses:							
General office department	Sales		15,000		7,500	4,500	3,000
Purchasing department	Purchase requisitions			9,400	3,900	3,400	2,100
Total expenses applicable to selling departments		71,800			36,100	17,700	18,000

Illustration 23–5

BETA HARDWARE STORE
Departmental Income Statement
Year Ended December 31, 19—

	Hardware department	Housewares department	Appliances department	Combined
Sales	$119,500	$71,700	$47,800	$239,000
Cost of goods sold	73,800	43,800	30,200	147,800
Gross profit on sales	45,700	27,900	17,600	91,200
Gross profit percentages	38.2%	38.9%	36.8%	38.2%
Operating expenses:				
Salaries expense	15,600	7,000	7,800	30,400
Rent expense	6,000	1,400	3,600	11,000
Heating and lighting expense	1,000	200	600	1,800
Advertising expense	500	300	200	1,000
Depreciation expense, equipment	400	100	200	700
Supplies expense	300	200	100	600
Insurance expense	900	600	400	1,900
Share of general office department expenses	7,500	4,500	3,000	15,000
Share of purchasing department expenses	3,900	3,400	2,100	9,400
Total operating expenses	36,100	17,700	18,000	17,800
Net income (loss)	$ 9,600	$10,200	$ (400)	$ 19,400

of departmental net incomes is most likely heard in companies where indirect expenses represent a large portion of total expenses. Those who criticize departmental net income numbers usually suggest the substitution of what are known as *departmental contributions to overhead*. A department's contribution to overhead is the amount its revenues exceed its direct costs and expenses. Illustration 23–6 shows the departmental contributions to overhead for Beta Company.

Compare the performance of the appliance department as it is shown in Illustrations 23–5 and 23–6. Illustration 23–5 shows an absolute loss of $400 resulting from the department's operations. On the other hand, Illustration 23–6 shows a positive contribution to overhead of $9,500, which is 19.9% of sales. While this contribution is not as good as for the other departments, it appears much better than the $400 loss. Which is the better basis of evaluation? To resolve the matter, one must critically review the bases used for allocating the indirect expenses to departments. In the final analysis, however, a department is usually considered profitable when it has a positive contribution to overhead.

Illustration 23–6

BETA HARDWARE STORE
Income Statement Showing Departmental Contributions to Overhead
Year Ended December 31, 19—

	Hardware department	Housewares department	Appliances department	Combined
Sales	$119,500	$71,700	$47,800	$239,000
Cost of goods sold	73,800	43,800	30,200	147,800
Gross profit on sales	45,700	27,900	17,600	91,200
Direct expenses:				
Salaries expense	15,600	7,000	7,800	30,400
Depreciation expense, equipment	400	100	200	700
Supplies expense	300	200	100	600
Total direct expenses	16,300	7,300	8,100	31,700
Departmental contributions to overhead	$ 29,400	$20,600	$ 9,500	$ 59,500
Contribution percentages	24.6%	28.7%	19.9%	24.9%
Indirect expenses:				
Rent expense				$ 11,000
Heating and lighting expense				1,800
Advertising expense				1,000
Insurance expense				1,900
General office department expense				15,000
Purchasing department expense				9,400
Total indirect expenses				40,100
Net income				$ 19,400

ELIMINATING THE UNPROFITABLE DEPARTMENT

When a department's net income shows a loss or when its contribution to overhead appears very poor, management may consider the extreme action of eliminating the department. However, in considering this extreme action, neither the net income figure nor the contribution to overhead provides the best information on which to base a decision. Instead, consideration should be given to the department's *escapable expenses* and *inescapable expenses*. Escapable expenses are those that would be avoided if the department were eliminated; inescapable expenses are those that would continue even though the department were eliminated. For example, the management of Beta Company is considering whether to eliminate its appliances department. An evaluation of the inescapable expenses and escapable expenses of the appliances department reveals the following:

	Escapable expenses	Inescapable expenses
Salaries expense	$ 7,800	
Rent expense		$3,600
Heating and lighting expense		600
Advertising expense	200	
Depreciation expense, equipment		200
Supplies expense	100	
Insurance expense (merchandise and equipment)	300	100
Share of office department expenses	2,200	800
Share of purchasing department expenses	1,000	1,100
Totals	$11,600	$6,400

If the appliances department is discontinued, its $6,400 of inescapable expenses will have to be borne by the remaining departments; thus, until the appliances department's annual loss exceeds $6,400, Beta Company is better off continuing the unprofitable department. That is, the cost saving is only $6,400, while the departmental contribution lost would be $9,500. In addition, another factor must be weighed when considering the elimination of an unprofitable department. Often, the existence of a department, even though unprofitable, contributes to the sales and profits of the other departments. In such a case, a department might be continued even when its losses exceed its inescapable expenses.

CONTROLLABLE COSTS AND EXPENSES

Net income figures and contributions to overhead are used in judging departmental efficiencies, but is either a good index of how well a department manager has performed? The answer is that neither may be a good index. Since many expenses entering into the calculation of a department's net income or into its contribution to overhead may be beyond the control of the department's manager, neither net income nor contribution to overhead is the best means of judging how well the manager has performed. Instead, the performance of a manager should be evaluated in terms of *controllable costs and expenses.*

What is the distinguishing characteristic of controllable costs and expenses? The critical factor is that the manager must have the power to determine or at least strongly influence the amounts to be expended. Controllable costs and expenses are not the same thing as direct costs and expenses. Direct costs and expenses are easily traced and therefore chargeable to a specific department, but the amounts expended may or may not be under the control of the department's manager. For example, a department manager often has little or no control over the amount of equipment assigned to the department and the resulting depreciation expense. Also, the manager has no control over his or her own salary.

On the other hand, a department manager commonly has some control over the employees and the amount of work they do. Also the manager normally has some control over supplies used in the department.

When controllable costs and expenses are used in evaluating a manager's efficiency, statistics are prepared showing the department's output and its controllable costs and expenses. The statistics of the current period are then compared with prior periods and with planned levels, to judge the manager's performance.

The concepts of *controllable costs* and *uncontrollable costs* must be defined with reference to a particular manager and within a definite time period. Without these two reference points, all costs are controllable; that is, all costs are controllable at some level of management if the time period is long enough. For example, a cost such as property insurance may not be controllable at the level of a department manager, but it is subject to control by the executive who is responsible for obtaining insurance coverage for the concern. Likewise the executive responsible for obtaining insurance coverage may not have any control over insurance expense resulting from insurance contracts presently in force. But when a contract expires, the executive is free to renegotiate and thus has control over the long run. Thus, it is recognized that all costs are subject to the control of some managers at some point in time. Revenues are likewise subject to the control of some managers.

RESPONSIBILITY ACCOUNTING

The concept of controllable costs and expenses provides the basis for a system of responsibility accounting. In *responsibility accounting,* each manager is held responsible for the costs and expenses that fall under the manager's control. Prior to each period of activity, plans are developed that specify the expected costs or expenses under the control of each manager. Those plans are called *responsibility accounting budgets.* To secure the cooperation of each manager and to be sure that the budgets represent reasonable goals, each manager should be closely involved in the preparation of his or her budget.

The accounting system is then designed to accumulate costs and expenses so that timely reports can be made to each manager of the costs for which the manager is responsible. These reports, called *performance reports* compare actual costs and expenses to the budgeted amounts. Managers use these reports to focus their attention on the specific areas in which actual costs exceed budgeted amounts. With this information in hand, they proceed to take corrective action.

Performance reports are also used to evaluate the effectiveness of each manager. The reports allow managers to be evaluated in terms of their ability to control costs and to keep costs within budgeted amounts. Importantly, managers are not held responsible for costs over which they have no control. Further consideration is given to performance reports in Chapter 26.

A responsibility accounting system must reflect the fact that control over costs and expenses applies to several levels of management. For example, consider the partial organization chart shown in Illustration 23–7. In Illustration 23–7, the lines connecting the various managerial positions represent lines of authority. Thus, while each department manager is responsible for the controllable costs and expenses incurred in his or her department, those same costs are subject to the general control of the plant manager. More generally, those costs are also subject to the control of the vice president of production, and of the president, and finally of the board of directors.

At the lowest levels of management, responsibilities and costs over which control is exercised are limited. Consequently, performance reports

Illustration 23–7

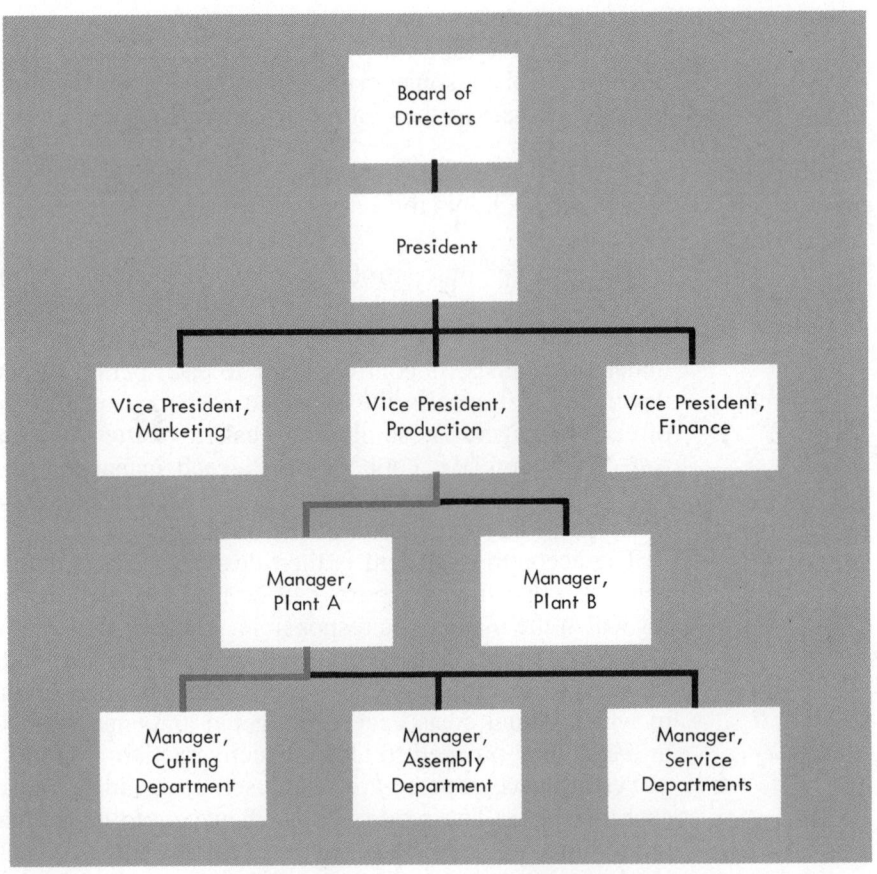

for this management level cover only those costs over which the department managers exercise control. Moving up the management hierarchy, responsibilities and control broaden, and reports to higher level managers are broader and cover a wider range of costs. However, reports to higher-level managers normally do not contain the details reported to their subordinates. Rather, the details reported to lower-level managers are normally summarized on the reports to their superiors. The details are summarized for two reasons: (1) lower level managers are primarily responsible and (2) too many details can be confusing. If reports to higher-level managers contain too much detail, they may draw attention away from the broad, more important issues confronting the company.

Illustration 23–8 shows summarized performance reports for three of the management levels depicted in Illustration 23–7. Observe in Illustration 23–8 how the costs under the control of the cutting department manager are totaled and included among the controllable costs of the plant manager. Similarly, the costs under the control of the plant manager

Illustration 23–8   Performance Reports

	For the month of July		
	Budgeted amount	Actual amount	Over (under) budget
Controllable costs			
Vice president, production:			
Salaries, plant managers..............	$ 80,000	$ 80,000	$ –0–
Quality control costs	21,000	22,400	1,400
Office costs	29,500	28,800	(700)
Plant A	276,700	279,500	2,800
Plant B...........................	390,000	380,600	(9,400)
Totals	$797,200	$791,300	$(5,900)
Manager, Plant A:			
Salaries, department managers	$ 75,000	$ 78,000	$ 3,000
Depreciation	10,600	10,600	–0–
Insurance.........................	6,800	6,300	(500)
Cutting department	79,600	79,900	300
Assembly department	61,500	60,200	(1,300)
Service Department 1	24,300	24,700	400
Service Department 2	18,900	19,800	900
Totals	$276,700	$279,500	$ 2,800
Manager, cutting department:			
Raw materials	$ 26,500	$ 25,900	$ (600)
Direct labour	32,000	33,500	1,500
Indirect labour	7,200	7,000	(200)
Supplies..........................	4,000	3,900	(100)
Other controllable costs	9,900	9,600	(300)
Totals	$ 79,600	$ 79,900	$ 300

are totaled and included among the controllable costs of the vice president, production. In this manner, a responsibility accounting system provides information that is relevant to the control responsibilities of each management level.

In conclusion, it should be said that the ability to produce vast amounts of raw data mechanically and electronically has far outstripped our ability to use the data. What is needed is the ability to select the data that is meaningful for planning and control. This is recognized in responsibility accounting, and every effort is made to get the right information to the right person at the right time, and the right person is the person who can control the cost or revenue.

JOINT COSTS

Joint costs are encountered in some manufacturing concerns and are introduced here because they have much in common with indirect expenses. A *joint cost* is cost incurred to secure two or more essentially different products. For example, a meat-packing company incurs a joint cost when it buys a pig from which it will get bacon, hams, shoulders, liver, heart, hide, pig feet, and a variety of other products. Likewise, a sawmill incurs joint costs when it buys a log and saws it into portions of Clears, Select Structurals, No. 1 Common, No. 2 Common, and other grades of lumber. In both cases, as with all joint costs, the problem is one of allocating the costs to the several joint products.

A joint cost may be, but is not commonly, allocated on some physical basis, such as the ratio of kilograms, square feet, or litres of each joint product to total kilograms, square feet, or gallons of all joint products flowing from the cost. The reason this method is not commonly used is that the resulting cost allocations may be completely out of keeping with the market values of the joint products and thus may cause certain of the products to sell at a profit and other products to show a loss. For example, a sawmill bought for $120,000 a number of logs which when sawed produced a million cubic metres (m^3) of lumber in the grades and amounts shown in Illustration 23–9.

Observe in Illustration 23–9 that the logs produced 200,000 m^3 of No. 3 Common lumber and that this is $\frac{2}{10}$ of the total lumber produced from the logs. If the No. 3 lumber is assigned $\frac{2}{10}$ of the $120,000 cost of the logs, it will be assigned $24,000 of the cost ($120,000 $\times$ $\frac{2}{10}$ = $24,000); and since this lumber can be sold for only $12,000, the assignment will cause this grade to show a loss. As a result, as in this situation, to avoid always showing a loss on one or more of the products flowing from a joint cost, such costs are commonly allocated to the joint products *in the ratio of the market values of the joint products at the point of separation.*

The ratios of the market values of the joint products flowing from

Illustration 23–9

Grade of Lumber	Produc-tion in m³	Market Price per 1,000 m³	Market Value of Production of each Grade	Ratio of Market Value of each Grade to Total
Structural	100,000	$360	$ 36,000	36/150
No. 1 Common	300,000	180	54,000	54/150
No. 2 Common	400,000	120	48,000	48/150
No. 3 Common	200,000	60	12,000	12/150
	1,000,000		$150,000	

the $120,000 of log cost are shown in the last column of Illustration 23–9. If these ratios are used to allocate the $120,000 cost, the cost will be apportioned between the grades as follows:

Structural:	$120,000 × 36/150 =	$ 28,800
No. 1 Common:	$120,000 × 54/150 =	43,200
No. 2 Common:	$120,000 × 48/150 =	38,400
No. 3 Common:	$120,000 × 12/150 =	9,600
		$120,000

Observe that if the No. 3 Common is allocated a share of the $120,000 joint cost based on market values by grades, it is allocated $9,600 of the $120,000. Furthermore, when the $9,600 is subtracted from the grade's $12,000 market value, $2,400 remains to cover other after-separation costs and provide a profit. The allocation of joint costs among the products is essentially arbitrary. Therefore it is imprudent to use allocated costs in making managerial decisions. The important fact is whether or not the total operation is profitable; for example, the total revenue obtained from cutting and selling the logs is greater than the total costs.

GLOSSARY

Controllable costs and expenses.   Costs for which the manager has the power to determine or strongly influence amounts to be expended.

Cost centre.   A unit of a business that incurs costs or expenses but does not directly generate revenues.

Departmental accounting.   Accounting for the parts, or subunits, of a business, especially referring to the development of subunit information for the use of internal managers.

Departmental contributions to overhead. The amount by which a department's revenues exceed its direct costs and expenses.

Direct costs or expenses. Costs that are easily traced to or associated with a cost object, for example, costs incurred by a department for the sole benefit of the department.

Escapable expenses. Costs that would end with an unprofitable department's elimination.

Indirect costs or expenses. Costs that are not easily traced to a cost object, for example, costs incurred for the joint benefit of more than one department.

Inescapable expenses. Expenses that would continue even though the department were eliminated.

Joint cost. A single cost incurred to secure two or more essentially different products.

Performance reports. Managerial reports which compare actual costs to budgeted amounts.

Productive departments. Subunits of a business, the operations of which involve manufacturing or selling the goods or services of a business.

Profit centre. A unit of a business that incurs costs and generates revenues.

Responsibility accounting. An accounting system designed to accumulate controllable costs in timely reports to be given to each manager determined responsible for the costs and also to be used in judging the performance of each manager.

Responsibility accounting budget. A plan that specifies the expected costs and expenses falling under the control of a manager.

Segmental reporting. Providing information about the subunits of a business, especially published information about a company's operations in different industries or geographical areas.

Service departments. Departments that do not manufacture or produce revenue but which supply other departments with essential services.

Uncontrollable cost. A cost that a specific manager cannot control within a given period of time.

QUESTIONS FOR CLASS DISCUSSION

1. What is the difference, if any, between segmental reporting and departmental accounting?

2. What are five items of segmental information about operations in different industries that may be required disclosures in the annual report of a company?

3. What are four basic issues confronted by the accountant in developing information on broad industrial segments?

4. Why is a business divided into departments?
5. What are two primary goals of departmental accounting?
6. Differentiate between productive departments and service departments.
7. Name several examples of service departments.
8. Are service departments analyzed as cost centres or as profit centres? Why?
9. How is a departmental sales analysis sheet used in determining sales by departments?
10. Differentiate between direct and indirect expenses.
11. Suggest a basis for allocating each of the following expenses to departments:
    a. Salary of a supervisory employee.   e. Janitorial services.
    b. Rent.   f. Advertising.
    c. Heat.   g. Expired insurance.
    d. Electricity used in lighting.   h. Taxes.
12. How is a departmental expense allocation sheet used in allocating expenses to departments?
13. How reliable are the amounts shown as net incomes for the various departments of a store when expenses are allocated to the departments?
14. How is a department's contribution to overhead measured?
15. As the terms are used in departmental accounting, what are:
    a. Escapable expenses?   b. Inescapable expenses?
16. What are controllable costs and expenses?
17. Why should a manager be closely involved in preparing his or her responsibility accounting budget?
18. In responsibility accounting, who is the right person to be given timely reports and statistics on a given cost?
19. What is a joint cost? How are joint costs normally allocated?

MULTIPLE CHOICE

1. Department C of a large firm has been operating at a loss for the past five years. In determining whether or not to close that department, management should compare departmental losses with:
    a. Direct costs.
    b. Indirect costs.
    c. Inescapable costs.
    d. Controllable costs.
    e. Uncontrollable costs.

2. Joint Products A and B are produced in a single operation forming Material M. Three hundred litres of Material M, costing $450, produce 200 litres of Product A that sells for $2 per litre, and 100 litres of Product B that sells for $6 per litre. If the cost of 300 litres of Material M is allocated to

the joint products in proportion to the market values of the products at the point of separation, Product A's share of the $450 cost is:

   a. $300.
   b. $270.
   c. $180.
   d. $150.
   e.   Some other amount.

3.   A company rents a small building consisting of 10,000 square metres of space for $15,000 per year, and it allocates the rent to its three departments on the basis of the amount and value of the space occupied by each. Department 1 occupies 2,000 square metres of ground-floor space, Department 2 occupies 3,000 square metres of ground-floor space, and Department 3 occupies 5,000 square metres of second-floor space. If rents for comparable floor space in the neighborhood average $2.20 for ground-floor space and $1.10 for second-floor space, Department 1 should be charged an annual rent expense in the amount of:

   a. $4,400.
   b. $4,000.
   c. $3,000.
   d. $2,200.
   e.   Some other amount.

4.   A sawmill bought a number of logs for $40,000. When sawed, the boards produced a million cubic metres (m^3) in the following grades:

      Type 1—400,000 m^3 priced to sell at $0.10 per m^3.
      Type 2—400,000 m^3 priced to sell at $0.06 per m^3.
      Type 3—200,000 m^3 priced to sell at $0.04 per m^3.

What will be the total cost apportioned to types 1 and 2, respectively?

   a. $16,000; $16,000.
   b. $13,333; $ 4,444.
   c. $40,000; $24,000.
   d. $22,222; $13,333.
   e.   Some other amounts.

5.   A departmental income statement indicates that Department X (or Departments X, Y, Z) is losing $5,000 a year after all direct and indirect expenses are allocated. Assume that the sales of one department do not affect the sales of other departments. An analysis of Department X's expenses indicates that of total expenses of $25,000, $18,000 are escapable and $7,000 are inescapable expenses. At what point should department X be eliminated?

   a.   Eliminate Department X now because it is losing money.
   b.   Eliminate Department X when its gross profit on sales falls below company standards.
   c.   Eliminate Department X when its contribution to overhead is less than $18,000.
   d.   Eliminate Department X when the department's annual loss exceeds $7,000.

  e. Department X should not be eliminated as long as indirect expenses are allocated to it.

6. In 198A, the shoe department of Lee's Department store had sales of $188,000; cost of goods sold of $132,500; indirect expenses of $13,250; and direct expenses of $27,500. The shoe department's contribution to overhead percentage is:

  a. 7.8%.
  b. 14.9%.
  c. 29.5%.
  d. 66.7%.
  e. 85.4%.

MINI DISCUSSION CASES

Case 23–1 You have just been hired by the Old Fashioned Sales Emporium Ltd. as the manager of their ready-wear clothing department. Part of the arrangement is that you will receive, as a bonus, a percentage of any increase in the department's net profit.

  By the end of your first year as manager, you have increased the department's sales by 20%, increased the department's gross profit on sales by 24%, and decreased the direct expenses by 6%. However, instead of receiving high praise and your bonus for your efforts, the president has asked you to explain why your department's net profits have decreased.

  Upon investigation, you discover that the bookkeeper has always allocated depreciation, advertising, building maintenance costs, and office expenses to the various departments on the basis of sales revenues. In addition, you determine that the overall sales revenues were about the same level as last year and that overall expenses have increased by about 10%.

Required:

  Make a case to the president diplomatically explaining your situation and make any suggestions you consider necessary in order to render the reporting system more useful.

Case 23–2 *a.* Under what circumstances would the method(s) of allocating joint costs be important? Why?
  b. Which parties would be most concerned about the method chosen to allocate joint costs? Why?

CLASS EXERCISES

Exercise 23–1 *Required:*

  Answer the following questions about the segmental information contained in the 1985 annual report of Moore Corporation shown in the Appendix at the end of the book: *(a)* What are the industrial geographics into which Moore Corporation's operations are divided? *(b)* What were the 1985 net sales (1) to outside parties and (2) to other segments of Moore Corporation? *(c)* Which segment earned the largest operating profit in 1985? *(d)* In which segment did Moore Corporation have the largest investment of identifiable assets at the end of 1985?

Exercise 23–2   A company rents for $30,000 per month all the space in a building, which is assigned to its departments as follows:

Department A: 200 sq. m. of first-floor space

Department B: 100 sq. m. of first-floor space

Department C: 60 sq. m. of second-floor space

Department D: 80 sq. m. of second-floor space

Department E: 160 sq. m. of second-floor space

The company allocates 60% of the total rent to the first floor and 40% to the second floor, and then allocates the rent of each floor to the departments on that floor on the basis of the space occupied.

Required:

Determine the monthly rent to be allocated to each department.

Exercise 23–3   A company rents for $72,000 per year all the space in a small building, and it occupies the space as follows:

Department A: 250 sq. m. of first-floor space

Department B: 150 sq. m. of first-floor space

Department C: 400 sq. m. of second-floor space

Required:

Determine the rent expense to be allocated to each department under the assumption that first-floor space rents for twice as much as second-floor space in the city in which this company is located.

Exercise 23–4   Thomas Cross works part-time in the men's shoe department and in the men's clothing department of James Bay Department Store. His work consists of waiting on customers who enter either department and of straightening and rearranging merchandise in either department as needed after it has been shown to customers. The store allocates his $6,000 in annual wages to the two departments in which he works. Last year the division was based on a sample of the time Cross spent working in the two departments. To gain the sample, observations were made on several days throughout the year of the manner in which Cross spent his time while at work. Following are the results of the observations:

Observed manner in which employee spent his time	Elapsed time in minutes
Selling in men's shoe department	1,850
Straightening and rearranging merchandise in men's shoe department	350
Selling in men's clothing department	1,425
Straightening and rearranging merchandise in men's clothing department	375
Doing nothing while waiting for a customer to enter one of the selling departments	250

Required:

Prepare a calculation to show the shares of the employee's wages that should be allocated to the departments.

Exercise 23–5

Bearing Company has two service departments, the office department and the purchasing department. It also has two sales departments, One and Two. During the past year the departments had the following direct expenses: general office department, $3,800; purchasing department, $2,800; Department One, $10,000; and Department Two, $7,000. The departments occupy the following amounts of floor space: office, 600 square metres; purchasing, 400 square metres; One, 1,200 square metres; and Two, 800 square meters. During the year Department One had three times as many dollars of sales as did Department Two, and the purchasing department processed twice as many purchase orders for Department One as it did for Department Two.

Required:

Prepare an expense allocation sheet for Bearing Company on which the direct expenses are entered by departments, the year's $72,000 of rent expense is allocated to the departments on the basis of floor space occupied, office department expenses are allocated to the sales departments on the basis of sales, and purchasing department expenses are allocated on the basis of purchase orders processed.

Exercise 23–6

Mark Masson is the manager of the appliance department of a department store. A 19D income statement for the department included the following:

Revenues:		
Appliance sales	$730,000	
Appliance service	210,000	$940,000
Costs and expenses:		
Cost of appliances sold	295,000	
Cost of parts sold	76,000	
Wages (hourly)	115,000	
Manager's salary	35,000	
Payroll expenses	37,000	
Supplies	42,000	
Depreciation, fixtures	7,000	
Depreciation, building	16,000	
Utilities	9,000	
Interest on long-term debt	11,000	
Income taxes allocated	120,000	
Total costs and expenses		763,000
Departmental net income		$177,000

Required:

Which of the income statement items do you think should be excluded from a report to be used in evaluating Mr. Masson's performance? State your reasons. If the exclusion of some items is questionable, list those items and explain why.

Exercise 23–7

Field's Realty Company has just completed a subdivision containing 15 buildings lots, of which 10 lots are for sale at $30,000 each and 5 are for sale at $40,000 each. The land for the subdivision cost $125,000, and the company spent $275,000 on street and sidewalk improvements.

Required:

Assume that the land and improvement costs are to be assigned to the lots as joint costs and determine the share of the costs to assign to a lot in each price class.

PROBLEMS

Problem 23–1

This 'N That Company occupies all the space in a two-story building, and it has an account in its ledger called "Building Occupancy" to which it charged the following during the past year:

Depreciation, building	$12,000
Interest, building mortgage	17,500
Taxes, building and land	5,400
Heating expenses	1,700
Lighting expense	600
Cleaning and maintenance	12,000
Total	$49,200

The building has 600 square metres of floor space on each of its two floors, a total of 1,200 square metres; and the bookkeeper divided the $49,200 by 1,200 and charged the selling departments on each floor with $41 of occupancy cost for each square metre of floor space occupied.

Frank Rey, the manager of a second-floor department occupying 200 square metres of floor space, saw the $41 per square metres, or $8,200 of occupancy cost, charged to his department and complained. He cited a recent real estate board study which showed average rental charges for like space, including heat but not including lights, cleaning, and maintenance, as follows:

Ground-floor space	. . . .	$45 per sq. m.
Second-floor space	. . . .	$30 per sq. m.

Required:

Prepare a computation showing how much building occupancy cost you think should have been charged to Frank Rey's department last year.

Problem 23–2   Horseshoe Supply Company began its operations one year ago with two selling departments and one office department. The year's operating results are:

HORSESHOE SUPPLY COMPANY
Departmental Income Statement
For Year Ended December 31, 19—

	Dept. A	Dept. B	Combined
Revenue from sales	$80,000	$50,000	$130,000
Cost of goods sold	52,000	30,000	82,000
Gross profit from sales	$28,000	$20,000	$ 48,000
Direct expenses:			
Sales salaries	$10,500	$ 6,000	$ 16,500
Advertising	900	675	1,575
Store supplies used	400	200	600
Depreciation of equipment	1,075	575	1,650
Total direct expenses	$12,875	$ 7,450	$ 20,325
Allocated expenses:			
Rent expense	$ 4,800	$ 2,400	$ 7,200
Heating and lighting expense	1,200	600	1,800
Share of office department expenses	4,800	3,000	7,800
Total allocated expenses	$10,800	$ 6,000	$ 16,800
Total expenses	$23,675	$13,450	$ 37,125
Net income	$ 4,325	$ 6,550	$ 10,875

The company plans to open a third selling department which it estimates will produce $30,000 in sales with a 35% gross profit margin and will require the following direct expenses: sales salaries, $4,500; advertising, $450; store supplies, $175; and depreciation of equipment, $350.

A year ago, when operations began, it was necessary to rent store space in excess of requirements. This extra space was assigned to and used by Departments A and B during the year; but when the new department, Department C, is opened it will take one fourth of the space presently assigned to Department A and one sixth of the space assigned to Department B.

The company allocates its general office department expenses to its selling departments on the basis of sales, and it expects the new department to cause a $525 increase in general office department expenses.

The company expects Department C to bring new customers into the store who in addition to buying goods in the new department will also buy sufficient merchandise in the two old departments to increase their sales by 5% each. And although the old departments' sales are expected to increase, their gross profit percentages are not expected to change. Likewise, their direct expenses, other than supplies, are not expected to change. The supplies used will increase in proportion to sales.

Required:

Prepare a departmental income statement showing the company's expected operations with three selling departments.

Problem 23–3   Humboldt Company is considering the elimination of its unprofitable Department B. The company's income statement for last year appears as follows:

HUMBOLDT COMPANY
Income Statement
For Year Ended December 31, 19—

	Dept. A	Dept. B	Combined
Sales	$76,500	$45,900	$122,400
Cost of goods sold	46,750	34,325	81,075
Gross margin on sales	$29,750	$11,575	$ 41,325
Operating expenses:			
Direct expenses:			
Advertising	$ 1,175	$ 895	$ 2,070
Store supplies used	325	215	540
Depreciation of store equipment	850	475	1,325
Total direct expenses	$ 2,350	$ 1,585	$ 3,935
Allocated expenses:			
Sales salaries	$11,050	$ 6,630	$ 17,680
Rent expense	2,625	1,575	4,200
Bad debts expense	380	230	610
Office salaries	2,600	1,560	4,160
Insurance expense	200	150	350
Miscellaneous office expenses	325	200	525
Total allocated expenses	$17,180	$10,345	$ 27,525
Total expenses	$19,530	$11,930	$ 31,460
Net income (loss)	$10,220	$ (355)	$ 9,865

If Department B is eliminated:

1. The company has one office clerk who earns $80 per week or $4,160 per year and four salesclerks each of whom earns $85 per week or $4,420 per year. At present the salaries of two and one-half salesclerks are charged to Department A and one and one-half salesclerks to Department B. It is the opinion of management that two salesclerks may be dismissed if Department B is eliminated, leaving only two full-time clerks in Department A, and making up the difference by assigning the office clerk to part-time sales work in the department. It is felt that although the office clerk has not devoted half of his time to the office work of Department B, if he devotes the same amount of time to selling in Department A during rush hours as he has to the office work of Department B, it will be sufficient to carry the load.

2. The lease on the store building is long term and cannot be changed; therefore, the space presently occupied by Department B will have to be used by and charged to Department A. Likewise, Department A will have to make whatever use of Department B's equipment it can, since the equipment has little or no sales value.

3. The elimination of Department B will eliminate the Department B advertising expense, losses from bad debts, and store supplies used. It will also eliminate 80% of the insurance expense, the portion on merchandise, and 25% of the miscellaneous office expenses presently allocated to Department B.

Required:

1. List in separate columns the amounts of Department B's escapable and inescapable expenses.
2. Under the assumption that Department A's sales and gross profit will not be affected by the elimination of Department B, prepare an income statement showing what the company can expect to earn from the operation of Department A after Department B is eliminated.

Problem 23–4 Richard and Kay Carmean own a farm that produces potatoes. Last year after preparing the following income statement, Richard remarked to Kay that they should have fed the No. 3 potatoes to the pigs and thus avoided the loss from the sale of this grade.

RICHARD AND KAY CARMEAN
Income from the Production and Sale of Potatoes
For Year Ended December 31, 19—

| | Results by Grades | | | Combined |
	No. 1	No. 2	No. 3	
Sales by grades:				
No. 1, 300,000 kgs. @ $0.045 per kg.	$13,500			
No. 2, 500,000 kgs. @ $0.04 per kg.		$20,000		
No. 3, 200,000 kgs. @ $0.03 per kg.			$6,000	
Combined				$39,500
Costs:				
Land preparation, seed, planting, and cultivating @ $0.01422 per kg.	$ 4,266	$ 7,110	$2,844	$14,220
Harvesting, sorting, and grading @ $0.01185 per kg.	3,555	5,925	2,370	11,850
Marketing @ $0.00415 per kg.	1,245	2,075	830	4,150
Total costs	$ 9,066	$15,110	$6,044	$30,220
Net income or (loss)	$ 4,434	$ 4,890	$ (44)	$ 9,280

On the foregoing statement Richard and Kay divided their costs among the grades on a per kilogram basis. They did this because with the exception of marketing costs, their records did not show costs per grade. As to marketing costs, the records did show that $4,020 of the $4,150 was the cost of placing the No. 1 and No. 2 potatoes in bags and hauling them to the warehouse of the produce buyer. Bagging and hauling costs were the same for both grades. The remaining $130 of marketing costs was the cost of loading the No. 3 potatoes into trucks of a potato starch factory that bought these potatoes in bulk and picked them up at the farm.

Required:

Prepare an income statement that will show better the results of producing and marketing the potatoes.

Problem 23–5   Hansen Retail Company has three selling departments, X, Y, and Z, and two service departments, general office and purchasing. At the end of an accounting period its bookkeeper brought together the following information for use in preparing the year-end statements:

Sales, purchases, and inventories:

	Dept. X	Dept. Y	Dept. Z
Sales	$95,400	$51,200	$73,400
Purchases	67,900	35,300	41,800
January 1 (beginning) inventory	12,300	8,500	10,200
December 31 (ending) inventory	14,500	9,400	7,300

Direct departmental expenses:

Hansen Retail Company treats salaries, supplies used, and depreciation as direct departmental expenses. The payroll, requisition, and plant asset records showed the following amounts of these expenses by departments:

	Salaries expense	Supplies used	Depreciation of equipment
General office	$ 9,345	$ 235	$ 625
Purchasing department	6,160	195	375
Department X	10,360	385	850
Department Y	5,510	215	450
Department Z	8,140	295	500
	$39,515	$1,325	$2,800

Indirect expenses:

The concern incurred the following amounts of indirect expenses:

Rent expense	$6,600
Advertising expense	5,500
Expired insurance	750
Heating and lighting expense	1,750
Janitorial expense	2,100

Hansen Retail Company allocates the foregoing expenses to its departments as follows:

a.   Rent expense on the basis of the amount and value of floor space occupied. The general office and purchasing departments occupy space in the rear of the store which is not as valuable as space in the front; consequently, $600 of the total rent is allocated to these two departments in proportion to the space occupied by each. The remainder of the rent is divided between the selling departments in proportion to the space occupied. The five departments occupy these amounts of space: General Office, 60 square metres; Purchasing Department, 40 square metres; Department X, 300 square metres; Department Y, 150 square metres; and Department Z, 150 square metres.

b.   Advertising expense on the basis of sales.

c.   Expired insurance on the basis of equipment book values. The book values of the equipment in the departments are General Office, $3,500; Purchasing

Department, $2,000; Department X, $9,000; Department Y, $5,000; and Department Z, $5,500.

d. Heating and lighting and janitorial expenses on the basis of floor space occupied.

Service department expenses:

Hansen Retail Company allocates its general office department expenses to its selling departments on the basis of sales, and it allocates purchasing department expenses on the basis of purchases.

Required:

1. Prepare a departmental expense allocation sheet for the concern.
2. Prepare a departmental income statement showing sales, cost of goods sold, expenses, and net incomes by departments and for the entire store.
3. Prepare a second departmental income statement showing departmental contributions to overhead and overall net income.

Problem 23–6   Kabel Company's Sorel plant is managed by Jean Thibeault, who is responsible for all costs of the Sorel operation other than his own salary. The plant is divided into two production departments and an office department. The widgets and the gidgets departments manufacture different products and have separate managers; the office department is managed by the plant manager. Kabel Company prepares a monthly budget for each of the production departments (widgets and gidgets) and then accumulates costs in a manner that assigns all of the Sorel plant costs to the departments.

The department budgets and cost accumulations for the month of August were as follows:

	Budget		Actual costs		
	Widgets dept.	Gidgets dept.	Widgets dept.	Gidgets dept.	Combined
Raw materials	$195,000	$140,000	$209,000	$143,500	$352,500
Wages	110,000	100,000	116,600	103,200	219,800
Salary, department manager	25,000	22,000	25,000	23,000	48,000
Supplies used	10,000	9,000	8,600	9,900	18,500
Depreciation of equipment	6,000	5,000	6,000	5,800	11,800
Heating and lighting	20,000	10,000	25,000	12,500	37,500
Rent on building	24,000	12,000	24,000	12,000	36,000
Share of office dept. costs........	49,000	49,000	46,800	46,800	93,600
	$439,000	$347,000	$461,000	$356,700	$817,700

Office department costs consisted of the following:

	Budget	Actual
Salary—plant manager	$45,000	$45,000
Other salaries	38,000	36,500
Other costs	15,000	12,100

Each department manager is responsible for the purchase and maintenance of equipment in the department. Heating and lighting cost and building rent are allocated to the production departments on the basis of relative space used by those departments.

Required:

Prepare responsibility accounting performance reports on the managers of each production department and on the plant manager.

ALTERNATE PROBLEMS

Problem 23–1A

Prairie Department Store has in its ledger an account called "Building Occupancy Costs" to which it charged the following last year:

Building rent	$54,000
Lighting expense	2,000
Cleaning and maintenance	10,000
Total	$66,000

The store occupies all the space in a building having selling space on three levels—basement level, street level, and second-floor level. Each level has 500 square metres of selling space, a total of 1,500 square metres; and the bookkeeper divided the $66,000 of building occupancy cost by 1,500 and charged each selling department with $44 of building occupancy cost for each square metre of space occupied.

When Ray Burchette, the manager of a basement-level department having 150 square metres of floor space, saw the $44 per square metre of building occupancy cost charged to his department, he complained. In this complaint he cited a recent local real estate study which showed average charges for like space, including heat but not including lights and janitorial service, as follows:

Basement-level space	$20 per sq. m.
Street-level space	$60 per sq. m.
Second-floor-level space	$40 per sq. m.

Required:

Prepare a computation showing the amount of building occupancy cost you think should be charged to Ray Burchette's department.

Problem 23–2A

Valley Retail Company began business last year with two selling departments and a general office department. It had the following results for the year:

VALLEY RETAIL COMPANY
Departmental Income Statement
For Year Ended December 31, 19—

	Dept. 1	Dept. 2	Combined
Sales	$120,000	$60,000	$180,000
Cost of goods sold	84,000	36,000	120,000
Gross profit from sales	$ 36,000	$24,000	$ 60,000
Direct expenses:			
Sales salaries	$ 12,500	$ 7,200	$ 19,700
Advertising expense	1,125	750	1,875
Store supplies used	600	300	900
Depreciation of equipment	1,025	550	1,575
Total direct expenses	$ 15,250	$ 8,800	$ 24,050
Allocated expenses:			
Rent expense	$ 5,400	$ 3,600	$ 9,000
Heating and lighting expense	1,080	720	1,800
Share of general office expenses	7,000	3,500	10,500
Total allocated expenses	$ 13,480	$ 7,820	$ 21,300
Total expenses	$ 28,730	$16,620	$ 45,350
Net income	$ 7,270	$ 7,380	$ 14,650

The company plans to add a third selling department which it estimates will produce $40,000 in sales with a 35% gross profit margin. The new department will require the following estimated direct expenses: sales salaries, $4,500; advertising expense, $450; store supplies, $250; and depreciation on equipment, $525.

When the company began its operations, it was necessary to rent a store room having selling space in excess of requirements. This extra space was assigned to and used by Departments 1 and 2 during the year; but when Department 3 is opened, it will take over one third the space presently assigned to Department 1 and one sixth the space assigned to Department 2. The space reductions are not expected to affect the operations or sales of the old departments.

The company allocates its general office department expenses to its selling departments on the basis of sales. It expects the new department to cause a $950 increase in general office department expenses.

The company expects the addition of Department 3 to bring new customers to the store who, in addition to buying Department 3 merchandise, will also do sufficient buying in the old departments to increase their sales by 5% each. It is not expected that the increase in sales in the old departments will affect their gross profit percentages nor any of their direct expenses other than supplies. It is expected the supplies used will increase in proportion to sales.

Required:

Prepare a departmental income statement showing the company's expected operating results with three departments.

Problem 23–3A

Whisper Sales is considering the elimination of its unprofitable Department A, which lost $2,285 last year as the income statement shows.

WHISPER SALES
Income Statement
For Year Ended December 31, 19—

	Dept. A	Dept. B	Combined
Sales	$68,500	$137,600	$206,100
Cost of goods sold	45,800	79,100	124,900
Gross profit on sales	22,700	58,500	81,200
Operating expenses:			
Direct expenses:			
Advertising expense	1,225	1,650	2,875
Store supplies expense	350	425	775
Depreciation expense, equipment	950	1,200	2,150
Total direct expenses	2,525	3,275	5,800
Indirect expenses:			
Sales salaries expense	15,600	26,000	41,600
Rent expense	2,000	2,800	4,800
Bad debts expense	250	375	625
Office salaries expense	4,160	6,240	10,400
Insurance expense	150	225	375
Miscellaneous office expenses	300	450	750
Total indirect expenses	22,460	36,090	58,550
Total operating expenses	24,985	39,365	64,350
Net income (loss)	$ (2,285)	$ 19,135	$ 16,850

If Department 1 is eliminated—

a. Its advertising, store supplies, and bad debts expenses will be eliminated. Also, two thirds of its insurance expense, the portion on its merchandise, and 20% of the miscellaneous office expenses presently allocated to Department A will be eliminated.

b. The company has one office clerk and four salesclerks who each earn $200 per week or $10,400 per year. At present the salaries of two and one-half salesclerks are allocated to Department B and one and one-half salesclerks to Department A. Management feels that two salesclerks may be dismissed if Department A is eliminated, leaving two full-time salesclerks in Department B, and making up the difference by assigning the office clerk to part-time sales work in the department. Management feels that if the office clerk devotes the same amount of time to selling in Department B as she has to the office work of Department A, this will be sufficient to carry the load.

c. The lease on the store is long term and cannot be changed; therefore, the space presently occupied by Department A will have to be used by and charged to Department B.

d. One half of Department A's store equipment can be sold at its book value, and this will eliminate one half of the department's depreciation expense. However, Department B will have to make whatever use it can of the other half of the department's equipment and be charged with the depreciation, since it has little or no sale value.

Required:

List in separate columns and total the amounts of Department A's escapable and inescapable expenses. Should Whisper eliminate Department A? Why?

Problem 23–4A

Ed Sample produced and sold a half million kilograms of apples last year, and he prepared the following statement to show the results:

ED SAMPLE
Income from the Sale of Apples
For Year Ended December 31, 19—

	Results by Grades			Combined
	No. 1	No. 2	No. 3	
Sales by grades:				
No. 1, 200,000 kgs. @ $0.11 per kg.	$22,000			
No. 2, 200,000 kgs. @ $0.07 per kg.		$14,000		
No. 3, 100,000 kgs. @ $0.04 per kg.			$ 4,000	
Combined sales				$40,000
Costs:				
Tree pruning and orchard care @				
$0.021 per kg.	$ 4,200	$ 4,200	$ 2,100	$10,500
Fruit picking, grading, and sorting				
@ $0.0252 per kg.	5,040	5,040	2,520	12,600
Marketing @ $0.0084 per kg.	1,680	1,680	840	4,200
Total costs	$10,920	$10,920	$ 5,460	$27,300
Net income or (loss)	$11,080	$ 3,080	$(1,460)	$12,700

Upon completing the statement, Mr. Sample thought a wise course of future action might be to leave the No. 3 apples on the trees to fall off and be plowed under when he cultivated between the trees, and thus avoid the loss from their sale. However, before doing so he consulted you.

When you examined the statement, you recognized that Mr. Sample had divided all his costs by 500,000 and allocated them on a per kilogram basis. You asked him about the marketing costs and learned that $3,960 of the $4,200 was incurred in placing the No. 1 and No. 2 fruit in boxes and delivering them to the warehouse of the fruit buyer. The cost for this was the same for both grades. You also learned that the remaining $240 was for loading the No. 3 fruit on the trucks of a cider manufacturer who bought this grade of fruit in bulk at the orchard for use in making apple cider.

Required:

Prepare an income statement that will reflect better the results of producing and marketing the apples.

Problem 23–5A

Toys 4U has three selling departments, A, B, and C, and two supporting departments, the general office and the purchasing department. Its accountant brought together the following information for use in allocating expenses to the departments:

Direct departmental expenses:

The store's direct departmental expenses for its annual accounting period which ended December 31, 19X, as shown by its payroll, requisition, and plant asset records were:

	Salaries expense	Supplies expense	Depr. of equipment	Equipment insurance
General office	$16,665	$ 195	$ 565	$185
Purchasing department	11,710	160	345	115
Department A	15,240	275	780	260
Department B	10,860	210	395	130
Department C	12,440	230	460	155
Totals	$66,915	$1,070	$2,545	$845

Indirect expenses:

The store incurred these indirect expenses:

Rent expense	$14,500
Advertising expense	6,000
Heating and lighting expense	5,200
Janitorial expense	10,400

The store allocates its indirect expenses to its departments as follows:

a. Rent expense on the basis of the amount and value of the floor space occupied. The general office and purchasing departments occupy space on a balcony at the rear of the store which is not as valuable as the space occupied by the selling departments; consequently, $1,500 of the total rent is allocated to these two departments in proportion to the space occupied. The remainder of the rent is divided between the selling departments in proportion to the space they occupy. The departments occupy the following amounts of space: general office, 150 square metres; purchasing department, 100 square metres; Department A, 625 square metres; Department B, 250 square metres; and Department C, 375 square metres.

b. Advertising expenses on the basis of sales which were Department A, $180,000; Department B, $84,000; and Department C, $136,000.

c. Heating and lighting and janitorial expenses on the basis of square metres of space occupied.

Supporting department expenses:

The store allocates its general office department expenses to its selling departments on the basis of sales, and it allocates purchasing department expenses on the basis of purchases. Purchases were Department A, $124,400; Department B, $62,200; and Department C, $93,300.

Required:

Prepare a departmental expense allocation schedule for the concern.

Problem
23–6A
Combustion Power, Ltd.'s Trail plant is managed by Sue Pedersen, who is responsible for all costs of the Trail operation other than her own salary. The plant is divided into two production departments and an office department. The casting and the polishing departments manufacture different products and have separate managers; the office department is managed by the plant manager. Combustion Power prepares a monthly budget for each of the production departments (casting and polishing) and then accumulates costs in a manner that assigns all of the Trail plant costs to the departments.

The department budgets and cost accumulations for the month of July were as follows:

	Budget		Actual costs		
	Casting dept.	Polishing dept.	Casting dept.	Polishing dept.	Combined
Raw materials	$230,000	$280,000	$223,500	$287,600	$ 511,100
Wages	168,000	198,000	173,900	192,900	366,800
Salary, department manager	26,000	28,000	27,500	28,000	55,500
Supplies used	7,500	8,000	9,600	9,200	18,800
Depreciation of equipment	14,000	10,000	14,000	11,000	25,000
Heating and lighting	16,000	24,000	19,440	29,160	48,600
Rent on building	10,000	15,000	10,000	15,000	25,000
Share of office dept. costs	60,000	60,000	66,000	66,000	132,000
	$531,500	$623,000	$543,940	$638,860	$1,182,800

Office department costs consisted of the following:

	Budget	Actual
Salary—plant manager	$48,000	$48,000
Other salaries	50,000	54,000
Other costs	22,000	30,000

Each department manager is responsible for the purchase and maintenance of equipment in the department. Heating and lighting cost and building rent are allocated to the production departments on the basis of relative space used by those departments.

Required:

Prepare responsibility accounting performance reports on the managers of each production department and on the plant manager.

PROVOCATIVE PROBLEMS

Provocative
Problem 23–1,
Land Deal
Partnership
Kevin Langfeld, Larry Fellingham, and John Tomassini entered into a partnership for the purpose of developing and selling a plot of land currently owned by Langfeld. Fellingham invested $52,000 cash in the partnership, Langfeld invested his land at its $60,000 fair market value, and Tomassini invested $8,000; and they agreed to share losses and gains equally. Tomassini was to provide the necessary real estate expertise to make the project a success. The

partnership installed streets and water mains costing $60,000 and divided the land into 14 building lots. They priced Lots 1, 2, 3, and 4 for sale at $12,000 each; Lots 5, 6, 7, 8, 9, 10, 11, and 12 at $14,000 each; and Lots 13 and 14 at $16,000 each. The partners agreed that Tomassini could take Lot 13 at cost for his personal use. The remaining lots were sold, and the partnership dissolved. Determine the amount of partnership cash each partner should receive in the dissolution.

Provocative Problem 23–2, Powerflow Company

The Powerflow Company bookkeeper prepared the following income statement for March of the current year:

POWERFLOW COMPANY
Income Statement
For March 19—

	Motor department	Compressor department	Combined
Sales	$40,000	$60,000	$100,000
Cost of goods sold	28,600	42,900	71,500
Gross profit on sales	$11,400	$17,100	$ 28,500
Warehousing expenses	$ 2,950	$ 2,950	$ 5,900
Selling expenses	5,600	6,100	11,700
General and administrative expenses	1,525	1,525	3,050
Total expenses	$10,075	$10,575	$ 20,650
Net income	$ 1,325	$ 6,525	$ 7,850

The company is a wholesaler of motors and compressors and is organized on a departmental basis. However, the company manager does not feel that the bookkeeper's statement reflects the profit situation in the company's two selling departments, and he has asked you to redraft it with any supporting schedules or comments you think desirable. Your investigation reveals the following:

1. The company sold 500 motors and 400 compressors during March. The bookkeeper apportioned cost of goods sold between the two departments on an arbitrary basis. A compressor actually costs the company twice as much as a motor.

2. A motor and a compressor are of approximately the same weight and bulk. However, because there are two styles of motors and three styles of compressors, the company must carry a 50% greater inventory of compressors, than motors.

3. The company occupies its building on the following bases:

	Area of space	Value of space
Warehouse	80%	60%
Motor sales office	5%	10%
Compressor sales office	5%	10%
General office	10%	20%

4. Warehousing expenses for March consisted of the following:

Wages expense	$3,000
Depreciation of building	2,000
Heating and lighting expenses	500
Depreciation of warehouse equipment	400
Total	$5,900

The bookkeeper had charged all of the building's depreciation plus all of the heating and lighting expenses to warehousing expenses.

5. Selling expenses for March consisted of the following:

	Motor department	Compressor department
Sales salaries	$4,000	$4,500
Advertising	1,500	1,500
Depreciation of office equipment	100	100
Totals	$5,600	$6,100

Sales salaries and depreciation were charged to the two departments on the basis of actual amounts incurred. Advertising was apportioned by the bookkeeper. The company has an established advertising budget based on dollars of sales which it followed rather closely in March.

6. General and administrative expenses for March consisted of the following:

Salaries and wages	$2,800
Depreciation of office equipment	200
Miscellaneous office expenses	50
Total	$3,050

Provocative Problem 23–3, Air Conditioner Sales Corporation

Air Conditioner Sales Corporation wholesales automobile air conditioners for small imported cars. Operations of the company during the past year resulted in the following:

	Standard	Deluxe
Units sold	900	300
Selling price per unit	$300	$400
Cost per unit	160	210
Sales commission per unit	45	60
Indirect selling and administrative expenses	75	100

Indirect selling and administrative expenses totaled $97,500 and were allocated between the sales of Standard and Deluxe units on the basis of their relative sales volumes. The Standard model produced $270,000 of revenue, and the Deluxe model produced $120,000; thus, the Standard model was assigned 27/39 of the $97,500 of indirect expenses and the Deluxe model was assigned 12/39. After allocating the total indirect expenses to the two models, the indirect expenses per unit were determined by dividing the total by the number of units sold. Hence, the Standard model's cost per unit was $75 and the Deluxe model's cost per unit was $100.

Management of Air conditioner Sales Corporation is attempting to decide between three courses of action and asks you to evaluate which of the three courses is most desirable. The three alternatives are (1) through advertising push the sales of the Standard model, (2) through advertising push the sales of the Deluxe model, or (3) do no additional advertising, in which case sales of each model will continue at present levels. The demand for air conditioners is fairly stable, and an increase in the number of units of one model sold will cause an equally large decrease in the sales of the other model. However, through the expenditure of $3,000 for advertising, the company can shift the sale of 150 units of the Standard model to the Deluxe model, or vice versa, depending upon which model receives the advertising attention.

Should the company advertise; and if so, which model? Back your position with income statements.

ANALYTICAL AND REVIEW PROBLEMS

Problem 23–1 A&R

Many accountants and analysts hold that whatever method is used for common costs or joint costs allocation it is arbitrary and an exercise in futility. Allocation obscures rather than illuminates the essential data on which evaluation and decision must be made. Consequently, allocation of costs should only be made where it is absolutely necessary, for example, amount of cost to be matched with the current period (cost of goods sold) and the amount of cost to be carried to future period(s) as inventory. Allocation for evaluation of performance should, however, not be made because such allocations are at best meaningless and at worst misleading and obscure the facts of a situation.

Required:

Do you agree with the view expressed? Discuss your answer.

Problem 23–2 A&R

It has been stated that in eliminating a profit centre, you eliminate all of the revenues but not all of the costs.

Required:

Do you agree? Support your answer with an illustration.

Problem 23–3 A&R

To allocate or not to allocate; that is the question.

Required:

Make a case for allocation and a case against allocation of common and/or joint costs.

Planning and Controlling Business Operations

PART EIGHT

Cost-Volume-Profit Analysis

24

After studying Chapter 24, you should be able to:

Describe the different types of cost behavior experienced by a typical company.

State the assumptions that underlie cost-volume-profit analysis and explain how these assumptions restrict the usefulness of the information obtained from the analysis.

Prepare and interpret a scatter diagram of past costs and sales volume.

Calculate a break-even point for a single-product company and graphically plot its costs and revenues.

Describe some extensions that may be added to the basic cost-volume-profit analysis of break-even point.

Calculate a composite sales unit for a multiproduct company and a break-even point for such a company.

Define or explain the words and phrases listed in the chapter Glossary.

Cost-volume-profit analysis is a means of predicting the effect of changes in costs and sales levels on the income of a business. In its simplest form it involves the determination of the sales level at which a company neither earns a profit nor incurs a loss, or in other words, the point at which it breaks even. For this reason cost-volume-profit analysis is often called break-even analysis. However, the technique can be expanded to answer additional questions, such as: What sales volume is necessary to earn a desired net income? What net income will be earned if unit selling prices are reduced in order to increase sales volume? What net income will be earned if a new machine that will reduce unit labour costs is installed? What net income will be earned if we change the sales mix? When the technique is expanded to answer such additional questions, the descriptive phrase ''cost-volume-profit analysis'' is more appropriate than ''break-even analysis.''

COST BEHAVIOUR

Conventional cost-volume-profit analyses require that costs be classified as either fixed or variable. Some costs are definitely fixed in nature. Others are strictly variable. But, when costs are examined, some are observed to be neither completely fixed nor completely variable.

Fixed Costs

A *fixed cost* remains unchanged in total amount over a wide range of production levels. For example, if the factory building is rented for, say, $1,000 per month, this cost remains the same whether the factory operates on a one-shift, two-shift, or an around-the-clock basis. Likewise, the cost is the same whether 100 units of product are produced in a month, 1,000 units are produced, or any other number up to the full production capacity of the plant. Note, however, that while the total amount of a fixed cost remains constant as the level of production changes, fixed costs per unit of product decrease as volume increases. For example, if rent is $1,000 per month and 2 units of product are produced in a month, the rent cost per unit is $500; but if production is increased to 10 units per month, rent cost per unit decreases to $100. Likewise it decreases to $2 per unit if production is increased to 500 units per month.

When production volume is plotted on a graph, units of product are shown on the horizontal axis and dollars of cost are shown on the vertical axis. Fixed costs are then depicted as a horizontal line, since the total amount of fixed costs remains constant at all levels of production. This is shown on the graph in Illustration 24–1 where the fixed costs remain at $32,000 at all production levels up to 2,000 units of product.

Illustration 24–1

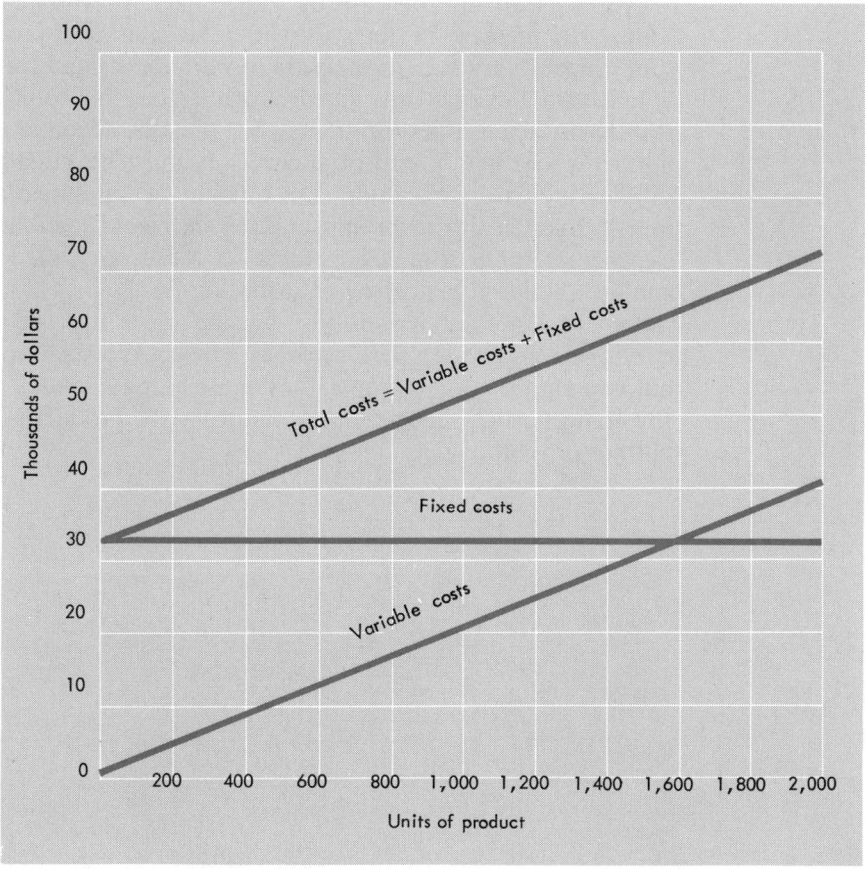

Variable Costs

A *variable cost* changes in total amount as production volume changes. For example, the cost of the material that enters into a product is a variable cost. If material costing $20 is required in the production of one unit of product, total material costs are $20 if one unit of product is manufactured, $40 if two units are manufactured, $60 if three units are manufactured, and so on for any number of units. In other words, the variable cost per unit of production remains constant while the total amount of variable cost changes in direct proportion to the level of production. Variable costs appear on a graph as a straight line with a positive slope; the line rises as the production volume increases, as in Illustration 24–1.

Semivariable Costs and Stair-Step Costs

All costs are not necessarily either fixed or variable. For example, some costs increase in steps. Consider the salaries of production supervisors. Supervisory salaries may be more or less fixed for any production volume from zero to the maximum that can be completed on a one-shift basis. Then, if an additional shift must be added to increase production, a whole new group of supervisors must be hired and supervisory salaries increase by a lump-sum amount. Total supervisory costs then remain fixed at this level until a third shift is added when they increase by another lump sum. Costs such as these are called *stair-step costs* and are shown graphically in Illustration 24–2.

In addition to stair-step costs, some costs may be semivariable or curvilinear in nature. *Semivariable costs* go up with volume increases, but when plotted on a graph, they must be plotted as a curved line (see Illustration 24–2). These costs change with production-level changes, but not proportionately.

Illustration 24–2

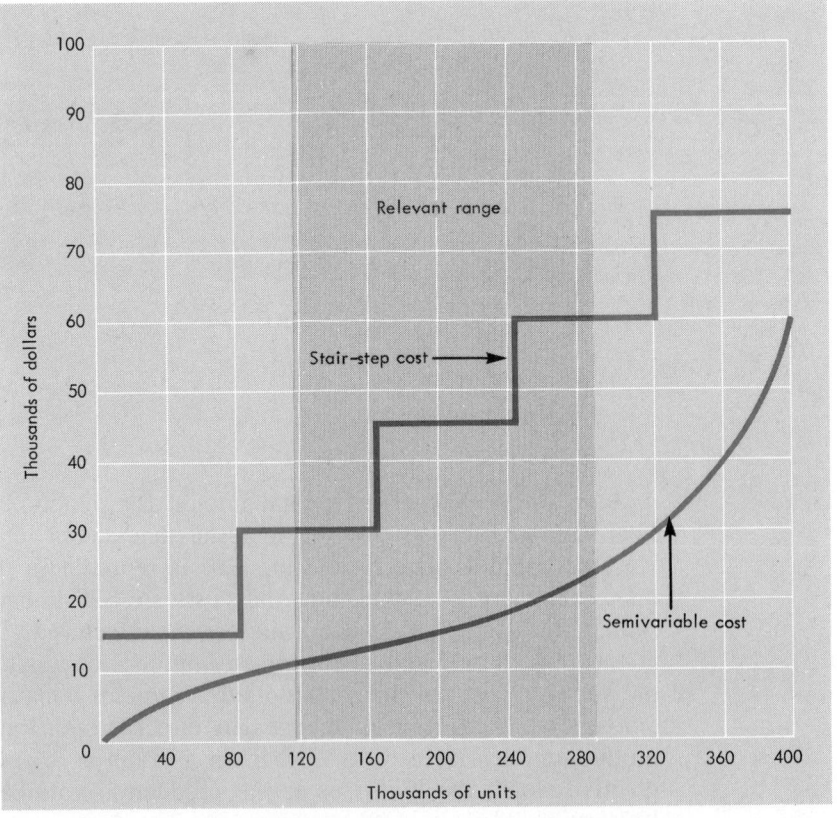

For example, at low levels of production, the addition of more labourers may allow each labourer to specialize so that the whole crew becomes more efficient. Each new labourer increases the total cost, but the increased production more than compensates for the increased cost so that the cost per unit is reduced. Eventually, however, the addition of more labourers in a given plant may cause inefficiencies; labourers may begin to waste time bumping into each other. Thus, the addition of a new labourer may add some production but the cost per unit increases.

Cost Assumptions

Conventional *cost-volume-profit analysis* is based on relationships that can be expressed as straight lines. Costs are assumed to be either fixed or variable. With the costs depicted as straight lines, the lines are then analysed in order to answer a variety of questions. The reliability of the answers rests on three basic assumptions. If a cost-volume-profit analysis is to be reliable:

1. The per unit selling price must be constant. (The selling price per unit must remain the same regardless of production level.)
2. The costs classified as "variable" must behave as variable costs; that is, the actual (variable) cost per unit of production must remain constant.
3. The costs classified as "fixed" must remain constant over wide changes in the level of production.

When these assumptions are met, costs and revenues may be correctly represented by straight lines. However, the actual behaviour of costs and revenues often is not completely consistent with these assumptions, and if the assumptions are violated significantly, the results of cost-volume-profit analysis will not be reliable. Nevertheless, there are at least two reasons why these assumptions tend to provide reliable analyses.

AGGREGATING COSTS MAY SUPPORT ASSUMPTIONS. While individual variable costs may not act in a truly variable manner, the process of adding such costs together may offset such violations of the assumption. In other words, the assumption of variable behaviour may be satisfied in respect to total variable costs even though it is violated in respect to individual variable costs. Similarly, the assumption that fixed costs remain constant may be satisfied for total fixed costs even though individual fixed costs may violate the assumption.

RELEVANT RANGE OF OPERATIONS. Another reason why the assumptions that revenues, variable costs, and fixed costs can be reasonably represented as straight lines is that the assumptions are only intended to apply over the *relevant range of operations*. The relevant range of operations, as plotted in Illustration 24–2, is the normal operating range for the business. It excludes the extremely high and low levels that are not apt to be encountered. Thus, a specific fixed cost is expected to be truly fixed only within the relevant range. It may be that beyond the limits of the relevant range, the fixed cost would not remain constant.

The previous discussion defined variable costs and fixed costs in terms of levels of production activity. However, in cost-volume-profit analysis, the level of activity is usually measured in terms of sales volume, whether stated as sales dollars or number of units sold. Thus, an additional assumption is frequently made that the level of production is the same as the level of sales, or if they are not the same, that the difference will not be enough to materially damage the reliability of the analysis. That is, there will be no significant changes in the quantity or the value levels of the inventories.

It must also be recognized that cost-volume-profit analysis yields approximate answers to questions concerning the interrelationships of costs, volumes, and profits. So long as management understands that the answers provided are approximations, cost-volume-profit analysis can be a useful managerial tool.

Estimating Cost Behaviour

The process of estimating the behaviour of a company's costs requires judgment and, to the extent past data is available, a careful examination of past experience. Initially, the individual costs should be reviewed and classified as fixed or variable based on the accountant's understanding of how each cost is likely to behave. Some costs may be classified quite easily. For example, raw material costs of a manufacturer or cost of goods sold of a merchandiser are undoubtedly variable costs. Similarly, a constant monthly rent expense or the monthly salaries of administrative personnel are clearly fixed costs.

MIXED COSTS.   Although some costs are easily classified as variable or fixed, the behaviour of other costs may be less obvious. For example, compensation to sales personnel might include a constant monthly salary plus a commission based on sales. A cost of this type is called a *mixed cost* (see Illustration 24–3). Instead of classifying a mixed cost as variable or fixed, it should be divided into separate fixed and variable components so that each can be classified correctly.

SCATTER DIAGRAMS.   Classifying costs as fixed or variable should be based, if possible, on an analysis of past experience. One helpful technique of analyzing past experience is to display past data on a *scatter diagram,* such as is shown in Illustration 24–4. In preparing a scatter diagram, volume in dollars or units is measured on the horizontal axis and cost is measured on the vertical axis. The cost and volume of each period are entered as a single point on the diagram.

Illustration 24–4 shows a scatter diagram of a company's total costs and sales for each of 12 months. Each point shows the total costs incurred

Illustration 24–3 Mixed Cost

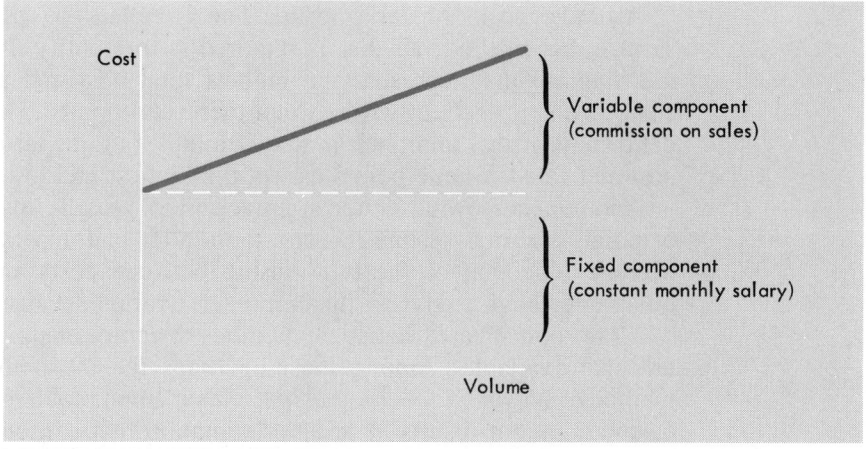

and the sales volume during a given month. For example, in one month, sales amounted to $30,000 and total costs were $26,000. These results were entered on the diagram as the point labeled A.

ESTIMATED LINE OF COST BEHAVIOUR. In Illustration 24–4, observe the ***estimated line of cost behaviour.*** This line attempts to reflect

Illustration 24–4

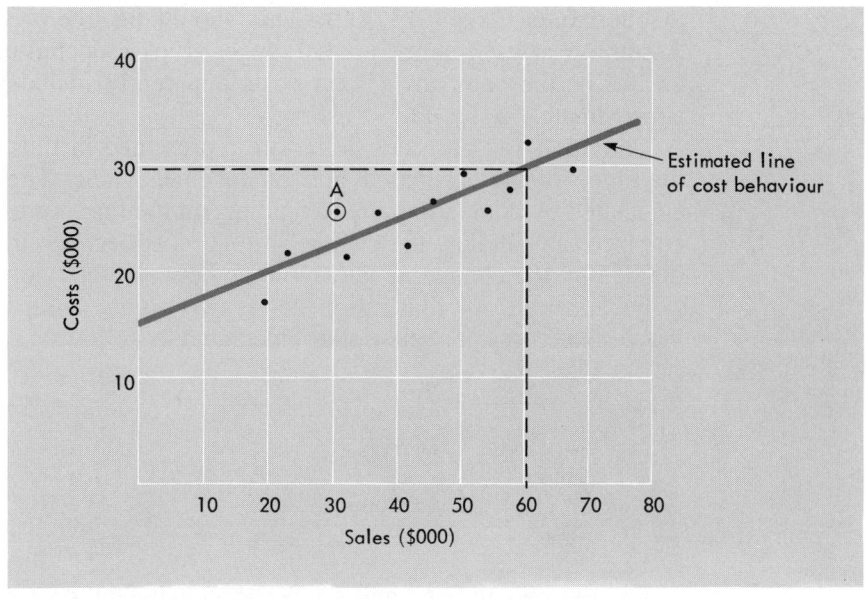

the average relationship between total costs and sales volume. Several alternative methods can be used to derive this line.

A crude means of deriving this line is called the *high-low method.* To use this method, all that is required is to identify the two points in the diagram that represent the highest total cost and the lowest total cost. A line is then drawn between these two points. The most obvious deficiency of this approach is that it totally ignores all of the available cost and sales volume points except the highest and lowest.

Another, somewhat better approach is to visually inspect the scatter of points and draw a line through the scatter that appears to provide an average reflection of the relationship between costs and volume. For quick and rough analyses, this approach is often satisfactory.

More sophisticated statistical methods of approximating cost behaviour are also available. Among these, perhaps the most often used is the method of *least-squares regression.* This method requires fairly extensive calculations but results in an approximation that can be described as a line that best fits the actual cost and sales volume experience of the company. These calculations are usually performed with the aid of specially designed computer software thus obviously facilitating the procedures. The concepts for least-squares regressions are typically covered in statistics courses and are applied to accounting data in more advanced cost accounting courses.

Return to Illustration 24–4 and observe that the sales volume each month ranged from approximately $20,000 to $67,000. If the estimated line of cost behaviour is extended too far beyond this range, it is likely to be an unreliable basis for predicting actual costs. Note, however, that the line has been extended downward to the point at which it intersects the horizontal axis ($15,000). This should be interpreted as follows: Assuming sales volume in the range of past operations ($20,000 to $67,000), the company's total costs apparently include fixed costs of approximately $15,000.

Variable costs per sales dollar are represented in Illustration 24–4 by the slope of the estimated line of cost behaviour. The slope may be calculated by comparing any two points on the line. To estimate variable cost per sales dollar, the change in total cost between the two points is divided by the change in sales volume between the two points.

For example, in Illustration 24–4, two points could be selected and the variable cost per sale dollar calculated as follows:

	Sales	Cost
First point	$60,000	$30,000
Second point	–0–	15,000
Changes	$60,000	$15,000

Or, the calculation may be performed by taking two pairs of data and similarly determining the following without the aid of a graph.

$$\frac{\text{Change in cost}}{\text{Change in sales}} = \frac{\$15,000}{\$60,000} = \$0.25 \text{ of cost per sales dollar}$$

An analysis of past experience may allow the accountant to estimate total fixed costs and variable costs per unit of volume without making a detailed classification of each individual cost. However, the accountant will have greater confidence in the analysis if individual costs are classified and the results are tested against observations of past experience. In testing the classifications, scatter diagrams may be prepared for individual costs, total variable costs, total fixed costs, and total costs.

BREAK-EVEN POINT

A company's *break-even point* is the sales level at which it neither earns a profit nor incurs a loss. It may be expressed either in units of product or in dollars of sales. To illustrate, assume that Alpha Company sells a single product for $100 per unit and incurs $70 of variable costs per unit sold. If the fixed costs involved in selling the product are $24,000, the company breaks even on the product as soon as it sells 800 units or as soon as sales volume reaches $80,000. This breakeven point may be determined as follows:

1. Each unit sold at $100 recovers its $70 variable costs and contributes $30 toward the fixed costs.
2. The fixed costs are $24,000; consequently, 800 units ($24,000 ÷ $30 = 800) must be sold to pay the fixed costs.
3. And 800 units at $100 each produce an $80,000 sales volume.

The $30 amount by which the sales price exceeds variable costs per unit is this product's *contribution margin per unit*. In other words, the contribution margin per unit is the amount that the sale of one unit contributes toward recovery of the fixed costs and then toward a profit. That is, the amount by which the selling price of a unit exceeds its variable cost.

Also, the contribution margin of a product expressed as a percentage of its sales price is its *contribution rate*. For instance, the contribution rate of the $100 product of this illustration is 30% ($30 ÷ $100 = 30%).

With contribution margin and contribution rate defined, it is possible to set up the following formulas for calculating a break-even point in units and in dollars:

$$\text{Break-even point in units} = \frac{\text{Fixed costs}}{\text{Contribution margin per unit}}$$

$$\text{Break-even point in dollars} = \frac{\text{Fixed costs}}{\text{Contribution rate}}$$

Application of the second formula to figures for the product of this illustration gives this result:

$$\text{Break-even point in dollars} = \frac{\$24,000}{30\%} = \frac{\$24,000}{0.30} = \$80,000$$

Although the solution in the present example comes out evenly, a contribution rate should be carried out several decimal places to avoid minor rounding errors when calculating the break-even point in dollars. In solving the exercises and problems at the end of this chapter, for example, calculations of contribution rate should be carried to six decimal places unless the requirements state otherwise. Calculated either way, Alpha Company's break-even point may be verified with an income statement, as in Illustration 24–5. Observe in the illustration that revenue from sales exactly equals the sum of the fixed and variable costs at the break-even point. Recognizing this will prove helpful in understanding the material that follows in this chapter.

BREAK-EVEN GRAPH

A cost-volume-profit analysis may be shown graphically as in Illustration 24–6. When presented in this form, the graph is commonly called a break-even graph or break-even chart. On such a graph the horizontal axis shows units sold, the vertical axis shows both dollars of sales and dollars of costs; and costs and revenues are plotted as straight lines. The illustrated graph shows the break-even point of Alpha Company. A break-even graph is prepared as follows:

1. The line representing fixed costs is plotted at the fixed cost level. Note that it is a horizontal line, since the fixed costs are the same at all sales levels. Actually, the fixed costs line is not essential to the analysis; however, it contributes important information and is commonly plotted on a break-even chart.

Illustration 24–5

ALPHA COMPANY
Income Statement
At the Break-Even Point

Sales (800 units at $100 each)		$80,000
Costs:		
Fixed costs	$24,000	
Variable costs (800 units at $70 each)	56,000	80,000
Net income		$ –0–

2. Next the sales line is projected from the point of zero units and zero dollars of sales to the point of maximum sales shown on the graph. In choosing the maximum number of units to be shown, a better graph results if the number chosen is such that it will cause the break-even point to appear near the centre of the graph.

3. Next the variable cost plus fixed cost line is plotted. Note that it begins at the fixed cost level and, as a result, shows total costs at all production levels. At the zero sales level there are no variable costs, only fixed costs. However, at any level above zero sales all the fixed costs are present and so are the variable costs for that level. Also observe that the variable cost plus fixed cost line intersects the sales line at the break-even point. It intersects at this point because at the break-even point the revenue from sales exactly equals the sum of the fixed and variable costs, or in other words, the total costs.

Illustration 24–6

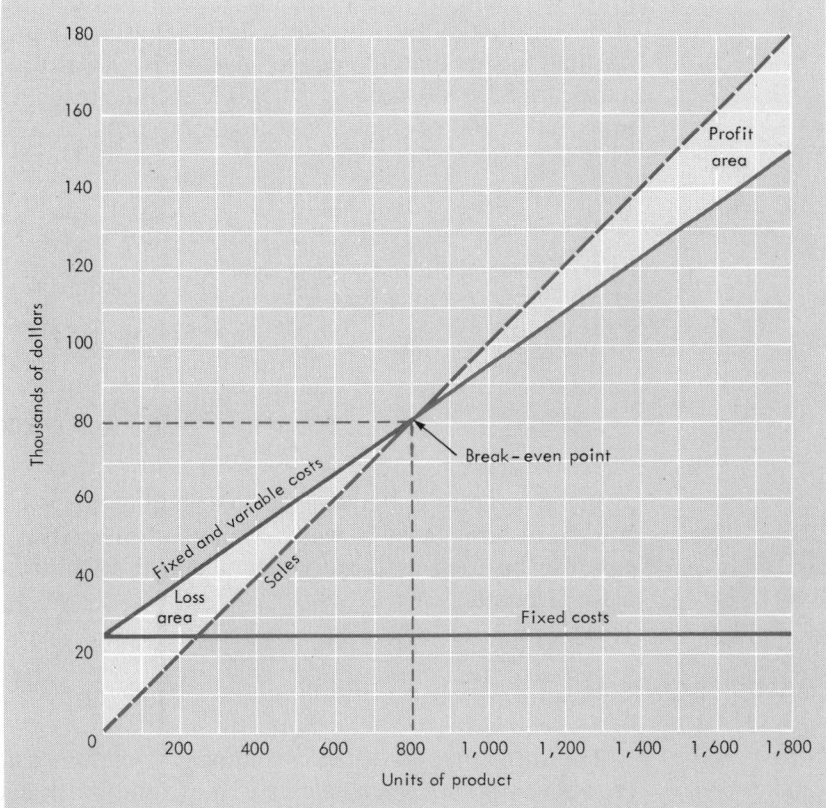

In reading a break-even chart, the vertical distance between the sales line and the total cost line represents a loss to the left of the break-even point and a profit to the right of it. The amount of profit or loss at any given sales level can be determined from the graph by measuring the vertical distance between the sales line and the total cost line at the given level.

SALES REQUIRED FOR A DESIRED NET INCOME

A slight extension of the concept behind the break-even calculation will produce a formula that may be used in determining the sales level necessary to produce a desired net income. The formula is:

$$\text{Sales at desired income level} = \frac{\text{Fixed costs} + \text{Net income} + \text{Income taxes}}{\text{Contribution rate}}$$

To illustrate the formula's use, assume that Alpha company of the previous example, the company having $24,000 of fixed costs and a 30% contribution rate, has set a $20,000 after-tax income goal for itself. Assume further that in order to have a $20,000 net income, the company must earn $28,500 and pay $8,500 in income taxes. Under these assumptions, $175,000 of sales are necessary to produce a $20,000 net income. This is calculated as follows:

$$\text{Sales at desired income level} = \frac{\text{Fixed costs} + \text{Net income} + \text{Income taxes}}{\text{Contribution rate}}$$

$$= \frac{\$24,000 + \$20,000 + - \$8,500}{30\%}$$

$$= \frac{\$52,500}{30\%} = \$175,000$$

In the formula just given, the contribution rate was used as the divisor, and the resulting answer was in dollars of sales. The contribution margin can also be used as the divisor; when it is, the resulting answer is in units of product.

MARGIN OF SAFETY

The difference between a company's current sales and sales at its break-even point, when sales are above the break-even point, is known as its margin of safety. The *margin of safety* is the amount that sales may decrease before the company will incur a loss. It may be expressed in units of product, dollars, or as a percentage of sales. For example, if current sales are $100,000 and the break-even point is $80,000, the margin of safety is $20,000, or 20%, of sales, calculated as follows:

$$\frac{\text{Sales} - \text{Break-even sales}}{\text{Sales}} = \text{Margin of safety}$$

or

$$\frac{\$100{,}000 - \$80{,}000}{\$100{,}000} = 20\% \text{ margin of safety}$$

INCOME FROM A GIVEN SALES LEVEL

Cost-volume-profit analysis goes beyond break-even analysis and can be used to answer other questions. For example, what income will result from a given sales level? To understand the analysis used in answering this question, recall the factors that enter into the calculation of income. When expressed in equation form, they are:

$$\text{Sales} - (\text{Fixed costs} + \text{Variable costs}) = \text{Income}$$

or

$$\text{Income} = \text{Sales} - (\text{Fixed costs} + \text{Variable costs})$$

This equation may be used to calculate the income that will result at a given sales level. For example, assume that Alpha Company of the previous illustrations wishes to know what income will result if its sales level can be increased to $200,000. That would be 2,000 units of its product at $100 per unit. To determine the answer, recall that the variable costs per unit of this product are $70 and note that the $70 is 0.7 of the product's selling price. Consequently, variable costs for 2,000 units of the product are 0.7 of the selling price of these units, or (0.7 × $200,000) = $140,000. Alpha Company's fixed costs are $24,000. Therefore, if these known factors are substituted in the equation for determining income, the equation will read:

$$\begin{aligned}
\text{Income} &= \$200{,}000 - [\$24{,}000 + (0.7 \times \$200{,}000)] \\
&= \$200{,}000 - \$164{,}000 \\
&= \$36{,}000
\end{aligned}$$

The $36,000 is "before-tax" income; and as a result, if Alpha Company wishes to learn its after-tax income from the sale of 2,000 units of its product, it will have to apply the appropriate tax rates to the $36,000.

OTHER QUESTIONS

A company may wish to know what would happen to its break-even point if it reduced the selling price of its product in order to increase sales. Or it might wish to know what would happen if it installed a new machine that would increase its fixed costs but which would reduce variable costs. These are two of several possible questions involving changes in selling prices and costs. At first glance such changes seem to violate the basic assumptions on which cost-volume-profit analysis is based. But this is not true. A constant selling price, truly variable costs, and truly fixed costs are assumed to hold for any analysis involving the assumed price and costs. However, changes may be made, and if made, the new price and new costs are assumed to remain constant for the analyses involving that price and those costs. The fact that changes can be made in these factors is helpful for planning purposes because the effect of changes can be predicted before the changes are actually made.

To illustrate the effect of changes, assume that Alpha Company is considering the installation of a new machine that will increase the fixed costs of producing and selling its product from $24,000 to $30,000. However, the machine will reduce the variable costs from $70 per unit of product to $60. The selling price of the product will remain unchanged at $100, and the company wishes to know what its break-even point will be if the machine is installed. Examination of the costs shows that the installation will not only increase the company's fixed costs but it will also change the contribution margin and contribution rate of the company's product. The new contribution margin will be $40, that is, ($100 − $60) = $40, and the new contribution rate will be $40, that is, ($40 ÷ $100) = 0.4, or 40%. Consequently, if the machine is installed, the company's new break-even point will be:

$$\text{Break-even point in dollars} = \frac{\$30,000}{0.4} = \$75,000$$

In addition to their use in determining Alpha Company's break-even point, the new fixed costs and the new contribution rate may be used to determine the sales level needed to earn a desired net income. They may also be used to determine the expected income at a given sales level or to answer other questions the company will want to answer before installing the new machine.

MULTIPRODUCT BREAK-EVEN POINT

The break-even point for a company selling a number of products can be determined by using a hypothetical unit made up of units of each of the company's products in their expected *sales mix*. Such a hypothetical unit is really a composite unit and is treated in all analyses as though it were a single product. To illustrate the use of such a hypothetical unit, assume that Beta Company sells three products, A, B, and C; and it wishes to calculate its break-even point. Unit selling prices for the three products are Product A, $5; Product B, $8; and Product C, $4. The sales mix or ratio in which the products are expected to be sold is 4:2:1, and the company's fixed costs are $48,000. Under these assumptions a composite unit selling price for the three products can be calculated as follows:

4 units of Product A at $5 per unit	$20
2 units of Product B at $8 per unit	16
1 unit of Product C at $4 per unit	4
Selling price of a composite unit	$40

Also, if the variable costs of selling the three products are Product A, $3.25; Product B, $4.50; and Product C, $2, the variable costs of a composite unit of the products are:

4 units of Product A at $3.25 per unit	$13
2 units of Product B at $4.50 per unit	9
1 unit of Product C at $2.00 per unit	2
Variable costs of a composite unit	$24

With the variable costs and selling price of a composite unit of the company's products calculated, the contribution margin for a composite unit may be determined by subtracting the variable costs of a composite unit from the selling price of such a unit, as follows:

$$\$40 - \$24 = \$16 \text{ contribution margin per composite unit}$$

The $16 contribution margin may then be used to determine the company's break-even point in composite units. The break-even point is:

$$\text{Break-even point in composite units} = \frac{\text{Fixed costs}}{\text{Composite contribution margin per unit}}$$

$$\text{Break-even point in composite units} = \frac{\$48,000}{\$16}$$

$$\text{Break-even point} = 3,000 \text{ composite units}$$

The company breaks even when it sells 3,000 composite units of its products. However, to determine the number of units of each product it must sell to break even, the number of units of each product in the composite unit must be multiplied by the number of composite units needed to break even, as follows:

Product A: $4 \times 3,000 = 12,000$ units
Product B: $2 \times 3,000 = 6,000$ units
Product C: $1 \times 3,000 = 3,000$ units

The accuracy of all these computations can be verified by preparing an income statement showing the company's revenues and costs at the break-even point. Such a statement is shown in Illustration 24–7.

Illustration 24–7

BETA COMPANY
Income Statement
At the Break-Even Point

Sales:		
Product A (12,000 units at $5)		$ 60,000
Product B (6,000 units at $8)		48,000
Product C (3,000 units at $4)		12,000
Total sales		120,000
Costs:		
Fixed costs	$48,000	
Variable costs:		
Product A (12,000 units at $3.25)	$39,000	
Product B (6,000 units at $4.50)	27,000	
Product C (3,000 units at $2.00)	6,000	
Total variable costs	72,000	
Total costs		120,000
Net income		$ –0–

A composite unit made up of each of a company's products in their expected sales mix may be used in answering a variety of cost-volume-profit questions. In making all such analyses, it is assumed that the product mix will remain constant at all sales levels just as the other factors entering into an analysis are assumed to be constant. Nevertheless, this does not prevent changes in the assumed sales mix in order to learn what would happen if the mix were changed. However, changes in the sales mix will require a recomputation of the composite unit selling price and composite unit variable costs for each change in the mix.

EVALUATING THE RESULTS

Cost-volume-profit analyses have their greatest use in predicting what will happen when changes are made in selling prices, product mix, and the various cost factors. However, in evaluating the results of such analyses, several points should be kept in mind. First, the analyses are used to predict future results. Therefore, the data used in the formulas and on the graphs are assumed or forecast data. Consequently, the results of the analyses are no more reliable than the data used. Second, cost-volume-profit analyses as presented here are based on the assumptions that in any one analysis selling price will remain constant, sales mix will not change, fixed costs are truly fixed, and variable costs are truly variable. These assumptions do not always reflect reality. Therefore, at best, the answers obtained through cost-volume-profit analyses are approximations. However, if this is recognized, cost-volume-profit analyses can be useful to management in making decisions.

The cost-volume-profit analyses presented in this chapter are based on the assumption that revenues and costs may be expressed as straight lines; and as pointed out, such an assumption does not always hold. Therefore, it should be noted that cost-volume-profit analyses based on curvilinear relationships are also possible. However, the use of curvilinear relationships requires rather sophisticated mathematics, and a discussion of this is deferred to a more advanced text.

GLOSSARY

Break-even point.   The sales level at which a company neither earns a profit nor incurs a loss.

Contribution margin per unit.   The dollar amount that the sale of one unit contributes toward recovery of fixed costs and then toward a profit.

Contribution rate.   The contribution margin per unit expressed as a percentage of sales price.

Cost-volume-profit analysis.   A method of predicting the effects of changes in costs and sales level on the income of a business.

Estimated line of cost behaviour.   A line that attempts to reflect the average relationship between cost and volume.

Fixed cost.   A cost that remains unchanged in total amount over a wide range of production levels.

High-low method.   A crude technique for deriving an estimated line of cost behaviour that connects the highest and lowest costs shown on a scatter diagram with a straight line.

Least-squares regression.   A sophisticated method of deriving an estimated line of cost behaviour; the resulting estimate can be described as a line that best fits the actual cost and volume data of a company.

Margin of safety.   The amount by which a company's current sales exceed the sales necessary to break even.

Mixed cost.   A cost that includes two components, one of which is fixed and one of which is variable.

Relevant range of operations.   The normal operating range for the business, which excludes extremely high and low levels of production that are not apt to be encountered.

Sales mix.   The ratio in which a company's different products are sold.

Scatter diagram.   A graph used to display the relationship between costs and volume in which the cost and volume for each period is shown as a point on the diagram.

Semivariable cost.   A cost that changes with production volume but not in the same proportion.

Stair-step cost.   A cost that remains constant over a range of production, then increases by a lump sum if production is expanded beyond this range, then remains constant over another range of production increases, and so forth.

Variable cost.   A cost that changes in total amount proportionately with production-level changes.

QUESTIONS FOR CLASS DISCUSSION

1.   Why is cost-volume-profit analysis used?

2.   What is fixed cost? Name two fixed costs.

3.   When there are fixed costs in manufacturing a product and the number of units manufactured is increased, do fixed costs per unit increase or decrease? Why?

4.   What is a variable cost? Name two variable costs.

5.   What is a semivariable cost?

6.   The reliability of cost-volume-profit analysis rests upon three basic assumptions. What are they?

7.   What two factors tend to make it possible to classify costs as either fixed or variable?

8.   What is a mixed cost? How should a mixed cost be classified for the purpose of cost-volume-profit analysis?

9.   How are scatter diagrams used in the process of estimating the behaviour of a company's costs?

10.   What is the primary weakness of the high-low method of deriving an estimated line of cost behaviour?

11.   What is the break-even point in the sale of a product?

12.   A company sells a product for $90 per unit. The variable costs of producing and selling the product are $54 per unit. What is the product's contribution margin per unit? What is its contribution rate?

13.   If a straight line is begun at the fixed cost level on a break-even graph and the line rises at the variable cost rate, what does the line show?

14.   When a break-even graph is prepared, why are the fixed costs plotted as a horizontal line?

15. What is a company's margin of safety?

16. What is meant by the sales mix of a company?

17. If a company produces and sells more than one product, the reliability of cost-volume-profit analysis depends on an additional assumption in regard to sales mix. What is that assumption?

MULTIPLE CHOICE

1. Cost-volume-profit analysis is based on three assumptions. Which one of the following is not one of these assumptions?
    - *a.* Fixed costs remain constant over wide changes in production level.
    - *b.* Semivariable costs change proportionately with changes in production volume, throughout the relevant range.
    - *c.* Variable costs per unit of production remain constant as production volume changes.
    - *d.* Selling price per unit remains constant as production volume changes.
    - *e.* None of the above are necessary assumptions of cost-volume-profit analysis.

2. Marnan Company has fixed costs of $56,000. Its product sells for $25 per unit and variable costs amount to $15 per unit. For 198A Marnan Company wishes to earn a before-tax return that equals 10% of fixed costs. How many units must it sell to derive this income level?
    - *a.* 560.
    - *b.* 4,107.
    - *c.* 5,600.
    - *d.* 6,160.
    - *e.* 7.040.

3. A Company manufactures and sells a product for $80 per unit. The annual fixed costs of manufacturing and selling the product are $45,840, and the variable costs are $60 per unit. The company's break-even point in dollars is:
    - *a.* $57,300.
    - *b.* $61,120
    - *c.* $76,400.
    - *d.* $183,360.
    - *e.* Some other amount.

4. The product mix of B Company is 3 units of A, 2 units of B, and 1 unit of C. Selling prices for each product are $10, $20, and $30, respectively. Variable cost per unit are $6, $12, and $18, respectively. Fixed costs are $160,000. What is the break-even point in composite units?
    - *a.* 1,111.
    - *b.* 1,600.
    - *c.* 2,666.

    d. 4,000.

    e. 5,000.

5. Y Company's product has a contribution margin of $11.25 and a contribution rate of 22.5%. What price does Y charge for its product?

    a. $15.

    b. $20.

    c. $30.

    d. $40.

    e. $50.

6. Acme Corporation manufactures records which sell for $5.00. Fixed costs are $28,000 and variable costs are $3.60 per unit. Acme can buy a newer record press that will increase fixed costs by $8,000 per year, but variable costs will be decreased by $0.40 per unit. What effect would the purchase of the new press have on the break-even point of Acme?

    a. 4,444 unit increase.

    b. 9,850 unit decrease.

    c. 5,714 unit increase.

    d. 4,444 unit decrease.

    e. The purchase of the machine will have no effect on the break-even point.

MINI DISCUSSION CASES

Case 24–1   "Cost-volume-profit analysis is useless because none of the revenues or costs ever behave according to our assumptions. None of the costs are really either fixed or variable but wander all over the place. No one can give me a good estimate of what our profits will be at any sales volume level."

The above comments were made by a very frustrated general manager who was attempting to make his company more profitable.

Required:

a. Do you agree with the above comments with respect to cost-volume-profit analysis? Why?

b. Advise the manager about how he could use cost-volume-profit analysis more advantageously in managing his operations.

Case 24–2   Explain how cost-volume-profit analysis can be used in a multiproduct firm. How do changes in the sales mix affect the analysis and what can be done to compensate for these changes?

CLASS EXERCISES

Exercise 24–1   The past experience of a company discloses the following information about a particular cost and sales volume.

Period	Sales	Cost X
1	$20,000	$ 8,900
2	27,500	11,200
3	18,750	9,000
4	28,750	10,700
5	23,750	9,800
6	15,000	8,000

Required:

Prepare a scatter diagram of the cost and volume data, estimate the line of cost behaviour, and decide whether the cost is a variable, fixed, or mixed cost.

Exercise 24–2   Ranger Company manufactures a single product that it sells for $91 per unit. The variable costs of manufacturing the product are $75 per unit, and the annual fixed costs incurred in manufacturing it are $56,320.

Required:

Calculate the company's

a. Contribution margin.
b. Contribution rate.
c. Break-even point for the product in units.
d. Break-even point in dollars of sales.

Exercise 24–3   *Required:*

Prepare an income statement for Ranger Company's operations (Exercise 24–2), showing sales, fixed costs, and variable costs at the break-even point. Also, if Ranger Company's fixed costs increased by $7,200, calculate how many additional sales (in dollars) would be necessary to break even.

Exercise 24–4   Assume that Ranger Company of Exercise 24–2 wishes to earn a $32,000 annual after-tax income from the sale of its product, and that it must pay 50% of its income in income taxes.

Required:

Calculate

a. The number of units of its product it must sell to earn a $32,000 after-tax income from the sale of the product.
b. Calculate the number of dollars of sales that are needed to earn a $32,000 after-tax income.

Exercise 24–5   The sales manager of Ranger Company (Exercise 24–2) thinks that within two years annual sales of the company's product will reach 5,500 units while the sales price will go up to $96. Variable costs are expected to increase only $2 per unit, and fixed costs are not expected to change.

Required:

Calculate the company's

a. Before-tax income from the sale of these units.
b. Calculate its after-tax income from the sale of the units.

Exercise 24–6   X-Ray Company markets Products X and Y which it sells in the ratio of four units of Product X at $3 per unit to each two units of Product Y at $10 per unit. The variable costs of marketing Product X are $2.12 per unit, and the variable costs for Product Y are $5.18 per unit. The annual fixed costs for marketing both products are $16,450.

Required:

Calculate

a.   The selling price of a composite unit of these products.
b.   The variable costs per composite unit.
c.   The break-even point in composite units.
d.   The number of units of each product that will be sold at the break-even point.

PROBLEMS

Problem 24–1   Sloop Company has collected the following monthly total cost and sales volume data related to its recent operations.

Period	Costs	Sales
1	$30,000	$36,000
2	32,500	28,000
3	25,000	16,000
4	22,500	24,000
5	20,000	12,000
6	35,000	40,000
7	40,000	52,000
8	32,500	32,000
9	31,000	48,000
10	37,500	60,000
11	37,500	48,000
12	37,500	52,000

Required:

1.   Design a diagram with sales volume marked off in $8,000 intervals on the horizontal axis and cost marked off in $5,000 intervals on the vertical axis. Record the cost and sales data of Sloop Company as a scatter of points on the diagram.
2.   Based on your visual inspection of the scatter diagram, draw an estimated line of cost behaviour that appears to show the average relationship between cost and sales.
3.   Based on the estimated line of cost behaviour, estimate the amount of Sloop Company's fixed costs.
4.   Use the estimated line of cost behaviour to approximate cost when sales volume is $20,000 and when sales volume is $60,000. Calculate an estimate of variable cost per sales dollar.

Problem 24–2   Beaufort Company manufactures a number of products, one of which, Product P, is produced and sold quite independently from the others, and sells for

$675 per unit. The fixed costs of manufacturing Product P are $77,700, and the variable costs are $490 per unit. In solving requirements 1(b) and 4 (below), the calculation of a contribution rate should be carried to six decimal places.

Required:

1. Calculate the company's break-even point in the sale of Product P *(a)* in units and *(b)* in dollars of sales.
2. Prepare a break-even graph for Product P. Use 1,000 as the maximum number of units on your graph.
3. Prepare an income statement showing sales, fixed costs, and variable costs for Product P at the break-even point.
4. Determine the sales volume in dollars that the company must achieve to earn a $22,200 after-tax (50% rate) income from the sale of Product P.
5. Determine the after-tax income the company will earn from a $513,000 sales level for Product P.

Problem 24–3   Baytown Company incurred a $4,000 loss last year in selling 4,000 units of its Product A, as the following income statement shows:

BAYTOWN COMPANY
Last Year's Income Statement for Product A

Sales		$100,000
Costs:		
Fixed	$24,000	
Variable	80,000	104,000
Net loss from sale of Product A		$ (4,000)

The production manager has pointed out that the variable costs of Product A can be reduced 25% by installing a machine to do a labour operation presently done by hand. However, the new machine will increase fixed costs by $6,400 annually.

Required:

1. Calculate last year's dollar break-even point for Product A.
2. Calculate the dollar break-even point for Product A under the assumption the new machine is installed.
3. Prepare a break-even chart under the assumption the new machine is installed. Use 6,000 as the maximum number of units on your chart.
4. Prepare an income statement showing expected annual results with the new machine installed, no change in the selling price of Product A, and no change in the number of units sold. Assume a 50% income tax rate.
5. Calculate the sales level required to earn a $12,000 per year after-tax income with the new machine installed and no change in the selling price of Product A. Prepare an income statement showing the results at this sales level.

Problem 24–4   Last year Willis Company earned an unsatisfactory 2.5% after-tax return from the sale of 50,000 packages of its Product M at $1 each. The company buys Product M in bulk and packages it for resale. Following are last year's costs for the product:

Costs of bulk Product M (sufficient for 50,000 packages) ... $25,000
Packaging materials and other variable packaging costs ...   5,000
Fixed costs..   17,500
Income tax rate 50%

It has been suggested that if the selling price of the product is reduced 10% and a slight change made in its packaging, the number of units sold can be doubled. The packaging change will increase packaging costs 10% per unit, but doubling the sales volume will gain a 5% reduction in the product's bulk purchase price. The packaging and volume changes will not affect fixed costs.

Required:

1. Calculate the dollar break-even points for Product M at the $1 per unit sales price and at $0.90 per unit.
2. Prepare a break-even chart for the sale of the product at each price. Use 100,000 units as the upper limit of your charts.
3. Prepare a condensed comparative income statement showing the results of selling the product at $1 per unit and the estimated results of selling it at $0.90 per unit.

Problem 24–5   Badlands Company sells two products, A and B, which are produced and sold independently. Last year the company sold 8,000 units of each of these products at $120 per unit, earning $105,000 from the sale of each as the following condensed income statement shows:

	Product A	Product B
Sales	$960,000	$960,000
Costs:		
Fixed costs	$150,000	$600,000
Variable costs	600,000	150,000
Total costs	$750,000	$750,000
Income before taxes	$210,000	$210,000
Income taxes (50% rate) ...	105,000	105,000
Net income	$105,000	$105,000

Required:

1. Calculate the break-even point for each product in units.
2. Prepare a break-even graph for each product. Use 10,000 as the maximum number of units on each graph.
3. Prepare a condensed income statement showing in separate columns the net income the company will earn from the sale of each product under the assumption that without a change in selling prices, the number of units of each product sold declines to 5,926 units.
4. Prepare a second condensed income statement showing in separate columns the net income the company will earn if the number of units of each product increases 25%.

Problem 24–6   Shiner Company manufactures and sells three products, X, Y, and Z. Product X sells for $16 per unit; Product Y sells for $9 per unit; and Product Z sells for $7 per unit. Their sales mix is in the ratio of 3:7:4, and the variable costs of manufacturing and selling the products have been: Product X, $12; Product Y, $6; and Product Z, $5. The fixed costs of manufacturing the three products are $139,400. A special material called Defluss has been used in manufacturing both Products X and Y; however, a new material called Sulfex has just become available, and if it is substituted for Defluss it will reduce the variable cost of manufacturing Product X by $0.75 and Product Y by $0.25. However, fixed costs will go up to $144,000 because of special equipment needed to process Sulfez.

Required:

1. Determine the company's break-even point in dollars and the number of units of each product sold at the break-even point under the assumption that Defluss is used in manufacturing Products X and Y. Show all pertinent calculations.
2. Determine the company's break-even point in dollars and the number of units of each product sold at the break-even point under the assumption that the new Sulfez material is used in manufacturing Products X and Y.

   Show all pertinent calculations.

ALTERNATE PROBLEMS

Problem 24–1A

Cradle Company has collected the following monthly total cost and sales volume data related to its recent operations.

Period	Costs	Sales
1	$33,000	$44,000
2	36,000	35,000
3	28,000	20,000
4	25,000	30,000
5	22,000	16,000
6	39,000	49,000
7	44,000	64,000
8	36,000	40,000
9	34,000	59,000
10	41,000	73,000
11	41,000	59,000
12	41,000	64,000

Required:

1. Design a diagram with sales volume marked off in $8,000 intervals on the horizontal axis and cost marked off in $5,000 intervals on the vertical axis. Record the cost and sales data of Cradle Company as a scatter of points on the diagram.
2. Based on your visual inspection of the scatter diagram, draw an estimated line of cost behaviour that appears to show the average relationship between cost and sales.
3. Based on the estimated line of cost behaviour, estimate the amount of Cradle Company's fixed costs.

4. Use the estimated line of cost behaviour to approximate cost when sales volume is $32,000 and when sales volume is $80,000. Calculate an estimate of variable cost per sales dollar.

Problem 24–2A

Among the products sold by Kennan Company is Product Y, which is produced and sold independently from the other products of the company, and which sells for $320 per unit. The fixed costs of selling Product Y are $39,000, and the variable costs are $260 per unit.

Required:

1. Calculate the company's break-even point in the sale of Product Y *(a)* in units and *(b)* in dollars of sales.
2. Prepare a break-even graph for Product Y, using 1,000 as the maximum number of units on the graph.
3. Prepare an income statement showing sales, fixed costs, and variable costs for Product Y at the break-even point.
4. Determine the sales volume in dollars required to achieve a $3,000 after-tax (50% rate) income from the sale of Product Y.
5. Determine the after-tax income the company will earn from a $313,600 sales level for Product Y.

Problem 24–3A

Athens Company lost $1,000 last year in selling 2,000 units of its Product A, as the following income statement shows:

ATHENS COMPANY
Last Year's Sales of Product A

Sales		$100,000
Costs:		
Fixed	$26,000	
Variable	75,000	101,000
Net loss from sales of Product A ...		$ (1,000)

The company has discovered that if it will install a new machine, it can save enough piece-rate labour and spoiled materials to reduce the variable costs of manufacturing Product A by 20%. However, the new machine will increase fixed costs $2,400 annually.

Required:

1. Calculate last year's dollar break-even point for Product A.
2. Calculate the dollar break-even point under the assumption the new machine is installed.
3. Prepare a break-even chart under the assumption the new machine is installed. Use 3,000 as the maximum number of units on your chart.
4. Prepare an income statement showing expected annual results with the new machine installed, no change in Product A's price, and sales at last year's level. Assume a 50% income tax rate.
5. Calculate the sales level required to earn a $10,000 per year after-tax income with the new machine installed and no change in the selling price of Product A. Prepare an income statement showing the results at this sales level.

Problem 24–4A

Last year Commerce Company sold 20,000 units of its product at $20 per unit. To manufacture and sell the product required $100,000 of fixed manufacturing costs and $20,000 of fixed selling and administrative expenses. Last year's variable costs and expenses per unit were as follows:

Material	$8.00
Direct labour (paid on a piece-rate basis)	3.00
Variable manufacturing overhead costs	0.60
Variable selling and administrative expenses	0.40

A new material has just come on the market that will cut the material cost of producing the product in half if substituted for the material presently being used. The substitution will have no effect on the product's quality; but it will give the company a choice in pricing the product. (1) The company can maintain the present per unit price, sell the same number of units, and make an extra $4 per unit profit as a result of the substitution. Or (2) it can reduce the product's price $4 per unit to an amount equal to the material savings, and because of the reduction, increase the number of units sold by 60%. If the latter choice is made, the fixed manufacturing overhead and fixed selling and administrative expenses will not change and the remaining variable costs and expenses will vary with volume.

Required:

1. Calculate the break-even point in dollars for each alternative.
2. Prepare a break-even chart for each. The company's capacity is 40,000 units, and this should be used as the upper limit of your charts.
3. Prepare a comparative income statement showing sales, total fixed costs, and total variable costs and expenses, operating income, income taxes (50% rate), and net income for each alternative.

Problem 24–5A

Double Company has two essentially unrelated divisions, each of which produces a single product. The two products, Q and R, are produced and sold independently. Coincidentally, each product sold last year at a price of $125, and 7,000 units of each product were sold.

Last year's income statements for the two products are as follows:

	Product Q	Product R
Sales	$875,000	$875,000
Costs:		
Fixed costs	560,000	140,000
Variable costs	140,000	560,000
Total costs	700,000	700,000
Income before taxes	175,000	175,000
Income taxes (40% rate)	70,000	70,000
Net income	$105,000	$105,000

Required:

1. Calculate the break-even point for each product in units.
2. Prepare a break-even graph for each product. Use 10,000 as the maximum number of units on each graph.

3. Prepare a condensed income statement showing in separate columns the net income the company will earn from the sale of each product under the assumption that without a change in selling prices, the number of units of each product sold declines to 4,167 units.
4. Prepare a second condensed income statement showing in separate columns the net income the company will earn if the number of units of each product increases 100%.

Problem 24–6A

Spooner Company manufactures and sells three products, X, Y, and Z that sell for $24 per unit, $20 per unit, and $16 per unit, respectively. Their sales mix is in the ratio of 2:5:8, and the variable costs of manufacturing and selling the products have been Product X, $16; Product Y, $14; and Product Z, $10. Fixed manufacturing, selling, and administrative costs amount to $488,800.

The management of Spooner Company is considering the possible purchase of a new machine to be used in the manufacture of Products Y and Z. If the machine is purchased, fixed manufacturing costs will increase by $99,200. However, variable costs of Product Y will decrease by $2 per unit and variable costs of Product Z will decrease by $1 per unit.

Required:

1. Determine the company's break-even point in dollars and the number of units of each product sold at the break-even point assuming the new machine is not purchased. Show all pertinent calculations.
2. Determine the company's break-even point in dollars and the number of units of each product sold at the break-even point assuming that the new machine is purchased. Show all pertinent calculations.

PROVOCATIVE PROBLEMS

Provocative Problem 24–1, Crazy Company

Crazy Company manufactures and sells Loops, Scoups, and Dangles. Last year's sales mix for the three products was in the ratio of 6:1:3, with combined sales totaling 12,000 units. Loops sell for $120 each and have a 20% contribution rate. Scoups sell for $100 each and have a 25% contribution rate, and Dangles sell for $90 each and have a 40% contribution rate. The fixed costs of manufacturing and selling the products amounts to $161,214. The company estimates that combined sales of the three products will continue at the 12,000 unit level next year. However, the sales manager is of the opinion that if the company's advertising and sales efforts are slanted further toward Scoups and Dangles during the coming year, with no increases in the amounts of money expended, the sales mix of the three products can be changed to the ratio of 3:3:4.

Required:

Should the company change its sales mix through advertising and sales efforts? What effect will the change have on the composite contribution rate of the three products? What effect will it have on the company's break-even point? Back your answers with figures.

Provocative Problem 24–2, Bancroft Company

Bancroft Company operated at near capacity during 198A, and a 20% annual increase in the demand for its product is expected. As a result the company's management is trying to decide how to meet this demand. Two alternatives are being considered. The first calls for changes that will increase variable costs to 55% of the selling price of the company's product but will not change fixed costs. The second calls for a capital investment that will increase fixed costs 15% but will not affect variable costs.

Bancroft Company's income statement for 198A provided the following summarized information:

Sales		$450,000
Costs:		
Variable costs	$216,000	
Fixed costs	160,000	376,000
Income before taxes		$ 74,000

Which alternative do you recommend? Back your recommendation with income statement information and any other data you consider relevant.

Provocative Problem 24–3, Paper Products Company

Paper Products Company produces a high-protein content cattle feed additive at its Waldport plant. The plant produced at near capacity last year with the results shown in the following condensed income statement:

Sales (300,000 kg.)	$600,000
Cost of goods manufactured and sold (fixed, $100,000; variable, $240,000)	340,000
Gross margin	$260,000
Selling and administrative expenses (fixed, $80,000; variable, $60,000)	140,000
Income before taxes	$120,000

Worldwide Company has offered a five-year contract to buy 200,000 kilograms of the additive annually at $1.60 per kilogram for export sales. Delivery on the contract would require a plant addition that would double fixed manufacturing costs. The contract would not affect present fixed selling expenses nor fixed and variable administrative expenses. However, variable selling expenses on the export sales would be reduced by 60%. Variable manufacturing costs would vary with volume.

Required:

Management is not certain it should enter into the contract, and it has asked for your opinion, including the following:

1. An estimated income statement for the first year following the plant addition, assuming no change in domestic sales.
2. A comparison of break-even sales levels before the plant addition and after the contract expiration. Assume after-contract sales and expense levels, other than fixed manufacturing costs, will be at the same levels as last year.
3. A statement showing net income after the contract expiration but at sales and expense levels of last year, other than fixed manufacturing costs.

ANALYTICAL AND REVIEW PROBLEMS

Problem 24–1
A&R

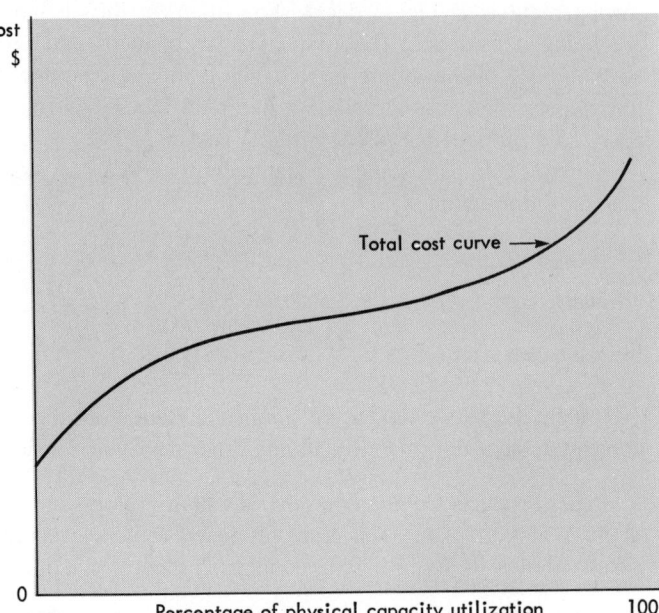

Required:

Utilizing the above diagram of cost/volume relationship, demonstrate your understanding of *(a)* the relevant range and *(b)* cost behaviour. (Hint: Identify the relevant ranges by lettering the appropriate points on the diagram.)

Problem 24–2
A&R

Fixed and variable costs are also viewed as capacity and activity costs.

Required:

Discuss the basis for the alternate view of fixed and variable costs.

Problem 24–3
A&R

For companies using full costing (fixed and variable costs are included in the overhead rate in estimating the cost of goods manufactured) reported net income tends to correlate with the level of production. On the other hand, companies using variable costing (only variable costs are included in the overhead rate in costing cost of goods manufactured) net income tends to correlate with the level of sales.

Required:

Do you agree with the above statements? Set up a numerical example to support or disprove the above statements.

The Master Budget:
A Formal Plan for the Business

25

After studying Chapter 25, you should be able to:

Explain the importance of budgeting.

Describe the specific benefits derived from budgeting.

List the sequence of steps required to prepare a master budget.

Prepare each budget in a master budget and explain the importance of each budget to the overall budgeting process.

Integrate the individual budgets into planned financial statements.

Define or explain the words and phrases listed in the chapter Glossary.

The process of managing a business consists of two basic elements: planning and control. If a business is to accomplish the variety of objectives expected of it, management must first carefully plan the activities and events the business should enter into and accomplish during future weeks, months, and years. Then, as the activities take place, they must be monitored and controlled so that actual events conform as closely as possible to the plan.

The management functions of planning and control are perhaps equally important to the long-run success of a business. Nevertheless, most business failures appear to result from inadequate planning. Countless pitfalls can be avoided if management carefully anticipates the future conditions within which the business will operate and if it prepares a detailed plan of the activities the business should pursue. Furthermore, the plans for future business activities should be formally organized and preserved. This process of planning future business actions and expressing those plans in a formal manner is called *budgeting*. Correspondingly, a *budget* is a formal statement of future plans. Since the economic or financial aspects of the business are primary matters of consideration, budgets are usually expressed in monetary terms.

THE MASTER BUDGET

When the plan to be formalized is a comprehensive or overall plan for the business, the resulting budget is called a *master budget.* As an overall plan, the master budget should include specific plans for expected sales, the units of product to be produced, the materials or merchandise to be purchased, the expense payments to be made, the long-term assets to be purchased, and the amount of cash to be borrowed, if any. The planned activities of each subunit of the business should be separately organized and presented within the master budget. Thus, the master budget for a business consists of several subbudgets, all of which articulate or join with each other to form the overall, coordinated plan for the business. As finally presented, the master budget typically includes sales, expense, production, equipment, and cash budgets. Also, the expected financial results of the planned activities may be expressed in terms of a planned income statement for the budget period and a planned balance sheet for the end of the budget period.

BENEFITS FROM BUDGETING

All business managements engage in planning; some degree of planning is absolutely necessary if business activities are to continue. However, a typical characteristic of poor management is sloppy or incomplete planning. But, if management plans carefully and formalizes its plans completely enough, that is, if management engages in a thorough budgeting process, it may expect to obtain the following benefits.

Study, Research, and a Focus on the Future

When a concern plans with sufficient care and detail to prepare a budget, the planning process usually involves thorough study and research. Not only should this result in the best conceivable plans but it should also instill in executives the habit of doing a reasonable amount of research and study before decisions are made. In short, budgeting tends to promote good decision-making processes. In addition, the items of interest to a budgetary investigation lie in the future. Thus, the attention of management is focused on future events and the associated opportunities available to the business. The pressures of daily operating problems naturally tend to take precedence over planning, thereby leaving the business without carefully thought-out objectives. Budgeting counteracts this tendency by formalizing the planning process; it makes planning an explicit responsibility of management.

The Basis for Evaluating Performance

The control function of management requires that performance be evaluated in light of some norms or objectives. On the basis of this evaluation, appropriate corrective actions can be implemented. In evaluating performance, there are two alternative norms or objectives against which actual performance can be compared: (1) past performance or (2) expected (budgeted) performance. Although past performance is sometimes used as the basis of comparison, budgeted performance is generally superior for determining whether actual performance is acceptable or in need of corrective action. Past performance fails to take into account all of the environmental changes that may affect the performance level. For example, in the evaluation of sales performance, past sales occurred under economic conditions that may have been dramatically different from those that apply to the current sales effort. Economywide fluctuations, competitive shifts within the industry, new product line developments, increased or decreased advertising commitments, and so forth, all tend to invalidate comparisons between past performance and present performance. On the other hand, budgeted (anticipated) performance levels are developed after a research and study process that attempts to take such environmental factors into account. Thus, budgeting provides the benefit of a superior basis for evaluating performance and a more effective control mechanism.

Coordination

Coordination requires that a business be operated as a whole rather than as a group of separate departments. When a budget plan is prepared, each department's objectives are determined in advance, and these objectives are coordinated. For example, the production department is budgeted to produce approximately the number of units the selling department can sell. The purchasing department is budgeted to buy raw materials on the basis of budgeted production; and the hiring activities of the personnel department are arranged to take into account budgeted production levels. Obviously, the departments and activities of an enterprise must be closely coordinated if the business operations are to be efficient and profitable. Budgeting provides this coordination.

Communication

In a very small firm, adequate communication of business plans might be accomplished by direct contact between the employees. Frequent conversations could perhaps serve as the means of communicating management's plans for the business. However, oral conversations often leave ambiguities and potential confusion if not backed up by documents that clearly state the content of the plans. Further, businesses need not be very large before informal conversations become inadequate. When a budget is prepared, the budget becomes a means of informing the organization not only of plans that have been approved by management but also of actions management wishes the organization to take during the budget period.

A Source of Motivation

As previously mentioned, budgets provide the standards against which actual performance is evaluated. Because of this, the budget and the manner in which it is used can significantly affect the attitudes of those who are to be evaluated. If management is not careful, the budgeting process may have a negative impact on the attitudes of employees. Budgeted levels of performance must be realistic. Also, the personnel who will be evaluated in terms of a budget should be consulted and involved in preparing the budget. Finally, the subsequent evaluations of performance must not be given critically, without offering the affected employees an opportunity to explain the reasons for performance failures. These three factors are important: (1) If the affected employees are consulted when the budget is prepared, (2) if obtainable objectives are budgeted, and (3) if the subsequent evaluations of performance are made fairly with opportunities provided to explain performance deficiencies, budgeting can be a positive, motivating force in the organization. Budgeted performance levels can provide goals that individuals will attempt to attain or even exceed as they fulfill their responsibilities to the organization.

THE BUDGET COMMITTEE

The task of preparing a budget should not be made the responsibility of any one department; and the budget definitely should not be handed down from above as the "final word." Rather, budget figures and budget estimates should be developed from "the bottom up." For example, the sales department should have a hand in preparing sales estimates. Similarly, the production department should have initial responsibility for preparing its own expense budget. Otherwise, production and salespeople may say the budget figures are meaningless because they were prepared by front office personnel who know little if anything of sales and production problems.

Although budget figures should be developed from "the bottom up," the preparation of a budget needs central guidance. This is commonly supplied by a budget committee consisting of department heads or other high-level executives who are responsible for seeing that budget figures are realistic and coordinated. If a department submits budget figures that do not reflect proper performance, the figures should be returned to the department with the budget committee's comments. The originating department then either adjusts the figures or defends them. It should not change the figures just to please the committee, since it is important that all parties agree that the figures are reasonable and attainable.

THE BUDGET PERIOD

Budget periods normally coincide with accounting periods. This means that in most companies the budget period is one year in length. However, in addition to their annual budgets, many companies prepare long-range budgets that set forth major objectives for periods of 3 to 5 or 10 years in advance. These long-range budgets are particularly important in planning for major expenditures of capital to buy plant and equipment. Additionally, the financing of major capital projects, for example, by issuing bonds, by issuing stock, by retaining earnings, and so forth, can be anticipated and planned as a part of preparing long-range budgets.

Long-range budgets of 2, 3, 5, and 10 years should reflect the planned accomplishment of long-range objectives. Within this context, the annual master budget for a business reflects the objectives that have been adopted for the next year. The annual budget, however, is commonly broken down into quarterly or monthly budgets. Short-term budgets of a quarter or a month are useful yardsticks that allow management to evaluate actual performance and to take corrective actions promptly. After the quarterly or monthly results are known, the actual performance is com-

Illustration 25–1

CONSOLIDATED STORES, INC.
Income Statement with Variations from Budget
For Month Ended April 30, 19—

	Actual	Budget	Variations
Sales	$63,500	$60,000	$+3,500
Less: Sales returns and allowances	1,800	1,700	+100
Sales discounts	1,200	1,150	+50
Net sales	60,500	57,150	+3,350
Cost of goods sold:			
Merchandise inventory, April 1, 19—	42,000	44,000	−2,000
Purchases, net	39,100	38,000	+1,100
Freight-in	1,250	1,200	+50
Goods for sale	82,350	83,200	−850
Merchandise inventory, April 30, 19—	41,000	44,100	−3,100
Cost of goods sold	41,350	39,100	+2,250
Gross profit	19,150	18,050	+1,100
Operating expenses:			
Selling expenses:			
Sales salaries	6,250	6,000	+250
Advertising expense	900	800	+100
Store supplies used	550	500	+50
Depreciation on store equipment	1,500	1,600	
Total selling expenses	9,300	8,900	+400
General and administrative expenses:			
Office salaries	2,000	2,000	
Office supplies used	165	150	+15
Rent	1,100	1,100	
Expired insurance	200	200	
Depreciation of office equipment	100	100	
Total general and administrative expenses	3,565	3,550	+15
Total operating expenses	12,865	12,450	+415
Income from operations	$ 6,285	$ 5,600	$ +685

pared to the budgeted amounts in a report similar to that disclosed in Illustration 25–1.

Many businesses follow the practice of ''continuous'' budgeting, and are said to prepare *rolling budgets*. As each monthly or quarterly budget period goes by, these firms revise their entire set of budgets, adding new monthly or quarterly sales, production, expense, equipment, and cash budgets to replace the ones that have elapsed. Thus, at any point in time, monthly or quarterly budgets are available for a full year in advance.

PREPARING THE MASTER BUDGET

As indicated in the previous discussion, the master budget consists of a number of budgets that collectively express the planned activities of the business. The number of arrangement of the budgets included in the master budget depend on the size and complexity of the business. However, a master budget typically includes:

1. Operating budgets.
   - *a.* Sales budget.
   - *b.* For merchandising companies: ***Merchandise purchases budget.***
   - *c.* For manufacturing companies:
     - (1) Production budget (stating the number of units to be produced).
     - (2) Manufacturing budget.
   - *d.* Selling expense budget.
   - *e.* General and administrative expense budget.
2. ***Capital expenditures budget,*** which includes the budgeted expenditures for new plant and equipment.
3. Financial budgets.
   - *a.* Budgeted statement of cash receipts and disbursements, called the cash budget.
   - *b.* Budgeted income statement.
   - *c.* Budgeted balance sheet.

In addition to these budgets, numerous supporting calculations or schedules may be required.

Some of the budgets listed above cannot be prepared until other budgets on the list are first completed. For example, the merchandise purchases budget cannot be prepared until the sales budget is available, since the number of units to be purchased depends upon how many units are to be sold. As a consequence, preparation of the budgets within the master budget must follow a definite sequence, as follows:

First: The sales budget must be prepared first because the operating and financial budgets depend upon information provided by the sales budget.

Second: The remaining operating budgets are prepared next. For manufacturing companies, the production budget must be prepared prior to the manufacturing budget, since the number of units to be manufactured obviously affects the amounts of materials, direct labour, and overhead to be budgeted. Other than this, the budgets for manufacturing costs or merchandise costs, general and administrative expenses, and selling expenses may be prepared in any sequence.

Third: If capital expenditures are anticipated during the budget period, the capital expenditures budget is prepared next. This budget usually depends upon long-range sales forecasts more than it does upon the sales budget for the next year.

Fourth: Based upon the information provided in the above budgets, the budgeted statement of cash receipts and disbursements is prepared. If this budget discloses an imbalance between disbursements and planned receipts, the previous plans may have to be revised.

Fifth: The budgeted income statement is prepared next. If the plans contained in the master budget result in unsatisfactory profits, the entire master budget may be revised to incorporate any corrective measures available to the firm.

Sixth: The budgeted balance sheet for the end of the budget period is prepared last. An analysis of this statement may also lead to revisions in the previous budgets. For example, the budgeted balance sheet may disclose too much debt resulting from an overly ambitious capital expenditures budget, and revised plans may be necessary.

PREPARATION OF THE MASTER BUDGET ILLUSTRATED

The following sections explain the procedures involved in preparing the budgets that comprise the master budget. Northern Company, a wholesaler of a single product, provides an illustrative basis for the discussion. The September 30, 198A, balance sheet for Northern Company is presented in Illustration 25–2. The master budget for Northern Company is prepared on a monthly basis, with a budgeted balance sheet

Illustration 25–2

NORTHERN COMPANY
Balance Sheet
September 30, 198A

Assets		Equities	
Cash	$ 20,000	Accounts payable	$ 58,200
Accounts receivable	42,000	Loan from bank	10,000
Inventory (9,000 units at $6)	54,000	Accrued income taxes payable	
Equipment*	200,000	(due October 15, 198A)	20,000
Less: Accumulated depreciation	(36,000)	Common stock	150,000
		Retained earnings	41,800
Total assets	$280,000	Total equities	$280,000

* The equipment is being depreciated on a straight-line basis over 10 years. Estimated salvage value is $20,000.

prepared for the end of each quarter. Also, a budgeted income statement is prepared for each quarter. In the following sections, Northern Company budgets are prepared for October, November, and December 198A.

Sales Budget

The *sales budget* provides an estimate of goods to be sold and revenue to be derived from sales. It is the starting point in the budgeting procedure, since the plans of all departments are related to sales and expected revenue. The sales budget commonly grows from a reconciliation of forecast business conditions, plant capacity, proposed selling expenses such as advertising, and estimates of sales. Since people normally feel a greater responsibility for reaching goals they have had a hand in setting, the sales personnel of a concern are often asked to submit, through the sales manager, estimates of sales for each territory and department. The final sales budget is then based on these estimates as reconciled for forecast business conditions, selling expenses, and so forth.

During September 198A, Northern Company sold 7,000 units of product at a price of $10 per unit. After obtaining the estimates of sales personnel and considering the economic conditions affecting the market for Northern Company's product, the sales budget (Illustration 25–3) is established for October, November, and December 198A. Since the purchasing department must base December 198A purchases on estimated sales for January 198B, the sales budget is expanded to include January 198B.

Observe in Illustration 25–3 that the sales budget is more detailed than simple projections of total sales; both unit sales and unit prices are forecast. Some budgeting procedures are less detailed, expressing the budget only in terms of total sales volume. Many sales budgets are far more detailed than the one illustrated. The more detailed sales budgets may show units and unit prices for each of many different products, classified by salesperson and by territory or by department.

Illustration 25–3

NORTHERN COMPANY
Monthly Sales Budget
October 198A–January 198B

	Budgeted unit sales		Budgeted unit price		Budgeted total sales
September 198A (actual)	7,000	×	$10	=	$ 70,000
October 198A	10,000	×	10	=	100,000
November 198A	8,000	×	10	=	80,000
December 198A	14,000	×	10	=	140,000
January 198B	9,000	×	10	=	90,000

Merchandise Purchases Budget

A variety of sophisticated techniques have been developed to assist management in making inventory purchase decisions. All of these techniques recognize that the number of units to be added to inventory depends upon the budgeted sales volume. Whether a company manufactures or purchases the product it sells, budgeted future sales volume is the primary factor to be considered in most inventory management decisions.

The amount of merchandise or materials to be purchased each month is determined as follows:

Budgeted sales for the month	XXX
Add the budgeted end-of-month inventory	XXX
Required amount of available merchandise	XXX
Deduct the beginning-of-month inventory	(XXX)
Inventory to be purchased	XXX

The calculation may be made in either dollars or in units. If the calculation is in units and only one product is involved, the number of dollars of inventory to be purchased may be determined by multiplying units to be purchased by the cost per unit.

After considering the cost of maintaining an investment in inventory and the potential cost associated with a temporary inventory shortage, Northern Company has decided that the number of units in its inventory at the end of each month should equal 90% of the next month's sales. In other words, the inventory at the end of October should equal 90% of the budgeted November sales, the November ending inventory should equal 90% of the expected December sales, and so on. Also, the company's suppliers have indicated that the September 198A per unit cost of $6 can be expected to remain unchanged through January 198B. Based on these factors the company prepared the merchandise purchases budget of Illustration 25–4.

The calculations in Northern Company's merchandise purchases budget differ slightly from the basic calculation previously given in that the first lines are devoted to determining the desired end-of-month inventory. Also, budgeted sales are added to the desired end-of-month inventory instead of vice versa, and on the last lines the number of dollars of inventory to be purchased is determined by multiplying units to be purchased by the cost per unit.

It was previously mentioned that some budgeting procedures are designed to provide only the total dollars of budgeted sales. Likewise, the merchandise purchases budget may not state the number of units to be purchased, and may be expressed only in terms of the total cost of merchandise to be purchased. In such situations, it is assumed that there is a constant relationship between sales and cost of goods sold. For

Illustration 25–4

NORTHERN COMPANY **Merchandise Purchases Budget** **October, November, and December 198A**			
	October	November	December
Next month's budgeted sales (in units)	8,000	14,000	9,000
Ratio of inventory to future sales	×90%	×90%	×90%
Desired end-of-month inventory	7,200	12,600	8,100
Budgeted sales for the month (in units)	10,000	8,000	14,000
Required units of available merchandise . . .	17,200	20,600	22,100
Deduct beginning-of-month inventory	(9,000)	(7,200)	(12,600)
Number of units to be purchased	8,200	13,400	9,500
Budgeted cost per unit	×$6	×$6	×$6
Budgeted cost of merchandise purchases . .	$49,200	$80,400	$57,000

example, Northern Company expects that cost of goods sold will equal 60% of sales. (Note that the budgeted sales price is $10 and the budgeted unit cost is $6.) Thus, its cost of purchases can be budgeted in dollars on the basis of budgeted sales without requiring information on the number of units involved.

Production Budgets and Manufacturing Budgets

Since Northern Company does not manufacture the product it sells, its budget for acquiring goods to be sold is a merchandise purchases budget (Illustration 25–4). If Northern Company had been a manufacturing company, a production budget rather than a merchandise purchases budget would be required. In a *production budget* the number of units to be produced each month is shown. For Northern Company such a budget would be very similar to a merchandise purchases budget. It would differ in that the number of units to be purchased each month (see Illustration 25–4) would be described as the number of units to be manufactured each month. Also, it would not show costs, since a production budget is always expressed entirely in terms of units of product and does not include budgeted production costs. Such costs are shown in the manufacturing budget, which is based on the production volume shown in the production budget.

A *manufacturing budget* shows the budgeted costs for raw materials, direct labour, and manufacturing overhead. In many manufacturing companies, the manufacturing budget is actually prepared in the form of three subbudgets: a raw materials purchases budget, a direct labour budget, and a manufacturing overhead budget. These budgets show the total budgeted cost of goods to be manufactured during the budget period.

Selling Expense Budget

The responsibility for preparing a budget of selling expenses typically falls on the vice president of marketing or the equivalent sales manager. Although budgeted selling expenses should affect the expected amount of sales, the typical procedure is to prepare a sales budget first and then to budget selling expenses. Estimates of selling expenses are based on the tentative sales budget and upon the experience of previous periods adjusted for known changes. After the entire master budget is prepared on a tentative basis, it may be decided that the projected sales volume is inadequate. If so, subsequent adjustments in the sales budget would generally require that corresponding adjustments be made in the selling expense budget.

Northern Company's selling expenses consist of commissions paid to sales personnel and a $24,000 per year salary, paid on a monthly basis to the sales manager. Sales commissions amount to 10% of total sales and are paid during the month the sales are made. The selling expense budget for Northern Company is presented in Illustration 25–5.

Illustration 25–5

NORTHERN COMPANY
Selling Expense Budget
October, November, and December 198A

	October	November	December	Total
Budgeted sales	$100,000	$80,000	$140,000	$320,000
Sales commission percentage . .	×10%	×10%	×10%	×10%
Sales commissions	10,000	8,000	14,000	32,000
Salary for sales manager ($24,000/12 = $2,000 per month)	2,000	2,000	2,000	6,000
Total selling expenses	$ 12,000	$10,000	$ 16,000	$ 38,000

General and Administrative Expenses

General and administrative expenses usually are the responsibility of the office manager, who should therefore be charged with the task of preparing the budget for these items. The amounts of some general and administrative expenses may depend upon budgeted sales volume. However, most of these expenses depend more upon other factors, such as management policies and inflationary influences, than they do upon monthly fluctuations in sales volume. Although interest expense and income tax expense are frequently classified as general and administrative expenses, they generally cannot be budgeted at this point in the budgeting sequence. Interest expense must await preparation of the cash budget, which determines the need for loans, if any. Income tax expense must await preparation of the budgeted income statement, at which time taxable income and income tax expense can be estimated.

General and administrative expenses for Northern Company include administrative salaries amounting to $54,000 per year and depreciation of $18,000 per year on equipment (see Illustration 25–2). The salaries are paid each month as they are earned. Illustration 25–6 shows the budget for these expenses.

Illustration 25–6

	NORTHERN COMPANY **General and Administrative Expense Budget** **October, November, and December 198A**					
		October	*November*	*December*	*Total*	
Administrative salaries ($54,000/12 = $4,500)		$4,500	$4,500	$4,500	$13,500	
Depreciation of equipment ($18,000/12 = $1,500)		1,500	1,500	1,500	4,500	
		$6,000	$6,000	$6,000	$18,000	

Capital Expenditures Budget

The capital expenditures or plant and equipment budget lists equipment to be scrapped and additional equipment to be purchased if the proposed production program is carried out. The purchase of additional equipment requires funds; and anticipating equipment additions in advance normally makes it easier to provide the funds. Also, at times, estimated production may exceed plant capacity. Budgeting makes it possible to anticipate this and either revise the production schedule or increase plant capacity. Planning plant and equipment purchases is called capital budgeting, and this is discussed in more detail in Chapter 27.

Northern Company does not anticipate any sales or retirements of equipment through December 198A. However, management plans to acquire additional equipment for $25,000 cash near the end of December 198A.

Cash Budget

After tentative sales, merchandise purchases, expenses, and capital expenditures budgets have been developed, the *cash budget* is prepared. This budget is especially important; a company should have at all times enough cash to meet needs, but it should not hold too much cash. Too much cash is undesirable because it often cannot be profitably invested. A cash budget requires management to forecast cash receipts and disbursements, and usually results in better cash management. Also, it enables management to arrange well in advance for loans to cover any anticipated cash shortages.

In preparing the cash budget, anticipated receipts are added to the beginning cash balance, and anticipated expenditures are deducted. If the resulting cash balance is inadequate, the required additional cash is provided in the budget through planned increases in loans.

Much of the information that is needed to prepare the cash budget can be obtained directly from the previously prepared operating and capital expenditures budgets. However, further investigation and additional calculations may be necessary to determine the amounts to be included.

Illustration 25–7 shows the cash budget for Northern Company. October's beginning cash balance was obtained from the September 30, 198A, balance sheet (Illustration 25–2).

Budgeted sales of Northern Company are shown in Illustration 25–3. An investigation of previous sales records indicates that 40% of Northern Company's sales are for cash. The remaining 60% are credit sales,

Illustration 25–7

NORTHERN COMPANY
Cash Budget
October, November, and December 198A

	October	November	December
Beginning cash balance	$ 20,000	$ 20,000	$ 22,272
Cash receipts from customers	82,000	92,000	104,000
Total	102,000	112,000	126,272
Cash disbursements:			
Payments for merchandise	58,200	49,200	80,400
Sales commissions (Illustration 24–5)	10,000	8,000	14,000
Salaries: Sales (Illustration 24–5)	2,000	2,000	2,000
Administrative (Illustration 24–6) ..	4,500	4,500	4,500
Accrued income taxes payable	20,000		
Dividends ($150,000 × 0.02)		3,000	
Interest on loan from bank:			
$10,000 × 0.01 = $100	100		
$22,800 × 0.01 = $228		228	
Purchase of equipment			25,000
Total cash disbursements	94,800	66,928	125,900
Balance	7,200	45,072	372
Additional loan from bank	12,800		19,628
Repayment of loan from bank		(22,800)	
Ending cash balance	20,000	22,272	20,000
Loan balance, end of month	$ 22,800	$ –0–	$ 19,628

and customers can be expected to pay for these sales in the month after the sales are made. Thus, the budgeted cash receipts from customers are calculated as follows:

	September	October	November	December
Sales	$70,000	$100,000	$80,000	$140,000
Credit sales percentage	×60%	×60%	×60%	×60%
Accounts receivable, end of month	$42,000	$ 60,000	$48,000	$ 84,000
Cash sales percentage		×40%	×40%	×40%
Cash sales		$ 40,000	$32,000	$ 56,000
Collections of accounts receivable		42,000	60,000	48,000
Total cash receipts		$ 82,000	$92,000	$104,000

Observe in the calculation that the October cash receipts consist of $40,000 from cash sales ($100,000 × 40%) plus the collection of $42,000 of accounts receivable as calculated in the previous column. Also, note that each month's total cash receipts are listed on the second line of Illustration 25–7.

Northern Company's purchases of merchandise are entirely on account, and full payments are made regularly in the month following purchase. Thus, in Illustration 25–7, the cash disbursements for purchases are obtained from the September 30, 198A, balance sheet (Illustration 25–2) and from the merchandise purchases budget (Illustration 25–4), as follows:

September 30, accounts payable equal October payments	$58,200
October purchases equal November payments	49,200
November purchases equal December payments	80,400

Sales commissions and all salaries are paid monthly, and the budgeted cash disbursements for these items are obtained from the selling expense budget (Illustration 25–5) and the general and administrative expense budget (Illustration 25–6).

As indicated in the September 30, 198A, balance sheet (Illustration 25–2), accrued income taxes are paid in October. Estimated income tax expense for the quarter ending December 31 is 40% of net income and is due in January 198B.

Northern Company pays 2% quarterly cash dividends, and the November payment of $3,000 is the planned disbursement for this item. Also, Northern Company has an agreement with the bank whereby additional loans are granted at the end of each month if they are necessary to maintain a minimum cash balance of $20,000 at the end of the month. Interest is paid at the end of each month at the rate of 1% per month, and if the cash balance at the end of a month exceeds $20,000, the excess is used to repay the loans to the bank. Illustration 25–7 indicates that the $10,000 loan from the bank at the end of September was not sufficient to provide a $20,000 cash balance at the end of October, and, as a result, the loan was increased by $12,800 at the end of October. The entire loan was repaid at the end of November, and $19,628 was again borrowed at the end of December.

Budgeted Income Statement

One of the final steps in preparing a master budget is to summarize the effects of the various budgetary plans on the income statement. The necessary information to prepare a budgeted income statement is drawn primarily from the previously prepared budgets or from the investigations that were made in the process of preparing those budgets.

For many companies, the volume of information that must be summarized in the budgeted income statement and the budgeted balance sheet is so large that a work sheet must be used to accumulate all of the budgeted transactions and to classify them in terms of their impact on the income statement and/or on the balance sheet. However, the transactions and account balances of Northern Company are few in number, and the budgeted income statement (and balance sheet) can be prepared simply by inspecting the previously discussed budgets and recalling the information that was provided in the related discussions. Northern Company's budgeted income statement is shown in Illustration 25–8.

Illustration 25–8

NORTHERN COMPANY
Budgeted Income Statement
For Three Months Ended December 31, 198A

Sales (Illustration 25–3, 32,000 units at $10)		$320,000
Cost of goods sold (32,000 units at $6)		192,000
Gross profit		128,000
Operating expenses:		
Sales commissions (Illustration 25–5)	$32,000	
Sales salaries (Illustration 25–5)	6,000	
Administrative salaries (Illustration 25–6)	13,500	
Depreciation on equipment (Illustration 25–6)	4,500	
Interest expense (Illustration 25–7)	328	(56,328)
Net income before income taxes		71,672
Income tax expense ($71,672 × 40%)		(28,669)
Net income		$ 43,003

Budgeted Balance Sheet

If a work sheet is used to prepare the budgeted income statement and balance sheet, the first two columns of the work sheet are used to list the estimated post-closing trial balance of the period prior to the budget period. Next, the budgeted transactions and adjustments are entered in the second pair of work sheet columns in the same manner as end-of-period adjustments are entered on an ordinary work sheet. For example, if the budget calls for sales on account of $250,000, the name of the Sales account is entered on the work sheet in the Account Titles column below the names of the post-closing trial balance accounts; and then Sales is credited and Accounts Receivable is debited for $250,000 in the second pair of money columns. After all budgeted transactions and adjustments are entered on the work sheet, the estimated post-closing trial balance amounts in the first pair of money columns are combined with the budget amounts in the second pair of columns and are sorted to the proper Income Statement and Balance Sheet columns of the work sheet. Finally, the information in these columns is used to prepare the budgeted income statement and budgeted balance sheet.

As previously mentioned, the transactions and account balances of Northern Company are few in number, and its budgeted balance sheet, shown in Illustration 25–9, can be prepared simply by inspecting the

Illustration 25–9

NORTHERN COMPANY
Budgeted Balance Sheet
December 31, 198A

Assets

Cash (Illustration 25–7)		$ 20,000
Accounts receivable (page 1033)		84,000
Inventory (Illustrations 25–4, 8, 100 units at $6)		48,600
Equipment (Illustrations 25–2 and 25–7)	$225,000	
Less: Accumulated depreciation (Illustrations 25–2 and 25–6)	40,500	184,500
Total assets		$337,100

Liabilities and Shareholders' Equity

Liabilities		
Accounts payable (Illustration 25–4)	57,000	
Accrued income taxes payable (Illustration 25–8)	28,669	
Bank loan payable (Illustration 25–7)	19,628	$105,297
Shareholders' equity:		
Common stock (Illustration 25–2)	150,000	
Retained earnings (see discussion)	81,803	231,803
Total liabilities and shareholders' equity		$337,100

previously prepared budgets and recalling the related discussions of those budgets.

Observe that the retained earnings balance in Illustration 25–9 is $81,803. This amount was determined as follows:

Retained earnings, September 30, 198A (Illustration 25–2)	$41,800
Net income for three months ended December 31, 198A (Illustration 25–8)	43,003
Total	84,003
Dividends declared in November, 198A (Illustration 25–7)	(3,000)
Retained earnings, December 31, 198A	$81,803

GLOSSARY

Budget.   A formal statement of future plans, usually expressed in monetary terms.

Budgeting.   The process of planning future business actions and expressing those plans in a formal manner.

Capital expenditures budget.   A listing of the plant and equipment to be purchased if the proposed production program is carried out. Also called the plant and equipment budget.

Cash budget.   A forecast of cash receipts and disbursements.

Manufacturing budget.   A statement of the estimated costs for raw materials, direct labour, and manufacturing overhead associated with producing the number of units estimated in the production budget.

Master budget.   A comprehensive or overall plan for the business that typically includes budgets for sales, expenses, production, equipment, cash, and also a planned income statement and balance sheet.

Merchandise purchases budget.   An estimate of the units (or cost) of merchandise to be purchased by a merchandising company.

Production budget.   An estimate of the number of units to be produced during a budget period.

Rolling budgets.   A sequence of revised budgets that are prepared in the practice of continuous budgeting.

Sales budget.   An estimate of goods to be sold and revenue to be derived from sales; serves as the usual starting point in the budgeting procedure.

QUESTIONS FOR CLASS DISCUSSION

1.   What is a budget? What is a master budget?

2.   What are the benefits from budgeting?

3.   How does the process of budgeting tend to promote good decision making?

4. What are the two alternative norms or objectives against which actual performance is sometimes compared and evaluated? Which of the two is generally superior?

5. Why should each department be asked to prepare or at least to participate in the preparation of its own budget estimates?

6. What are the duties of the budget committee?

7. What is the normal length of a master budget period? How far in advance are long-range budgets generally prepared?

8. What is meant by the terms *continuous budgeting* and *rolling budgets?*

9. What are the three primary types of budgets that make up the master budget?

10. In comparing merchandising companies and manufacturing companies, what differences show up in the operating budgets?

11. What is the sequence that is followed in preparing the set of budgets that collectively makes up the master budget?

12. What is a sales budget? A selling expense budget? A capital expenditures budget?

13. What is the difference between a production budget and a manufacturing budget?

14. What is a cash budget? Why must it be prepared after the operating budgets and the capital expenditures budget?

MULTIPLE CHOICE

1. Which of the following budgets is needed before a cash budget can be prepared?
    a. Capital expenditures budget.
    b. Sales budget.
    c. Merchandise purchases budget.
    d. General and administrative expense budget.
    e. All of the above.

2. Budgeting an amount for interest expense will depend most directly upon:
    a. The number of receivables outstanding.
    b. The cash budget which determines loans.
    c. The budgeted income statement.
    d. The budgeted balance sheet.
    e. The opinions of management.

3. Which of the following would not be used in the preparation of a cash budget for October?
    a. Beginning cash balance on October 1.
    b. Budgeted sales and collections for October.
    c. Estimated depreciation expense for October.

    d. Budgeted salaries expense for October.

    e. Budgeted capital equipment purchases for October.

4. In October a sporting goods store purchased $3,500 worth of ski boots. The store had $1,500 worth on hand at the beginning of October, and to cover part of anticipated November sales they expect to have $1,000 worth of ski boots on hand at the end of the month of October. What were their budgeted sales of ski boots for October?

    a. $2,500.

    b. $3,500.

    c. $4,000.

    d. $4,500.

    e. $5,000.

5. Rayon Company had the following credit sales during 198A: September, $12,500; October, $18,000; November, $15,000; December, $16,000. Experience has shown that payment for the credit sales is received as follows: 10% in the month of sale, 60% in the first month after sale, 20% in the second month after sale, and 10% is uncollectible. How much will Rayon Company collect from credit sales in November?

    a. $9,100.

    b. $13,500.

    c. $14,200.

    d. $14,800.

    e. $16,200.

6. M & O Company is trying to decide how many units of merchandise to order each month. The company's policy is to have 20% of the next month's sales on hand at the end of the current month. Projected sales for August, September, and October are 15,000 units. 10,000 units, and 20,000 units, repectively. How many units must be ordered in September?

    a. 7,000.

    b. 10,000.

    c. 11,000.

    d. 12,000.

    e. 14,000.

MINI DISCUSSION CASES

Case 25–1   Your friend says to you that "budgeting is simple. All that's needed is to take the current year's results and increase them by 10% or by whatever the estimated inflation rate is expected to be."

Required:

Respond to your friend's comments.

Case 25–2   You have just been hired as the accountant for a small manufacturing company consisting of about 25 plant employees and 8 office and sales staff. When you enquire about preparing a budget for the next fiscal year, your boss, the owner-manager, says that he has never used a budget because he always knows what he's going to do and has a pretty good idea of what it is going to cost.

Required:

Explain the benefits of a formal budget to your boss.

CLASS EXERCISES

Exercise 25–1   The sales budget of Coast Department Store's Department B calls for $8,400 of sales during March. The department expects to begin March with a $6,700 inventory and end the month with a $5,500 inventory. Its cost of goods sold averages 65% of sales.

Required:

Prepare a merchandise purchases budget for Department B showing the amount of goods to be purchased during March.

Exercise 25–2   Simon Company manufactures a product called Zipalls. The company's management estimates there will be 3,800 units of Zipalls in the March 31 finished goods inventory, that 12,500 units will be sold during the year's second quarter, that 16,000 units will be sold during the third quarter, and that 20,000 units will be sold during the fourth quarter. Management also believes the concern should begin each quarter with units in the finished goods inventory equal to 30% of the next quarter's budgeted sales.

Required:

Prepare a production budget showing the units of Zipalls to be manufactured during the year's second quarter and third quarter.

Exercise 25–3   A company has budgeted the following cash receipts and cash disbursements from operations during the second quarter of 19A:

	Receipts	Disbursements
April ...	$250,000	$170,000
May	90,000	200,000
June ...	170,000	130,000

According to a credit agreement with the bank, the company promises to maintain a minimum, end-of-month cash balance of $20,000. In return, the bank has agreed to provide the company the right to receive loans up to $100,000 with interest of 12% per year, paid monthly on the last day of the month. If the loan must be increased during the last ten days of a month to provide enough cash to pay bills, interest will not begin to be charged until the end of the month.

The company is expected to have a cash balance of $20,000 and a loan balance of $10,000 on March 31, 198A.

Required:

Prepare a monthly cash budget for the second quarter of 19A.

Exercise 25–4   Using the following information, prepare a cash budget showing expected cash receipts and disbursements for the month of June and the balance expected on June 30.

1. Beginning cash balance on June 1, $33,000.
2. Budgeted sales for June: $250,000; 40% are collected in the month of sale, 50% in the next month, 5% in the following month, and 5% are uncollectible.
3. Sales for May: $300,000.
4. Sales for April: $200,000.
5. Budgeted merchandise purchases for June: $150,000; 50% are paid in month of purchase; 50% are paid in the month following purchase.
6. Merchandise purchased in May: $100,000.
7. Budgeted cash disbursements for salaries in June: $64,000.
8. Depreciation expense in June: $4,000.
9. Other cash expenses budgeted for June: $18,000.
10. Budgeted taxes payable in June: $42,000.
11. Budgeted interest payable on bank loan in June: $2,400.

Exercise 25–5   Based on the information provided in Exercise 24–4 and the additional information which follows, prepare a budgeted income statement for the month of June and a budgeted balance sheet for June 30.

1. Cost of goods sold is 55% of sales.
2. The inventory at the end of May was $45,000.
3. Salaries payable on May 31 was $10,000 and is expected to be $12,000 on June 30.
4. The Equipment account shows a balance of $384,000. On May 31, Accumulated Depreciation had a balance of $92,000.
5. The $2,400 cash payment of interest represents the 1% monthly expense on a bank loan of $240,000.
6. Income taxes payable on May 31 amounted to $42,000, and the income tax rate applicable to the company is 48%.
7. The 5% of sales which prove to be uncollectible are debited to Bad Debts Expense and credited to Allowance for Doubtful Accounts during the year of sale. However, specific accounts that prove to be uncollectible are not written off until the second month after the sale, at which time all accounts not yet collected are so written off.
8. The only balance sheet accounts other than those implied by the previous discussion are Common Stock, which shows a balance of $100,000, and Retained Earnings, which showed a balance of $103,000 on May 31.

PROBLEMS

Problem 25–1

Welling Manufacturing Company manufactures a steel product called a "sand tap." Each "sand tap" requires 80 kilograms of steel and is produced in a single operation by a stamping process. The concern's management estimates there will be 1,500 units of the product and 100,000 kilograms of steel on hand on March 31 of the current year, and that 12,000 units of the product will be sold during the year's second quarter. Management also believes that due to the possibility of a strike in the steel industry, the concern should begin the third quarter with a 300,000-kilogram steel inventory and 2,000 finished "sand taps." Steel can be purchased for approximately $0.24 per kilogram.

Required:

Prepare a second-quarter production budget and a second-quarter steel purchases budget for the company.

Problem 25–2

During the latter part of February, the owner of Cottonwood Store approached the bank for a $10,000 loan to be made on April 1 and repaid 60 days thereafter with interest at 12%. The owner planned to increase the store's inventory by $10,000 during March and needed the loan to pay for the merchandise during April. The bank's loan officer was interested in Cottonwood Store's ability to repay the loan and asked the owner to forecast the store's May 31 cash position.

On March 1 Cottonwood Store was expected to have a $4,100 cash balance, $28,000 of accounts receivable, and $14,600 of accounts payable. Its budgeted sales, purchases, and cash expenditures for the following three months are as follows:

	March	April	May
Sales	$24,000	$25,000	$23,000
Merchandise purchases	25,500	15,000	14,000
Payroll	2,400	2,400	2,400
Rent	1,000	1,000	1,000
Other cash expenses	1,200	1,100	1,300
Repayment of bank loan			10,200

The budgeted March purchases include the inventory increase. All sales are on account; and past experience indicates 80% is collected in the month following the sale, 15% in the next month, 4% in the next, and the remainder is not collected. Application of this experience to the March 1 accounts receivable balance indicates $22,500 of the $28,000 will be collected during March, $4,000 during April, and $1,000 during May. All merchandise is paid for in the month following its purchase.

Required:

Prepare cash budgets for March, April, and May for Cottonwood Store under the assumption the bank loan will be paid on May 31.

Problem 25–3

Lyndale Company has a cash balance of $25,000 on June 1, 19A. The product sold by the company sells for $25 per unit. Actual and projected sales are:

April, actual	$200,000
May, actual	150,000
June, estimated	250,000
July, estimated	200,000
August, estimated	180,000

Experience has shown that 50% of the billings are collected in the month of sale, 30% in the second month, 15% in the third month, and 5% will prove to be uncollectible.

All purchases are payable within 15 days. Thus, approximately 50% of the purchases in a month are due and payable in the next month. The unit purchase cost is $16. Lyndale Company's management has established a policy of maintaining an end-of-month inventory of 100 units plus 50% of the next month's unit sales, and the June 1 inventory is consistent with this policy.

Selling and general administrative expenses (excluding depreciation) for the year amount to $360,000 and are distributed evenly throughout the year.

Required:

Prepare a monthly cash budget for June and July, with supporting schedules showing cash receipts from collections of receivables and cash payments for merchandise purchases.

Problem 25–4

Shore Company buys merchandise at $6.40 per unit and sells it at $12 per unit. Sales personnel are paid a commission of 10% of sales. The September 19A income statement of Shore Company as is follows:

SHORE COMPANY
Income Statement
For September 19A

Sales	$120,000
Cost of goods sold	64,000
Gross profit	56,000
Expenses:	
Sales commissions	12,000
Advertising	7,200
Store rent	2,400
Administrative salaries	4,500
Depreciation expense	1,200
Other expenses	3,400
Total	30,700
Net income	$ 25,300

The management of Shore Company expects the September results to be repeated during October, November, and December. However, certain changes are being considered. Management believes that if selling price is reduced to $10.50 and advertising expenses are increased by 50%, unit sales will increase at a rate of 10% each month during the last quarter of 19A. If these changes are made, merchandise will still be purchased at $6.40 per unit. Sales personnel will continue to earn a commission of 10%, and the remaining expenses will remain constant.

Required:

Prepare a budgeted income statement that shows in three columns the planned results of operations for October, November, and December 19A, assuming the changes are implemented. Based on the budgeted income statements, decide whether management should make the changes.

Problem 25–5   Shortly before the end of 19A, Gough Company's management prepared a budgeted balance sheet for December 31, 19A, as follows:

GOUGH COMPANY LTD.
Balance Sheet
At End of December 31, 19A

Assets		**Equities**	
Cash	$ 5,000	Accounts payable	$ 8,000
Accounts receivable	15,000	Loan from bank	5,000
Inventory	75,000	Taxes payable (due March	
Equipment	60,000	15, 19B)	12,000
Accumulated depreciation	(6,000)	Common stock	75,000
		Retained earnings	49,000
Total assets	$149,000	Total equities	$149,000

In the process of preparing a master budget for January, February, and March 19B, the following information has been obtained:

1. The product sold by XYZ Company is purchased for $30 per unit and resold for $45 per unit. Although the inventory level on December 31, 19A (2,500 units), is smaller than desired, management has established a new inventory policy for 19B whereby the end-of-month inventory should be 80% of the next month's expected sales (in units). Budgeted unit sales are January, 10,000; February, 9,000; March, 12,000; and April, 12,000.

2. Total sales each month are 50% for cash and 50% on account. Of the credit sales, 80% are collected in the first month after the sale and 20% in the second month after the sale. Similarly, 80% of the Accounts Receivable balance on December 31, 19A, should be collected during January and 20% should be collected in February. Losses from bad debts are insignificant.

3. Merchandise purchased by the company is paid for as follows: 70% in the month after purchase and 30% in the second month after purchase. Similarly, 70% of the Accounts Payable balance on December 31, 19A, will be paid during January and 30% will be paid during February.

4. Sales commissions amounting to 10% of sales are paid each month. Additionally, the salary of the sales manager is $22,000 per year.

5. Repair expenses amount to $800 per month and are paid in cash. General administrative salaries amount to $108,000 per year.

6. The equipment shown in the December 31, 19A, balance sheet was purchased one year ago. It is being depreciated over ten years according to the straight-

line method. Regarding new purchases of equipment, management has decided to take a full month's depreciation (rounded to the nearest dollar) during the month the equipment is purchased, and to use straight-line depreciation over ten years, assuming no salvage value. The company plans to purchase additional equipment worth $10,000 in January, $5,000 in February, and $15,000 in March.

7. The company plans to acquire some land in March at a cost of $100,000. The land will not require a cash outlay until the last day of March. Thus, if a bank loan is necessary, the first payment of interest will be due at the end of April.

8. XYZ Company has an arrangement with the bank whereby additional loans are available as they are needed at a rate of 10% per year, paid monthly. If part or all of a loan is repaid during a month, the payment will be made on the last day of the month, along with any interest that is due. XYZ Company has agreed to maintain an end-of-month cash balance of at least $5,000.

9. Disregard income taxes that would normally be payable in February and March.

Required:

Prepare a master budget for the first quarter of 19B, with the operating budgets, capital expenditures budget, and the cash budget prepared on a monthly basis. The budgeted income statement should show operations for the first quarter, and the budgeted balance sheet should be prepared as of March 31, 19B. The operating budgets included in the master budget should include a sales budget (showing both budgeted unit sales and dollar sales), a merchandise purchases budget, a selling expense budget, and a general and administrative expense budget. Round all amounts to the nearest dollar.

ALTERNATE PROBLEMS

Problem 25–1A

Big Bend Sales Company sells three products that it purchases in their finished ready-for-sale state. The products' March 1 inventories are Product X, 3,900 units; Product Y, 3,750 units; and Product Z, 6,300 units. The company's manager is disturbed because each product's March 1 inventory is excessive in relation to immediately expected sales. Consequently, he has set as a goal a month-end inventory for each product that is equal to one half the following month's expected sales. Expected sales in units for March, April, May, and June are as follows:

Expected sales in units

	March	April	May	June
Product X	5,000	4,600	5,000	3,800
Product Y	2,800	2,800	3,400	3,600
Product Z	6,000	5,400	5,200	5,800

Required:

Prepare purchases budgets in units for the three products for each of March, April, and May.

Problem 25–2A

Oceanic Company expects to have a $5,800 cash balance on December 31 of the current year. It also expects to have a $35,200 balance of accounts receivable and $20,900 of accounts payable. Its budgeted sales, purchases, and cash expenditures for the following three months are as follows:

	January	February	March
Sales	$24,000	$18,000	$27,000
Purchases	14,000	17,300	18,000
Payroll	2,400	2,400	2,800
Rent	1,000	1,000	1,000
Other cash expenses	1,200	1,600	1,400
Purchase of store equipment	—	5,000	—
Payment of quarterly dividend	—	—	4,000

All sales are on account; and past experience indicates that 85% will be collected in the month following the sale, 10% in the next month, and 4% in the third month. Notwithstanding these expectations for future sales, an analysis of the December 31 accounts receivable balance indicates that $28,000 of the $35,200 balance will be collected in January, $5,200 in February, and $1,600 in March.

Purchases of merchandise on account are paid in the month following each purchase; likewise, the store equipment will be paid for in the month following its purchase.

Required:

Prepare cash budgets for the months of January, February, and March.

Problem 25–3A

The actual and projected monthly sales of Frantz Company are as follows:

September 19A, actual	$240,000
October 19A, actual	160,000
November 19A, estimated	190,000
December 19A, estimated	230,000
January 19B, estimated	210,000

Experience has shown that 40% of the sales are collected in the month of sale, 40% are collected in the first month after the sale, 18% in the second month after the sale, and 2% prove to be uncollectible.

Merchandise purchased by the Frantz Company is paid for 10 days after the date of purchase. Thus, approximately one third of the purchases in a month are due and paid for in the next month. Frantz Company pays $25 per unit of merchandise and subsequently sells the merchandise for $50 per unit. Frantz Company always plans to maintain an end-of-month inventory of 250 units plus 60% of the next month's unit sales, and the October 31, 19A, inventory is consistent with this policy.

In addition to cost of goods sold, Frantz Company incurs other operating expenses (excluding depreciation) of $582,000 per year, and they are distributed evenly throughout the year. On October 31, 19A, the company has a cash balance of $40,000.

Required:

Prepare a monthly cash budget for November and December, with supporting schedules showing cash receipts from collections of receivables and cash payments for merchandise purchases. Round all amounts to the nearest dollar.

Problem 25–4A

Northfield Company buys merchandise at $22 per unit and sells it at $36 per unit. Sales personnel are paid a commission of 10% of sales. The June 19A income statement of Northfield Company is as follows:

NORTHFIELD COMPANY
Income Statement
For June 19A

Sales	$396,000
Cost of goods sold	242,000
Gross profit	154,000
Expenses:	
Sales commissions	39,600
Advertising	21,000
Store rent	6,000
Administrative salaries	9,000
Depreciation expense	3,000
Other expenses	7,500
Total	86,100
Net income	$ 67,900

The management of Northfield Company expects the June results to be repeated during July, August, and September. However, certain changes are being considered. Management believes that if the selling price is reduced to $32 and advertising expenses are increased by 40%, unit sales will increase at a rate of 10% each month during the third quarter of 19A. If these changes are made, merchandise will still be purchased at $22 per unit. Sales personnel will continue to earn a commission of 10%, and the remaining expenses will remain constant.

Required:

Prepare a budgeted income statement that shows in three columns the planned results of operations for July, August, and September 19A, assuming the changes are implemented. Based on the budgeted income statements, decide whether management should make the changes.

Problem 25–5A

During March 19A, the management of Cloud Corporation prepared a budgeted balance sheet for March, 19A, which is presented below.

CLOUD CORPORATION
Budgeted Balance Sheet
At March 31, 19A

Assets		Equities	
Cash	$ 14,500	Accounts payable	$ 25,000
Accounts receivable	46,500	Loan from bank	15,000
Inventory	68,000	Taxes payable (due	
Equipment	170,000	June 15, 19A)	32,000
Accumulated depreciation	(17,000)	Common stock	125,000
		Retained earnings	85,000
Total assets	$282,000	Total equities	$282,000

In the process of preparing a master budget for April, May, and June 19A; the following information has been obtained:

a. The product sold by Cloud Corporation is purchased for $17 per unit and resold for $26 per unit. Although the inventory level on March 31 (4,000 units) is less than desired, management has established a new inventory policy whereby the end-of-month inventory should be 70% of the next month's expected sales (in units). Budgeted unit sales are: April, 15,000; May, 12,500; June, 18,000; July, 18,000.

b. Total sales each month are 40% for cash and 60% on account. Of the credit sales, 80% are collected in the month after sale and 20% in the second month after sale. Similarly, 80% of the accounts receivable on March 31 should be collected during April and 20% should be collected in May. Bad debt losses are insignificant.

c. Merchandise purchased by the company is paid for as follows: 70% in the month after purchase and 30% in the second month after purchase. Similarly 70% of the accounts payable balance on March 31 will be paid in April, and 30% will be paid in May.

d. Sales commissions amounting to 10% of sales are paid each month. Additionally, the sales manager is paid $30,000 per year.

e. Repair expenses amount to $1,400 per month and are paid in cash. General administrative salaries amount to $240,000 annually.

f. The equipment shown on the March 31, 19A balance sheet was purchased one year ago. It is a company policy to depreciate equipment over 10 years using the straight-line method assuming no salvage value and to take a full month's depreciation (rounded to the nearest dollar) in the month of purchase. The company plans to purchase additional equipment costing $22,000 in April; $12,000 in May; and $28,000 in June.

g. The company plans to acquire some land in June at a cost of $215,000. The land will not require a cash outlay until the last day of June. Thus, if a bank loan is necessary, the first interest payment will not be due until the end of July.

h. Cloud Corporation has an arrangement with the bank whereby additional loans are available as needed, at an annual rate of 12%, paid monthly. If part, or all of a loan is repaid, it is done at the end of the month along with any interest that is due. Cloud Corporation has agreed to maintain an end-of-month cash balance of at least $15,000.

i. The income tax rate is 40%. However, tax on the income for the second quarter of 19A will not be paid until July.

Required:

Prepare a master budget for the second quarter of 19A, with the operating budgets, capital expenditures budget, and the cash budget prepared on a monthly basis. The budgeted income statement should show operations for the second quarter, and the budgeted balance sheet should be prepared as of June 30, 19A. The operating budgets included in the master budget should include a sales budget (showing both budgeted unit sales and dollars sales), a merchandise purchases budget, and a general and administrative expense budget. Round all amounts to the nearest dollar.

PROVOCATIVE PROBLEMS

Provocative Problem 25–1, Fibretool Corporation

Fibretool Corporation produces a Product X which requires 4 kilograms of fibreglass per unit of X. The owner of Fibretool Corporation is in the process of negotiating with the bank for the approval to make loans as they are needed by the company. One of the important items in their discussion has been the question of how much cash will be needed to pay for purchases of fibreglass. Fibretool Corporation purchases fibreglass on account, and the resulting payables are paid in cash as follows: 60% during the month after purchase and 40% during the second month after purchase. The company plans to manufacture enough units of X to maintain an end-of-month inventory of finished units equal to 70% of the next month's sales, and enough fibreglass is purchased each month to maintain an end-of-month inventory equal to 50% of the next month's production requirements. Budgeted sales (in units) are as follows: February, 4,000; March, 6,000; April, 7,000; and May, 8,000. On January 31, 19A, the following data are available: finished units of Product X on hand, 2,800; kilograms of fibreglass on hand, 10,800; and Accounts Payable, $140,000 due in February plus $60,000 due in March.

In recent months the price of fibreglass has varied substantially, and the owner estimates that during the next few months the price could range from $10 to $15 per kilogram.

Required:

You are asked to assist the owner by estimating the cash payments to be made in February, in March, and in April. In preparing your answer, you should prepare separate estimates based on a $10 price and a $15 price.

Provocative Problem 25–2, Starship Corporation

The Starship Corporation has budgeted the following monthly sales volumes: October, 25,000; November, 15,000; December, 15,000; and January, 36,000 units. The company policy is to maintain an end-of-month finished goods inventory equal to 5,000 units plus 20% of the next month's budgeted sales in units. Consistent with this policy, the October 1 inventory was 10,000 units. An analysis of Starship Corporation's manufacturing costs show the following:

Material cost per unit $7.30
Direct labour cost per unit $3.80
Fixed manufacturing overhead costs . . . . $23,000 per month
Variable manufacturing overhead costs . . . . . $3.20 per unit manufactured

Required:

Prepare production budgets and manufacturing budgets for the months of October, November, and December.

ANALYTICAL AND REVIEW PROBLEM

Problem 25–1
A&R

Matthew (Matt) Brady and Dellaire (Dell) Grady were invited by the Arctic Twins for a weekend of skiing during the spring break. During the weekend Mr. Arctic made good on his promise to give Dell another "lesson" on the computer. The lesson was really a demonstration of how the computer is used to plan four or five years ahead under a variety of assumptions. Mr. Arctic loaded the "multiplan" program into his minicomputer and put in the financial statements of Assumed Company. The statements appeared on the screen, Mr. Arctic explained the assumptions he was putting into the machine, and with the press of the button projected five-year income statements as well as balance sheets at the end of each year appeared on the screen. He had these printed out and repeated the process with a set of different assumptions. Mr. Arctic also demonstrated projections with graphs and bar charts. Amazed and astonished at the speed and the alternatives in presenting financial data, Matt and Dell thanked Mr. Arctic for the demonstration.

On the way back to the University, Matt and Dell contemplated Mr. Arctic's remark at the conclusion of the demonstration which was, "the computer is nothing; the assumptions made are king."

Required:

What do you think Mr. Arctic meant by the above remark? Explain fully.

Flexible Budgets; Standard Costs

26

After studying Chapter 26, you should be able to:

State the deficiencies of fixed budgets.

Prepare flexible budgets and state their advantages.

State what standard costs represent, how they are determined, and how they are used in the evaluation process.

Calculate material, labour, and overhead variances, and state what each variance indicates about the performance of a company.

Explain the relevance of standard cost accounting to the management philosophy known as "management by exception."

Define or explain the words and phrases listed in the chapter Glossary.

The development of a master plan for a business was discussed in Chapter 25; consideration was also given to the importance of controlling subsequent operations. This function of control was recognized as one of the two basic functions of management. In order to control business operations, management must obtain information or feedback regarding how closely actual operations conform to the plans. To the extent possible, the comparison of actual performance with planned performance should direct management's attention toward the reasons why actual performance differs from planned performance. Flexible budgets and standard costs are important techniques that are used to help management determine why actual performance differs from the plan.

FIXED BUDGETS AND PERFORMANCE REPORTS

In preparing a master budget as discussed in Chapter 25, the initial step is to determine the expected sales volume for the budget period. All of the subsequent budget procedures are based on this specific estimate of sales volume. The amount of each budgeted cost is based on the assumption that a specific or fixed amount of sales will take place. When a budget is based on a single estimate of sales or production volume, the budget is called a *fixed* or *static budget.* In budgeting the total amount of each cost, a fixed budget gives no consideration to the possibility that the actual sales or production volume may be different from the fixed or budgeted amount.

If a company uses only fixed budgets, the comparison of actual performance with the budgeted performance is presented in a *performance report* such as that shown in Illustration 26–1.

The budgeted sales volume of London Manufacturing Company is 10,000 units (see Illustration 26–1). Also, to simplify the discussion, production volume is assumed to equal sales volume; no beginning or ending inventory is maintained by the company. In evaluating London Manufacturing Company's operations, management should be interested in answering such questions as: Why is the actual income from operations $13,400 higher than the budgeted amount? Are the prices being paid for each expense item too high? Is the manufacturing department using too much raw material? Is it using too much direct labour? The performance report shown in Illustration 26–1 provides little help in answering questions such as these. Since the actual sales volume was 2,000 units higher than the budgeted amount, it may be assumed that this increase caused total dollar sales and many of the expenses to be higher. But other factors may have influenced the amount of income, and the fixed budget performance report fails to provide management much information beyond the fact that the sales volume was higher than budgeted.

Illustration 26–1

LONDON MANUFACTURING COMPANY
Fixed Budget Performance Report
For Month Ended November 30, 198A

	Fixed budget	Actual perfor- mance	Variances
Sales: In units	10,000	12,000	
In dollars	$100,000	$125,000	$25,000F
Cost of goods sold:			
Raw materials	10,000	13,000	3,000U
Direct labour	15,000	20,000	5,000U
Overhead:			
Factory supplies	2,000	2,100	100U
Utilities	3,000	4,000	1,000U
Depreciation of machinery	8,000	8,000	—
Supervisory salaries	11,000	11,000	—
Selling expenses:			
Sales commissions	9,000	10,800	1,800U
Shipping expenses	4,000	4,300	300U
General and administrative expenses:			
Office supplies	5,000	5,200	200U
Insurance expense	1,000	1,200	200U
Depreciation of office equipment	7,000	7,000	—
Administrative salaries	13,000	13,000	—
Total expenses	88,000	99,600	11,600U
Income from operations	$ 12,000	$ 25,400	$13,400F

F = Favourable variance; that is, compared to the budget, the actual cost or revenue contributes to a higher income.
U = Unfavourable variance; that is, compared to the budget, the actual cost or revenue contributes to a lower income.

FLEXIBLE BUDGETS

To help answer questions such as those mentioned above, many companies prepare *flexible* or *variable budgets*. In contrast to fixed budgets, which are based on one fixed amount of budgeted sales or production, flexible budgets recognize that different levels of activity should produce different amounts of cost.

PREPARING A FLEXIBLE BUDGET

To prepare a flexible budget, each type of cost is examined to determine whether it should be classified as a variable cost or as a fixed cost.

Recall from Chapter 24 that the total amount of a variable cost changes in direct proportion to a change in the level of activity. Thus, variable cost per unit of activity remains constant. On the other hand, the total amount of a fixed cost remains unchanged regardless of changes in the level of activity (within the relevant or normal operating range of activity).[1]

After each cost item is classified as variable or fixed, each variable cost is expressed as a constant amount of cost per unit of sales (or per sales dollar). Fixed costs are, of course, budgeted in terms of the total amount of each fixed cost that is expected, regardless of the sales volume that may occur within the relevant range.

Illustration 26–2 shows how the fixed budget of London Manufacturing Company is reformulated as a flexible budget. Compare the first column of Illustration 26–2 with the first column of Illustration 26–1. Notice that seven of the expenses have been reclassified as variable costs; the remaining five expenses have been reclassified as fixed costs. This classification results from an investigation of each expense incurred by London Manufacturing Company, and the classification should not be misunderstood. It does not mean that these particular expenses are always variable costs in every company. For example, office supplies expense may frequently be a fixed cost, depending upon the nature of the company's operations. Nevertheless, London Manufacturing Company's accountant investigated this item and concluded that the office supplies cost behaves as a variable cost.

Observe in Illustration 26–2 that the variable costs of London Manufacturing Company are listed together, totaled, and subtracted from sales. As explained in Chapter 24, the difference between sales and variable costs is identified as the contribution margin. The budgeted amounts of fixed costs are then listed and totaled.

In Illustration 26–2, Columns 2 and 3 show the flexible budget amounts that may be applied to any volume of sales that occurs. The last two columns merely illustrate what form the flexible budget takes when the budget amounts are applied to particular sales volumes.

Recall from Illustration 26–1 that London Manufacturing Company's actual sales volume for November 198A was 12,000 units. This was 2,000 units more than the 10,000 units originally forecast in the master budget. The effect of this sales increase on the income from operations can be determined by comparing the budget for 10,000 units with the budget for 12,000 units (see Illustration 26–2). At a sales volume of 12,000 units, the budgeted income from operations is $22,400, whereas the budget for sales of 10,000 units shows income from operations of $12,000. Thus, if sales volume is 12,000 rather than 10,000 units, man-

---

[1] In Chapter 24, it was recognized that some costs are neither strictly variable nor strictly fixed. However, in the present discussion, it is assumed that all costs can be reasonably classified as being either variable or fixed.

Illustration 26-2

LONDON MANUFACTURING COMPANY
Flexible Budget
For Month Ending November 30, 198A

	Fixed budget	Flexible budget Variable cost per unit	Total fixed cost	Flexible budget for unit sales of 12,000	Flexible budget for unit sales of 14,000
Sales: In units	10,000			12,000	14,000
In dollars	$100,000	$10.00		$120,000	$140,000
Variable costs:					
Raw materials	10,000	1.00		12,000	14,000
Direct labour	15,000	1.50		18,000	21,000
Factory supplies	2,000	0.20		2,400	2,800
Utilities	3,000	0.30		3,600	4,200
Sales commissions	9,000	0.90		10,800	12,600
Shipping expenses	4,000	0.40		4,800	5,600
Office supplies	5,000	0.50		6,000	7,000
Total variable costs	48,000	4.80		57,600	67,200
Contribution margin..................	52,000	$ 5.20		62,400	72,800
Fixed costs:					
Depreciation of machinery	8,000		$ 8,000	8,000	8,000
Supervisory salaries	11,000		11,000	11,000	11,000
Insurance expense	1,000		1,000	1,000	1,000
Depreciation of office equipment........................	7,000		7,000	7,000	7,000
Administrative salaries	13,000		13,000	13,000	13,000
Total fixed costs	40,000		$40,000	40,000	40,000
Income from operations	$ 12,000			$ 22,400	$ 32,800

agement should expect income from operations to be higher by $10,400 ($22,400–$12,000). In other words, the difference between the $25,400 actual income from operations (see Illustration 26–1) and the $12,000 income from operations shown on the master budget can be analyzed, as follows:

Actual income from operations (12,000 units)		$ 25,400
Income from operations on master budget (10,000 units) ...		12,000
Difference to be explained		13,400
Income from operations:		
On the flexible budget for 12,000 units	$22,400	
On the budget for 10,000 units	12,000	
Additional income caused by increase in sales volume		(10,400)
Unexplained difference		$ 3,000

This $3,000 unexplained difference is the amount by which the actual income from operations exceeds budgeted income from operations as shown on the flexible budget for a sales volume of 12,000 units. As management seeks to determine what steps should be taken to control London Manufacturing Company's operations, the next step is to determine what caused this $3,000 unexplained difference. Information to help answer this question is provided by a flexible budget performance report.

FLEXIBLE BUDGET PERFORMANCE REPORT

A *flexible budget performance report* is designed to analyze the difference between actual performance and budgeted performance, where the budgeted amounts are based on the actual sales volume or level of activity. The report should direct management's attention toward those particular

Illustration 26–3

LONDON MANUFACTURING COMPANY
Flexible Budget Performance Report
For Month Ended November 30, 198A

	Flexible budget	Actual performance	Variances
Sales (12,000 units)	$120,000	$125,000	$5,000F
Variable costs:			
Raw materials	12,000	13,000	1,000U
Direct labour	18,000	20,000	2,000U
Factory supplies	2,400	2,100	300F
Utilities	3,600	4,000	400U
Sales commissions	10,800	10,800	
Shipping expenses	4,800	4,300	500F
Office supplies	6,000	5,200	800F
Total variable costs	57,600	59,400	1,800U
Contribution margin	62,400	65,600	3,200F
Fixed costs:			
Depreciation of machinery	8,000	8,000	
Supervisory salaries	11,000	11,000	
Insurance expense	1,000	1,200	200U
Depreciation of office equipment	7,000	7,000	
Administrative salaries	13,000	13,000	
Total fixed costs	40,000	40,200	200U
Income from operations	$ 22,400	$ 25,400	$3,000F

F = Favourable variance; that is, compared to the budget, the actual cost or revenue contributes to a higher income.

U = Unfavourable variance; that is, compared to the budget, the actual cost or revenue contributes to a lower income.

costs or revenues where actual performance has differed substantially from the budgeted amount.

The flexible budget performance report for London Manufacturing Company is presented in Illustration 26–3.

Observe in Illustration 26–3 the $5,000 favourable variance in total dollar sales. Since the actual number of units sold amounted to 12,000 and the budget was also based on unit sales of 12,000, the $5,000 variance must have resulted entirely from a difference between the average price per unit and the budgeted price per unit. Further analysis of the $5,000 variance is as follows:

Average price per unit, actual	$125,000/12,000 = $10.42
Budgeted price per unit	$120,000/12,000 = 10.00
Favourable variance in price per unit	$5,000/12,000 = $ 0.42

The variances in Illustration 26–3 direct management's attention toward the areas in which corrective action may be necessary to control London Manufacturing Company's operations. In addition, students should recognize that each of the cost variances can be analyzed in a manner similar to the above discussion of sales. Each of the expenses can be thought of as involving the use of a given number of units of the expense item and paying a specific price per unit. Following this approach, each of the cost variances shown in Illustration 26–3 might result in part from a difference between the actual price per unit and the budgeted price per unit (a price variance); and they may also result in part from a difference between the actual number of units used and the budgeted number of units to be used (a quantity variance). This line of reasoning, called variance analysis, is discussed more completely in the following section on standard costs.

STANDARD COSTS

In Chapter 22 it was said that there are two basic types of manufacturing cost systems, job order and process, but there are a large number of variations of the two. A **standard cost system,** that is, one based on *standard* or *budgeted costs,* is such a variation.

The costs of a job or a process as discussed in Chapter 22 were historical costs—historical in the sense that they had been incurred and were "history" by the time they were recorded. Such costs are useful; but to judge whether or not they are reasonable or what they should be, management needs a basis of comparison. Standard costs offer such a basis.

Standard costs are the costs that should be incurred under normal conditions in producing a given product or part or in performing a particular service. They are established by means of engineering and accounting studies made before the product is manufactured or the service is performed. Once established, standard costs are used to judge the reasonableness of the actual costs incurred when the product or service is produced. Standard costs are also used to replace responsibilities when actual costs vary from standard.

Accountants speak of **standard material cost, standard labour cost,** and **standard overhead cost,** and this terminology is used in this chapter. However, it should be observed that standard material, labour, and overhead costs are really budgeted material, labour, and overhead costs.

ESTABLISHING STANDARD COSTS

Great care and the combined efforts of people in accounting, engineering, personnel administration, and other management areas are required to establish standard costs. Time and motion studies are made of each labour operation in a product's production or in performing a service. From these studies, management learns the best way to perform the operation and the standard labour time required under normal conditions for its performance. Exhaustive investigations are commonly made of the quantity, grade, and cost of each material required; and machines and other productive equipment are subject to detailed studies in an effort to achieve maximum efficiencies and to learn what costs should be.

However, regardless of care exercised in establishing standard costs and in revising them as conditions change, actual costs incurred in producing a given product or service commonly vary from standard costs. When this occurs, the difference in total cost is likely to be a composite of several cost differences. For example, the quantity and/or the price of the material used may have varied from the standard. Also, the labour time and/or the labour price may have varied. Likewise, overhead costs may have varied.

VARIANCES

When actual costs vary from standard costs, the differences are called **variances.** Variances may be favourable or unfavourable. A favourable variance is one in which actual cost is less than standard cost, and an unfavourable variance is one in which actual cost is greater than standard.

When variances occur, they are isolated and studied for possible remedial action and to place responsibilities. For example, assume the standard material cost for producing 2,000 units of Product A is $800, but material costing $840 was used in producing the units. The $40 variance may have resulted from paying a price higher than standard for the material. Or, a greater quantity of material than standard may have been used. Or, there may have been some combination of these causes. The price paid for a material is a purchasing department responsibility; consequently, if the variance was caused by a price greater than standard, responsibility rests with the purchasing department. On the other hand, since the production department is usually responsible for the amount of material used, if a quantity greater than standard was used, responsibility normally rests with the production department. However, if more than a standard amount of material was used because the material was of a grade below standard, causing more than normal waste, the purchasing department is again responsible because it bought a substandard grade.

ISOLATING MATERIAL AND LABOUR VARIANCES

As previously stated, when variances occur, they are isolated and studied in order to take possible remedial action and to place responsibilities. For example, assume the XL Company has established the following standard costs per unit for its Product Z:

Material (1 kg. per unit at $1 per kg.) .... $ 1.00
Direct labour (1 hr. per unit at $9 per hr.) 9.00
Overhead ($4 per standard direct labour hour) .. 4.00
Total standard cost per unit $14.00

Material Variances

Assume further that during May, XL Company completed 3,500 units of Product Z, using 3,600 kilograms of material costing $1.05 per kilogram, or $3,780. Under these assumptions the actual and standard material costs for the 3,500 units are:

Actual cost: 3,600 kg. at $1.05 per kg. $3,780
Standard cost: 3,500 kg. at $1 per kg. 3,500
Material cost variance (unfavourable) .... $ 280

Observe that the actual material cost for these units is $280 above their standard cost. The causes of this unfavourable material cost variance may be discovered in the following manner:

```
Quantity variance:
    Actual units at the standard price  . . . . . .   3,600 kgs. at $1.00 = $3,600
    Standard units at the standard price  . . . .    3,500 kgs. at $1.00 =   3,500
        Variance (unfavourable)  . . . . . . . . . .     100 kgs. at $1.00 =              $100

Price variance:
    Actual units at the actual price  . . . . . . . .   3,600 kgs. at $1.05 =   3,780
    Actual unts at the standard price  . . . . . . .   3,600 kgs. at $1.00 =   3,600
        Variance (unfavourable)  . . . . . . . . . .   3,600 kgs. at $0.05 =                180
        Material cost variance
            (unfavourable)  . . . . . . . . . . . . . .                                      $280
```

The analysis shows that $100 of the excess material cost resulted from using 100 more kilograms than standard, and $180 resulted from a unit purchase price that was $0.05 above standard. With this information management can go to the responsible individuals for explanations.

Labour Variances

Labour cost in manufacturing a given part or in performing a service depends on a composite of the number of hours worked (quantity) and the wage rate paid (price). Therefore, when the labour cost for a task varies from standard, it too may be analysed into a *quantity variance* and a *price variance*.

For example, the direct labour standard for the 3,500 units of Product Z is one hour per unit, or 3,500 hours at $9 per hour. If 3,400 hours costing $9.30 per hour were used in completing the units, the actual and standard labour costs for these units are:

```
Actual cost:    3,400 hrs. at $9.30 per hr.  . . . . . . . . .   $31,620
Standard cost:  3,500 hrs. at $9.00 per hr.  . . . . . . . . .    31,500
    Direct labour cost variance (unfavourable) . . . .   $    120
```

In this case actual cost is only $120 over standard, but isolating the quantity and price variances involved reveals the following:

```
Quantity variance:
    Standard hours at standard price . . . . .   3,500 hrs. at $9.00 = $31,500
    Actual hours at standard price  . . . . . . .   3,400 hrs. at $9.00 =   30,600
        Variance (favourable)  . . . . . . . . . .     100 hrs. at $9.00 =              $ 900

Price variance:
    Actual hours at actual price  . . . . . . . .   3,400 hrs. at $9.30 =   31,620
    Actual hours at standard price  . . . . . . .   3,400 hrs. at $9.00 =   30,600
        Variance (unfavourable) . . . . . . . . .   3,400 hrs. at $0.30 =              1,020
        Direct labour cost variance
            (unfavourable)  . . . . . . . . . . . . .                                      $ 120
```

The analysis shows a favourable quantity variance of $900, which resulted from using 100 fewer direct labour hours than standard for the units produced. However, this favourable variance was more than offset by a wage rate that was $0.30 above standard.

When a factory or department has workers of various skill levels, it is the responsibility of the foreman or other supervisor to assign to each task a worker or workers of no higher skill level than is required to accomplish the task. In this case, an investigation could reveal that workers of a higher skill level were used in producing the 3,500 units of Product Z. Hence, fewer labour hours were required for the work. However, because the workers were of a higher skill level, the wage rate paid them was higher than standard.

CHARGING OVERHEAD TO PRODUCTION

When standard costs are used, factory overhead is charged to production by means of a predetermined standard overhead rate. The rate may be based on the relationship between overhead and standard labour cost, standard labour hours, standard machine-hours, or some other measure of production. For example, XL Company charges its Product Z with $4 of overhead per standard direct labour hour; and since the direct labour standard for Product Z is one hour per unit, the 3,500 units manufactured in May were charged with $14,000 of overhead.

Before going on, recall that only 3,400 actual direct labour hours were used in producing these units. Then, note again that overhead is charged to the units, not on the basis of actual labour hours but on the basis of standard labour hours. Standard labour hours are used because the amount of overhead charged to these units should not be less than standard simply because less than the standard (normal) amount of labour was used in their production. In other words, overhead should not vary from normal simply because labour varied from normal.

ESTABLISHING OVERHEAD STANDARDS

A variable or flexible factory overhead budget is the starting point in establishing reasonable standards for overhead costs. A flexible budget is necessary because the actual production level may vary from the expected level; when this happens, certain costs vary with production, but others remain fixed. This may be seen by examining XL Company's flexible budget shown in Illustration 26–4.

Observe in Illustration 26–4 that XL Company's flexible budget has been used to establish standard costs for four production levels, ranging from 70% to 100% of capacity. When actual costs are known, they should be compared with the standards for the level actually achieved

Illustration 26–4

XL COMPANY
Flexible Overhead Costs Budget
For Month Ended May 31, 198A

	Budget amounts	Production levels			
		70%	80%	90%	100%
Production in units	1 unit	3,500	4,000	4,500	5,000
Standard direct labour hours		3,500	4,000	4,500	5,000
Budgeted factory overhead:					
Fixed costs:					
Building rent..........................	$2,000	$ 2,000	$ 2,000	$ 2,000	$ 2,000
Depreciation, machinery	2,400	2,400	2,400	2,400	2,400
Supervisory salaries	3,600	3,600	3,600	3,600	3,600
Totals	$8,000	8,000	8,000	8,000	8,000
Variable costs:					
Indirect labour	$0.80	2,800	3,200	3,600	4,000
Indirect materials.....................	0.60	2,100	2,400	2,700	3,000
Power and lights	0.40	1,400	1,600	1,800	2,000
Maintenance	0.20	700	800	900	1,000
Totals	$2.00	7,000	8,000	9,000	10,000
Total factory overhead		$15,000	$16,000	$17,000	$18,000

and not with the standards at some other level. For example, if the plant actually operated at 70% capacity during May, actual costs incurred should be compared with standard costs for the 70% level. Actual costs should not be compared with costs established for 80% or 90% levels.

In setting overhead standards after the flexible overhead budget is prepared, management must determine the expected operating level for the plant. This can be 100% of capacity, but it seldom is. Errors in scheduling work, breakdowns, and, perhaps, the inability of the sales force to sell all the product produced are factors that commonly reduce the operating level to some point below full capacity.

After the flexible budget is set up and the expected operating level is determined, overhead costs at the expected level are related to, for example, labour hours at this level to establish the standard overhead rate. The rate thus established is then used to apply overhead to production. For example, assume XL Company decided that 80% of capacity is the expected operating level for its plant. The company then would calculate a $4 per direct labour hour overhead rate by dividing the budgeted $16,000 of overhead costs at the 80% level by the 4,000 standard direct labour hours required to produce the product manufactured at this level.

OVERHEAD VARIANCES

As previously stated, when standard costs are used, overhead is applied to production on the basis of a predetermined overhead rate. Then, at the end of a cost period the difference between overhead applied and overhead actually incurred is analysed, and variances are calculated to determine what was responsible for the difference.

Overhead variances are computed in several ways. A common way divides the difference between overhead applied and overhead incurred into (1) the **volume variance** and (2) the **controllable variance.**

Volume Variance

The *volume variance* is the difference between (1) *the amount of overhead budgeted at the actual operating level achieved during the period* and (2) *the standard amount of overhead charged to production during the period*. For example, assume that during May, XL Company actually operated at 70% of capacity. It produced 3,500 units of Product Z, which were charged with overhead at the standard rate. Under this assumption the company's volume variance for May is:

Volume variance:	
Budgeted overhead at 70% of capacity	$15,000
Standard overhead charged to production (3,500 standard	
labour hours at the $4 per hour standard rate)	14,000
Variance (unfavourable).....................................	$ 1,000

To understand why this volume variance occurred, reexamine the flexible budget of Illustration 26–4. Observe that at the 80% level the $4 per hour overhead rate may be subdivided into $2 per hour for fixed overhead and $2 per hour for variable overhead. Furthermore, at the 80% (normal) level, the $2 for fixed overhead exactly covers the fixed overhead. However, when this $4 rate is used for the 70% level, and again subdivided, the $2 for fixed overhead will not cover all the fixed overhead because $8,000 is required for fixed overhead, and 3,500 hours at $2 per hour equals only $7,000. In other words, at this 70% level the $4 per hour standard overhead rate did not absorb all the overhead incurred; it lacked $1,000, the amount of the volume variance. Or again, the volume variance resulted simply because the plant did not reach the expected operating level.

An unfavourable volume variance tells management that the plant did not reach its normal operating level; and when such a variance is large, management should investigate the cause or causes. Machine breakdowns, failure to schedule an even flow of work, and a lack of sales orders are common causes. The first two may be corrected in the factory, but the third requires either more orders from the sales force or a downward adjustment of the operating level considered to be normal.

Controllable Variance

The ***controllable variance*** is the difference between (1) *overhead actually incurred* and (2) *the overhead budgeted at the operating level achieved.* For example, assume that XL Company incurred $15,300 of overhead during May. Since its plant operated at 70% of capacity during the month, its controllable overhead variance for May is:

Controllable variance:	
Actual overhead incurred	$15,300
Overhead budgeted at operating level achieved	15,000
Variance (unfavourable)....................	$ 300

The controllable overhead variance measures management's efficiency in adjusting controllable overhead costs (normally variable overhead)

Illustration 26–5

XL COMPANY
Factory Overhead Variance Report
For Month Ended May 31, 198A

Volume variance:
Normal production level.........................	80%	of capacity.
Production level achieved	70%	of capacity.
Volume variance.............................	$1,000 (unfavourable)	

Controllable variance:

	Budget	Actual	Favourable	Unfavourable
Fixed overhead costs:				
Building rent	$2,000	$2,000		
Depreciation, machinery ...	2,400	2,400		
Supervisory salaries	3,600	3,600		
Total fixed	8,000	8,000		
Variable overhead costs:				
Indirect labour	2,800	3,050		$250
Indirect materials	2,100	2,050	$ 50	
Power and lights	1,400	1,500		100
Maintenance	700	700		
Total variable	$7,000	$7,300		
Total controllable variances			50	350
Net controllable variance (unfavourable)			300	
			$350	$350

to the operating level achieved. In this case, management failed by $300 to maintain overhead costs at the amount budgeted for the 70% level.

The controllable overhead variance measures management's efficiency in adjusting overhead costs to the operating level achieved. However, an overhead variance report is a more effective means for showing just where management achieved or failed to achieve the budgeted expectations. Such a report for XL Company appears in Illustration 26–5.

Combining the Volume and Controllable Variances

The volume and controllable variances may be combined to account for the difference between overhead actually incurred and overhead charged to production. For example, XL Company actually incurred $15,300 of overhead during May and charged $14,000 to production. Its overhead variances may be combined as follows to account for the difference:

Volume variance:		
Overhead budgeted at operating level achieved	$15,000	
Standard overhead charged to production (3,500 standard		
hours at $4 per hour)	14,000	
Variance (unfavourable)		$1,000
Controllable variance:		
Actual overhead incurred	15,300	
Overhead budgeted at operating level achieved	15,000	
Variance (unfavourable)		300
Excess of overhead incurred over overhead charged		
to production		$1,300

CONTROLLING A BUSINESS THROUGH STANDARD COSTS

Business operations are carried on by people, and control of a business is gained by controlling the actions of the people responsible for its revenues, costs, and expenses. When a budget is prepared and standard costs established, control is maintained by taking appropriate action when actual costs vary from standard or from the budget.

Reports like the ones shown in this chapter are a means of calling management's attention to these variations, and a review of the reports is essential to the successful operation of a budget program. However, in making the review, management should practice the control technique known as **management by exception.** Under this technique, management gives its attention only to the variances in which actual costs are significantly different from standard; it ignores the cost situations in which performance is satisfactory. In other words, management concentrates its attention on the exceptional or irregular situations and pays little or no attention to the normal.

Many companies develop standard costs and apply variance analysis only when dealing with manufacturing costs. In these companies, the master budget includes selling, general, and administrative expenses; but the subsequent process of controlling these expenses is not based upon the establishment of standard costs and variance analysis. However, other companies have recognized that standard costs and variance analysis may help control selling, general, and administrative expenses just as well as manufacturing costs. Students should understand that the previous discussions of material and labour cost variances can easily be adapted to many selling, general, and administrative expenses.

STANDARD COSTS IN THE ACCOUNTS

Standard costs can be used solely in the preparation of management reports and need not be taken into the accounts. However, in most standard cost systems such costs are recorded in the accounts to facilitate both the record-keeping and the preparation of reports.

No effort will be made here to go into the record-keeping details of a standard cost system. This is reserved for a course in cost accounting. Nevertheless, when standard costs are taken into the accounts, entries like the following (the data for which are taken from the discussion of material variances on pages 1059–60) may be used to enter standard costs into the Goods in Process account and to separately identify variances in variance accounts.

May	31	Goods in Process............................	3,500.00	
		Material Quantity Variance	100.00	
		Material Price Variance	180.00	
		Materials		3,780.00
		To charge production with 3,600 kilograms of material at $1.05 per kilogram.		

Variances taken into the accounts are allowed to accumulate in the variance accounts until the end of an accounting period. If at that time the variance amounts are immaterial, they are closed directly to Cost of Goods Sold. However, if the amounts are material, they may be prorated between Goods in Process, Finished Goods, and Cost of Goods Sold.

GLOSSARY

Budgeted costs. Estimated costs for an activity level or an accounting period from which standard costs may be developed.

Controllable variance. The difference between overhead actually incurred and the overhead budgeted at the operating level achieved.

Fixed budget. A budget based on a single estimate of sales or production volume that gives no consideration to the possibility that the actual sales or production volume may be different from the assumed amount.

Flexible budget. A budget that provides budgeted amounts for all levels of production within the relevant range.

Flexible budget performance report. A report designed to analyse the difference between actual performance and budgeted performance, where the budgeted amounts are based on the actual sales volume or level of activity.

Performance report. A financial report that compares actual cost and/or revenue performance with budgeted amounts and designates the differences between them as favourable or unfavourable variances.

Price variance. A difference between actual and budgeted revenue or cost caused by the actual price per unit being different from the budgeted price per unit.

Quantity variance. The difference between actual cost and budgeted cost that was caused by a difference between the actual number of units used and the number of units budgeted.

Standard costs. The costs that should be incurred under normal conditions in producing a given product or part or in performing a particular service.

Static budget. A synonym for fixed budget.

Variable budget. A synonym for flexible budget.

Volume variance. The difference between the amount of overhead budgeted at the actual operating level achieved during the period and the standard amount of overhead charged to production during the period.

QUESTIONS FOR CLASS DISCUSSION

1. What is a *fixed* or *static* budget?
2. What limits the usefulness of fixed budget performance reports?
3. What is the essential difference between a fixed budget and a flexible budget?
4. What is the initial step in preparing a flexible budget?
5. Is there any sense in which a variable cost may be thought of as being constant in amount? Explain.

6. A particular type of cost may be classified as variable by one company and fixed by another company. Why might this be appropriate?

7. What is meant by contribution margin?

8. What is a flexible budget performance report designed to analyze?

9. In cost accounting, what is meant by a *variance?*

10. A cost variance often consists of a price variance and a quantity variance. What is a price variance? What is a quantity variance?

11. What is the purpose of a *standard cost?*

12. What department is usually responsible for a material price variance? What department is generally responsible for a material quantity variance?

13. What is a *predetermined standard overhead rate?*

14. In analyzing the overhead variance, explain what is meant by a *volume variance?*

15. In analysing the overhead variance, explain what is meant by a *controllable variance?*

16. What is the relationship between standard costs, variance analysis, and *management by exception?*

MULTIPLE CHOICE

1. A company's flexible budget for 12,000 units of production showed sales, $48,000; variable costs, $18,000; and fixed costs, $16,000. The net income you would expect the company to earn if it produces and sells 15,000 units is:

    a. $0.
    b. $14,000.
    c. $17,500.
    d. $21,500.
    e. $26,000.

2. Job B was budgeted to need three hours of labour at $8 per hour. However, it was completed in two hours by a person who worked for $9 per hour. What is the labour cost variance?

    a. $2 unfavourable.
    b. $3 unfavourable.
    c. $6 favourable.
    d. $8 unfavourable.
    e. $9 unfavourable.

3. A company has established five pounds of Material M at $2 per pound as the standard amount and cost per unit for the material in its Product A, and the company has just finished 100 units of the product, using 520 pounds of Material M that cost $988. The quantity variance in producing these units was:

    b. $40 unfavourable.

    b. $12 favourable.

    c. $40 favourable.

    d. $52 favourable.

    e. Some other variance.

4. The standard material cost to produce one unit of Product M is 1 pound of material at a standard price of $50 per pound. In manufacturing 8,000 units, 8,250 pounds of material were used at a cost of $52 per pound. What is the material cost variance?

    a. $16,500 unfavourable.

    b. $16,000 unfavourable.

    c. $29,000 favourable.

    d. $29,000 unfavourable.

    e. $13,000 unfavourable.

5. XY Zipper Company charged overhead to production at a rate of $3.75 per direct labour-hour for the month of December. This figure was based on 90% capacity or 900 direct labour-hours. XY Zipper Company operated, however, at only 80% capacity or 800 direct labour-hours. Budgeted overhead at 80% of capacity is $3,150. Overhead actually incurred was $3,800. The volume variance for December was:

    a. $150 favourable.

    b. $150 unfavourable.

    c. $225 unfavourable.

    d. $375 unfavourable.

    e. $800 unfavourable.

6. Hanger Company's flexible budget shows $9,000 of overhead at 75% of capacity, which was the operating level achieved during May. However, the company applied overhead to production during May at a rate of $2 per direct labour-hour based on a budgeted operating level of 6,120 direct labour-hours (90% of capacity). If overhead actually incurred was $9,473 during May, the controllable variance for the month was:

    a. $473 unfavourable.

    b. $473 favourable.

    c. $1,200 favourable.

    d. $1,200 unfavourable.

    e. $727 favourable.

MINI DISCUSSION CASES

Case 26–1   The Evans Dinghy Company has just completed its best year ever showing a profit of $150,000 on sales of 800 units. However, Mr. Evans, the president, is a little perplexed because according to his budget, which was based on sales of 750 units, profit was estimated at $115,000.

The company sells its dinghies for $1,850 and has a standard cost per dinghy of $1,450. Selling, general, and administrative expenses were not significantly different from the budget. Obviously, the additional 50 units sold at a standard gross profit of $400 does not account for all of the increased profit.

Required:

Provide Mr. Evans with an explanation for the difference between his expected and actual profit.

Case 26–2

Rod Collinge, the foreman for the shaping department, has just received the monthly variance report for his department. It shows an unfavourable labour quantity variance of $4,360. The standard labour cost for his department is $10.50 per hour.

Required:

As the production manager looking at the unfavourable report, what additional information would you want to have before taking remedial action?

CLASS EXERCISES

Exercise 26–1

A company manufactures and sells wooden desks and generally operates eight hours a day, five days per week. On the basis of this general information, classify the following costs as fixed or variable. In those instances where further investigation might reverse your classification, comment on the possible reasons for treating the item in the opposite manner.

a.	Wood planks.	*h.*	Depreciation on saws.
b.	Nails and glue.	*i.*	Fire insurance on property.
c.	Paint.	*j.*	Supplies for office.
d.	Direct labour.	*k.*	Sales commissions.
e.	Hydro to run saws.	*l.*	Packaging expenses.
f.	President's salary.	*m.*	Utilities (gas and water).
g.	Repair expense on saws.	*n.*	Shipping expenses.

Exercise 26–2

Cadena Company's fixed budget for the second quarter of 19A is presented below.

Sales (8,500 units)		$ 119,000
Cost of goods sold:		
Materials	$22,100	
Direct labour	24,650	
Production supplies	3,400	
Depreciation	2,800	
Plant manager's salary	3,000	(55,950)
Gross profit		$ 63,050
Selling expenses:		
Sales commissions	$ 9,860	
Packaging expense	2,550	(12,410)
Administrative expenses:		
Administative salaries	$ 5,200	
Insurance expense	1,400	
Office rent expense	3,400	
Executive salaries	7,900	(17,900)
Income from operations		$ 32,740

Required:

Recast the budget as a flexible budget and show the budgeted amounts for 8,000 units and 9,000 units of production.

Exercise 26–3

Outdoor Furniture Company has just completed 300 units of its deluxe picnic table using 14,500 board feet of lumber costing $3,045. The company's material standards for one unit of this table are 50 board feet of lumber at $0.20 per board foot.

Required:

Isolate the material variances incurred in manufacturing these tables.

Exercise 26–4

Outdoor Furniture Company takes its standard costs into its cost records. As a result, in charging material costs to Goods in Process, it also takes any variances into its accounts.

Required:

1. Under the assumption that the materials used to manufacture the tables of Exercise 26–3 were charged to Goods in Process on March 5, give the entry to charge the materials and to take the variances into the accounts.
2. Under the further assumption that the material variances of Exercise 26–3 were the only variances of the year and were considered immaterial, give the year-end entry to close the variance accounts.

Exercise 26–5

A company has established the following standard costs for one unit of its product:

Material (1 unit @ $5 per unit)	$ 5
Direct labour (1 hr. @ $9 per hr.)	9
Factory overhead (1 hr. @ $4 per hr.)	4
Standard cost	$18

The $4 per direct labour hour overhead rate is based on a normal 80% of capacity operating level and the following monthly flexible budget information:

	Operating levels		
	75%	80%	85%
Budgeted production in units	7,500	8,000	8,500
Budgeted overhead:			
Fixed overhead	$16,000	$16,000	$16,000
Variable overhead	15,000	16,000	17,000

During the past month the company operated at 75% of capacity, producing 7,500 units of product with the following overhead costs:

Fixed overhead costs	$16,000
Variable overhead costs	15,250
Total overhead costs	$31,250

Required:

Isolate the overhead variances into a volume variance and a controllable variance.

PROBLEMS

Problem 26–1

Craven Company's master (fixed) budget for 19A was based on an expected production and sales volume of 9,200 units, and included the following operating items:

CRAVEN COMPANY
Fixed Budget
For Year Ended December 31, 19A

Sales		$184,000
Cost of goods sold:		
Materials.....................................	$46,000	
Direct labour	27,600	
Machinery repairs (variable cost)	1,380	
Depreciation of plant	5,000	
Utilities (40% of which is a variable cost)	9,200	
Supervisory salaries	12,000	(101,180)
Gross profit		$ 82,820
Selling expenses:		
Packaging	$ 4,600	
Shipping	6,900	
Sales salary (an agreed-upon, annual salary)	14,000	(25,500)
General and administrative expenses:		
Insurance expense	$ 3,000	
Salaries	21,000	
Rent expense	16,000	(40,000)
Income from operations		$ 17,320

Required:

1. Prepare a flexible budget for the company and show detailed budgets for sales and production volumes of 8,400 units and 10,000 units.
2. A consultant to the company has suggested that developing business conditions in the area are reaching a crossroads, and that the effect of these events on the company could result in a sales volume of approximately 11,300 units. The president of Craven Company is confident that this is within the relevant range of existing production capacity but is hesitant to estimate the impact of such a change on operating income. What would be the expected increase in operating income?
3. In the consultant's report, the possibility of unfavourable business events was also mentioned, in which case production and sales volume for 19A would likely fall to 8,000 units. What amount of income from operations should the president expect if these unfavourable events occur?

Problem 26–2   Refer to the discussion of Craven Company in Problem 26–1. Craven Company's actual statement of income from 19A operations is as follows:

CRAVEN COMPANY
Statement of Income from Operations
For Year Ended December 31, 19A

Sales (10,000 units)		$190,000
Cost of goods sold:		
Materials	$45,000	
Direct labour	31,000	
Machinery repairs	1,000	
Depreciation of plant	5,000	
Utilities (50% of which was a variable cost)	11,040	
Supervisory salaries	11,700	(104,740)
Gross profit		$ 85,260
Selling expenses:		
Packaging	$ 4,500	
Shipping	7,900	
Sales salary	14,000	(26,400)
General and administrative expenses:		
Insurance expense	$ 3,100	
Salaries	21,500	
Rent expense	16,000	(40,600)
Income from operations		$ 18,260

Required:

1. Using the flexible budget you prepared for Problem 26–1, present a flexible budget performance report for 19A.
2. Explain the sales variance.

Problem 26–3   Gull Manufacturing Company makes a single product for which it has established the following standard costs per unit:

Material (5 kgs. @ $0.50 per kgs.)	$ 2.50
Direct labour (1 hr. @ $9 per hr.)	9.00
Factory overhead (1 hr. @ $3.25 per hr.)	3.25
Total standard cost	$14.75

The $3.25 per direct labour hour overhead rate is based on a normal, 90% of capacity, operating level and the following flexible budget information:

	Operating levels		
	80%	90%	100%
Production in units	1,600	1,800	2,000
Standard direct labour hours	1,600	1,800	2,000
Fixed factory overhead	$3,600	$3,600	$3,600
Variable factory overhead ..	$2,000	$2,250	$2,500

During March the company operated at 80% of capacity, producing 1,600 units of product which were charged with the following standard costs:

Material (8,000 kgs. @ $0.50 per kg.)	$ 4,000
Direct labour (1,600 hrs. @ $9 per hr.)	14,400
Factory overhead costs (1,600 hrs. @ $3.25 per hr.)	5,200
Total standard cost	$23,600

Actual costs incurred during March were:

Material (8,100 kgs.)	$ 3,969
Direct labour (1,550 hrs.)	14,415
Fixed factory overhead costs	3,600
Variable factory overhead costs	2,115
Total actual costs	$24,099

Required:

Isolate the material and labour variances into price and quantity variances and isolate the overhead variance into the volume variance and the controllable variance.

Problem 26–4   Weberville Company has established the following standard costs per unit for the product it manufactures:

Material (4 kgs. @ $1.50 per kg.)	$ 6.00
Direct labour (3 hrs. @ $9 per hr.)	27.00
Overhead (3 hrs. @ $4.50 per hr.)	13.50
Total standard cost	$46.50

The $4.50 per direct labour hour overhead rate is based on a normal, 85% of capacity, operating level and the following flexible budget information for one month's operations.

	Operating levels		
	80%	85%	90%
Production in units	1,600	1,700	1,800
Standard direct labour hours	4,800	5,100	5,400
Budgeted factory overhead:			
Fixed costs:			
Rent of factory building	$ 5,400	$ 5,400	$ 5,400
Depreciation expense, machinery	4,800	4,800	4,800
Taxes and insurance	600	600	600
Supervisory salaries	4,500	4,500	4,500
Total fixed costs	15,300	15,300	15,300
Variable costs:			
Indirect materials	1,920	2,040	2,160
Indirect labour	3,600	3,825	4,050
Power	960	1,020	1,080
Maintenance	720	765	810
Total variable costs	7,200	7,650	8,100
Total factory overhead costs	$22,500	$22,950	$23,400

During May the company operated at 90% of capacity, produced 1,800 units of product, and incurred the following actual costs:

Material (7,250 kgs. @ $1,48 per kg.)		$10,730
Direct labor (5,300 hrs. @ $9.30 per hr.)		49,290
Overhead costs:		
Rent of factory building	$5,400	
Depreciation expense, machinery	4,800	
Taxes and insurance	600	
Supervisory salaries	4,500	
Indirect materials.........................	2,100	
Indirect labour	3,930	
Power	1,065	
Maintenance	900	23,295
Total costs		$83,315

Required:

1. Isolate the material and labour variances into quantity and price variances and isolate the overhead variance into the volume variance and the controllable variance.
2. Prepare a factory overhead variance report showing the volume and controllable variances.

Problem 26–5   Ranger Company has established the following standard costs for one unit of its product:

Material (3 kgs. @ $2.50 per kg.)	$ 7.50
Direct labour (½ hr. @ $9 per hr.)	4.50
Overhead (½ hr. @ $5.20 per hr.)	2.60
Total standard cost	$14.60

The $5.20 per direct labour hour overhead rate is based on a normal, 80% of capacity, operating level, and at this level the company's monthly output is 4,000 units. However, production does vary slightly, and each 1% variation results in a 50-unit increase or decrease in the production level. Following are the company's budgeted overhead costs at the 80% level for one month.

RANGER COMPANY
Budgeted Monthly Factory Overhead at 80% Level

Fixed costs:		
Depreciation expense, building	$2,000	
Depreciation expense, machinery	1,600	
Taxes and insurance	400	
Supervision	2,400	
Total fixed costs		$ 6,400
Variable costs:		
Indirect materials...................	$1,600	
Indirect labour	960	
Power	640	
Repairs and maintenance	800	
Total variable costs		4,000
Total overhead costs		$10,400

During July of the current year the company operated at 70% of capacity and incurred the following actual costs:

Material (10,620 kgs.)	$25,488
Direct labour (1,700 hrs.)	15,555
Depreciation expense, building	2,000
Depreciation expense, machinery	1,600
Taxes and insurance	400
Supervision	2,400
Indirect materials...................	1,450
Indirect labour	800
Power	590
Repairs and maintenance	720
Total costs	$51,003

Required:

1. Prepare a flexible overhead budget for the company showing the amount of each fixed and variable cost at the 70%, 80%, and 90% levels.
2. Isolate the material and labour variances into quantity and price variances and isolate the overhead variance into the volume variance and the controllable variance.
3. Prepare a factory overhead variance report showing the volume and controllable variances.

ALTERNATE PROBLEMS

Problem
26–1A

In the process of preparing a master budget for 19A, Prichard Company assumed a sales volume of 18,000 units. The resulting budgeted income statement included the following items that comprise income from operations.

PRICHARD COMPANY
Fixed Budget
For Year Ended December 31, 19A

Sales		$ 315,000
Cost of goods sold:		
Raw materials	$72,000	
Direct labour	41,004	
Factory supplies	4,194	
Depreciation of plant	7,800	
Utilities (of which $6,000 is a fixed cost)	11,796	
Salary of plant manager	18,000	(154,791)
Gross profit		$ 160,209
Selling expenses:		
Packaging	$37,998	
Sales commissions	25,200	
Shipping	14,202	
Salary of vice president–marketing	14,000	
Promotion (variable)	15,750	(107,150)
General and administrative expenses:		
Depreciation	$ 7,000	
Consultant's fees (annual retainer)	14,500	
Administrative salaries	32,500	(54,000)
Income from Operations		$ (941)

Required:

1. Prepare a flexible budget for the company, showing specific budget columns for sales and production volumes of 20,000 units and 22,000 units.
2. What would be the expected increase in income from operations if sales and production volume were 21,200 units rather than 18,000 units?
3. Although the management of Prichard Company believes that the master budget was a conservative estimate of sales and production volume, it is possible that the level of activity could fall to 16,000 units. What would be the effect on income from operations if this occurs?

Problem
26–2A

Refer to the discussion of Prichard Company in Problem 26–1A. Prichard Company's actual statement of income from 19A operations is as follows:

PRICHARD COMPANY
Statement of Income from Operations
For Year Ended December 31, 19A

Sales (20,000 units)		$390,000
Cost of goods sold:		
Raw materials	$78,000	
Direct labour	49,000	
Factory supplies	4,900	
Depreciation of plant	7,800	
Utilities (of which 50% is a fixed cost) . . .	12,400	
Salary of plant manager	18,000	(170,100)
Gross profit		$219,900
Selling expenses:		
Packaging	$39,000	
Sales commissions	31,200	
Shipping	14,950	
Salary of vice president–marketing	14,000	
Promotion (variable)	18,250	(117,400)
General and administrative expenses:		
Depreciation	$ 7,000	
Consultant's fees	16,300	
Administrative salaries	31,250	(54,550)
Income from Operations		$ 47,950

Required:

1. Using the flexible budget you prepared for Problem 26–1A, present a flexible budget performance report for 19A.
2. Explain the sales variance.

Problem 26–3A

A company has established the following standard costs for one unit of its product:

Material (3 kgs. @ $5 per kg.)	$15.00
Direct labour (3 hrs. @ $10.50 per hr.) . . .	31.50
Overhead (3 hrs. @ $3 per hr.)	9.00
Total standard cost	$55.50

The $3 per direct labour hour overhead rate is based on a normal, 90% of capacity, operating level for the company's plant and the following flexible budget information for April.

	Operating levels		
	80%	90%	100%
Production in units	800	900	1,000
Direct labour hours	2,400	2,700	3,000
Fixed factory overhead	$4,500	$4,500	$4,500
Variable factory overhead . . .	$3,200	$3,600	$4,000

During April the company operated at 80% of capacity, producing 800 units of product having the following actual costs:

Material (2,350 kgs. @ $5.10 per kg.) $11,985
Direct labour (2,500 hrs. @ $10.20 per hr.) . .   25,500
Fixed factory overhead costs   4,500
Variable factory overhead costs   3,325

Required:

Isolate the material and labour variances into price and quantity variances and isolate the overhead variance into the volume variance and the controllable variance.

Problem 26–4A

Frankford Company has established the following standard costs per unit for the product it manufactures:

Material (4 kgs. @ $0.75 per kg.) . . . . $ 3.00
Direct labour (2 hrs. @ $10.50 per hr.) . . .   21.00
Overhead (2 hrs. @ $7.50 per hr.) 15.00
Total standard cost $39.00

The $7.50 per direct labour hour overhead rate is based on a normal, 80% of capacity, operating level and the following flexible budget information for one month's operations.

	Operating levels		
	75%	80%	85%
Production in units	1,500	1,600	1,700
Standard direct labour hours	3,000	3,200	3,400
Budgeted factory overhead:			
Fixed costs:			
Depreciation, building	$ 3,600	$ 3,600	$ 3,600
Depreciation, machinery	5,100	5,100	5,100
Taxes and insurance	900	900	900
Supervisory salaries	4,800	4,800	4,800
Total fixed costs	14,400	14,400	14,400
Variable costs:			
Indirect materials	2,250	2,400	2,550
Indirect labour	4,500	4,800	5,100
Power	1,125	1,200	1,275
Maintenance	1,125	1,200	1,275
Total variable costs	9,000	9,600	10,200
Total factory overhead . . .	$23,400	$24,000	$24,600

During August the company operated at 75% of capacity, produced 1,500 units of product, and incurred the following actual costs:

Material (5,900 kgs. @ $0.78 per kg.)		$ 4,602
Direct labour (3,060 hrs. @ $10.35 per hr.) ...		31,671
Overhead costs:		
Depreciation expense, building	$ 3,600	
Depreciation expense, machinery	5,100	
Taxes and insurance	900	
Supervisory salaries	4,800	
Indirect materials	2,205	
Indirect labour	4,680	
Power	1,155	
Maintenance	1,020	23,460
Total		$59,733

Required:

1. Isolate the material and labour variances into price and quantity variances and isolate the overhead variance into the volume variance and the controllable variance.
2. Prepare a factory overhead variance report showing the volume and controllable variances.

Problem
26–5A

Prince Company has established the following standard costs for one unit of its product:

Material (3 kgs. at $2.50 per kg.) ...	$ 7.50
Direct labour (1 hr at $12 per hr.) ...	12.00
Overhead (1 hr. at $7.80 per hr.) ...	7.80
Total standard cost	$27.30

The $7.80 per direct labour hour overhead rate is based on a normal, 80% of capacity, operating level, and at this level the company's monthly output is 4,000 units. Following are the company's budgeted overhead costs at the 80% level for one month:

PRINCE COMPANY
Budgeted Monthly Factory Overhead
At 80% Level

Fixed costs:		
Depreciation expense, building	$1,500	
Depreciation expense, machinery ...	1,200	
Taxes and insurance	300	
Supervision	1,800	
Total fixed costs		$4,800
Variable costs:		
Indirect materials	1,200	
Indirect labour	720	
Power	480	
Repairs and maintenance	600	
Total variable costs		3,000
Total overhead costs		$7,800

During July of the current year, the company operated at 70% of capacity and incurred the following actual costs:

Material (10,620 kgs.)	$25,488
Direct labour (850 hrs.)	10,370
Depreciation expense, building	1,500
Depreciation expense, machinery . . .	1,200
Taxes and insurance	300
Supervision	1,800
Indirect materials	1,090
Indirect labour	600
Power	445
Repairs and maintenance	540
Total costs	$43,333

Required:

1. Prepare a flexible overhead budget for the company showing the amount of each fixed and variable cost at the 70%, 80%, and 90% levels.
2. Isolate the material and labour variances into quantity and price variances and isolate the overhead variance into the volume variance and the controllable variance.
3. Prepare a factory overhead variance report showing the volume and controllable variances.

PROVOCATIVE PROBLEMS

Provocative
Problem 26–1,
Potter
Company

Potter Company's manager plans to sell artistic, clay pots for $9 each. Each pot should require 2 kilograms of a specially processed clay that the company expects to purchase for $1.50 per kilogram. The pots ought to be produced at the rate of five pots per direct labour hour, and the company should be able to hire the needed labourers for $10.50 per hour. Each pot will be packaged in a cardboard container that weighs one-half kilogram, and the company will seek to buy cardboard for $0.20 per kilogram.

If actual sales and production volume range from 80,000 to 120,000 pots, the manager would expect the company to incur administrative and sales personnel salaries of $60,000, depreciation of $10,000, utilities expenses of $8,000, and insurance expense of $6,000.

In 19A, Potter Company actually produced and sold 100,000 pots at $11.50 each. It used 225,000 kilograms of clay, purchased at $1.54 per kilogram. Labourers were paid $10.65 per hour and worked 22,000 hours to produce the pots. Cardboard was purchased for $0.18 per kilogram and 48,000 kilograms were used. All other expenses occurred as planned.

Although the above facts are all available to the manager, he has expressed considerable confusion over the matter of evaluating the operating performance of the company. He recognizes that the actual operating income was different from the expected amount but is not able to sort out which items caused the change. He has also expressed interest in learning the magnitude of the impact of price changes in specific items purchased by the company as well as any other factors that might be of help in evaluating the company's performance. Can you help the manager?

Provocative
Problem 26–2,
Machine
Products
Company

Ray Sauls has been an employee of Machine Products Company for nine years, the last seven of which he has worked in the casting department. Eight months ago he was made foreman of the department, and since then has been able to end a long period of internal dissention, high employee turnover, and inefficient operation in the department. Under Ray's supervision the department's production has increased, employee morale has improved, absenteeism has dropped, and for the past two months the department has regularly been beating its standard for the first time in years.

However, a few days ago Jack Payne, an employee in the department, suggested to Ray that the company install new controls on the department's furnace similar to those developed by a competitor. The controls would cost $15,000 installed and would have a 10-year life and no salvage value. They should increase production 10%, reduce maintenance costs $500 per year, and do away with the labour of one person.

Ray's answer to Jack was, "Forget it. We are doing OK now; we don't need the extra production; and besides, jobs are hard to find and if we have to let someone go, who'll it be?"

Do you think standard costs had anything to do with Ray's answer to Jack? Explain. Do you agree with Ray's answer? Should Ray be the person to make a decision such as this? How can a company be sure that suggestions such as Jack's are not lost in the chain of command?

Provocative
Problem 26–3,
Rayburn
Company

Rayburn Company manufactures Frebolas. They have a seasonal demand and cannot be stored for long periods; consequently, the number of units manufactured varies with the season. In accounting for costs, the company charges actual costs incurred to a goods in process account maintained for the product, which it closes at the end of each quarter to Finished Goods. At the end of last year, which was an average year, the following cost report was prepared for the company manager:

RAYBURN COMPANY
Quarterly Report of Costs for Frebolas
Year Ended December 31, 19—

	1st quarter	2d quarter	3d quarter	4th quarter
Materials	$ 31,200	$ 38,900	$ 15,700	$ 7,900
Direct labour	93,400	116,000	47,000	23,600
Fixed overhead costs	42,000	42,000	42,000	42,000
Variable overhead costs	51,200	63,900	25,900	13,000
Total manufacturing costs	$217,800	$260,800	$130,600	$86,500
Production in units	40,000	50,000	20,000	10,000
Cost per unit	$ 5.445	$ 5.216	$ 6.530	$ 8.650

The manager has asked you to explain why unit costs for the product varied from a low of $5.216 in the second quarter to a high of $8.650 in the last quarter, and to suggest a better way to accumulate or allocate costs. The manager feels that the quarterly reports are needed for purposes of control, so attach to your explanation a schedule showing what last year's material, labour, and overhead costs per unit would have been had your suggestion or suggestions been followed for the year.

ANALYTICAL AND REVIEW PROBLEM

Problem 26–1 A&R

While on vacation Miss McKenna, president of McKenna Works, took in a seminar on ''Reporting to Top Management.'' One of the seminars was on the use of P/V charts, which Miss McKenna thought would have applicability to her firm.

Upon returning, Miss McKenna summoned the controller, Mr. Pollice, to her office, told him of the seminar and asked for a report on how soon such a reporting procedure could be implemented at McKenna Works. The next day a memorandum arrived accompanied by a break-even chart (reproduced below) based on standard budgeted costs and representative of the cost breakdown, and the cost-volume-profit relationship under the current selling price and cost structure.

The president studied the chart and filed it away for reference at month-end. On April 3, on arrival at work, the president found the March Income Statement on her desk (reproduced below). It was not long before Mr. Pollice was on the carpet trying to explain the apparent discrepancy between the income statement and the break-even chart.

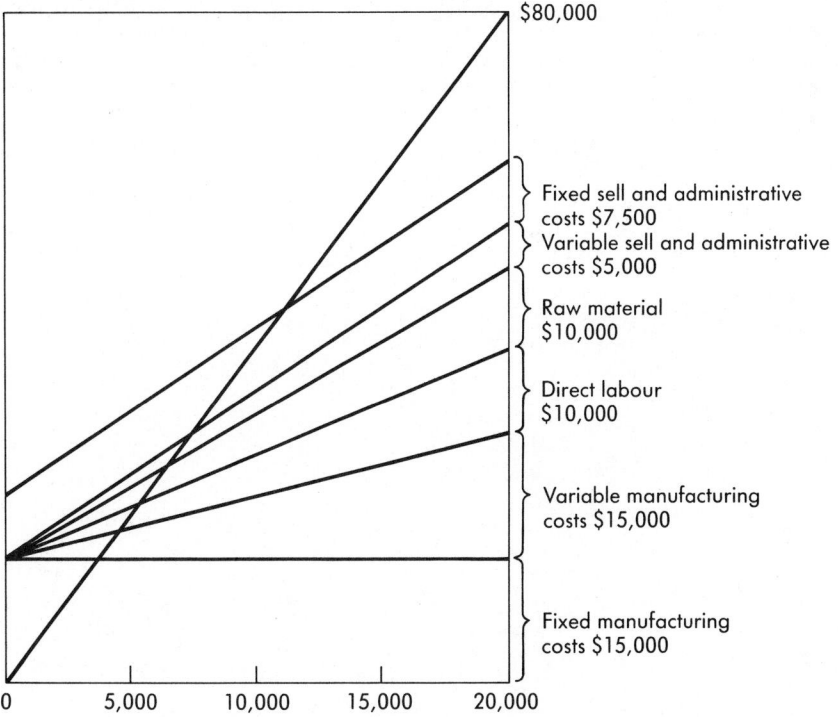

McKENNA WORKS LIMITED
Income Statement
For the Month Ending March 31, 1980

Sales 14,000 units @ $4		$56,000
Cost of sales at standard $2.50 . . .		35,000
		$21,000
Selling and administrative costs . . .		11,000
"Normal" net income		$10,000
Variances:*		
Material price and usage	$500 cr.	
Labour rate and efficiency	300 dr.	
Budget variance	800 cr.	1,000
		$11,000

* The company uses standard absorption costing.

Miss McKenna was heard saying, "I don't know what kind of accounting you are practicing—I can't understand how when the break-even chart indicates that at 14,000 unit sales volume net income should be $5,500 and you show in the income statement an amount that is double—you expect me to have confidence in your reporting? You had better go back to your office and examine your figures and come back with an explanation—and it had better be good, short and to the point."

Required:

As Mr. Pollice's assistant he has asked you to prepare the short (½ page) report to reconcile the income statement and break-even chart net incomes.

Capital Budgeting; Managerial Decisions

27

After studying Chapter 27, you should be able to:

Describe the impact of capital budgeting on the operations of a company.

Calculate a payback period on an investment and state the inherent limitations of this method.

Calculate a rate of return on an investment and state the assumptions on which this method is based.

Describe the information obtained by using the discounted cash flow method, the procedures involved in using this method, and the problems associated with its use.

Explain the effects of incremental costs on a decision to accept or reject additional business and on a decision whether to make or buy a given product.

State the meaning of sunk costs, out-of-pocket costs, and opportunity costs, and describe the importance of each type of cost to decisions such as whether to scrap or rebuild defective units or to sell a product as is or to process it further.

Define or explain the words and phrases listed in the chapter Glossary.

A business decision involves choosing between two or more courses of action, and the best choice normally offers the highest return on the investment or the greatest cost savings. Business managers at times make decisions intuitively, without trying to measure systematically the advantages and disadvantages of each possible choice. Often they make intuitive decisions because they are unaware of any other way to choose; but sometimes the available information is so sketchy or unreliable that systematic measurement is useless. Also, intangible factors such as convenience, prestige, and public opinion are at times more important than the factors that can be reduced to a quantitative basis. Nevertheless, in many situations it is possible to reduce the anticipated consequences of alternative choices to a quantitative basis and measure them systematically. This chapter will examine several areas of decision making in which more or less systematic methods of analysis are available.

CAPITAL BUDGETING

Planning plant asset investments is called *capital budgeting.* The plans may involve new buildings, new machinery, or whole new projects. In all such cases, a fundamental objective of business firms is to earn a satisfactory return on the invested funds. Capital budgeting often requires some of the most crucial and difficult decisions faced by management. The decisions are difficult because they are commonly based on estimates projected well into a future that is at best uncertain. Capital budgeting decisions are crucial because (1) large sums of money are often involved; (2) funds are committed for long periods of time; and (3) once a decision is made and a project is begun, it may be difficult or impossible to reverse the effects of that decision.

Capital budgeting involves the preparation of cost and revenue estimates for all proposed projects, an examination of the merits of each, and a choice of those worthy of investment. It is a broad field, and the discussion of this chapter must be limited to three ways of comparing investment opportunities. They are the **payback period,** the **return on average investment,** and **discounted cash flows.**

Payback Period

Generally an investment in a machine or other plant asset will produce a *net cash flow,* and the *payback period* for the investment is the time required to recover the investment through this net cash flow. For example, assume that Murray Company is considering several capital investments. One investment involves the purchase of a machine to be used in manufacturing a new product. The machine will cost $16,000, have an eight-year service life, and have no salvage value. The company estimates that 10,000 units of the machine's product will be sold each year, and the sales will result in $1,500 or after-tax net income, calculated as follows:

Annual sales of new product		$30,000
Deduct:		
Cost of materials, labour, and overhead other than		
depreciation on the new machine	$15,500	
Depreciation on the new machine	2,000	
Additional selling and administrative expenses	9,500	27,000
Annual before-tax income		3,000
Income tax (assumed rate, 50%)		1,500
Annual after-tax net income from new product sales		$ 1,500

Through annual sales of 10,000 units of the new product, Murray Company expects to gain $30,000 of revenue and $1,500 of net income. The net income represents an inflow of assets that will be available to pay back the new machine's cost. Also, since depreciation expense does not involve a current outflow of assets or funds, the amount of the annual depreciation charge represents an inflow of assets that will be available to pay back the machine's cost. The $1,500 of net income plus the $2,000 depreciation charge total $3,500, and together are the **annual net cash flow** expected from the investment. Thus, the annual net cash flow will pay back the investment in the new machine in 4.6 years, calculated as follows:

$$\frac{\text{Cost of new machine, \$16,000}}{\text{Annual net cash flow, \$3,500}} = 4.6 \text{ years to recover investment}$$

The answer just given is 4.6 years. Actually, when $16,000 is divided by $3,500, the result is just a little over 4.57; but 4.6 years is close enough. Remember that the calculation is based on estimated net income and estimated depreciation; consequently, it is pointless to carry the answer to several decimal places.

In choosing investment opportunities, a short payback period is desirable because (1) the sooner an investment is recovered the sooner the funds are available for other uses and (2) a short payback period also means a short ''bail-out period'' if conditions should change. However, the payback period should never be the only factor considered because it ignores the length of time revenue will continue to be earned after the end of the payback period. For example, one investment may pay back its cost in three years and cease to produce revenue at that point, while a second investment may require five years to pay back its cost but will continue to produce inflows of assets for another 15 years.

Rate of Return on Average Investment

The *rate of return on the average investment* in a machine is calculated by dividing the after-tax net income from the sale of the machine's product by the average investment in the machine.

In calculating the average investment, an assumption must be made as to the timing of the cost recovery from depreciation. If sales are earned evenly throughout the year, the cost recovery from depreciation may be assumed to occur at the middle of the year. Under these conditions, the average investment each year may be calculated as the average of the beginning-of-year book value and the end-of-year book value. If Murray Company's $16,000 machine is depreciated $2,000 each year, the average investment each year and the average investment over the life of the machine may be calculated as shown in Illustration 27–1.

More simply, the average investment may be calculated as:

$$\$16,000 \div 2 = \$8,000$$

Note that the above example is simplified by the fact that the machine has no salvage value. If the machine had a salvage value, the average investment would be calculated as (Original cost + Salvage value) ÷ 2.

After average investment is determined, the rate of return on average investment is calculated. As previously stated, this involves dividing the estimated annual after-tax net income from the sale of the machine's product by average investment. Since Murray Company expects an after-tax net income of $1,500, the expected rate of return is calculated as follows:

$$\$1,500 \div \$8,000 = 18\tfrac{3}{4}\% \text{ return on average investment}$$

In some investments, the revenue from the investment is not spread evenly over each year and may be received near the end of each year.

Illustration 27–1

Year	Beginning-of-year book value	Average investment each year	
1	$16,000	$15,000	
2	14,000	13,000	
3	12,000	11,000	
4	10,000	9,000	$\dfrac{\$64,000}{8}$ = $8,000 average investment over life of machine
5	8,000	7,000	
6	6,000	5,000	
7	4,000	3,000	
8	2,000	1,000	
Totals	$72,000	$64,000	

If the revenue is expected to be received at the year's end, the cost recovery from depreciation also occurs at the year's end. Thus, the average investment each year is the beginning-of-year book value. Referring back to Illustration 27–1, these assumptions result in the following calculation of average investment:

$72,000 ÷ 8 = $9,000 average investment over life of investment

Instead of adding the beginning-of-year book values and averaging over eight years, a shorter way to the same answer is to average the book values of the machine's first and last years in this manner:

$16,000 book value at beginning of (and throughout) first year
  2,000 book value at beginning of (and throughout) last year
$18,000
————
$18,000 ÷ 2 = $9,000 average investment over life of investment

Note that if the machine had a salvage value, the book value at the beginning of (and throughout) the last year would be the salvage value plus the depreciation expense of the last year.

Given a $9,000 average investment, the return on investment is:

$1,500 ÷ $9,000 = 16⅔% return on average investment

At this point the question naturally arises whether 16⅔% or 18¾% are good rates of return. Obviously, 18¾% appears better than 16⅔%. However, even this may not be true. A project that is expected to yield 18¾% may be much riskier than another project having a 16⅔% expected return. And, depending on other available investment alternatives, neither may be acceptable. In other words, a return must be judged in relation to other returns and the differing riskiness of the alternatives. However, when average investment returns are used in deciding between capital investments, the one having the least risk, the shortest payback period, and the highest return for the longest time is usually the best.

Rate of return on average investment is easy to calculate and understand and, as a result, has long been used in selecting investment opportunities. Furthermore, when the opportunities produce uniform cash flows, it offers a fair basis for selection. However, a comparison of *discounted cash flows* with amounts to be invested offers a better means of selection.

An understanding of discounted cash flows requires an understanding of the concept of present value. This concept was explained in Chapter 12, beginning on page 501. That explanation should be reviewed at this point by any student who does not fully understand it. The present value tables in Chapter 12, on pages 503 and 505, must be used to solve some of the problems that follow the present chapter.

Discounted Cash Flows

When a business invests in a new plant asset. it expects to secure a stream of future cash flows from the investment. Normally it will not invest unless the flows are sufficient to return the amount of the investment plus a satisfactory return on the investment. For example, assume that the cash flows from Murray Company's investment will be received at the end of each year. Will the investment in the machine return the amount of the investment plus a satisfactory return? If Murray Company considers a 10% compound annual return a satisfactory return on its capital investments, it can answer this question with the calculations of Illustration 27–2.

To secure the machine of Illustration 27–2, Murray Company must invest $16,000. However, from the sale of the machine's product it will recapture $2,000 of its investment each year in the form of depreciation; in addition, it will earn a $1,500 annual net income. In other words, the company will receive a $3,500 net cash flow from the investment each year for eight years. Therefore, in calculating the net cash flows only *cash* inflows and outflows are considered and noncash expenses, such as depreciation, are ignored.

The first column of Illustration 27–2 indicates that the net cash flows of the first year are received one year hence, and so forth for subsequent years. This means that the net cash flows are received at the end of the year. To simplify the discussion of this chapter and the problems at the end of the chapter, the net cash flows of a company's operations are generally assumed to occur at the end of the year. More refined calculations are left for consideration in an advanced course.

Illustration 27–2 Analysis of Proposed Investment in Machine

Years Hence	Net Cash Flows	Present Value of $1 at 10%	Present Value of Net Cash Flows
1	$3,500	0.9091	$ 3,181.85
2	3,500	0.8265	2,892.75
3	3,500	0.7513	2,629.55
4	3,500	0.6830	2,390.50
5	3,500	0.6209	2,173.15
6	3,500	0.5645	1,975.75
7	3,500	0.5132	1,796.20
8	3,500	0.4665	1,632.75

Total present value	$18,672.50
Amount to be invested	16,000.00
Positive net present value	$ 2,672.50

The annual net cash flows, shown in the second column of Illustration 27–2, are multiplied by the amounts in the third column to determine their present values, which are shown in the last column. Observe that the total of these present values exceeds the amount of the required investment of $16,000 by $2,672.50. Consequently, if Murray Company considers a 10% compound return satisfactory, this machine will recover its required investment, plus a 10% compound return, and $2,672.50 in addition.

Generally, when the cash flows from an investment are discounted at a satisfactory rate and have a present value in excess of the investment, the investment is worthy of acceptance. Also, when several investment opportunities are being compared and each requires the same investment and has the same risk, the one having the highest positive net present value is the best.

Shortening the Calculation

In Illustration 27–2 the present values of $1 at 10% for each of the eight years involved are shown. Each year's cash flow is multiplied by the present value of $1 at 10% for that year to determine its present value. Then, the present values of the eight cash flows are added to determine their total. This is one way to determine total present value. However, since in this case the cash flows are uniform, there are two shorter ways. One shorter way is to add the eight yearly present values of $1 at 10% and to multiply $3,500 by the total. Another even shorter way is based on Table 12–2, which shows the present value of $1 to be received periodically for a number of periods. In the case of the Murray Company machine, $3,500 is to be received annually for eight years. Consequently, to determine the present value of these annual receipts discounted at 10%, go down the 10% column of Table 12–2 to the amount opposite eight periods. This factor is 5.3349. Therefore, the present value of the eight annual $3,500 receipts is $3,500 multiplied by 5.3349, or $18,672.15. The $0.35 difference between this answer and the answer shown in Illustration 27–2 results from the fact that the numbers in Tables 12–1 and 12–2 are rounded.

Cash Flows Not Uniform

Present value analysis has its greatest usefulness when cash flows are not uniform. For example, assume a company can choose one capital investment from among Projects A, B, and C. Each requires a $12,000 investment and will produce cash flows as follows:

Years Hence	Annual Cash Flows		
	Project A	Project B	Project C
1	$ 5,000	$ 8,000	$ 1,000
2	5,000	5,000	5,000
3	5,000	2,000	9,000
	$15,000	$15,000	$15,000

Note that all three projects produce the same total cash flow. However, the flows of Project A are uniform, those of Project B are greater in the earlier years, while those of Project C are greater in the later years. Consequently, when present values of the cash flows, discounted at 10%, are compared with the required investments, the statistics of Illustration 27–3 result.

Note that an investment in Project A has a $434.50 positive net present value; an investment in Project B has a $907.90 positive net present value; and an investment in Project C has a $196.70 negative net present value. Therefore, if a 10% return is required, an investment in Project C should be rejected, since the investment's net present value indicates it will not earn such a return. Furthermore, as between Projects A and B, other things being equal, Project B is the better investment, since its cash flows have the higher net present value. Although the present value numbers in Illustration 27–3 show dollars and cents, present values of projected cash flows are always approximations. Hence, it would be appropriate to round such calculations to the nearest whole dollar.

Illustration 27–3

	Years Hence	Present Values of Cash Flows Discounted at 10%		
		Project A	Project B	Project C
	1	$ 4,545.50	$ 7,272.80	$ 909.10
	2	4,132.50	4,132.50	4,132.50
	3	3,756.50	1,502.60	6,761.70
Total present values		$12,434.50	$12,907.90	$11,803.30
Required investments		12,000.00	12,000.00	12,000.00
Net present values		$ +434.50	$ +907.90	$ −196.70

Salvage Value and Accelerated Depreciation

The $16,000 machine of the Murray Company example was assumed to have no salvage value at the end of its useful life. Often a machine is expected to have a salvage value, and in such cases the expected salvage value is treated as an additional cash flow to be received in the last year of the machine's life.

Also, in the Murray Company example, depreciation was deducted on a straight-line basis; but in actual practice, accelerated depreciation is used for tax purposes. Accelerated depreciation results in larger depreciation deductions in the early years of an asset's life and smaller deductions in the later years. This results in smaller income tax liabilities in the early years and larger ones in later years. However, this does not change the basic nature of a present value analysis. It only results in larger cash flows in the early years and smaller ones in later years, which normally make an investment more desirable. The income tax effects on capital budgeting are beyond the scope of this text.

Selecting the Earnings Rate

The selection of a satisfactory earnings rate for capital investments is always a top-management decision. Formulas have been devised to aid management. But, in many companies the choice of a satisfactory or required rate of return is largely subjective. Management simply decides that enough investment opportunities can be found that will earn, say, a 10% compound return; and this becomes the minimum below which the company refuses to make an investment of average risk.

Whatever the required rate, it is always higher than the rate at which money can be borrowed, since the return on a capital investment must include not only interest but also an additional allowance for risks involved. Therefore, when the rate at which money can be borrowed is around 10%, a required after-tax return of 15% may be acceptable in industrial companies, with a lower rate for public utilities and a higher rate for companies in which investment opportunities are unusually good or the risks are high.

Replacing Plant Assets

In a dynamic economy, new and better machines are constantly entering the market. As a result, the decision to replace an existing machine with a new and better machine is a common one. Often, the existing machine is in good condition and will produce the required product; but the new machine will do the job with a large savings in operating costs. In such a situation, management must decide whether the aftertax savings in operating costs justifies the investment.

The amount of after-tax savings from the replacement of an existing machine with a new machine is complicated by the fact that depreciation on the new machine for tax purposes normally is based on the book value for tax purposes of the old machine plus the cash given in the exchange. There can be other complications too. Consequently, a discussion of the replacement of plant assets is deferred to a more advanced course.

ACCEPTING ADDITIONAL BUSINESS

Costs obtained from a cost accounting system are average costs and also historical costs. They are useful in product pricing and in controlling operations. But, in a decision to accept an additional volume of business they are not necessarily the relevant costs. In such a decision the relevant costs are the additional costs, commonly called the *incremental* or *differential costs*.

For example, a concern operating at its normal capacity, which is 80% of full capacity, has annually produced and sold approximately 100,000 units of product with the following results:

Sales (100,000 units at $10)		$1,000,000
Materials (100,000 units at $3.50)	$350,000	
Labour (100,000 units at $2.20)	220,000	
Overhead (100,000 units at $1.10)	110,000	
Selling expenses (100,000 units at $1.40)	140,000	
Administrative expenses (100,000 units at $0.80)	80,000	900,000
Operating income		$ 100,000

The concern's sales department reports it has an exporter who has offered to buy 10,000 units of product at $8.50 per unit. The sale to the exporter is several times larger than any previous sale made by the company; and since the units are being exported, the new business will have no effect on present business. Therefore, in order to determine whether the order should be accepted or rejected, management of the company asks that statistics be prepared to show the estimated net income or loss that would result from accepting the offer. It received the following figures based on the average costs previously given:

Sales (100,000 units at $8.50)		$85,000
Materials (10,000 units at $3.50)	$35,000	
Labour (10,000 units at $2.20)	22,000	
Overhead (10,000 units at $1.10)	11,000	
Selling expenses (10,000 units at $1.40)	14,000	
Administrative expenses (10,000 units at $0.80)	8,000	90,000
Operating loss		$ (5,000)

If a decision were based on these average costs, the new business would likely be rejected. However, in this situation average costs are not relevant. The relevant costs are the added costs of accepting the new business. Consequently, before rejecting the order, the costs of the new business were examined more closely, and the following additional information was obtained: (1) Manufacturing 10,000 additional units of product would require materials and labour at $3.50 and $2.20 per unit just as with normal production. (2) However, the 10,000 units could be manufactured with overhead costs, in addition to those already incurred, of only $5,000 for power, packing, and handling labour. (3) Commissions and other selling expenses resulting from the sale would amount to $2,000 in addition to the selling expenses already incurred. And (4) $1,000 additional administrative expenses in the form of clerical work would be required if the order were accepted. Based on this added information, the statement of Illustration 27–4 showing the effect of the additional business on the company's normal business was prepared.

Illustration 27–4 shows that the additional business should be accepted. Present business should be charged with all present costs, and the additional business should be charged only with its incremental, or differential, costs. When this is done, accepting the additional business at $8.50 per unit will apparently result in $20,000 additional income before taxes.

Incremental or differential costs always apply to a particular situation at a particular time. For example, adding units to a given production volume may or may not increase depreciation expense. If the additional units require the purchase of more machines, depreciation expense is increased. Likewise, if present machines are used but the additional units shorten their life, more depreciation expense results. However, if present machines are used and their appreciation depends more on the passage of time or obsolescence rather than on use, additional depreciation expense might not result from the added units of product.

Illustration 27–4

	Present business		Additional business		Present plus the additional business
Sales		$1,000,000		$85,000	$1,085,000
Materials	$350,000		$35,000		$385,000
Labour	220,000		22,000		242,000
Overhead	110,000		5,000		115,000
Selling expenses	140,000		2,000		142,000
Administrative expense ...	80,000		1,000		81,000
Total		900,000		65,000	965,000
Operating income		$ 100,000		$20,000	$ 120,000

BUY OR MAKE

Incremental, or differential, costs are often a factor in a decision as to whether a given part or product should be bought or made. For example, a manufacturer has idle machines that can be used to manufacture one of the components (Part 417) of the company's product. This part is presently purchased at a $1.20 delivered cost per unit. The manufacturer estimates that to make Part 417 would cost $0.45 for materials, $0.50 for labour, and an amount of overhead. At this point a question arises as to how much overhead should be charged. If the normal overhead rate of the department in which the part would be manufactured is 100% of direct labour cost, and this amount is charged against Part 417, then the unit costs of making Part 417 would be $0.45 for materials, $0.50 for labour, and $0.50 for overhead, a total of $1.45. At this cost, the manufacturer would be better off to buy the part at $1.20 each.

However, on a short-run basis the manufacturer might be justified in ignoring the normal overhead rate and in charging Part 417 for only the additional overhead costs resulting from its manufacture. Among these additional overhead costs might be, for example, power to operate the machines that would otherwise be idle, depreciation on the machines if the part's manufacture resulted in additional depreciation, and any other overhead that would be added to that already incurred. Furthermore, if these added overhead items total less than $0.25 per unit, the manufacturer might be justified on a short-run basis in manufacturing the part. However, on a long-term basis, Part 417 should be charged a full share of all overhead.

Any amount of overhead less than $0.25 per unit results in a total cost for Part 417 that is less than the $1.20 per unit purchase price. Nevertheless, in making a final decision as to whether the part should be bought or made, the manufacturer should also consider such things as quality, the reactions of customers and suppliers, and other intangible factors. When these additional factors are considered, small cost differences may become a minor factor.

OTHER COST CONCEPTS

Sunk costs, out-of-pocket costs, and *opportunity costs* are additional concepts that may be encountered in managerial decisions.

A sunk cost is a cost resulting from a past irrevocable decision, and is sunk in the sense that it cannot be avoided. As a result, sunk costs are irrelevant in decisions affecting the future.

An out-of-pocket cost is a cost requiring a current outlay of funds. Material costs, supplies, heat, and power are examples. Generally, out-of-pocket costs can be avoided; consequently, they are irrelevant in decisions affecting the future.

Costs as discussed thus far have been outlays or expenditures made to obtain some benefit, usually goods or services. However, the concept of costs can be expanded to include **sacrifices made to gain some benefit.** For example, if a job that will pay a student $1,200 for working during the summer must be rejected in order to attend summer school, the $1,200 is an opportunity cost of attending summer school.

Obviously, opportunity costs are not entered in the accounting records; but they may be relevant in a decision involving rejected opportunities. For example, decisions to scrap or rebuild defective units or product commonly involve situations that involve both sunk costs and opportunity costs.

SCRAP OR REBUILD DEFECTIVE UNITS

Any costs incurred in manufacturing units of product that do not pass inspection are sunk costs and as such should not enter into a decision as to whether the units should be sold for scrap or be rebuilt to pass inspection. For example, a concern has 10,000 defective units of product that cost $1 per unit to manufacture. The units can be sold as they are for $0.40 each, or they can be rebuilt for $0.80 per unit, after which they can be sold for their full price of $1.50 per unit. Should the company rebuild the units or should it sell them in their present form? The original manufacturing costs of $1 per unit are sunk costs and are irrelevant in the decision; so, based on the information given, the comparative returns from scrapping or rebuilding are:

	As scrap	Rebuilt
Sales of defective units	$4,000	$15,000
Less: Cost to rebuild		(8,000)
Net return	$4,000	$ 7,000

From the information given, it appears that rebuilding is the better decision. This is true if the rebuilding does not interfere with normal operations. However, suppose that to rebuild the defective units the company must forgo manufacturing 10,000 new units that will cost $1 per unit to manufacture and can be sold for $1.50 per unit. In this situation the comparative returns may be analyzed as follows:

	As scrap	Rebuilt
Sale of defective units	$ 4,000	$15,000
Less: Cost to rebuild the defective units		(8,000)
Sale of new units	15,000	
Less: Cost to manufacture the new units ...	(10,000)	
Net return	$ 9,000	$ 7,000

If the defective units are sold without rebuilding, then the new units can also be manufactured and sold, with a $9,000 return from the sale of both the new and old units, as shown in the first column of the analysis. Obviously, this is better than forgoing the manufacture of the new units and rebuilding the defective units for a $7,000 net return.

The situation described here also may be analysed on an opportunity cost basis as follows: If to rebuild the defective units the company must forgo manufacturing the new units, then the return on the sale of the new units is an opportunity cost of rebuilding the defective units. This opportunity cost is measured at $5,000 (revenue from sale of new units, $15,000; less their manufacturing costs of $10,000 equals the $5,000 benefit that will be sacrificed if the old units are rebuilt); and an opportunity cost analysis of the situation is as follows:

	As scrap	Rebuilt
Sale of defective units	$4,000	$15,000
Less: Cost to rebuild the defective units		(8,000)
Less: Opportunity cost (return sacrificed by not manufacturing the new units)		(5,000)
Net return	$4,000	$ 2,000

Observe that it does not matter whether this or the previous analysis is made. Either way there is a $2,000 difference in favour of scrapping the defective units.

PROCESS OR SELL

Sunk costs, out-of-pocket costs, and opportunity costs are also encountered in deciding whether it is best to sell an intermediate product as it is or process it further and sell the product or products that result from the additional processing. For example, a company has 40,000 units of Product A that cost $0.75 per unit or a total of $30,000 to manufacture. The 40,000 units can be sold as they are for $50,000 or they can be processed further into Products X, Y, and Z at a cost of $2 per original Product A unit. The additional processing will produce the following numbers of each product, which can be sold at the unit prices indicated:

Product X	10,000 units at $3
Product Y	22,000 units at $5
Product Z	6,000 units at $1
Lost through spoilage	2,000 units (no salvage value)
Total	40,000 units

The net advantage of processing the product further is $16,000, as shown in Illustration 27–5.

Illustration 27–5

Revenue from further processing:		
Product X, 10,000 units at $3	$ 30,000	
Product Y, 22,000 units at $5	110,000	
Product Z, 6,000 units at $1	6,000	
Total revenue		$146,000
Less:		
Additional processing costs, 40,000 units at $2	80,000	
Opportunity cost (revenue sacrificed by not		
selling the Product A units)	50,000	
Total		130,000
Net advantage of further processing...................		$ 16,000

Note that the revenue available through the sale of the Product A units is an opportunity cost of further processing these units. Also notice that the $30,000 cost of manufacturing the 40,000 units of Product A does not appear in the Illustration 27–5 analysis. This cost is present regardless of which alternative is chosen; therefore, it is irrelevant to the decision. However, the $30,000 does enter into a calculation of the net income from the alternatives. For example, if the company chooses to further process the Product A units, the gross return from the sale of Products X, Y, and Z may be calculated as follows:

Revenue from the sale of Products X, Y, and Z		$146,000
Less:		
Cost to manufacture the Product A units	$30,000	
Cost to further process the Product A units	80,000	110,000
Gross return from the sale of Products X, Y, and Z		$ 36,000

DECIDING THE SALES MIX

When a company sells a combination of products, ordinarily some of the products are more profitable than others, and normally management should concentrate its sales efforts on the more profitable products. However, if production facilities or other factors are limited, an increase in the production and sale of one product may require a reduction in the production and sale of another. In such a situation management's job is to determine the most profitable combination or sales mix for the products and concentrate on selling the products in this combination.

To determine the best sales mix for its products, management must have information as to the contribution margin of each product, the facilities required to produce and sell each product, and any limitations on these facilities. For example, assume that a company produces and sells two products, A and B. The same machines are used to produce both products, and the products have the following selling prices and variable costs per units:

	Product A	Product B
Selling price	$5.00	$7.50
Variable costs	3.50	5.50
Contribution margin	$1.50	$2.00

If the amount of production facilities required to produce each product is the same and there is an unlimited market for Product B, The company should devote all its facilities to Product B because of its larger contribution margin. However, the answer differs if the company's facilities are limited to, say, 100,000 machine-hours of production per month and if one machine-hour is required to produce each unit of Product A but two machine-hours are required for each unit of Product B. Under these circumstances, if the market for Product A is unlimited, the company should devote all its production to this product because it produces $1.50 of contribution margin per machine-hour, while Product B produces only $1 per machine-hour.

Actually, when there are no market or other limitations, a company should devote all its efforts to its most profitable product. It is only when there is a market or other limitation on the sale of the most profitable product that a need for a sales mix arises. For example, if in this instance one machine-hour of production facilities are needed to produce each unit of Product A and 100,000 machine-hours are available, 100,000 units of the product can be produced. However, if only 80,000 units can be sold, the company has 20,000 machine-hours that can be devoted to the production of Product B, and 20,000 machine-hours will produce 10,000 units of Product B. Consequently, the company's most profitable sales mix under these assumptions is 80,000 units of Product A and 10,000 units of Product B.

The assumptions in this section have been kept simple. More complicated factors and combinations of factors exist. However, a discussion of these is deferred to a more advanced course.

GLOSSARY

Capital budgeting.   Planning plant asset investments; involves the preparation of cost and revenue estimates for all proposed projects, an examination of the merits of each, and a choice of those worthy of investment.

Discounted cash flows.   The present value of a stream of future cash flows from an investment, based on an interest rate that gives a satisfactory return on investment.

Incremental cost. An additional cost resulting from a particular course of action. Also called a *differential cost*.

Opportunity cost. A sacrifice made to gain some benefits; that is, in choosing one course of action, the lost benefit associated with an alternative course of action.

Out-of-pocket cost. A cost requiring a current outlay of funds.

Payback period. The time required to recover the original cost of an investment through net cash flows from the investment.

Rate of return on average investment. The annual, after-tax income from the sale of an asset's product divided by the average investment in the asset.

Sunk cost. A cost incurred as a consequence of a past irrevocable decision and that, therefore, cannot be avoided; hence, it is irrelevant to decisions affecting the future.

QUESTIONS FOR CLASS DISCUSSION

1. What is capital budgeting? Why are capital budgeting decisions crucial to the business concern making the decisions?

2. A successful investment in a machine will produce a net cash flow. Of what does this consist?

3. If depreciation is an expense, explain why, when the sale of a machine's product produces a net income, the portion of the machine's cost recovered each year through the sale of its product includes both the net income from the product's sale and the year's depreciation on the machine.

4. Why is a short payback period on an investment desirable?

5. What is the average amount invested in a machine during its life if the machine cost $28,000, has an estimated five-year life during which revenue is earned at the end of each year, and an estimated $3,000 salvage value? Assume straight-line depreciation.

6. Is a 15% return on the average investment in a machine a good return?

7. Why is the present value of the expectation of receiving $100 a year hence less than $100? What is the present value of the expectation of receiving $100 one year hence, discounted at 12%?

8. What is indicated when the present value of the net cash flows from an investment in a machine, discounted at 12%, exceeds the amount of the investment? What is indicated when the present value of the net cash flows, discounted at 12%, is less than the amount of the investment?

9. What are the incremental costs of accepting an additional volume of business?

10. A company manufactures and sells 250,000 units of product in this country at $5 per unit. The product costs $3 per unit to manufacture. Can you describe a situation under which the company may be willing to sell an additional 25,000 units of the product abroad at $2.75 per unit?

11. What is a sunk cost? An out-of-pocket cost? An opportunity cost? Is an opportunity cost typically recorded in the accounting records?

12. Any costs that have been incurred in manufacturing a product are sunk costs. Why are such costs irrelevant in deciding whether to sell the product in its present condition or to make it into a new product through additional processing?

MULTIPLE CHOICE

1. X Company paid $200,000 10 years ago for a specialized machine that is being depreciated at the rate of $10,000 per year. The company is considering using the machine in a new project which will have incremental revenues of $28,000 per year and annual cash expenses of $20,000. In analysing the new project, the $10,000 depreciation on the machine is an example of:
   a. An incremental cost.
   b. An opportunity cost.
   c. A variable cost.
   d. A sunk cost.
   e. An out-of-pocket cost.

2. Y Corporation inadvertently produced 10,000 defective transistor radios. The radios cost $8 each to be manufactured. As they are, a salvage company will purchase the defective units for $3 each. Y's production manager reports that the defects can be corrected for $3 per unit, enabling Y to sell them at their regular price of $12.50. Y should:
   a. Sell the radios for $3 per unit.
   b. Correct the defects and sell the radios at regular price.
   c. Be indifferent to this decision since the cost of repair equals the benefit of scrapping the radios.
   d. Sell 5,000 radios to the salvage company and repair the remainder.
   e. Do something else.

3. Product A requires 2½ machine-hours to be produced, Product B requires only 1½ machine-hours, and the company's productive capacity is limited to 120,000 machine-hours. Product A sells for $8 and has variable costs of $3. Product B sells for $6 and has variable costs of $1.50. The sales mix should be as follows:
   a. Only Product A should be produced.
   b. Only Product B should be produced.
   c. 50% of Product A and 50% of Product B should be produced.
   d. 62.5% of Product A and 37.5% of Product B should be produced
   e. 40% of Product A and 60% of Product B should be produced.

4. X Corporation is considering the purchase of a new piece of equipment costing $9,000. The projected after-tax net income is $500 after deducting $3,000 of depreciation. The revenue is to be received at the end of each year. The machine has a useful life of three years and no salvage value. X also considers a 12% return on investment satisfactory. The present values of $1 received periodically for a number of periods are:

Periods hence	12%
1	.893
2	1.690
3	2.402
4	3.037

    What is the net present value of the machine?
    - a. $8,407.
    - b. −$593.
    - c. $593.
    - d. $9,000.
    - e. None of the above is correct.

5. A company has the choice of either selling 1,000 defective units as scrap or rebuilding them. They could sell the defective units at $2.00 per unit or they could rebuild them at additional costs of $0.50 per unit for materials, $1.00 per unit for labour, and $0.75 per unit for overhead, and then sell the rebuilt units for $4.00 per unit. Which should the company do?
    - a. Sell the units as scrap.
    - b. Rebuild the units.
    - c. It does not matter because both alternatives have the same result.
    - d. Neither sell nor rebuild since both result in a loss. Instead, store the units permanently.
    - e. Some other answer.

6. Company X had the following results of operations for 198A:

Sales (8,000 units at $10)	$80,000
Materials and direct labour	48,000
Fixed overhead	8,000
Selling and administrative expenses	16,000
Operating income	$ 8,000

    A foreign company, whose sales will not affect X's domestic market, offers to buy 2,000 units at $7.50 per unit. In addition to variable manufacturing costs, sale of these units would increase overhead costs by $300 and increase selling and administrative costs by $800. If X accepts the offer, the effect on X Company's profits will be:
    - a. $2,400 increase.
    - b. $2,400 decrease.
    - c. $4,100 decrease.
    - d. $13,900 increase.
    - e. $1,900 increase.

MINI DISCUSSION CASES

Case 27–1   You have just presented your boss with a discounted cash flow analysis of a long-term investment proposal. However, he seems less than enthusiastic about the proposal because it shows a payback period of 4.5 years. Your boss feels that no project can be truly profitable if it has a payback period longer than three years.

Required:

a. Is your boss correct in his assumption about the payback period?
b. How would you go about convincing your boss that your project was worthy of adoption?

Case 27–2   Your company manufactures electric drills, which normally sell for a wholesale price of $18.50. The standard cost per drill includes: material, $4.80; labour, $4.00; and overhead (65% fixed), $6.00.

A buyer from Q-Mart has offered to purchase 8,000 drills at a special price of $13.50. Q-Mart is planning to offer the drills as part of their Canadawide "home fix-up" sale at a special price of $24.95. The usual suggested retail price of the drills is $39.95.

Required:

a. Assume that your plant has sufficient idle capacity to manufacture the order without interrupting the normal plant activity. Should the special order be accepted?
b. Assume that your plant has some idle capacity but that in order to produce the Q-Mart request, normal sales would need to be cut back by 4,500 units. Under these circumstances, should the special order be accepted?
c. What additional information would you like to have before you make a final decision under the conditions of both *(a)* and *(b)?* Explain why the information you would like is important to your decision.

CLASS EXERCISES

Exercise 27–1   Machine A cost $8,000 and has an estimated four-year life and no salvage value. Machine B cost $12,000 and has an estimated five-year life and a $2,000 salvage value.

Required:

Under the assumption that the average investment in each machine is the average of its yearly book values, calculate the average investment in each machine.

Exercise 27–2   A company is planning to purchase a machine and add a new product to its line. The machine will cost $200,000, have a four-year life, no salvage value, and will be depreciated on a straight-line basis. The company expects to sell 100,000 units of the machine's product each year with these results:

Sales		$500,000
Costs:		
Materials, labour, and overhead excluding depreciation on the new machine	$260,000	
Depreciation on new machine	50,000	
Selling and administrative expenses	150,000	460,000
Operating income		$ 40,000
Income taxes		20,000
Net Income		$ 20,000

Required:

Calculate (1) the payback period and (2) the return on the average investment in this machine.

Exercise 27–3   After evaluating the risk characteristics of the investment described in Exercise 27–2, the company concludes that it must earn at least a 12% compound return on the investment in the machine. Based on this decision, determine the total present value and net present value of the net cash flows from the machine the company is planning to buy.

Exercise 27–4   A company can invest in each of three projects, A, B, and C. Each project requires a $12,500 investment and will produce cash flows as follows:

Years Hence	Annual Cash Flows		
	Project A	Project B	Project C
1	$ 3,000	$ 5,000	$ 7,000
2	5,000	5,000	5,000
3	7,000	5,000	3,000
	$15,000	$15,000	$15,000

Required:

Under the assumption the company requires a 10% compound return from its investments, determine in which of the projects it should invest.

Exercise 27–5   A company has 10,000 units of Product X that cost $1 per unit to manufacture. The 10,000 units can be sold for $15,000, or they can be further processed at a cost of $7,000 into Products Y and Z. The additional processing will produce 4,000 units of Product Y that can be sold for $2 each and 6,000 units of Product Z that can be sold for $2.25 each.

Required:

Prepare an analysis to show whether the Product X units should be further processed.

PROBLEMS

Problem 27–1   A company is planning to add a new product to its line, the production of which will require new machinery costing $45,000 and having a five-year life and no salvage value. This additional information is available:

Estimated annual sales of new product	$150,000
Estimated costs:	
Materials	30,000
Labour	40,000
Overhead excluding depreciation on new machinery ...	38,000
Selling and administrative expenses	25,000
Income taxes	50%

Required:

Using straight-line depreciation, calculate (1) the payback period on the investment in new machinery, (2) the rate of return on the average investment, and (3) the net present value of the net cash flows discounted at 12%.

Problem 27–2   A company has an opportunity to invest in either of two projects. Project A requires an investment of $40,000 for new machinery having a five-year life and no salvage value. Project B requires an investment of $35,000 for new machinery having a seven-year life and no salvage value. The products of the projects differ; however, each will produce an estimated $3,000 after-tax profit for the life of the project.

Required:

Calculate the payback period, the return on average investment, and the net present value of the net cash flows from each project discounted at 10%. State which project you think is the better investment and why.

Problem 27–3   Twist'n Fix Company manufactures a small tool that it sells to wholesalers at $4 each. The company manufactures and sells approximately 100,000 of the tools each year, and a normal year's costs for the production and sale of this number of tools are as follows:

Materials	$ 60,000
Direct labour	150,000
Manufacturing overhead ...	75,000
Selling expenses..........	30,000
Administrative expenses ...	25,000
	$340,000

A mail-order concern has offered to buy 10,000 of the tools at $3.25 each to be marketed under the mail-order concern's trade name. If accepted, the order is not expected to affect sales through present channels.

A study of normal costs and their relation to the new business reveals the following: *(a)* Material costs are 100% variable. *(b)* The per unit direct labour costs for the additional units will be 50% greater than normal since their production will require overtime at time and one half. *(c)* Of a normal year's manufacturing overhead costs, two thirds will remain fixed at any production level from zero to 150,000 units and one third will vary with volume. *(d)* There will be no additional selling costs if the new business is accepted. *(c)* Acceptance of the new business will increase administrative costs by $1,500.

Required:

Prepare a comparative income statement that shows (1) in one set of columns the operating results and operating income of a normal year, (2) in the second set of columns the operating results and income that may be expected from the new business, and (3) in the third set of columns the combined results from normal and the expected new business.

Problem 27–4   Ft. York Company is considering a project that requires a $108,000 investment in machinery having a six-year life and no salvage value. The project will produce $36,500 at the end of each year for six years, before deducting depreciation on the new machinery and income taxes of 50%.

For analysis purposes, the company may choose between two alternative depreciation schedules, as follows:

Year	Straight-line depreciation schedule	Capital cost allowance
1	$10,800	$16,200
2	21,600	27,540
3	21,600	19,278
4	21,600	13,495
5	21,600	9,446
6	10,800	22,041

Required:

1. Calculate the company's cash flow from the project for each of the six years with depreciation calculated according to:
   a. The straight-line depreciation schedule.
   b. The capital cost allowance (CCA) schedule.
2. Calculate the net present value of the net cash flows discounted at 14%, assuming the straight-line depreciation schedule is used.
3. Calculate the net present value of the net cash flows discounted at 14%, assuming the CCA schedule is used.
4. Explain why the CCA method increases the net present value of this project.

Problem 27–5   Straiken Company's sales and costs for its two products last year were:

	Product X	Product Y
Unit selling price	$ 20	$ 18
Variable costs per unit	$ 12	$ 6
Fixed costs	$60,000	$80,000
Units sold	9,000	8,000

Through sales effort the company can change its sales mix. However, sales of the two products are so interrelated that a percentage increase in the sales of one product causes an equal percentage decrease in the sales of the other, and vice versa.

Required:

1. State which of its products the company should push, and why.
2. Prepare a columnar statement showing last year's sales, fixed costs, variable costs, and income before taxes for Product X in the first pair of columns, the results for Product Y in the second set of columns, and the combined results for both products in the third set of columns.
3. Prepare a like statement for the two products under the assumption that the sales of Product X are increased 20%, with a resulting 20% decrease in the sales of Product Y.
4. Prepare a third statement under the assumption that the sales of Product X are decreased 20%, with a resulting 20% increase in the sales of Product Y.

ALTERNATE PROBLEMS

Problem 27–1A

A company is considering adding a new product to its line. It estimates it can sell 20,000 units annually at $10 per unit. Manufacturing the product will require new machinery having an estimated five-year life, no salvage value, and a cost of $60,000. The new product will have a $4 per unit direct material cost and a $2 per unit direct labour cost. Manufacturing overhead chargeable to the new product, other than for depreciation on the new machinery, will be $33,000 annually. Also, $25,000 of additional selling and administrative expenses will be incurred annually in producing and selling the product, and income taxes will take 50% of the before-taxes profit.

Required:

Using straight-line depreciation, calculate (1) the payback period on the investment in new machinery, (2) the rate of return on the average investment, and (3) the net present value of the net cash flows discounted at 12%.

Problem 27–2A

A company has the opportunity to invest in either of two projects. Project X requires an investment of $56,000 for new machinery having a seven-year life and no salvage value. Project Y requires an investment of $60,000 for new machinery having a five-year life and no salvage value. Sales of the two projects will produce the following estimated annual results:

	Project X		Project Y	
Sales		$130,000		$150,000
Costs:				
Materials..................	$30,000		$36,000	
Labour	27,000		35,000	
Manufacturing overhead including depreciation on new machinery...............	38,000		44,000	
Selling and administrative expenses	25,000	120,000	25,000	140,000
Operating income		$ 10,000		$ 10,000
Income taxes		5,000		5,000
Net Income		$ 5,000		$ 5,000

Required:

Calculate the payback period, the return on average investment, and the net present value of the net cash flows from each project discounted at 12%. State which project you think is the better investment and why.

Problem 27–3A

Heatransfer Company annually sells 100,000 units of its product at $10 per unit. At the 100,000-unit production level the product costs $9 a unit to manufacture and sell, and at this level the company has the following costs and expenses:

Fixed manufacturing overhead costs	$100,000
Fixed selling expenses	50,000
Fixed administrative expenses	60,000
Variable costs and expenses:	
Materials ($2 per unit)	200,000
Labour ($2.50 per unit)	250,000
Manufacturing overhead ($1.50 per unit) ...	150,000
Selling expenses ($0.50 per unit)	50,000
Administrative expense ($0.40 per unit)	40,000

All the units the company presently sells are sold in this country. However, recently an exporter has offered to buy 10,000 units of the product for sale abroad, but he will pay only $8.90 per unit, which is below the company's present $9 per unit manufacturing and selling costs.

Required:

Prepare an income statement that shows (1) in one set of columns the revenue, costs, expenses, and income from selling 100,000 units of the product in this country; (2) in a second set of columns the additional revenue, costs, expenses, and income from selling 10,000 units to the exporter; and (3) in a third set of columns the combined results from both sources. (Assume that acceptance of the new business will not increase any of the company's fixed costs and expenses nor change any of the variable per unit costs and expenses.)

Problem 27–4A

Skylar Company is considering a project that requires a $75,000 investment in machinery having a five-year life and no salvage value. The project will produce $29,000 of income at the end of each year for six years, before deducting depreciation on the new machinery and income taxes of 50%.

For analysis purposes, the company may choose between two alternative depreciation schedules, as follows:

Year	Straight-line depreciation schedule	Capital cost allowance
1	$ 9,375	$15,000
2	18,750	24,000
3	18,750	14,400
4	18,750	8,640
5	9,375	12,960

Required:

1. Calculate the company's cash flow from the project for each of the five years with depreciation for tax purposes calculated according to:
   a. The straight-line depreciation schedule
   b. The capital cost allowance schedule.
2. Calculate the net present value of the net cash flows discounted at 12%, assuming the straight-line depreciation schedule is used.
3. Calculate the net present value of the net cash flows discounted at 12%, assuming the capital cost allowance schedule is used.
4. Explain why the capital cost allowance method increases the net present value of this project.

Problem 27–5A

Cross Cutter Company manufactures and sells a machine called a sectioner. Last year the company made and sold 1,400 sectioners, with the following results:

Sales (1,400 units @ $180)		$252,000
Costs and expenses:		
Variable:		
Materials.........................	$55,440	
Labour	45,360	
Factory overhead	37,800	
Selling and administrative expenses ...	25,200	
Fixed:		
Factory overhead	38,000	
Selling and administrative expenses ...	24,000	225,800
Income before Taxes		$ 26,200

The state highway department has asked for bids on 150 sectioners almost identical to Cross Cutter Company's machine, the only difference being a counter not presently installed on the Cross Cutters Company sectioner. To install the counter would require the purchase of a new machine costing $1,000, plus $4 per sectioner for additional material and $5 per sectioner for additional labour. The new machine would have no further use after the completion of the highway department contract, but it could be sold for $400. Sale of the additional units would not affect the company's fixed costs and expenses, but all variable costs and expenses, including variable selling and administrative expenses, would increase proportionately with the volume increase.

Required:

1. List with their total the unit costs of the material, labour, and so forth that would enter into the lowest unit price the company could bid on the special order without causing a reduction in income from normal business.
2. Under the assumption the company bid $159 per unit and was awarded the contract for the 150 special units, prepare an income statement showing (1) in one set of columns the revenues, costs, expenses, and income before taxes from present business; (2) in a second set of columns the revenue, costs, expenses, and income before taxes from the new business; and (3) in a third set of columns the combined results of both the old and new business.

PROVOCATIVE PROBLEMS

Provocative
Problem 27–1,
Coppernic
Company

Coppernic Company operates metal alloy producing plants, one of which is located at Sydney. The Sydney plant no longer produces a satisfactory profit due to its distance from raw material sources, relatively high hydro power costs, and lack of modern machinery. Consequently, construction of a new plant to replace the Sydney plant is under consideration.

The new plant would be located close to a raw material source and near low-cost hydroelectric power; but its construction would necessitate abandonment of the Sydney plant. The company president favours the move; but several members of the board are not convinced the Sydney plant should be abandoned in view of the great loss that would result.

You have been asked to make recommendations concerning the proposed abandonment and construction of the new plant. Data developed during the course of your analysis include the following:

Loss from abandoning the Sydney Plant. The land, buildings, and machinery of the Sydney plant have a $3,800,000 book value. Very little of the machinery can be moved to the new plant. Most will have to be scrapped. Therefore, if the plant is abandoned, it is estimated that only $800,000 of the remaining investment in the plant can be recovered through the sale of its land and buildings, the sale of scrap, and by moving some of its machinery to the new plant. The remaining $3,000,000 will be lost.

Investment in the new plant. The new plant will cost $12,000,000, including the book value of any machinery moved from Sydney and will have a 20-year life. It will also have double the 25,000-ton capacity of the Sydney plant, and it is estimated the 50,000 tons of metal alloy produced annually can be sold without a price reduction.

Comparative production costs. A comparison of the production costs per ton at the old plant with the estimated costs at the new plant shows the following:

	Old plant	New plant
Raw material, labour, and plant costs (other than depreciation)	$325	$275
Depreciation	18	12
Total costs per ton	$343	$287

The higher per ton depreciation charge of the old plant results primarily from depreciation being allocated to fewer units of product.

Prepare a report analyzing the advantages and disadvantages of the move, including your recommendation. You may assume that the Sydney plant can continue to operate long enough to recover the remaining investment in the plant; however, due to the plant's high costs, operation will be at the break-even point. Furthermore, a shortage of skilled personnel would not allow the company to operate both the Sydney plant and the new plant. Present any pertinent analyses based on the data given.

Provocative Problem 27–2, Rayburn Company

Rayburn Company has operated at substantially less than its full plant capacity for several years, producing and selling an average of 65,000 units of its product annually and receiving a per unit price of $12. Its costs at this sales level are as follows:

Direct materials	$266,500
Direct labour	208,000
Manufacturing overhead:	
Variable	81,250
Fixed	40,000
Selling and administrative expenses:	
Variable	39,000
Fixed	80,000
Income taxes	50%

After searching for ways to utilize the plant capacity of the company more fully, management has begun to consider the possibility of processing the product beyond the present point at which it is sold. If the product is further processed, it can be sold for $14 per unit. Further processing will increase fixed manufacturing overhead by $16,500 annually, and it will increase variable manufacturing costs per unit as follows:

Materials	$0.42
Direct labour	0.38
Variable manufacturing overhead	0.30
Total	$1.10

Selling the further processed product will not affect fixed selling and administrative expenses, but it will increase variable selling and administrative expenses by 10%. Further processing is not expected to either increase or decrease the number of units sold.

Should the company further process the product? Back your opinion with a simple calculation and also a comparative income statement showing present results and the estimated results of the further processed product.

Provocative
Problem 27–3,
Jamestown
Company

Jamestown Company manufactures and sells a common piece of industrial machinery, selling an average of 56,000 units of the machine each year. The company generally earns an after-tax (50% rate) net income of $16 per unit sold. Jamestown Company's production process involves assembling the several components of the machine, some of which are manufactured by the company and others of which are purchased from a variety of suppliers.

One of the components that has been manufactured by the company is a pump which is also available from other suppliers. Jamestown Company uses special equipment to make the pump, and the equipment has no alternative uses. The equipment has a $42,000 book value, a seven-year remaining life, and is depreciated at the rate of $6,000 per year. In addition to depreciation of the equipment, the costs to manufacture the pump are direct materials, $2.00; direct labour, $1.60; and variable overhead, $0.40.

One of Jamestown's suppliers has recently offered the company a contract to purchase pumps from the supplier at a delivered cost of $4.26 per unit. If the company decides to purchase the pumps, the special equipment used to manufacture them can be sold for cash at its book value (no profit or loss) and the cash can be invested in other projects that will pay a 12% compound after-tax return, which is the return the company demands on all its capital investments.

Should the company continue to manufacture the pump, or should it sell the special equipment and buy the pump? Back your answer with explanations and computations

ANALYTICAL AND REVIEW PROBLEMS

Problem 27–1
A&R

Five investment opportunities of equal cost offer the following cash flow patterns:

Year	A	B	C	D	E
1	$ 1,000	$ 3,000	$ 2,500	$ 2,000	$ 4,000
2	1,000	3,000	2,500	2,000	4,000
3	1,000	3,000	2,500	2,000	4,000
4	1,000	3,000	2,500	2,000	4,000
5	1,000	3,000	2,500	2,000	4,000
6	4,000	2,000	2,500	3,000	1,000
7	4,000	2,000	2,500	3,000	1,000
8	4,000	2,000	2,500	3,000	1,000
9	4,000	2,000	2,500	3,000	1,000
10	4,000	2,000	2,500	3,000	1,000
Total	$25,000	$25,000	$25,000	$25,000	$25,000

Required:

Rank the five alternatives in terms of desirability and justify your ranking.

Problem 27–2
A&R

George Disposal has been offered an opportunity to submit a bid for the right to provide a garbage disposal service for the local municipality. The contract would run for five years. Mr. Disposal estimates that his net cash receipts from the disposal business would amount to $75,000 annually. If his bid is accepted, Mr. Disposal would have to make an initial investment of $15,000 in specialized equipment.

Required:

What is the maximum amount that Mr. Disposal can afford to bid for the disposal service business, assuming that he requires a 15% return on his investment? (Do not consider income taxes.)

Tax Considerations in Business Decisions

28

After studying Chapter 28, you should be able to:

Explain the importance of tax planning.

Describe the steps an individual must go through to calculate his tax liability, and explain the difference between deductions to arrive at net income, deductions from net income, and tax credits.

Calculate the taxable income and net tax liability for an individual.

State the procedures used to determine the tax associated with capital gains and losses, dividends and interest.

Describe the differences between the calculations of taxable income and tax liability for corporations and for individuals.

Explain why income tax expenses shown in financial statements may differ from taxes actually payable.

Define or explain the terms and phrases listed in the chapter Glossary.

Not too many years ago, when tax rates were low, management could afford to ignore or dismiss as of minor importance the tax effects of a business decision; but today, when about half the income of a business must commonly be paid out in income taxes, this is no longer wise. Today, a successful management must constantly be alert to every possible tax savings, recognizing that it is often necessary to earn two "pretax dollars" in order to keep one "after-tax dollar," or that a dollar of income tax saved is commonly worth a two-dollar reduction in any other expense.

TAX PLANNING

When a taxpayer plans his affairs in such a way as to incur the smallest possible tax liability, he is engaged in tax planning. Tax planning consists of applying tax laws to all possible methods of conducting a transaction and then choosing the method that will incur the smallest tax liabilities.

Normally tax planning requires that a tax-saving opportunity be recognized at the time it arises. This is because although it is sometimes possible to take advantage of a previously overlooked tax saving, the common result of an overlooked opportunity is a lost opportunity.

Since effective tax planning requires an extensive knowledge of both tax laws and business procedures, it is not the purpose of this chapter to make expert tax planners out of elementary accounting students. Rather, the purpose is to make students aware of the merits of effective tax planning, recognizing that for complete and effective planning, the average student, business, or citizen should seek the advice of a public accontant, tax consultant, or other qualified person.

TAX EVASION AND TAX AVOIDANCE

In any discussion of taxes a clear distinction should be drawn between tax evasion and *tax avoidance*. Tax evasion is illegal and may result in heavy penalties; but tax avoidance is a perfectly legal and profitable activity.

Taxes are avoided by preventing a tax liability from coming into existence. This may be accomplished by any legal means, for example, by the way in which a transaction is completed, or the manner in which a business is organized, or by a wise selection from among the options provided in the Income Tax Act. It makes no difference how, so long as the means is legal and it prevents a tax liability from arising

In contrast, tax evasion involves the fraudulent denial and concealment of an existing tax liability. For example, taxes are evaded when taxable income, such as interest, dividends, tips, fees, or profits from the sale of stocks, bonds, and other assets, is unreported. Taxes are also evaded when items not legally deductible from income are deducted. For example, taxes are evaded when the costs of operating the family automobile are deducted as a business expense, or when charitable contributions not allowed or not made are deducted. Tax evasion is illegal and thus should be scrupulously avoided.

PROVINCIAL INCOME TAXES

All provinces levy income taxes. The provinces are free to impose whatever tax they choose, but to have the tax collected by the federal government, the provincial tax must be expressed as a percentage of the federal tax. Combined income tax rates, equal to the federal rates plus minimum provincial rates, are used throughout this chapter. Some provinces levy income taxes at rates higher than the minimums used in calculating the combined rates. However, other than noting the existence of provincial tax laws and that they increase the total tax burden and make tax planning even more important, the following discussion is limited to the federal income tax.

HISTORY AND OBJECTIVES OF THE FEDERAL INCOME TAX

The history of today's federal income tax legislation dates to 1917, when the Income War Tax Act was passed. This act, with numerous amendments, remained in effect until the Income Tax Act of 1948 became law in 1949. Widespread recognition of defects in the income tax system led, in 1962, to the appointment of the Royal Commission on Taxation. The Commission's report was published in 1967 and made serious criticism of the existing law and proposed some fundamental changes.

The need for general reform was made clear; and in 1969 the Government of Canada placed before Parliament, the Canadian people, and the provincial governments its major proposals for reform of the income tax structure. After considerable debate, on June 30, 1971, a Tax Reform Bill was presented to Parliament to replace the 1948 Act as of January 1972. The 1972 Act and its numerous amendments remain in effect today.

The original purpose of the federal income tax was to raise revenue, but over the years this original goal has been expanded to include the following and other nonrevenue objectives:

1. To achieve a fair distribution of the tax burden based upon ability to pay.
2. To promote steady economic growth and continuing prosperity.
3. To recognize modern social needs.
4. To interfere as little as possible with incentives to work and to invest.
5. To promote investment in the economy in the direction that meets the demands of consumers and foreign markets.

6. To spur economic ventures that involve exceptional risks and promise exceptional rewards.

7. To promote widespread understanding of and voluntary compliance with tax laws, combined with enough detail to block opportunities for abuse.

8. To adopt a tax system that can and will be used by the provinces as well as Canada.

Also, just as the objectives have expanded over the years, so have the rates and the number of people required to pay taxes. In 1917 the minimum rate was 4% and maximum for individuals was 29%. This contrasts with the 1985 minimum (federal and provincial) 9% rate for individuals and maximum of over 50%. Likewise, the total number of tax returns filed has grown from a few thousand in 1917 to well over 8,000,000 in recent years.

SYNOPSIS OF THE FEDERAL INCOME TAX

The following brief synopsis of the federal income tax is given at this point because it is necessary to know something about the federal income tax in order to appreciate its effect on business decisions.

Classes of Taxpayers

Federal income tax law recognizes three classes of taxpayers: individuals, corporations, and trusts. Members of each class must file returns and pay taxes on taxable income.

A business operated as a single proprietorship or partnership is not treated as a separate taxable entity under the law. Rather, a single proprietor must report the income from his business on his individual return; and each partner in a partnership is required to include his share of partnership net income on his individual return. In other words, the income of a single proprietorship or partnership, whether withdrawn from the business or not, is taxed as the individual income of the single proprietor or partners.

The treatment given corporations under the law is different, however. A business operated as a corporation must file a return and pay taxes on its taxable income. Also, if a corporation pays out in dividends some or all of its "after-tax income," its shareholders must report these dividends as income on their individual returns. Because of this, it is commonly claimed that corporation income is taxed twice, once to the corporation and again to its shareholders.

The Individual Income Tax

The amount of income tax an individual must pay each year depends upon his or her gross income, deductions, exemptions, and tax credits;

and it is calculated as in Illustration 28–1. Several items outlined in Illustration 28–1 require additional explanation:

TOTAL (GROSS) INCOME.   Income tax law defines *total (gross) income* as **all income from whatever source derived, unless expressly excluded by law.** Income, therefore, includes income from operating a business, which is defined as "the profit therefrom for the year," and is the same as net income determined by the application of generally accepted accounting principles, unless a departure from such principles is provided by law. One important departure is for capital cost allowance deductions as explained later in this chapter. Total income also includes gains from property sales, pensions, dividends, interest, rents, royalties, and compensation for services, such as salaries, wages, fees, commissions, bonuses, and tips. Actually, the answers to two questions are all that is required to determine whether an item should be included or excluded. The two questions are: (1) Is the item income? (2) Is it expressly excluded by law? If an item is income and not specifically excluded, it must be included.

Certain items are recognized as not being income, for example, gifts, inheritances, and in most cases the proceeds of life insurance policies paid upon the death of the insured. These are not income and are excluded. Other items such as the first $500 of fellowships, scholarships, and bursaries are specifically excluded. Also excluded are the gain on the sale of the taxpayer's principal residence, gains from gambling, windfall gains, and certain gains on the sale of personal property.

DEDUCTIONS TO ARRIVE AT NET INCOME.   The nature of allowable deductions from gross income fall into three classifications:

1.   Deductions which are a postponement of current period income to future periods. These include Canada or Quebec pension plan contributions, registered pension plan contributions, and registered retirement savings plan contributions.
2.   Deductions for the purpose of enhancing future income, and deductions to maintain current income. An example of the former is tuition fees paid to an educational institution. Union and professional fees and unemployment insurance contributions are examples of the latter.
3.   Adjustments for business losses of other years.

Deductions from Net Income

By legislative grace, an individual taxpayer is permitted certain deductions from net income. These are as follows:

1.   Personal exemption allowances:
     a.   For self.
     b.   For dependants.
     c.   Re age.

Illustration 28–1

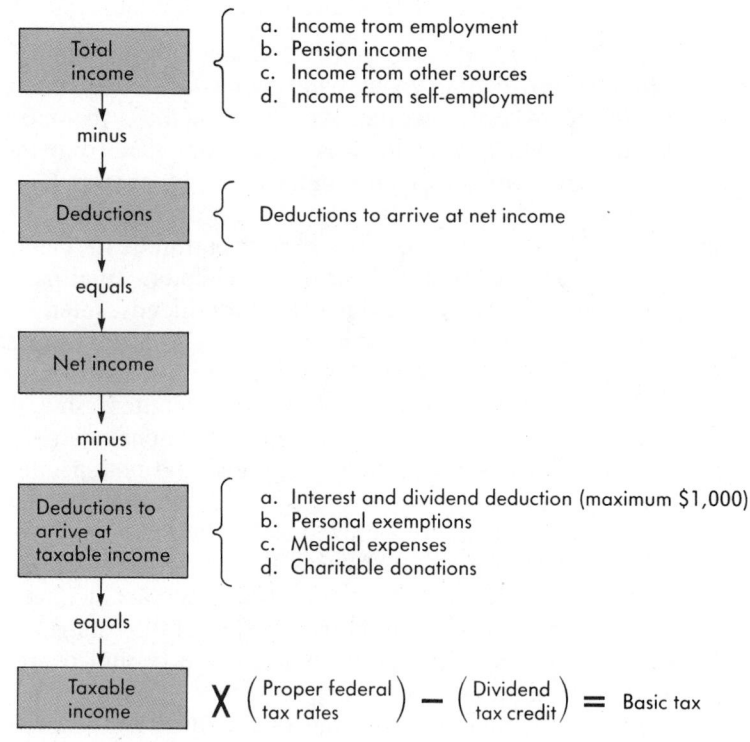

Total income
{
a. Income from employment
b. Pension income
c. Income from other sources
d. Income from self-employment
}

minus

Deductions
{
Deductions to arrive at net income
}

equals

Net income

minus

Deductions to arrive at taxable income
{
a. Interest and dividend deduction (maximum $1,000)
b. Personal exemptions
c. Medical expenses
d. Charitable donations
}

equals

Taxable income
$$\times \left(\begin{array}{c}\text{Proper federal}\\\text{tax rates}\end{array}\right) - \left(\begin{array}{c}\text{Dividend}\\\text{tax credit}\end{array}\right) = \text{Basic tax}$$

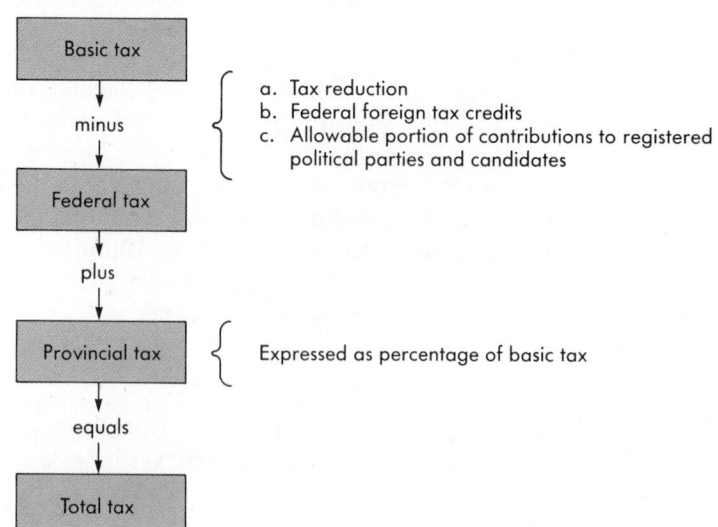

Basic tax

minus
{
a. Tax reduction
b. Federal foreign tax credits
c. Allowable portion of contributions to registered political parties and candidates
}

Federal tax

plus

Provincial tax
{
Expressed as percentage of basic tax
}

equals

Total tax

2. Investment income allowance:

    a. Re first $1,000 of Canadian interest and dividends.

3. Pension income allowance:

    a. Re first $1,000 of nongovernment pension.

4. Charitable donations:

    a. Up to 20% of net income.

5. Medical expenses

    a. Of self, spouse, and dependants, less 3% of net income.

6. Disability allowance.

7. Education deduction:

    a. $50 per month for every month in full-time attendance at a post-secondary institution.

Since 1974, personal expemption and disability allowances have been indexed. The adjusted exemptions for 1985 are as follows:

For single taxpayer	$4,140
For a dependant spouse	3,630
Children born in 1968 or later	710
Children born in 1967 or earlier	1,420
For age (65 at year-end) or disability (blind or confined to a bed or a wheelchair)	2,590

Investment Income Allowance

To encourage saving and investment in Canadian enterprise and to give partial recognition to the claim that corporate income is taxed twice (once as business income in the corporation and again as investment income when received as dividends by the shareholders), the law provides for special treatment of investment income received from qualifying domestic corporations. Beginning in 1974, individual taxpayers were allowed to deduct in calculating taxable income up to $1,000 of Canadian interest that had been included in net income. In 1975, this provision was extended to cover the first $1,000 of interest and dividend amounts from Canadian sources. In 1978, this provision was further extended to cover the first $1,000 of interest, dividends, and taxable capital gains on Canadian investments. In 1985, capital gains were exempted from taxation (in gradual steps up to $500,000 in a lifetime) so that capital gains were removed from this exemption. Thus, if a taxpayer's net income includes interests or dividends, he or she can claim an allowance equal to the lesser of such amounts or $1,000 in calculating his or her taxable income.

As explained above, Canadian source dividends may actually escape tax, because although they are included in the calculation of net income, they can be deducted again, up to $1,000, in the calculation of taxable income. The treatment of Canadian source dividends is further complicated by the gross-up and credit rules. These rules were initially introduced to eliminate the effects of double taxation of corporate income. The effect of these rules today is to effectively eliminate any personal tax liability on Canadian dividend income up to approximately $22,000. The rules work as follows:

1. Any dividends received from Canadian companies must be grossed up by 50% and included in net income in an amount equal to 150% of the amount actually received. (It is the first $1,000 of this grossed-up amount that is eligible for the investment income allowance.)

2. Once federal taxes payable have been calculated, this payable can be reduced by an amount equal to $22\frac{2}{3}\%$ of the grossed-up value of the dividend. This tax reduction is referred to as a *dividend tax credit.*[1]

Illustration 28–2

		Tax bracket		
		16%	*25%*	*34%*
A.	Dividend income	$6,000	$6,000	$6,000
	Add: 50%	3,000	3,000	3,000
	Net income	9,000	9,000	9,000
	Investment income allowance	1,000	1,000	1,000
	Taxable income	8,000	8,000	8,000
	Federal income tax	1,280	2,000	2,720
	Less: dividend tax credit ($22\frac{2}{3}\%$ of 9,000)	(2,040)	(2,040)	(2,040)
	Basic federal tax	(760)*	(40)*	680
	Dividends received	6,000	6,000	6,000
	Tax to pay	760	40	(680)
	Net cash remaining	$6,760	$6,040	$5,320
B.	Interest income	$6,000	$6,000	$6,000
	Investment income allowance	1,000	1,000	1,000
	Taxable income	5,000	5,000	5,000
	Basic federal tax	800	1,250	1,700
	Interest received	6,000	6,000	6,000
	Tax to pay	800	1,250	1,700
	Net cash remaining	$5,200	$4,750	$4,300
C.	Ordinary income	$6,000	$6,000	$6,000
	Basic federal tax	960	1,500	2,040
	Net cash remaining	$5,040	$4,500	$3,960

* This money would not actually be refunded but would reduce taxes payable on other forms of income.

[1] Beginning in 1987, the "gross-up" will be $33\frac{1}{3}\%$ and the $\frac{1}{3}$ "gross-up" will also be the dividend tax credit.

The investment income allowance and the dividend gross-up and tax credit rules make dividends from Canadian sources a particularly attractive form of income to Canadian taxpayers. The effects of this situation are strongest in low-income tax brackets. This is demonstrated in Illustration 28–2, which contrasts cash remaining after taxes assuming *(a)* dividend income, *(b)* interest income, and *(c)* ordinary (perhaps employment) income in three different tax brackets.

Income Tax Rates

Once taxable income has been determined, the federal tax payable on this income must be calculated. Canadian income tax rates are progressive in nature. Each additional segment or bracket of taxable income is subject to a higher rate than the preceding segment or bracket. The rates applied to taxable income in 1985 are shown in Illustration 28–3.

It is generally recognized that our Canadian income tax rates are steeply progressive. Proponents claim that this is only fair, since the taxpayers most able to pay, those with higher incomes, are subject to higher rates. Opponents claim that the high rates stifle initiative. For example, a young executive earning $35,000 of taxable income per year, upon being offered a new job with additional responsibilities and a $5,000 salary increase, might turn the new job down, feeling that the after-tax increase in pay would be insufficient to compensate for the additional responsibilities.

Whether or not our progressive income tax rates stifle initiative is open to debate, but there is no question that the rates do cause high-income taxpayers to search for tax-saving opportunities.

Illustration 28–3   1985 Rates of Federal Income Tax

Taxable income	Tax	Taxable income	Tax
$1,295 or less ..	6%	$12,950	$ 2,176 + 20% on next $ 5,180
1,295	$ 78 + 16% on next $1,295	18,130	3,212 + 23% on next 5,180
2,590	285 + 17% on next 2,590	23,310	4,403 + 25% on next 12,950
5,180	725 + 18% on next 2,590	36,260	7,641 + 30% on next 25,900
7,770	1,191 + 19% on next 5,180	62,160	15,411 + 34% on remainder

Tax Credits

The initial federal tax figure is reduced by the dividend tax credit discussed earlier to generate a basic federal tax figure. There are then several other credits which may be used to reduce this liability. The most common such credits are discussed briefly below.

1. General tax reduction $100 or the amount of *basic federal tax,* whichever is less.
2. Residents of Quebec reduce their federal liability by 16.5% of basic tax. This is because the provincial government of Quebec finances certain services for its residents that are provided by the federal government in all other provinces.
3. Contributions made to federal political parties or to candidates for federal seats trigger a tax credit equal to:

75% of the first	$ 100 =	$ 75
50% of the next	450 =	225
⅓ of the next	600 =	200
	$1,150	$500 Maximum credit

Provincial Taxes

All provinces except Quebec assess personal taxes on the same basis as the federal government. Their tax rates are expressed as a percentage of basic tax and are collected on their behalf by Revenue Canada. In 1985, the provincial tax rates and the top marginal combined federal/provincial rates were as follows:

1985 Income Tax Rates

Province	Provincial percentage of basic federal tax*	Top marginal combined federal/provincial*
Newfoundland	60.0%	56.10%
Prince Edward Island	52.5	53.55
Nova Scotia	56.5	54.91
New Brunswick	58.0	55.42
Quebec	N/A†	62.10
Ontario	48.0	52.02
Manitoba	54.0	57.73
Saskatchewan	50.5	54.93
Alberta	43.5	50.49
British Columbia	44.0	53.47
Northwest Territories	43.0	50.32
Yukon	45.0	51.00
Nonresident	47.0	51.68

* This is a summary of basic tax rates and should be used only for comparative purposes. Many factors, such as tax credits, exemptions, surtaxes, the tax base, and rate reductions, can affect these basic rates.

† Quebec personal income tax is levied on a graduated scale

Quebec has a completely separate tax statute, and residents of Quebec must file separate tax returns before the end of April each year.

The province to which a person gives income tax is determined (except for some business income) by his/her province of residence on the last day of the year—for example, someone who moves to Nova Scotia on December 20th will have to pay Nova Scotia provincial tax rates on his/her full year's income but will have no liability to the province in which he/she resided for 97% of the year.

Prepayments

Individual taxpayers are required to pay income taxes on a pay-as-income-is-earned basis throughout each year. Then, before April 30, after the end of each year, every taxpayer must file a tax return reporting the amount of his or her income and the tax thereon. At that time the taxpayer may claim a refund for any overpayment or must pay any balance due. Penalties are assessed for a major underpayment.

The pay-as-you-earn basis works differently for employees and for those individuals whose sources of income are other than employment. The procedure by which employers withhold income taxes from the salary, wages, or other remuneration such as commissions paid the taxpayer by an employer has been discussed in a previous chapter. Payment by those in self-employment and those individuals whose income is from sources other than employment needs further discussion.

Individual taxpayers, who earn the bulk of their income from sources other than employment, are required to pay their income taxes in quarterly installments based on the estimated income for the current taxation year. The estimate is based on one of two bases:

1. The taxpayer's ascertained income of the preceding year.
2. A different amount based on known altered circumstances.

Using the estimated amount, the taxpayer computes his/her estimated tax obligation for the year and remits one quarter of the latter amount to the Receiver General of Canada on or before each of March 31, June 30, September 30, and December 31.

Special Treatment of Capital Gains and Losses

From a tax-saving point of view, one of the most important features of Canadian federal income tax laws is the special treatment given gains from capital asset sales and exchanges. Prior to 1985, the effect of this special treatment was a tax on net capital gains which was one half the tax on an equal amount of income from some other source, commonly called ordinary income. The May 1985 budget proposed a tax exemption for net capital gains realized by individuals of up to a lifetime limit of $500,000 ($250,000 of net taxable capital gains). The exemption will be phased in over six years as follows:

1985	$ 20,000
1986	50,000
1987	100,000
1988	200,000
1989	300,000
1990	500,000

In 1985, for example, an individual may have a capital gain of $12,000, which would, because of the exemption, not be taxable. It would, however, lower the lifetime exemption available to $488,000 ($500,000 – $12,000). If an individual had a capital gain in 1985 of $25,000; $20,000 would be exempt and serve to lower the lifetime exemption to $480,000; while one half of the remaining $5,000 would be taxable at the normal 1985 rates for ordinary income.

Capital gains may be realized on such *capital assets* as investment in stocks and bonds, personal property (if the selling price of the asset is more than $1,000), and depreciable property used in a business.

A *capital gain* on the sale of a capital asset occurs when the proceeds of the sale exceed the cost base of the asset sold, and a *capital loss* occurs when the asset's cost base exceeds the proceeds. A depreciable asset sold at more than its book value, but at cost or less than cost results in a portion or all of depreciation previously charged against the asset to be treated as ordinary income. A capital gain results if the depreciable asset is sold at more than its *capital cost* and the gain is equal to the proceeds less cost.

To illustrate the recognition of a capital gain on the disposal of a depreciable asset, assume that an apartment building, which cost $260,000 and on which $50,000 of depreciation has accumulated, is sold for $280,000. The basis of the asset is cost, $260,000; therefore, the capital gain is $20,000 ($280,000 – $260,000). The $50,000 difference between the cost of the asset ($260,000) and its book value ($210,000) is referred to as recaptured depreciaion or capital cost allowance (discussed later in this chapter) and is taxable as ordinary income.

Any capital losses realized would be deducted from the capital gains in determining the net capital gains that would be applied against the exemption. Gains on the sale of a principal residence continue to be tax free; however, only one principal residence is allowed per married couple in the taxation year. Gains on the sale of a second residence such as a cottage would be taxable to the extent that they exceed the exemption.

Individual Income Tax Computation

The Canadian income tax system is based on self-assessment, and its success relies, to a marked extent, on the cooperation of the individual taxpayers. Every taxpayer is required to complete and file his/her yearly income tax return in which he/she must supply information as to income earned, deductions and exemptions claimed, and his/her calculation of income tax payable for the completed calendar year.

An individual taxpayer's tax computation, demonstrating the main features of income tax legislation, is shown in Illustration 28–4. The computation is based on assumed data for a hypothetical taxpayer, resident in the province of Ontario, Mr. James Evans, a publisher's representative, who is married and has two daughters ages two and four. Mrs. Evans teaches school and files a separate return. Mr. Evans claims, on his return, the two dependent daughters as well as the charitable donations. The assumed data are as follows:

Income:
Income from employment	$38,200.00
Dividend income from Canadian corporations	800.00
Interest on bonds and on bank account	450.00
Taxable benefit from personal use of employer's car	1,500.00
Gain on shares of stock	1,820.00
Loss on shares of stock	460.00

Expenditures:
Donations to church and charitable organizations	720.00
Contributions to a registered pension fund	1,910.00
Contributions to a registered retirement savings plan	1,590.00
Canada Pension Plan contribution	379.80
Unemployment insurance contribution	562.12
Contribution to registered political party	100.00

The Corporation Income Tax

For income tax purposes, the taxable income of a corporation organized for profit is calculated in much the same way as the taxable income of an individual. However, there are important differences, five of which follow:

1. Dividends received by a public corporation from another Canadian corporation are exempt from tax.
2. Dividends received by a private corporation from another Canadian corporation are subject to two sets of rules: one for dividends received from a subsidiary (more than 50% ownership) and the other for dividends from nonsubsidiary corporations. Dividends from subsidiaries are exempt from tax. Dividends received by private corporations from nonsubsidiary corporations are subject to a special 25% tax which is fully refunded to the corporation as dividends are paid to shareholders. For every $4 of dividends paid, $1 of tax is refunded.
3. Corporations may deduct capital losses from capital gains, but not from other income; and like individual taxpayers, they may carry losses back three years and forward until absorbed by capital gains.

Illustration 28–4

MR. JAMES EVANS
Income Tax Computation
For the Year 1985

Incomes:

Employment	$38,200.00	
Less: Employment expense allowance	500.00	$37,700.00
Dividends (gross-up by ½)		1,200.00
Interest		450.00
Taxable benefit from use of employer's car		1,500.00
Net capital gain ½ ($1,820 − $460)		680.00
		41,530.00

Deductions:

Canada Pension Plan contribution	379.80	
Unemployment insurance contribution	562.12	
Contribution to registered pension plan	1,910.00	
Contribution to registered retirement savings plan	1,590.00	4,441.92
Net income		37,088.08

Deductions from net income:

1. Personal exemptions:		
Self	4,140.00	
Two dependent children under 18	1,420.00	
2. Investment income allowance	1,000.00	
3. Charitable donations	720.00	
4. Capital gains exemption	680.00	
Total deductions		7,960.00
Taxable income		$29,129.08

Federal tax:

Tax on $23,310	4,403.00	
Tax on ($29,129.08 − $23,310 @ 25%)	1,454.77	
	5,857.77	
Less: Dividend tax credit (22⅔% × $1,200)	272.04	
Basic federal tax	5,585.73	
Less: Federal tax reduction	100.00	
	5,485.73	
Less: Political contribution credit (75% × $100)	75.00	
Federal tax		$ 5,410.73
Ontario provincial tax (48% of $5,585.73)		2,681.15
Total income tax liability		$ 8,091.88

In 1985, the federal government introduced a surtax on "Basic federal tax" in excess of $6,000. In this example the basic tax is less than $6,000, and thus the surtax is not applicable.

4. Personal deductions for the taxpayer and his/her dependants do not apply to a corporation, and a corporation does not have certain other deductions of an individual, such as for personal medical expenses.

5. In addition, the big difference between the corporation and the individ-

ual income tax is that the corporation tax rate is not progressive but consists of a general federal tax rate and a general provincial tax rate. In 1985 the federal tax rate was 46%; however, in the case of private corporations it was subject to adjustments, for example, the small business deduction and manufacturing and processing profits deduction. The provincial rates vary from province to province, and in 1985 ranged from 10% to 16% of taxable income earned in the province. Because of the complexity of corporate taxation and variation in effective rates not only from province to province but from corporation to corporation, for purposes of this chapter a 50% combined federal and provincial tax rate is assumed for all corporations except those qualifying for the small business deduction. A 25% tax rate is assumed for these. Additionally, corporations qualifying for the small business deduction pay a special tax of 12½% on dividends paid to all individuals and paid to corporations that do not control the payer corporation.

Corporations also must pay income tax as income is earned. Payments are made in 12 monthly installments and are based on a corporation's actual income of the preceding fiscal year or on the preceding year's income adjusted for known altered circumstances. The monthly payments commence on the last day of the first month of the fiscal year in which the income is earned. For example, a corporation with a September 1 to August 31 fiscal year must make its first payment on the year's tax on September 30, and a corporation with a fiscal year beginning on January 1 must make its first payment on January 31.

TAX EFFECTS OF BUSINESS ALTERNATIVES

Alternative decisions commonly have different tax effects. Following are several examples illustrating these effects.

Form of Business Organization

The difference between individual and corporation tax rates commonly affects one of the basic decisions a businessperson must make; namely, that as to the legal form his or her business should take. Should it be a single proprietorship, partnership, or corporation? The following factors influence the decision:

1. As previously stated, a corporation is a taxable entity. Its income is taxed at corporation rates, and any portion distributed in dividends is taxed again as individual income to its shareholders. On the other hand, the income of a single proprietorship or partnership, whether withdrawn or left in the business, is taxed only once as individual income of the proprietor or partners.

2. In addition, a corporation may pay salaries to shareholders who work for the corporation, and the sum of these salaries is a tax-deductible expense in arriving at the corporation's taxable income. In a partnership or a single proprietorship on the other hand, salaries of the partners or the proprietor are nothing more than allocations of income.

In arriving at a decision as to the legal form a business should take, a business executive, with the foregoing points in mind, must estimate the tax consequences of each form and select the best. For example, assume that Ralph Jones is choosing between the single proprietorship and corporate forms, and that he estimates the business will have annual gross sales of $250,000, with cost of goods sold and operating expenses, other than his own salary as manager, of $190,000. Assume further that $20,000 per year is his salary for managing the business and that Mr. Jones plans to withdraw virtually all profits from the business. Under these assumptions, Mr. Jones's tax situation will be as shown in Illustration 28–5.

Under the assumptions of Illustration 28–5, Mr. Jones will incur $537 less tax overall under the corporate format than as a proprietorship. However, his personal after-tax income is slightly less under the corporate format due to the retention of $750 by the corporation. This is due to the tax on dividends paid which makes the distribution of the entire corporate income extremely difficult to calculate efficiently. Other factors such as ease of formation, lack of shareholder's liability, or the necessity of funds for growth may become deciding factors.

Growth is commonly financed through retained earnings; and when it is, organizing a business as a corporation may prove advantageous, since income retained in a business organized as a corporation is not taxed as individual income to its shareholders, but the income of a single proprietorship is so taxed whether retained in the business or withdrawn. It is especially advantageous to retain earnings in the business rather than pay out dividends at the higher-income tax brackets.

When earnings are retained in a corporation to finance growth, the growth normally results in an increase in the price of the corporation's stock, and the owners of the stock may capture the retained earnings in the form of capital gains upon the sale of the stock. However, whether such gains ultimately result in a tax savings depends upon the tax bracket of the taxpayer at the time he/she realizes the capital gains.

Method of Financing

When a corporation is in need of additional financing, it is often to its advantage to borrow the funds rather than to issue shares, since interest on debt is a tax-deductible expense but dividends are not. For example, assume that a corporation with a 50% tax rate needs $100,000 for an expansion, and that it can earn 15% on the $100,000, before

Illustration 28–5

	Proprietorship		Corporation	
Operating results under each form:				
Estimated sales		$250,000		$250,000
Cost of goods sold and operating expenses other than owner-manager's salary	$190,000		$190,000	
Salary of owner-manager	nil	190,000	20,000	210,000
Before-tax income		60,000		40,000
Corporate income tax*		nil		13,250
Net income		$ 60,000		$ 26,750
Owner's after-tax income under each form:				
Single proprietorship net income		$ 60,000		$ nil
Salary		nil		20,000
Dividends received from net income		nil		26,000
Total receipts		60,000		46,000
Total personal tax†		18,456		4,669
Owner's after-tax income		$ 41,554		$ 41,331
*Calculation of corporate income tax assuming a dividend paid of $26,000:				
Corporate tax at 25% of net income				$ 10,000
Special dividend tax on dividends paid (12½% × $26,000)				3,250
				$ 13,250
†Calculation of individual's tax (assuming deductions and exemptions totaling $8,000):				
Taxable income		$ 52,000		$ 51,000
Federal taxes		12,363		12,063
Dividend tax credit		nil		8,841
Basic federal tax		12,363		3,222
Federal tax reduction		nil		100
		12,363		3,122
Federal surtax		159		nil
		12,522		3,122
Provincial tax at 48% of basic tax		5,934		1,547
Total personal tax		$ 18,456		$ 4,669
Total personal and corporate tax		$ 18,456		$ 17,919

interest and taxes. If the company secures the funds by issuing 7% preferred shares, it will earn $15,000 before taxes and $7,500 after taxes, and the after-tax earnings will little more than cover the preferred dividends. However, if it borrows the $100,000 at, say 9%, the $9,000[2] of interest on the loan will be a tax-deductible expense, and as a result the company will have only $6,000 of taxable earnings from the expansion.

_____

[2] Interest on debt is usually higher than the dividend rate on preferred shares.

Furthermore, since the tax on $6,000 is 50% of that amount, the company will have $3,000 left for its common shareholders.

Although, due to taxes, it is commonly to the advantage of a limited company to borrow rather than to issue shares, other factors are often involved. For example, borrowed capital may be difficult to obtain, especially if the owners are supplying a very small portion of total financing. Also, borrowing exposes the corporation to greater risks than does raising capital through the sale of shares.

In addition to a choice between borrowing funds and issuing shares, taxes are also a factor in a decision as whether to buy or lease assets. Taxes enter into such decisions because a leasing arrangement may offer rental deductions in excess of depreciation and interest.

NET INCOME AND TAXABLE INCOME

The taxable income of a business commonly differs from its reported net income. It differs because (1) net income is determined by the application of GAAP, (2) while tax rules are used in determining taxable income, and (3) the rules differ from GAAP on some points. For example:

1. The application of accounting principles requires that the full amount of any material gains from capital asset sales and exchanges be taken into reported net income, but for tax purposes only 50% of the net gains from such sales commonly enters into taxable income.[3]
2. Accounting principles require an estimate of future costs, such as costs of making good on guarantees; they also require a deduction of such costs from revenue in the year the guaranteed goods are sold. However, tax rules do not permit the deduction of such costs until they are actually incurred.
3. Reported net income also differs from taxable income because the taxpayer uses a method or procedure for accounting purposes that he/she feels fairly reflects periodic net income but is required to use a different method of procedure for tax purposes. For example, the last-in, first-out inventory method of cost allocation may be used for accounting purposes but is not permitted for tax purposes. Likewise, many companies use straight-line depreciation for accounting purposes but are required to use a different procedure, called capital cost allowances, for tax purposes.

CAPITAL COST ALLOWANCES

Depreciation accounting has been greatly influenced by income tax laws. The 1948 Income Tax Act replaced the complex body of rules

---

[3] The capital gains exemption applies only to individuals. Thus, corporations are taxable on capital gains.

that had developed for the purpose of limiting the amount of depreciation allowed for tax purposes. The act defined and set a limit on amounts which could be deducted, for tax purposes, in respect to the cost of depreciable assets. These amounts are known as *capital cost allowances* (CCA).

The capital cost allowances are identical in nature and purpose with the accountants' concept of depreciation and are based on the declining-balance method, discussed in Chapter 10. For tax purposes, the taxpayer may claim the maximum allowed or any part thereof in any year regardless of the depreciation method and the amounts he/she uses in the accounting records.

Although capital cost allowances are based on the declining-balance method, certain procedures have been set out by the Regulations of the Act. The more important of these are as follows:

1. All depreciable assets are grouped into a comparatively small number of classes and a maximum rate allowed is prescribed for each group. The assets most commonly in use are set out below according to the class to which they belong, with the maximum rate of allowance for each such class.

   Class 3 (5%): Brick, cement, and stone buildings.

   Class 6 (10%): Frame, log, stucco, and corrugated iron buildings.

   Class 7 (15%): Ships, scows, canoes, and rowboats.

   Class 10 (30%): Automobiles, trucks, and tractors.

   Class 8 (20%): Machinery, equipment, and furniture.

2. The assets of a designated class are considered to form a separate pool of costs. The costs of asset additions are added to their respective pools of undepreciated capital cost. When assets are disposed of, the proceeds (up to the original cost) received from disposal are deducted from the proper pool. The balance of each pool of costs is also diminished by the accumulated capital cost allowances claimed. A capital cost allowance is claimed on the balance, referred to as the undepreciated capital cost (UCC), in the pool at the end of the fiscal year. However, when there are net additions to the pool, only one half of the amount added is used in the calculation of CCA. The effect is that the assets are assumed to have been acquired halfway through the fiscal year.

3. "Losses" and "gains" on disposal of individual assets disappear into the pool of undepreciated capital costs except when an asset is sold for more than its capital cost. In this case, proceeds of disposal in excess of the capital cost of the asset are normally treated as a capital gain. Where the proceeds of disposal (excluding the capital gain, if any) exceed the undepreciated capital cost of the class immediately before the sale, the amount of the excess is treated

as a "recapture" of capital cost allowances previously made. Such a recapture is considered as ordinary income. When all of the assets in a class are disposed of and the proceeds are less than the undepreciated capital cost of the class immediately before the sale, the proceeds less the undepreciated capital cost may be deducted in determining the year's taxable income.

Companies must, with few exceptions, use capital cost allowances for tax purposes, but commonly use straight-line depreciation in their accounting records. A problem arising from this practice is discussed in the next section.

TAXES AND THE DISTORTION OF NET INCOME

When one accounting procedure is required for tax purposes and a different procedure is used in the accounting records, a problem arises as to how much income tax expense should be deducted each year on the income statement. If the tax actually incurred in such situations is deducted, reported net income often varies from year to year due to the postponement and later payment of taxes. Consequently, in such cases, since shareholders may be misled by these variations, many accountants are of the opinion that income taxes should be allocated in such a way that any distortion resulting from postponing taxes is removed from the income statement.

To appreciate the problem involved here, assume that a corporation has installed a $100,000 machine, the product of which will produce a half-million dollars of revenue in each of the succeeding four years and $80,000 of income before depreciation and taxes. Assume further that the company must pay income taxes at a 40% rate (round number assumed for easy calculation) and that it plans to use straight-line depreciation in its records but the capital cost allowance for tax purposes. If the machine has a four-year life and a $10,000 salvage value and if the maximum permitted capital cost allowance rate on this particular machine is 50%, annual depreciation calculated by each method will be as follows:

Year	Straight line	Declining balance
1	$22,500	$25,000
2	22,500	37,500
3	22,500	18,750
4	22,500	8,750*
Totals	$90,000	$90,000

* Use $8,750 in order to match salvage value. CCA allowed is $9,375.

And since the company has elected capital cost allowance for tax purposes, it will be liable for $22,000 of income tax on the first year's income, $17,000 on the second, $24,500 on the third, and $28,500 on the fourth. The calculation of these taxes is shown in Illustration 28–6.

Illustration 28–6

Annual income taxes	*Year 1*	*Year 2*	*Year 3*	*Year 4*	*Total*
Income before depreciation and income taxes	$80,000	$80,000	$80,000	$80,000	$320,000
Depreciation for tax purposes (declining balance)	25,000	37,500	18,750	8,750	90,000
Taxable income	$55,000	$42,500	$61,250	$71,250	$230,000
Annual income taxes (40% of taxable income)	$22,000	$17,000	$24,500	$28,500	$ 92,000

Furthermore, if the company were to deduct its actual tax liability each year in arriving at income to be reported to its shareholders, it would report the amounts shown in Illustration 28–7.

Observe in Illustrations 28–6 and 28–7 that total depreciation, $90,000, is the same whether calculated by the straight-line or the declining-balance method. Also note that the total tax liability for the four years, $92,000, is the same in each case. Then note the distortion of the final income figures in Illustration 28–7 due to the postponement of taxes.

Illustration 28–7

Income after deducting actual tax liabilities	*Year 1*	*Year 2*	*Year 3*	*Year 4*	*Total*
Income before depreciation and income taxes	$80,000	$80,000	$80,000	$80,000	$320,000
Depreciation per books (straight line)	22,500	22,500	22,500	22,500	90,000
Income before taxes	57,500	57,500	57,500	57,500	230,000
Income taxes (actual liability of each year)	22,000	17,000	24,500	28,500	92,000
Remaining income	$35,500	$40,500	$33,000	$29,000	$138,000

If this company should report successive annual income figures of $35,500, $40,500, $33,000, and then $29,000, some of its shareholders might be misled as to the company's earnings trend. Consequently, in cases such as this many accountants think income taxes should be allocated so that the distortion caused by the postponement of taxes is removed from the income statement. These accountants advocate that—

> When one accounting procedure is used in the accounting records and a different procedure is used for tax purposes, the tax expense deducted on the income statement should not be the actual tax liability but the amount that would be payable if the procedure used in the records were also used in calculating the tax.

If the foregoing is applied in this case, the corporation will report to its shareholders in each of the four years the amounts of income shown in Illustration 28–8.

Illustration 28–8

Net income that should be reported to shareholders	Year 1	Year 2	Year 3	Year 4	Total
Income before depreciation and income taxes	$80,000	$80,000	$80,000	$80,000	$320,000
Depreciation per books (straight line)	22,500	22,500	22,500	22,500	90,000
Income before taxes	57,500	57,500	57,500	57,500	230,000
Income taxes (amounts based on straight-line depreciation)	23,000	23,000	23,000	23,000	92,000
Net income	$34,500	$34,500	$34,500	$34,500	$138,000

In examining Illustration 28–7, recall that the company's tax liabilities are actually $22,000 in the first year, $17,000 in the second, $24,500 in the third, and $28,500 in the fourth, a total of $92,000. Then observe that when this $92,000 liability is allocated evenly over the four years, the distortion of the annual net incomes due to the postponement of taxes is removed from the published income statements.

ENTRIES FOR THE ALLOCATION OF TAXES

When income taxes are allocated as in Illustration 28–8, the tax liability of each year and the deferred taxes are recorded with an adjusting entry. The adjusting entries for the four years of Illustration 28–7 and the entries in general journal form for the payment of the taxes (without explanations) are as follows:

Year 1	Income Tax Expense	23,000		
	Income Taxes Payable		22,000	
	Deferred Income Taxes		1,000	
	Income Taxes Payable	22,000		
	Cash		22,000	
Year 2	Income Tax Expense	23,000		
	Income Taxes Payable		17,000	
	Deferred Income Taxes		6,000	
	Income Taxes Payable	17,000		
	Cash		17,000	
Year 3	Income Tax Expense	23,000		
	Deferred Income Taxes	1,500		
	Income Taxes Payable		24,500	
	Income Taxes Payable	24,500		
	Cash		24,500	
Year 4	Income Tax Expense	23,000		
	Deferred Income Taxes	5,500		
	Income Taxes Payable		28,500	
	Income Taxes Payable	28,500		
	Cash		28,500	

Note: To simplify the illustration, it is assumed here that the entire year's tax liability is paid at one time. However, corporations are usually required to pay estimated taxes on a monthly basis.

In the entries the $23,000 debited to Income Taxes Expense each year is the amount that is deducted on the income statement in reporting annual net income. Also, the amount credited to Income Taxes Payable each year is the actual tax liability of that year.

Observe in the entries that since the actual tax liability in each of the first two years is less than the amount debited to Income Taxes Expense, the difference is credited to *Deferred Income Taxes*. Then note that in the last two years, since the actual liability each year is greater than the debit to Income Taxes Expense, the difference is debited to Deferred Income Taxes. Now observe in the following illustration of the company's Deferred Income Taxes account that the debits and credits exactly balance each other out over the four-year period:

Deferred Income Taxes				
Year	Explanation	Debit	Credit	Balance
1			1,000	1,000
2			6,000	7,000
3		1,500		5,500
4		5,500		–0–

In passing, it should be observed that many accountants believe the interests of government, business, and the public would be better served if there were more uniformity between taxable income and reported net income. However, since the federal income tax is designed to serve other purposes than raising revenue, it is apt to be some time before this is achieved.

GLOSSARY

Basic federal tax. Taxable income multiplied by the applicable federal tax rate(s).

Capital asset. Any item of property except (1) inventories, (2) trade notes and accounts receivable, (3) real property and depreciable property used in a trade or business, (4) copyrights or similar property, and (5) any government obligation due within one year and issued at a discount.

Capital cost. The cost of a capital asset.

Capital cost allowance. Depreciation of capital assets allowed for tax purposes.

Capital gain or loss. The difference between the proceeds from the sale of a capital asset and the original cost of the asset.

Corporate income tax. A tax levied by the federal and provincial authority on the taxable income of corporations.

Deferred income taxes. The difference between the income tax expense in the financial statements and the income taxes payable according to tax law, resulting from financial accounting and tax accounting timing differences with respect to expense or revenue recognition.

Dividend tax credit. The income tax act provides for special treatment of dividend income from Canadian corporations in order to alleviate the impact of double taxation.

Total (gross) income. All income from whatever source derived, unless expressly excluded by law.

Marginal tax rate. The rate that applies to the next dollar of income to be earned.

Provincial income tax. Income tax levied by each of the provinces. The tax is calculated (except for Quebec) as a percentage of basic federal tax.

Tax avoidance. A legal means of preventing a tax liability from coming into existence.

Tax credit. A direct reduction in the amount of tax liability.

QUESTIONS FOR CLASS DISCUSSION

1. Jackson expects to have $500 of income in a 50% bracket; consequently, which should be more desirable to him:
   a. A transaction that will reduce his income tax by $100?
   b. A transaction that will reduce an expense of his business by $150?

2. Why must a taxpayer normally take advantage of a tax-saving opportunity at the time it arises?

3. Distinguish between tax avoidance and tax evasion. Which is legal and desirable?

4. What are some of the nonrevenue objectives of the federal income tax?

5. What nonrevenue objective is gained by granting a lower tax rate to small corporations?

6. What questions must be answered in determining whether an item should be included or excluded from gross income for tax purposes?

7. Name several items that are not income for tax purposes.

8. What justification is given for permitting an individual to claim a dividend tax credit on dividends from domestic corporations?

9. What is a capital gain?

10. An individual has had capital asset transactions that have resulted in nothing but capital gains. What special tax treatment may be given these gains?

11. For tax purposes, what is "ordinary income"?

12. Why do tax planners try to have income emerge as a capital gain?

13. It is often a wise tax decision for the owner of an incorporated business to forgo the payment of dividends from the earnings of his business. Why?

14. Why does the taxable income of a business commonly differ from its net income?

MINI DISCUSSION CASES

Case 28–1   It has often been said that it is better for an individual to receive $100 as dividend income rather than as interest income.

Required:

Do you agree with this statement? Why?

Case 28–2   You have a client who operates a business as a proprietorship and who insists on buying an expensive new car every two years or so. He says that the reason for buying the car is that he can charge the expense against his business income. This reduces his income tax liability. In this way the car costs far less because the government helps pay for the car, and he pays much less income tax.

Required:

Assume that the car is legitimately used for business. Is your client's reasoning correct? Why?

CLASS EXERCISES

Exercise 28–1   List the letters of the following items and write after each either the word included or excluded to indicate whether the item should be included or excluded from gross income for income tax purposes.

a. A portable TV set having a $100 fair market value which was received as a door prize.
b. Tips received while working as a parking lot attendant.
c. Cash inherited from a deceased aunt.
d. Scholarship received from a university.
e. Unemployment insurance benefits.
f. Workers' compensation insurance received as the result of an accident while working on a part-time job.
g. Gain on the sale of a personal automobile bought and rebuilt.
h. Dividends from shares in domestic corporations received by an individual.
i. Dividends from shares in domestic public corporations received by a corporation.
j. Interest on a savings account.

Exercise 28–2   During 1985 Ted Hall, who is married and has two dependent children over 16 years of age, earned $19,200 as an employee of an electronics company. He had $2,690 of income tax, $451.44 of unemployment insurance, and $300.60 of Canada Pension Plan taxes withheld from his pay cheques. He also received $200 in dividends from a domestic corporation in which he owned shares. During the year Ted made a number of small charitable donations: however, he did not retain any receipts. Show the calculation of Ted's taxable income in the manner outlined in the chapter. Then using the rate schedule of Illustration 28–3, show the calculations of net income tax payable or refund due Ted. (Assume that Ted Hall resides in British Columbia.)

Exercise 28–3   A taxpayer who had no other investment income received $7,500 in dividends. Use the rate schedule of Illustration 28–3 and determine the amount of federal income tax the taxpayer will have to pay from this transaction under each of the following unrelated assumptions:

a. The taxpayer had $18,000 of taxable income from other sources.
b. The taxpayer had $62,000 of taxable income from other sources.
c. The taxpayer had $96,000 of taxable income from other sources.

PROBLEMS

Problem 28–1   Ted Moss has operated Mesa Sales for a number of years with the following average annual results:

MESA SALES
Income Statement
For an Average Year

Sales		$380,000
Cost of goods sold	$225,000	
Operating expenses	115,000	340,000
Net income		$ 40,000

Mr. Moss is unmarried and without dependents and has been operating Mesa Sales as a single proprietorship. He has been withdrawing $18,000 each year to pay his personal living expenses. His total deductions and personal exemptions amount to $6,000. He has no income other than from Mesa Sales.

Required:

1. Assume that Mr. Moss is considering the incorporation of his business beginning with the 1985 tax year and prepare a comparative income statement for the business showing its net income as a single proprietorship and as a corporation. Assume that if he incorporates, Mr. Moss will pay $18,000 per year to himself as a salary.

2. Use the rate schedule of Illustration 28–3 and determine the amount of federal income tax Mr. Moss will have to pay for himself and for his business under each of the following assumptions: *(a)* the business is not incorporated; *(b)* the business is incorporated, pays Mr. Moss a $18,000 annual salary as manager, and also pays him $18,000 per year in dividends; and *(c)* the business is incorporated, pays Mr. Moss a $18,000 salary, but does not pay any dividends.

Problem 28–2   Ted Pace is a practicing lawyer. Some of the information contained in his 1985 income tax return follows:

Income from law practice	$52,000
Dividend income from Canadian corporation	1,800
Interest income	1,420
Capital gains	4,200
Capital losses	2,800
Registered Retirement Savings Plan contributions	4,000
Canada Pension Plan contributions	760
Personal exemptions	7,000

Required:

Compute Mr. Pace's quarterly income tax payments for the current year. Assume that Mr. Pace's circumstances and expectations have not changed from the previous year. Show supporting computations. (Assume that Mr. Pace resides in Nova Scotia.)

Problem 28–3

Part 1. At the beginning of his taxation year, Dale Isley purchased an apartment building for $300,000. The building is of frame and stucco construction. Mr. Isley took maximum capital cost allowance for each year and resold the building four years after purchase.

Required:

For each of the following selling prices, determine the amount of profit or loss realized and state how the profit or loss affected Mr. Isley's taxable income: *(a)* $330,000; *(b)* $230,000; *(c)* $190,000.

Part 2. In 19A, Mr. Dale Isley started a trucking business and purchased the following trucks: No. 1 for $19,200; No. 2 for $23,600; and No. 3 for $21,200. In 19B he purchased truck No. 4 for $25,600 and truck No. 5 for $22,800 and sold truck No. 1 for $9,200. No truck purchases or disposals took place in 19C.

Required:

Calculate the maximum capital cost allowance for the year 19C.

Problem 28–4

Early in January 19A, Deeplake Corporation installed a new machine in its plant that cost $360,000 and was estimated to have a four-year life and a $24,000 salvage value. The machine enabled the company to add a new product to its line that produces $240,000 of income annually before depreciation or capital cost allowance and income taxes. The company allocates income taxes in its reports to its shareholders, since it uses straight-line depreciation in its accounting records and for tax purposes, deducts the maximum capital cost allowance each year of an asset's life, until salvage value is reached.

Required:

1. Prepare a schedule showing 19A, 19B, 19C, and 19D, and total net income for the four years after deducting maximum capital cost allowances and actual taxes. Assume a 40% income tax rate and that the maximum capital cost allowance rate of the asset of this problem is 50%.

2. Prepare a second schedule showing each year's net income and the four-year total after deducting straight-line depreciation and actual taxes.
3. Prepare a third schedule showing income reported to shareholders with straight-line depreciation and allocated taxes.
4. Set up a T-account for Deferred Income Tax and show therein the entries that result from allocating the income taxes.

ALTERNATE PROBLEMS

Problem 28–1A

Richard Hall is married with no dependent children. He has no income other than from Valley Sales, a profitable single proprietorship business that Mr. Hall owns and which averages $400,000 annually in sales, with a 40% gross profit and $100,000 of operating expenses. Hall's total deductions and personal exemptions amount to $6,000. In the past, Mr. Hall has withdrawn $25,000 annually from the business for personal living expenses plus sufficient additional cash to pay the income tax on his return.

Mr. Hall thinks he can save taxes by reorganizing his business into a corporation beginning with the 1985 tax year. If the corporation is organized Mr. Hall will own all of the outstanding shares and the corporation will pay him $28,000 per year salary for managing the business.

Required:

1. Prepare a comparative income statement for the business showing its net income as a single proprietorship and as a corporation.
2. Use the rate schedule of Illustration 28–3 and determine the amount of income taxes Hall will pay for himself and for the business under each of the following assumptions: *(a)* the business remains a single proprietorship; *(b)* the business is incorporated, pays Mr. Hall a $28,000 salary, but pays no dividends; *(c)* the business is incorporated, pays Mr. Hall a $28,000 salary, and pays $15,000 in dividends. (Assume that Mr. Hall resides in Ontario and if incorporated the company would qualify for the small corporation tax rate.)

Problem 28–2A

David Douglas is a practicing accountant. He is married with no dependent children. Some of the information contained in his last year's income tax return follows:

Income from the accounting practice	$43,000
Dividend income from Canadian corporations	1,400
Interest income	1,300
Capital gains	4,200
Capital losses	1,600
Wife's income	1,600
Registered Retirement Savings Plan contributions	5,500
Canada Pension Plan contributions	760
Donations	880

Required:

Compute the current year's quarterly payment that Mr. Douglas must make. Assume that the circumstances and expectation Mr. and Mrs. Douglas have have not changed from the previous year. Show supporting computations. (Mr. and Mrs. Douglas reside in the province of Newfoundland.)

Problem 28–3A

Part 1. At the beginning of his taxation year, Lee Hall purchased an apartment building for $500,000. The building is of brick construction. Mr. Hall took maximum capital cost allowance for each year and resold the building three years after purchase.

Required:

For each of the following selling prices, determine the amount of profit or loss realized and state how the profit or loss affected Mr. Hall's taxable income: *(a)* $515,000; *(b)* $482,000; *(c)* $443,000.

Part 2. At the beginning of 19A the undepreciated capital cost allowance of Class 10 assets was $78,800. During 19A, additions to the class amounted to $49,200. In 19B, proceeds from disposal of Class 10 assets amounted to $14,600. No purchase or disposal transactions took place during 19C.

Required:

Calculate the maximum capital cost allowance on Class 10 assets for the year 19C.

Problem 28–4A

At a cost of $262,500, Green Hill Corporation installed a new machine in its plant early in January 19A, so that it could add a new product to its line. It estimated the new machine would have a four-year life, a $21,000 salvage value, and its product would produce $236,250 of income each year before capital cost allowance or depreciation and income taxes at an assumed 40% rate. The company uses straight-line depreciation for its accounting records. It also allocates income taxes in its reports to shareholders, because for tax purposes, it deducts the maximum capital cost allowance each year of an asset's life until salvage value is reached.

Required:

1. Prepare a schedule showing 19A, 19B, 19C, and 19D and total net income for the four years from the sale of the new product after deducting maximum capital cost allowances and actual income taxes. Assume that the maximum capital cost allowance rate of the asset of this problem is 40%.
2. Prepare a second schedule showing each year's income and total net income after deducting straight-line depreciation and actual income taxes.
3. Prepare a third schedule showing income reported to shareholders with straight-line depreciation and allocated income taxes.
4. Set up a T-account for Deferred Income Tax and showing the entries that result from allocating the income taxes with respect to this machine.

PROVOCATIVE PROBLEMS

Provocative
Problem 28–1,
Ithaca
Corporation

Tedrow Grey and his wife own all the outstanding shares of Ithaca Corporation, a company Tedrow organized several years ago and which is growing rapidly and needs additional capital.

Bob Brown, a friend of the Greys, examined the following comparative income statement, which shows the corporation's net income for the past three years and which was prepared by its bookkeeper. He expressed a tentative willingness to invest $50,000 in the corporation by purchasing a portion of its unissued shares.

ITHACA CORPORATION
Comparative Income Statement
For the Years 19A, 19B, and 19C

	19A	19B	19C
Sales	$700,000	$750,000	$825,000
Costs and expenses other than depreciation and income taxes	$425,000	$450,000	$500,000
Depreciation expense	105,000	110,000	125,000
Income taxes	65,000	70,000	75,000
Total costs and expenses	$595,000	$630,000	$700,000
Net Income	$105,000	$120,000	$125,000

However, before making a final decision, Bob Brown asked permission for his own accountant to examine the accounting records of the corporation. Permission was granted, the examination was made, and the accountant prepared the following comparative income statement covering the past three years.

ITHACA CORPORATION
Comparative Income Statement
For the Years 19A, 19B, and 19C

	19A	19B	19C
Sales	$700,000	$750,000	$825,000
Costs and expenses other than depreciation	$425,000	$450,000	$500,000
Depreciation expense*	105,000	110,000	125,000
Total costs and expenses	$530,000	$560,000	$625,000
Income before income taxes	$170,000	$190,000	$200,000
Applicable income taxes	85,000	95,000	100,000
Net Income	$ 85,000	$ 95,000	$100,000

* The corporation deducted $145,000 of depreciation on its 19A tax returns, $160,000 on its 19B returns, and $175,000 on its 19C returns.

Tedrow was surprised at the difference in annual net incomes reported on the two statements and immediately called for an explanation from the accountant who set up the corporation's accounting system and who prepares the annual tax returns of the corporation and the Greys.

Required:

Explain why there is a difference between the net income figures on the two income statements. Prepare a statement that will justify the amounts shown on the corporation bookkeeper's statement. Account for the difference in the reported net incomes. Assume a 50% income tax rate.

Provocative Problem 28–2, Haul-a-way Ltd.

Haul-a-way Ltd., is about to invest $160,000 in a fleet of light trucks (Class 10 asset). The new trucks will be purchased in January 1985 and are expected to have a five-year life and no salvage value; you, the company's accountant, have prepared the following statement showing the expected results from the services provided by the new trucks. The statement is based on the assumption that the new trucks will be depreciated on a straight-line basis and that the company must pay out 40% of its before-tax earnings in income taxes.

FLAT BED, INC.
Expected Results from Sale of New Product

	1985	1986	1987	1988	1989	Totals
Sales	$375,000	$375,000	$375,000	$375,000	$375,000	$1,875,000
All costs other than depreciation and income taxes	250,000	250,000	250,000	250,000	250,000	1,250,000
Income before depreciation and income taxes	125,000	125,000	125,000	125,000	125,000	625,000
Depreciation expense	32,000	32,000	32,000	32,000	32,000	160,000
Income before income taxes	93,000	93,000	93,000	93,000	93,000	465,000
Income taxes	37,200	37,200	37,200	37,200	37,200	186,000
Net income	$ 55,800	$ 55,800	$ 55,800	$ 55,800	$ 55,800	$ 279,000

When the company president examined your statement, he said he knew that regardless of how calculated, the company could charge off no more than $160,000 of depreciation on the new trucks during their five-year life. Furthermore, he said he could see that this would result in $465,000 of earnings before taxes for the five years, $186,000 of income taxes, and $279,000 of net income. Nevertheless, he continued that he had been talking to a friend on the golf course a few days back and the friend had tried to explain the tax advantage of using capital cost allowance deductions. He said he did not understand all the friend had tried to tell him; and as a result he would like for you to prepare an additional statement that calculates income after actual tax payments but based on CCA deductions.

Required:

The president expressed the belief that straight-line depreciation was the best method to use in financial statements. As a consequence, he wants you to explain the impact that the use of CCA for tax purposes will have on the income statements. Prepare the information for the president.

ANALYTICAL AND REVIEW PROBLEMS

Problem 28–1
A&R

Using the data given in the chapter, determine the federal and provincial income taxes for Mr. James Evans under the following conditions:

a. Assume that Mr. Evans resides in *your* province.
b. Use current year's amounts for:
  1. Personal deductions.
  2. Canada Pension Plan.
  3. Unemployment Insurance.
c. Use current year's federal and provincial income tax rates.

Problem 28–2
A&R

Income tax returns of Vachon Corporation reflected the following:

	Year Ended Dec. 31		
	19A	19B	19C
Royalty income	$ 60,000		
Investment income	30,000	$20,000	$40,000
Rent income	10,000	10,000	10,000
	$100,000	$30,000	$50,000
Deductible expenses	30,000	20,000	20,000
Taxable income	$ 70,000	$10,000	$30,000

Assume the average income tax rate for each year was 40%.

The only differences between taxable income on the tax returns and the pretax accounting income relate to royalty income. For accounting purposes, royalty income was recognized ratably (equally) over the three-year period.

Required:

Give journal entries such as would appear at the end of each year to reflect income tax and allocation. (CGA adapted)

Problem 28–3
A&R

The following are excerpts from the consolidated statements of financial positions, at December 31, 1985, and 1984, of Imperial Oil Limited and Stelco Inc.:

IMPERIAL OIL LIMITED

	1984	1985
Sources of capital employed:		
Long-term debt and other obligations (10, 18)	$1,184	$1,219
Commitments and contingent liabilities (12)		
Deferred income taxes (6)	$1,544	$1,610

STELCO INC.

	1985	1984
Other liabilities:		
Long-term debt (Note 11)	$572,156	$555,200
Deferred income taxes	239,537	250,626

Additionally, in the notes to the financial statements of Imperial Oil, (no explanatory note with regard to deferred taxes appears in the Stelco statement) the following appears:

Note 6. **Deferred income taxes.** The company complies with income-tax laws and pays income taxes when due. Deferred income taxes are not a tax liability under the law. They result from differences between income-tax legislation and conventional accounting treatments of certain revenues and expenses. The major difference results from the substitution of legislated allowances on capital costs for depreciation and amortization expenses.

From the presentation on the statement of financial position and notes thereto Stelco appears to consider deferred income taxes as a liability, while Imperial Oil does not.

Required:

Do you agree with Stelco's apparent position or with Imperial Oil's position? Explain your answer.

Microcomputer Software for Accounting Applications

This chapter prepared by Mr. John W. Yu, M.Sc., C.G.A., C.D.P.

29

After studying Chapter 29, you should be able to:

Explain how microcomputers can be used in the accounting process.

Describe the principles and applications of accounting and business programs.

Explain the key features found in accounting programs, spreadsheet programs, database programs, and word processing programs. Describe how these programs are used in businesses.

Describe examples of microcomputer programs used for accounting and business applications.

Define or explain the words and phrases listed in the chapter Glossary.

Chapter 6 gave a brief explanation of computerized data processing and microcomputers. This chapter expands on the material in Chapter 6, focusing on business data processing applications using microcomputers. This chapter will familiarize readers with the use of microcomputer programs for accounting. Although it provides a comprehensive introduction to the field, it does not teach specific skills or review specific programs in great detail. The material is presented in the context of decision making with the focus on software programs that assist this process. Therefore, the material covers principles and applications of accounting and business programs. "Guided tours" of selected microcomputer programs are used for illustration. The chapter assumes readers have no prior experience with microcomputers. Those who do have should use the headings and subheadings to guide them to any unfamiliar topics and concepts.

OVERVIEW OF COMPUTER SYSTEMS

Computers are used in virtually every facet of daily life. It is rare to find a professional accountant whose work is not affected by computers. In most successful enterprises, big and small, computers provide timely and accurate information that helps managers operate the business and make decisions. Many large corporations would find it impossible to operate more than a day or two without their computer systems.

Benefits from Computers

In addition to providing timely and accurate information, computers can also help streamline the operation of a business, reduce operating costs, and provide information economically and reliably. For example, with a computerized accounts receivable system, an accountant can track outstanding invoices more readily and accurately, thereby improving the company's cash flow. Using a computerized inventory system, a company can exercise better control over inventory levels and reduce unnecessary stock, thereby improving its profit margin. A properly developed computer system relieves accountants from many of the computational and informational management chores, thus freeing them to attend to the more important tasks of planning and control.

Development of Computers

The earliest form of a computation device is the Chinese abacus, invented about 5,000 years ago. Charles Babbage is generally recognized as the person who invented the first computer. The **difference engine,** built by Babbage in 1822, was a steam-driven mechanical calculator. In 1946, Mauchly and Eckert, both Americans, built an electronic digital computer called the ENIAC. Sperry Rand Corporation built the UNIVAC I

(Universal Automatic Computer I) to handle the 1952 U.S. census. Until the mid-1970s, computers were very large and expensive to acquire and operate. Microcomputers were first introduced in the mid-1970s after Intel Corporation invented the microprocessor in 1971. The Apple mircocomputer was introduced in 1977 and marked the beginning of a new era in computing. In August 1981, IBM introduced the IBM PC and made the microcomputer a standard piece of business equipment.

Although accounting applications were among the first business applications to be automated, the only accountants affected were those who worked for companies that could afford an expensive computer system. The microcomputer is the first computer that is readily available and affordable to large segments of the public. Medium to small businesses, which conduct a large percentage of the economic activities in an industrialized society, are suddenly able to afford computers. Accountants are finding that more and more of their employers or clients need and expect assistance in selecting and using microcomputers.

Uses of Microcomputers

Microcomputers can be used in almost every facet of a business. Virtually any task that is done with a pen and paper or calculator can be done on a microcomputer. Some application programs are designed to perform specific tasks such as accounting; some are designed to provide general facilities, such as calculating work sheets or keeping lists of information.

For instance, microcomputers can be used to:

1. Keep financial records and prepare financial statements.
2. Prepare and analyze trial balances.
3. Record and manage accounts receivables and payables.
4. Record payroll and issue payroll cheques.
5. Record and manage inventories.
6. Create and monitor budgets.
7. Track costs.
8. Prepare business projections.
9. Prepare reports and documents.

Microcomputers have many uses in the operation and management of a business, whether small or large. Various programs used will be discussed in this chapter including the following:

General ledger programs are designed to keep the financial records of a business. General ledger programs perform functions similar to general ledgers kept manually.

Accounts receivable and **accounts payable programs** can be used to accurately record accounts receivable and accounts payable.

Payroll programs can be used to alleviate many of the payroll record-keeping chores of a business employing more than a dozen employees.

Inventory programs are used to record and manage inventories and to provide timely and accurate inventory counts and reduce inventory stocking costs. Microcomputer programs such as **database and management programs** can also be used to manage inventories.

Spreadsheet programs can be used to create and monitor budgets and to track costs. Variance analysis can be easily performed using such programs. Spreadsheet programs can also be used to prepare business projections, such as sales and revenue forecasts, cash flow requirement planning, and cost projections.

Word processing programs are examples of microcomputer programs designed to assist in the preparation of written business reports and documents, including proposals, legal contracts, status reports, and general correspondence. Word processing programs not only perform the functions of an electronic typewriter, they can also check spelling and display thesaurus references.

To summarize, better management decisions can be made with accurate and timely information. Microcomputers, if used effectively, can provide this information.

Components of Microcomputers

A basic understanding of the microcomputer's hardware and software components will help readers learn more about the use of the microcomputer for business applications. A glossary of commonly used technical terms is included at the end of this chapter. The bibliography at the end of this chapter provides a list of selected additional readings.

HARDWARE. Like a stereo system, a microcomputer system is made up of components: hardware and software. In a microcomputer system, the *hardware* components are equivalent to the electronics of a stereo system; the software components can be compared to the songs recorded on a record or cassette tape.

Most microcomputer systems have the following hardware components:

1. A **system unit** composed of a microprocessor, *memory,* and supporting electronic circuits. This system unit is usually encased in a box. The microprocessor is the **brain** of the microcomputer and performs calculations. Memory serves as a **scratch pad;** it holds information needed by the microprocessor. Memory is measured in units of K-bytes. Each *byte* can hold one character, and a K-byte holds 1,024 characters. For example, a microcomputer with

256K bytes of memory can hold 262,144 characters for use by the microprocessor.

2. **Disk storage** is accomplished by one or more floppy disk drives or hard disk drives. A *floppy disk* can hold an amount of information equivalent to approximately 120 typed pages. A *hard disk* can hold information equivalent to that contained on 30 to 60 floppy disks.

3. A **keyboard** is used for data and command entries. The layout of a computer keyboard is similar to that of a typewriter.

4. A **display monitor** is used for displaying information. The display monitor is a TV-like device. The microcomputer relays the results of calculations or information processing through the display monitor. Also, when data or commands are typed on the keyboard, they are **echoed** on the display monitor for the user's verification.

5. A **printer** is used for hard copy output. The printer has a printing mechanism similar to that of a typewriter and prints results of calculations or information processing on paper.

SOFTWARE. There are two kinds of *software* that run on a microcomputer: (1) operating systems and (2) application programs. A computer requires an operating system in order to work. This system is a collection of computer programs designed to control the hardware components. For example, the IBM PC, a popular microcomputer, uses the operating system called PC-DOS (Personal Computer—Disk Operating System). *Application programs,* on the other hand, are designed to perform specific business tasks; for example, keeping the financial records of a business, saving and printing a document, and keeping track of accounts receivable. We will learn more about application programs in this chapter.

The IBM PC and Compatibles

There are many different microcomputers on the market. The various makes of microcomputers use different operating systems and are incompatible with one another. That is, a computer program that runs on one make of microcomputer with a particular operating system does not run on another type with a different operating system.

Of the many different makes, the IBM PC dominates. And many microcomputers are designed to be compatible with the IBM PC. These compatibles use the operating system MS-DOS (Microsoft Disk Operating System), which is compatible with PC-DOS. Because of the wide acceptance of the IBM PC and compatibles, there is a good collection of application programs that run on these microcomputers. In general, most application programs written to operate under PC-DOS will run on microcomputers that use MS-DOS. This chapter will focus on application programs that run under PC-DOS.

OVERVIEW OF THE OPERATING SYSTEM

The operating system is an integrated set of computer programs designed to control the operation of the computer hardware. The operating system for the IBM PC and compatible microcomputers is designed by Microsoft Corporation. This operating system is generally referred to as *DOS*. In order to use the microcomputer, the user must instruct it using commands called DOS commands.

DOS Commands

The operating system of a microcomputer is commonly stored on a floppy disk called a DOS disk. The disk must be mounted in a floppy disk drive when the computer is turned on so that DOS can be loaded into the microcomputer. The user can then direct DOS to perform desired operations or load an application program. The following is a brief description of some commonly used DOS commands.

COPY.   Duplicates one or more files from one disk to another disk.

DIR[ectory].   Lists the name of all files on a disk.

DISKCOPY.   Duplicates the contents of a floppy disk to another disk. It is common practice to use the DISKCOPY command to prepare a working copy of an application program.

ERASE.   Deletes one or more files on a disk.

FORMAT.   Prepares a new disk so that it will be able to accept data.

RENAME.   Changes the name of a file on a disk.

APPLICATION PROGRAMS FOR BUSINESS

There are numerous application programs that run on the IBM PC and compatible microcomputers. These application programs include accounting and business software, graphics software, statistical software, education software, and games. The main concern in this chapter is the accounting and business software. These application programs can be grouped into four categories: accounting, spreadsheet, database, and word processing programs. Accounting programs are used to manage the accounting records of a business. Spreadsheet programs are used to calculate columnar work sheets and to perform "what-if" analyses. Database programs enable information, such as inventory or customer lists, to be filed and managed. Word processing programs are useful for preparing documents, business proposals, and correspondence.

Features of Accounting Programs

Accounting programs can be used to computerize a company's accounting system. Automated transaction processing is faster and more accurate than manual methods. Accounting programs can be used to manage the major accounting applications of general ledger, accounts payable, accounts receivable, inventory, payroll, and job costing. The better built accounting systems **integrate** these major accounting applications.

The term *integrate* refers to an accounting system that links the general ledger, accounts payable, accounts receivable, inventory, payroll, and job costing programs. Information (usually in the form of transactions) can be posted from one program to another automatically (without re-keying). Almost all integrated accounting systems available on microcomputers permit individual programs to run independently as well as enable the user to add programs later. Accounting systems that are not integrated require information to be re-keyed from one program to another. Such systems are not as desirable as integrated ones.

Basic Principles of Accounting Programs

An accounting system is usually made up of a collection of programs that accept and keep financial transactions. Most accounting systems provide menus that are displayed on the screen. By selecting one of the choices presented in a *menu,* users can direct the accounting system to take a specific action—for example, accept new transactions from the keyboard, post a batch of transactions into the general ledger, or print a set of financial statements. A computerized accounting system stores information in *files.* A file is a collection of related information saved on a disk. In general, three types of files are used:

1. **Profile file.** A file that keeps permanent information on the company, such as company name, address, and fiscal periods.
2. **Master file.** A file that keeps the information essential for the operation of the accounting program. The information stored in a *master file* is permanent, and it is usually organized into accounts.

The following are examples of the various master files:
a. The master file of a general ledger program keeps information on the **chart of accounts** and the account balances.
b. The master file of an accounts payable keeps information on the **vendors** and account balances.
c. The master file of an accounts receivable keeps information on the **customers** and account balances.
d. The master file of an inventory system keeps information on the **inventory** items, cost, markup, and count.

3. **Transaction file.** A file that holds detailed information on transactions. The information stored in a *transaction file* is not permanent. A transaction file is purged after all the totals have been distributed to the master file and an audit trail has been printed. The transaction file of a general ledger holds the journal entries, whereas that of an accounts receivable holds records of invoices and payment receipts.

An integrated accounting system is generally designed so that a transaction only needs to be entered into the system once. A transaction is the entry of a single value (either debit or credit) into the computer files. Therefore, a journal entry is represented by two transactions; for example:

Journal entry on paper:

```
Interest Expense  ......................................  500.00
      Bond Interest Payable  ..............................          500.00
```

Transactions:

The following illustrates how to enter the above journal entry into a computerized accounting system. The text on the left would appear on the screen as ''prompts'' to the accountant. The actual keystrokes used to enter the figures are shown in boldface.

```
Transaction Number [    1]
Account          [    750]
Amount    Dr.[   50000]    Cr.[              ]

Transaction Number [    2]
Account          [    550]
Amount    Dr.[          ]    Cr.[    50000]
```

Most accounting systems have built-in facilities to control the posting of transaction entries so the general ledger is always in balance. For an integrated accounting system, transaction files (say, in the general ledger program and accounts receivable program) are cross-referenced by account numbers so account balances from one program can be posted to another automatically.

For some accounting systems (e.g., ACCPAC, a popular accounting system), transactions are entered into an accounting system via a *video form,* also known as a **video screen,** or **input screen.** A video form is functionally equivalent to a paper form. Some accounting systems use on-screen dialogues instead of video forms—instead of ''filling'' a video form, users type the answers to the questions presented on the screen.

General Ledger Programs

The general ledger (G/L) is the heart of any integrated accounting system. Like the manually kept general ledger, it keeps all the financial records of a business. The master file of a general ledger program is the chart of accounts. The major activities carried out by the general ledger program can be grouped into four types:

1. Transaction processing.
2. Account posting.
3. Working paper printing.
4. Financial statement preparation.

Illustration 29–1 shows the flow of activities of a typical general ledger program.

Some general ledger programs provide flexible numbering for the chart of accounts, while some use account names rather than account numbers. Many programs can handle data identified by department. Department codes are usually coded into account numbers. Some general

Illustration 29–1 General Ledger Activity Chart

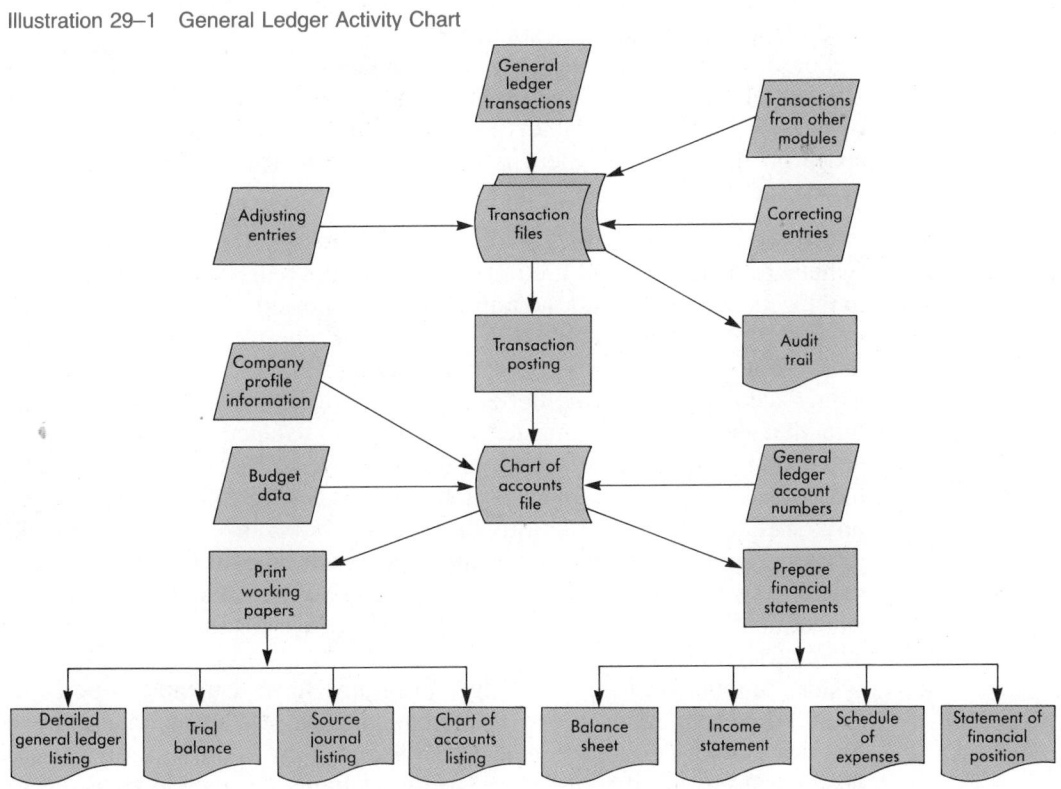

ledger programs use fixed account number ranges; for example, account numbers 100 to 199 are reserved for assets, 200 to 299 for liabilities, and so on. Although most businesses can work within this constraint, it is an undesirable feature of an accounting program. All except the very basic general ledger programs can handle a large number of accounts. A general ledger program that can handle only a small number of accounts is usually not worthwhile.

TRANSACTION PROCESSING. Many general ledger programs use transaction batches. A transaction *batch* is a group of transactions usually but not necessarily related by activity or by date. Transaction batches are held in the transaction file until posted to the general ledger. Transactions held in the transaction file can be edited anytime prior to posting to the master file of the general ledger. For an integrated accounting system, the general ledger program also accepts transaction batches from other programs, such as accounts receivable or accounts payable. Some general ledger programs accept transactions directly into the transaction file without going through batches. Many general ledger programs can handle transactions that recur monthly. Many expenses that occur once a year but are distributed on a monthly basis can be structured as recurring transactions; for example, monthly distribution of insurance costs, fixed asset depreciation, and payable accruals.

For most general ledger programs running on a hard disk, the maximum number of transactions per fiscal period is only limited by the amount of hard disk space available. Because of the limited amount of storage space on floppy disks, there is usually some restriction on the number of transactions per fiscal period.

ACCOUNT POSTING. Transactions held in the transaction file (whether batched or not) are not reflected in the balances of the accounts in the general ledger until the transactions are posted. The posting process is similar to that in a manual system; that is, the totals from the books of original entry are posted to (entered into) the appropriate general ledger accounts. In a computerized general ledger, transactions are posted into the general ledger master file, and the balances of the accounts updated. For general ledger programs that use transaction batches, any batch that is not in balance will not be posted. Some general ledger programs will post transactions that are not in balance but will provide the appropriate warning or error message. Such general ledger programs usually have a built-in means of keeping the general ledger in balance by automatically creating correcting transactions in an error-correcting account.

All computerized general ledger programs have a means to perform year-end posting. This process automatically closes the income and expense accounts to the retained earnings accounts at the end of a fiscal year. Usually, the income and expense accounts are then **zeroed** out in the general ledger to start the new fiscal year.

Transactions are posted to the general ledger without the use of subsidiary ledgers. Instead of subsidiary ledgers, many general ledger programs allow the grouping of transactions into **source journals;** each source journal being equivalent to a subsidiary ledger. These source journals, such as cash disbursement, cash receipts, and payroll distribution, are not separate entities, but merely names associated with transactions.

WORKING PAPER PRINTING.   Most accounting systems print an audit trail and working papers on demand. Printed journal listings provide the audit trail for internal control purposes. To enforce an audit trail, many general ledger programs require that the posted transactions be printed before they can be purged (deleted) from the transaction file. The transaction listing forms part of the working file for the auditor.

Other working papers produced by most general ledger programs include:

1.   Detailed general ledger listing.
2.   Trial balance.
3.   Listing of the source journals.
4.   Chart of account listing.

As explained in Chapter 6, in a manual accounting system of any size, transaction details are usually kept in subsidiary ledgers. To review transactions, the subsidiary ledgers must be examined. In a computerized general ledger, transactions are reviewed by examining a printout called the **general ledger listing,** which provides a list of all transactions posted to the general ledger accounts. Most general ledger programs permit the user to select all accounts or ranges of accounts for the general ledger listing. Some programs permit the listing of transactions for specified fiscal periods.

With a manual system, a **trial balance** is prepared at the end of an accounting period after all of the regular entries have been entered into the general ledger. As described in Chapter 2, a trial balance is a work sheet used to verify that the debits equal the credits in the general ledger. A trial balance is used to review accounting balances and prepare adjusting entries before the financial statements are prepared. Doing a trial balance by hand can be time-consuming and frustrating, particularly if it does not balance. A computerized general ledger system can produce a trial balance by a few simple keystrokes. Because the general ledger is always in balance, the debits and credits in such a trial balance always match. The trial balance in a general ledger system is used to review account balances. Almost all general ledger systems permit the listing of the trial balance at any time.

Source journals are used in general ledger programs to group transactions of the same nature, much the same way subsidiary ledgers do. Most general ledger programs provide a facility to print a **source journal**

listing, which shows all the transactions belonging to the same source journal.

The **chart of accounts listing** is a handy reference when entering transactions into the transaction file. All general ledger programs provide a means of listing the chart of accounts on the printer. The information printed usually includes all the general ledger accounts in numeric sequence (or alphabetical order if numbers are not used for accounts), account name, and type.

FINANCIAL STATEMENT PREPARATION.　One of the major differences between general ledger programs is in the preparation of financial statements. Many general ledger programs provide standard formats for financial statements as well as some means of customizing these statements. Some formats offer very limited capabilities in customizing financial statements; others offer powerful but complex commands. A kind of specification language for the user to indicate required statement format is often provided in the program. A specification language is similar to a programming language—it is used to control how financial statements appear. Unfortunately, most specification languages require practice before they can be mastered. The ability to customize financial reports is one of the most important features to consider in selecting a computerized general ledger program. Such a function must be easy to use but powerful enough to meet all a company's statement preparation needs. Financial statement formats available from most general ledger programs include:

1. Balance sheet.
2. Income statement.
3. Schedule of expenses.
4. Statement of changes in financial position.

All the popular general ledger programs provide a means of producing statements that compare the current period with prior periods. Some of the more sophisticated general ledger programs include the capability to produce financial statements for any prior period (within certain limits) as well as for the current period. Many programs provide a means to enter budget figures into the general ledger accounts and to produce statements comparing the actual figures with the budget.

The ability to group several accounts into one entry in the financial statements is an important feature. For example, in a balance sheet, it may be desirable to show the total for all current asset accounts in one line. Different general ledger programs offer various capabilities to show subtotals and totals. For the income statement, subtotals and totals should be provided for gross income, cost of goods sold, administrative and selling expenses, and net income. For the balance sheet, subtotals and totals should be provided for current assets, fixed assets, and total assets on the asset side; and current liabilities, long-term liabilities, equity, and retained earnings on the liabilities and equity side. In general, the more sophisticated the financial statement preparation capabilities of the general ledger program, the harder the program is to learn. Ideally, the general ledger program should combine sophisticated format control with ease of use.

Accounts Receivable Programs

Managing accounts receivable is a critical activity for many enterprises. In many integrated accounting systems, the accounts receivable program can be used separately. Later, when the general ledger program is added, the accounts receivable program can be integrated into the general ledger program with relative ease. Some businesses start computerizing their accounting systems by installing the accounts receivable program first. The following are activities carried out by the accounts receivable program:

1. Invoice processing.
2. Payment receipts.
3. Report printing.
4. Interface to the general ledger.

Illustration 29–2 shows the flow of activities in a typical accounts receivable program. The customer file contains the key information for an accounts receivable program. This information usually includes customer number, customer name, address, telephone number, contact person, year-to-date sales, and credit limit. The customer file should be able to handle the company's total number of customers. The customer file in some accounts receivable programs has a very limited capacity. On a hard disk, the maximum number of vendors and invoices is only limited by the amount of space available. Many small businesses can work quite comfortably within this space. Floppy disks, however, place more restrictions on how many transactions can be stored. A good accounts receivable program should show the user how to determine the maximum number of transactions permissible for either a hard or floppy disk.

INVOICE PROCESSING. There are basically three types of accounts receivable transactions: (1) invoices, (2) cash receipts, and (3) adjustments. As with general ledger programs, some accounts receivable programs require that invoices and adjustments be entered in batches. Others allow direct entry into the transaction file. In either case, the entries in the transaction file can be modified before they are posted to the customer file. In order to provide an audit trail, transactions posted to the customer file are usually printed. Invoice information that needs to be entered includes customer number, invoice number, invoice date, and invoice amount.

PAYMENT RECEIPTS. Two methods of accounting for payment receipts are normally used. One is the **open item** method, in which payment

Illustration 29–2 Accounts Receivable Activity Chart

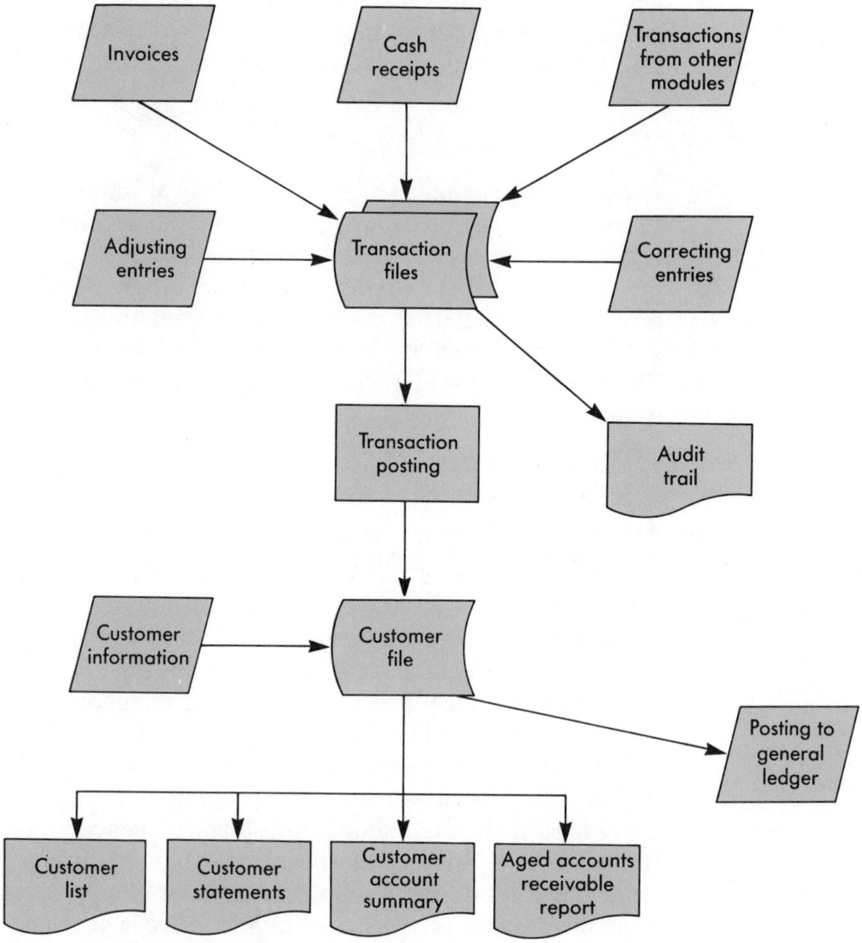

receipts are matched to open invoices. The other is the **balance forward** method, in which payment receipts are applied to customers' account balances. Many accounts receivable programs can handle either method. To record a payment for the open item method, the payment receipts must be credited against an open invoice. In this case, the customer number and invoice number must be specified. If the balance forward method is used, the customer number is the key for recording the payment. The accounts receivable program must also provide a means of recording miscellaneous cash transactions, including cash sales and interest.

REPORT PRINTING. Reports generated by an accounts receivable program are usually in fixed format; it is rare that the report format can be altered. Reports commonly available include the following:

1. Customer list.
2. Customer statements.
3. Customer account summary.
4. Aged accounts receivable report.

Customer List. This is an alphabetical listing of customer information in the customer file, including customer name, address, and other related information.

Customer Statements. Many accounts payable programs can print customer statements for notifying customers of the status of their accounts. It is important that the program provide a means of designing customized statements because preprinted forms vary considerably.

Customer Account Summary. This summary is used to review the status of individual customers. Most accounts receivable programs permit listing by selected ranges of customer numbers or customer names. The summary should include outstanding balances, credit limits, and last transaction dates.

Aged Accounts Receivable Report. This report is used to review overdue customer accounts. Some programs have fixed aged periods, usually 30, 60, 90, and 120 days. Other programs provide more flexibility and permit the user to specify several aged periods.

INTERFACE TO GENERAL LEDGER. An accounts receivable program that is part of an integrated accounting system can automatically post general ledger entries resulting from accounts receivable transactions. The general ledger entries are usually posted to the receivable control account, a cash account, and possibly an interest account and a discount account. Some integrated accounting systems have predetermined general ledger accounts for posting from the accounts receivable program; others allow these accounts to be specified at system setup time.

Accounts Payable Program

Any business that handles a large number of cheques and has a multitude of vendors should consider using a computerized accounts payable program. An accounts payable program can be used to optimize the timing of payments and to take maximum advantage of early payment discounts. It can also be used to plan cash requirements. Many accounts receivable programs also print cheques and cheque registers. In many integrated accounting systems, the accounts payable program can run separately or as one part of the integrated accounting system. In the latter case, the accounts payable program accumulates and summarizes general ledger entries that result from accounts payable transactions. Usually only the totals are posted to the general ledger control accounts. In this manner, the accounts payable program keeps the accounts payable subsidiary ledger used in manual accounting systems. The major activities carried out by the accounts payable program are:

1. Payment invoice processing.
2. Cheque processing.
3. Report printing.
4. Interface to the general ledger.

Illustration 29–3 shows the flow of activities of a typical accounts payable program.

The vendor file contains the key information for an accounts payable program including vendor number, vendor name, address, telephone number, contact person, and terms of payment. It is important that the vendor file be able to handle the total number of vendors for the business. The vendor file in some accounts payable programs has a very limited capacity. The maximum number of vendors and invoices are more limited if the vendor file is stored on a floppy disk than if it is stored on a hard disk. A good accounts payable program should show the user how to calculate the maximum number of vendors and invoices permissible for either a hard or floppy disk.

Illustration 29–3   Accounts Payable Activity Chart

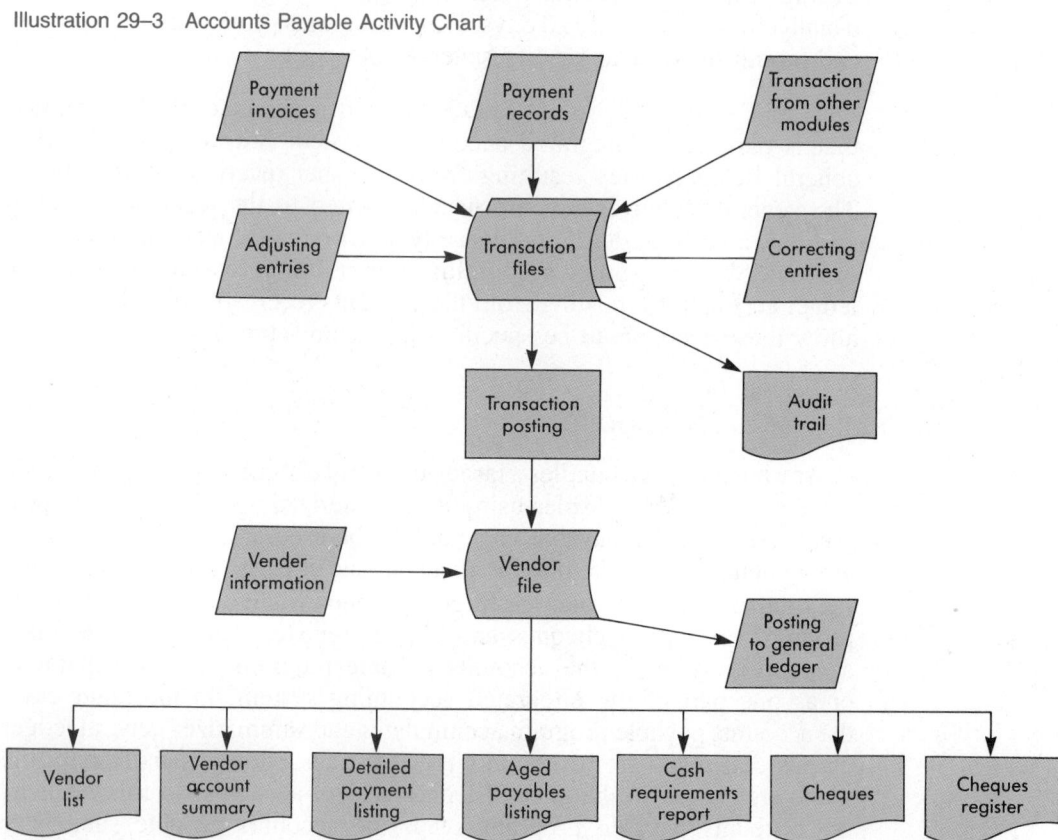

PAYMENT INVOICE PROCESSING. Accounts payable transactions are basically of two types: purchase invoices and adjustments. As with general ledger programs, while some accounts payable programs require that purchase invoices and adjustments be entered in batches, other programs allow direct entry into the transaction file. In either case, the entries in the transaction file can be modified before they are posted to the accounts payable master file. Once posted, reversing entries are required to remove or modify the effect of the posted transactions. In processing accounts payable, similar to processing accounts receivable, two methods of recording payment invoices are normally used. One is the **open item** method in which every transaction has a unique invoice number and payments are recorded against specific invoices. The other method is the **balance forward** method under which payments are applied against the vendor's account balance instead of specific invoices. Invoice information that needs to be entered includes: vendor number, invoice number, date invoice received, date due, total amount, and discount option.

CHEQUE PROCESSING. Usually, cheque processing includes the printing of payment cheques and payment advice notices. Not all accounts payable programs include a cheque processing function. The program should permit users to customize the format of cheques and payment advice notices.

REPORT PRINTING. The printing of an audit trail is an important safeguard that should be provided by the accounts payable program. Other reports commonly available include the following:

1. Vendor list.
2. Vendor account summary.
3. Detailed payment listing.
4. Aged payables listing.
5. Cash requirement report.

Vendor List. This is a listing of vendor information in alphabetical order from the vendor file. Vendor information printed includes vendor name, address, phone number, and contact person.

Vendor Account Summary. Usually, accounts payable programs provide a means to print a vendor account summary for selected vendors. Selection is either by vendor number or vendor name. The summary should at least include year-to-date purchases, total payment outstanding, and last payment date.

Detailed Payment. This listing is a printout of all outstanding payment invoices and associated transactions in the vendor accounts. Usually, only vendors with amounts owing are listed.

Aged Payable Listing. Most account payable programs provide some means to age outstanding payables. An aged payable listing is one such means. This report lists all outstanding payables, aged either by fixed time intervals (usually 30, 60, and 90 days) or by user specification.

Cash Requirement Report. One of the most useful reports from an accounts payable program is the cash requirement report. This report is used to plan cash requirements to pay the outstanding payables.

INTERFACE TO GENERAL LEDGER. For an accounts payable program that is part of an integrated accounting system, this facility automatically summarizes and posts general ledger entries resulting from accounts payable transactions.

Features of Spreadsheet Programs

Spreadsheet programs are used to replace columnar work sheets which are constructed using pencil, paper, and a calculator. Chapter 4 introduced the process of preparing a trial balance using a work sheet. This process can be simplified if the trial balance is prepared on an electronic spreadsheet. Electronic *spreadsheets* can also be used in many other business activities, including cash flow projection, tax planning, budgeting, sales and profit forecasting, income statements, and balance sheets. Spreadsheet programs are most useful for "what-if" analyses; that is, by changing some of the key parameters in a spreadsheet, the entire spreadsheet can be recalculated in a few seconds. For example, using a "what-if" analysis, a financial analyst can examine the effect of interest rate changes on a stock portfolio. Spreadsheet programs are ideally suited for financial planning.

The first spreadsheet program, VisiCalc®, was invented in 1978 by Robert Frankston and Dan Bricklin. In 1980, Sorcim Corporation introduced SuperCalc. Mitch Kapor and Jonathan Sachs of Lotus Development Corporation introduced the popular Lotus® 1-2-3 in 1983. By then, spreadsheet programs had proved their usefulness in the business environment. Until the introduction of VisiCalc, accountants had to prepare work sheets manually, assisted only by a calculator. With a paper work sheet, any change requires manual recalculation of all the affected entries. Sometimes, the amount of recalculation can be extensive and time-consuming. For this reason, a complicated work sheet (e.g., a 24-month cash projection) can take hours to prepare and refine. With an electronic spreadsheet, once the formulas have been entered, any changes involving recalculation can be made quickly and automatically.

Many spreadsheet programs are multifunction and integrated. Usually multifunction spreadsheet programs can display graphs and manage data records as well as calculate spreadsheets. If changes made on a spreadsheet are reflected automatically in associated graphs and data records, then the functions of spreadsheet, graph display, and data management are said to be integrated. Most spreadsheet programs have the following features:

1. A large number of columns and rows (e.g., 256 columns by 8,192 rows). The intersection of a column and a row is called a *cell.*
2. Keys (called cursor keys) to control the positioning of the active cell. The active cell is the cell in which data is entered from the keyboard.
3. **Commands** to make changes to (edit) spreadsheets.
4. A **menu** of commands that enables the user to format the screen display, save and print spreadsheets, and perform many other functions.
5. *Formulas* that use arithmetic and logical operators to calculate a value in a cell.
6. A set of built-in *functions* to accomplish complex arithmetic, financial, or logical calculations. For example, present value of a stream of future cash payments can be instantly computed by means of a built-in present value function that incorporates the formula and performs the calculation.
7. Display of information in the form of bar graphs, line graphs, and pie charts.
8. A means to sort and look up data records stored in a spreadsheet.

Basic Principles of Spreadsheet Programs

A spreadsheet program stores information in cells. A cell is the intersection of a column and a row. Columns are identified by alphabets—the first column is column A, the second column is column B, and so on. (Some spreadsheet programs, notably Multiplan, use numbers instead of alphabets to name columns.) Rows are identified by numbers—the first row is row 1, the second row is row 2, and so on. Therefore, the entry found in cell D6 is the entry in the fourth column, sixth row of the spreadsheet. Illustration 29–4 shows an example of a paper worksheet. Illustration 29–5 is an example of an equivalent electronic spreadsheet. Illustration 29–6 shows the same spreadsheet displaying the formulas stored in the cells.

On a **paper work sheet,** an entry is always shown as a label or a number, even though the number may be the result of a complicated formula. Footnotes are used to document complicated formulas used in the work sheet. On a **electronic spreadsheet,** an entry in a cell may be a label, a number, or a formula. If a cell contains a formula, the user can have either the formula or the result of the calculation shown on the spreadsheet.

TYPES OF FILES.   Electronic spreadsheets are stored on disks as files. Most spreadsheet programs have several types of files:

Spreadsheet File.   This file stores all the values and formulas of a spreadsheet. It also stores characteristics of the spreadsheet, including the appearance (display format) of the columns and rows. Changes can

Illustration 29–4   Example of a Paper Worksheet

LARRY OWEN, LAWYER
Trial Balance
July 31, 19—

Cash	$1,185	
Prepaid rent	900	
Office supplies	60	
Office equipment	4,000	
Accounts payable		$ 260
Unearned legal fees		450
Larry Owen, capital		5,000
Larry Owen, withdrawals	200	
Legal fees earned		1,500
Office salaries expense	800	
Telephone expense	30	
Heating and lighting expense	35	
Totals	$7,210	$7,210

Illustration 29–5   Example of an Electronic Spreadsheet (display computed results)

```
  ¦  A  ¦¦  B  ¦¦  C  ¦¦  D  ¦¦  E  ¦¦  F  ¦
 1
 2                          LARRY OWEN, LAWYER
 3                            Trial Balance
 4                            July 31, 19--
 5
 6  Cash                            $1,185
 7  Prepaid rent                       900
 8  Office supplies                     60
 9  Office equipment                 4,000
10  Accounts payable                              260
11  Unearned legal fees                           450
12  Larry Owen, capital                         5,000
13  Larry Owen, withdrawals            200
14  Legal fees earned                           1,500
15  Office salaries expense            800
16  Telephone expense                   30
17  Heating and lighting expense        35
18                                  ------   ------
19       Totals                     $7,210   $7,210
20                                  ======   ======
```

Illustration 29–6   Example of an Electronic Spreadsheet (displaying formulas)

```
      |  A  ||  B  ||.  C  ||  D  ||    E    ||   F   |
  1
  2                          LARRY OWEN, LAWYER
  3                            Trial Balance
  4                            July 31, 19--
  5
  6   Cash                               1185
  7   Prepaid rent                        900
  8   Office supplies                      60
  9   Office equipment                   4000
 10   Accounts payable                              260
 11   Unearned legal fees                           450
 12   Larry Owen, capital                          5000
 13   Larry Owen, withdrawals            200
 14   Legal fees earned                            1500
 15   Office salaries expense            800
 16   Telephone expense                   30
 17   Heating and lighting expense        35
 18                                  ----------  ---------
 19        Totals                   SUM(E6:E17) SUM(F6:F17)
 20                                  ==========  =========
```

be made to a spreadsheet file by retrieving it to the screen and keying in changes to its content or format.

Print File.   This file stores the spreadsheet as it appears in printed output. A print file of a spreadsheet (or some part of it) may be merged with a document produced with a word processing program. Thus, a user can integrate both text and spreadsheet into a report.

Graph File.   This file stores the graph as it appears on the monitor screen. Some spreadsheet programs require that a graph file be saved on disk first before the graph is printed. Other programs can print a graph directly without using a graph file.

BUILT-IN FUNCTIONS.   All spreadsheet programs provide built-in functions to calculate arithmetic or financial formulas, including the more complex ones. The following functions are found in all spreadsheet programs:

Arithmetic Functions.   These include functions used to compute the sum, average, maximum, minimum, and standard deviation of numbers stored in a range of cells. Another arithmetic function useful to accountants is the square root of a number. Trigonometric functions such as sine, cosine, and tangent are also usually provided.

Logical Functions.   These functions provide the means to compare values in cells or to test for certain conditions. The most commonly used logical function is the IF function.

Financial Functions.   These functions are essential to the accountant and are used to calculate present values, future values, internal rate of returns, and annuity payments.

Special Functions. Most spreadsheet programs have their own set of special functions. Some are used to look up values in columns of cells, and others are used to test for error conditions in a cell.

Most spreadsheet programs can print the spreadsheet with cells showing computed results as well as underlying formulas. It is important to be able to print the formulas used in a spreadsheet so that the logic and accuracy of the formulas can be checked. Printing the formulas also provides documentation and an audit trail.

SPREADSHEET COMMANDS. All spreadsheet programs provide commands for the user to control the program's operation. The power of a spreadsheet program is measured by the number and variety of commands it can recognize. The functions provided by commands include the capacity to:

1. Erase the content of cells or the entire spreadsheet.
2. Insert and delete rows or columns.
3. Retrieve, save, and delete spreadsheets on disk.
4. Copy formulas from cells to cells.
5. Specify the appearance of numbers or text in cells; for example, displaying numbers as dollar amounts or centering labels.
6. Display and print bar graphs, line graphs, and pie charts.
7. Print spreadsheets on paper.
8. Sort columns of numbers.
9. Look up a specific value in a column or row of numbers.

MACROS. Some spreadsheet programs provide a facility to **automate** any sequence of spreadsheet commands or tasks. This facility is called a ***macro***. A macro is essentially a small file of commands in a user-built sequence of steps; each step represents an instruction to the spreadsheet program. Activating a macro usually involves pressing one or two keys. Each time a macro is activated, the spreadsheet program carries out all the stored steps as if the instructions had been typed in one by one. For example, printing a spreadsheet on paper can take several steps. A macro can be built to store all the steps involved. Then, when users want to print a spreadsheet, all they have to do is activate the printing macro. In general macros are used to: (1) reduce the number of keystrokes involved in repetitive tasks and (2) build spreadsheets for inexperienced users by "hiding" all the complex commands and keystrokes in what appears to be a single command.

DATA MANAGEMENT. Some spreadsheet programs contain powerful data management functions. Data management functions enable users to sort tables of information (data tables) into ascending or descending order; search for specific values in data tables; and extract records from data tables according to specified selection criteria. Statistical values, such as totals, averages, and standard deviations from data tables, can also be computed.

Applications of Spreadsheet Programs

Integrated spreadsheet programs can be used to prepare and analyze the following:

1. Comparative financial statements.
2. Ratio analysis on financial statements.
3. Budgets.
4. Cash flow projections.
5. Loan amortizations.
6. Inventory management systems.
7. Sales and revenue forecasts.
8. Investment portfolio schedules.
9. Fixed assets management.
10. Accounts receivable aging.
11. Accounts payable management.
12. Capital budgeting.
13. Project management (including Gantt charts).

Features of Database Programs

No business can operate without information and some system of information management. Consequently, information is stored in manila files, which are arranged in filing cabinets in some sort of order (e.g., chronological or alphabetical). While accounting and spreadsheet programs are designed to store and manipulate numeric data, database programs are specifically designed to manage administrative and business data. For example, a database program can store the names and addresses of customers, employees, or vendors. It can also store mailing lists for sales promotion, personnel data, and information on prospective clients or customers.

A *database* is a collection of related data stored in a file or a set of files; it can be visualized as an electronic filing cabinet. As with paper files, database records are stored in some logical order. Searching through conventional files for specific information can consume a lot of time. Searching through a database, on the other hand, is fast and usually more reliable.

Database programs have been available on large computers for many years. dBASE II® was perhaps the first widely accepted database program on microcomputers and has been updated several times, most recently as dBASE III PLUS®. Introduced in 1980 by Ashton-Tate, it was an instant success. Many other programs followed, including R:Base 4000,

Knowledgeman®, and Revelation. Database programs provide capabilities different from those provided by other business programs. Stored data can be selectively retrieved and correlated; for example, if vendor information is stored in a database file, the user can rapidly retrieve and print information on vendors by selected criteria such as city or province. Notice that users cannot select vendors using these criteria if vendor information is stored only in an accounts payable file. Accounting programs should not be used to store information that does not reflect the company's accounting records. For example, information on prospective clients clearly does not belong in any accounting file, yet it can be just as important for the business; such information belongs in a database. Most database programs have the following features:

1. Capacity for a large number of data records.
2. Commands to define the contents (structure) of data records.
3. Commands to add, change, and delete data records in a database.
4. A means to sort data records according to some specified criteria.
5. Commands to retrieve data records using one or more selection criteria.
6. A means to print reports selecting records from a database.

BASIC PRINCIPLES OF DATABASE PROGRAMS.   A database program stores information in **database files** which consist of **data records.** A data record contains all the information for a particular entity; for example, if the database file is used to keep track of prospective clients, a data record can be made up of all relevant information on a prospective client. A data record is also made up of *fields*. Each field contains an individual piece of data for each data record; for example, the name of a prospective client can form a field and so can the address of a prospective client.

Most database programs classify fields by field types, of which the most common are character, numeric, and logical. A **character field** holds character information, such as names and addresses. A **numeric field,** on the other hand, contains numbers and can be used in calculations; for example, age and annual salary are stored in numeric fields. A **logical field** contains a logical value, usually "true" or "false"; for example, a field containing information on whether the prospective client has a credit problem is a logical field—it contains only the logical value true or false. Some database programs require that fields be of fixed lengths; that is, when a field is set up, the user must tell the program how many characters or digits the field can hold. Other database programs allow any number of characters or digits to be entered into a field.

Most database programs provide a means to generate reports, which contain information retrieved from the database according to some selection criteria and presented in a predefined format.

Features of Word Processing Programs

Word processing programs are important tools for business. Many people have the misconception that word processing programs are only useful to clerical staff. But word processing programs are equally valuable for managers or accountants.

The most significant feature of a word processing program is that it lets the user change (edit) a report or document without retyping it. Blocks of text can be moved within the document (cut and pasted) or between documents. Repetitive text, such as standard paragraphs in form letters, can be easily copied and combined. The format (e.g., margin or pagination) of a document can be changed with a few keystrokes. Users save additional time because only the changes need to be reread in an edited document.

All word processing programs perform *word-wrap* automatically at the end of a line, thus freeing the writer from having to determine where the line should end. Lines are adjusted automatically to subsequent additions or deletions. Most word processing programs start a new page automatically when a page is full, but also permit the writer to begin a new page at will. Some programs permit multiple columns of text to be typed on a page without the laborious calculation and setting of tabs required on a typewriter. Other functions enable the writer to generate a table of contents or to index automatically; this operation is particularly useful for long reports. Word processing programs can help managers and accountants organize and express ideas and refine a draft without constant recourse to clerical help.

A word processing program is more than just an electronic typewriter, particularly when it is used in conjunction with other microcomputer programs. For example, in a financing proposal, users may wish to include a cash flow projection spreadsheet that they developed using a spreadsheet program. The most efficient (and error-proof) method is to **import** the cash flow spreadsheet electronically into the financial proposal without retyping. Word processing programs can also be used to improve the quality of reports. Many of these programs provide a built-in electronic dictionary and thesaurus. By pressing a key, the user can command the dictionary to check the spelling of a word, a page, or the entire document. An online thesaurus provides instant access to a range of word choices. In situations where standard paragraphs are used in different documents, word processing programs are particularly invaluable. These programs produce form letters by combining (merging) a letter with a name and address list. Standard forms, such as invoices, purchase orders, pay notifications, and inventory lists, can be filled electronically.

Laser printers further enhance office word processing. By linking a word processing program with a laser printer, a document will have typeset quality without the delay and expense of professional printing.

This desktop electronic publishing system lends itself to the direct production of such documents as a company annual report, a prospectus, a price list, or a sales promotion flyer.

There are a good collection of word processing programs available for the IBM PC and compatibles. WordStar® from MicroPro International Corporation was perhaps the first full-function word processing program initially available on the CP/M operating system. It was later converted to operate under MS-DOS and PC-DOS. Other popular word processing programs include WordStar 2000; WordPerfect; Multimate; Volkswriter; EasyWriter II; IBM's DisplayWrite 1, 2, and 3; and Microsoft Word.

Some of the purposes for which a word processing program can be used include the following:

1. Preparation of report and proposals.
2. Preparation of form letters.
3. Preparation of legal contracts.
4. Typing of business correspondence.
5. Preparation of annual reports and financial statements.

BASIC PRINCIPLES OF WORD PROCESSING PROGRAMS. Word processing programs store documents in computer files. A word processed document is any piece of text prepared using a word processing program and stored electronically on a hard or floppy disk. It can be a one-page letter, a multipage proposal, or a large report. A word processing document can be retrieved from disk and modified. A document is made up of characters, words, lines, paragraphs, and pages. Because word processing programs can recognize words, they can search for and replace selected words throughout an entire document. Some word processing programs create a backup file each time an existing file is replaced.

All word processing programs provide commands that let the user control the appearance (format) of documents. Usually there are commands to underline text, boldface text, center a title or a page, and so on. Commands are also used to control the printing of documents. The quality of a word processing program depends largely on the power and variety of commands. Word processing programs with easy-to-use commands are preferable.

GUIDED TOURS OF ACCOUNTING AND BUSINESS PROGRAMS

This section provides a guided tour of selected accounting and business programs to illustrate the principles and features described in the previous section. Two examples are described for each of the applications of accounting programs, spreadsheet programs, database programs, and word processing programs. The features of the selected programs described in this section are current as of this writing. However, microcomputer programs are frequently updated and improved. Readers interested in the features of a particular program should check the most recent documentation from the software publisher.

Guided Tours of Two Accounting Programs

ACCPAC is one of the best known names in accounting software in Canada. It features a comprehensive set of accounting modules designed for small to medium-sized businesses. Bedford has a newer history. It is a very simple accounting program designed for small businesses. ACCPAC and Bedford are completely different in design philosophy and serve different needs.

ACCPAC/EASYBUSINESS SYSTEMS. The ACCPAC accounting series, first released in 1979, is made up of eight integrated accounting modules developed by Basic Software Group of Vancouver, B.C., now part of Computer Associates International, Inc., of San Jose, California. (In the United States, ACCPAC is marketed under the trade name Easy-Business Systems.) The eight *modules* are General Ledger, Accounts Receivable, Accounts Payable, Inventory Control, Order Entry, Retail Invoicing, Payroll, and Job Costing.

Two utility programs, EasyPlus and EasyPlus Networking can be used to facilitate the operation of the modules. EasyPlus is a windowing software that allows up to 10 ACCPAC modules to run concurrently. EasyPlus Networking is used to operate the ACCPAC modules in a local network environment. ProPac, a time, billing, and receivable module, can also be used in accounting practice. Each module can run on a standalone basis. The minimum hardware requirement is 256K bytes of memory and two floppy disk drives. However, 512K bytes of memory and a hard disk are required to take full advantage of the integrated capability of the ACCPAC series. The EasyPlus windowing program is ideal when several integrated modules are used; for example, there can be accounts receivable in one window and order entry in another window of the same screen. It is possible to flip back and forth between different windows and transfer data between windows.

The accounts receivable module can handle both the open item or the balance forward method. As previously stated, the size of the customer file is only limited by the amount of disk space available. A maximum of 20 General Ledger accounts can be specified for distribution to the general ledger. The aging periods can be specified. Customer notifications and mailing labels can be generated. There are comprehensive controls over customer accounts including interest rates, recurring charges, credit limits, and discounts. A flexible facility is provided to custom design customer notifications. The accounts payable module can only handle open item accounts. This module can distribute data to seven G/L accounts. Users can specify up to four aging periods for the aged cash

Illustration 29–7   Example of an ACCPAC On-Screen Menu

```
THE UNIVERSAL CORPORATION
ACCPAC General Ledger Master Menu

Please select activity from the following:

1. G/L Account Maintenance
2. Transaction Batch Maintenance
3. Account Posting
4. Reports
5. Housekeeping
6. Print Financial Statement
7. Fetch Report Specification

Press ESCAPE to exit.
```

requirement report and the overdue payables report. Cheques and payment advice can be generated. A flexible facility is provided to custom-design cheques and payment notices.

ACCPAC uses on-screen menus extensively. Users select an activity by pressing one key. Illustration 29–7 is an example of an on-screen menu from the ACCPAC general ledger module.

A submenu is presented if the activity selected involves several further choices. Illustration 29–8 is an example of a submenu used in the ACCPAC general ledger module.

All data entry is handled through **video forms,** which are electronic

Illustration 29–8   Example of an ACCPAC Submenu

```
THE UNIVERSAL CORPORATION
G/L Account Maintenance Menu

Please select activity from the following:

    1. Add Accounts
    2. Delete Accounts
    3. Modify Existing Accounts

    4. View Accounts

    5. Edit Historical Data
    6. Edit Budget Data

    7. Export/Import Accounts

Press ESCAPE to exit.
```

Illustration 29–9   Example of an ACCPAC Video Form

```
THE UNIVERSAL CORPORATION
Enter/Edit Batch of Transactions

   Batch Number [2   ] has      Transactions.
   _____

   Transaction Number [     ]

   Period       [  ]
   Source       [ ]
   Date         [  /  /  ]
   Reference    [      ]
   Description  [                              ]

   Account      [      ] Dept.[      ]
   Amount    Dr.[              ]    Cr.[           ]

  Press ESCAPE to exit.
```

equivalents of paper forms except that users key in information in response to on-screen prompts. Each module has very similar menus. After learning to use one module, users will have no problem learning to use others. Illustration 29–9 is an example of an ACCPAC video form used to enter transactions into the G/L transaction file.

ACCPAC: THE GENERAL LEDGER MODULE. The general ledger module of ACCPAC (ACCPAC/GL) illustrates how ACCPAC works. The major features of ACCPAC/GL include:

1. The number of accounts and transactions on each floppy disk used to hold G/L data is limited to 300 accounts and 1,500 transactions in total. If fewer than 300 accounts are used, the total number of transactions will increase (e.g., for 150 accounts, the number of transactions increases to 1,900).
2. If a hard disk is used, the number of accounts is limited to 65,000; the total number of transactions is limited only by the amount of space available on the disk.
3. Up to 24 months of net balance of transactions for every account can be stored. Each account can contain 37 net balances: 12 for current period, 12 for previous year, 12 for budget, and 1 year-to-date.
4. Up to 12 alphanumeric digits can be used for the account number: 6 for the account code and 6 (optional) for department code. There is no restriction on how the account numbers are used. The account numbers can be enumerated in any order desired.

5.   Good audit trails are provided by requiring transactions to be printed before posting or purging.

6.   Recurrent entries can be stored for repetitive use.

7.   ACCPAC/GL is completely integrated with other ACCPAC modules; that is, transactions can be obtained from the Accounts Receivable, Accounts Payable, Inventory Control, Payroll, and Job Costing modules.

8.   ACCPAC/GL provides interface (through ASCII files) to other computer programs such as dBASE III. It can export information in standard Lotus 1-2-3 (.WKS files) and SuperCalc4 (.CAL files) spreadsheet format.

9.   Multiple companies can be consolidated through the use of Export/Import functions.

10.   Flexible budgeting is provided with built-in mini-spreadsheet functions.

11.   Comprehensive control over the layout of the financial statements and reports is also provided.

12.   Prior year and prior period adjustments can be made easily without affecting current operations.

13.   Automatic year-end closing of income and expense accounts to retained earnings at the end of a fiscal year can be made.

Transactions are entered into the G/L using batches. Only those batches that are in balance can be posted. Batches that are out of balance cannot be posted into the G/L.

BEDFORD INTEGRATED ACCOUNTING.   Bedford Integrated Accounting was published and released in 1985 by Bedford Software Limited of Burnaby, B.C. Bedford Integrated Accounting is made up of six integrated functions: General Ledger, Accounts Receivable, Accounts Payable, Payroll, JobCost, and System. These functions must operate together and cannot run as stand-alone programs. Bedford runs on the IBM PC and compatibles and require two floppy drives and 256K bytes of memory. All the programs fit on one floppy disk, but Bedford can also take advantage of a hard disk.

The Bedford accounting system operates completely in memory. All programs and master files are loaded into memory when the system is started. Unlike ACCPAC, journal entries that are entered in any of Bedford's programs are stored in a General Journal. Only the General Journal is kept on disk and updated on exit from the Bedford programs. Because everything is stored in memory, the programs are fast and give instantaneous response in most cases. Unlike most accounting software, Bedford does not recognize formal accounting periods as such. As long as the general journal has not been purged, and there is disk space to hold the detailed transactions, the user can have as many ''accounting periods'' as needed in a fiscal year.

Both accounts payable and accounts receivable programs use the open item method. The accounts payable program can print cheques and handle manual cheques. It provides summary as well as detailed reports on aged accounts payable. Users can control the aging periods. The accounts receivable program works similar to the accounts payable program. Bedford uses a very simple video screen for entering transactions. Illustration 29–10 shows an example of a transaction entry screen.

Illustration 29–10 Example of Bedford Transaction Entry Screen

```
 _____
|                                                    |
| GENERAL   PAYABLE   RECEIVABLE   PAYROLL   JOBCOST   SYSTEM |
| _____ |
|                                                    |
|   Comment   ............................           |
|   Source                                           |
|   Account                                          |
|     Amount                                         |
|   Project                                          |
|     Amount                                         |
|_____|
```

All transactions are kept in the General Journal file. To keep the General Journal always in balance, the user cannot leave a journal entry unless the debit amount entered equals the credit amount. The major features of Bedford include the following:

1. Regardless of the amount of memory or disk space available, there can be no more than 500 G/L accounts, 999 vendor accounts, 999 customer accounts, 999 employee records, or 999 project records.

2. The maximum number of journal entries is determined by the amount of space available on the data disk.

3. No monthly account totals are stored; for example, only the opening balance and the year-to-date totals are stored in the master files. All transaction details are stored in the general journal file. When the general journal is purged, the opening balances of the master files are updated.

4. No prior-year information is stored. The programs cannot handle budget information.

5. The format of financial statements is predefined and cannot be changed. The users can, however, control the totals and subtotals by specifying account types in the chart of accounts.

6. Account numbers are three digits with predefined ranges:

Asset accounts:	100–199
Liability accounts:	200–299
Equity accounts:	300–399
Revenue accounts:	400–499
Expense accounts:	500–599

7. Audit trail is provided through the printing of the General Journal and General Ledger Listings.
8. All the programs are integrated. Transactions can be obtained from the Accounts Receivable, Accounts Payable, Payroll, and JobCost programs.
9. Some reports can be "exported" to word processing programs in ASCII format, to Lotus 1-2-3 in standard 1-2-3 work sheet format, and to other computer programs through DIF (Data Interchange Format) files.
10. Access control is provided by setting an individual password for each program.
11. Automatic year-end closing of income and expense accounts to retained earnings at the end of a fiscal year is provided.

In summary, Bedford is designed for small businesses. Because there are no comparative statements, no budget data, and no monthly totals, it is unsuitable for businesses that require more comprehensive accounting controls and reports.

Guided Tour of Two Spreadsheet Programs

Lotus 1-2-3 is the most popular spreadsheet program; SuperCalc4 is a well-built spreadsheet program. Both provide very similar functions, although they have different designs. Either will serve the needs of the accountant well.

LOTUS 1-2-3.   Lotus 1-2-3 provides three integrated functions: spreadsheet, graphics, and data management. Lotus 1-2-3 was first released in 1982 by Lotus Development Corporation of Cambridge, Massachusetts. The current version of Lotus 1-2-3 is Release 2, which features many improvements over Release 1A. Lotus 1-2-3 requires a minimum of 256K bytes of memory and two floppy disk drives. The Lotus 1-2-3 program itself takes up 192K bytes of memory. Thus, because Lotus 1-2-3 stores the current spreadsheet in memory, users need more than 256K bytes of total memory to work with a large spreadsheet. Although a hard disk is not required, it would be preferable, particularly to store a large number of spreadsheets. Spreadsheets constructed using Lotus 1-2-3 are called "worksheets." The Lotus 1-2-3 (Release 2) worksheet has a maximum size of 8,192 rows by 256 columns. When the Lotus 1-2-3, using the Lotus Access System, is loaded for the first time, the Access Screen will be presented (see Illustration 29–11).

If the 1-2-3 is selected, the user will enter the spreadsheet program of Lotus 1-2-3. The operation of Lotus 1-2-3 is controlled through commands, which are presented via a command menu and can be activated by pressing the slash (/) key. Illustration 29–12 shows the Lotus 1-2-3 work sheet and the command menu. Notice that the second command line is a submenu and displays the submenu for the command that the cursor is resting on. In Illustration 29–12, the second command line

Illustration 29–11 Lotus Access Screen

```
  ┌─────┐
  │1-2-3│ PrintGraph  Translate  Install  View  Exit
  └─────┘
      Enter 1-2-3 -- Lotus Worksheet/Graphics/Database program
```

```
                    1-2-3 Access System
                Lotus Development Corporation
                      Copyright 1985
                     All Rights Reserved
                        Release 2


     The Access system lets you choose 1-2-3, PrintGraph, the
     Translate utility, the Install program, and View of 1-2-3
     from the menu at the top of this screen.  If you're using a
     diskette system, the Access system may prompt you to change
     disks.  Follow the instructions below to start a program


     o  Use [RIGHT] or [LEFT] to move the menu pointer (the
        highlight bar at the top of the screen) to the program you
        want to use.


     o  Press [RETURN] to start the program.


     You can also start a program by typing the first letter of
     the menu choice.
     Press [HELP] for more information.
```

(starting with **Global**) is the submenu for the command **Worksheet.** The user selects a command by pressing the first letter of the command or by moving the cursor to the command and pressing the RETURN key. For example, to select the command **File,** the letter F is pressed. If the command contains more than one action, a submenu will be presented. Illustration 29–13 shows the submenu from the command File.

Users can construct very complex formulas using mathematical and logical operators. One of the powerful features of Lotus 1-2-3 is its rich collection of prebuilt functions that can be used either by themselves in cells or as part of formulas. Functions in Lotus 1-2-3 all begin with the symbol @. For example, **@PV** is a function that computes present values. There are seven major types of functions: financial, date, logical, statistical, database statistical, mathematical, and special functions.

1. *Financial functions* are used to calculate formulas such as present values, future values, and annuity payments.

Illustration 29–12   Lotus 1-2-3 Worksheet and Command Menu

```
A1:                                                                    MENU
Worksheet  Range  Copy  Move  File  Print  Graph  Data  System  Quit
Global, Insert, Delete, Column, Erase, Titles, Window, Status, Page
           A         B         C         D         E         F         G         H
 1
 2
 3
 4
 5
 6
 7
 8
 9
10
11
12
13
14
15
16
17
18
19
20
07-Jun-86   12:45 PM
```

2. *Date functions* are used to enter dates into cells and perform calculations using dates.
3. *Logical functions* are used to test for specified conditions such as the existence of a certain value in a cell.
4. *Statistical functions* are used to calculate statistical values such as sum, average, and standard deviation.
5. *Database statistical functions* are statistical functions that operate on data tables.
6. *Mathematical functions* are used to compute mathematical formulas such as sine, cosine, tangent, square root, and exponents.
7. *Special functions* include table lookup functions such as **HLOOKUP,** which is used to look up a value in a data table arranged in rows.

The Lotus 1-2-3 worksheet can be used to perform any calculations that involve columns and rows of numbers. Illustration 29–14 is an example of a comparative income statement prepared in a Lotus 1-2-3 worksheet.

Cell D17 (total expenses for 1986) contains the formula **@SUM(D12..D15).** This is a Lotus 1-2-3 formula that calculates the sum of the contents of cells D12, D13, D14, and D15. The value **507,000**

Illustration 29–13   Submenu from the File Command

```
A1:
Retrieve  Save  Combine  Xtract  Erase  List  Import  Directory
Erase the current worksheet and display the selected worksheet
          A        B        C        D        E        F        G
  1
  2
  3
  4

 20
```

is the result of this summation. Cell D19 (net income for 1986) contains the formula **D8 − D19,** which is equal to revenue (cell D8) minus total expenses (cell D19). Similarly, the percent change of revenue in cell F8 is calculated by the formula **(D8 − E8)/E8*100,** which represents the difference between the 1986 revenue (cell D8), and the 1985 revenue (cell E8) divided by the 1985 revenue (cell E8), then multiplied by 100 to yield the percentage change of 7.94.

Illustration 29–14   Example of a Lotus 1-2-3 Worksheet

```
A1:

          A        B          C          D          E          F
  1                      XYZ Computer Rental Ltd.
  2                      Comparative Income Statement
  3
  4                                          Year ended December 31
  5
  6                                   1986       1985     % Change
  7
  8   Revenue:                    $680,000   $630,000       7.94
  9
 10   Expenses:
 11
 12             Salaries          410,000    389,000        5.40
 13             Office rent        35,000     32,000        9.38
 14             Advertising        12,000     10,000       20.00
 15             Depreciation       50,000     48,000        4.17
 16                              --------   --------     --------
 17   Total expenses             507,000    479,000        5.85
 18                              --------   --------     --------
 19   Net income               $173,000   $151,000       14.57
 20                              ========   ========     ========
```

The macro facility in Lotus 1-2-3 is very powerful. Macros are user-built command sequences that automate repetitive worksheet tasks. Spreadsheet *templates* can be built for use by other Lotus 1-2-3 users. A template is a prebuilt worksheet application that accepts data input from the user and calculates and displays the result automatically. Lotus 1-2-3 provides data management functions that can be used to manage client data bases, inventory lists, personnel databases, accounts receivable, and accounts payable. Lotus 1-2-3 can also be used to display and print bar graphs, pie charts, and line graphs using values calculated in the worksheets. To print a graph, the user has to store the graph in a graph file and use a graph printing program (named PrintGraph). Lotus does not have a facility to print a wide spreadsheet sideways. However, the program SIDEWAYS from Funk Software, Inc., of Cambridge, Massachusetts, can be used to do so.

SUPERCALC4.   There are several versions of SuperCalc, the most current being SuperCalc4. First introduced in 1980 by Sorcim Corporation, SuperCalc has undergone several major changes. The latest, SuperCalc4, was released in June 1986 by Computer Associates International, Inc., of San Jose, California. It incorporates many features found in Lotus 1-2-3. SuperCalc4 provides three integrated functions: spreadsheet, graphics, and data management. The integration of graphics with spreadsheet is particularly well done in this program. SuperCalc4 requires 256K bytes of memory and two floppy disk drives. If more memory is present in the microcomputer, SuperCalc4 will use it automatically. Three sizes of spreadsheets are provided: small (254 rows by 63 columns), medium (2,000 rows by 127 columns), and large (9,999 rows by 255 columns). If large spreadsheets are used, a hard disk is recommended to speed up spreadsheet retrieval and calculations.

As with Lotus 1-2-3, the operation of SuperCalc4 is controlled through commands. SuperCalc4 commands, called slash commands, are presented in a menu when the slash key is pressed. Illustration 29–15 shows the SuperCalc4 spreadsheet area and the command menu. Notice that there are two lines of commands in the command menu at the bottom of the screen, starting with the command **Arrange** and ending with the command **/more.** A brief explanation of the selected command is displayed as the last line of the screen, headed by the word MENU. The explanation in Illustration 29–15 is for the command **Arrange.** As you move the cursor from command to command, the explanation changes.

SuperCalc4 has a rich collection of built-in functions consisting of eight categories: logical, calendar, financial, index, statistical, data management, arithmetic, and trigonometric. Lotus 1-2-3 and SuperCalc4 do not have an identical set of built-in functions, but most of them share similar names and perform similar actions. SuperCalc4 contains powerful but easy to use macro facilities that can be used to automate many of the frequently used spreadsheet commands. Unlike those of Lotus 1-2-3, SuperCalc4 macros can be learned in a short time by a novice.

Illustration 29–15   SuperCalc4 Spreadsheet Area and Command Menu

```
     ¦ A  ¦¦  B  ¦¦  C  ¦¦  D  ¦¦  E  ¦¦  F  ¦¦  G  ¦¦  H  ¦¦
   1
   2
   3
   4
   5
   6
   7
   8
   9
  10
  11
  12
  13
  14
  15
  16
  17
  18
  19
  20
  Arrange  Blank  Copy  Delete  Edit  Format  Global  Insert  Load  Move  Name
  Output  Protect  Quit  Save  Title  Unprotect  View  Window  Zap  /more
    2>/
  MENU  Sort spreadsheet (entire or partial) by a column or row
```

The data management function of SuperCalc4 is comparable to that of Lotus 1-2-3, including a similar set of statistical data management functions. SuperCalc4 provides more types of graphs, including bar graphs, pie charts, line graphs, stacked bar graphs, and high-low graphs. The printing and plotting of graphs are handled directly without needing to go through a graph printing program as in Lotus 1-2-3. SuperCalc4 comes with a utility program—SIDEWAYS—which can be used to print a wide spreadsheet sideways. The program SIDEWAYS is produced by Funk Software, Inc.

Guided Tour of Two Database Programs

dBASE III is one of the most popular database programs running on microcomputers. PFS:FILE is a very simple information filing and retrieval program. While it takes several days to learn dBASE III, it only takes a few hours to learn PFS:FILE.

dBASE III.   dBASE III, a powerful database management program, was first introduced as dBASE II by Ashton-Tate of Los Angeles, California. The program has undergone many changes; The most current version of dBASE III is dBASE III Plus. dBASE III can be used to create simple or complex databases. Several accounting systems are built using dBASE III, the most notable being The Champion from Data Base Research Corporation. Complex inventory systems can also be built using dBASE III. In spite of its power, dBASE III is relatively easy to use. It only takes users a few hours to learn to build their first database.

dBASE III provides a programming language that enables users to create any computer application involving the recording of information and subsequent analysis. It can be used to build applications, to manage inventory, to manage order entry and billing, to maintain employee records and payroll, and to keep customer and vendor records. Many specialized applications have been built using dBASE III, including medical, dental, real estate, and construction systems. dBASE III requires a minimum of 256K bytes of memory and two floppy disk drives; however, more than 256K bytes of memory is recommended. Although a floppy disk can be used to store the databases, dBASE III performs best with a hard disk. This is particularly true if the database contains several hundred records. When the user starts up dBASE III, a copyright screen will be presented. At the bottom of the screen, will be the dBASE III command prompt, which appears as a period (.), indicating that dBASE III is ready to accept a command.

dBASE III contains an extensive amount of HELP information the user can access through the Main Help Menu. dBASE III also has a facility called **the Assistant,** which is an extensive set of menus and submenus designed to assist the user. dBASE III works with files, records, and several types of fields: character, numeric, date, logical, and memo. The most commonly used field types are character and numeric. The user can specify the width of a field. Numeric fields can be specified with number of decimal places.

To create a database, the user types the command **CREATE.** dBASE III will prompt the user for the name of the file, followed by a blank form which is used to define the database structure. Illustration 29–16 shows an example of a completed screen defining the structure for a database called EMPLOYEE. Notice that dBASE III adds the suffix **.DBF** to the filename indicating that this is a database file.

After a database has been created, dBASE III provides the option of keying in data records immediately. The command **APPEND** is used to add records to a database. Illustration 29–17 shows an example of a completed record.

Commands are used to manage, edit, scan, or print the database. For instance, users may initiate a search for records that meet specific conditions. Using the EMPLOYEE database, a user might wish to search records that meet specific conditions. For example, he/she might wish to search for all employee records with position numbers between 200 and 299, and hourly wage rates of less than $20. The dBASE III command for this search would read:

.DISPLAY ALL FOR POSITION>200 .AND. <300 .AND. HRLY_RATE>20.00

Illustration 29–16   Example of a dBASE III Database Structure

```
b:\EMPLOYEE.DBF                              Bytes remaining:   3880
                                             Fields defined:      11

     field name   type     width  dec     field name   type     width  dec
     ======================================     ======================================
  1  SIN_NUM      Numeric      9    0
  2  JOB_NUM      Numeric      5    0
  3  LAST_NAME    Char/text   20
  4  GIVEN_NAME   Char/text   20
  5  ADDRESS      Char/text   20
  6  CITY         Char/text   10
  7  PROVINCE     Char/text   10
  8  POSTALCODE   Char/text    6
  9  PHONE        Numeric      7    0
 10  HRLY_RATE    Numeric      5    2
 11  OVTME_RATE   Numeric      5    2
 12               Char/text
```

A database can be reorganized using the **MODIFY** command. Users can design their own reports. Reports can also be in table format. Arithmetic can be performed in the reports since subtotals and totals are easy to specify. Mailing labels can be generated using the report formatting function of dBASE III. dBASE III enables users to work with up to 10 databases concurrently. This means that data can be used from one database as a lookup table to process another database. One of the most powerful features of dBASE III is its ability to "join" two databases to form a third using the **JOIN** command. By keeping the two databases separate, the task of keeping the databases current is simplified. But, when users need to generate a report that requires data from both databases, they may use the **JOIN** command to create a third database temporarily.

Illustration 29–17   A Completed dBASE III Data Entry Form

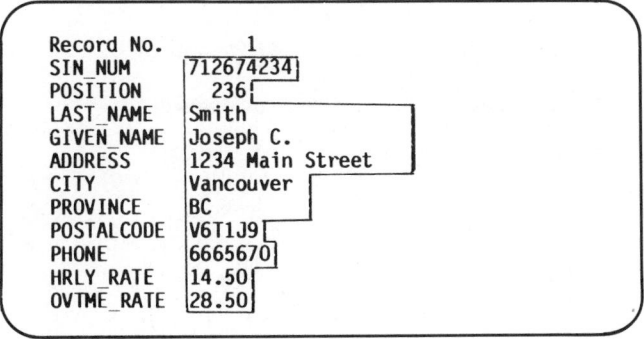

```
     Record No.        1
     SIN_NUM       712674234
     POSITION          236
     LAST_NAME     Smith
     GIVEN_NAME    Joseph C.
     ADDRESS       1234 Main Street
     CITY          Vancouver
     PROVINCE      BC
     POSTALCODE    V6T1J9
     PHONE         6665670
     HRLY_RATE     14.50
     OVTME_RATE    28.50
```

In summary, dBASE III is a truly versatile program ideally suited to the needs of the accountant.

PFS:FILE. PFS:FILE is a simple information filing program. Strictly speaking, PFS:FILE cannot be called a database program. It lacks many of the database management functions found in other more sophisticated programs. The main advantage of PFS:FILE is its simplicity and ease of use. PFS:FILE is published by Software Publishing Corporation of Mountain View, California, and is part of a family of integrated microcomputer programs, including PFS:WRITE (word processing), PFS:REPORT (report generator), and PFS:GRAPH (graphics). All these programs are easy to use. The files of one may be accessed by any other program in the series.

PFS:FILE requires 256K bytes of memory and two floppy disk drives. A floppy disk (360K byte) can hold up to 2,475 very simple PFS:FILE forms. With a hard disk, there is no limit on the number of forms users can create. When PFS:FILE is started up, the user is presented with the main menu as shown in Illustration 29–18. As can be seen from this main menu, there are six functions in PFS:FILE: **Design file, Add forms, Copy, Search/Update, Print,** and **Remove.**
To create a new file (database), users select the first choice on the main menu: Design file. This allows them to create a form "freehand" the way a form is designed using a typewriter. Illustration 29–19 shows the Design File menu.
A new form is created by selecting the first choice of the design File Menu—Create a new file. A blank screen will be presented and then the data can be keyed in. Illustration 29–20 shows an example of a form designed using PFS:FILE.
Users can just as easily create a multipage form. Once a form is designed,

Illustration 29–18   PFS:File Main Menu

```
    ----------------------
          PFS:FILE MAIN MENU
    ----------------------


    1. Design file          5. Print

    2. Add forms            6. Remove

    3. Copy                 7. Exit

    4. Search/Update



                Selection:

                Disk or filename:
```

Illustration 29–19   Design File Menu

```
            DESIGN FILE MENU

    1. Create a new file

    2. Add, delete, or move items

    3. Change existing item names

    4. Specify formulas for calculated items


            Selection:
```

users can use the **Add forms** function of the main menu to enter forms. They will be presented with a blank form which they designed using the **Design File** menu. Users can print any form once entered and can modify or delete any form stored on disk. They can also search through forms for specific information meeting one or more criteria. If a summary report of forms on file is needed, the program PFS:REPORT must be used. PFS:FILE is easy to learn and simple to use. It takes one to two hours to learn to use all its functions and is ideal for filing simple forms on the microcomputer.

Guided Tour of Two Word Processing Programs

Two of the more popular word processing programs are WordPerfect and WordStar. WordPerfect is perhaps one of the best word processing programs for the business user. It contains a comprehensive set of features designed to facilitate and improve report writing and presentation. Word-Star is the classic and first computer word processing program on the

Illustration 29–20   Example of a Form Designed Using PFS:FILE

```
                    Employee Record
                    ---------------

   Social Insurance #:          Date of employment:

   Job Title:                   Position #:

   Last name:                   Given names:
   Address:
   City:            Province:   Postal Code:
   Phone:

   Hourly rate:                 Overtime rate:
```

microcomputer. Although this program is awkward to use and dated, it still has a large and committed following.

WORDPERFECT®   WordPerfect is one of the most efficient word processing programs available on microcomputers. It provides a comprehensive set of word processing functions, including support of over 200 printers. It can also work with several of the popular laser printers. First published in 1982 by Satellite Software International of Orem (now WordPerfect Corporation), Utah, WordPerfect has undergone many dramatic improvements. The current version is Version 4.1, released in September 1985. WordPerfect Version 4.1 requires a minimum of 256K bytes of memory and two floppy disk drives. However, to take full advantage of WordPerfect, a hard disk is recommended. This is particularly true if the dictionary and the thesaurus are being used. They each come on a floppy disk. Without a hard disk, the user faces the minor inconvenience of changing floppy disks. When users start up WordPerfect, they see a blank screen. At the bottom of the screen, a status line is displayed. It reads:

Doc 1   Pg   1   Ln   1   Pos 10

This display indicates that WordPerfect is ready to accept the typing. WordPerfect uses the 10 function keys found on the left-hand side of the keyboard as command keys. These function keys are used in four levels: by themselves, or in conjunction with the ALT, SHIFT, or CNTRL key. Thus, 40 functions are readily accessible. A standard format is preset with top and bottom, left and right margins, tab positions, number of lines per page, and so on. WordPerfect displays the effect of any command entered.

The word processing capabilities of WordPerfect match those of dedicated word processing computers. WordPerfect offers accountants several useful features to assist in writing reports. An electronic thesaurus helps users find the **right** word by displaying synonyms and other words of similar idea. Illustration 29–21 shows an example of a thesaurus lookup. The Speller in WordPerfect comes with a dictionary of over 100,000 words. Words and technical terms, even acronyms, can be added to make as many supplementary dictionaries as needed (e.g., for use with a specific type of report or document). Spell-checking can be carried out at three levels: word, page, and the entire document. To activate the Speller, the Spell command key is pressed. The Speller can perform two additional types of dictionary lookup that can be useful for users who ''half-know'' a spelling; for example, users can provide the beginning or ending of the word, or even its phonetic spelling. During spell-checking, if WordPerfect encounters a word not found in its dictionary or the supplementary dictionary specified, it will prompt the user for action.

WordPerfect can also generate a table of contents for the document

Illustration 29–21   Example of a WordPerfect Thesaurus Lookup

```
It is expected

expect=(v) =================================================
| 1 A .anticipate        |                   |                   |
|   B .await             |                   |                   |
|   C .envision          |                   |                   |
|   D .foresee           |                   |                   |
|                        |                   |                   |
| 2 E .demand            |                   |                   |
|   F .exact             |                   |                   |
|   G .require           |                   |                   |
|                        |                   |                   |
| 3 H .assume            |                   |                   |
|   I .imagine           |                   |                   |
|   J .presume           |                   |                   |
|   K .suppose           |                   |                   |
|                        |                   |                   |
| Replace Word; 2 View Doc; 3 Look up Word; 4 Clear Column: 0
```

automatically. It can also generate an index for a report or document using a similar technique. WordPerfect can be used to create a multicolumn newsletter, glossary, inventory list, or any document that requires several (up to five) columns of text on a page. Newspaper-style columns suitable for newsletters or parallel columns suitable for inventory lists can be used. Footnotes or endnotes can also be created. WordPerfect generates the footnote or endnote numbers automatically.

WordPerfect can be used to generate form letters by merging the body of the letter with a name and address list. The same feature used to merge letters can also be used to merge forms, such as invoices or pay notifications, or to generate labels. The mathematics feature of Word-Perfect enables the user to create a simple financial statement and will calculate totals and subtotals. In summary, WordPerfect is a versatile program for the accountant with writing and reporting responsibilities. It has more refinements than most other word processing programs and can be learned quickly. It can enhance report writing activities and improve the quality of reports and other documents.

WORDSTAR®.   WordStar is one of the best known word processing programs available for microcomputers. Released in 1978, it was one of the first fully developed word processing programs, and, until recently, was commonly accepted as the standard against which other programs were measured. Originally developed for the CP/M operating system by MicroPro International Corporation, it was later converted to operate under the IBM PC and compatibles. In 1984, MicroPro introduced a new word processing program called WordStar 2000, which was based on WordStar but incorporated many new features. WordStar comes with two companion programs—MailMerge and CorrectStar. MailMerge can be used to merge names and addresses with form letters. CorrectStar is used to check spelling. WordStar can be operated with only one floppy disk drive and 64K bytes of memory. However, to take full advantage of WordStar with CorrectStar, users should have at least two floppy disk drives.

Most word processing programs use command keys to control text format. WordStar, however, requires the user to key in coded commands, which are then embedded in the text to specify text format. For example, to boldface a word, the user puts a ^B at the beginning of the word, and another ^B at the end of the word using the command **^PB.** To control the format of a page, WordStar uses commands called **dot commands.** The command **.PA** is used to start a new page.

WordStar is not an easy program to use, and its commands are difficult to remember. Because the effect of text formatting (e.g., underline or boldface) is not shown on the screen, users must be familiar with the program to visualize the document's format on the screen. Spell-checking involves a separate step and is inconvenient to use. However, because WordStar was the first generally accepted word processing program on the microcomputer, quite a few businesses and microcomputer users still find it effective. WordStar is still the most popular microcomputer program used by the typesetting and printing businesses.

OTHER BUSINESS SOFTWARE

The previous section reviewed eight different microcomputer programs. There are many more on the market, and still others are added to the list monthly. This section provides a brief annotated selection for reference. The information presented below is current as of June 1986.

Accounting Programs

K-I-S, published by EPO Business Systems Ltd., of Vancouver, British Columbia, is an integrated accounting system that comes with General Ledger, Accounts Receivable, and Accounts Payable. K-I-S is designed for use by small business. It can be used on two floppy disk systems or hard disk systems. K-I-S uses a common document entry program to accept transactions which are then posted to the General Ledger, Accounts Receivable, or Accounts Payable modules. Passwords can be used to control access to a particular company's accounting records.

Only account balances of the current year are kept. Prior year account balances and budget figures cannot be handled.

Niakwa, published by Modern Accounting of Vancouver, British Columbia, is a client-accounting program designed for the accountant in public practice. It is a general ledger program that enables the accountant to keep accounting information and generate financial statements for many clients. The strength of Niakwa lies in the ease of transaction processing. Financial statement formats can be stored in the system libraries and used in conjunction with the financial records of different clients. Custom financial statements can be created for specific clients and stored in client libraries.

Peachtree, published by Peachtree Software, Inc., of Atlanta, Georgia, is an integrated accounting system with General Ledger, Accounts Receivable, Accounts Payable, Fixed Assets, Inventory Control, Job Costing, Sales Analysis, and Invoicing. For several years, IBM sold Peachtree in its microcomputer product centres as the accounting system for use with the IBM PC. The Peachtree General Ledger can be operated with two floppy disk drives, and menus are used to guide the user through the General Ledger functions. Budget totals, prior-year totals, and current totals are kept. Transactions are entered in batches; out-of-balance batches cannot be posted to the General Ledger.

BPI Enterprise Series, first introduced in 1979, is published by BPI Systems, Inc., of Austin, Texas. In 1981, the BPI Entry Series, composed of General Accounting, Accounts Receivable, Payroll, Inventory Control, and JobCost, was released and sold under the IBM label in IBM Product Centres. The BPI Enterprise Series is the current version and contains five integrated modules of General Ledger, Accounts Receivable, Accounts Payable, Payroll, and Network Support. BPI Enterprise must be used with a hard disk because all five modules take up 2.5 megabytes to store. Menus enable the user to control accounting activities. The General Ledger is an interactive system—transactions are entered directly into the accounts instead of batched in a transaction file. It stores historical balances, budget information, and current balances. It also provides a General Journal of up to 12 accounts distributions and 10 lines of description.

Spreadsheet Programs

Multiplan, published by Microsoft Corporation of Bellevue, Washington, is a popular spreadsheet program that runs on many different microcomputers, including the Apple II, Apple Macintosh, the Wang PC, the IBM PC and compatibles, and all CP/M microcomputers. Unlike Lotus 1-2-3 or SuperCalc4, Multiplan does not have graphics or data mangement functions and does not provide a macro facility.

Symphony, published by Lotus Development Corporation of Cambridge, Massachusetts, is an integrated program featuring spreadsheet, graphics, data management, word processing, and telecommunications. It features very powerful spreadsheet capabilities and is particularly suitable for users who build complex spreadsheets. Symphony is a very large program and requires a minimum of 320K bytes of memory to run; 640K bytes are recommended for large spreadsheets. Although it can be used with two floppy disk drive systems, a hard disk is preferable. Symphony shares many common spreadsheet features with Lotus 1-2-3, but it contains more spreadsheet functions and more powerful macro facilities than Lotus 1-2-3. The word processing facility of Symphony is not too powerful and lacks many of the features commonly available in the popular standalone word processing programs.

VisiCalc, the first spreadsheet program that ran on microcomputers, was published by VisiCorp of San Jose, California, but is now owned by Lotus Development Corporation. It has been claimed that all spreadsheet programs share some design features with VisiCalc. Like Multiplan, VisiCalc runs on many different microcomputers. It does not provide graphics or data management functions.

Database Programs

DB Master, published by Stoneware Inc., of San Rafael, California, is a popular database program that runs on the Apple II. It is a powerful program that requires some effort to master.

Framework, published by Ashton-Tate of Culver City, California, is an integrated program featuring database, spreadsheet, word processing, graphics, and telecommunications. Framework is text oriented and contains powerful database capabilities. It is ideally suited for professionals who deal with ideas and the printed word.

KnowledgeMan, published by Micro Data Base Systems, Inc., of Lafayette, Indiana, is an integrated program featuring database, spreadsheet, and statistical analysis. Unlike other microcomputer database programs, KnowledgeMan uses a powerful command language similar to IBM's SQL (Structured Query Language).

Revelation, published by COMOS, Inc., of Seattle, Washington, is a powerful database program that contains a flexible programming language. However, the program can be operated at several levels ranging from novice to sophisticated.

R:Base 4000, published by Microrim, Inc., of Bellevue, Washington, is a database program that features easy-to use commands. It provides powerful "relational" database enquiry command.

Word Processing Programs

The **DisplayWrite** series, published by IBM Corporation of Boca Raton, Florida, is made up of three different word processing programs aimed at three levels of users. DisplayWrite 1 is designed for "light-duty'' word processing. DisplayWrite 2 is designed for ''professional'' use. DisplayWrite 3 is the most advanced of the series and features many sophisitcated word processing features.

EasyWriter II, published by Sorcim IUS of Computer Associates International, Inc., of San Jose, California, is an easy-to-use word processing program suitable for the novice and sophisticated users. It has many powerful word processing features and is part of the integrated family of programs that includes EasySpeller II, EasyFiler, and EasyPlanner.

MultiMate is a popular word processing program designed to look like a Wang word processing system. MultiMate, originally published by MultiMate International Corporation of Torrance, California, is now owned by Ashton-Tate of Culver City, California. Unlike many other word processing programs, it is page oriented and operates like an electronic typewriter. It contains powerful but easy-to-use functions. The most current version of Multimate is MultiMate Advantage.

Microsoft Word, published by Microsoft Corporation of Bellevue, Washington, is a powerful word processing program with many advanced features, including good support for laser printers. The program is easy to learn; most commands in Microsoft Word are activated by one keystroke. It runs on the IBM PC and compatibles as well as the Apple Macintosh.

Volkswriter deluxe, published by Lifetree Software, Inc., of Monterey, California, is an easy-to-use but powerful word processing program that uses menus extensively. Text entry and editing commands are entered via the function keys. It keeps multiple formats for documents, thereby enabling the user to print a document in several formats. Volkswriter is particularly suitable for first-time users.

BIBLIOGRAPHY

There are a number of good books on the evaluation and use of business software. The following is an annotated selection.

Cobb, D. F., and L. Anderson. *1-2-3 for Business*. Que Corporation, 1984.
Designed for accountants: contains many useful spreadsheet templates.

Hixson, A. C. *A Buyer's Guide to Microcomputer Business Software: Accounting and Spreadsheets*. Reading, Mass.: Addison-Wesley, 1984.
Covers a broad spectrum of accounting and spreadsheet programs. The software is not reviewed in depth.

LeBlond, G. T., and D. F. Cobb. *Using 1-2-3*. Que Corporation, 1983.
This is very well-written book that explains, through examples, how to use Lotus 1-2-3.

Lotus Books (TM). *The Lotus Guide to Learning 123: Includes Release 2*. Reading, Mass.: Addison-Wesley, 1985.

This book is a hands-on guide for the new Lotus 1-2-3 user. It is designed to augment the *Lotus 1-2-3 Users Manual.*

McClelland, T. *Dynamics of WordPerfect.* Homewood, Ill.: Dow Jones-Irwin, 1986.

A how-to-use book on WordPerfect: provides good explanations of major functions.

One Point (TM). *Computerizing Your Accounting System.* Rochelle Park, N.J.: Hayden Book Company, 1985.

Reviews the features of microcomputer accounting programs using ACCPAC (EasyBusiness) as the benchmark.

Reizer, A., S. Chinn, and A. J. Townsend. *Dynamics of dBASE III.* Homewood, Ill.: Dow Jones-Irwin, 1986.

Describes an application approach to database management, including an introductory section and an advanced section on dBASE III. Programming in dBASE III is also covered. The book is well written and easy to follow.

Yasuda P., and V. Frederick. *Using Microcomputers.* Menlo Park, Calif.: Benjamin/Cummings, 1986.

Introduces the novice to fundamental software concepts and applications. Application examples are used to illustrate the concepts. Software illustrated includes WordStar, PFS:FILE, PFS:WRITE, PFS:GRAPH, Lotus 1-2-3, and BASIC.

Yu, J., and D. Harrison. *Dynamics of SuperCalc4.* Homewood, Illinois: Dow Jones-Irwin, 1987.

Provides detailed explanation on how to use SuperCalc4 for the novice and sophisticated. The coverage of SuperCalc4 macro facility is indepth and extensive. This book has a business application emphasis and contains many spreadsheet templates for financial and management applications.

GLOSSARY

Application program. Computer program designed to solve specific problems or produce specific results. ACCPAC General Ledger is an example of a computer program designed to keep accounting records for a business.

Batch. A collection of transactions that are entered together into the computer as one entity.

Byte. The amount of computer memory needed to store one character. Microcomputer memory is usually measured in K-bytes. For example, 256K bytes.

Cell. A location on the spreadsheet uniquely identified by the intersection of a column and a row. A cell stores the smallest unit of information on a spreadsheet.

Configure. To set up a computer program or system to operate in a certain way.

Database. One or more computer files containing related data for a specific purpose.

DOS (Disk Operating System). An integrated set of computer programs designed to control the operation of computer equipment.

File. A collection of related data stored on a disk in a computer.

Floppy disk. A flexible (''floppy'') magnetic medium used to store computer files.

Formula. Mathematical expression used in spreadsheet programs to calculate a value.

Function. Pre-built formula in spreadsheet programs used to provide convenient means to compute complex calculations.

Hard disk. A rigid magnetic medium used to store computer files.

Hardware. Those components of microcomputer that you can feel and touch. Contrast with *software*.

Integrated. Computer programs that can share information without re-keying.

Macro. A set of user-defined commands.

Master file. A data file containing key information that is not changed very often. Contrast with *transaction file*.

Memory. The ''working space'' or temporary storage for computer programs and word processing files.

Menu. A list of options provided on the screen for choosing a particular function or setting.

Module. A module is a computer program that can operate either as a standalone entity or as part of an integrated system. For example, the Accounts Payable program is a module of ACCPAC.

Software. Computer programs that control and direct the microcomputer to perform specific tasks.

Spreadsheet. An electronic work sheet used to replace paper-based columnar work sheets. A spreadsheet is constructed using a computer application program called a *spreadsheet program*.

Template. Prebuilt spreadsheet containing formulas to be used by someone else.

Transaction file. A data file containing information that is changed frequently.

Video form. A data entry form displayed electronically on a computer screen.

Window. A self-contained portion of a video screen used to display related information.

Word processing. An electronic means of typing information and ideas into a readable form.

Word-wrap. The automatic positioning of a word at the end of the current line or the beginning of the next line by a word processing program.

QUESTIONS FOR CLASS DISCUSSION

1. What benefits can be obtained by using a computer in a business?

2. Name 10 uses of microcomputers in accounting.

3. You are an accountant for a small business. The owner asks you to explain the potential uses and benefits of your spreadsheet program. Outline your response.

4. What is a master file? What is a transaction file? Give an example of each to show how they are related.

5. What are some of the key features to look for in a general ledger program?

6. Why are integrated accounting programs more desirable than others?

7. What is a database program? For what purposes can a database program be used by the accountant?

8. It is commonly believed that word processing programs are designed for use by a typist. Why should an accountant learn to use a word processing program?

9. Name five differences between the general ledger function of ACCPAC and Bedford.

10. Of the seven types of built-in functions provided by Lotus 1-2-3, financial functions and statistical functions are the most commonly used by the accountant. Briefly describe the capabilities of financial and statistical functions.

11. The owner of a small business has decided to purchase a database program to help the office keep track of information. Two possibilities have been suggested: dBASE III and PFS:FILE. How would you determine which program would be most useful.

MINI DISCUSSION CASE

Case 29–1   Steve Krassman worked as a welder and foreman in shipyards for many years. Three years ago, Steve decided to try running his own business. He started a small welding and fabricating plant near the harbour. Krassman Fabrications, Inc., started with a crew of five. Currently, a crew of 20 operates the plant in three shifts. The business specializes in fabricating steel containers and structures for cargo ships that visit the harbour. Many of the jobs are one to two working days in duration. A quotation is usually provided before work starts on a job.

For the first year, Steve kept all his business records on scraps of paper filed chronologically. However, because he was too busy running the plant, he had difficulty keeping track of his invoices and payment. In the second year, Steve hired an accountant, Barbara Smith, to look after the financial records of the business. In the meantime, Steve expanded into steel fabrication for some of the local shipyards.

Now, after a year, Barbara is having difficulty keeping all the records current. Overdue invoices are not followed up in a timely manner because the aging of accounts receivable alone can take Barbara a whole day. Furthermore, Steve wants to have a better handle on the finances of the business. He now feels he needs monthly financial statements. But it takes Barbara most of a day to work out a trial balance work sheet even if the work sheet balances. Consequently, interim financial statements are not produced on time.

Because of the rapid expansion, there is a constant shortage of working cash. Barbara knows that better management of cash, including more frequent cash flow projections, must be done. To ensure repeat business, Steve wants to keep track of the arrival and departure dates of about 200 regular clients' ships in order to schedule work better and respond to requests faster.

Barbara thinks a microcomputer would help with her work, and she asks your advice.

Required:

1. How could a microcomputer help Steve Krassman run his business?
2. What features does Barbara need in an accounting program?
3. What factors should Barbara and Steve consider in deciding whether they need a spreadsheet program?
4. What factors should they consider in deciding whether they need a database program? How would a database program be used at Krassman?

Moore Corporation Limited
1985 Annual Report

Report to shareholders

Moore continued to establish a strong base for future growth in 1985 while achieving new levels of performance in overall operating results.

Sales and earnings exceeded those of the previous year reflecting generally favourable business conditions and the dedicated efforts of Moore employees at all levels.

The Corporation is in the forefront of an information revolution and new and advanced products and services are required to meet the changing needs of the market.

Substantial progress was made during the year in establishing state-of-the-art printing processes, in renewed emphasis on training and in developing market directed products and services.

The forward thrust of the Corporation is symbolized by the new Moore logo adopted in 1985 for use throughout the Moore worldwide organization.

Financial

Sales at $2.1 billion increased from $2.0 billion in 1984. Growth in value-added products more than offset planned reductions in lower margin products, and selling prices remained generally firm throughout the year.

Net earnings of $137 million rose 8.7% from $126 million in 1984. Net earnings were $1.53 per subdivided share compared with $1.43 for the previous year. Net earnings per sales dollar increased to 6.6¢ compared to 6.2¢ in 1984 and 5.4¢ in 1983.

Unrealized exchange adjustments of $14 million reduced earnings by 16¢ per share compared to a reduction of $6 million and 7¢ per share in 1984. The increase reflects a major devaluation of the Mexican peso and a continuing decline in the value of the Brazilian cruzeiro in relation to the United States dollar.

Income from operations of $234 million was up 16.3% from $201 million last year and is 51.4% higher than the $155 million earned in 1983. The 1985 performance reflects improved productivity, lower paper costs and growth in value-added products and services. Operating income continued to be adversely affected by unfavourable year to year variations in foreign exchange rates and the continuing cost of establishing a storefront marketing organization in the United States.

The balance sheet continues to reflect the strong financial condition of the Corporation. Working capital increased $30 million to $553 million at December 31, 1985 and the current ratio remained strong at 2.9:1. Capital expenditures were a record $95 million.

Dividends and capital stock

Following the subdivision of the common shares in April, 1985, the quarterly dividend was established at 18¢ per common share, or an indicated annual rate of 72¢. Dividends declared in 1985 were 70$^{2}/_{3}$¢ per share compared to 66$^{2}/_{3}$¢ in 1984.

Since dividends are payable in United States dollars, shareholders converting their dividends to Canadian currency again benefited from the strength of the United States dollar in relation to the Canadian dollar.

The number of issued common shares increased by 1,208,450 during the year as shareholders took advantage of the Dividend Reinvestment Plan.

Investing for growth

Moore continues to invest in programs to further enhance the Corporation's position as a premier provider of information-related products and services required by businesses, governments and other enterprises for efficient management of their daily activities.

The record capital expenditure program reflects an acceleration of plans to provide state-of-the-art manufacturing equipment, processes and facilities to meet changing customer needs.

Acquisitions were made in the United States, Canada, Sweden and Australia. A label company was acquired in the United States which provides an opportunity to move rapidly into the fast-growing continuous form bar code and pressure sensitive label market. The Canadian acquisition provides specialized mailing list and data base management services for publishers, advertising agencies and major corporations. The Swedish company entered the marketing of computer supplies. In Australia, two new interests provide credit management and electronic printing services. The diversity of these acquisitions illustrates how Moore pursues its corporate objective of providing the most complete line of information processing and communication products and systems.

Preparing for the future

Investment in research and development has long been a Moore tradition. The Corporation is in the forefront of significant changes in printing technology, developing proprietary printing systems which are being installed in Moore plants throughout the world.

Extensive activity continues at the Moore Research Center in the development of new software, printing and material processing technologies.

Advanced business information products and communication systems demand increased skills. Accordingly, new training programs provide information to enhance the Corporation's significant investment in people. Moore sales representatives and technical support personnel provide a total service, making available to customers the full capability of every part of the Moore organization. The Corporation continues to benefit from the two-year-old Productivity and Cost Evaluation program which emphasizes employee participation, training, communications and improved productivity.

The accelerating pace of business within Moore is also reflected in changes in the internal management structure of the Corporation.

The office of Chief Operating Officer has been introduced at the Corporate level to promote synergy, coordinate management and enhance development of the operating units to maximize growth.

Adoption of the new logo, which uses the single word "Moore" as a recurring identification for all operating units, symbolizes Moore's advance into new business information processing and communications systems.

Operations

While forms and forms based systems continue to be the primary focus for Moore, considerable emphasis is being placed on developing value-added products and services to ensure future growth. These programs are centred in the use of bar codes, electronic printing of variable information, information distribution services, forms management and data based management services that assist business in the processing and communication of information.

The business forms and systems units in the United States, Canada and Brazil turned in particularly strong performances in 1985. European and Australian results were below expectation, but programs in place are expected to produce sharply higher sales and earnings in 1986.

Operating results of the Response Graphics Division in the United States, which offers timely delivery of computer based printing to the direct mail, lottery and games industries and to other businesses, declined from the record levels achieved in 1984. In 1986, the outlook is for renewed growth.

The Data Management Services Division in the United States, which offers data based publishing, on-line computer services and printed products to real estate and other businesses, continued its growth trend with another year of outstanding performance.

The storefront marketing organization in the United States operated at a loss during the year, reflecting a period of intense competition within the microcomputer retail industry and the longer than anticipated period required for the reorganization of this new program. This division was placed under new management effective January 1, 1986. The Corporation's objective of serving customers' total information processing requirements encompasses a Moore presence in the growing multibillion dollar market for microcomputers and supplies. Every effort will be made to move this operation toward a satisfactory level of performance in 1986.

While Moore's principal method of selling is through direct representatives, telemarketing and catalog marketing of computer supplies and forms have spread quickly and successfully throughout the Moore organization and are now used by most of the operating units around the world.

Moore participates in the custom packaging industry with plants in the United Kingdom and Canada. The United Kingdom packaging subsidiary had an excellent year, surpassing its operating objectives.

During the year, Retirement Plans covering employees in the United States and Canada were revised to provide improved benefits. In addition, a contributory Savings Plan with employer matching contributions and profit sharing features was introduced effective August 1, 1985 in the United States and January 1, 1986 in Canada.

Outlook

Forecasts of another year of stable prices and modest growth in the United States and Canadian economies and indications of renewed growth in other industrial nations hold prospects for further gains in sales and earnings in 1986.

The Corporation's firm commitment to profitable growth, while building for the future, will be continued with emphasis on productivity improvement, employee training and on being a low cost producer of its products and services.

Opportunities to augment growth through acquisitions that support Moore's traditional business and broaden the base of service to customers will be pursued at the operating and corporate levels.

Management

M. Keith Goodrich was appointed Executive Vice President and Chief Operating Officer and a Director of the Corporation effective January 1, 1986. Mr. Goodrich was formerly President of the United States Business Forms & Systems Division and Executive Vice President of Moore Business Forms, Inc. Other management changes are included on page 33 of this report.

Appreciation

Having attained the retirement age set by the Corporation for Directors, Edwin H. Heeney will not stand for re-election. Appreciation is expressed for his valued counsel and many contributions as a Director and as Chairman of the Audit Committee of the Board.

The outstanding efforts, enhanced skills and dedication of Moore employees throughout the world are reflected in the continued growth and development of the Corporation. This dedication will ensure Moore's ability to confidently satisfy its thousands of customers, worldwide, with quality products to meet their current and future needs.

D. W. Barr
*Chairman of the
Board*
February 18, 1986

J. W. Sinclair
*President and Chief
Executive Officer*

Consolidated balance sheet

Moore
Corporation
Limited

As at December 31
Expressed in United States currency
in thousands of dollars

Assets	1985	1984
Current assets		
Cash	$ 6,122	$ 5,183
Short-term securities, at cost which approximates market value	146,689	138,917
Accounts receivable, less allowance for doubtful accounts $11,349 ($11,466 in 1984)	390,455	362,357
Inventories (note 2)	281,266	272,901
Prepaid expenses	14,481	11,340
Total current assets	839,013	790,698
Fixed assets		
Land	15,359	13,346
Buildings	157,976	148,841
Machinery and equipment	545,816	467,359
	719,151	629,546
Less: accumulated depreciation	341,884	310,474
	377,267	319,072
Investment in associated corporation (note 3)	32,519	23,706
Other assets (note 4)	72,367	54,238
	$1,321,166	$1,187,714

Liabilities		1985	1984
	Current liabilities		
	Bank loans (note 5)	$ 26,658	$ 39,951
	Accounts payable and accruals (note 6)	222,665	195,084
	Dividends payable	16,176	14,791
	Accrued income taxes	20,340	17,884
	Total current liabilities	285,839	267,710
	Long-term debt (note 7)	49,307	53,644
	Deferred income taxes and liabilities (note 8)	67,186	58,316
	Equity of minority shareholders in subsidiary corporations	11,443	12,226
		413,775	391,896
Shareholders' equity			
	Common shares (note 9)		
	Authorized: 120,000,000 shares without par value		
	Issued: 89,930,573 shares (88,722,123 shares in 1984)	115,944	96,183
	Unrealized foreign currency translation adjustments (note 10)	(79,061)	(97,434)
	Retained earnings	870,508	797,069
		907,391	795,818
		$1,321,166	$1,187,714

Approved by the Board of Directors:

Director   Director

**Consolidated statement
of earnings**

For the year ended December 31
Expressed in United States currency and except
earnings per share in thousands of dollars

	1985	1984	1983
Sales	$2,067,710	$2,020,801	$1,813,573
Cost of sales	1,312,244	1,342,669	1,216,270
Selling, general and administrative expenses	468,521	425,998	387,426
Depreciation	41,933	38,574	34,104
Interest expense	10,668	12,080	20,971
	1,833,366	1,819,321	1,658,771
Income from operations	234,344	201,480	154,802
Investment and other income	25,650	24,923	31,552
Earnings before income taxes, minority interests and unrealized exchange adjustments	259,994	226,403	186,354
Income taxes (note 14)	108,011	92,618	79,974
Minority interests	997	2,030	1,725
Unrealized exchange adjustments	14,303	6,022	6,065
Net earnings	$ 136,683	$ 125,733	$ 98,590
Earnings per share (notes 9 and 15)	$1.53	$1.43	$1.16

**Consolidated statement
of retained earnings**

For the year ended December 31
Expressed in United States currency
in thousands of dollars

	1985	1984	1983
Balance at beginning of year	$ 797,069	$ 729,880	$ 688,178
Net earnings	136,683	125,733	98,590
	933,752	855,613	786,768
Dividends 70²/₃¢ per share (66²/₃¢ in 1984 and 1983) (note 9)	63,244	58,544	56,888
Balance at end of year	$ 870,508	$ 797,069	$ 729,880

**Consolidated statement of
changes in cash resources**

Moore
Corporation
Limited

For the year ended December 31
Expressed in United States currency
in thousands of dollars

	1985	1984	1983
Cash resources provided by (applied to)			
Operations	$ 182,321	$146,596	$ 82,095
Investment	(111,145)	(84,866)	(48,653)
Financing	11,321	13,640	9,393
Dividends	(63,244)	(58,544)	(56,888)
Increase (decrease) in cash resources before			
unrealized exchange adjustments	19,253	16,826	(14,053)
Unrealized exchange adjustments	2,751	(7,200)	(5,146)
Increase (decrease) in cash resources			
(note 16(a))	22,004	9,626	(19,199)
Cash resources at beginning of year	104,149	94,523	113,722
Cash resources at end of year	$ 126,153	$104,149	$ 94,523
Operations			
Net earnings	$ 136,683	$125,733	$ 98,590
Items not affecting cash resources (note 16(b))	62,726	46,991	47,599
Decrease (increase) in working capital			
other than cash resources (note 16(c))	(17,088)	(26,128)	(64,094)
	$ 182,321	$146,596	$ 82,095
Investment			
Expenditure for fixed assets	$ (94,505)	$ (67,151)	$ (56,809)
Sale of fixed assets	13,696	9,005	4,226
Addition to long-term receivables	(15,833)	(3,529)	(8,164)
Reduction in long-term receivables	2,814	3,637	2,246
Long-term investments	(3,437)	(8,540)	(3,474)
Sale of long-term investment	–	2,046	2,876
Acquisitions, net of cash resources	(11,820)	(11,936)	–
Sale of subsidiary, net of cash resources	–	–	10,082
Deferred charges	(1,579)	(8,587)	(688)
Investment in associated corporation	(1,865)	–	–
Dividends from associated corporation	1,284	1,027	1,052
Other	100	(838)	–
	$(111,145)	$ (84,866)	$ (48,653)
Financing			
Addition to long-term debt	$ 6,724	$ 5,303	$ 2,831
Reduction in long-term debt	(14,324)	(30,914)	(9,378)
Issue of common shares	19,761	40,248	16,558
Other	(840)	(997)	(618)
	$ 11,321	$ 13,640	$ 9,393

**Notes to consolidated
financial statements**

Moore
Corporation
Limited

*Year ended December 31, 1985
Expressed in United States currency*

1 Summary of accounting policies

Accounting principles:
Moore Corporation Limited is incorporated under
the laws of the Province of Ontario, Canada.
    The consolidated financial statements are pre-
pared in accordance with accounting principles
generally accepted in Canada.

Translation of foreign currencies:
The consolidated financial statements are
expressed in United States currency because the
greater part of the net assets and earnings are
located or originate in the United States. Except for
the foreign currency financial statements of subsidiaries in countries with highly inflationary
economies, Canadian and other foreign currency
financial statements have been translated into
United States currency on the following bases:
    All assets and liabilities at the year-end rates
    of exchange;
    Income and expenses at average exchange
    rates during the year.
    Net unrealized exchange adjustments arising on
translation of foreign currency financial statements
are charged or credited directly to shareholders'
equity and shown as unrealized foreign currency
translation adjustments.
    The foreign currency financial statements of
subsidiaries in countries with highly inflationary
economies are translated into United States currency on the following bases:
    Current assets, excluding inventory, current
    liabilities, pension liabilities, long-term receiv-
    ables and long-term debt, at the year-end rates of
    exchange;
    All other assets, liabilities, accumulated depreci-
    ation and related charges against earnings and
    share capital, at historical rates of exchange;
    Income and expenses, other than depreciation
    and cost of sales, at average exchange rates
    during the year.
    Net unrealized exchange adjustments arising on
translation of foreign currency financial statements
of subsidiaries in countries with highly inflationary
economies are charged to earnings as unrealized
exchange adjustments.
    Realized exchange losses or gains are included in
earnings.
    Unrealized exchange losses or gains related to
monetary items with a fixed or ascertainable life
extending beyond the end of the following fiscal

year are deferred and amortized over the remaining
life of the asset or liability.

Inventories:
Inventories of raw materials and work in process
are valued at the lower of cost and replacement
cost and inventories of finished goods at the lower
of cost and net realizable value. The cost of the
principal raw material inventories and the raw
material content of finished goods inventories in
Canada and the United States is determined on the
last-in, first-out basis. The cost of all other inventories is determined on the first-in, first-out basis.

Fixed assets and depreciation:
Fixed assets are stated at historical cost after
deducting investment tax credits and other grants
on eligible capital assets. Depreciation is provided
on a basis that will amortize the cost of depreciable
assets over their estimated useful lives using the
straight-line method. All costs for repairs and
maintenance are expensed as incurred.
    The estimated useful lives of buildings range
from 20 to 50 years and of machinery and
equipment from 3 to 17 years.
    Gains or losses on the disposal of fixed assets are
included in earnings and the cost and accumulated
depreciation related to these assets are removed
from the accounts.

Investment in associated corporations:
The Corporation accounts for its investment in
associated corporations by the equity method.

Goodwill:
Goodwill is amortized by the straight-line method
over periods not exceeding forty years.

Amortization of deferred costs:
Deferred production engineering costs are amortized over varying periods not exceeding five years.

Income taxes:
Income taxes are accounted for on the tax allocation basis which relates income taxes to the
accounting income for the year.
    No provision has been made for taxes on
undistributed earnings of subsidiaries not currently
available for paying dividends inasmuch as such
earnings have been reinvested in the business.

2 Inventories

	1985	1984
	(in thousands)	
Raw materials	$108,426	$115,309
Work in process	24,985	21,969
Finished goods	142,287	129,952
Other	5,568	5,671
	$281,266	$272,901

The excess of the current cost over the last-in, first-out cost of those inventories determined on the latter basis is approximately $49,000,000 at December 31, 1985 (1984-$65,000,000).

3 Investment in associated corporation

The investment in associated corporation represents a 45% ownership in Toppan Moore Company, Ltd. in Japan. Dividends received from this corporation in 1985 were $1,284,000 (1984-$1,027,000; 1983-$1,052,000) and its undistributed earnings included in retained earnings are $21,578,000 (1984-$18,450,000; 1983-$13,683,000).

4 Other assets

Other assets include goodwill of $22,592,000 (1984-$16,237,000), net of accumulated amortization of $6,806,000 (1984-$3,193,000); investments in United States tax benefit transfers of $3,563,000 (1984-$7,838,000); taxes being amortized over a five-year period, of $4,221,000 (1984-$4,743,000), net of accumulated amortization of $5,288,000 (1984-$2,624,000), and a long-term receivable of $5,756,000 (1984-$4,687,000) related to the sale of F. N. Burt Company, Inc. in 1983.

5 Unused lines of credit

The unused lines of credit outstanding at December 31, 1985 for short-term financing are $41,000,000 (1984-$32,000,000), of which $20,000,000 is for the support of commercial paper borrowings. There were no commercial paper borrowings outstanding at the end of either year.

6 Accounts payable and accruals

	1985	1984
	(in thousands)	
Trade accounts payable	$100,402	$ 80,575
Other payables	22,598	22,014
	123,000	102,589
Accrued payrolls	43,928	39,290
Accrued retirement plan payments	10,510	16,899
Other accruals	45,227	36,306
	99,665	92,495
	$222,665	$195,084

7 Long-term debt

	1985	1984
	(in thousands)	
Moore Corporation Limited		
Bank loan payable in Canadian dollars due 1989	$ 10,609	$ 11,156
6% Subordinated Debentures due 1994 ($1,868,000 Cdn. in 1985 and 1984)	1,336	1,416
Other	214	276
Moore Business Forms, Inc.		
7.9% Senior Notes due 1996	14,000	15,000
Industrial Development Revenue Bonds bearing interest at 6.85% and 9.5% due 2004	7,350	7,350
Other loan and capital lease commitments	796	1,340
Moore Paragon S.A.		
Bank and other loans payable in French francs bearing interest at 8.25% to 11.75% due 1987 to 1999. Loans amounting to $4,064,000 (1984-$2,420,000) are secured	7,909	5,631
	$ 42,214	$ 42,169

Note 7 continued

	1985	1984
Balance forward	**$ 42,214**	$ 42,169
Moore Formularios Limitada		
Bank and other loans payable in United States dollars bearing		
interest at 10.0% and 10.25% due 1987 and 1990	**1,116**	1,456
Capital lease commitments	**2,268**	762
Other subsidiaries		
Secured loans	**1,777**	796
Unsecured loans	**1,932**	8,461
	$ 49,307	$ 53,644

The sinking fund obligations with respect to the retirement of the 6% Subordinated Debentures for the years 1986 to 1993 inclusive were satisfied in prior years.

The bank loan agreement of the Corporation provides options either to borrow any currency freely traded on the London Interbank Eurocurrency Market, with interest determined at $^3/_8$ of 1% per annum over the London Interbank Offered Rate existing from time to time, or to borrow Canadian dollars through bankers acceptances at market interest rates existing from time to time plus a fee of $^1/_2$ of 1% per annum of the face value of the acceptances. At December 31, 1985, the interest rate on this bank loan was 9.17%.

The long-term debt of other subsidiaries bears interest at rates ranging from 5.1% to 27.5%. These debts mature on varying dates to 1992. Loans amounting to $3,709,000 (1984–$4,035,000) are payable in currencies other than United States dollars and loans of $1,777,000 (1984–$796,000) are secured by assets of six (1984–five) subsidiaries. The long-term debt of other subsidiaries in 1984 includes $4,300,000 which was repaid by Moore Business Forms de Mexico, S.A. de C.V. in 1985.

The cost of assets subject to lien approximated $18,000,000 (1984–$21,000,000), the liens being primarily mortgages against fixed assets.

Payments of $5,380,000 (1984–$3,351,000) on long-term debt due within one year are included in current liabilities. For the years 1987 through 1990 payments required on long-term debt are as follows:
1987–$5,068,000; 1988–$4,015,000;
1989–$13,859,000 and 1990–$2,787,000.

8 Deferred income taxes and liabilities

Deferred income taxes amount to $59,410,000 (1984–$51,478,000). Deferred liabilities include $4,321,000 (1984–$3,516,000) for pensions under unfunded retirement plans of certain overseas subsidiaries (note 11).

9 Common shares

Each of the 40,000,000 issued and unissued common shares of the Corporation were subdivided into three common shares effective April 18, 1985.

The following share capital information is presented after giving effect to such subdivision.

	Authorized number of shares	Issued Number of shares	Issued Amount
Balance, January 1, 1983	120,000,000	84,688,062	$ 39,377,000
Optional Stock Dividend and Dividend Reinvestment Plan		775,761	10,916,000
Exercise of executive stock options		101,820	1,015,000
Conversion of $5,708,000 Cdn. principal amount of			
6% Convertible Subordinated Debentures		291,108	4,627,000
Balance, December 31, 1983	120,000,000	85,856,751	55,935,000
Optional Stock Dividend and Dividend Reinvestment Plan		1,253,121	15,683,000
Exercise of executive stock options		33,750	313,000
Conversion of $30,951,000 Cdn. principal amount of			
6% Convertible Subordinated Debentures		1,578,501	24,252,000
Balance, December 31, 1984	120,000,000	88,722,123	96,183,000
Optional Stock Dividend and Dividend Reinvestment Plan		1,168,130	19,392,000
Exercise of executive stock options		40,320	369,000
Balance, December 31, 1985	120,000,000	89,930,573	$115,944,000

Since stock dividends are now subject to the same Canadian income and withholding tax treatment as cash dividends, the Stock Dividend option in the Corporation's Optional Stock Dividend and Dividend Reinvestment Plan has been deleted. The Plan now only provides for dividend reinvestment whereby the amount of the dividend otherwise receivable in cash (less any applicable withholding tax) is used to acquire shares at a 5% discount from an average market value.

Pursuant to the terms of the 1985 Long Term Incentive Plan approved by the shareholders of the Corporation on April 4, 1985, 3,000,000 common shares of the Corporation were reserved for issuance. This new Plan replaces the 1976 Executive Stock Option Plan which expires in 1986. Under the terms of this Plan, stock options, stock appreciation rights, restricted stock awards and performance awards may be granted to certain key employees. The exercise price under all options involving the common shares of the Corporation shall not be less than 100% of fair market value of the shares covered by the option on the date of grant. Options may be exercised at such times as are determined at the date they are granted and expire not more than ten years from the date granted. On February 19, 1985, options under the terms of the 1976 Plan were granted to purchase 127,950 shares of the Corporation and on November 6, 1985, options under the terms of the 1985 Plan were granted to purchase 246,400 shares of the Corporation. Details of the stock option activity in 1985 are as follows:

Years options granted	1985	1983	1981	1979	1976	Total
Number of common shares under option						
Outstanding December 31, 1984		186,750	47,580	48,150	21,000	303,480
Options granted–1976 Plan	127,950					127,950
–1985 Plan	246,400					246,400
Options lapsed		(11,250)				(11,250)
Options exercised		(3,000)	(14,720)	(13,600)	(9,000)	(40,320)
Outstanding December 31, 1985	246,400 127,950	172,500	32,860	34,550	12,000	626,260
Option price per share						
Canadian currency	$26.44 $22.23	$18.23	$11.91	$12.65	$11.65	

The number of shares available for stock option grants pursuant to the terms of the 1976 Executive Stock Option Plan were 127,950 common shares as at January 1, 1985 and 11,250 common shares as at December 31, 1985. Under the terms of the 1985 Long Term Incentive Plan there were 2,753,600 common shares available for grants as at December 31, 1985.

10 **Unrealized foreign currency translation adjustments**

	1985	1984	1983
	(in thousands)		
Balance at beginning of year	**$97,434**	$69,504	$50,667
Adjustments for the year	**(18,373)**	27,930	18,837
Balance at end of year	**$79,061**	$97,434	$69,504

The adjustments for each year result from the variation from year to year in the rates of exchange at which foreign currency net assets are translated to United States currency.

11 **Retirement programs**

The Corporation and its subsidiaries have several retirement programs covering substantially all of the employees in Canada, the United States, the United Kingdom, South Africa, Australia and New Zealand.

In 1985, revised programs were adopted in Canada and the United States that improved the retirement plan benefits earned to January 1, 1985, incorporated a different method of calculating benefits earned after this date and introduced a new contributory savings plan that supplements the basic retirement plan. Also, in the actuarial valuation of the United States retirement plan a change in the actuarial method (from entry age normal to projected pro-rata unit credit) and in assumptions (decrease in average retirement age from 63.9 to 62.3) occurred. The combined effect of these changes mainly accounts for a decrease of approximately $5,900,000 in the Canadian and United States retirement plan expense in 1985 compared with the previous year. The additional expense associated with the new savings plan was $7,859,000.

Based upon the latest reports of independent consulting actuaries on the Corporation's retirement plans all vested benefits are fully funded. As a result of the new method of calculating benefits in the United States retirement plan along with the fixing of the accrued benefits earned to January 1, 1985 in both the Canadian and United States plans, no obligation arises for pension benefits expected to accrue and vest in the future which are related to prior service. At December 31, 1984 this obligation, based upon the actuarial method and Canadian and United States retirement plan provisions in effect at that time, approximated $85,000,000. The actuarial method used for the valuation of the retirement plans in the United Kingdom, South Africa, Australia and New Zealand produces no unfunded past service obligations.

In some international subsidiaries, where either state or funded retirement plans exist, there are certain small supplementary unfunded plans. In addition, pensionable service prior to establishing funded contributory retirement plans in other international subsidiaries, covered by former discretionary non-contributory retirement plans, was assumed as a prior service obligation. The deferred liability for pensions at December 31, 1985, referred to in note 8, relates primarily to the unfunded portion of this prior service obligation and the small supplementary unfunded plans.

The following data, as set out in the table below, with respect to the Corporation's retirement plans in Canada, the United States, the United Kingdom, South Africa, Australia and New Zealand is based upon the latest reports of independent consulting actuaries on such retirement plans.

The value of the net assets of those plans has been determined on a full accrual, market value basis and the amount funded and expensed each year includes an amount to cover current service costs and an amount to amortize any past service costs.

	January 1 1985	January 1 1984
	(in thousands)	
Actuarial present value of accumulated plan benefits of which $248,755,000 (1984 – $185,641,000) are vested	$280,968	$206,149
Net assets available for benefits	327,335	313,415
Assumed interest rate used in calculating accumulated plan benefits	7.5%	7.5%

12 Post-retirement health care and life insurance benefits

In addition to providing pension benefits, the Corporation and its subsidiaries provide health care and life insurance benefits for certain retired employees. Substantially all of the Corporation's employees in Canada and the United States become eligible for these benefits if they reach normal retirement age while working for the Corporation.

The cost of these health care and life insurance benefits is recognized as an expense as claims are incurred. In 1985, the costs for these benefits approximate $1,900,000 (1984 – $1,200,000).

13 Consolidated statement of earnings information

	1985	1984	1983
	(in thousands)		
Interest expense			
Interest on long-term debt	$ 5,657	$ 6,182	$ 7,717
Other interest	5,011	5,898	13,254
	$10,668	$12,080	$20,971
Investment and other income			
Interest on short-term investments	$14,863	$13,985	$23,795
Equity in earnings of associated corporations	4,412	4,474	3,350
Income on tax incentive investments	2,760	2,972	919
Gain on sale of long-term investment	–	1,344	1,822
Miscellaneous	3,615	2,148	1,666
	$25,650	$24,923	$31,552
Rent	$39,251	$36,226	$33,808
Repairs and maintenance	38,026	33,493	30,444
Communications	29,188	26,241	27,937
Taxes other than income and payroll taxes	23,896	19,093	22,733
Retirement programs, including in 1985 savings plan expense of $7,859,000.	20,565	17,488	17,786
Research and development	18,599	16,825	14,807
Amortization of goodwill	2,871	1,243	580

14 Income taxes

The components of earnings before income taxes and the provision for income taxes for the three years ended December 31, 1985 are as follows:

Earnings before income taxes	1985	1984	1983
	(in thousands)		
Canada	$ 33,439	$ 34,313	$ 25,155
United States	158,962	128,482	104,427
Other countries	67,593	63,608	56,772
	$259,994	$226,403	$186,354

Provision for income taxes	1985 Current	1985 Deferred	1984 Current	1984 Deferred	1983 Current	1983 Deferred
	(in thousands)					
Canada (federal and provincial)	$12,595	$ (310)	$13,184	$ (404)	$10,947	$ (500)
United States						
Federal	58,362	8,683	42,280	10,804	37,062	6,092
State	9,615	(54)	8,258	821	6,103	23
Other countries	13,966	1,882	12,296	2,078	13,652	1,837
Withholding taxes on inter-company dividends	3,272	–	3,301	–	4,758	–
	$97,810	$10,201	$79,319	$13,299	$72,522	$7,452

Deferred income taxes in each of the three years arose from a number of differences of a timing nature between income for accounting purposes and taxable income in the jurisdictions in which the Corporation and its subsidiaries operate. These timing differences include the variation between tax and accounting depreciation, state income taxes in the United States and other items. Investments made in accordance with tax incentives to encourage expenditure on capital equipment generated additional deferred income taxes in the three years.

The effective rates of tax for each year compared with the statutory Canadian rates were as follows:

	1985	1984	1983
Canadian combined federal and provincial statutory rate	50.6%	50.4%	50.3%
Increase (decrease) in the statutory rate resulting from:			
Corporate surtax	0.8	–	0.8
Manufacturing and processing rate reduction	(6.0)	(5.5)	(5.9)
Inventory allowance	(1.2)	(1.3)	(1.5)
Tax exempt investment income	(7.5)	(6.4)	(2.2)
Weighted effect of higher United States tax rate	7.0	6.3	3.2
Weighted effect of lower tax rate in other countries	(3.5)	(4.1)	(4.3)
Withholding taxes	1.3	1.5	2.5
Total consolidated effective tax rate	41.5%	40.9%	42.9%

15 Earnings and fully diluted earnings per share

The earnings per share calculations are based on the weighted average number of common shares outstanding during the year.

If it were assumed that at the beginning of the year all outstanding stock options had been exercised with the funds derived therefrom yielding an annual return of 4.3% net of tax and, in 1984 and 1983, the 6% Convertible Subordinated Debentures had been converted into common shares, the earnings per share for the year would have been $1.52 (1984 – $1.43; 1983 – $1.14) (note 19).

16 Consolidated statement of cash resources information

(a) Increase (decrease) in cash resources by component	1985	1984	1983
	(in thousands)		
Cash	$ 939	$ (589)	$ (4,920)
Short-term securities	7,772	20,839	(200,340)
Bank loans	13,293	(10,624)	186,061
	$ 22,004	$ 9,626	$ (19,199)

(b) Items not affecting cash resources	1985	1984	1983
	(in thousands)		
Depreciation	$ 41,933	$ 38,574	$ 34,104
Equity in earnings of associated corporations	(4,412)	(4,474)	(3,350)
Minority interests in earnings	997	2,030	1,725
Deferred income taxes	10,392	4,498	7,762
Unrealized exchange adjustments	14,303	6,022	6,065
Other	(487)	341	1,293
	$ 62,726	$ 46,991	$ 47,599

(c) Decrease (increase) in working capital other than cash resources	1985	1984	1983
	(in thousands)		
Accounts receivable	$(28,098)	$ (4,980)	$(24,303)
Inventories	(8,365)	(17,453)	(23,791)
Prepaid expenses	(3,141)	(1,026)	(323)
Deferred taxes	–	8,801	(278)
Accounts payable and accruals	27,581	2,906	7,572
Dividends payable	1,385	484	193
Accrued income taxes	2,456	2,515	(7,738)
Working capital adjustment from acquisitions	(72)	(2,318)	–
Working capital adjustment from divestiture	–	–	(3,222)
Unrealized exchange adjustments	(8,834)	(15,057)	(12,204)
	$(17,088)	$(26,128)	$(64,094)

17 Lease commitments

At December 31, 1985, long-term lease commitments require approximate future rentals as follows:

1986	$34,230,000	1989	$12,977,000
1987	24,435,000	1990	9,588,000
1988	18,246,000	1991 and thereafter	8,907,000

25

18 **Segmented information**

The Corporation and its subsidiaries have operated predominantly in one industry segment during the three years ended December 31, 1985, that being the provision of products and services which facilitate the recording, retention, processing, retrieval and communication of business informa-tion. Transfers of product between geographic segments are generally accounted for on a basis that results in a fair profit being earned by each segment. The export of product from Canada is insignificant.

Geographic segments
(in thousands)

1985	Canada	United States	Europe	Other	Consolidated
Total revenue	$188,887	$1,432,619	$237,834	$218,705	$2,078,045
Intergeographical segment sales	(109)	(8,064)	(1,978)	(184)	(10,335)
Sales to customers outside the enterprise	$188,778	$1,424,555	$235,856	$218,521	$2,067,710
Segment operating profit	$ 31,007	$ 173,503	$ 11,245	$ 32,062	$ 247,817
Interest expense					(10,668)
General corporate expense					(2,805)
Income from operations					$ 234,344
Identifiable assets	$105,803	$ 823,681	$217,853	$141,757	$1,289,094
Intersegment eliminations					(25,409)
Corporate assets including investment in associated corporation					57,481
Total assets					$1,321,166
Depreciation expense	$ 3,550	$ 27,381	$ 5,924	$ 5,078	$ 41,933
Capital expenditures	$ 8,505	$ 50,679	$ 17,653	$ 17,668	$ 94,505
1984	Canada	United States	Europe	Other	Consolidated
Total revenue	$199,357	$1,403,759	$227,404	$200,631	$2,031,151
Intergeographical segment sales	(120)	(8,727)	(1,503)	–	(10,350)
Sales to customers outside the enterprise	$199,237	$1,395,032	$225,901	$200,631	$2,020,801
Segment operating profit	$ 29,755	$ 148,082	$ 10,523	$ 28,150	$ 216,510
Interest expense					(12,080)
General corporate expense					(2,950)
Income from operations					$ 201,480
Identifiable assets	$100,608	$ 747,118	$170,075	$123,576	$1,141,377
Intersegment eliminations					(17,092)
Corporate assets including investment in associated corporation					63,429
Total assets					$1,187,714
Depreciation expense	$ 3,692	$ 25,579	$ 5,103	$ 4,200	$ 38,574
Capital expenditures	$ 5,605	$ 44,777	$ 8,000	$ 8,769	$ 67,151
1983	Canada	United States	Europe	Other	Consolidated
Total revenue	$185,516	$1,216,481	$245,724	$174,855	$1,822,576
Intergeographical segment sales	(88)	(7,376)	(1,539)		(9,003)
Sales to customers outside the enterprise	$185,428	$1,209,105	$244,185	$174,855	$1,813,573
Segment operating profit	$ 26,314	$ 114,404	$ 12,814	$ 21,423	$ 174,955
Interest expense					(20,971)
General corporate income					818
Income from operations					$ 154,802
Identifiable assets	$ 90,091	$ 672,217	$194,417	$119,296	$1,076,021
Intersegment eliminations					(13,071)
Corporate assets including investment in associated corporation					57,555
Total assets					$1,120,505
Depreciation expense	$ 3,445	$ 21,981	$ 5,286	$ 3,392	$ 34,104
Capital expenditures	$ 3,983	$ 35,919	$ 5,208	$ 11,699	$ 56,809

19 **Differences between Canadian and United States generally accepted accounting principles**

The continued registration of the common shares of the Corporation with the Securities and Exchange Commission and listing of the shares on the New York Stock Exchange requires compliance with the integrated disclosure rules of the Securities and Exchange Commission.

The accounting policies in note 1 and accounting principles generally accepted in Canada are consistent in all material aspects with United States generally accepted accounting principles except in the following areas:

Translation of foreign currencies:
Under United States generally accepted accounting principles the unrealized exchange losses or gains related to monetary items with a fixed or ascertainable life would be included in income as they occur.

Prior period adjustment:
Under United States generally accepted accounting principles the litigation settlement in 1984 would have been charged to earnings during that year rather than being treated as a prior period adjustment.

Earnings and fully diluted earnings per share:
The calculation of primary earnings per share under United States generally accepted accounting principles would include the common share equivalent of any outstanding stock options granted where the average market price for the year exceeds the option price and, in 1984 and 1983, the common share equivalent of the 6% Convertible Subordinated Debentures. Under United States generally accepted accounting principles the calculation of fully diluted earnings per share would include the dilutive effect, if any, of any common shares issued during the period on conversion of debentures or the exercise of stock options with effect from the beginning of the period. Also, the calculation of fully diluted earnings per share would include the additional dilutive effect of outstanding options if the market price at the close of the period is higher than the average market price used in computing primary earnings per share.

The above described United States generally accepted accounting principles would have the following income statement effect:

	1985	1984	1983
	(in thousands)		
Net earnings as determined under Canadian generally accepted accounting principles	**$136,683**	$125,733	$98,590
Add (Deduct):			
Unrealized exchange loss	**(97)**	(119)	–
Prior period adjustment	–	(5,916)	(973)
Net earnings as determined under United States generally accepted accounting principles	**$136,586**	$119,698	$97,617
Primary and fully diluted earnings per share	**$1.53**	$1.36	$1.13

Management's statement on financial reporting

All of the information in this annual report has been approved by the Board of Directors and all the financial information contained herein conforms to the accompanying consolidated financial statements, which have been prepared by management in accordance with accounting principles generally accepted in Canada.

The Corporation maintains a system of internal control which is designed to provide reasonable assurance that assets are safeguarded and that reliable financial records are maintained.

The consolidated financial statements have been examined by the Corporation's independent auditors, Price Waterhouse, and their report is included herein.

The Audit Committee of the Board of Directors is composed entirely of outside directors and meets periodically with the Corporation's independent auditors, management and the Corporation's Director of Internal Audit to discuss the scope and results of audit examinations with respect to adequacy of internal controls and financial reporting of the Corporation.

Auditors' report

To the Shareholders of
Moore Corporation Limited:
We have examined the consolidated balance sheets of Moore Corporation Limited as at December 31, 1985 and 1984 and the consolidated statements of earnings, retained earnings and changes in cash resources for each of the three years in the period ended December 31, 1985. Our examinations were made in accordance with generally accepted auditing standards, and accordingly included such tests and other procedures as we considered necessary in the circumstances.

In our opinion, these consolidated financial statements present fairly the financial position of the Corporation as at December 31, 1985 and 1984 and the results of its operations and the changes in its cash resources for each of the three years in the period ended December 31, 1985 in accordance with generally accepted accounting principles applied on a consistent basis.

Price Waterhouse
Chartered Accountants
Toronto, Canada
February 18, 1986

Distribution of revenue

Moore
Corporation
Limited

	1985	1984	1983
Sales and investment and other income	100.0%	100.0%	100.0%
Used as follows:			
Wages, salaries and employee benefits	31.7	31.0	32.7
Materials, supplies and services	53.2	55.4	54.8
Depreciation	2.0	1.9	1.8
Income, property and other taxes	5.8	5.1	4.9
Allocated to minority interests	.1	.1	.1
Unrealized exchange adjustments	.7	.3	.3
Dividends	3.0	2.9	3.1
Retained in business	3.5	3.3	2.3

Quarterly financial information

*Expressed in United States currency
and except per share amounts in
thousands of dollars (unaudited)*

	1985				1984			
	Fourth quarter	Third quarter	Second quarter	First quarter	Fourth quarter	Third quarter	Second quarter	First quarter
Sales	$562,287	$511,090	$494,429	$499,904	$529,417	$494,363	$497,281	$499,740
Cost of sales	347,280	330,230	312,030	322,704	334,775	331,395	335,761	340,738
Income from operations	71,783	53,981	55,529	53,051	63,405	46,031	45,304	46,740
Net earnings	41,415	31,318	31,736	32,214	39,738	29,983	28,166	27,846
Per share	$0.46	$0.35	$0.36	$0.36	$0.45	$0.34	$0.32	$0.32
Net earnings based on United States generally accepted accounting principles (note 19)	$ 41,318	$ 31,318	$ 31,736	$ 32,214	$ 44,454	$ 19,059	$ 28,254	$ 27,931
Per share	$0.46	$0.35	$0.36	$0.36	$0.50	$0.22	$0.32	$0.32

**Market price of common shares
and related security holder matters**

The principal trading markets of the common shares of the Corporation in Canada and the United States are Toronto and New York, respectively. The common shares of the Corporation are also listed on the Montreal Stock Exchange.

Each of the 40,000,000 issued and unissued common shares of the Corporation were subdivided into three common shares effective April 18, 1985.

The information in the following table is presented after giving effect to such subdivision and sets forth the reported high and low sales prices of the common shares of the Corporation on the Toronto, Montreal and New York stock exchanges, as reported by The Toronto Stock Exchange Trading Summary, Montreal Stock Exchange and the New York Stock Exchange Monthly Market Statistics Report, respectively.

	1985							1984
	Fourth quarter	Third quarter	Second quarter	First quarter	Fourth quarter	Third quarter	Second quarter	First quarter
Toronto Stock Exchange *(Canadian currency)*								
High	$30.25	$29.25	$27.25	$24.33	$20.08	$18.33	$16.92	$18.17
Low	24.50	23.75	22.62	19.67	17.42	16.50	14.83	15.33
Montreal Stock Exchange *(Canadian currency)*								
High	30.12	29.12	27.25	24.29	20.08	18.42	16.77	18.08
Low	24.62	23.75	22.62	19.67	17.46	16.54	14.88	15.38
New York Stock Exchange *(United States currency)*								
High	21.75	21.87	20.00	17.71	15.25	14.08	12.79	14.58
Low	18.00	17.50	16.67	14.87	13.17	12.50	11.58	12.00
Dividends paid per common share *(United States currency)*	18¢	18¢	18¢	16⅔¢	16⅔¢	16⅔¢	16⅔¢	16⅔¢

On February 3, 1986, the closing price per share of the Corporation's common shares was $28.50 (Cdn.) and $28.62 (Cdn.) on the Toronto Stock Exchange and Montreal Stock Exchange respectively and $19.87 (U.S.) on the New York Stock Exchange.

On February 3, 1986, the number of shareholders of record was 13,365.

There are no restrictions on the export or import of capital which affect the remittance of dividends, interest or other payments to non resident holders of the Corporation's securities.

The Investment Canada Act replaced the Foreign Investment Review Act with its passage into law on June 6, 1985. The Act requires review by the Government of Canada of the acquisition by, or transfer to, non-Canadians of direct or indirect control of a Canadian business entity, such as the Corporation. The Act does not apply to the purchase of shares or securities of a corporation where such purchases would not give the purchaser at least one-third of the voting shares.

Withholding taxes at the rate of 25% are imposed on the payment of interest and cash dividends to non residents of Canada. Under the Canada/United States tax treaty, such rate is generally reduced from 25% to 15%.

Ten-year summary

Moore
Corporation
Limited

*Expressed in United States currency
and except per share amounts
in thousands of dollars*

Income statistics	1985	1984	1983
Sales	$2,067,710	$2,020,801	$1,813,573
Income from operations	234,344	201,480	154,802
Per dollar of sales	11.3¢	10.0¢	8.5¢
Income taxes	108,011	92,618	79,974
Percent of pretax earnings	41.5%	40.9%	42.9%
Earnings before extraordinary items	136,683	125,733	98,590
Per dollar of sales	6.6¢	6.2¢	5.4¢
Per share	$1.53	$1.43	$1.16
Net earnings	136,683	125,733	98,590
Per dollar of sales	6.6¢	6.2¢	5.4¢
Per share	$1.53	$1.43	$1.16
Dividends	63,244	58,544	56,888
Per share	70²/₃¢	66²/₃¢	66²/₃¢
Earnings retained in business	73,439	67,189	41,702

Balance sheet and other statistics	1985	1984	1983
Current assets	$ 839,013	$ 790,698	$ 755,790
Current liabilities	285,839	267,710	251,181
Working capital	553,174	522,988	504,609
Ratio of current assets to current liabilities	2.9:1	3.0:1	3.0:1
Fixed assets (net)	377,267	319,072	303,666
Long-term debt	49,307	53,644	82,235
Ratio to equity	0.1:1	0.1:1	0.1:1
Shareholders' equity	907,391	795,818	716,311
Per share	$10.09	$8.97	$8.34
Total assets	1,321,166	1,187,714	1,120,505
Number of shareholders of record at year-end	13,369	13,597	16,135
Number of employees	27,331	26,457	26,100

Per share data reflects the three for one
subdivision of the common shares effective
April 18, 1985.

	1982	1981	1980	1979	1978	1977	1976
	$1,847,076	$1,879,063	$1,804,781	$1,541,048	$1,323,362	$1,183,890	$1,053,427
	178,407	192,801	207,599	191,853	164,134	158,477	142,559
	9.7¢	10.3¢	11.5¢	12.4¢	12.4¢	13.4¢	13.5¢
	95,509	99,806	106,198	97,554	86,653	86,427	77,497
	48.3%	47.0%	48.7%	48.4%	50.5%	52.6%	52.1%
	87,508	107,986	108,821	100,635	82,830	74,673	66,057
	4.7¢	5.7¢	6.0¢	6.5¢	6.3¢	6.3¢	6.3¢
	$1.04	$1.28	$1.29	$1.20	$0.99	$0.89	$0.79
	87,508	107,986	108,821	100,635	81,182	73,640	64,845
	4.7¢	5.7¢	6.0¢	6.5¢	6.1¢	6.2¢	6.2¢
	$1.04	$1.28	$1.29	$1.20	$0.88	$0.88	$0.77
	56,286	50,476	45,961	40,352	36,987	33,624	33,624
	66⅔¢	59⅓¢	54¢	47⅓¢	43⅓¢	39⅓¢	39⅓¢
	31,222	57,510	62,860	60,283	44,195	40,016	31,221

	1982	1981	1980	1979	1978	1977	1976
	$ 912,355	$ 728,831	$ 688,347	$628,947	$522,727	$502,484	$453,166
	437,215	251,179	236,434	223,398	182,099	197,297	137,617
	475,140	477,652	451,913	405,549	340,628	305,187	315,549
	2.1:1	2.9:1	2.9:1	2.8:1	2.9:1	2.5:1	3.3:1
	302,777	308,235	308,290	296,887	288,605	284,793	268,361
	91,161	96,750	106,283	111,291	96,614	90,780	90,417
	0.1:1	0.1:1	0.2:1	0.2:1	0.2:1	0.2:1	0.2:1
	676,888	668,635	630,288	563,801	504,288	461,202	416,976
	$7.99	$7.95	$7.50	$6.71	$6.00	$5.49	$4.96
	1,272,457	1,081,744	1,037,950	963,926	848,971	816,873	748,106
	17,991	18,370	18,999	18,547	19,993	20,059	20,036
	26,218	27,703	27,839	28,317	26,748	27,045	25,964

Index

1220